# FACE IT

As animation software becomes more advanced and graphics become more refined, the opportunity to create informative detail becomes more achievable in your characters. You can't give every character the same facial contours anymore. Today's graphic engines and hi-definition screens enhance detail, and the features in your character can make or break the believability of your game or movie.

*Face It* provides you with the resources that you need to ensure an accurate character model. By examining the skulls of people of different ages, ethnicities, and geographical areas, authors Patricia Beckmann-Wells and Scott Wells showcase the intricacies of the human head and face and show you how to apply that to your models.

This *Second Edition* features new and updated tutorials as well as a new chapter discussing facial variation over time. Whether it be a Caucasian woman in her 50s or an African man in his late 20s, you'll know how to properly shape a forehead, an eye socket, and even cheekbones to ensure the 100% accuracy of your 3D character.

# FACE IT

## A Visual Reference for Multi-Ethnic Facial Modeling

Second Edition

PATRICIA BECKMANN-WELLS

TUTORIALS BY SCOTT WELLS

CRC Press
Taylor & Francis Group
Boca Raton London New York

CRC Press is an imprint of the
Taylor & Francis Group, an **informa** business

Second edition published 2025

by CRC Press
2385 NW Executive Center Drive, Suite 320, Boca Raton FL 33431

and by CRC Press
4 Park Square, Milton Park, Abingdon, Oxon, OX14 4RN

*CRC Press is an imprint of Taylor & Francis Group, LLC*



First edition published by Focal Press 2013



ISBN: 978-1-032-77741-2 (hbk)
ISBN: 978-1-032-76444-3 (pbk)
ISBN: 978-1-003-48455-4 (ebk)

DOI: 10.1201/9781003484554

Typeset in Avenir
by Apex CoVantage, LLC

# CONTENTS

# ABOUT THE AUTHORS

**Dr. Patricia Beckmann-Wells** is a researcher and creative director whose research for *Face It* has led to roles as a consultant for the *Epic Games Unreal Metahuman* project and speaking engagements with Pixar, Walt Disney Animation Studios, and SIGGRAPH on Informed Identity in character design.

Recently, Dr. Beckmann-Wells was invited to speak at the AgBO + Slamdance Summer showcase hosted by the Russo Brothers (of *Everything Everywhere All at Once* fame) as a member of the featured roundtable discussion of "AI and independent filmmaking." She has also been selected for the Metamorph AI Directors club of award-winning filmmakers for her storytelling skills and creative use of artificial intelligence pipelines with original art.

Dr. Beckmann-Wells's career includes executive leadership roles at Dreamworks SKG and Walt Disney Animation Studios, where she has been responsible for art asset pipeline development and international training, and artist roles at Warner Brothers Digital, Film Roman, ITE Denmark, as well as her own studio as a content creator. *Patricia* has been a frequent Chair of SIGGRAPH, founding the 'FJORG!' animation marathon. She also founded the animation department at the Savannah College of Art and Design (SCAD) and consulted on the first bachelor's degree at the Gnomon School of Visual Arts. She chose to enter education as a professor to pursue her creative work and motivate diverse student populations to create their authentic voice.

Her animated films and projection mapping have received international acclaim in over 200 festivals, premiering at venues like Slamdance, the Los Angeles Contemporary Museum of Art (LACMA), CERN, Supernova Digital Animation Festival, and Anima Zagreb, among others. Her current film *Mombomb, Part 1* is winning awards internationally in the visual effects, story, and short film categories. *Patricia* was chosen for LUNAFEST, sponsored by Luna Bars, and her film *Family Tale* traveled with LUNAFEST, raising money for breast cancer patients. Her film *Propolis, Part 7* premiered at Slamdance Film Festival in Park City, Utah, and she continues with the festival as a judge for Series Shorts and DIG (Digital, Interactive, Gaming).

Furthermore, the Interactive Media Arts program she founded at IVC was awarded a Commendation from the City of Irvine for its excellence. Dr. Patricia Beckmann-Wells also received the Greater Irvine Chamber Distinguished Educator Award.

**Scott Wells** is a digital character artist and traditional sculptor with over 30 years of experience in games, film, and television.

Scott is a lead character artist at Treyarch on the *Call of Duty: Black Ops* franchise where he oversees character portrait, hair authoring, facial shape capture as well as talent casting, facial rig development, and performance solving. Previously, he was a senior artist on the Character Body Art Team. His projects at Treyarch are *Call of Duty: Black Ops: Cold War, COD: Black Ops 1–4*, and *007: Quantum of Solace*.

Before Treyarch, Scott was a creature modeler at Rhythm & Hues (R&H), where he worked on several film and television projects. His film credits at R&H include *Night at the Museum, The Golden Compass, Evan Almighty*, and *Superman Returns*.

He has a Master of Fine Arts in Animation from The Savannah College of Art and Design (2005) and a Bachelor of Fine Arts in Illustration from The University of Massachusetts Dartmouth (1991).

Scott has been a guest lecturer at Pixar and has taught as an adjunct professor of Digital Media at SCAD and as an advanced modeling instructor at the Gnomon School of Visual Effects in Hollywood, CA. He has also acted as a professional adviser for students at the Academy of Art San Francisco and Cal State LA.

Scott has been recognized individually for his work with two Emmy nominations, a Telly award, and an MIMC award.

# 1

CHAPTER 1

# THE BASIC SKULL

DOI: 10.1201/ 9781003484554-1

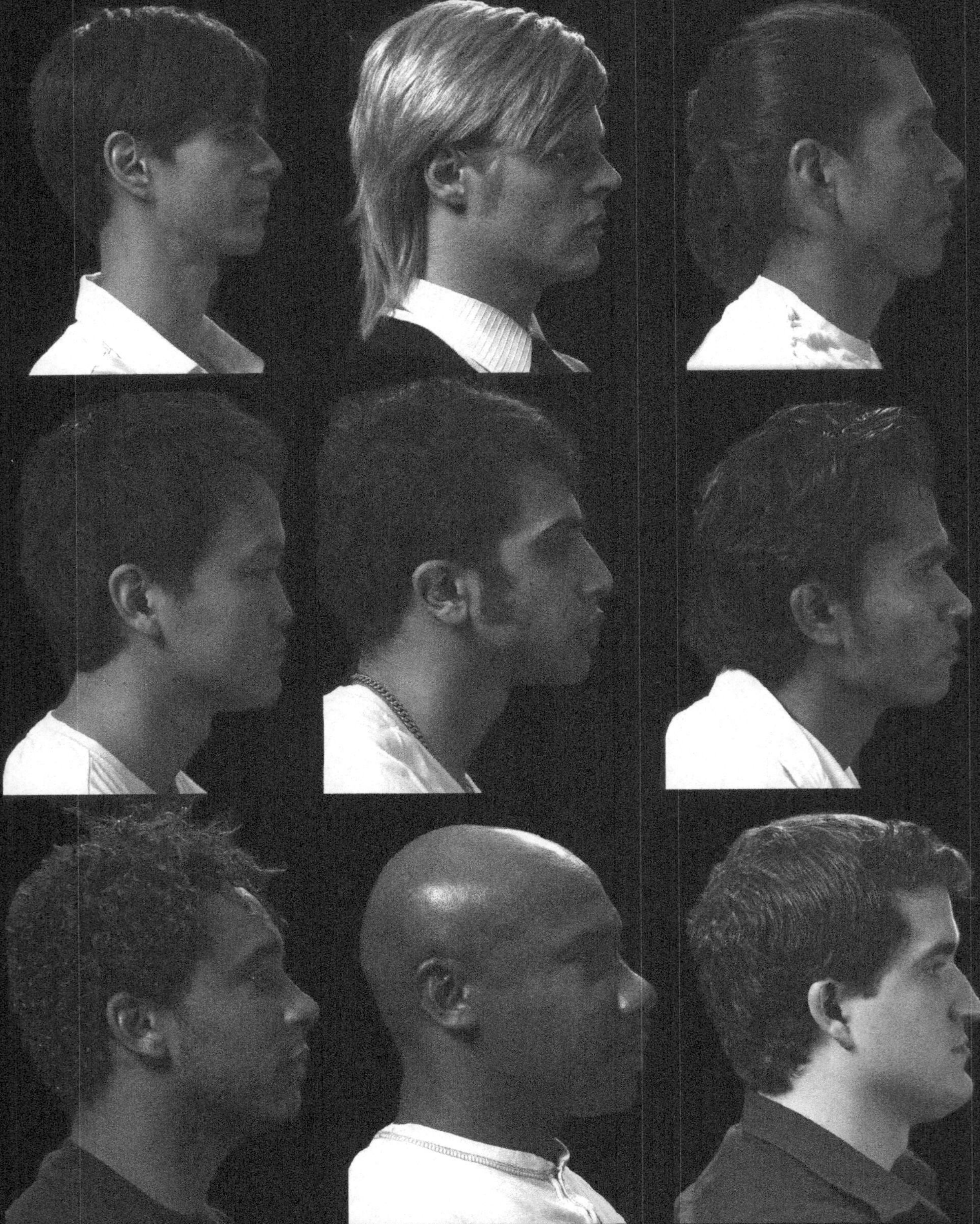

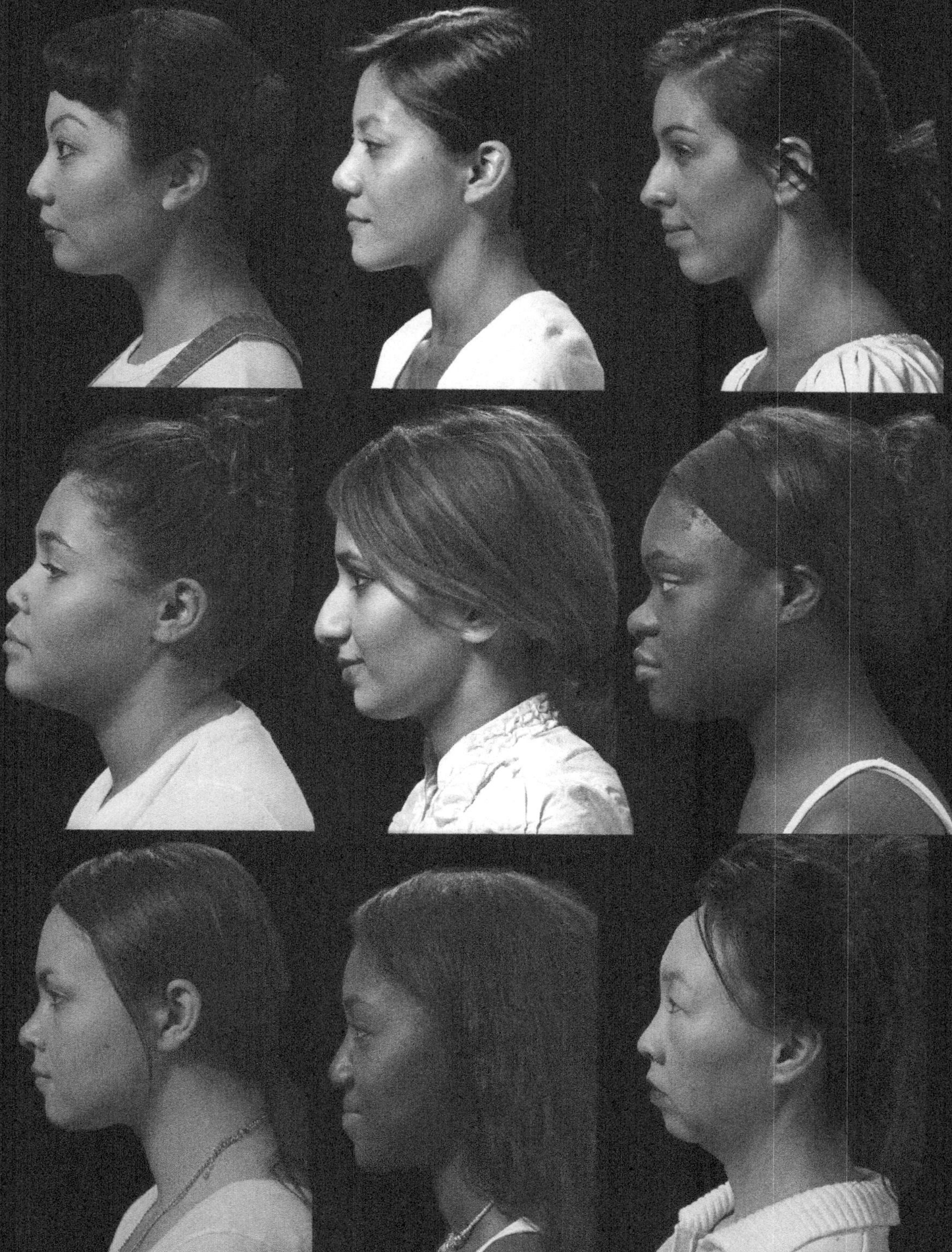

*We are all very much alike—but our faces portray unique differences, as demonstrated by these people who claim ancestry from around the world.*

# THE HUMAN FACE

All humans have a common ancestry. Our faces and bodies may portray unique differences, but we are all very much alike. A clear explanation of where we all come from is not yet agreed upon by human society—though social and behavioral anthropologists, religious institutions, science fiction writers, and cultural philosophers have all chimed in. We cannot say for certain how and where our minute differences in physical construct originated. We only know that people from different parts of the world show tendencies common to the founding families of their communities. To mix things all up, humans have wandered off to new lands to make families in faraway communities each and every generation since humans could travel.

The author's perspective in this book is that the earth is one giant ball of meshed genes. In areas where lines of a family have existed for centuries, certain physical attributes may dominate a human settlement. These attributes are further enhanced by the diet of that region (for example, whether meat is a staple), how much sunlight is experienced in a common day, and what mutations survive in this environment. Forensic anthropology supplies us with rich information and empirical data on regional characteristics. These physical attributes are tools for character designers whose game, toy, and film products are now on the world stage. It is more important than ever for character designers to research the communities they wish to portray. Why? The people who live in those regions want to be respected through the accurate portrayal of their physical characteristics. People will bond with characters they identify with. The character designer is a critical link to creating international appeal.

In this text, we explore the unique features present in the human face, and provide comparison to skulls found near a model's claim of ancestral lineage. We will present models from all over the world for you to analyze for regional traits as a stepping stone into creating your own research. The results of our photo shoot study are fascinating. We consider this book an important snap shot in time cataloging what a piece the human looks like today. In another generation, our genes will have pooled again—taking us another giant step further away from regional identification.

In some cases, we can readily identify someone's ancestral lineage as having resided in regions around Asia, Africa, the Americas, or Europe, among others. In some cases, we cannot readily identify someone as having ancestors born in or near any region—as the model will show characteristics common to several regions. This is valuable to know too, as it makes us aware that we cannot stereotype a feature to a region. Our study will also explore what makes the typical female face unique to the typical male face. Structural differences between the two are sometimes very subtle, depending on the individual. We have provided the measurements of every face so that you can compare and contrast features on your favorite models.

The next generation born will make a huge change in our physical identity. Transportation has become much cheaper and safer. We have models in this text claiming globally opposite genetic heritage—lineage from countries as far away from each other as Ireland and Malaysia, or Africa, the Philippines, and the United States. We are no longer isolated communities of limited gene pools.

*A family from China.*

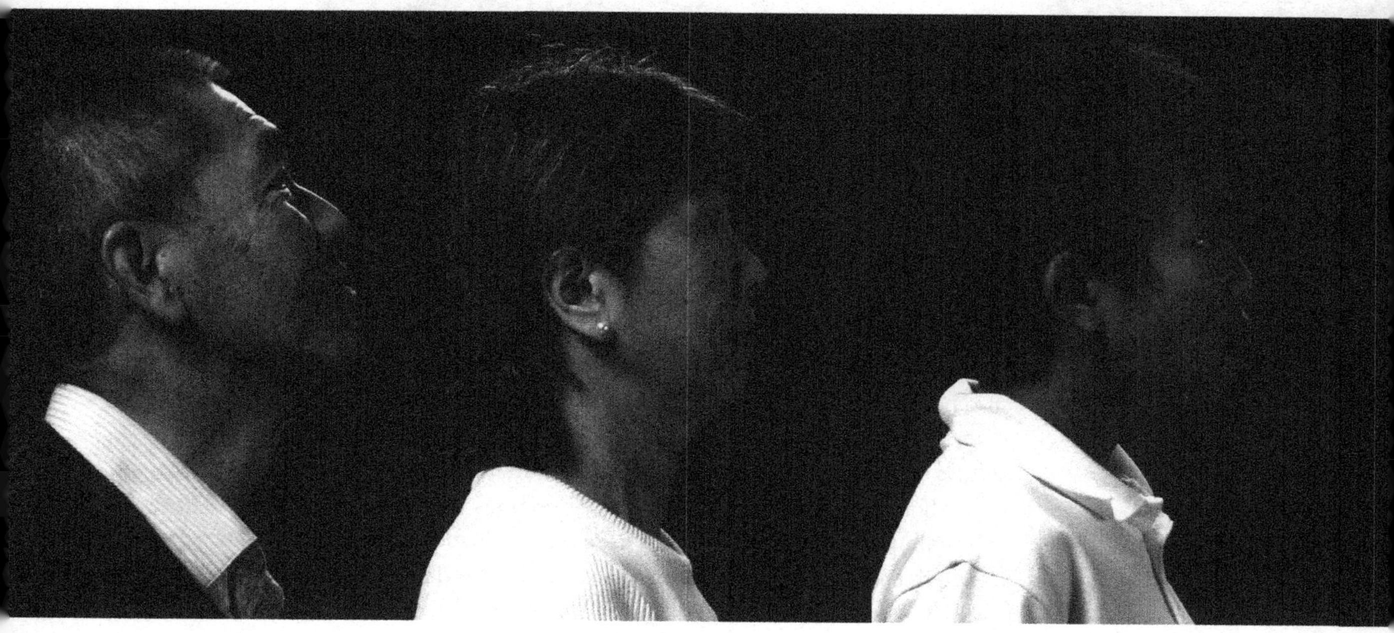

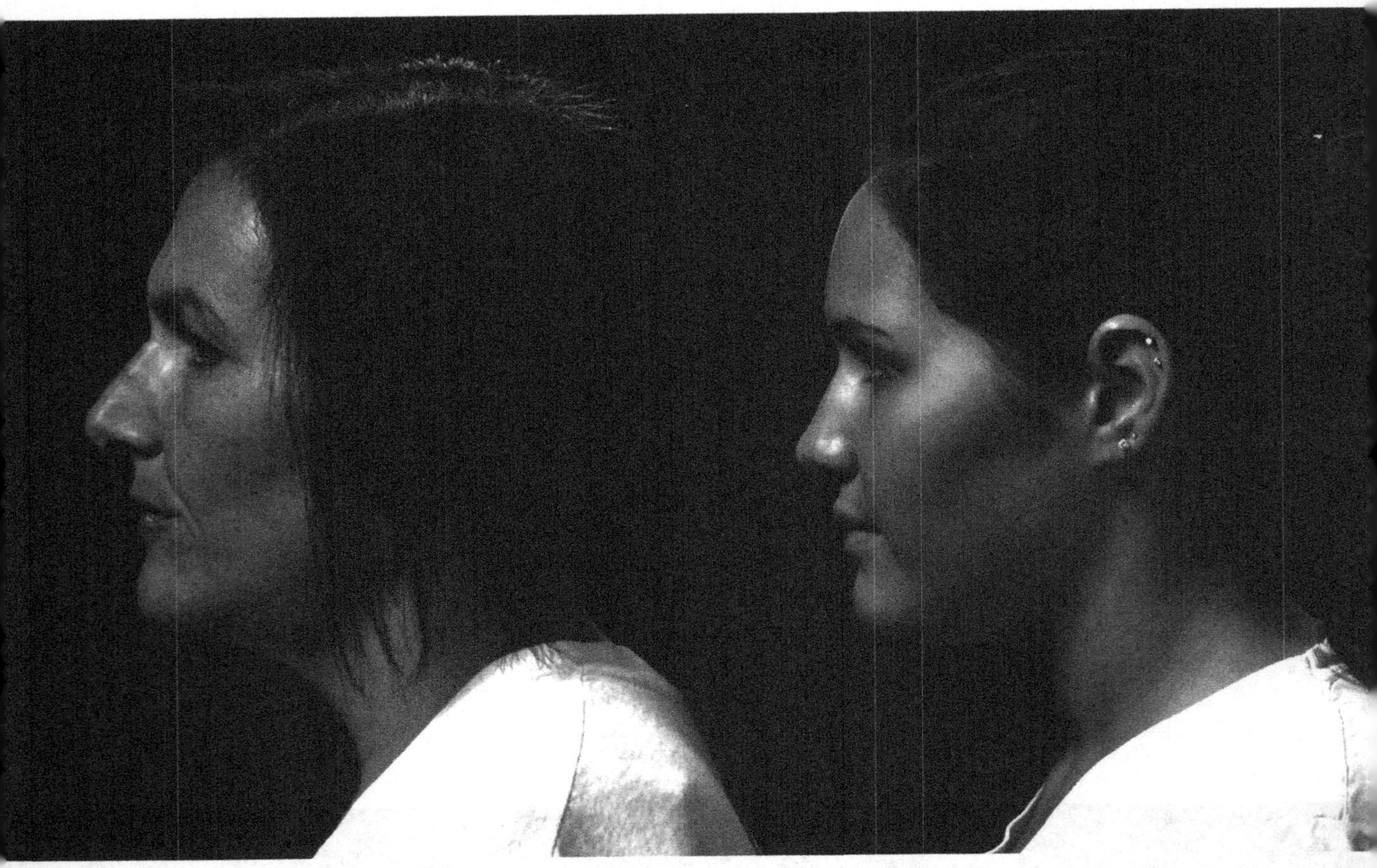

Mother and daughter.

It may appear unusual to you that we are organizing people by self-identified region of ancestry instead of ethnicity. Race is a recent classification of people, and some consider it an unfair method. Human evolution, racial mapping, and ethnicity are hotly debated topics amongst anthropologists. The authors of this text are not anthropologists. We are artists in search of research material to provide a greater depth to our character designs. We are in search of identifiable physical characteristics typical in some ancestral lineages, whose understanding will allow us to create a believable diversity in 3D character modeling. Our goal is to gather visual information about the many diverse populations living on earth and use this information to discover the rich details that make us each unique race. We do not create this text to identify one ethnicity with tiny noses, thin lips, or bulbous ear lobes. Rather, we seek to celebrate the unique features that provide information about how our ancestors traveled, and how these travels influence character design.

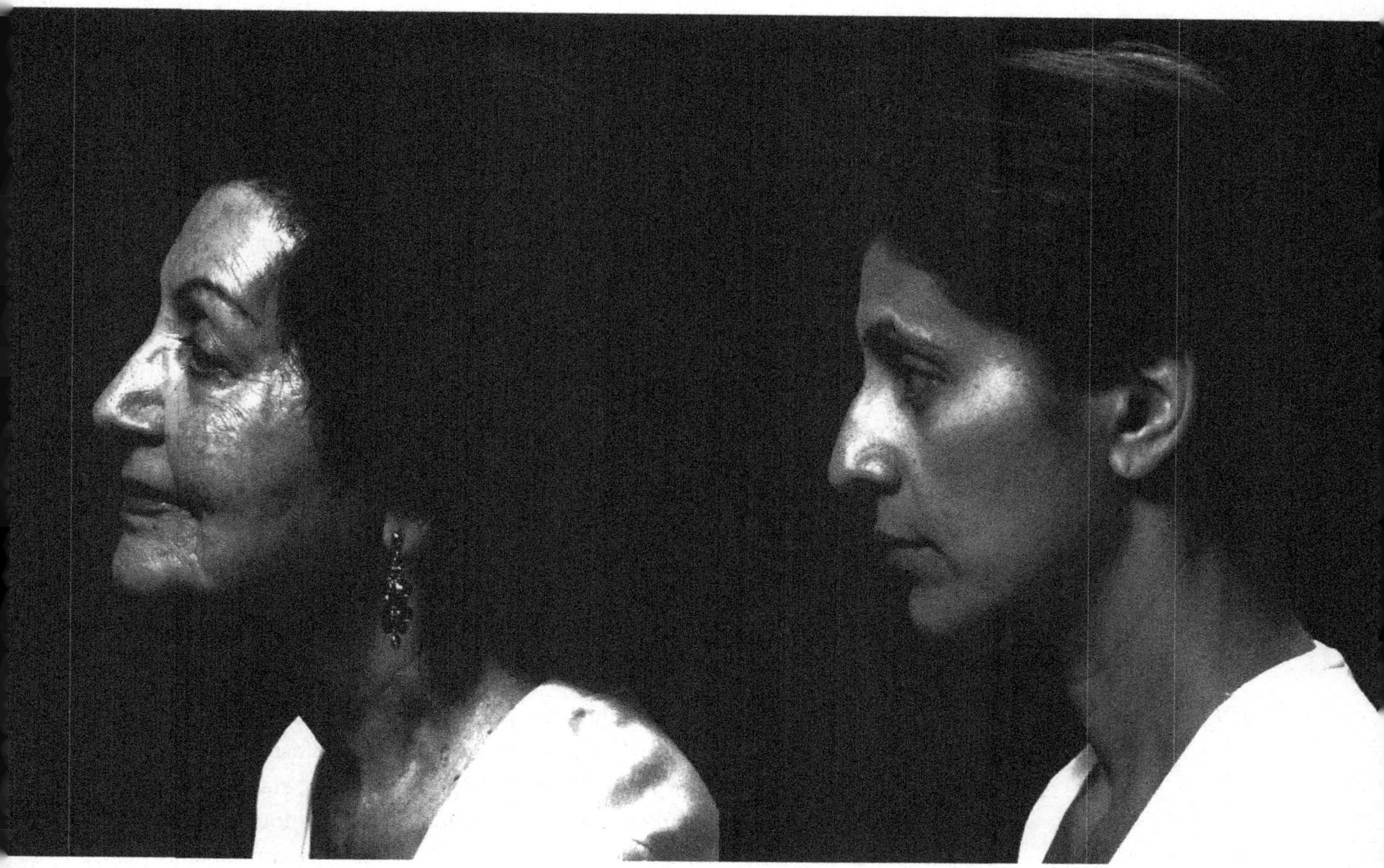

Mother and daughter.

Humans do not have physical differences based on which side of a country's border they are born on. The border was not always there. And, as in the case of Russia, borders can change in just one generation. So, we will avoid stating that a person looks a certain way because it is a common trait in a certain country. We will instead map our models to different regions in the world, and hope in time to grow a large database of such images that all artists can draw from. For the sake of our study, we will allow all of the models to self-identify their ancestral homes by the name of the country their parents came from. We were unable to cover every country in the world with our small sample, but we do have a disparate sample from around the globe. We hope this is enough to raise awareness of morphological variation in the human species.

Historically, the organization of regional ancestral lineage was based on a method of categorization initiated by Dr. W.W. Howells (1973, 1989, 1995) and his long-term study of craniometric variation in modern humans. He categorized ancestral lineage from six world regions: Europe, Sub-Saharan Africa, Australasia, Polynesia, the Americas, and the Far East.

Today, the United Nations has unofficially categorized member states into five geopolitical regional groups, and one non-UN member group. These groups are: the African group, the Asia-Pacific group, the Eastern European group, the Latin American and Caribbean group, the Western European and others group, and the non-UN state or territory. The groups span across continents, but Africa's region stays central to its continent.

Anthropologists once used Typology to categorize members of the human species by physical traits such as head shape, skin color, hair form, body build and stature back in the late 19th and early 20th centuries. Caleton S. Coon created the five classifications. The typological model divided people from different ethnic regions into races. He labeled them, in 1962, as: Negroid race, Caucasoid race, Mongoloid race, Australoid race, and Capoid race. Typology is now considered by some a contributor to racism and no longer used to categorize people.

Empirical evidence has shown that geographic variation actually has very little to do with why we look different from each other. Professor John Relethford, from the State University of York College at Oneonta, states that previous studies of genetic markers and mitochondrial DNA have found that the amount of variation among major geographic groupings of *Homo sapiens* is relatively low, accounting for roughly 10% of total variation (Relethford, 1994). These data were derived from six core areas: Europe, Sub-Saharan Africa, Australasia, Polynesia, the Americas, and the Far East. An additional set of analyses was performed using a three-region subset (Europe, Sub-Saharan Africa, and the Far East) to provide comparability with several genetic studies. Relethford (1994) determined that there is little limited variation in modern human skulls among major geographic regions.

---

Howells, W. W. 1973 *The Pacific Islanders.* London: Weidenfeld and Nicolson.

Howells, W. W. 1989 *Skull Shapes and the Map: Craniometric Analysis in the Dispersion of Modern Homo. Papers of the Peabody Museum of Archaeology and Ethnology, Vol. 79.* Cambridge: Harvard University Press.

Howells, W. W. 1995 *Who's Who in Skulls: Ethnic Identification of Crania From Measurements. Papers of the Peabody Museum of Archaeology and Ethnology, Vol. 82.* Cambridge: Harvard University Press.

Relethford (1994) states that a great deal of genetic variation is among individuals within groups, and physical differences are not due to variation among groups. This further negates the Typology system of racial classification. Authors Stringer and Andrews (1988) state that humans show "great morphological variation. However, in contrast to this, genetic variation between human populations is low overall" (p. 1264).

If we are all so similar, why is it we are able to distinguish the features of people from regions other than our own, and identify them as from a different part of the world? Our eye is finely tuned to this small percentage of genetic and sexual variation. Let's look at the structure of a basic human skull so that we have a common ground to base our comparisons.

# UNITED NATIONS REGIONAL GROUPS

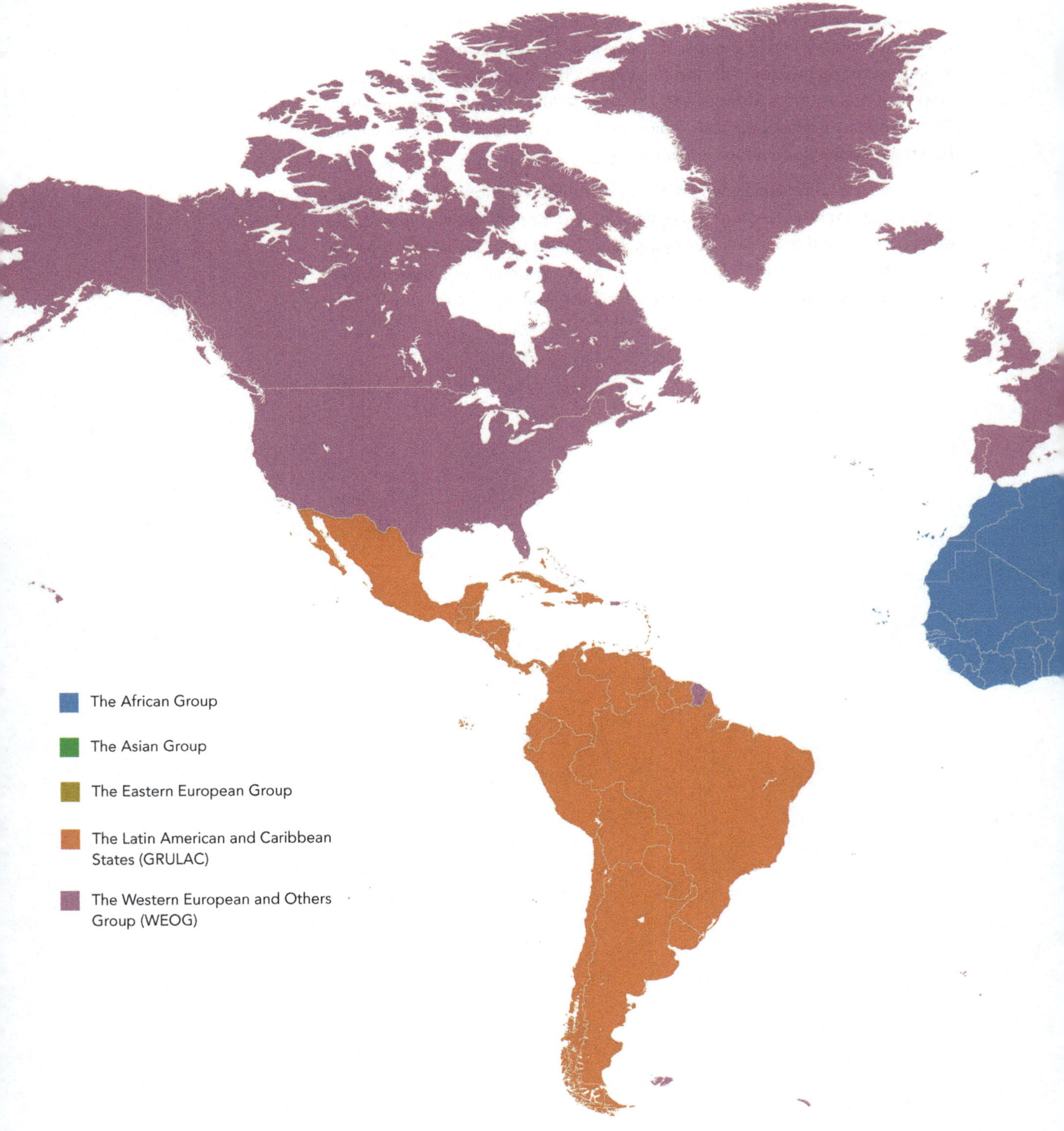

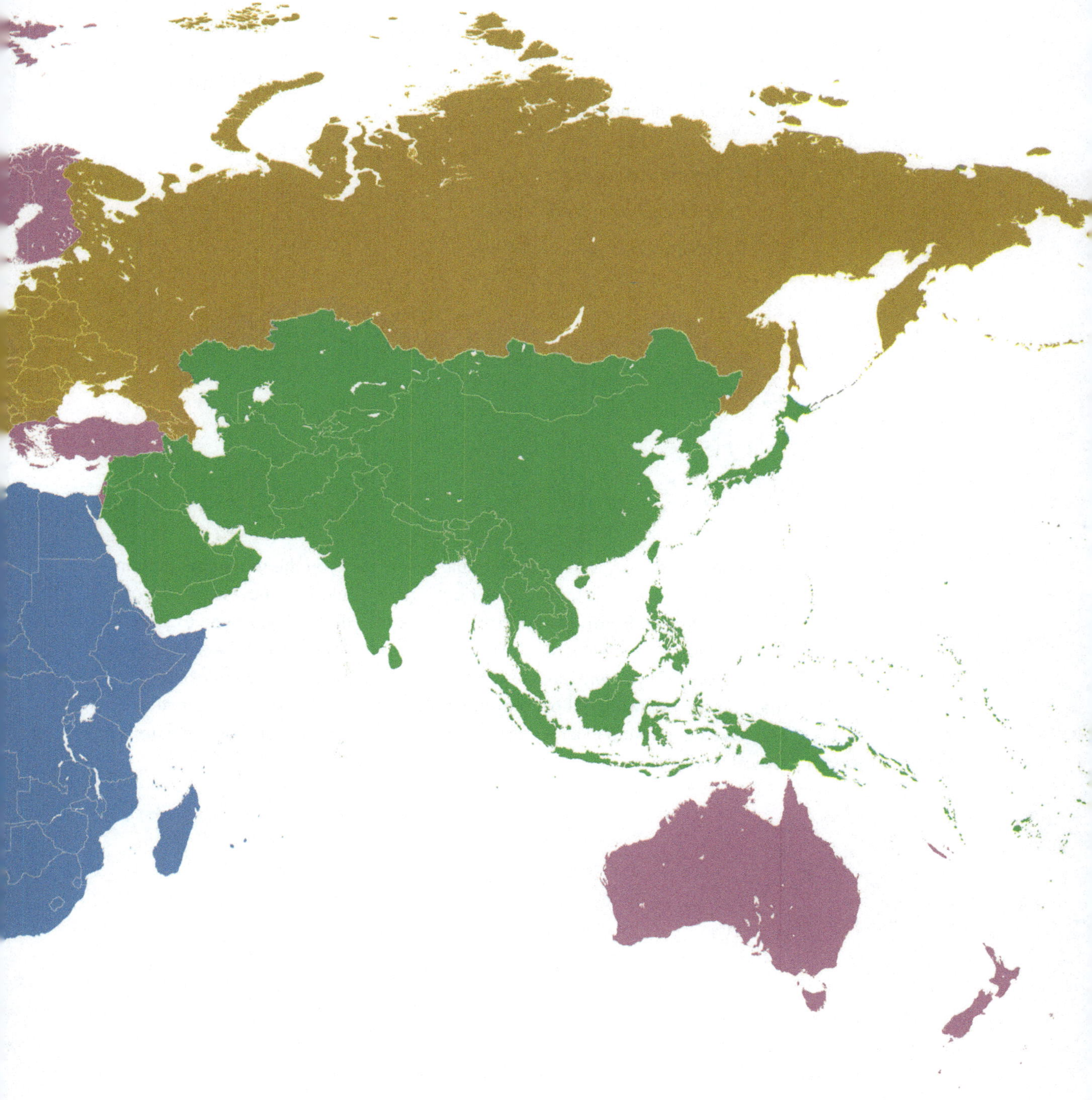

### VARIATIONS

Anatomists have determined from head and skull shape that there are three types of heads. Look for them in the following photos. They use a term for measurement of the head, cephalic index, to determine these head types. The three classifications are:

1. Dolichochocephalic: long head
2. Mesocephalic: medium head
3. Brachycephalic: broad head

## ANATOMY OF THE HUMAN HEAD: ESTABLISHING A VOCABULARY

These are three images of a human skull. I won't tell you the region this is from yet. It looks like a basic human skull right? How would you know what part of the world it came from? Markers exist on this skull that will allow you to identify features typical to human identity form different regions around the world. We hope to provide you with an introductory understanding of these markers so that you can be aware of how they structurally influence facial characteristics, and have been found in larger samples to provide evidence of characteristics typical to a region.

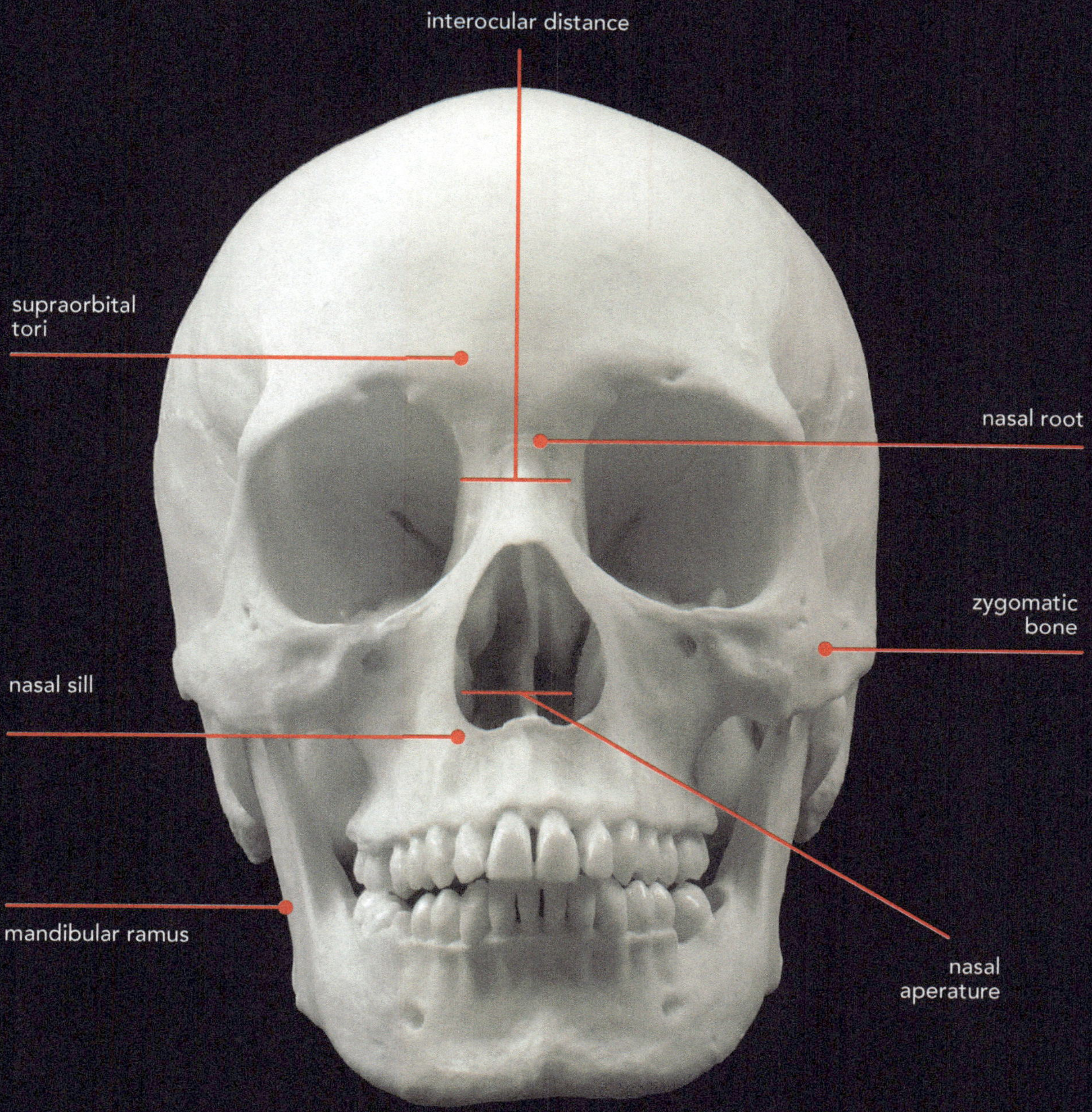


*A basic human skull, front view. Major terms demonstrated.*

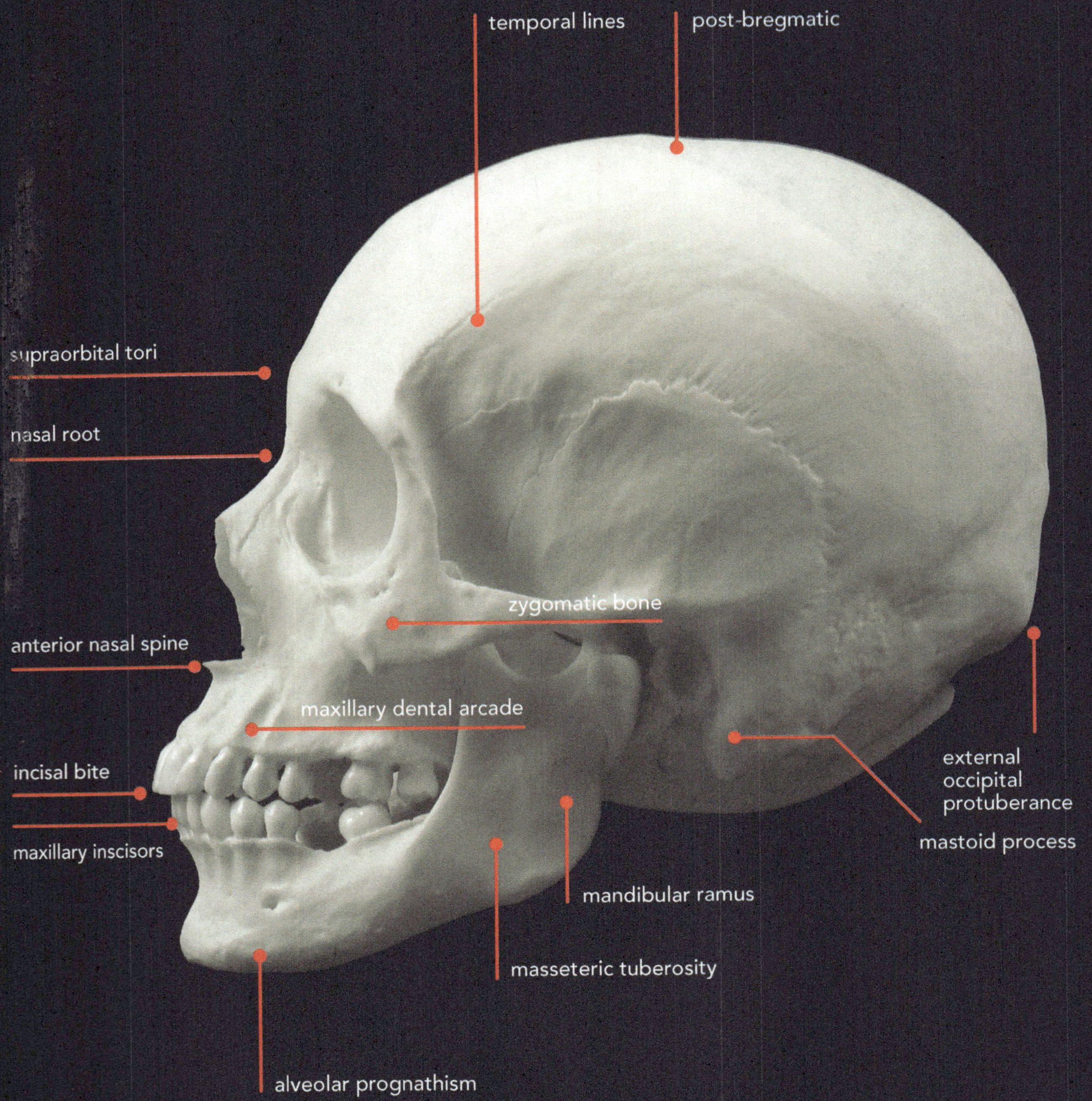
temporal lines
post-bregmatic
supraorbital tori
nasal root
zygomatic bone
anterior nasal spine
maxillary dental arcade
incisal bite
maxillary inscisors
external occipital protuberance
mastoid process
mandibular ramus
masseteric tuberosity
alveolar prognathism

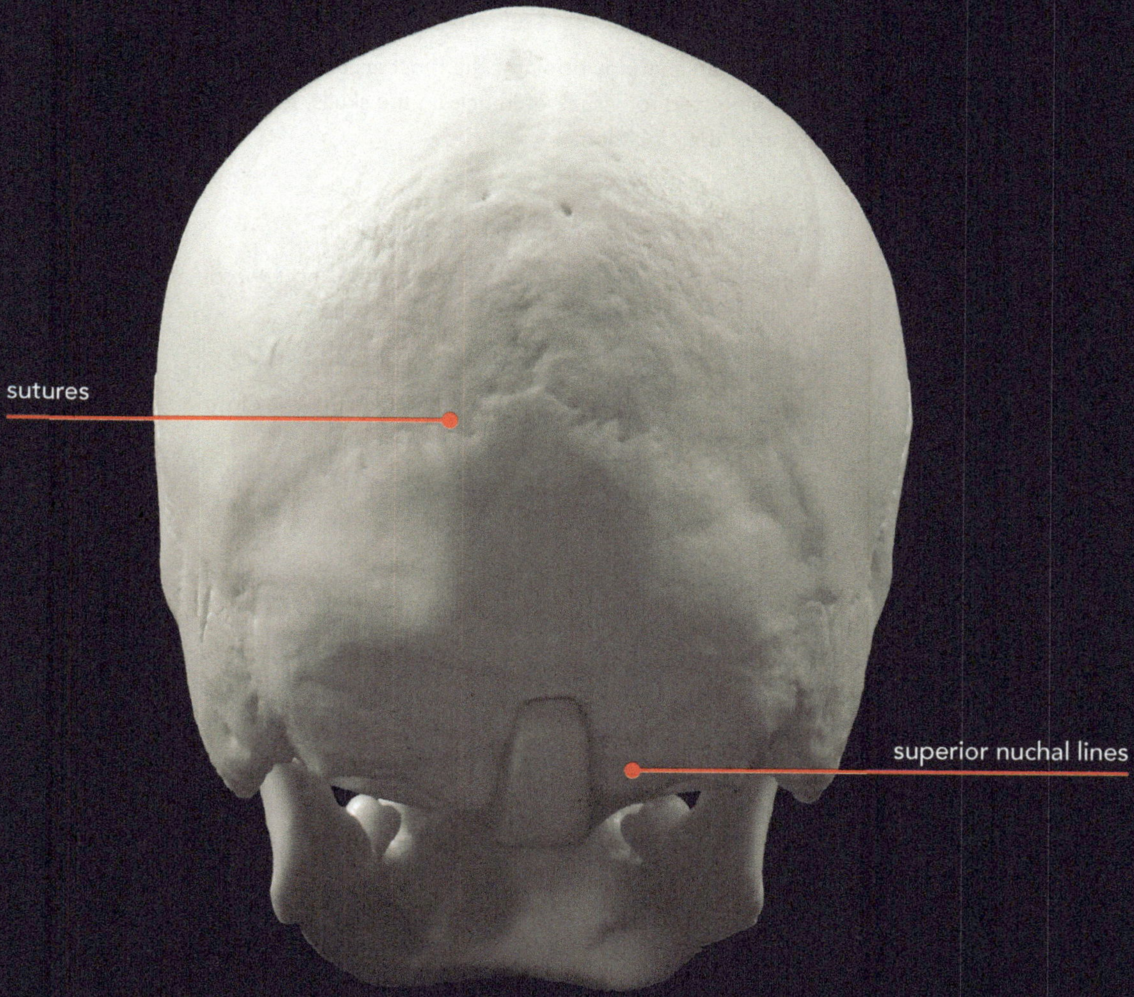


*A basic human skull, back view. Major terms demonstrated.*

# GENERAL TERMS

Please consult an anatomy book for the most accurate description of terms. The terms are listed for visual reference on the skulls, followed by a general description of their location.

- Anterior—toward the front of the body
- Lateral—extending away from the middle, moving towards the side of the body
- Median—midline, going through the center of the head
- Medial—extending towards the middle, moving away from the side of the body
- Posterior—toward the back of the body
- Superior—toward the top
- Inferior—toward the bottom

**Interocular distance:** this measurement is the distance between the eyes, and is also commonly referred to as the interpupillary distance.

**Nasal root:** the nasal root is found at the top of the nose. It is where the nasal bone meets the frontal bone.

**Zygomatic bone:** this is the term for the cheek bone.

**Nasal aperture:** the nasal aperture describes the width, length and depth of the nose, seen when looking upward at the nostrils.

**Anterior nasal spine:** this is at the bottom of the nose above the teeth, and is a small sharp protrusion from the skull.

**Nasal sill:** this is the floor of the nasal opening. It is best viewed upwards facing the nostrils. It is the bottom of the nose, with the nostrils above it and the tip of the nose above the nostrils.

**Maxillary dental arcade:** this is the bone that holds the upper teeth of the mouth.

**Maxillary incisors:** front teeth in the upper jaw.

**Incisal bite:** this refers to how the upper and lower teeth meet—the bite.

**Alveolar prognathism:** jaw protruding forward.

**Post-bregmatic depression:** a dent in the top of the skull.

**Sutures:** these are the fibrous joints in the skull. There are many of them that join together the many pieces of the skull.

**Nuchal lines:** these lines are four curved ridges on the occipital bone, found on the back bottom of the skull.

**External occipital protuberance:** this runs between the nuchal lines.

**Mastoid process:** this is the bony protrusion found behind the ear.

**Temporal lines:** these two lines cross the middle of the parietal bone.

**Supraorbital tori:** this is the bony ridge above the eye sockets.

**Masseteric tuberosities:** this refers to the rough surface on the mandible bone.

**Occipital condyles:** these are flat surfaces under the occipital bone.

**Supramastoidal crest:** this is the ridge that forms at the root of the zygomatic process of the temporal bone.

**Mandibular ramus:** part of the jaw.

Knowing these key terms and where these features are located will give us a starting place to compare other skulls too. This comparison will allow us to identify features that are different in different faces. We will often refer to this anatomical vocabulary when making observations about human faces. Memorize these terms and what they represent, as they will be used extensively in Chapter 2. Please find additional anatomy books that detail the human skull for additional information. We are artists, and specialists in anatomy will give you more information on specific bones than we can.

*A basic human skull and muscle mass, front view.*

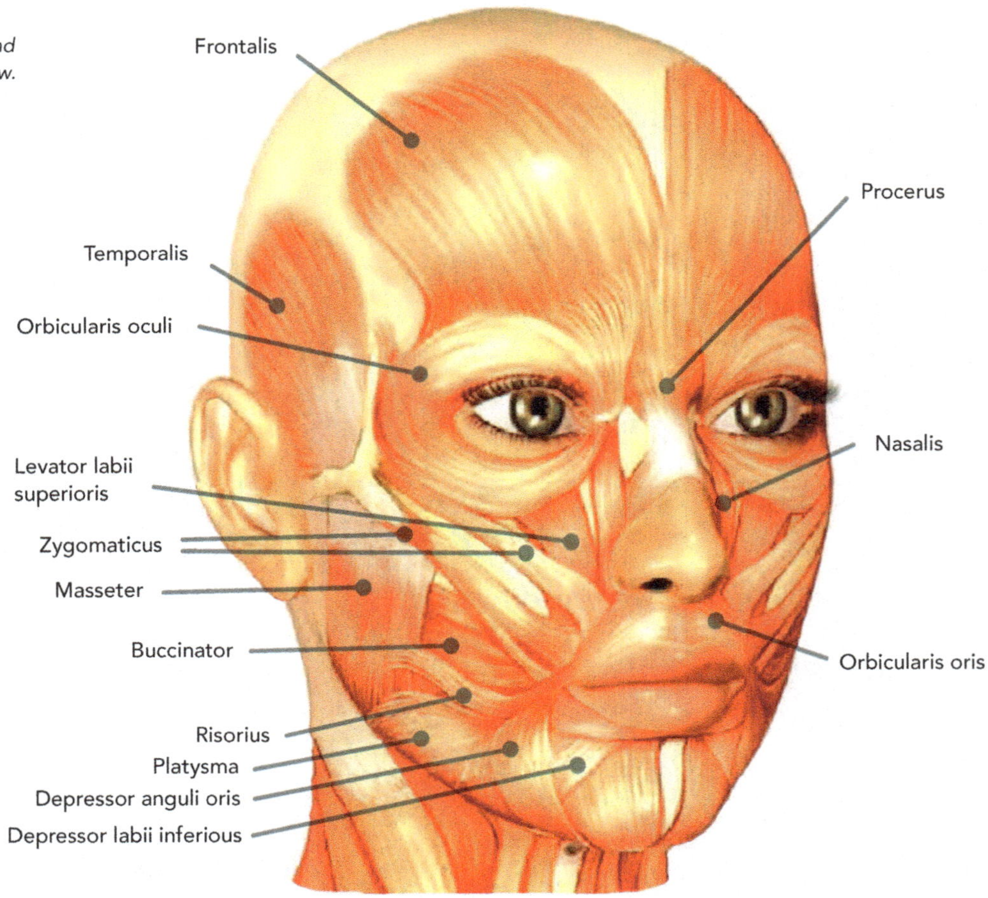

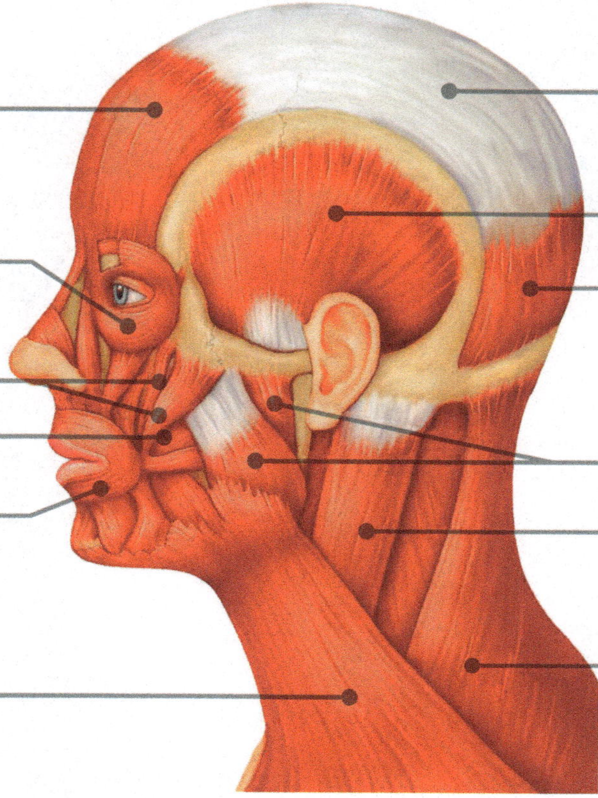


*A basic human skull and muscle mass, side view.*

These are illustrations of basic muscle groups attached to the skull. The size of these groups may vary in different faces. Fat deposits rest on top of these muscle groups, further impacting the facial features of our models. Facial anatomy is very extensive, and I urge you to couple your study of these faces with a facial anatomy text book. Our observations will only consult the basic skull.

## REFERENCES AND SUGGESTED READING

Coon, Carleton S. (1962), *The Origin of Races,* Alfred A. Knopf, Inc., 1st edition (June 1962) New York

Relethford, J.B. (1994), "Craniometric variation, genetic theory, and modern human origins," *American Journal of Physical Anthropology* 95: 53–62.

Stringer, C.B., and Andrews, P. (1988), "Genetic and fossil evidence for the origin of modern humans," *Science* 239: 1263–1268.

Gill, George W. and Rhine, Stanley, eds. (1990), *Skeletal Attribution of Race: Methods for Forensic Anthropology.* Maxwell Museum of Anthropology, Anthropological Papers No. 4 (Albuquerque, NM).

2

CHAPTER 2

# SKULLS

DOI: 10.1201/ 9781003484554-2

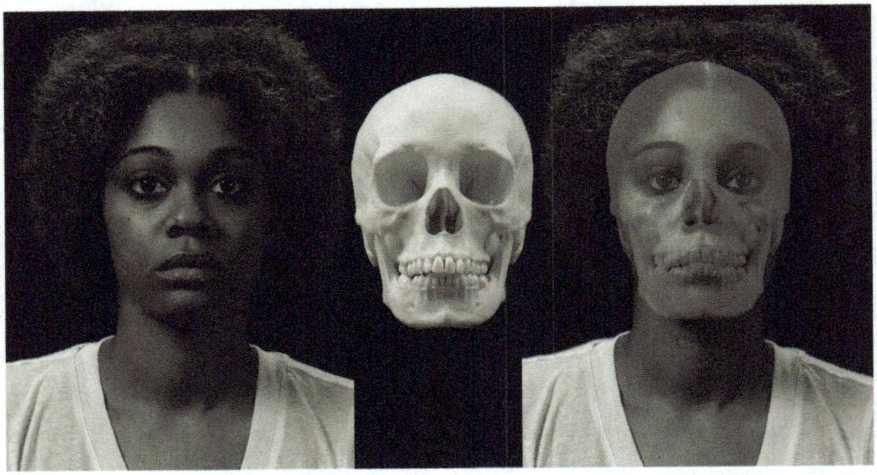

*The skull molds the face.*

# SKULLS FROM AROUND THE WORLD

Let's look at a sample of skulls collected from around the world. Note that skulls and their attributes need to be evaluated from a large sample. These attributes are not indicative of every human from that region. They are attributes measured and compared to a larger sample. Please see pages 65-67 for measurements for each of the skulls in the following sample.

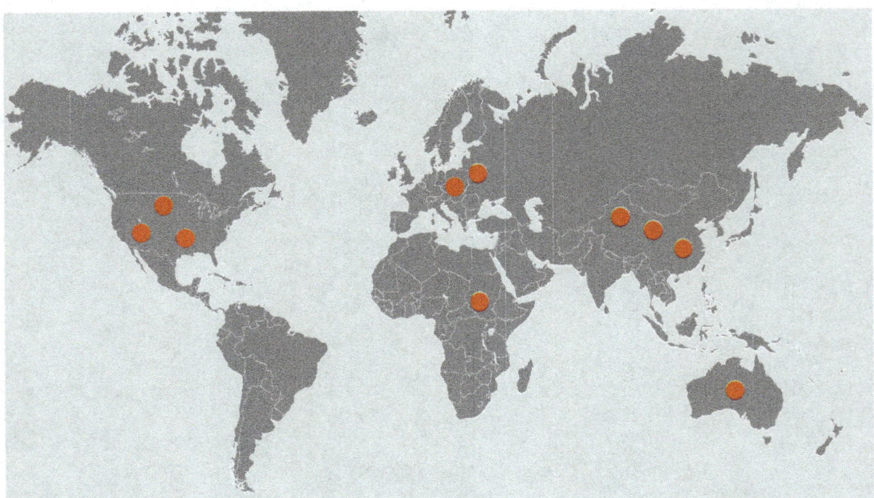

*Map of six regions, and a callout to each of the skulls identified. A pin denotes the region each one was found in.*

# AUSTRALIAN ABORIGINAL MALE SKULL

This skull was found in 1905 near the lower Darling River in New South Wales, Australia, and was known to be from a very stout 50-year old male of the Bindaboo Tribe.

**Features of this skull:**

The *interocular distance* is broad.

The *nasal root* is depressed and the *nasal angle* is obtuse.

The *zygomatic bones* retreat posteriorly from the plane of the face.

The *nasal aperture* is broad superiorly and inferiorly.

The *anterior nasal spine* is short, and the inferior margin of the nasal aperture has a bilateral gutter (right greater than left).

There is no *nasal sill.*

The *maxillary dental arcade* is rectangular.

There is moderate *alveolar prognathism.*

The *maxillary incisors* are peg-like (because of severe attrition).

There is no *post-bregmatic depression.*

The *calvarial sutures* are focally complex.

**Features of sex:**

There is marked prominence of the cranial sites for musculofacial attachment including especially:

- the nuchal lines
- the external occipital protuberance
- the mastoid processes of the temporal bones
- the temporal lines (slight)
- the supraorbital tori
- the masseteric tuberosities of the mandible
- the occipital condyles
- the supramastoidal crest

There is a broad ascending mandibular ramus. The nasion is markedly rough, and the supraorbital margins are blunted. The inferior border of the mandible is square.

www.boneclones.com, Dr. Evan Matshes, BSc MD.

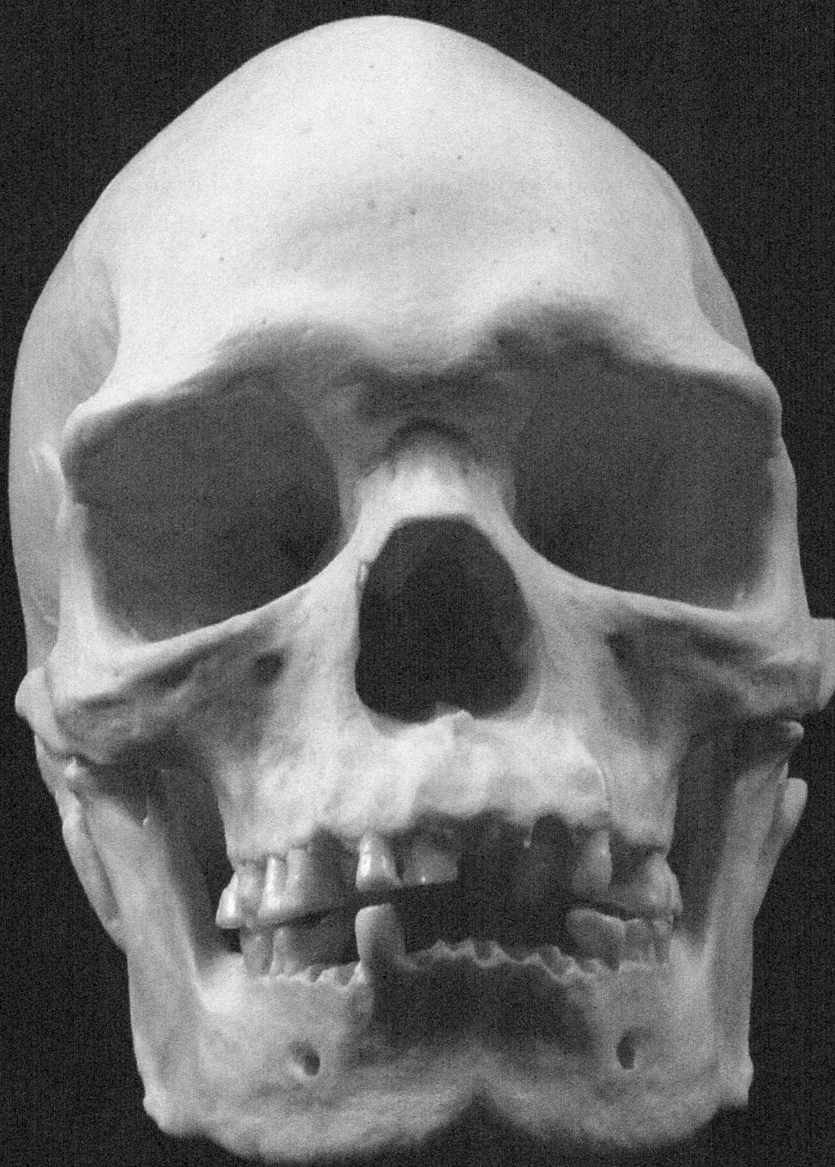

*Australian Aboriginal male.*

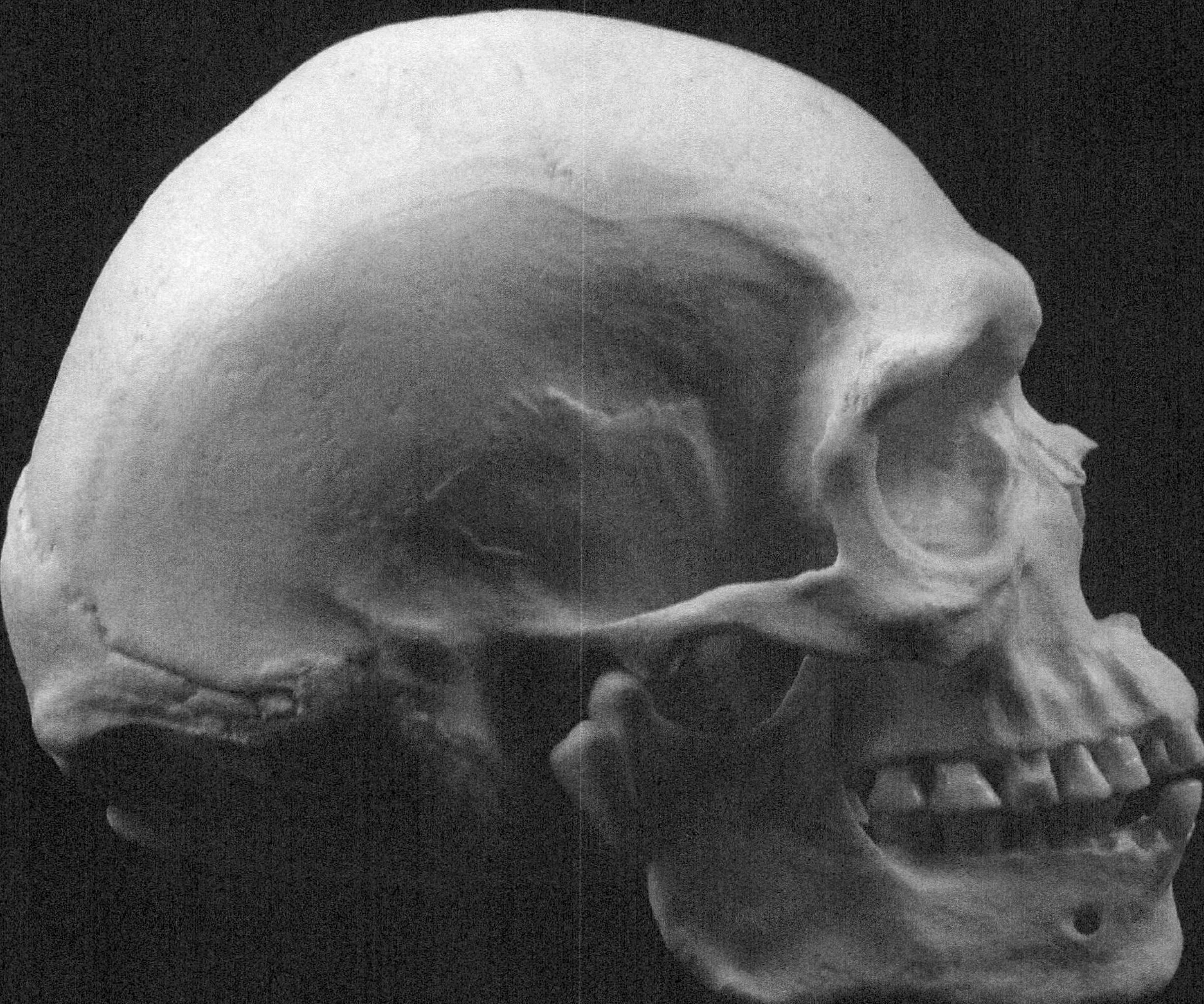

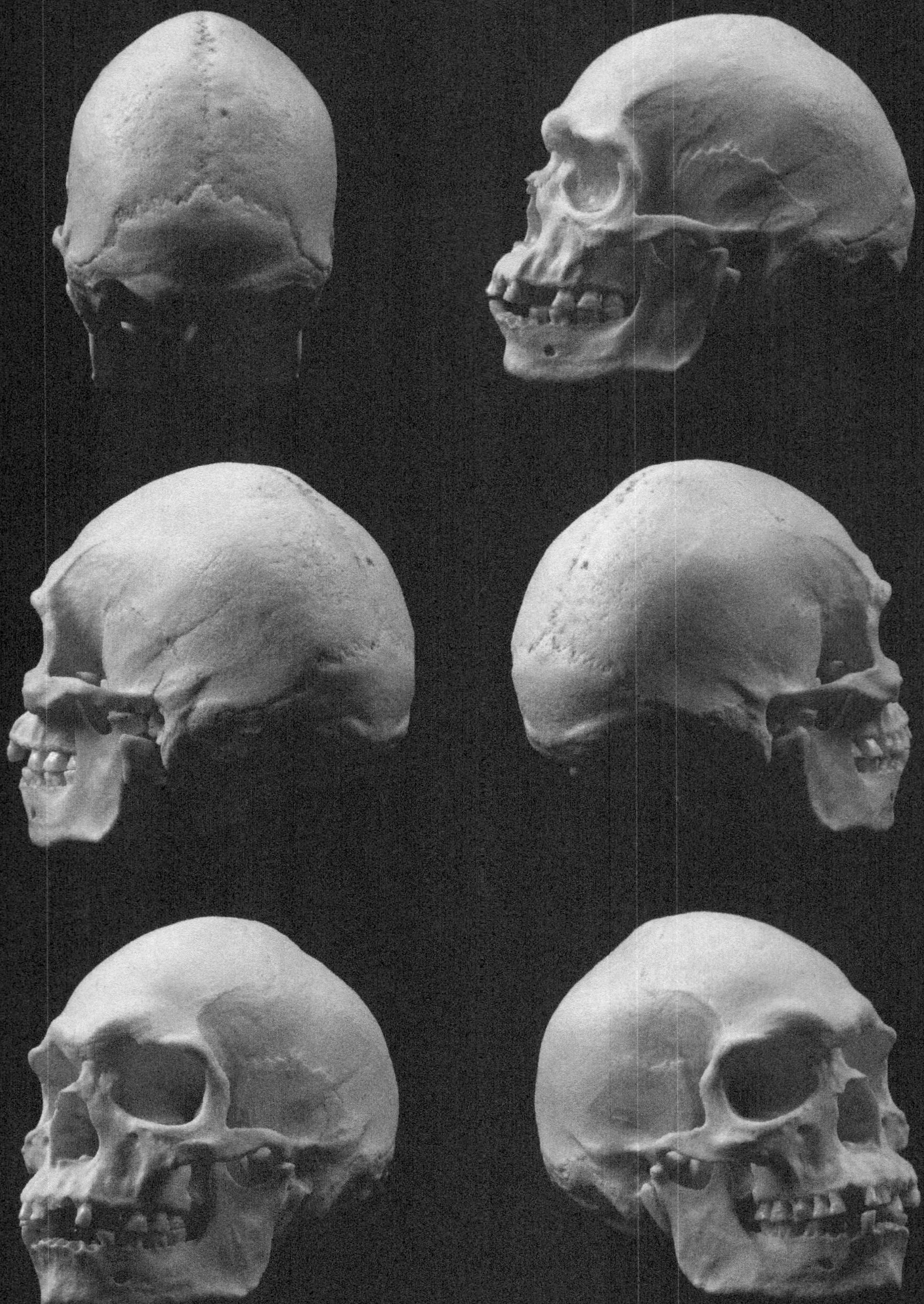

*Australian Aboriginal male.*

# AFRICAN AMERICAN FEMALE SKULL

**Features of this skull:**

The interocular distance is slightly widened.

The nasal root is not prominent and the nasal angle is obtuse.

The zygomatic bones retreat posteriorly from the plane of the face.

The nasal aperture is broad superiorly and inferiorly.

The anterior nasal spine is somewhat prominent, and the inferior margin of the nasal aperture has a sharp (nasal) sill, and a very slight suggestion of a right gutter.

The maxillary dental arcade has a rectangular shape.

There is moderate alveolar prognathism.

The maxillary incisors are blade-like, but there is the slightest suggestion of shoveling of the 1.2 [#7], 2.1 [#9], and 2.2 [#10] teeth.

There is no edge-on-edge incisal bite.

There is a slight post-bregmatic depression.

The calvarial sutures are predominantly simple.

**Features of the sex:**

There is no significant prominence of the cranial sites for musculofascial attachment.

Slight prominence is seen at:

- the external occipital protuberance
- the mastoid processes of the temporal bones
- the temporal lines
- the supramastoidal crests

There is a somewhat broad ascending mandibular ramus. The nasion is smooth, and the supraorbital margins are blunted. The inferior border of the mandible is somewhat rounded.

Estimated age: 40–60 years old.

www.boneclones.com, Dr. Evan Matshes, BSc MD.

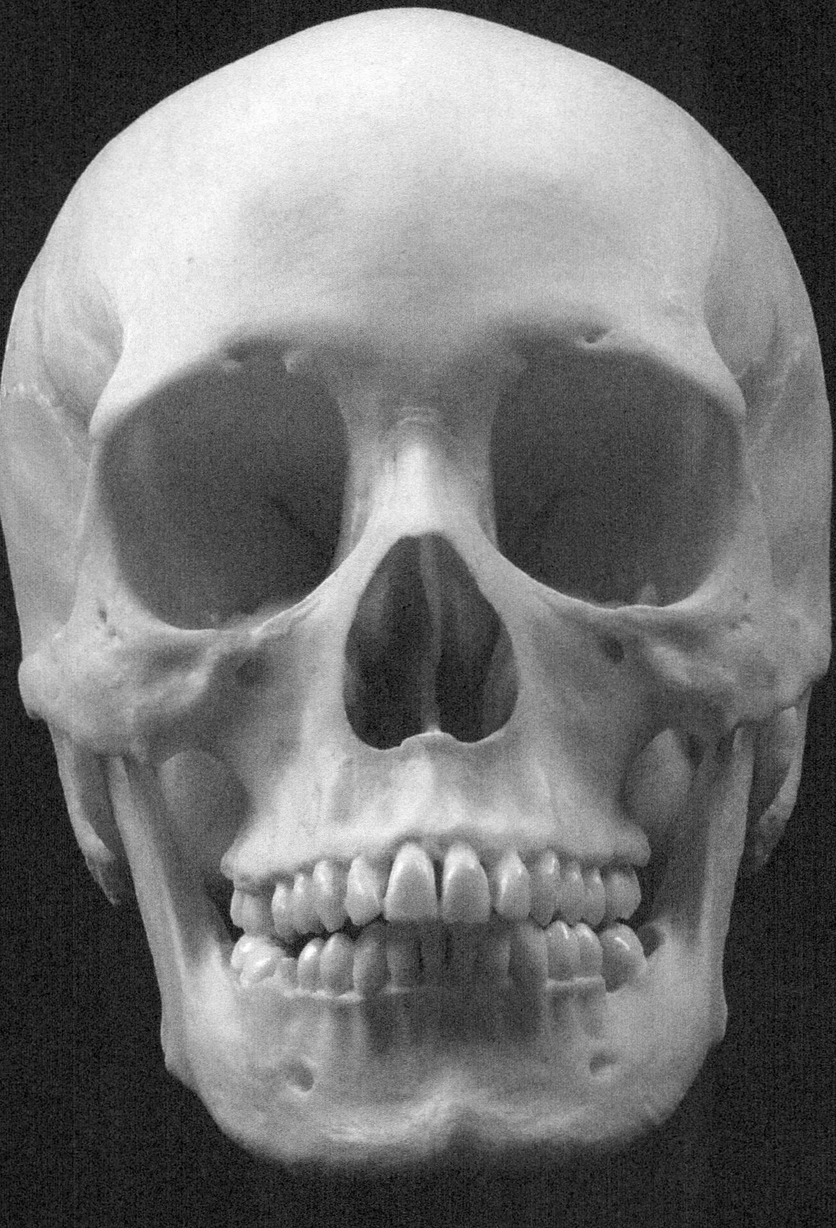

*African American female.*

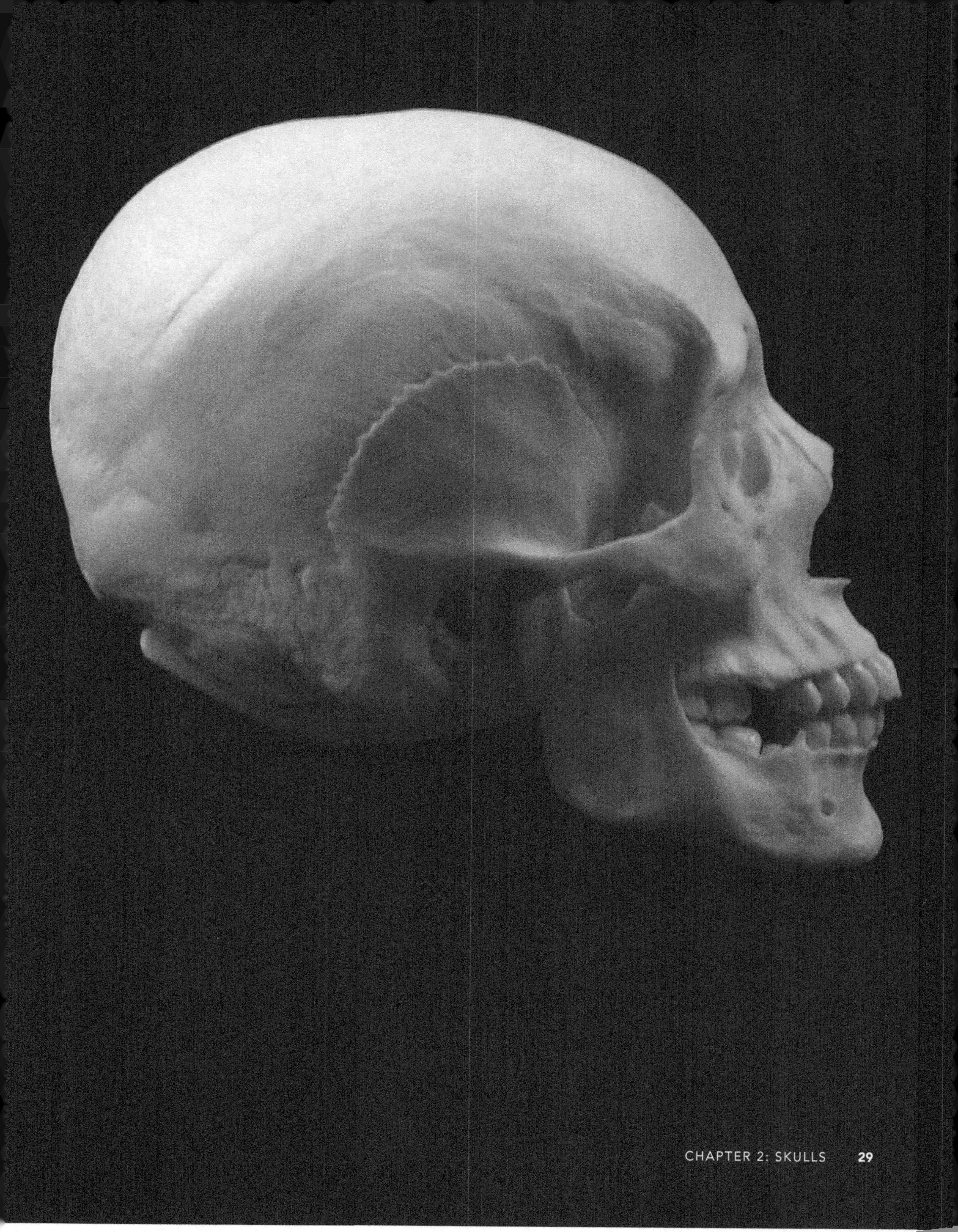

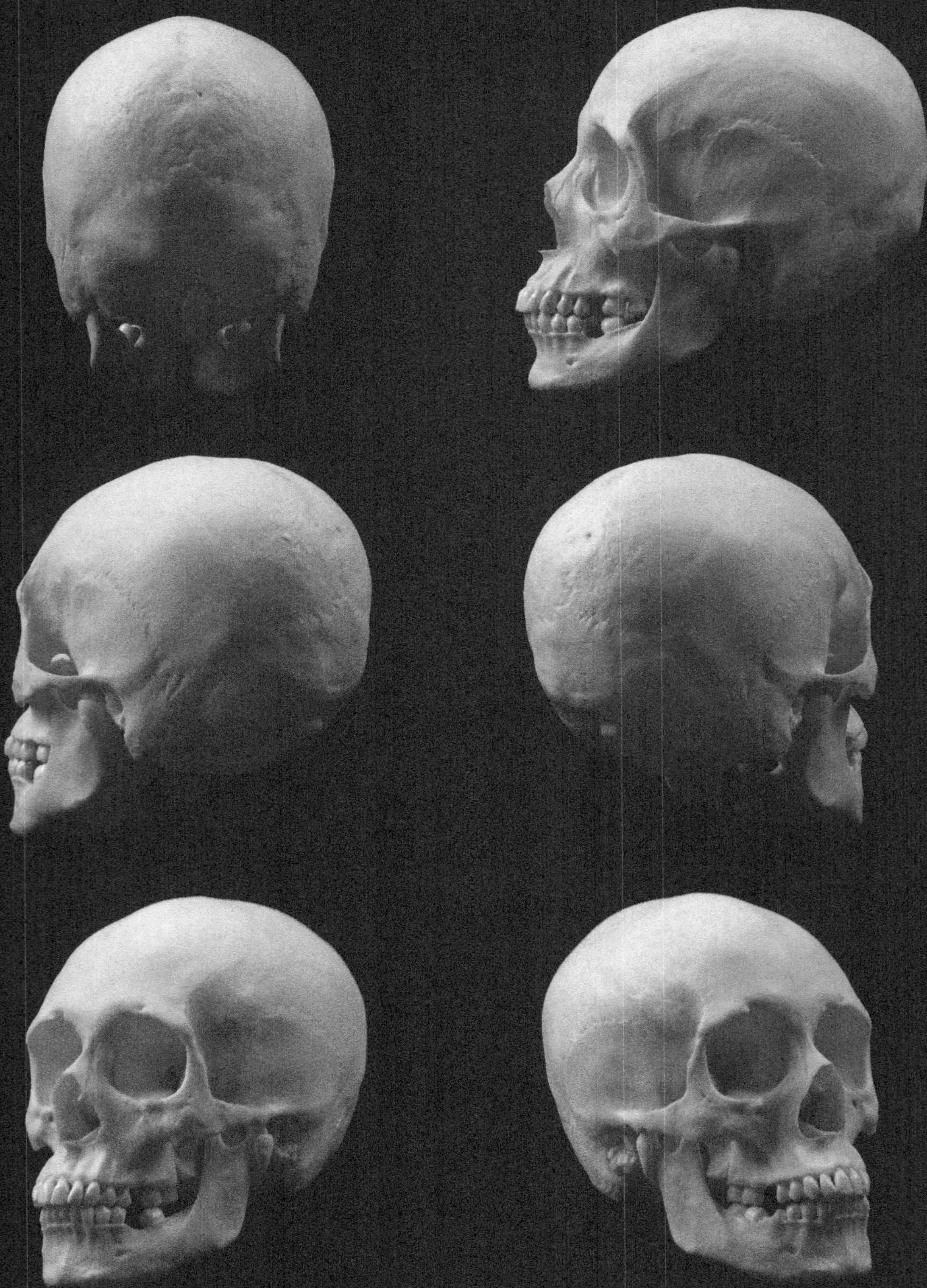

*African American female.*

# AFRICAN AMERICAN MALE SKULL

**Features of this skull:**

The interocular distance is broad.

The nasal root is depressed and the nasal angle is obtuse.

The zygomatic bones retreat posteriorly from the plane of the face.

The nasal aperture is narrow superiorly and broader inferiorly.

The anterior nasal spine is short, and the inferior margin of the nasal aperture has a bilateral gutter.

The maxillary dental arcade has a somewhat rectangular shape.

There is prominent alveolar prognathism, and the skull is elongated in the anteroposterior plane. The maxillary incisors are blade-like.

There is no edge-on-edge incisal bite.

There is a post-bregmatic depression.

The calvarial sutures are focally complex.

**Features of the sex:**

There is moderate prominence of the cranial sites for musculofascial attachment including especially:

- the nuchal lines
- the external occipital protuberance
- the mastoid processes of the temporal bones
- the temporal lines
- the supraorbital tori
- the masseteric tuberosities of the mandible
- the supramastoidal crest

There is a broad ascending mandibular ramus. The nasion is somewhat rough, and the supraorbital margins are blunted. The inferior border of the mandible is square.

Estimated age: 30–50 years old.

www.boneclones.com, Dr. Evan Matshes, BSc MD.

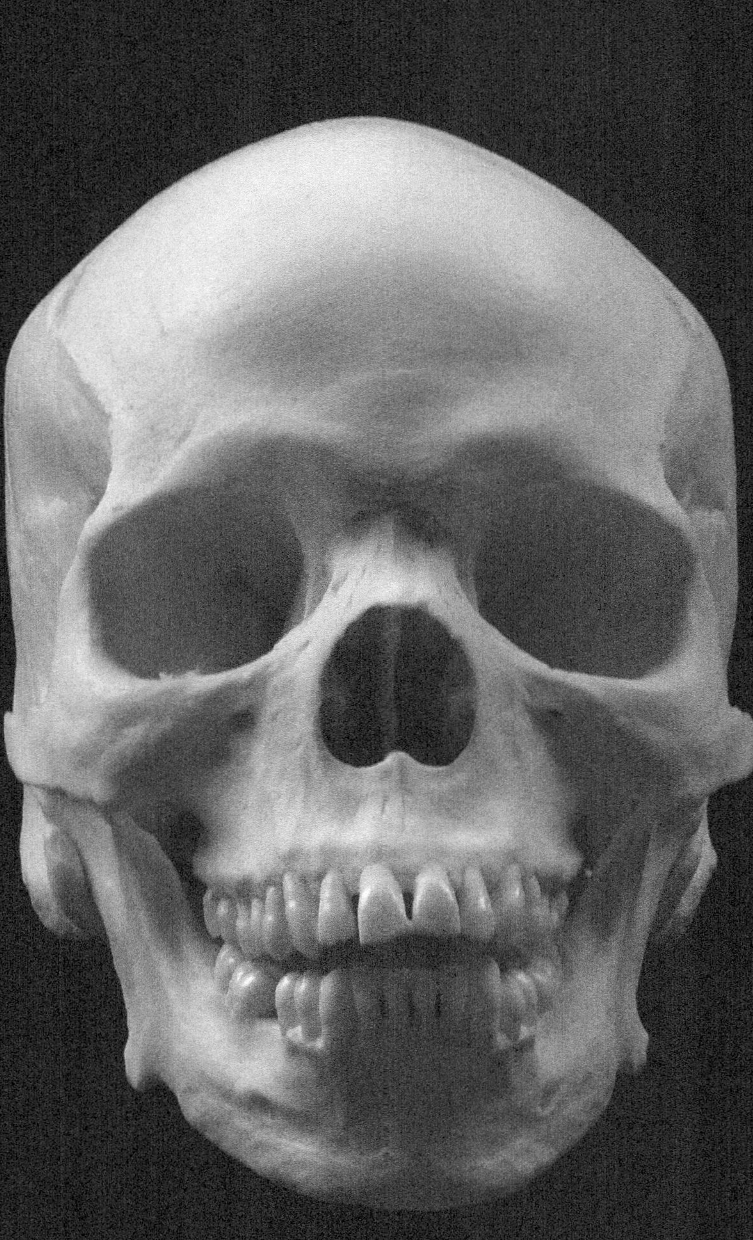

*African American male.*

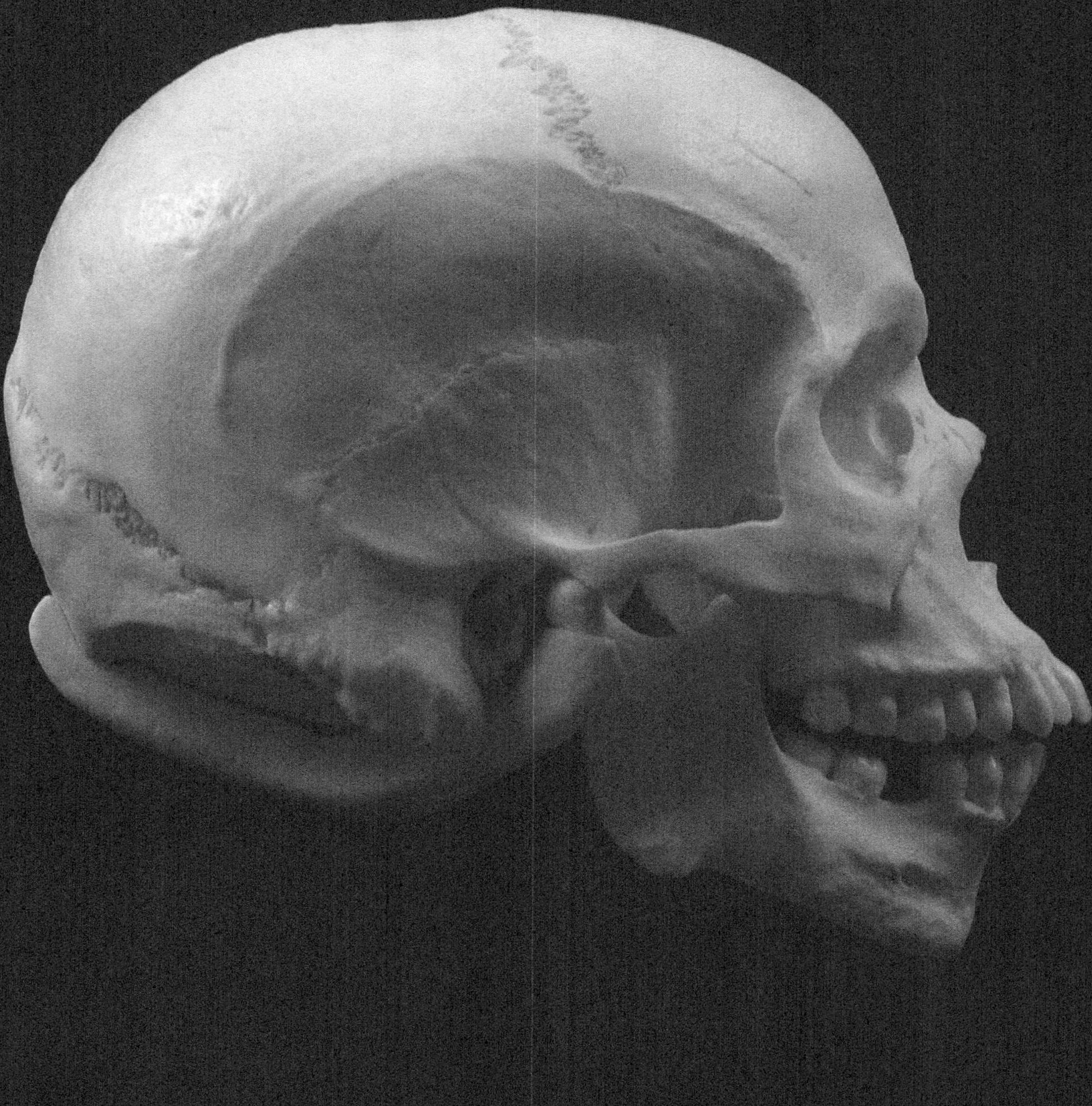

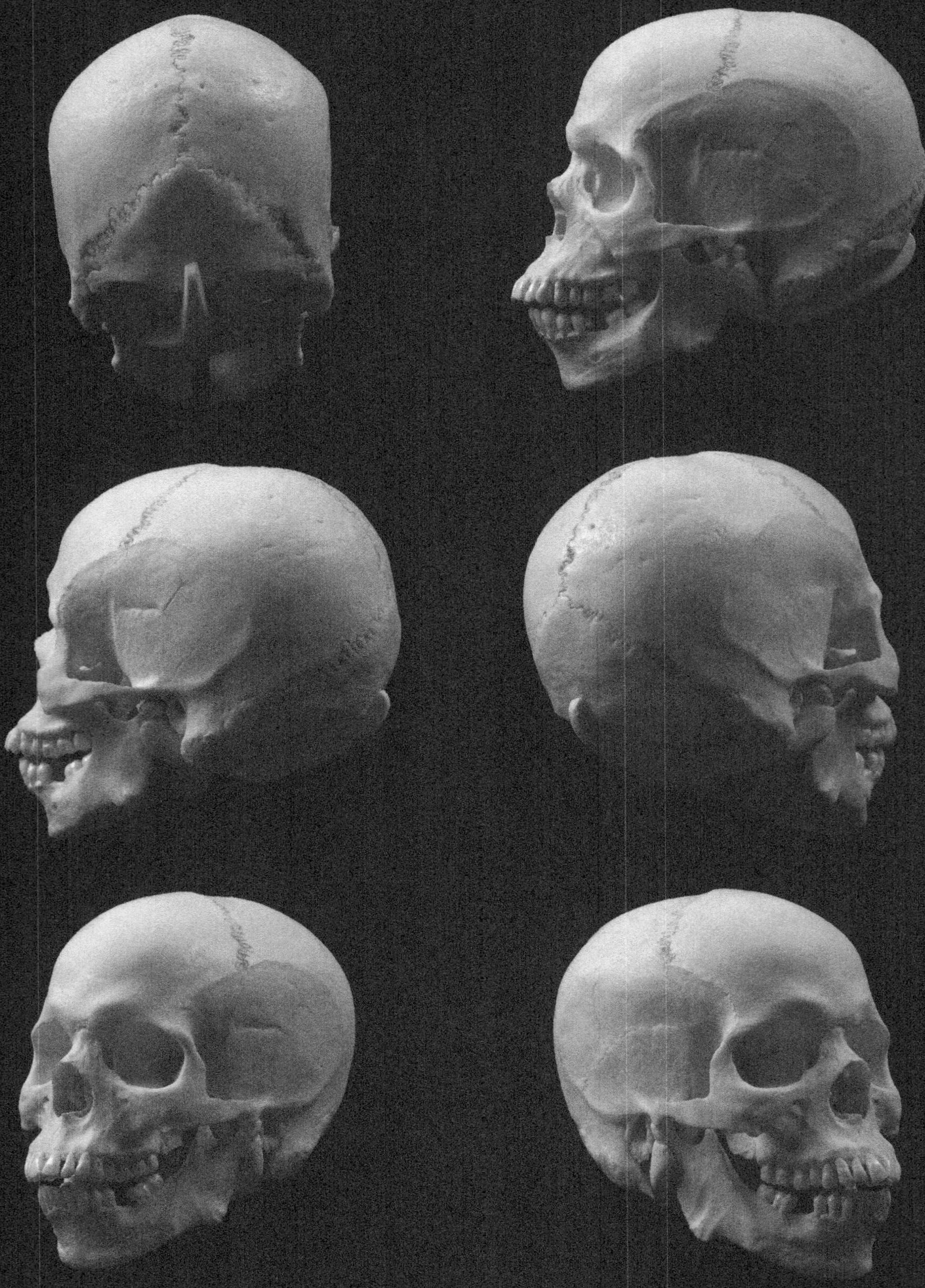

*African American male.*

# AFRICAN MALE SKULL

**Features of this skull:**

The interocular distance is broad.

The nasal root is depressed and the nasal angle is obtuse.

The zygomatic bones retreat posteriorly from the plane of the face.

The nasal aperture is markedly broad both superiorly and inferiorly.

The anterior nasal spine is short, and the inferior margin of the nasal aperture has a bilateral gutter, and there is no nasal sill. The maxillary dental arcade has a somewhat rectangular shape. There is mild to moderate alveolar prognathism.

The maxillary incisors are blade-like; however, there is a slight suggestion of shoveling on 2.1 [#9].

There is no edge-on-edge incisal bite.

There is no post-bregmatic depression.

The calvarial sutures are very slightly complex.

The skull is somewhat elongated in the antero-posterior plane.

**Features of the sex:**

There is moderate prominence of the cranial sites for musculofascial attachment including especially:

- the nuchal lines
- the external occipital protuberance
- the mastoid processes of the temporal bones
- the supraorbital tori
- the masseteric tuberosities of the mandible with gonial eversion bilaterally
- the supramastoidal crests

There is a broad ascending mandibular ramus. The nasion is smooth, and the supraorbital margins are blunted. The inferior border of the mandible is somewhat square.

Estimated age: 30–50 years old

www.boneclones.com, Dr. Evan Matshes, BSc MD.

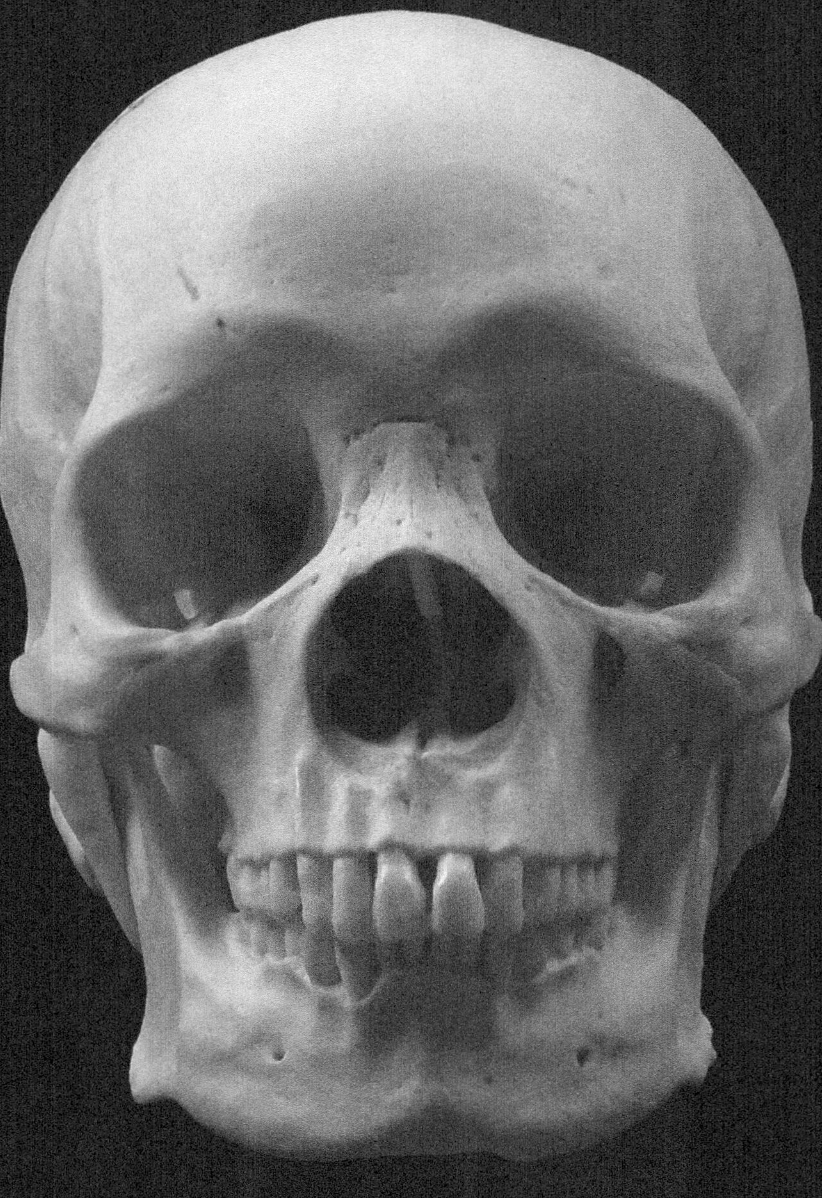

*African male.*

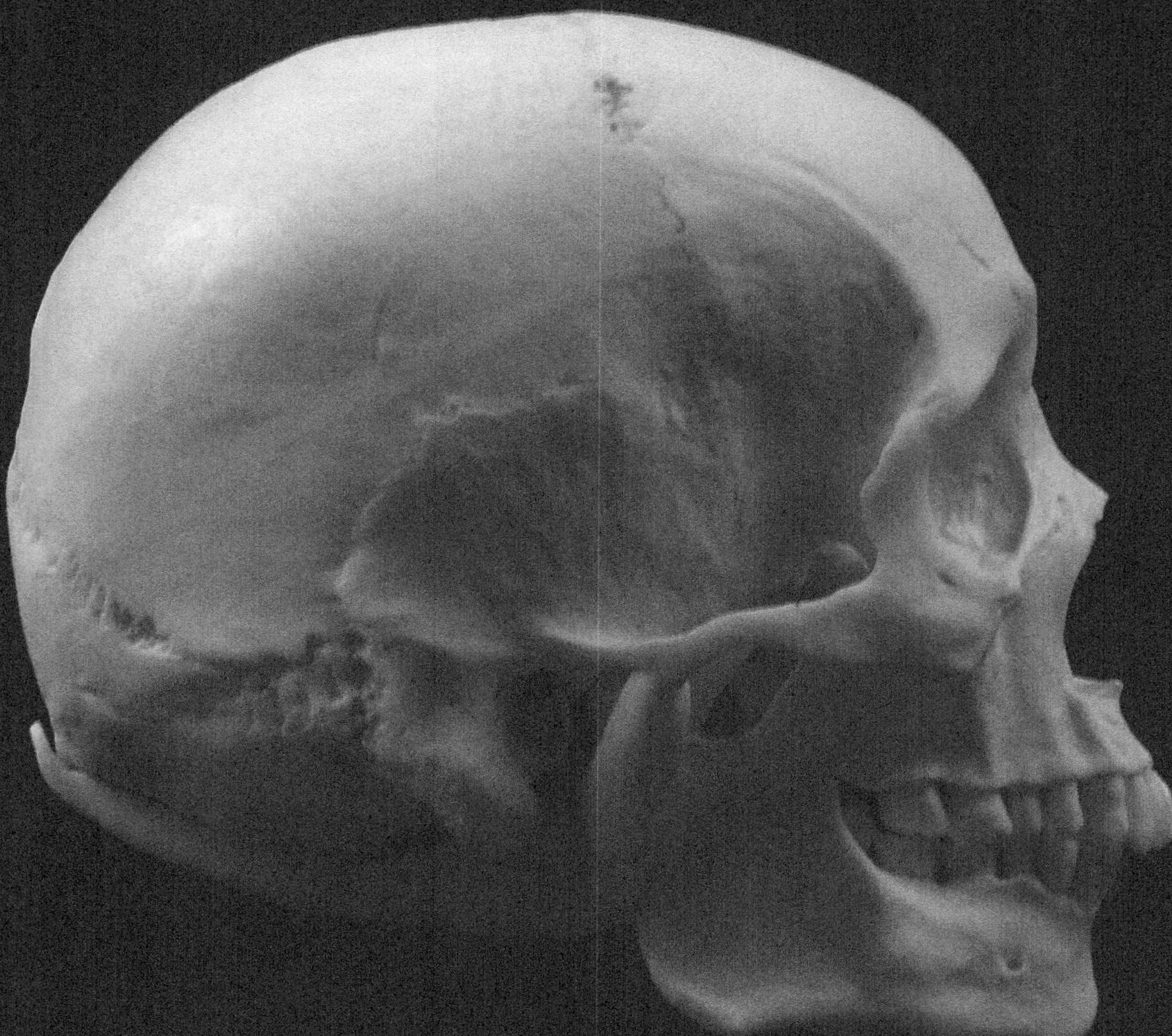

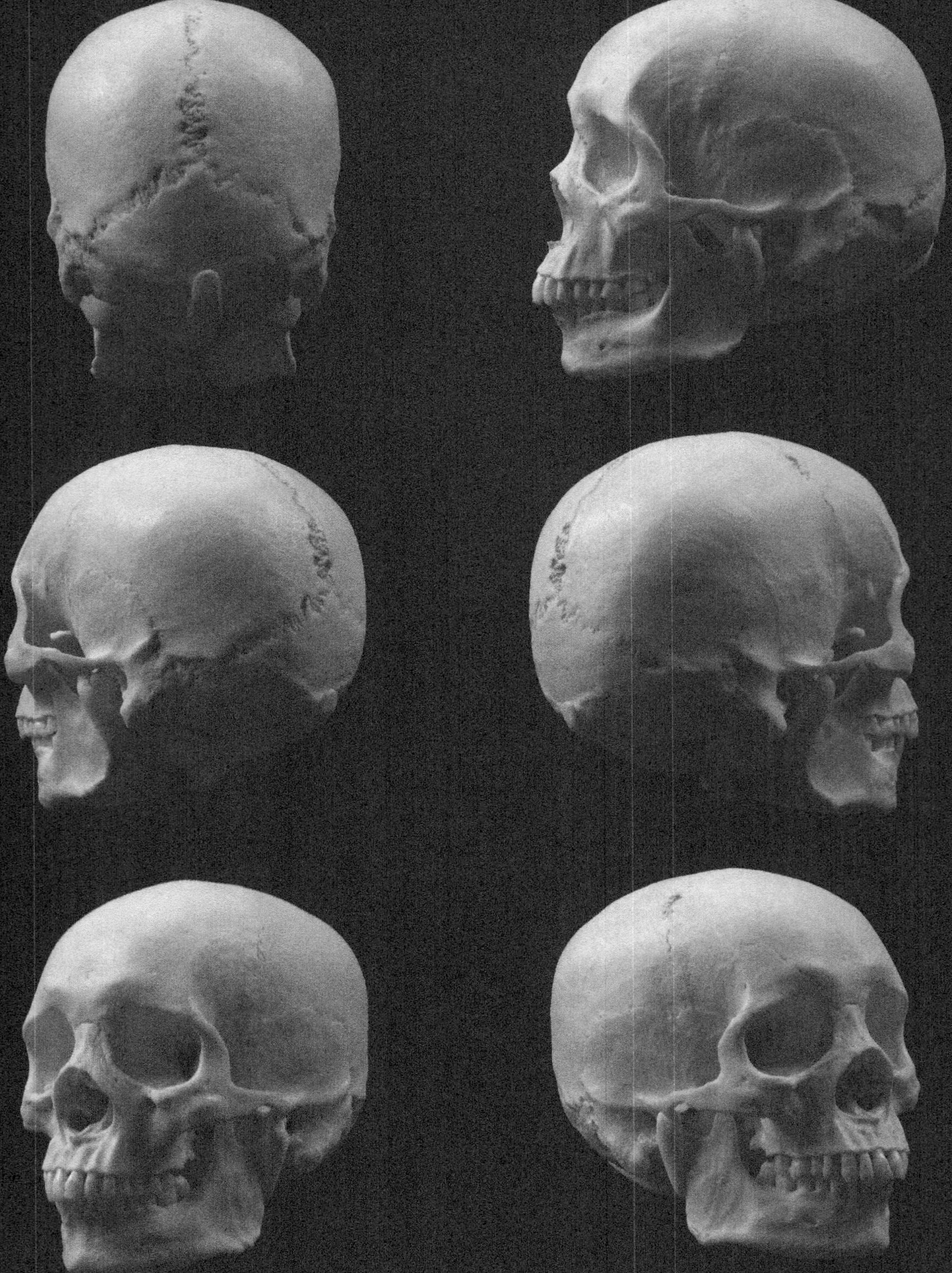

*African male.*

# ASIAN FEMALE SKULL

**Features of this skull:**

The interocular distance is not significantly widened.

The nasal root is flat and the nasal angle is obtuse.

The zygomatic bones retreat posteriorly from the plane of the face.

The nasal aperture is broad superiorly and inferiorly.

The anterior nasal spine is short, and the inferior margin of the nasal aperture is smooth on the left and somewhat sharp on the right, with the suggestion of a bilateral nasal gutter (right greater than left); there is no nasal sill.

The maxillary dental arcade is somewhat rounded.

There is mild to moderate alveolar prognathism.

The maxillary incisors are shovel-like.

There is no edge-on-edge incisal bite.

There is a slight post-bregmatic depression.

The calvarial sutures are complex.

**Features of the sex:**

There is mild prominence of the cranial sites for musculofascial attachment including especially:

- the nuchal lines
- the mastoid processes of the temporal bones
- the temporal lines
- the supraorbital tori
- the masseteric tuberosities of the mandible

There is a broad ascending mandibular ramus. The nasion is smooth, and the supraorbital margins are sharp. The inferior border of the mandible is somewhat squared.

Estimated age: 30–50 years old

www.boneclones.com, Dr. Evan Matshes, BSc MD.

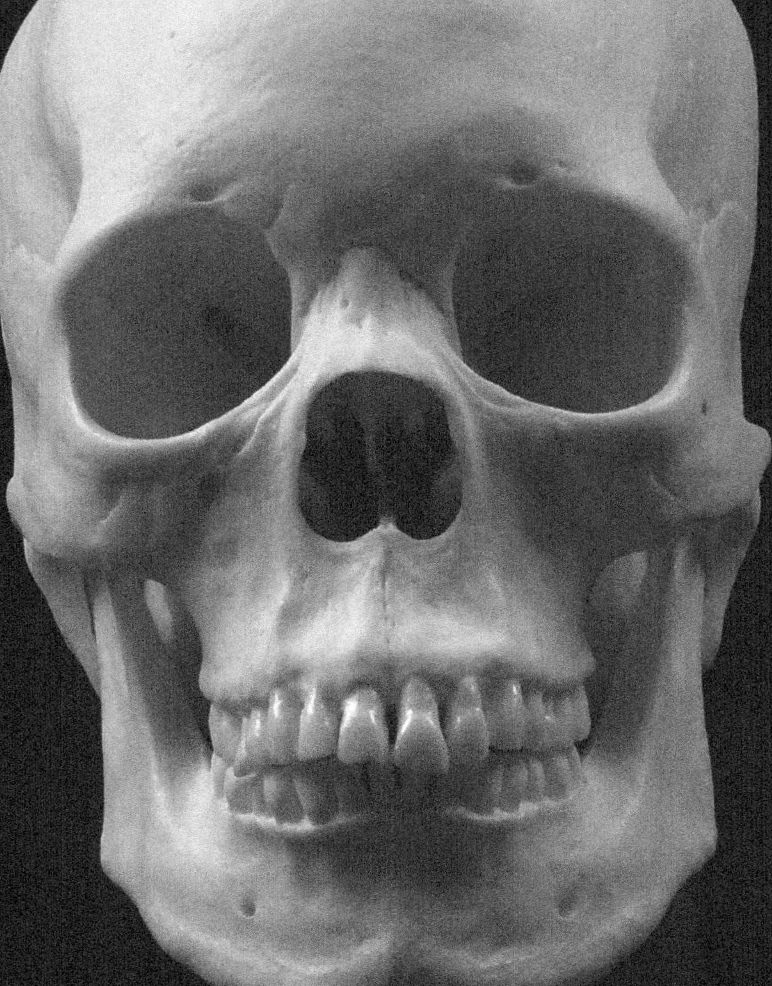

*Asian female.*

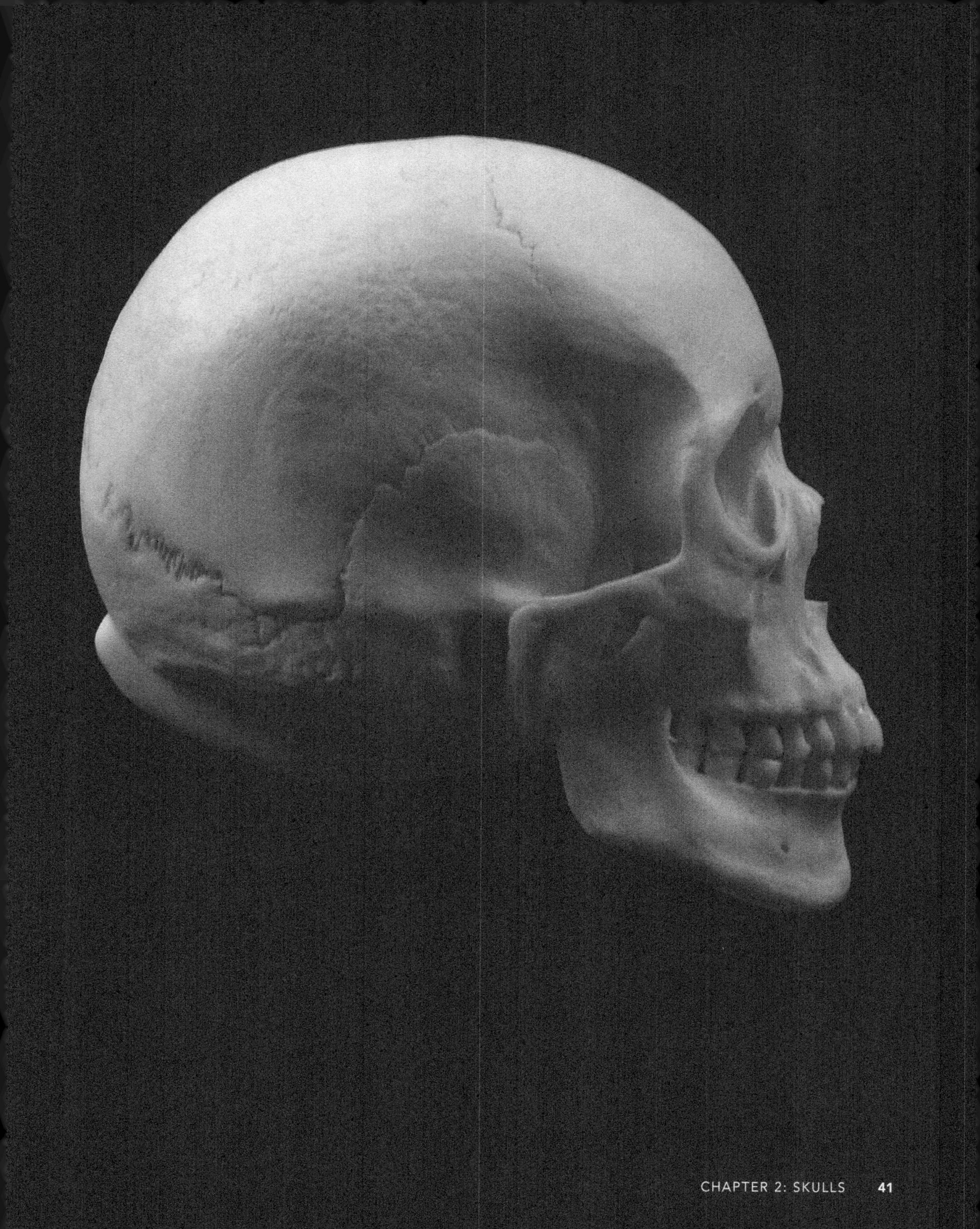

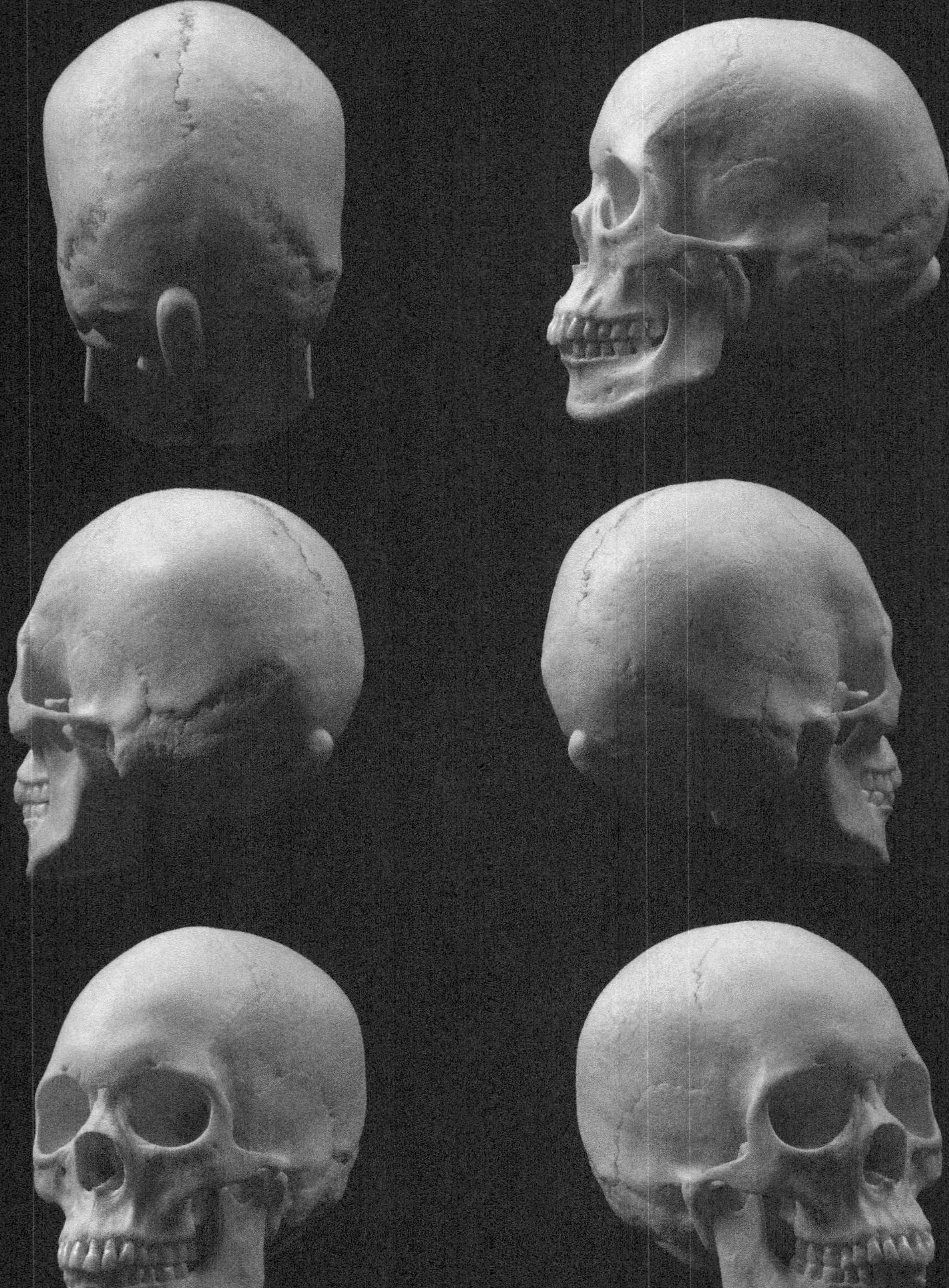

*Asian female.*

# ASIAN MALE SKULL

**Features of this skull:**

The interocular distance is broad.

The nasal root is flat and the nasal angle is obtuse.

The zygomatic bones are broad.

The nasal aperture is broad superiorly and inferiorly.

The anterior nasal spine is short, and the inferior margin of the nasal aperture is blunt; there is no gutter.

The maxillary dental arcade has somewhat of a rounded shape.

There is prominent alveolar prognathism.

The maxillary incisors are prominently shovel-shaped.

There is no edge-on-edge incisal bite.

There is a very slight post-bregmatic depression.

The calvarial sutures are focally complex.

**Features of the sex:**

There is mild prominence of the cranial sites for musculofascial attachment including especially:

- the nuchal lines
- the external occipital protuberance
- the mastoid processes of the temporal bones
- the temporal lines (slight)
- the supraorbital tori (prominent)
- the masseteric tuberosities of the mandible, with slight right gonial eversion (prominent)
- the occipital condyles
- the supramastoidal crest

There is a broad ascending mandibular ramus. The nasion is somewhat rough (difficult assessment due to metopic suture), and the supraorbital margins are blunted. The inferior border of the mandible is square.

Estimated age: 30–50 years old

www.boneclones.com, Dr. Evan Matshes, BSc MD.

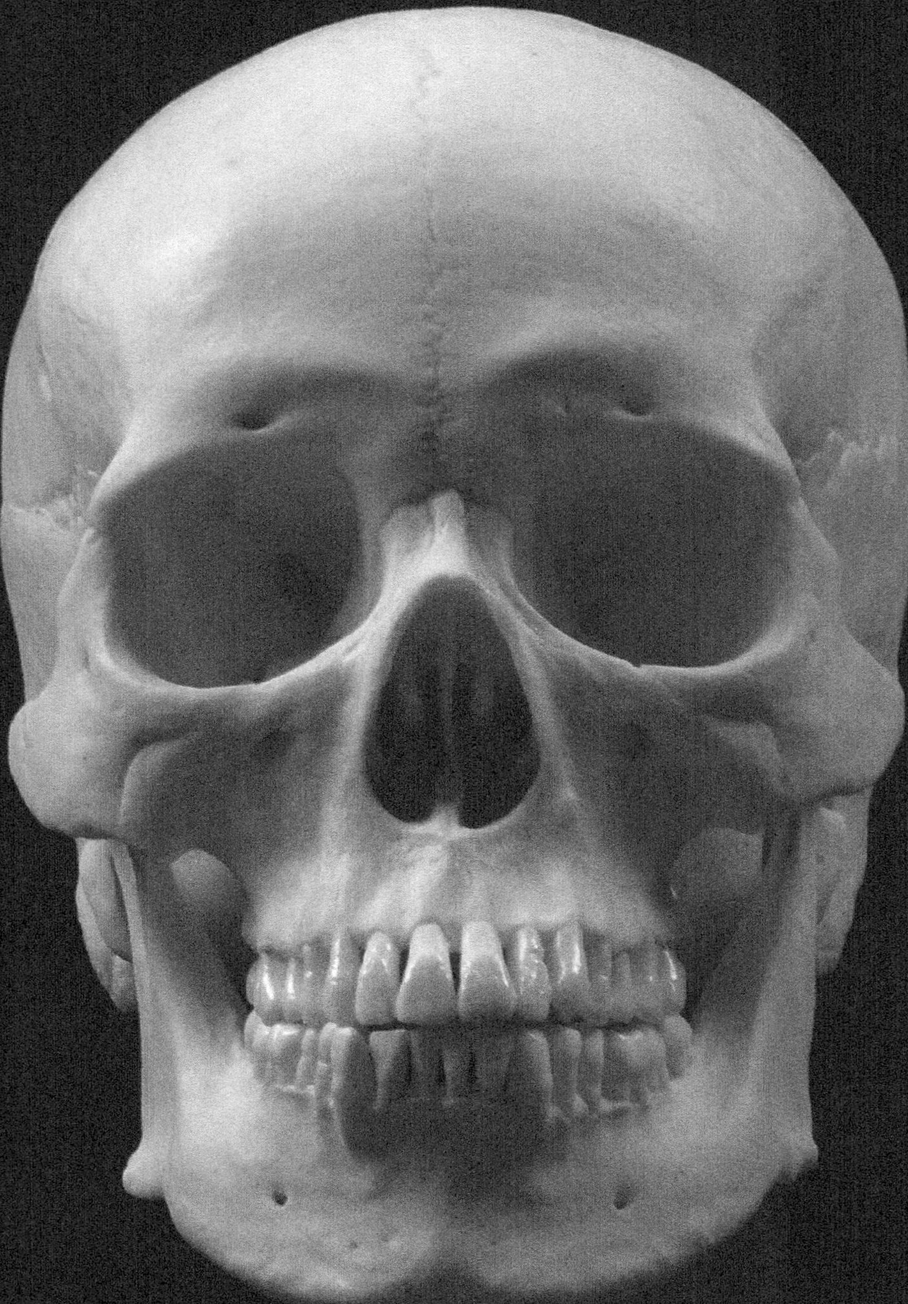

*Asian male.*

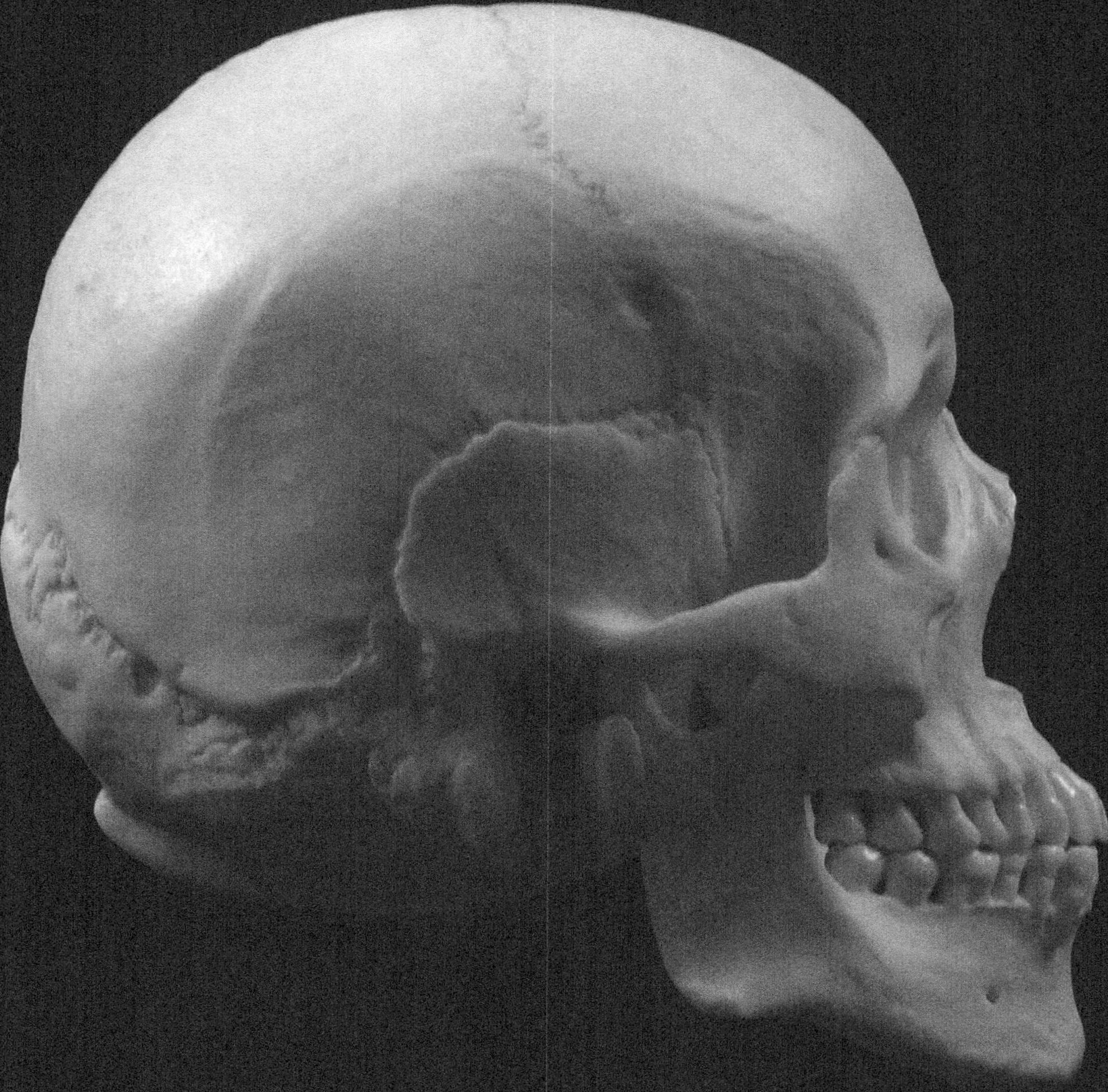

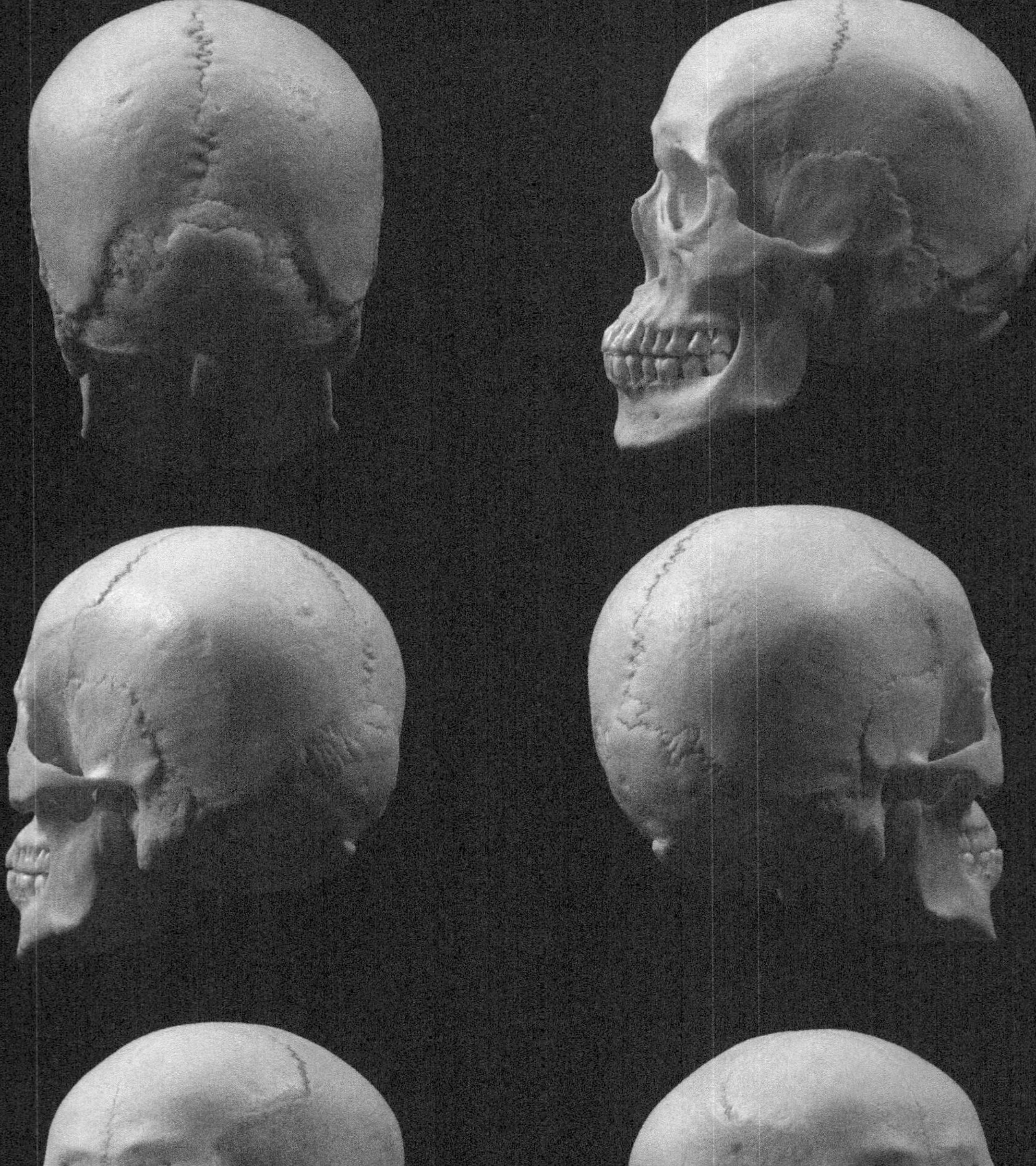

*Asian male.*

# ASIAN MALE ROBUST SKULL

**Features of this skull:**

The discriminate function analysis program, FORDISC 3.0, classifies the skull as American Indian with a posterior probability of 0.996. This classification is further substantiated by the presence of shovel-shaped incisors and multiple Wormian bones in lambdoidal suture. The face is broad, and the nasal aperture is wide. The nasal sill is smooth and guttered. Differentiation of Asian and American Indian is difficult, if not impossible, given the information available.

The nasal aperture is somewhat rounded, not vertical as in persons of European origin. The nasal sill flows inward across a mild gutter from the alveolar ridge. The nasal spine is present but not prominent. These are traits associated with persons of non-European origin.

**Posterior View of Skull** Multiple Wormian bones (sutural bones) can be seen within the lambdoidal suture. This condition is typical in individuals of Asian origin.

Note also the extremely large external occipital protuberance and crest-like inferior nuchal lines, both masculine traits.

**Features of the sex:**

The skull displays extreme masculine traits. The supraorbital ridge is large, the supraorbital margin is rounded, and the jaw is massive. The gonial angle is close to 90 degrees and strongly flared.

**Frontal View of Skull** The skull displays extremely masculine traits. The supraorbital ridge is large, the supraorbital margin is well-rounded, and the jaw is massive. The gonial angle is strongly flared.

**Lateral View of Neurocranium** The lateral and posterior views of the skull are also impressively masculine. The suprameatal crest (also called a "zygomatic arch extension") is sharply defined, and the mastoid processes are large. The external occipital protuberance is enormous, and the inferior nuchal lines are almost crest-like.

Estimated age: Early 20s

www.boneclones.com, Dr. Karen Ramey Burns, PhD.

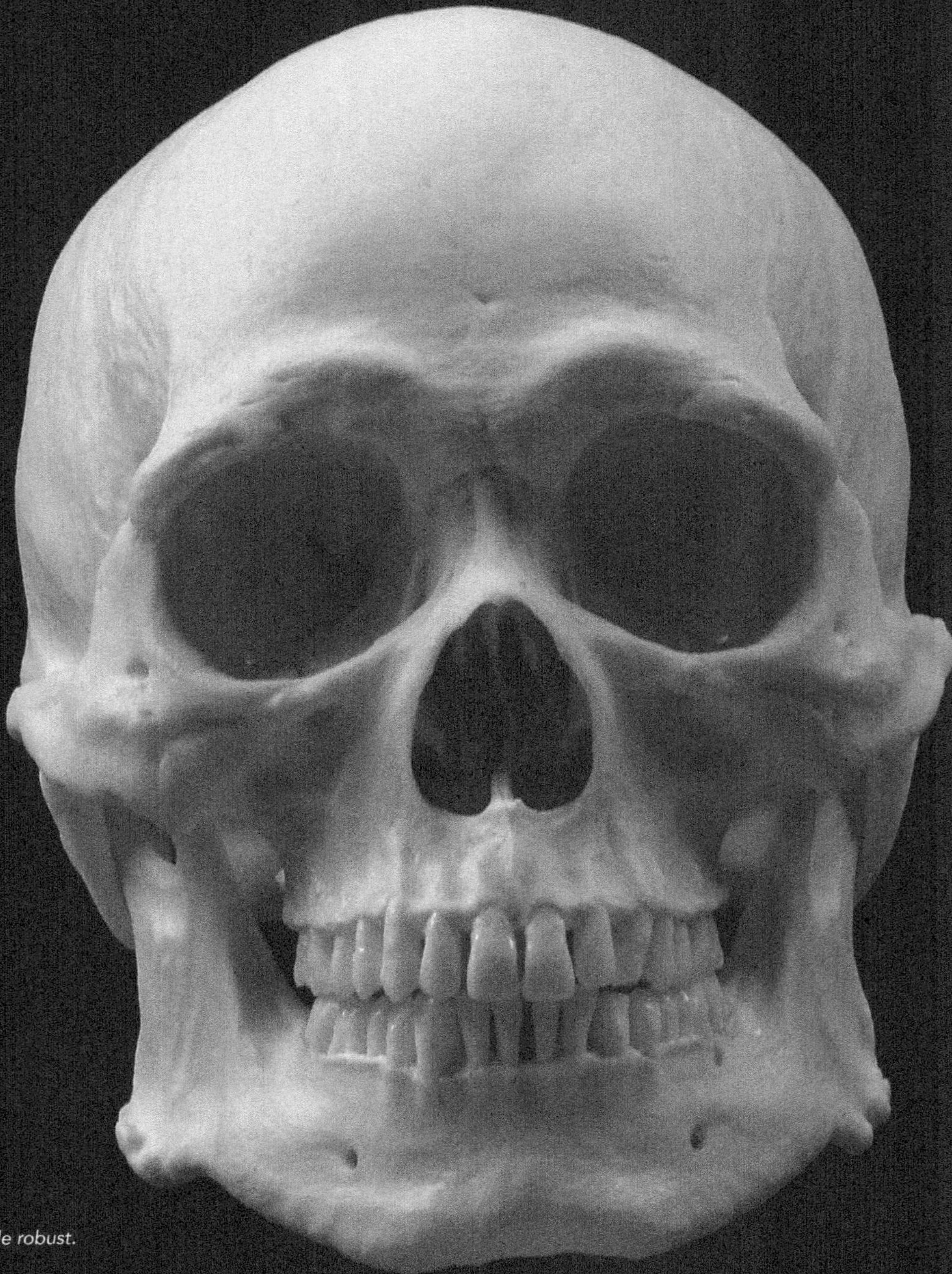

*Asain male robust.*

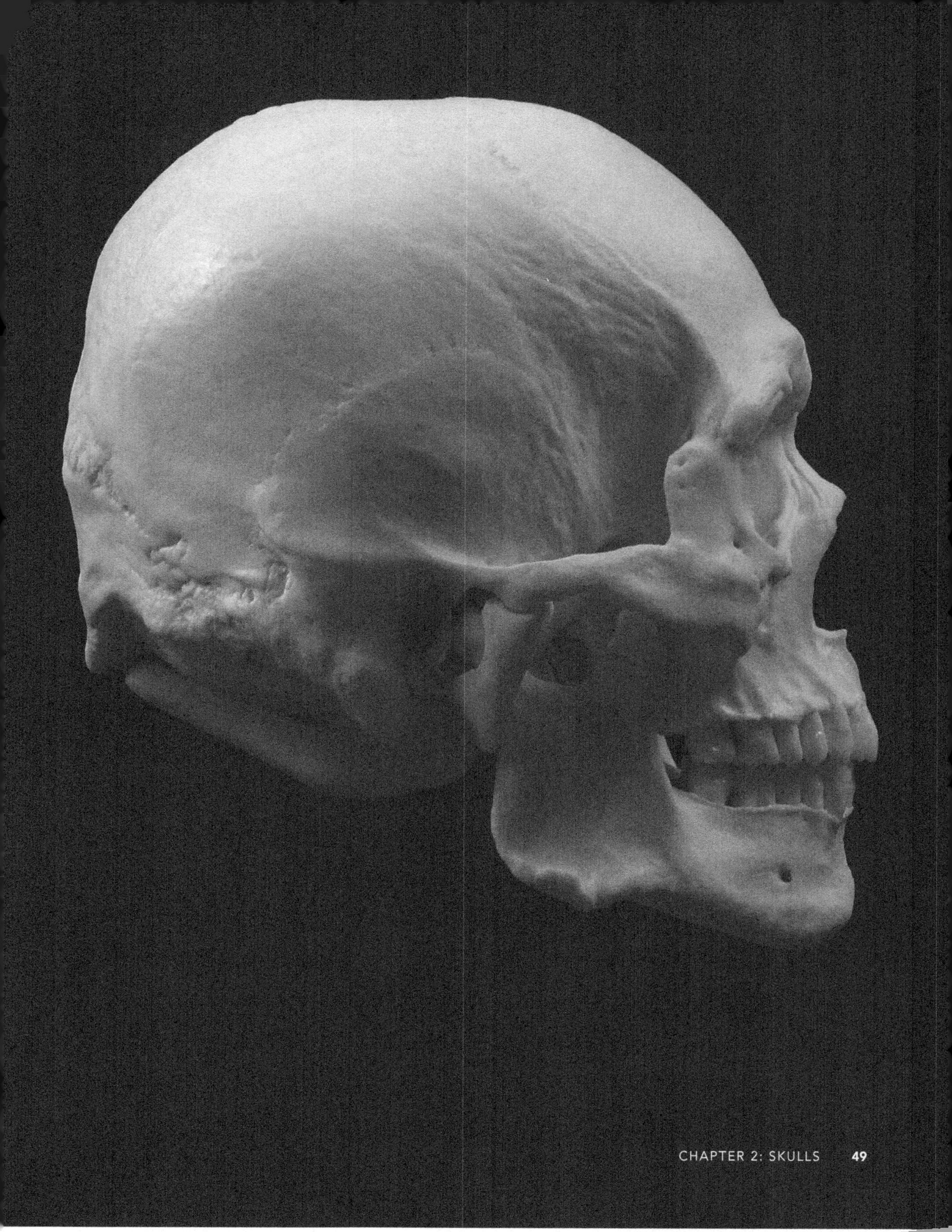

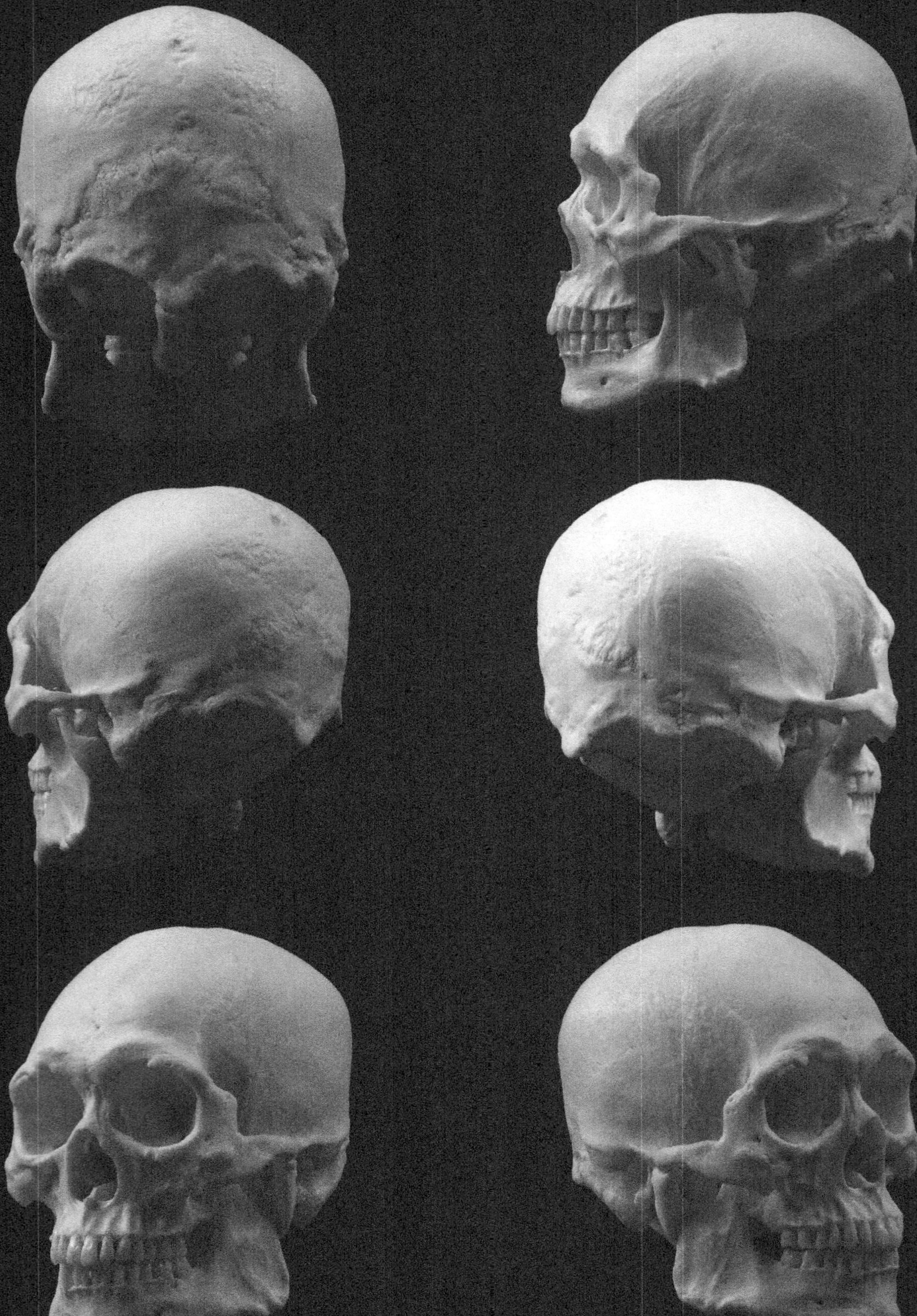

*Asain male robust.*

# AMERICAN INDIAN FEMALE SKULL

**Features of this skull:**

The interocular distance is not prominently widened. The nasal root is depressed and the nasal angle is obtuse. The robust zygomatic bones are broad. The nasal aperture is somewhat narrow superiorly and inferiorly. The anterior nasal spine is very short, and the inferior nasal margin is smooth and depressed; there are no gutters, nor is there a sill.

The maxillary dental arcade has a somewhat round-to-rectangular shape. There is no alveolar prognathism. Due to the severe degree of attrition, it is not possible to assess for a shovel-shape on the single remaining maxillary incisor (2.1 [#9]). There is no post-bregmatic depression. The calvarial sutures are complex.

**Features of the sex:**

There is mild prominence of the cranial sites for musculofascial attachment including especially:

- the nuchal lines
- the mastoid processes of the temporal bones (slight)
- the temporal lines (slight)
- the supraorbital tori (slight)
- the occipital condyles
- the supramastoidal crest

There is a broad ascending mandibular ramus. The gonion angles flare slightly. The nasion is smooth, and the supraorbital margins are blunted. The inferior border of the mandible is rounded.

Estimated age: 47–57 years old

www.boneclones.com, Dr. Evan Matshes, BSc MD.

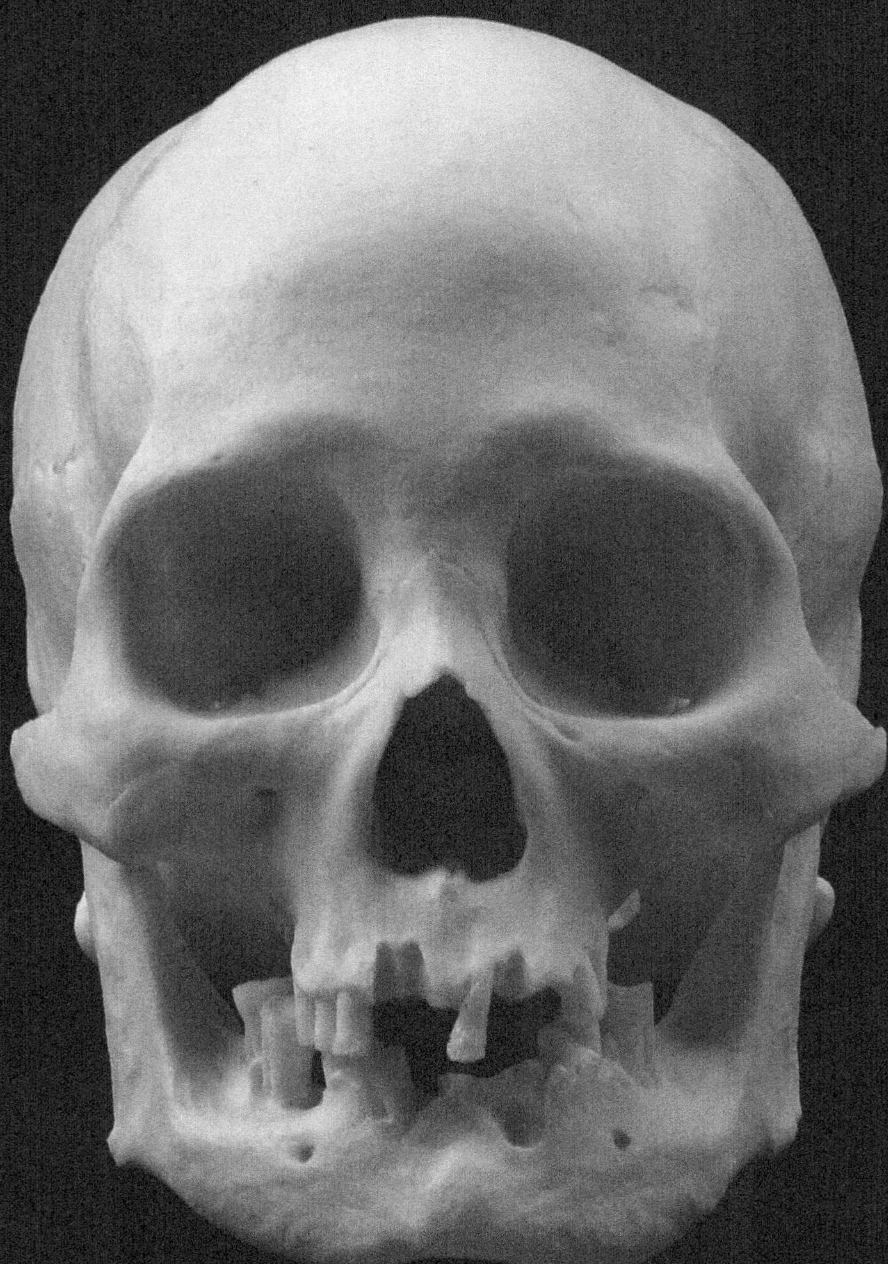

*American Indian female.*

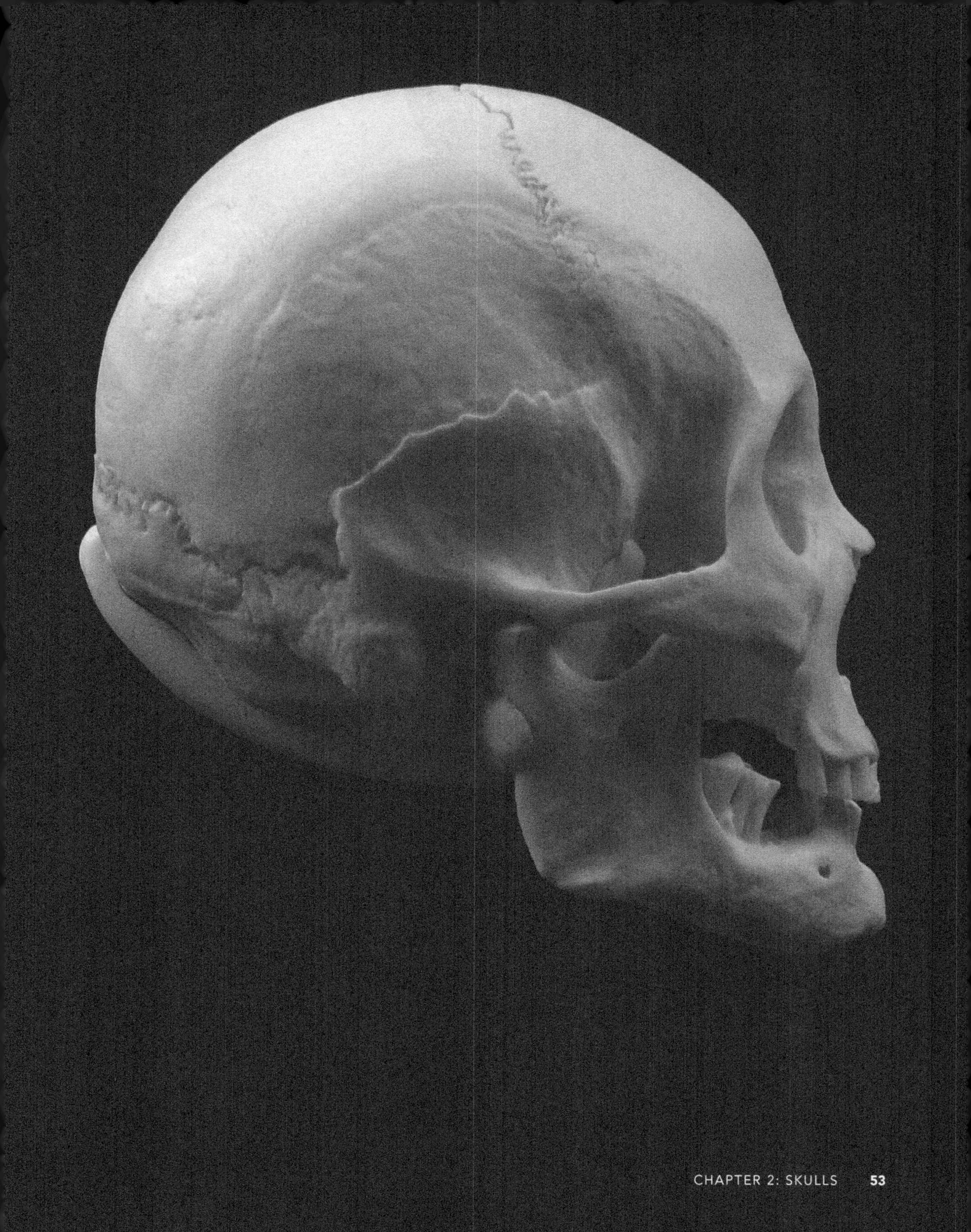

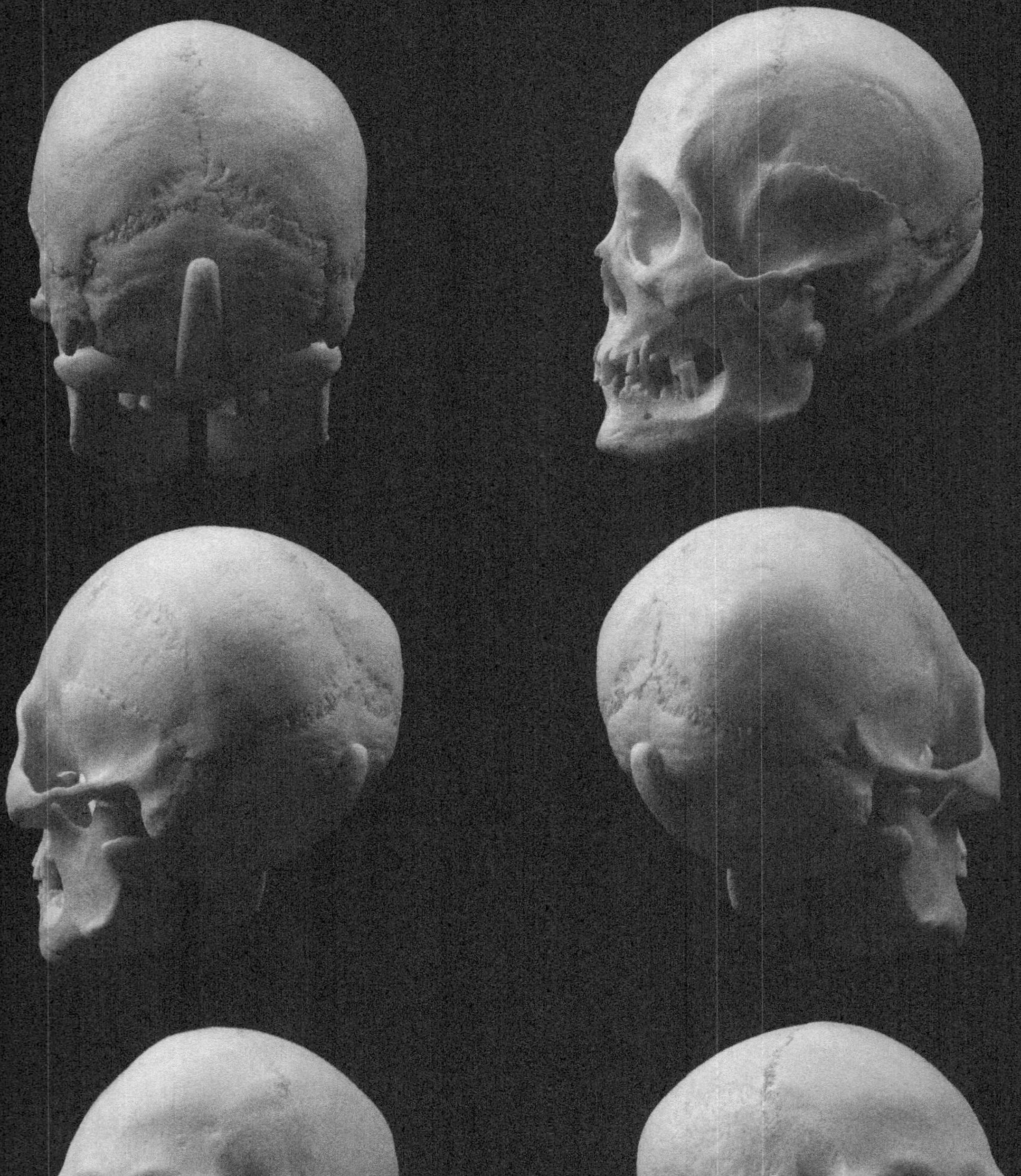

*American Indian female.*

# EUROPEAN FEMALE SKULL

**Features of this skull:**

The interocular distance is not prominently widened. The nasal root is prominent and the nasal angle is acute. The zygomatic bones retreat posteriorly from the plane of the face.

The nasal aperture is narrow superiorly and broader inferiorly. The anterior nasal spine is short, and the inferior margin of the nasal aperture has a sharp (nasal) sill with a very vague impression of bilateral gutters. The maxillary dental arcade has somewhat of a V shape.

There is very slight alveolar prognathism. The maxillary incisors are blade-like.

There is no edge-on-edge incisal bite. There is no post-bregmatic depression. The calvarial sutures are predominantly simple.

**Features of the sex:**

There is moderate prominence of the cranial sites for musculofascial attachment including especially:

- the nuchal lines
- the external occipital protuberance
- the mastoid processes of the temporal bones
- the temporal lines (slight)
- the supraorbital tori
- the masseteric tuberosities of the mandible
- the occipital condyles
- the supramastoidal crest (slight)

There is a somewhat broad ascending mandibular ramus. The nasion is rough, and the supraorbital margins are blunted. The inferior border of the mandible is somewhat square.

www.boneclones.com, Dr. Karen Ramey Burns, PhD.

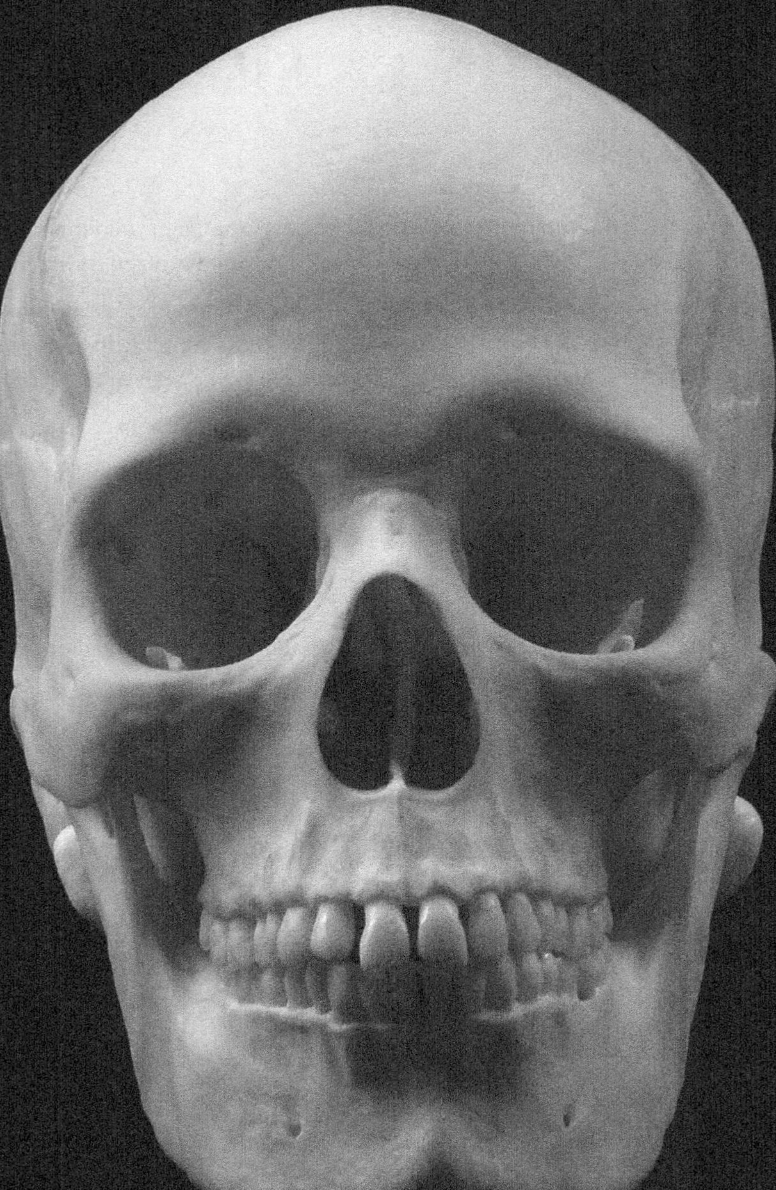

*European female.*

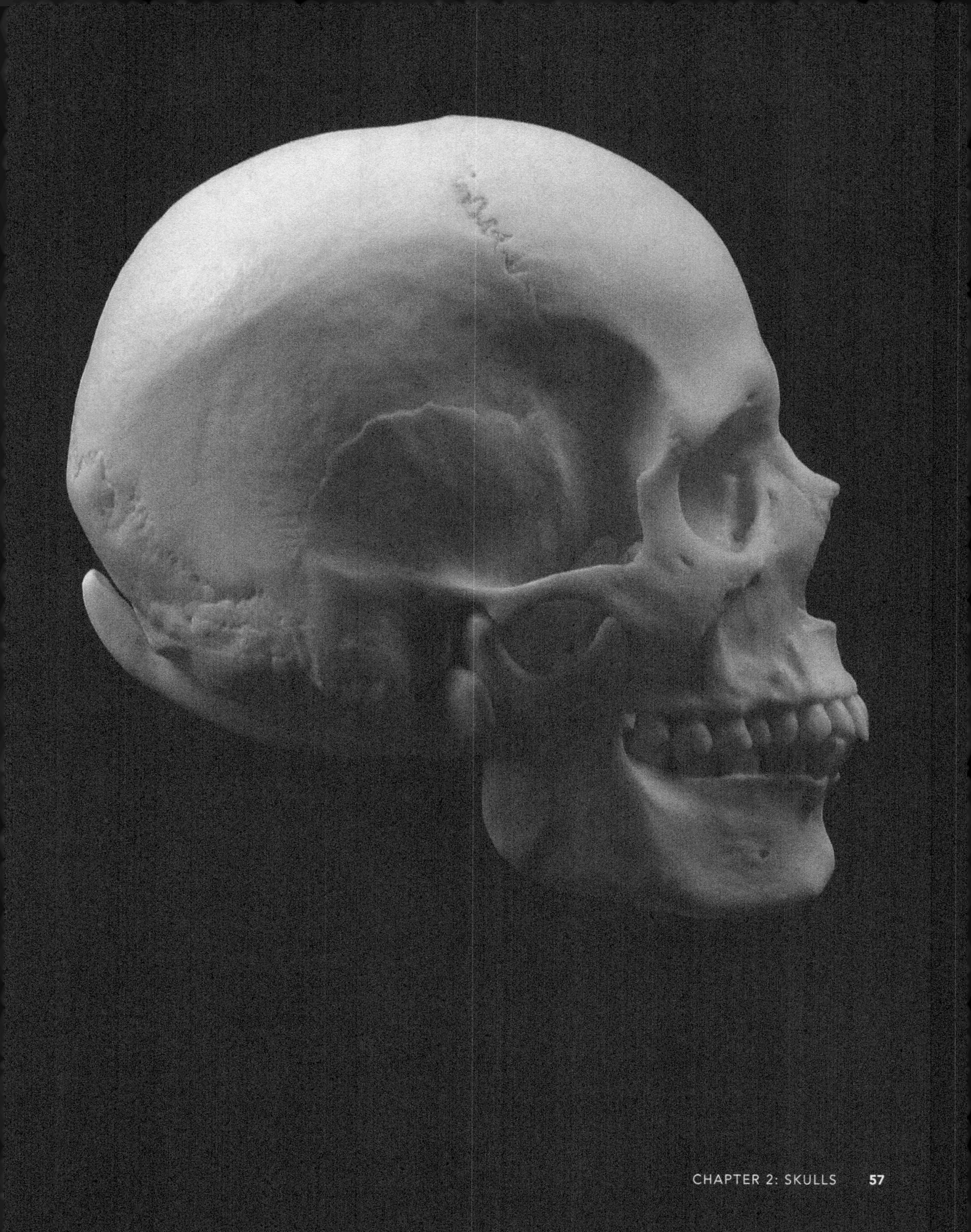

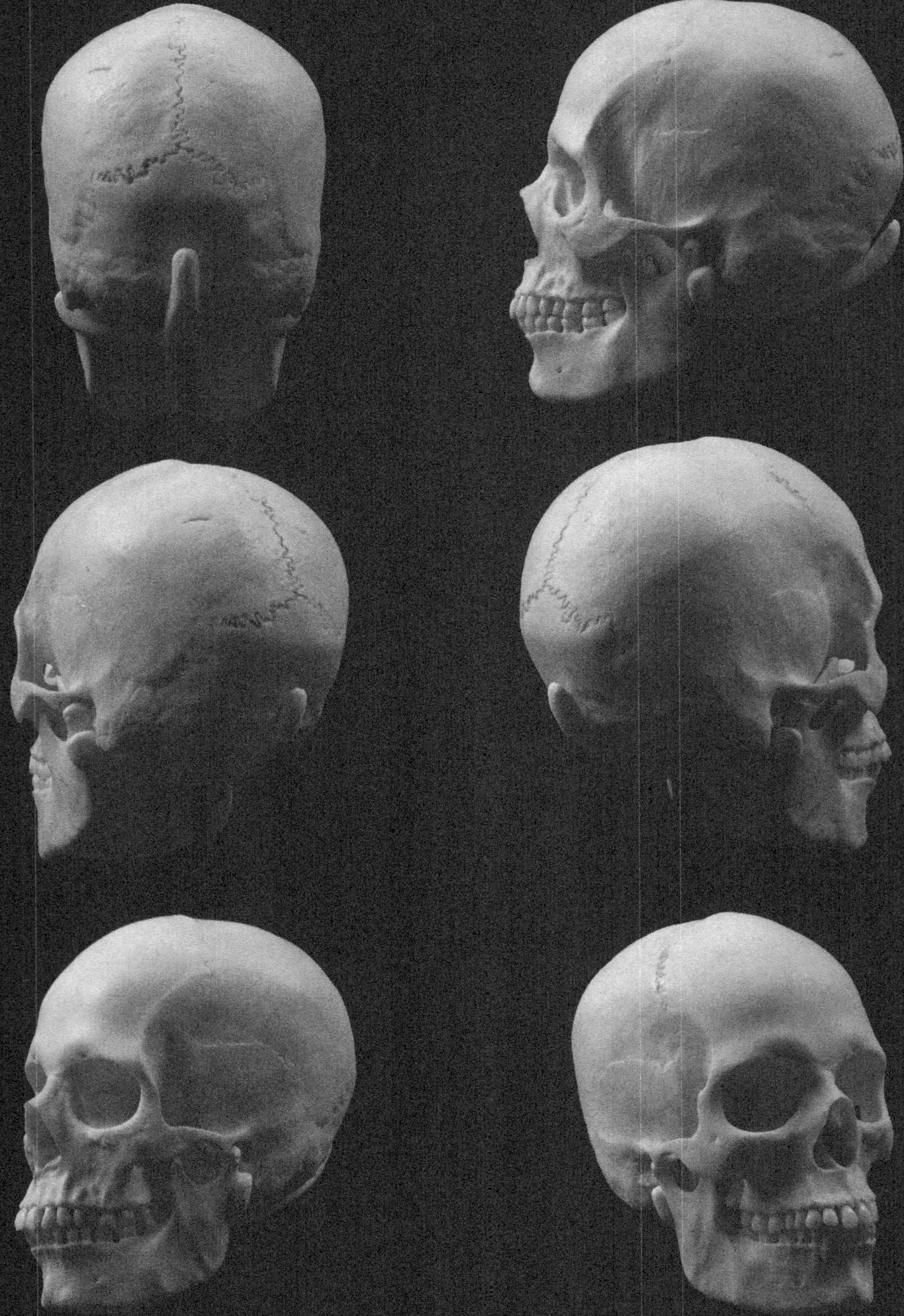

*European female.*

# EUROPEAN MALE SKULL

**Features of this skull:**

The interocular distance is not prominently widened. The nasal root is prominent and the nasal angle is acute. The zygomatic bones retreat posteriorly from the plane of the face.

The nasal aperture is narrow superiorly and broader inferiorly. The anterior nasal spine is short, and the inferior margin of the nasal aperture has a sharp (nasal) sill with a very vague impression of bilateral gutters. The maxillary dental arcade has somewhat of a V shape.

There is very slight alveolar prognathism. The maxillary incisors are blade-like.

There is no edge-on-edge incisal bite. There is no post-bregmatic depression. The calvarial sutures are predominantly simple.

**Features of the sex:**

There is moderate prominence of the cranial sites for musculofascial attachment including especially:

- the nuchal lines
- the external occipital protuberance
- the mastoid processes of the temporal bones
- the temporal lines (slight)
- the supraorbital tori
- the masseteric tuberosities of the mandible
- the occipital condyles
- the supramastoidal crest (slight)

There is a somewhat broad ascending mandibular ramus. The nasion is rough, and the supraorbital margins are blunted. The inferior border of the mandible is somewhat square.

Estimated age: 33–60 years old.

www.boneclones.com_Dr. Karen Ramey Burns, PhD.

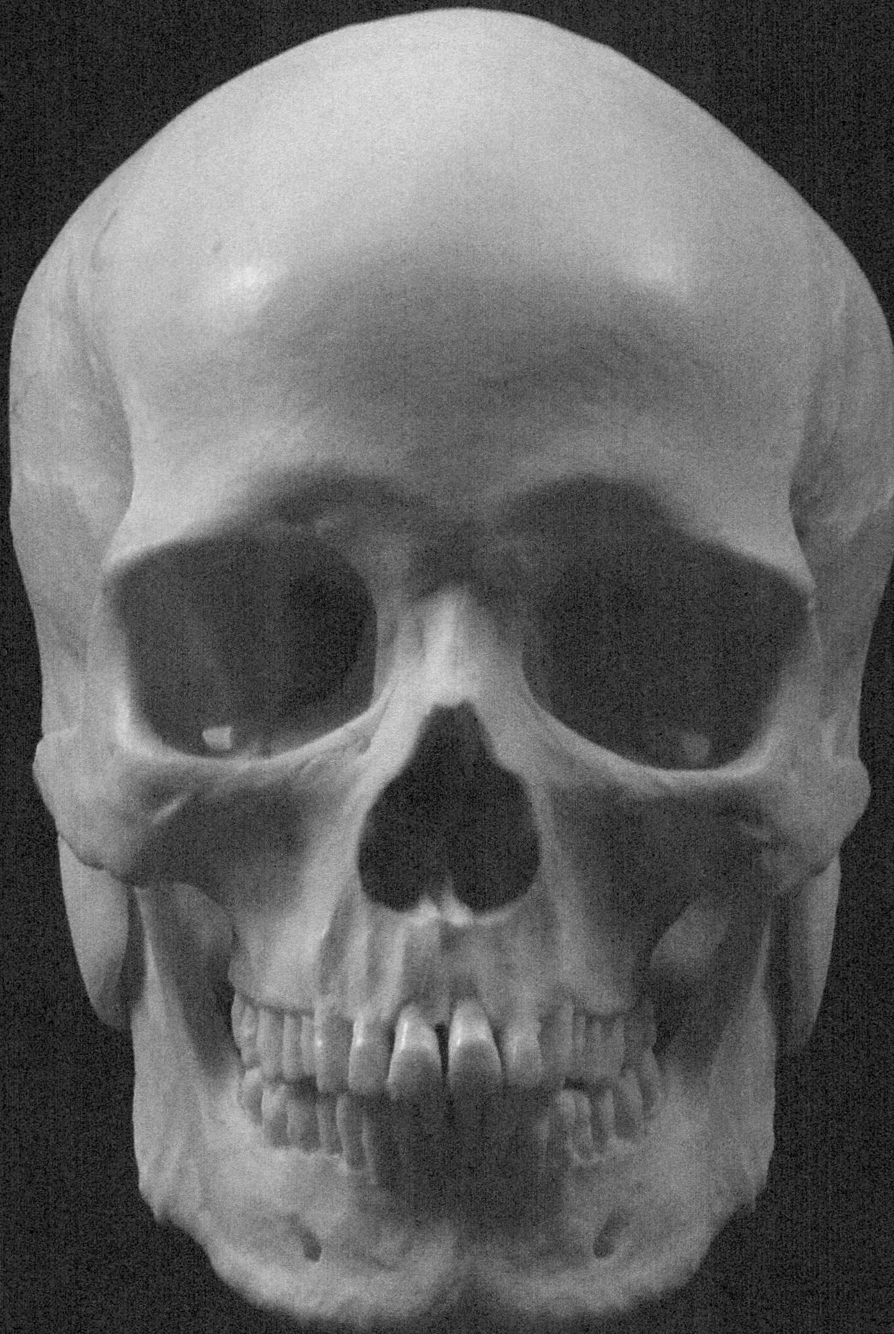

*European male.*

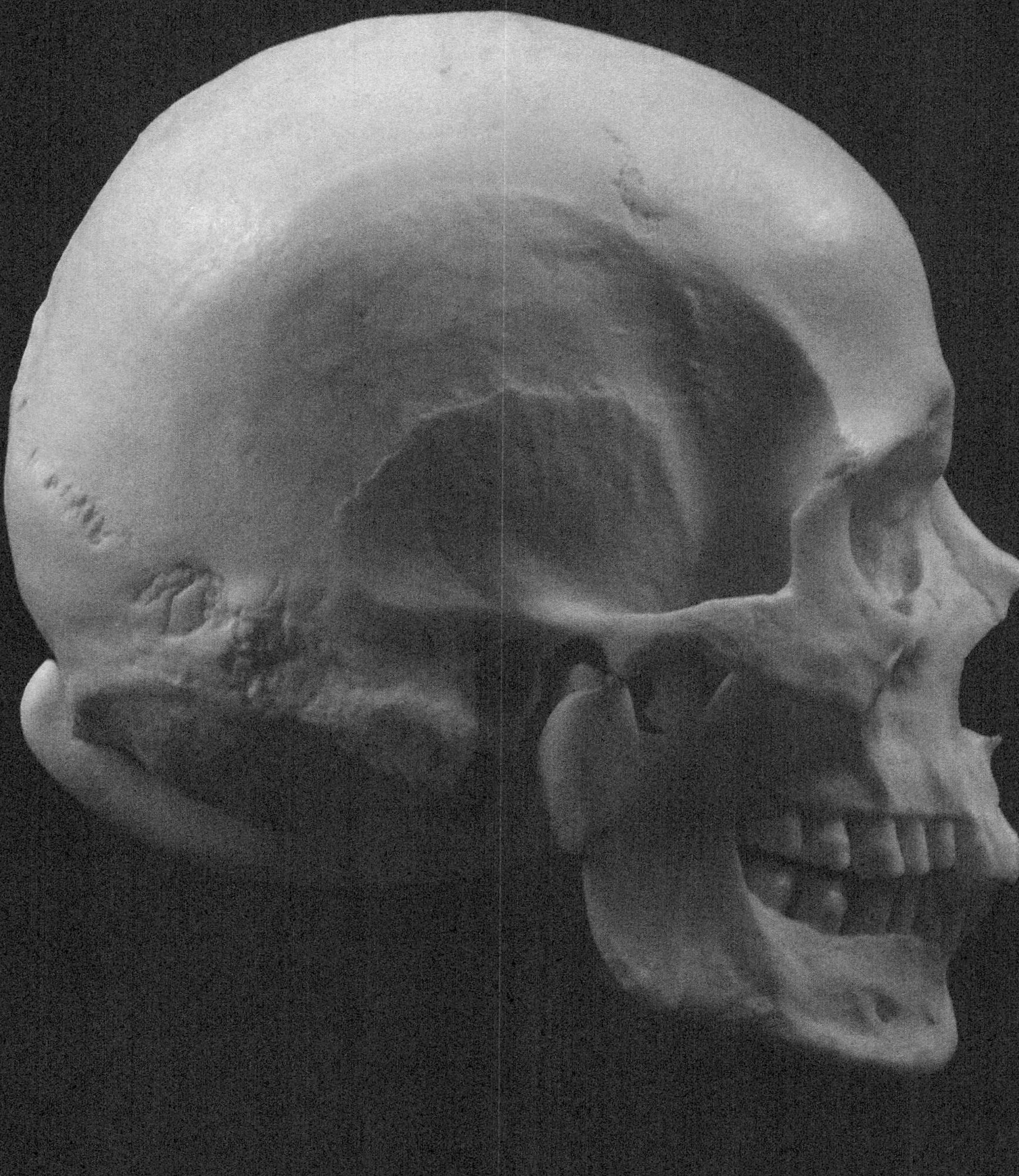

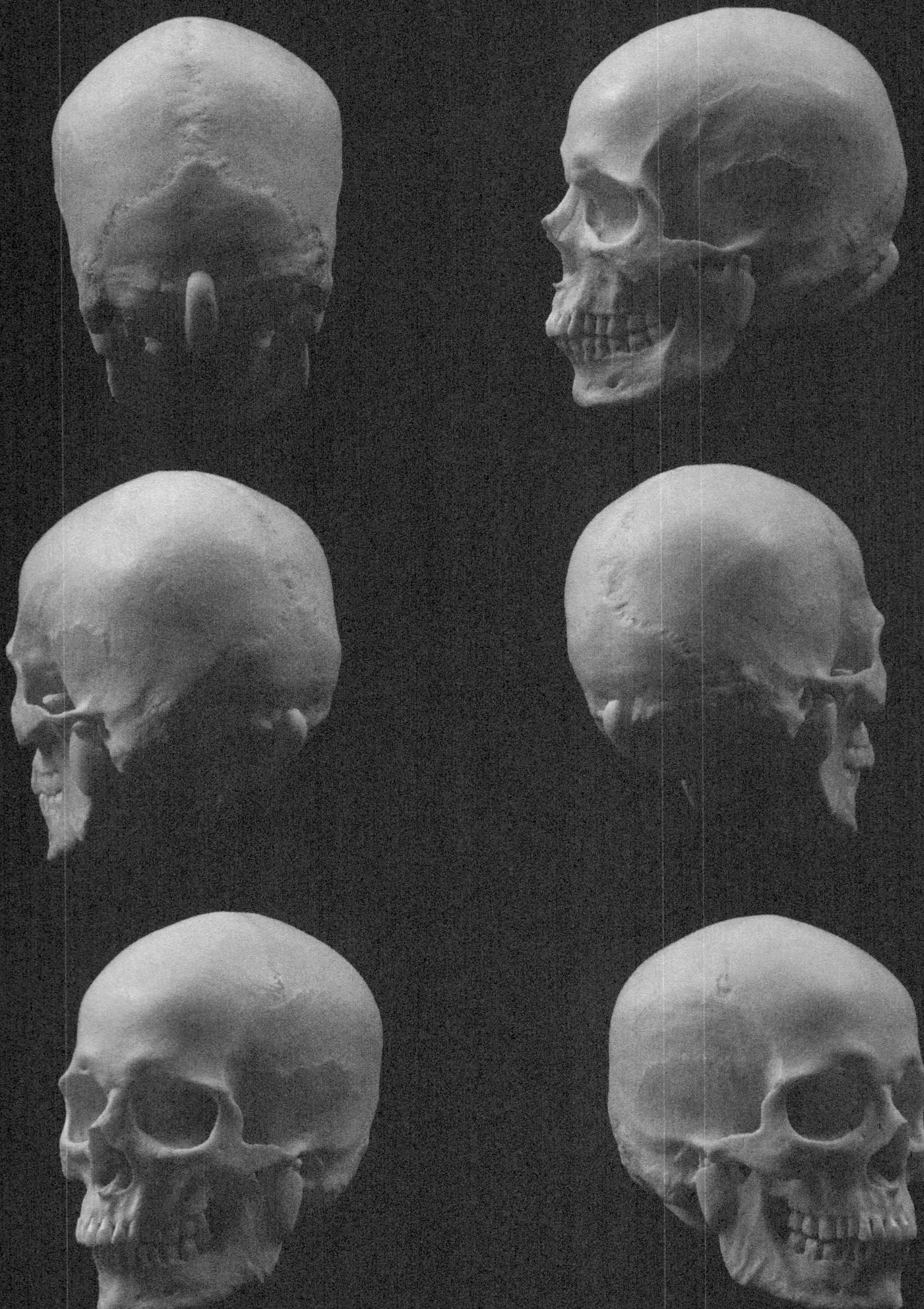

*European male.*

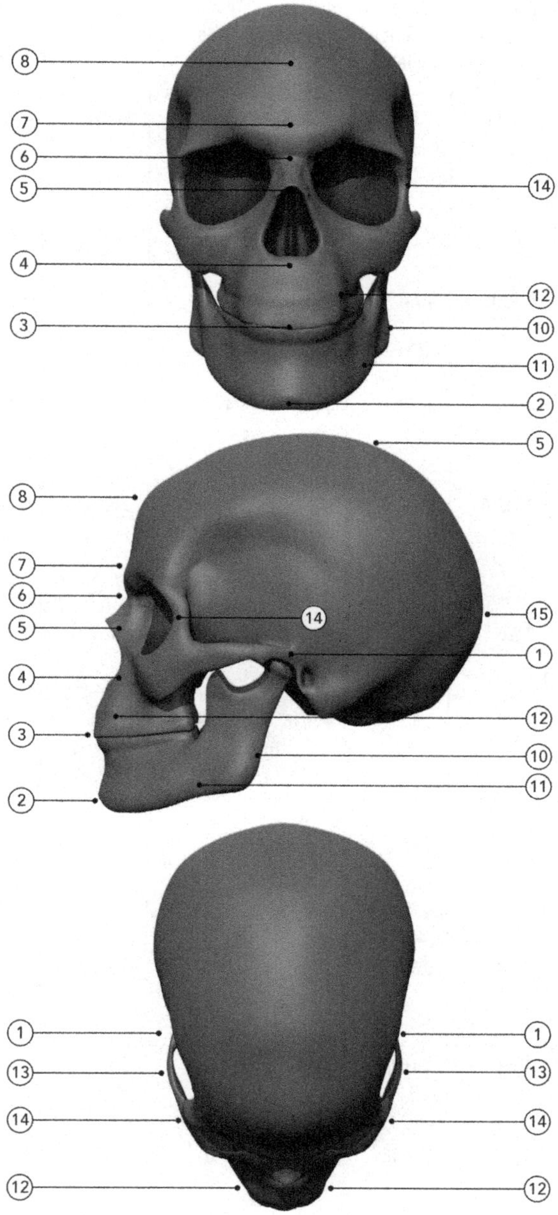


Take a look at this chart. The measurements of each skull are identified. Notice the disparity between each measurement and each skull. No two skulls are alike. Look at the female measurements as a whole, and compare them to the male measurements. Does one group appear larger? Does one group appear smaller? This chart should emphasize the value of measuring your subjects with calipers and recording the data.

| | European male | European female | African American female | African American male | Asian male | Asian female | Aboriginal male | American Indian female | African male | Robust Asian male |
|---|---|---|---|---|---|---|---|---|---|---|
| 1 left–1 right: Tragus* to tragus (point on zygomatic arch above condyle process of mandible) | 4 9/16 | 4 7/16 | 4 3/4 | 4 15/16 | 5 3/16 | 4 3/8 | 4 3/ 4 | 5 | 4 5/8 | 5 9/16 |
| 1–2: Tragus* to chin (defined as center of triangle of chin) | 4 9/16 | 4 9/16 | 4 7/8 | 4 15/16 | 5 1/4 | 4 9/16 | 5 1/ 4 | 4 7/8 | 4 3/4 | 5 3/8 |
| 1–3: Tragus to lower edge of top front teeth | 4 5/16 | 4 3/16 | 4 7/16 | 4 7/8 | 4 1/2 | 4 1/8 | 4 3/ 4 | 4 3/8 | 4 1/2 | 5 7/8 |
| 1–4: Tragus to base nasal cavity (not including anterior nasal spine) | 3 13/16 | 4 11/16 | 3 11/16 | 4 1/8 | 3 13/16 | 3 5/16 | 4 1/ 8 | 3 3/4 | 4 7/8 | 4 3/16 |
| 1–5: Tragus to top nasal cavity | 4 | 3 7/8 | 3 4/5 | 4 1/4 | 3 13/16 | 3 1/2 | 4 1/ 4 | 3 7/8 | 4 | 4 1/4 |
| 1–6: Tragus to nose bridge (furthest posterior point in silhouette or suture point between nasal bone & brow if area relatively flat) | 3 3/4 | 3 5/8 | 3 5/8 | 4 1/16 | 3 3/4 | 3 7/16 | 4 1/16 | 3 3/4 | 3 7/8 | 4 1/8 |
| 1–7: Tragus to brow center/high point in side silhouette | 3 7/8 | 3 3/4 | 3 3/4 | 4 1/4 | 4 1/8 | 3 9/8 | 4 1/4 | 3 7/8 | 4 1/16 | 4 3/8 |
| 1–8: Tragus to apex frontal eminence | 4 3/8 | 4 1/4 | 4 1/8 | 4 7/8 | 4 3/4 | 4 1/16 | 4 9/16 | 4 3/8 | 4 7/16 | 4 5/8 |
| 1–9: Tragus to crown | 5 3/16 | 4 13/16 | 5 1/16 | 5 1/2 | 5 1/2 | 5 1/8 | 5 1/16 | 5 3/16 | 5 7/8 | 5 7/16 |
| 10 left –10 right: Posterior Mandible width (end of vertical segment back of jaw) | 3 11/16 | 3 5/16 | 3 3/8 | 3 5/8 | 4 1/16 | 3 11/16 | 3 7/ 8 | 4 3/16 | 4 7/16 | 4 3/4 |
| 11 left – 11 right: Inferior Mandible width @ rear molar | 2 7/8 | 2 7/8 | 3 3/16 | 3 1/8 | 3 5/8 | 3 1/8 | 3 3/16 | 3 3/8 | 3 | 3 7/8 |

| | European male | European female | African American female | African American male | Asian male | Asian female | Aboriginal male | American Indian female | African male | Robust Asian male |
|---|---|---|---|---|---|---|---|---|---|---|
| 12 left – 12 right: Maxila width at canine | 1 1/2 | 1 7/16 | 1 1/2 | 1 11/16 | 1 1/2 | 1 1/2 | 1 5/ 8 | 1 7/8 | 1 5/8 | 1 11/16 |
| 13 left – 13 right: Zygomatic arch widest point | 4 13/16 | 4 5/8 | 4 15/16 | 5 5/16 | 5 3/8 | 4 5/8 | 5 1/ 4 | 5 5/16 | 4 15/16 | 6 |
| 14 left – 14 right: Middle orbital cavity width (at angle change in orbital bone, slightly outside opening) | 3 7/8 | 3 11/16 | 3 13/16 | 4 1/4 | 4 1/4 | 3 7/8 | 4 1/ 2 | 4 15/16 | 4 1/16 | 4 5/16 |
| 2–3: Chin to lower edge of top front teeth | 1 5/16 | 1 3/ 8 | 1 3/8t | 2 1/8 | 1 5/8 | 1 1/2 | 1 1/ 2 | 1 1/16 | 1 1/4 | 1 1/2 |
| 2–4: Chin to nasal cavity base | 2 3/16 | 2 3/8 | 2 3/8 | 3 1/8 | 2 3/4 | 2 3/4 | 2 1/ 2 | 2 | 2 1/4 | 2 5/8 |
| 2–5: Chin to nasal cavity top | 3 3/8 | 3 11/16 | 3 3/4 | 4 1/8 | 4 1/8 | 3 3/4 | 3 3/ 4 | 3 1/4 | 3 7/16 | 3 15/16 |
| 2–6 Chin to nose bridge | 4 1/16 | 4 1/8 | 4 3/8 | 4 3/4 | 5 7/8 | 4 3/8 | 4 3/ 8 | 4 1/8 | 4 3/16 | 4 1/2 |
| 2–8: Chin to frontal eminence apex | 5 3/4 | 5 3/4 | 5 15/16 | 6 5/8 | 6 3/4 | 4 13/16 | 6 1/ 8 | 6 1/8 | 5 3/4 | 6 1/2 |
| 2–7: Chin to center brow | 4 1/2 | 4 1/2 | 4 7/8 | 5 | 5 7/16 | 4 7/8 | 4 5/ 8 | 4 3/4 | 4 5/8 | 5 1/16 |
| 2–9: Chin to crown | 8 3/8 | 8 5/16 | 8 5/8 | 9 1/8 | 9 3/8 | 8 11/16 | 8 3/ 4 | 8 3/4 | 8 3/16 | 9 1/4 |
| 7–8: center brow to frontal eminence apex | 1 5/16 | 1 1/4 | 1 3/16 | 1 5/8 | 1 3/8 | 1 1/4 | 1 5/ 8 | 1 1/2 | 1 1/8 | 1 1/4 |
| 8–9: frontal eminence apex to crown | 4 1/4 | 4 | 4 1/16 | 4 13/16 | 4 1/2 | 4 9/16 | 3 7/ 8 | 4 1/4 | 3 7/16 | 4 7/16 |
| 9–15: crown to furthest point rear skull (occipital region) | 4 | 3 3/4 | 3 1/2 | 3 3/4 | 4 15/16 | 3 1/16 | 4 3/ 8 | 3 1/16 | 3 1/4 | 3 1/8 |
| 5–15: top nose to furthest point rear skull (occipital region) | 7 1/4 | 7 | 7 1/16 | 7 3/4 | 7 3/16 | 7 | 7 5/ 8 | 6 3/4 | 7 1/8 | 7 1/4 |

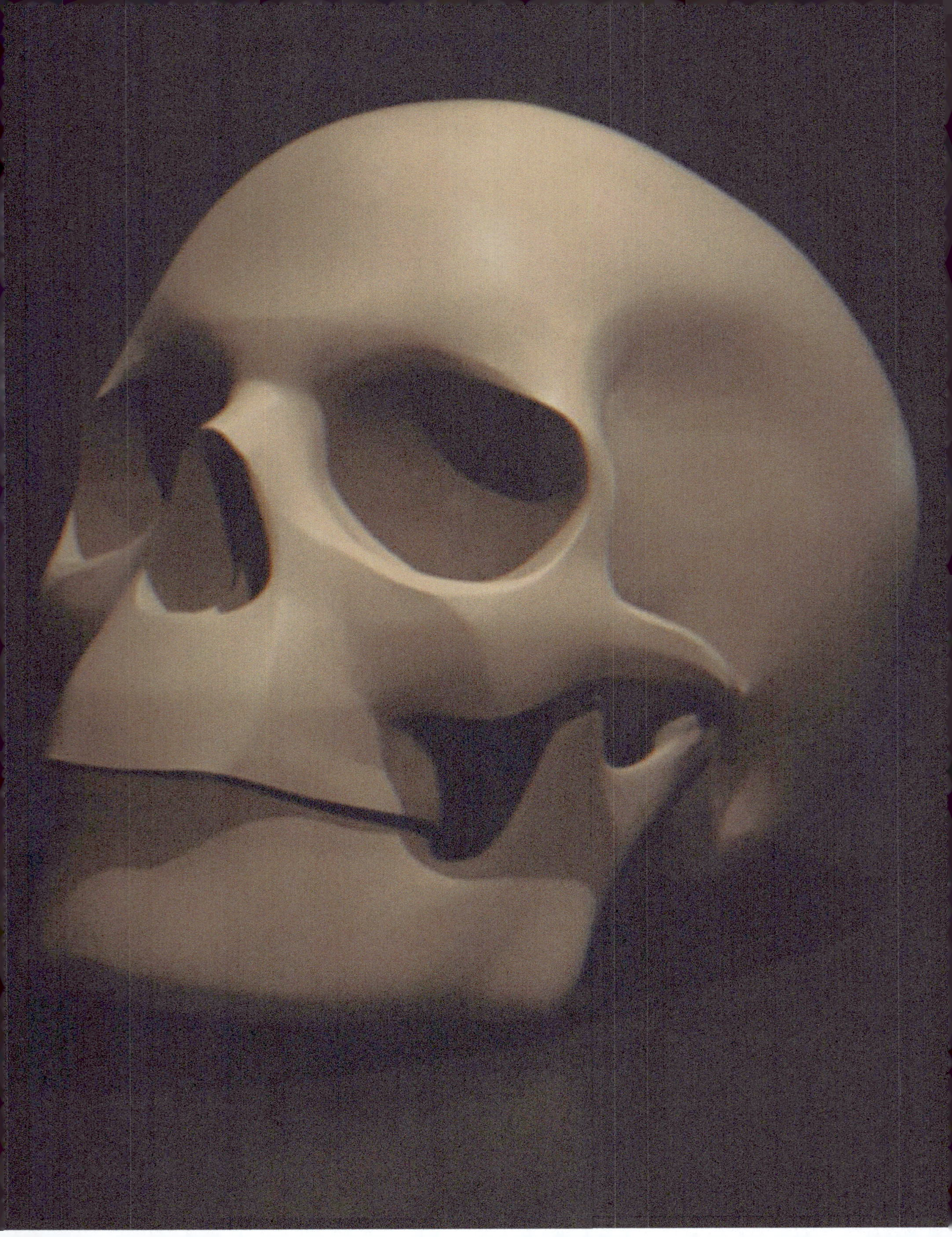

CHAPTER 2:
3D TUTORIAL

# THE BASIC SKULL

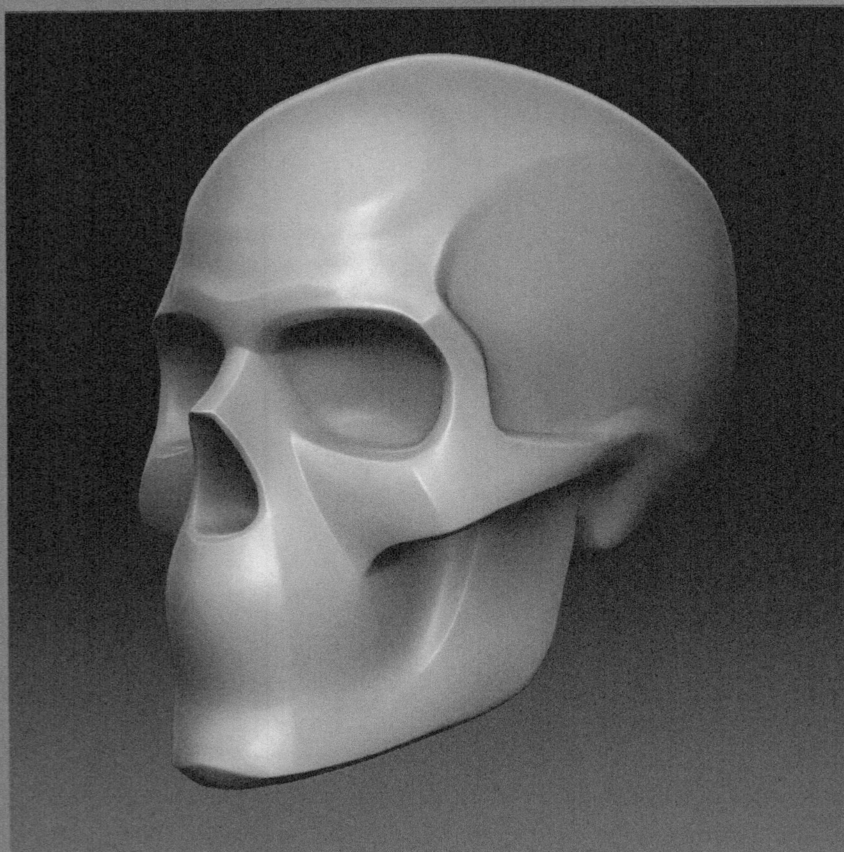

*Basic shape of the skull.*

The first tutorial is designed to get you thinking about bones, specifically the major bony landmark forms of the skull that lie under all the soft tissue and how they differ among diverse populations. In this tutorial, we are going to build a basic skull similar to the one shown in Figure 1.1, based on our Bone Clones reference. At the end of the tutorial, you will be directed to the resources to repeat this process for three more variants of the human skull. These are intended to be useful for you to refer back to in the future when observing different facial features.

For this tutorial, we will focus on the Asian male skull. At the end of the tutorial, you will repeat the process with the Asian female, African male, and American Indian female skulls. It is important to remember that there is no definitive set of facial characteristics that represent any population in their entirety. The majority of individuals you will observe may have some combination of features unique to themselves. These examples begin to give you tools for comparison, not absolute definitions.

When trying to identify characteristic differences related to ancestral populations, consider the following features:

- Relative robustness—gracile qualities of the cranium.

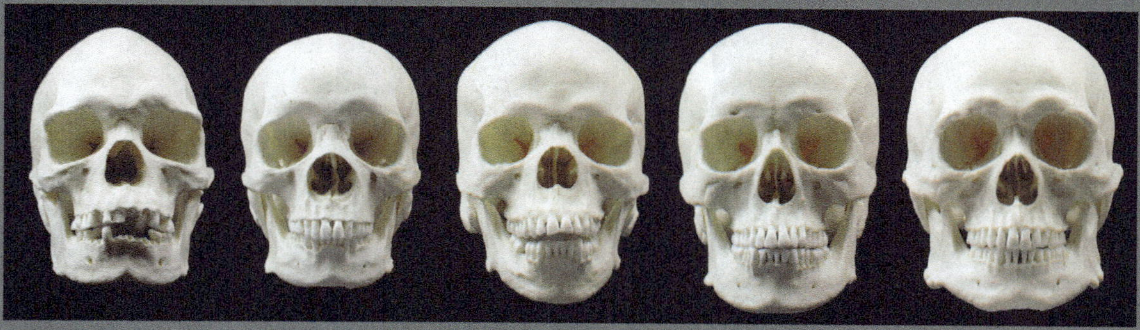

*Front views of Aboriginal, African male, African American male, Asian male, Asian robust male.*

- Nasal root: the bridge of the nose—does it insert high or low into the brow and what is the angle of the nasal bone in profile?

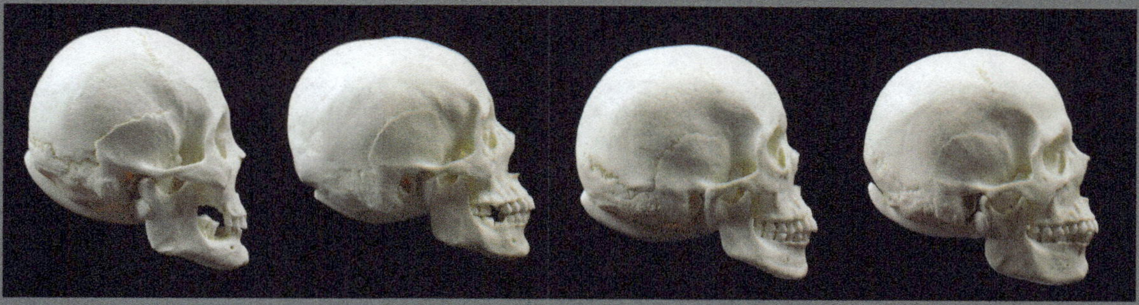

*American Indian female, African American female, Asian female, European female.*

- Interocular distance: basically, how wide the eyes set are, but also how far apart the medial edge of the left orbital opening is from the right (tear duct to tear duct in basic terms).

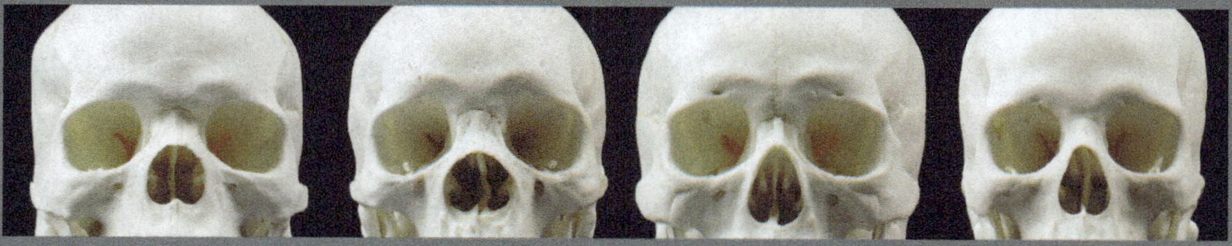

*Interocular distance, left to right: African American Male, African Male, Asian Male, European Male.*

- Relative squareness/roundness of the orbital cavities.

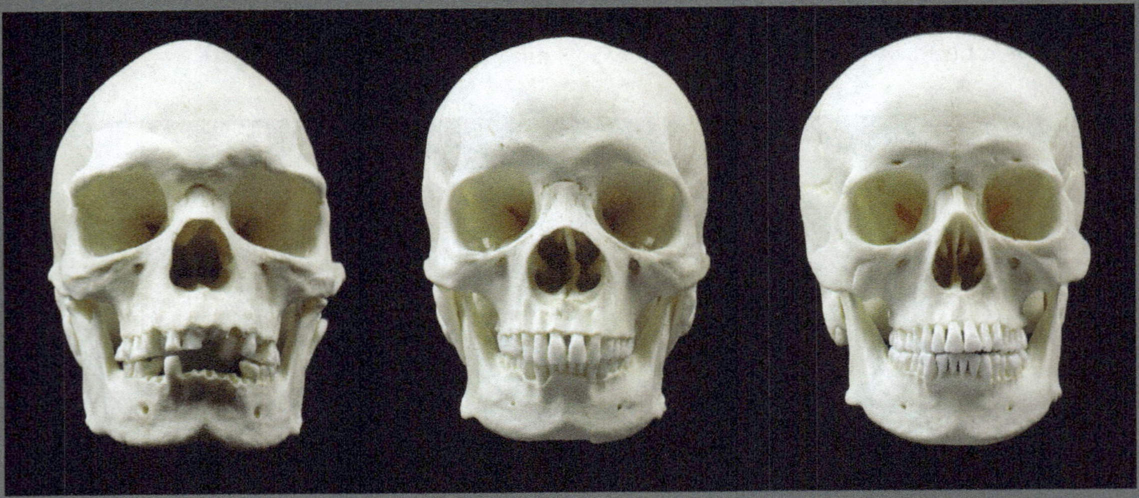

*Front view: Aboriginal, African and Asian skulls.*

- Sweep of the zygomatic bones—are they sweeping backward away from the front plane of the face or staying primarily in the plane of the face?

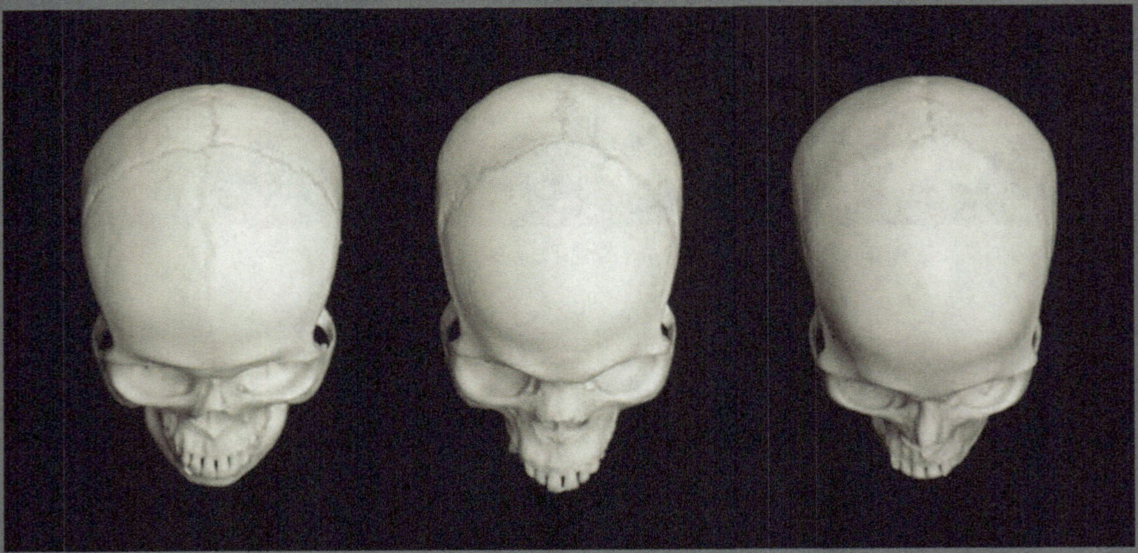

*View looking down: Asian, African, Caucasian.*

- Prognathism—basically how far forward are the upper and lower jaws relative to the rest of the skull? This can also involve the relative forward angle of the front teeth. In profile this would be the basic tilt of the face between the forehead and jaw

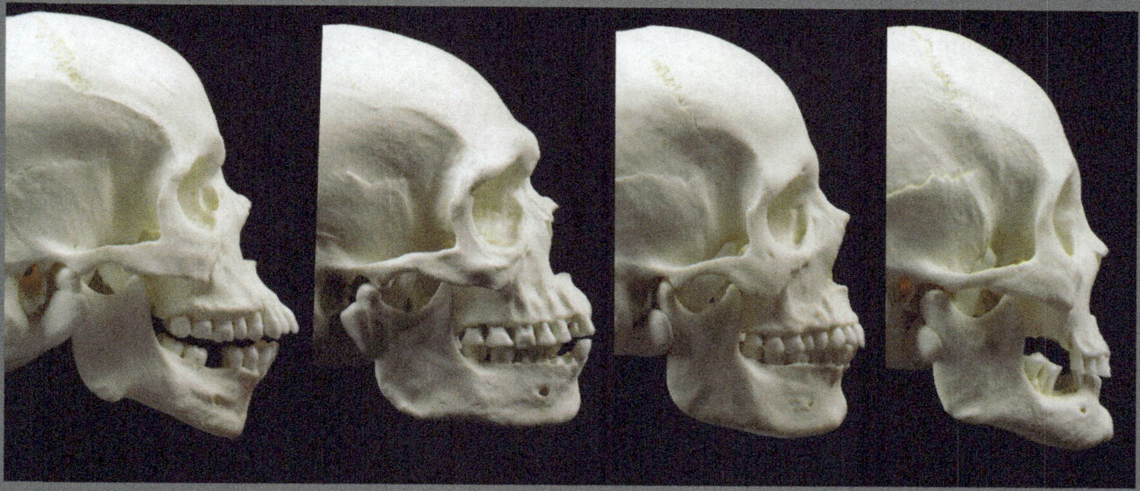

*Side view, Asian male, Caucasian male, African American male.*

- Supraorbital Tori—prominence of the brows —Asian male, African American male, Aboriginal male

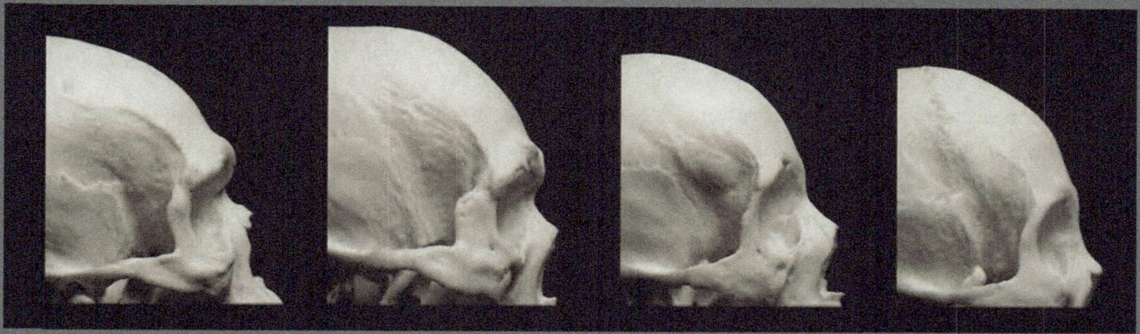

*Asian male, African American male, Aboriginal male.*

Use the following images as visual reference for the locations and basic forms listed above:

All the tutorials in this book are written non-application specific. The reader can approach these tutorials in the way that they are most comfortable with either digital or traditional techniques. A base model:

> **\tutorials\tutorial1\base_skull.obj**
>
> as well as image planes
>
> **\tutorials\tutorial1\image_planes**
>
> and corresponding markers
>
> **\tutorials\tutorial1\skull_markers**
>
> are provided for users of digital sculpting and modeling applications. Also included are measurements files
>
> \tutorials\tutorial1\skull_measurements\
>
> that can be used with calipers for the readers who are working in clay.

One of the trickier aspects in the digital model creation process is matching exactly source photography to a digital model in a synthetic camera. While there are various techniques and specialized tools used in studio environments, in the major digital sculpture applications you cannot exactly match real world cameras and the barrel distortion created by lenses. So, you should not expect to get an exact 1:1 relationship between your model and reference photographs. Ideally you want to know the focal length of the camera lens that the photos were shot with and try to match that as best you can. This is why (as you will see in the following tutorials) the authors recommend using reference photography in combination with the provided measurement markers along with your eye to evaluate the model. For traditional sculptors this will be more familiar.

# TUTORIAL: THE BASIC ASIAN MALE SKULL

As we are focusing on the larger landmark forms of the skull in this tutorial, as such we will not be diving into the small details. Once the student feels comfortable with their results, they should feel free to go into as much detail as they wish.

Open your application of choice. Import the following images as image planes for reference:

**\tutorials\tutorial1\front_asian_male.jpg**

**\tutorials\tutorial1\side_asian_male.jpg**

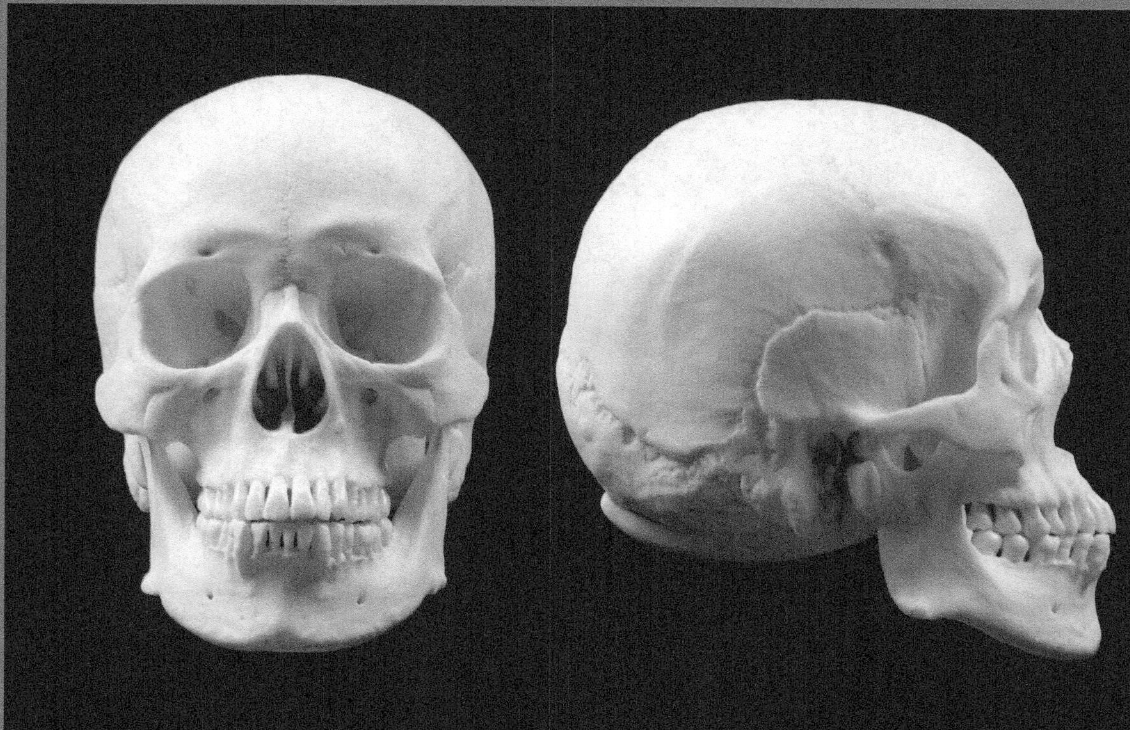

*Asian male skull.*

Now import:

**\tutorials\tutorial1\markers\asian_make_markers.obj**

If necessary, align the image plane to the marker geometry:

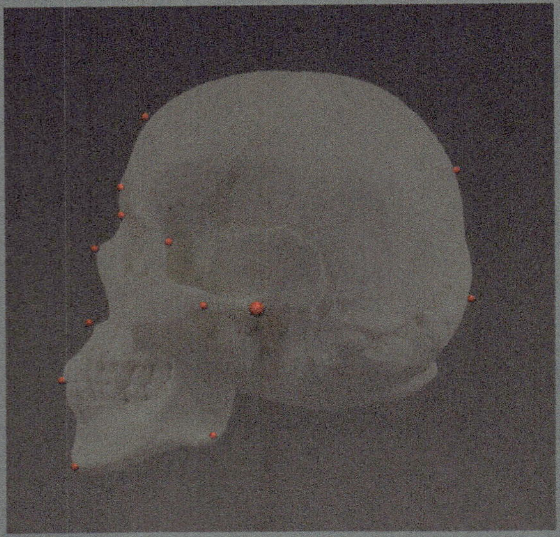

*Markers aligned with reference image.*

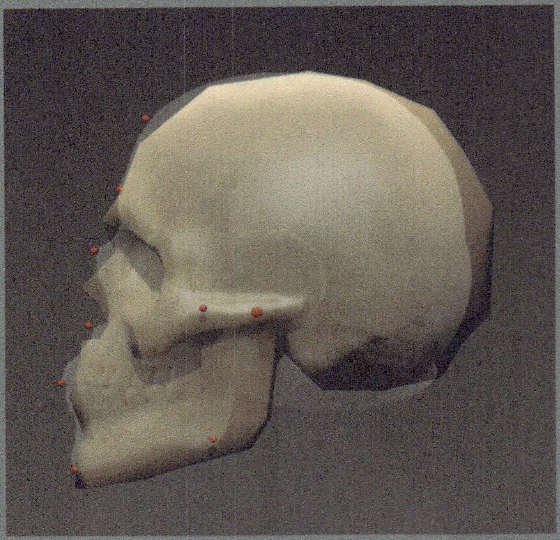

*Skull starter geometry basically aligned with markers.*

Import the file:

**\tutorials\tutorial1\base_skull.obj**

The skull starter geometry should very roughly sit within the marker geometry and the skull shape of the image plane. If for any reason it does not, move/scale the skull geometry with the side view image plane so that with the External Acoustic Meatus (ear hole) aligned between the image and model, the crown-to-chin height of the geometry matches the photo.

The starter skull geometry is generic in its proportions. Notice both the forward tilt of the face from brow to chin in this example (prognathism) as well as the depth of the anterior (front) plane of the cheek bones in the photo reference.

Using your applications geometry transform tool with a large diameter fall off, begin to match the basic silhouette of the geometry to the skull. Be careful to ignore the stand at the base of the skull in the photograph. Refine the silhouette by gradually reducing the size of your move tool to get the finer angles after the big forms are in place.

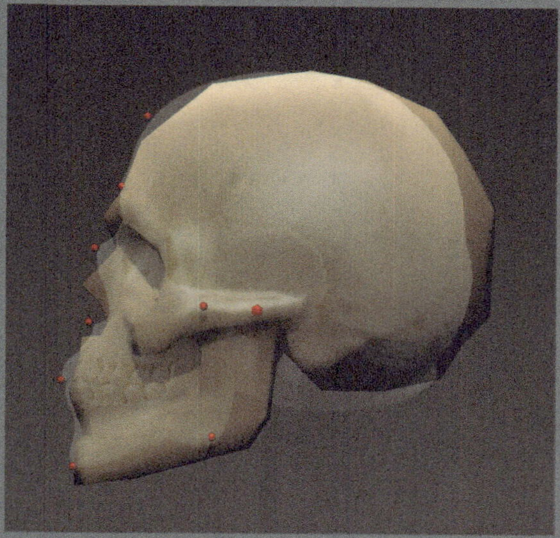

*Starting point.*

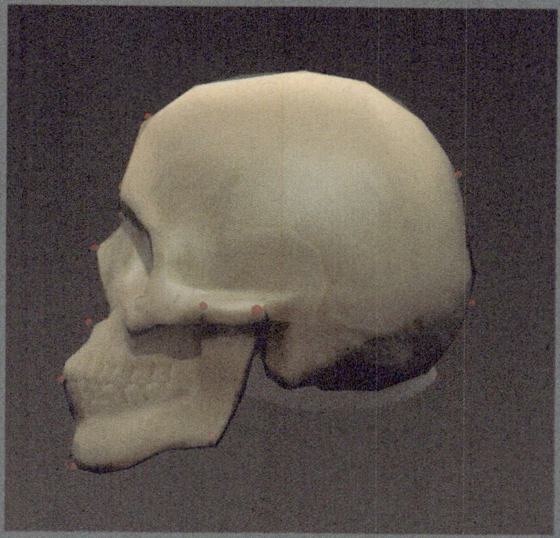

*First step - align silhouette.*

Once the profile is accurate, what is left is locating the depth of certain landmark points in horizontal space. To do this, we will use a combination of the front view, the markers, and the 3/4 view. The method that we are going to use is to have the imported markers overlaid on the starter skull with the front image plane offset to the side to evaluate your progress on reshaping the skull. The markers were generated from measurements of one side of the skull, so they are set up symmetrically. The skull is not perfectly symmetrical, so the positions of the markers are an approximate guide. The photographs should be your ultimate guide for evaluation.

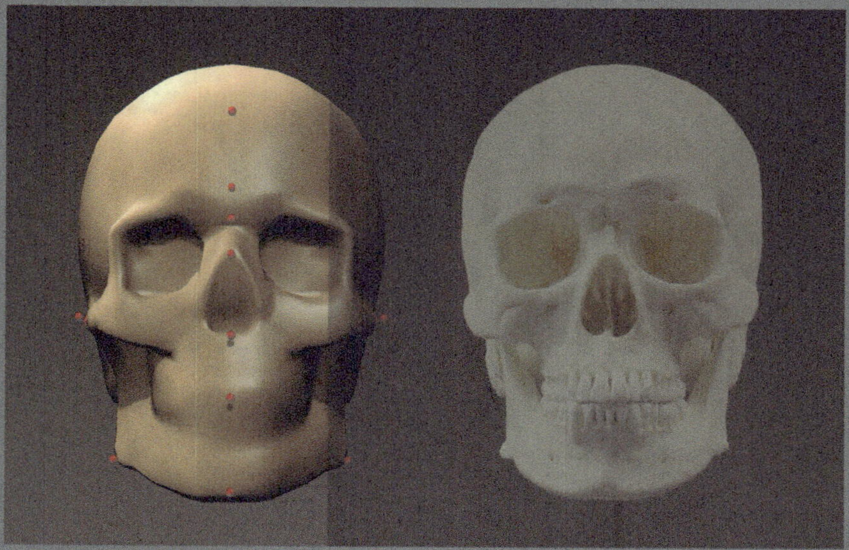

*Suggested setup for evaluating front view.*

You should switch back and forth between the front and side views to evaluate your progress. Once you're basically satisfied with your front and side views, you should import one or more of the front angle views to do a final evaluation before we move on to focus on finalizing the landmark forms.

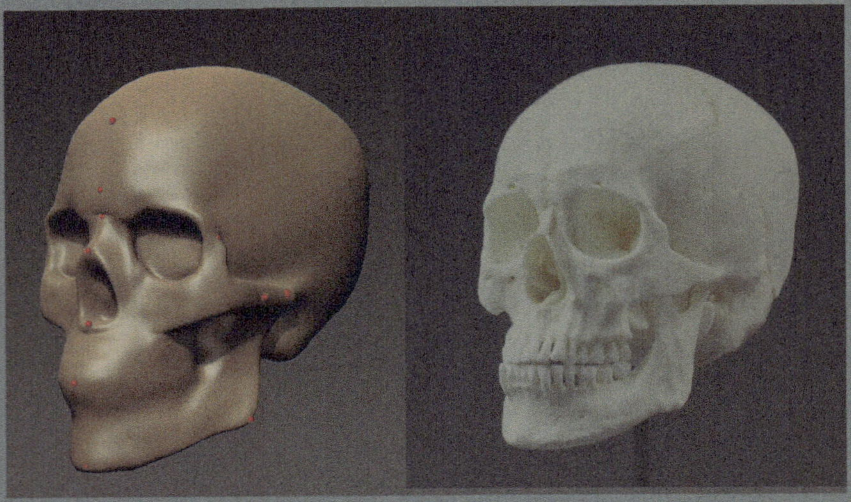

*Suggested setup for evaluating 3/4 view.*

What you should have at this point is a loose approximation of the Asian male skull. Now we are going to start to sculpt the planes and forms that will help you to begin to understand what's at the core of making each face look like a face and how the position and proportions vary.

The first area we are going to clearly define is the zygomatic region (cheek bone and most of eye socket). Referring to the images below and the reference photography of the Asian male skull, attempt to refine the region indicated:

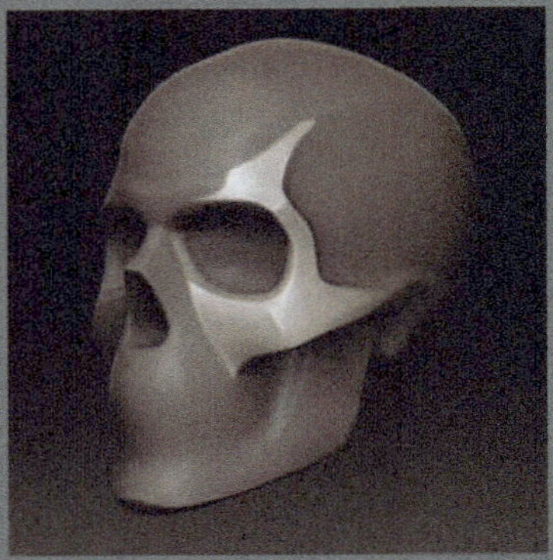

*Zygomatic region on skull.*

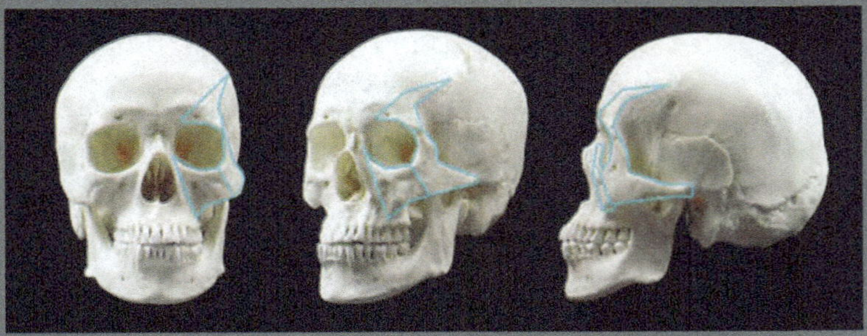

*Zygomatic region.*

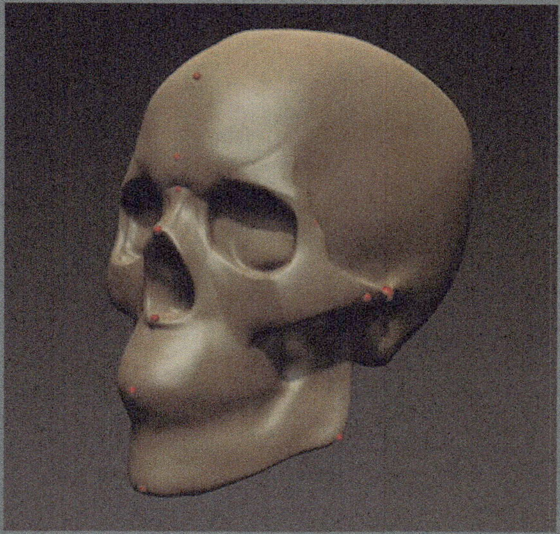

*Zygomatic blocked in.*

**A couple of important things to keep in mind as you work:**

The eye socket in this individual is fairly round. Eye sockets vary from round to square between sexes and ethnic groups. As mentioned earlier, the anterior plane of the cheek bone is fairly front facing. In the side view, the outer corner of the plane is not much further back than where it inserts at the maxilla. This "sweep" of the outer corner of the zygomatic will retreat more or less towards the rear of the skull in different ethnic groups.

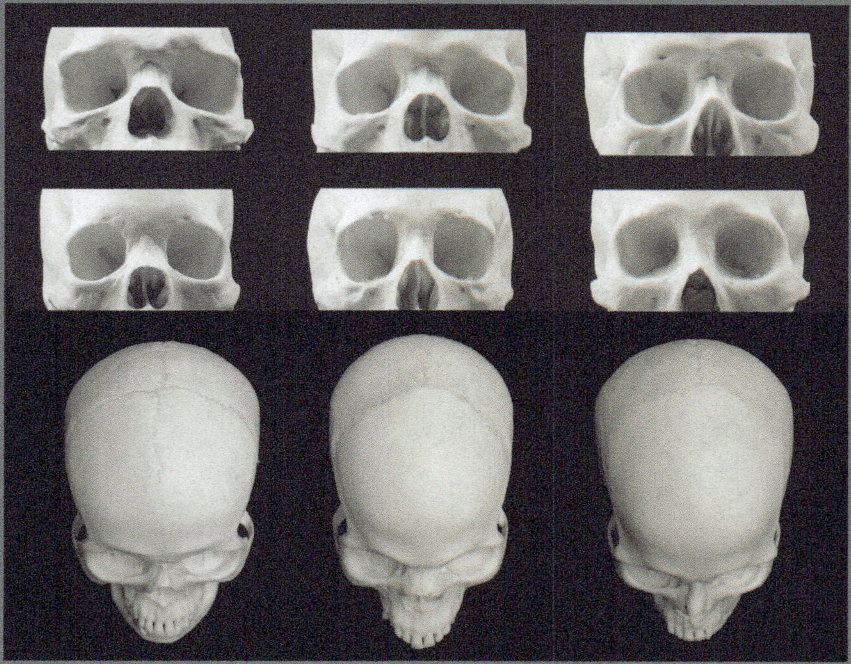

*Images demonstrating the shape of eye socket and zygomatic sweep.*

**Next we will define the planes of the nasal cavity.**

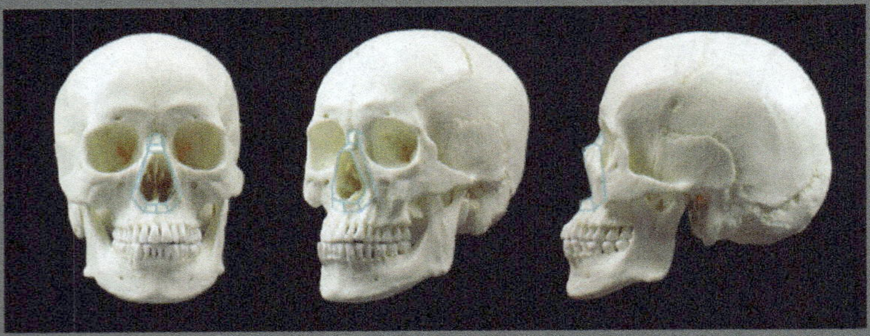

*Nasal cavity forms on skull.*

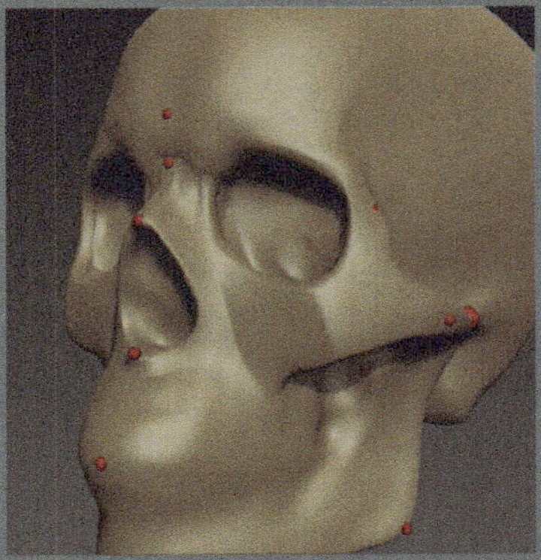

*Result: nasal cavity.*

**Now proceed to refining the brow and forehead region:**

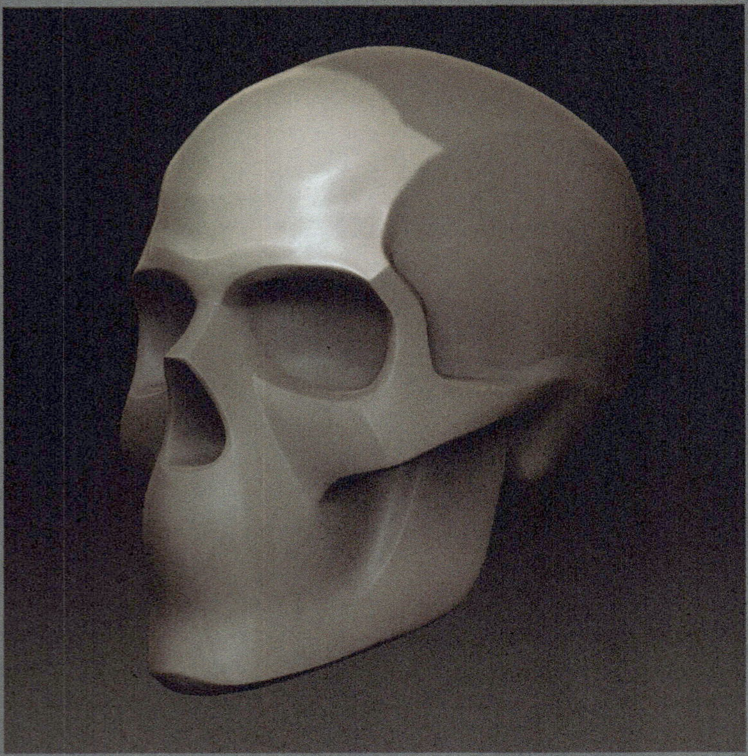

*Brow and forehead region highlighted.*

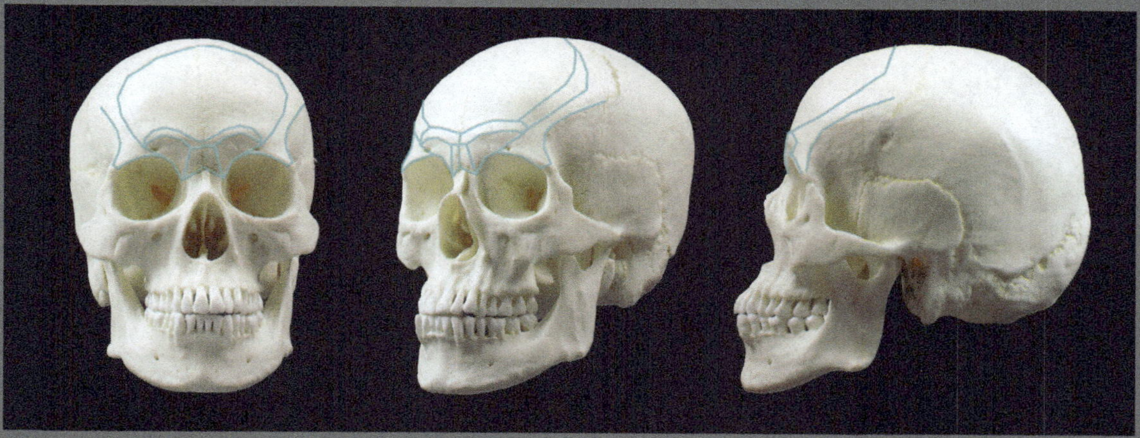

*Reference image.*

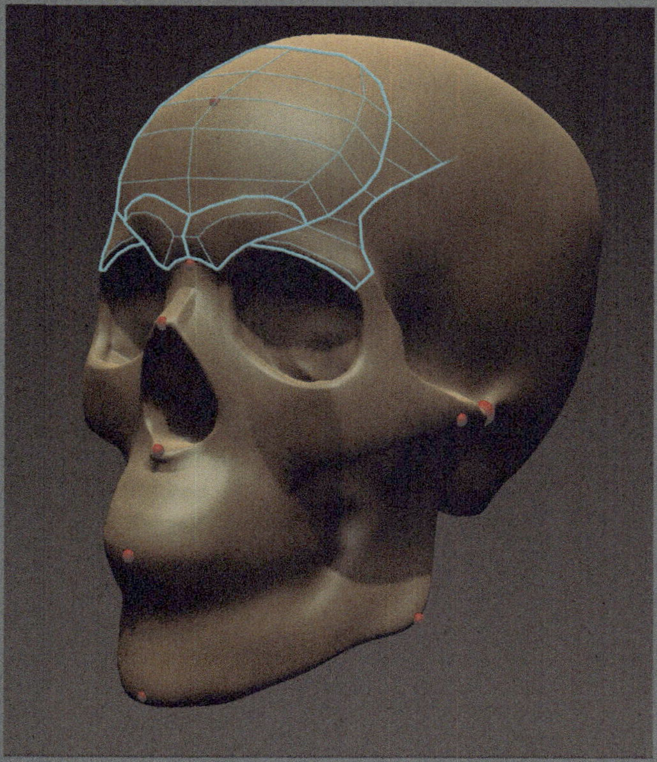

*Blue line.*

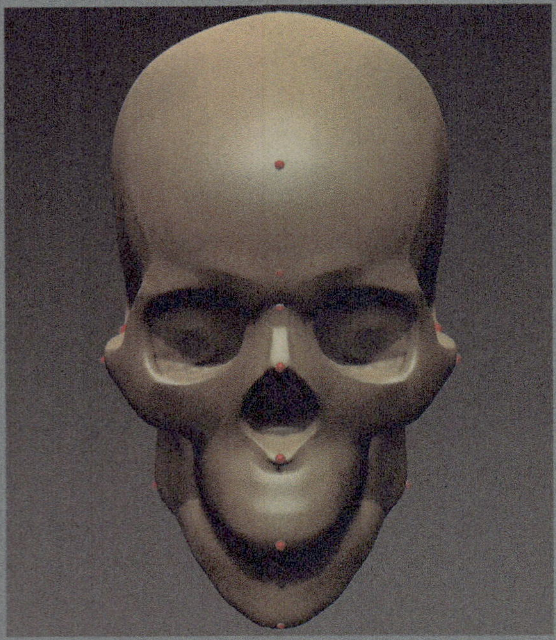

*Front view.*

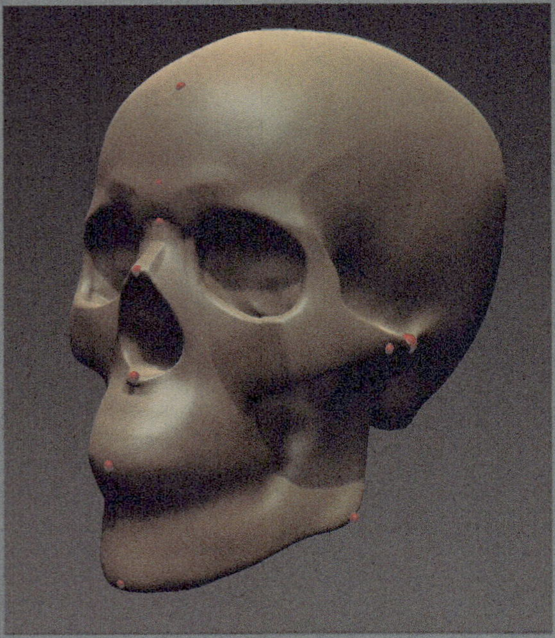

*Finished.*

**Next move on to the barrel of the mouth and jaw region:**

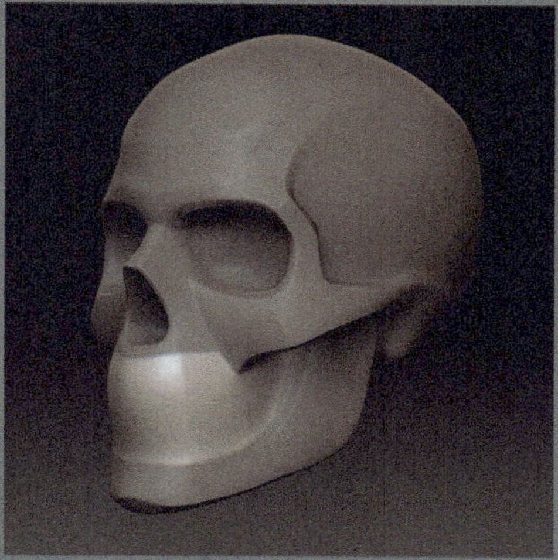

*Jaw region.*

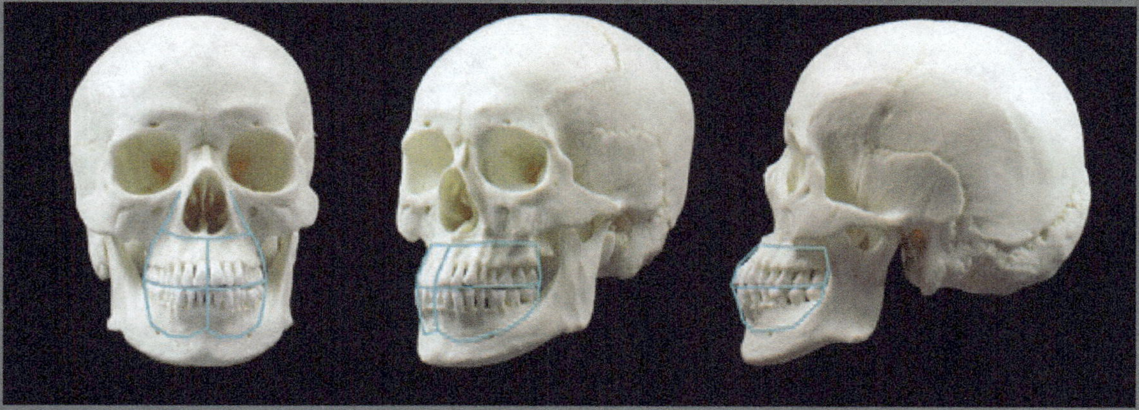

*Jaw planes on skull.*

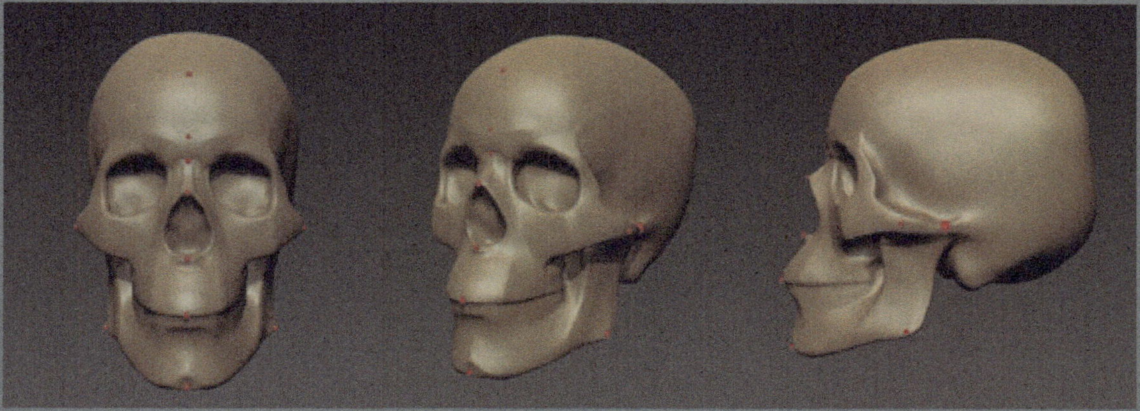

*Jaw planes added to model.*

Cranium

**While the focus of this book is primarily on the face, we will take a moment to look at the posterior forms of the skull:**

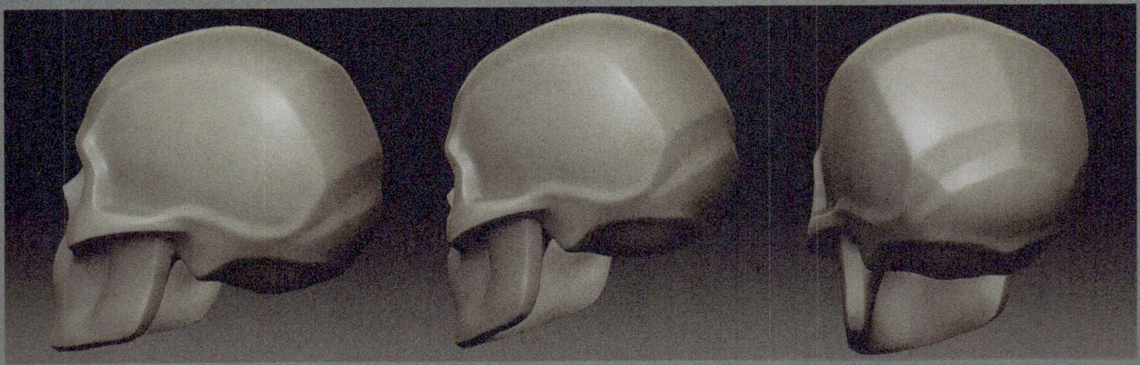

*Image of basic geometric forms of back of skull.*

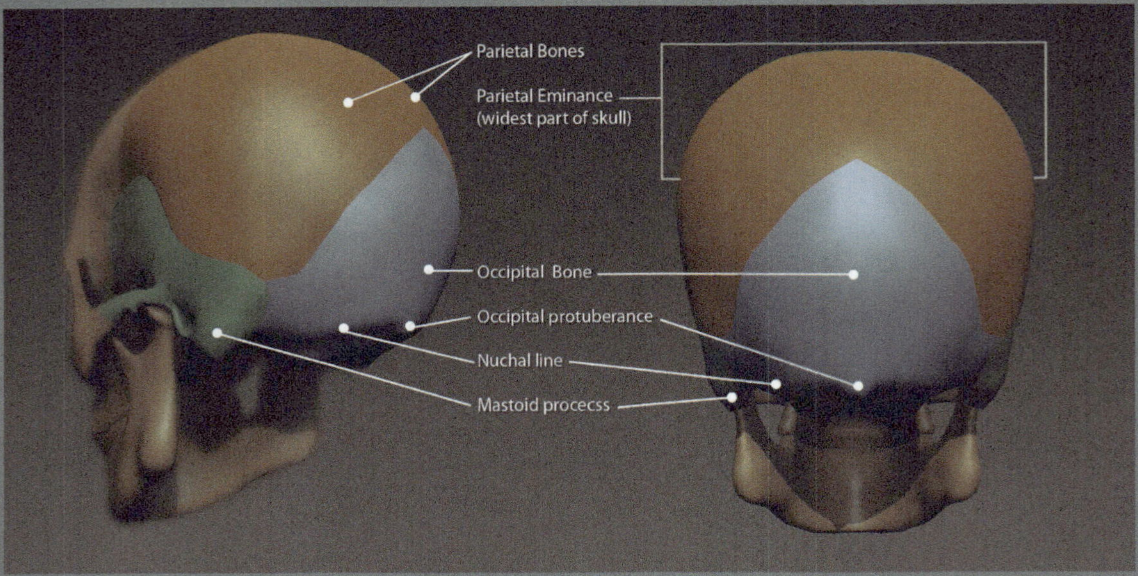


*Simple bones of the back of the skull.*

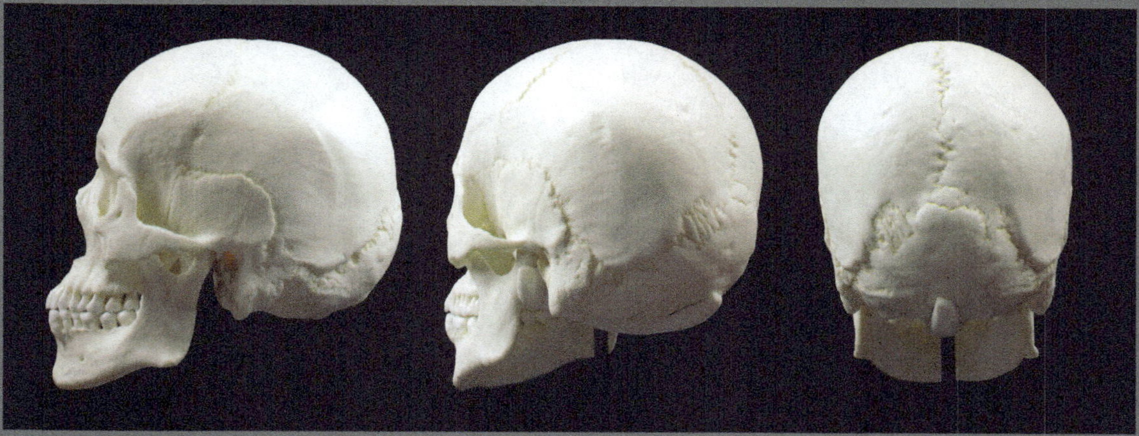

*Image of Asian male skull matching previous image.*

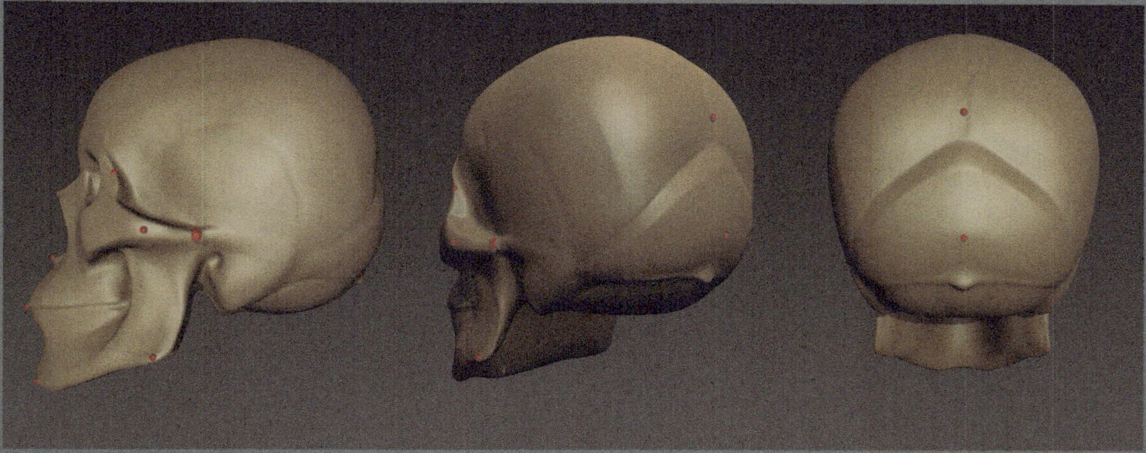

*Image of tutorial skull completed.*

Now that you have walked though one simple example, use the resources provided in the folder for this chapter's tutorial to complete three more skull studies of an Asian female and an African male and an Aboriginal male.

**\tutorials\tutorial1\male_caucasian_nose_baseform.obj**

**\tutorials\tutorial1\male_asian_nose_baseform.obj**

**\tutorials\tutorial1\male_african_american_nose_baseform.obj**

**\tutorials\tutorial1\asian_male.jpg**

**\tutorials\tutorial1\african_american_male.jpg**

# 3

# CHAPTER 3

# FEMALE FACES

DOI: 10.1201/ 9781003484554-3

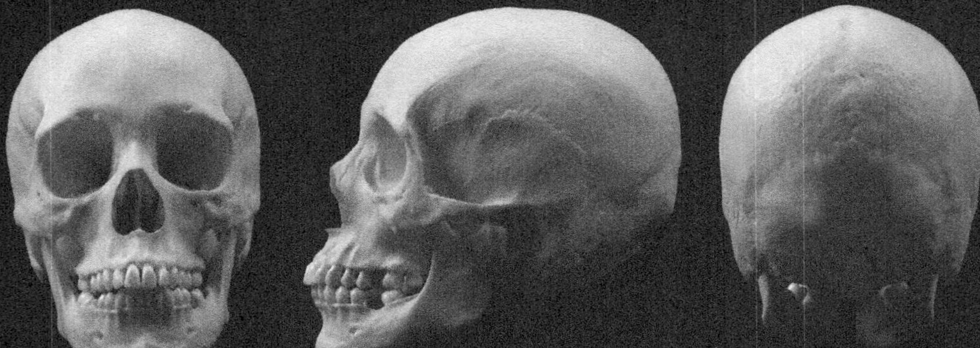

Female, African American

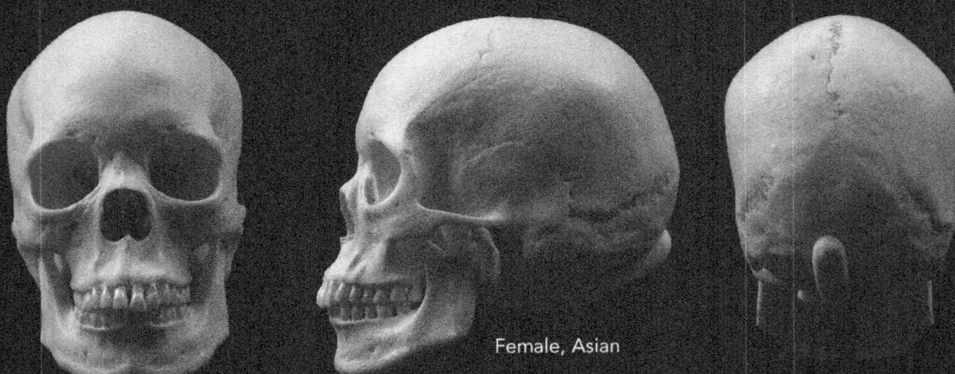

Female, Asian

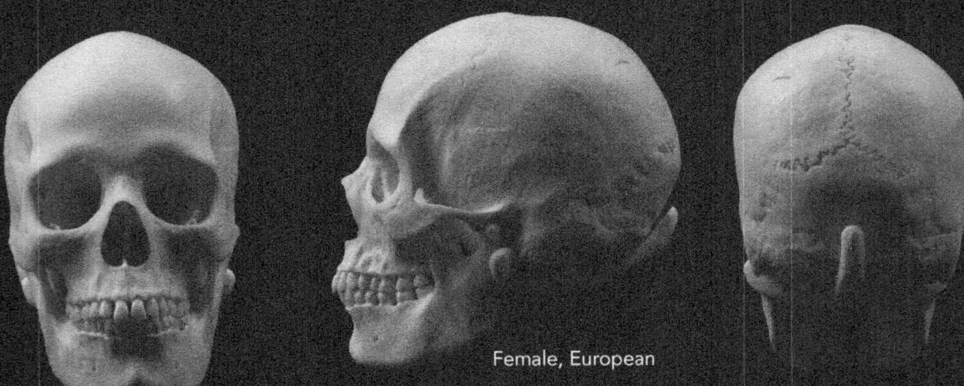

Female, European

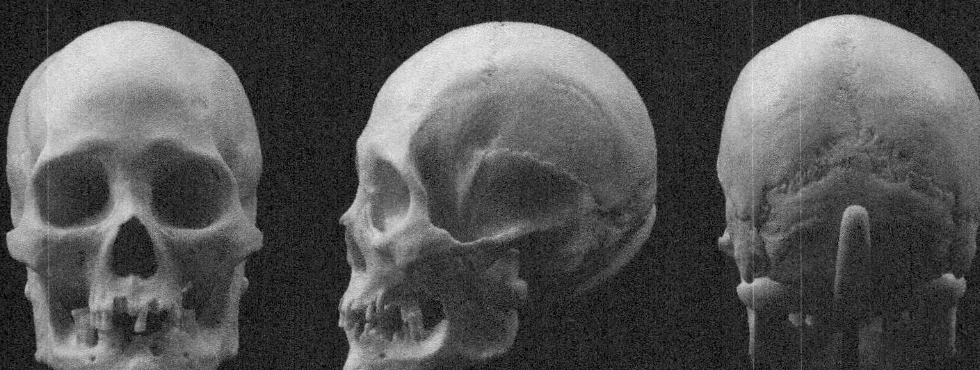

Female, Native American

*Female skulls from around the world.*

The female face is featured in this chapter. Each female will be featured in a turn-around. Each model's description will include measurements taken with calipers, and the country the person claims ancestry from.

Chapter 2 demonstrated the difference in size found between the sample male and female skulls we have. What did you notice?

The female face is usually smaller and softer than the male face. The forehead is a bit more upright and smooth. The female mandible is proportionally smaller, the angle of the jaw is less defined, and the chin is more pointed. Did you notice that even the teeth are smaller on the female than on the male counterpart?

# APPROXIMATE FEMALE ANCESTRY

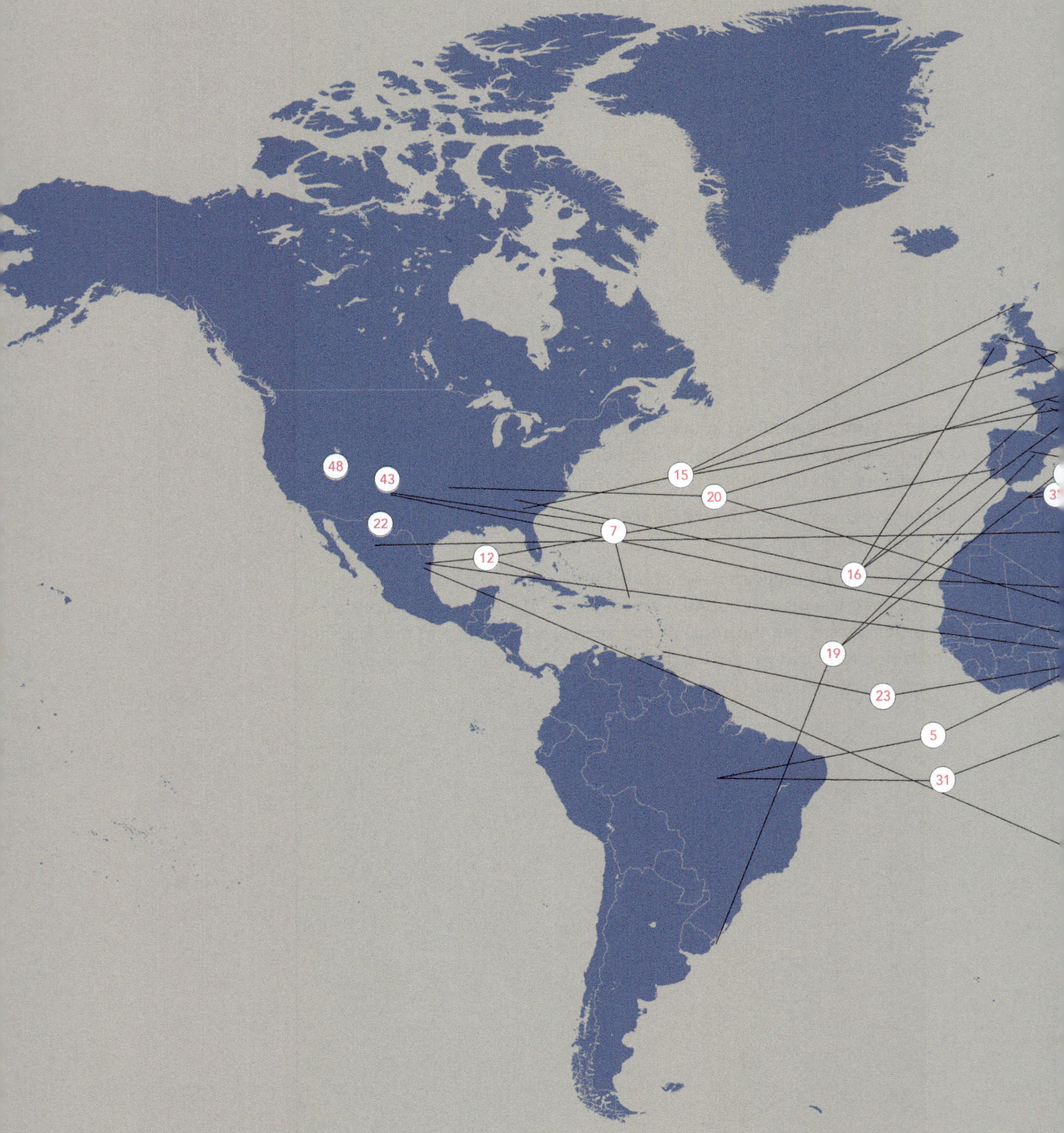

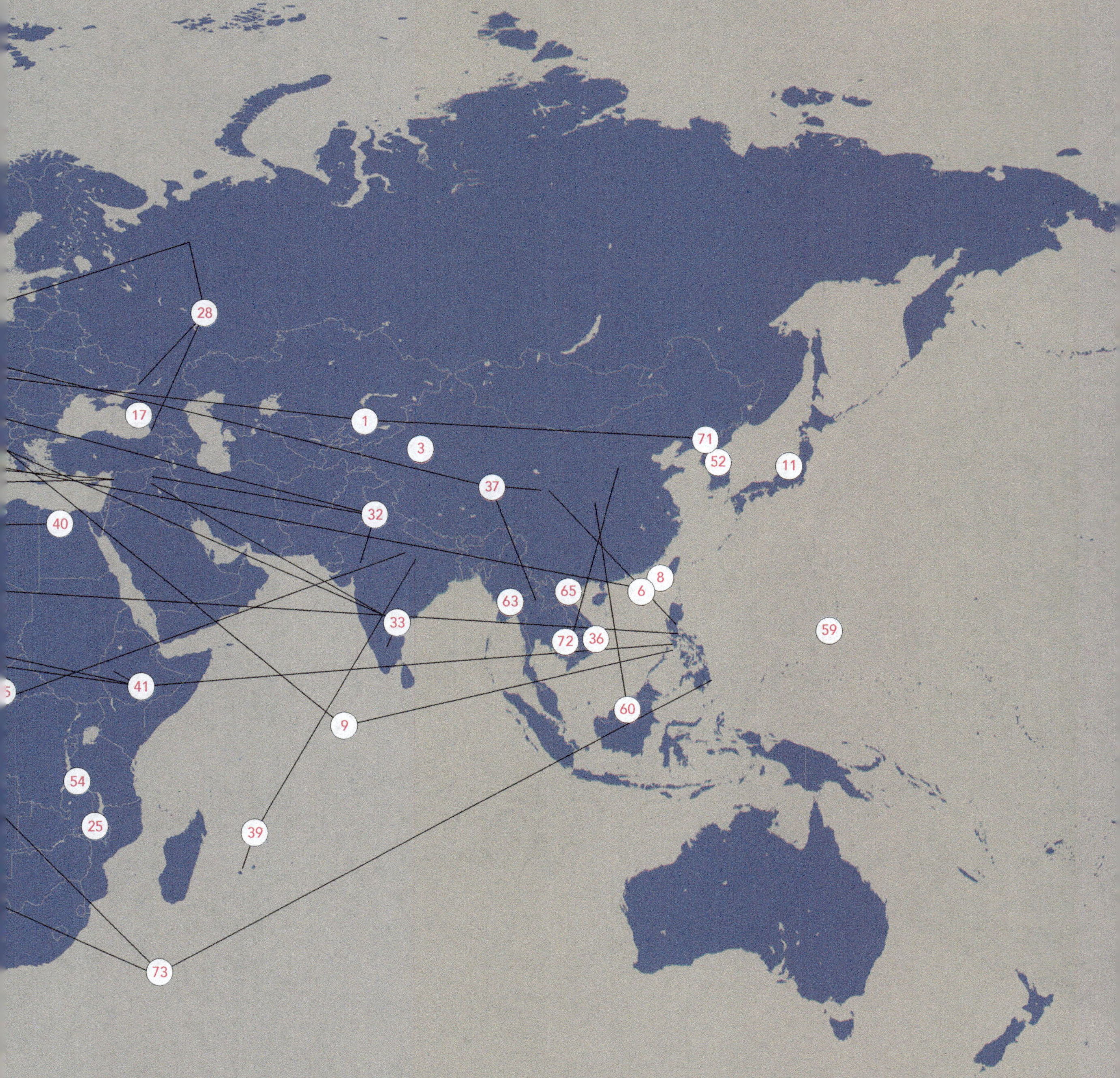


*Approximation of ancestry claimed by females.*

MAP REFERENCE:

1

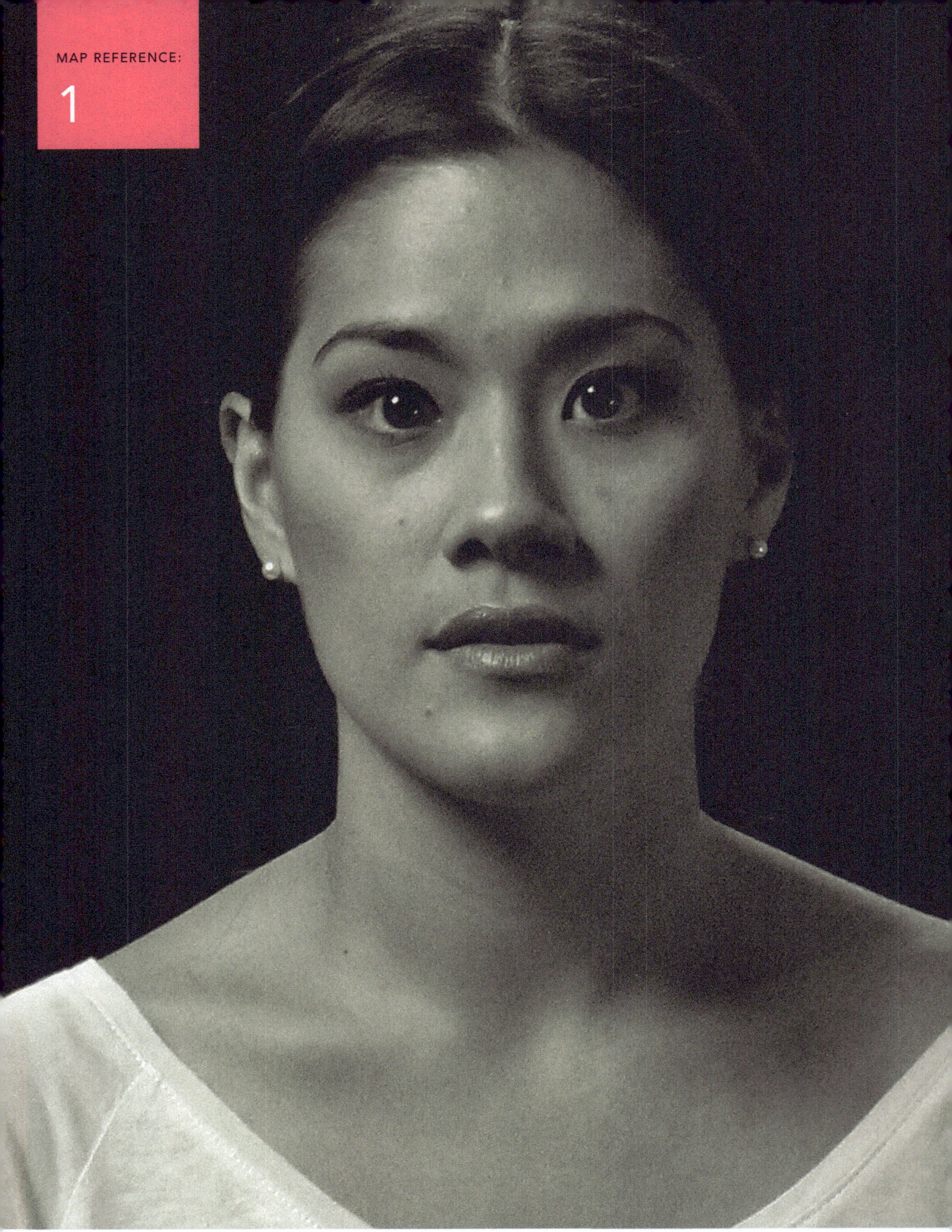

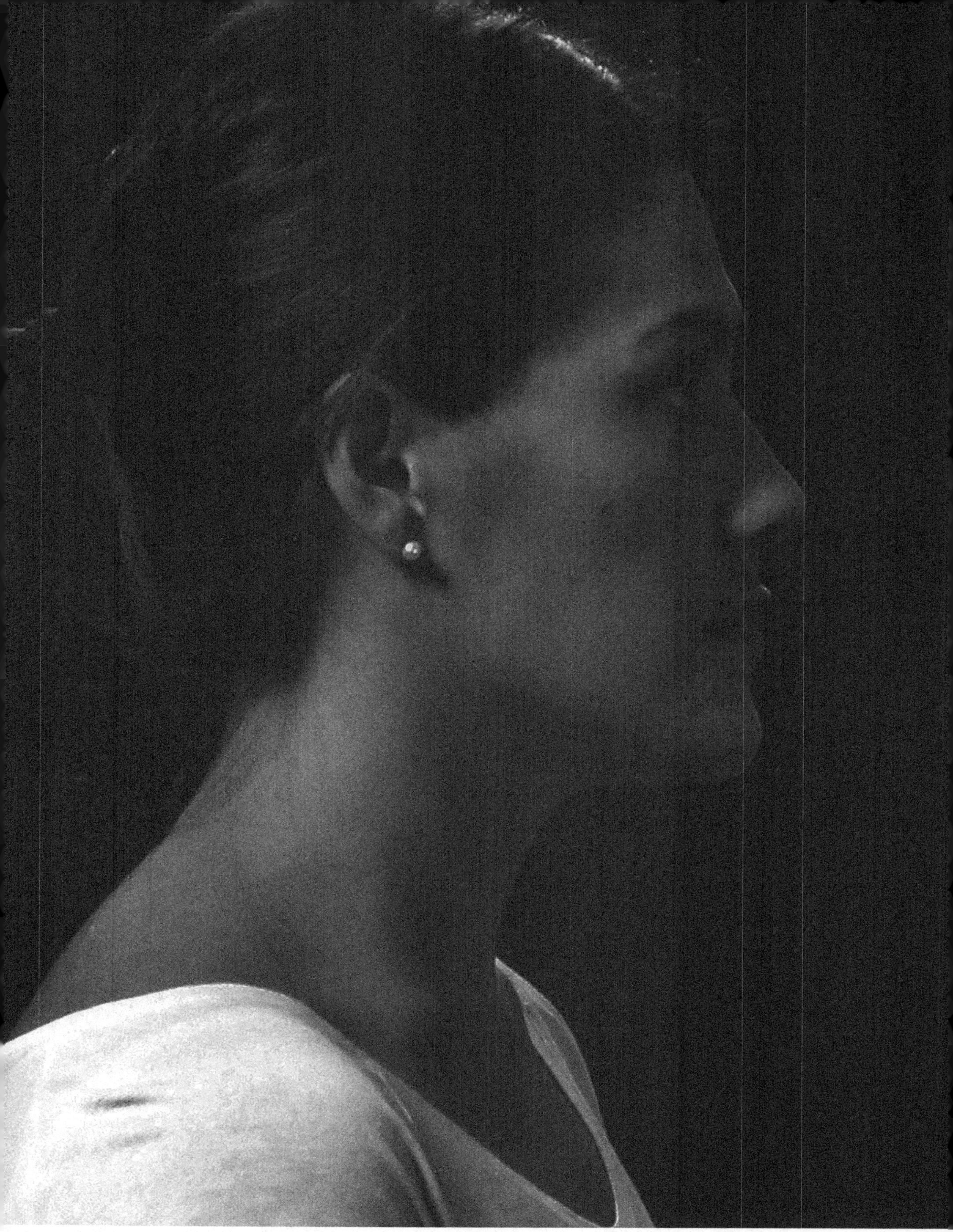

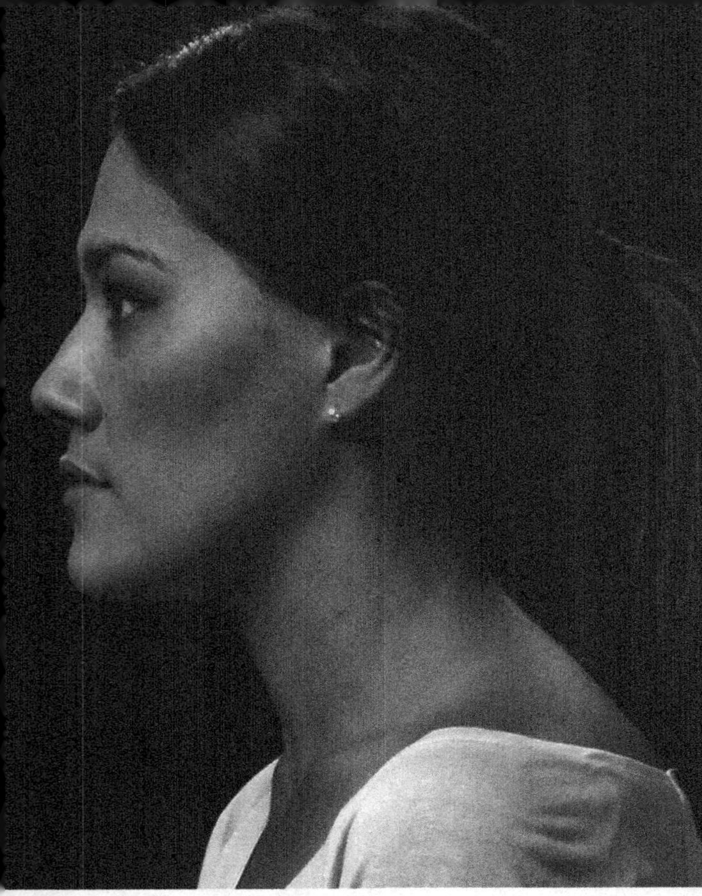

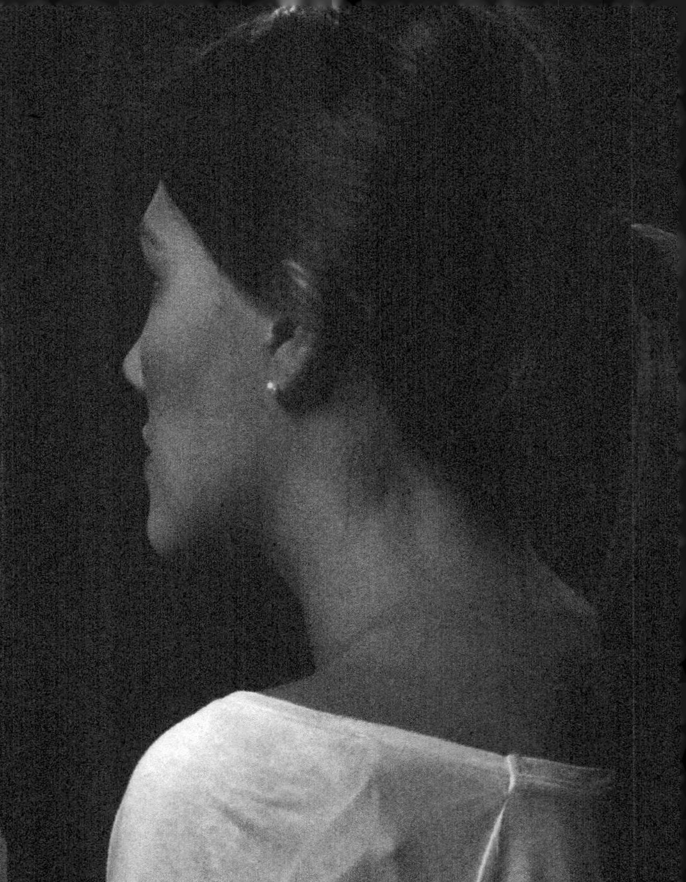

**Ethnicities claimed:**

Germany, Korea.

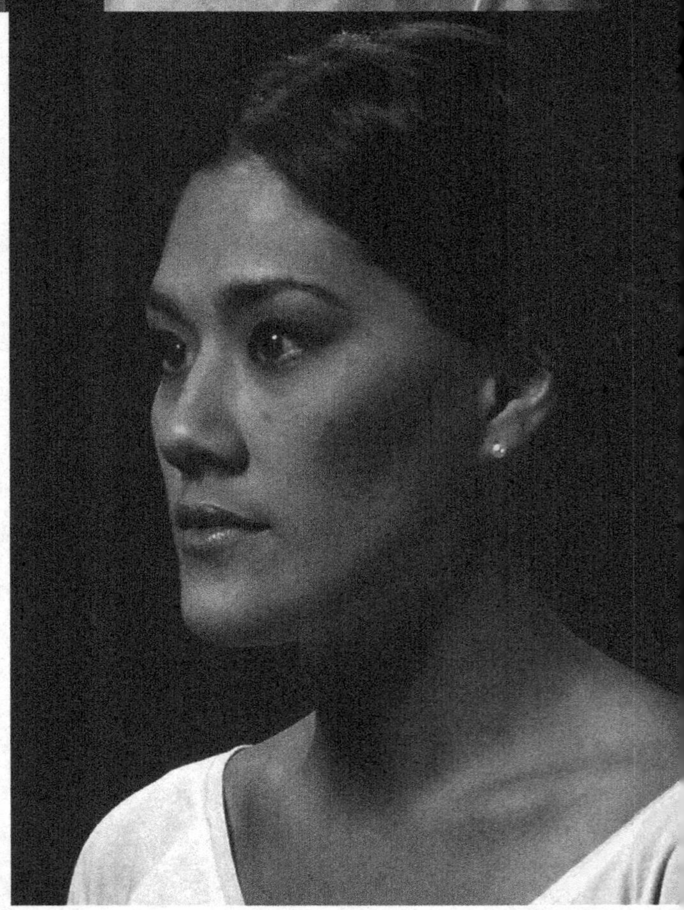

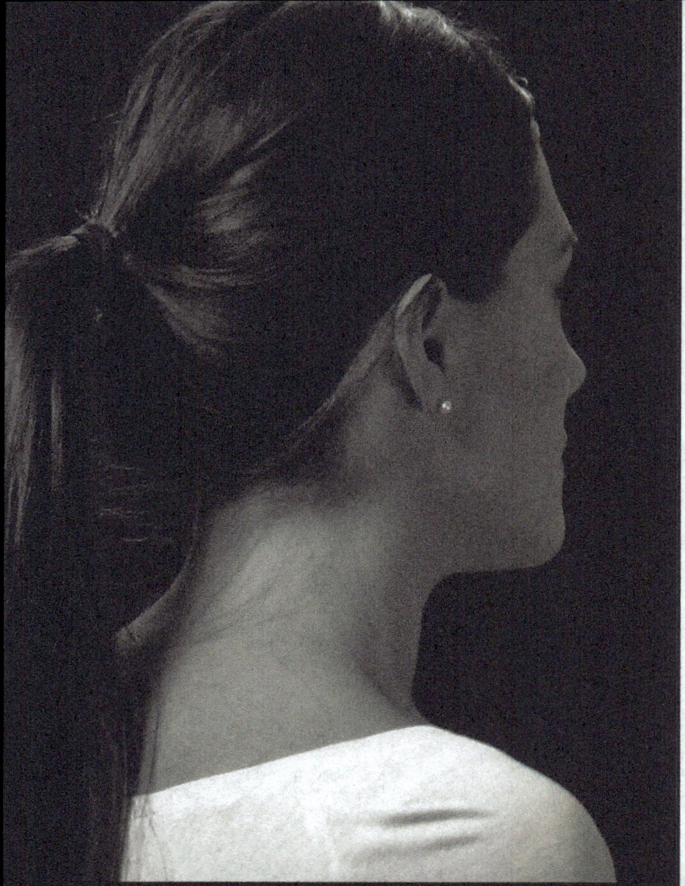

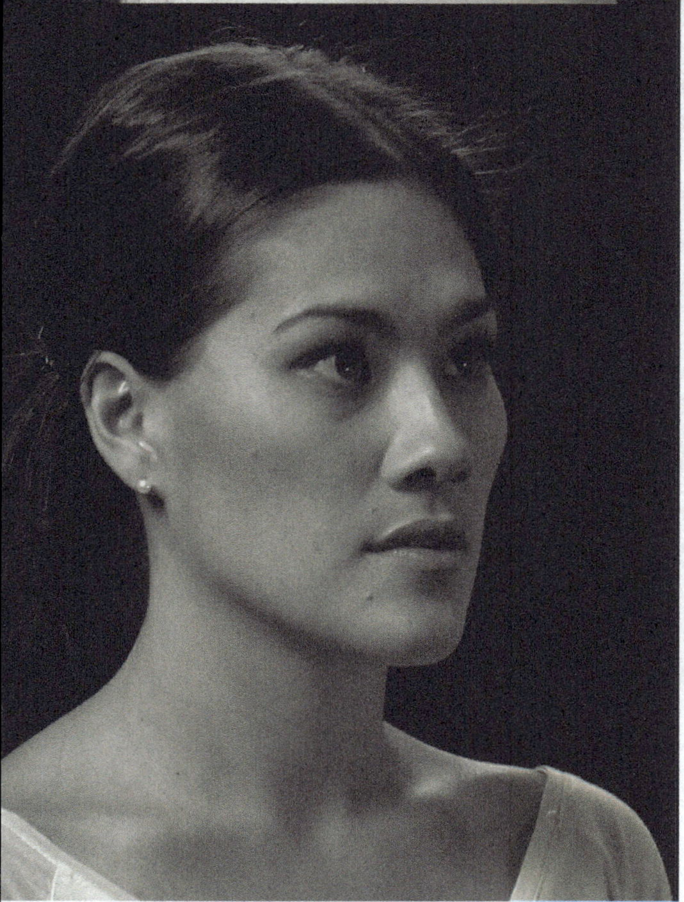

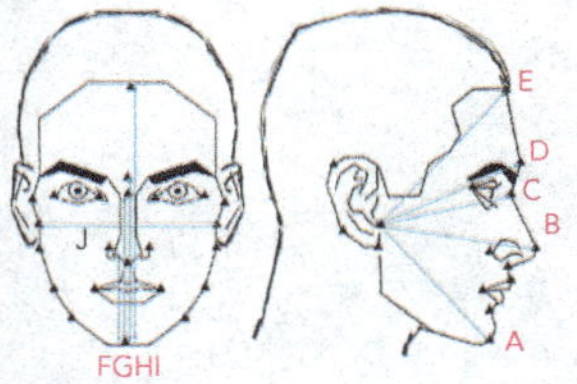


**Head measurements (in):**

A: 5 5/8
B: 5 1/8
C: 4 5/8
D: 5
E: 6 1/4
F: 3 1/2
G: 4 1/8
H: 5
I: 7 3/8
J: 5 1/5

MAP REFERENCE:

3

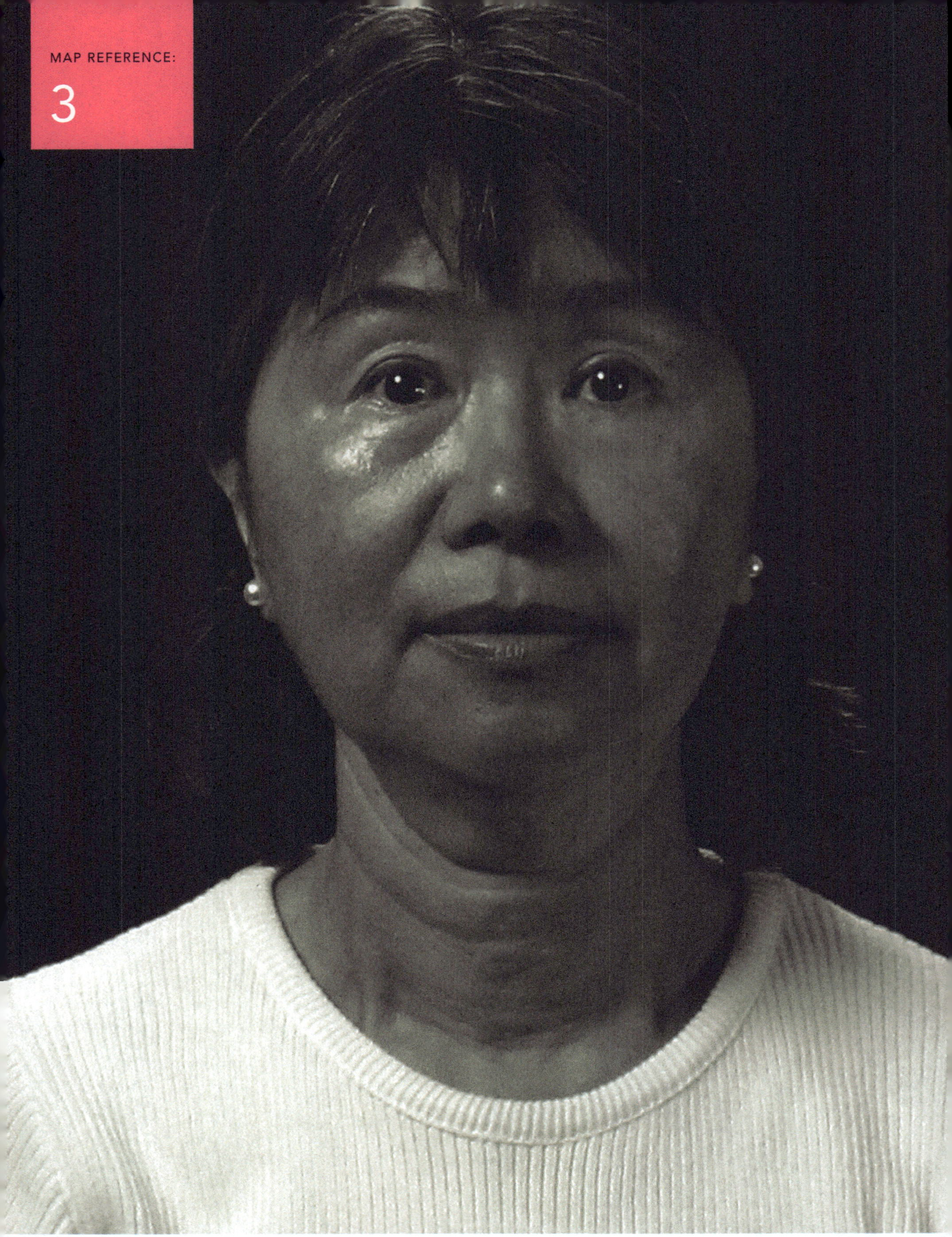

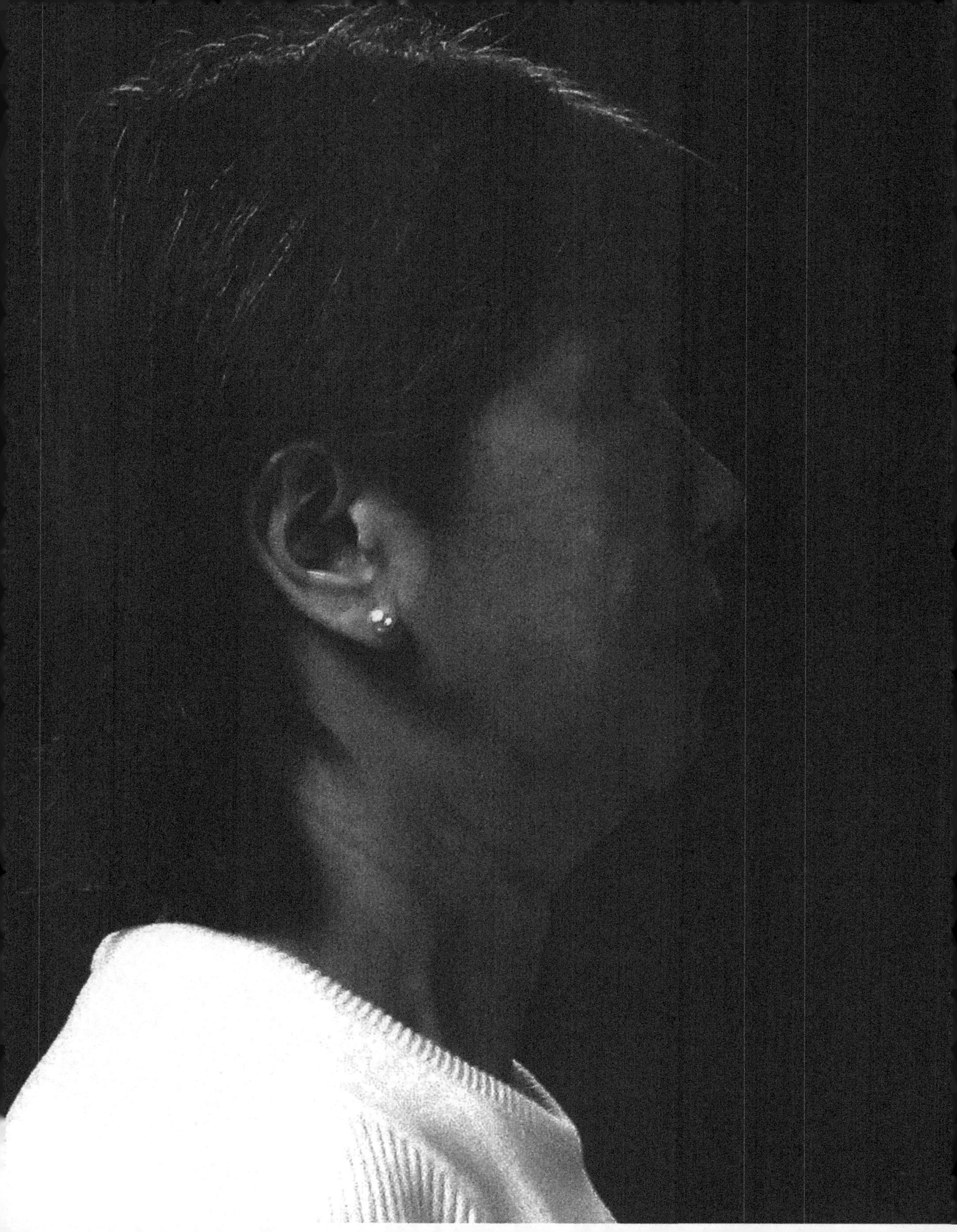

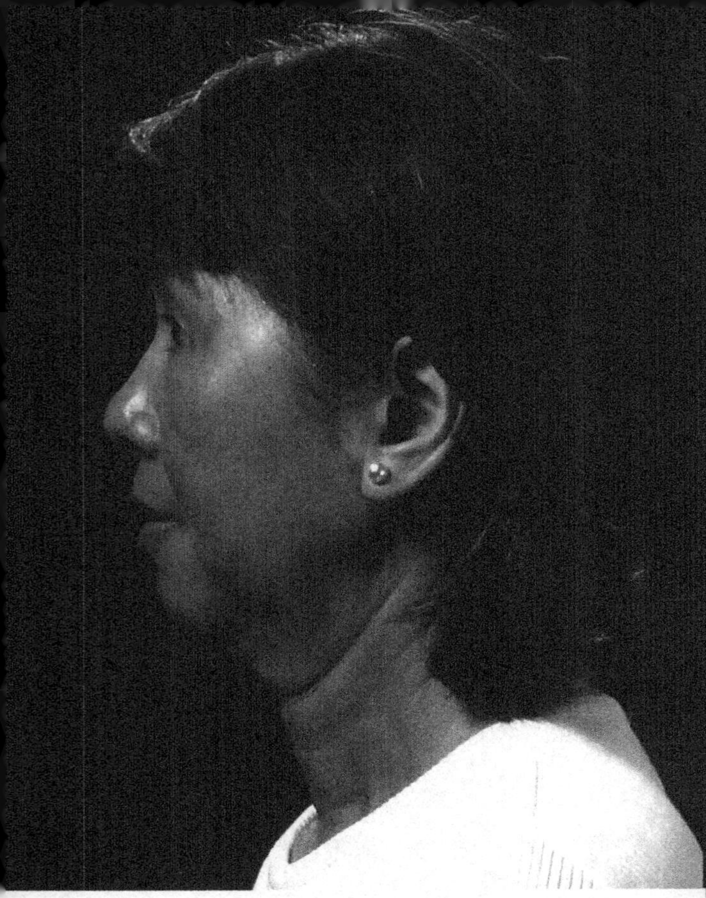

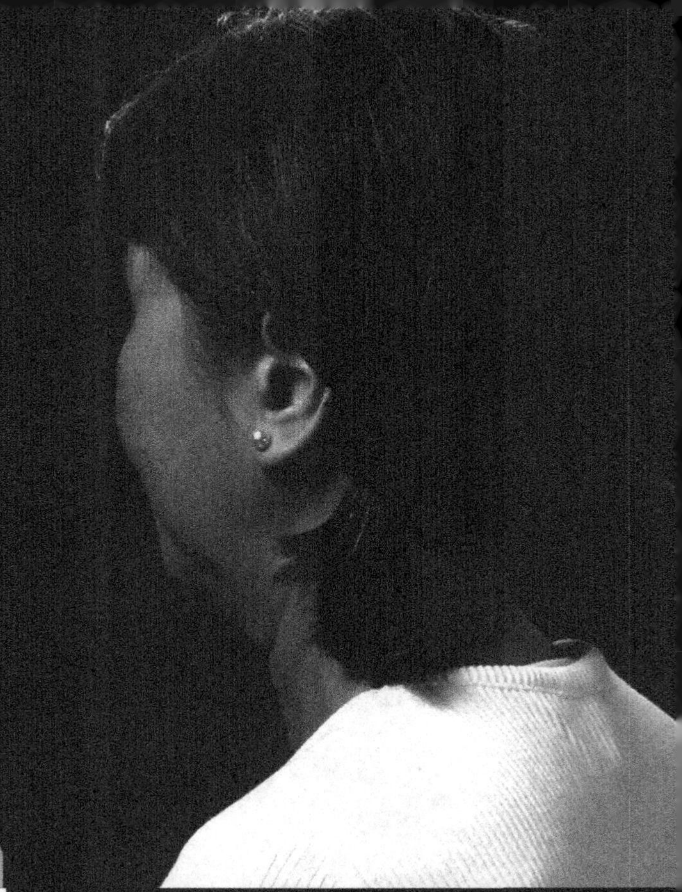

**Ethnicities claimed:**

China.

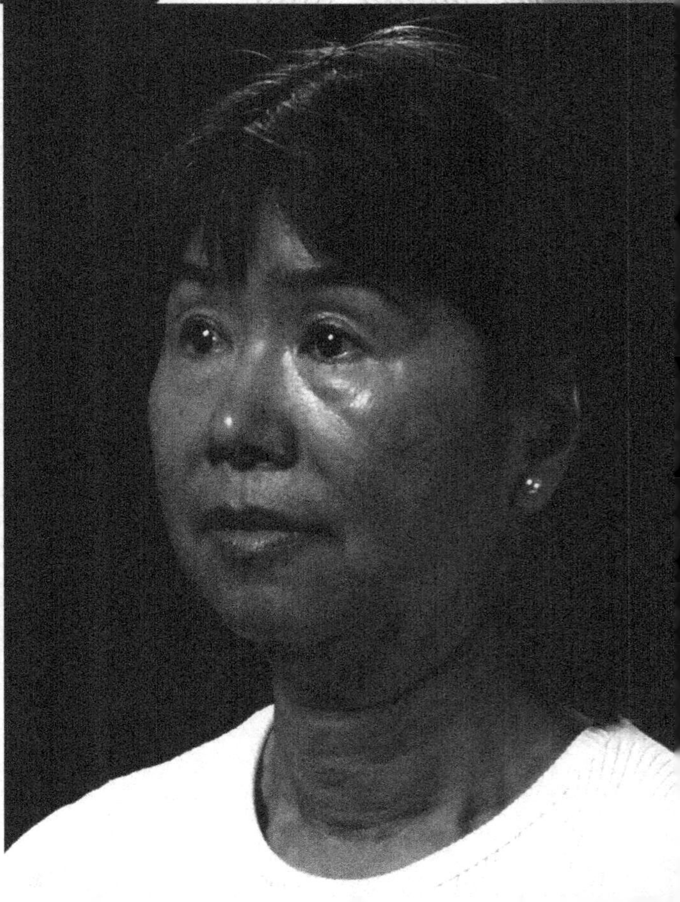

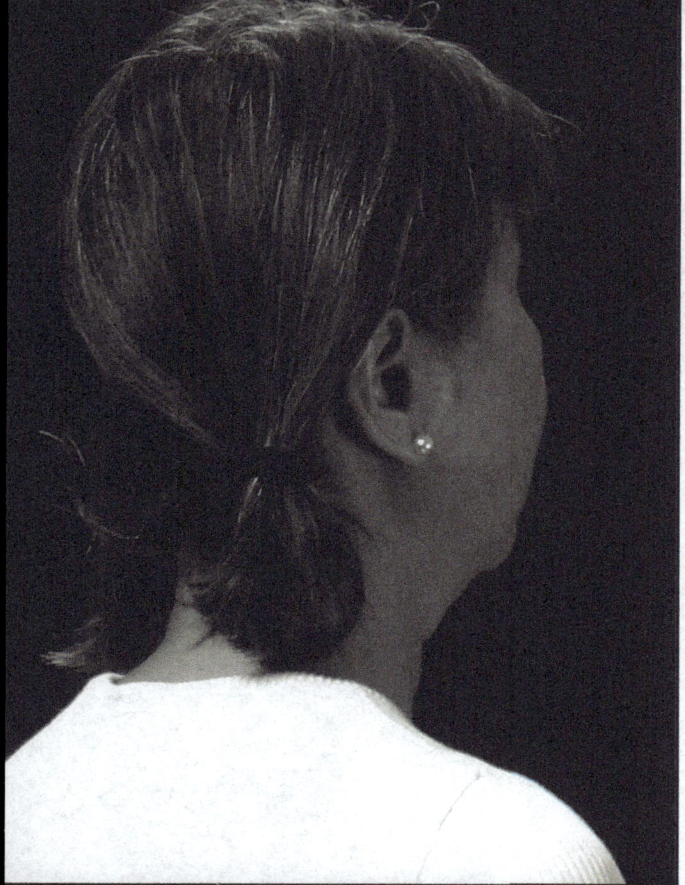

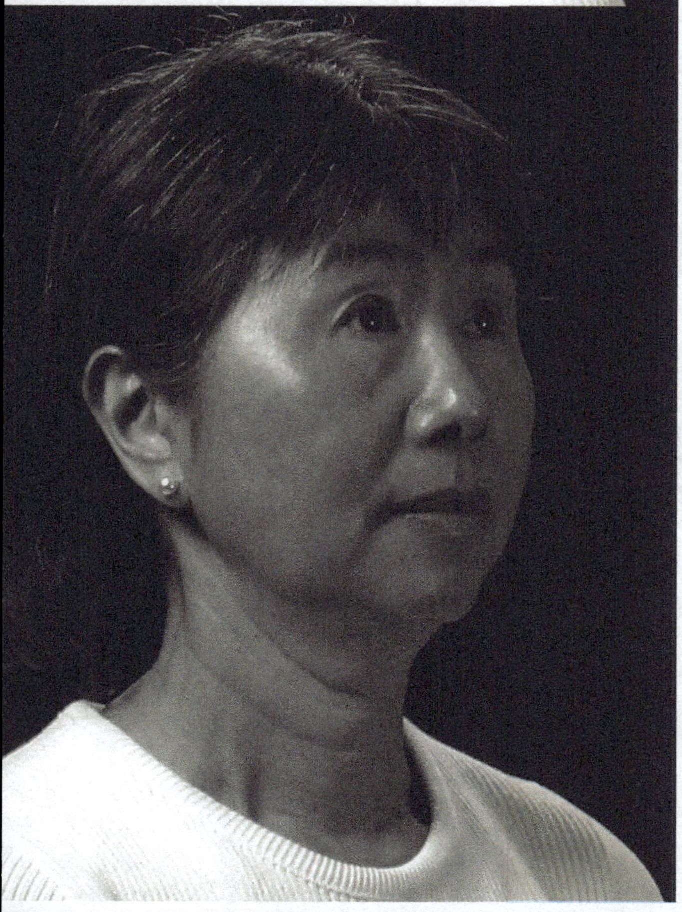

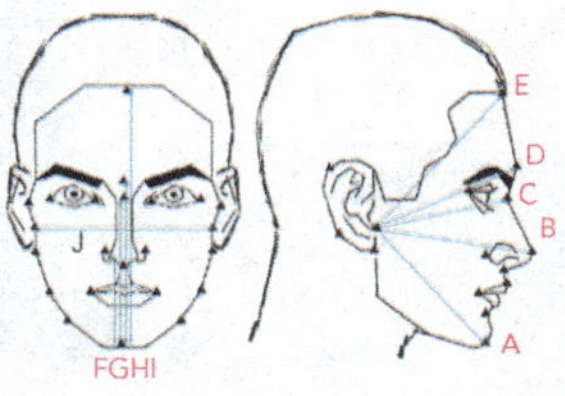


**Head measurements (in):**

A: 5
B: 5 1/8
C: 4 1/2
D: 4 7/8
E: 5 3/4
F: 3 3/8
G: 4 1/4
H: 5 1/8
I: 7 1/4
J: 4

MAP REFERENCE:

6

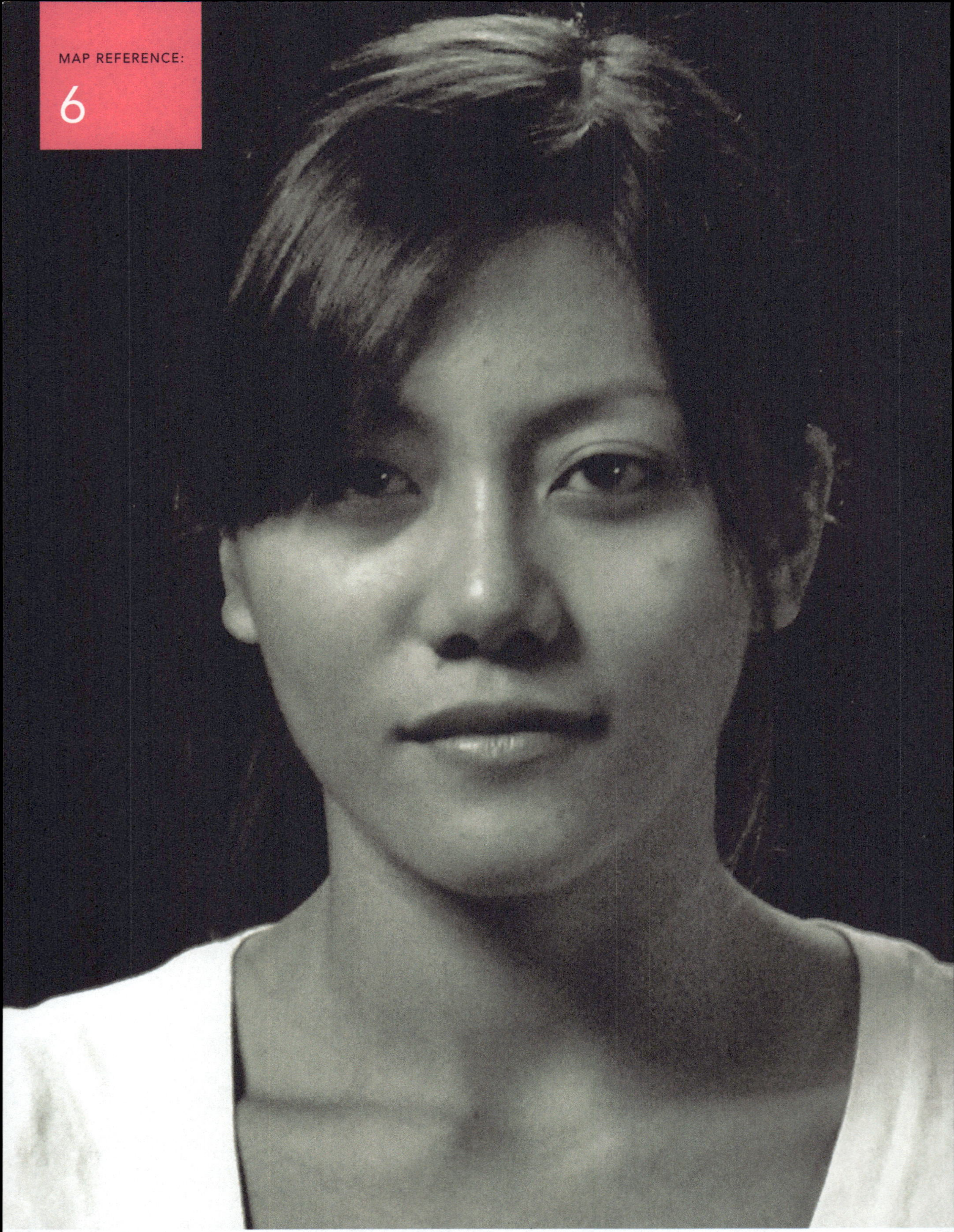

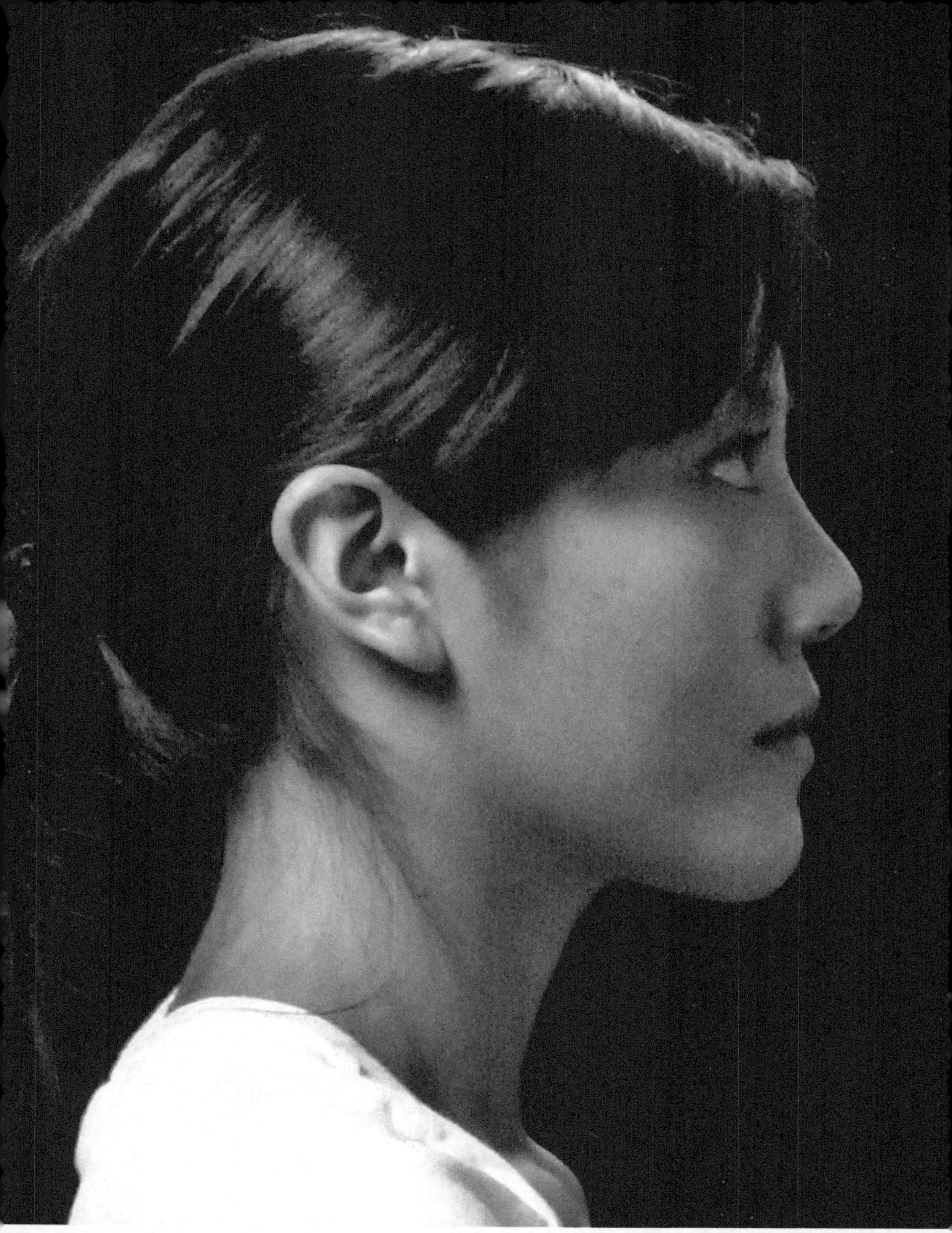

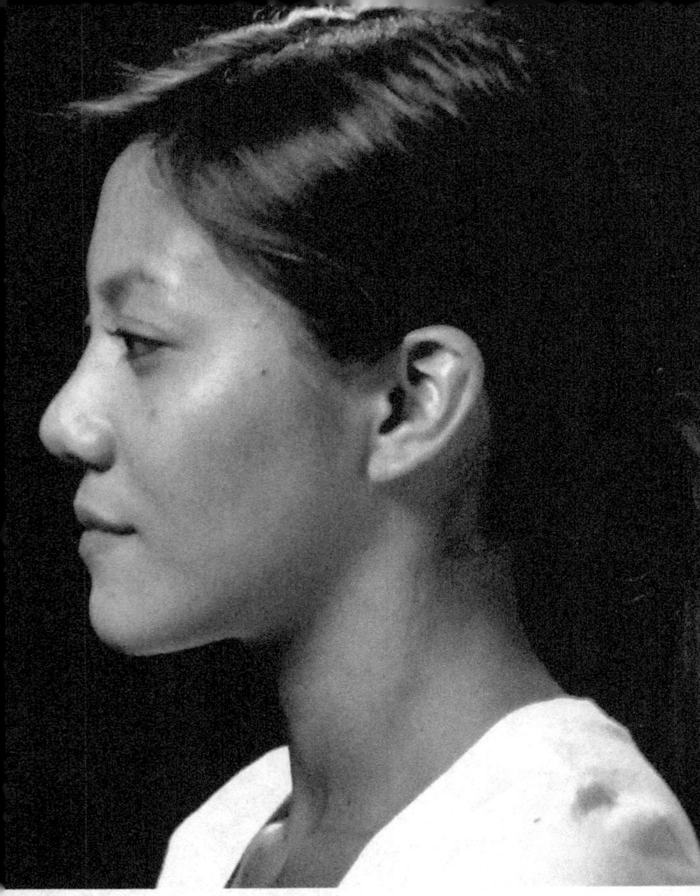

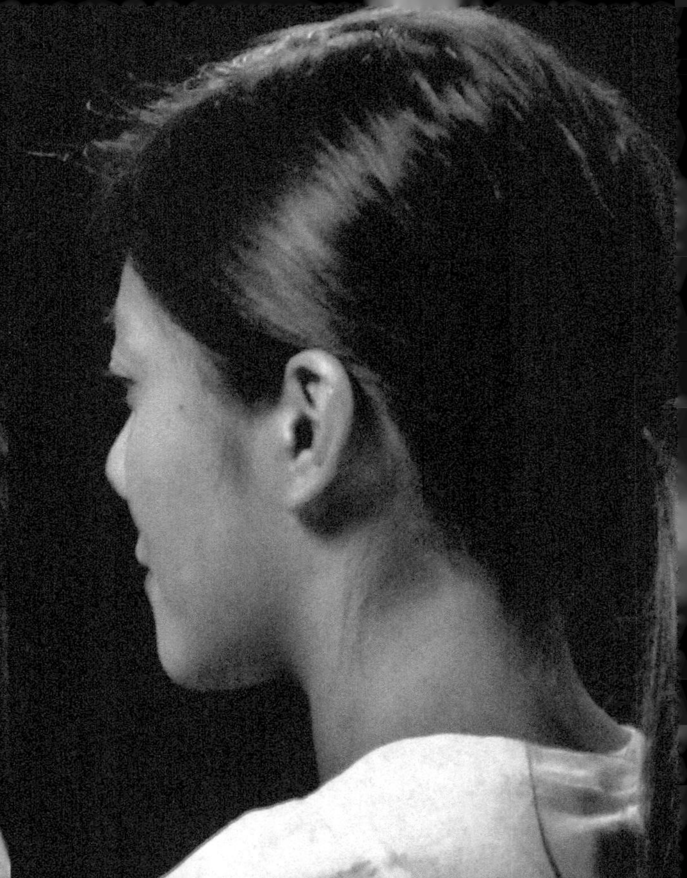

**Ethnicities claimed:**

Philippines, Spain, China.

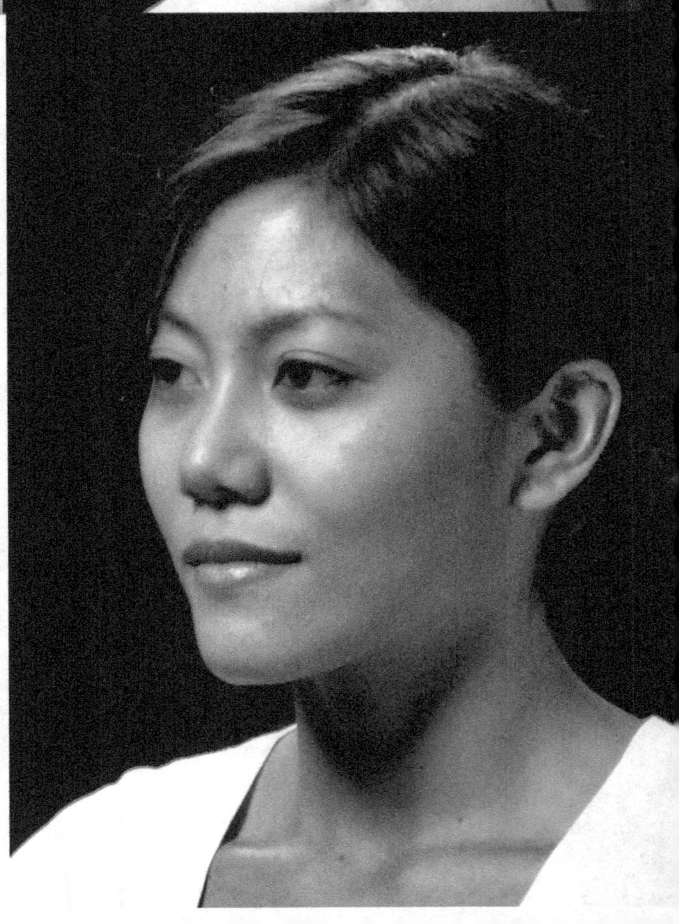

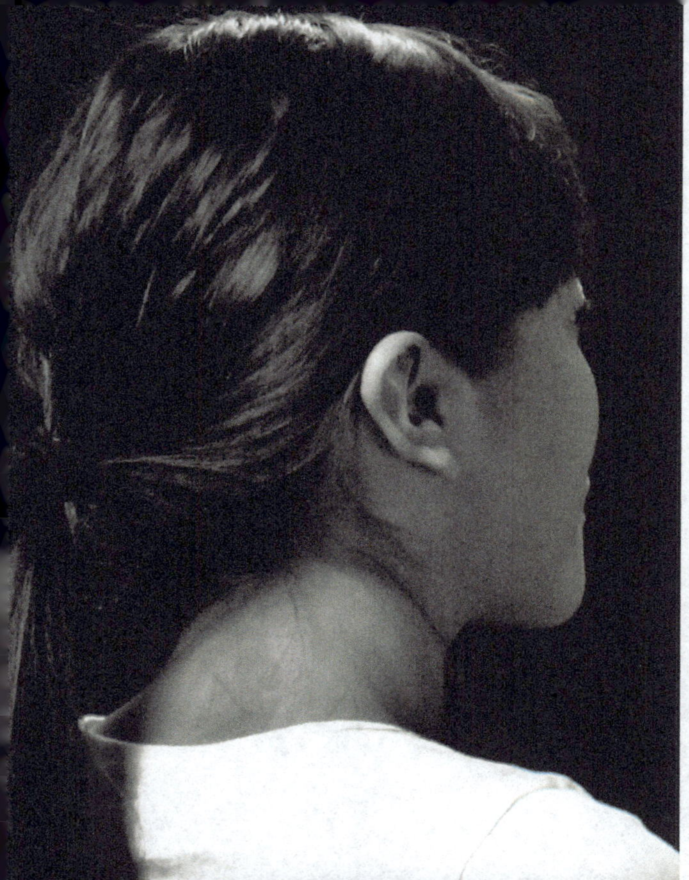

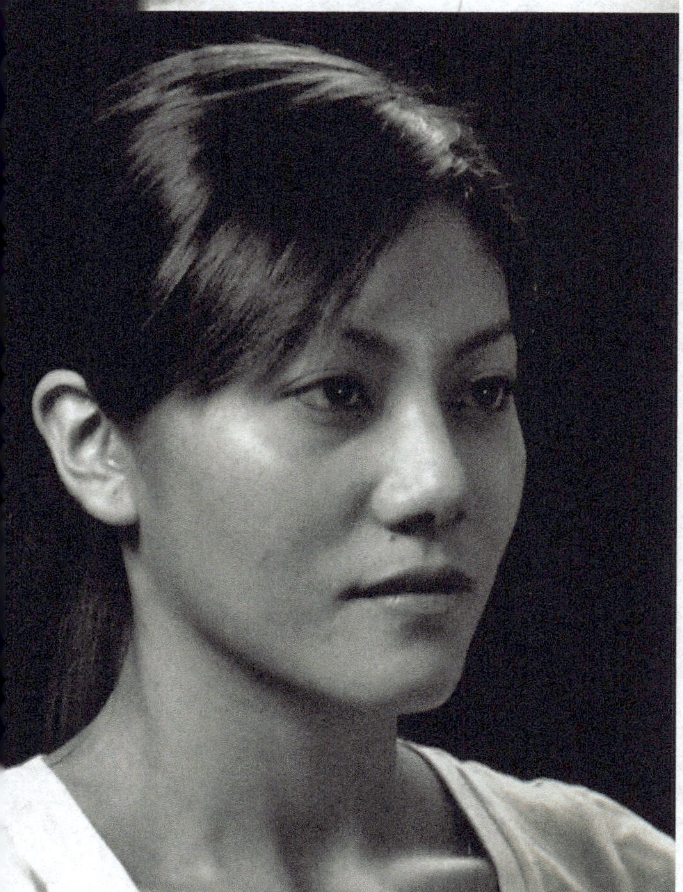

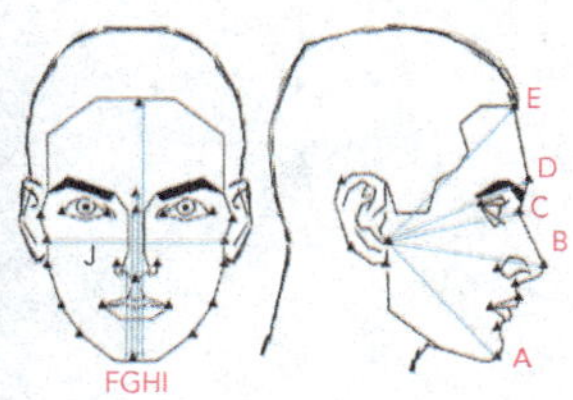


**Head measurements (in):**

A: 4 3/4
B: 5
C: 4 5/8
D: 5
E: 5 5/8
F: 3 3/8
G: 4 3/8
H: 5
I: 7 3/8
J: 5 1/8

MAP REFERENCE:

7

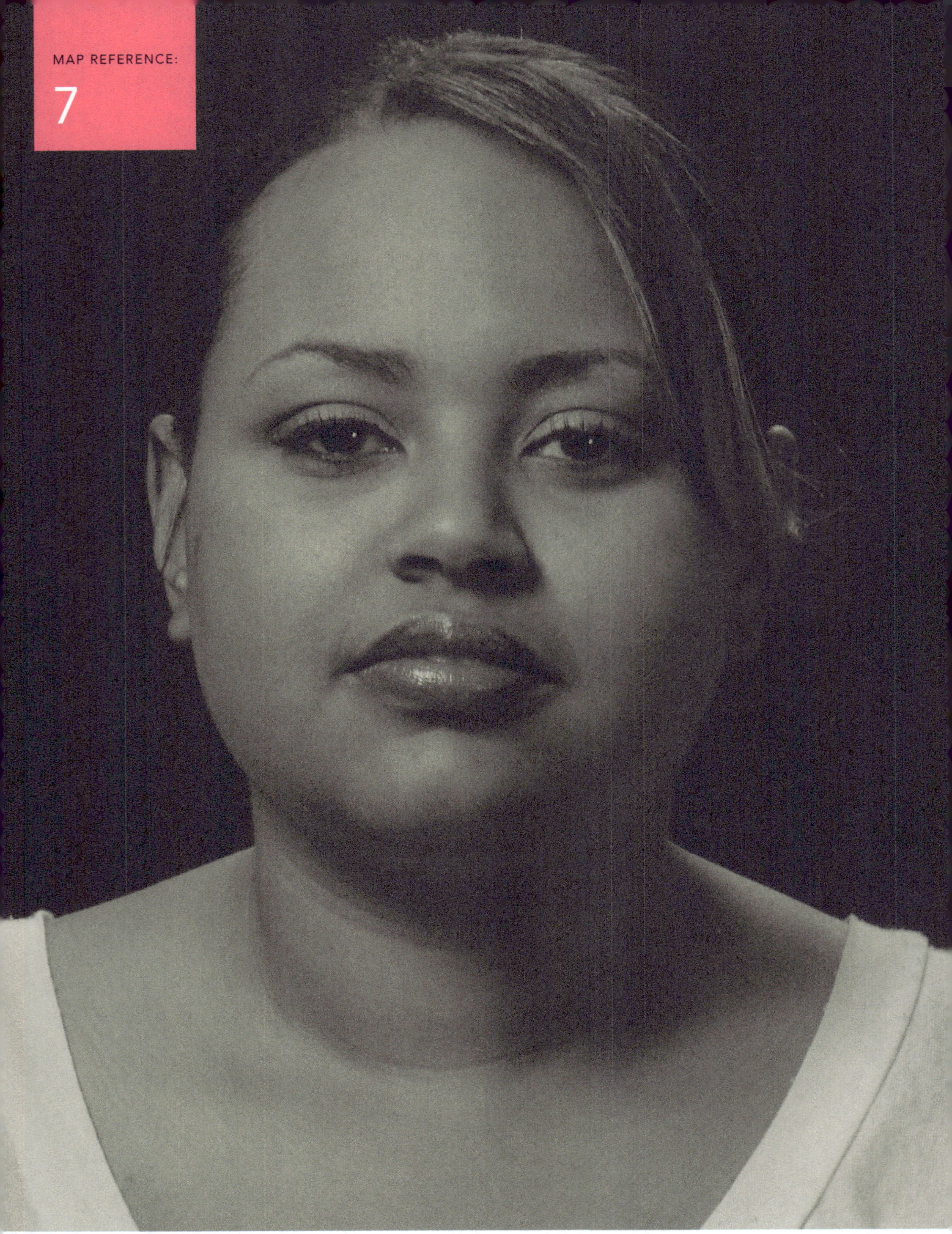

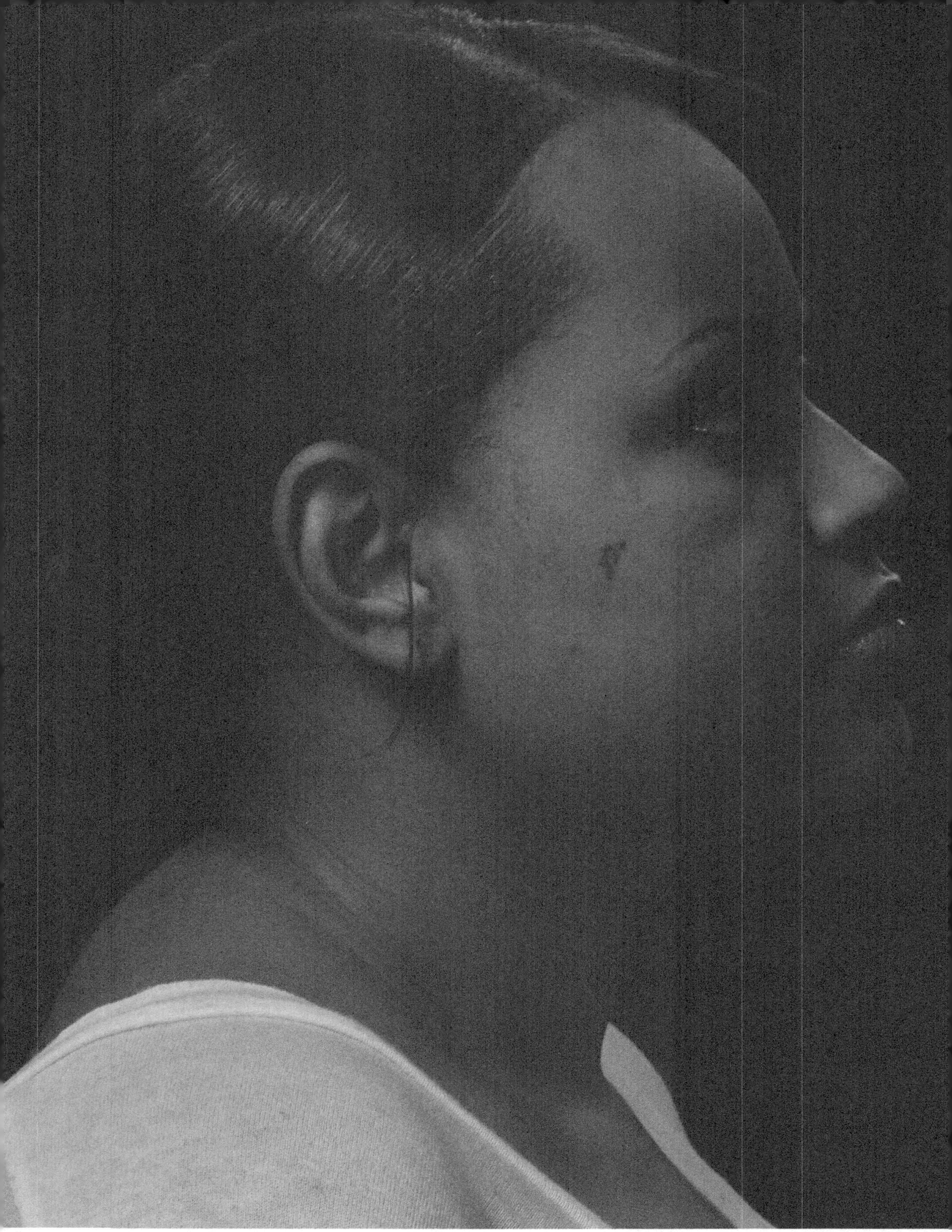

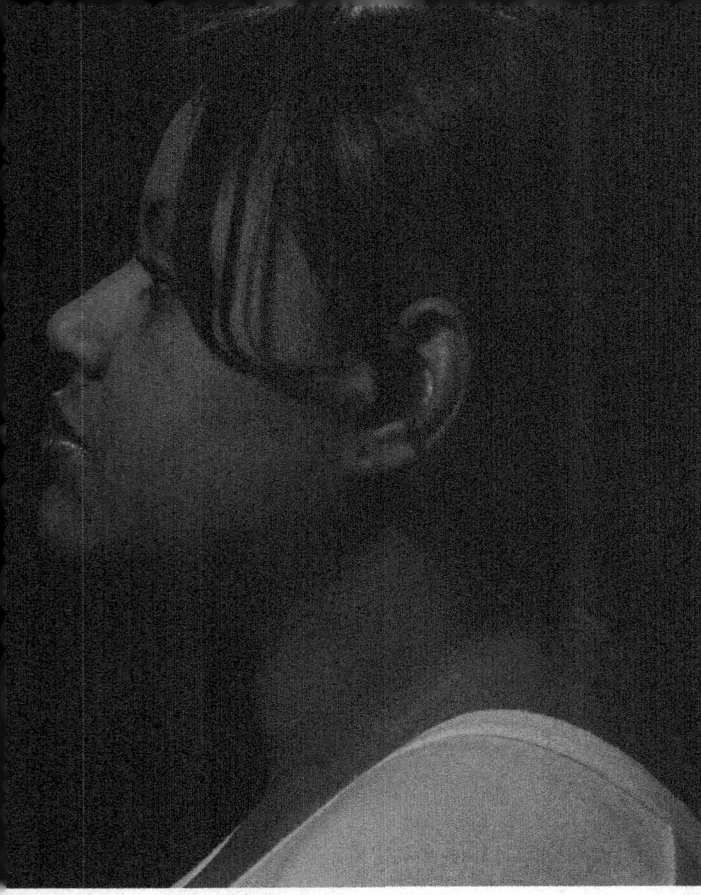

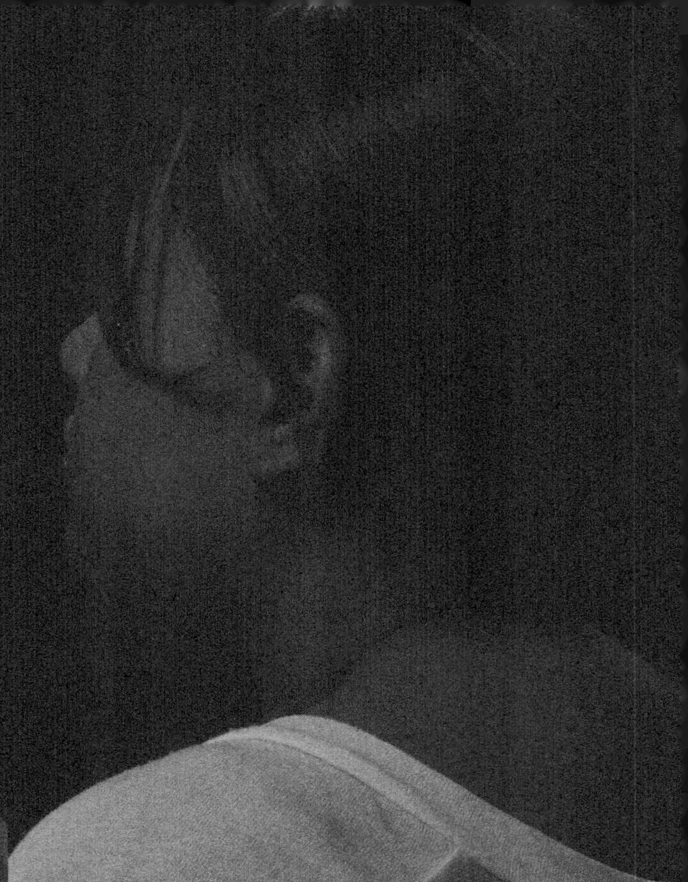

**Ethnicities claimed:**

Caya—Puerto Rico, America—Choctaw Indian.

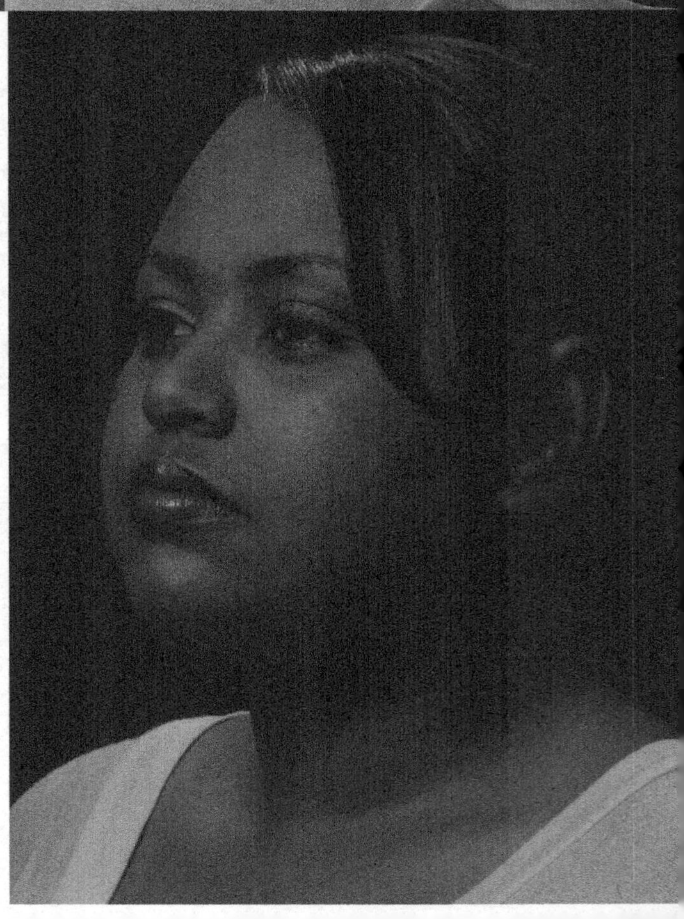

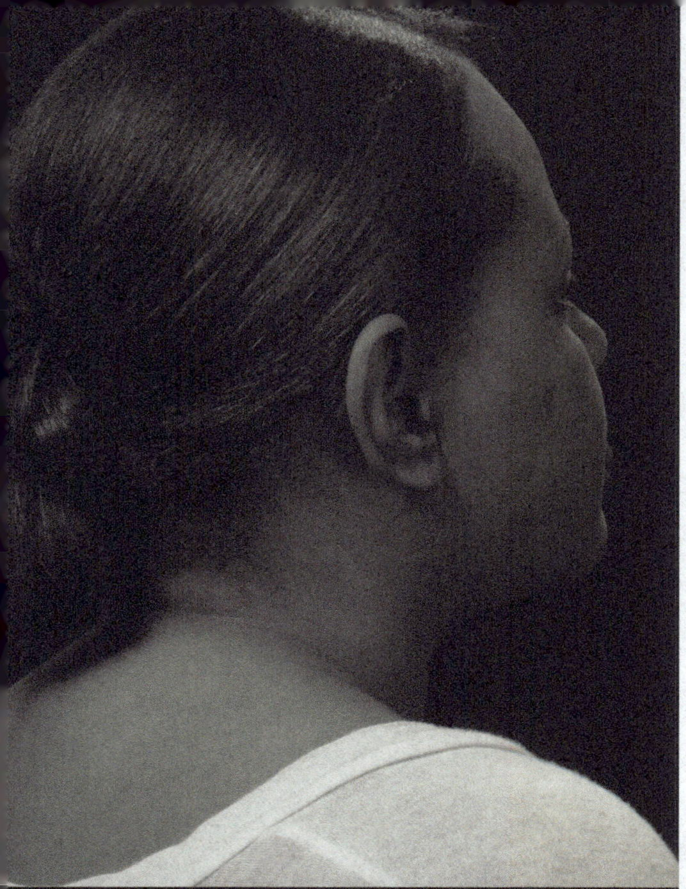

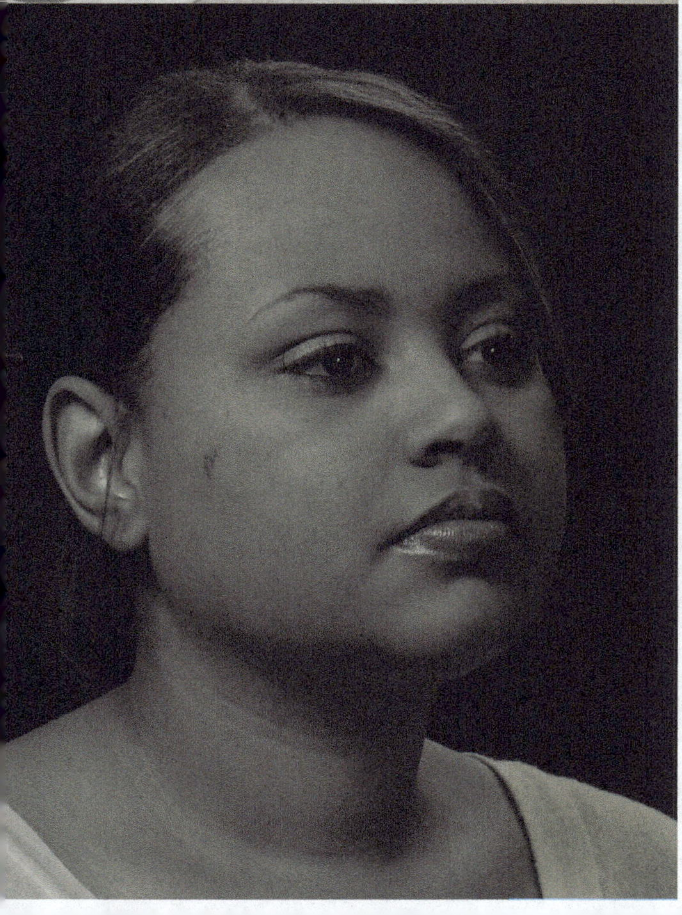

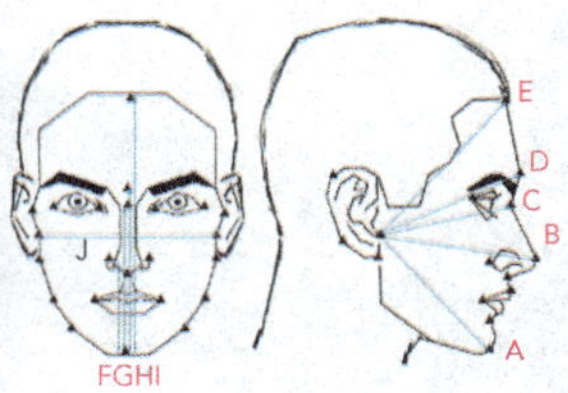


**Head measurements (in):**

A: 5 3/8
B: 5
C: 4 3/4
D: 4 5/8
E: 6 1/2
F: 3 3/8
G: 4
H: 4 3/4
I: 7 5/8
J: 5 1/2

MAP REFERENCE:

8

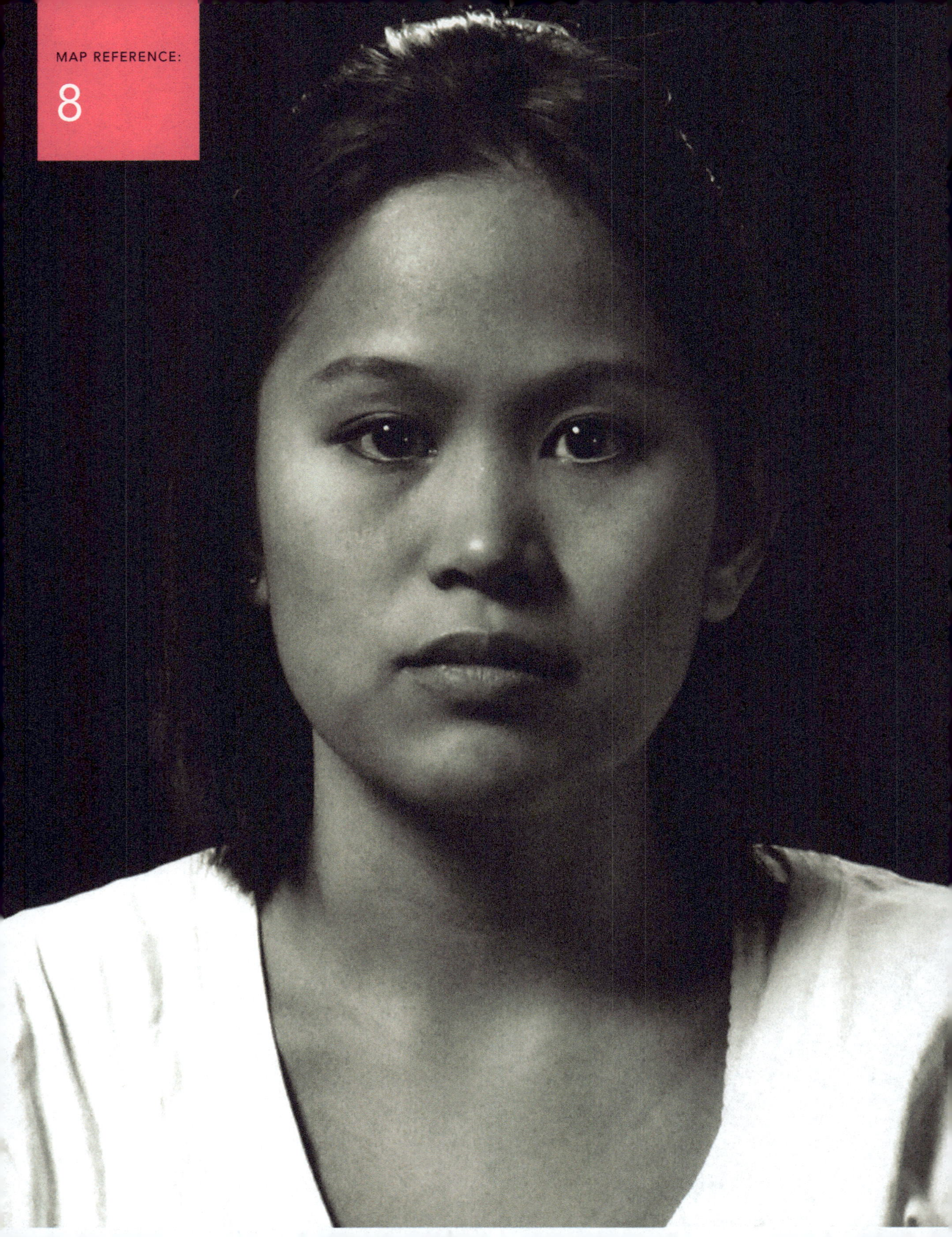

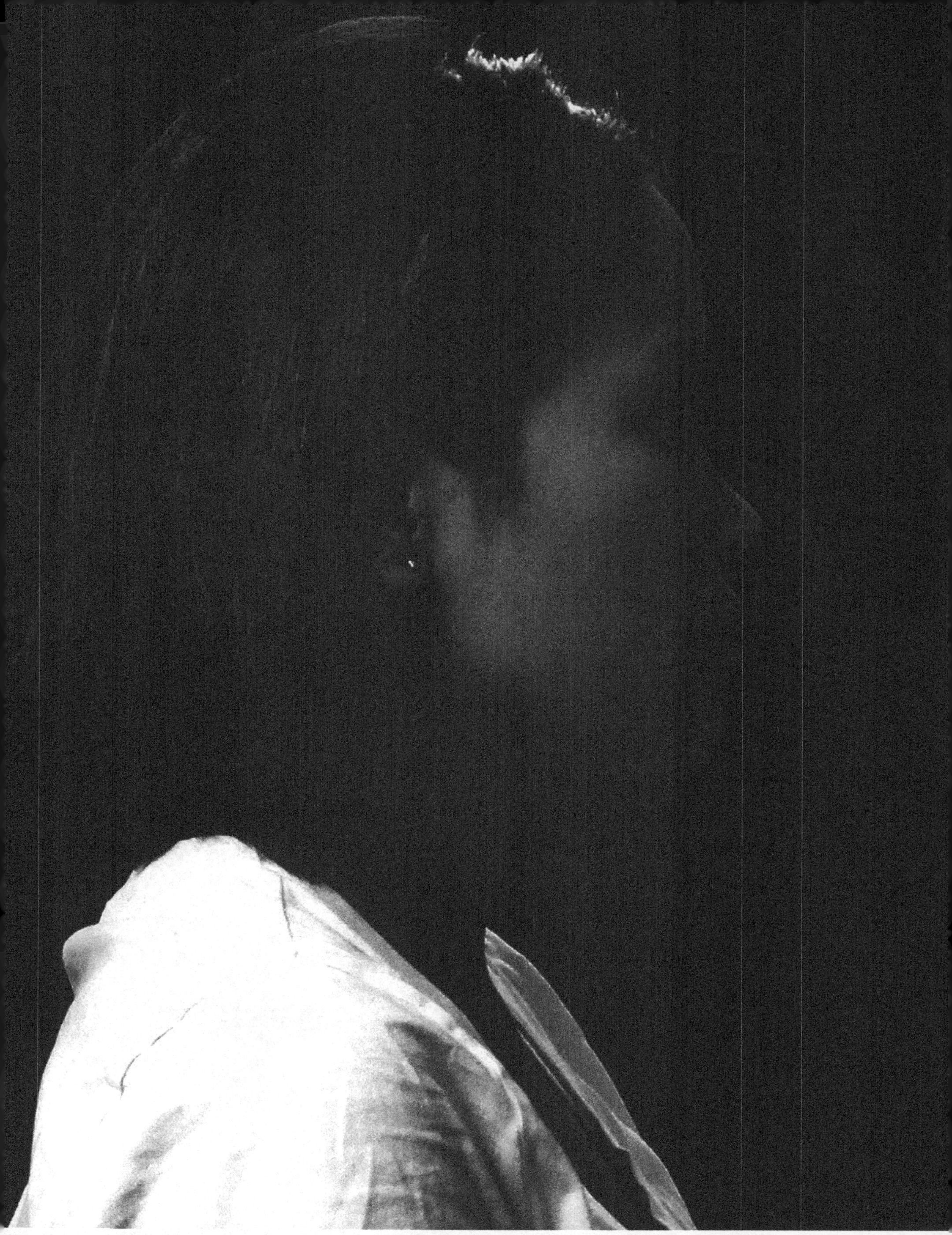

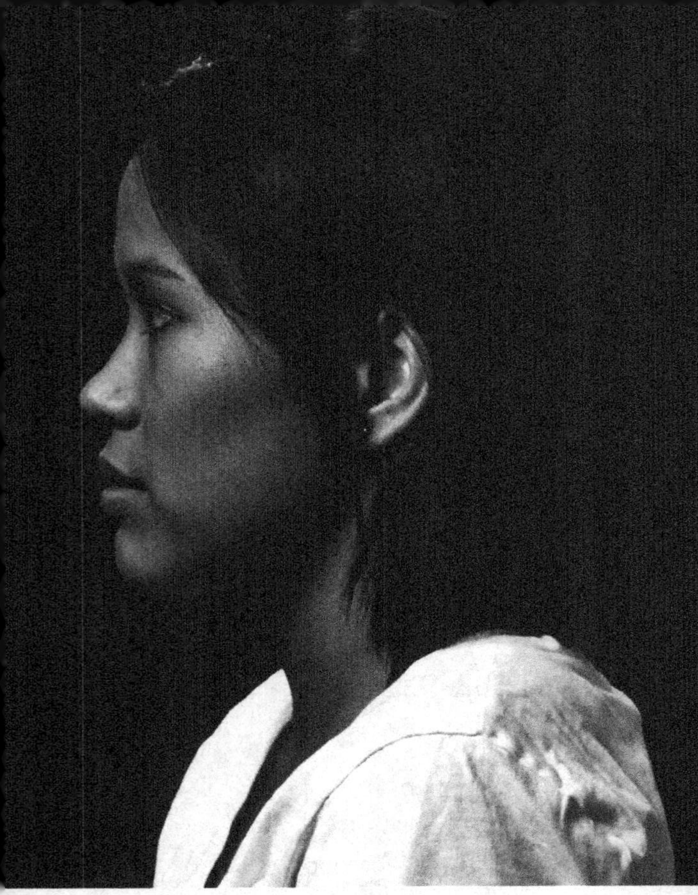

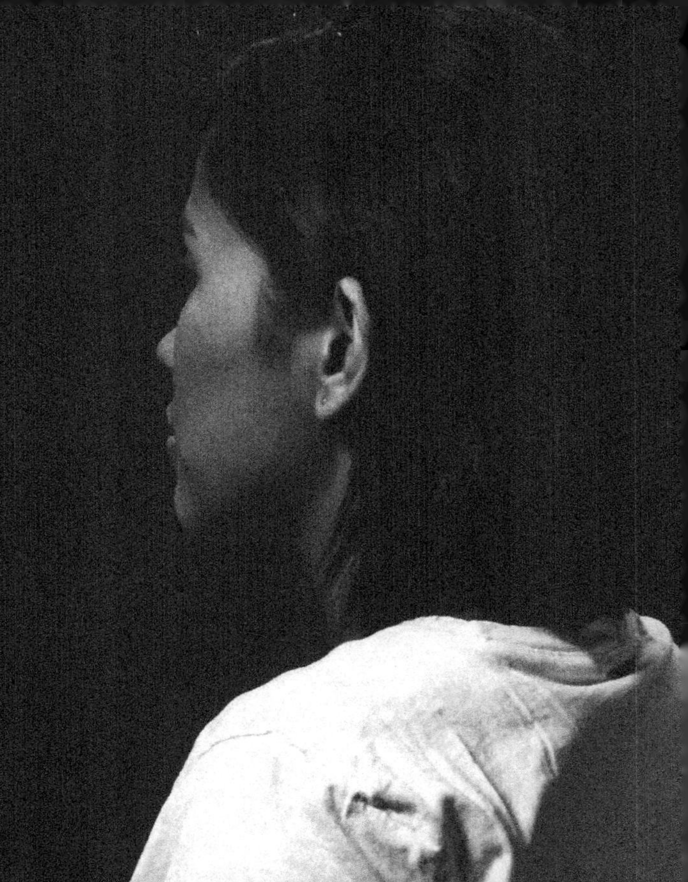

**Ethnicities claimed:**

Philippines, Spain, China.

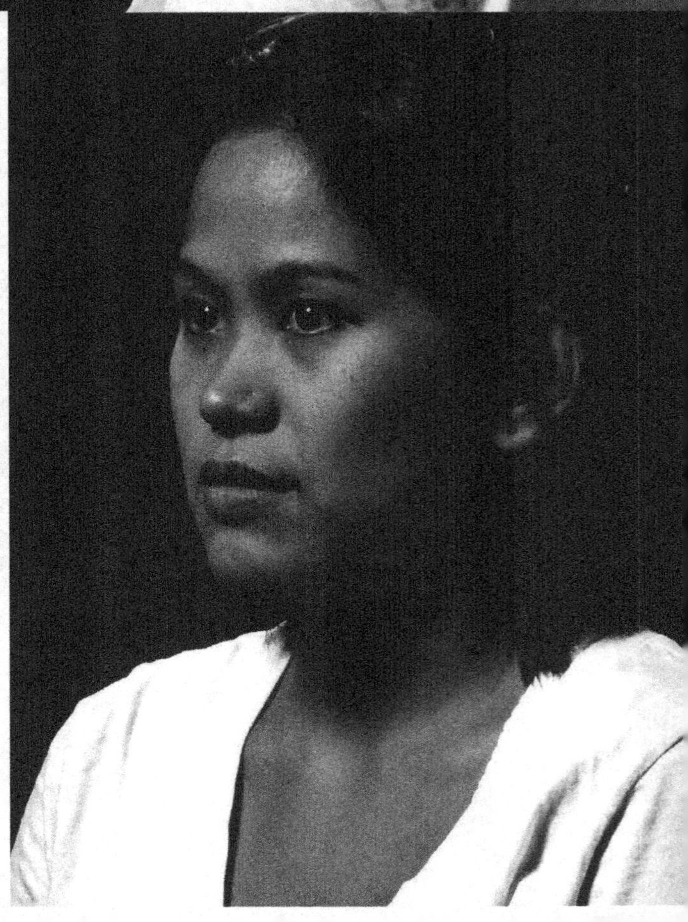

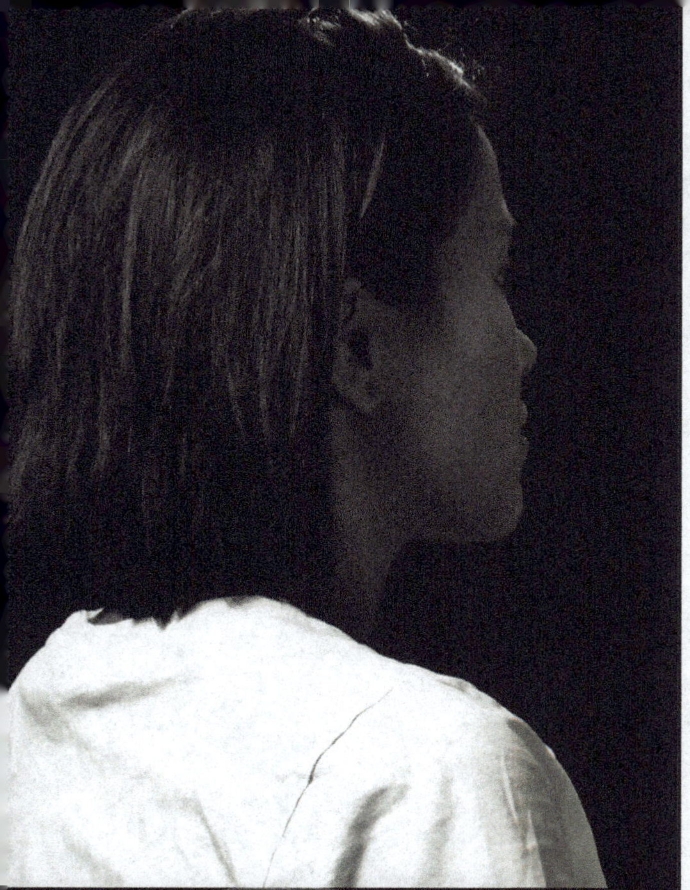

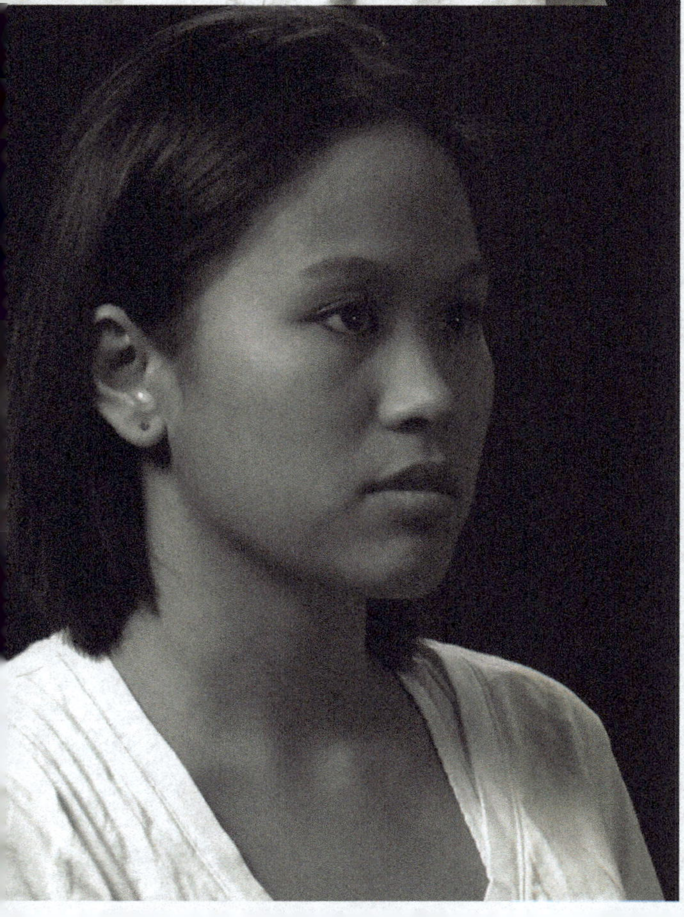

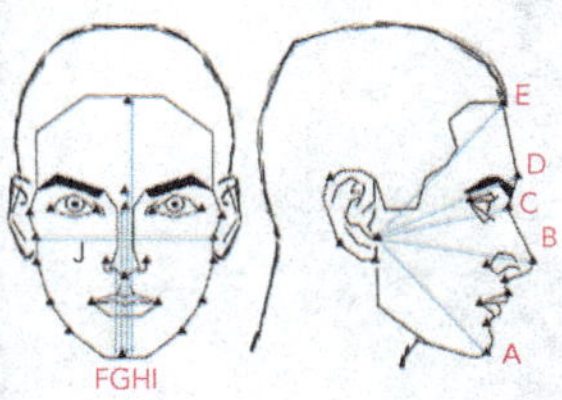


**Head measurements (in):**

A: 5 1/4
B: 4 1/4
C: 4 5/8
D: 4 3/4
E: 6 3/8
F: 3 3/8
G: 4 1/4
H: 5
I: 7 1/2
J: 5 5/8

MAP REFERENCE:

9

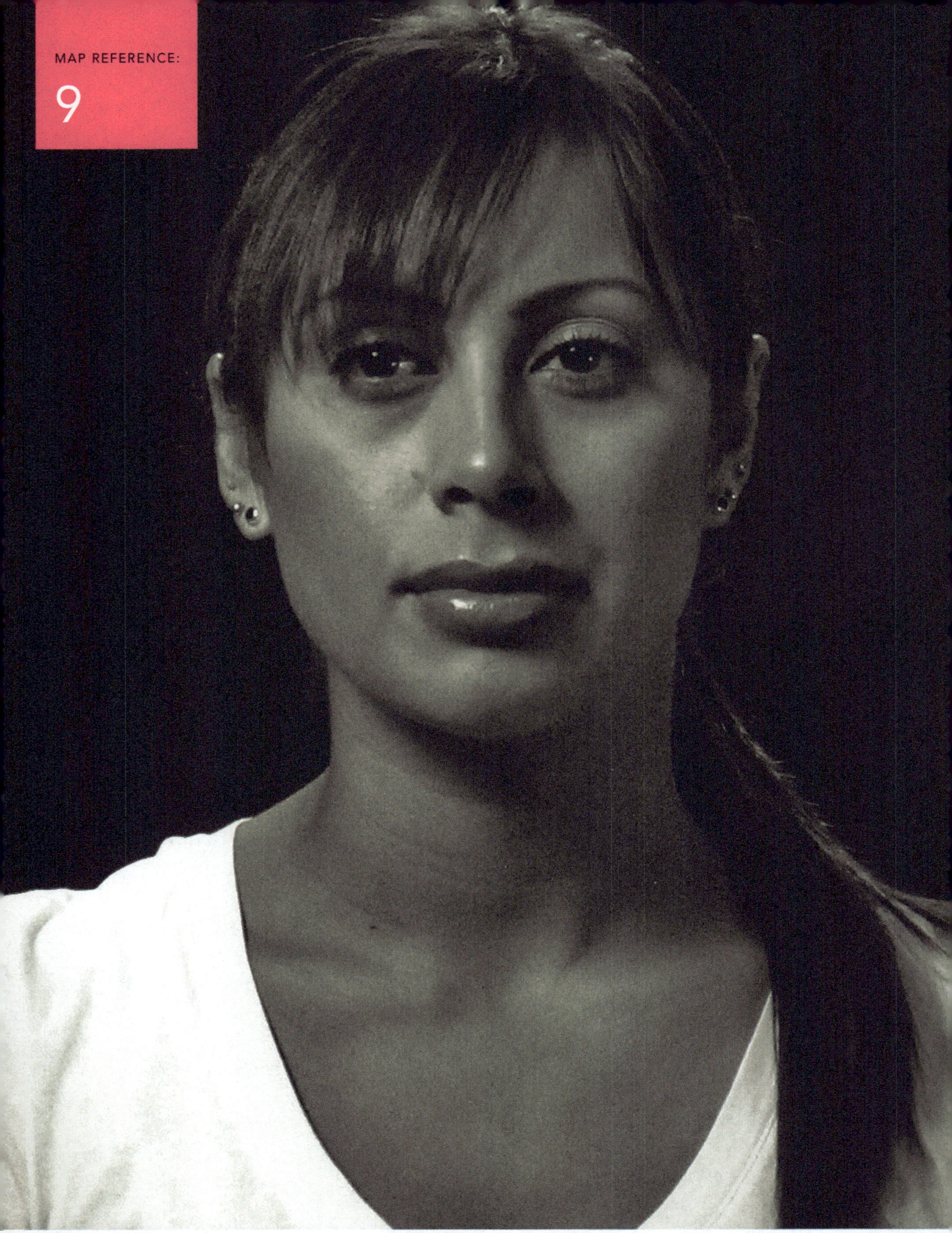

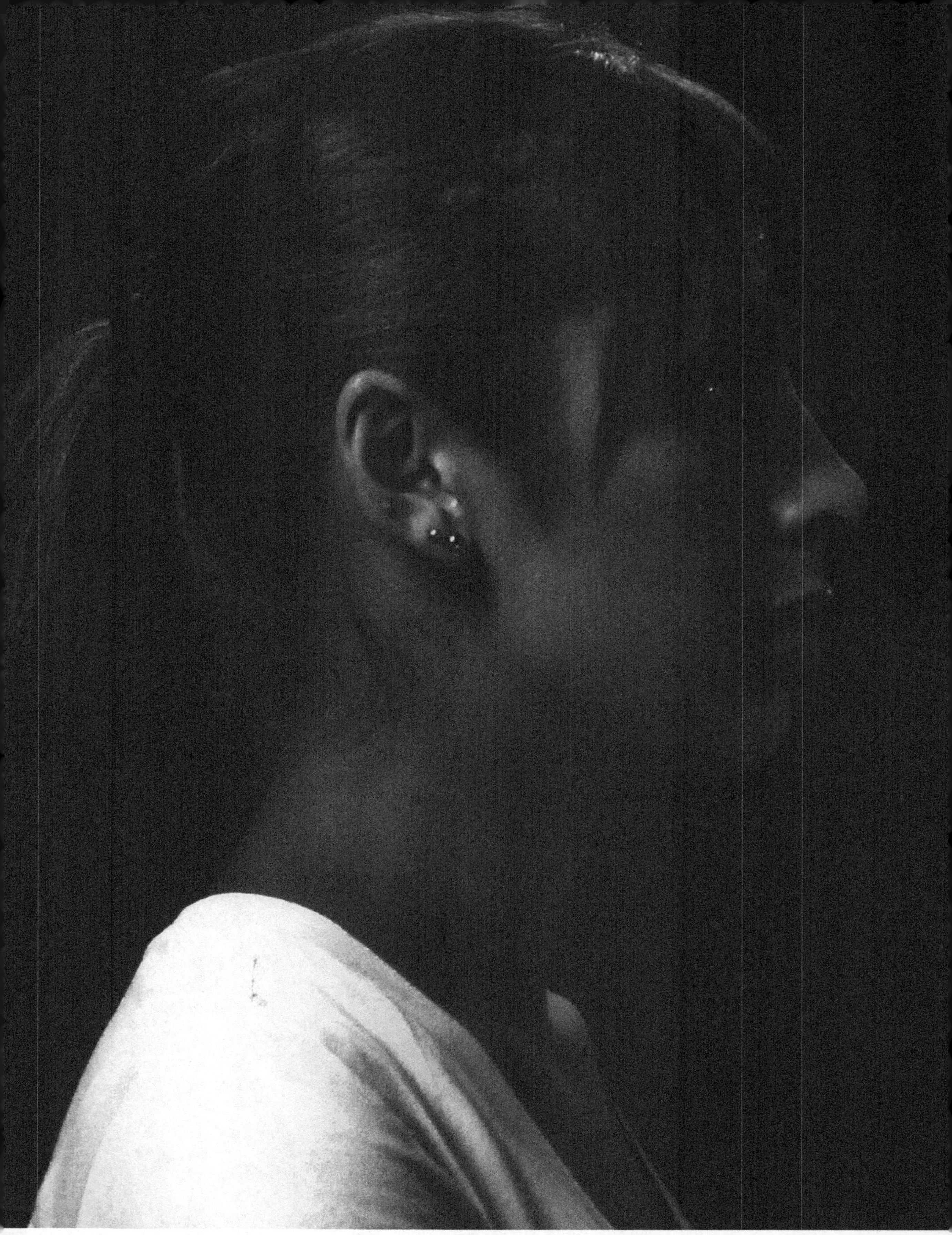

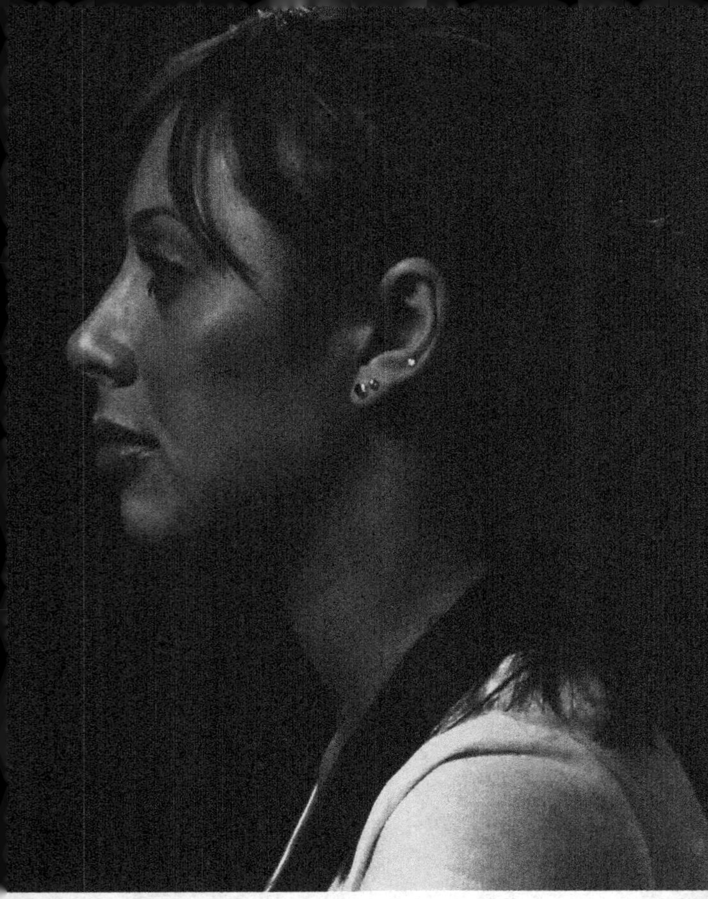

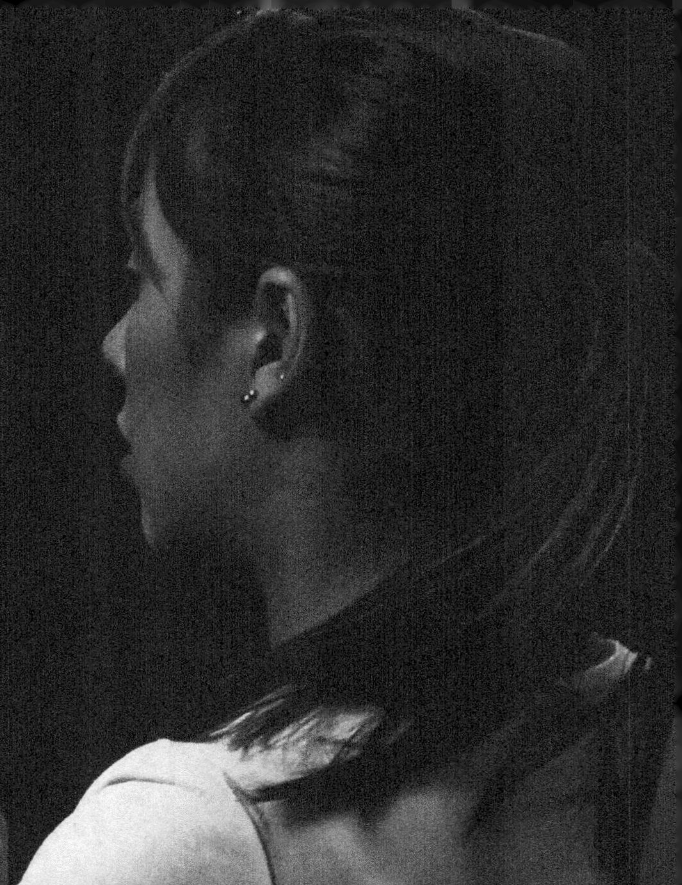

**Ethnicities claimed:**

Philippines, England.

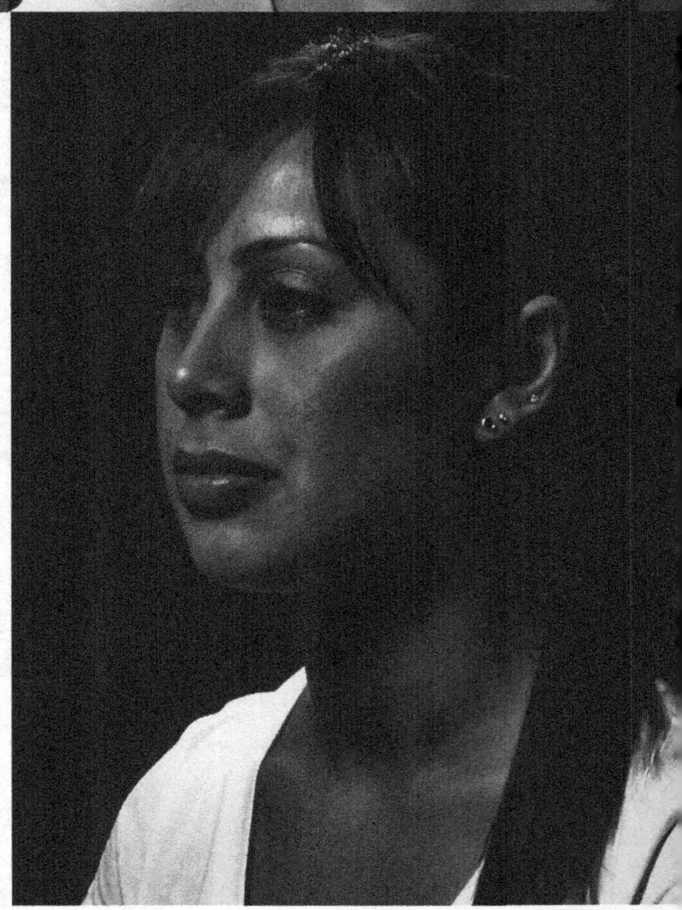

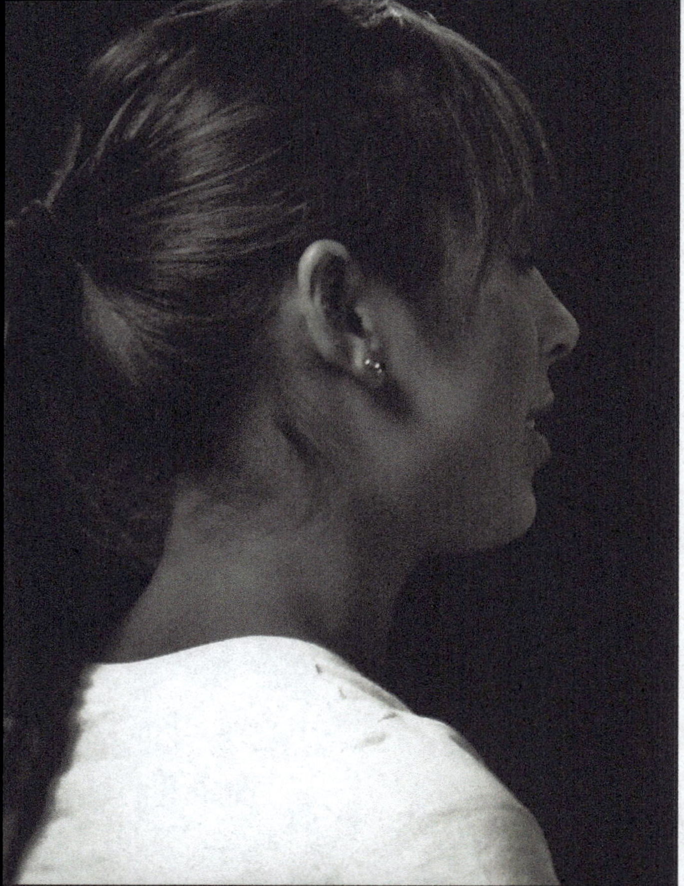

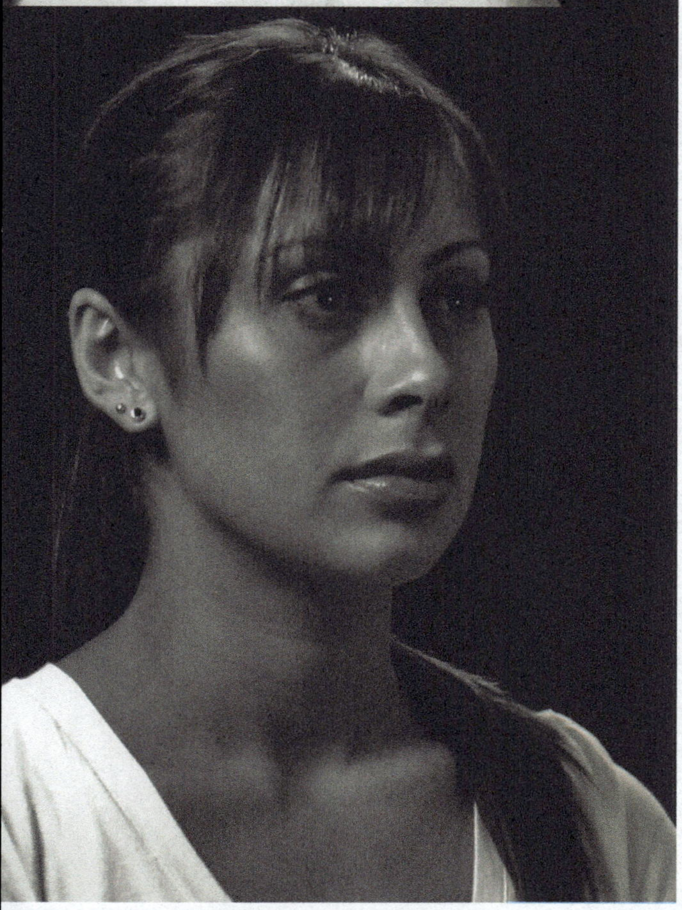

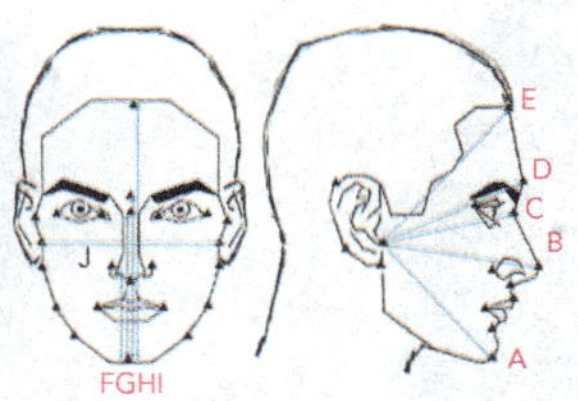


**Head measurements (in):**

A: 5 1/8
B: 4 7/8
C: 4 3/4
D: 4 3/4
E: 6 1/4
F: 3 1/2
G: 4 1/2
H: 5 1/4
I: 7 1/8
J: 5 3/8

MAP REFERENCE:

11

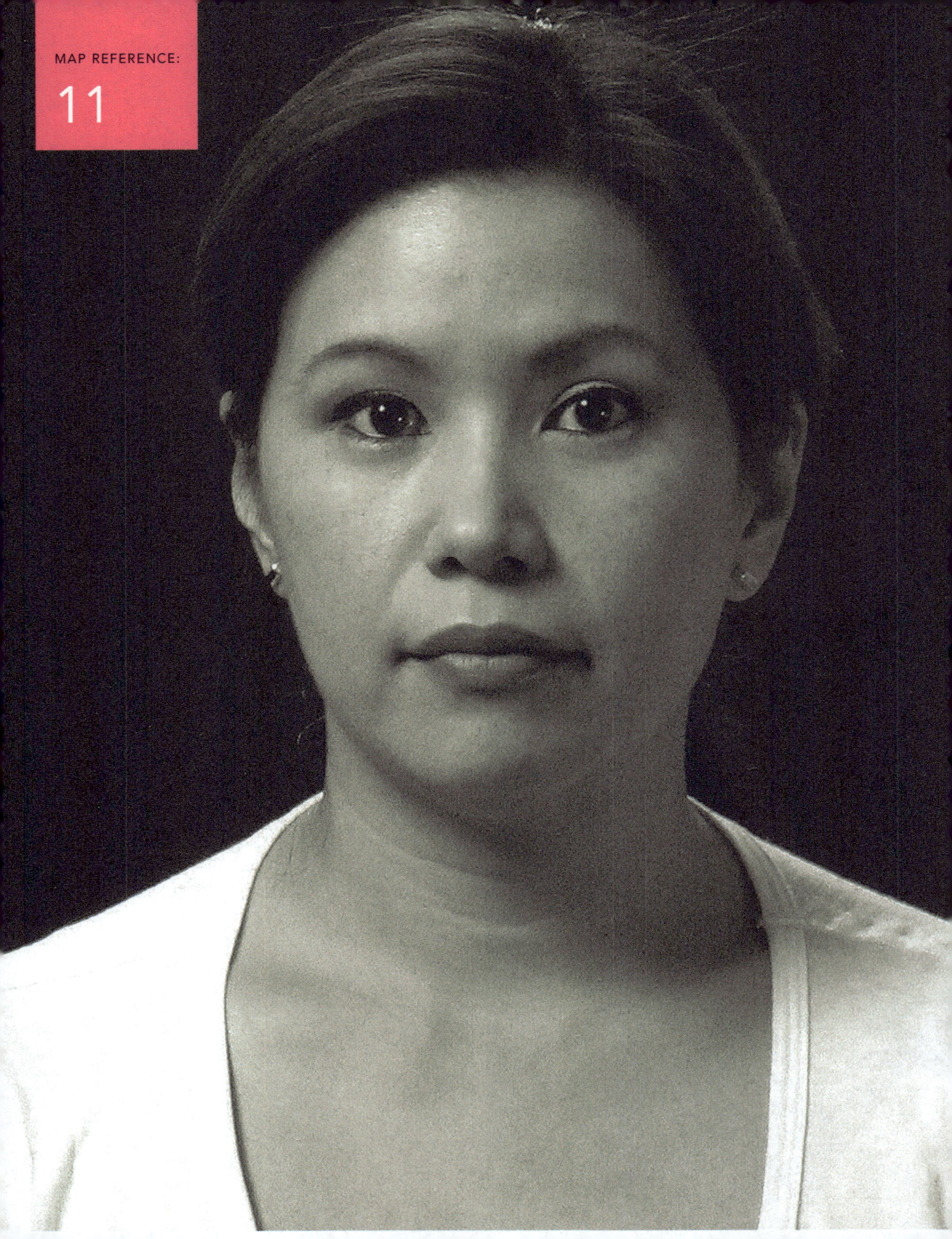

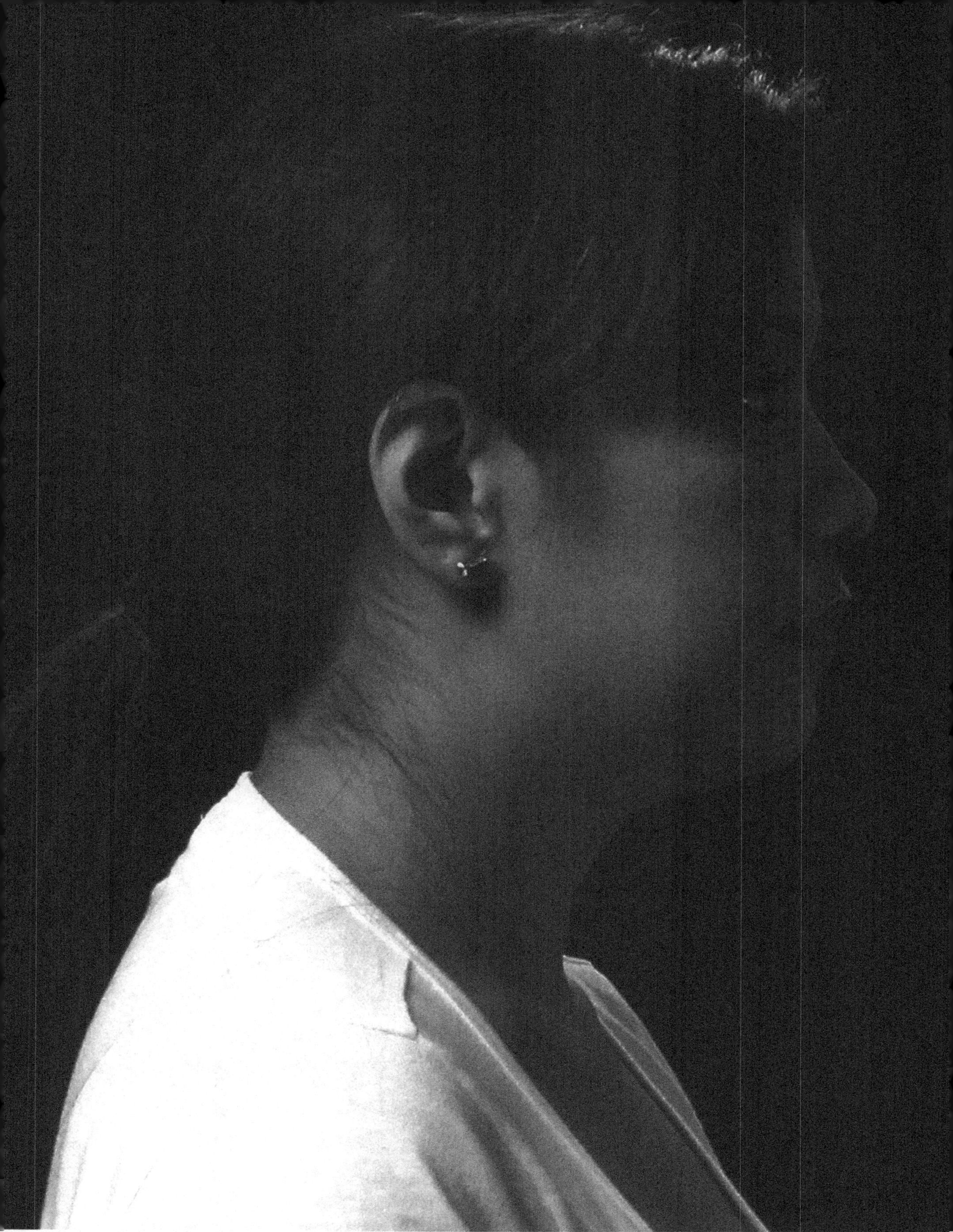

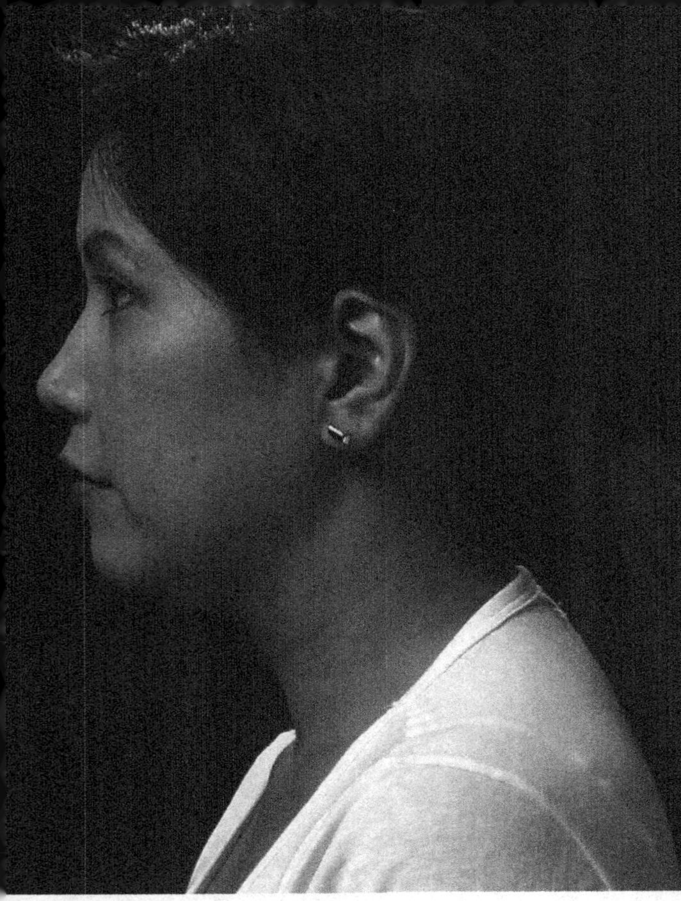

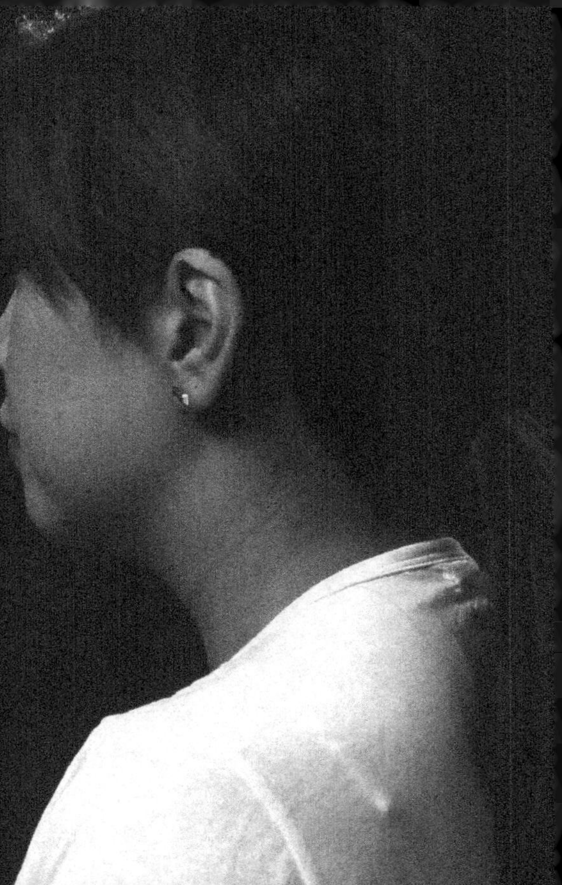

**Ethnicities claimed:**

Japan.

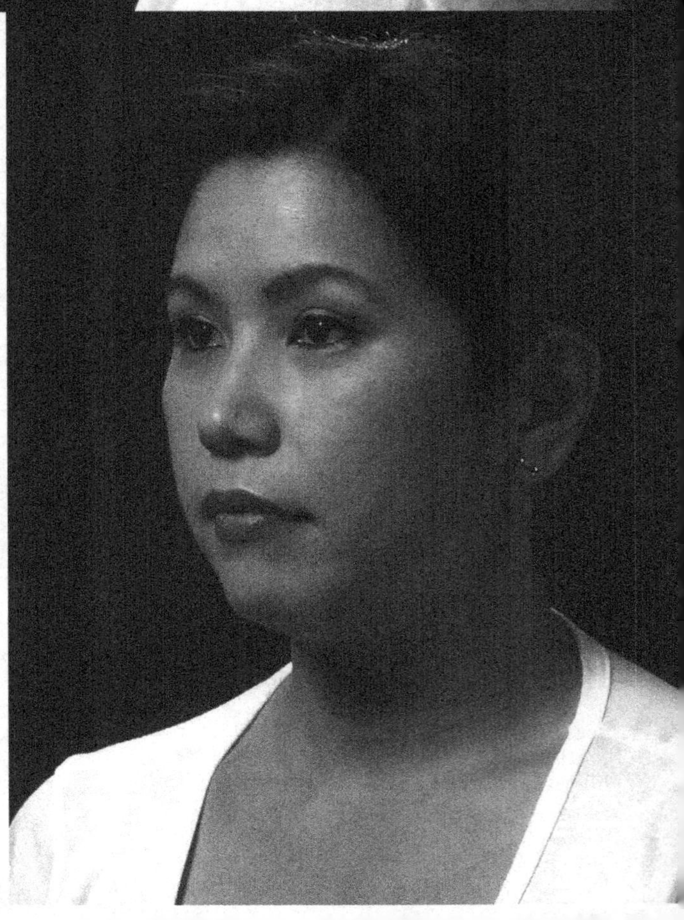

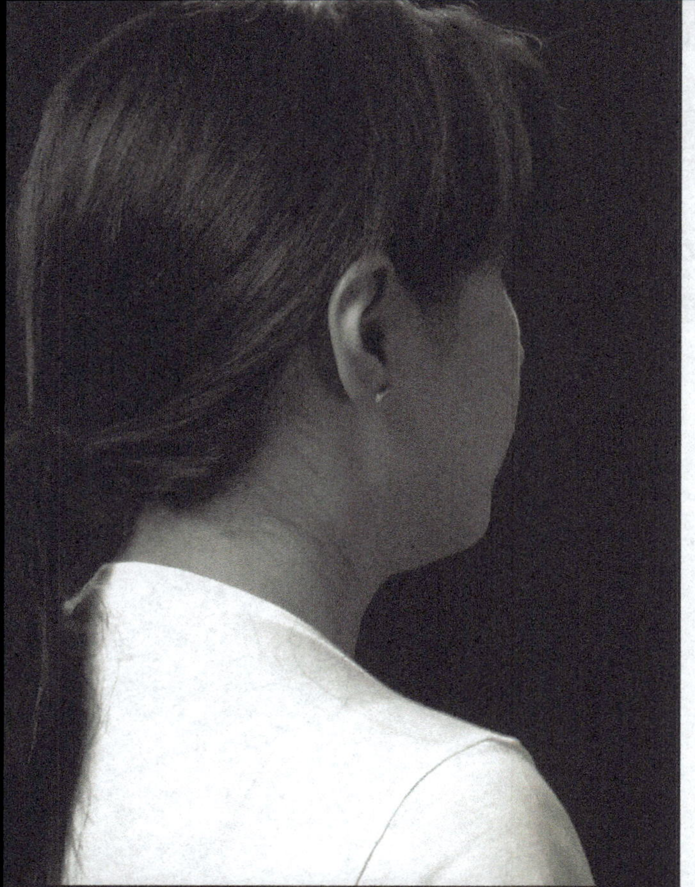

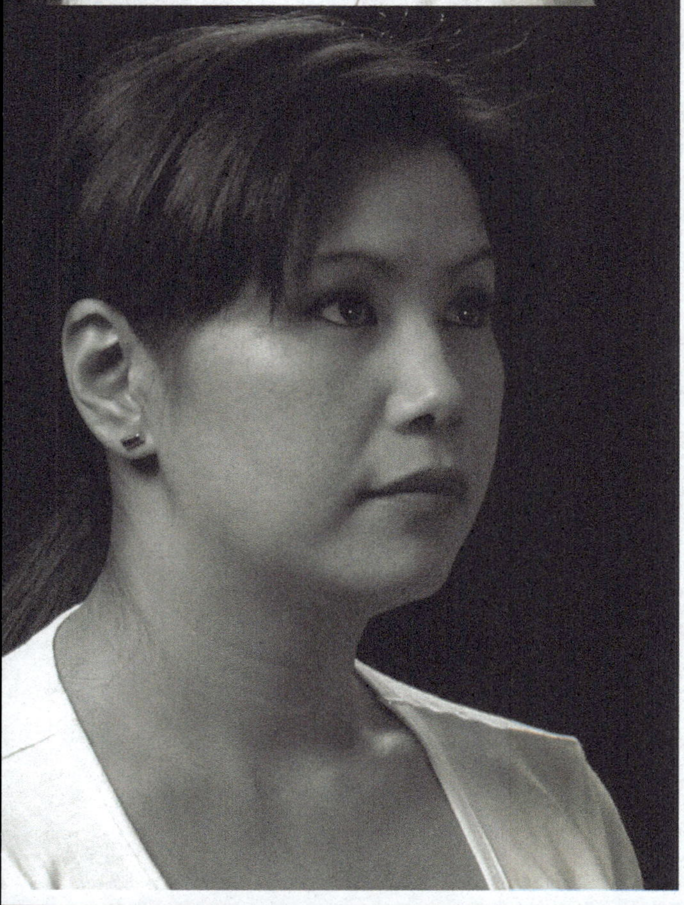

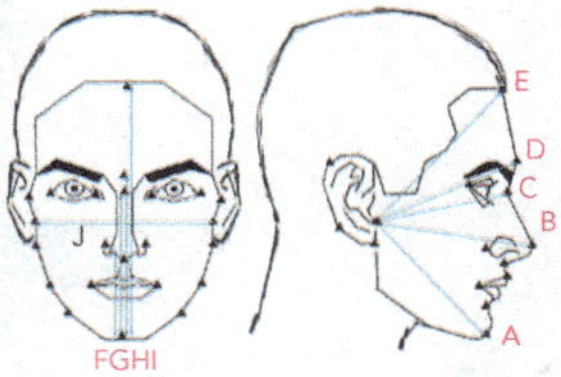


**Head measurements (in):**

A: 5 1/8
B: 5 3/8
C: 5
D: 5 1/2
E: 6
F: 3 3/8
G: 4 3/8
H: 5 3/8
I: 7 3/4
J: 5 5/8

MAP REFERENCE:

12

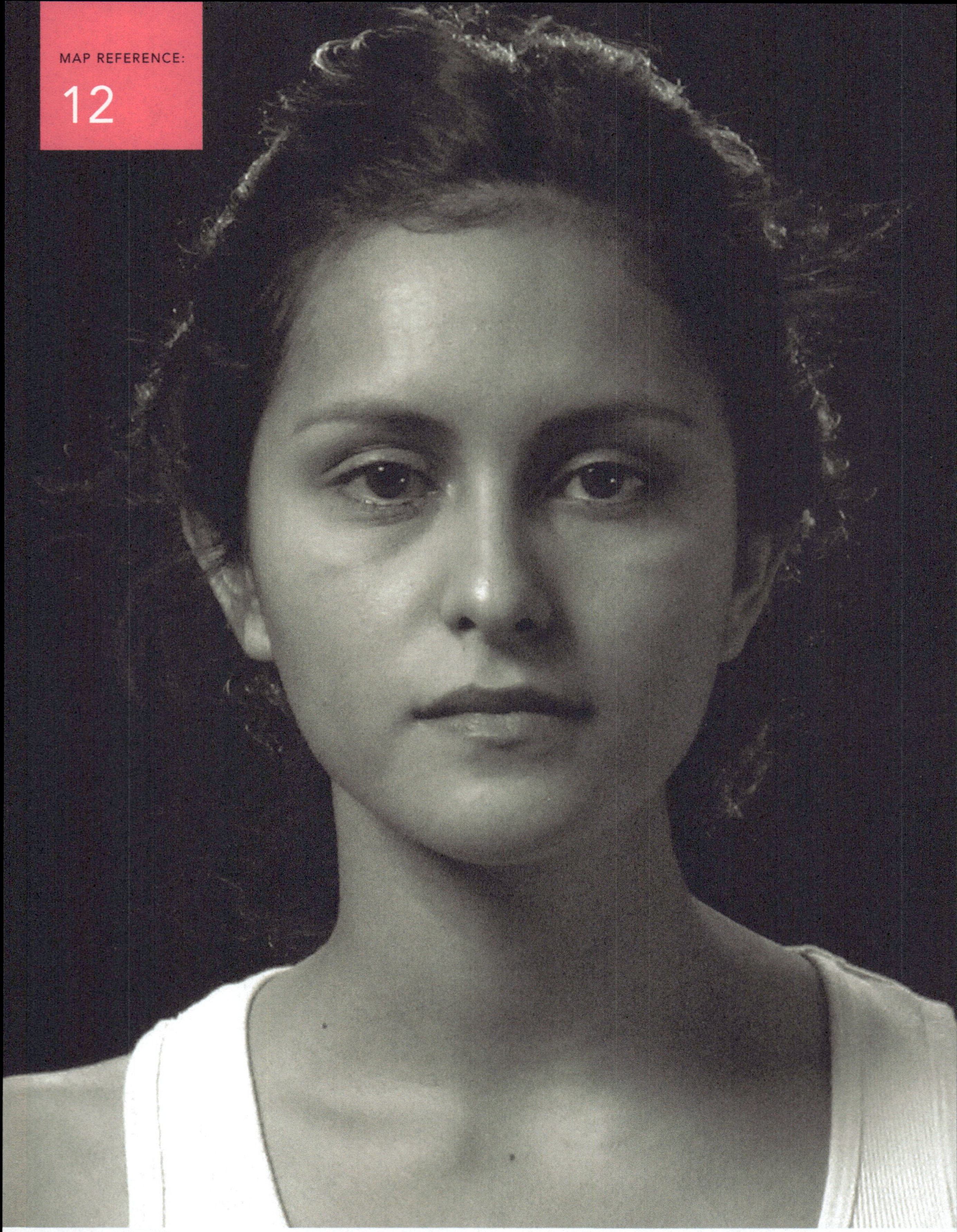

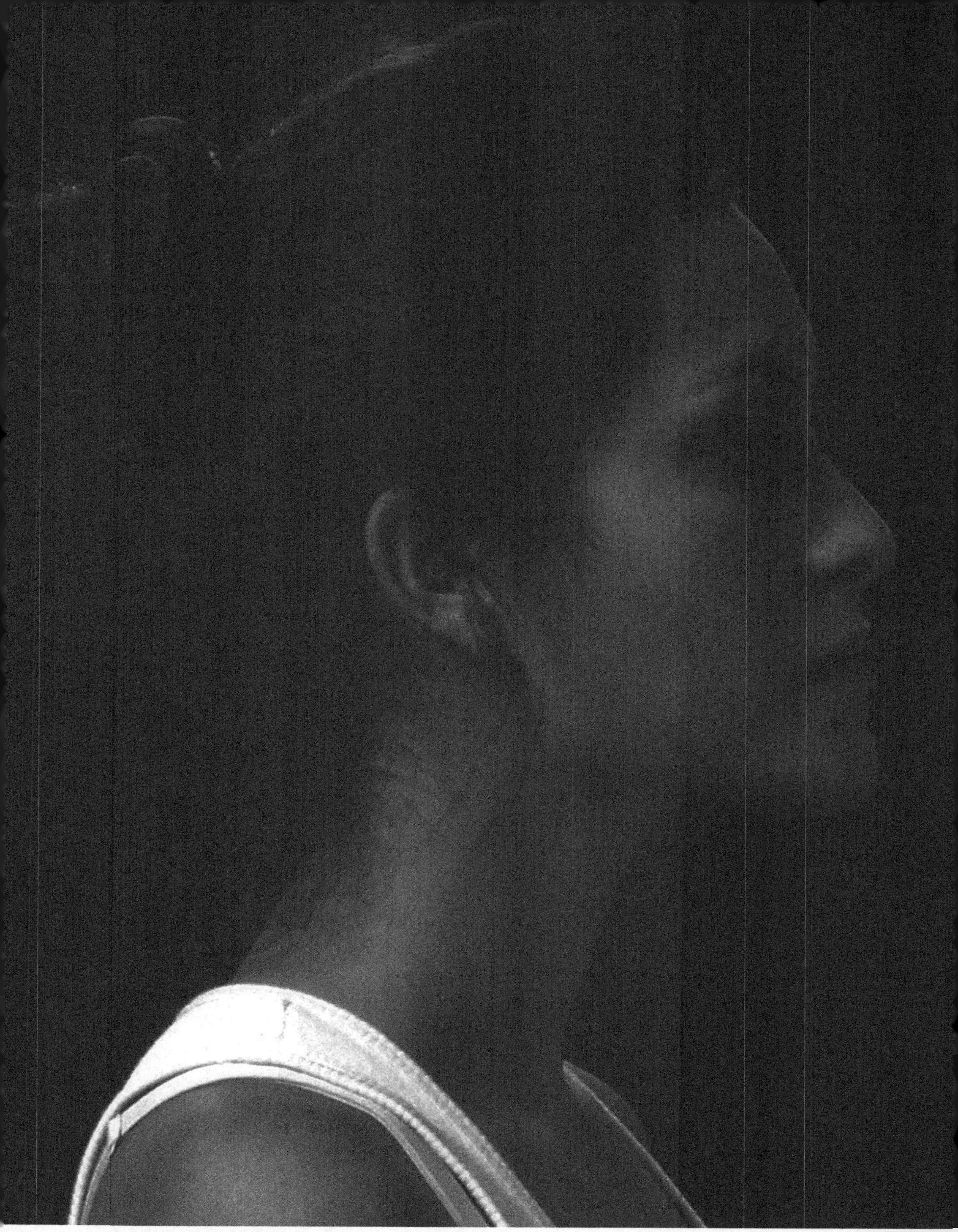

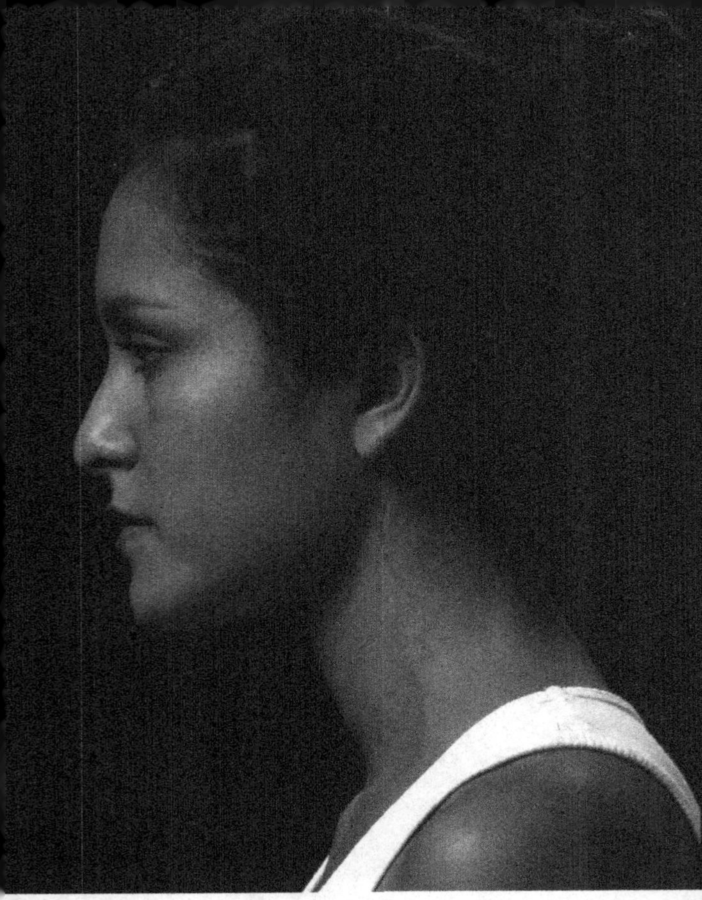

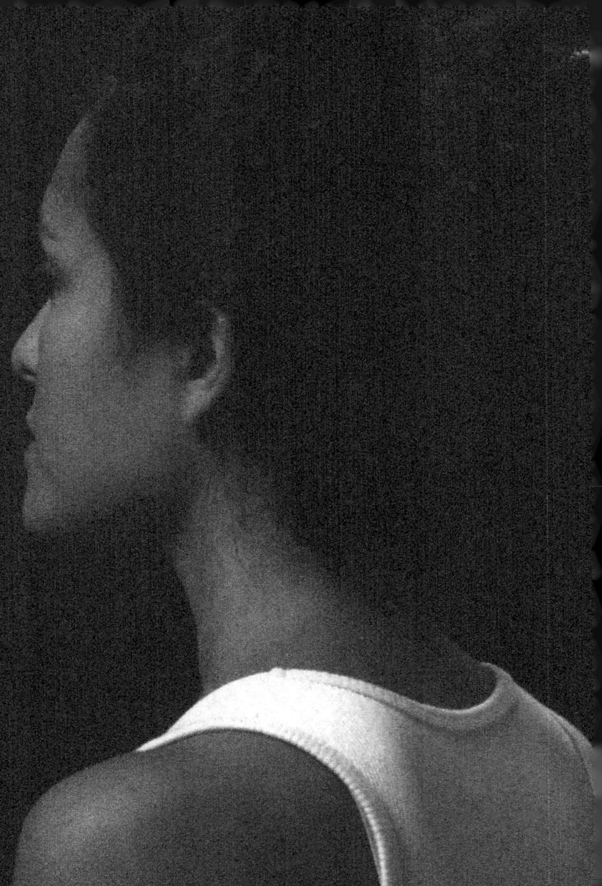

**Ethnicities claimed:**

Cuba, Spain, Mexico.

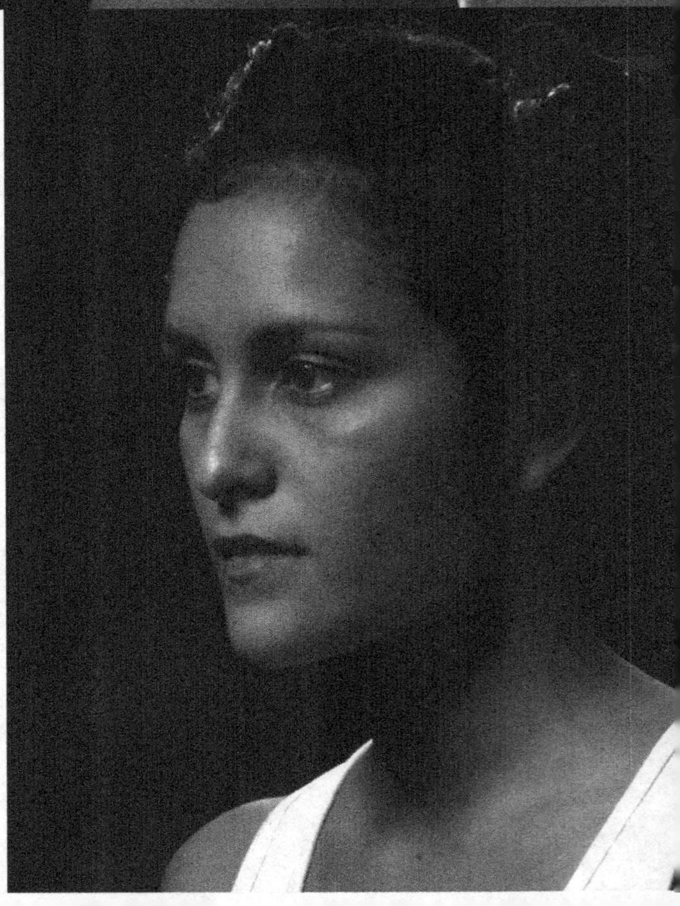

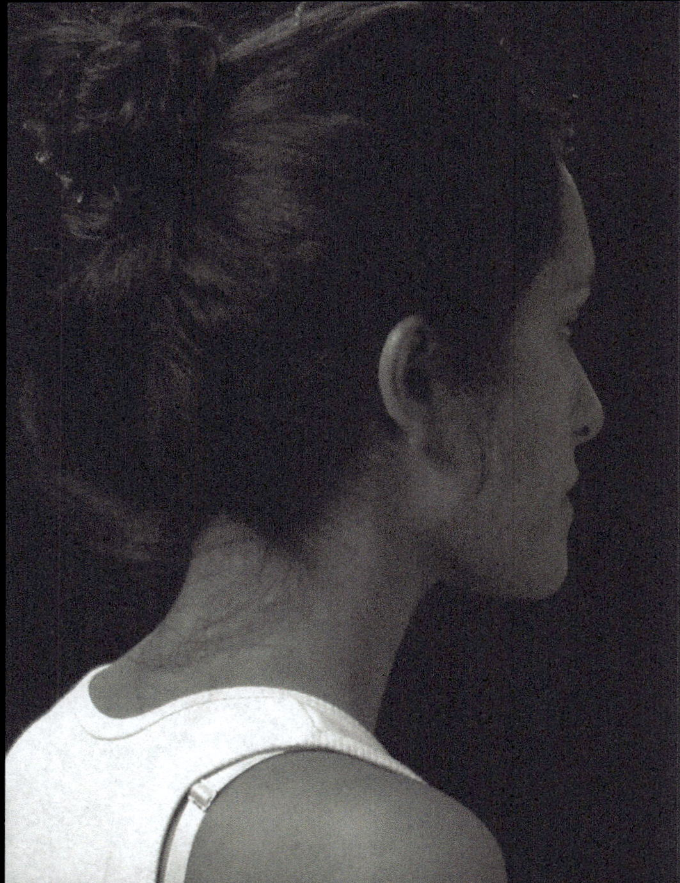

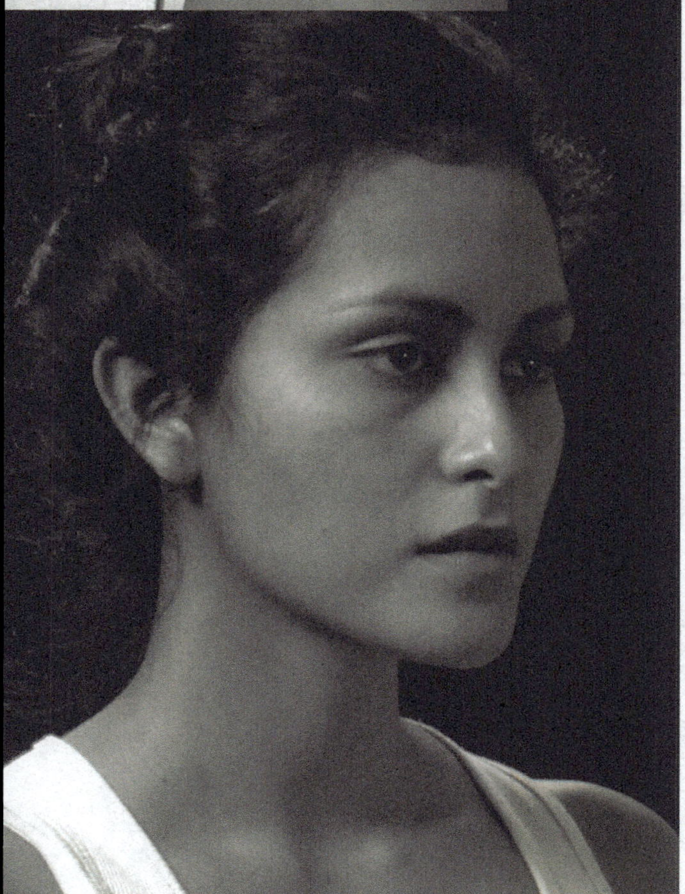

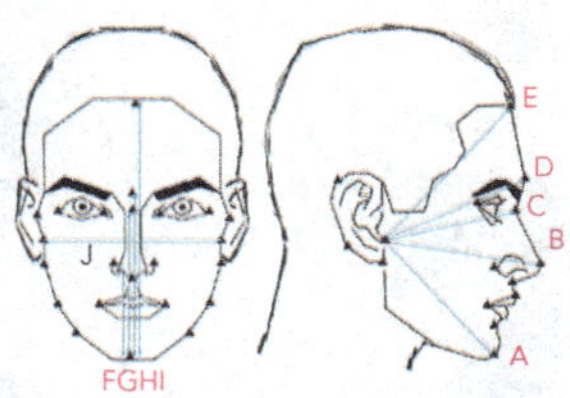


**Head measurements (in):**

A: 5 1/4
B: 4 1/2
C: 4 3/8
D: 4 3/4
E: 6 1/8
F: 3 3/8
G: 4 1/8
H: 5
I: 7 1/4
J: 5 1/8

MAP REFERENCE:

16

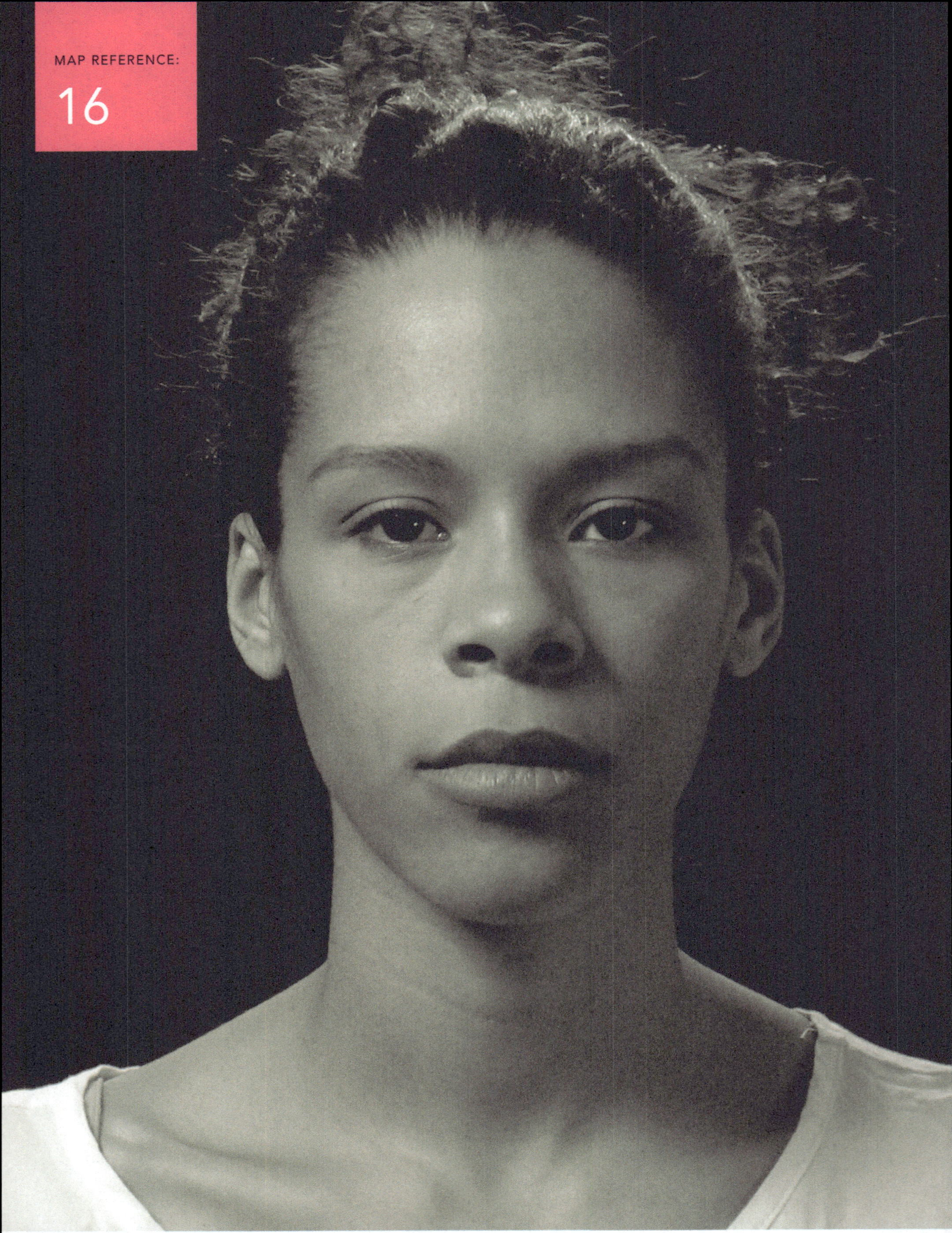

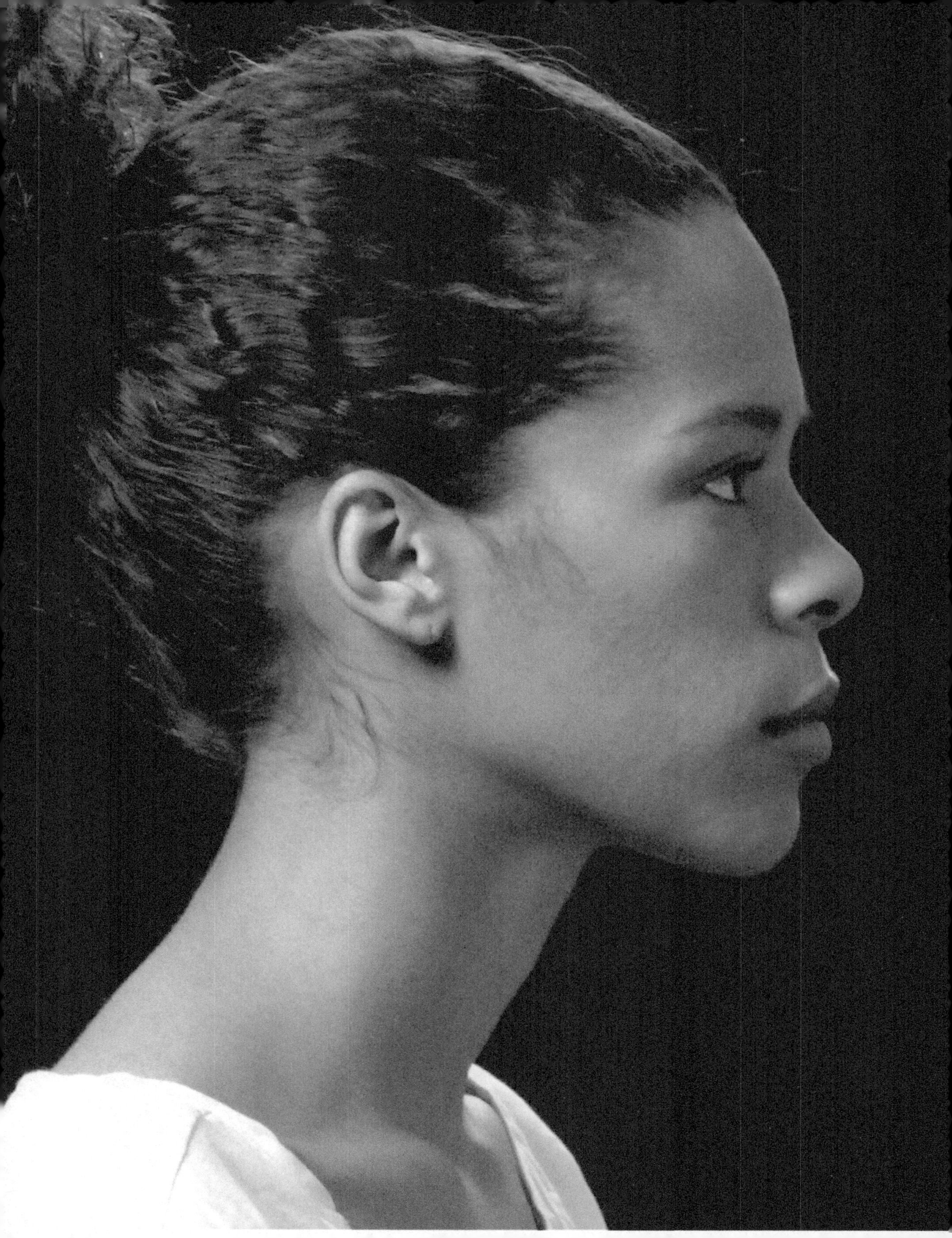

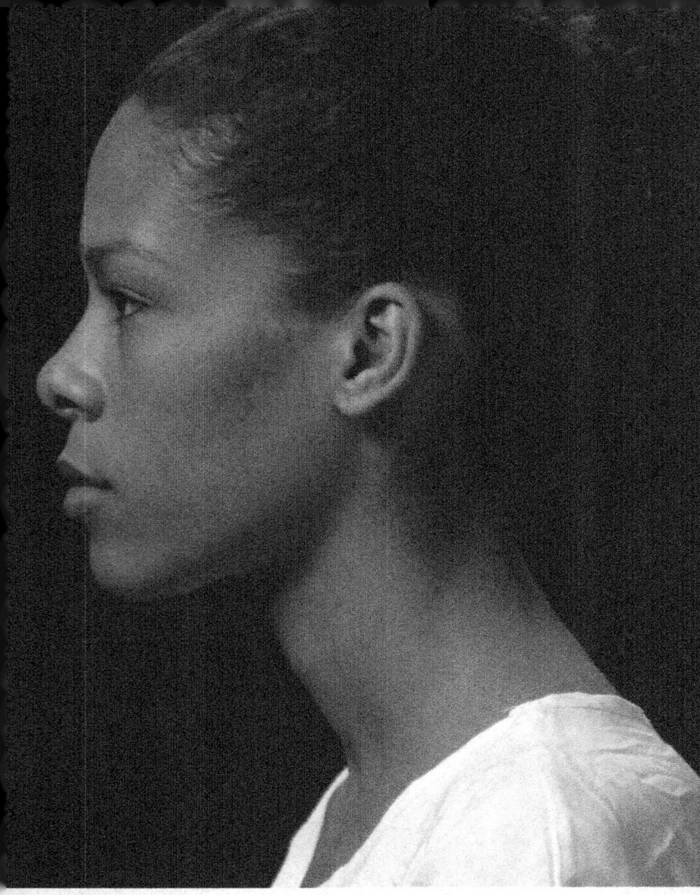

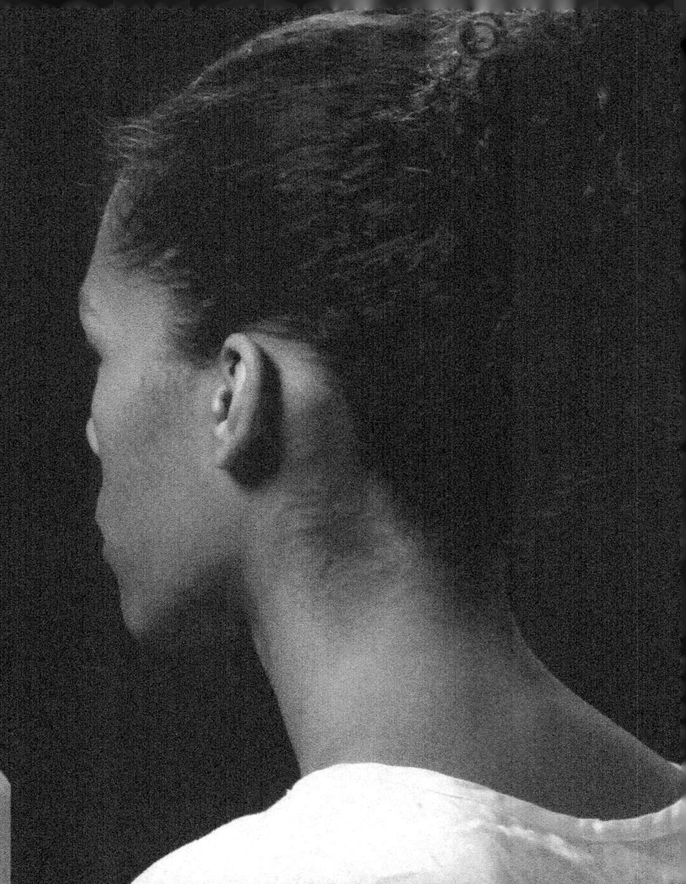

**Ethnicities claimed:**

United States—Creole, Philippines, Ireland, United States—African American, Poland, Czechoslovakia.

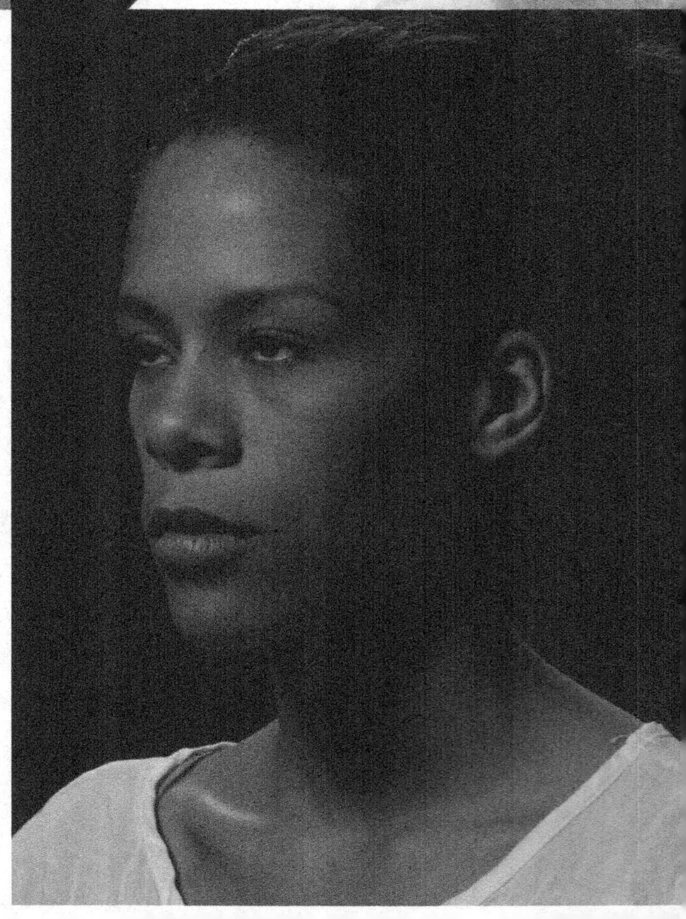

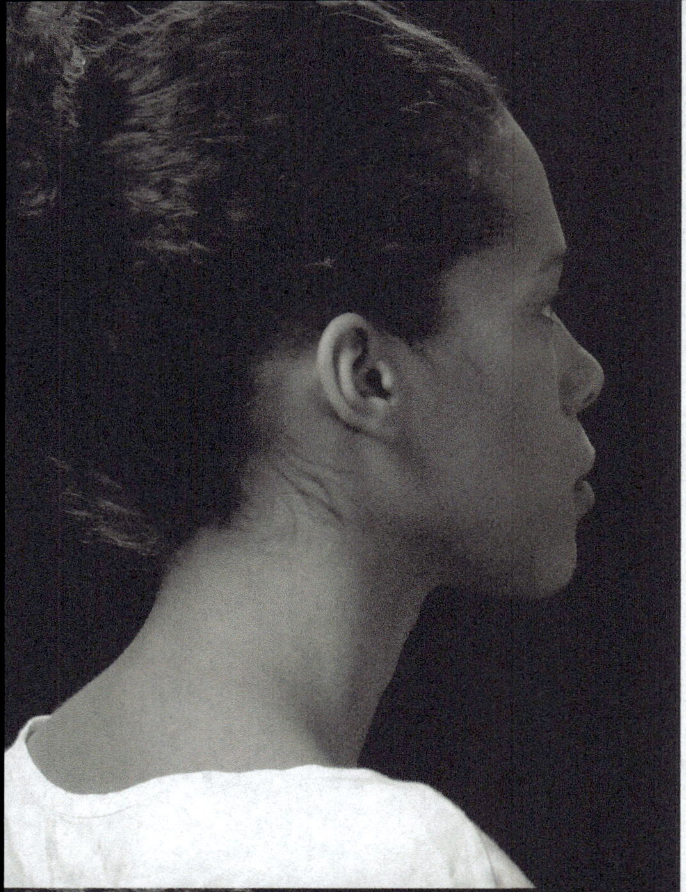

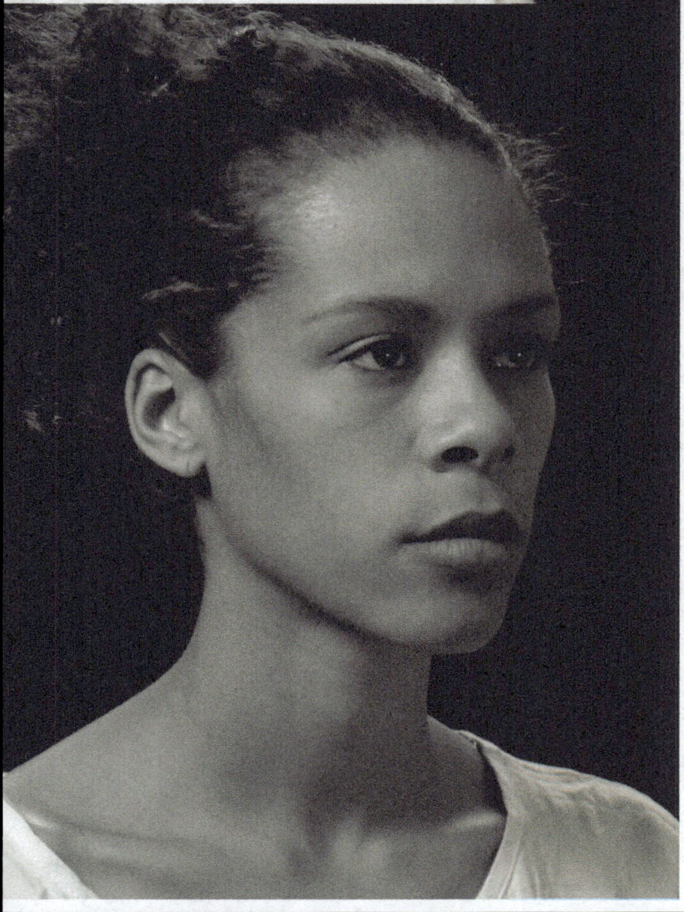

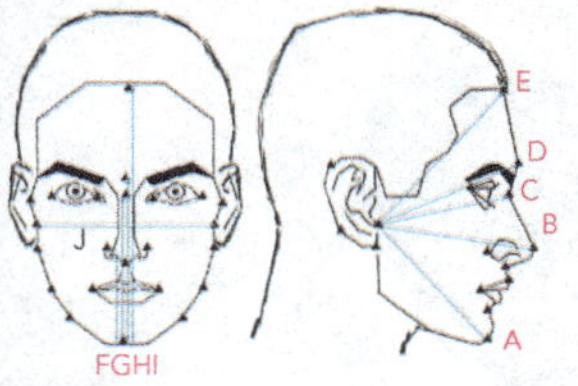


**Head measurements (in):**

A: 5 1/4
B: 5 3/8
C: 5
D: 5 1/8
E: 6 1/4
F: 3 1/4
G: 4 1/2
H: 5 1/4
I: 7 5/8
J: 5 3/4

MAP REFERENCE:

17

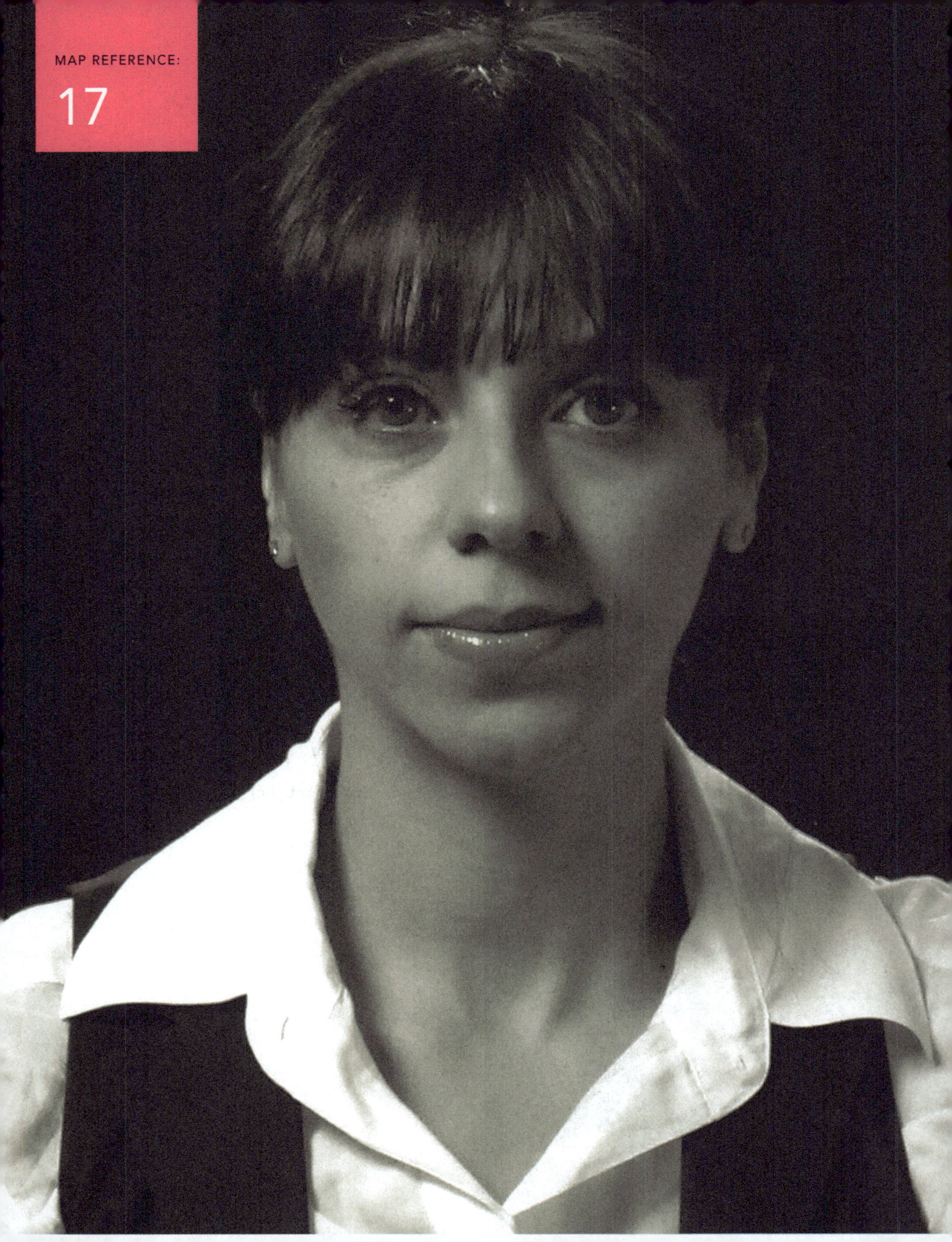

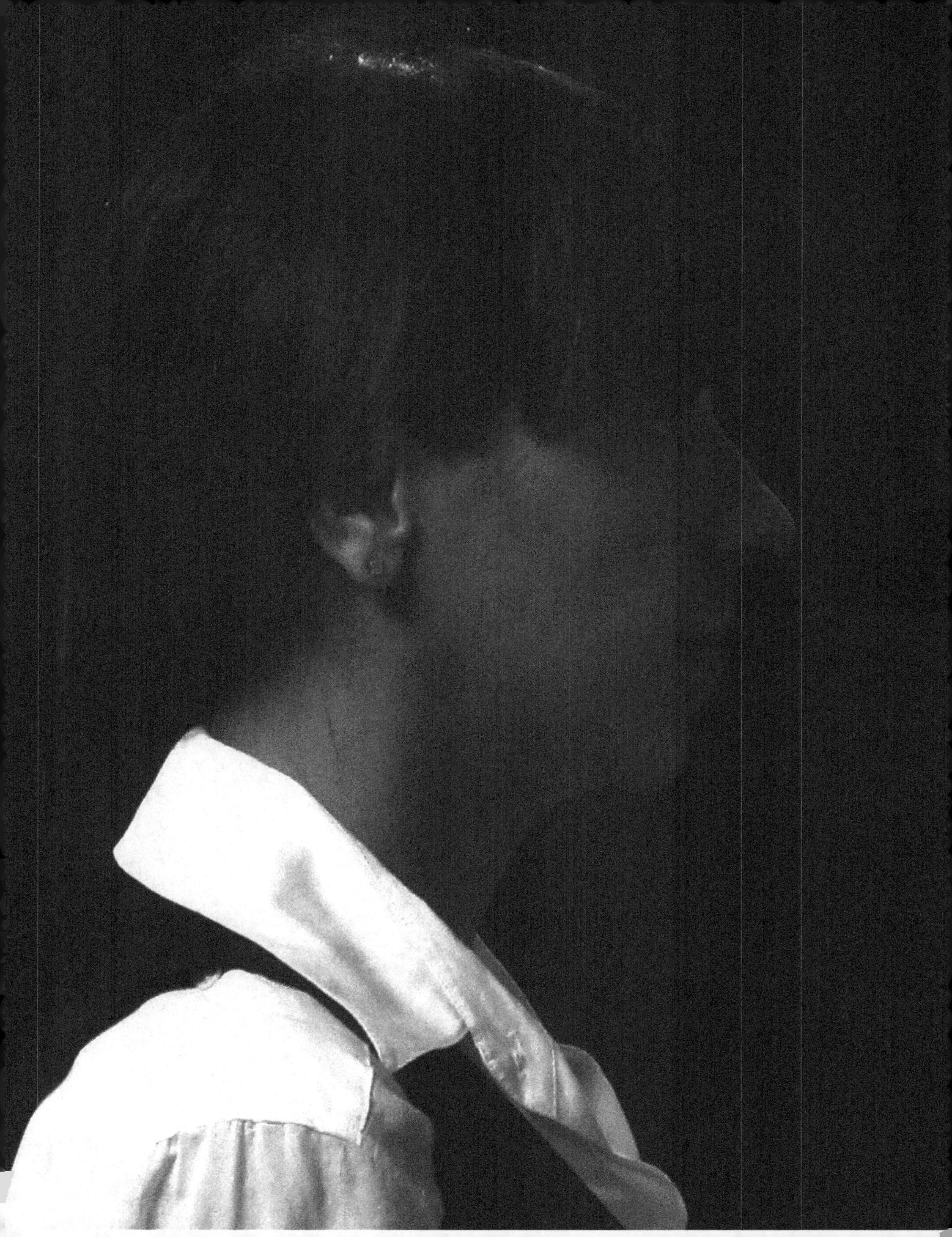

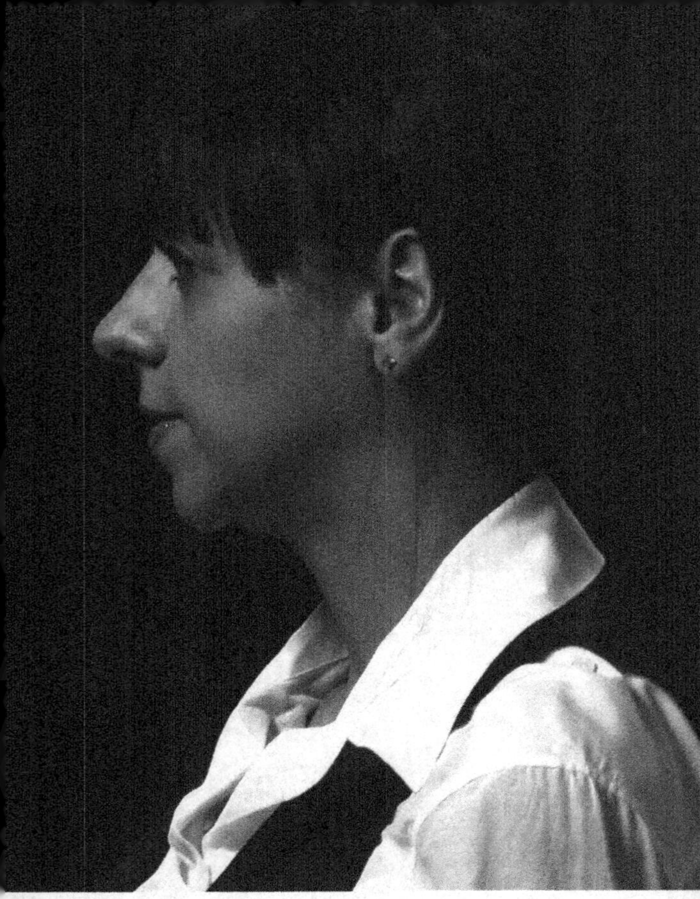

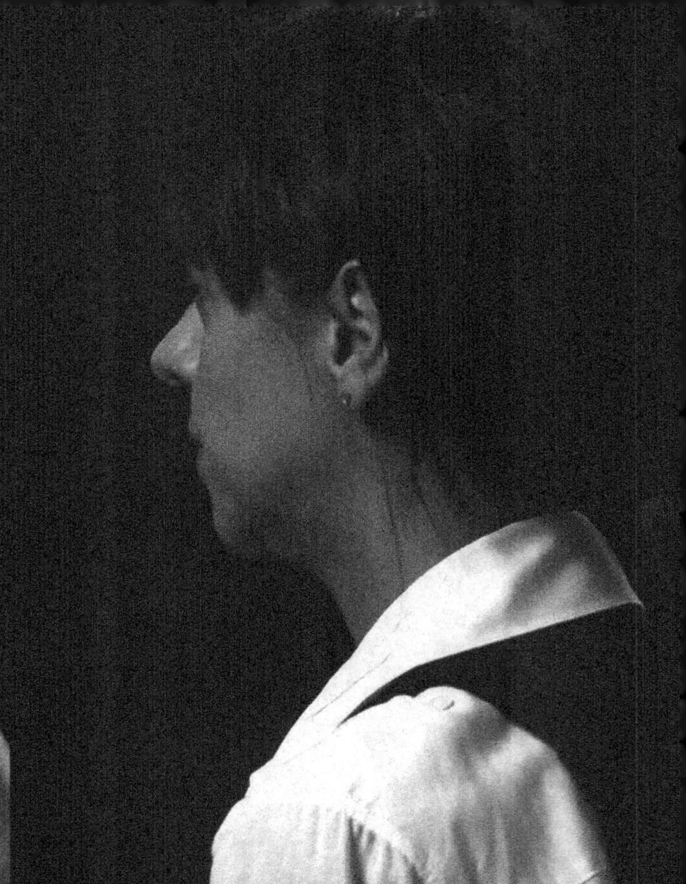

**Ethnicities claimed:**

Armenia.

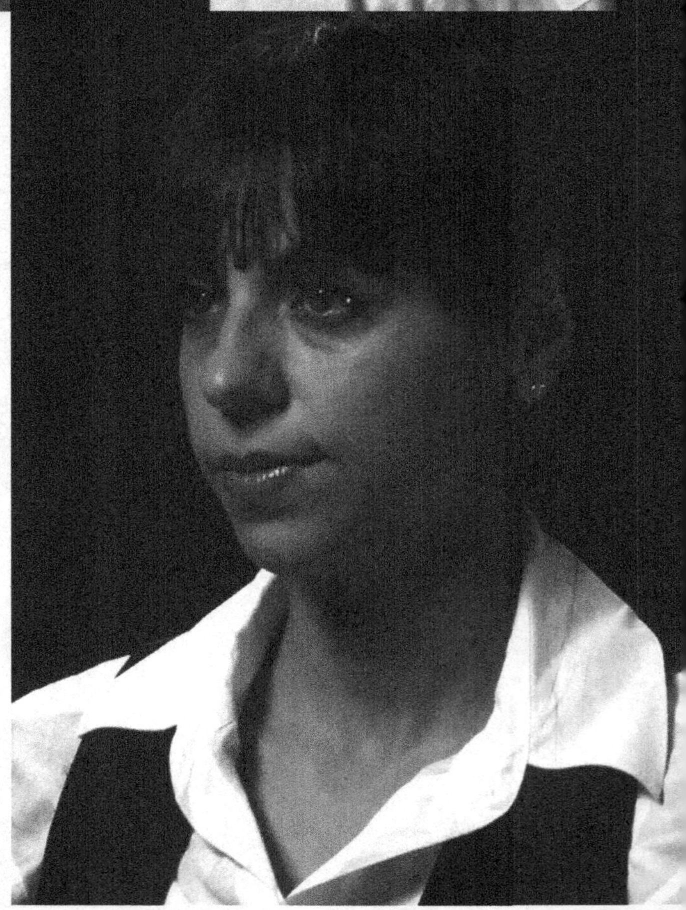

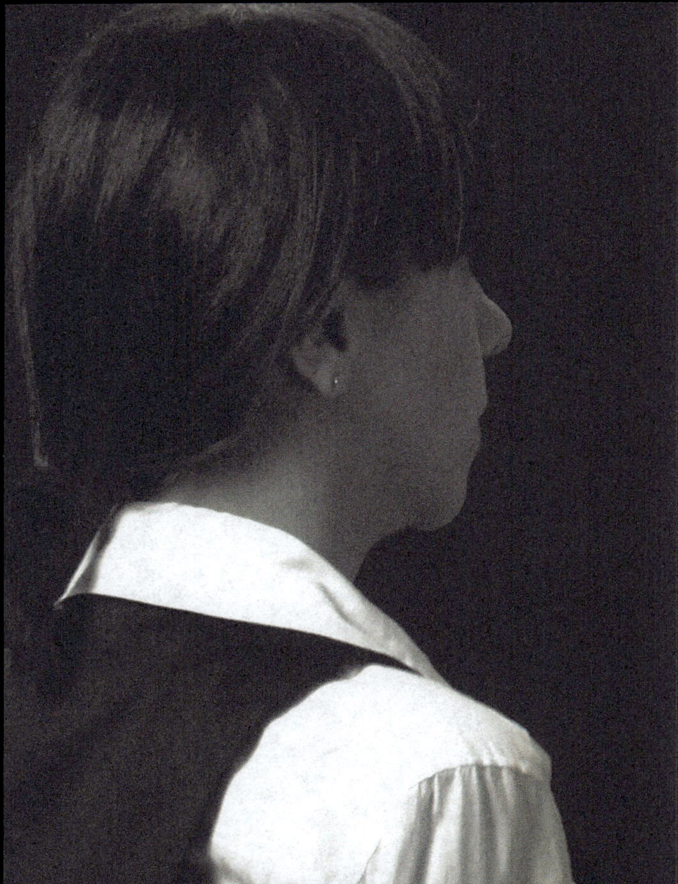

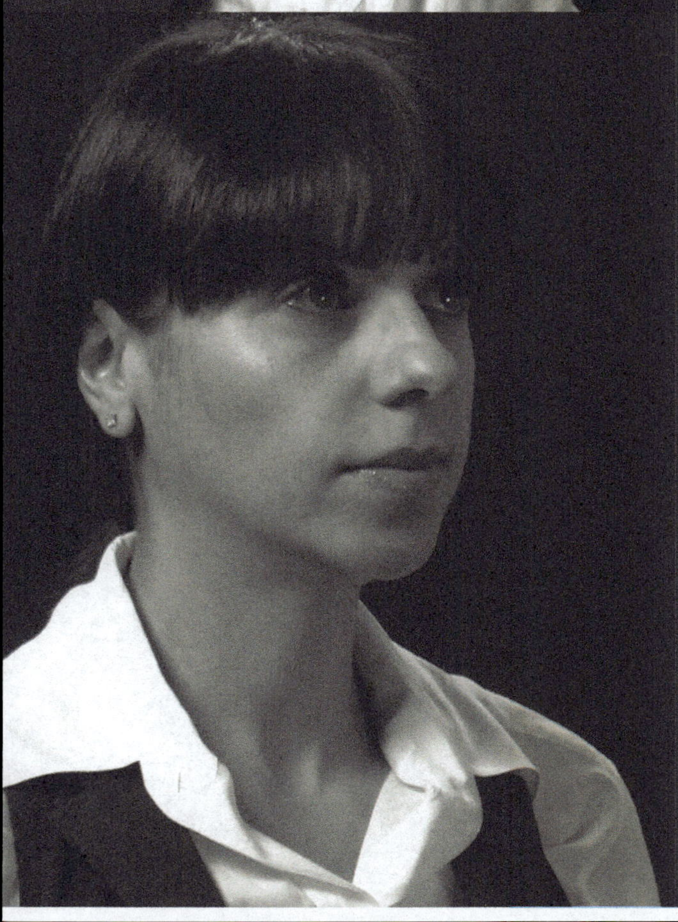

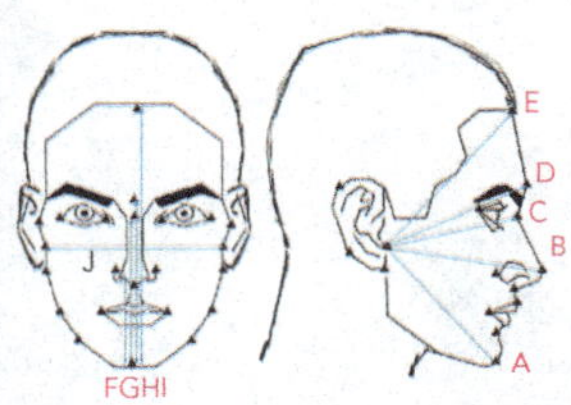


**Head measurements (in):**

A: 5
B: 5 1/4
C: 5
D: 5 1/8
E: 5 3/4
F: 3 1/2
G: 4
H: 4 7/8
I: 7
J: 5 3/4

MAP REFERENCE:

19

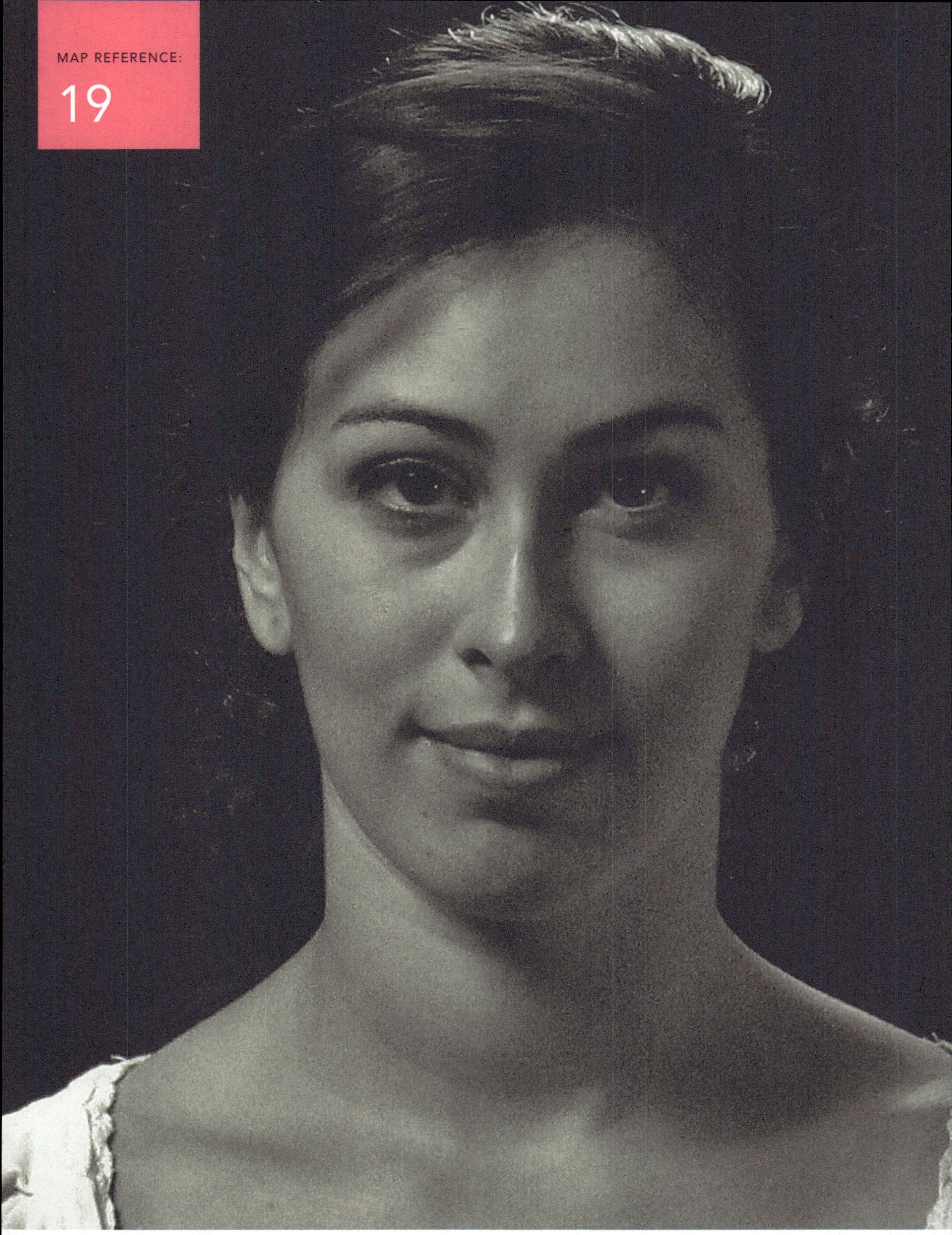

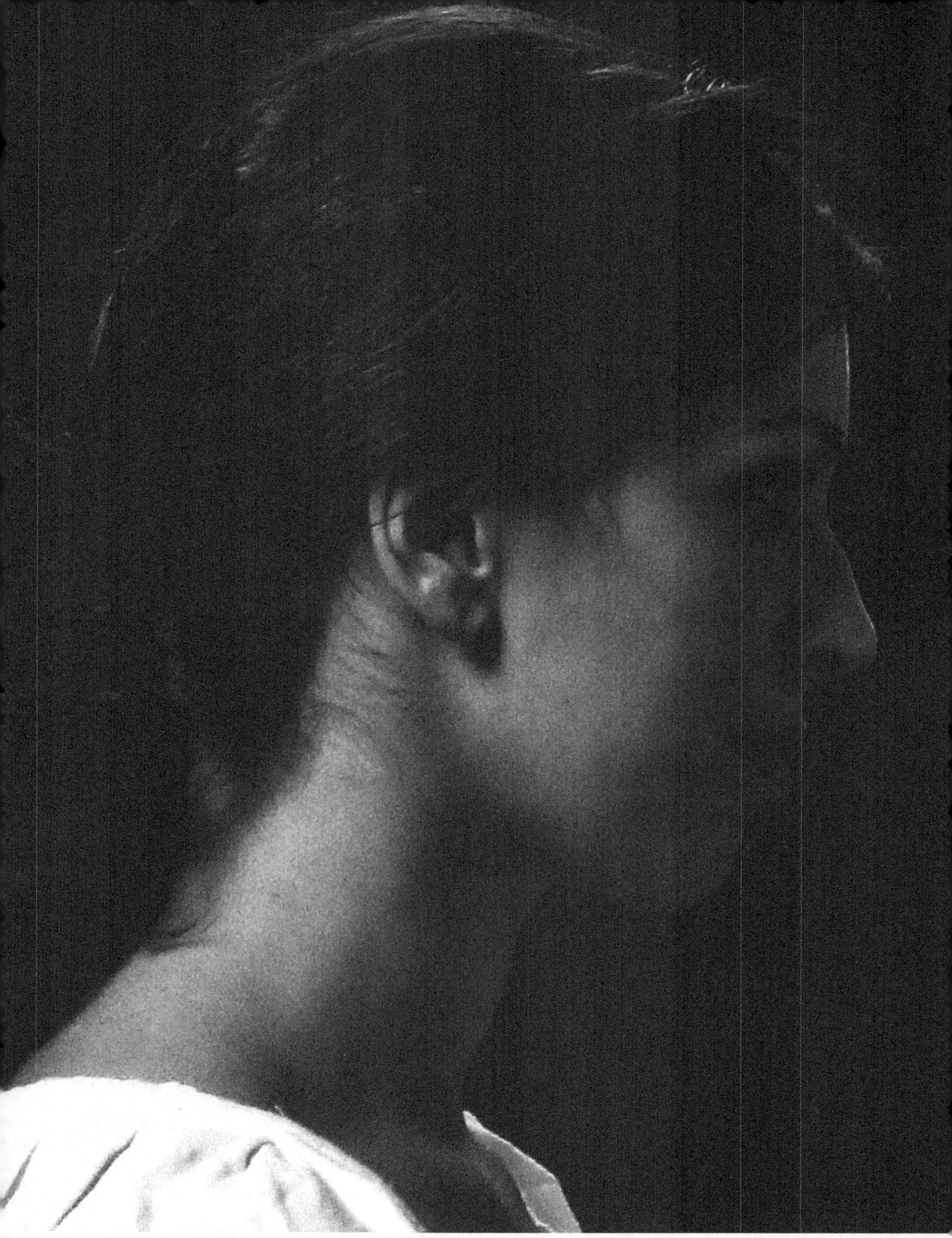

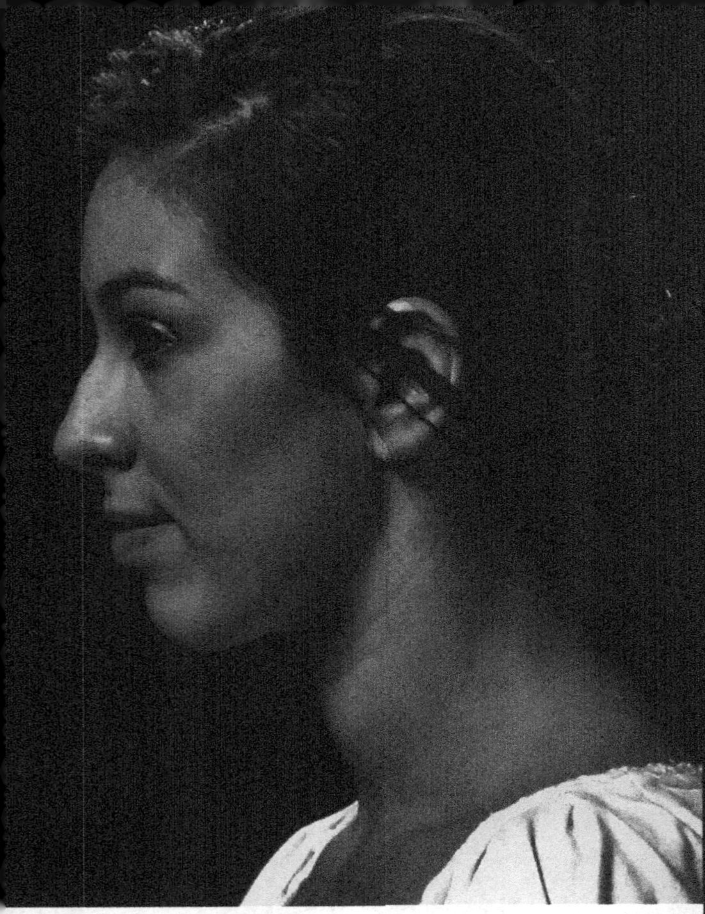

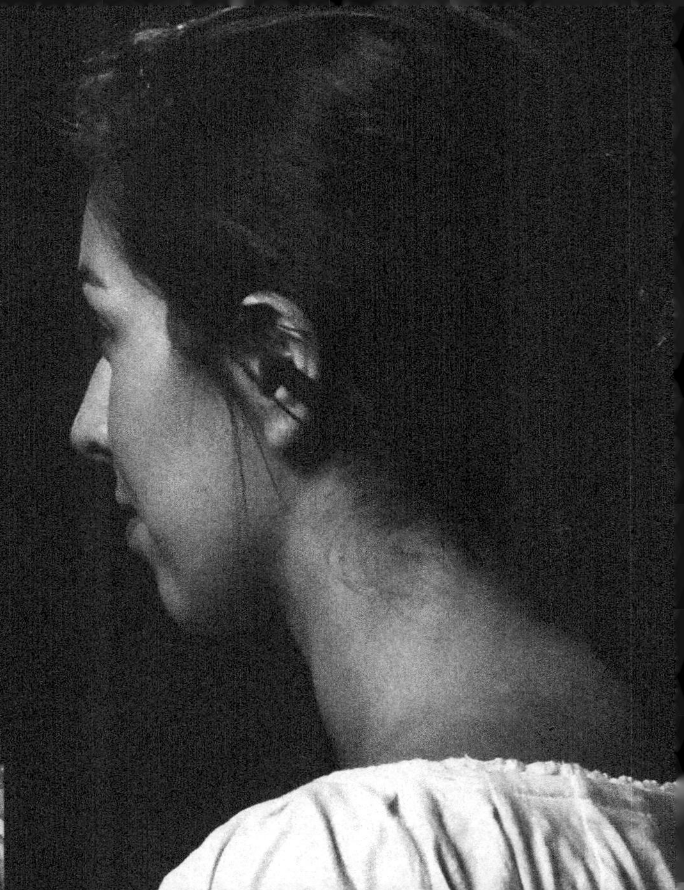

**Ethnicities claimed:**

Uruguay, South America, Spain, Italy.

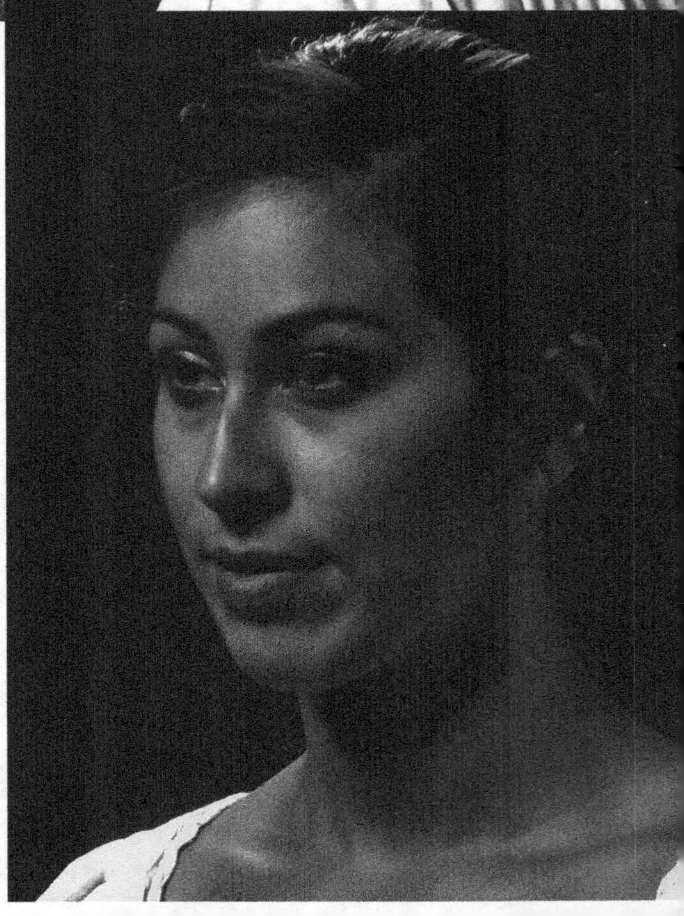

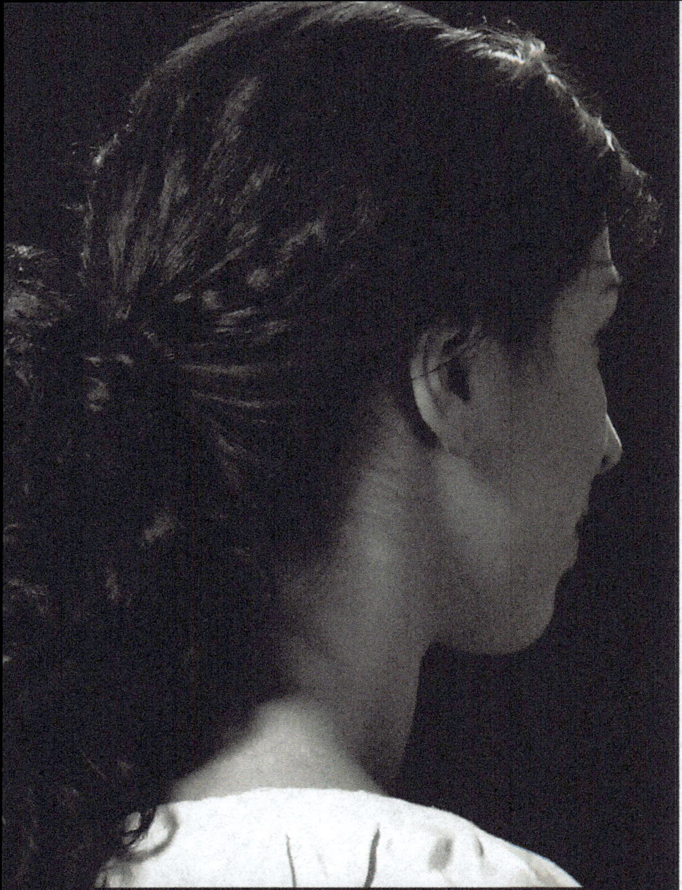

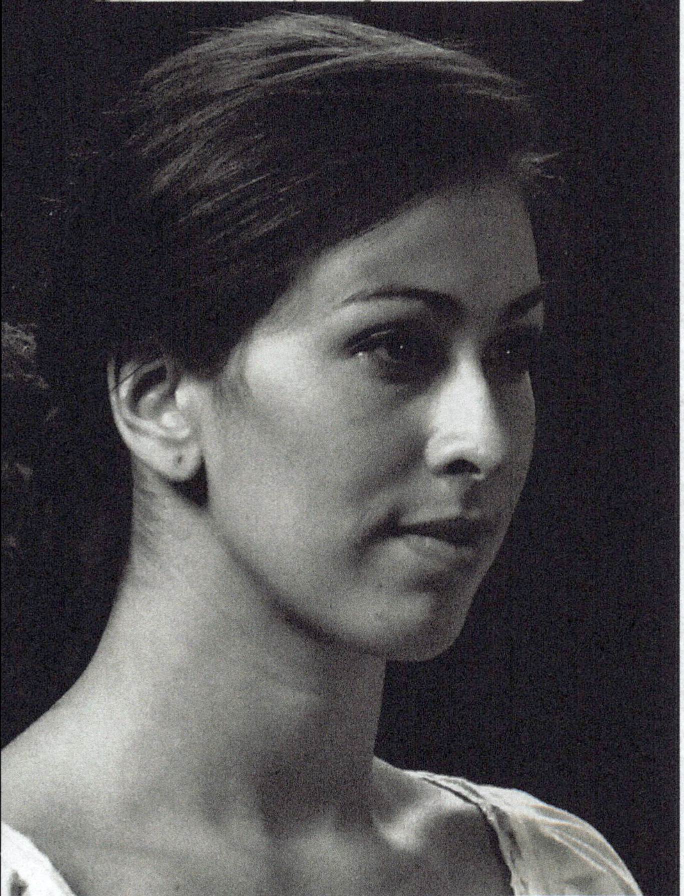

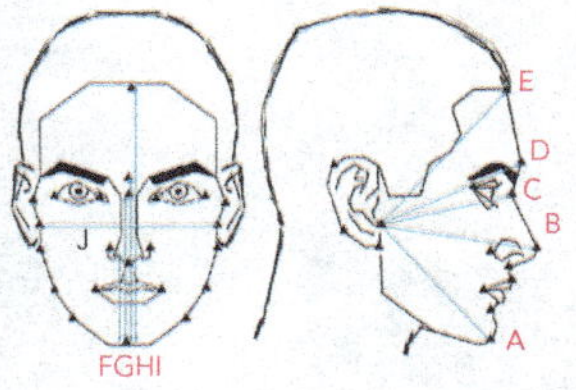


**Head measurements (in):**

A: 4 7/8
B: 4 3/4
C: 4 5/8
D: 4 3/4
E: 5 3/4
F: 3 5/8
G: 4 1/2
H: 5 1/8
I: 7 1/2
J: 5 1/4

MAP REFERENCE:

20

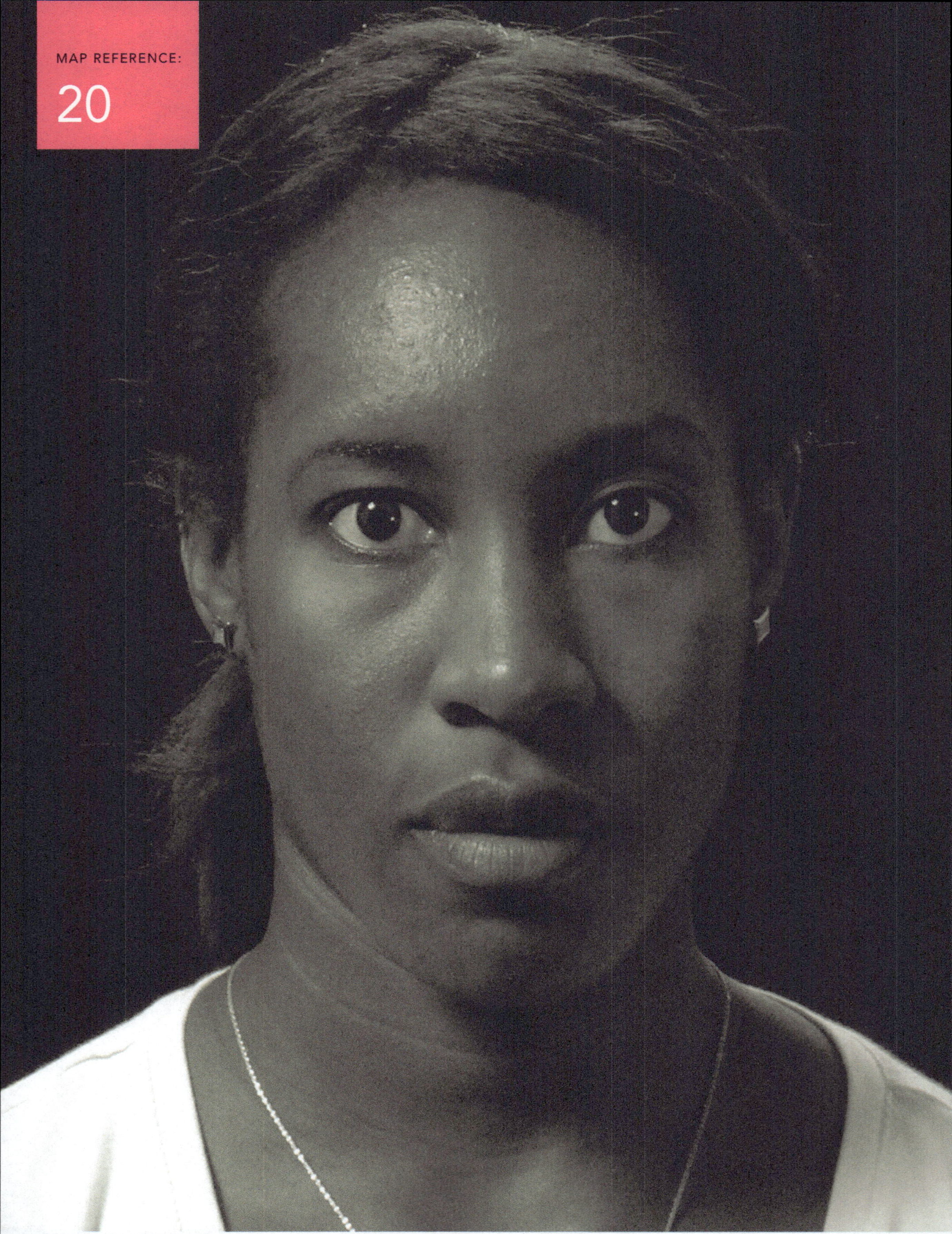

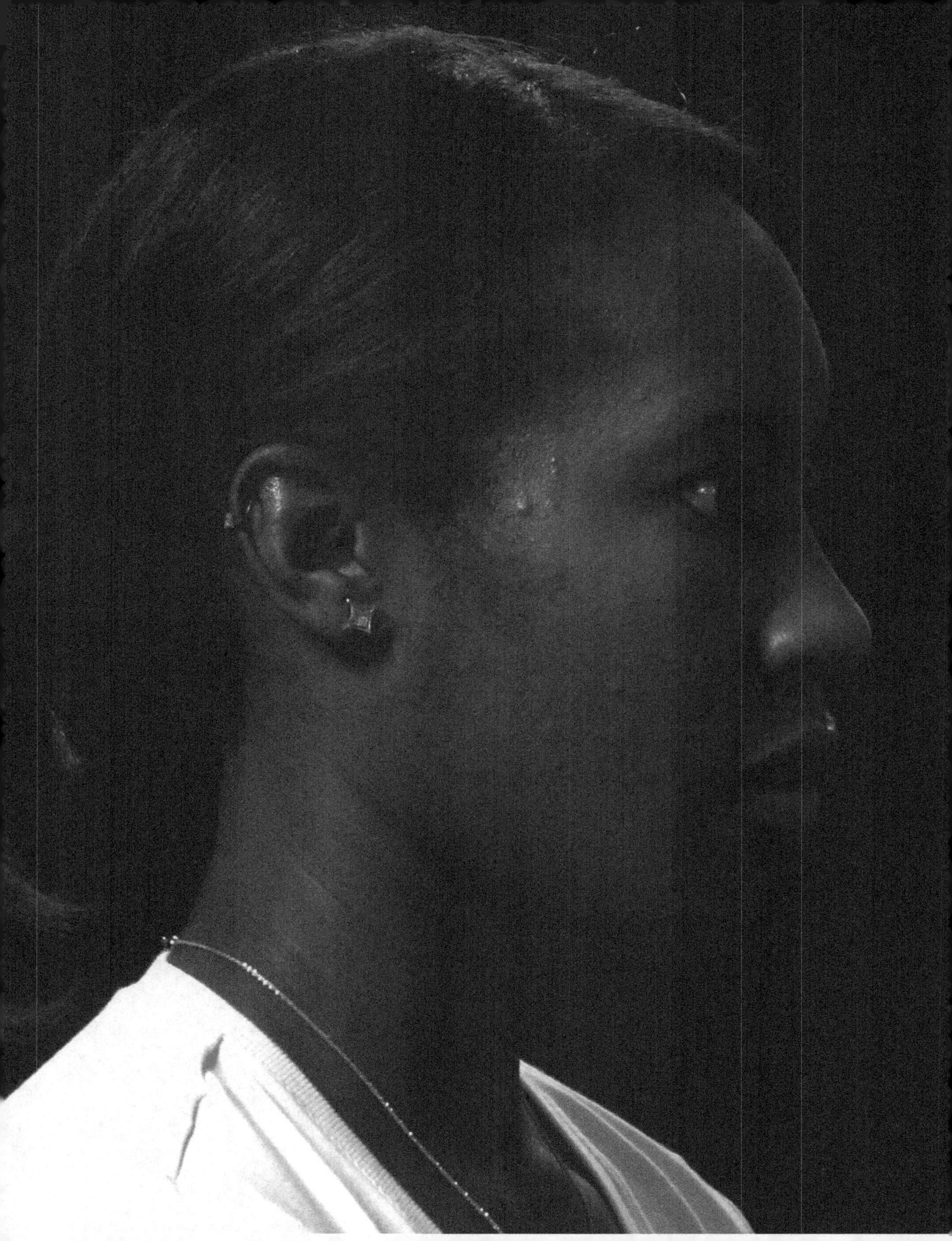

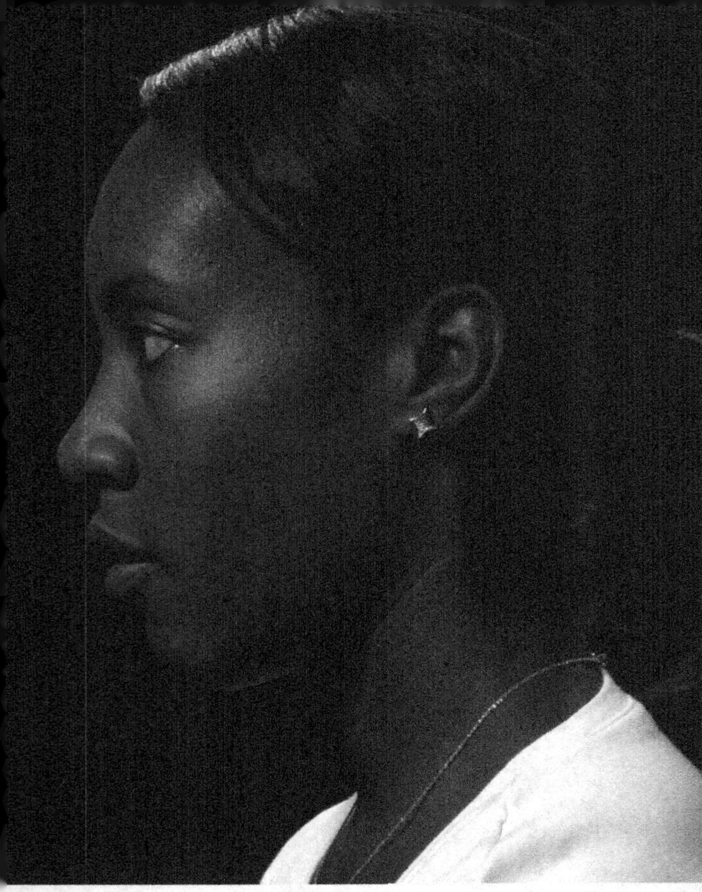

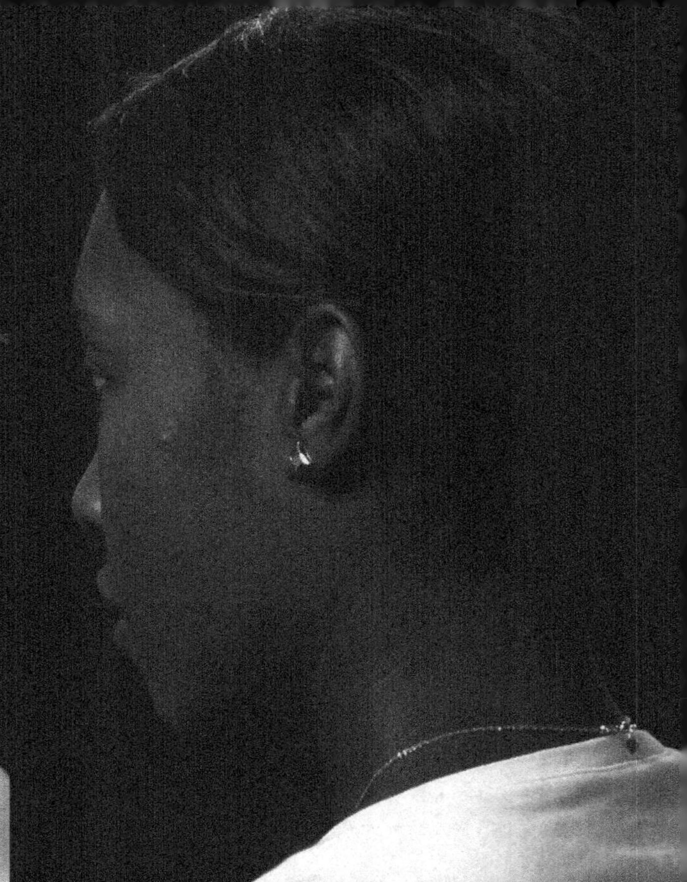

**Ethnicities claimed:**

United States—Cherokee, Africa, Europe.

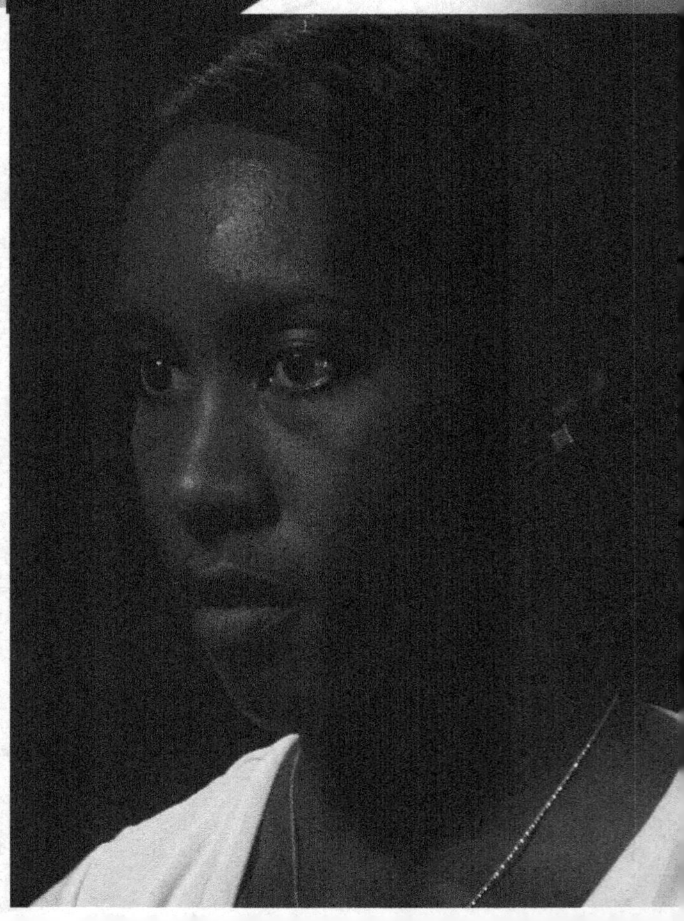

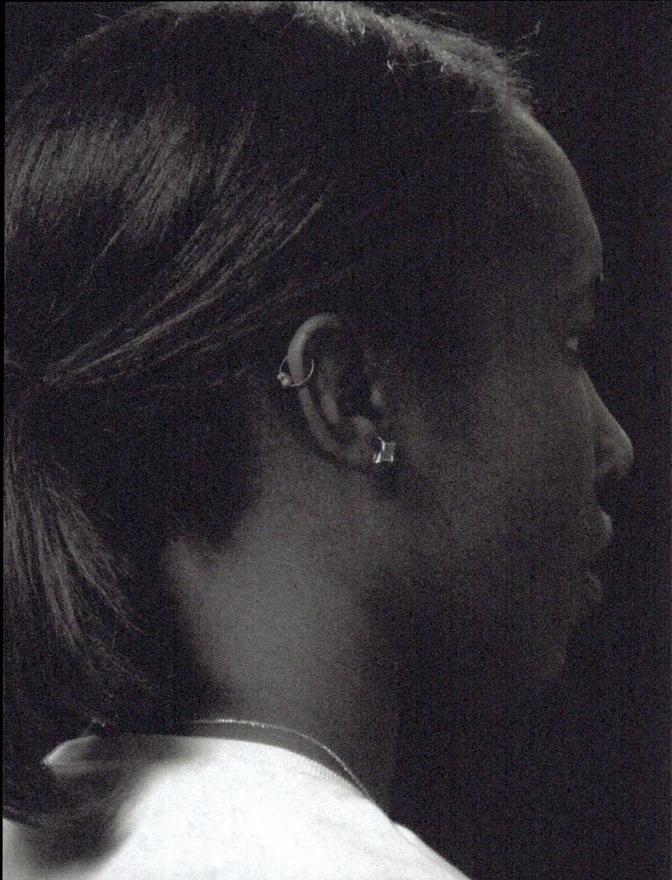

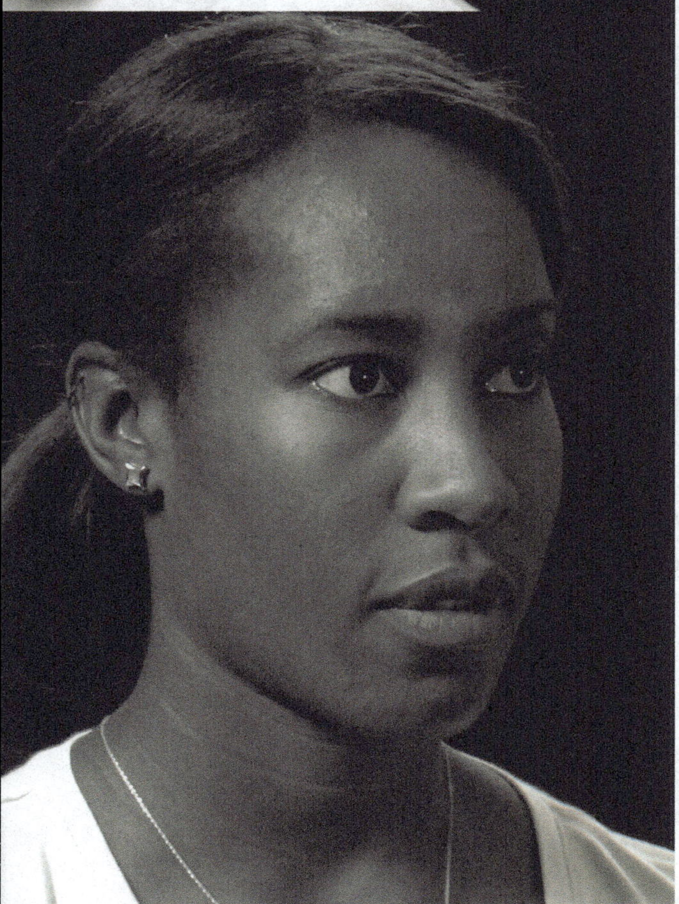

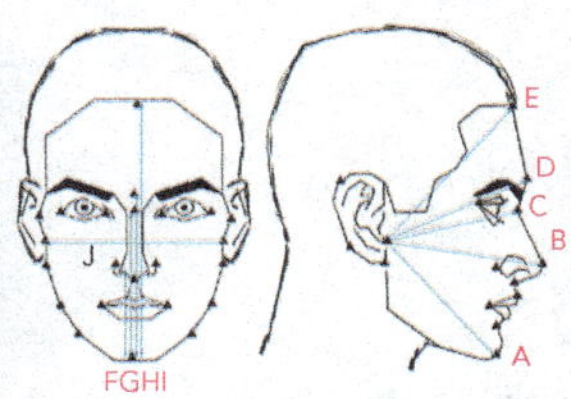


**Head measurements (in):**

A: 6
B: 5 1/4
C: 5 1/8
D: 5 5/8
E: 6 7/8
F: 4 1/4
G: 4 7/8
H: 6
I: 8 5/8
J: 5 1/2

MAP REFERENCE:
22

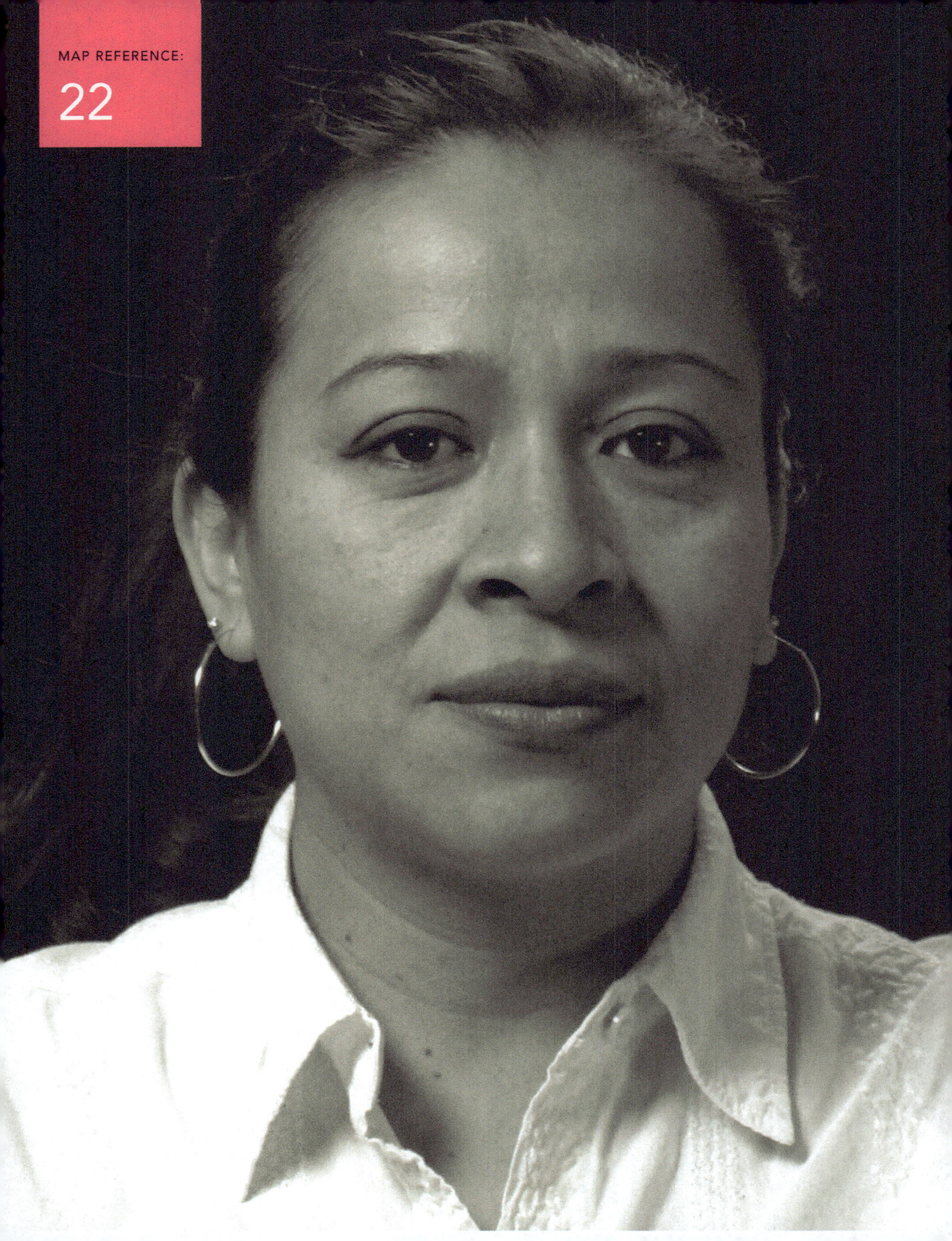

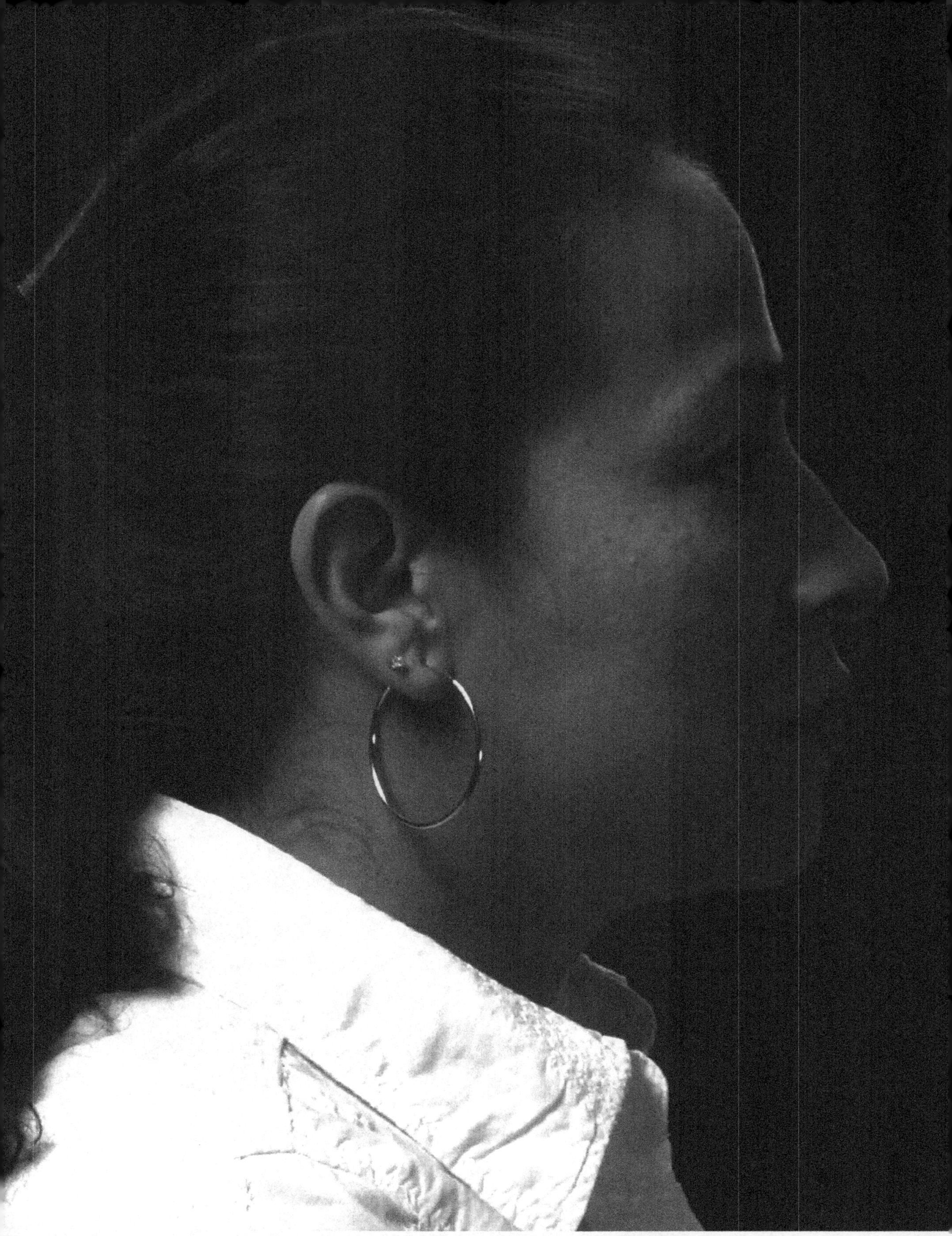

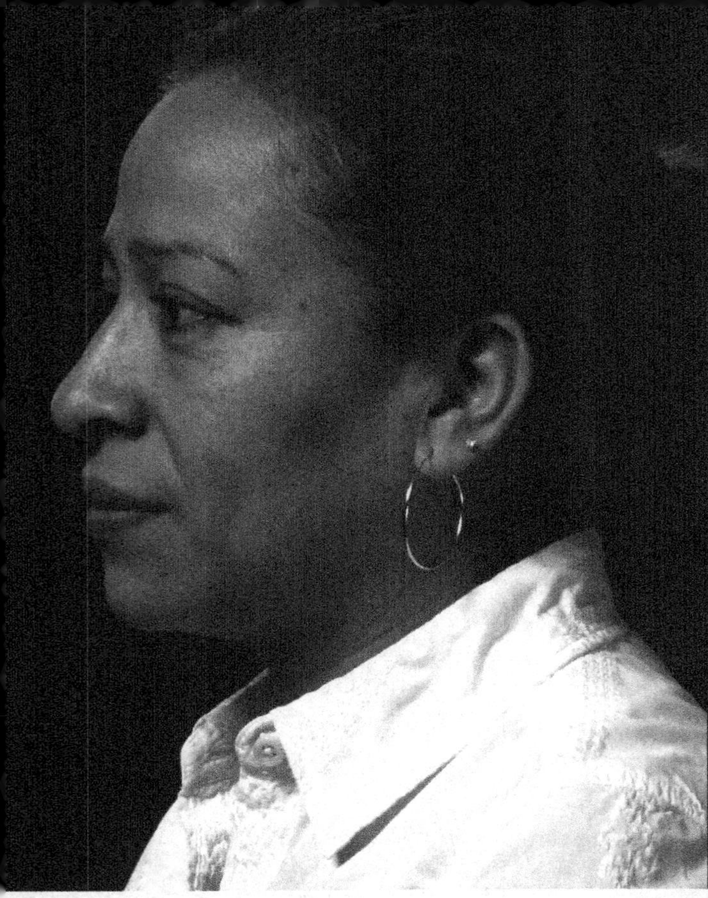

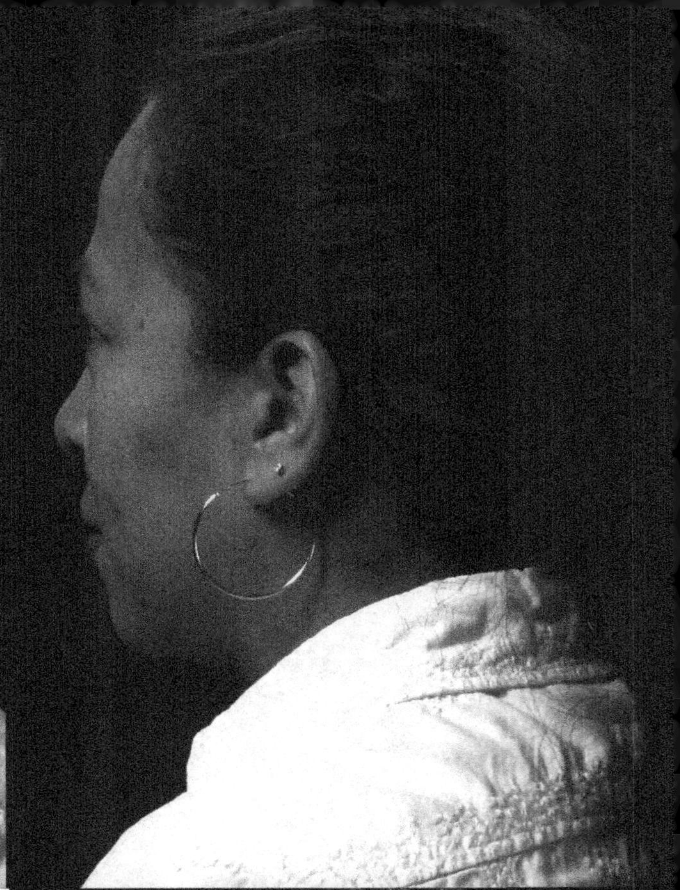

**Ethnicities claimed:**

Mexico.

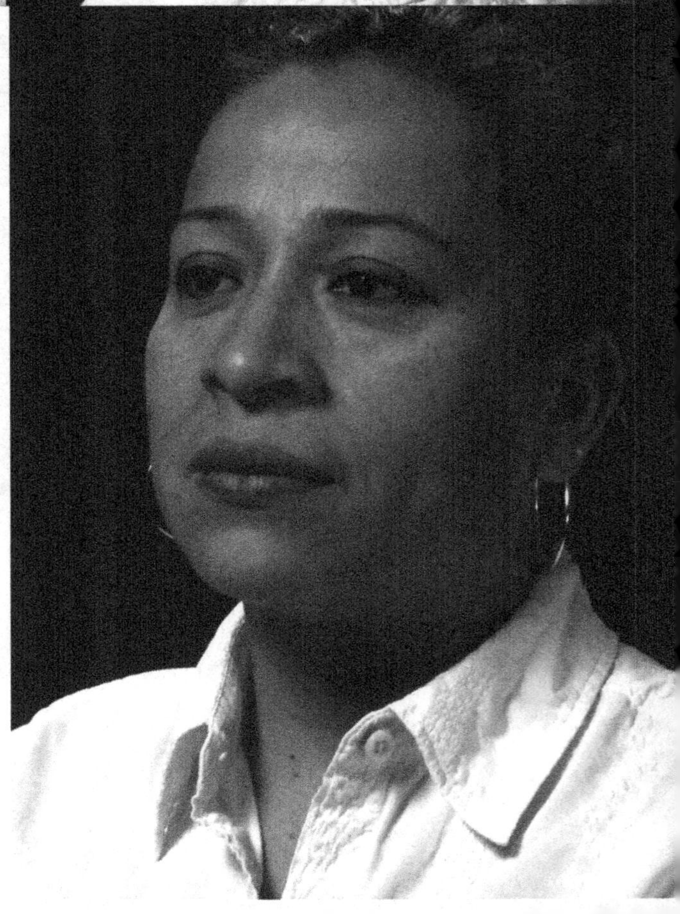

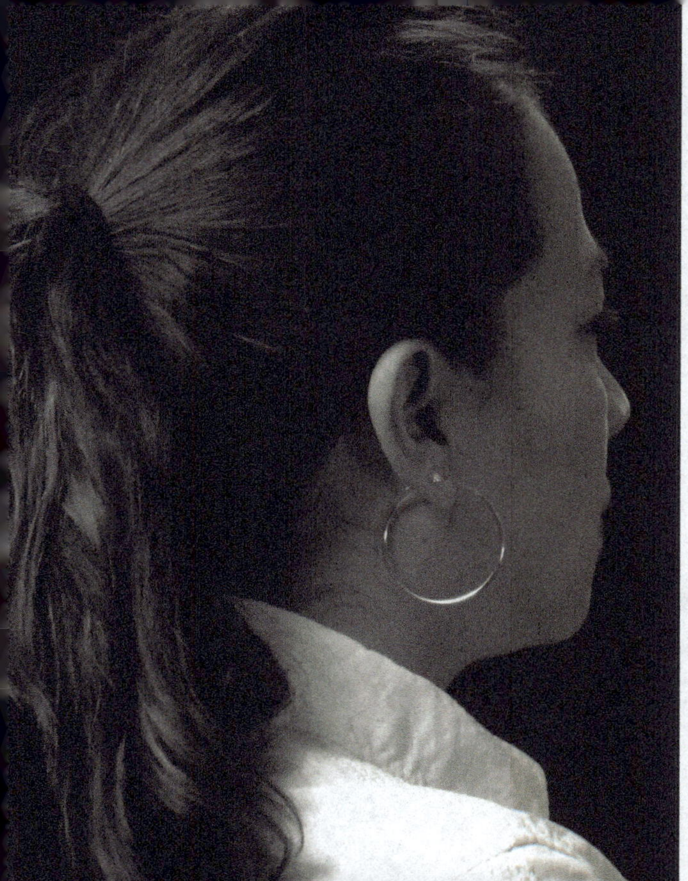

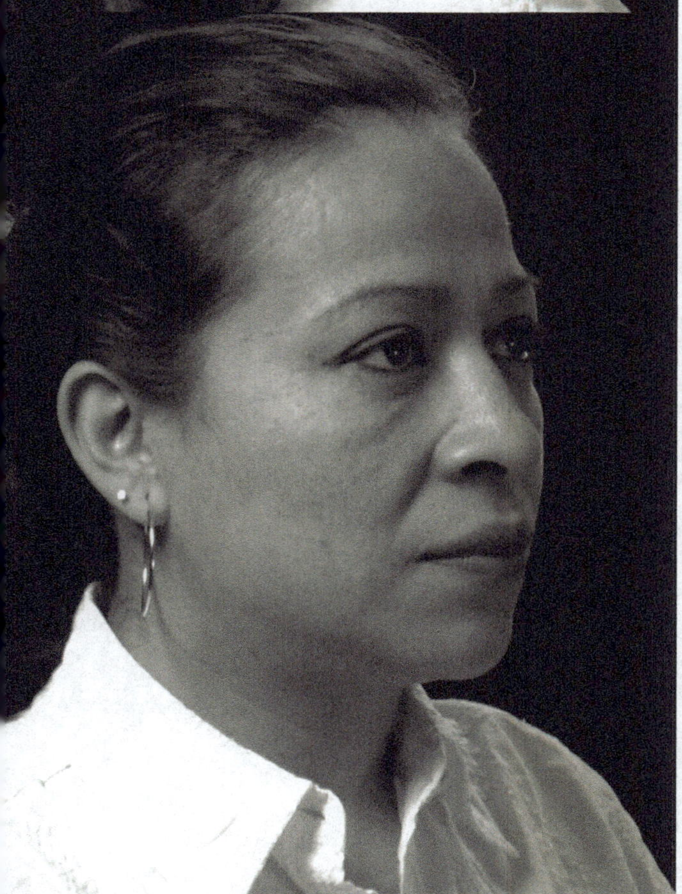

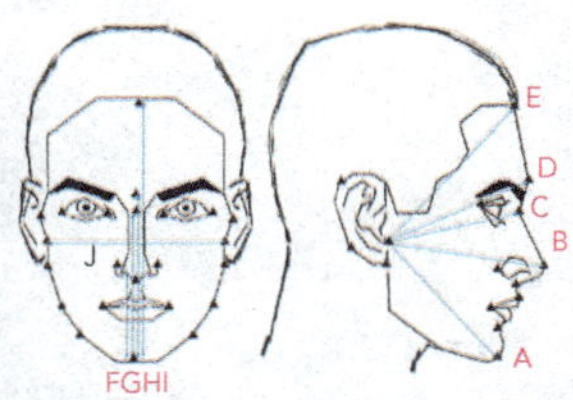


**Head measurements (in):**

A: 5 1/4
B: 5 1/8
C: 4 7/8
D: 5
E: 6 3/8
F: 3 3/8
G: 4 1/8
H: 5 3/8
I: 7 3/4
J: 5 3/4

MAP REFERENCE:

23

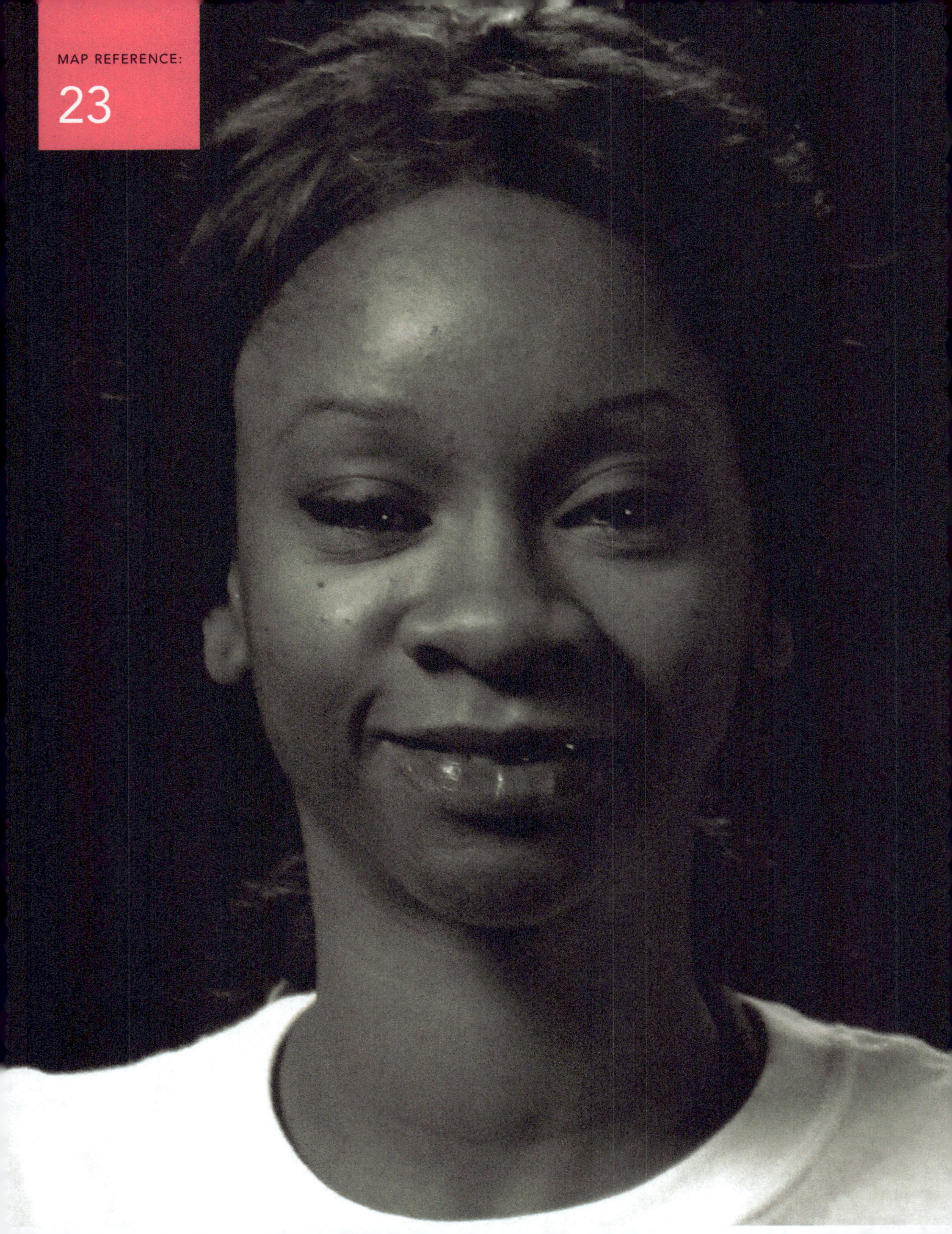

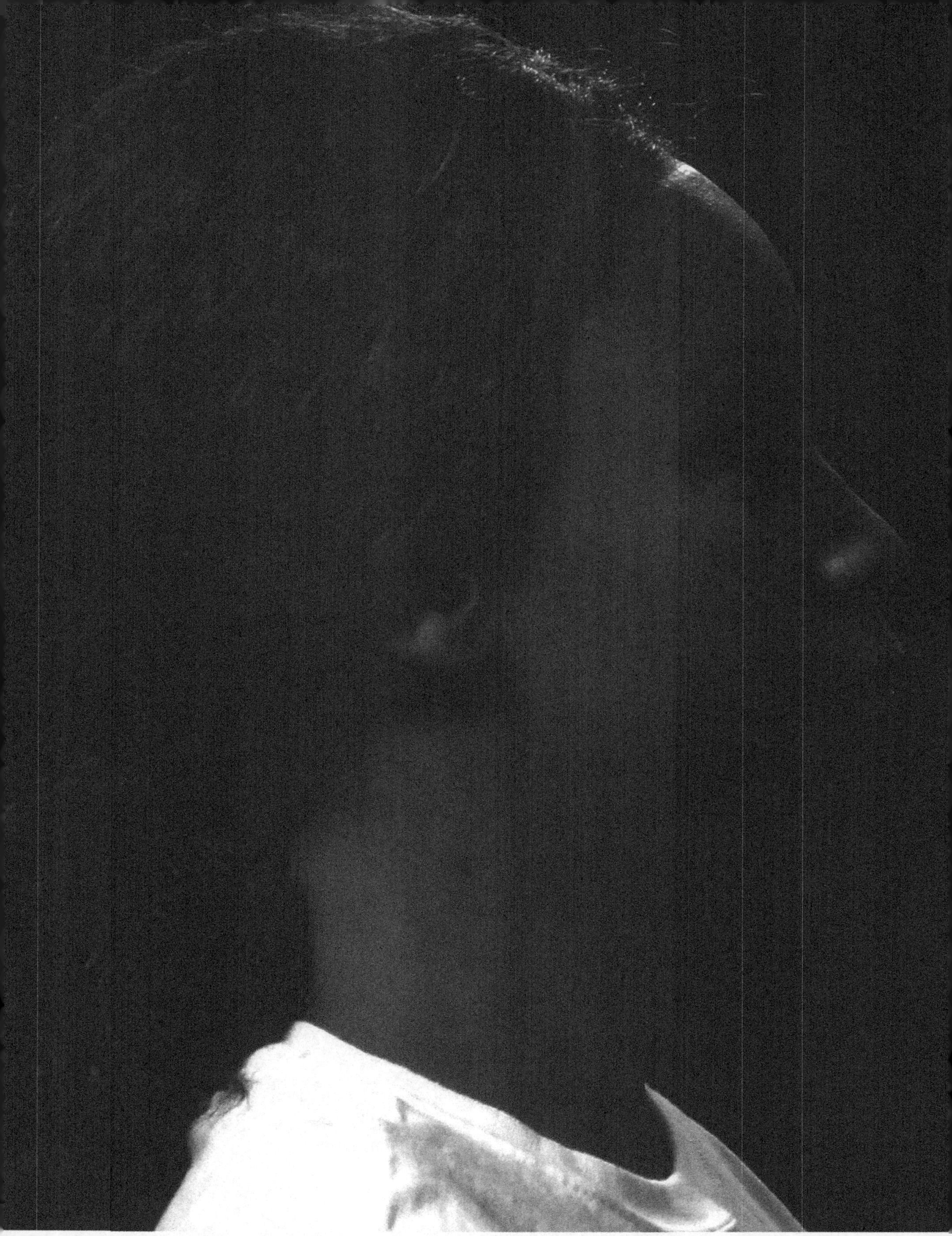

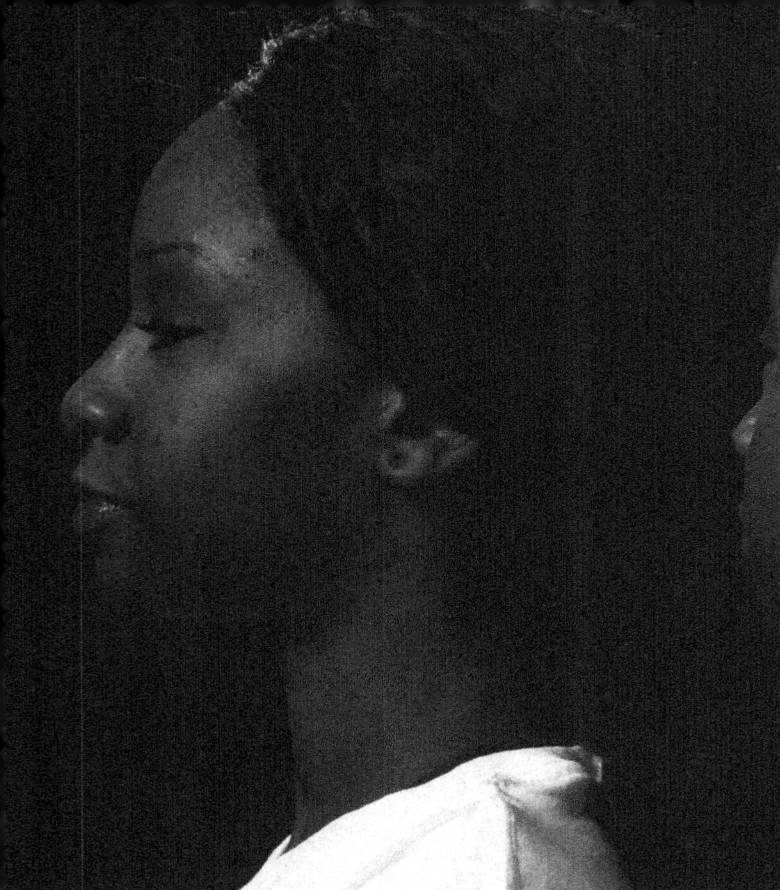

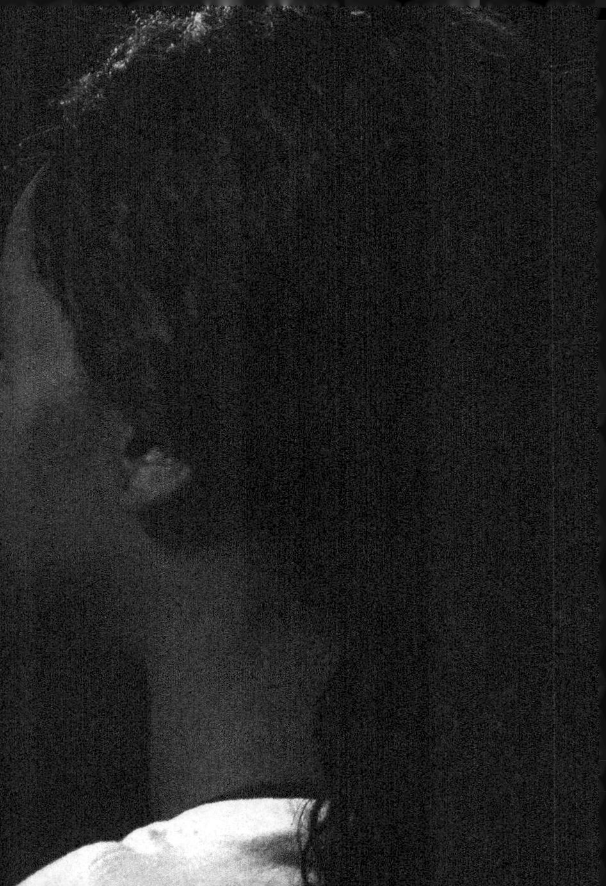

**Ethnicities claimed:**

Trinidad, Nigeria.

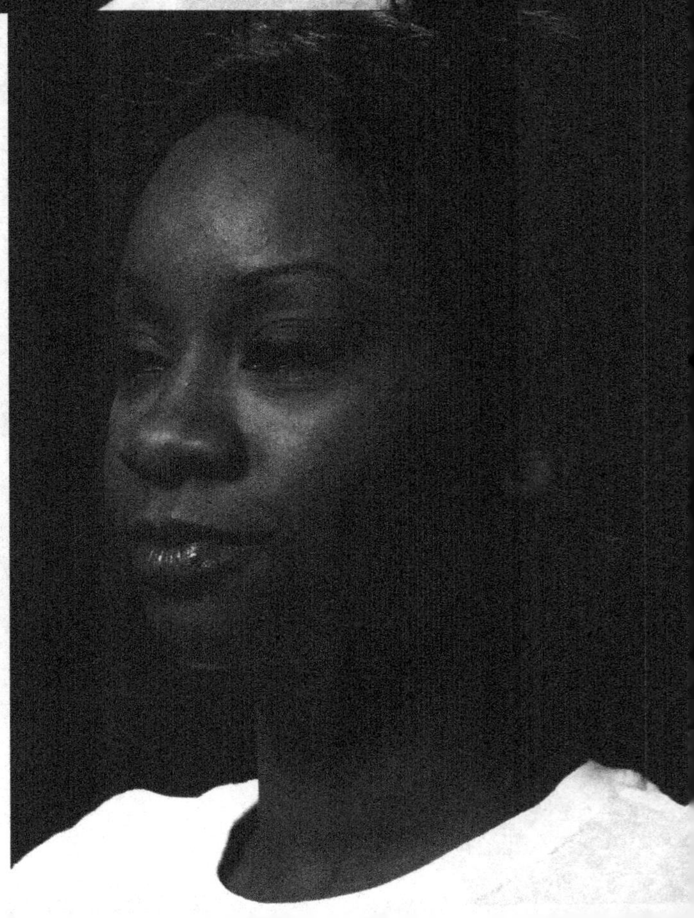

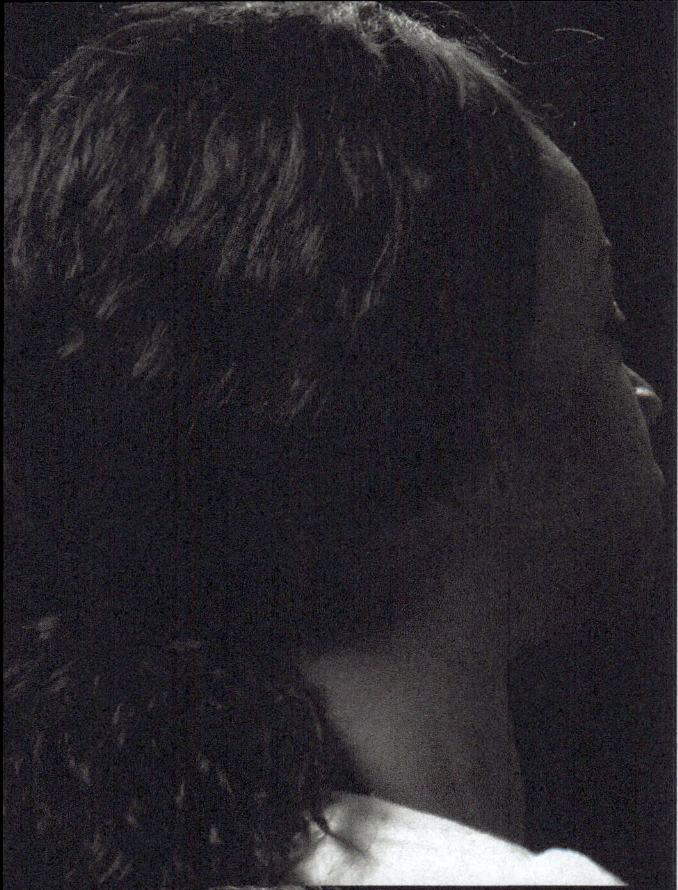

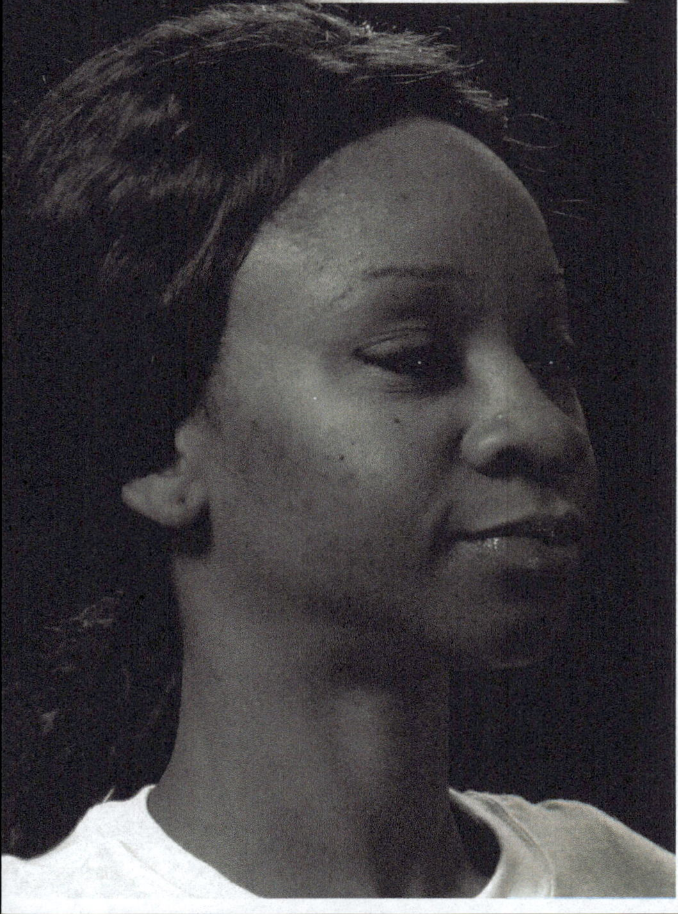

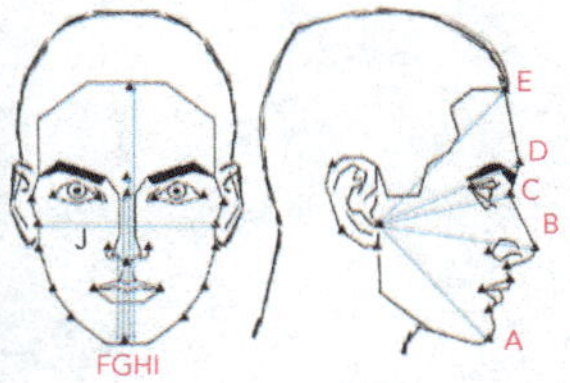


**Head measurements (in):**

A: 5 1/4
B: 5 1/4
C: 4 3/4
D: 5
E: 6 1/8
F: 3 1/2
G: 3 7/8
H: 5
I: 7 1/4
J: 5 3/8

MAP REFERENCE:

5

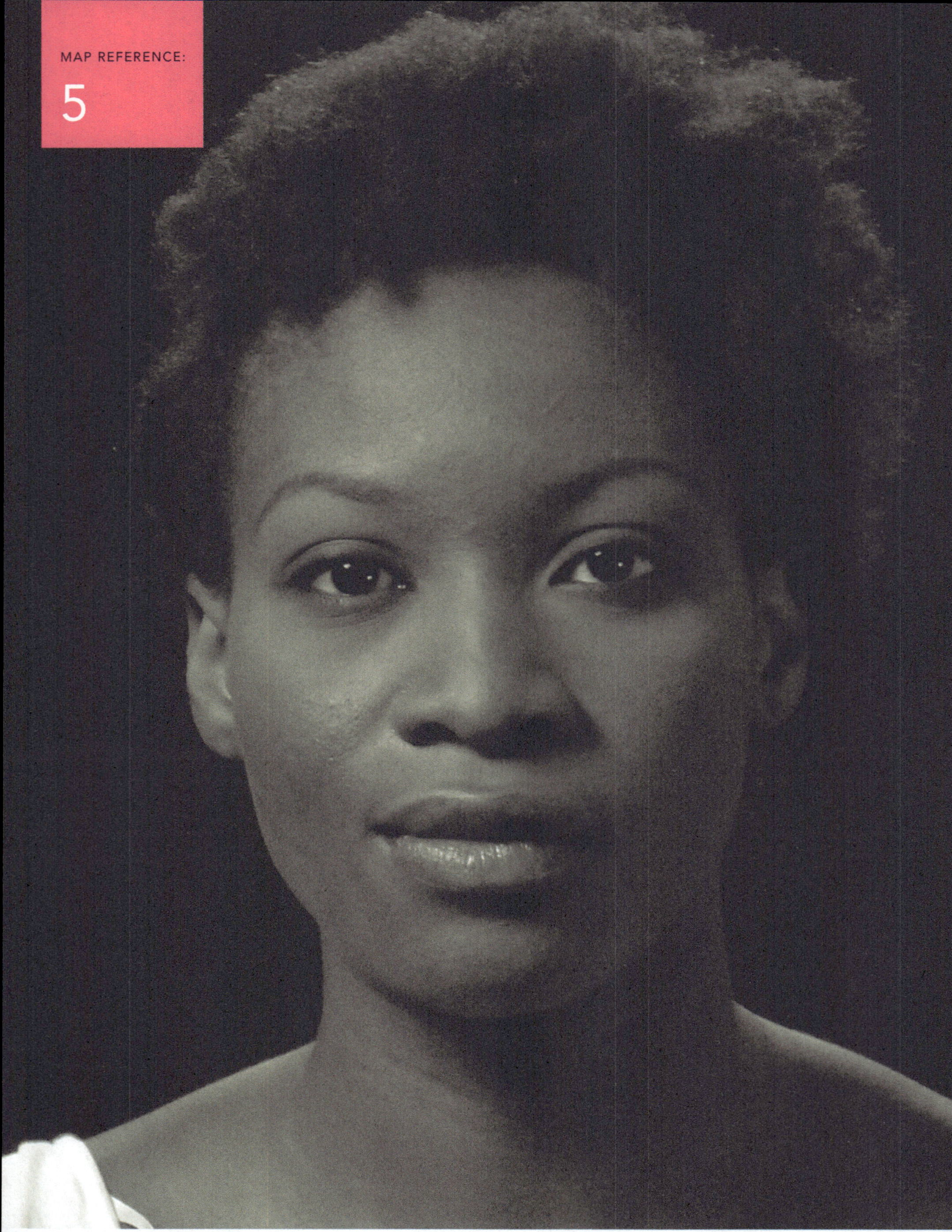

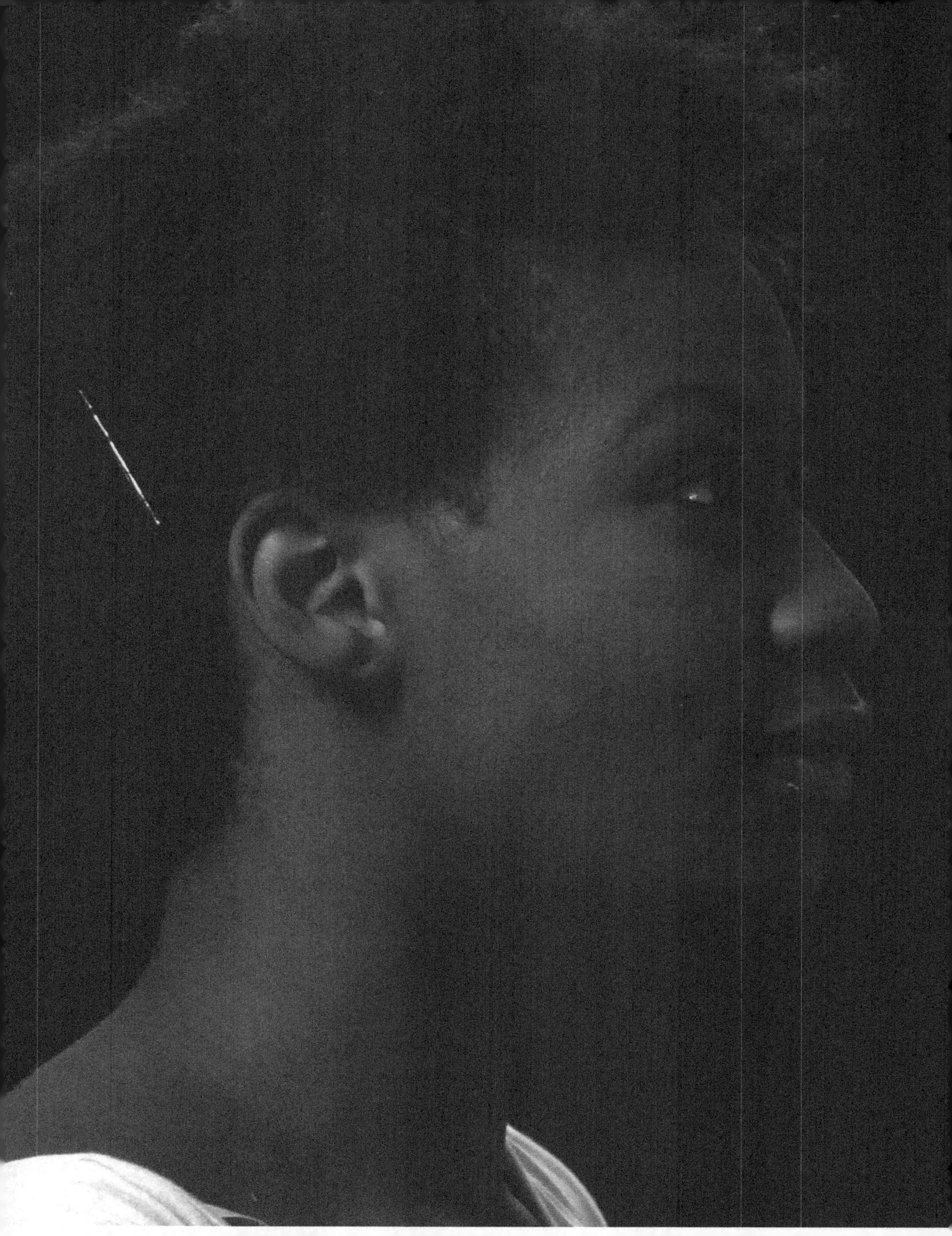

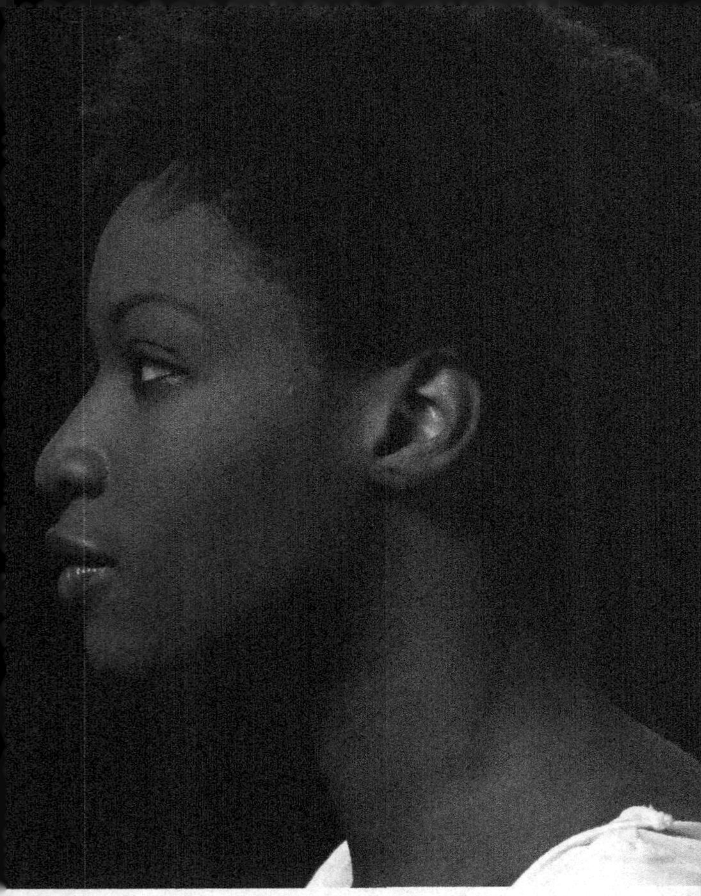

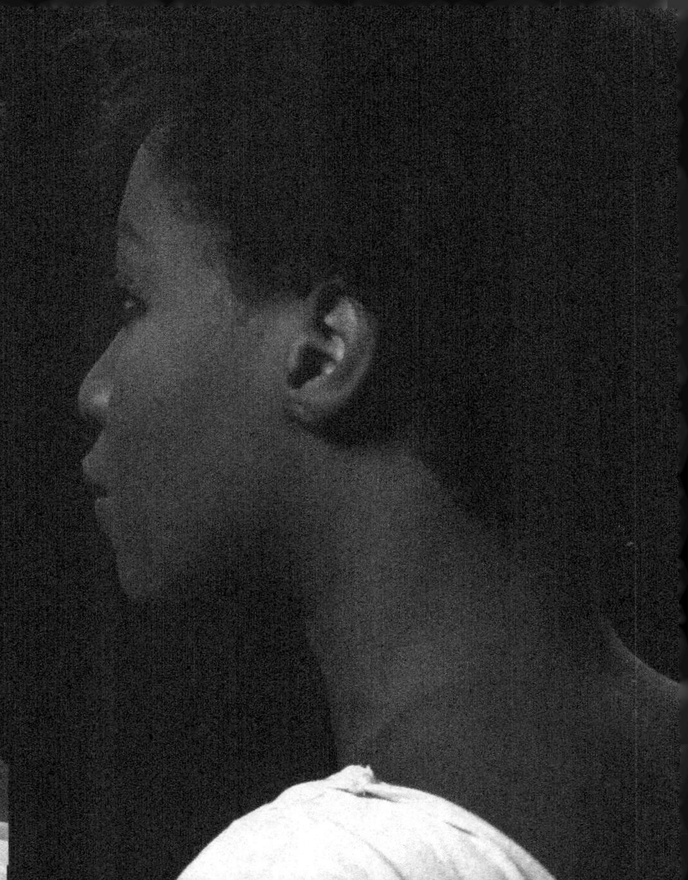

**Ethnicities claimed:**

Tiv, Yoruba, Brazil.

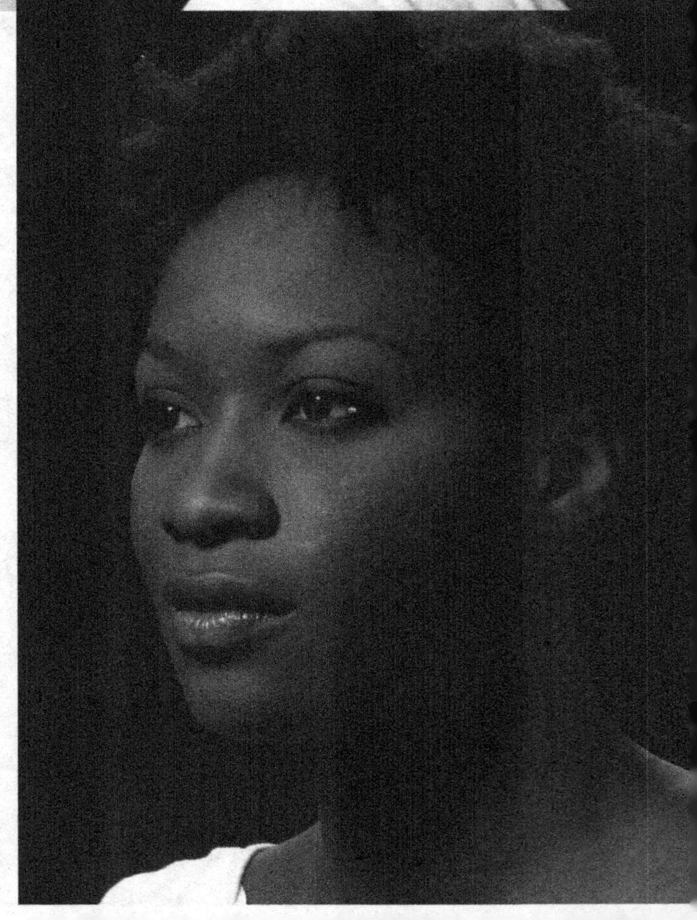

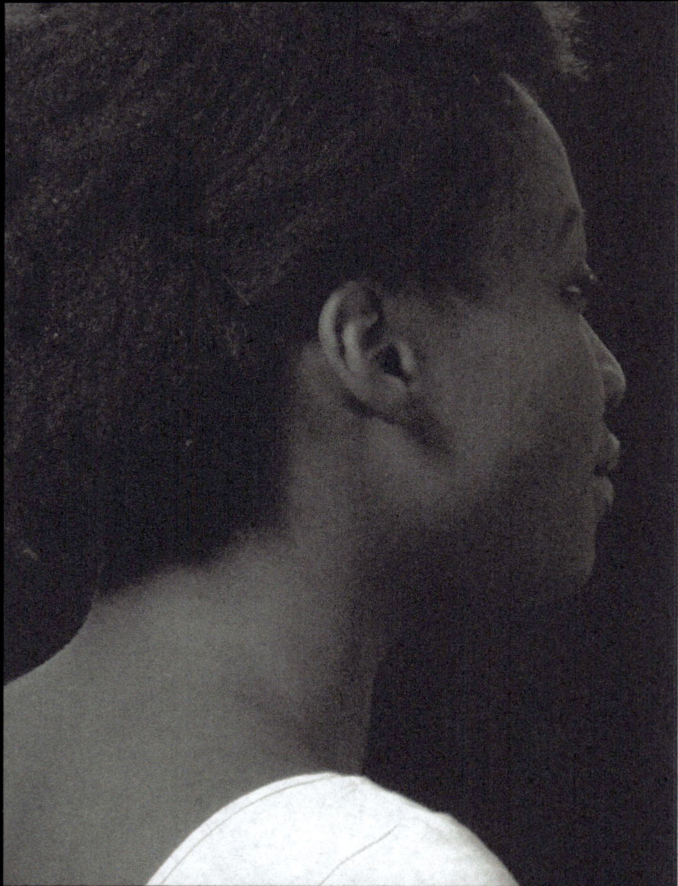

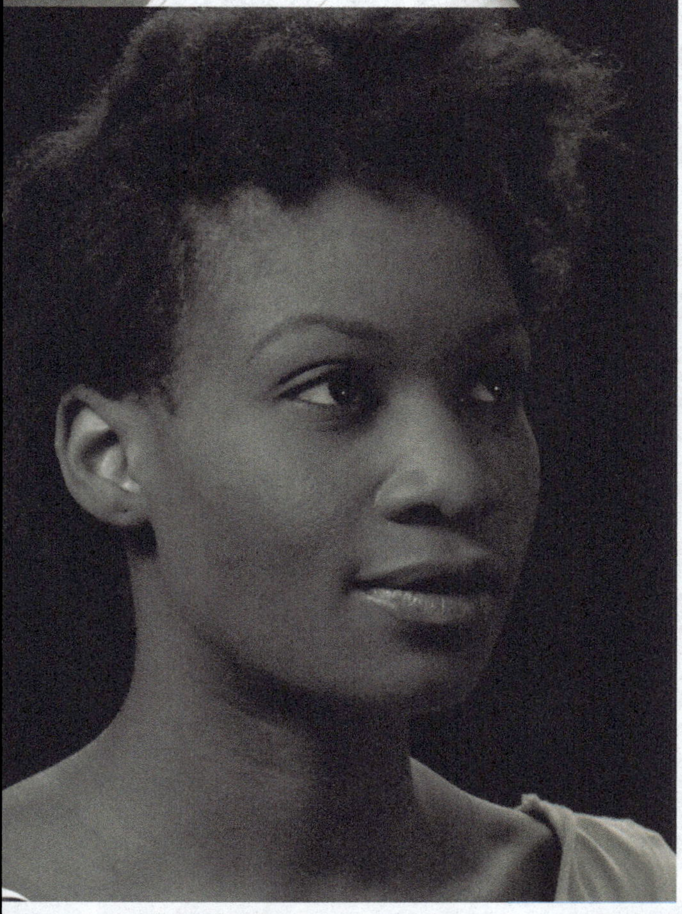

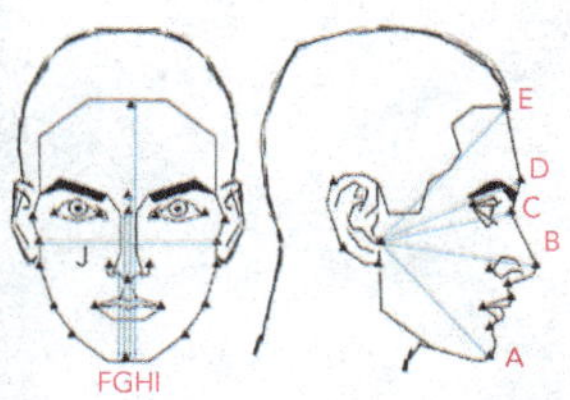



**Head measurements (in):**

A: 5 3/4
B: 4 5/8
C: 5
D: 4 7/8
E: 5 3/4
F: 3 1/2
G: 4 3/8
H: 5 3/8
I: 7 1/4
J: 5 5/8

MAP REFERENCE:

25

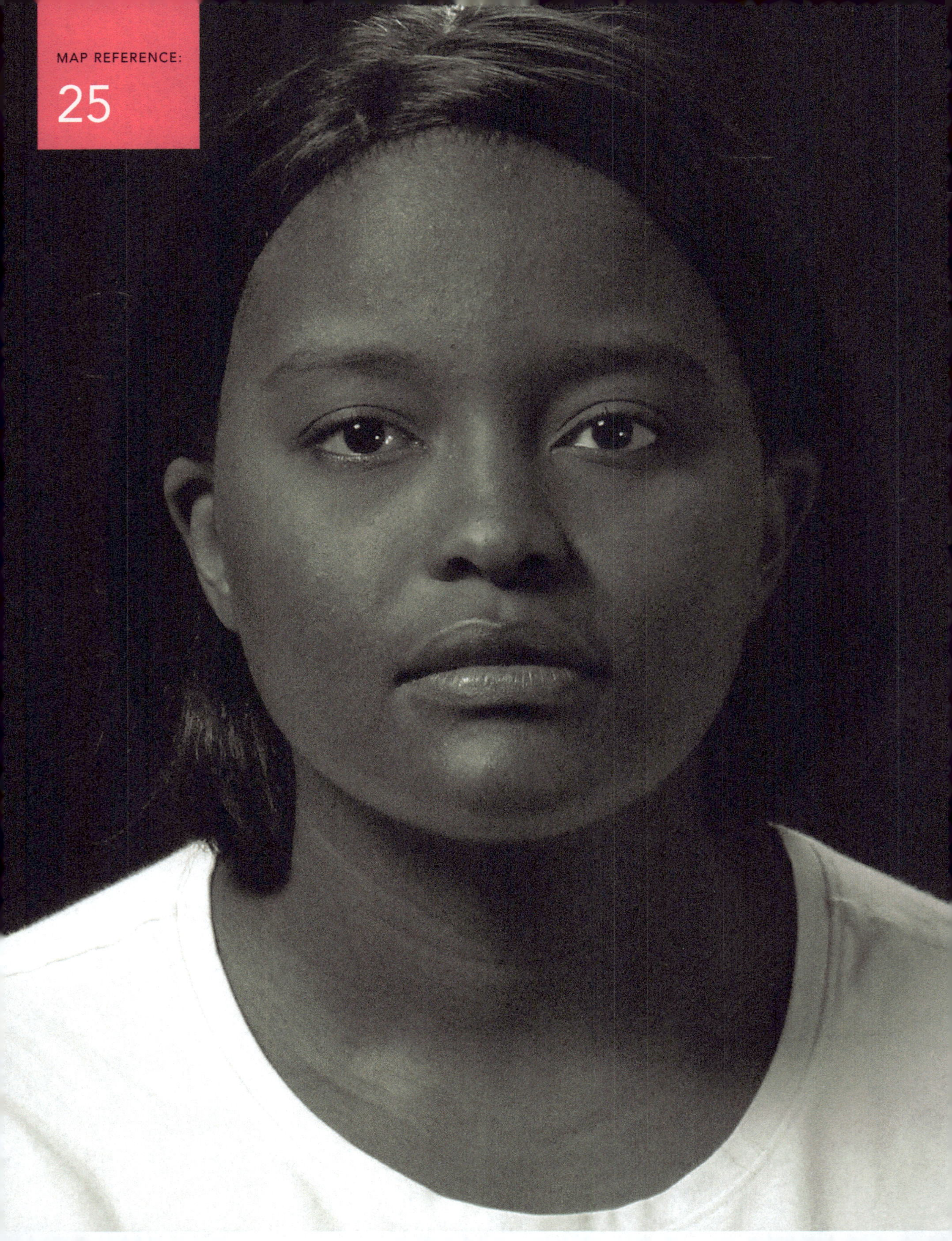

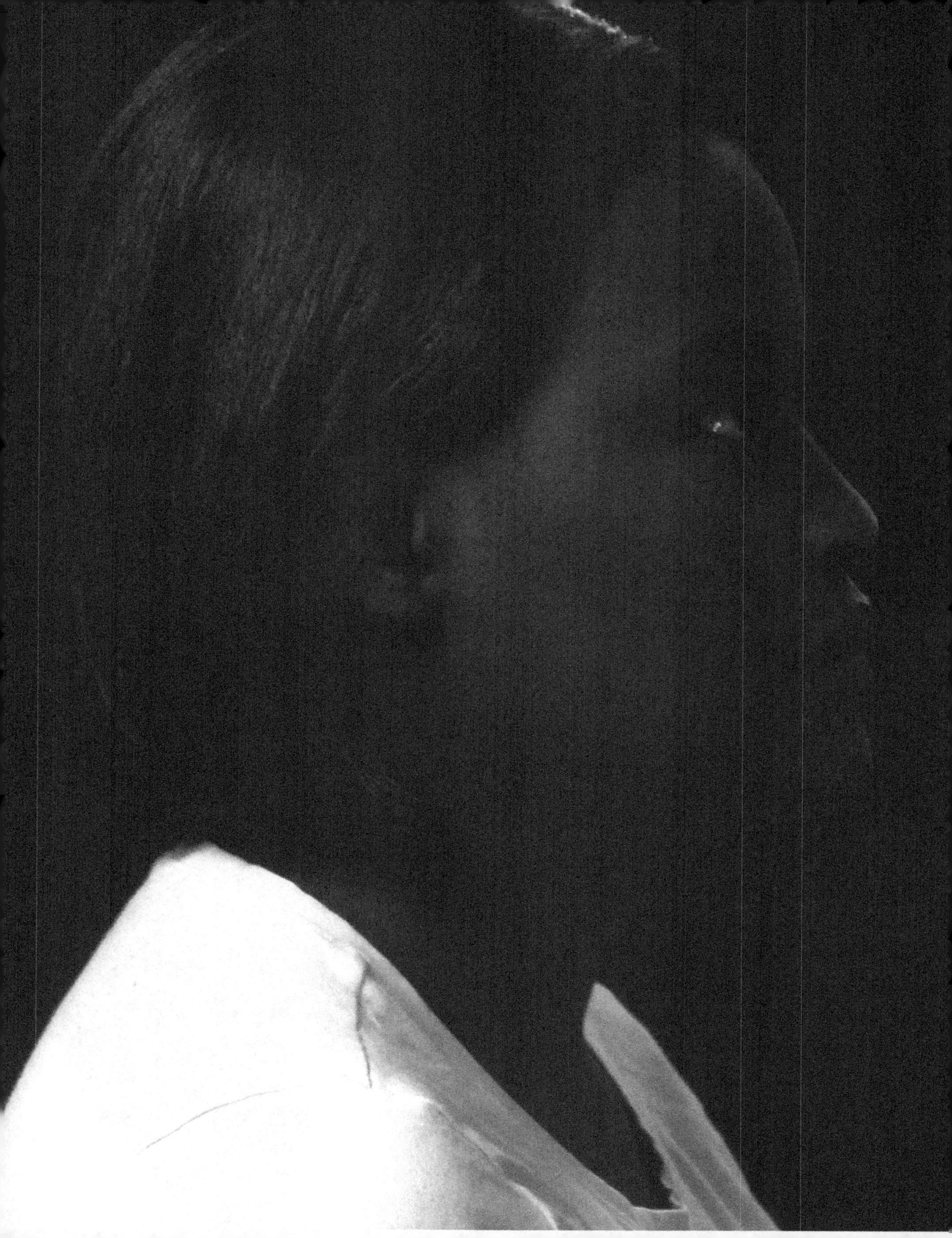

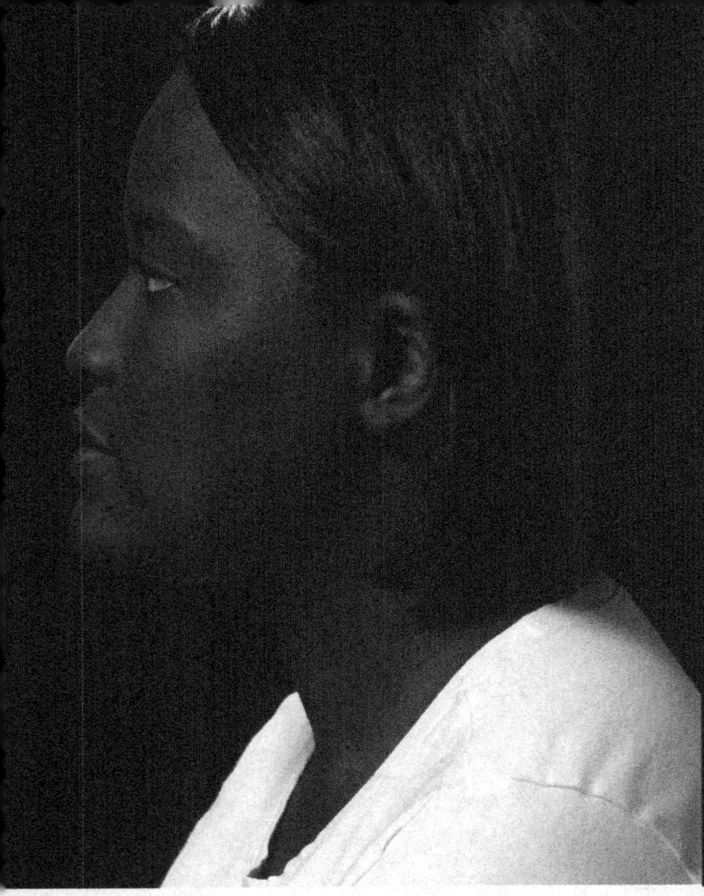

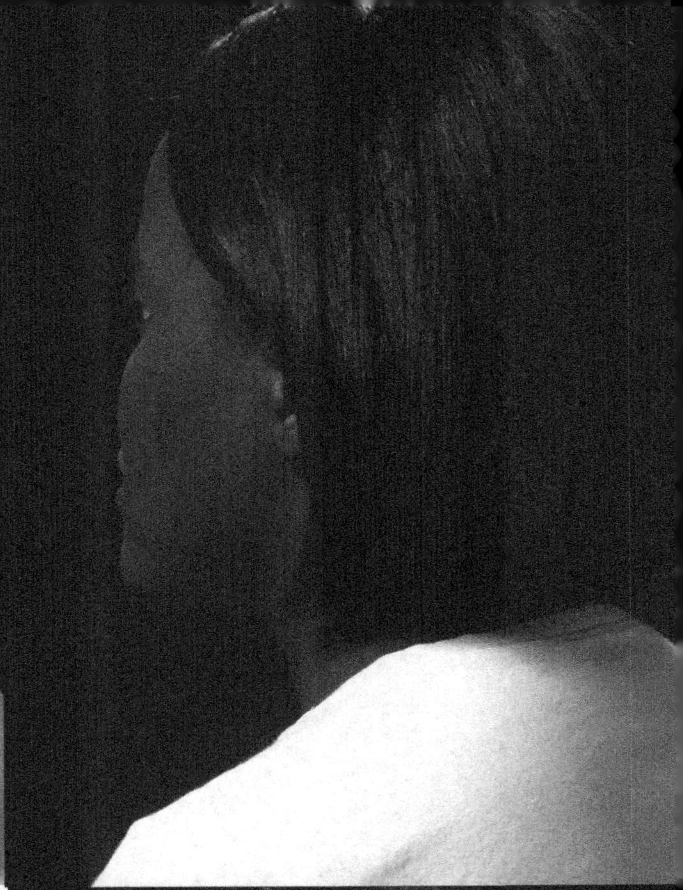

**Ethnicities claimed:**

Malawi.

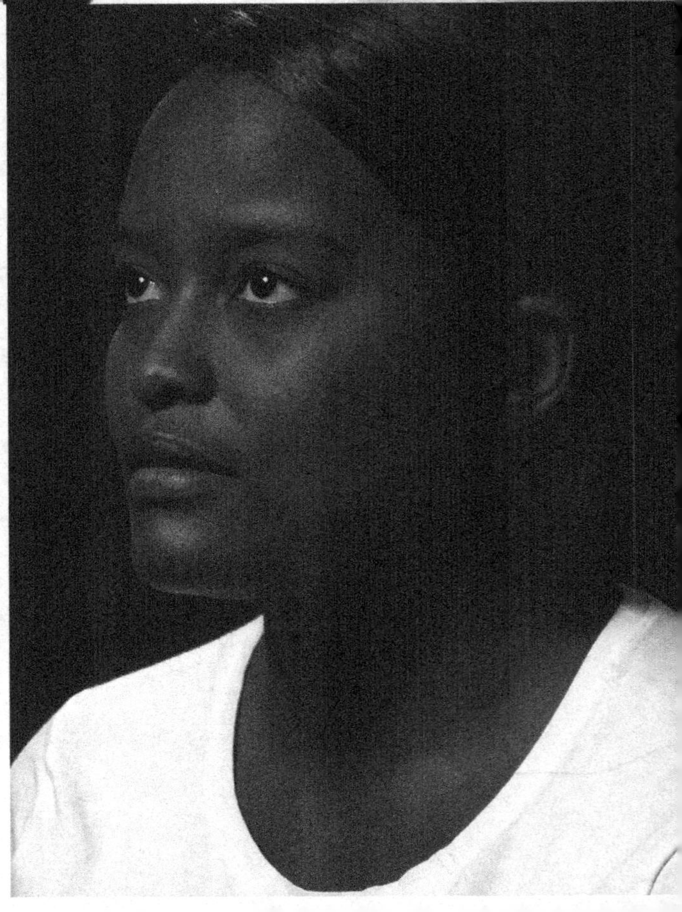

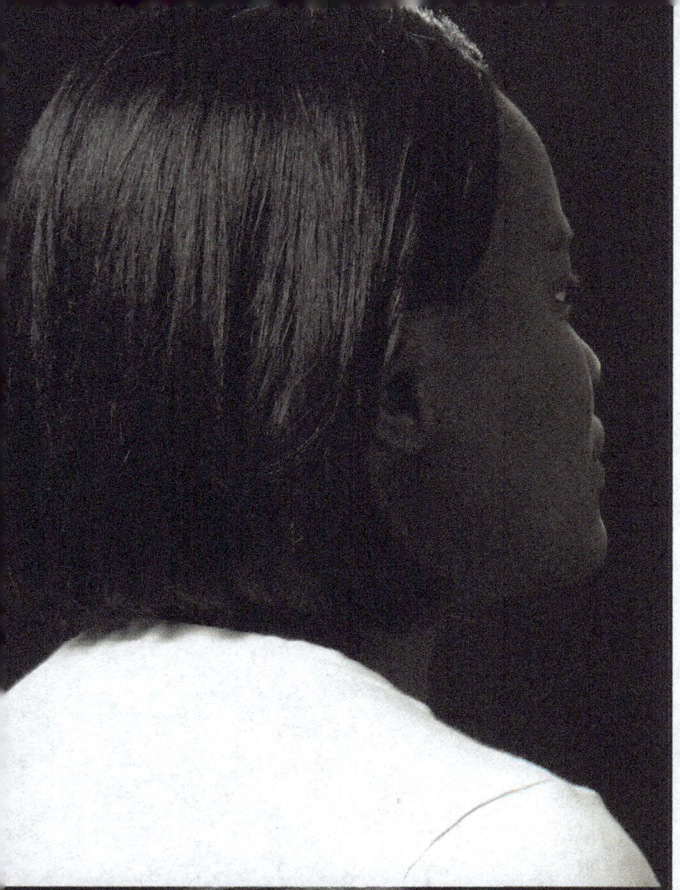

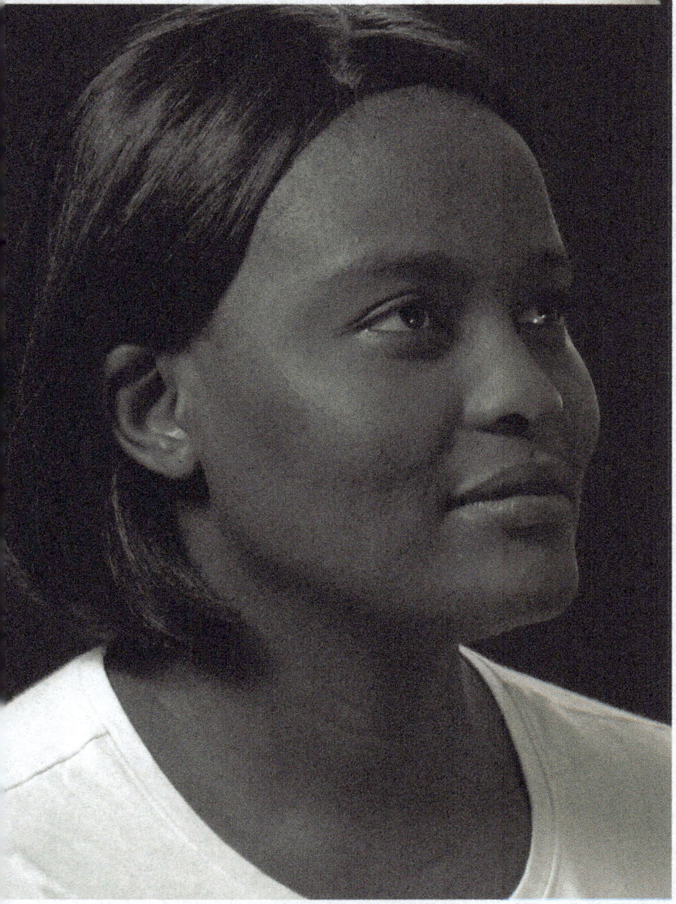

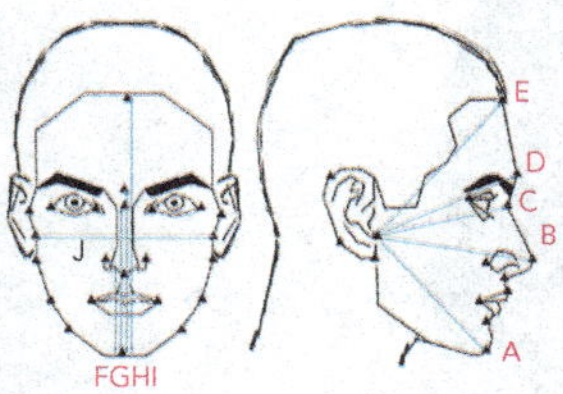


**Head measurements (in):**

A: 5 1/2
B: 5 1/2
C: 5
D: 5 1/2
E: 6 1/4
F: 3 3/8
G: 4 1/8
H: 5 1/8
I: 7 1/4
J: 5 3/4

MAP REFERENCE:

28

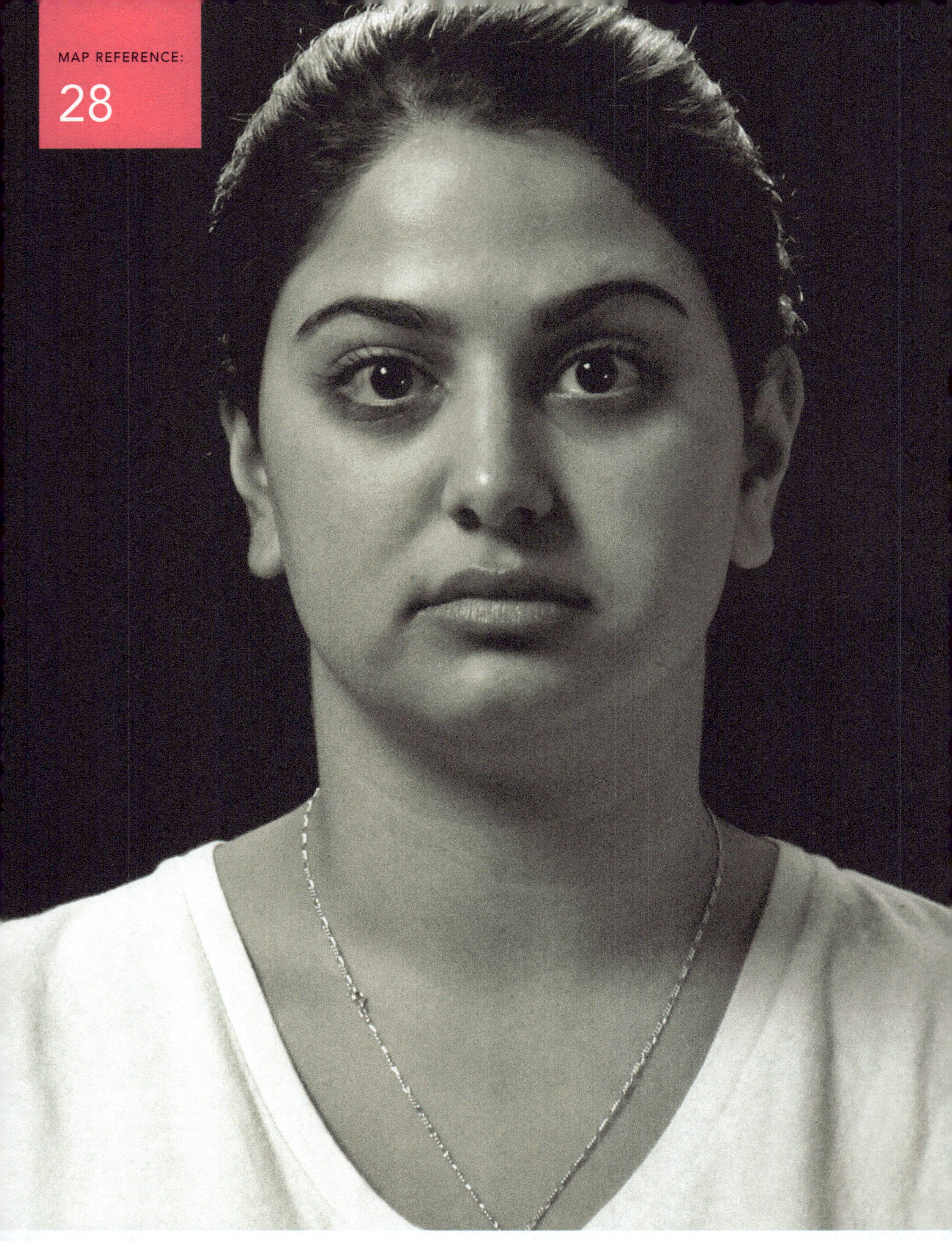

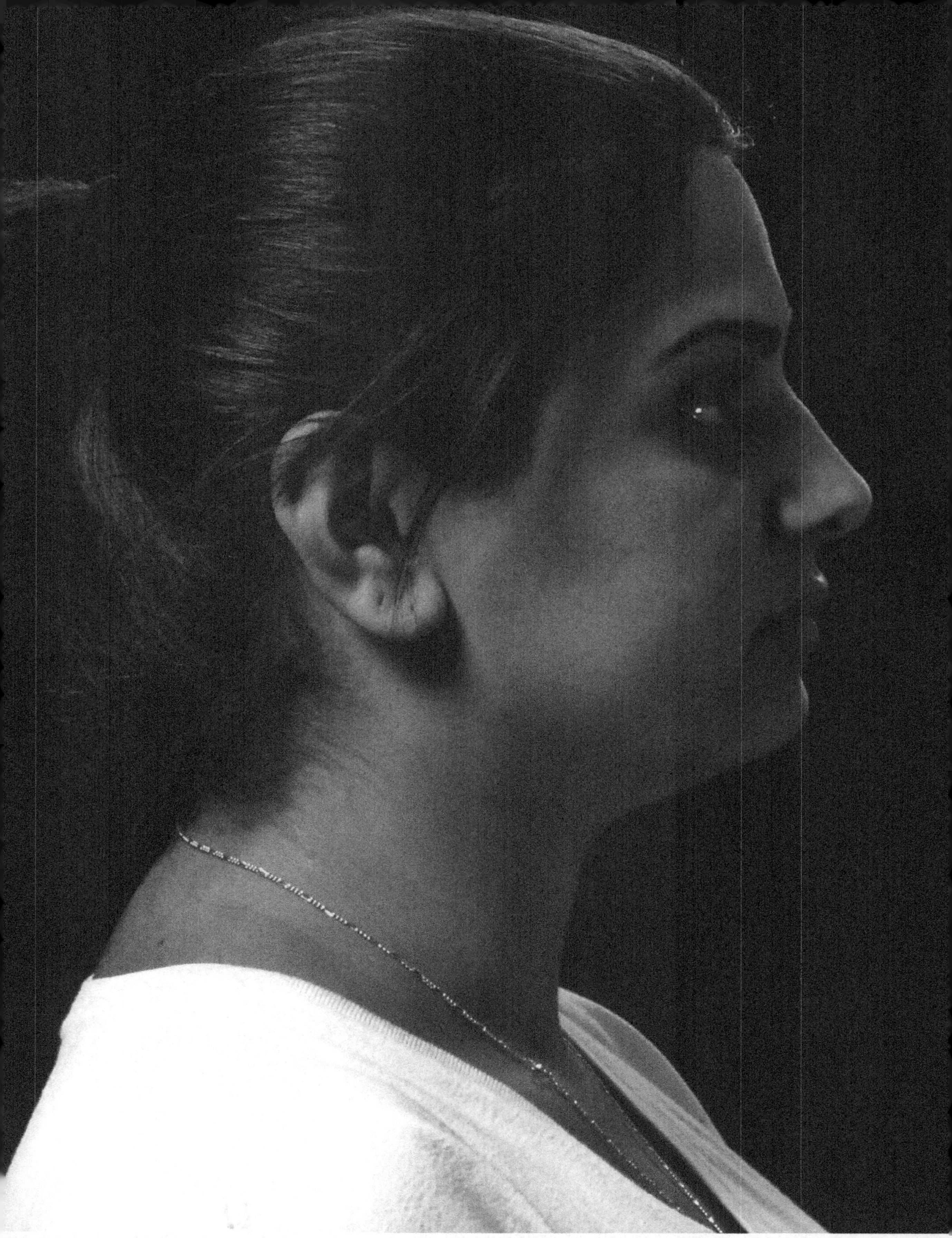

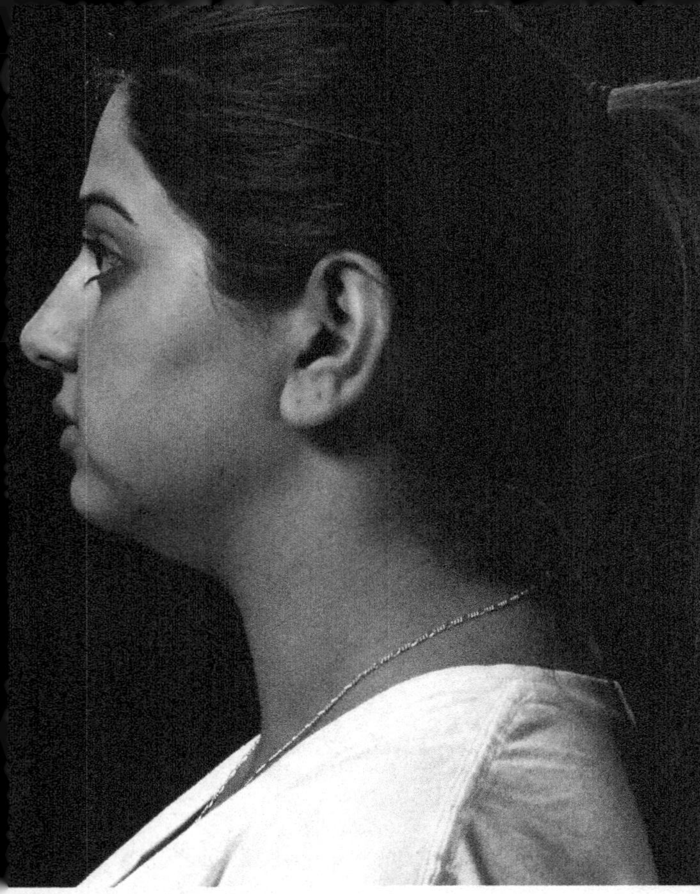

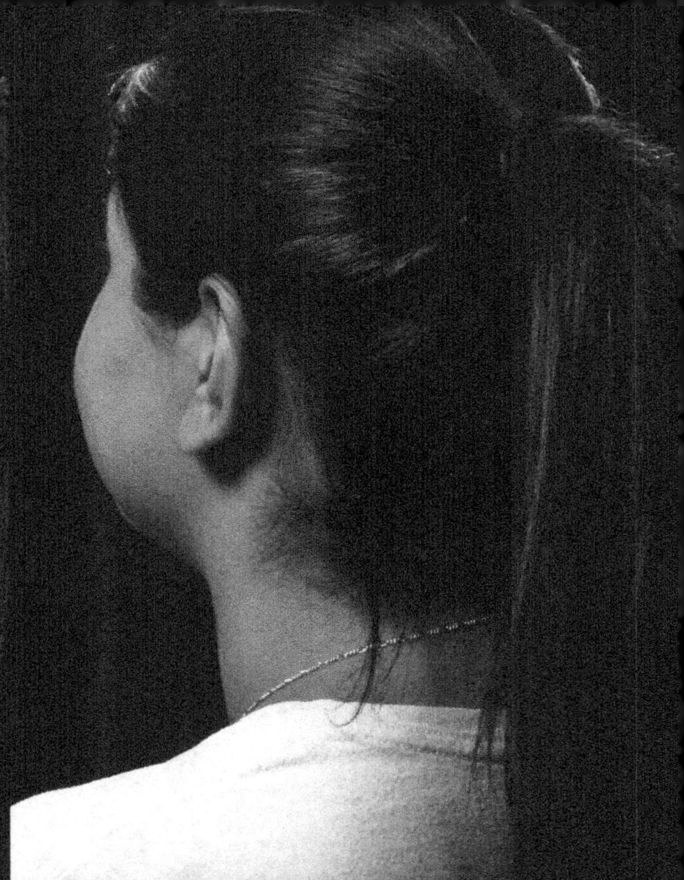

**Ethnicities claimed:**

Armenia, Georgia.

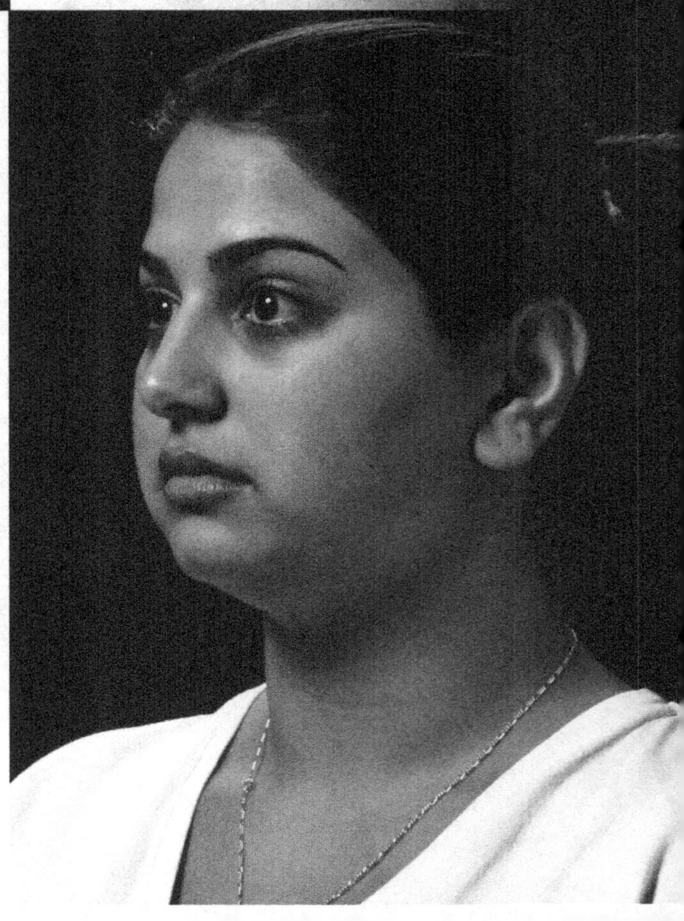

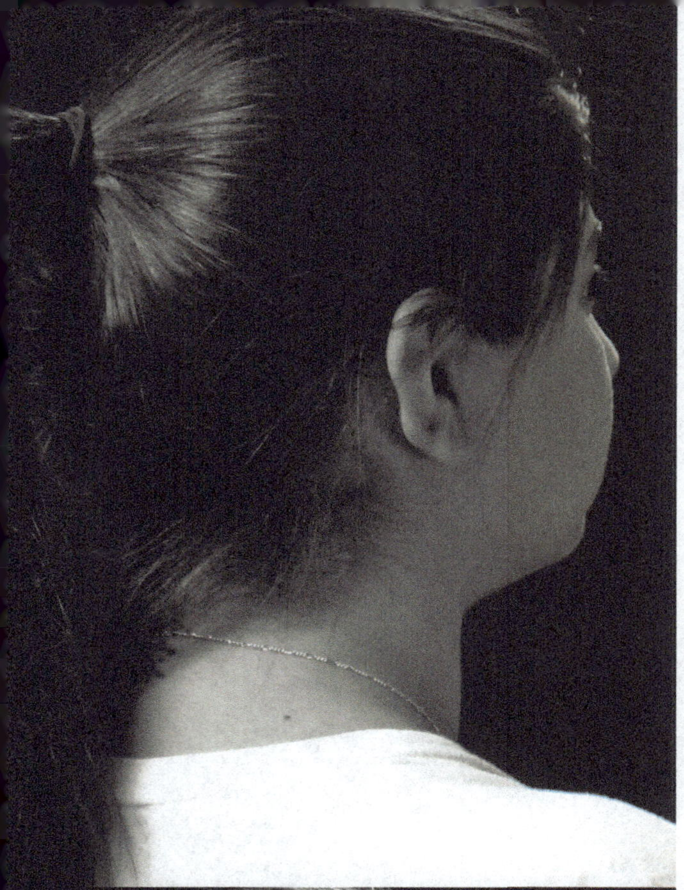

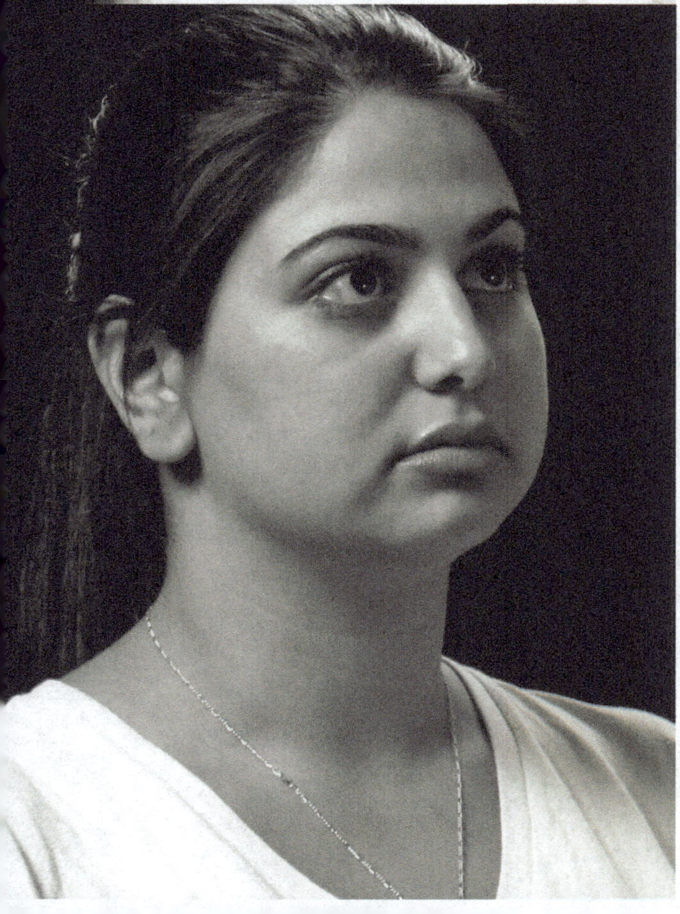

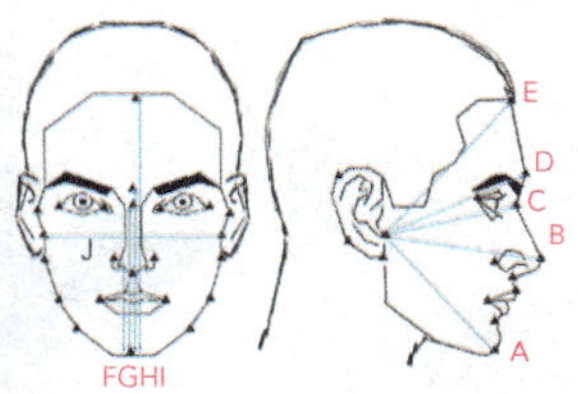


**Head measurements (in):**

A: 5
B: 5 1/2
C: 5
D: 5 1/4
E: 6 3/8
F: 3 1/8
G: 3 7/8
H: 4 7/8
I: 7 1/4
J: 5 1/2

MAP REFERENCE:

31

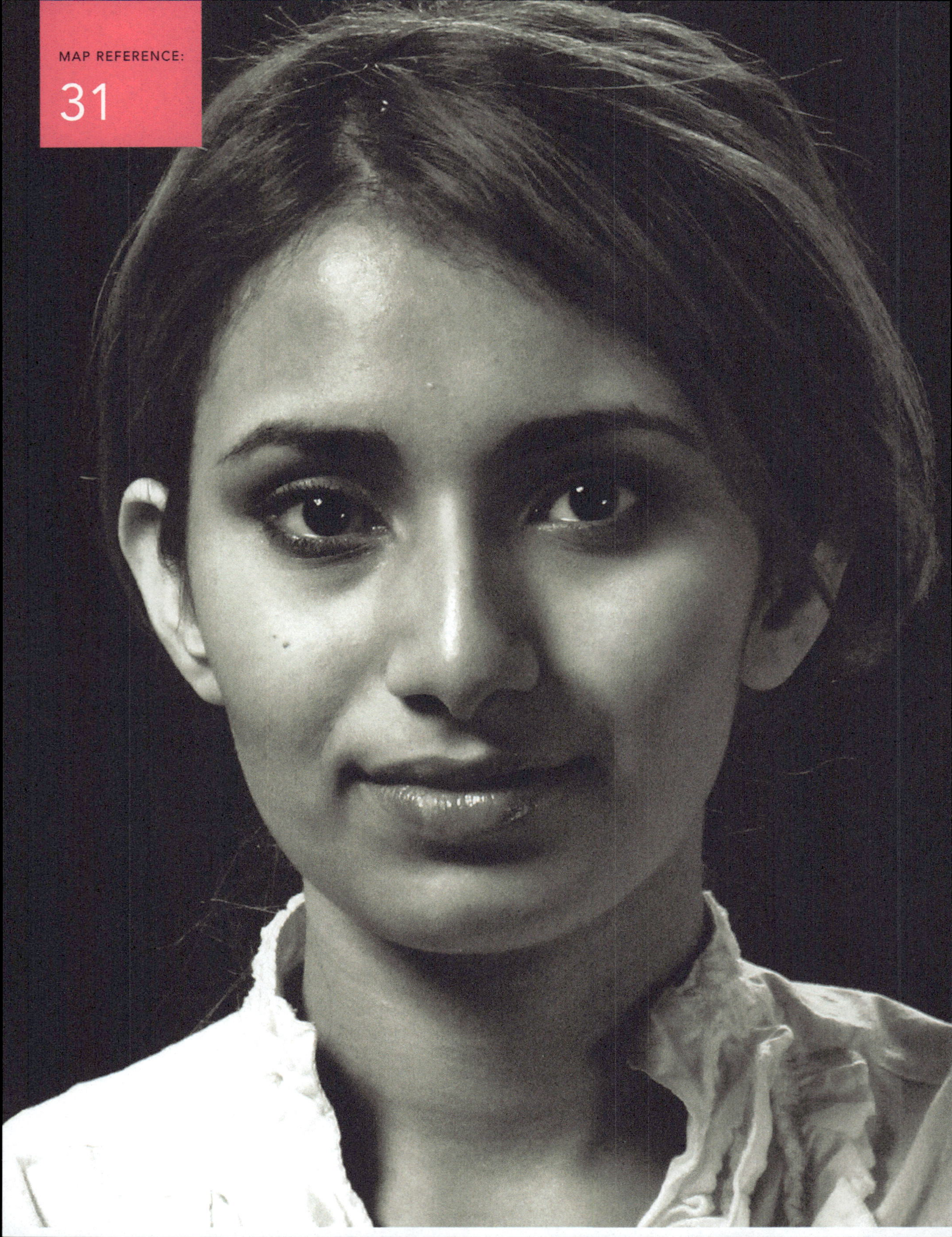

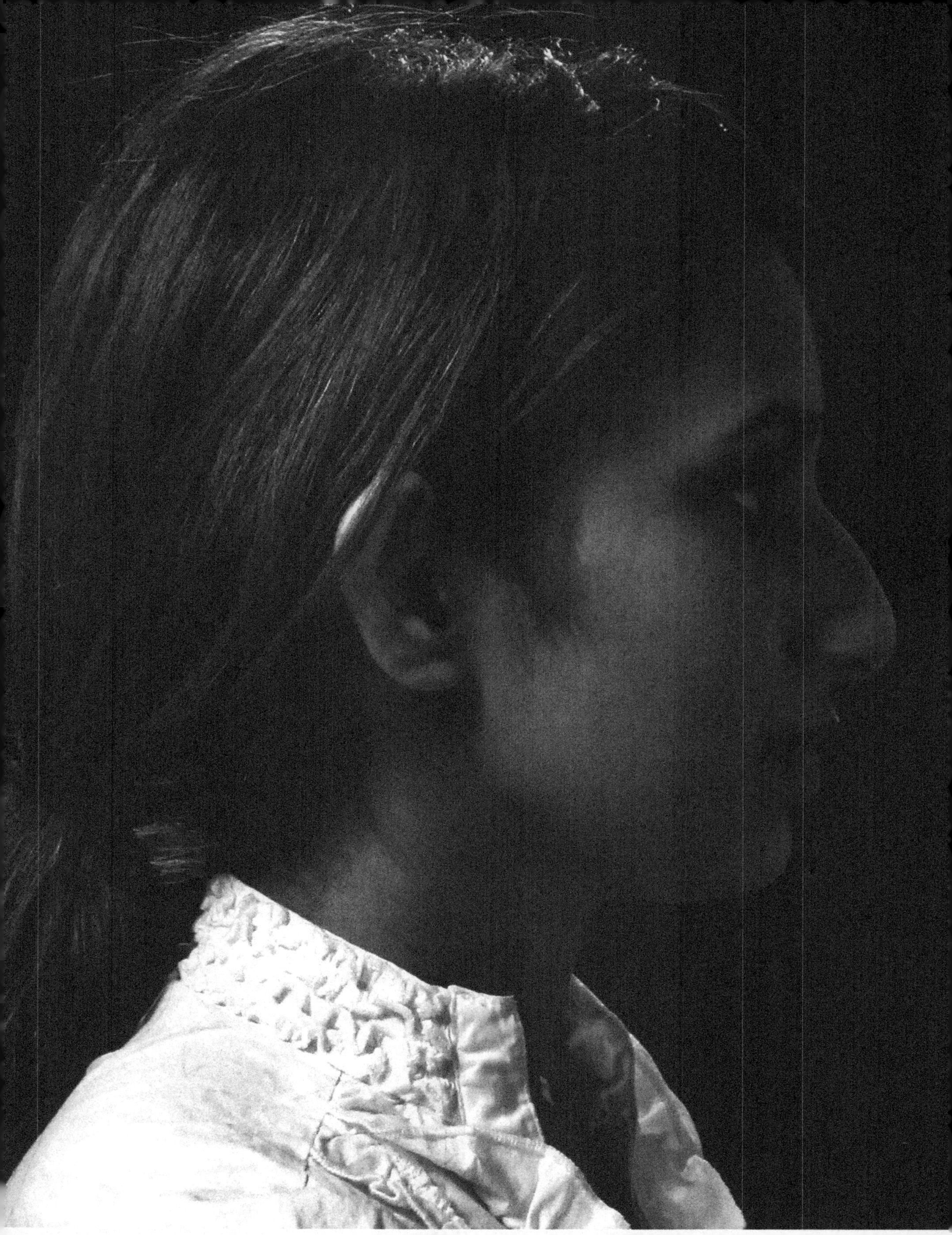

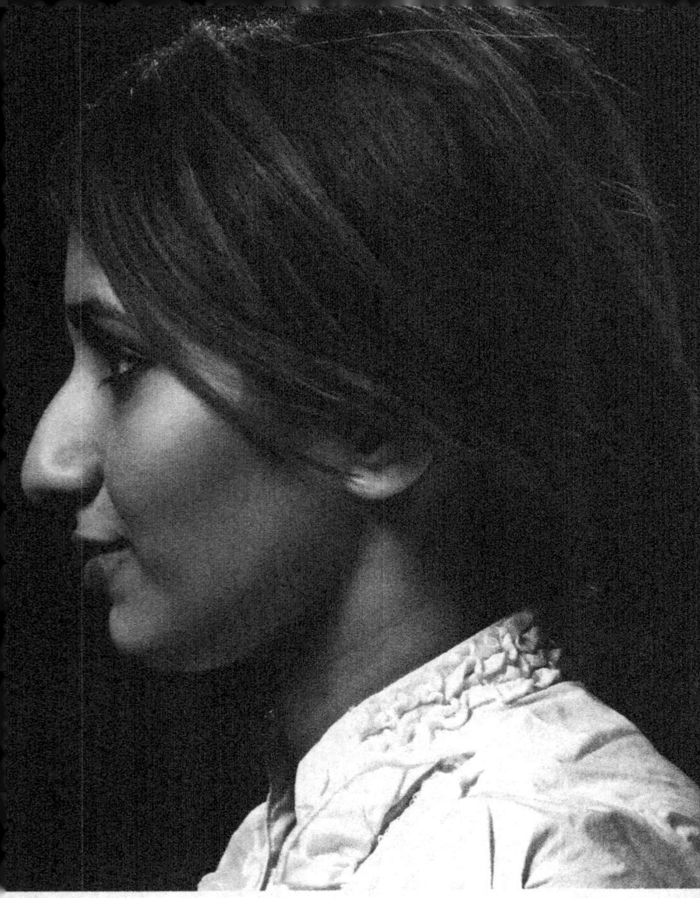

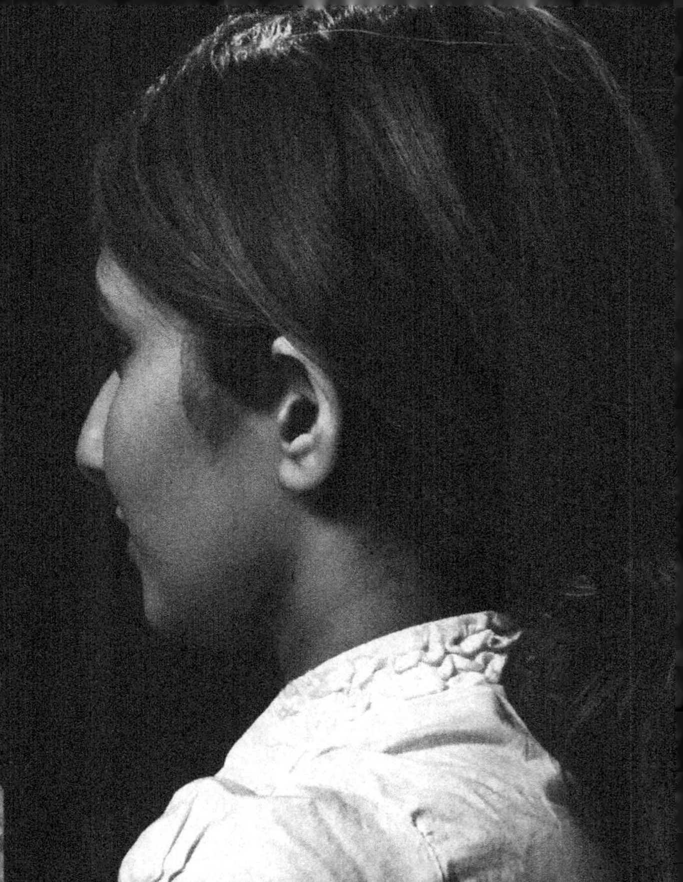

**Ethnicities claimed:**

Brazil, India.

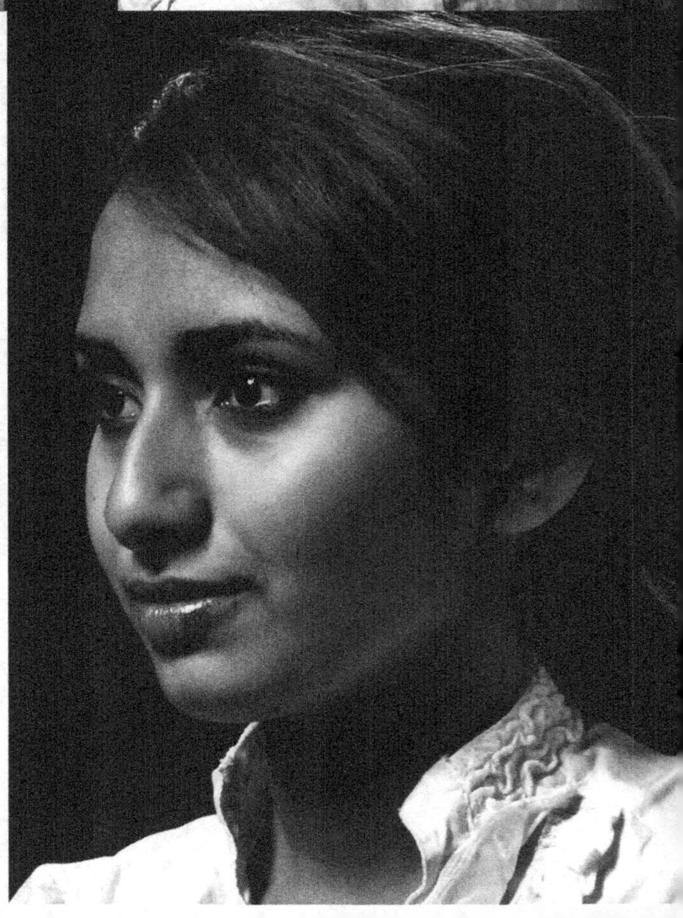

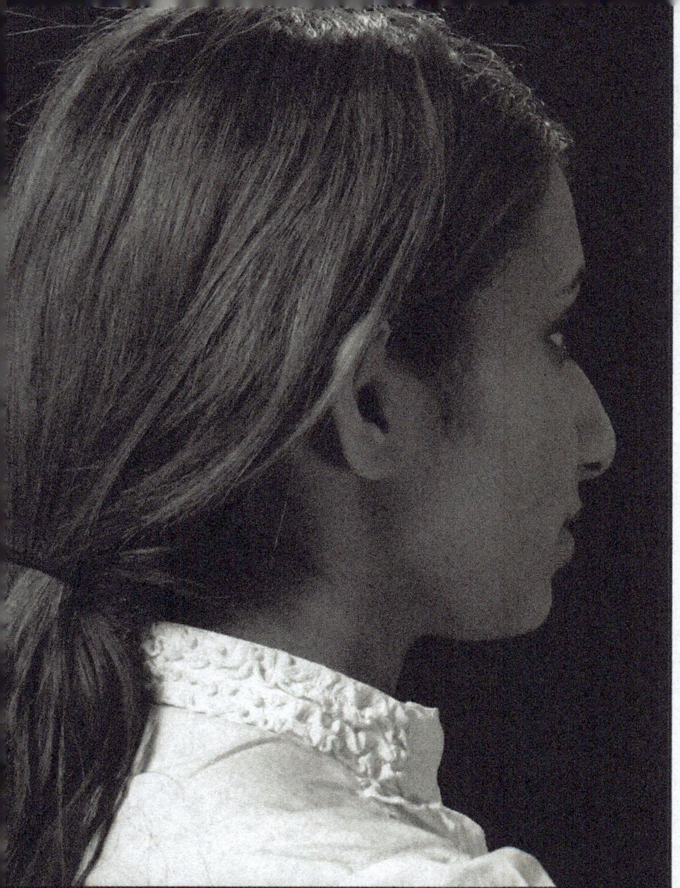

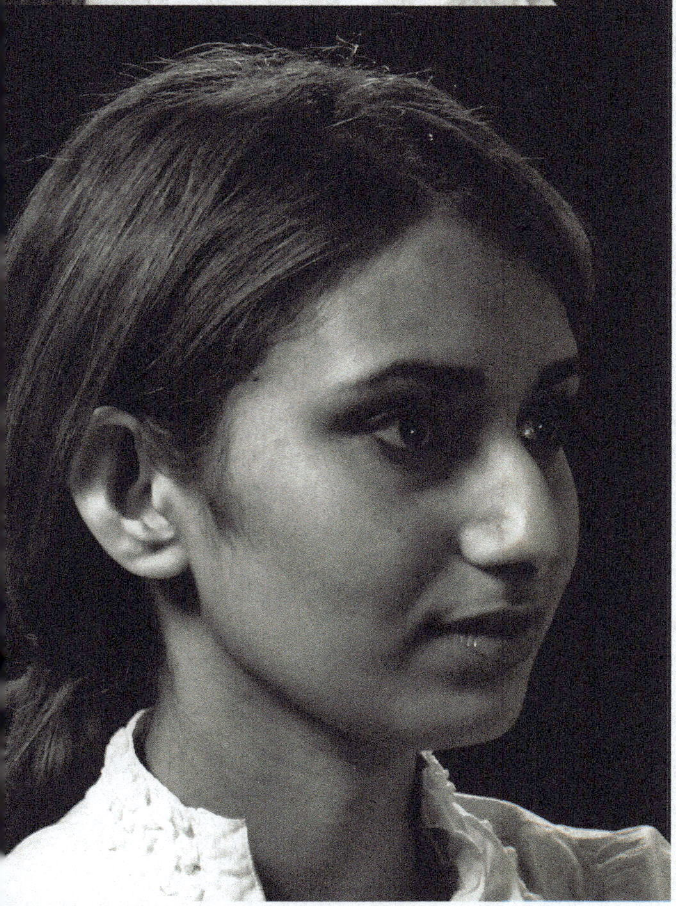

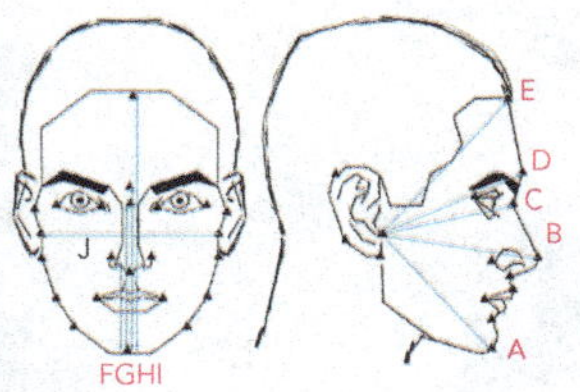


**Head measurements (in):**

A: 4 1/2
B: 4 3/4
C: 5
D: 5
E: 6
F: 3
G: 4 1/8
H: 5
I: 7 3/8
J: 5 1/2

MAP REFERENCE:

32

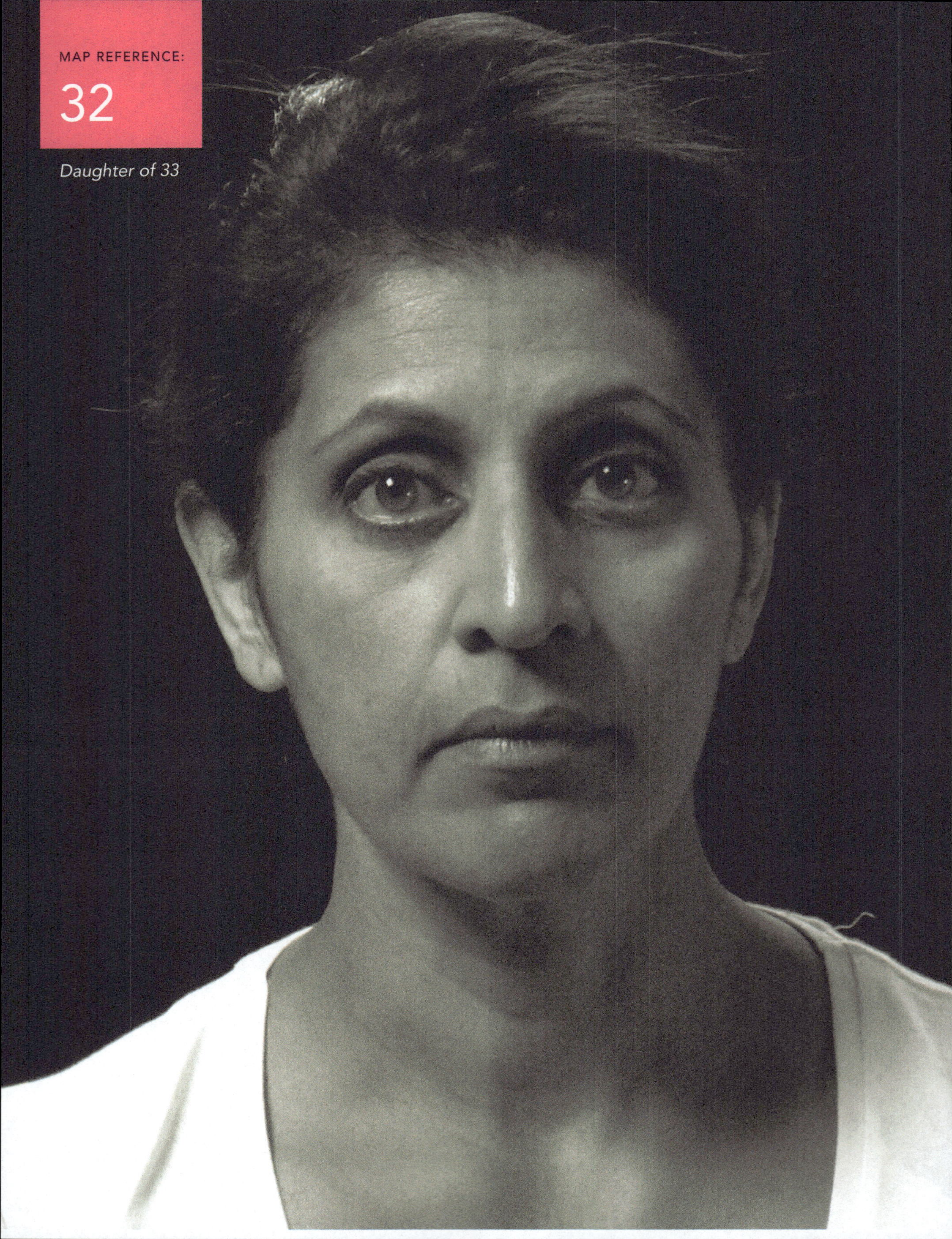

*Daughter of 33*

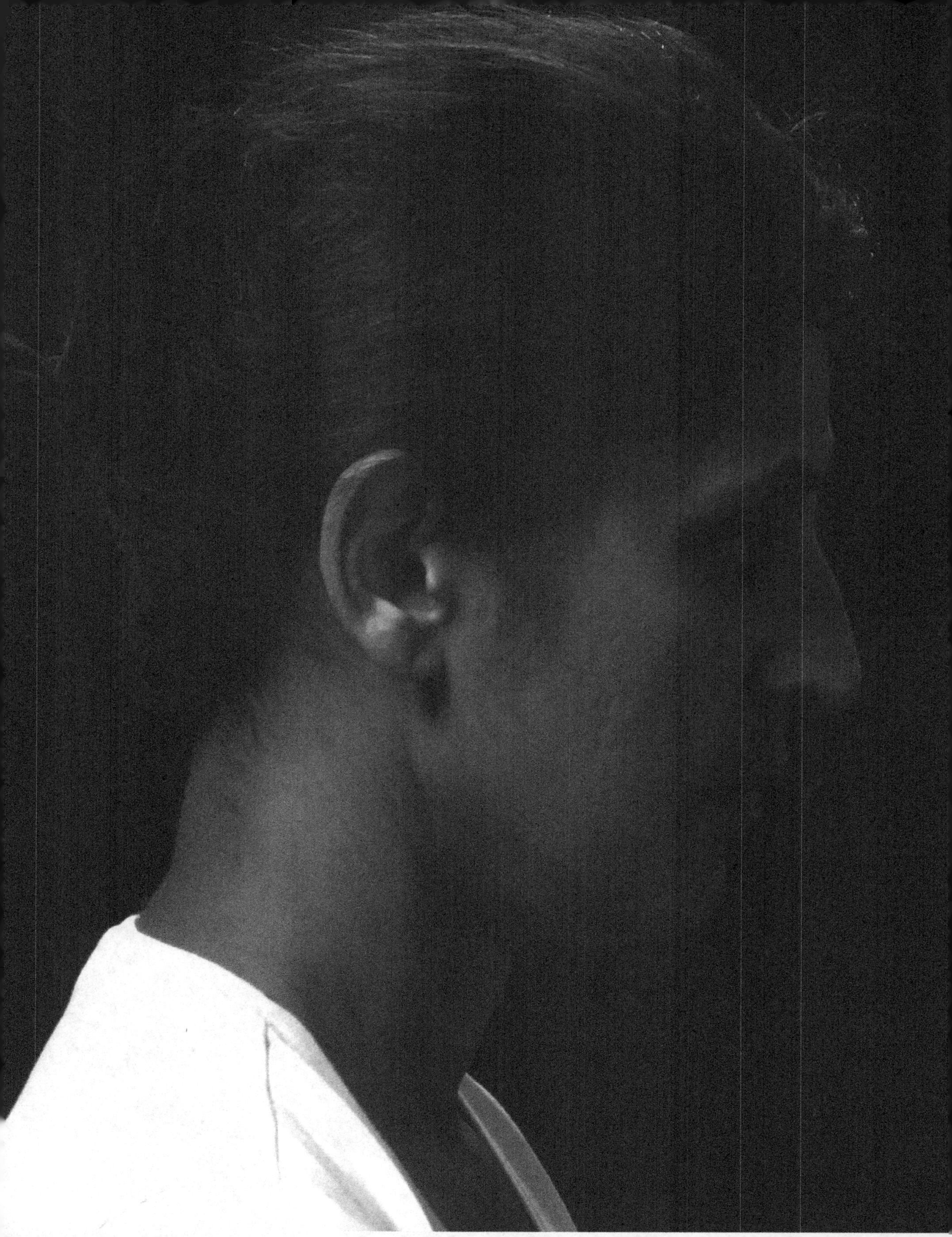

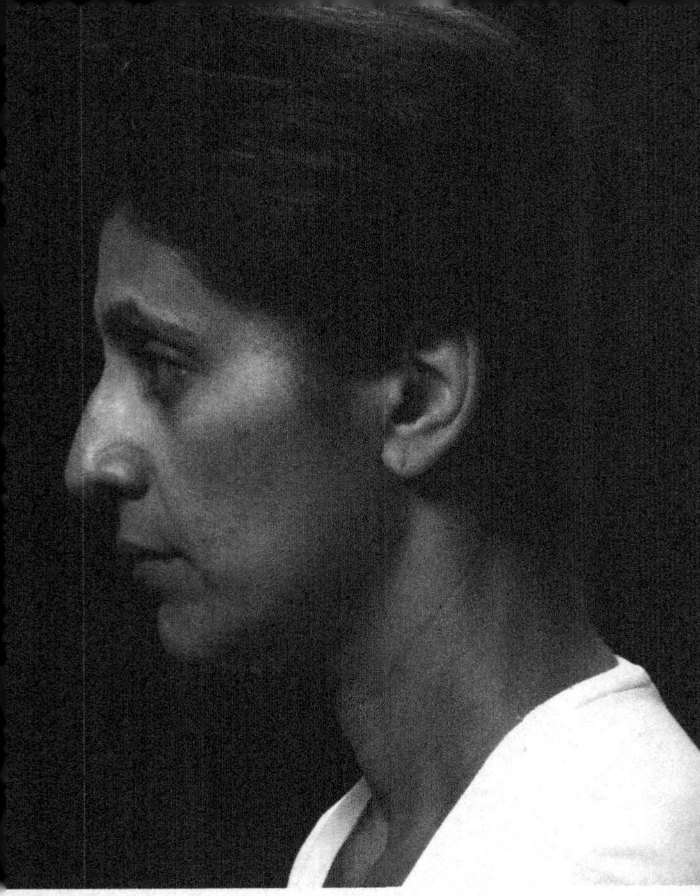

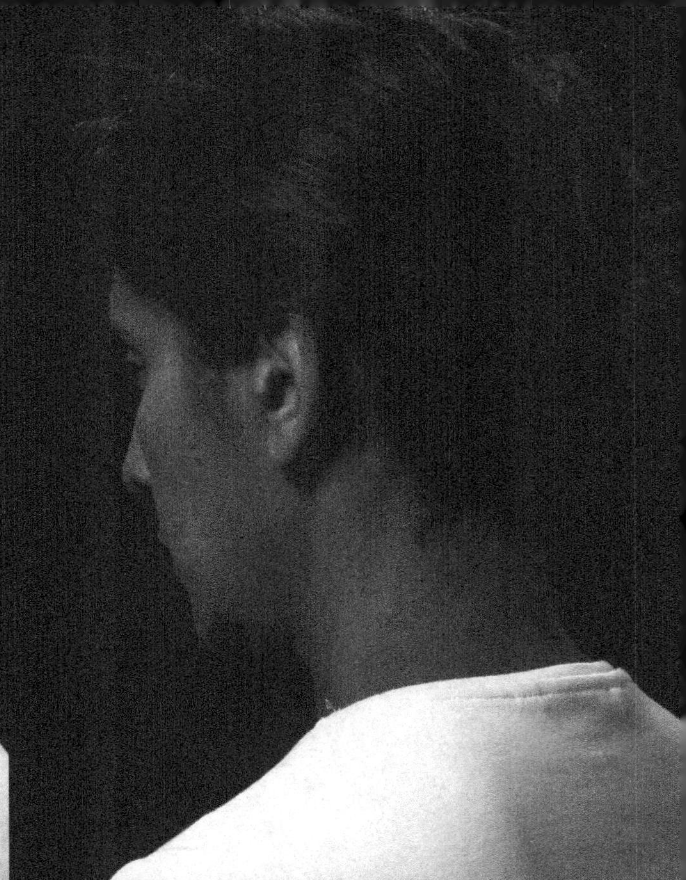

**Ethnicities claimed:**

Tamil (East India), Iraq, France, Malaylee (East India).

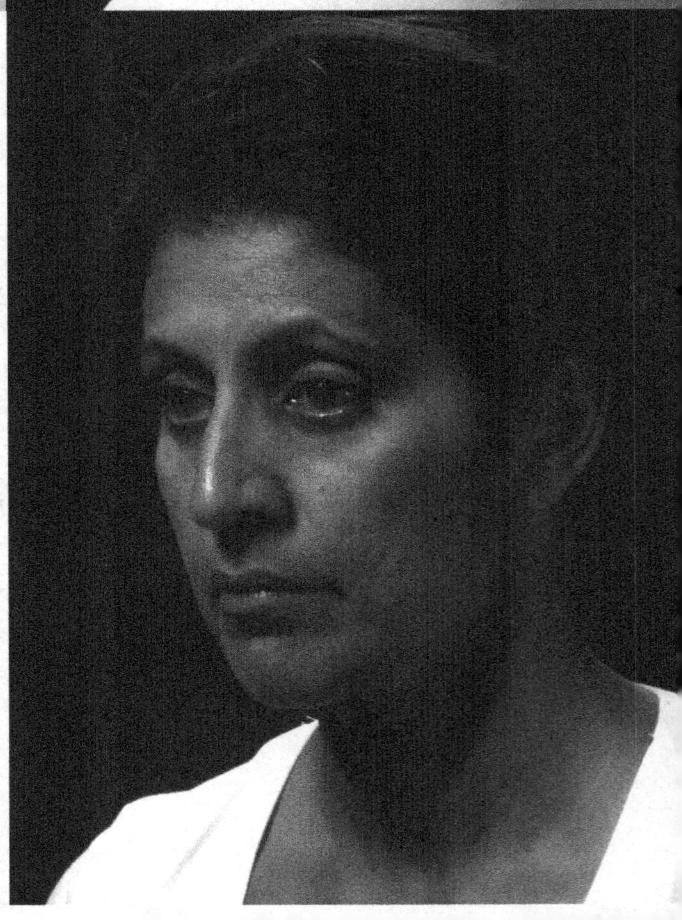

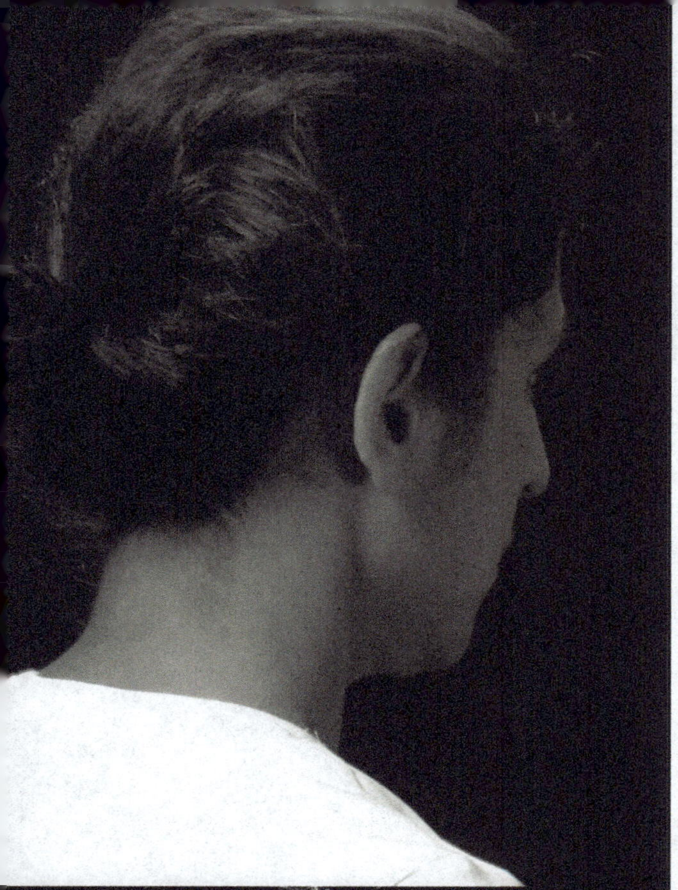

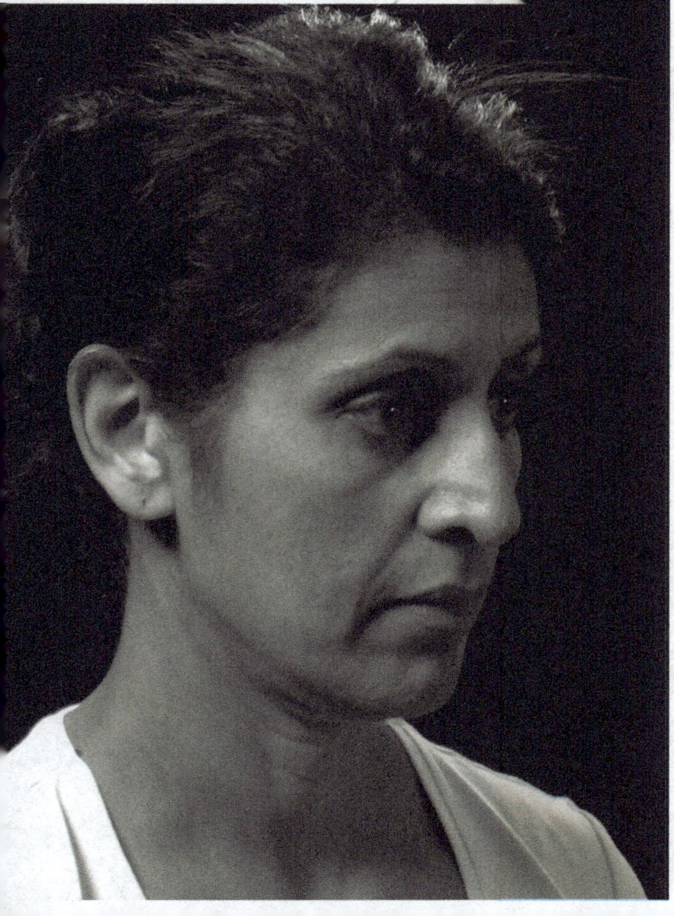

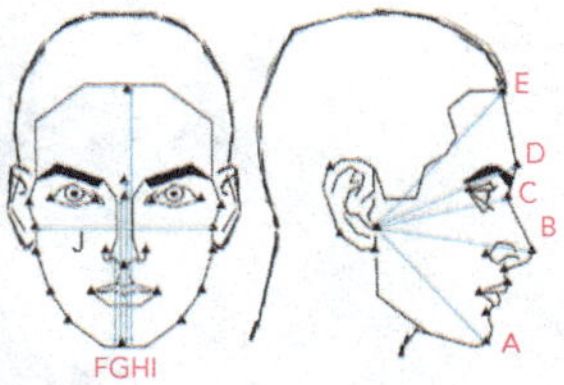


**Head measurements (in):**

A: 5 3/8
B: 5 1/2
C: 5 1/8
D: 5 1/4
E: 6 3/8
F: 3 5/8
G: 4 1/2
H: 5 5/8
I: 7 3/8
J: 5 5/8

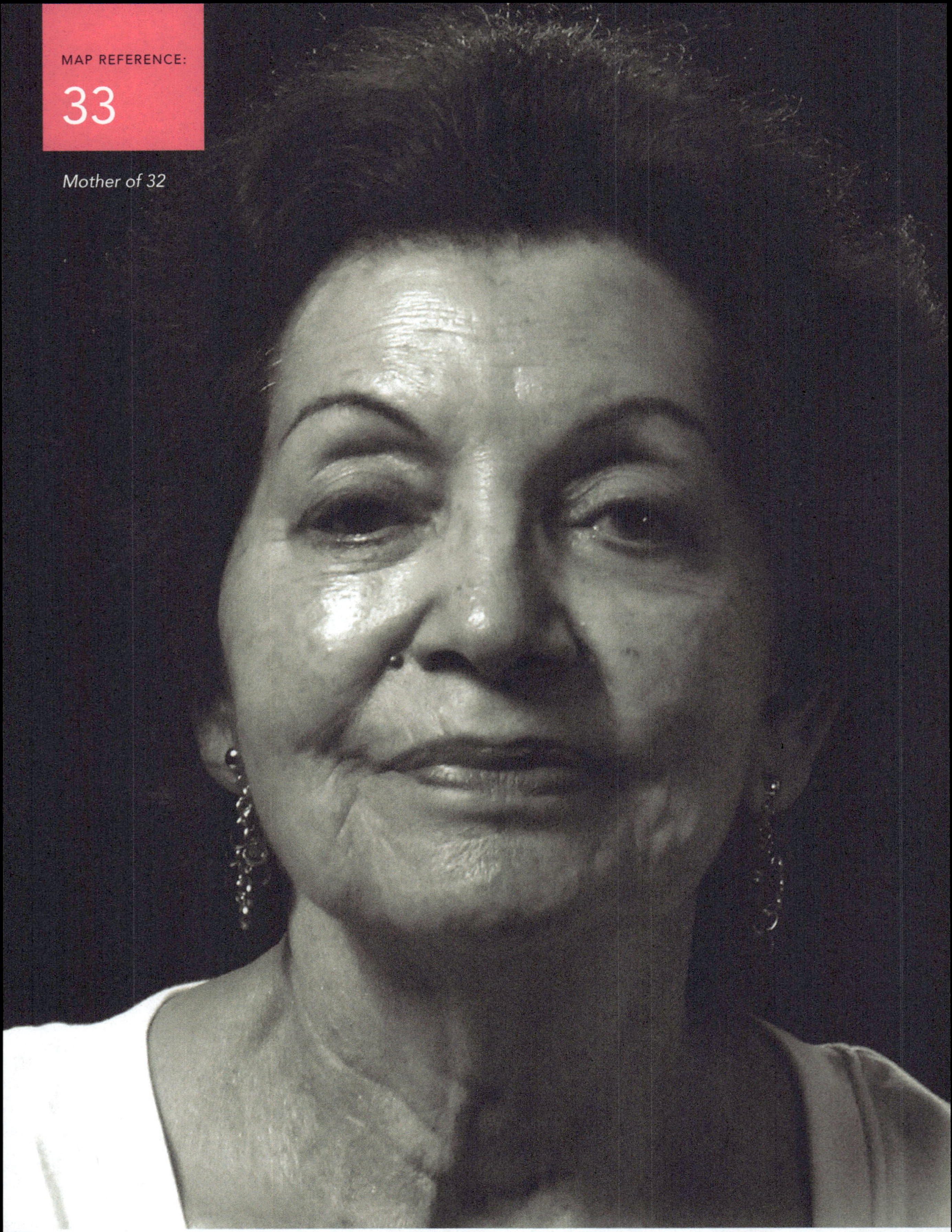

MAP REFERENCE:

33

*Mother of 32*

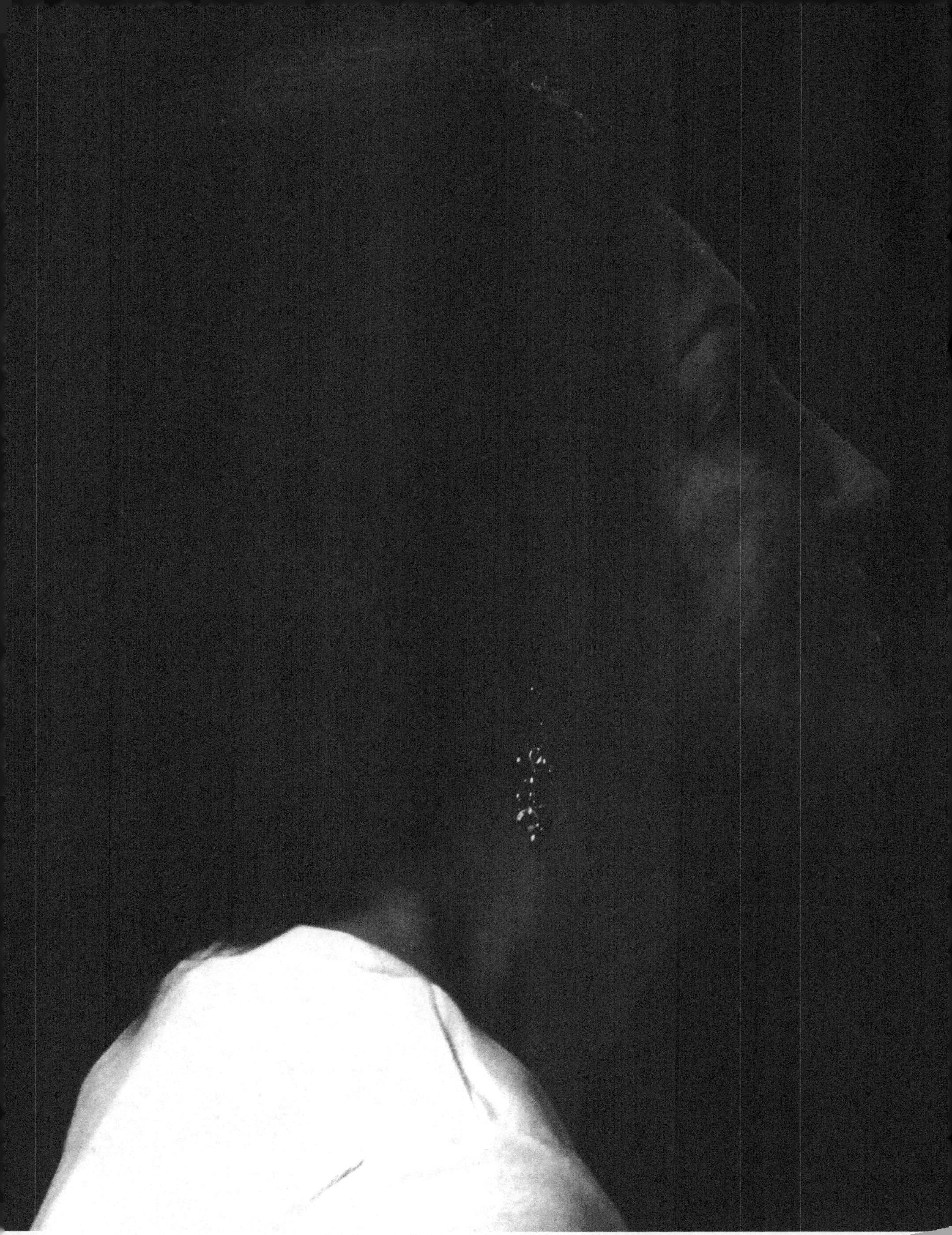

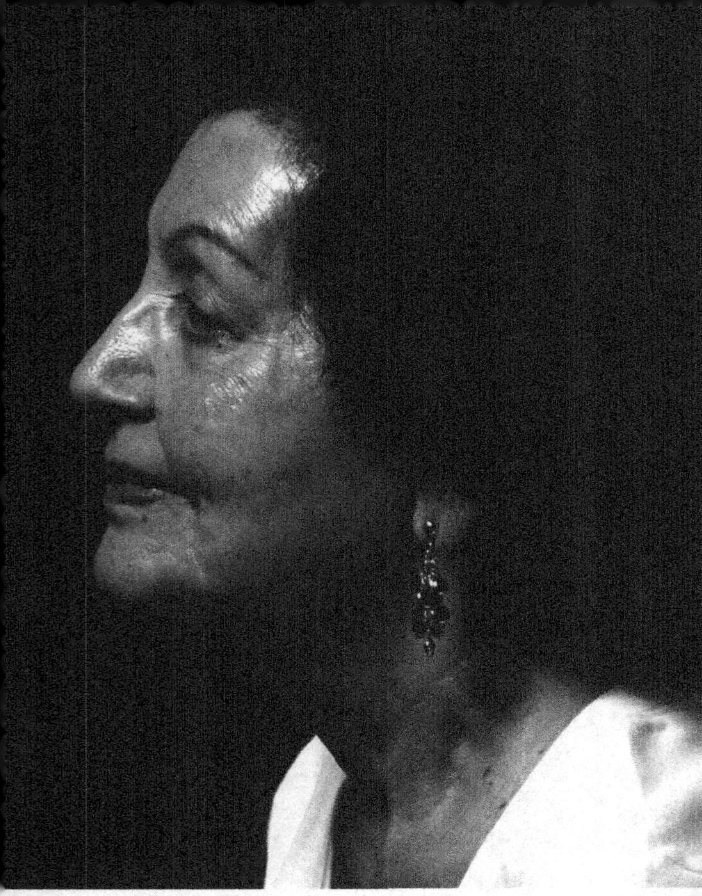

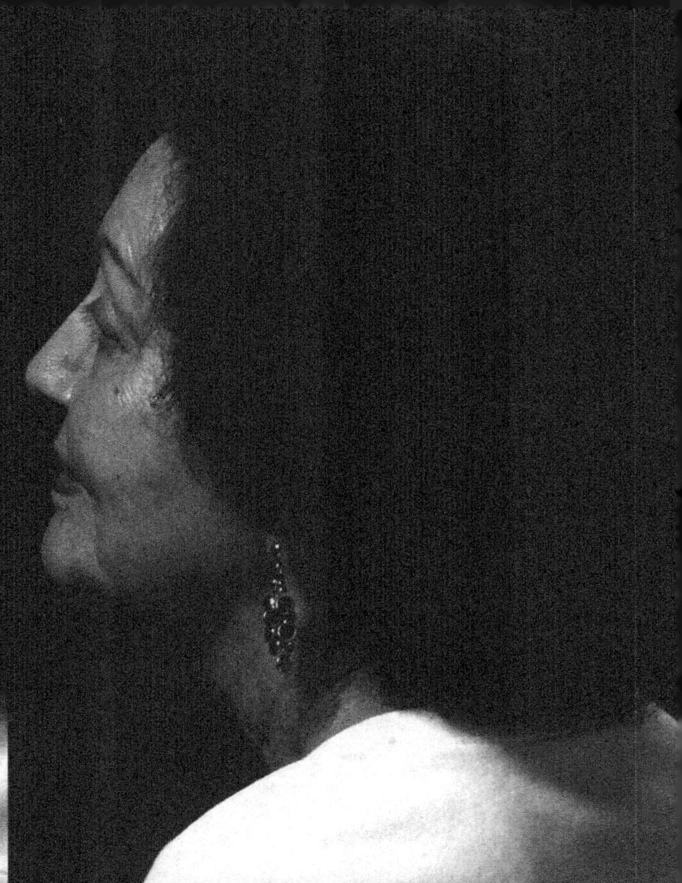

**Ethnicities claimed:**

Iraq, France, South India.

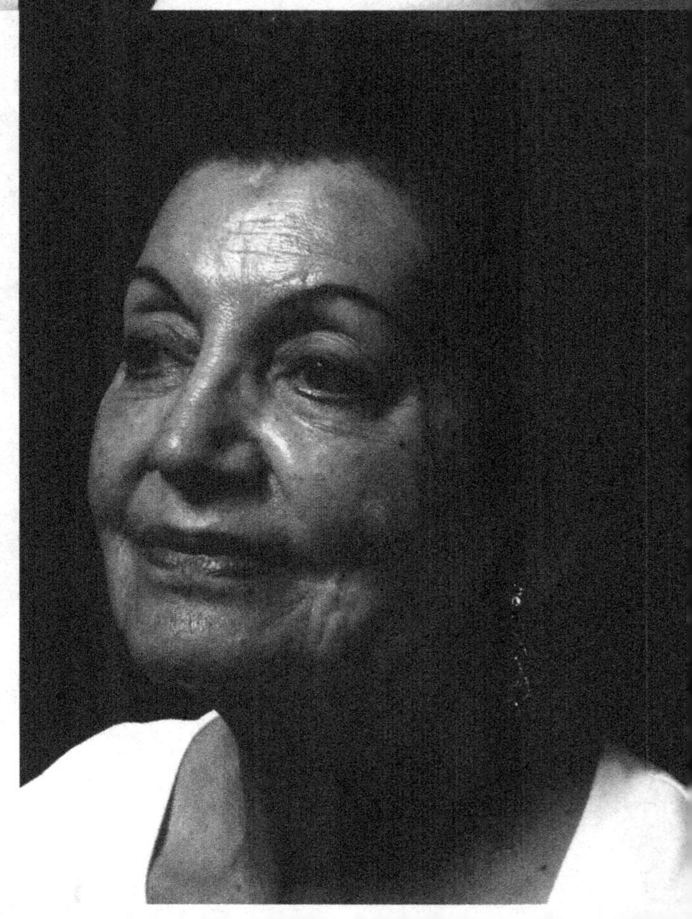

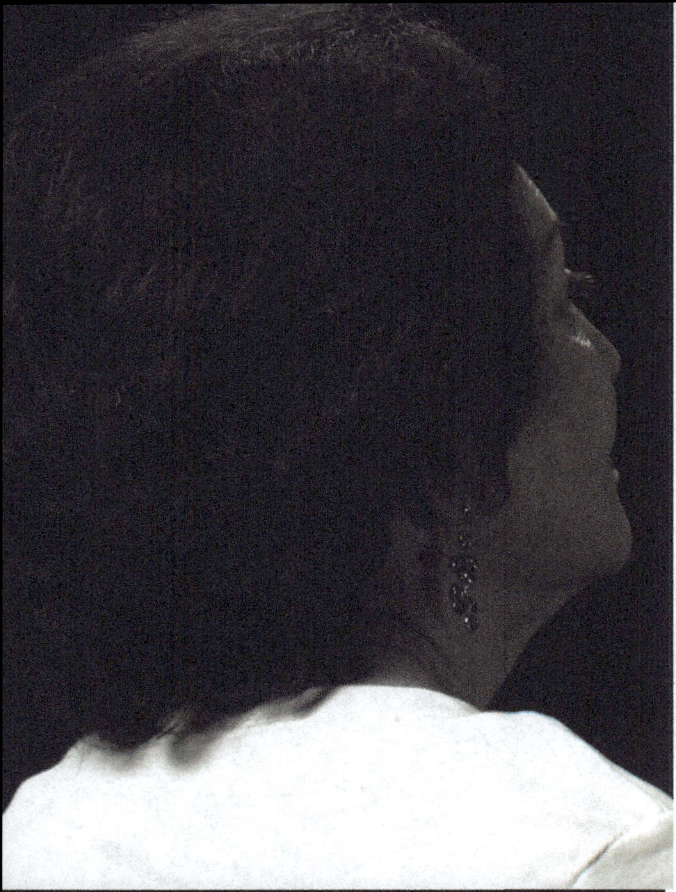

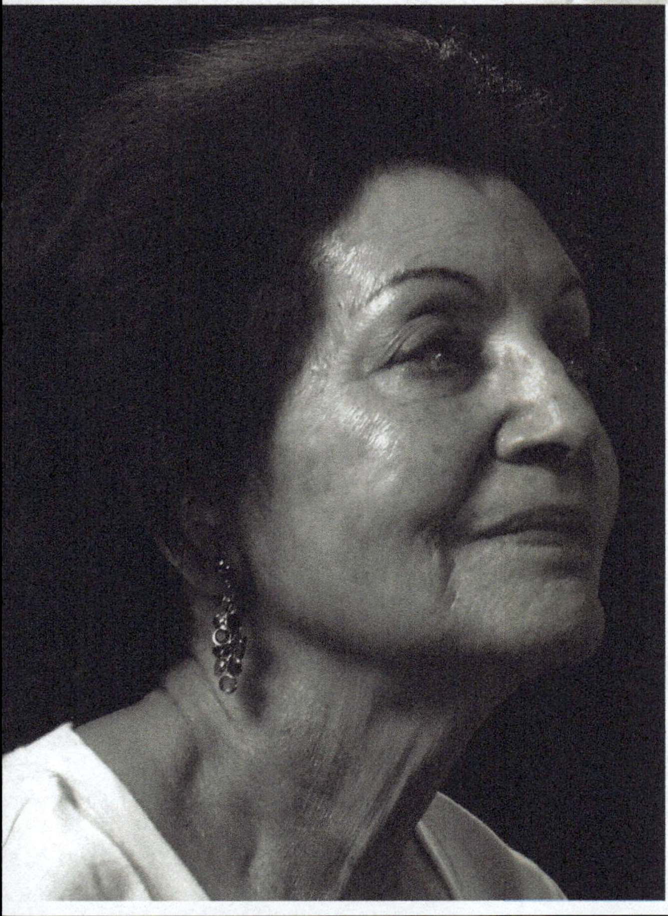

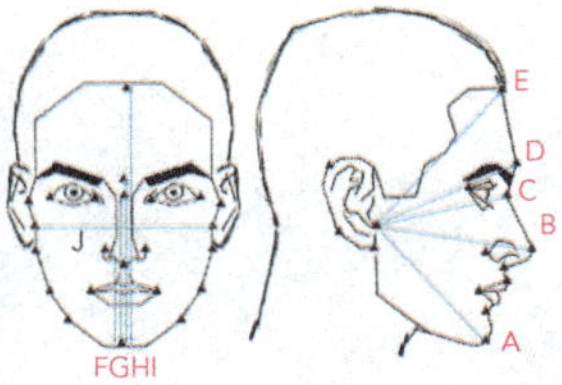


**Head measurements (in):**

A: 4 7/8
B: 5 1/8
C: 5
D: 5 1/8
E: 6 3/8
F: 3
G: 4
H: 5
I: 7 1/8
J: 5 7/8

MAP REFERENCE:

34

*Daughter of 35*

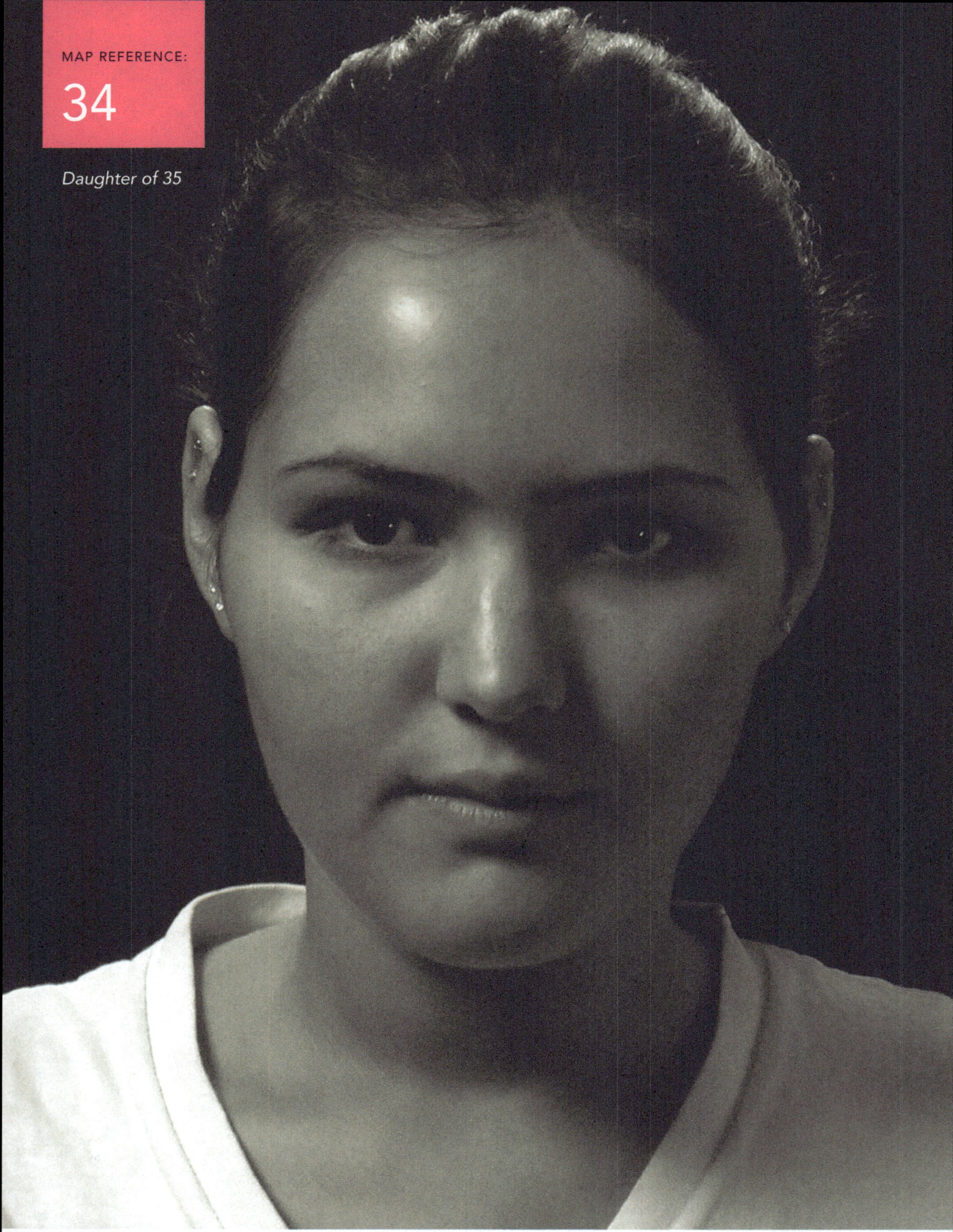

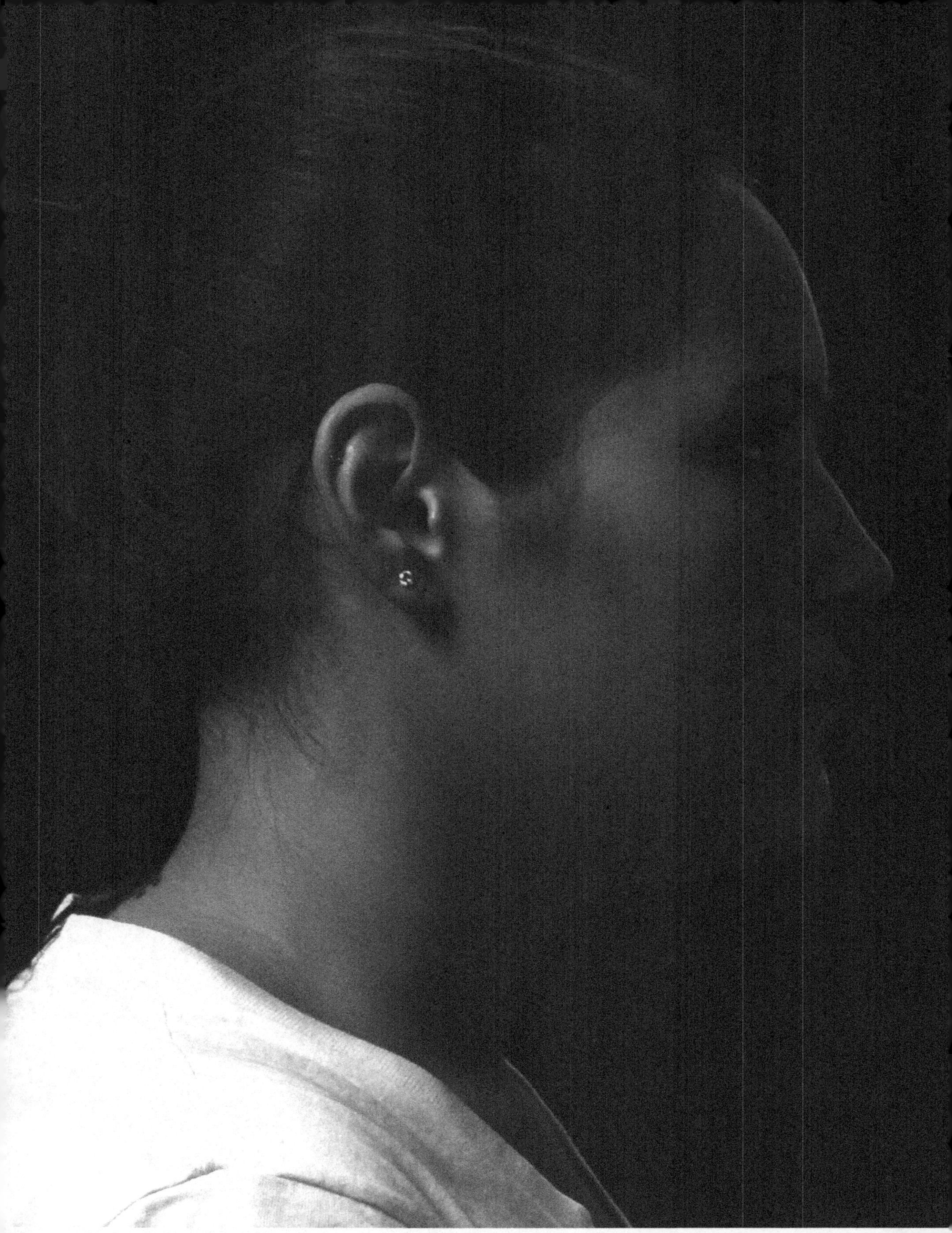

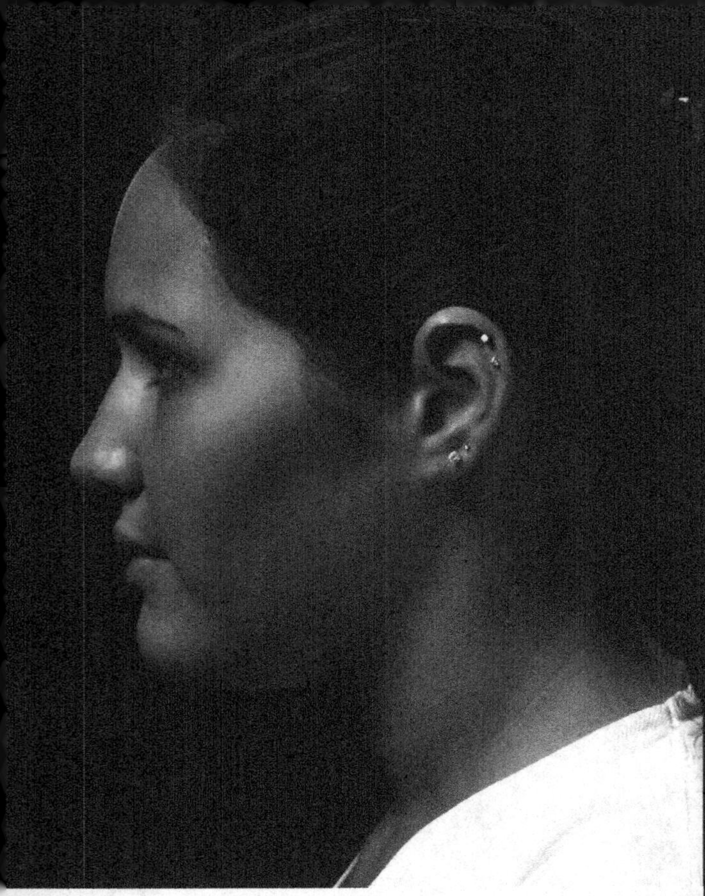

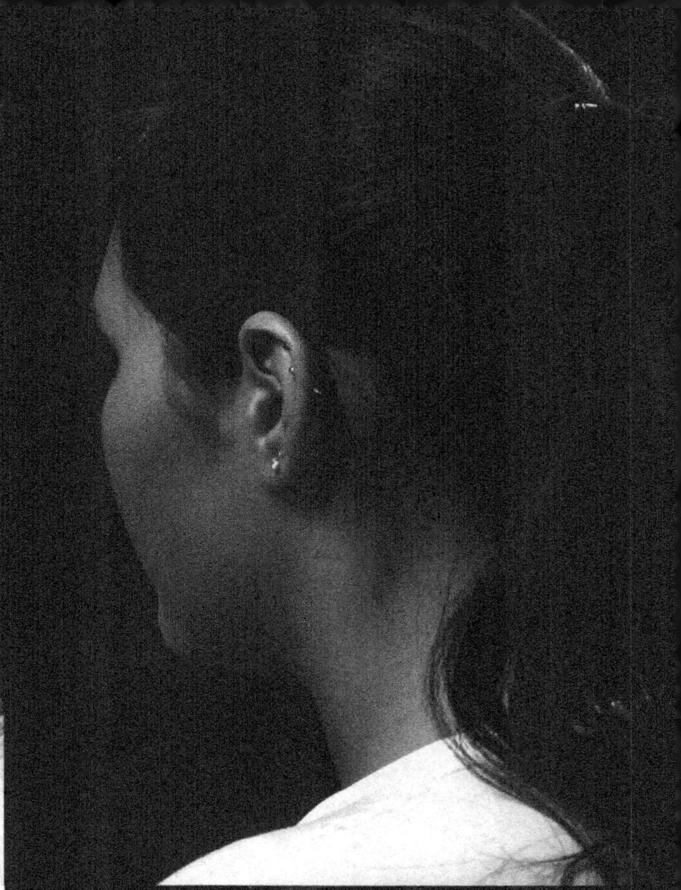

**Ethnicities claimed:**

Syria, Morocco.

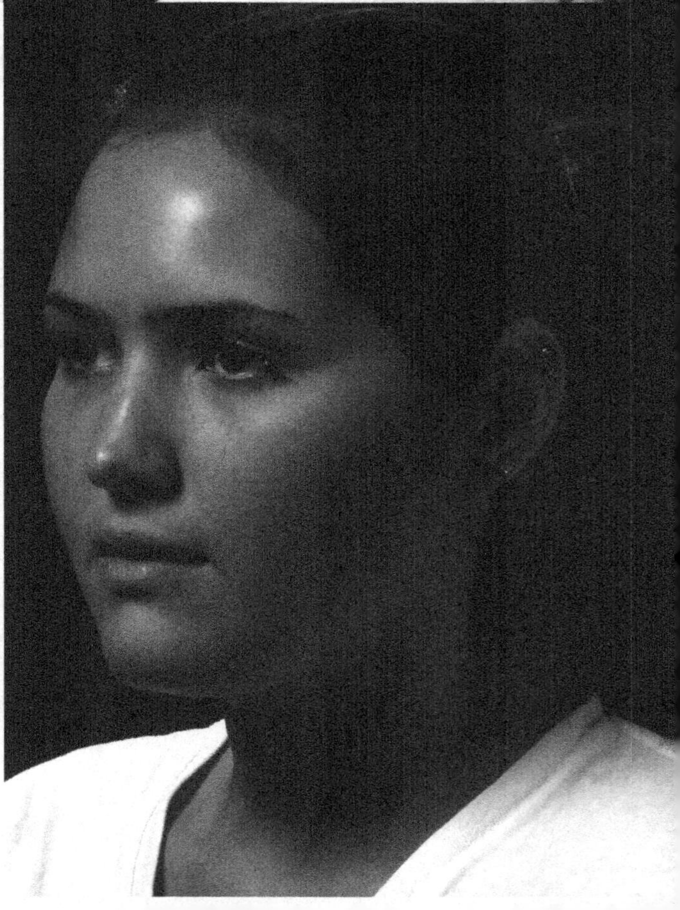

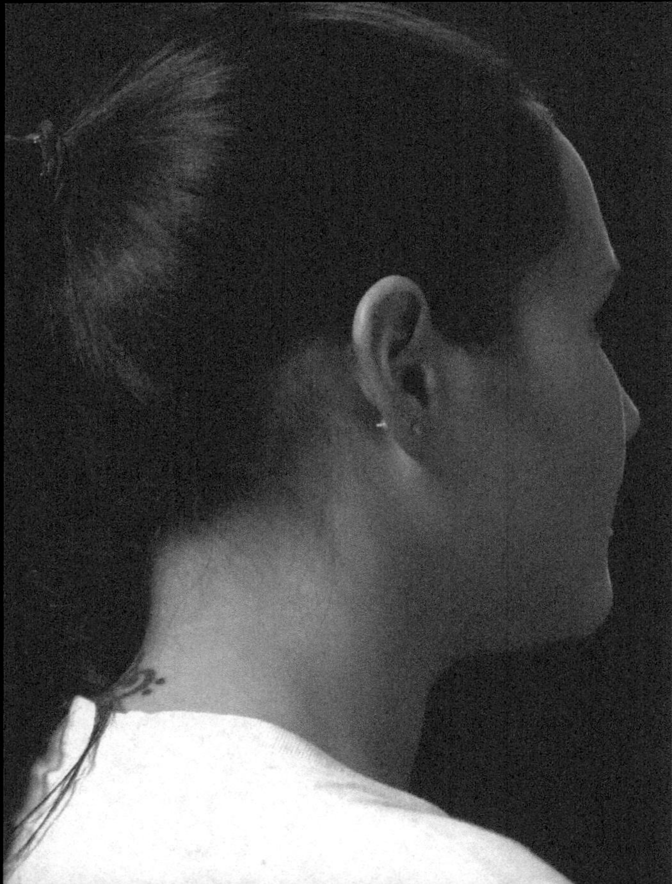

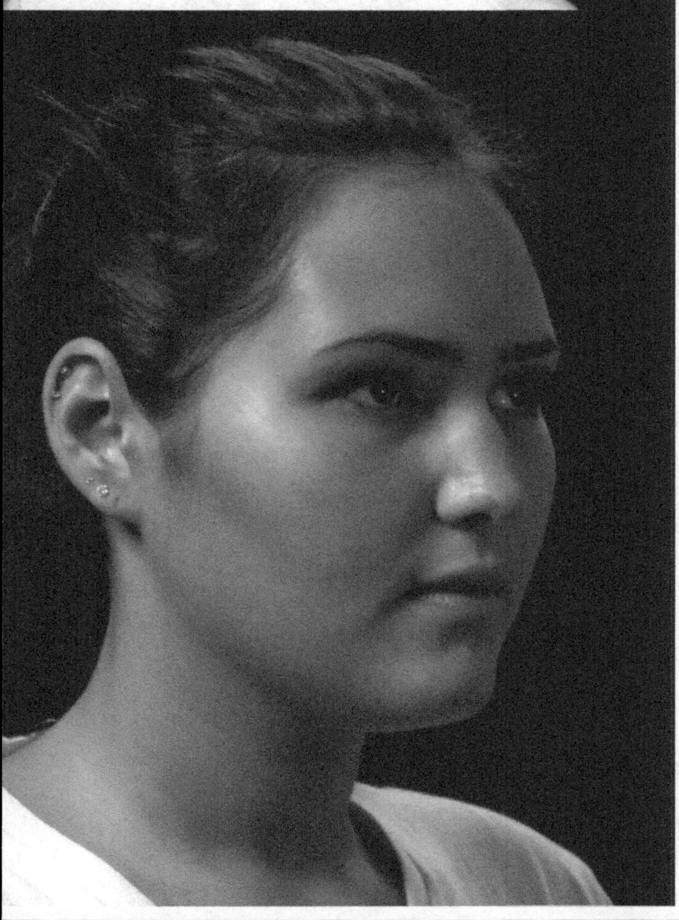

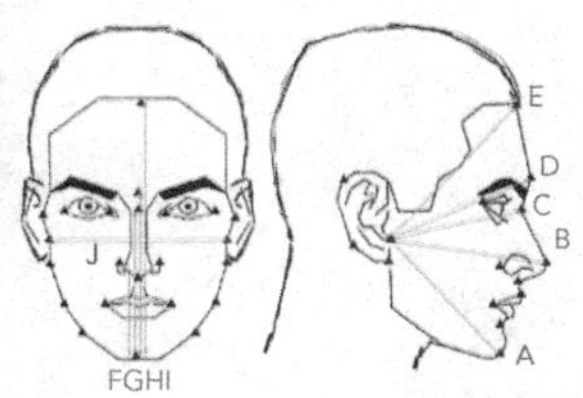


**Head measurements (in):**

A: 5 7/8
B: 5 5/8
C: 5 1/8
D: 5 3/4
E: 6 3/4
F: 3 1/2
G: 4 1/2
H: 5 1/8
I: 7 3/4
J: 5 3/8

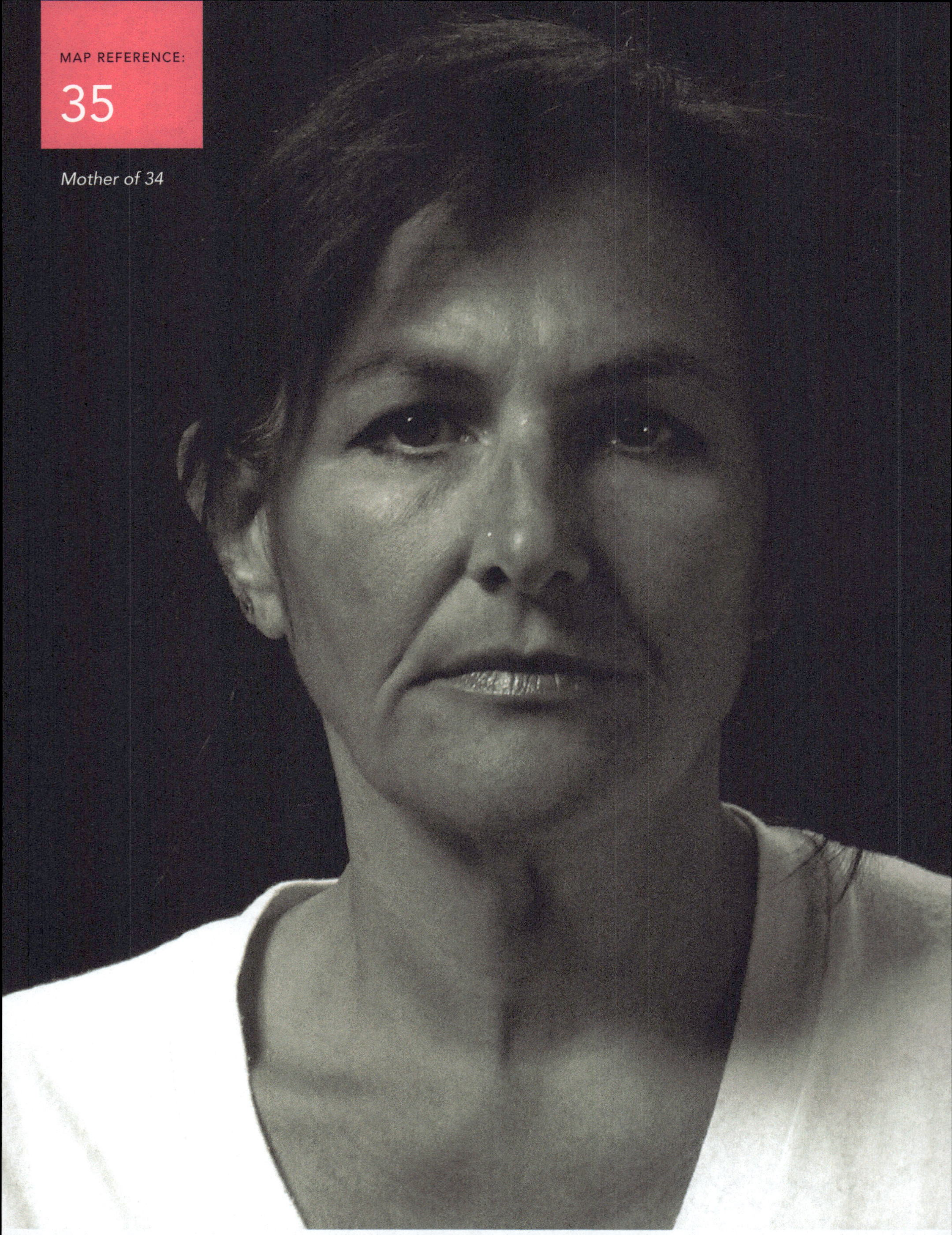

MAP REFERENCE:
35

*Mother of 34*

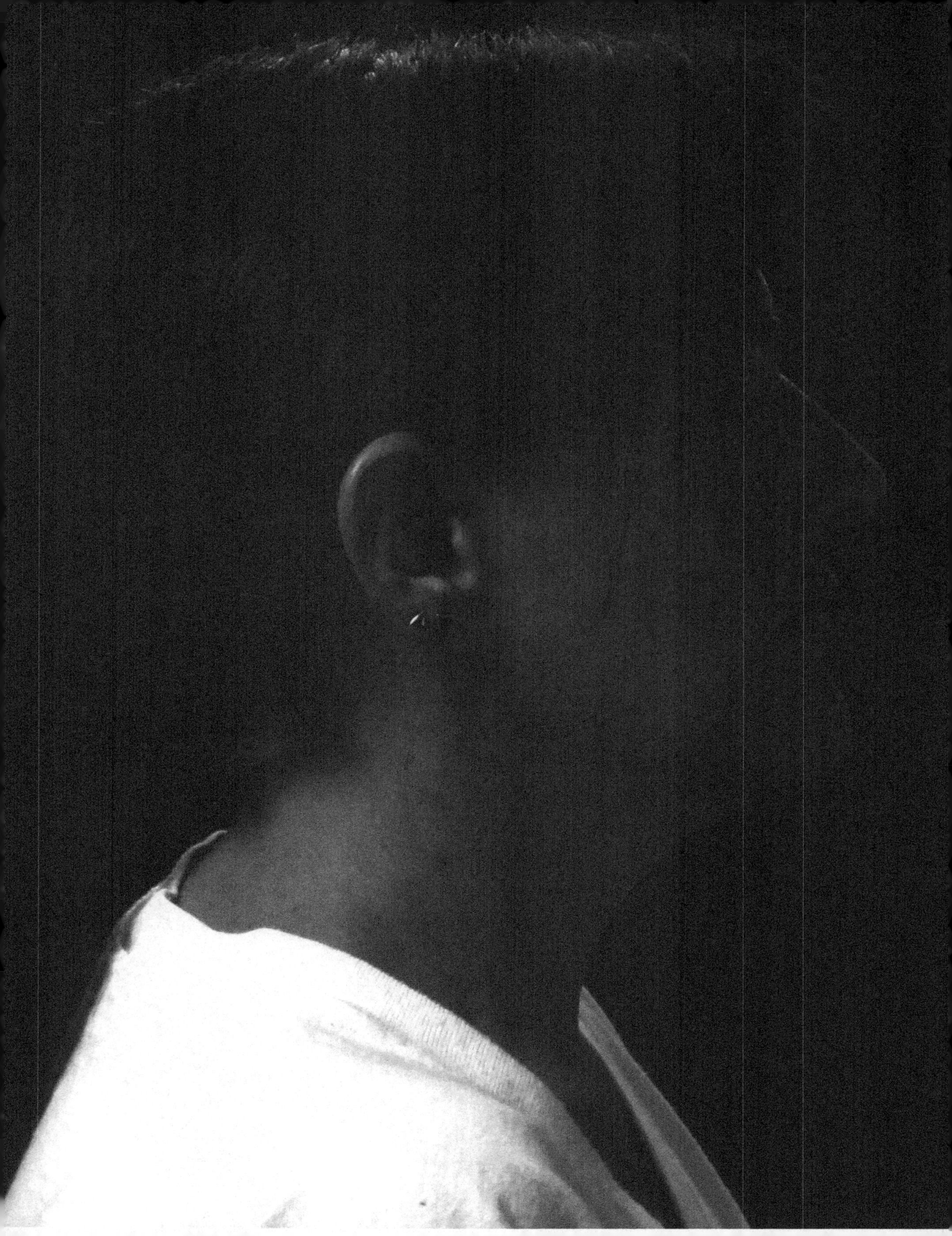

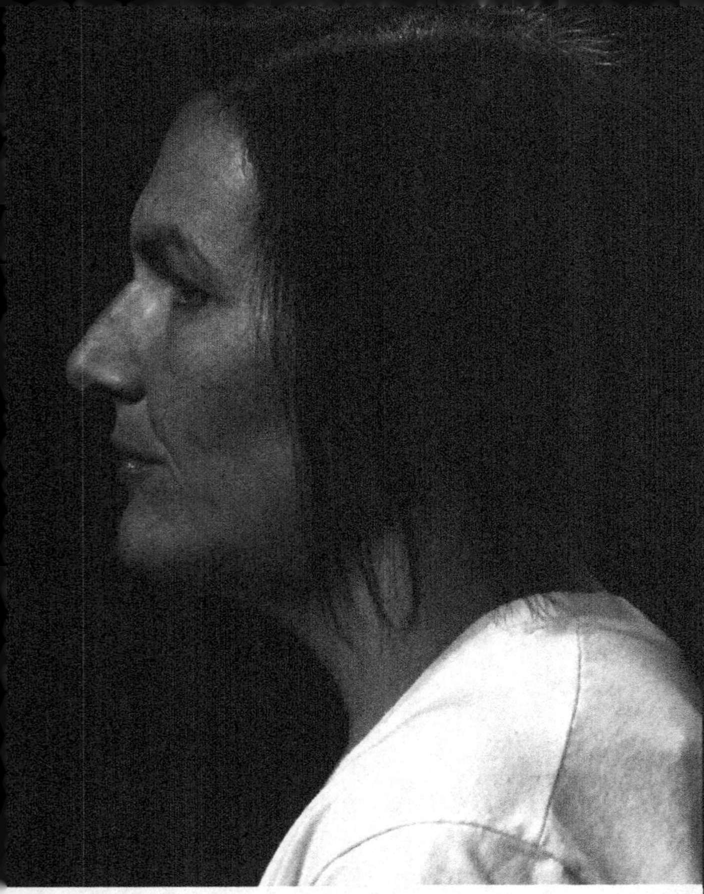

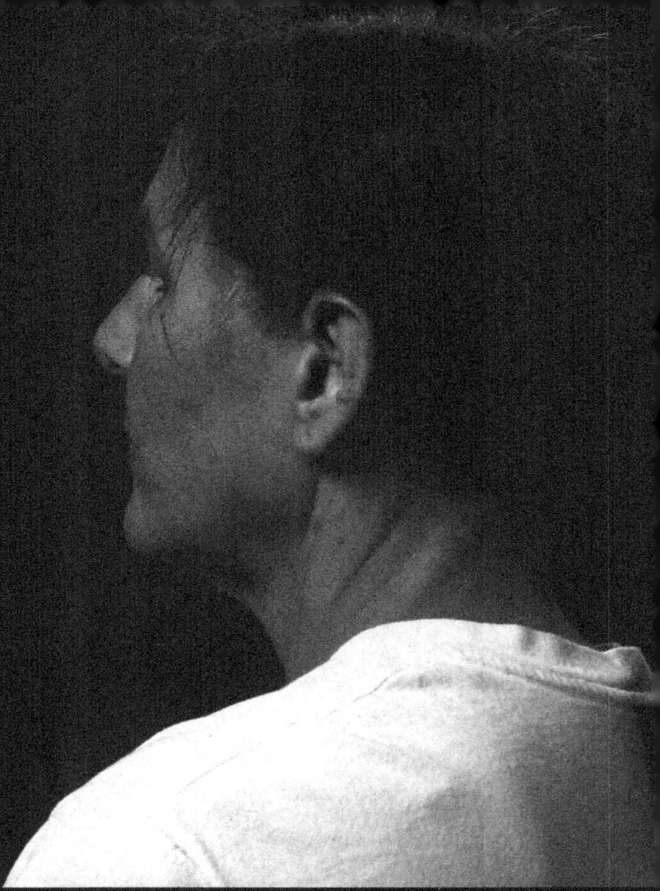

**Ethnicities claimed:**

Syria, Morocco.

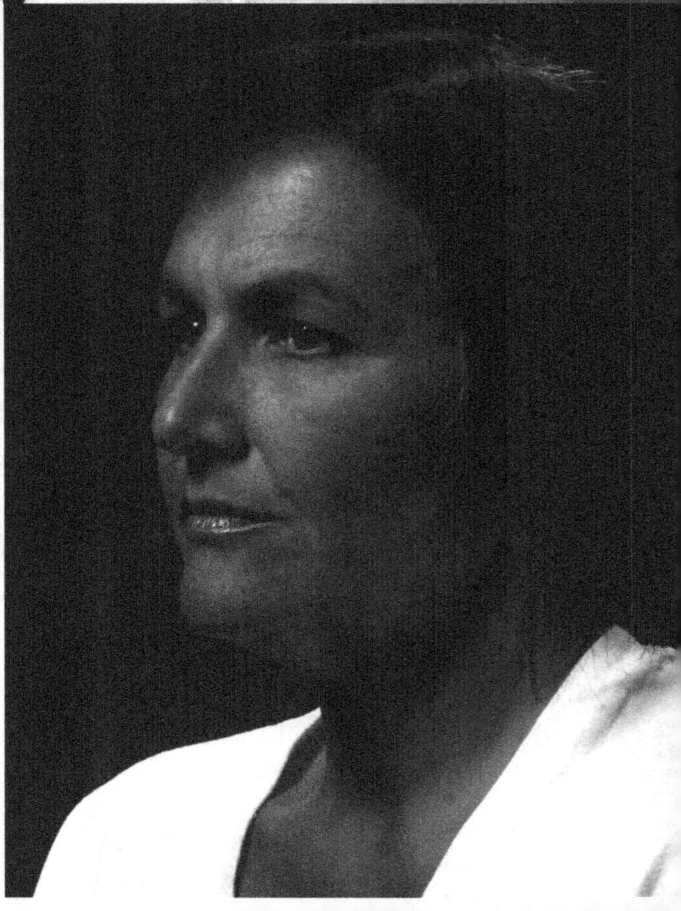

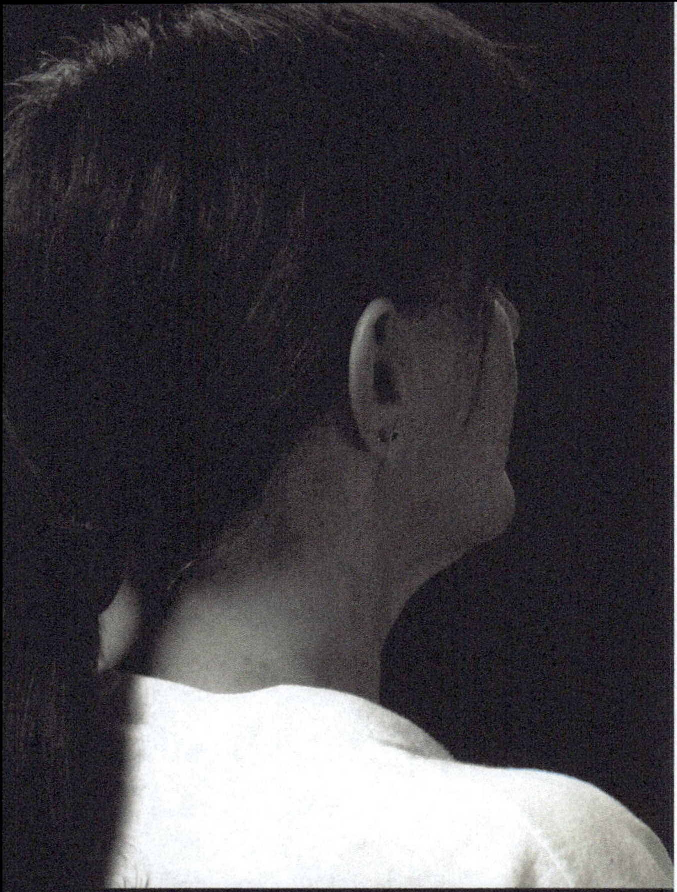

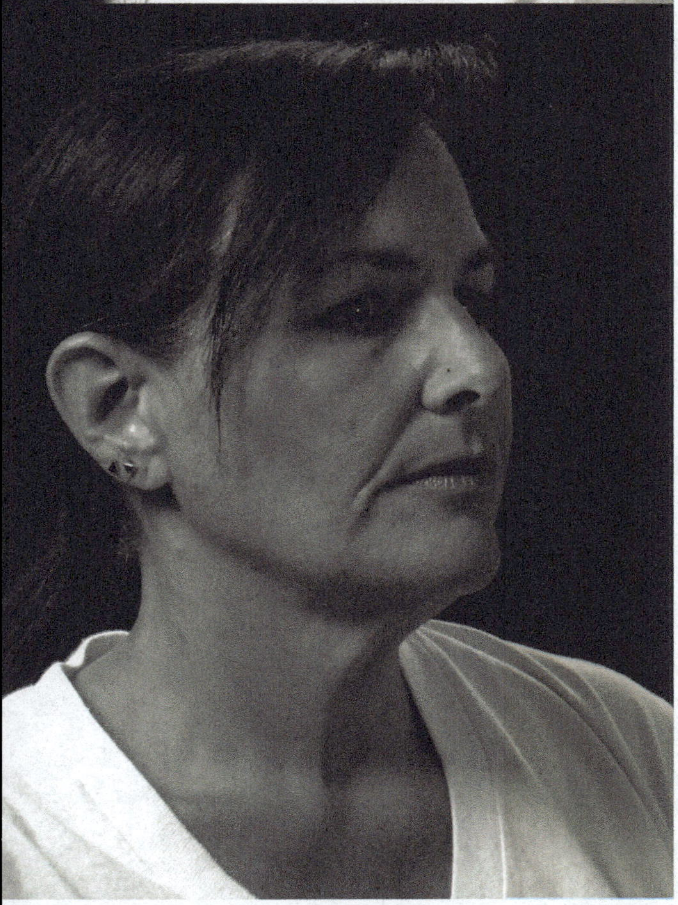

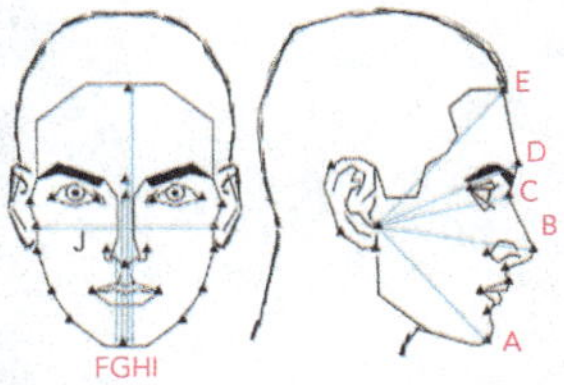


**Head measurements (in):**

A: 5 1/2
B: 4 3/4
C: 5 1/4
D: 5 1/2
E: 5 3/4
F: 3
G: 4 1/8
H: 5
I: 7
J: 6

MAP REFERENCE:

36

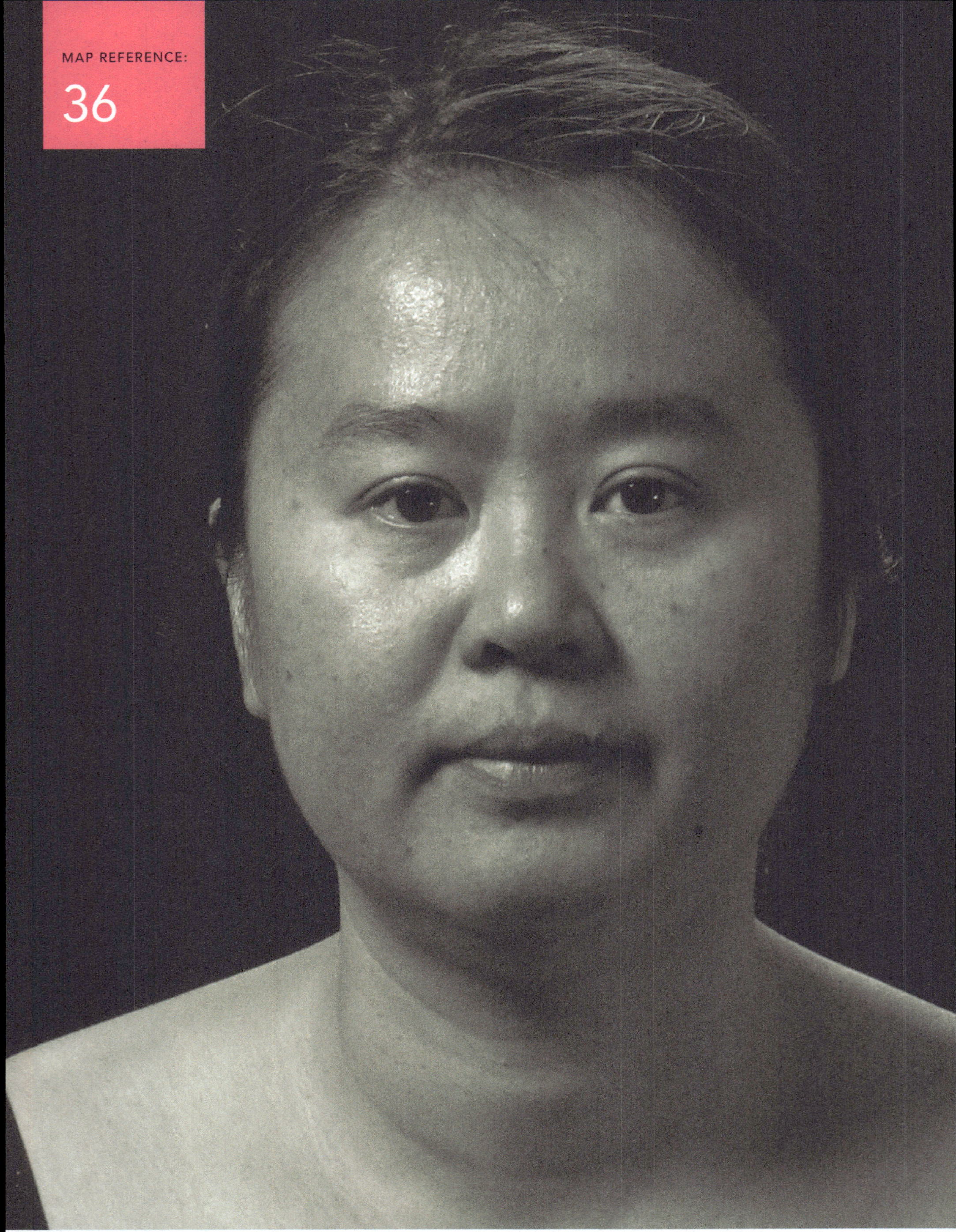

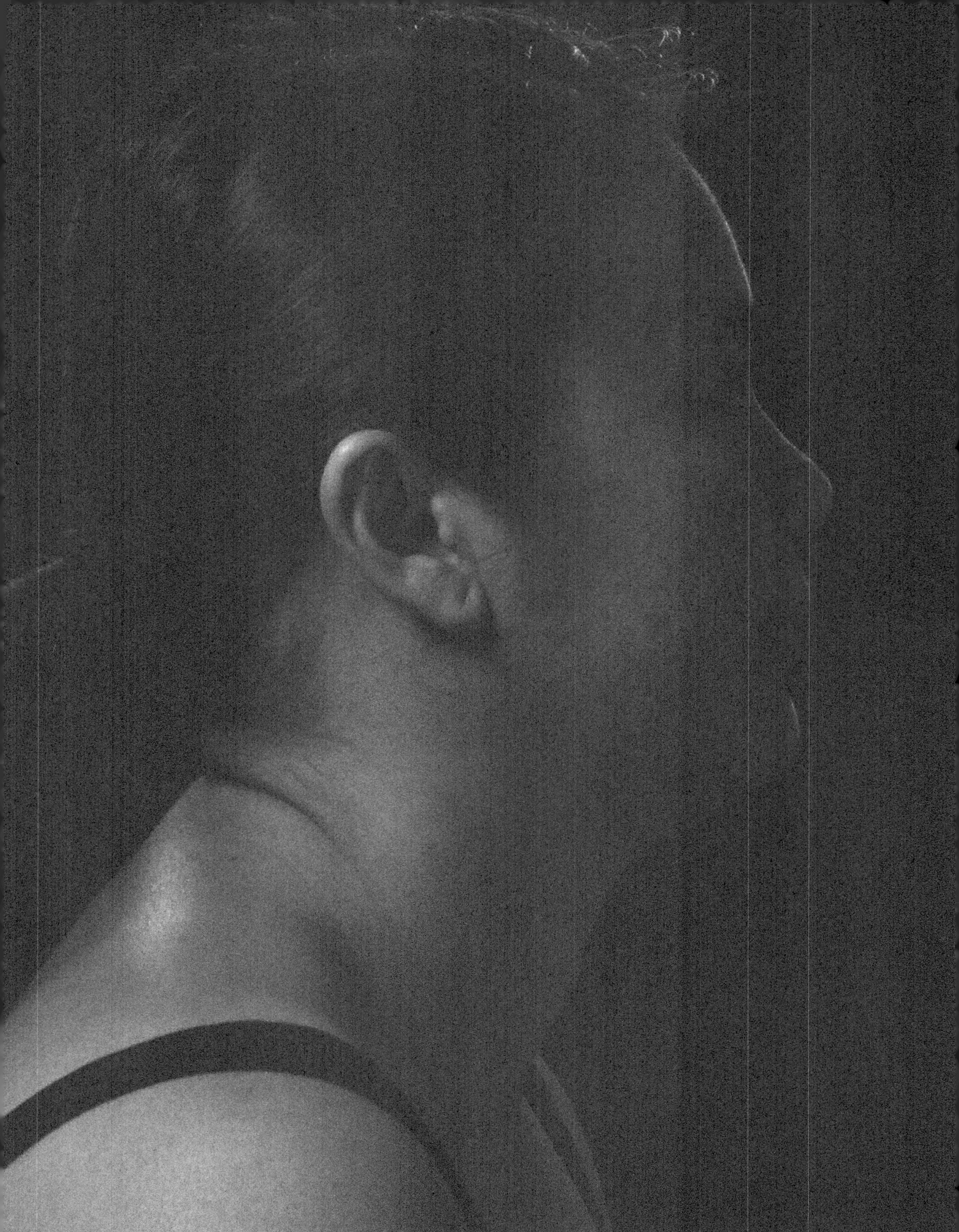

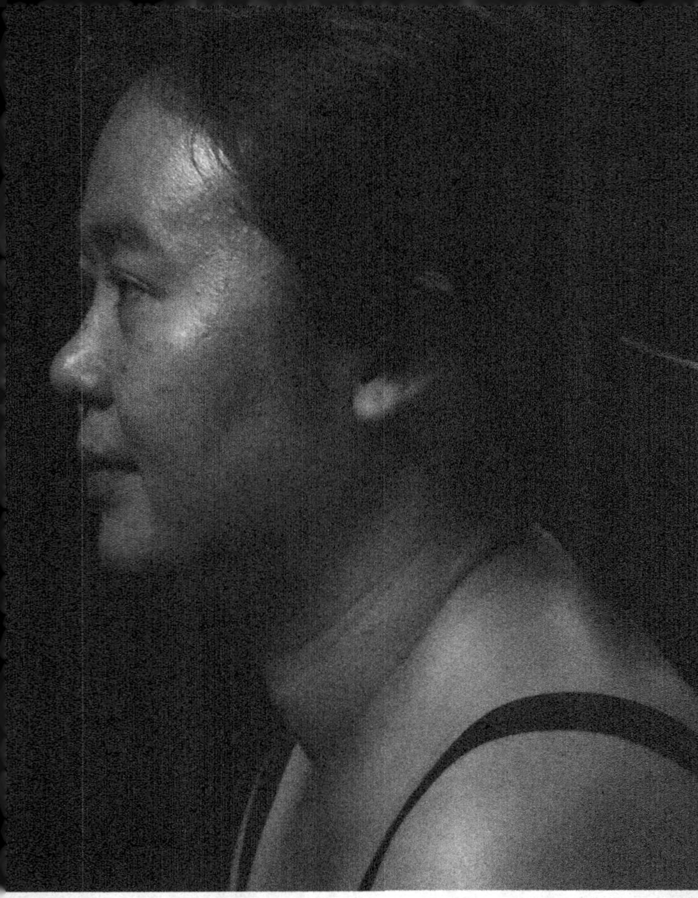

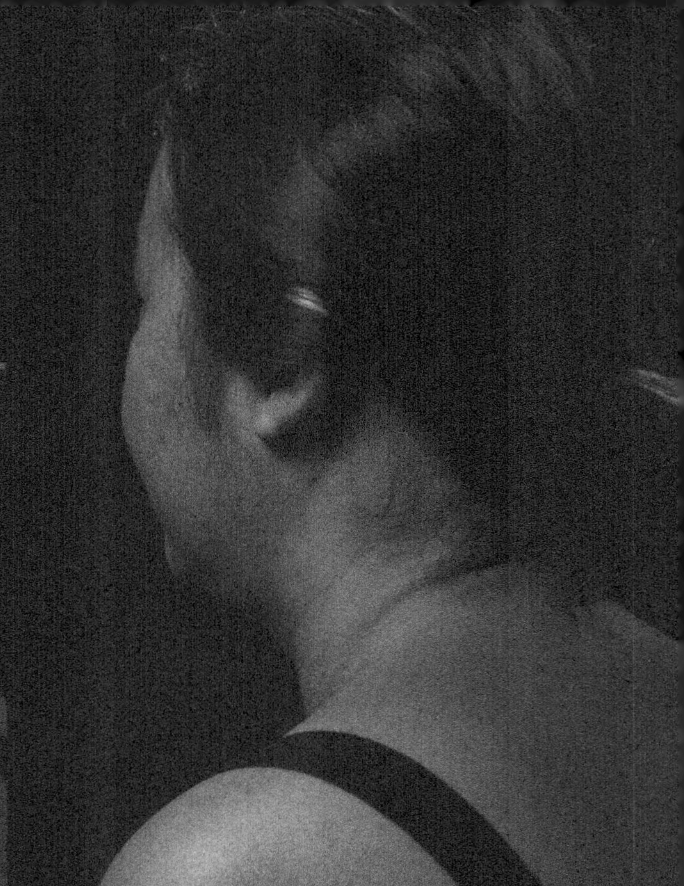

**Ethnicities claimed:**

Viet Nam.

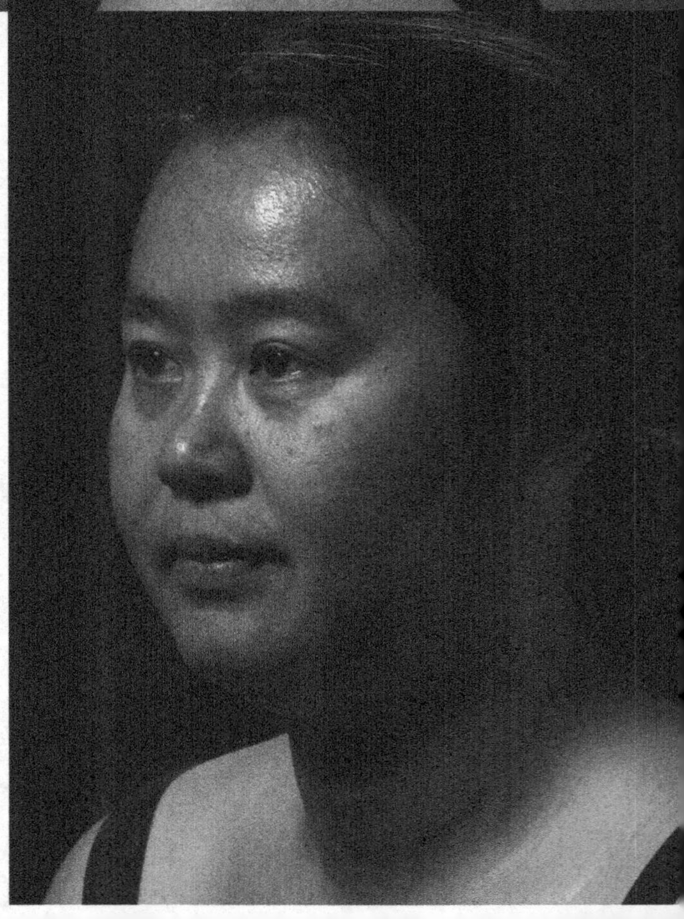

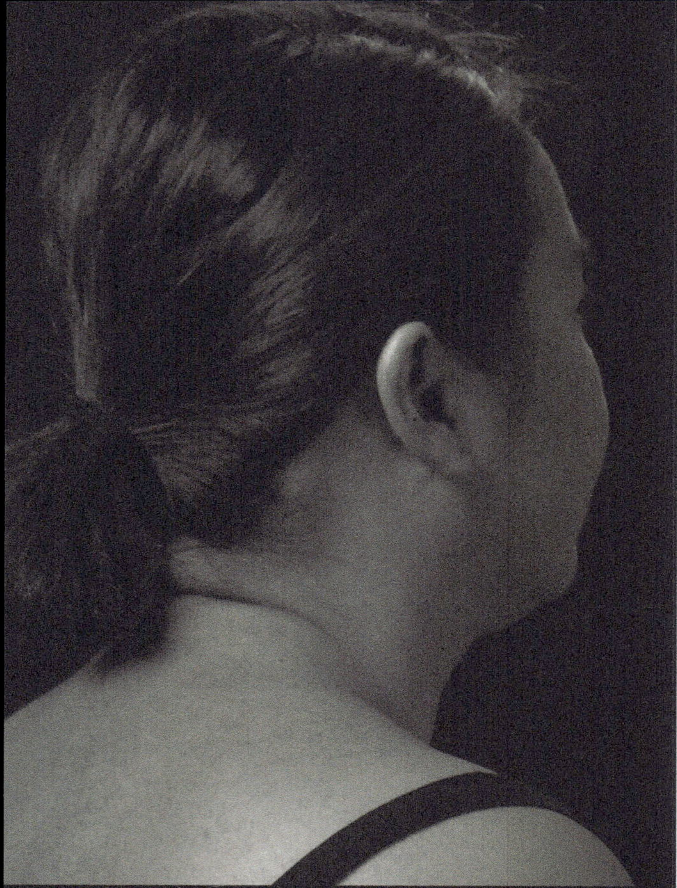

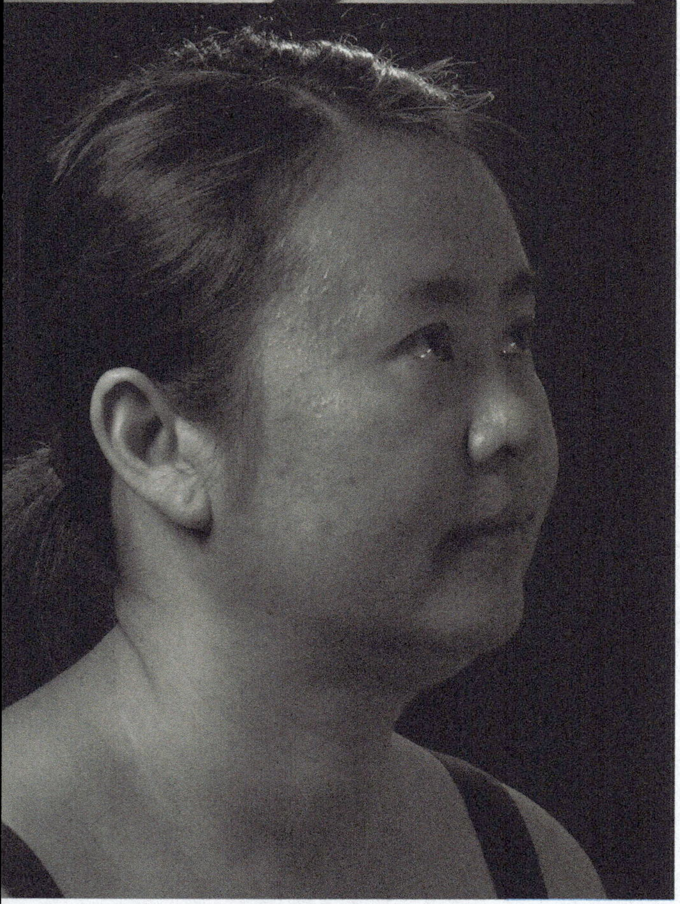

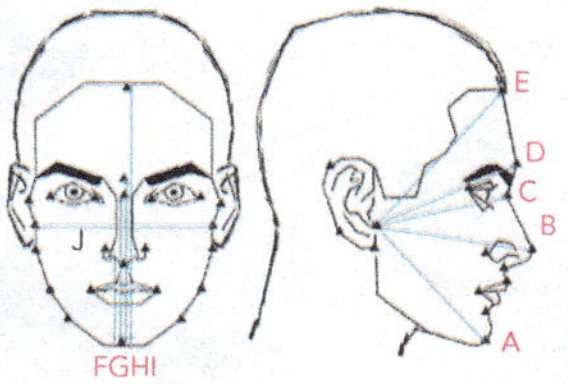


**Head measurements (in):**

A: 5 1/8
B: 5 1/8
C: 4 3/4
D: 5 1/8
E: 6 1/4
F: 3 3/8
G: 5
H: 5 1/4
I: 7 3/8
J: 5 3/4

MAP REFERENCE:

37

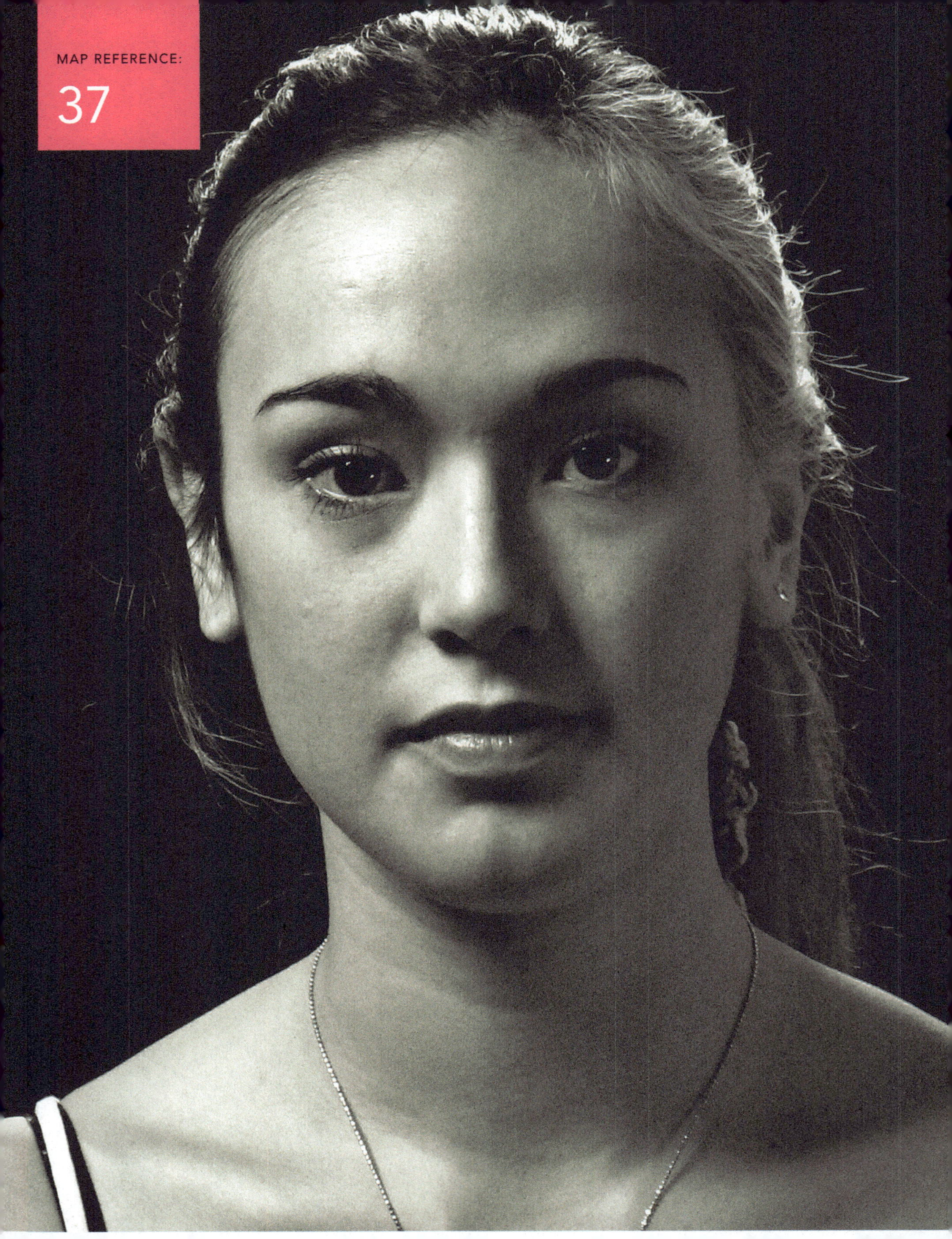

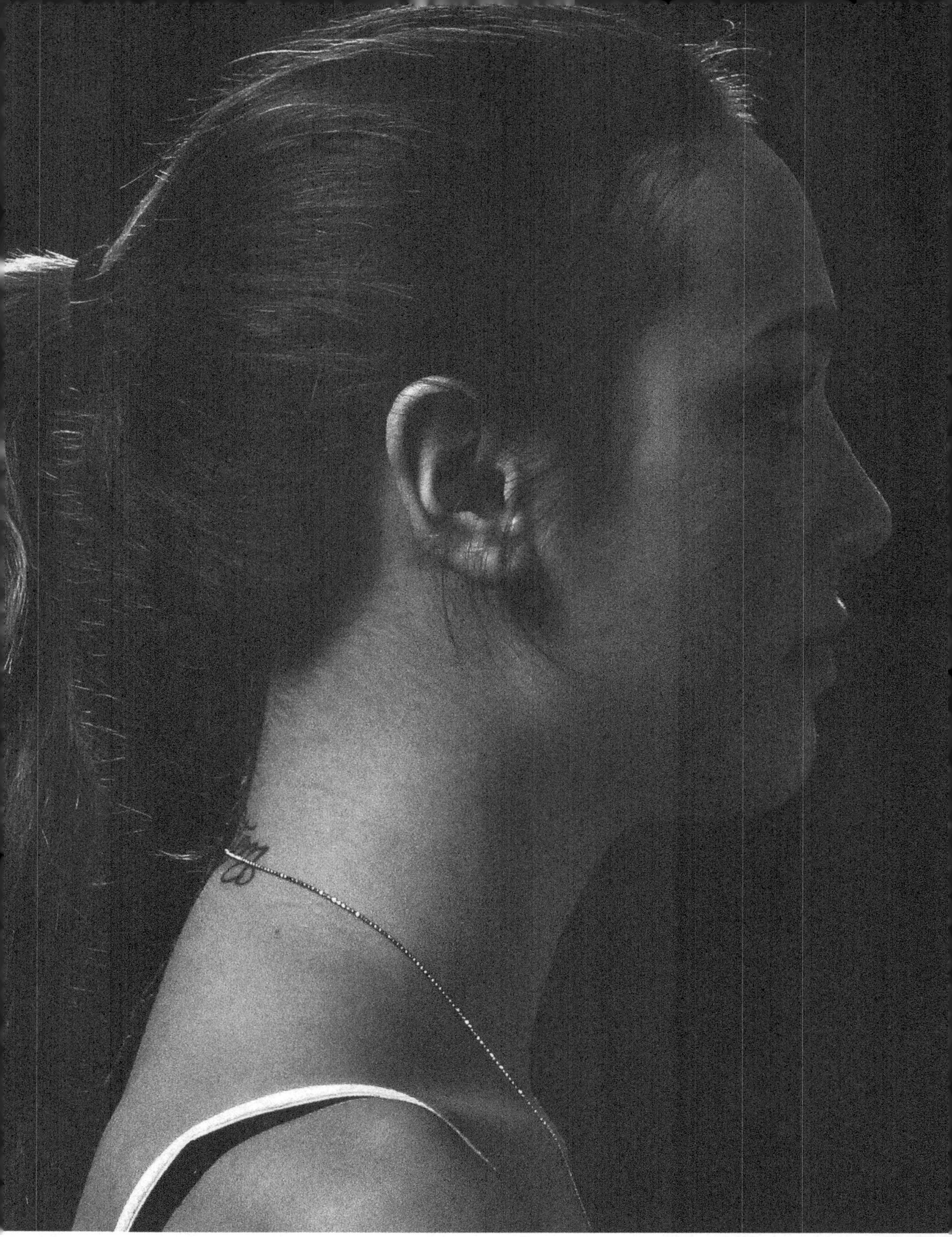

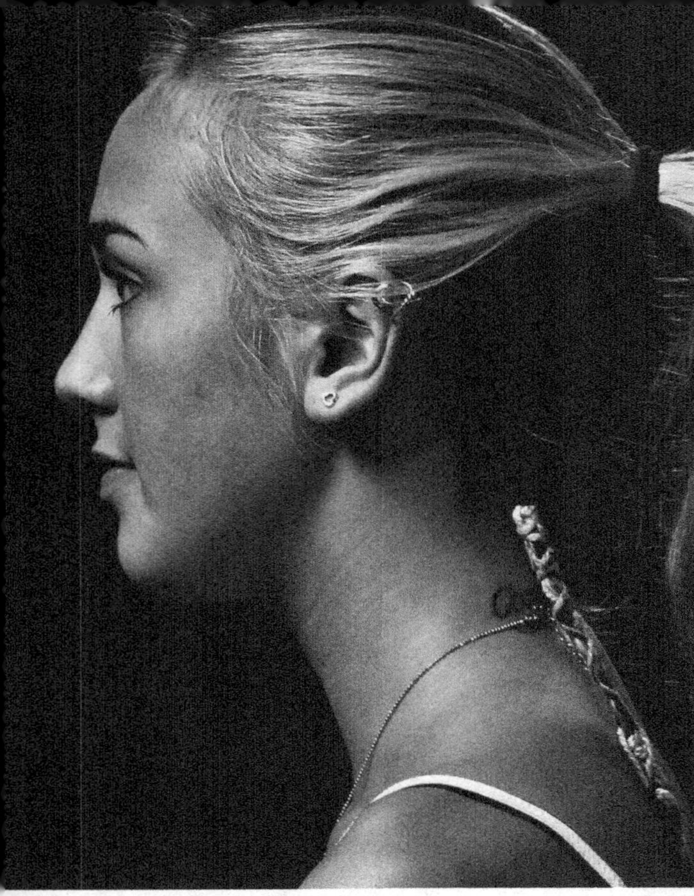

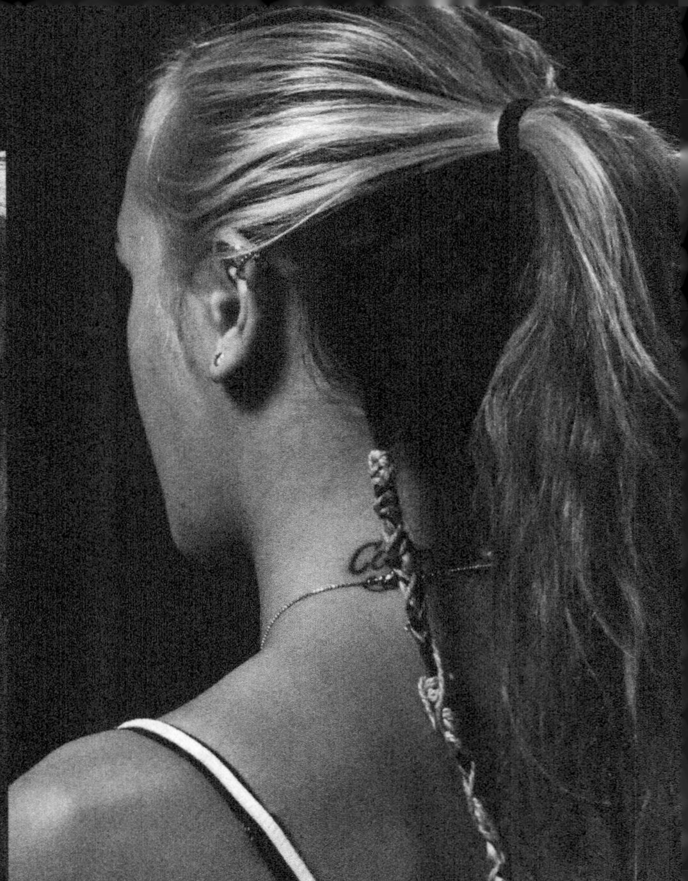

**Ethnicities claimed:**

England, Ireland, Scotland, Germany, China, Thailand.

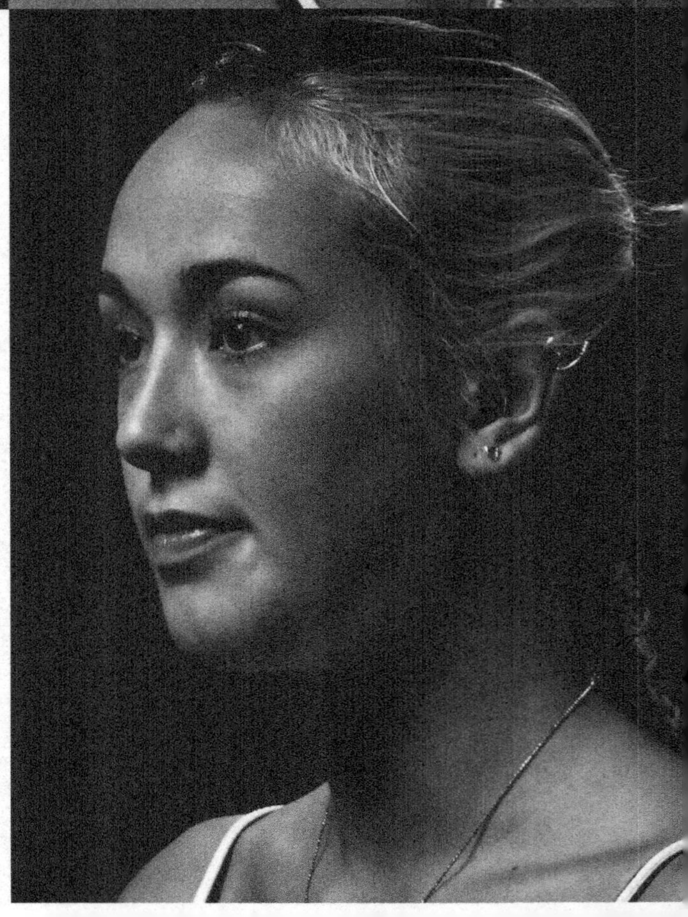

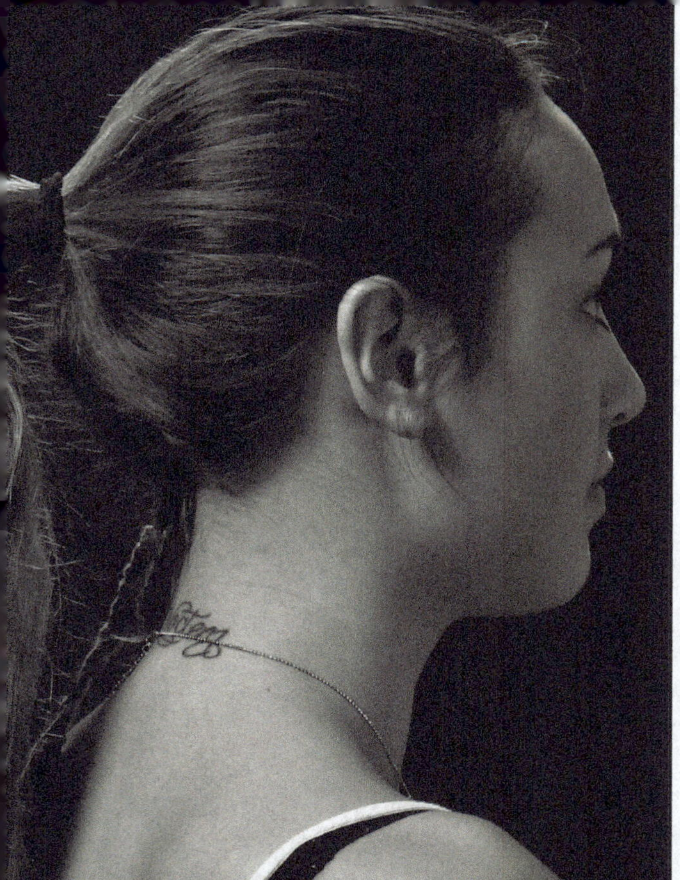

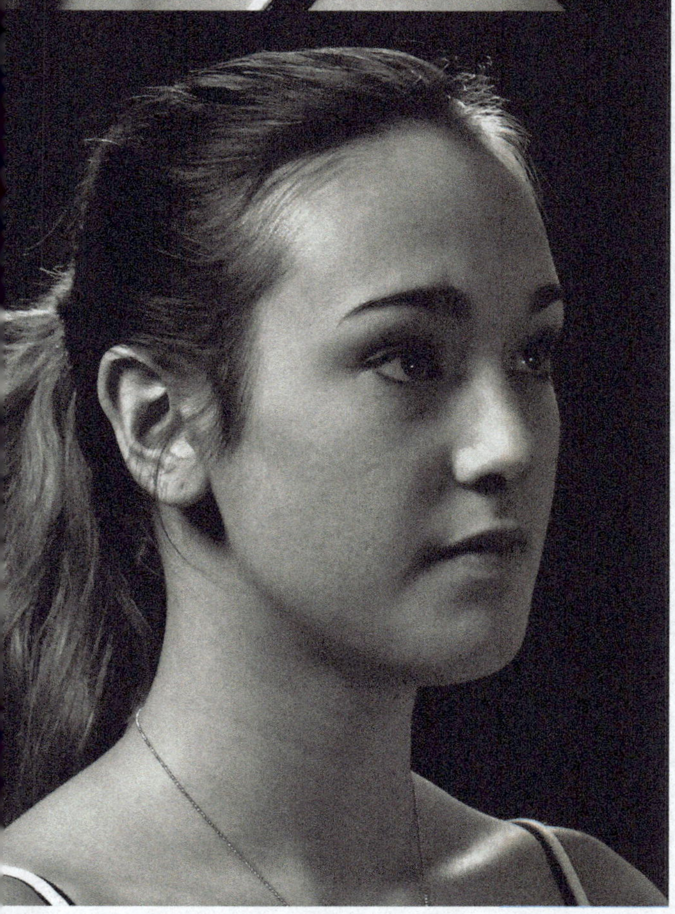

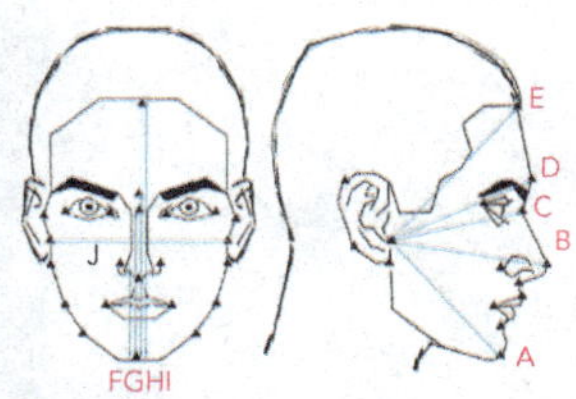


**Head measurements (in):**

A: 5
B: 4 7/8
C: 4 3/4
D: 5
E: 5 5/8
F: 3 5/8
G: 4 5/8
H: 5 3/8
I: 7 7/8
J: 5 5/8

MAP REFERENCE:

39

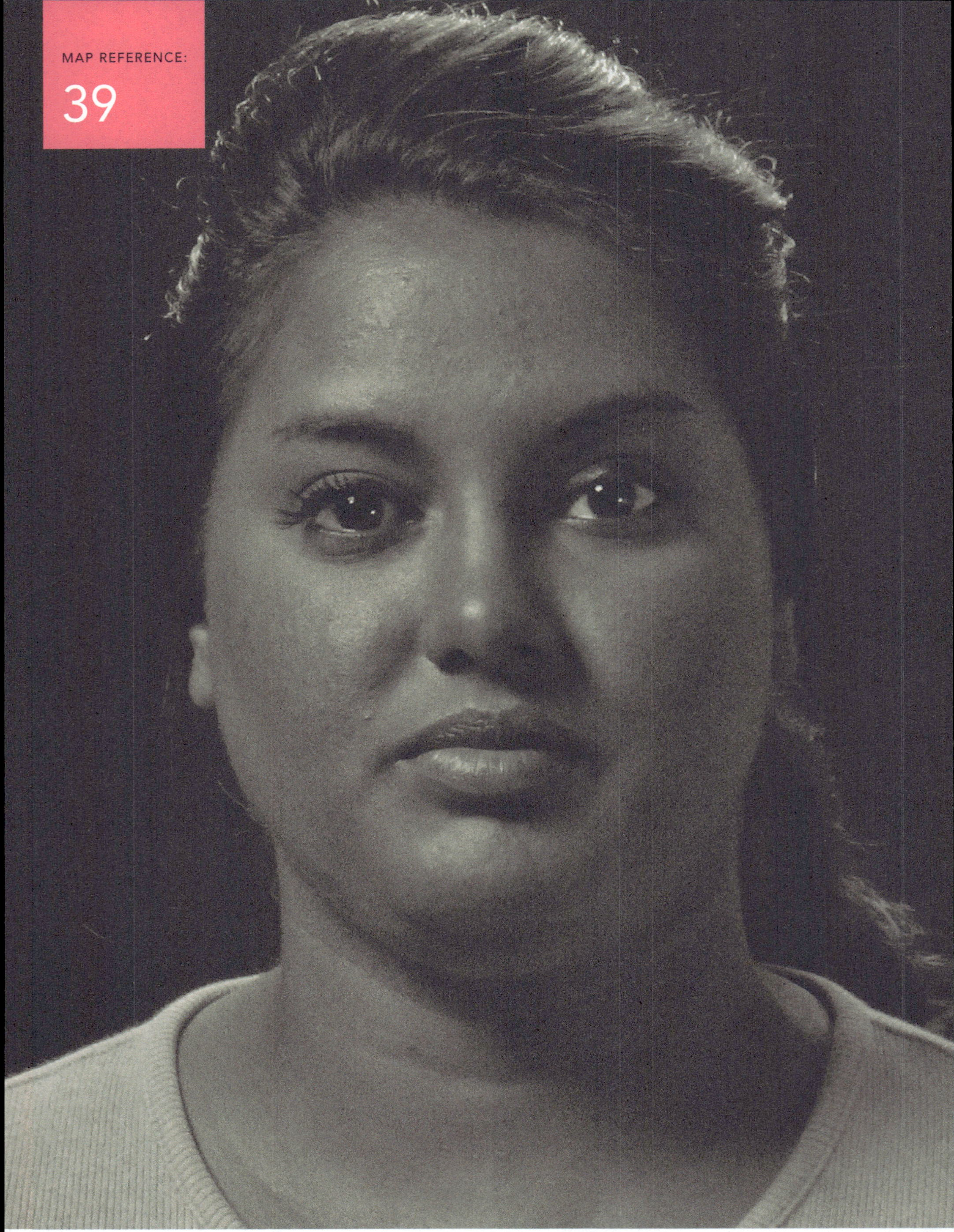

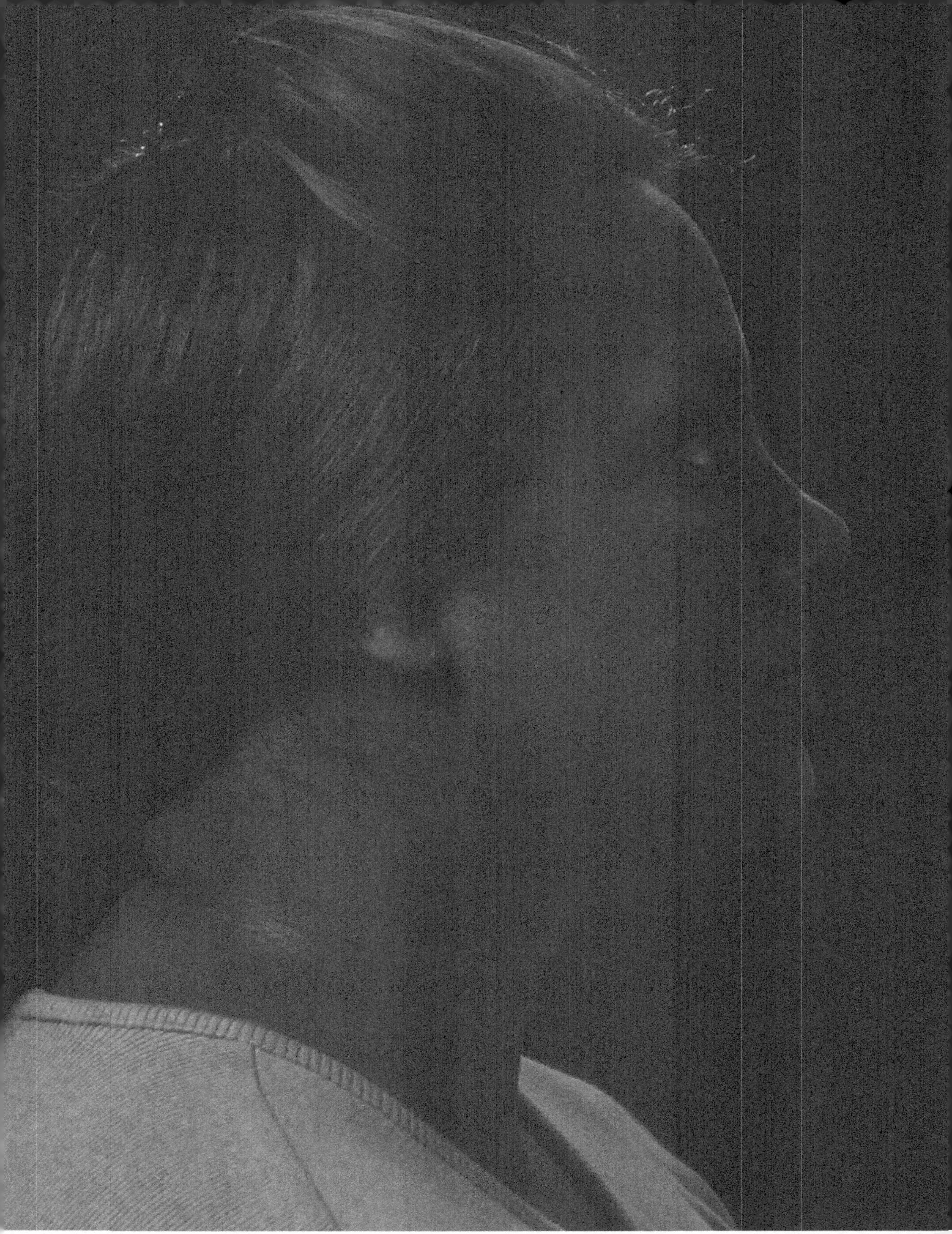

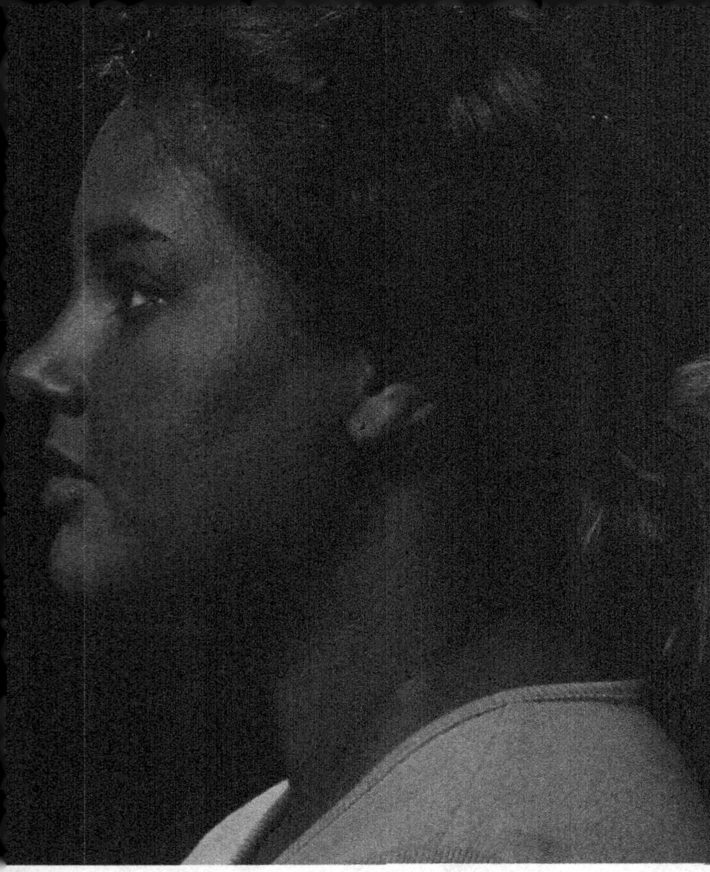

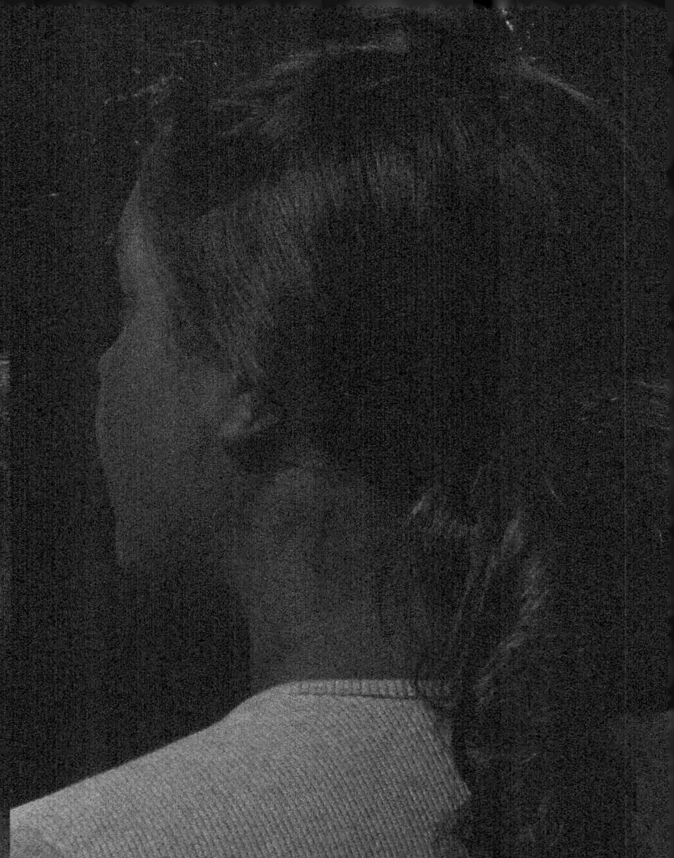

**Ethnicities claimed:**

India, Africa—Republic of Mauritius

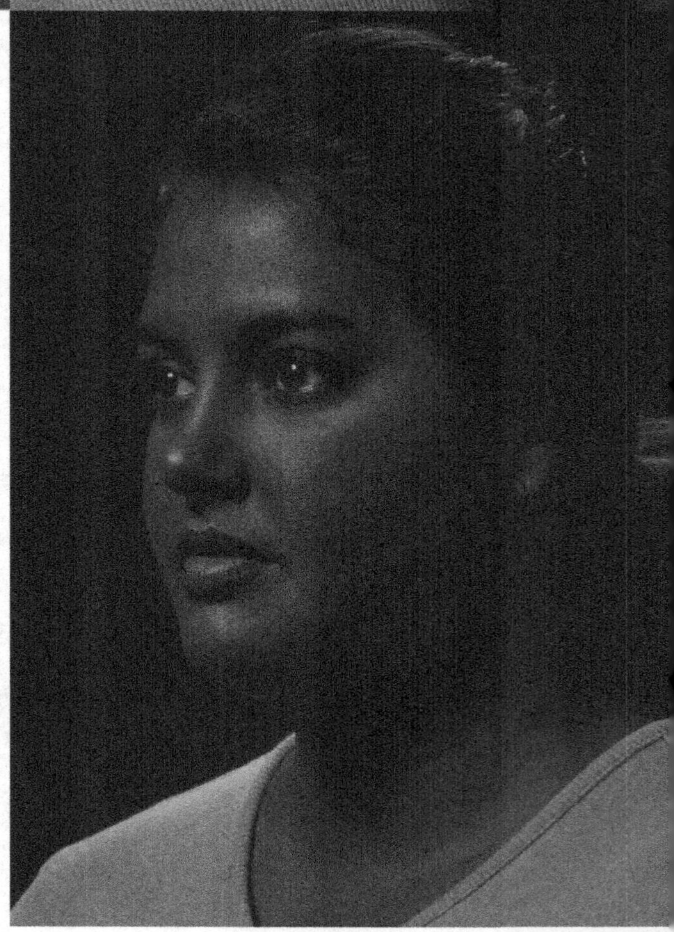

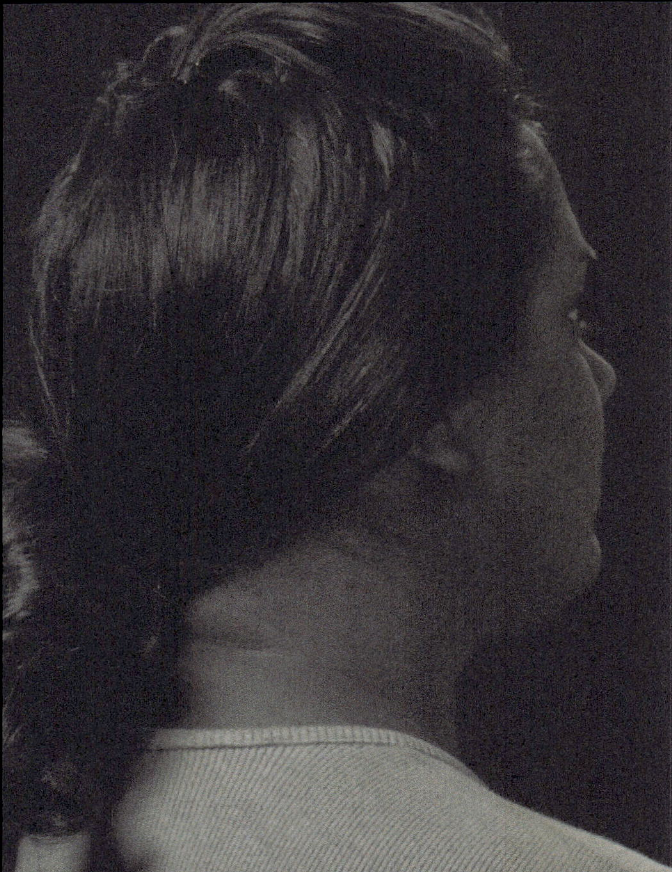

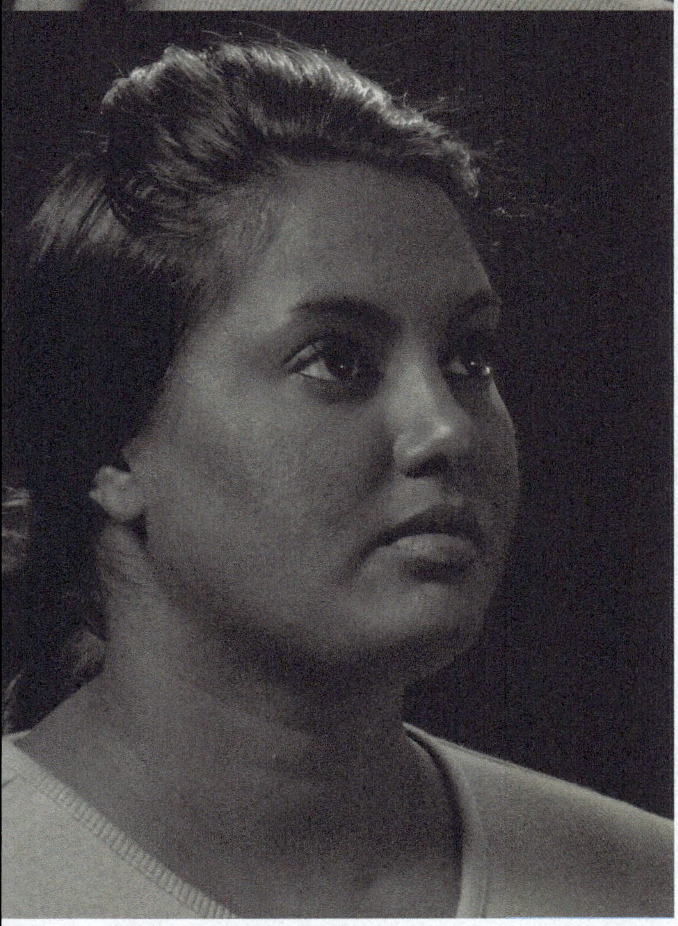

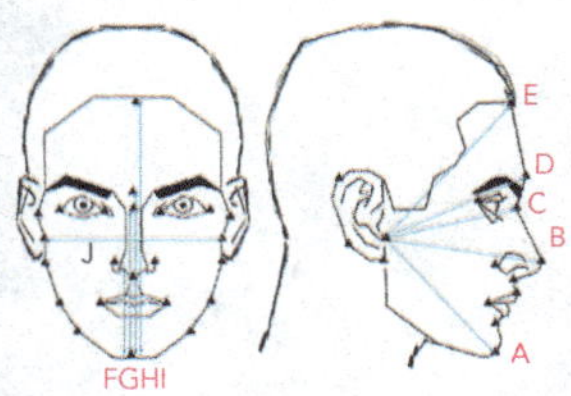


**Head measurements (in):**

A: 5 1/2
B: 4 7/8
C: 4 5/8
D: 4 7/8
E: 5 5/8
F: 3
G: 3 7/8
H: 4 5/8
I: 7
J: 5 5/8

MAP REFERENCE:

40

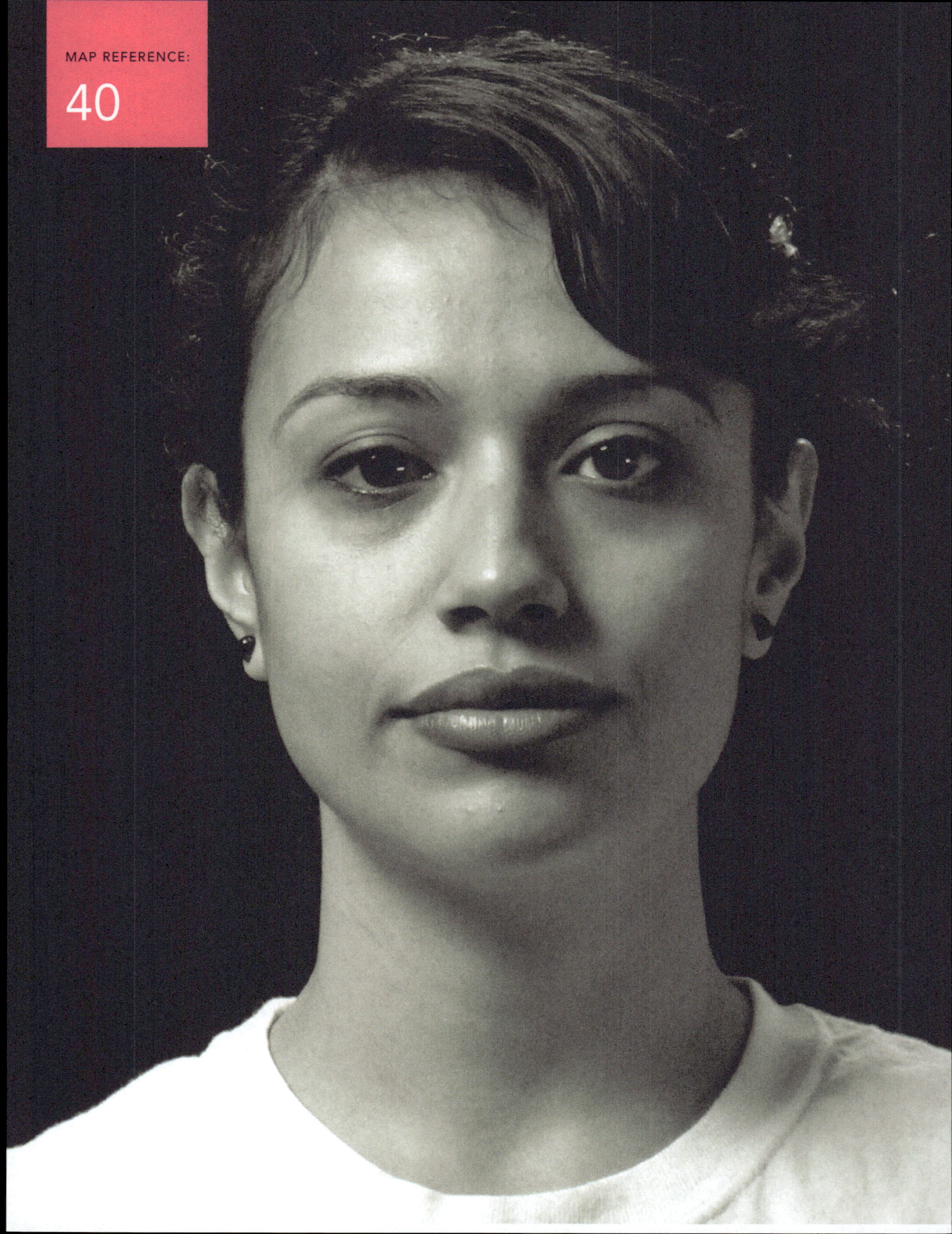

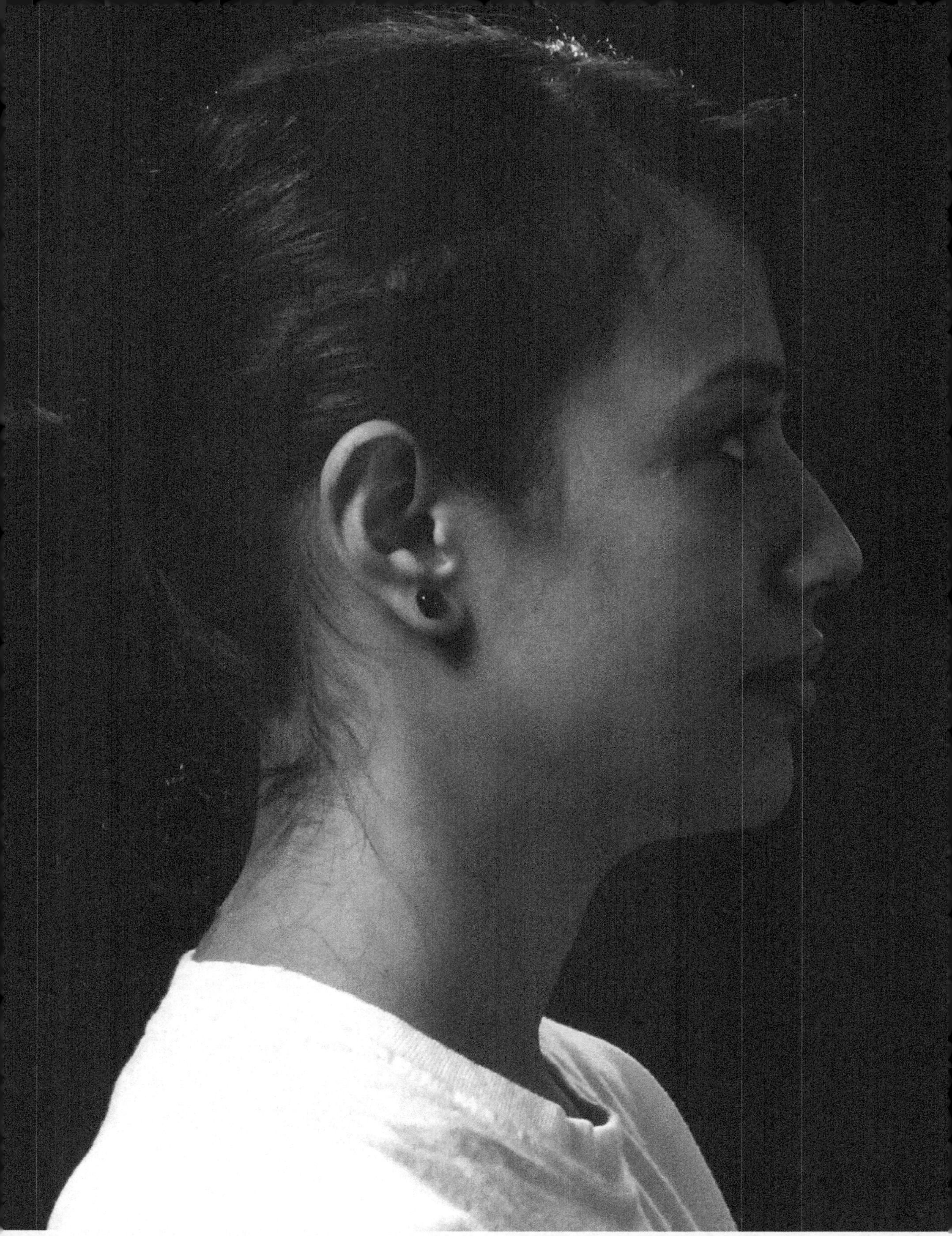

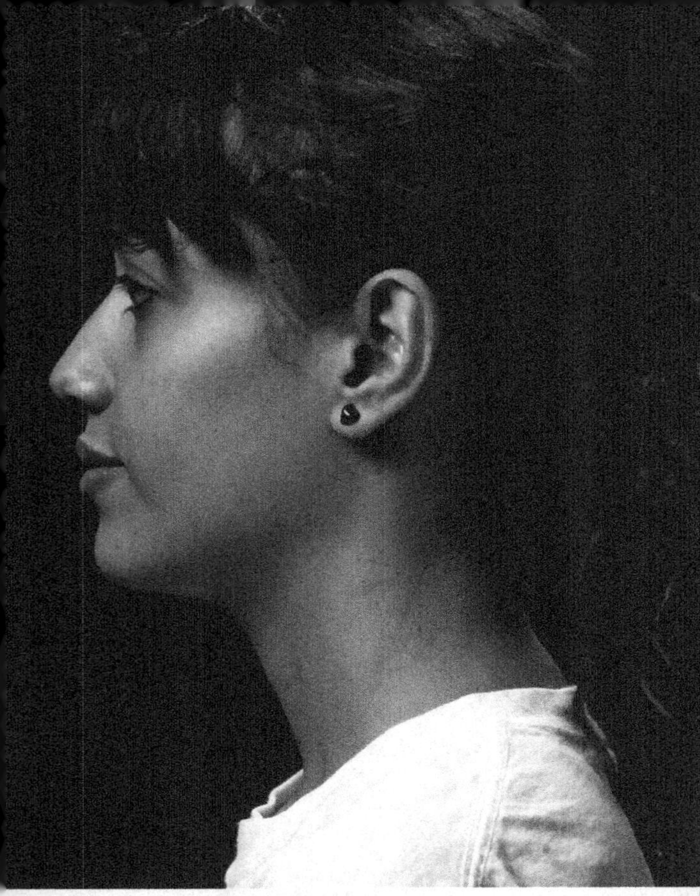

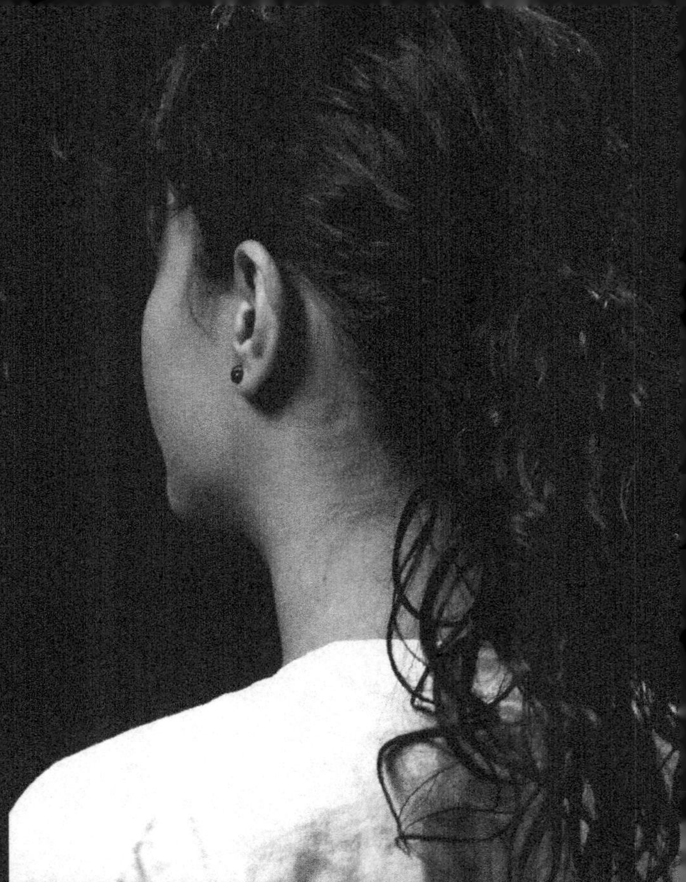

**Ethnicities claimed:**

Egypt, Mexico (Indian).

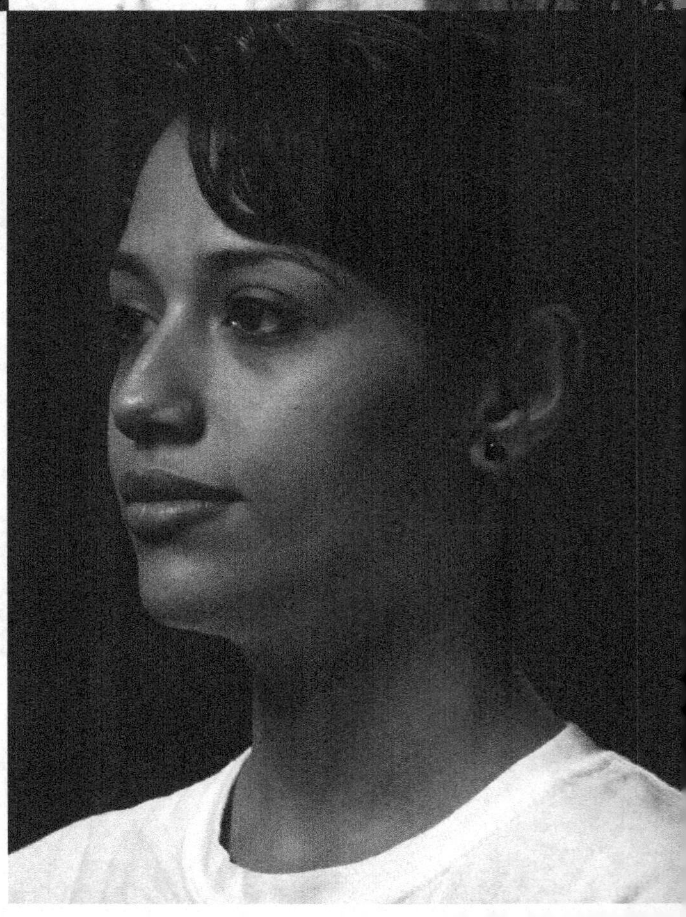

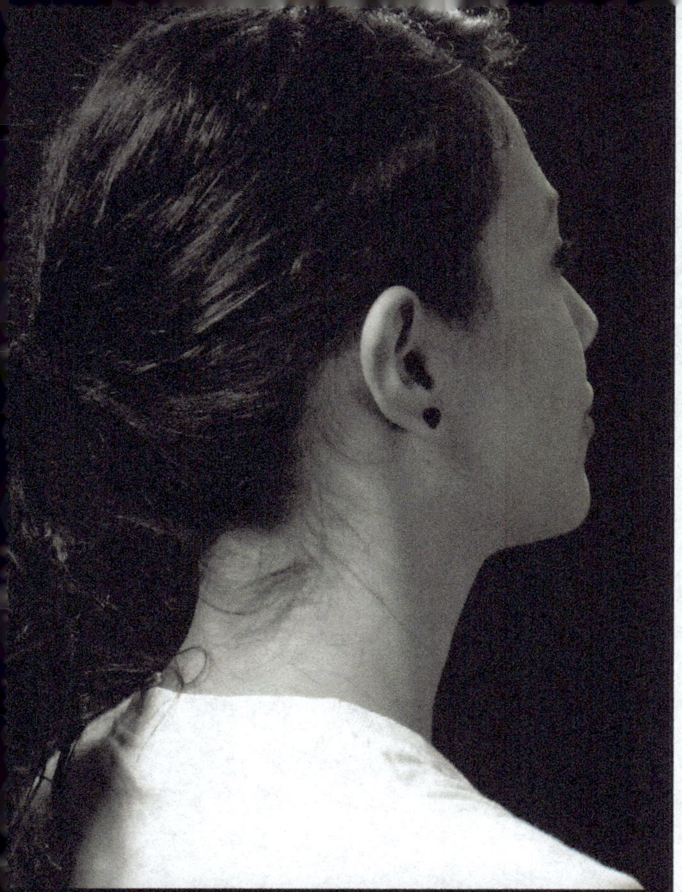

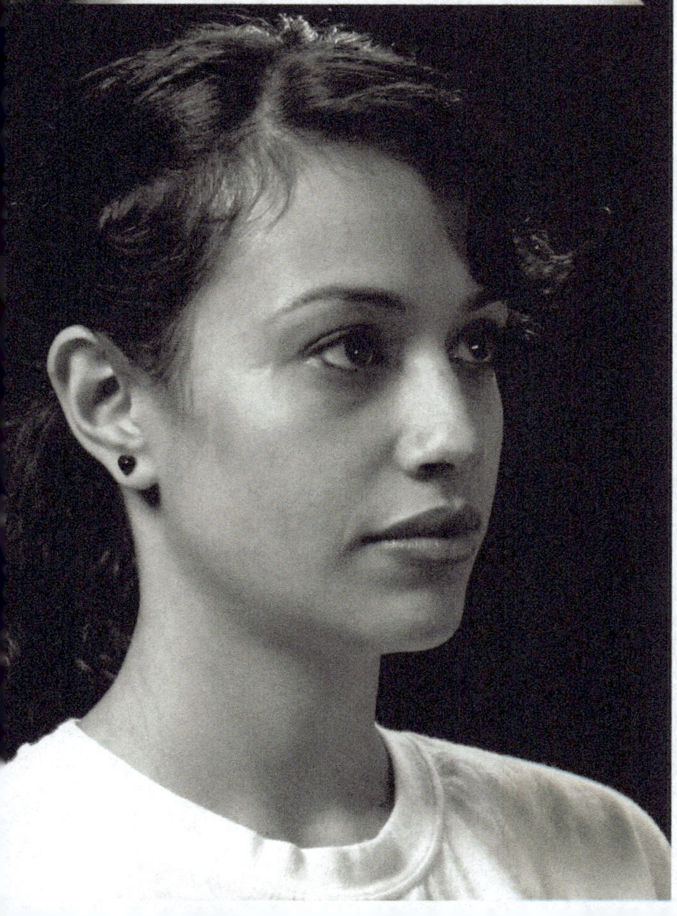

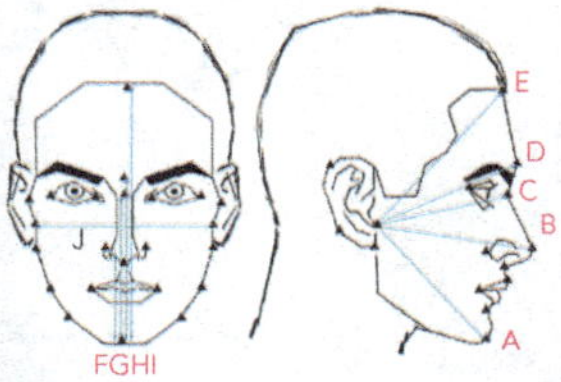


**Head measurements (in):**

A: 5 3/8
B: 4 7/8
C: 4 3/8
D: 5
E: 5 1/2
F: 3 1/4
G: 4 3/8
H: 4 7/8
I: 7 1/8
J: 5 5/8

MAP REFERENCE:

41

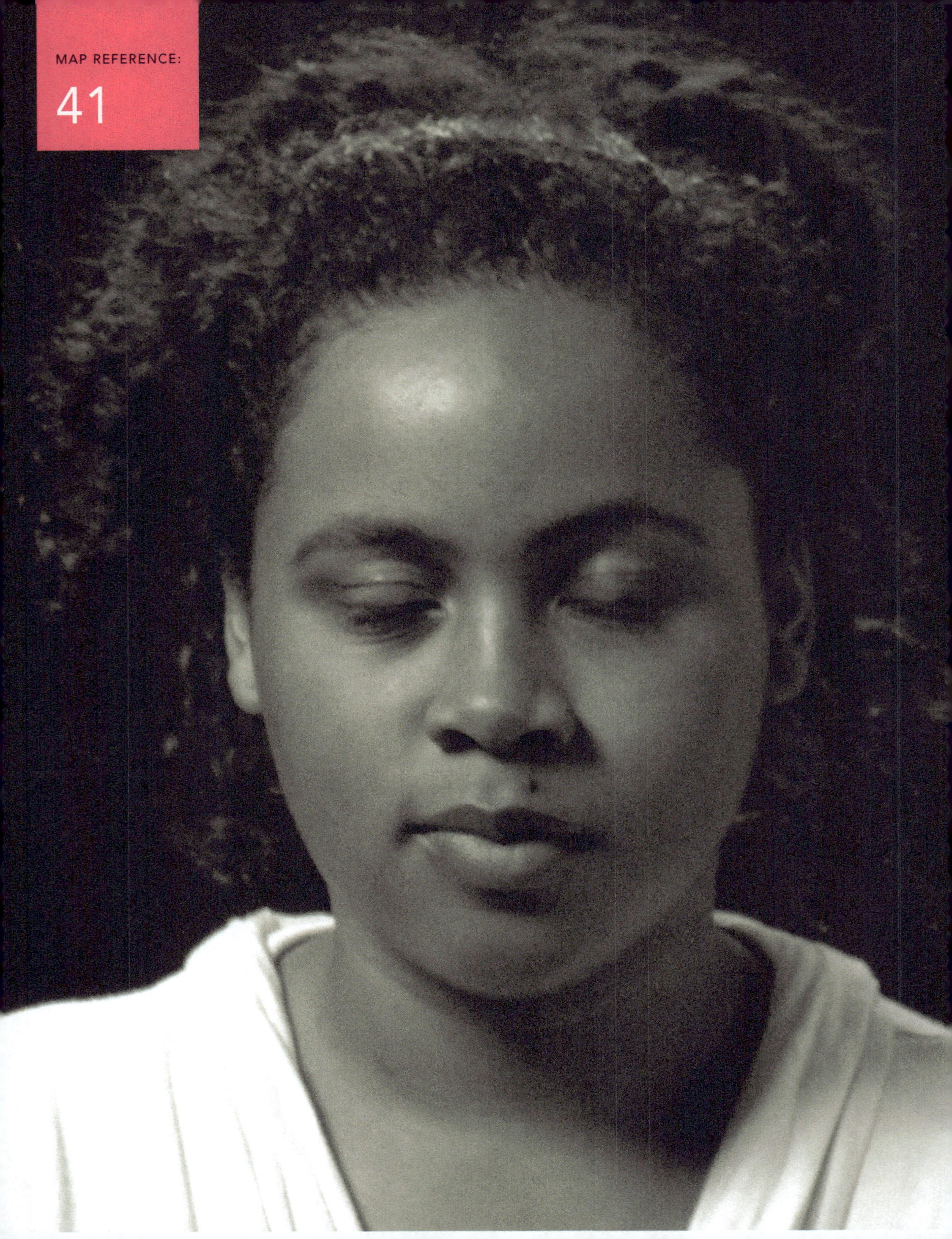

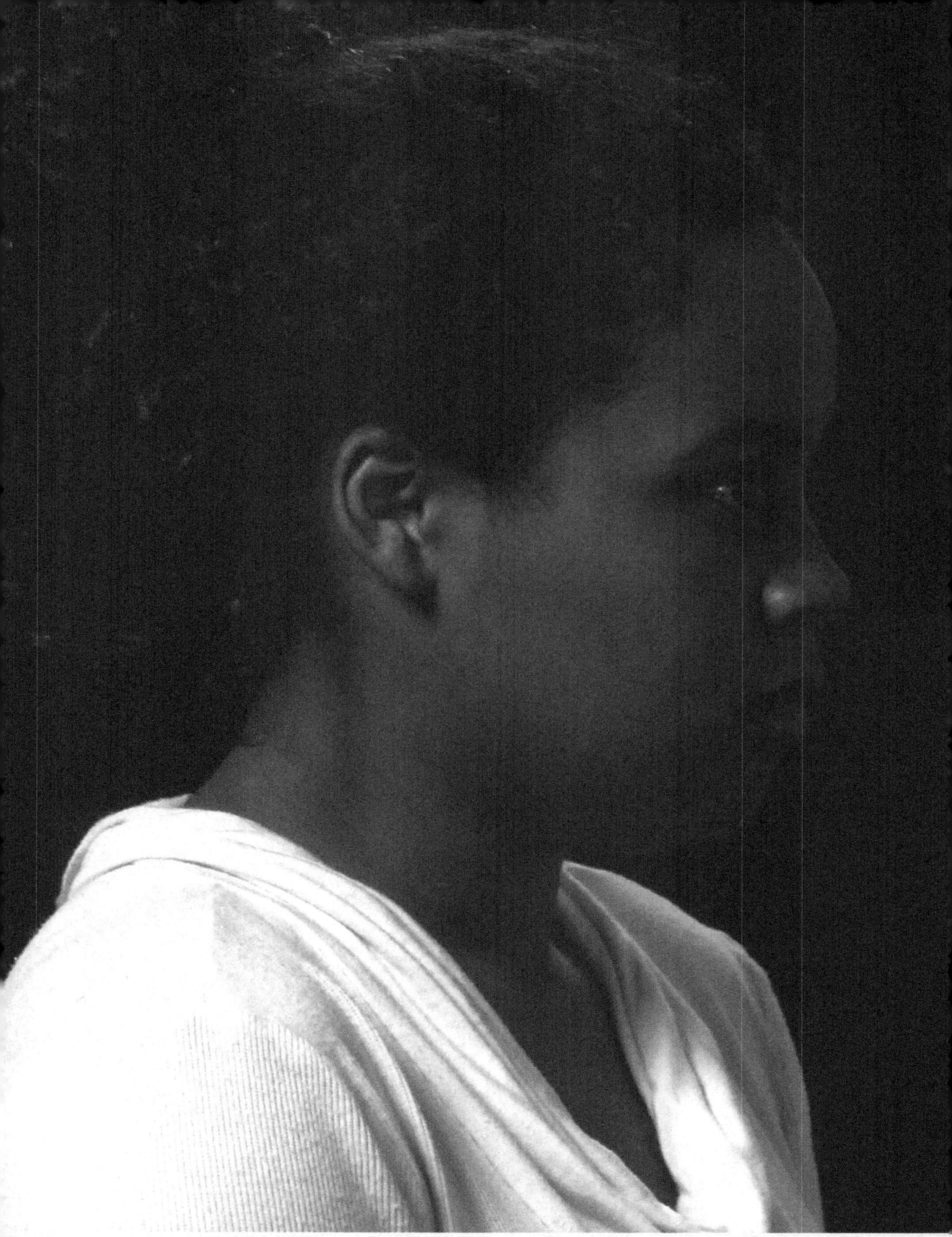

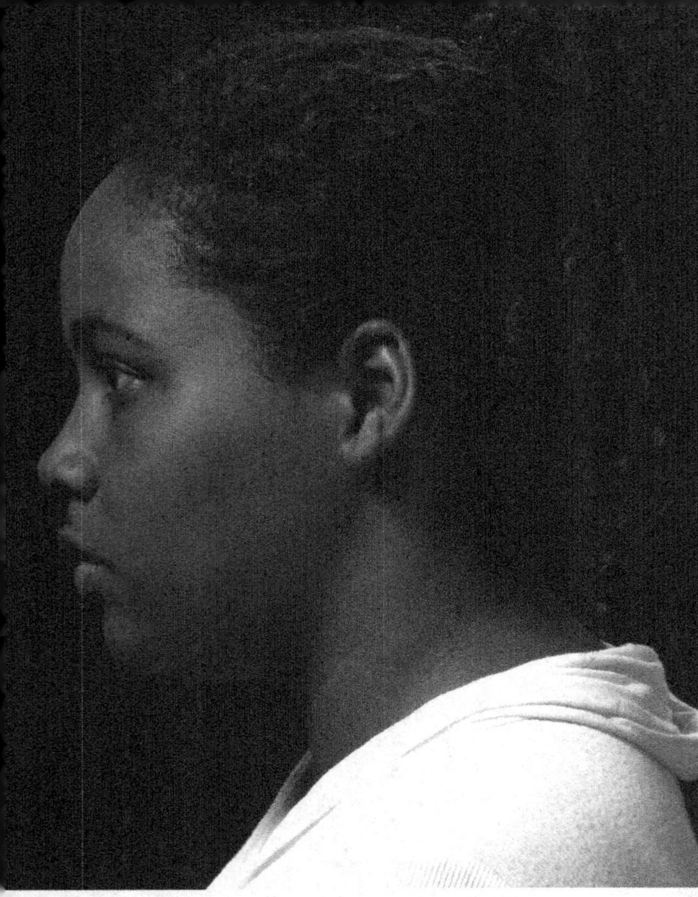

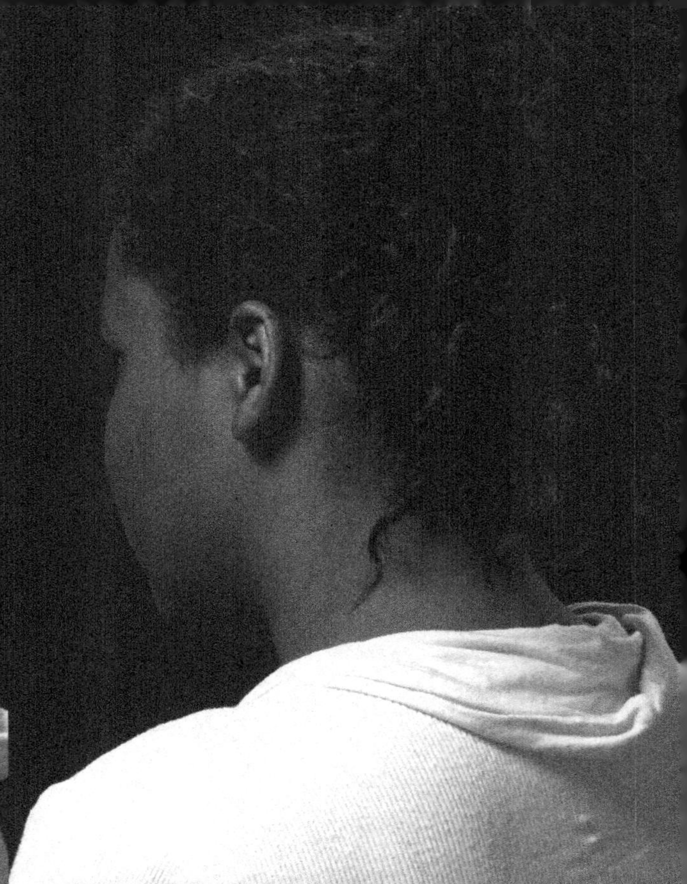

**Ethnicities claimed:**

Ethiopia, Mexico, Philippines, United States—Native American.

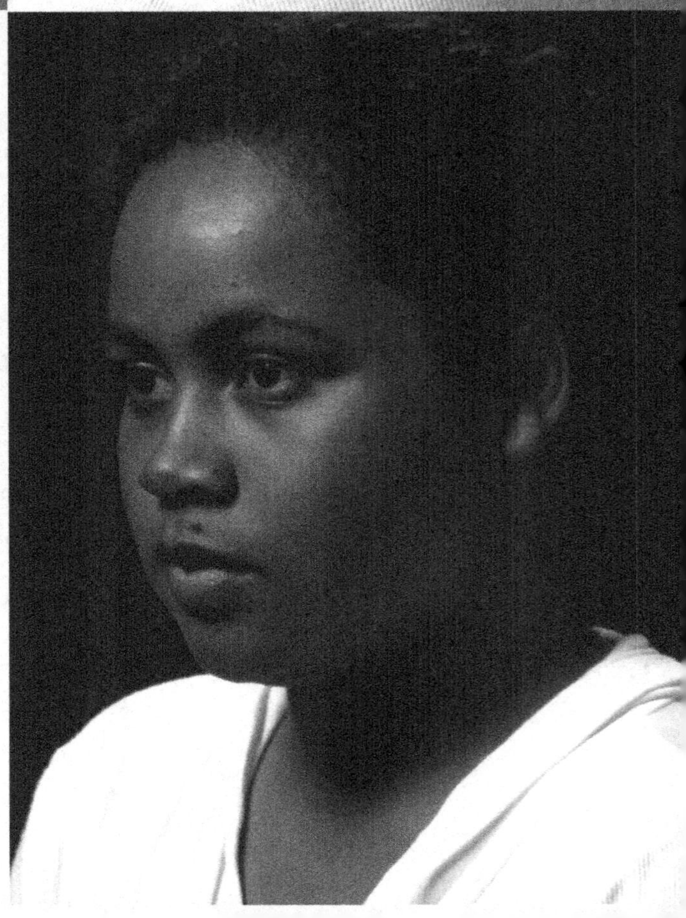

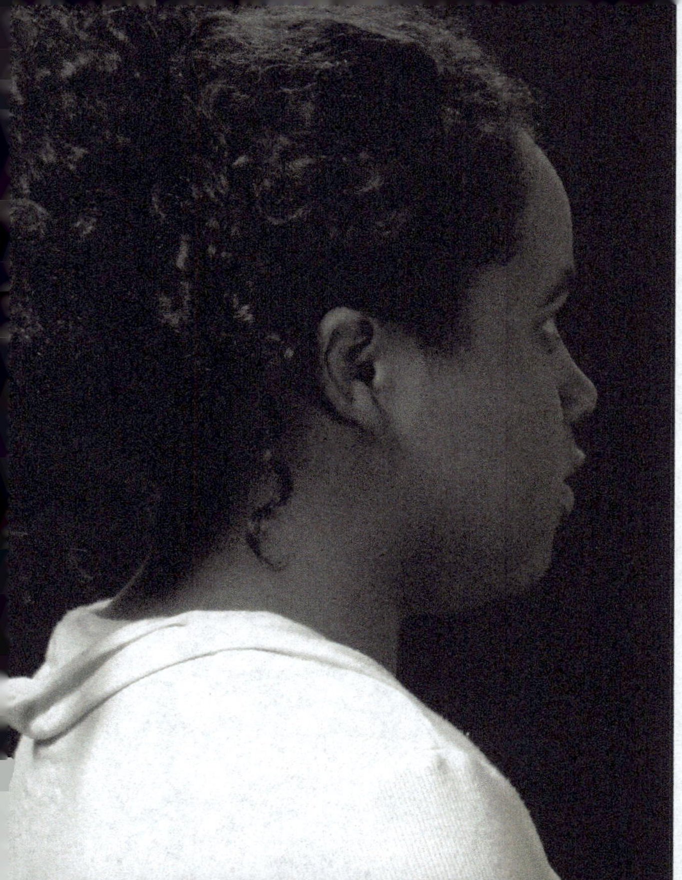

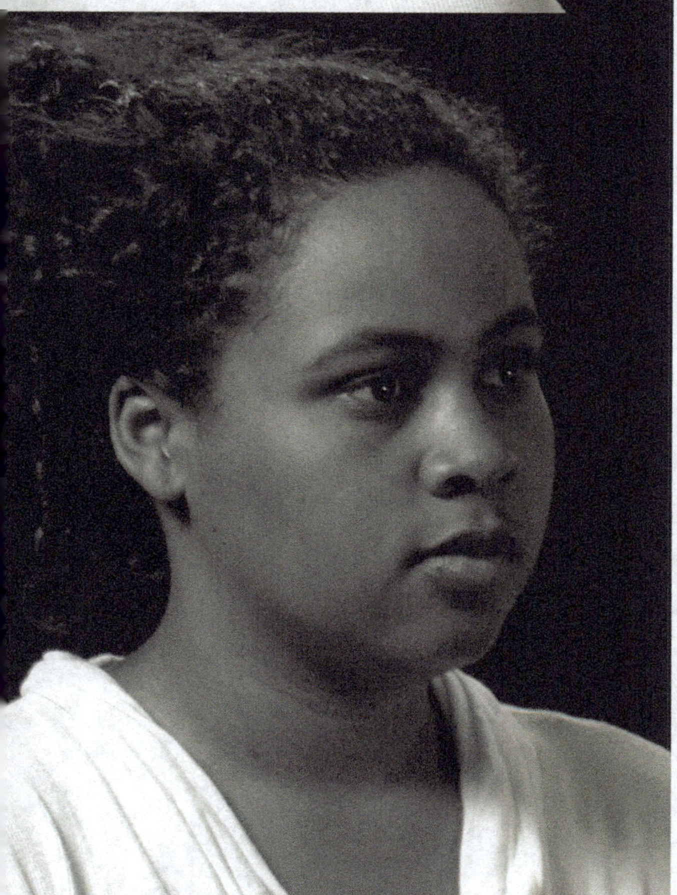

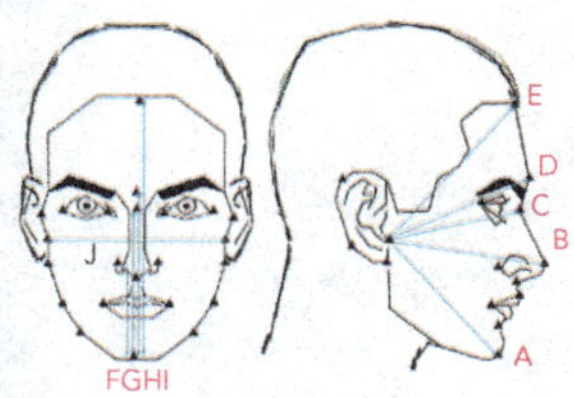


**Head measurements (in):**

A: 5 1/2
B: 5 1/2
C: 5
D: 5 3/8
E: 6 1/4
F: 3 3/8
G: 4 3/8
H: 5
I: 8
J: 5 7/8

MAP REFERENCE:

43

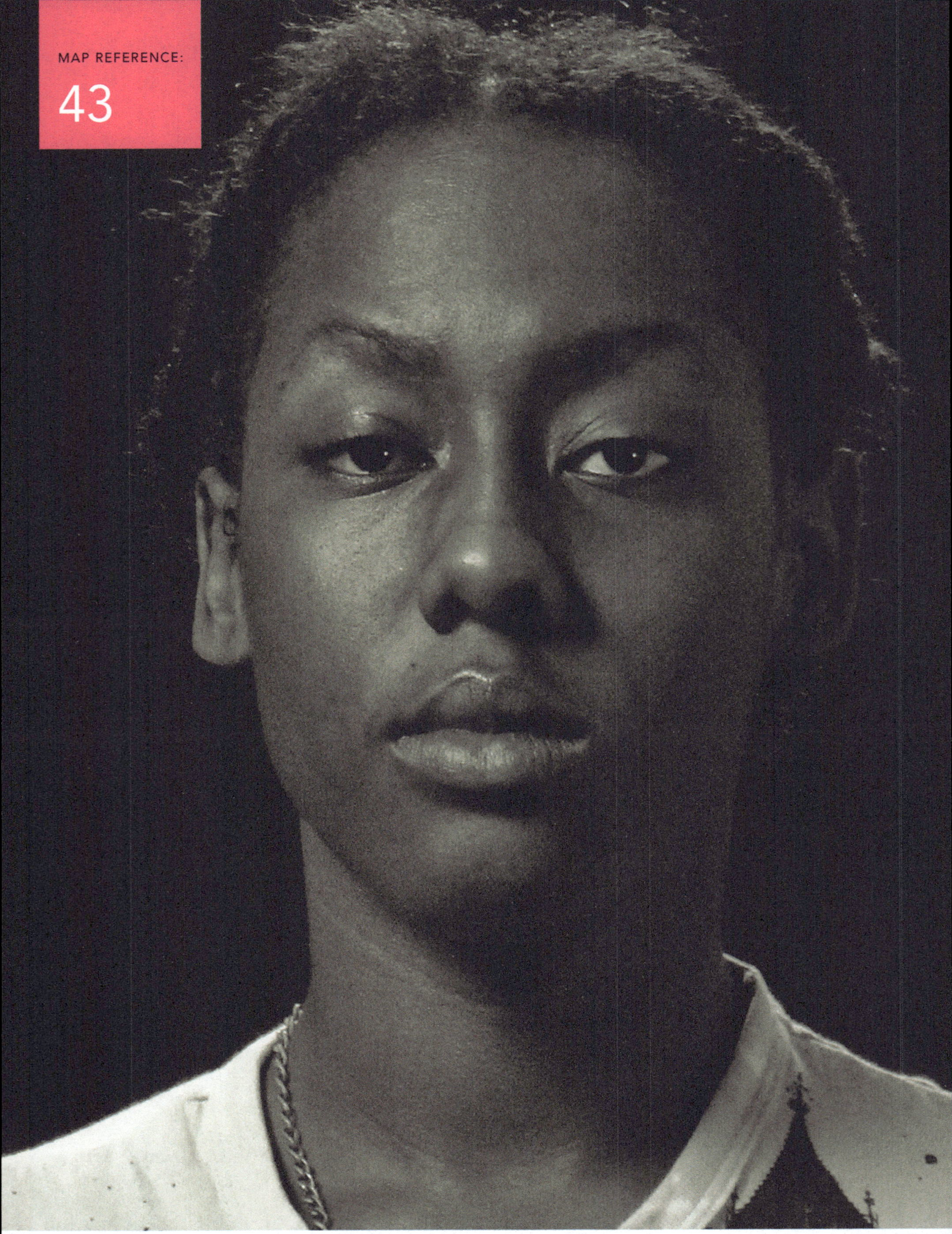

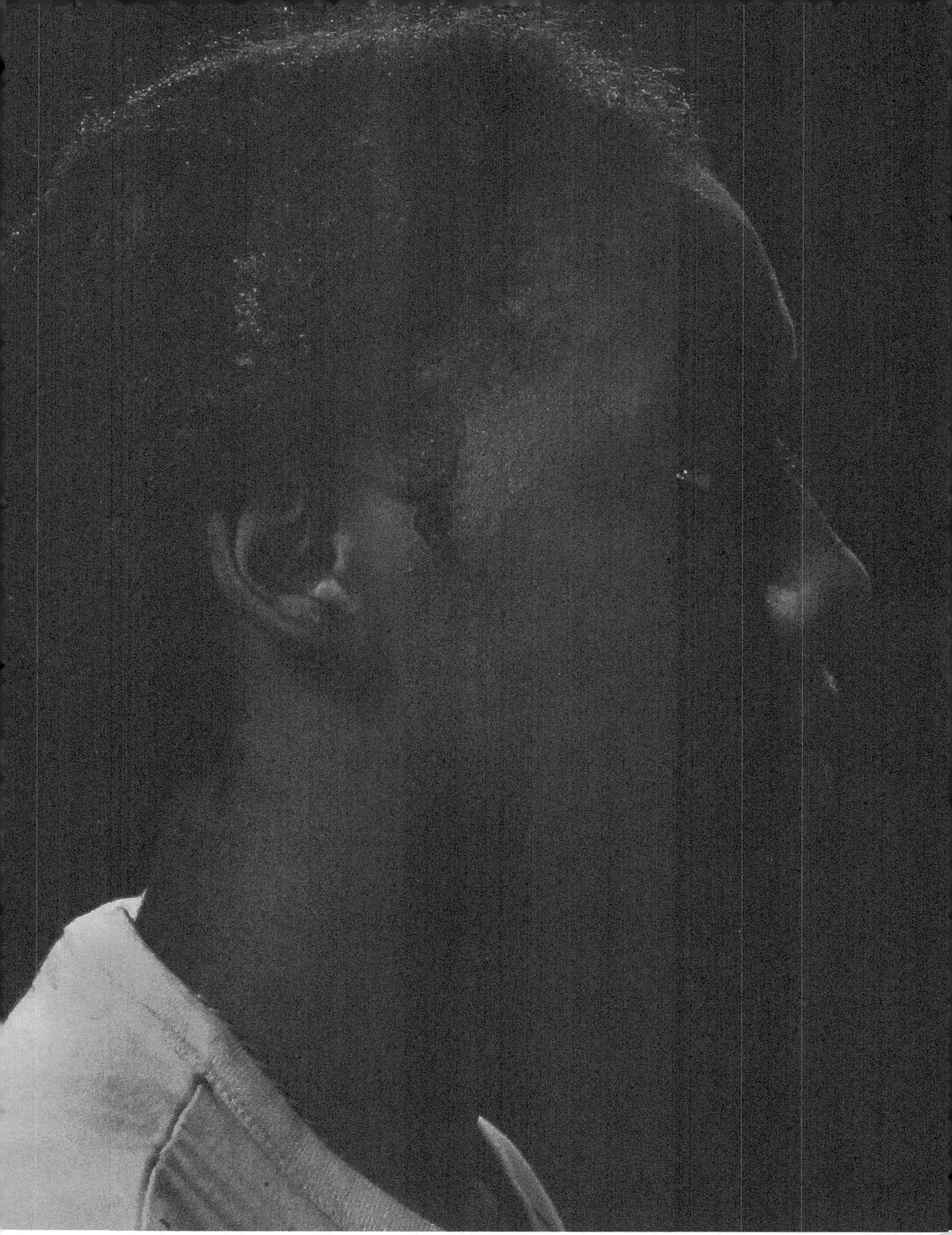

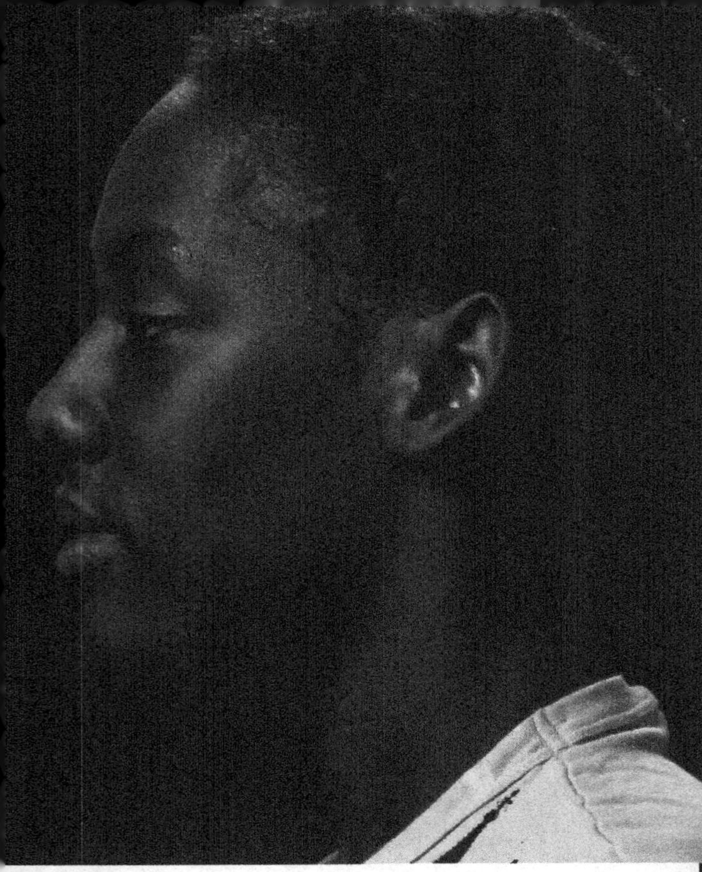

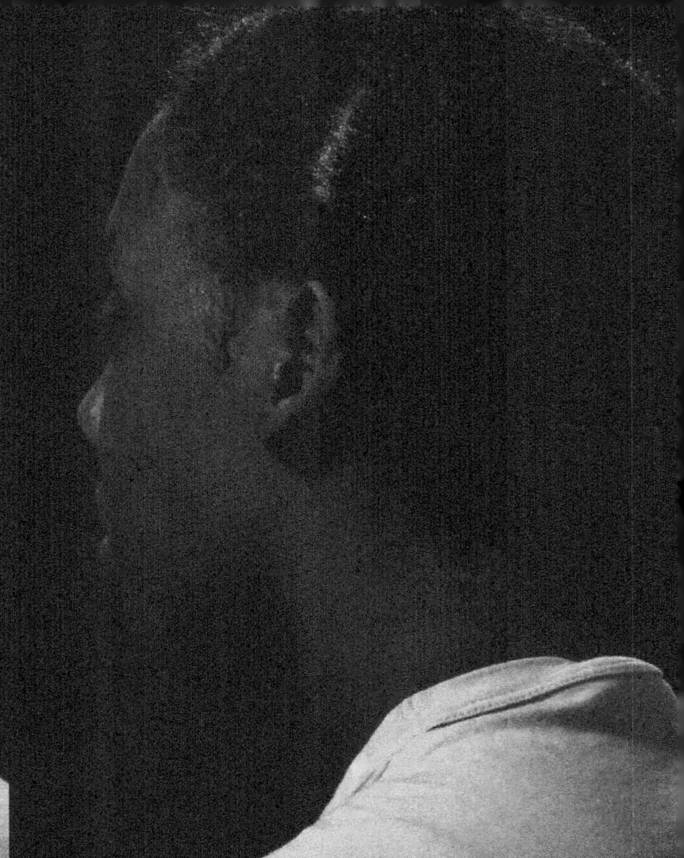

**Ethnicities claimed:**

African American, American Indian.

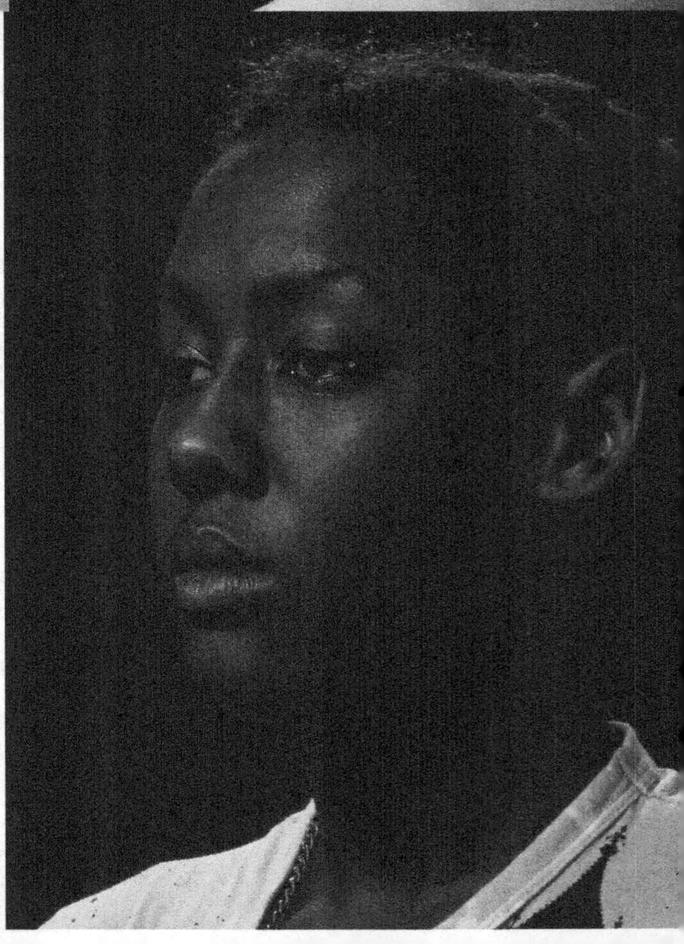

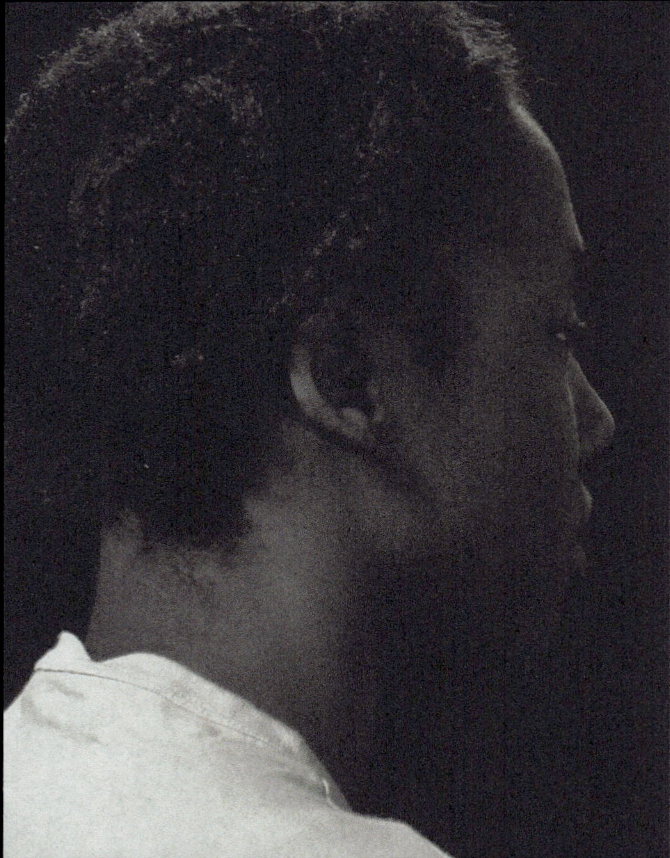

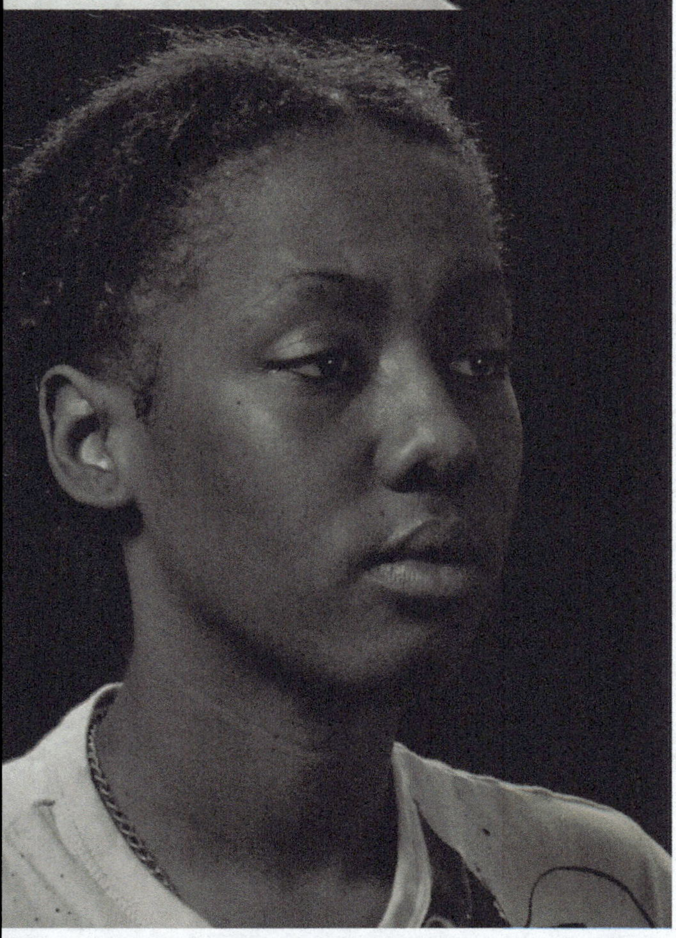

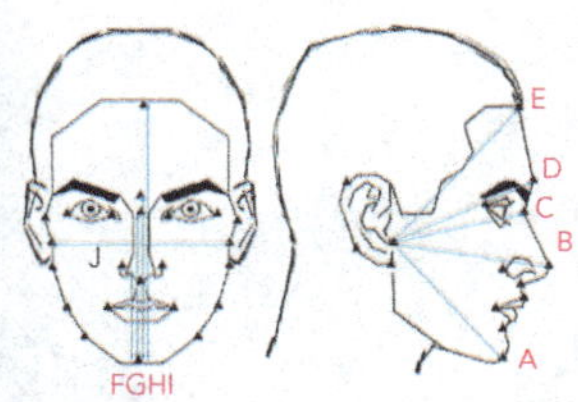


**Head measurements (in):**

A: 5 1/4
B: 5 1/8
C: 5
D: 5 1/4
E: 5 7/8
F: 3 1/8
G: 4 1/4
H: 5 1/4
I: 7 7/8
J: 5 7/8

MAP REFERENCE:

44

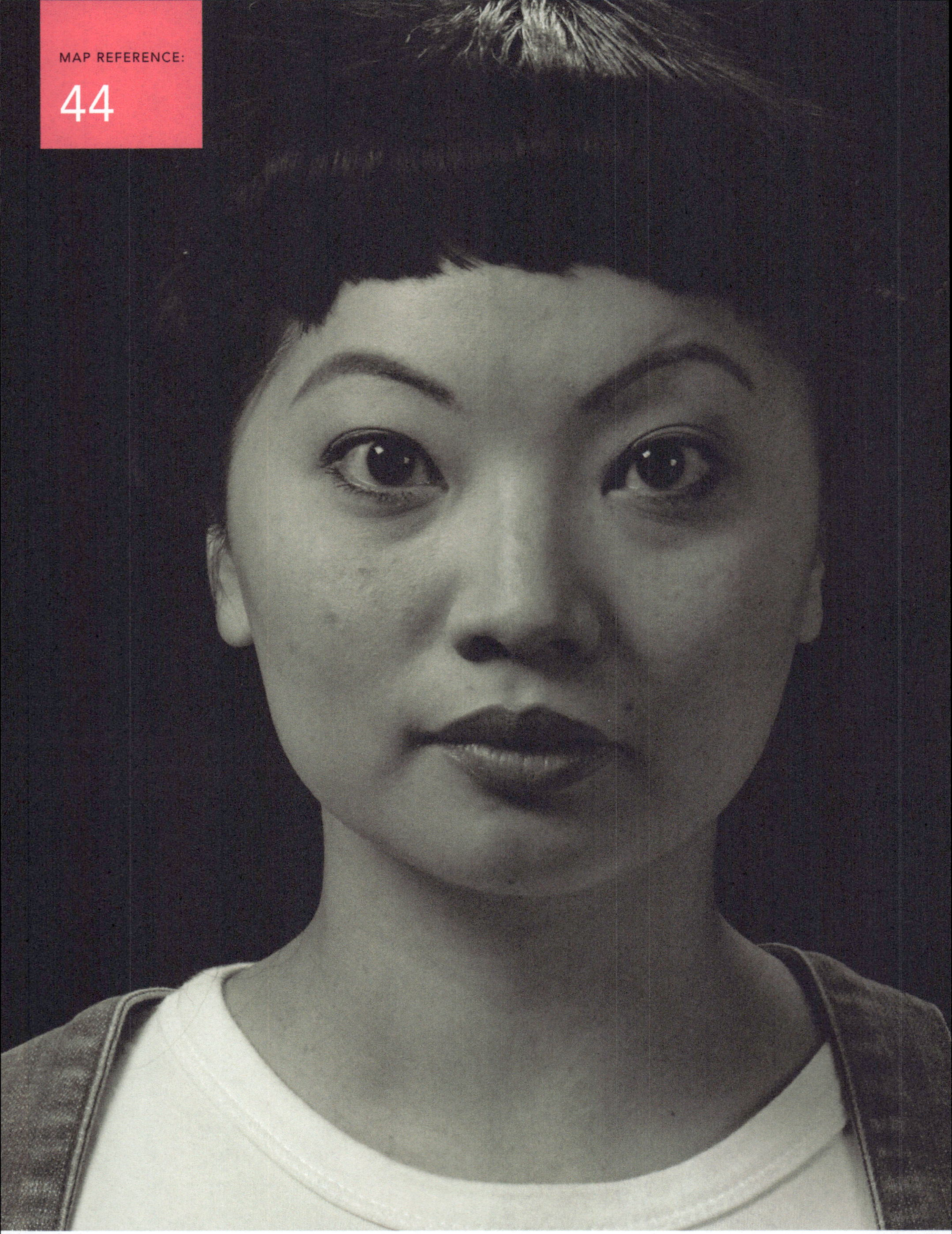

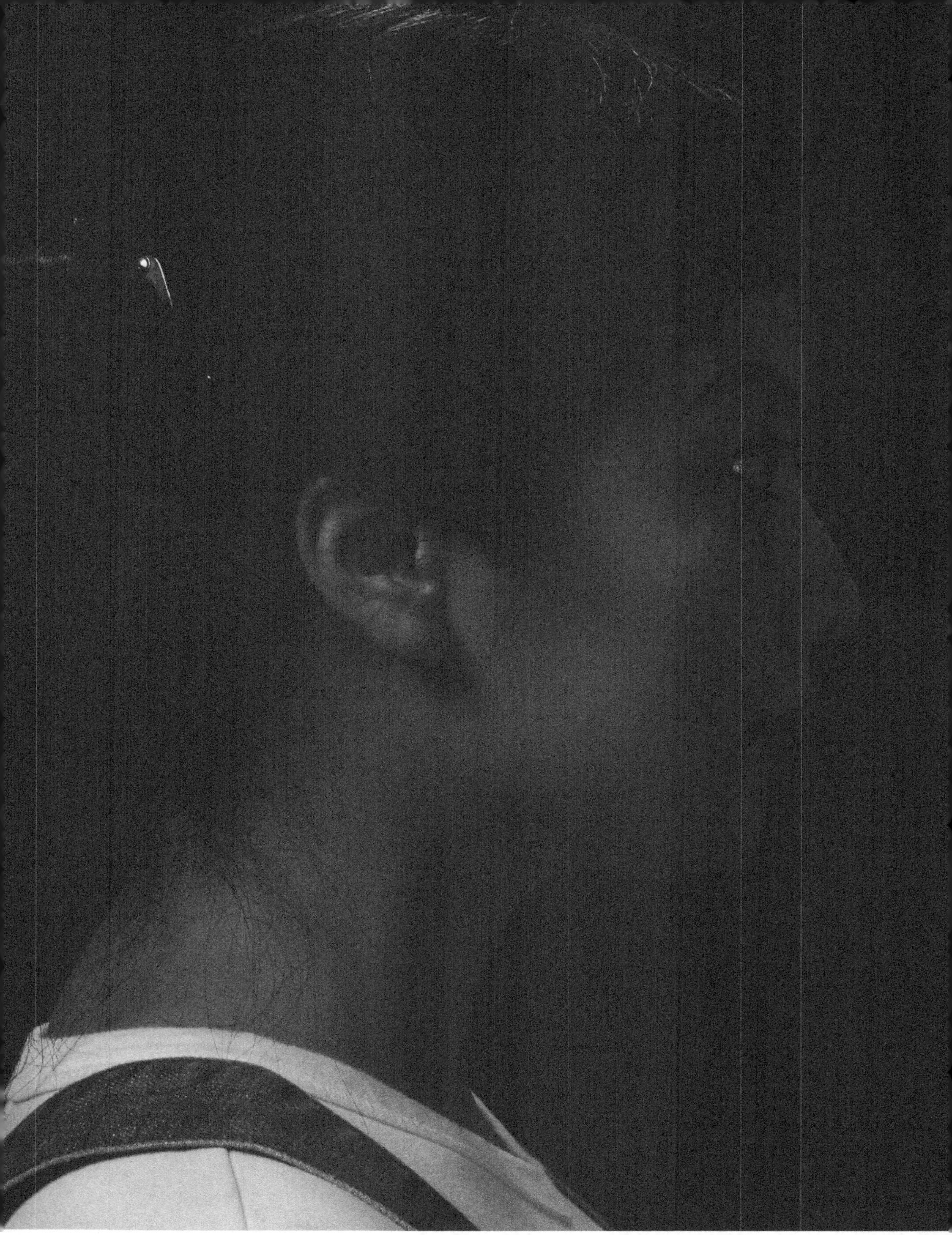

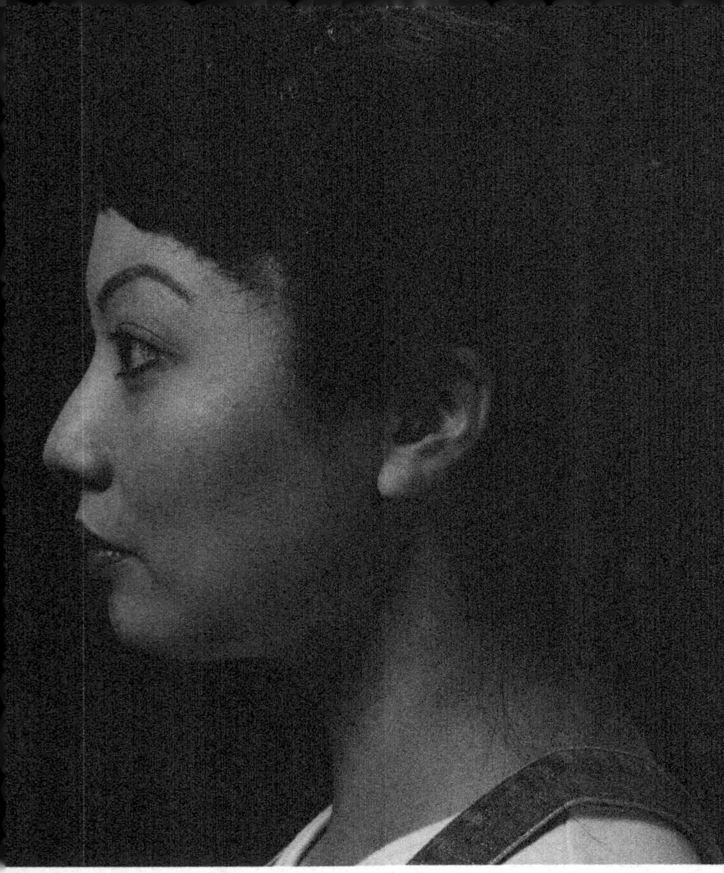

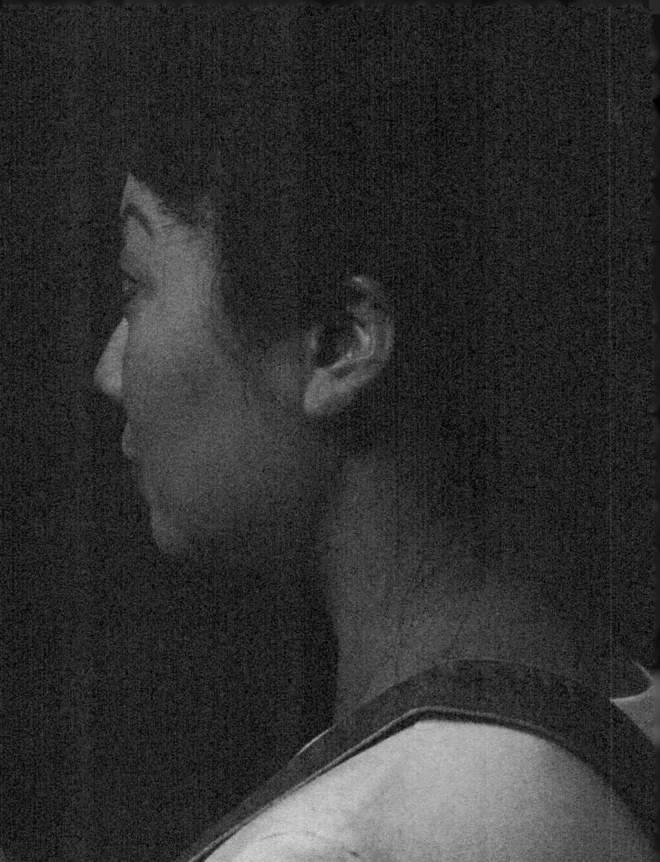

**Ethnicities claimed:**

China.

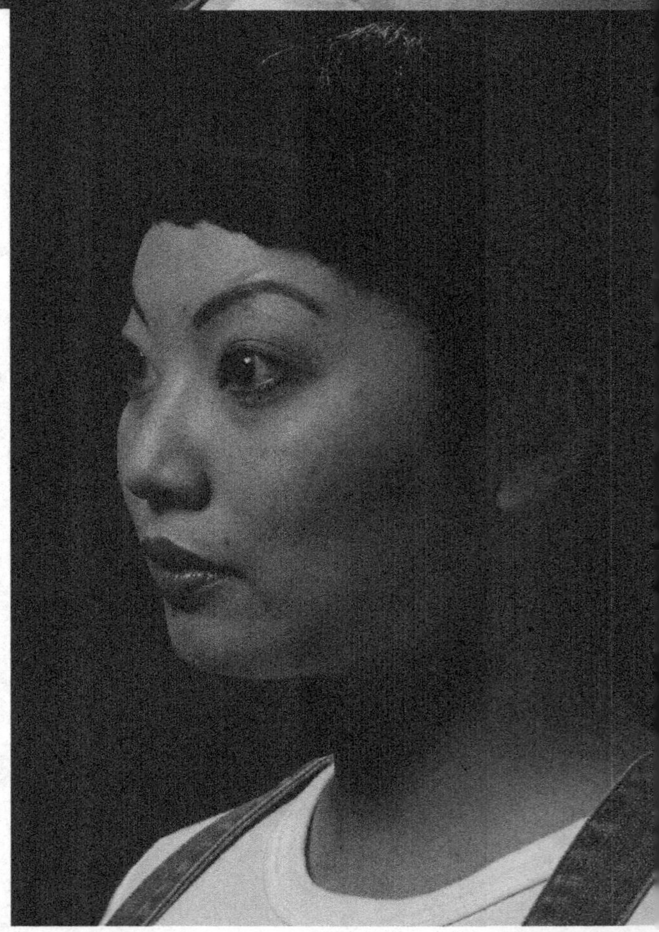

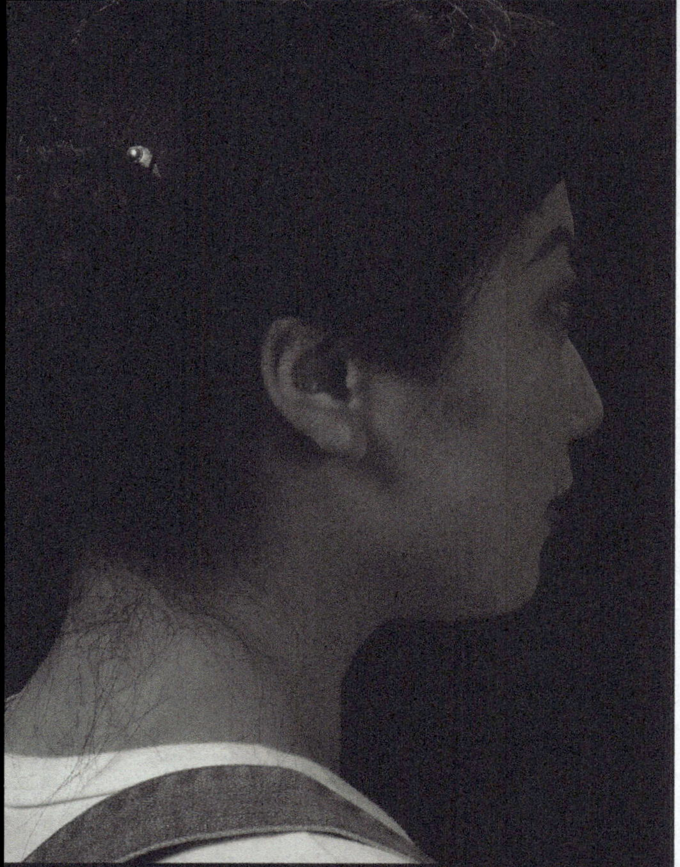

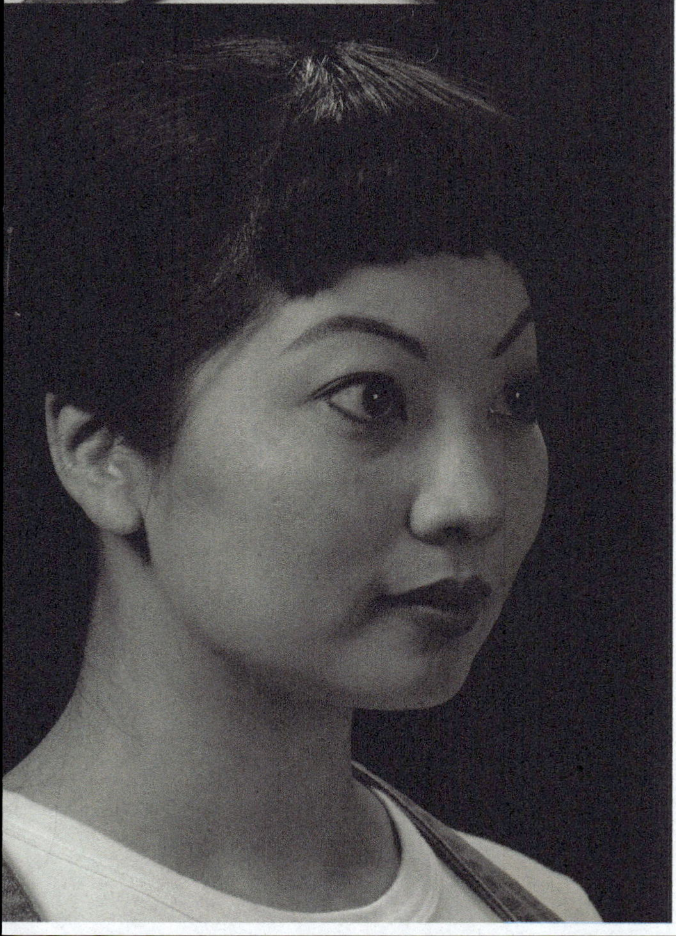

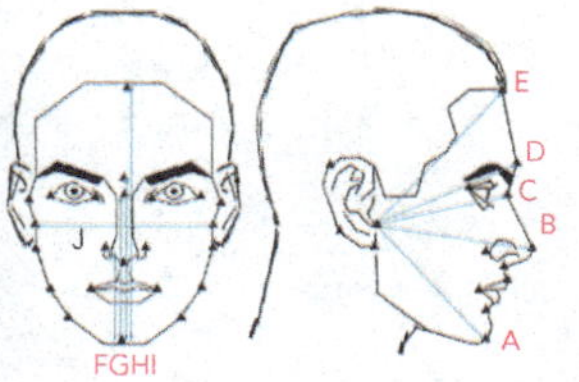


**Head measurements (in):**

A: 5 1/4
B: 5 1/2
C: 5 1/8
D: 5 3/8
E: 5 7/8
F: 3 1/4
G: 4 1/8
H: 4 7/8
I: 6 3/4
J: 6 1/8

MAP REFERENCE:

48

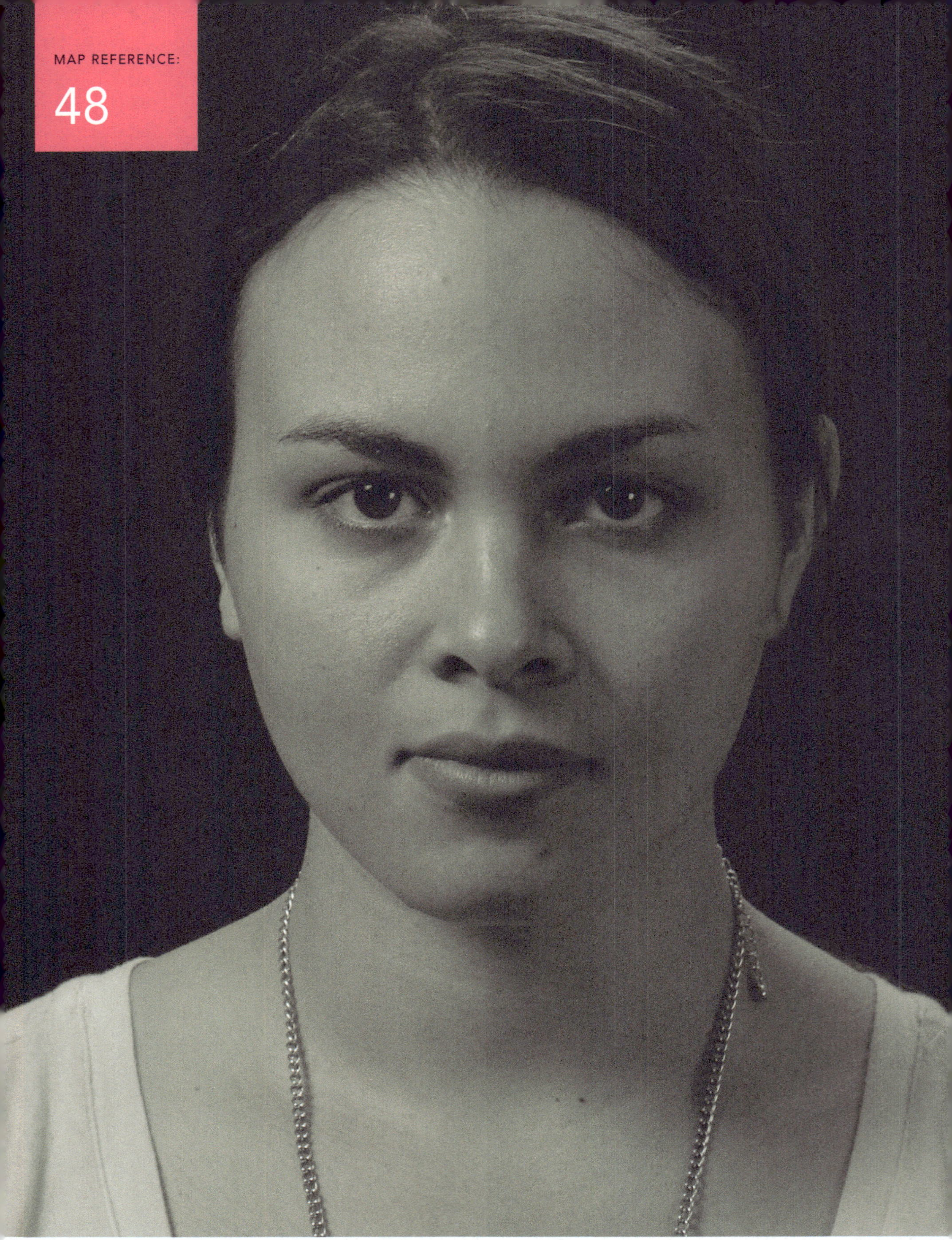

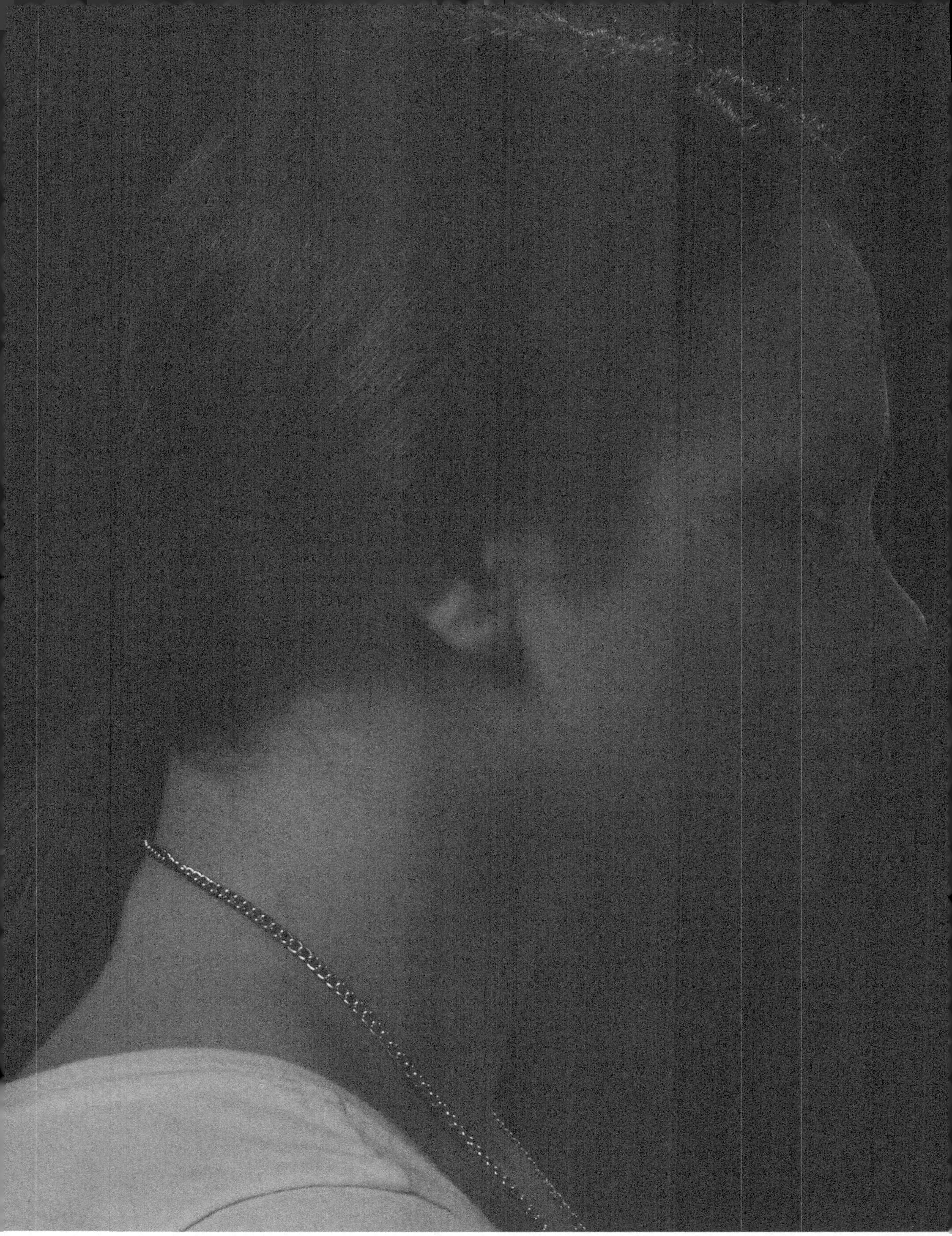

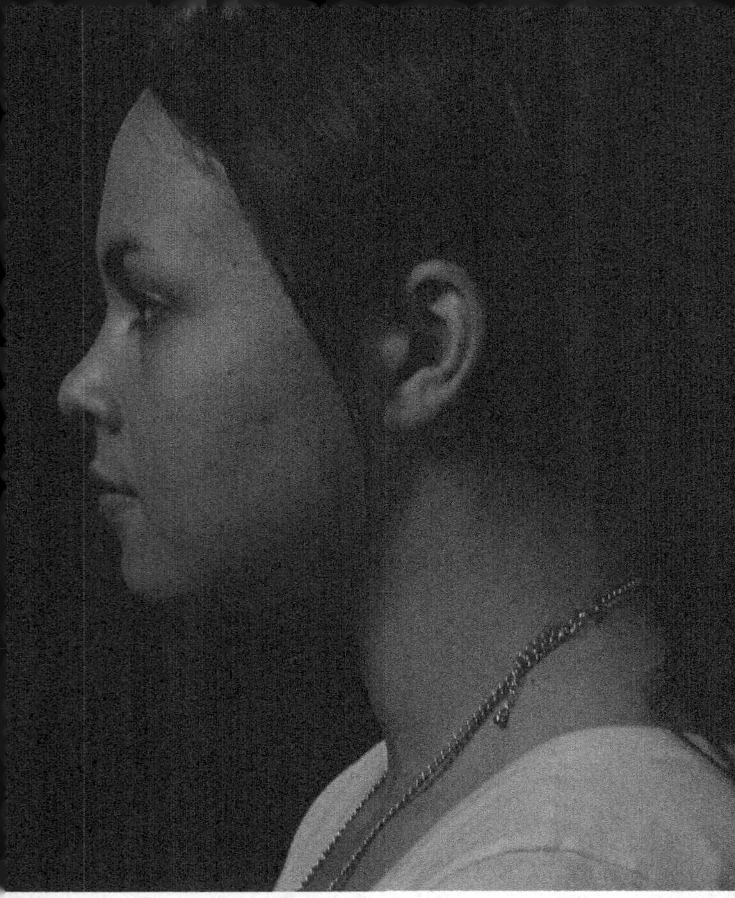

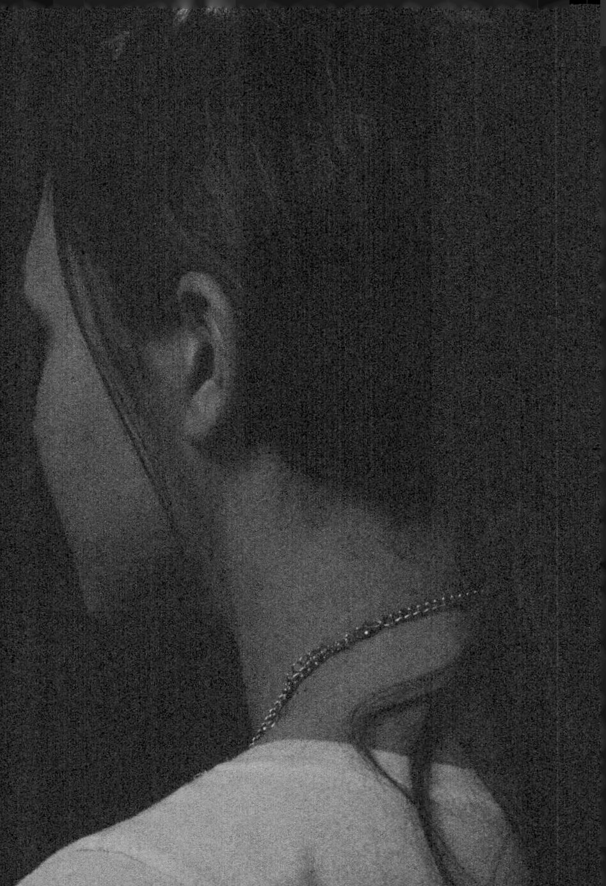

**Ethnicities claimed:**

United States—Navajo.

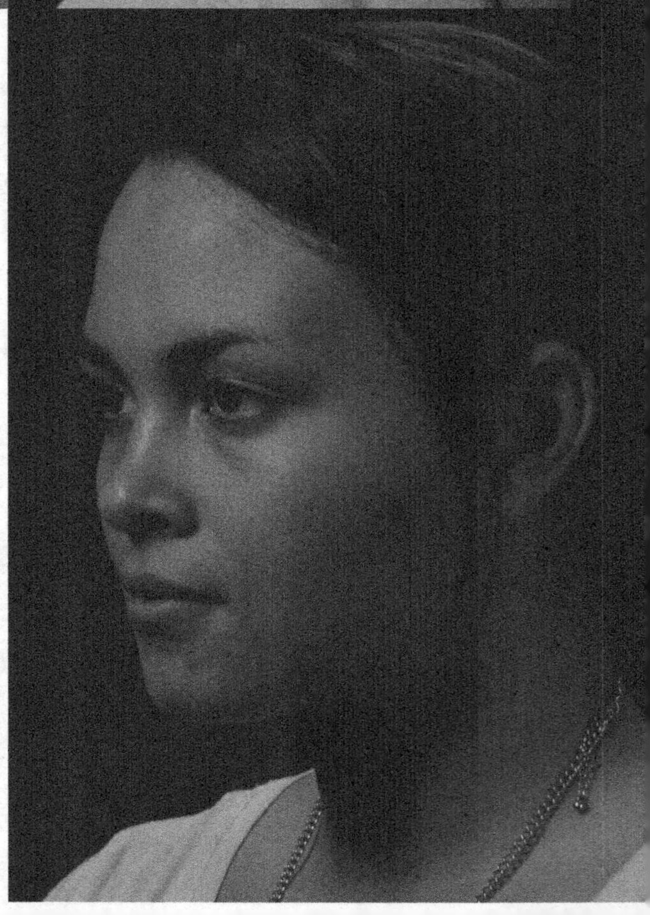

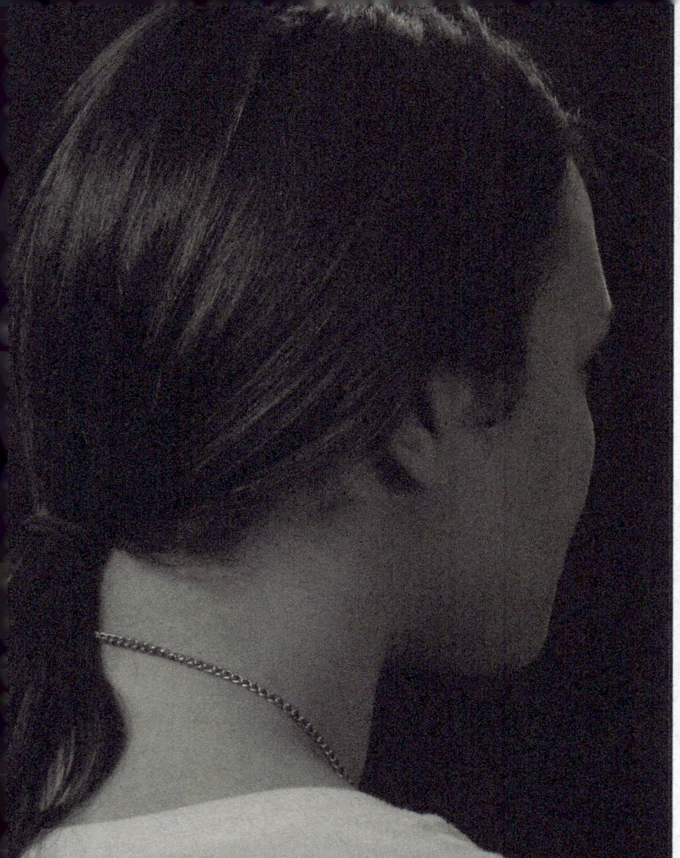

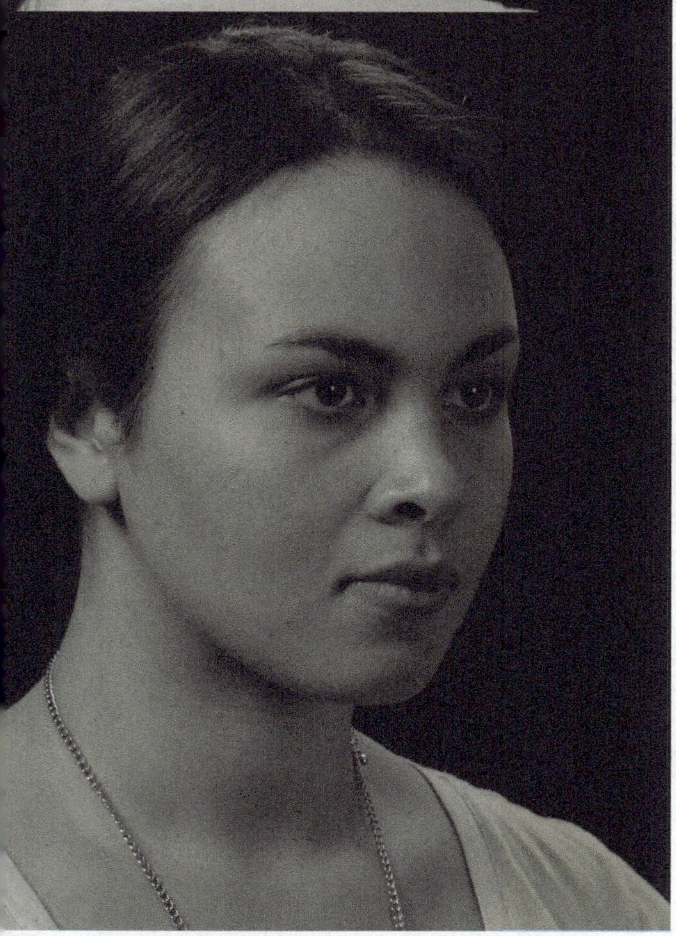

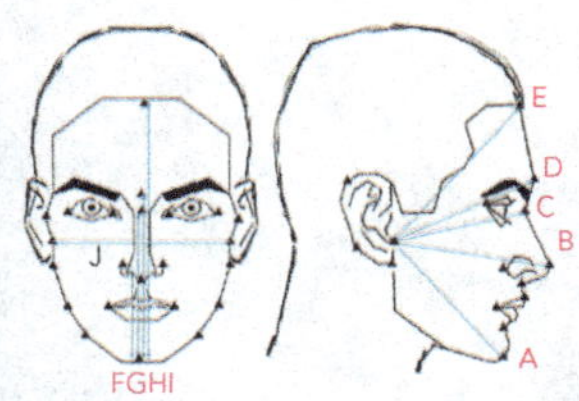


**Head measurements (in):**

A: 5 5/8
B: 5 1/2
C: 5 1/4
D: 5 3/4
E: 6 1/4
F: 3 1/2
G: 4 1/4
H: 4 7/8
I: 7 5/8
J: 5 7/8

MAP REFERENCE:

52

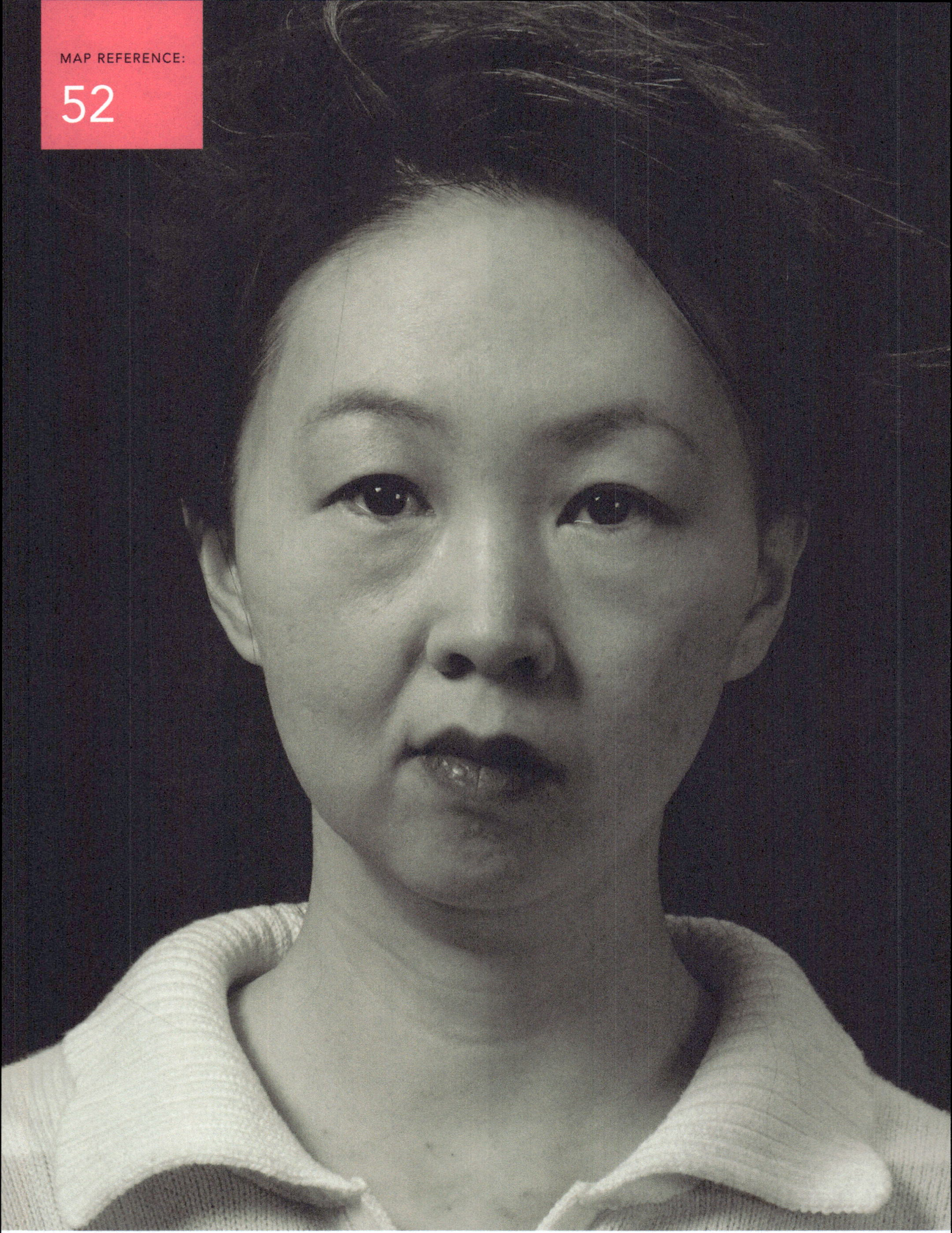

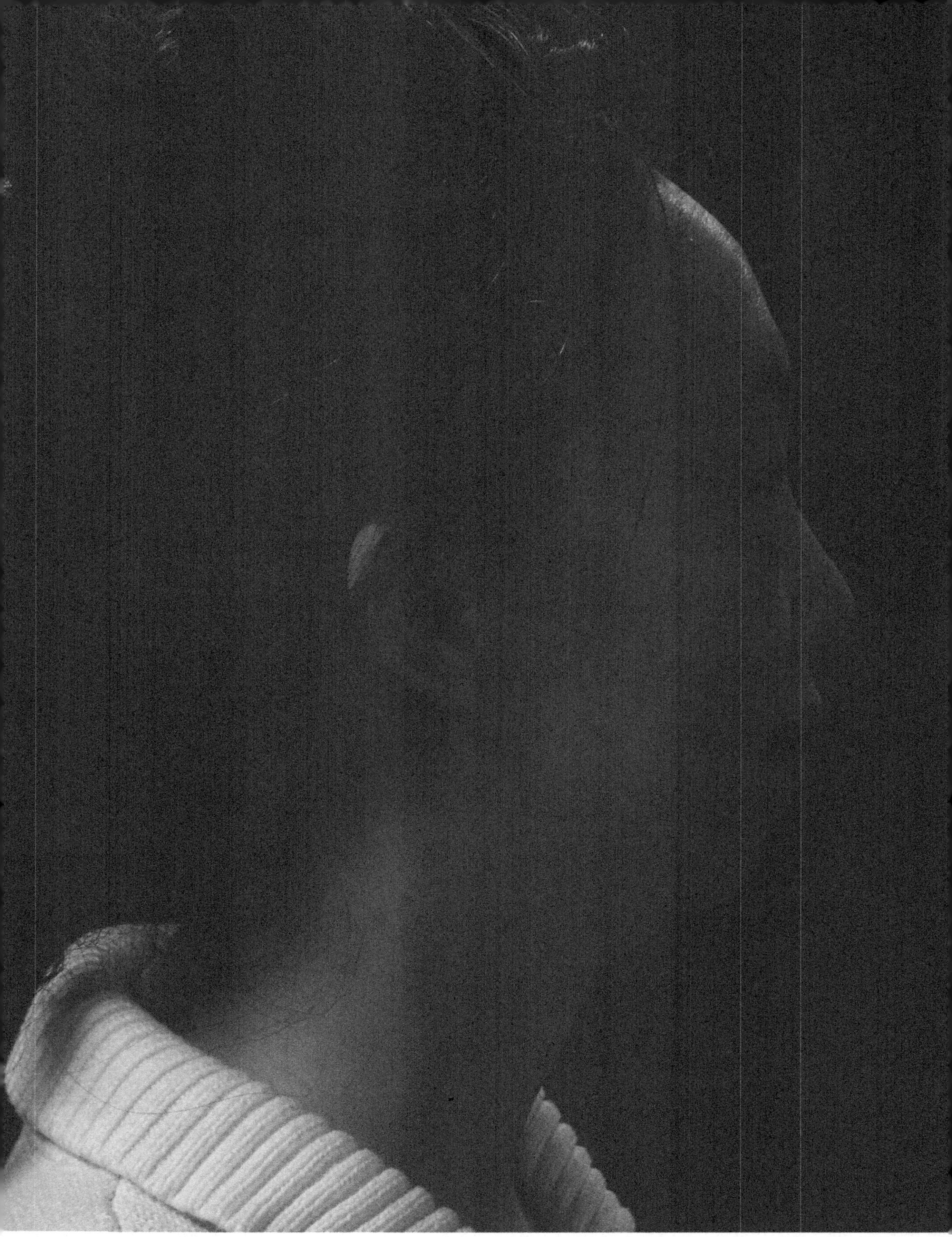

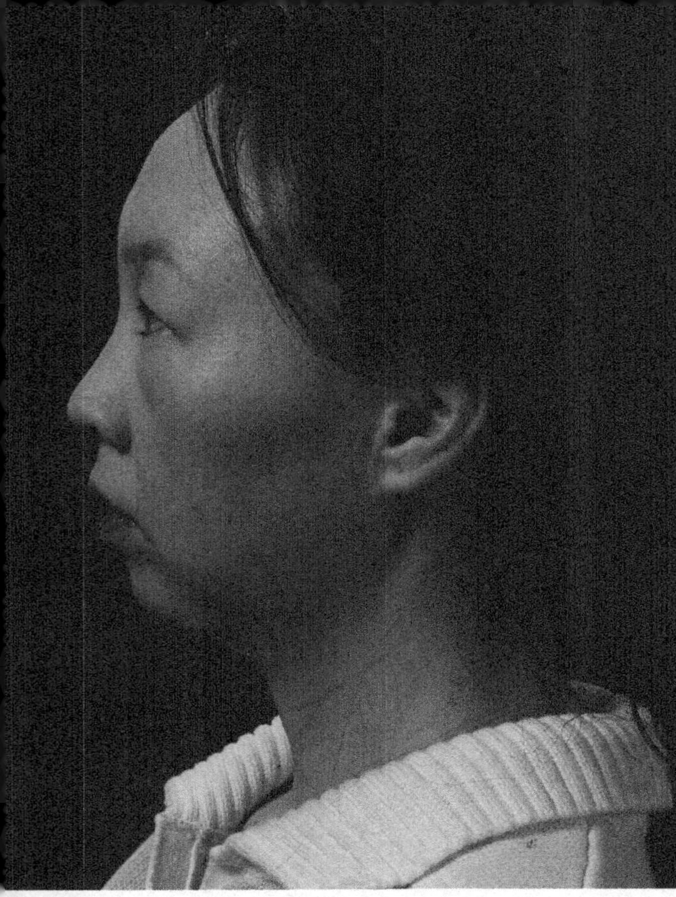

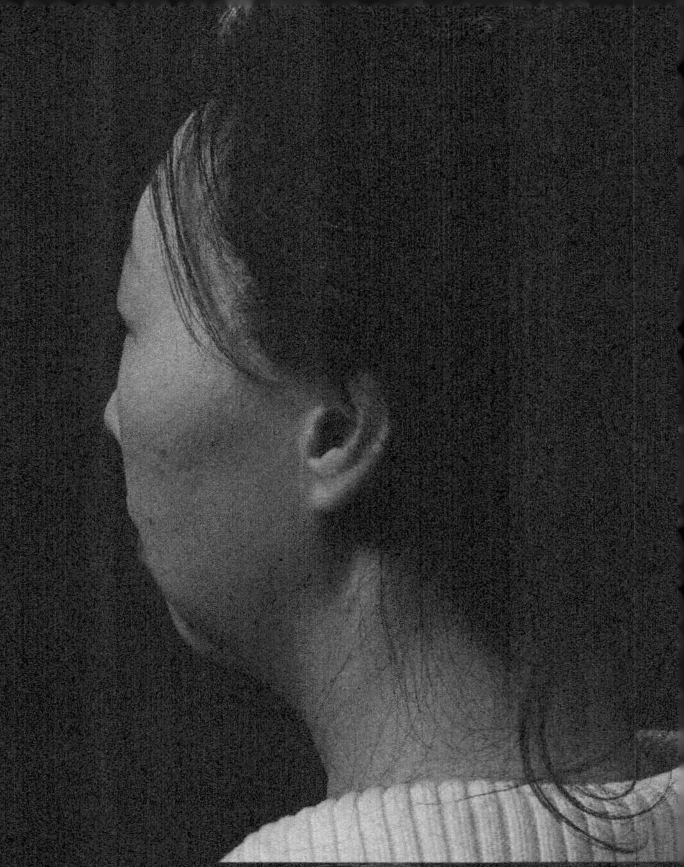

**Ethnicities claimed:**

Korea.

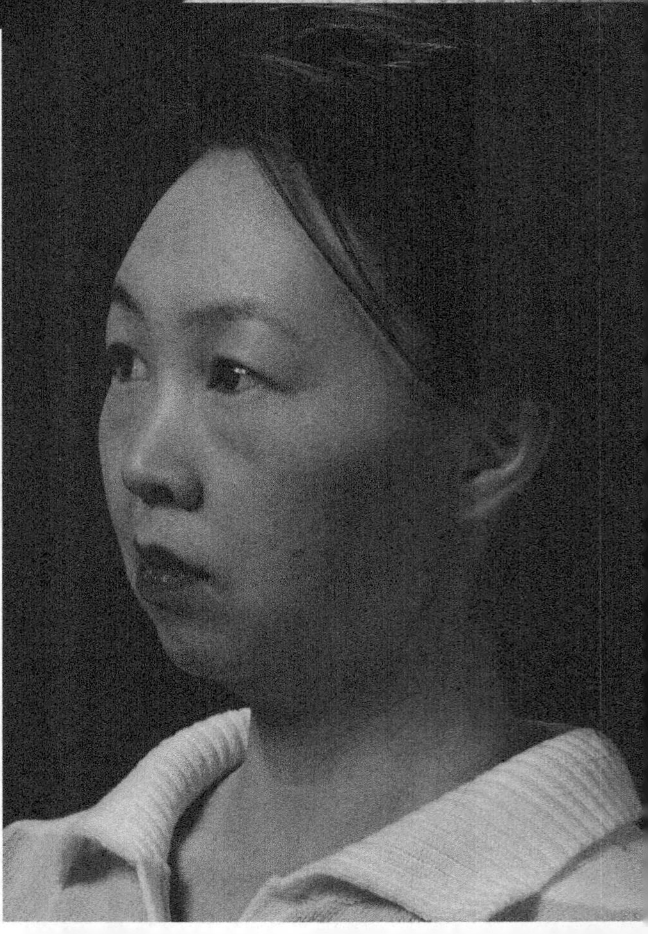

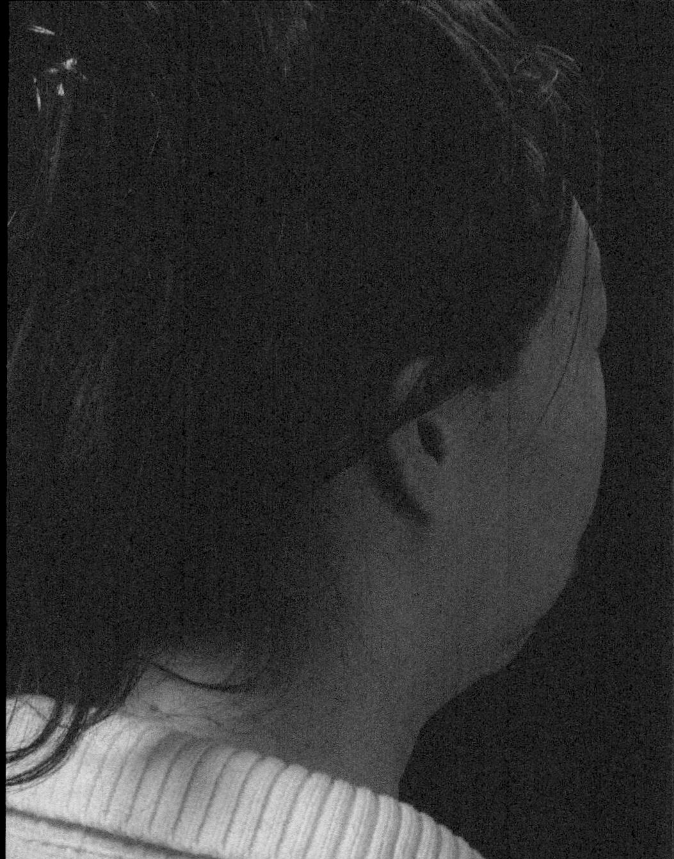

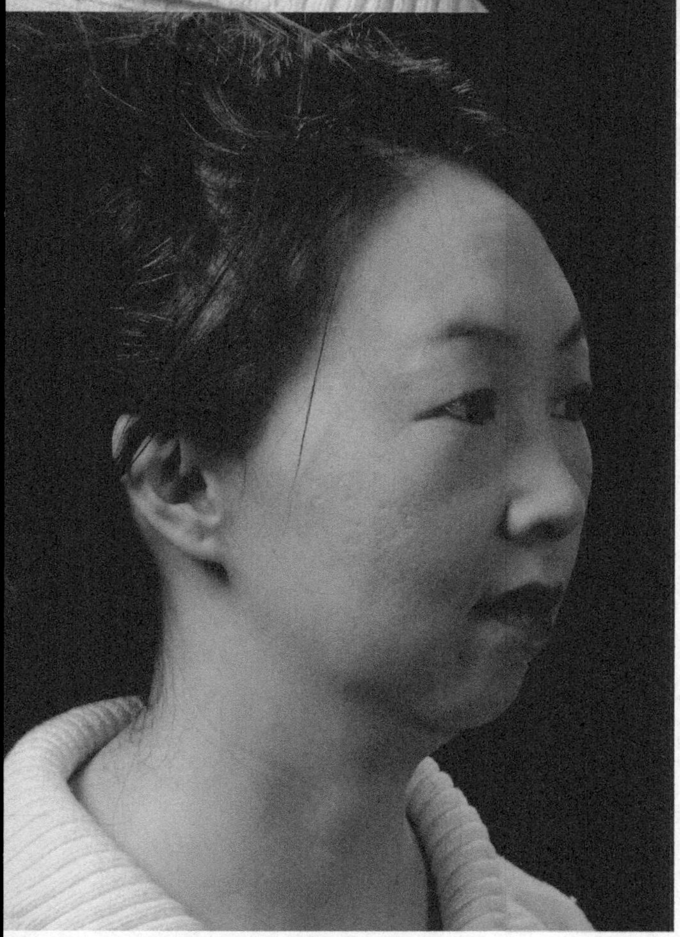

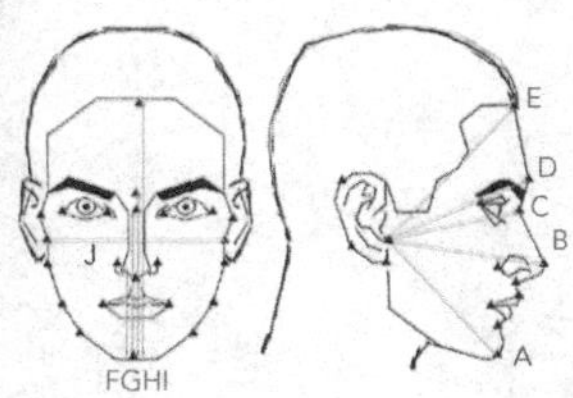


**Head measurements (in):**

A: 4 1/2
B: 4 1/4
C: 4 1/4
D: 4 5/8
E: 5 1/4
F: 3 1/4
G: 4 1/8
H: 4 5/8
I: 7
J: 5 3/8

MAP REFERENCE:

54

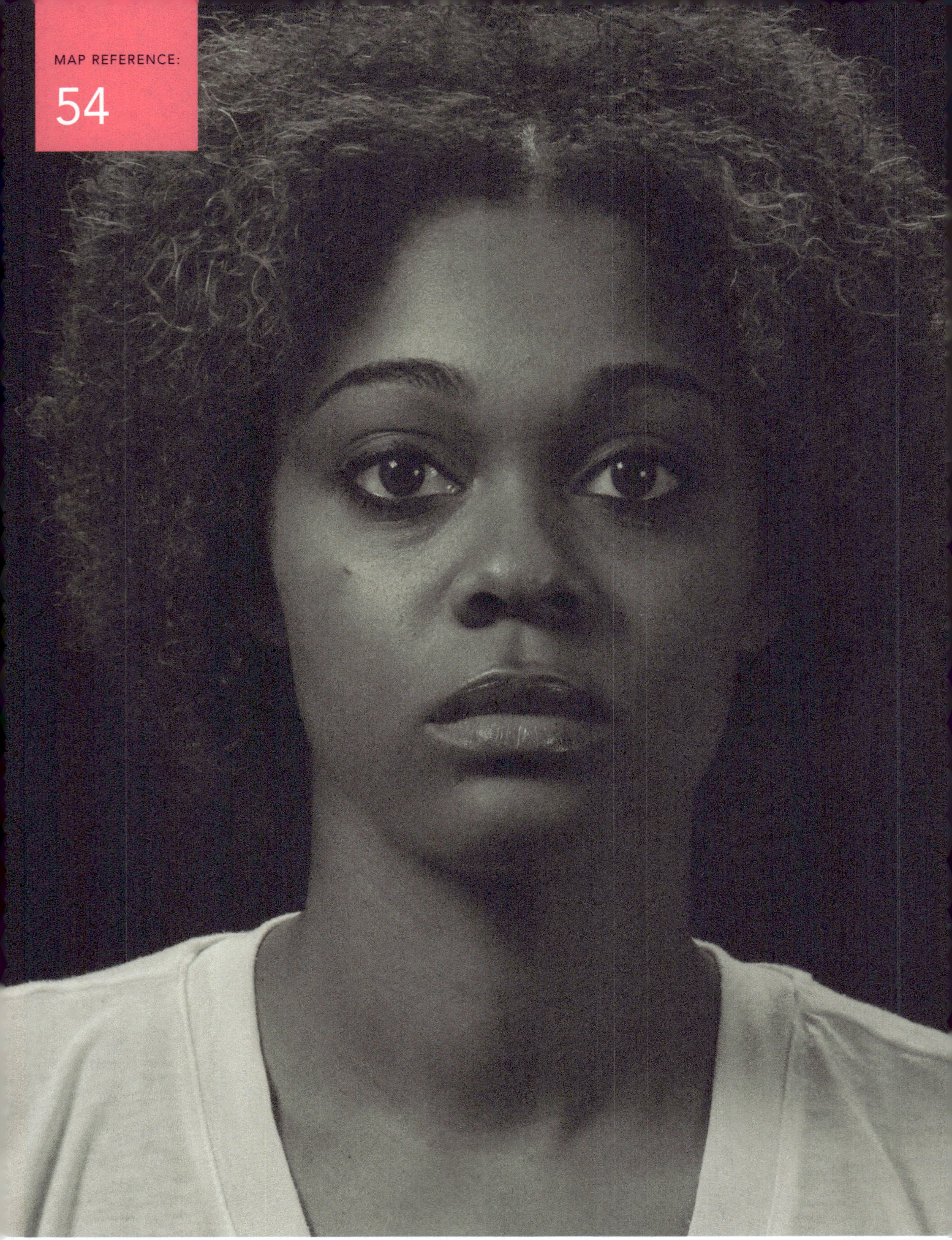

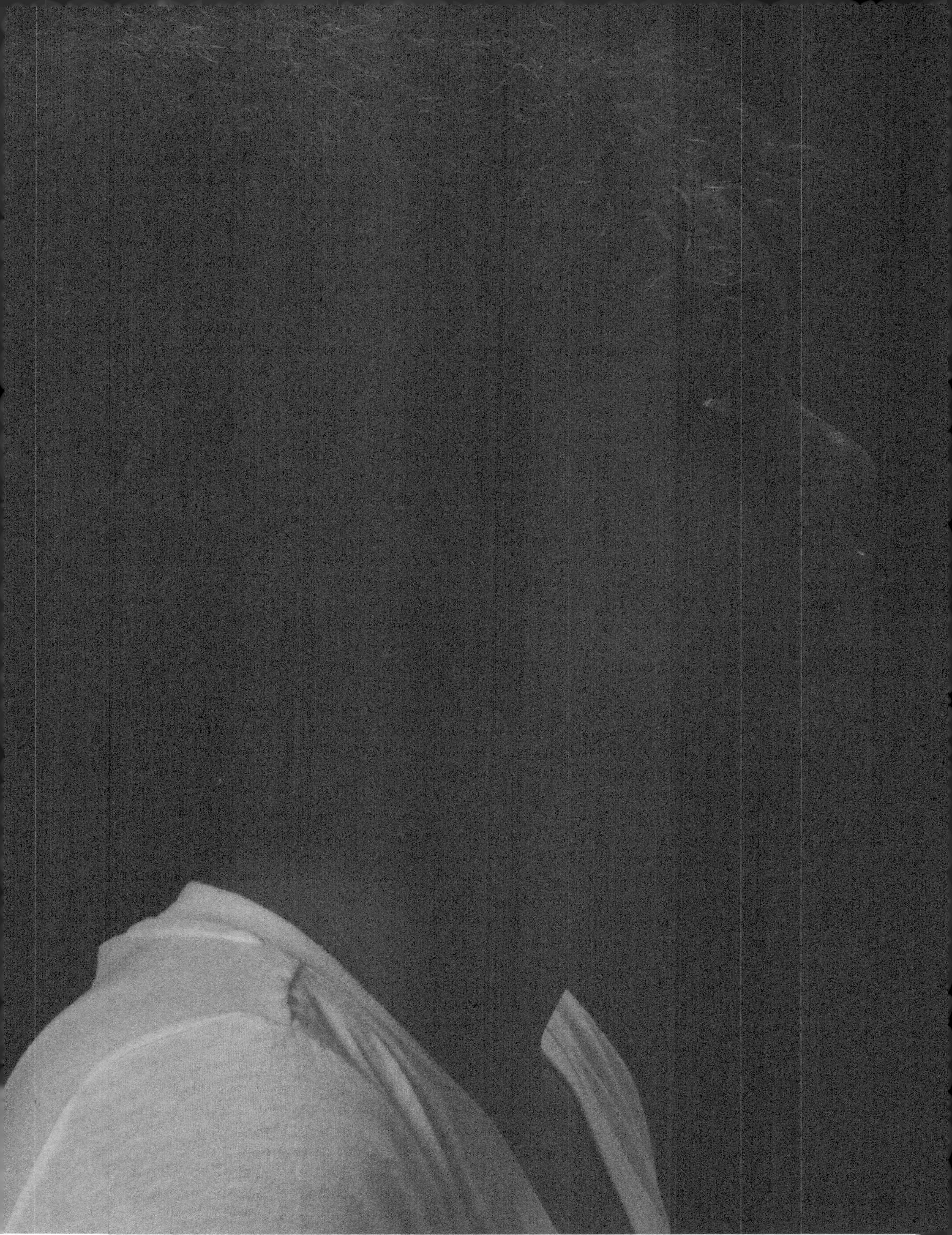

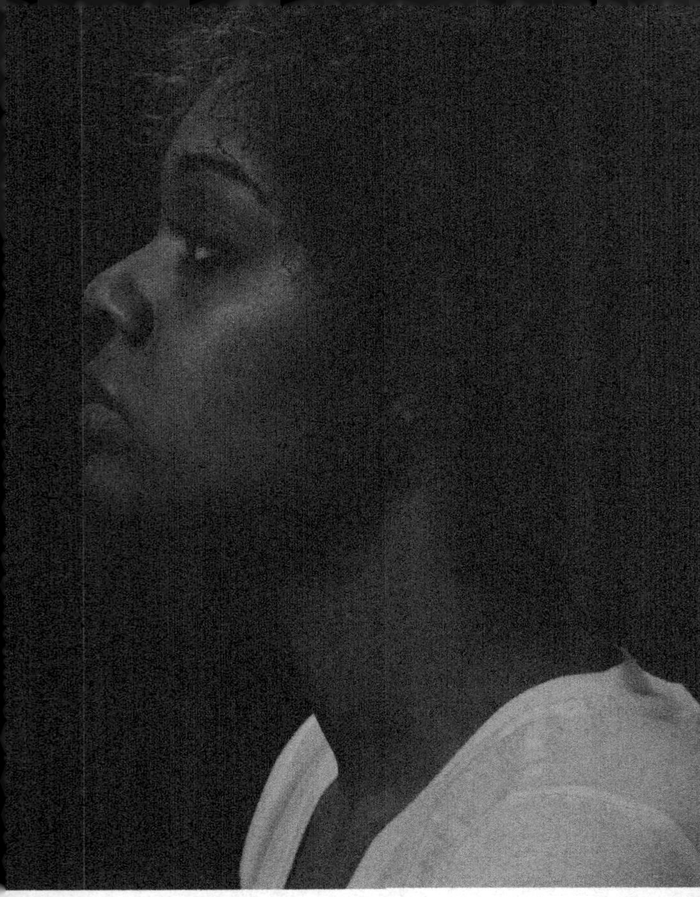

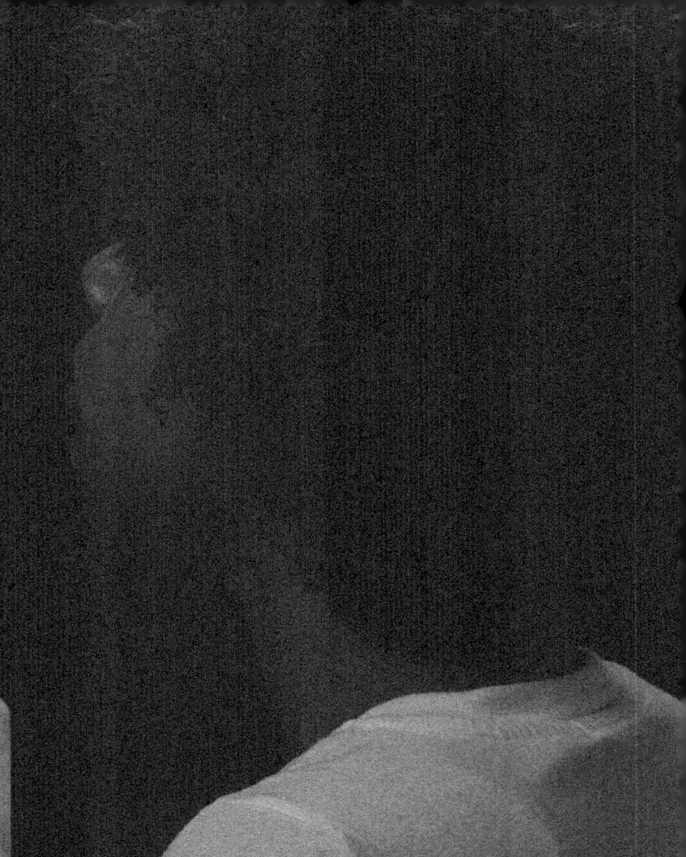

**Ethnicities claimed:**

Africa.

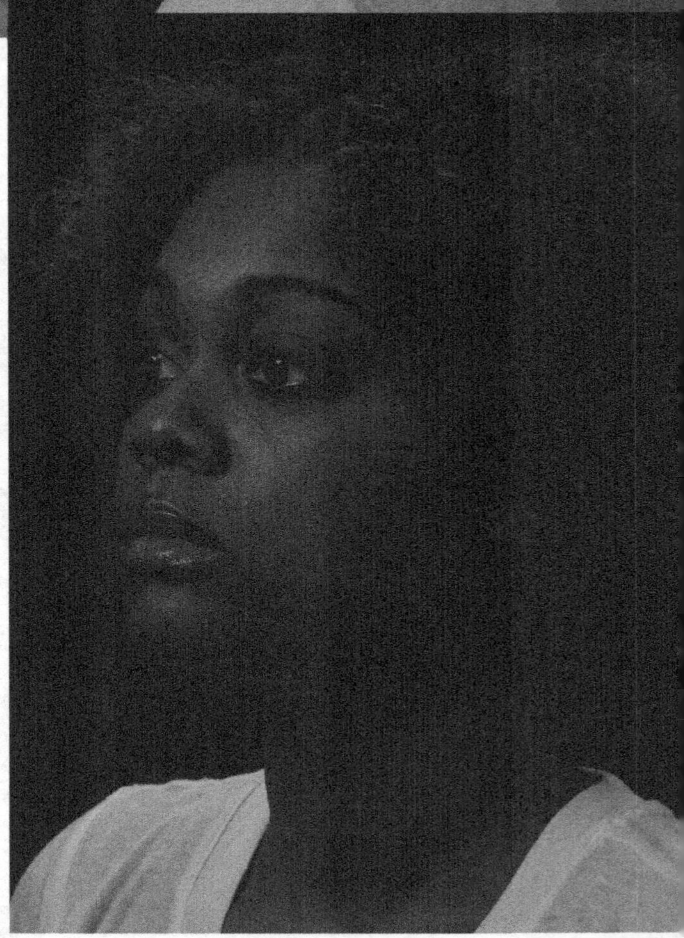

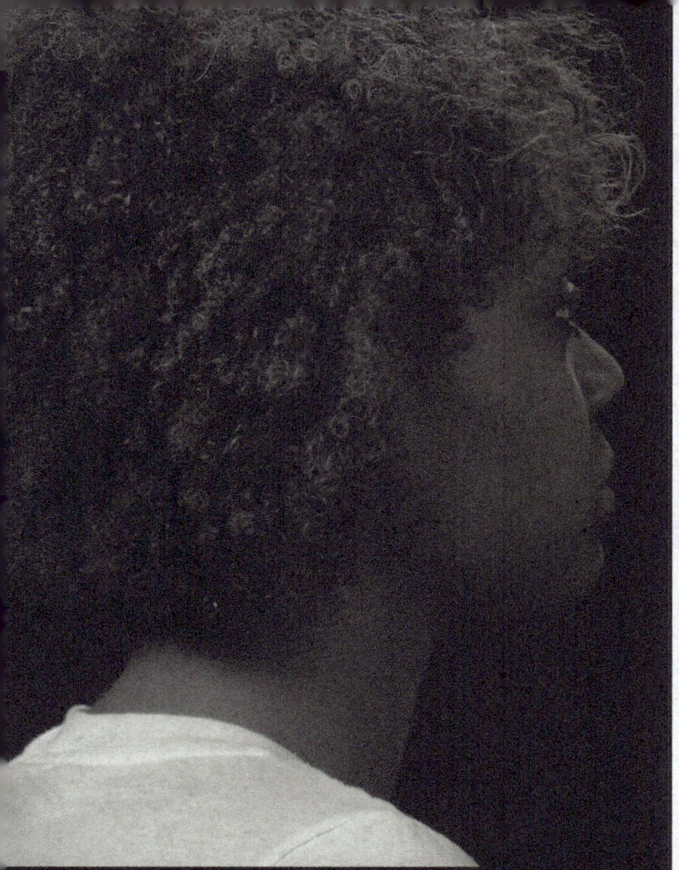

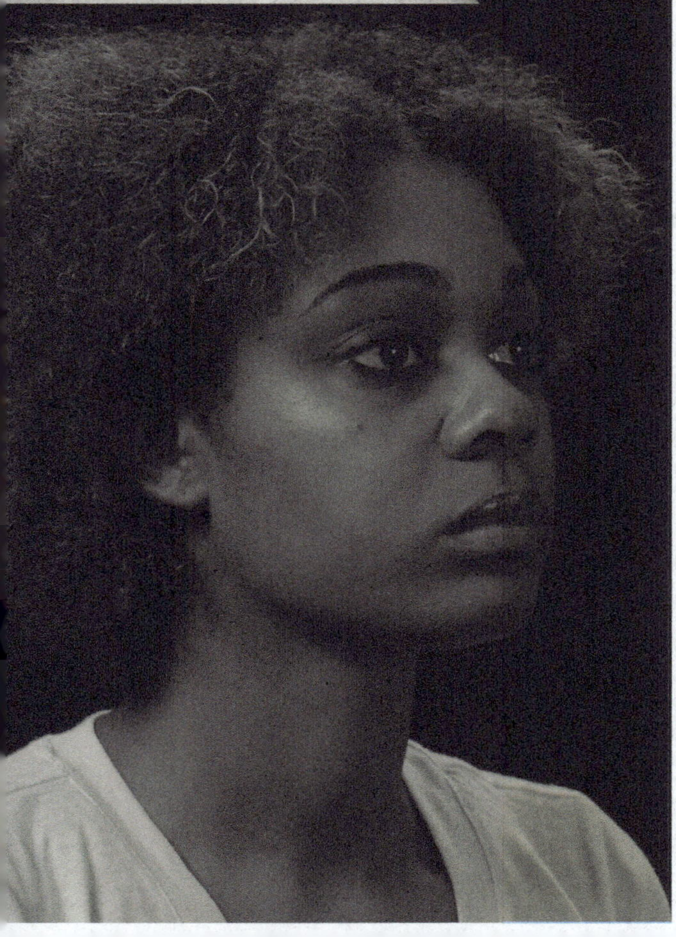

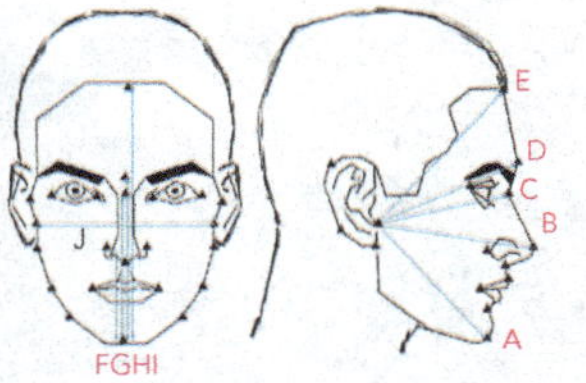



**Head measurements (in):**

A: 4 1/2
B: 4 5/8
C: 4 1/8
D: 4 3/4
E: 6
F: 3 5/8
G: 4 1/4
H: 4 7/8
I: 6 1/4
J: 4 7/8

MAP REFERENCE:

58

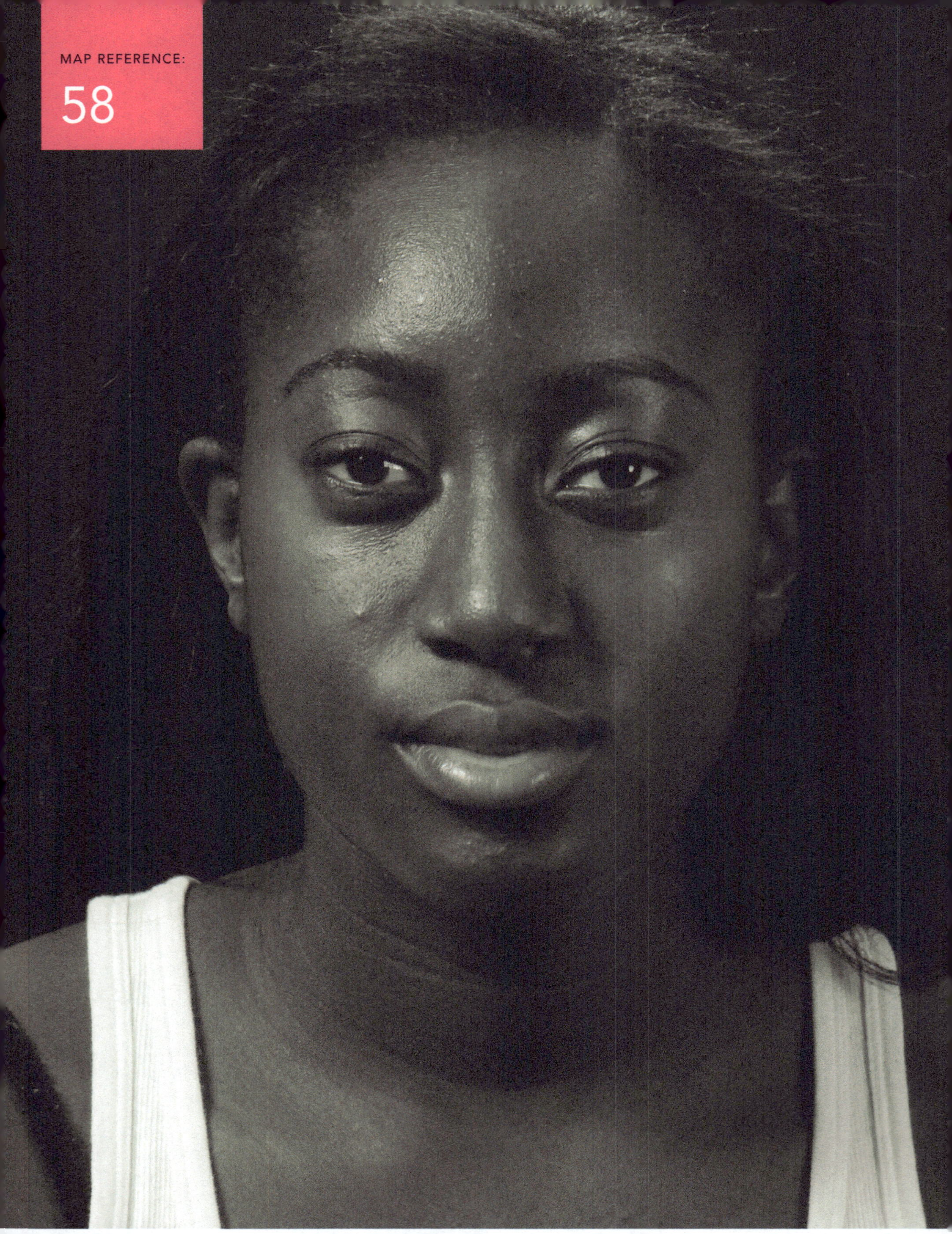

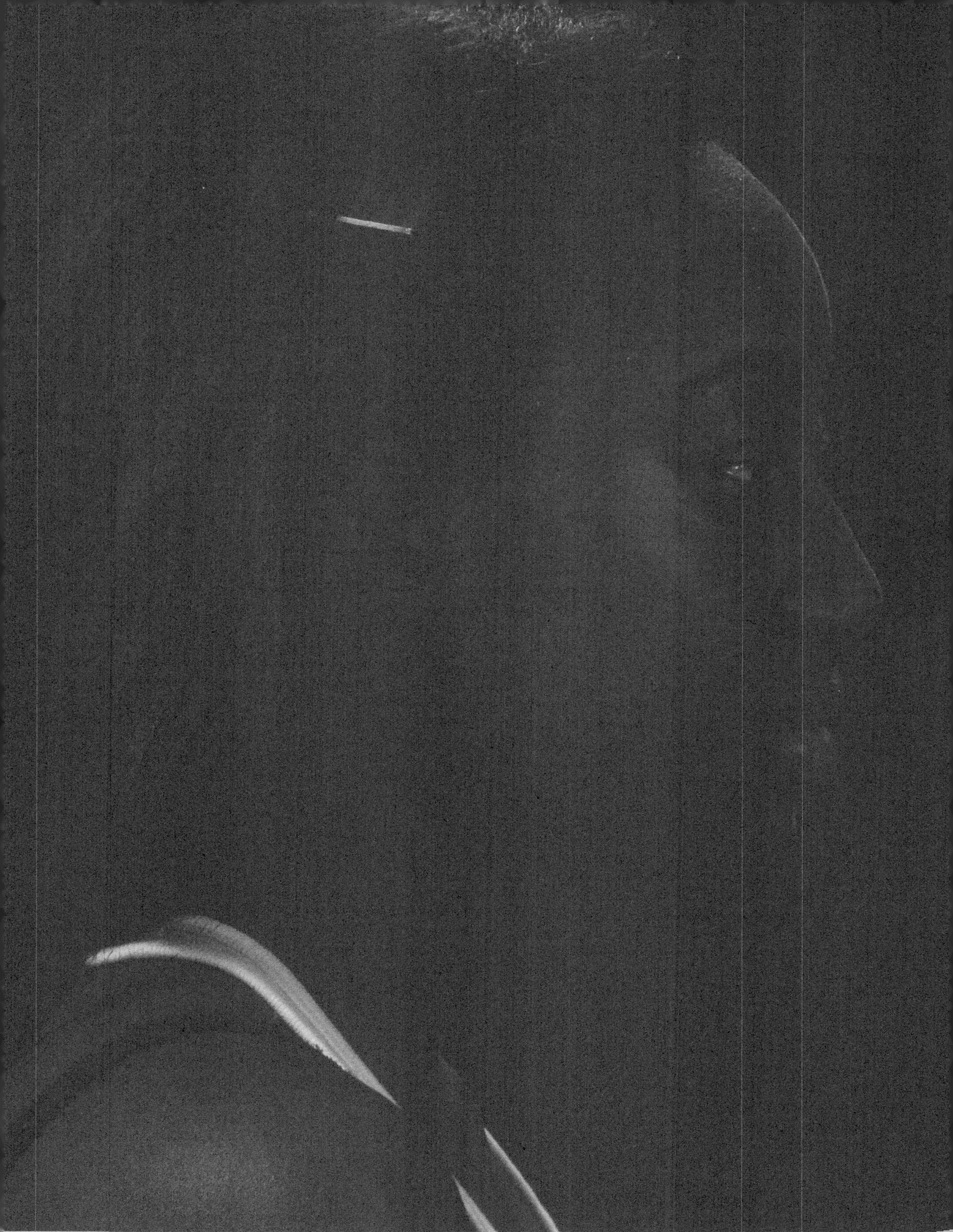

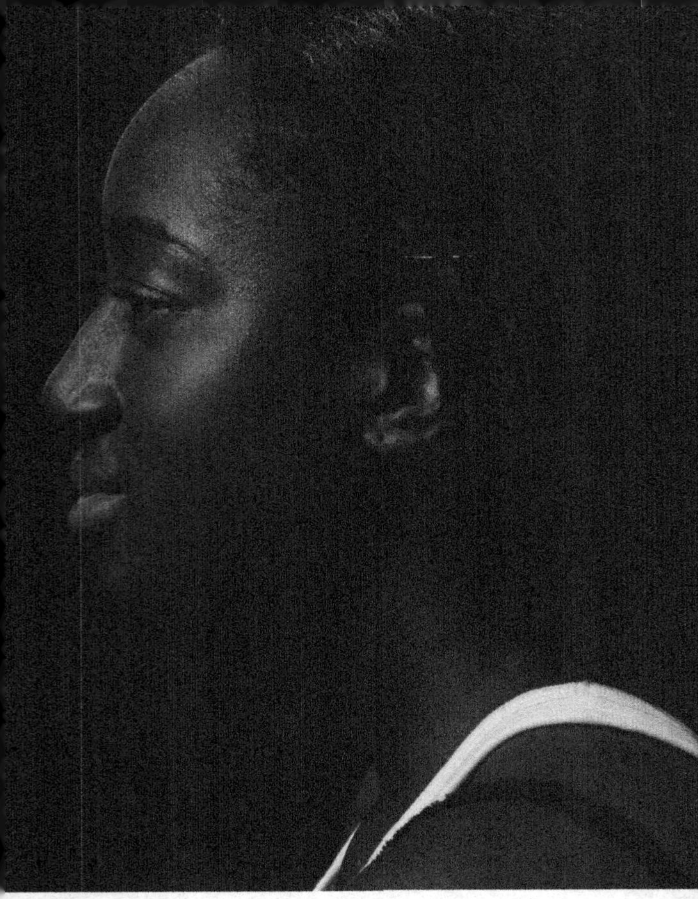

**Ethnicities claimed:**

Nigerian.

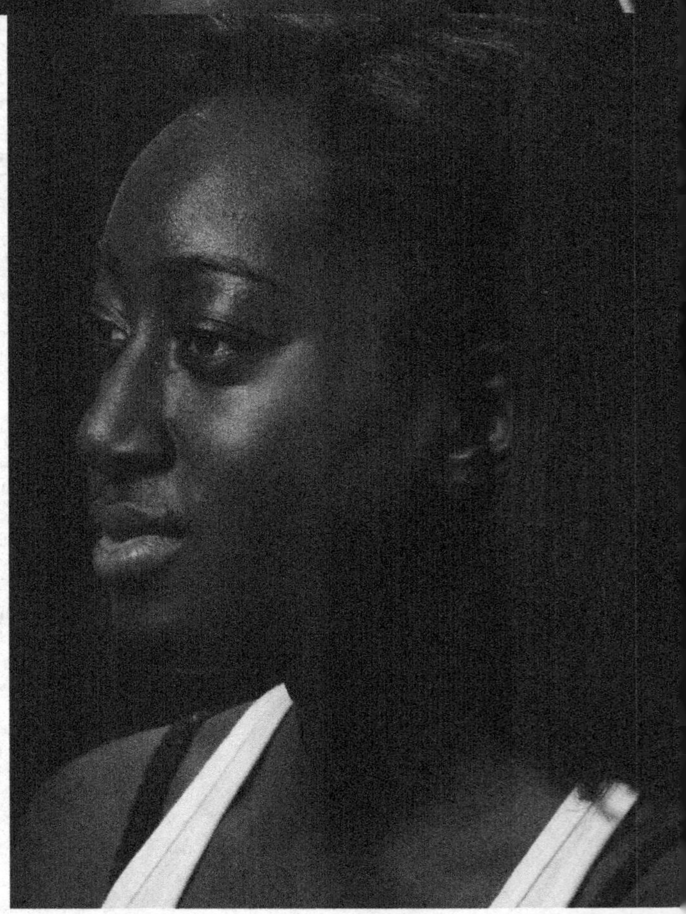

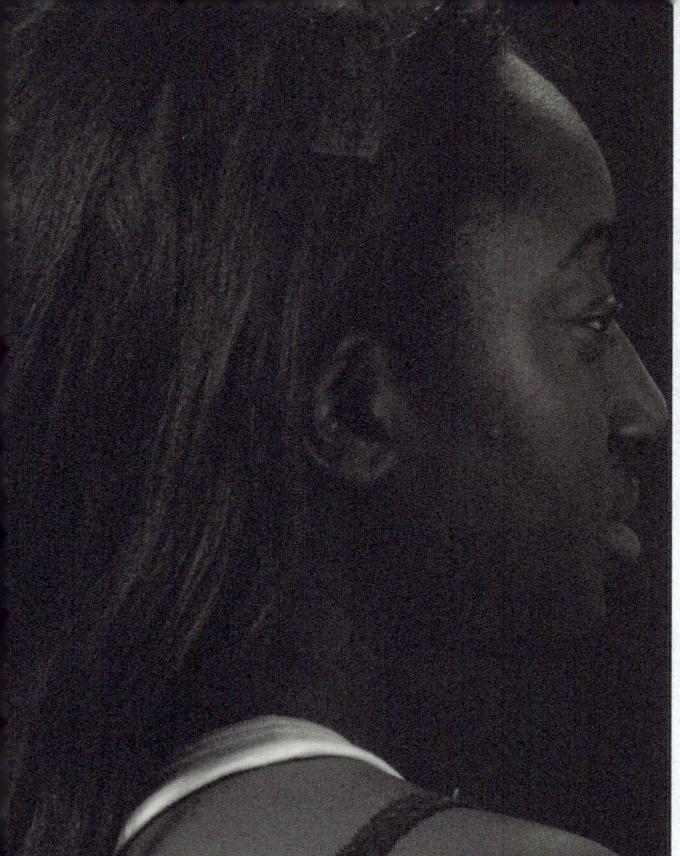

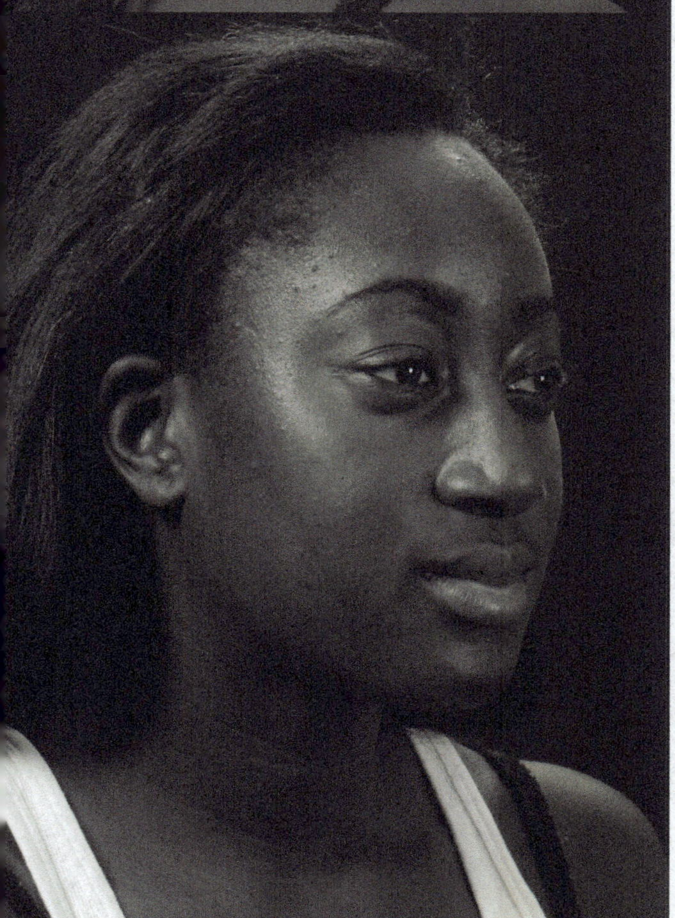

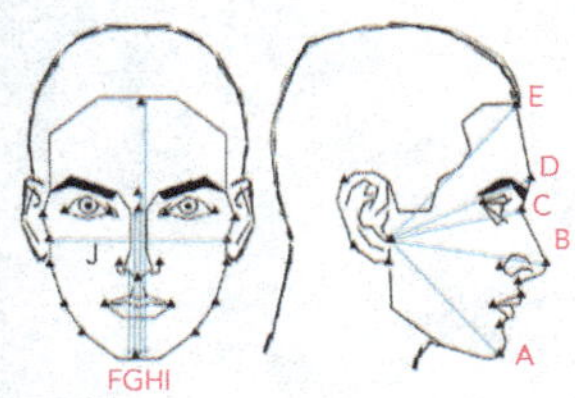


**Head measurements (in):**

A: 5 3/4
B: 4 3/4
C: 4 7/8
D: 4 15/16
E: 6
F: 3 1/2
G: 5
H: 5 5/8
I: 8 1/8
J: 5 3/8

MAP REFERENCE:

59

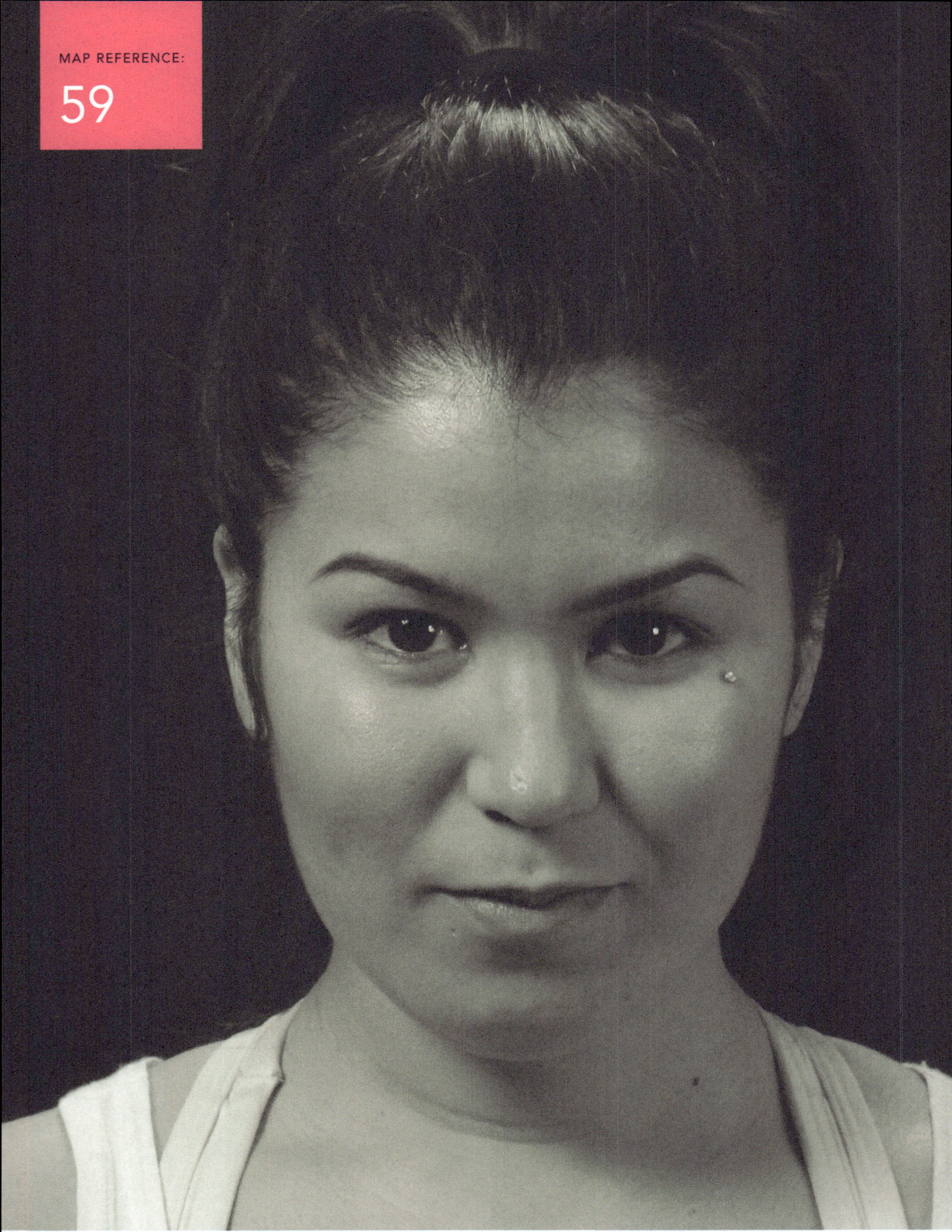

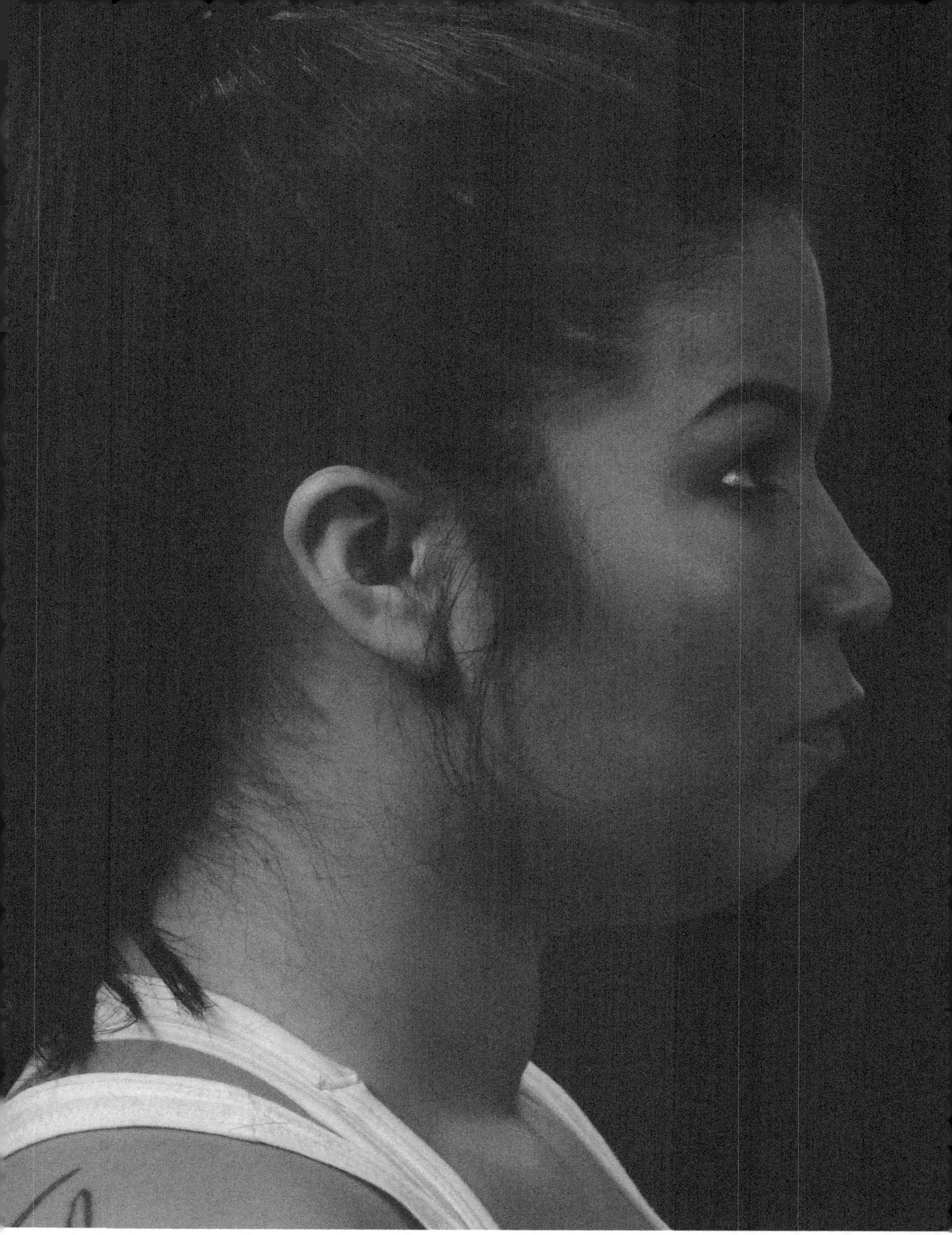

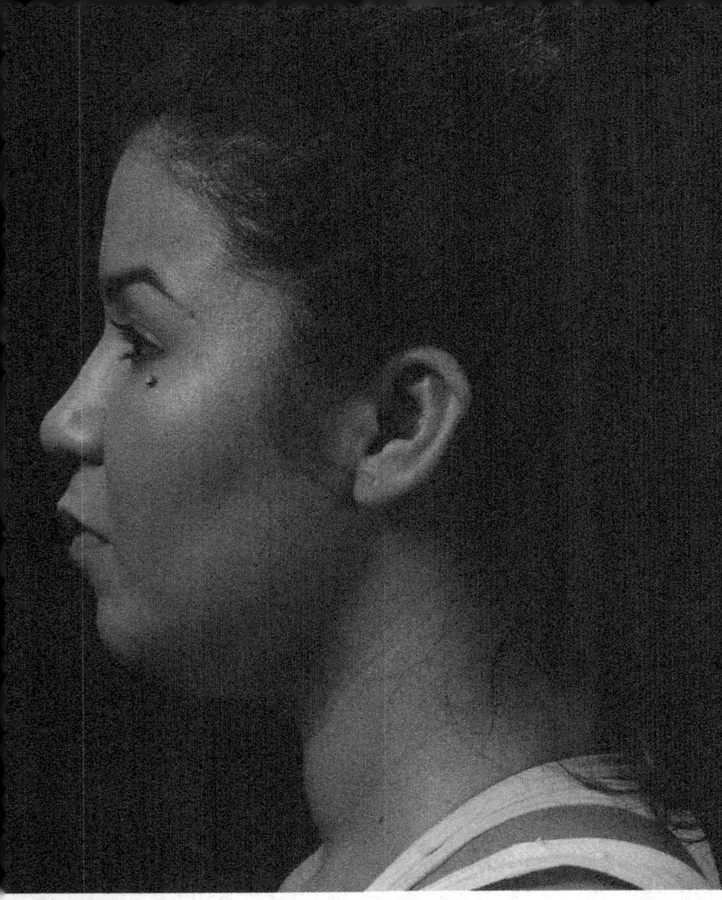

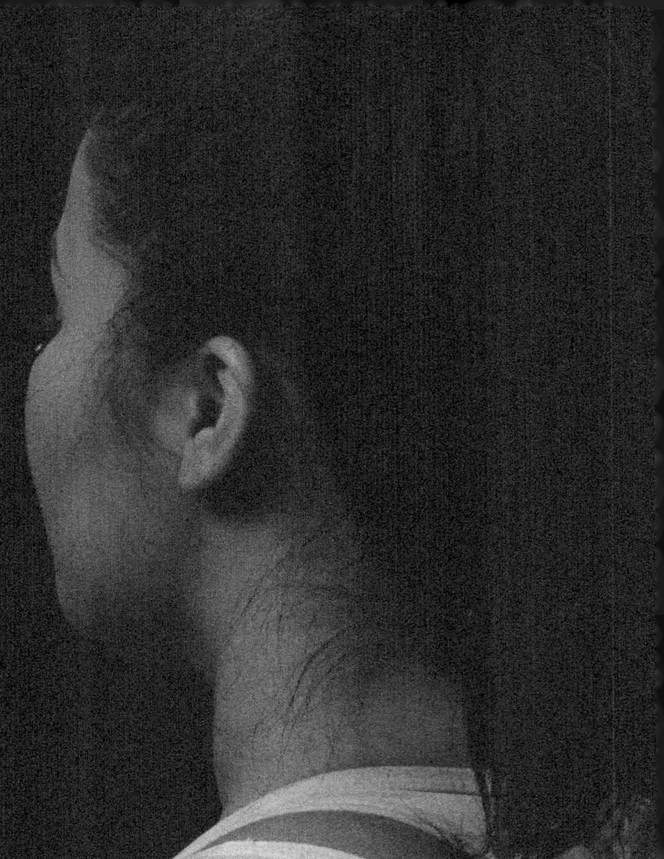

**Ethnicities claimed:**

Guam.

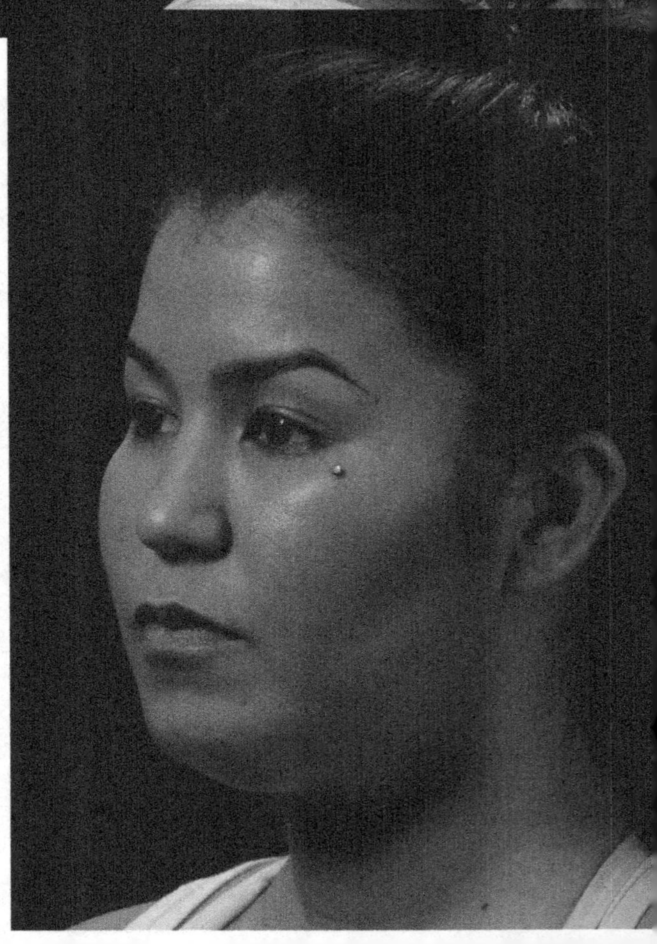

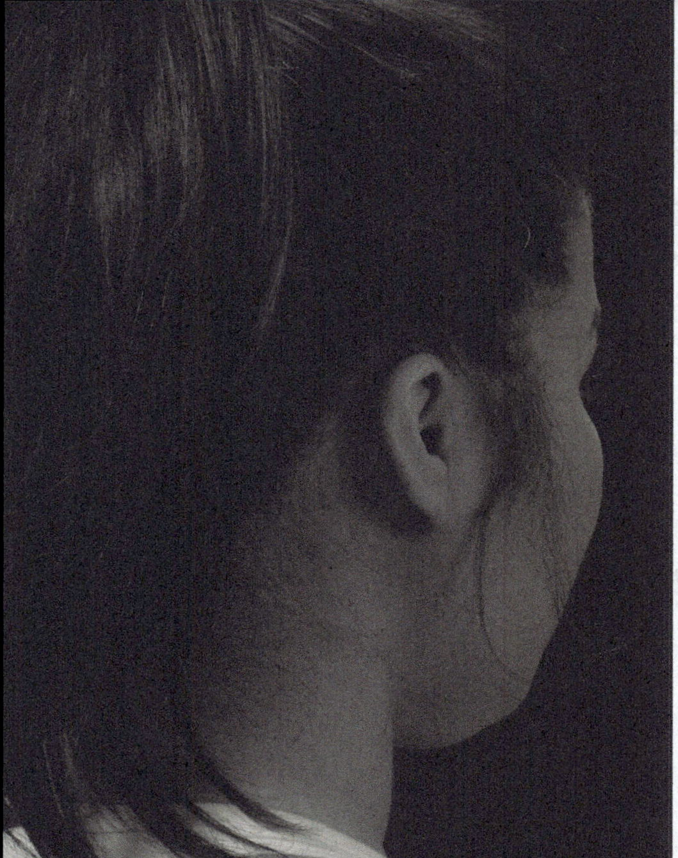

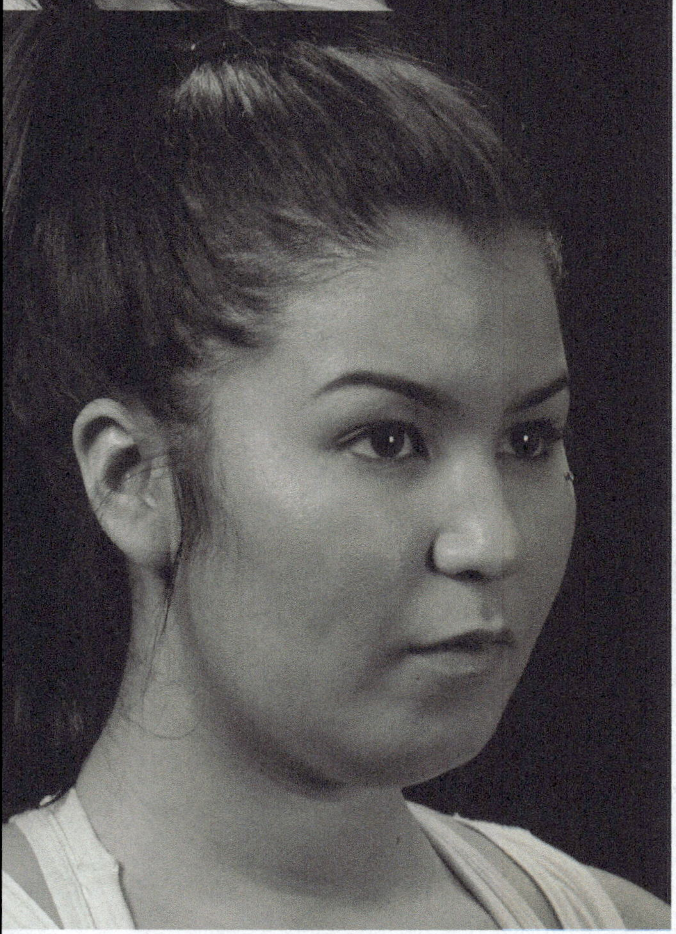

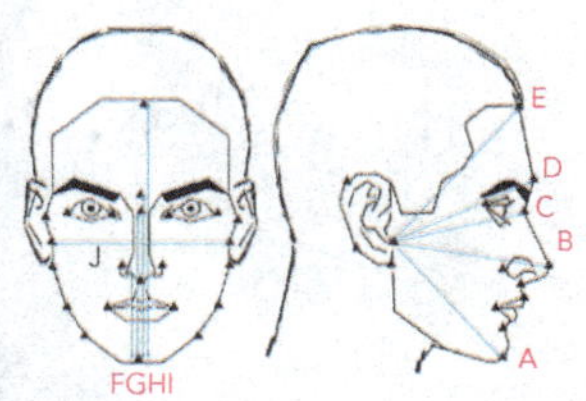


**Head measurements (in):**

A: 5
B: 4 1/2
C: 4 3/8
D: 4 3/4
E: 5 1/2
F: 3 5/8
G: 4 1/8
H: 4 3/4
I: 6 5/8
J: 4 1/2

MAP REFERENCE:
60

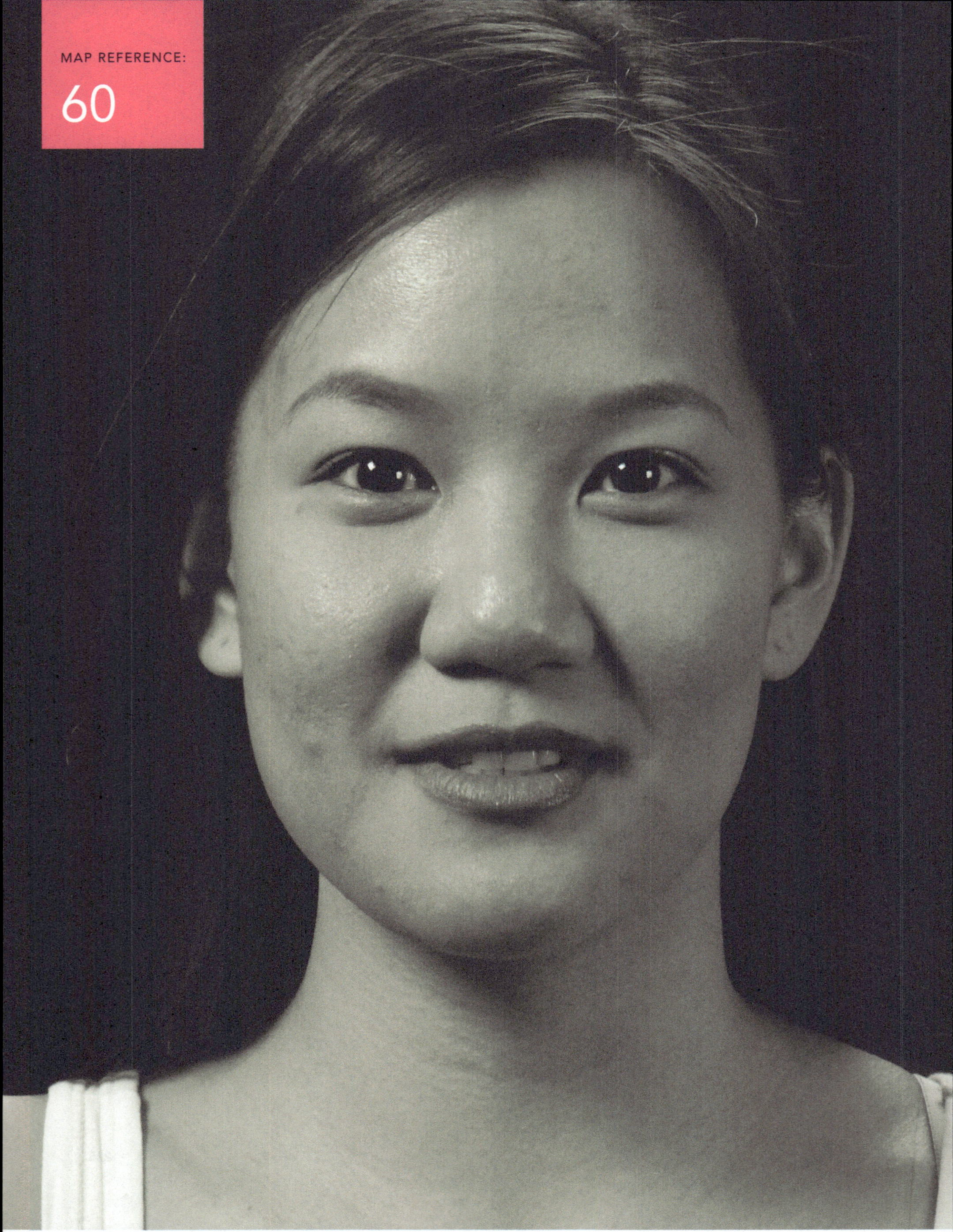

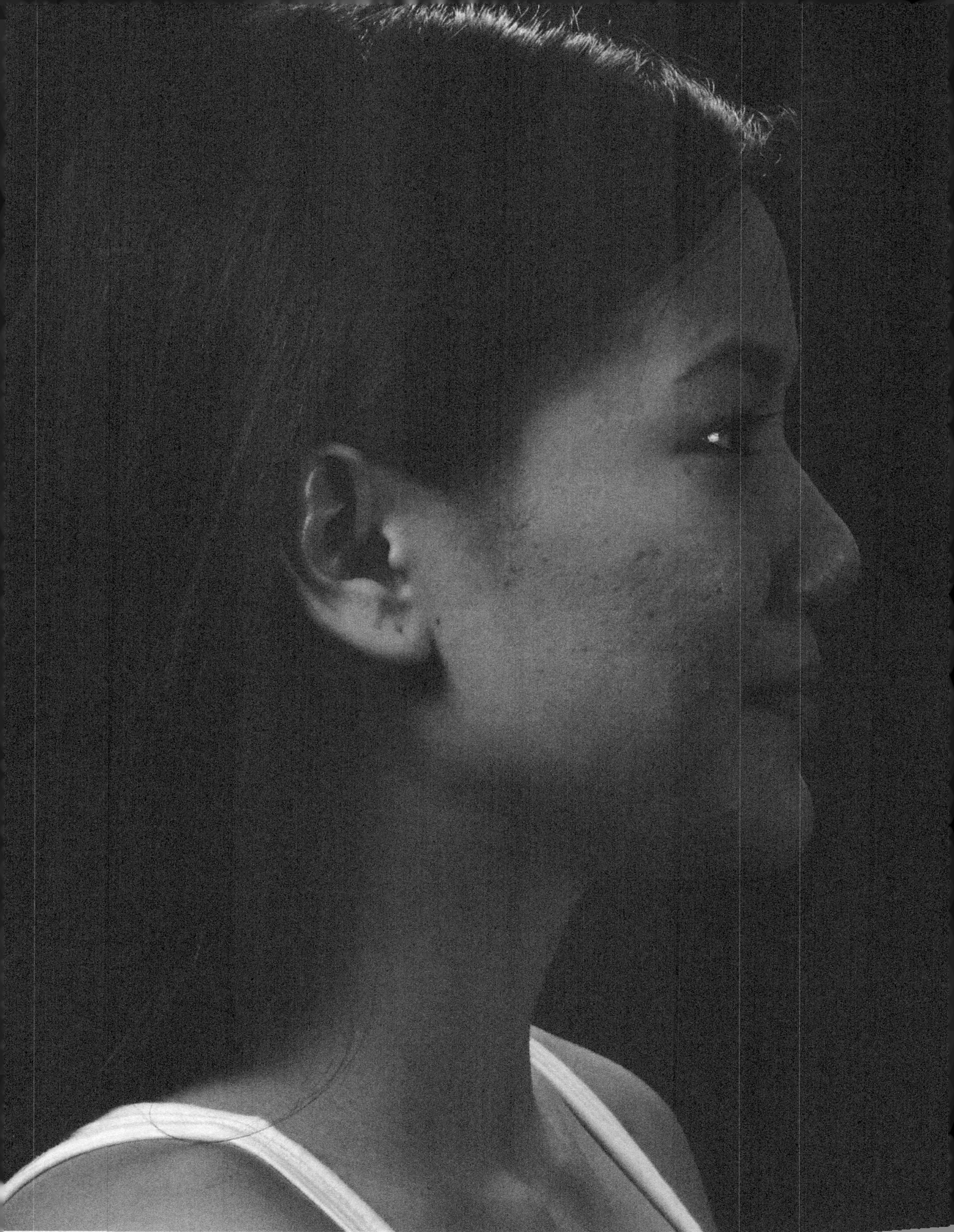

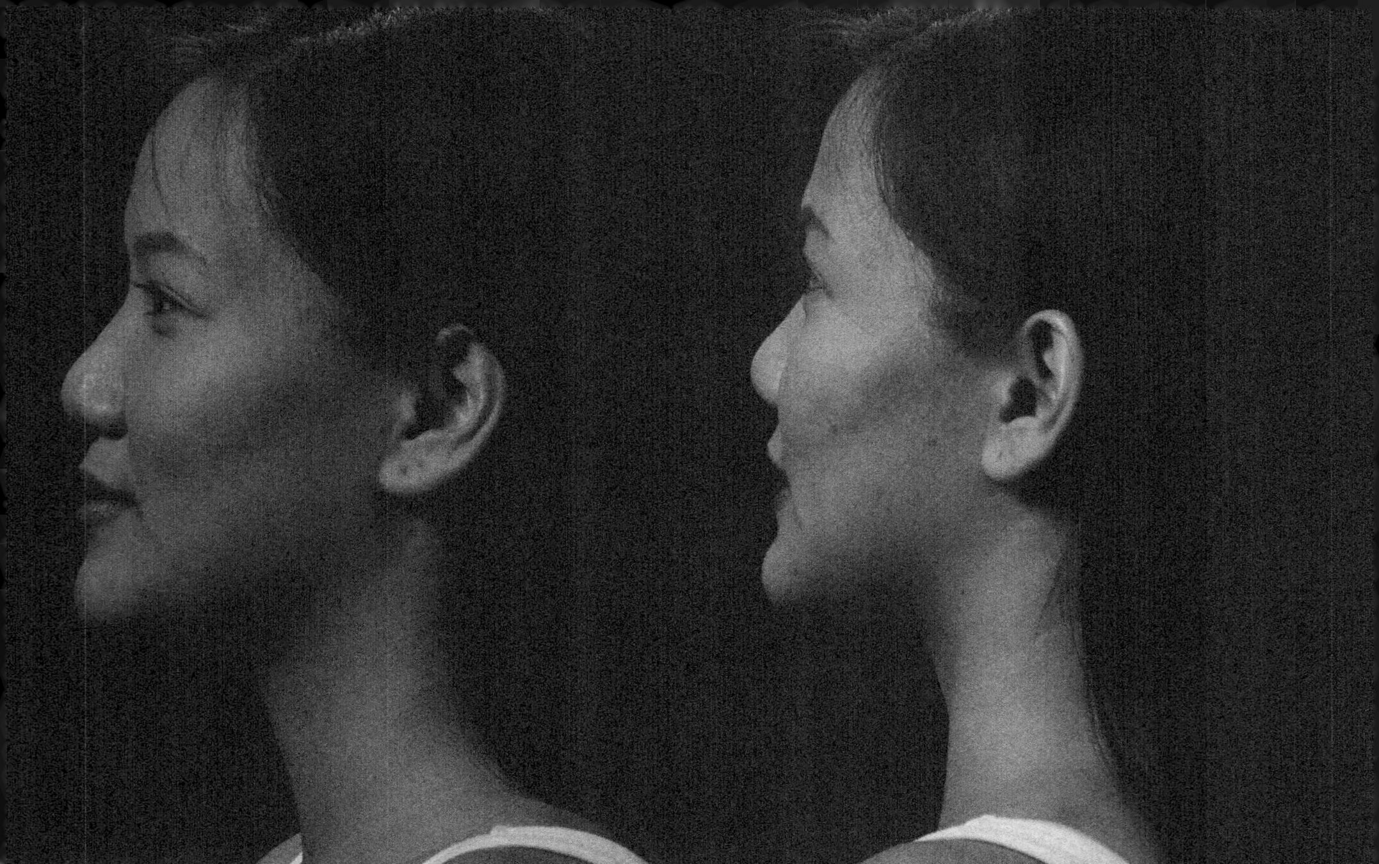

**Ethnicities claimed:**

Malaysia, China.

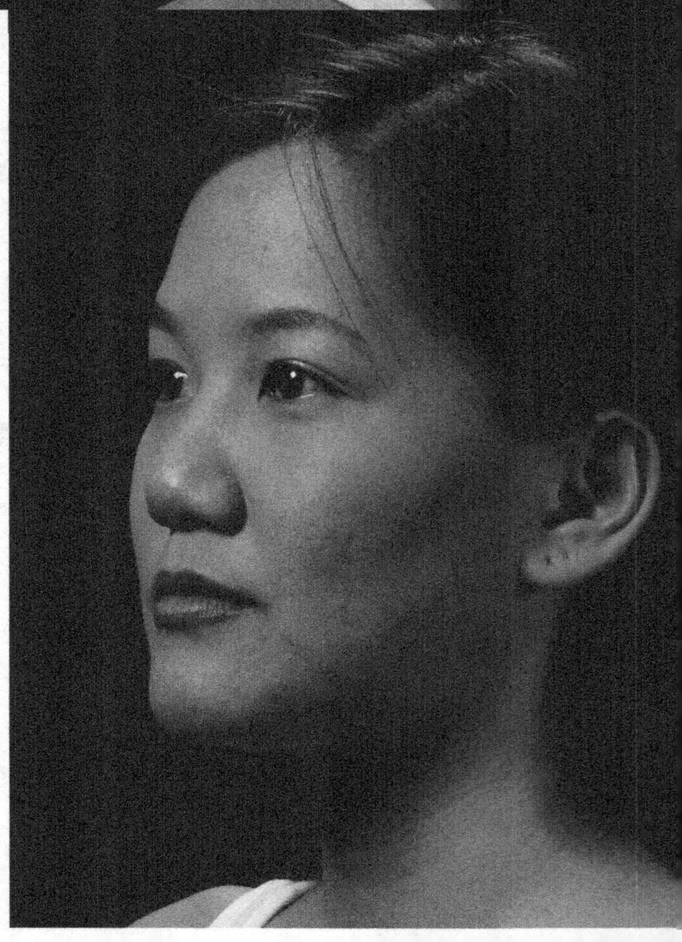

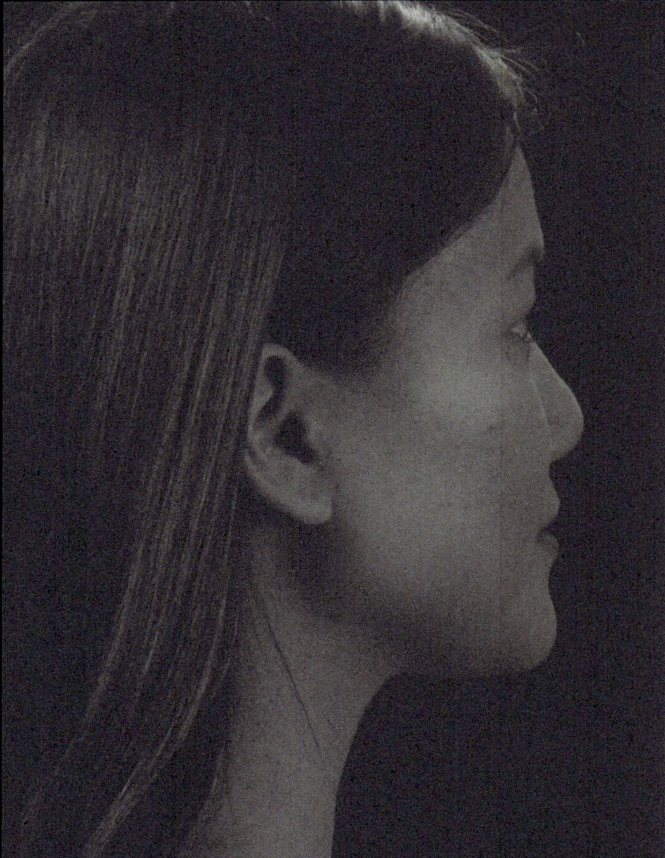

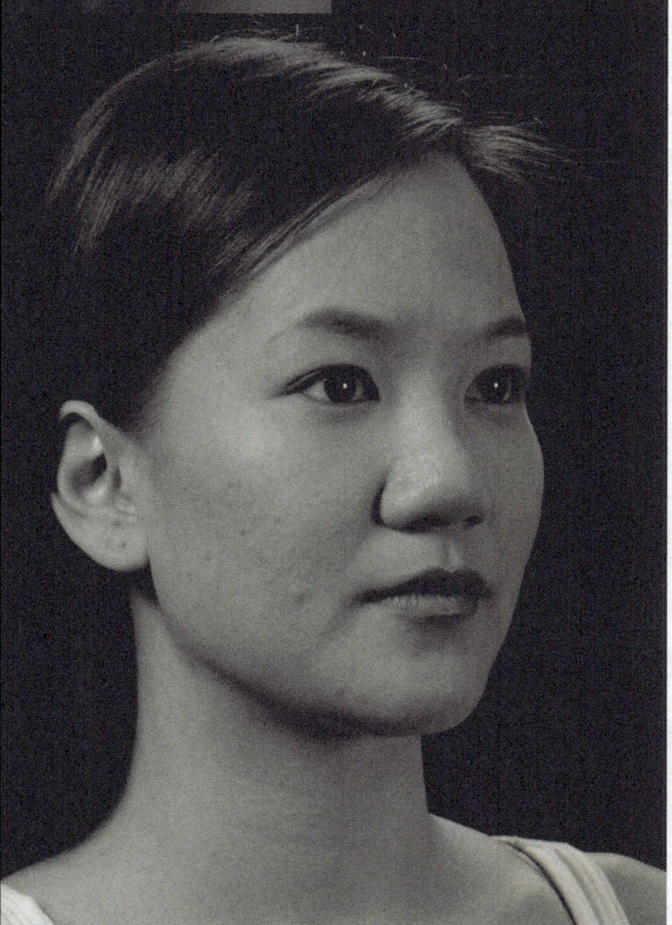

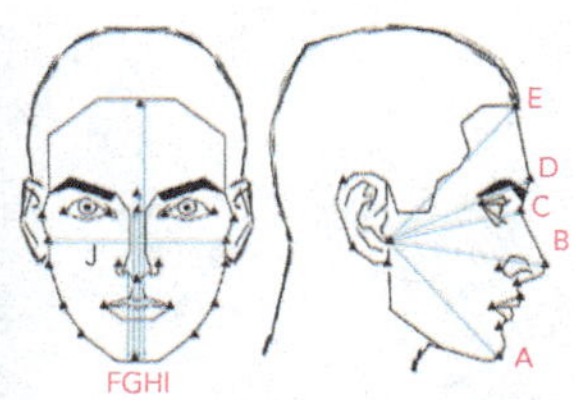


**Head measurements (in):**

A: 5 1/2
B: 5 1/8
C: 4 1/2
D: 5 1/8
E: 6 1/8
F: 3 1/4
G: 4 1/2
H: 5 1/4
I: 7 1/2
J: 5 3/8

MAP REFERENCE:

63

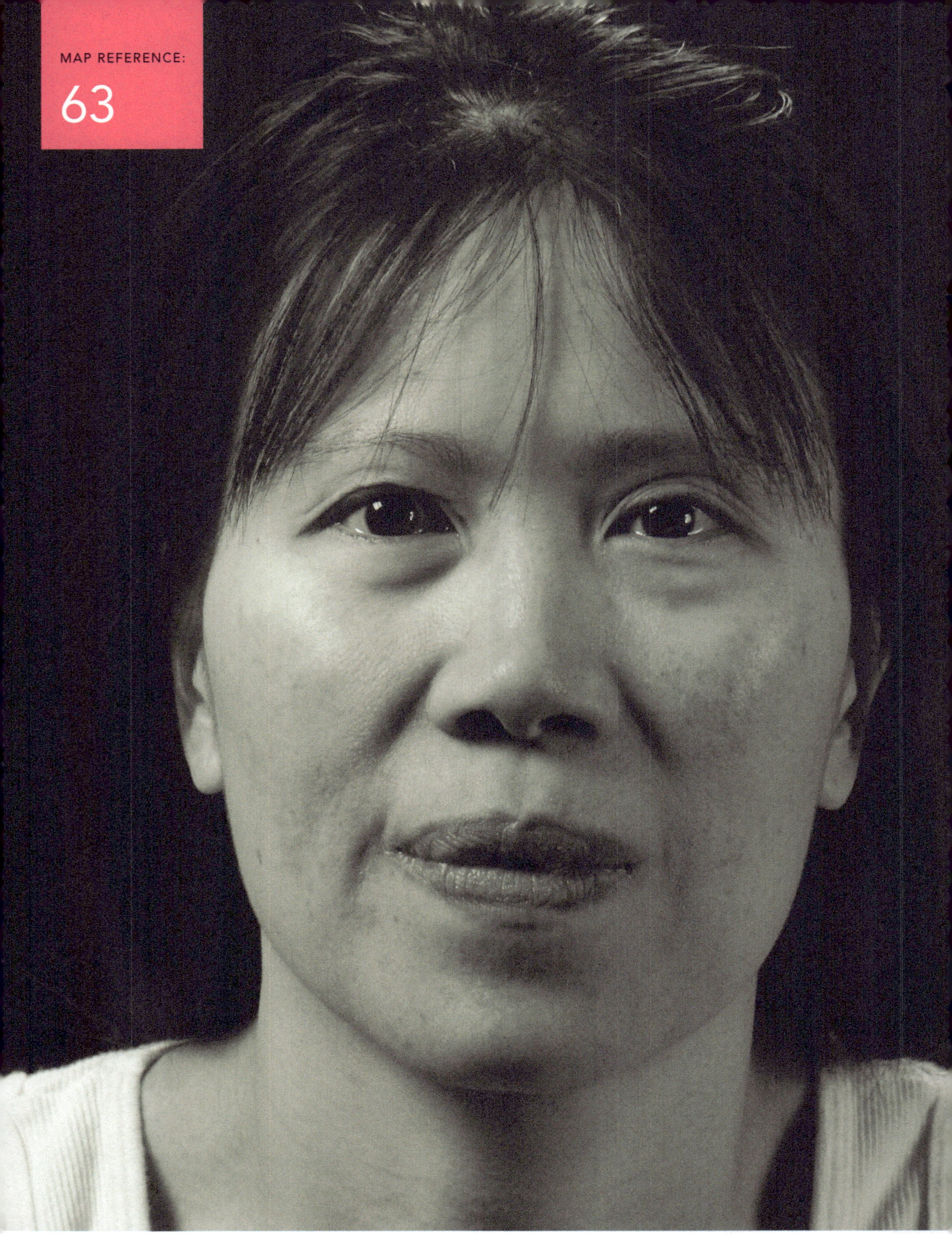

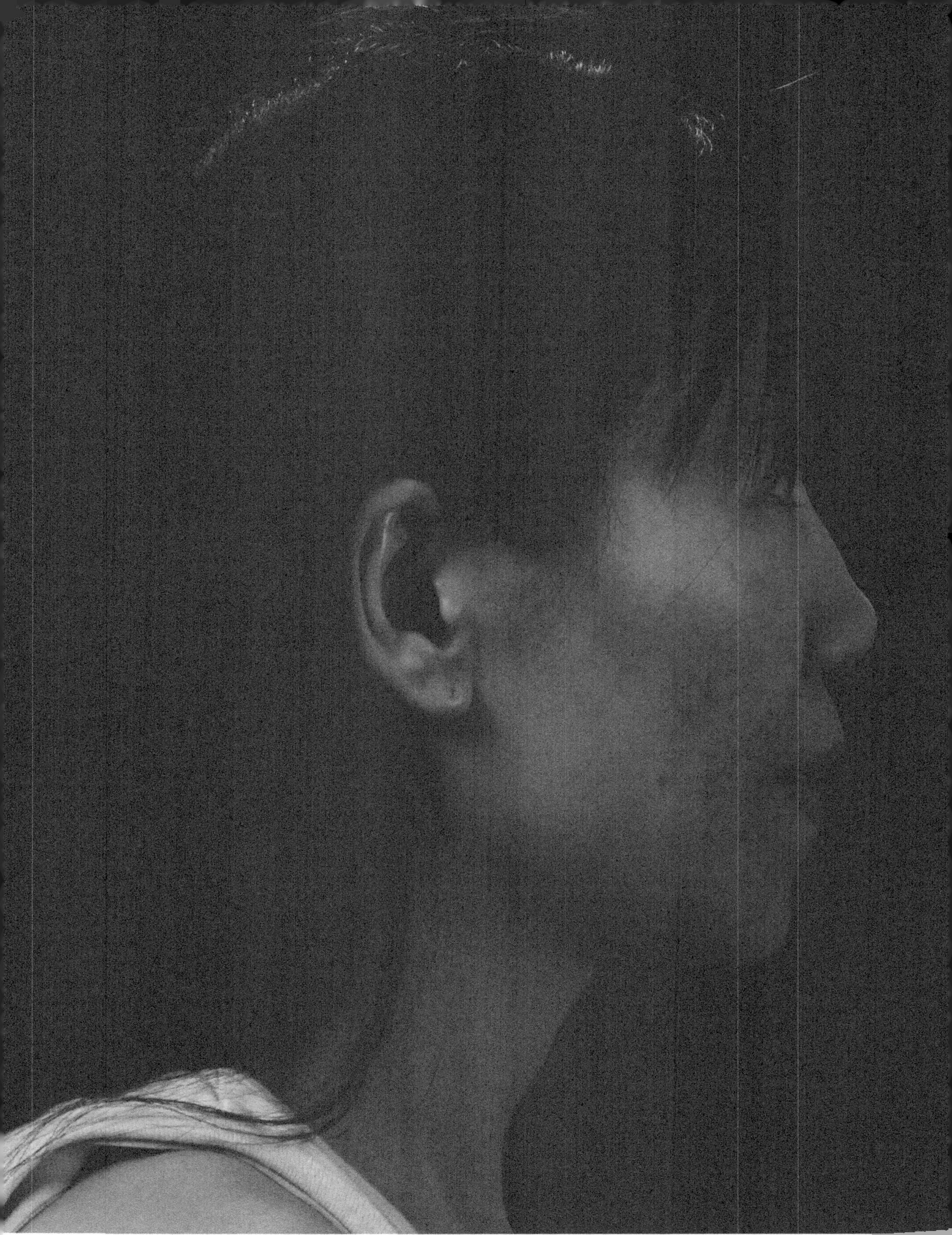

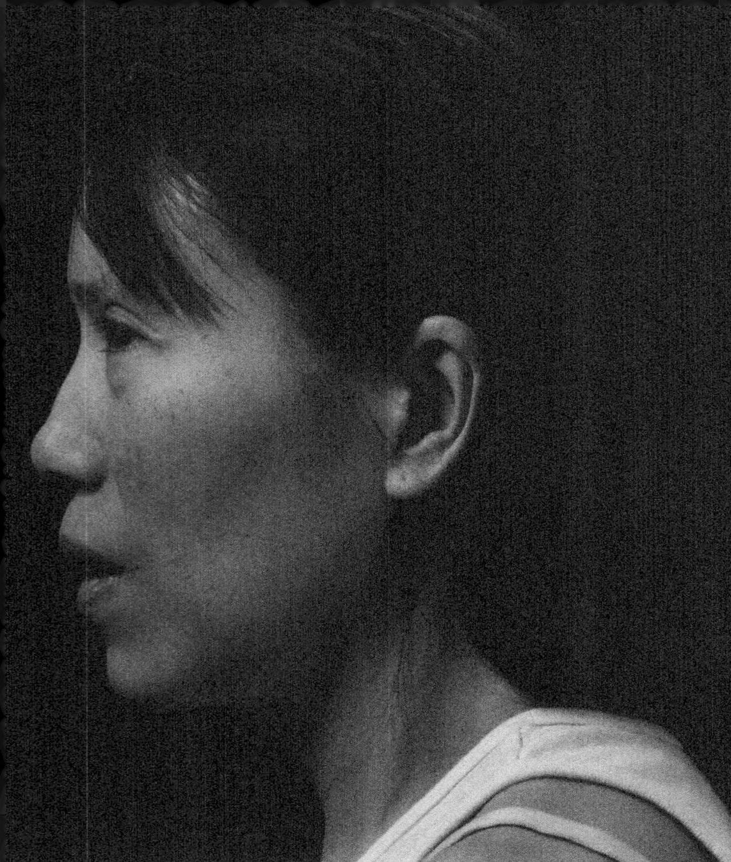

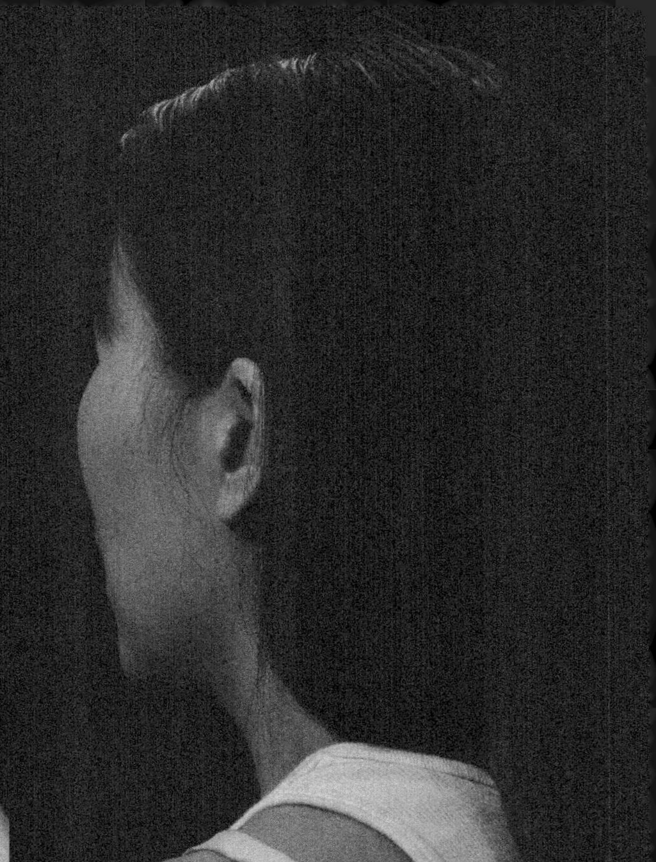

**Ethnicities claimed:**

Burma, Thailand.

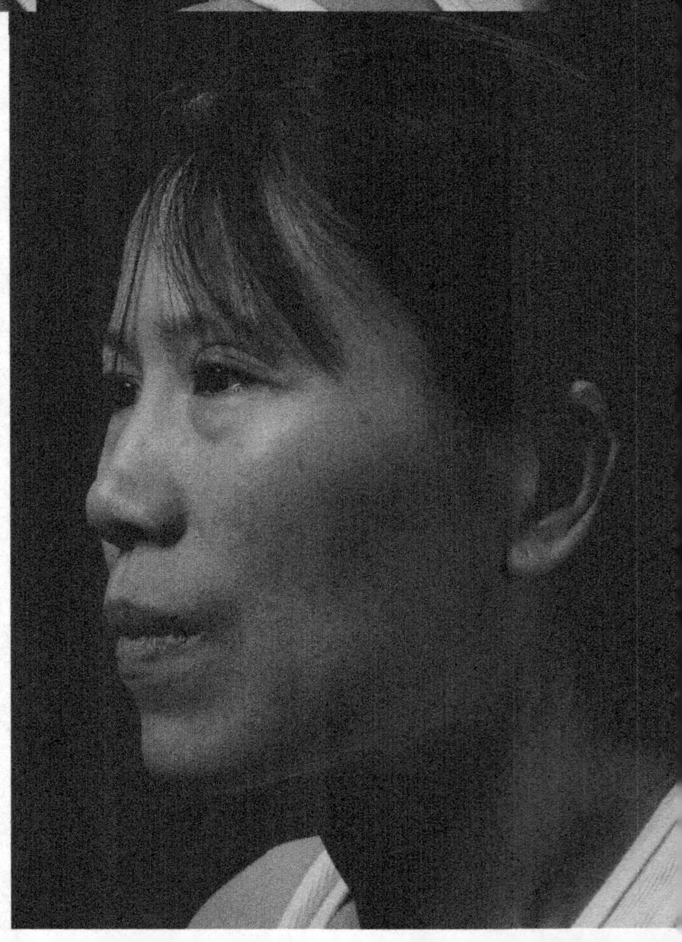

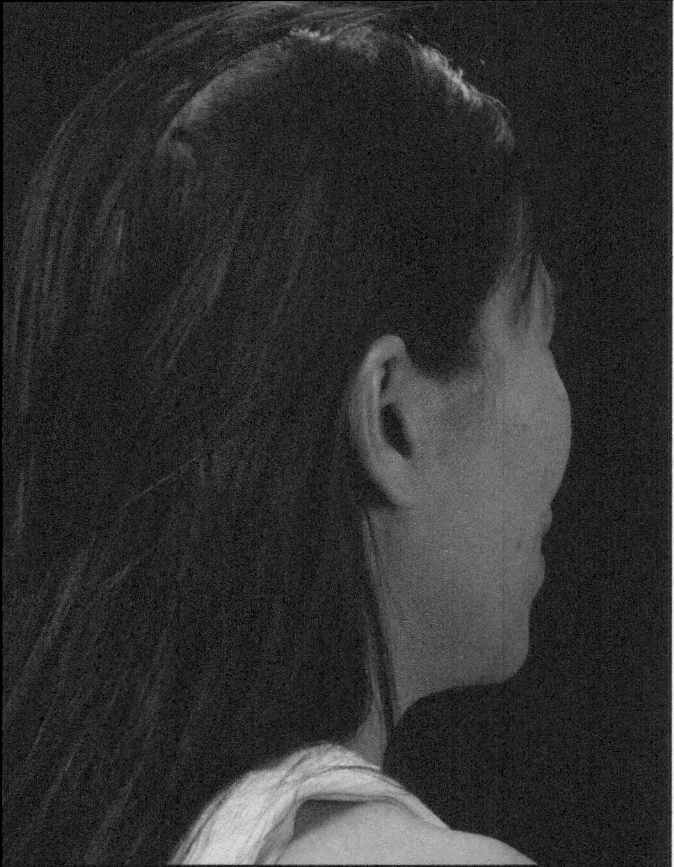

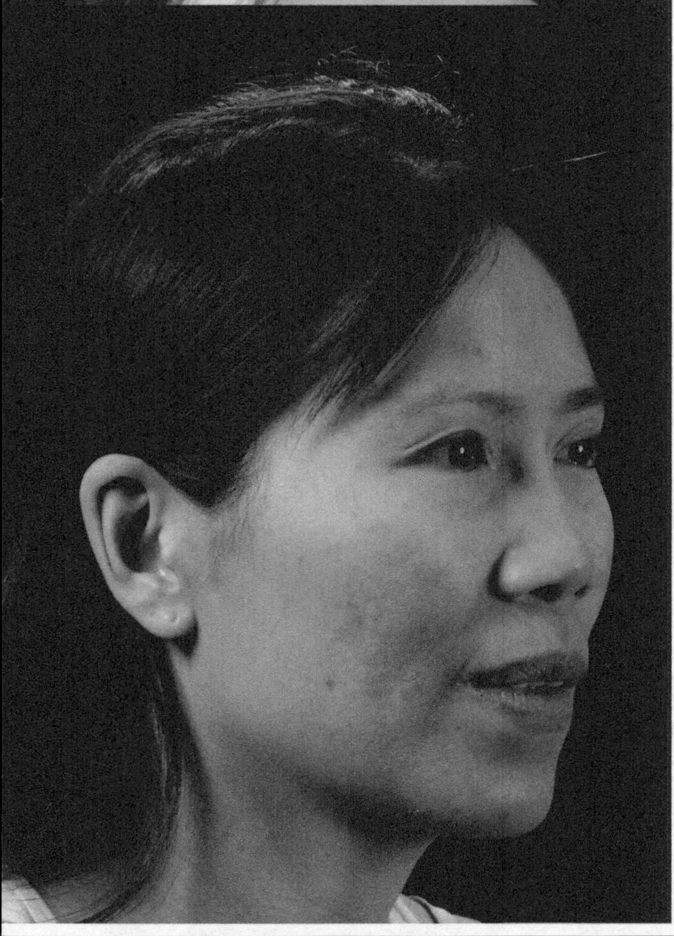

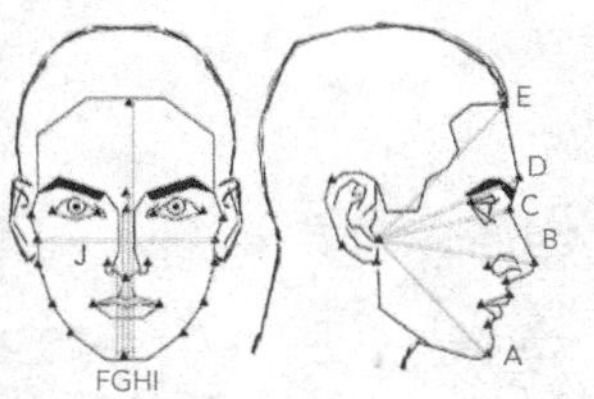


**Head measurements (in):**

A: 5 1/2
B: 4 3/4
C: 5
D: 5 3/8
E: 5 3/4
F: 3 5/8
G: 5 1/8
H: 5 3/8
I: 8
J: 5 1/2

MAP REFERENCE:

64

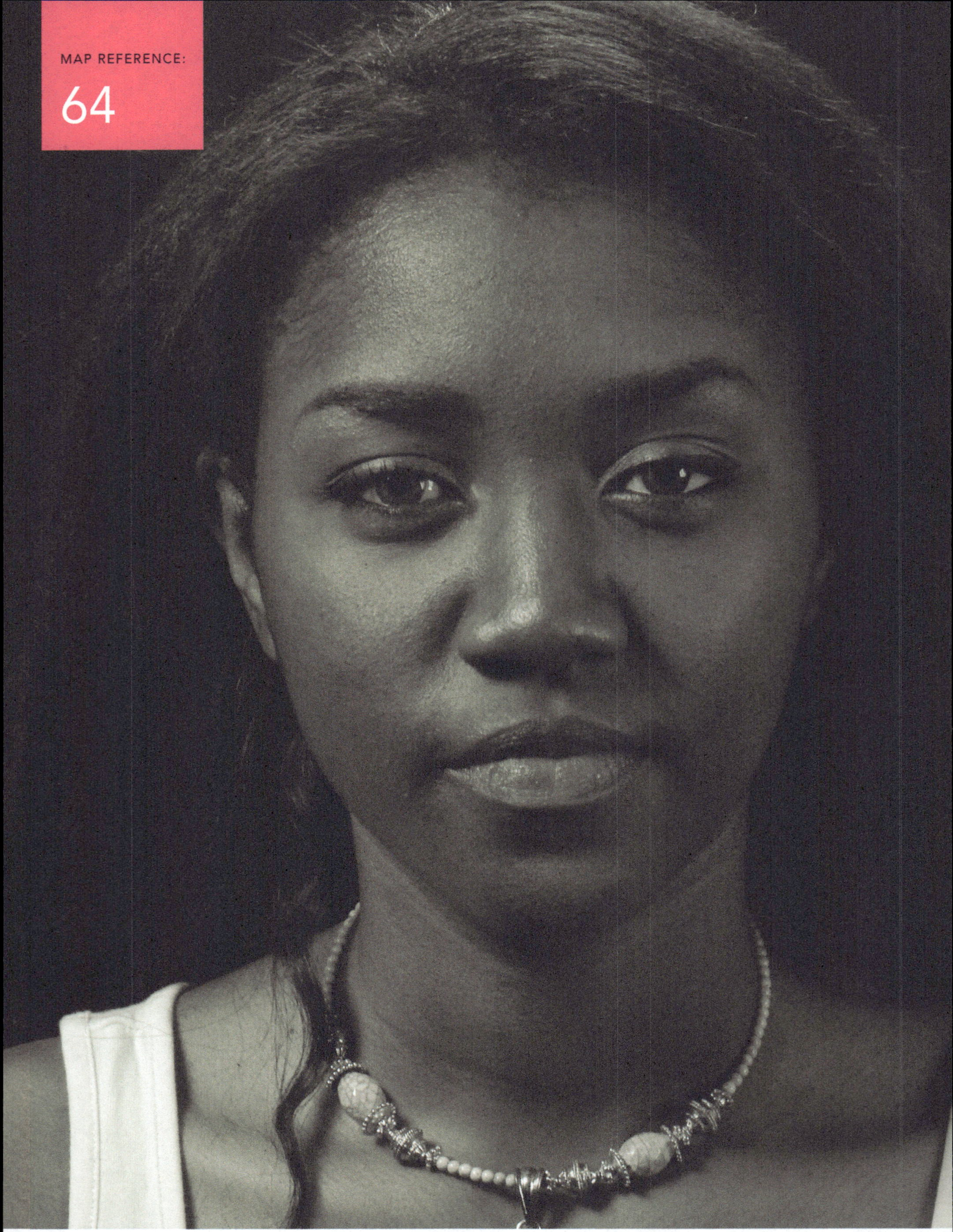

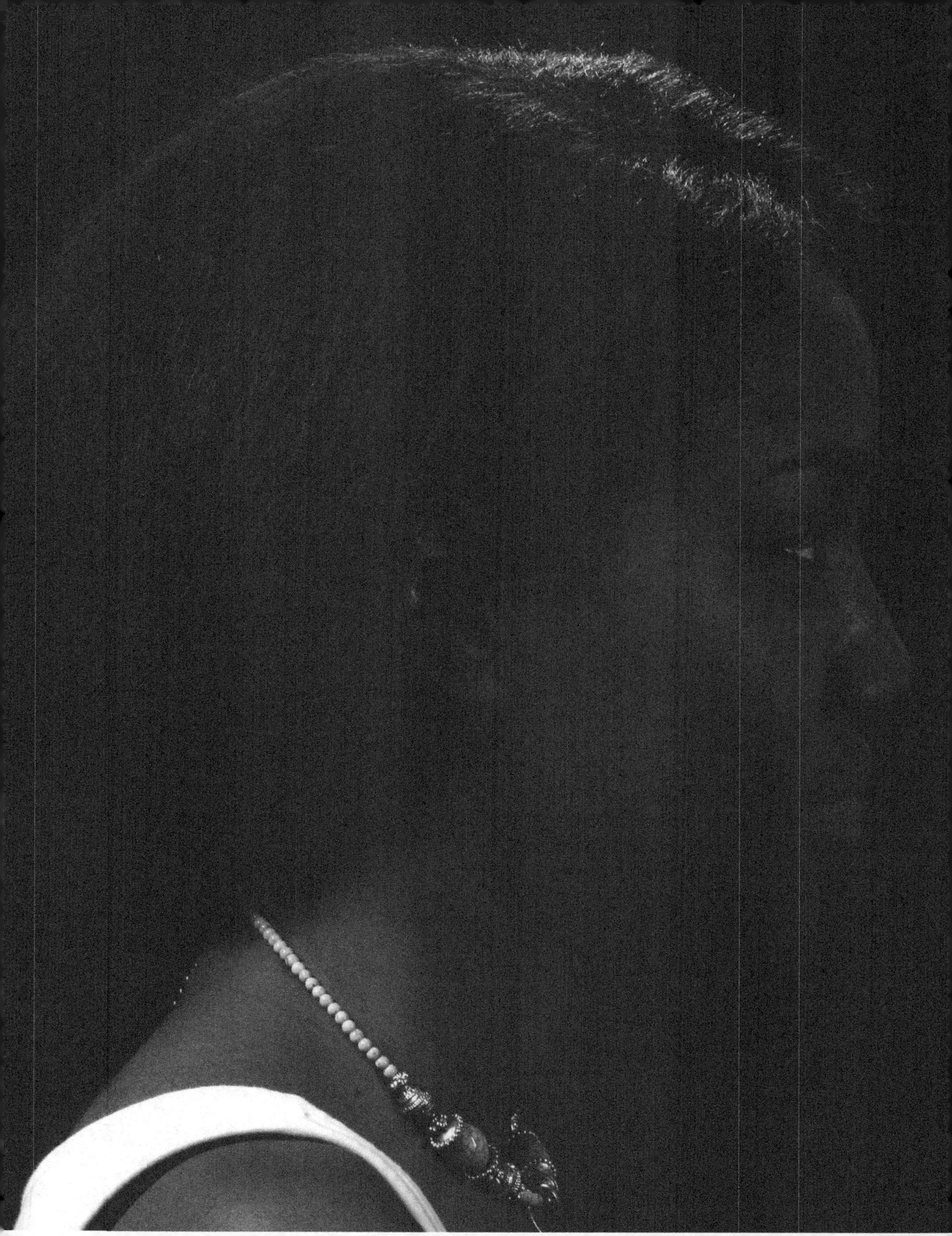

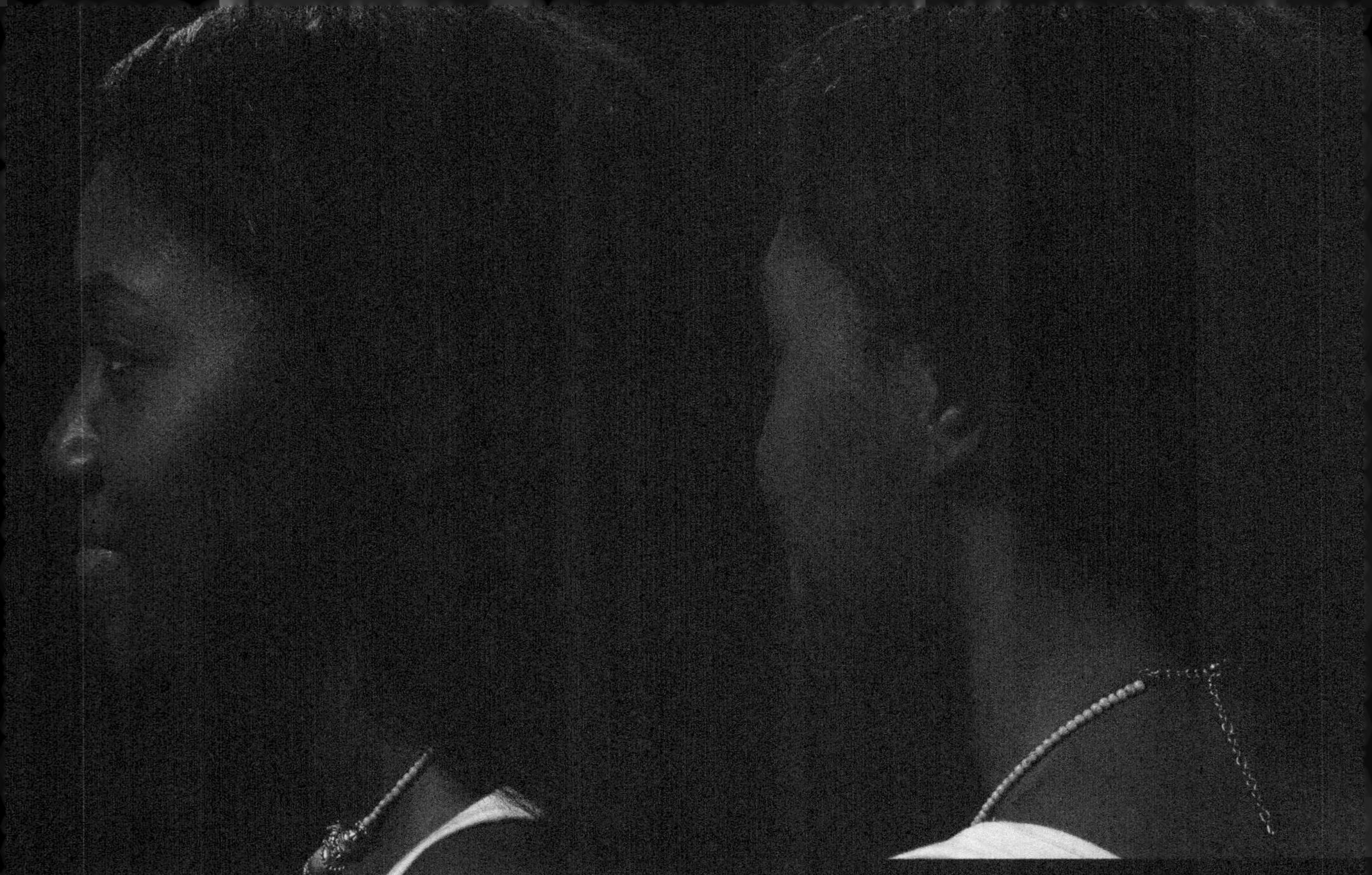

**Ethnicities claimed:**

Congo.

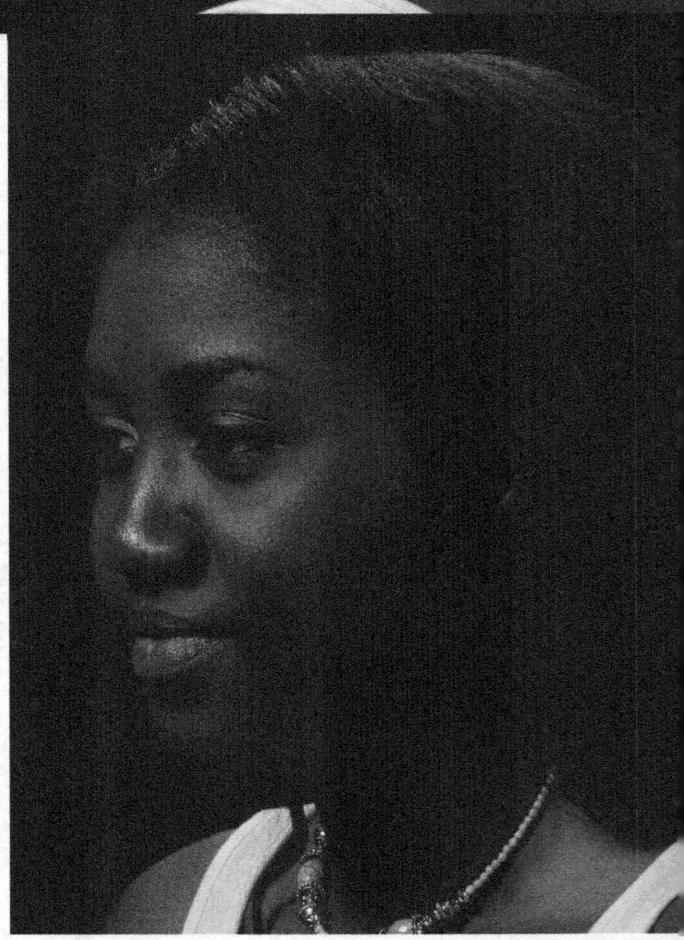

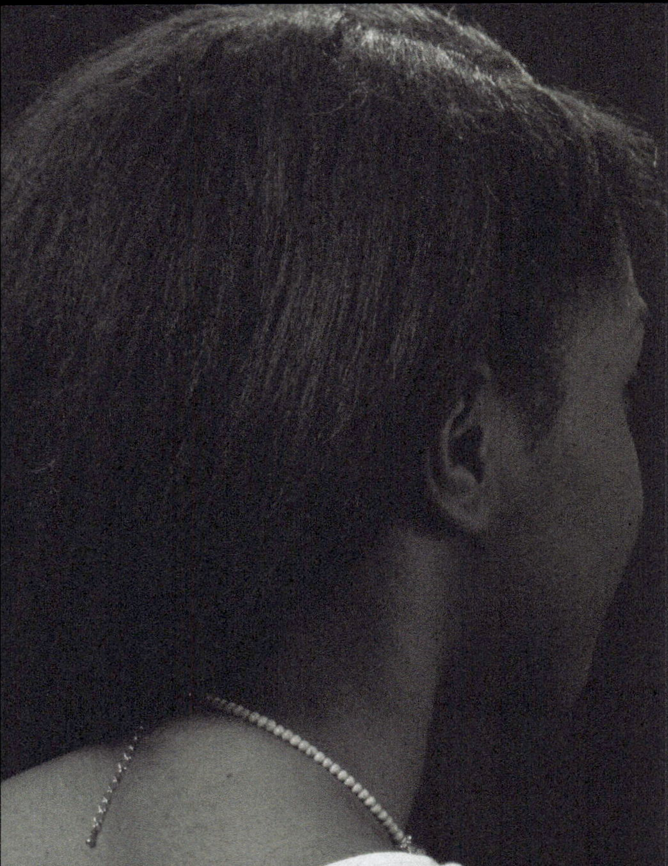

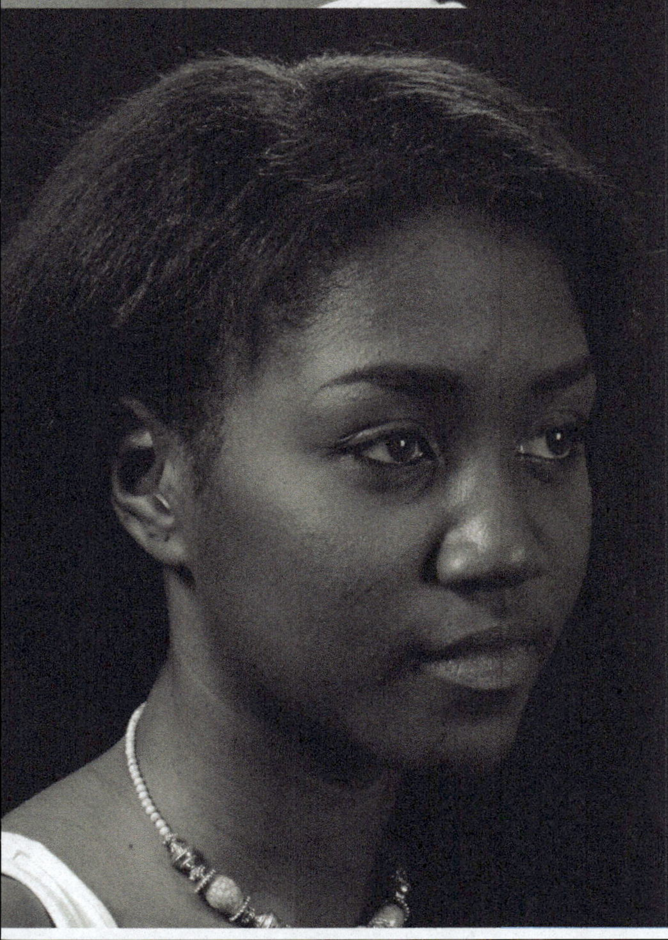

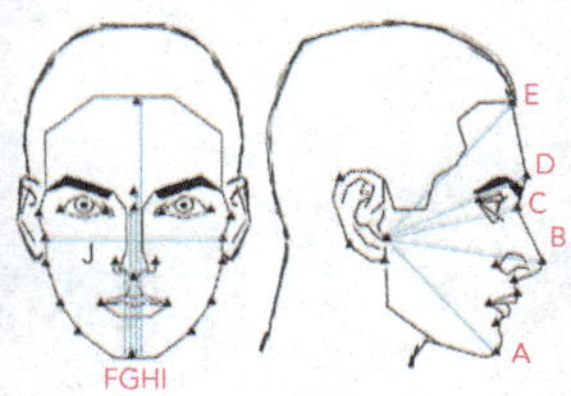


**Head measurements (in):**

A: 5 1/4
B: 5
C: 4 7/8
D: 5 1/8
E: 6
F: 3 3/8
G: 4 1/2
H: 5 3/8
I: 7 7/8
J: 5 1/8

MAP REFERENCE:

65

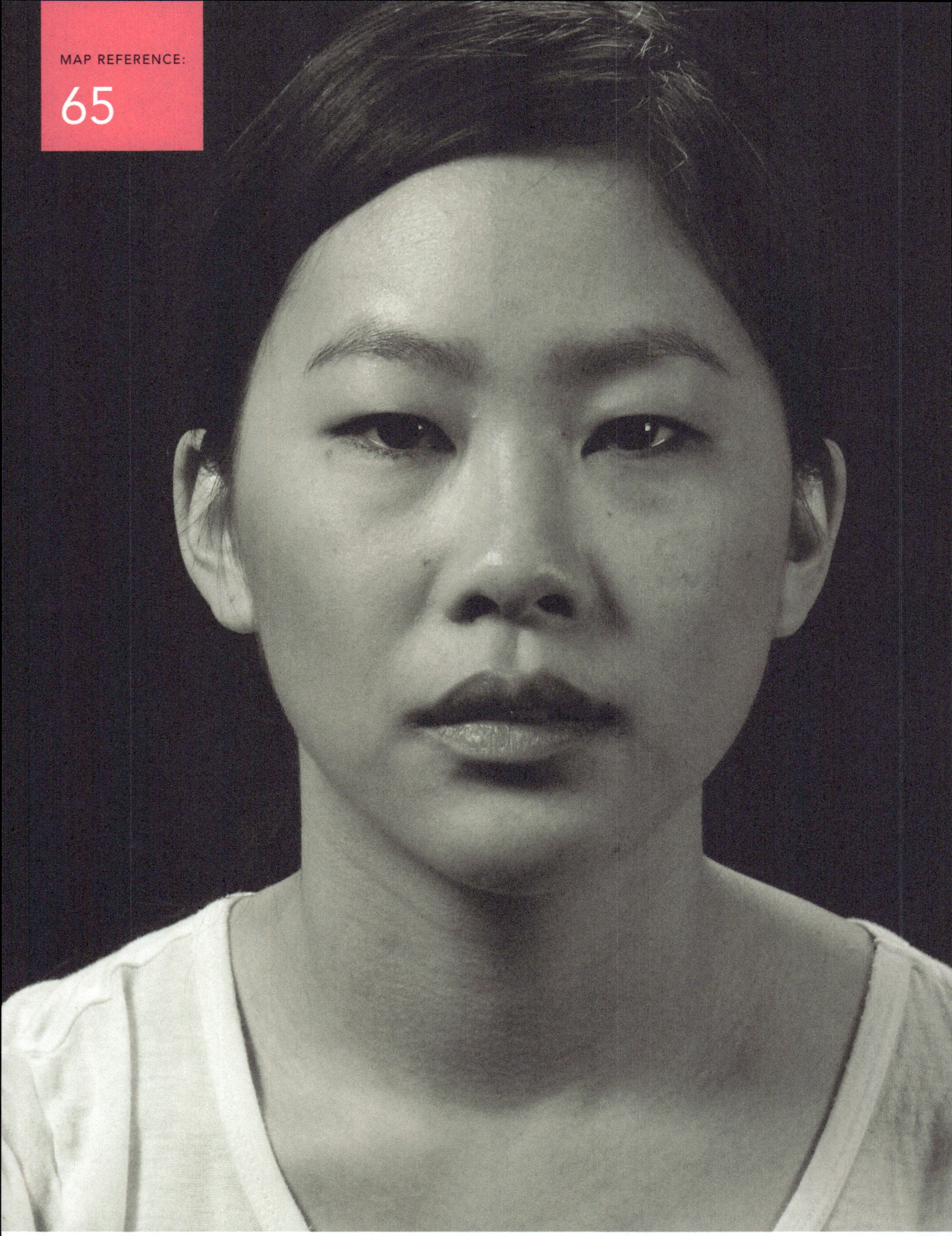

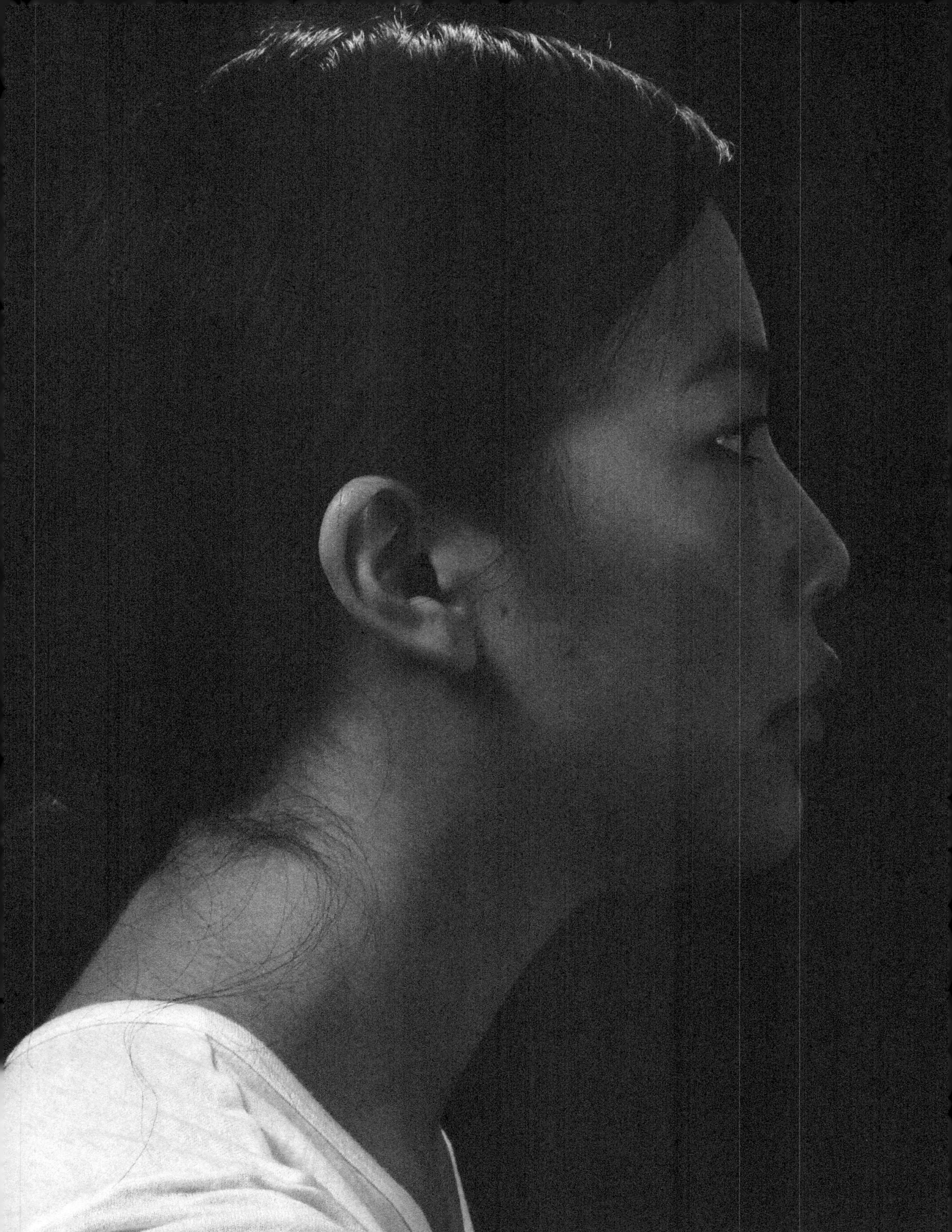

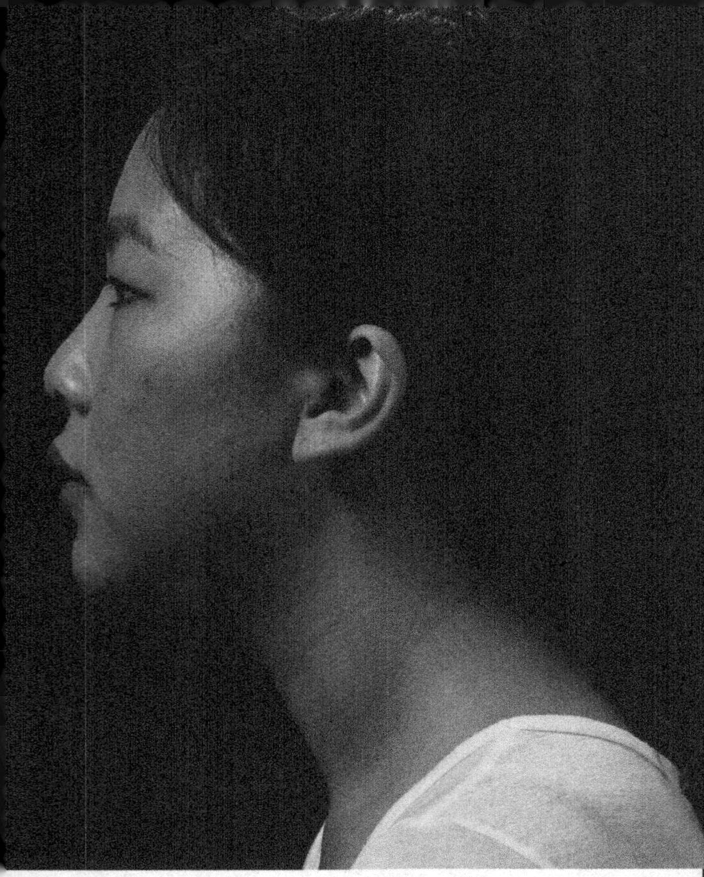

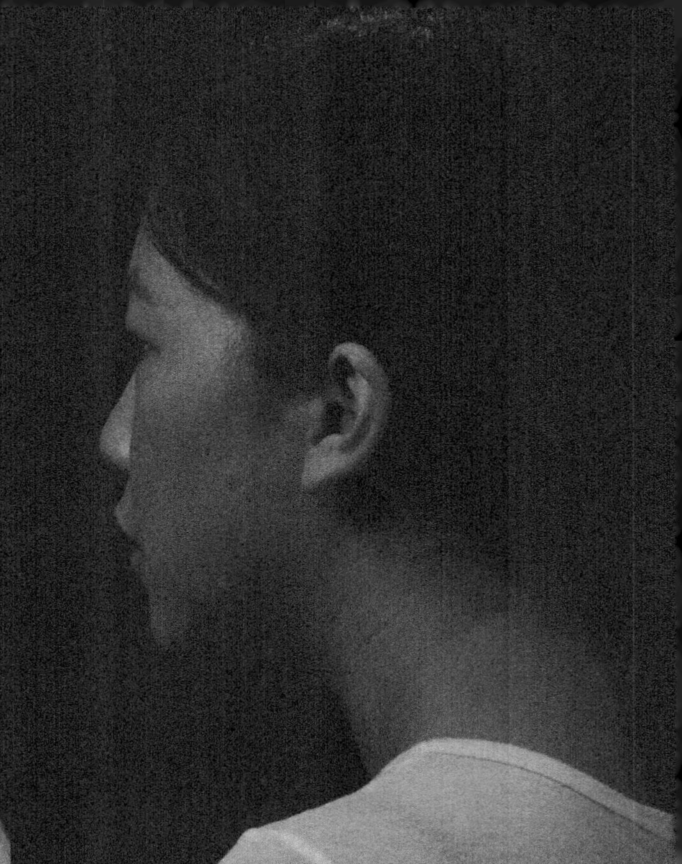

**Ethnicities claimed:**

Hmong Mountains—China.

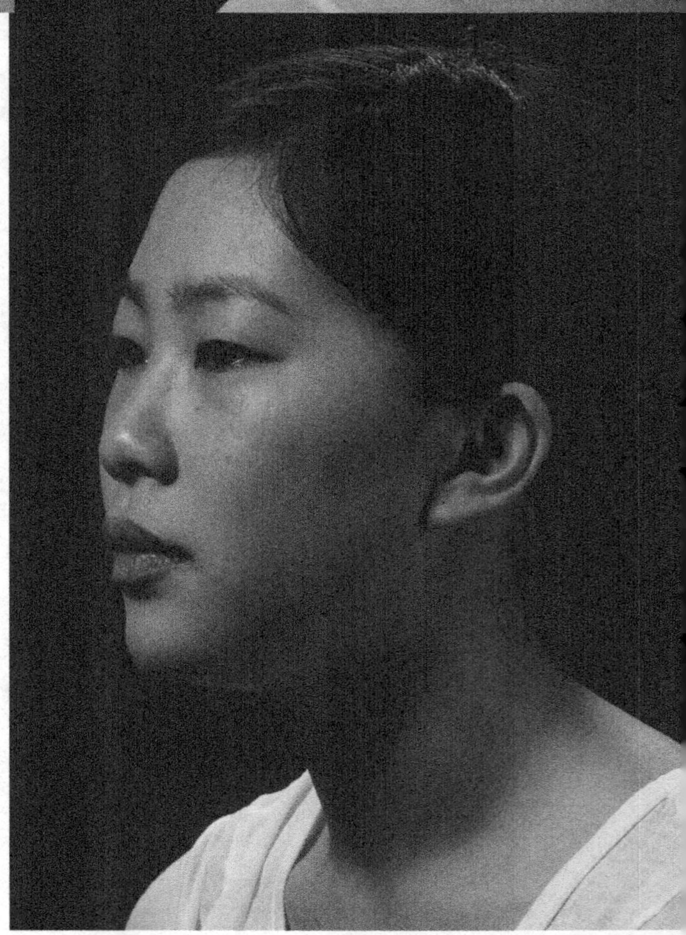

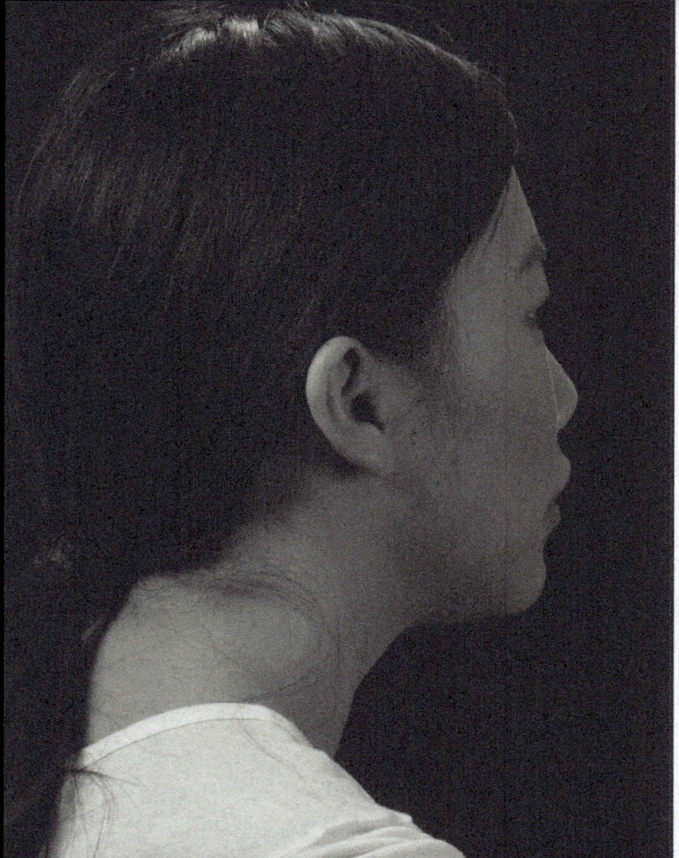

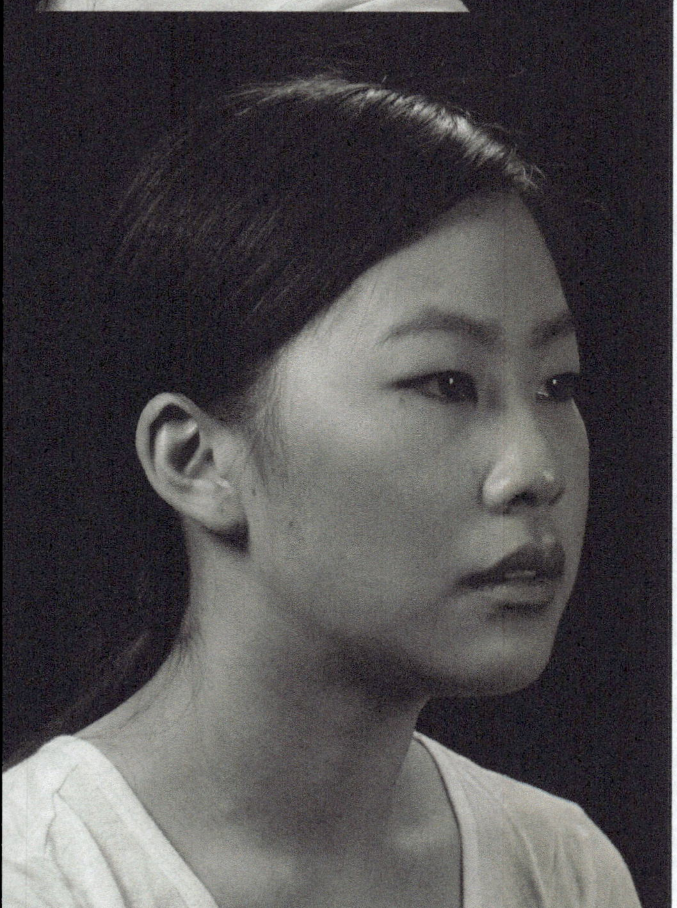

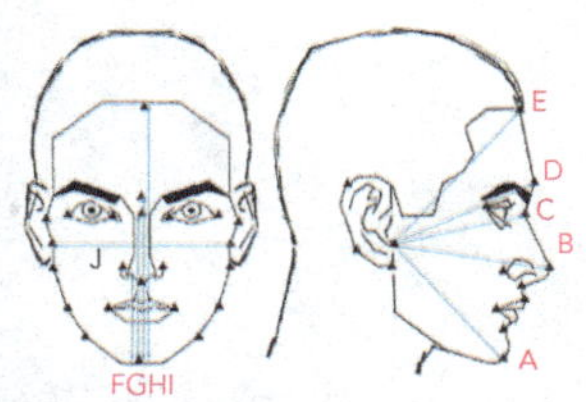


**Head measurements (in):**

A: 4 1/2
B: 4 3/8
C: 4 1/4
D: 4 5/8
E: 5 3/4
F: 3 1/4
G: 4 1/4
H: 4 7/8
I: 7 1/4
J: 5 1/2

MAP REFERENCE:

68

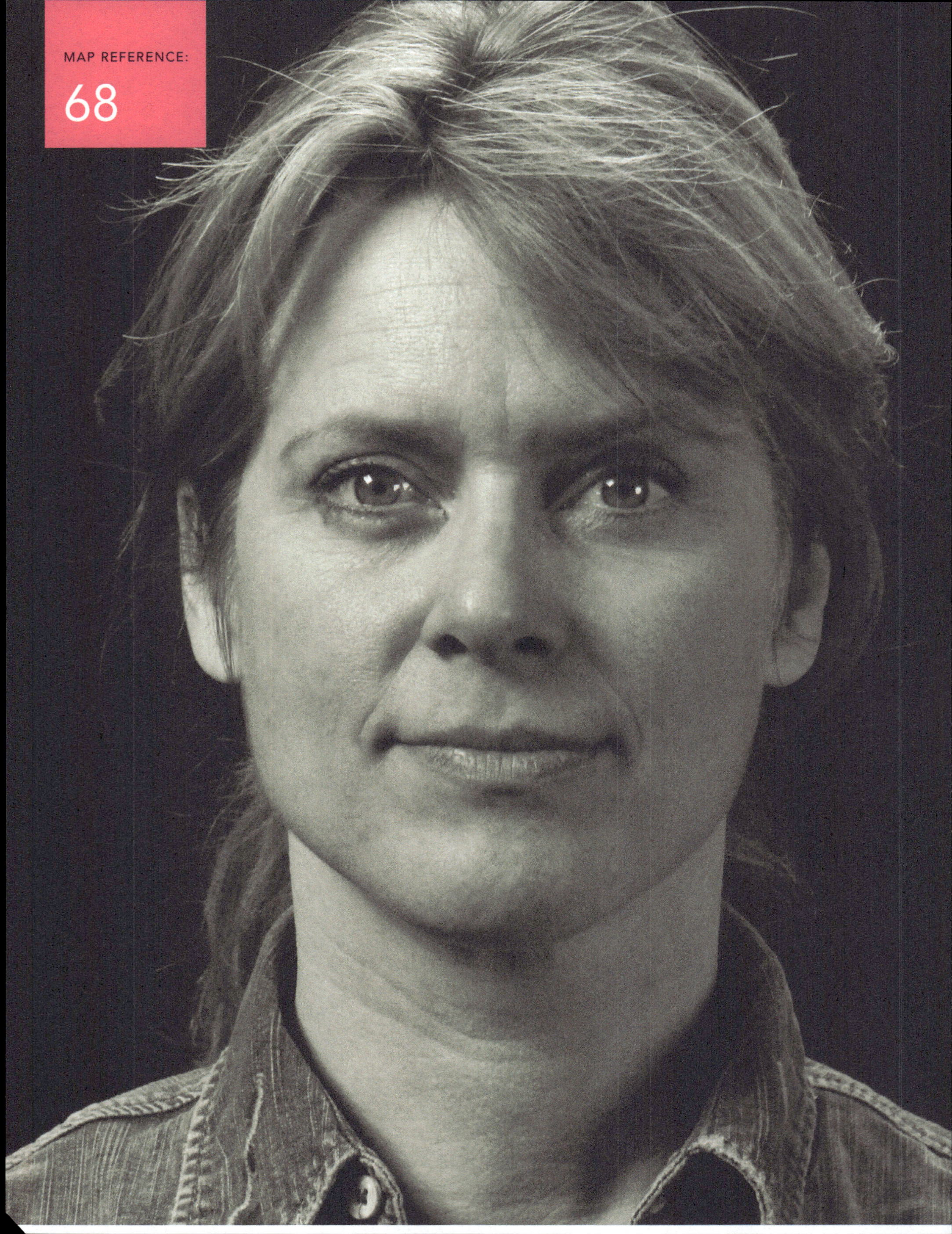

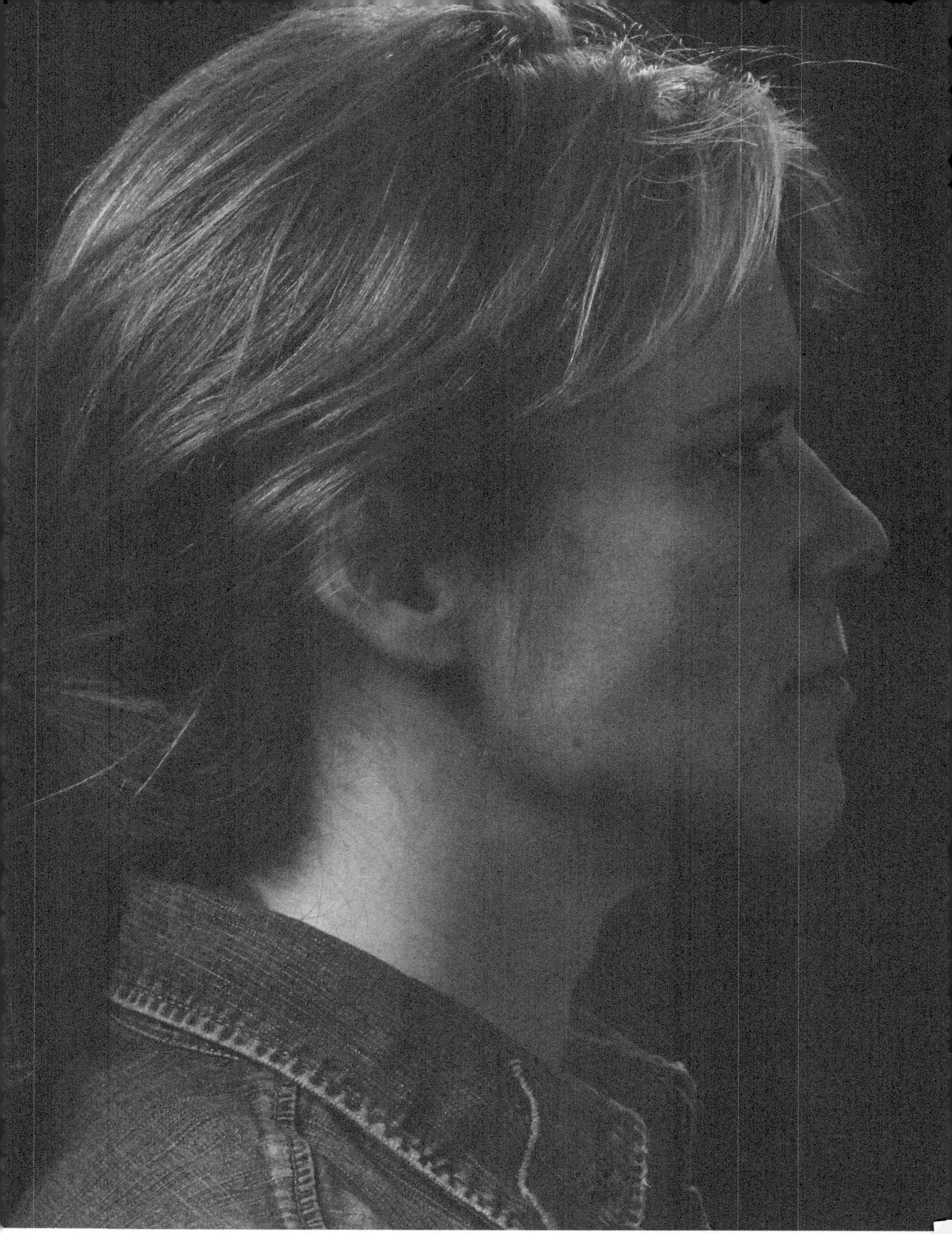

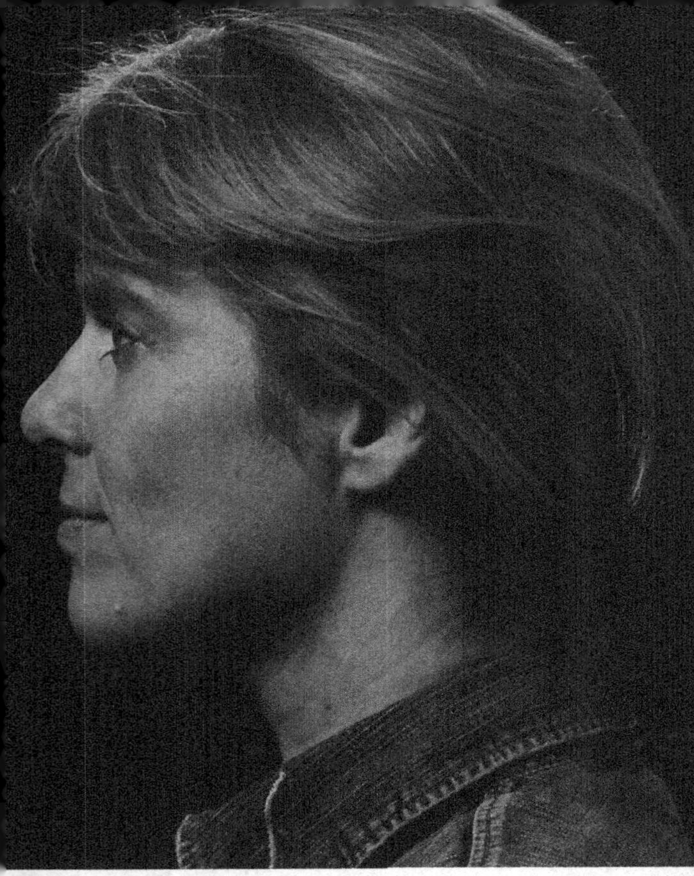

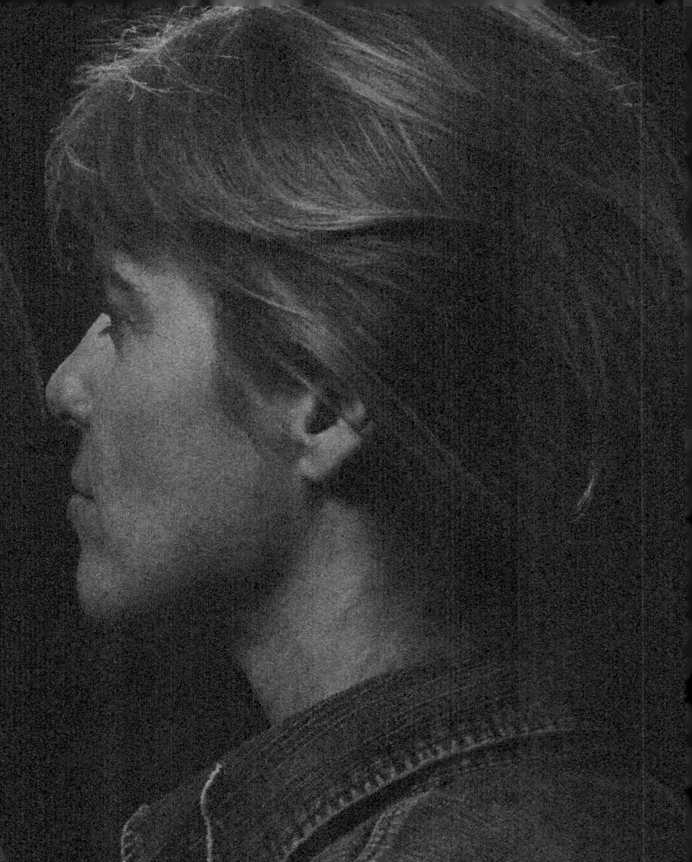

**Ethnicities claimed:**

Germany.

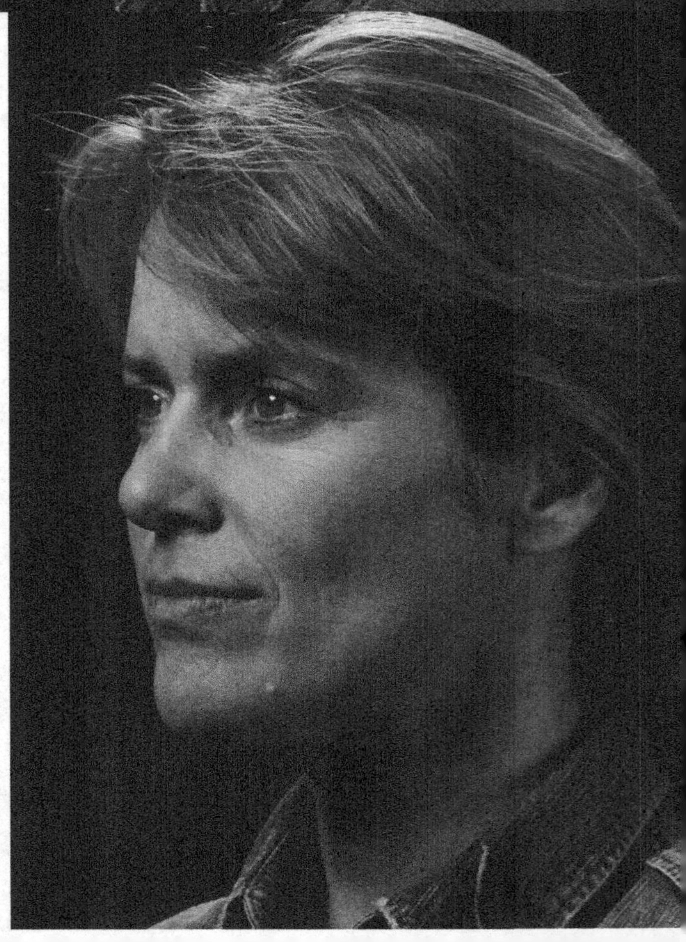

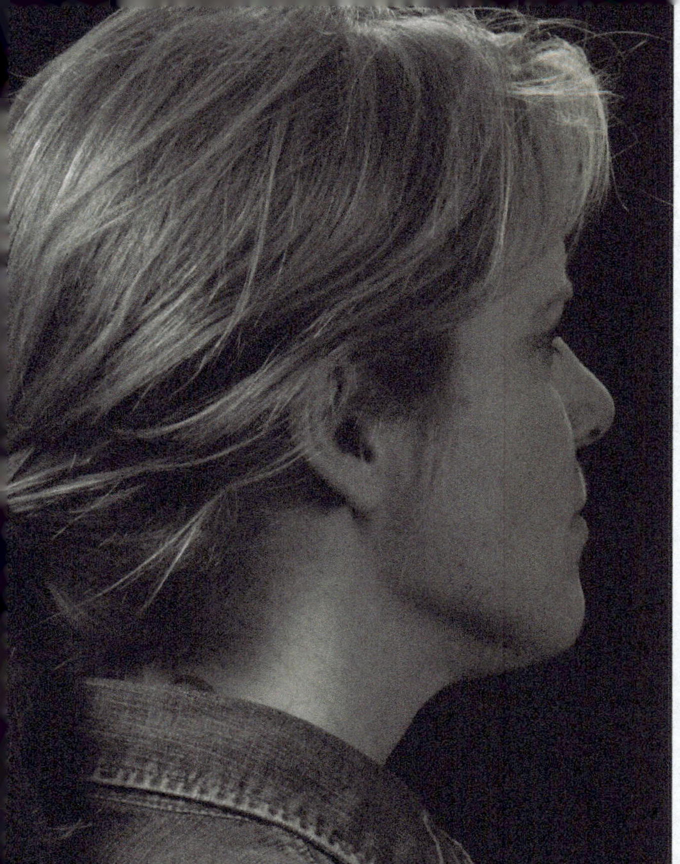

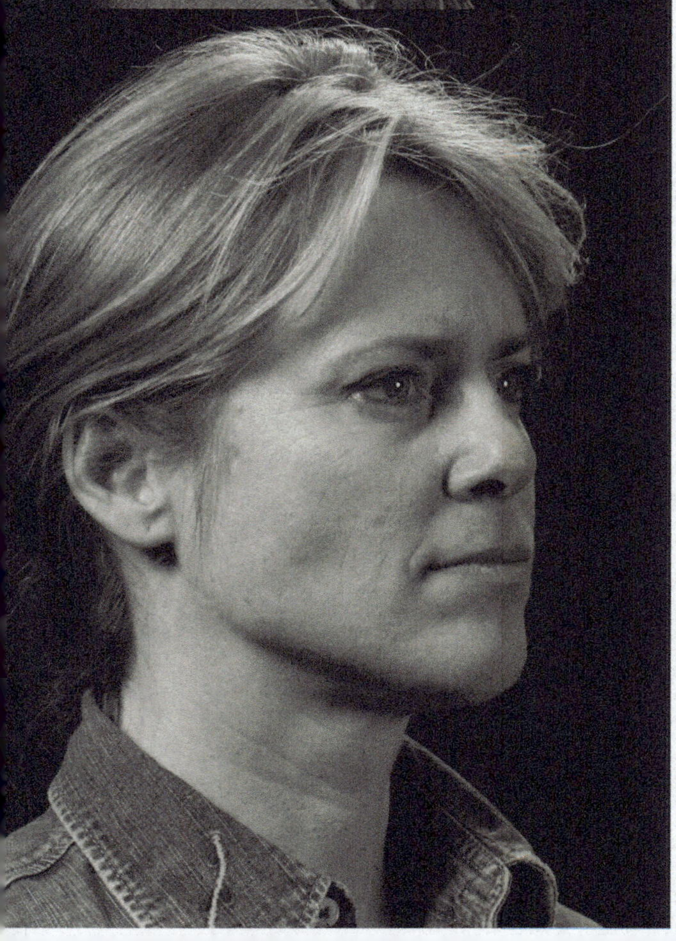

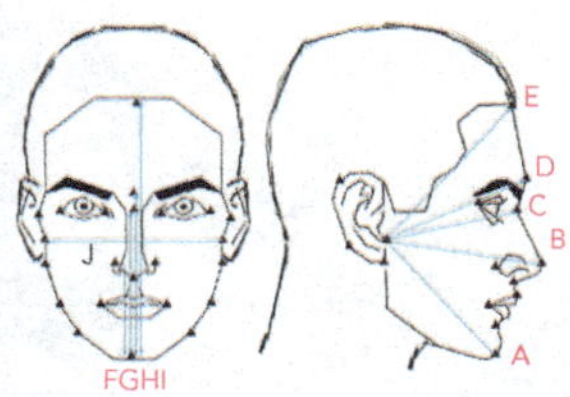


**Head measurements (in):**

A: 5 3/8
B: 5 3/16
C: 4 13/16
D: 5 3/16
E: 6 1/16
F: 3 1/16
G: 4 1/16
H: 4 7/8
I: 7
J: 5 1/4

MAP REFERENCE:

71

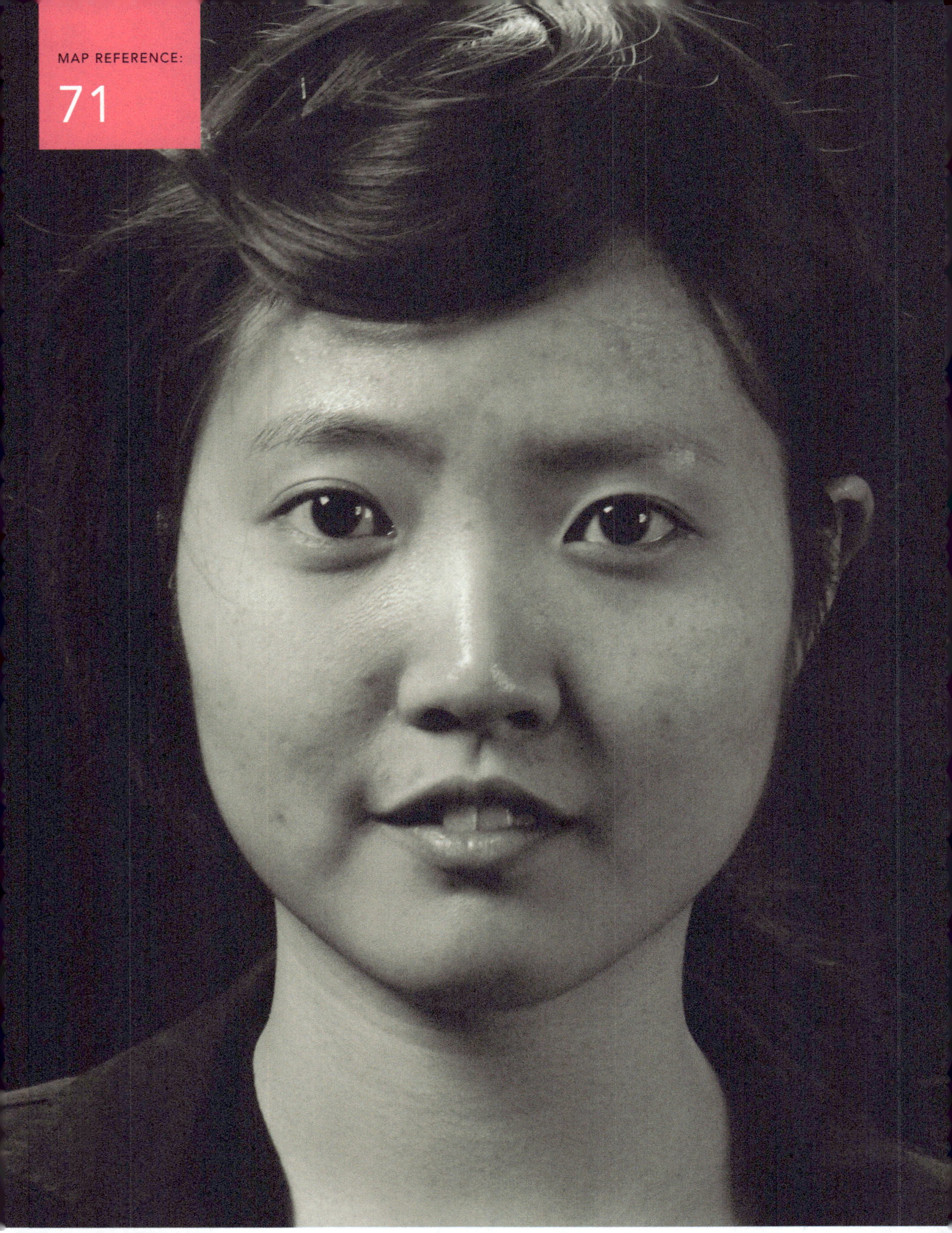

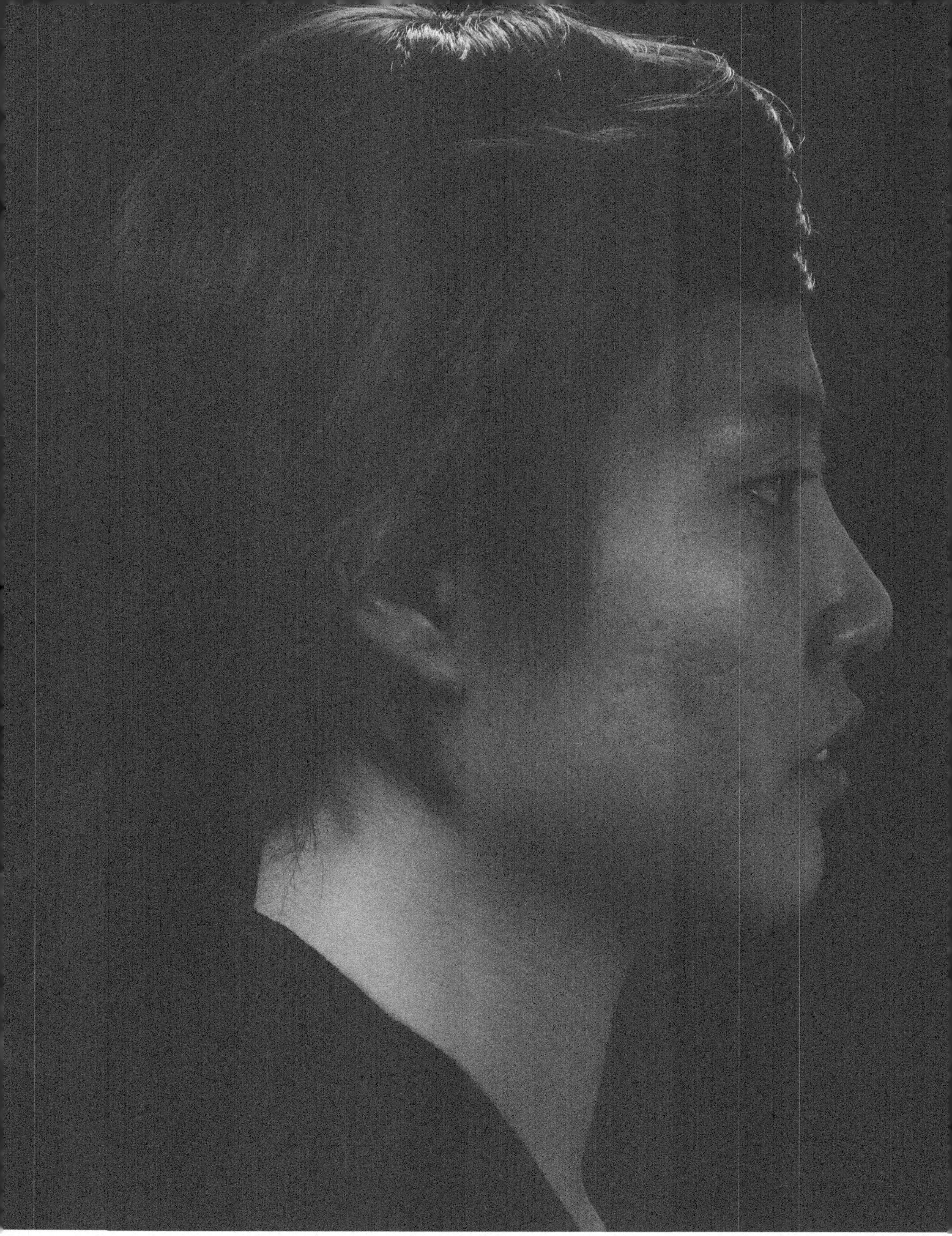

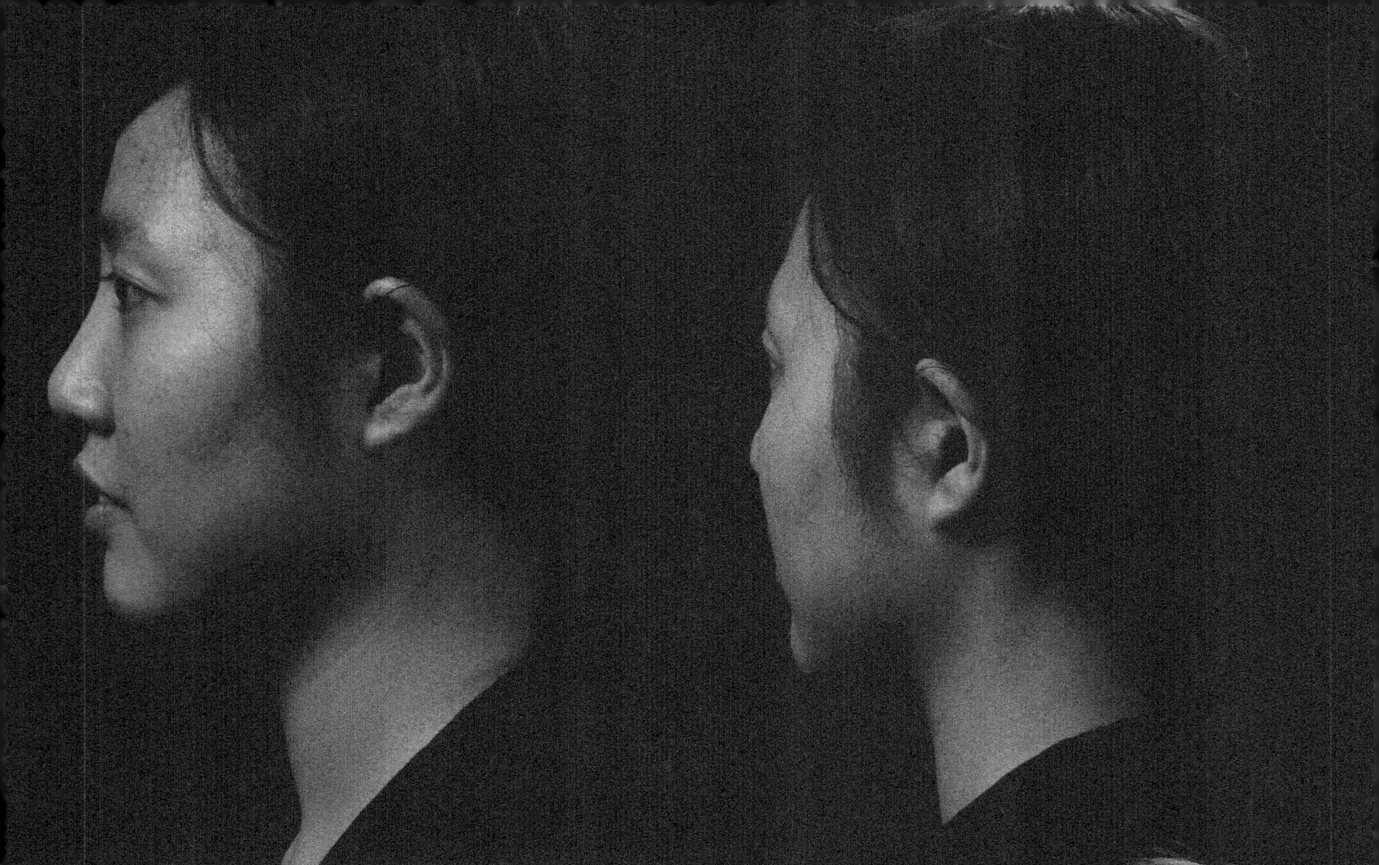

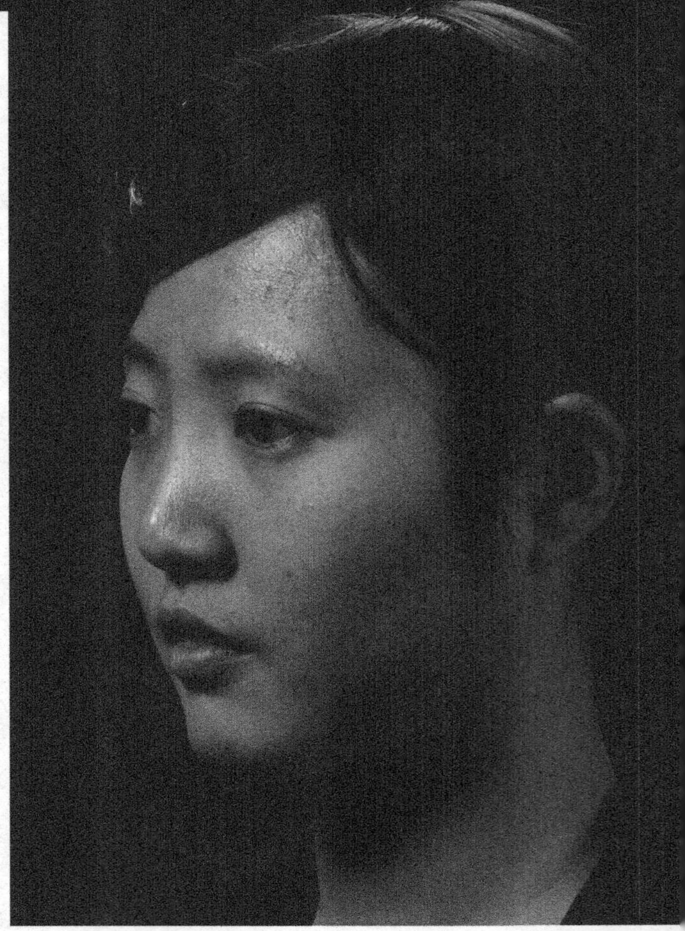

**Ethnicities claimed:**

Korea.

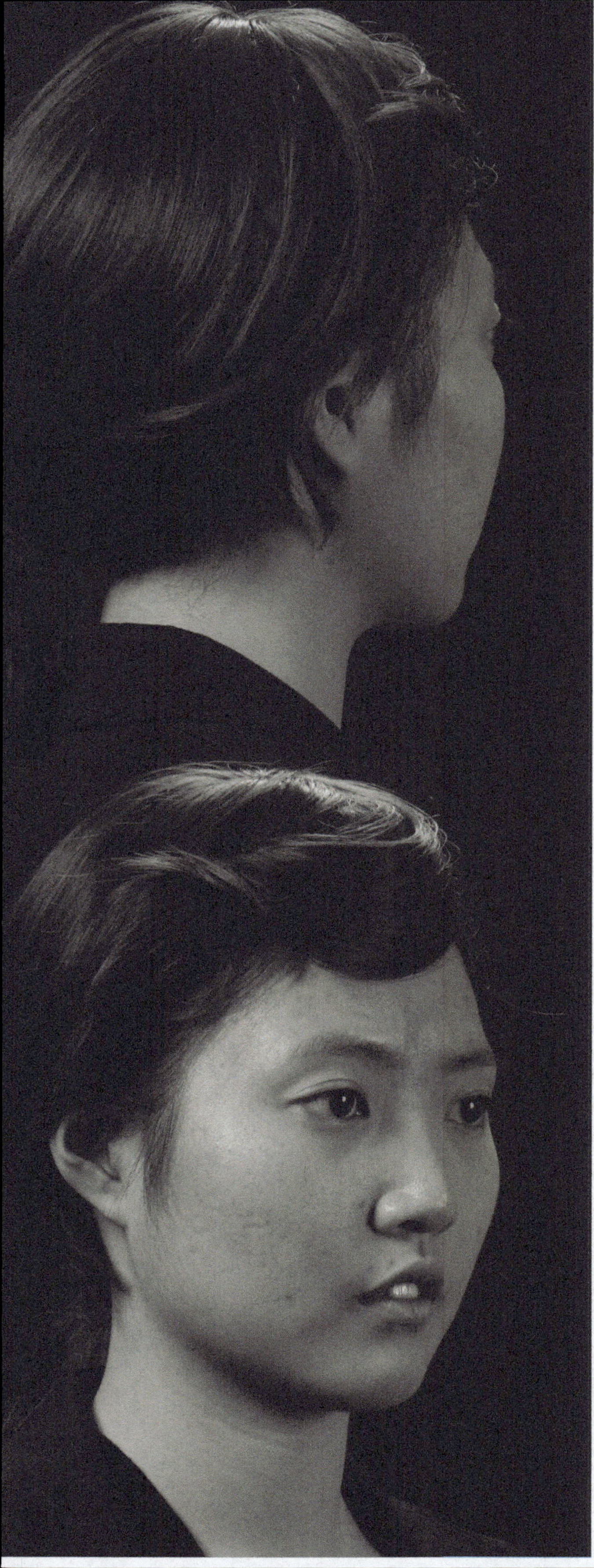

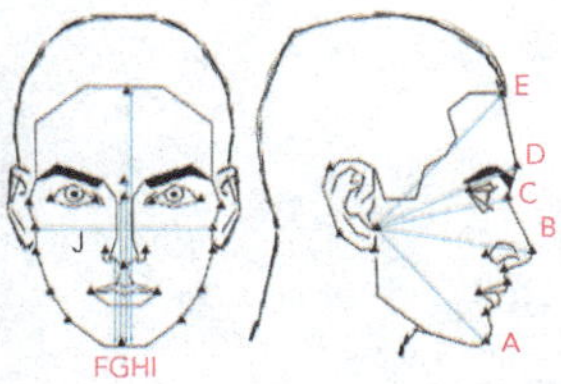


**Head measurements (in):**

A: 5 1/8
B: 5
C: 4 7/8
D: 5
E: 5 5/8
F: 3 1/8
G: 4 3/8
H: 5 1/4
I: 7 3/4
J: 5 1/2

MAP REFERENCE:

72

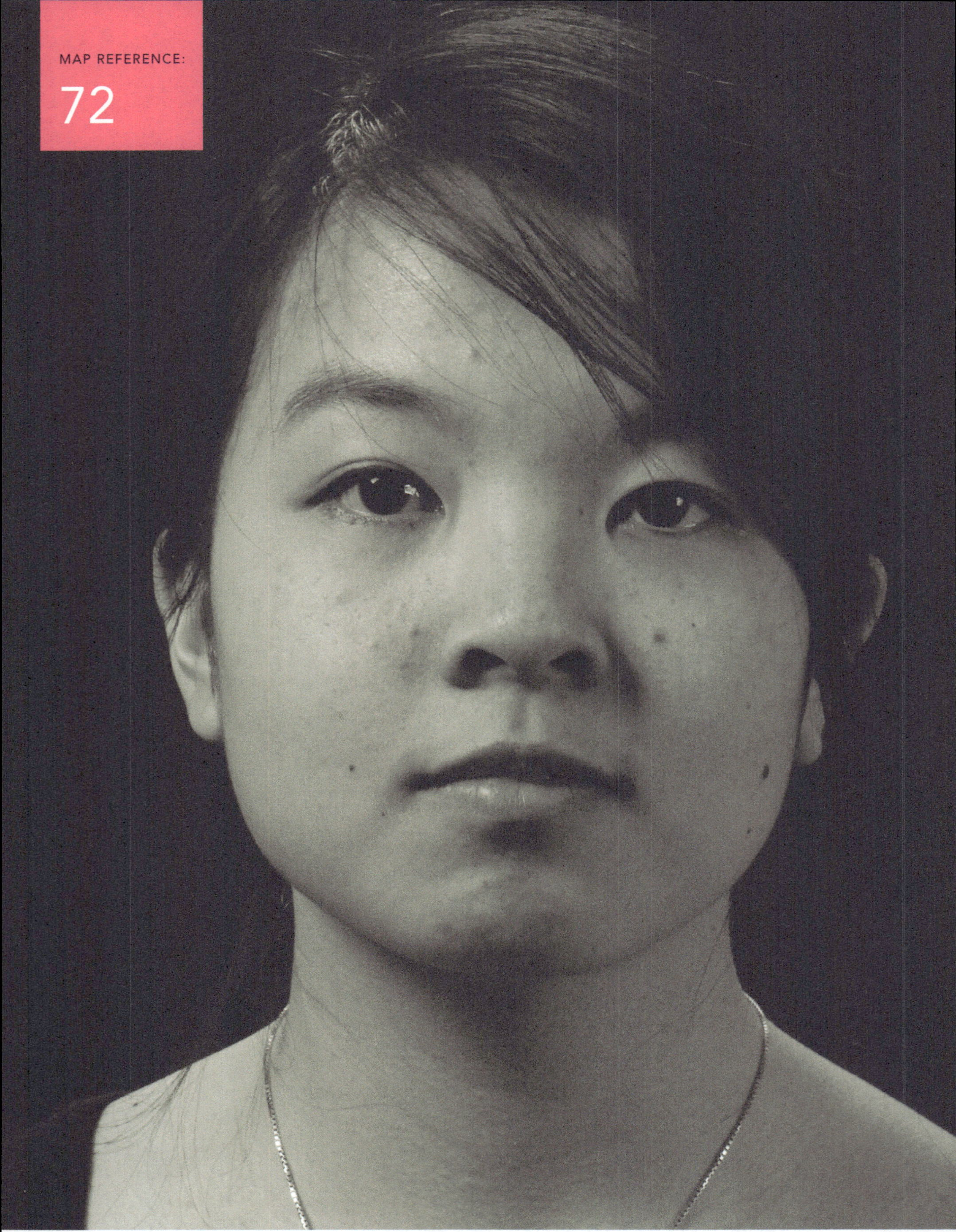

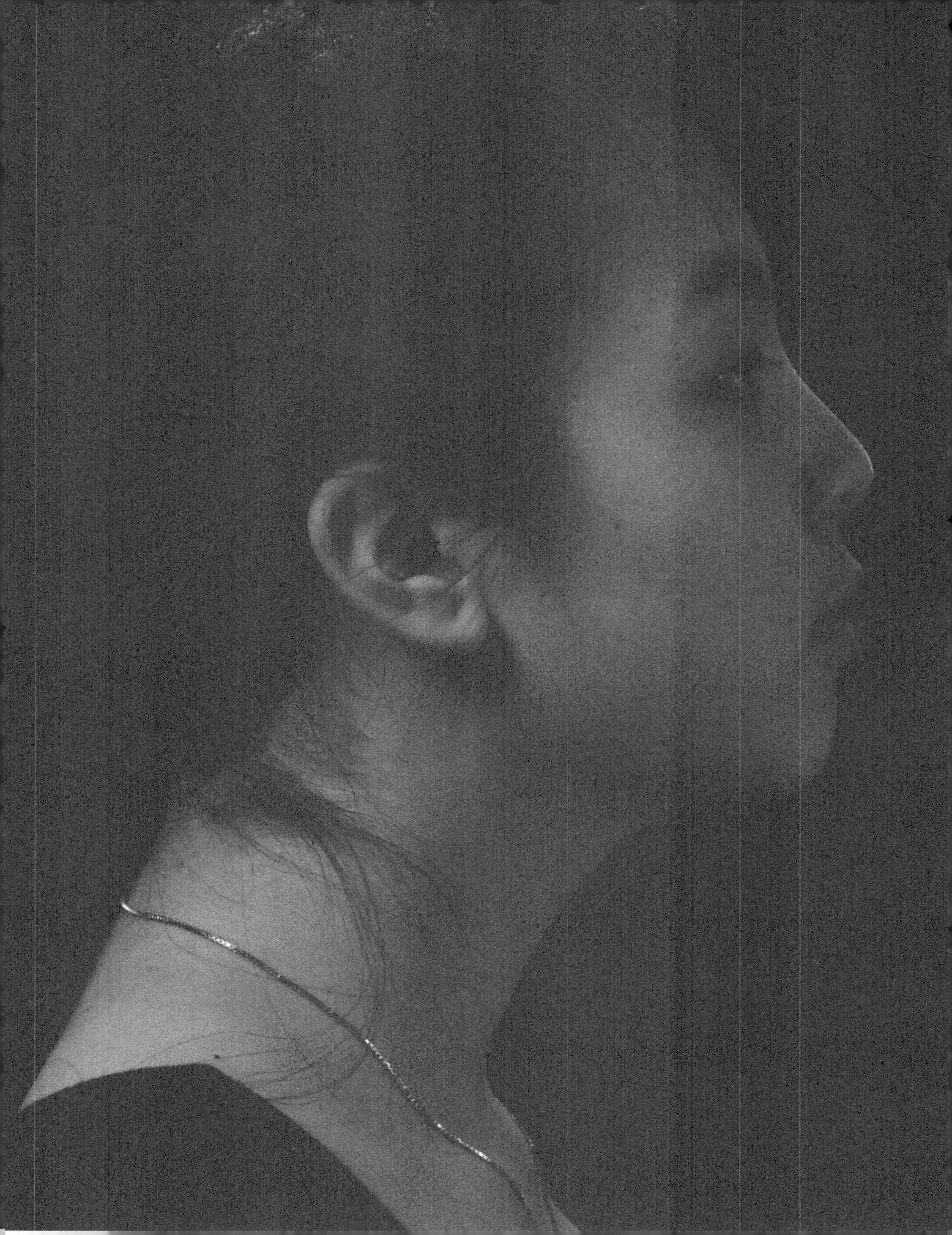

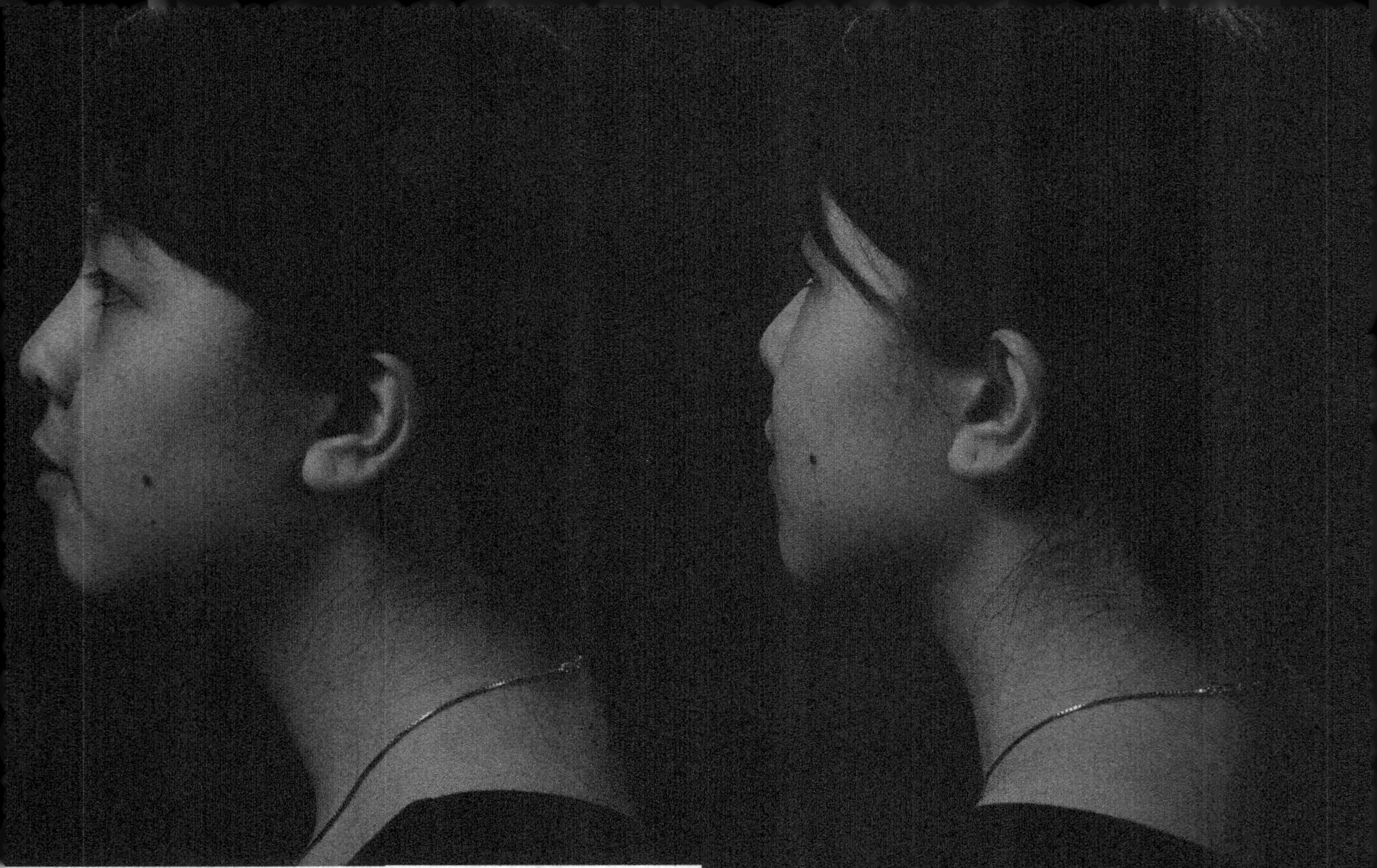

**Ethnicities claimed:**

Chinese, Cambodian.

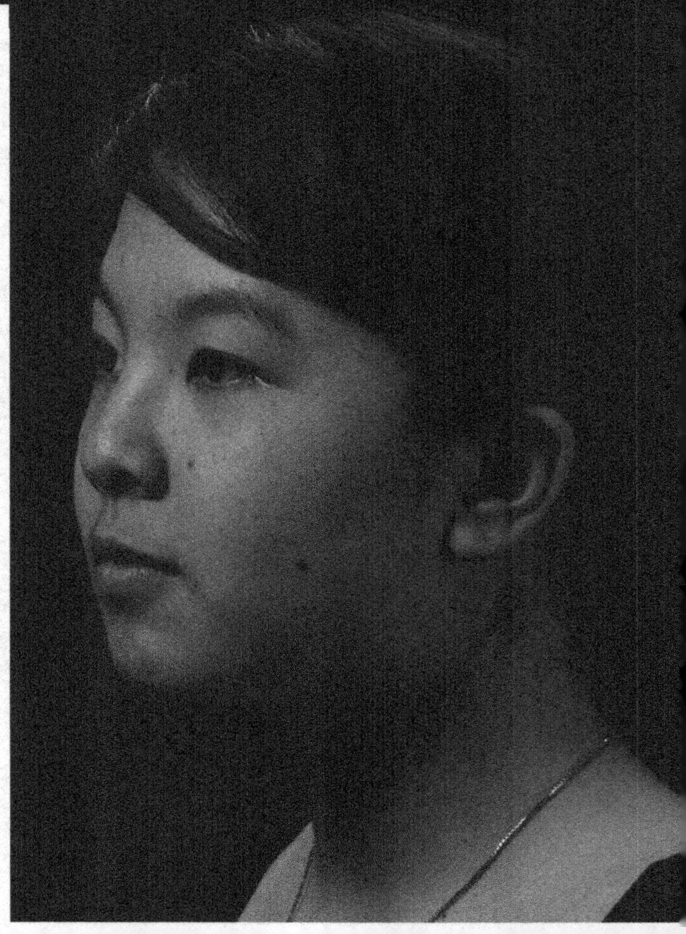

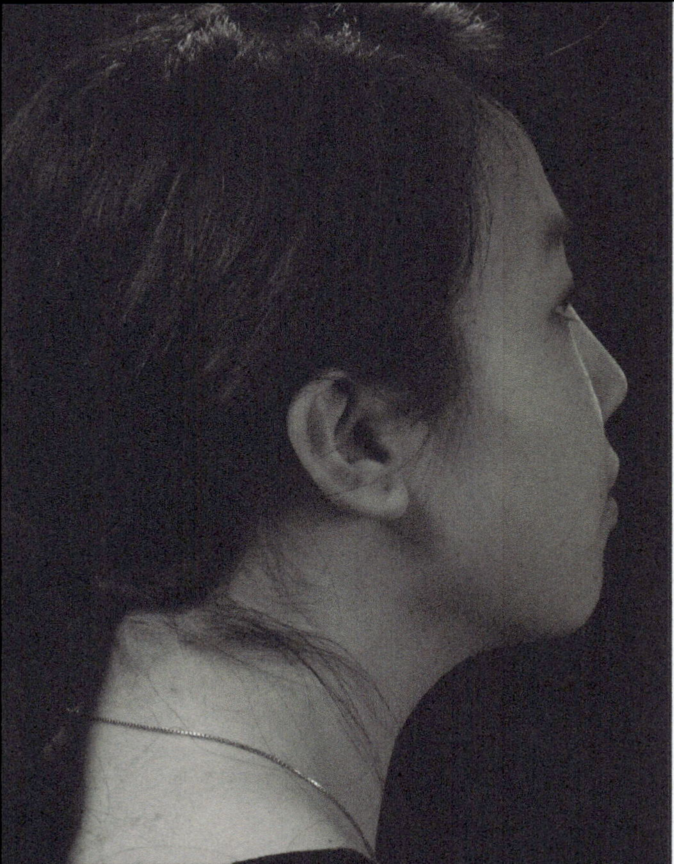

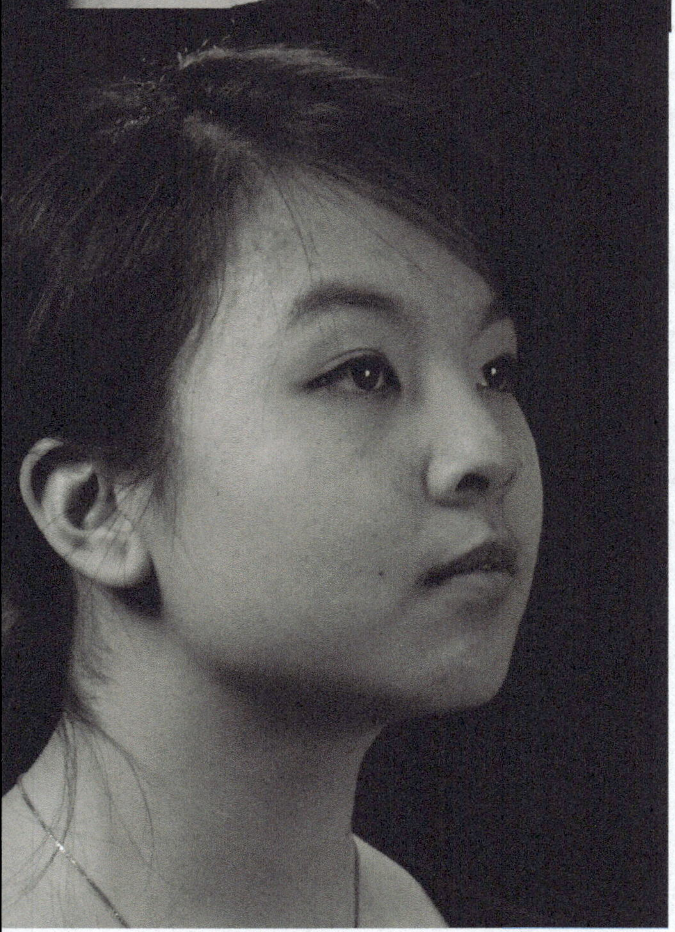

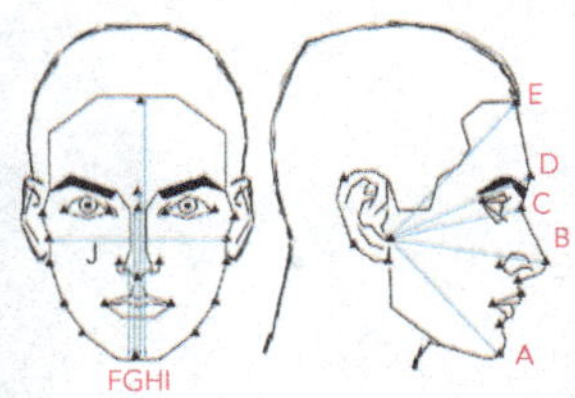


**Head measurements (in):**

A: 5 3/8
B: 5
C: 4 3/4
D: 4 5/8
E: 5 3/8
F: 3 1/8
G: 4 1/2
H: 5
I: 7 1/2
J: 5 1/4

MAP REFERENCE:

73

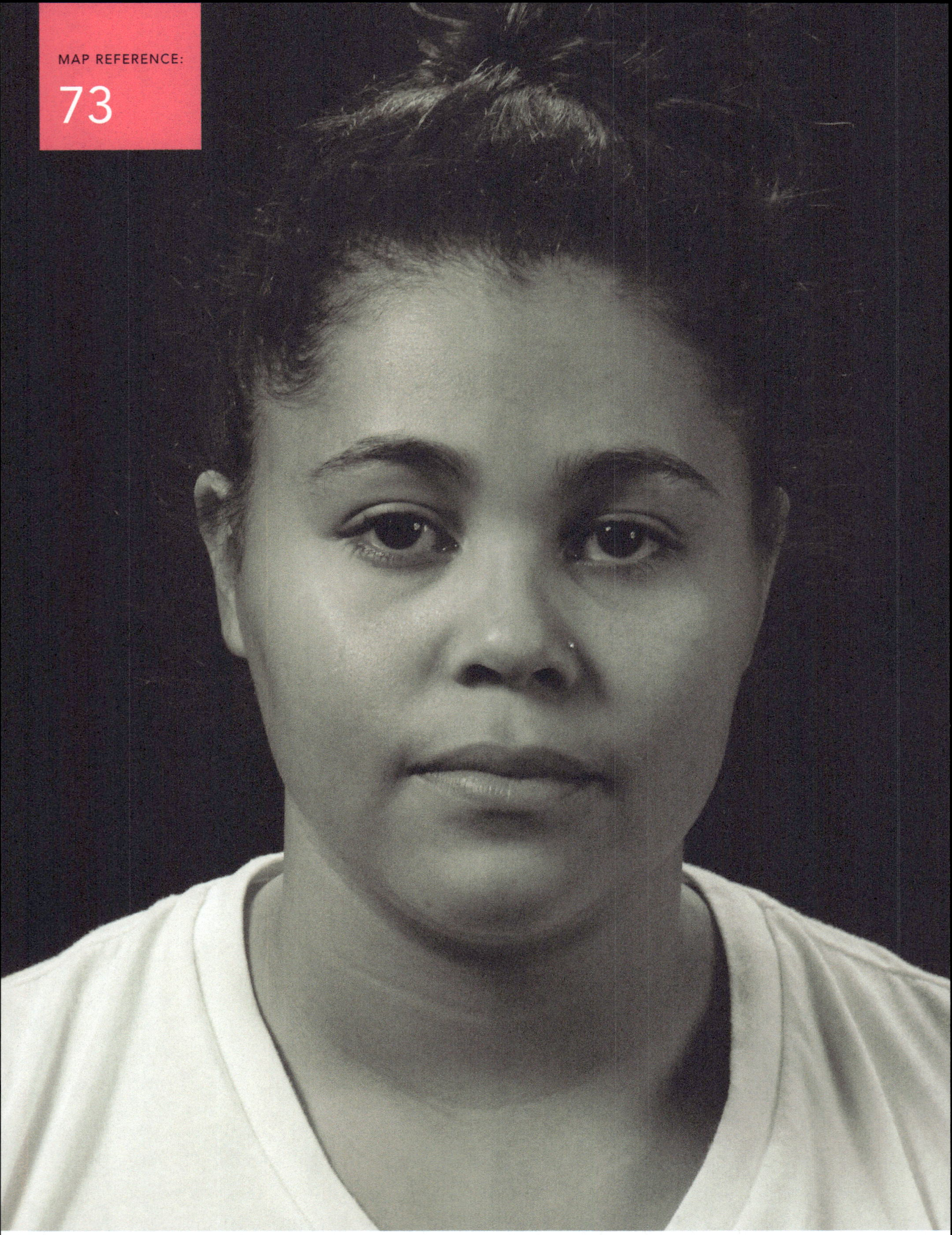

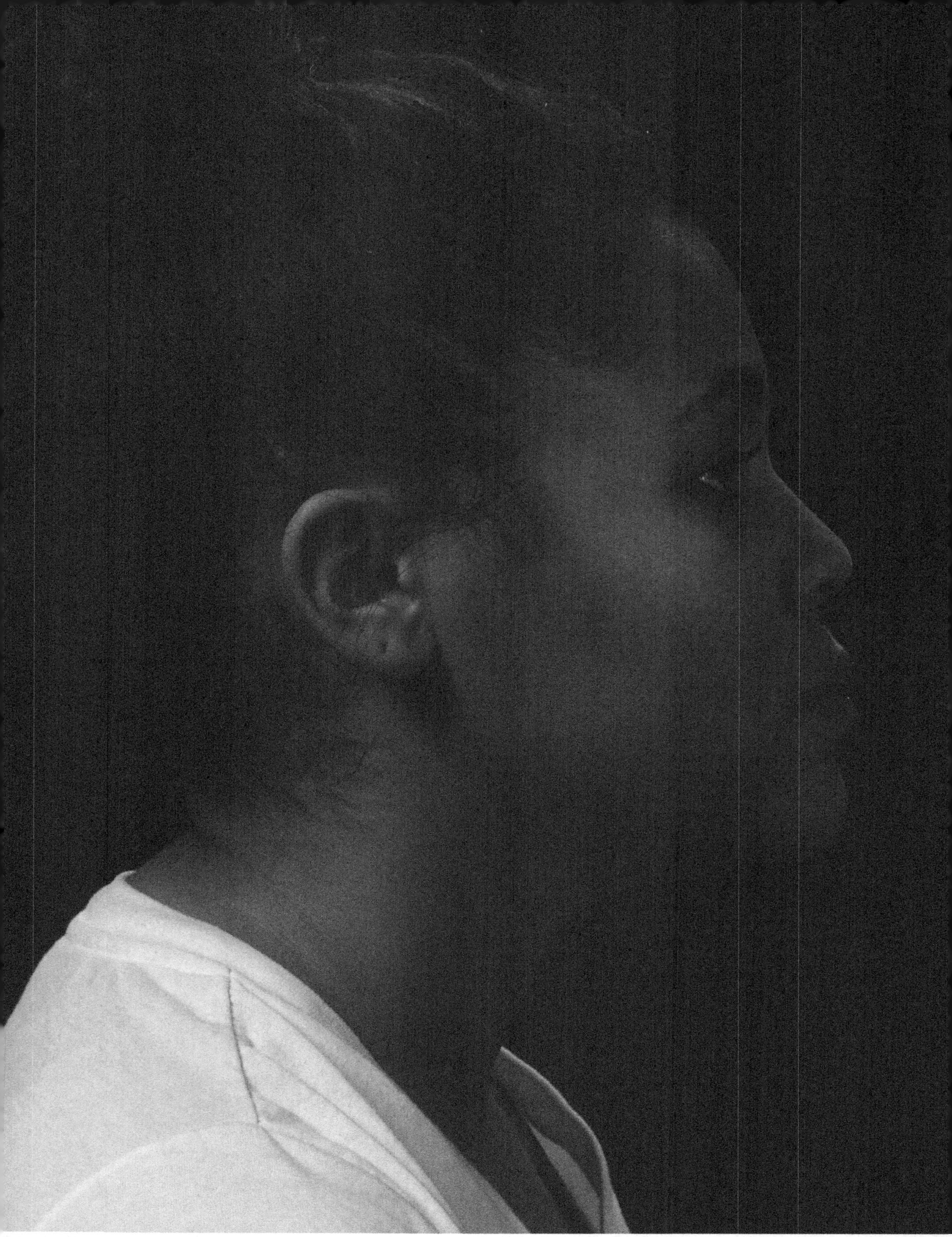

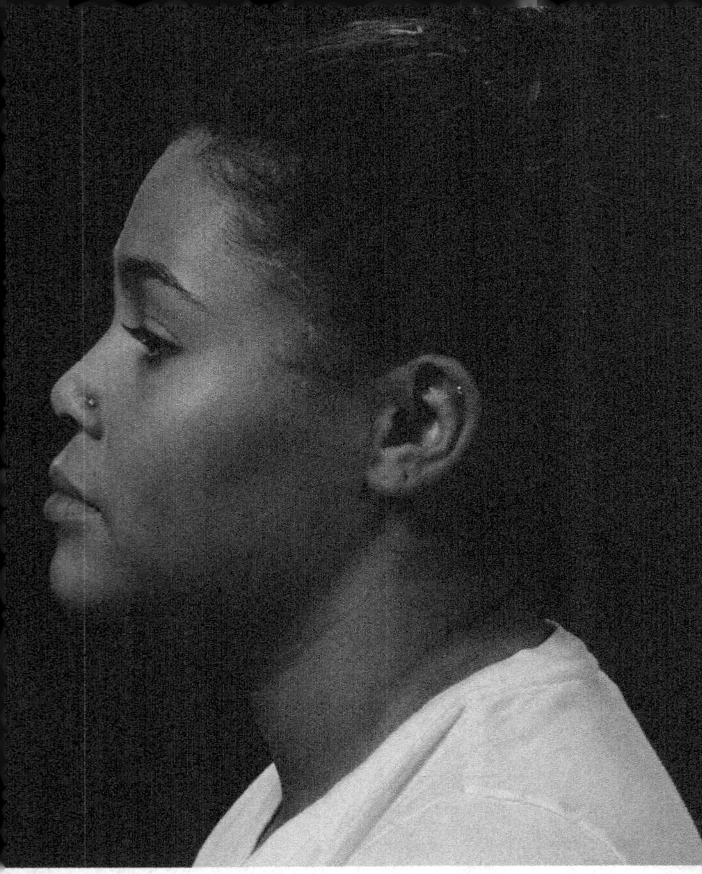

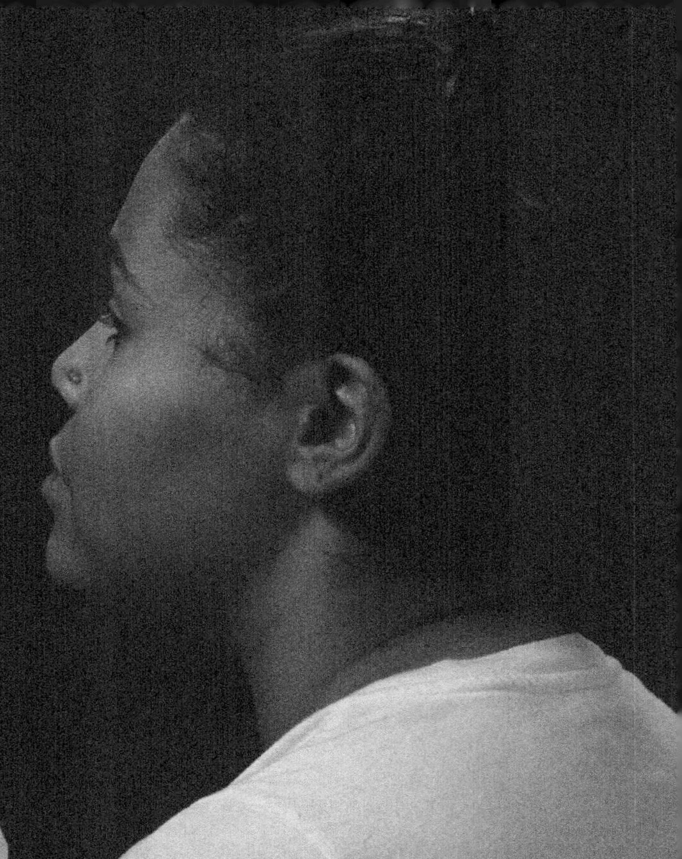

**Ethnicities claimed:**

Philippines, Mexico, United States—African American

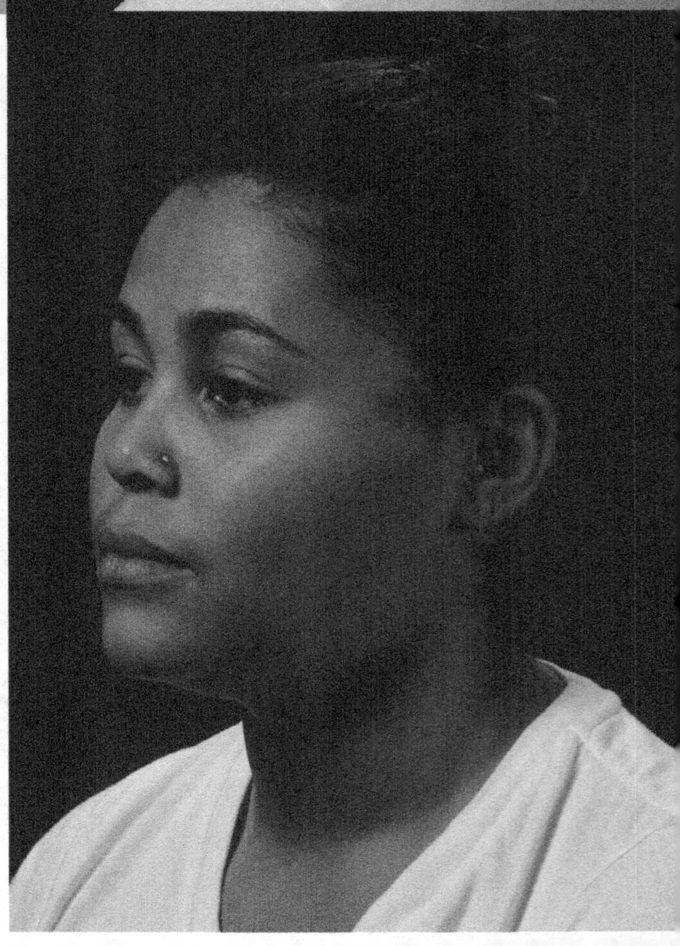

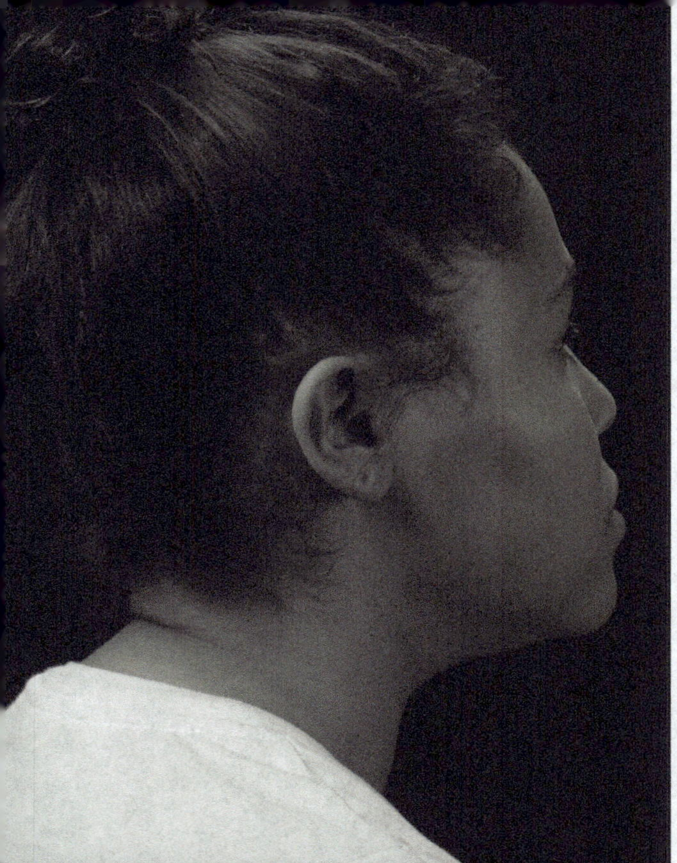

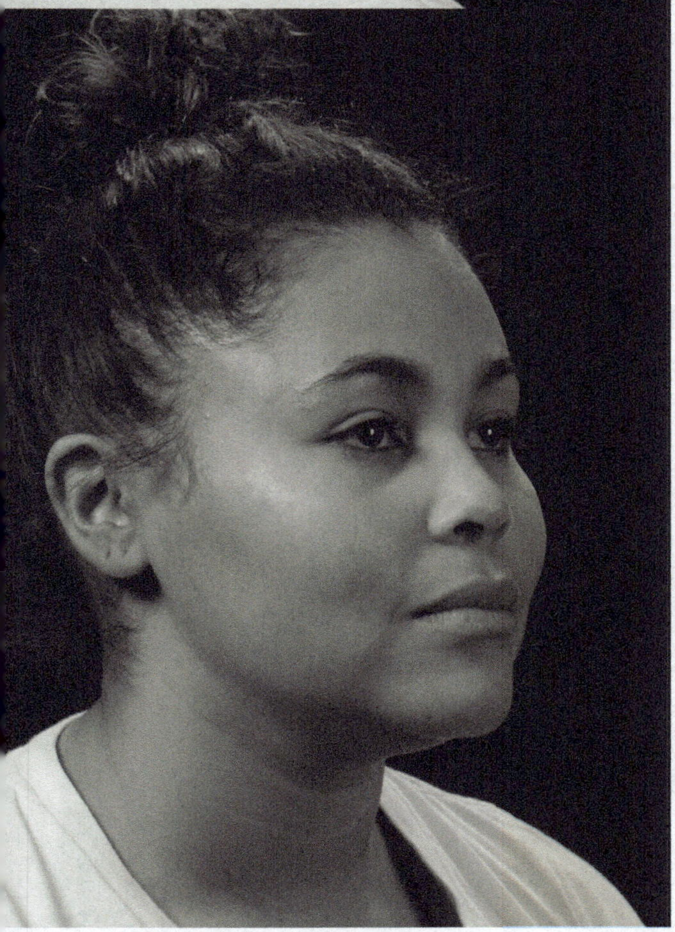

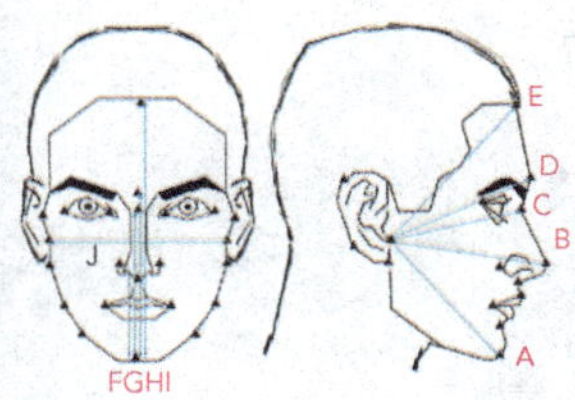


**Head measurements (in):**

A: 5 3/4
B: 5 1/4
C: 4 3/4
D: 5
E: 5 5/8
F: 3 1/8
G: 4 1/2
H: 4 7/8
I: 7 1/4
J: 5 1/4

MAP REFERENCE:

75

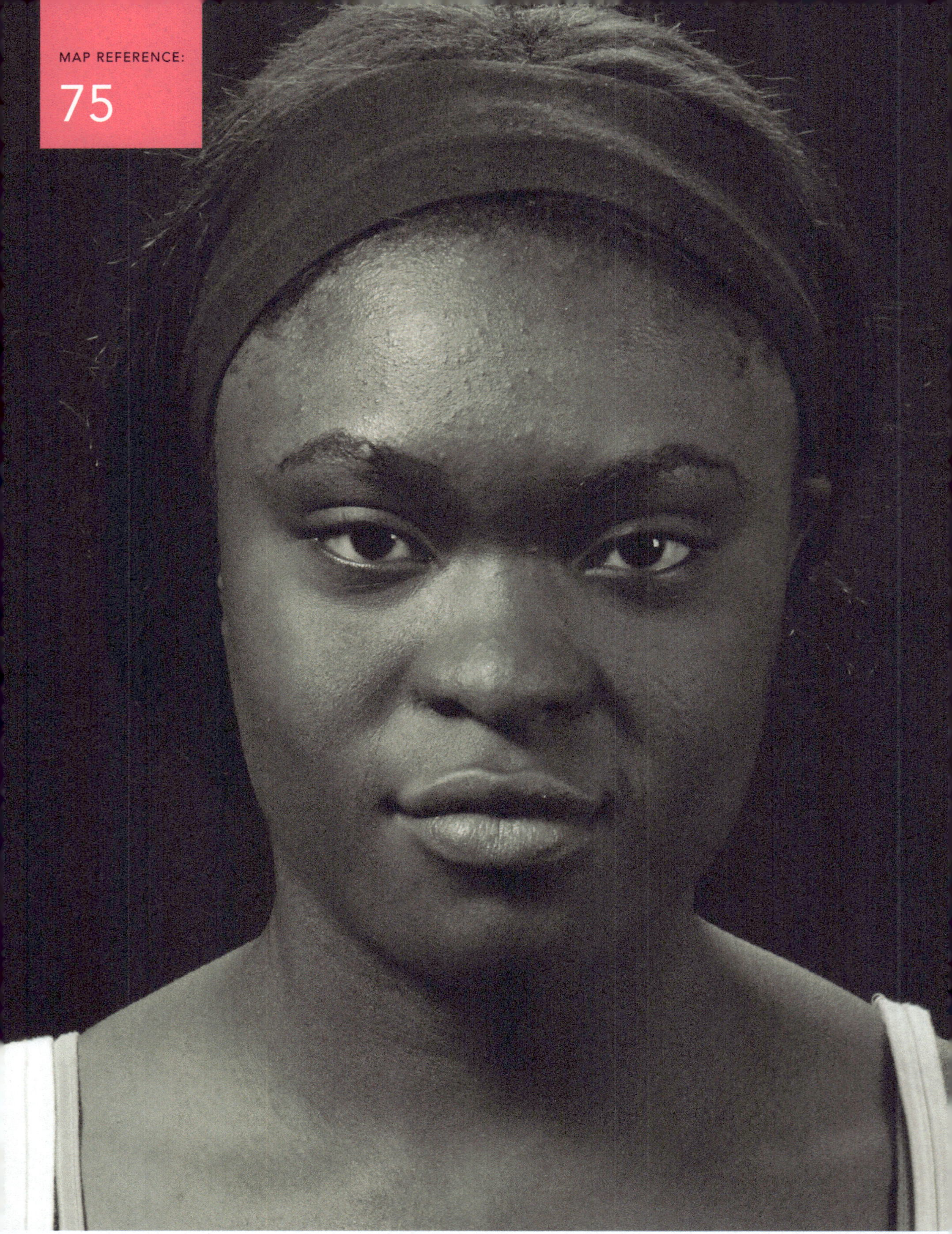

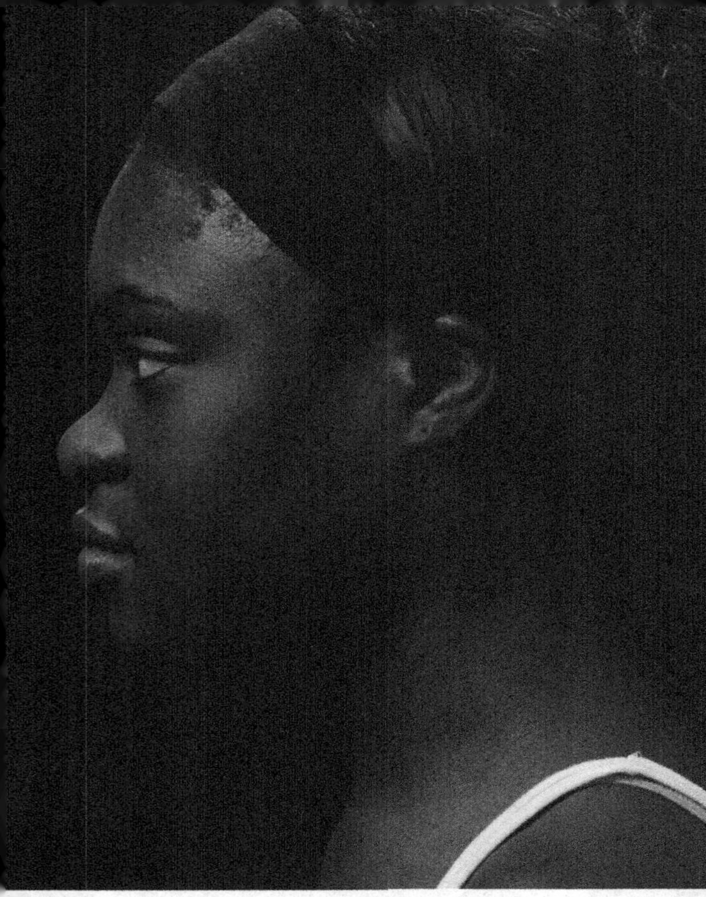

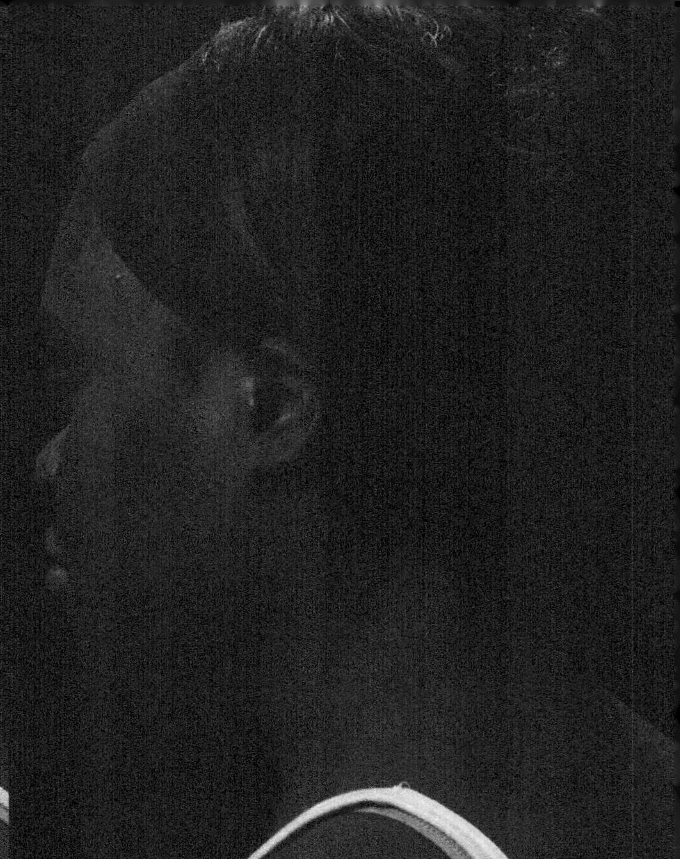

**Ethnicities claimed:**

United States—African American.

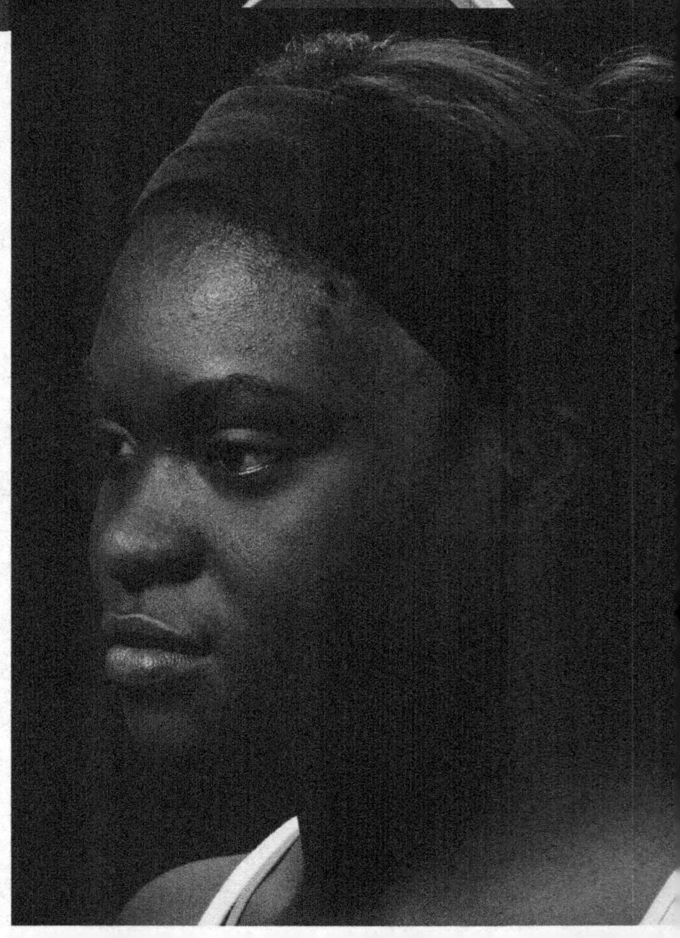

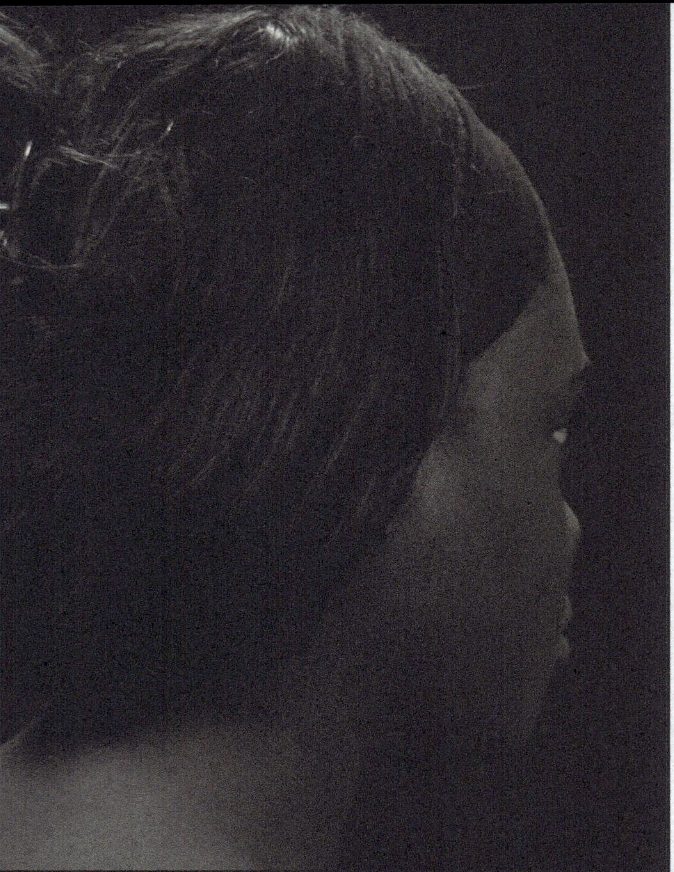

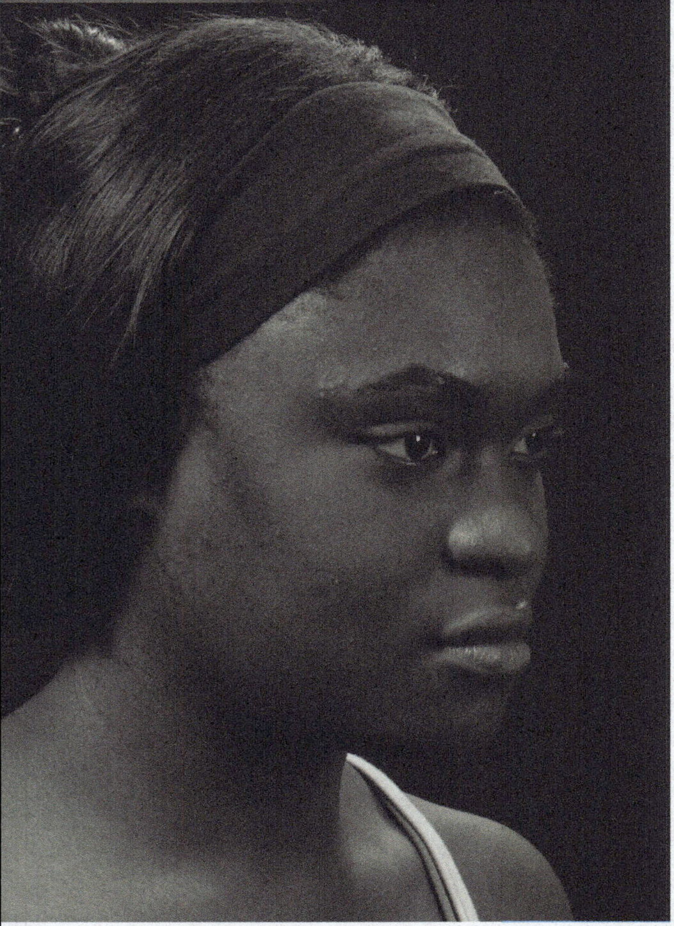

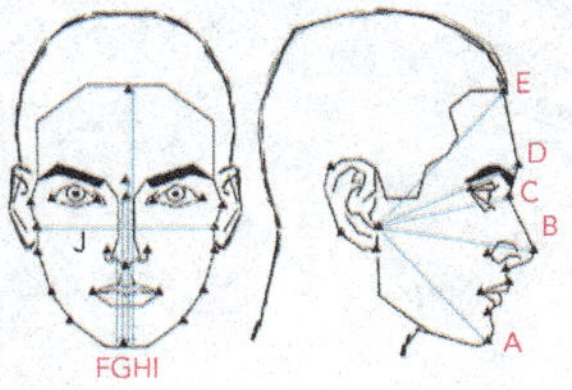


**Head measurements (in):**

A: 5 5/8
B: 5 1/2
C: 4 5/8
D: 5 1/4
E: 5 3/4
F: 3 3/8
G: 4 1/2
H: 4 7/8
I: 7 1/2
J: 5 5/8

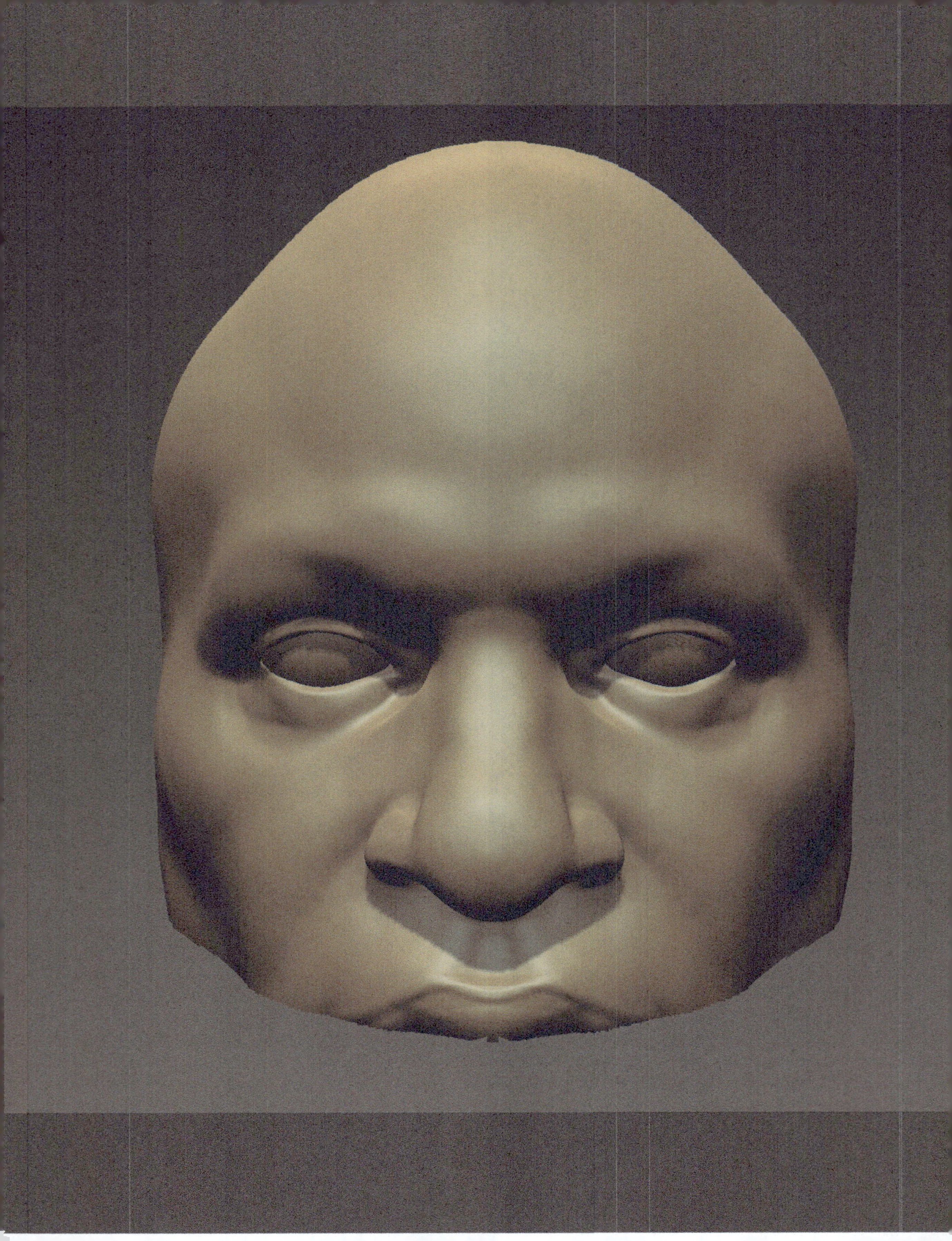

CHAPTER 3:
3D TUTORIAL

# THE NOSE

# 3.1 INTRODUCTION

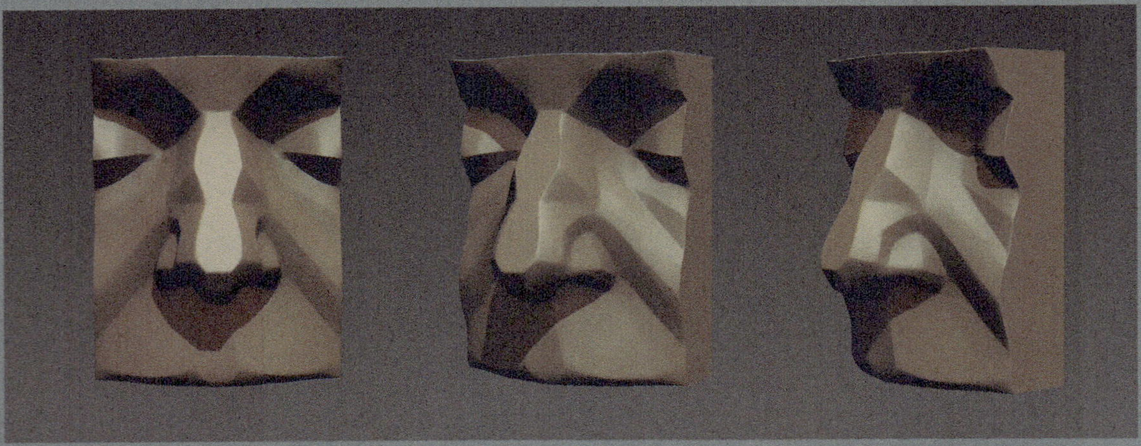

*Basic planes of the nose.*

Like all other aspects of anatomy, there are basic anatomical forms that make up all noses. What varies is the relative proportion and to a certain extent relative positions of those forms.

Figures 3.2 and 3.3 show the basic bone and cartilage anatomical elements that construct the shape of all human noses.

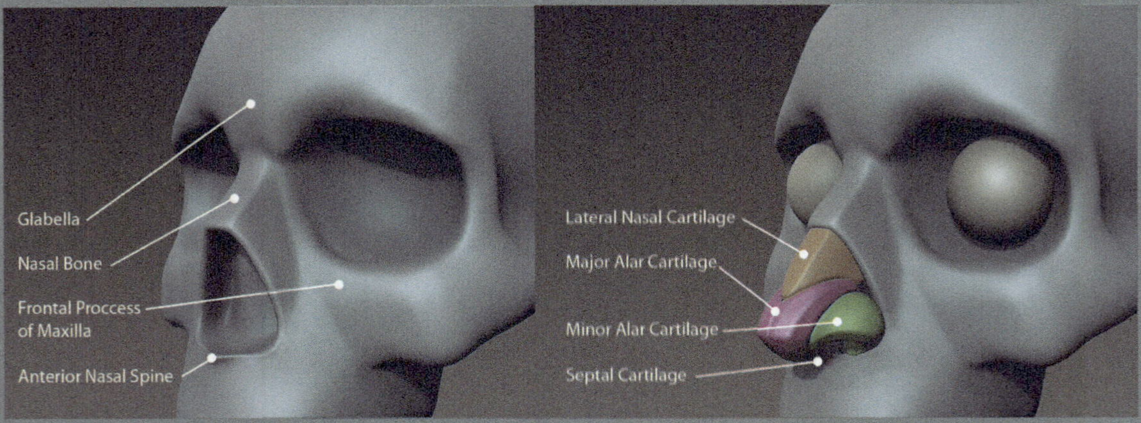


*Basic anatomy of the nose.*

In addition there are small muscles that will contribute to surface form depending on the individual and the facial expression. These muscles are the Nasalis, Procurus, Orbicularis Oculi, Corrugator and Levator Labii Superioris Alaeque:

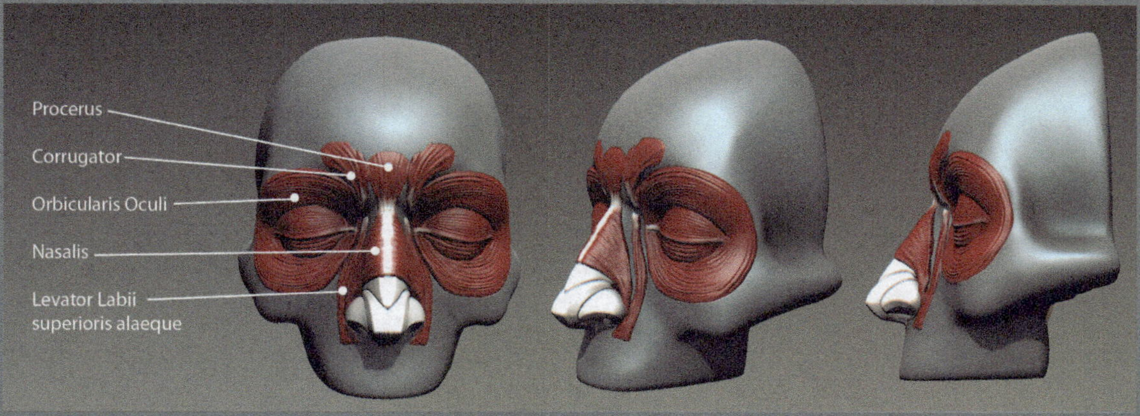


*Basic muscles.*

For the purposes of this tutorial, we are only concerned with how these muscles can affect surface form in a neutral facial pose. In Figure 3.4, you will see a simple example of how these forms translate into surface detail:

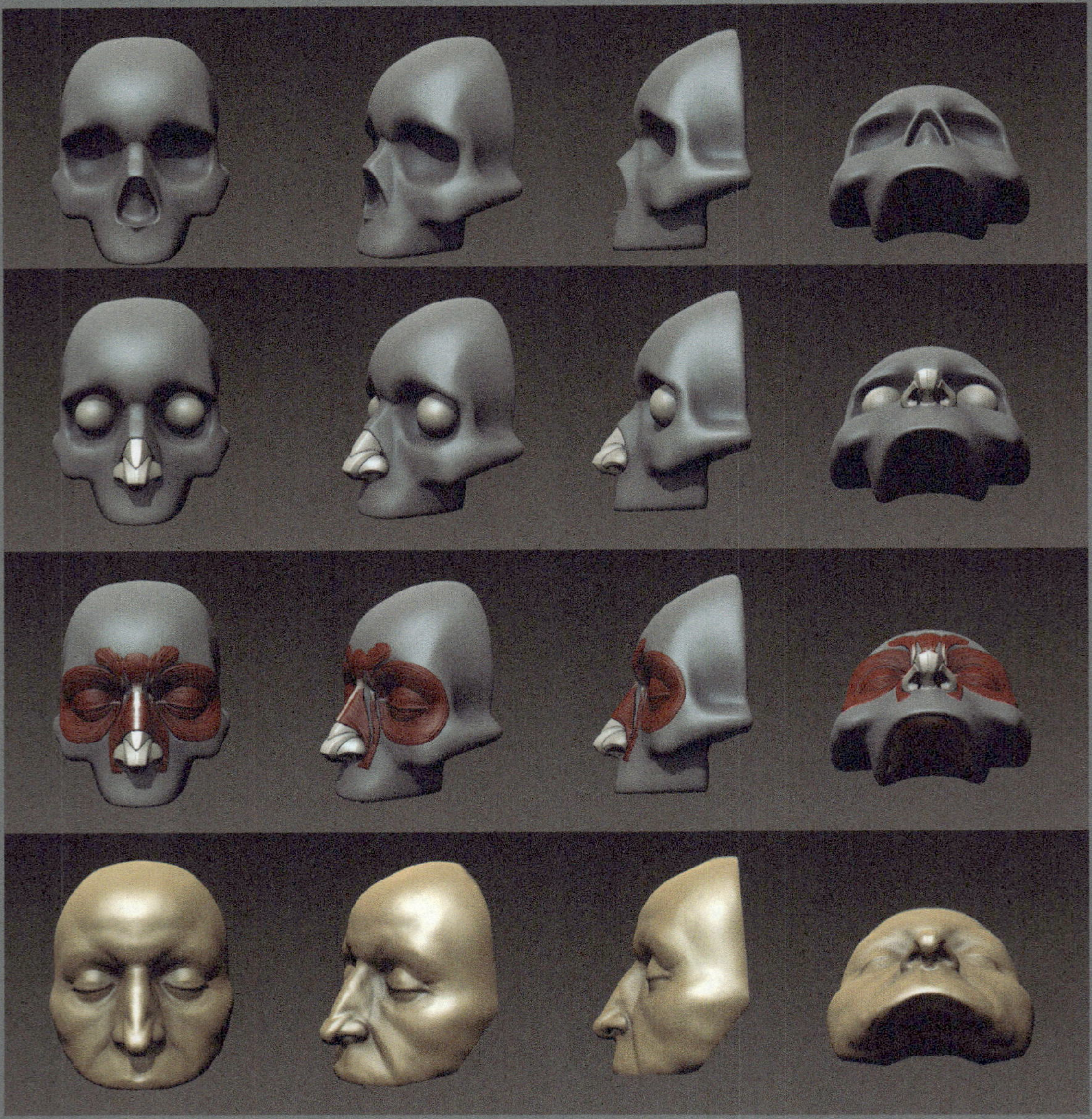

*Form relations.*

There are also intersecting forms surrounding the nose that you will need to consider. These will be shown in the tutorial below as well as in other tutorials in this book in more detail.

We will now walk through the construction of a basic nose using a basic version of our Bone Clones African American Female skull along with one of our female African American models.

***\tutorials\tutorial2\african_american_female.jpg,***
***\tutorials\tutorial2\african_american_female_skull.jpg***

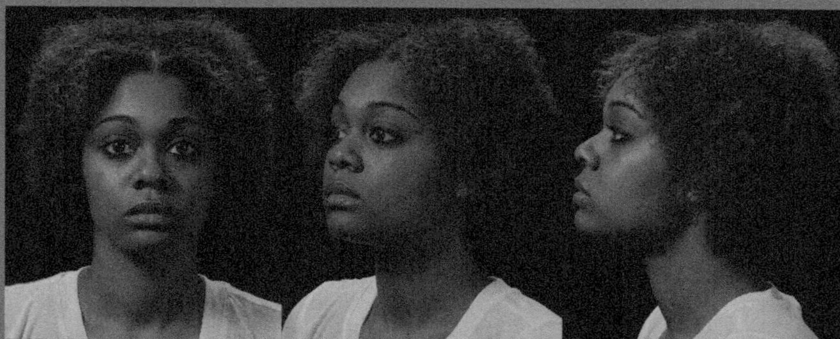

*Model reference.*

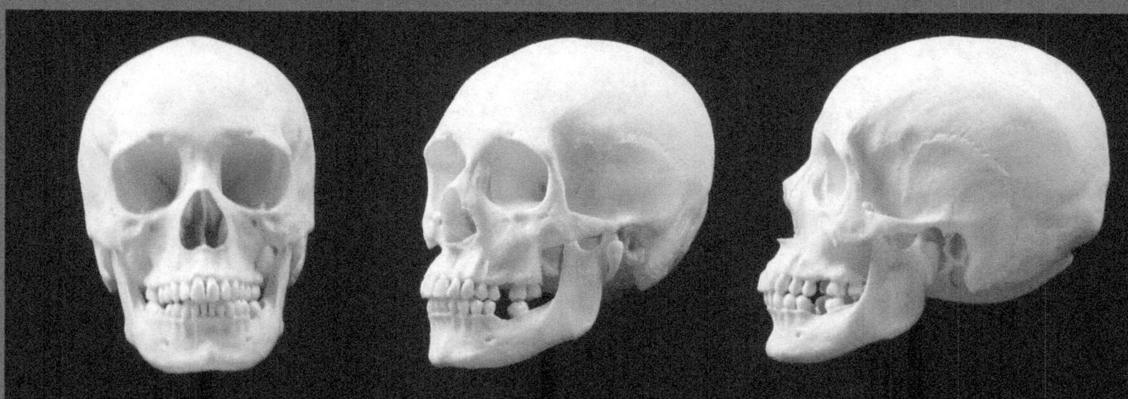

*Bone Clones African American skull.*

# TUTORIAL

Import \tutorials\tutorial2\female_african_nose_baseform.obj into your sculpting application. You may wish to assign a brightly colored material to the base form model so you can see it clearly where it penetrates your sculpt. Lock the base form model so you don't accidentally alter it.

Import ***\tutorials\tutorial2\base_nose_skin.obj*** model. You should see something like this:

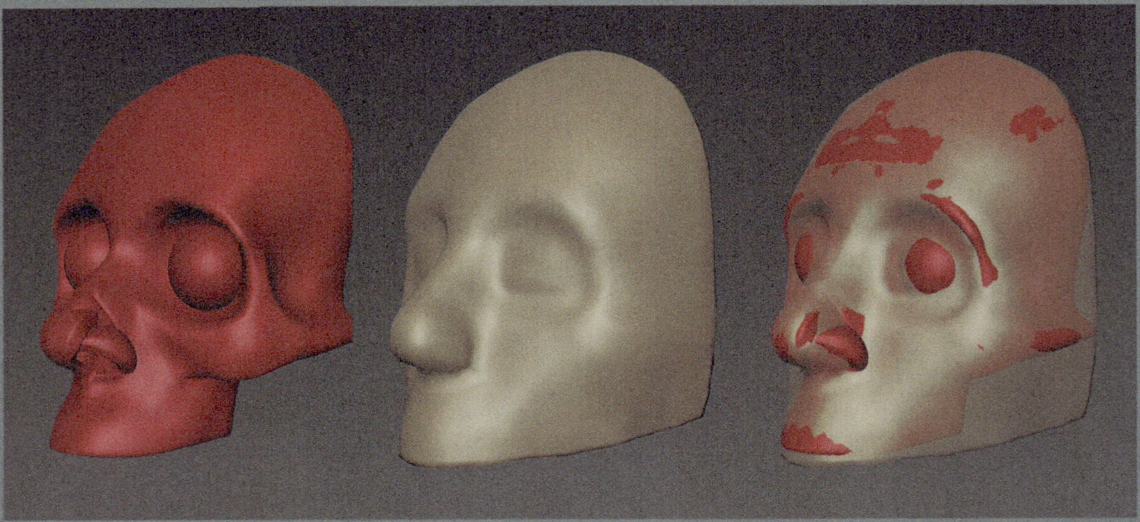

*Starting point of tutorial. Transparency added to skin object to show alignment.*

Skull measurements are provided (\tutorials\tutorial2\african_fem_skull_meas.txt) for traditional sculptors who want to block out the skull form in clay. You will need to approximate your own cartilage and eye forms using the photos provided.

While this tutorial may have a bit of a forensic reconstruction feel to it, what the goal really is, is to have you both thinking about the anatomical forms that rest directly below the skin surface and give you a tangible way to evaluate your work.

Subdivide the base skin model one to two times (less is better: keeping the polygon count as low as possible as you build up form is the best practice. You should increase subdivisions only when you no longer have enough resolution to create the forms you need). Begin by making the images of the model available to refer to either an image viewer onscreen, as image planes in your sculpture program or as printouts.

The first step will be to define the glabella, nasal bone, and the border of the orbital cavity. These landmarks will give you the structure to begin seating the features of the face within. Keep in mind that while the skull is representative of a *typical* African American female skull, it will only loosely correspond to the model's features. So use her photos as a loose guide, but in this exercise, focus on the base form geometry as a guide for positioning features.

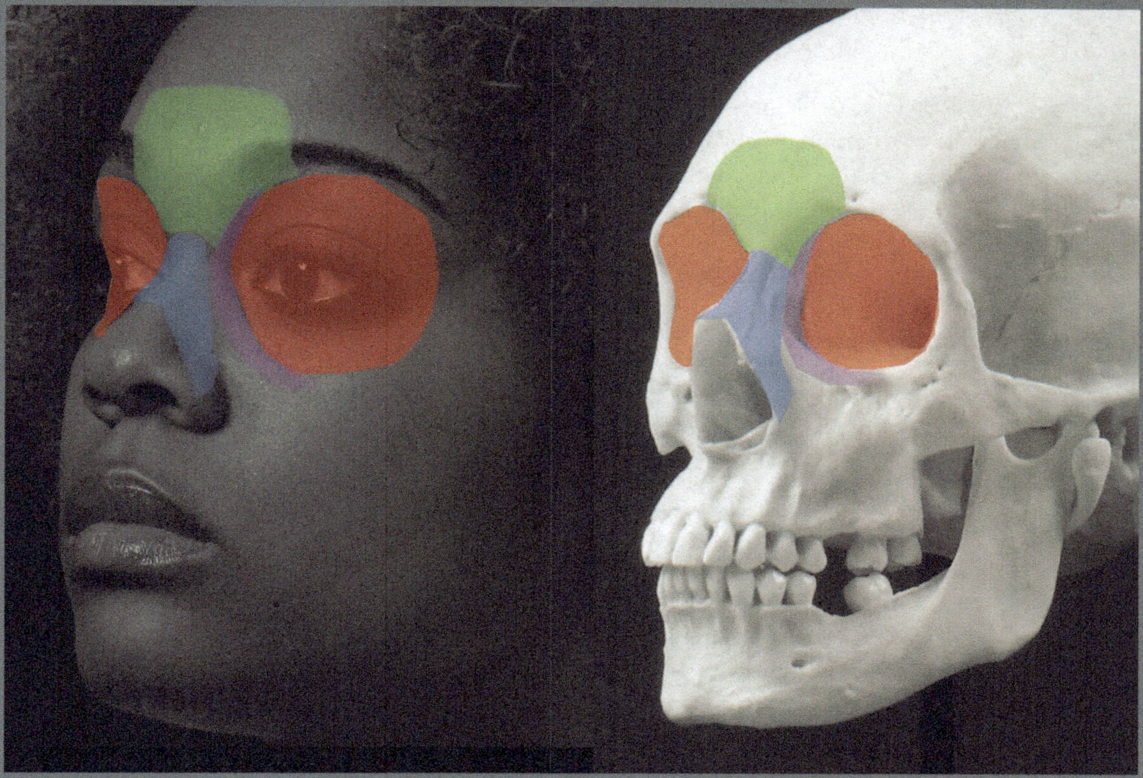

*Areas to focus on the skull, and model photo.*

You should make the overall shape of the skin geometry conform to the base form so that none of the skull is penetrating (with the exception of the nose cartilage forms for now). Once that is complete, focus your effort on the roughing-in the bony areas mentioned above. When complete, your first step should look something like this:

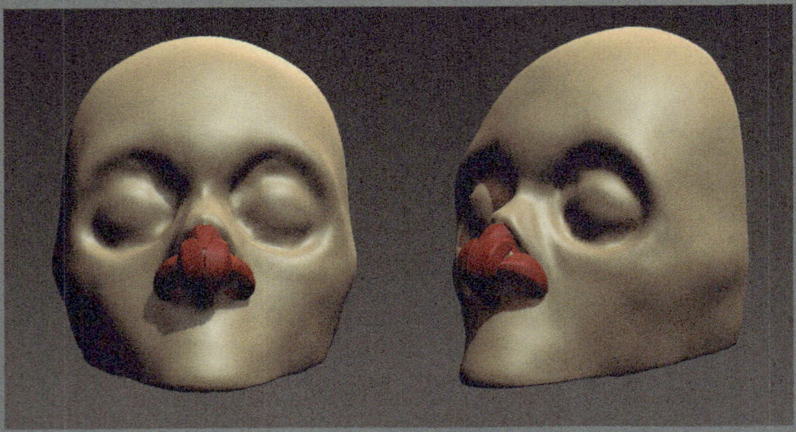

The next step will be to fill in the nose cartilage area, again using the base form as a template for the surface you are creating. Try adding one cartilage form at a time so that you get a feel for those forms and memorize them. Keep referring back to the model photos as reference for the surface forms that you are trying to create.

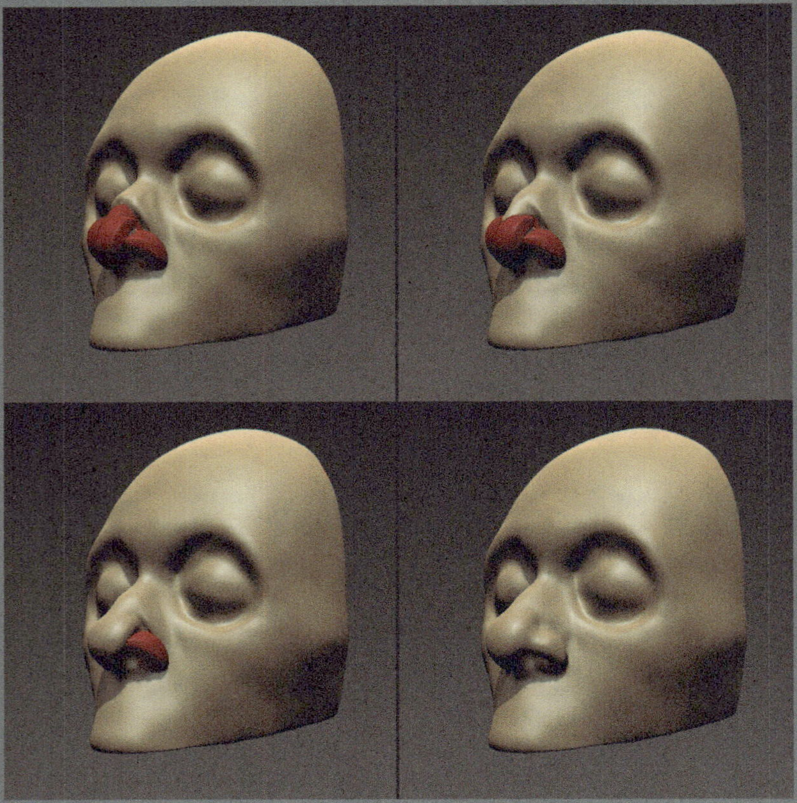

At this point, you have blocked out the basic nose forms. Now, we need to be concerned with the forms that surround the nose and how they interact. The first area we will address is the barrel of the mouth.

There is a decent amount of thickness to the flesh that covers the maxilla (upper jawbone/teeth), and there is a distinct barrel shape in most people of this form. The important thing to think about for now is the area where the nose and upper lip come together. The teardrop-shaped cleft in the center that runs to the base of the nose is called the Philtrum. The way the forms transition from the nostrils to the upper lip and the interconnection between the philtrum and the base of the nose are important things to observe carefully.

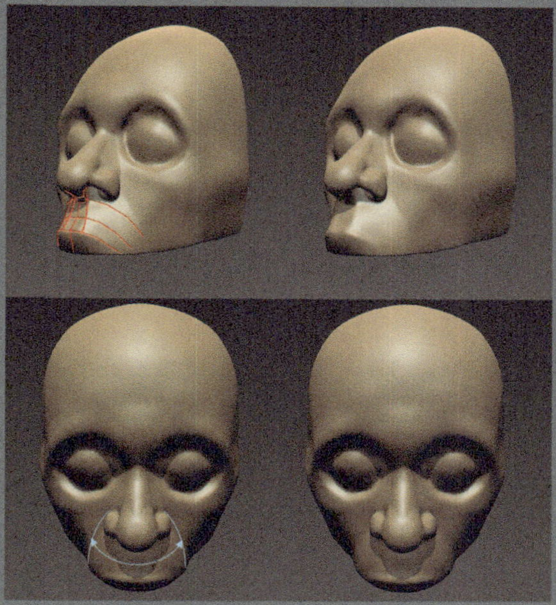

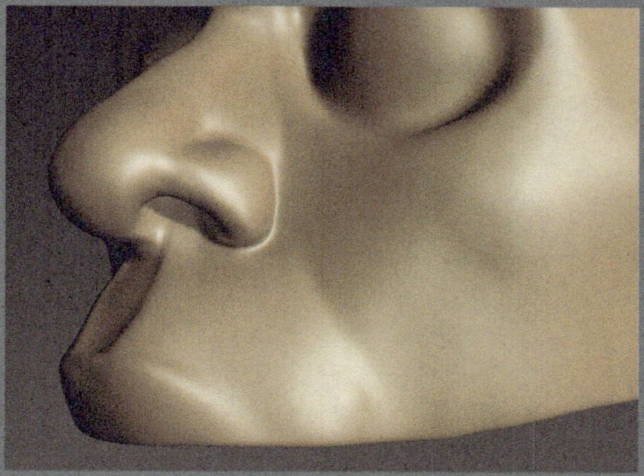

The final area we are going to look at is the nasal labial fold.

The nasal labial fold is the characteristic crease from the rear edge of the nostril to the region near the corners of the mouth. It includes a fat pad that covers the zygomatic muscles that travel from the cheek bone to the corner of the lips.

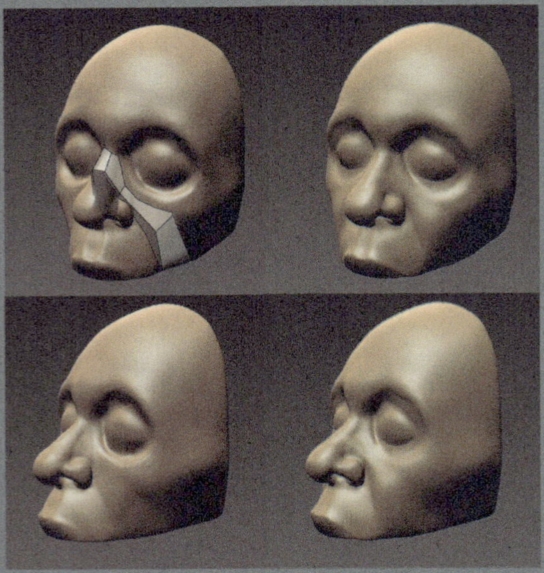

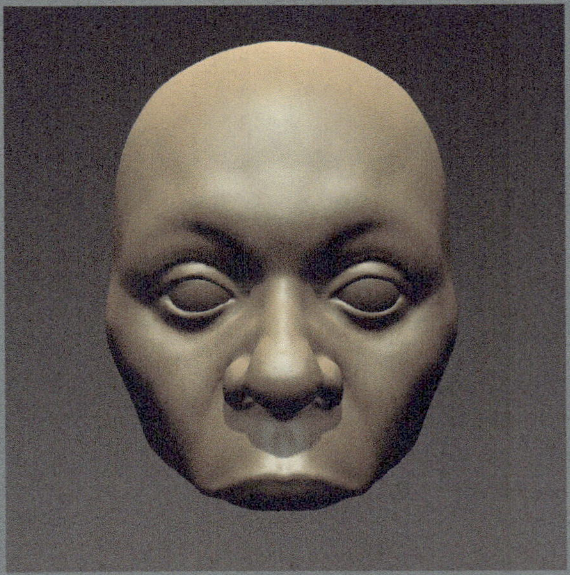

In the next tutorial, we will cover the eye, and we will revisit this project to finish the eye, brow cheek, and temple areas.

Now that you have walked though one example, use the resources provided in the folder for this chapter's tutorial to complete three more nose studies of an Asian male and an African American male. The Caucasian male resources files used at the beginning of this tutorial are also provided.

***\tutorials\tutorial2\male_asian_nose_baseform.obj***
***\tutorials\tutorial2\male_african_american_nose_baseform.obj***
***\tutorials\tutorial2\asian_male.jpg***
***\tutorials\tutorial2\african_american_male.jpg***

Noses can appear very differently in different individuals, but if you keep in mind the basic anatomy that makes up all noses, you should have the tools for evaluating and constructing what you see in your subjects.

# 4

CHAPTER 4

# MALE FACES

DOI: 10.1201/ 9781003484554-4

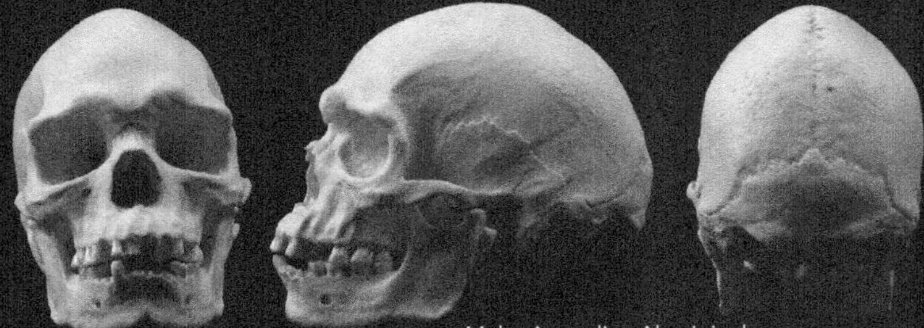

Male, Australian Aboriginal

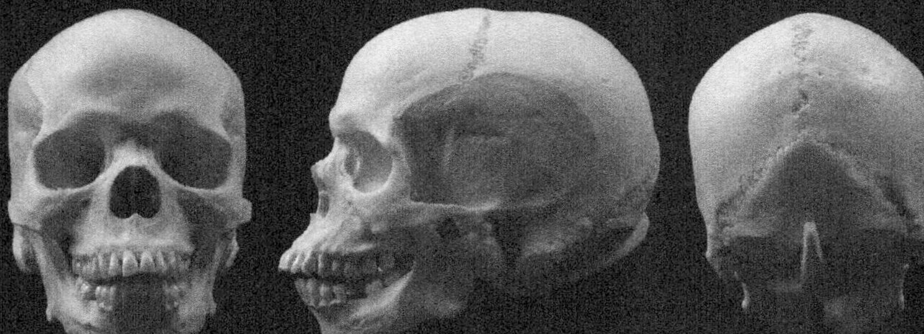

Male, African American

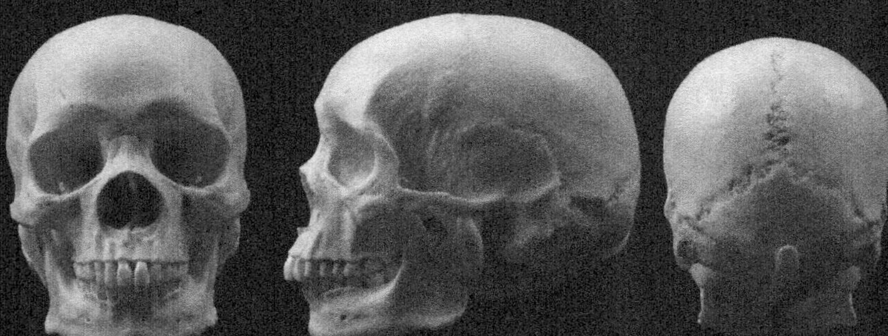

Male, Africa

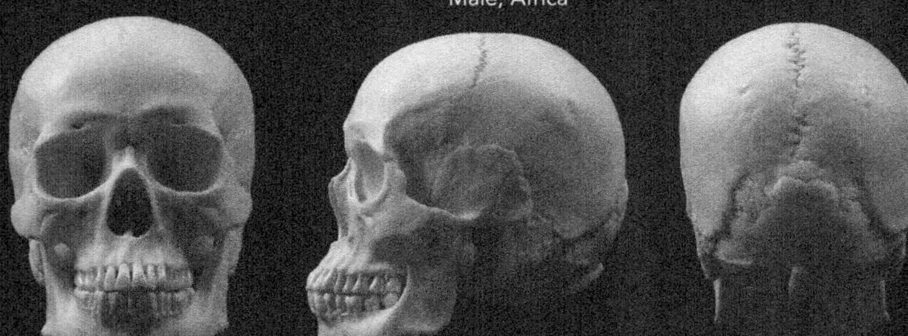

Male, Asian

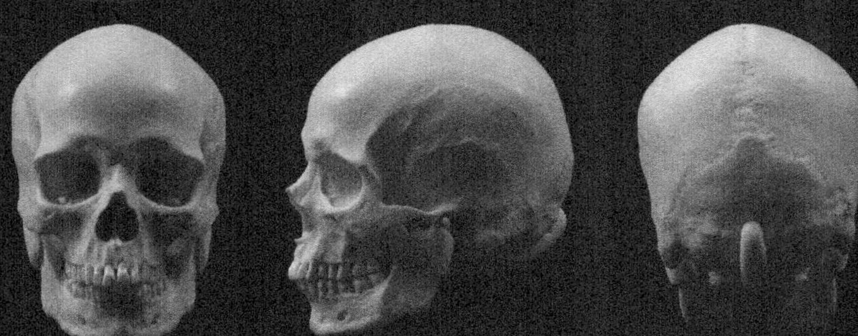

Male, European

*Male skulls from around the world.*

The male face is featured in this chapter. Each male will be featured in a turn-around. Each model's description will include measurements taken with calipers, and the country the person claims ancestry from.

You will notice when comparing the page of male skulls to the page of female skulls that the male skull is generally more angular than the female skull.  Notice the forehead. The male forehead is more sloping. The ridge area is more pronounced too. The lower half of the face is larger on the male than on the female. This can be seen in the acute angle of the jaw, the square, pronounced chin, and the greater mass of muscle tissue. Notice, though, that this mass is more muscular. There is less fat in the male face.

# APPROXIMATE MALE ANCESTRY

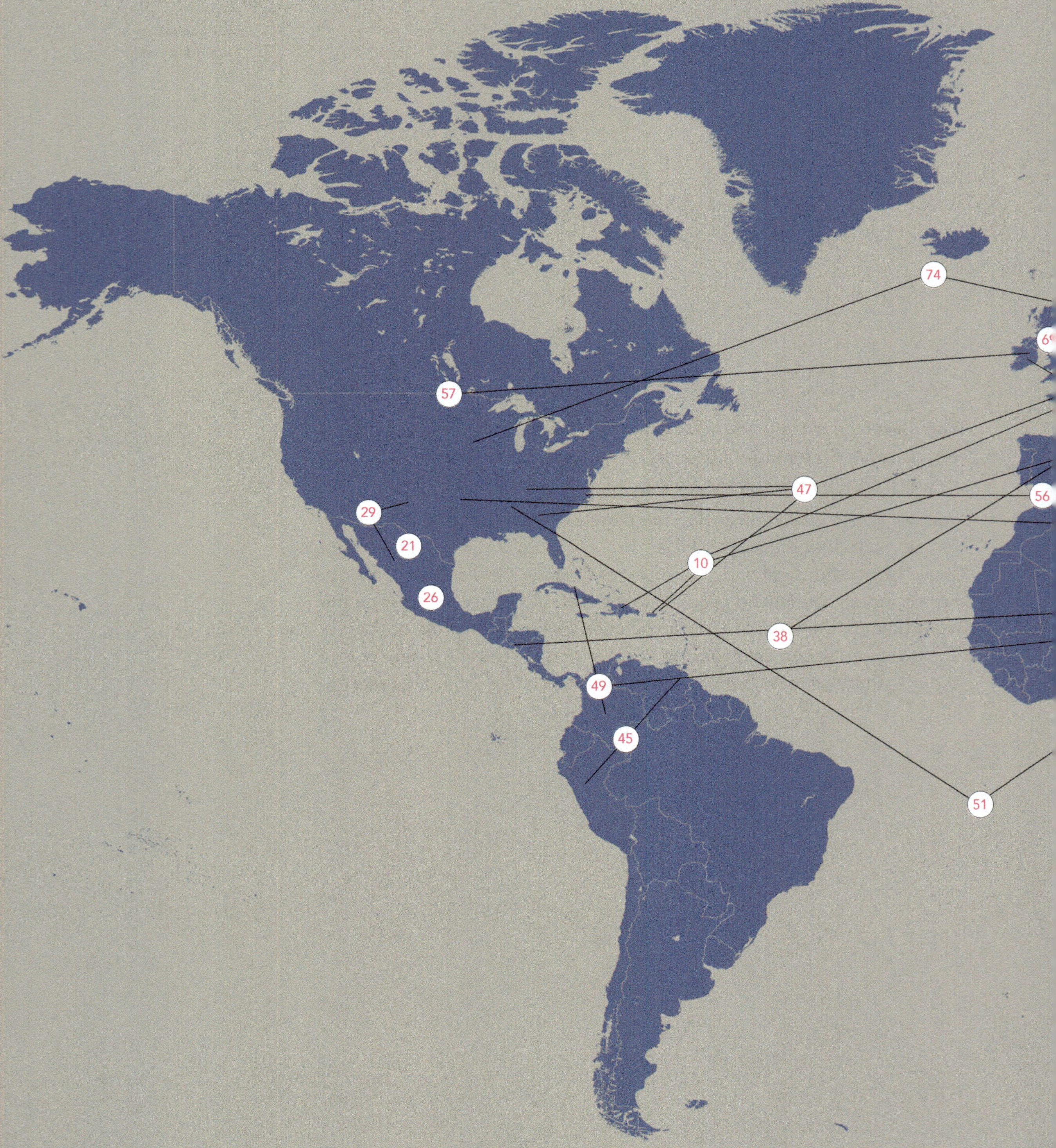

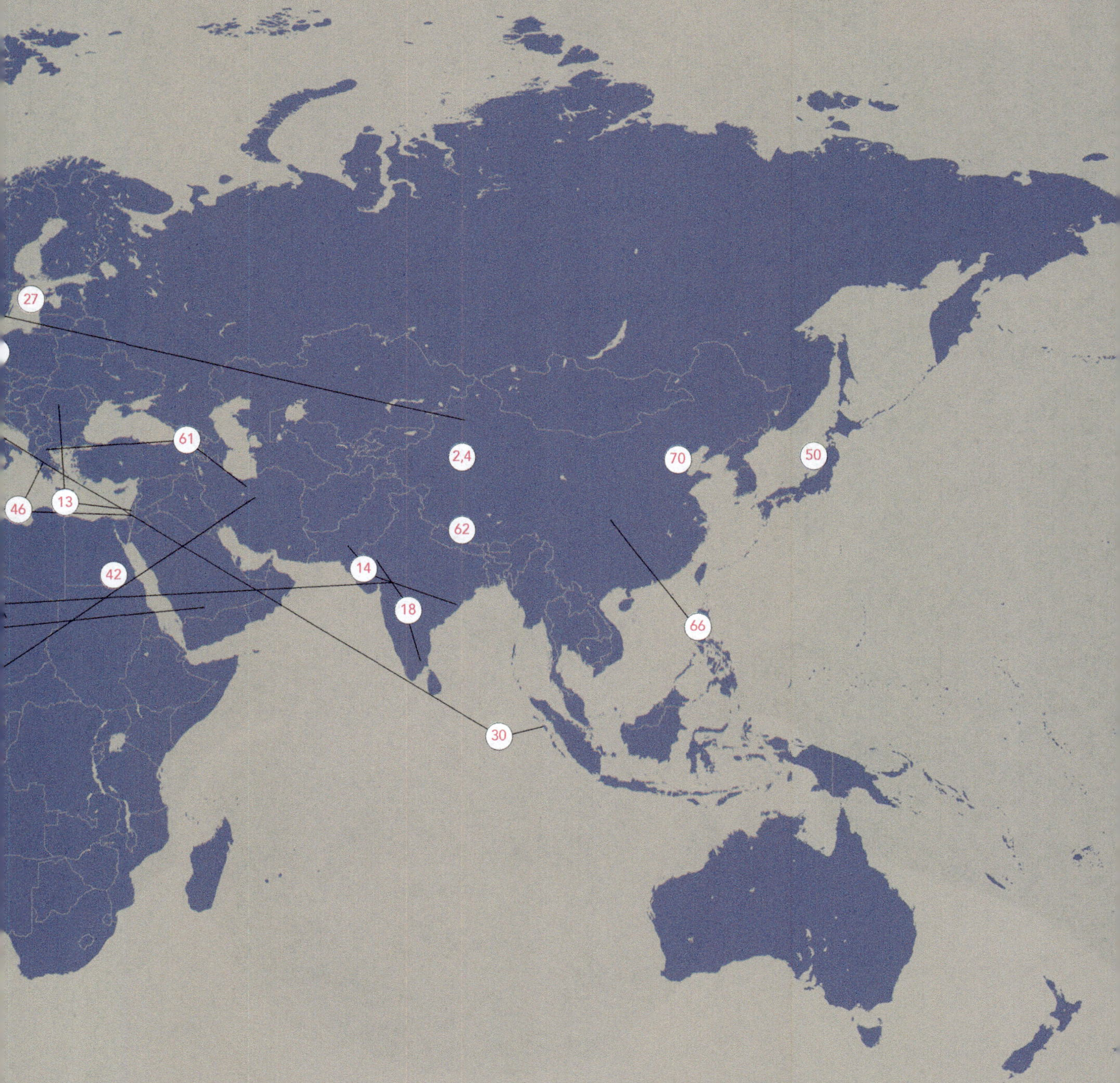


*Approximation of ancestry claimed by males.*

MAP REFERENCE:

2

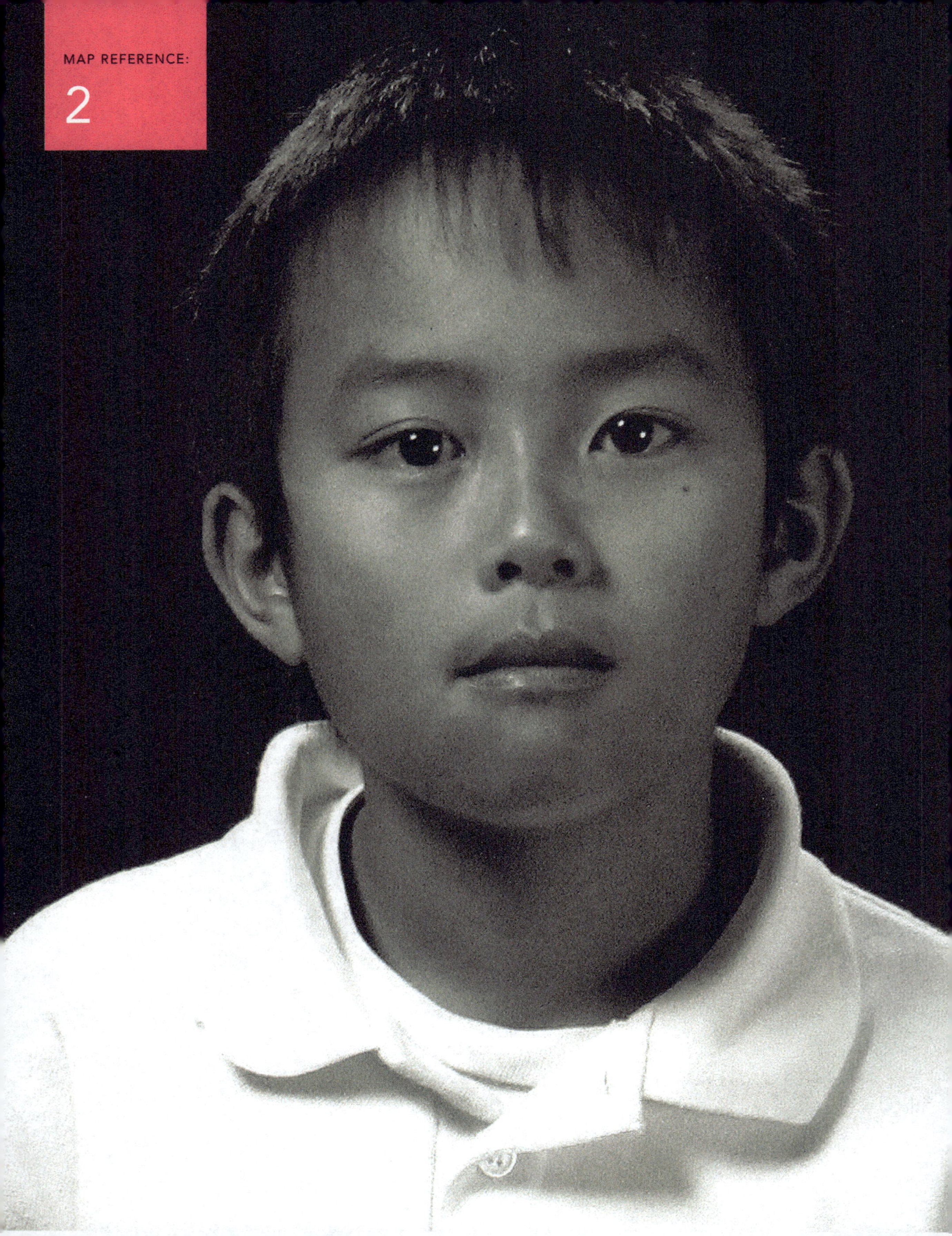

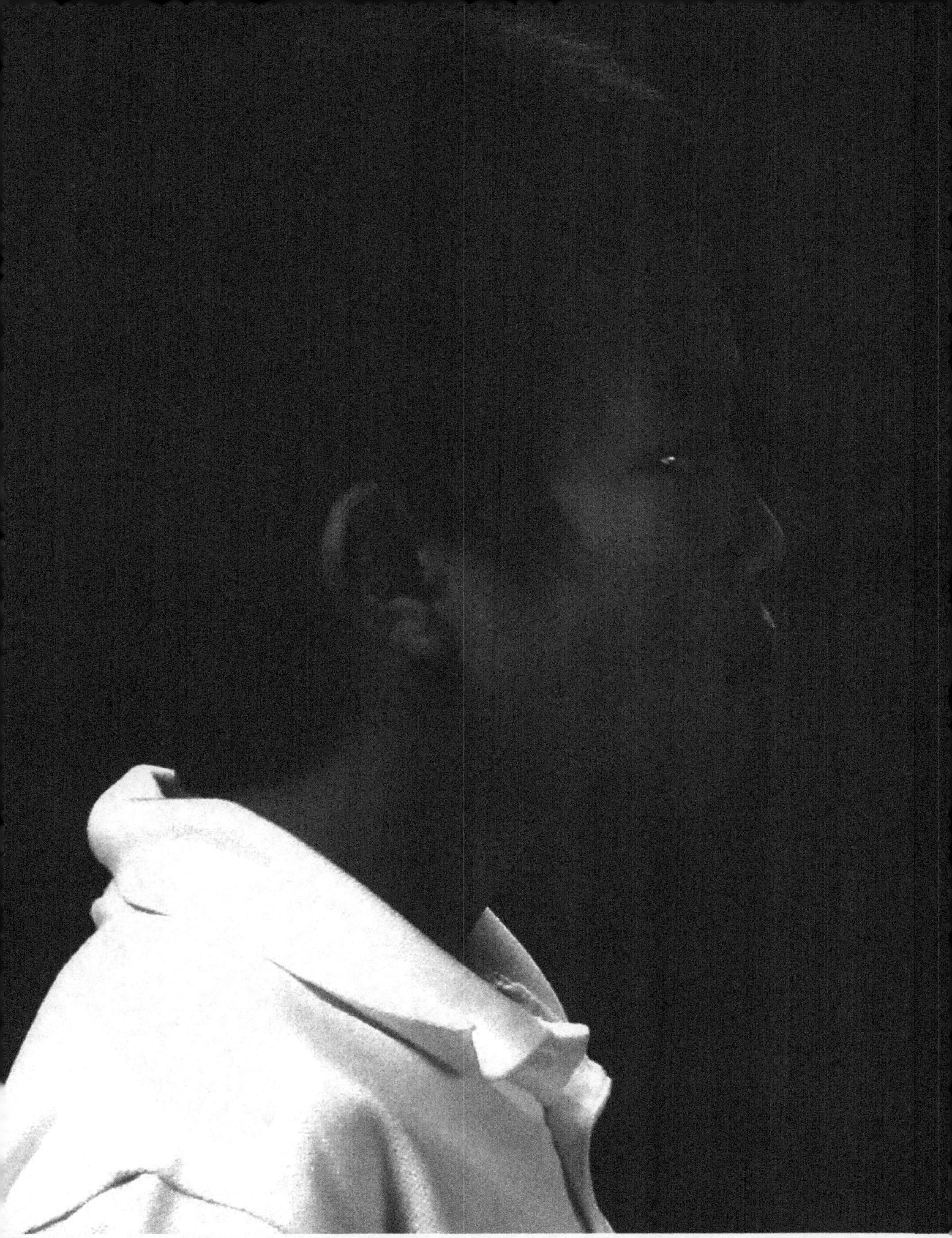

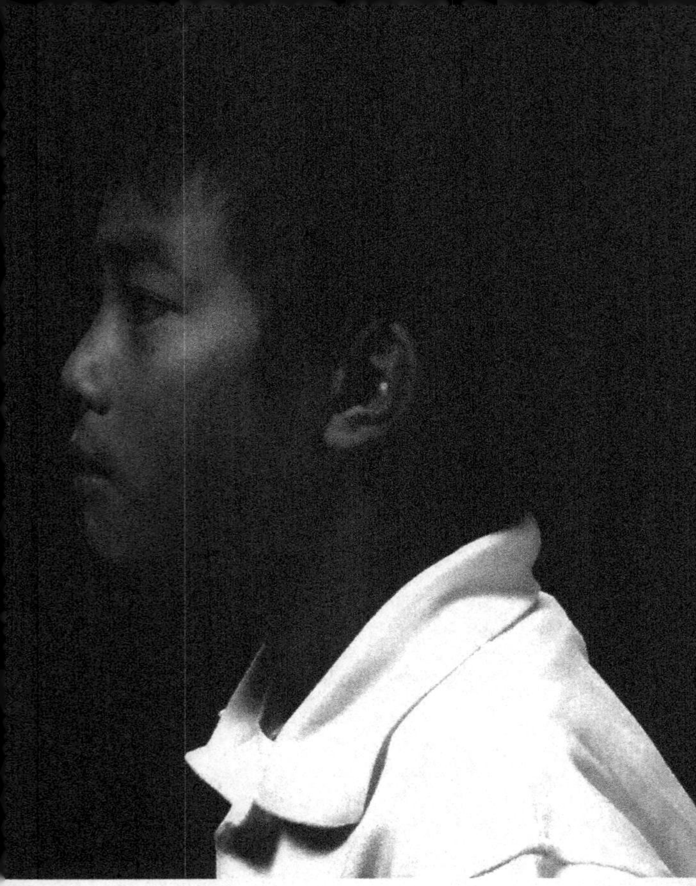

**Ethnicities claimed:**

China.

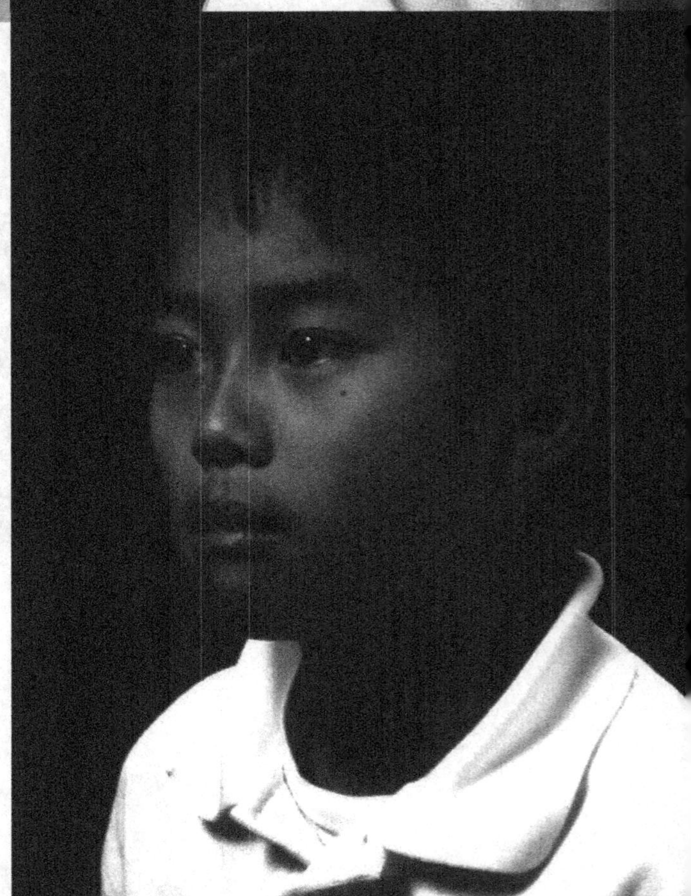

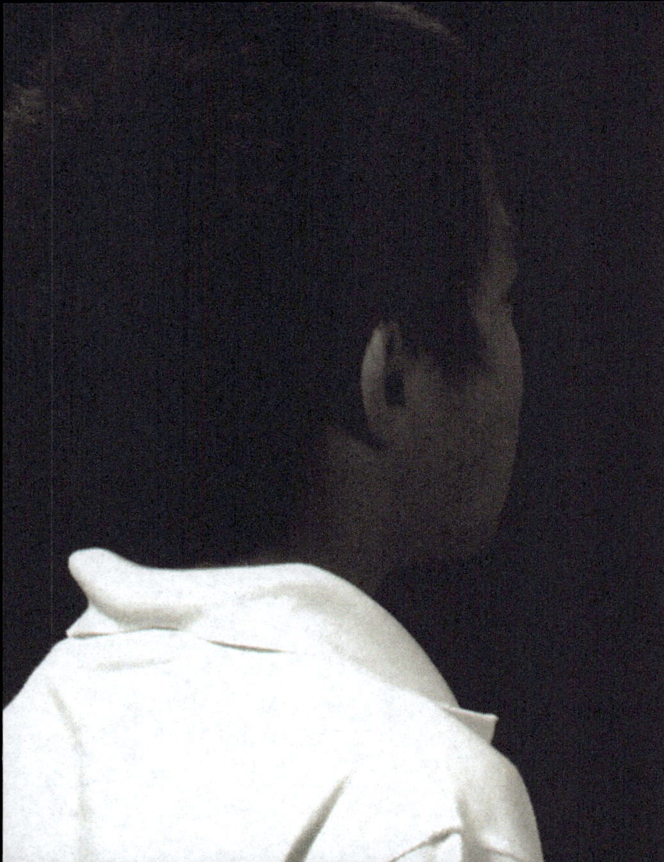

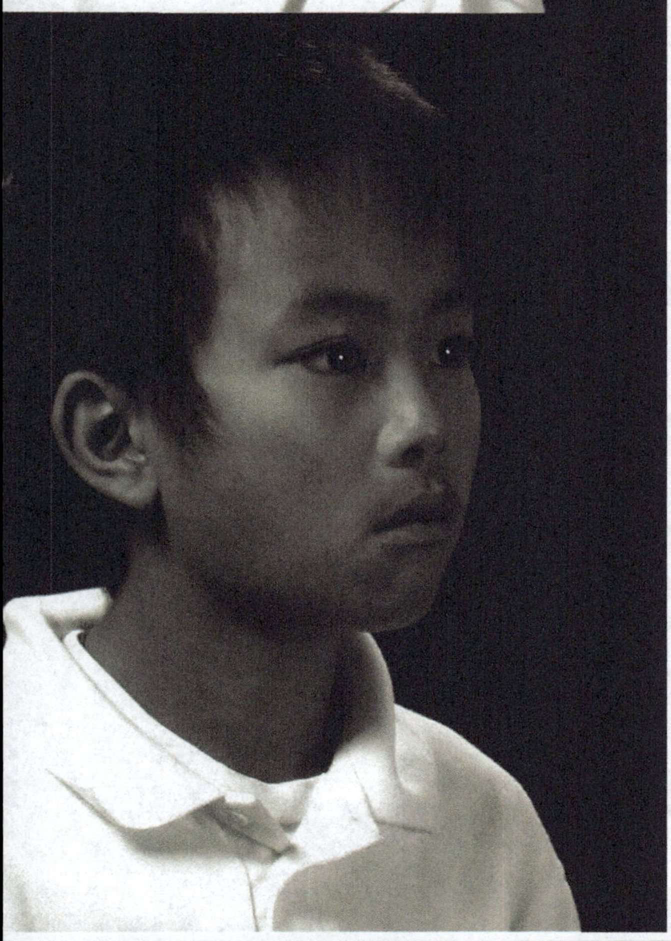

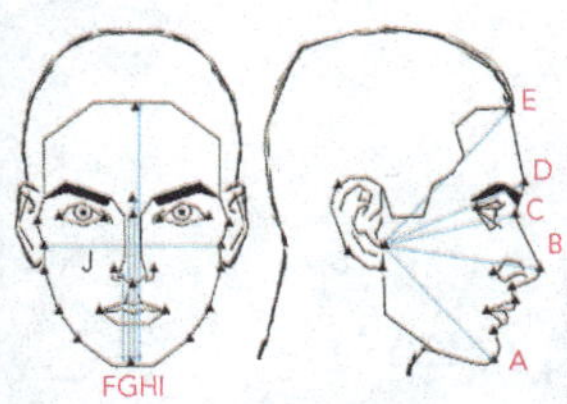


**Head measurements (in):**

A: 5
B: 4 3/8
C: 4 1/4
D: 4 3/8
E: 5 5/8
F: 3 1/2
G: 4
H: 4 7/8
I: 7 1/2
J: 5 3/8

MAP REFERENCE:

4

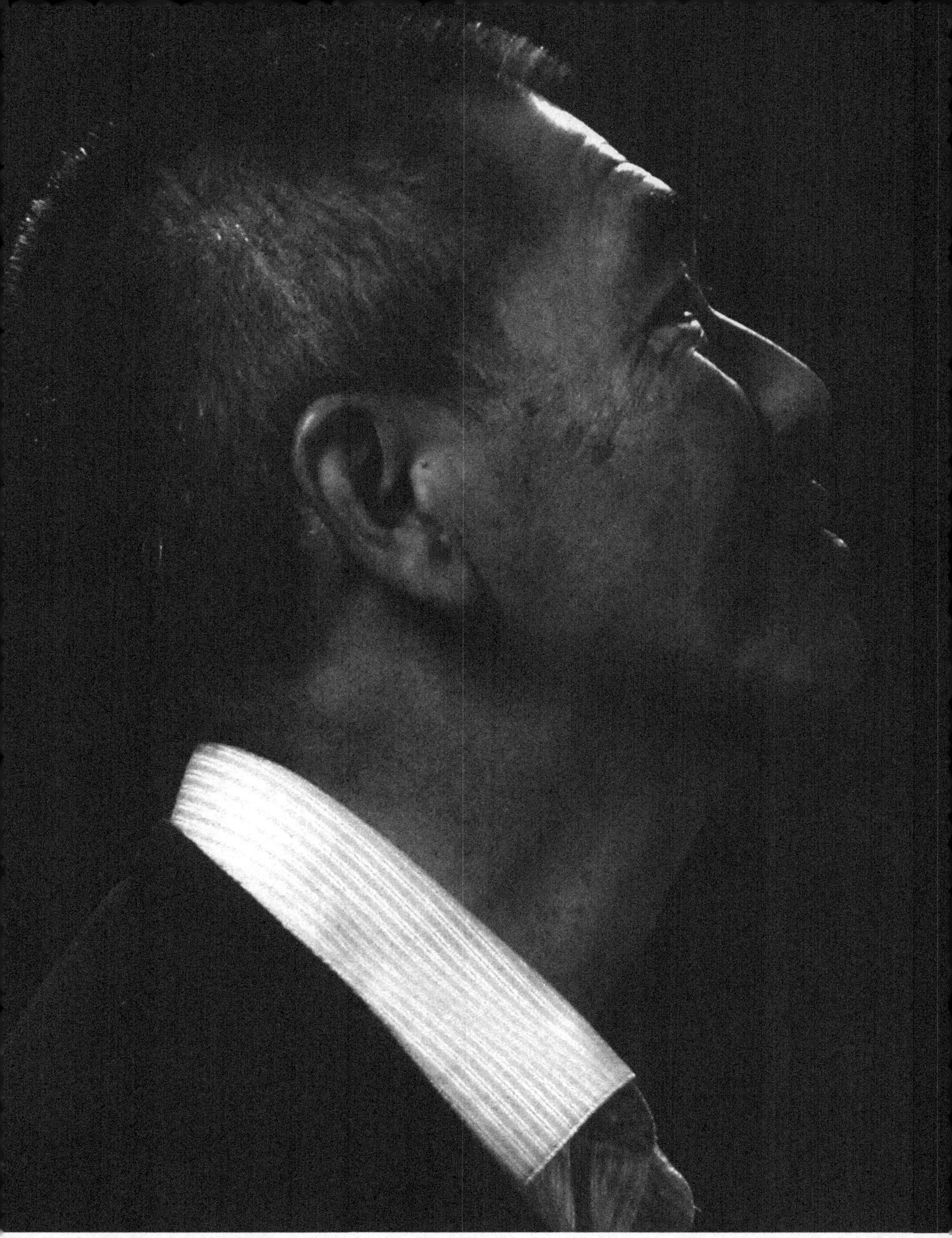

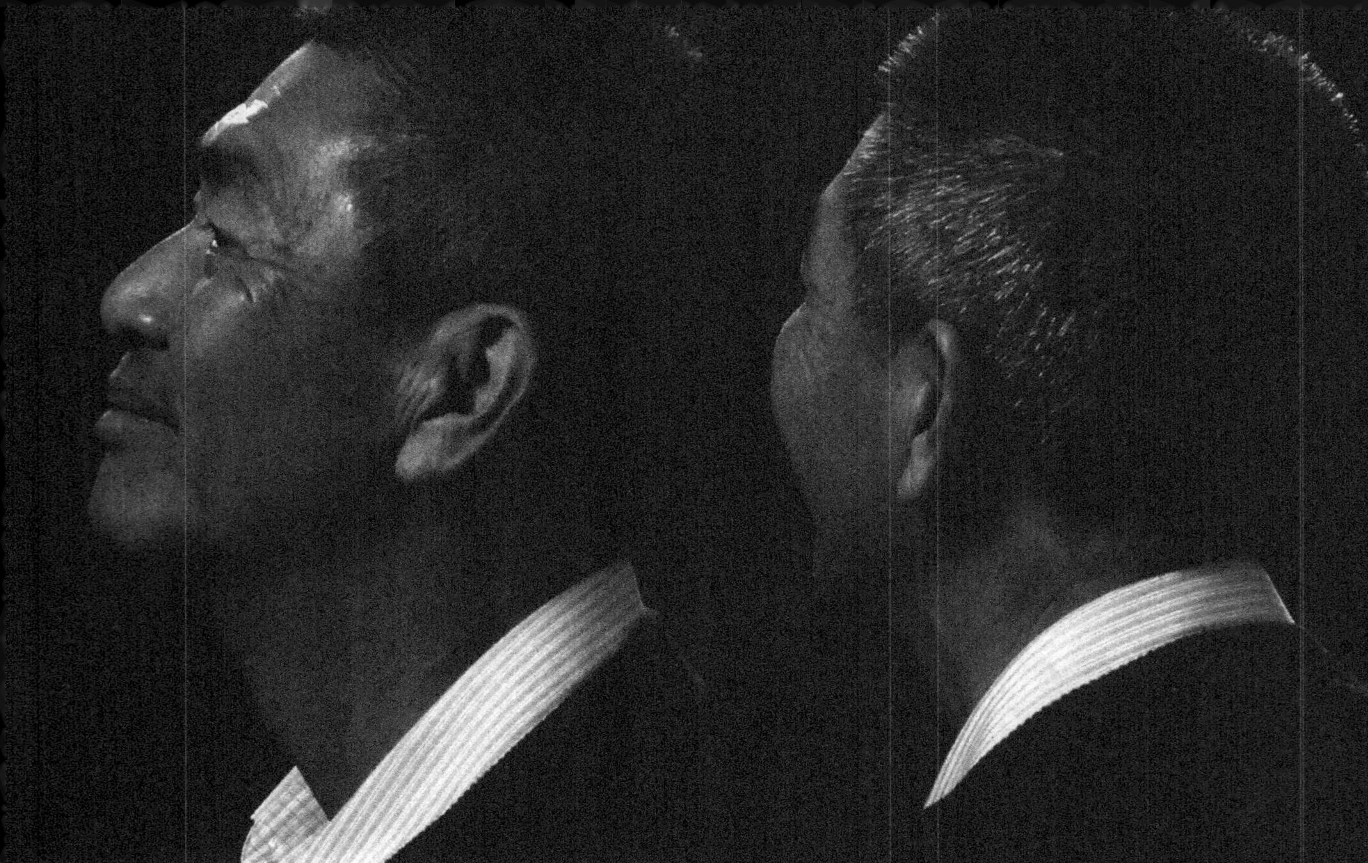

**Ethnicities claimed:**

China.

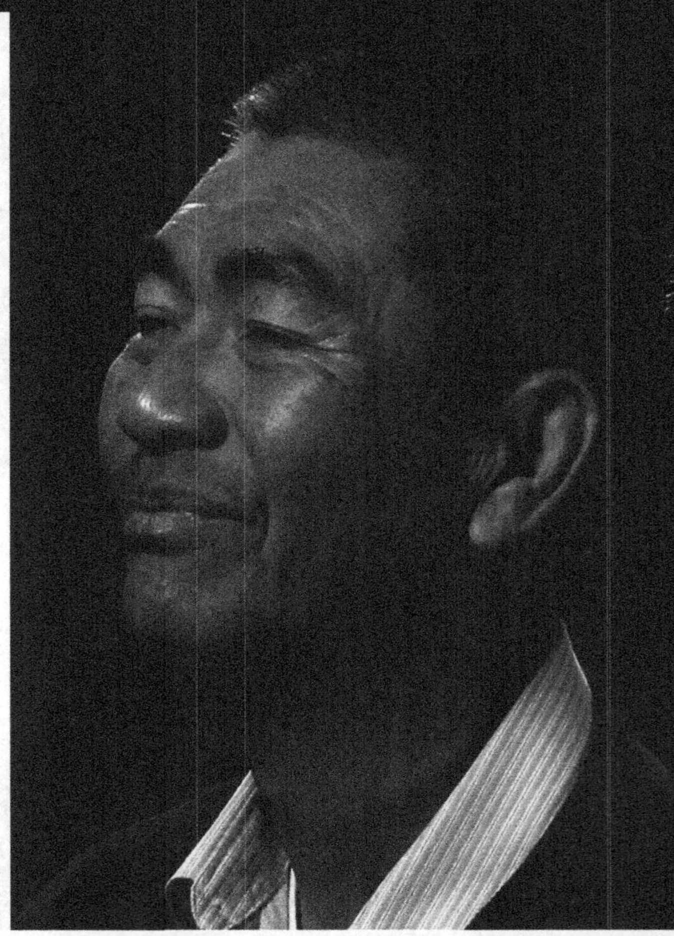

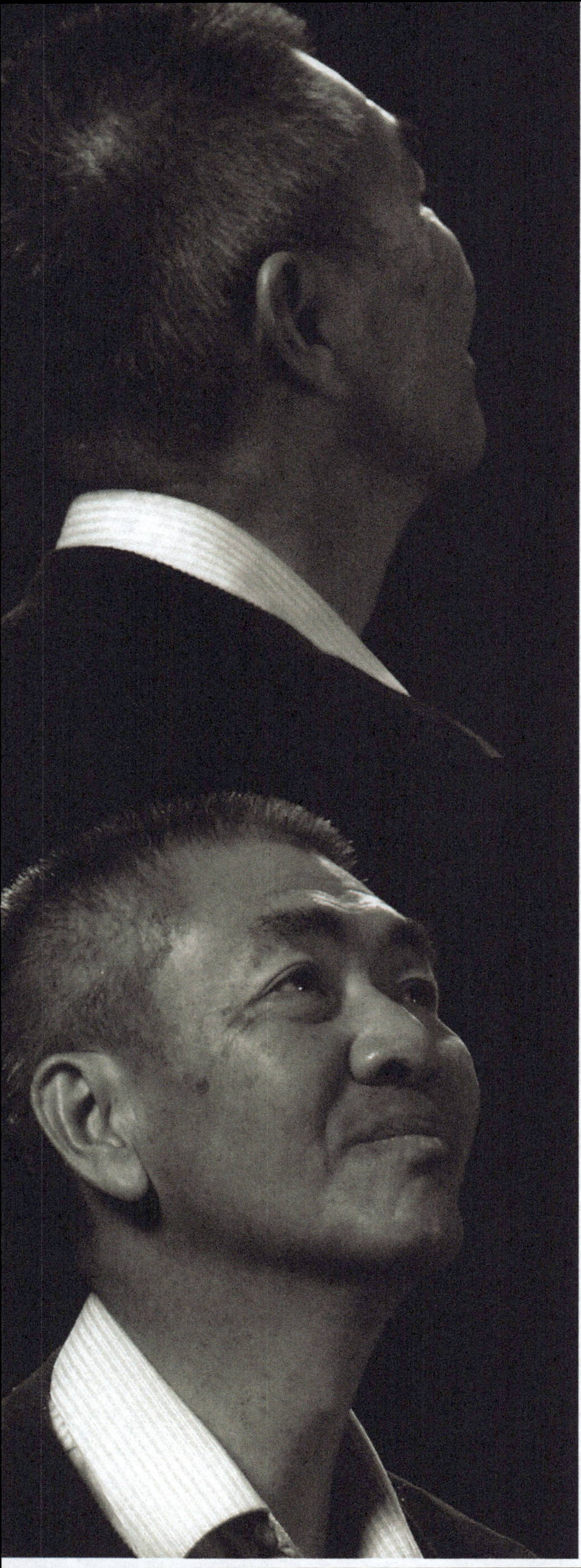

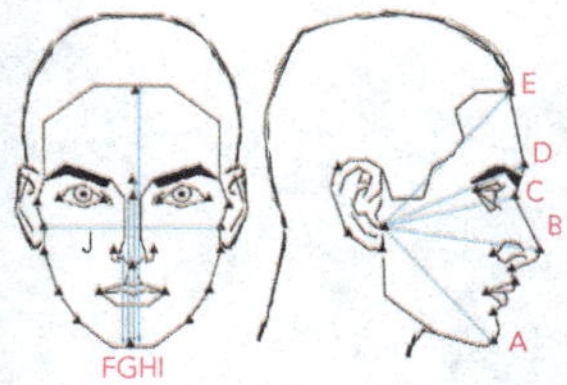


**Head measurements (in):**

A: 5 5/8
B: 5 1/2
C: 5 1/8
D: 5 1/2
E: 5 1/4
F: 3 1/4
G: 4 3/8
H: 5 3/4
I: 7 5/8
J: 6

MAP REFERENCE:

10

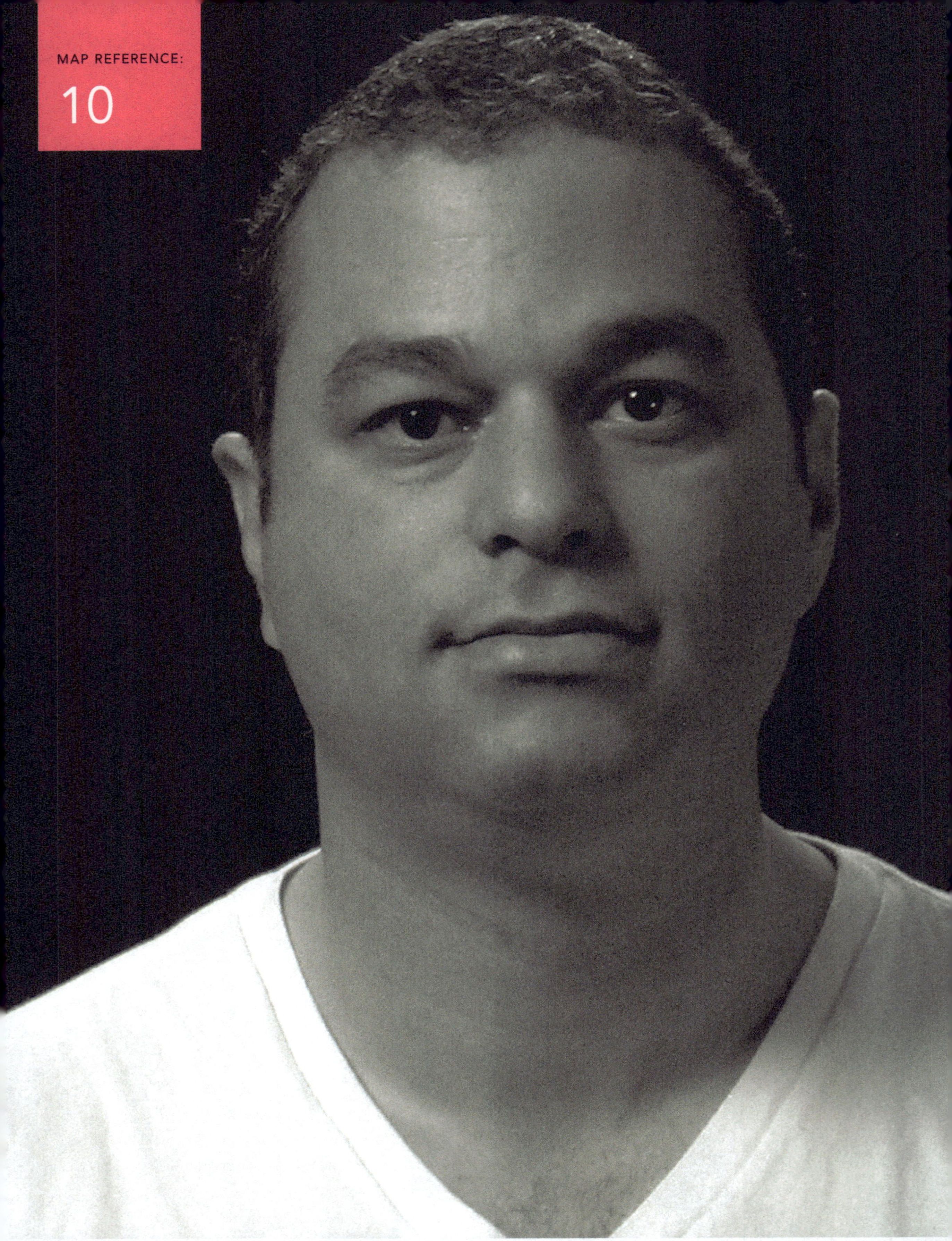

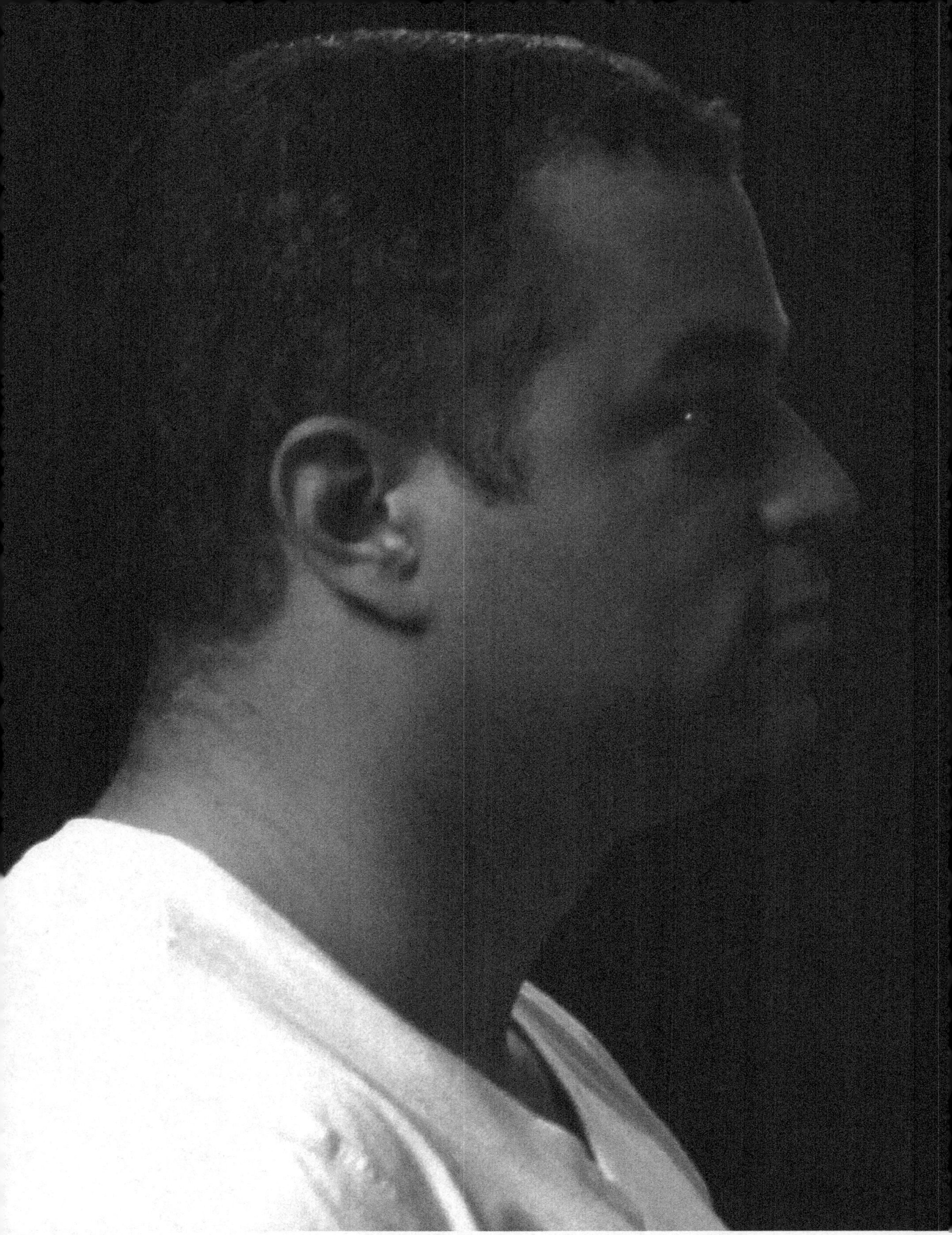

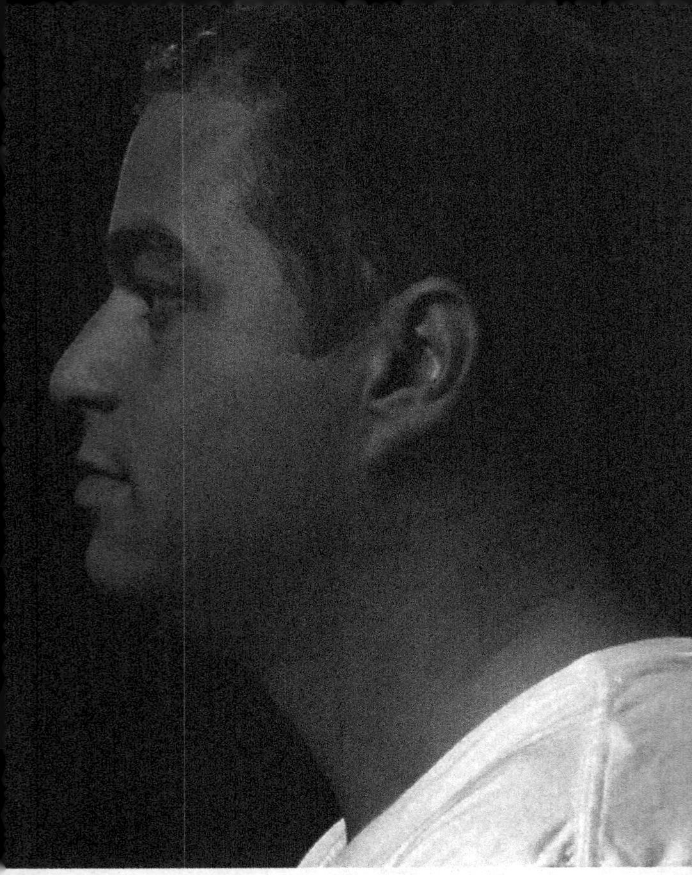

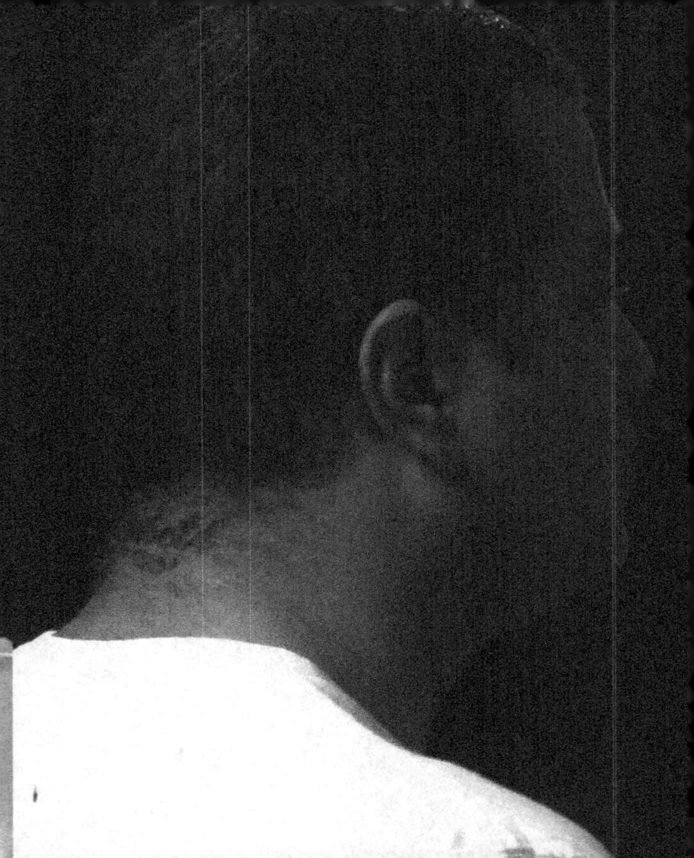

**Ethnicities claimed:**

Haiti, Puerto Rico, Italy, and Germany.

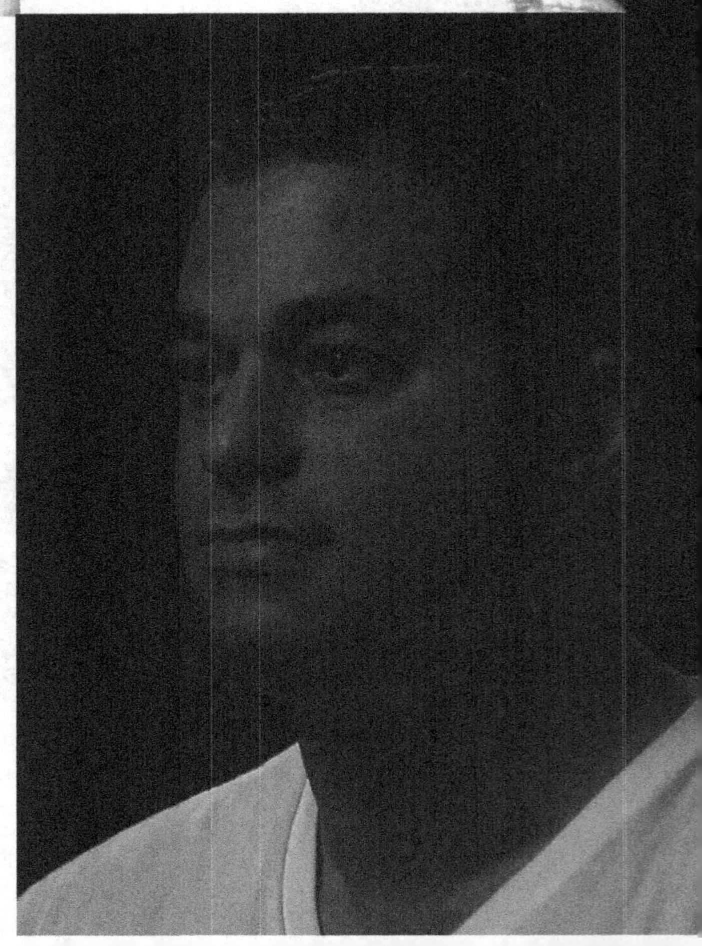

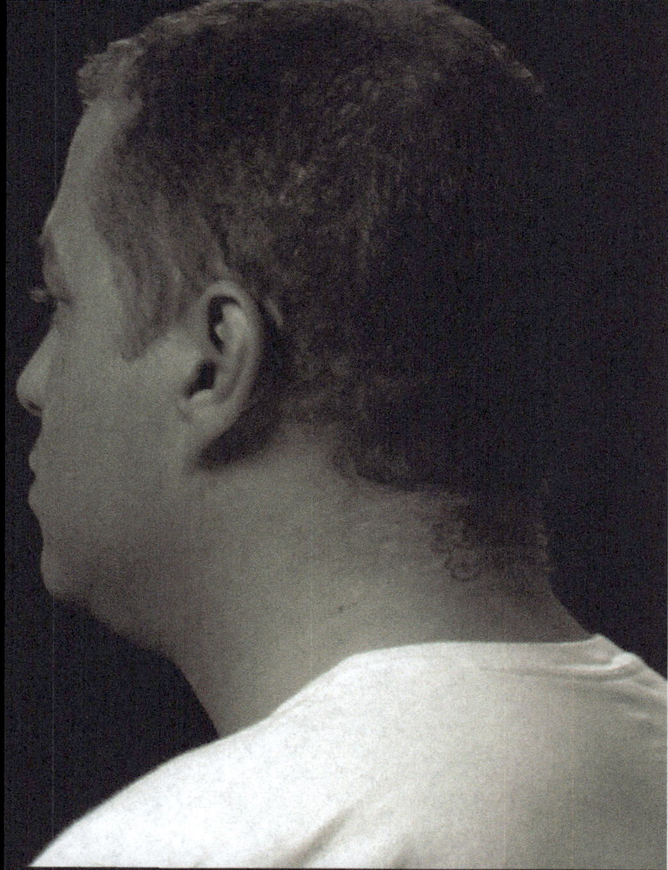

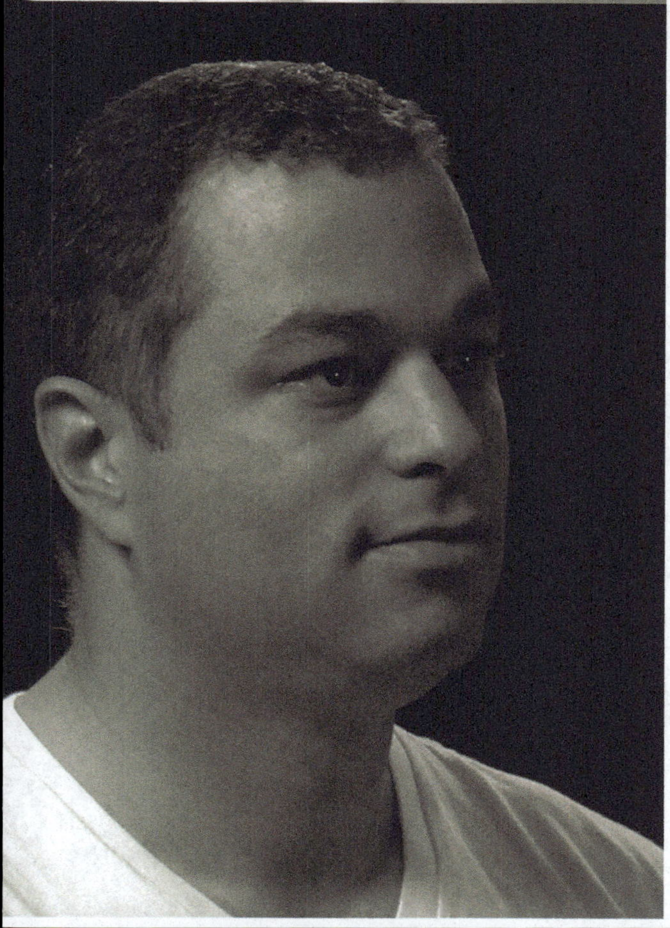

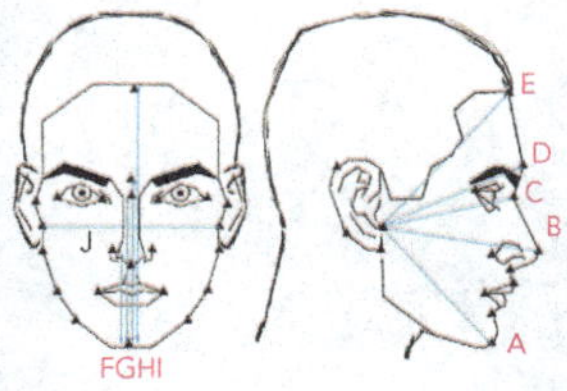


**Head measurements (in):**

A: 5 1/2
B: 5 5/8
C: 5
D: 5 1/2
E: 6 7/8
F: 3 3/8
G: 5 3/4
H: 5 3/8
I: 7 1/2
J: 6 1/4

MAP REFERENCE:

15

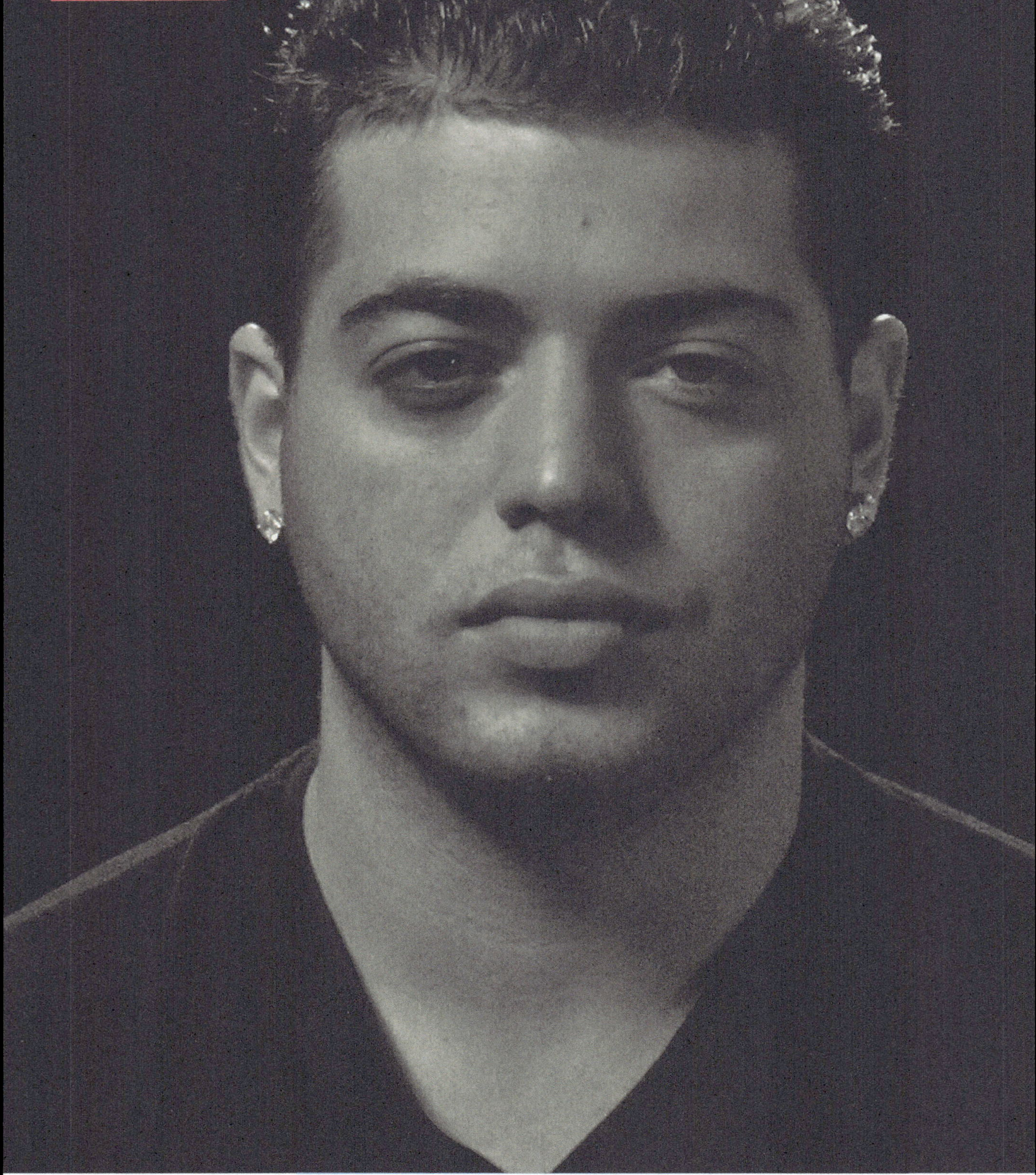

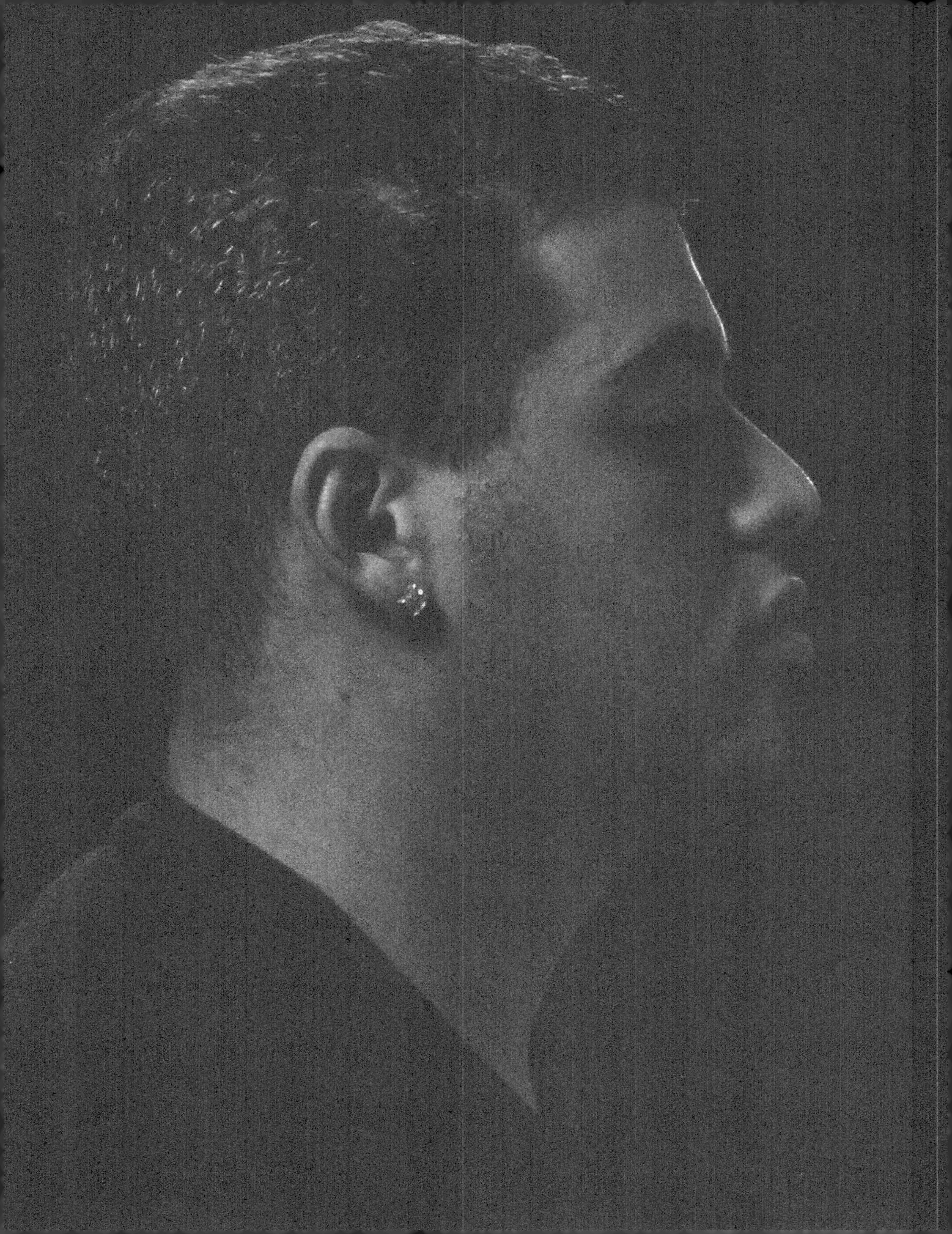

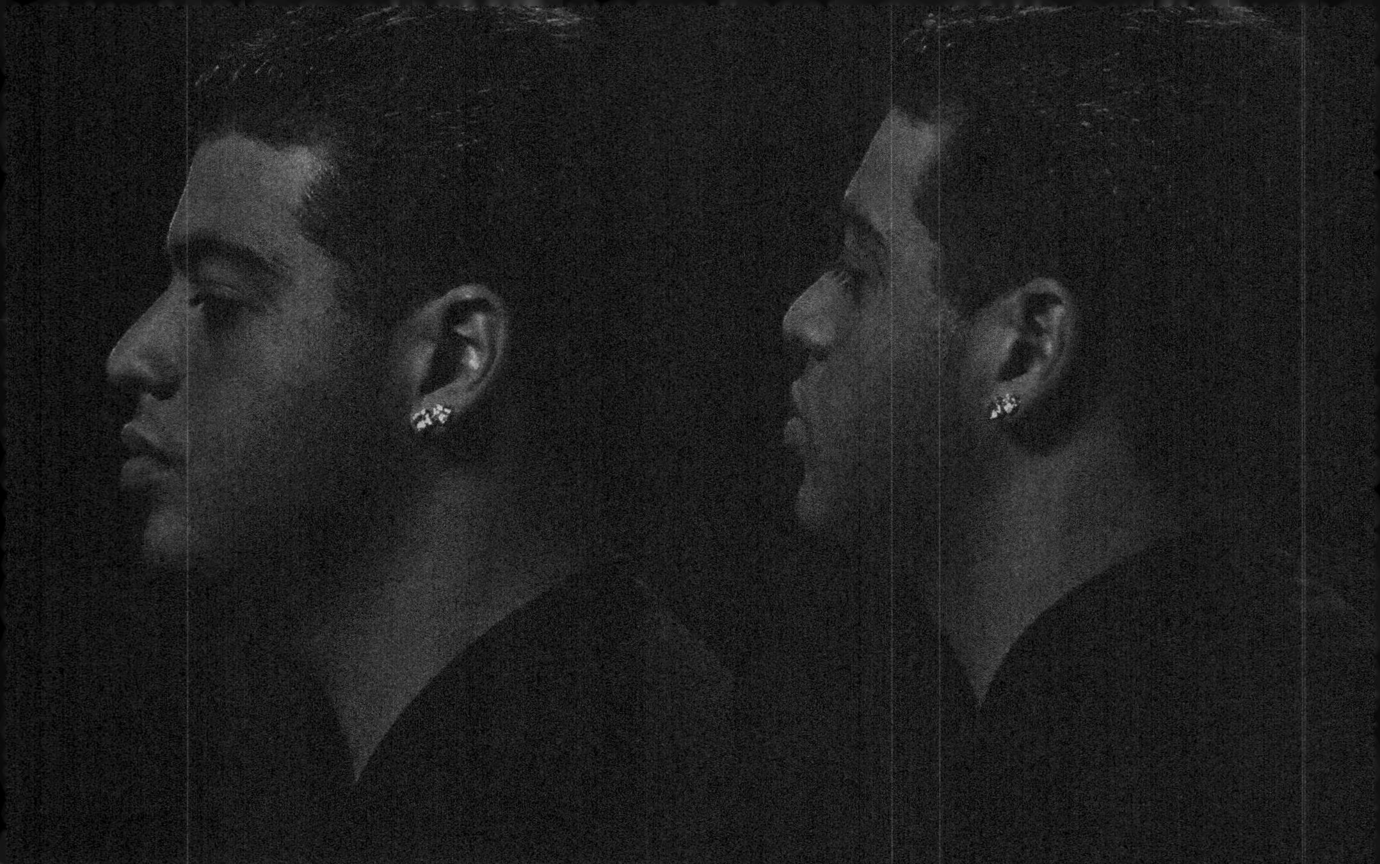

**Ethnicities claimed:**

Native American, African American, Creole, Russia, Italy, and Scotland.

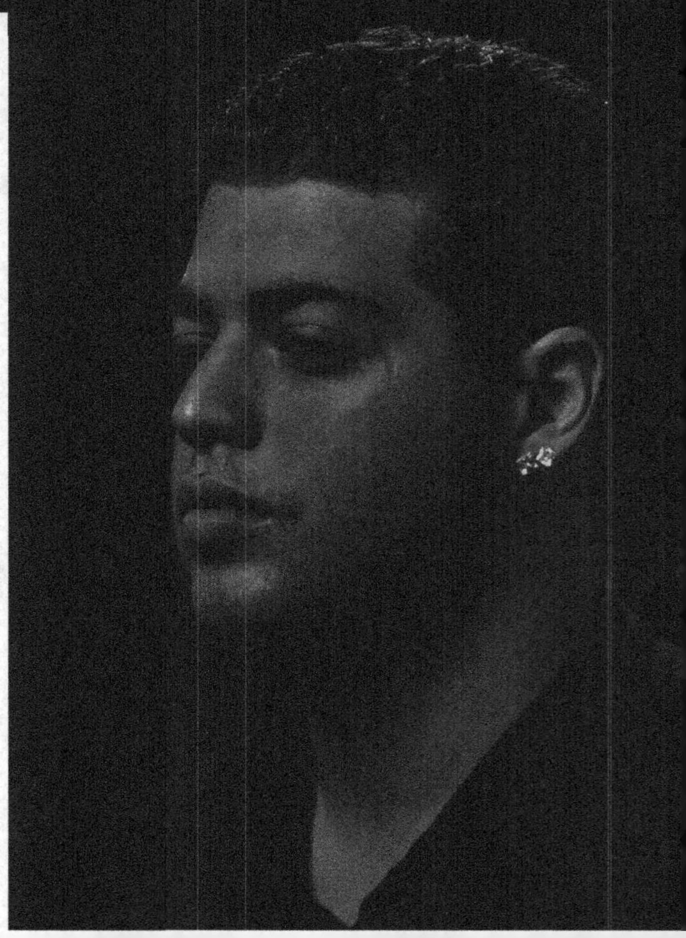

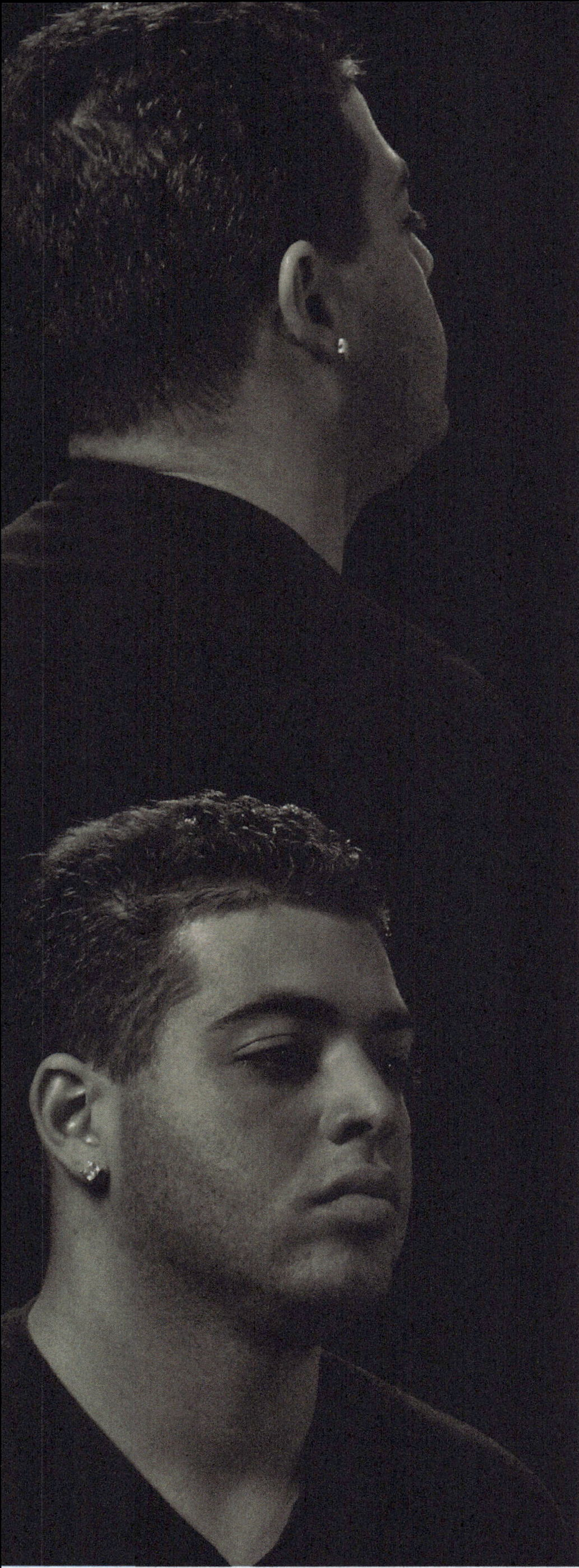

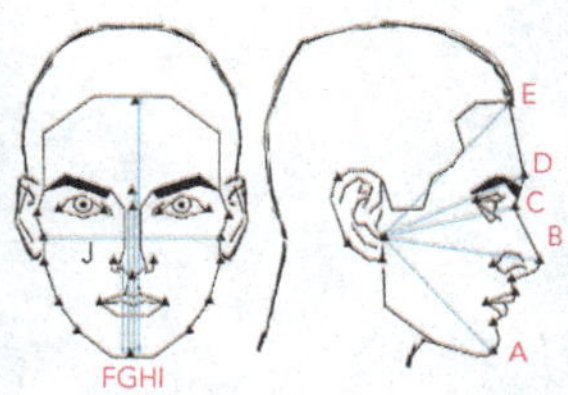


**Head measurements (in):**

A: 5 7/8
B: 5 3/8
C: 5 1/8
D: 5 1/8
E: 6 1/2
F: 3 5/8
G: 4 5/8
H: 5 1/4
I: 7 1/4
J: 6 1/4

MAP REFERENCE:

13

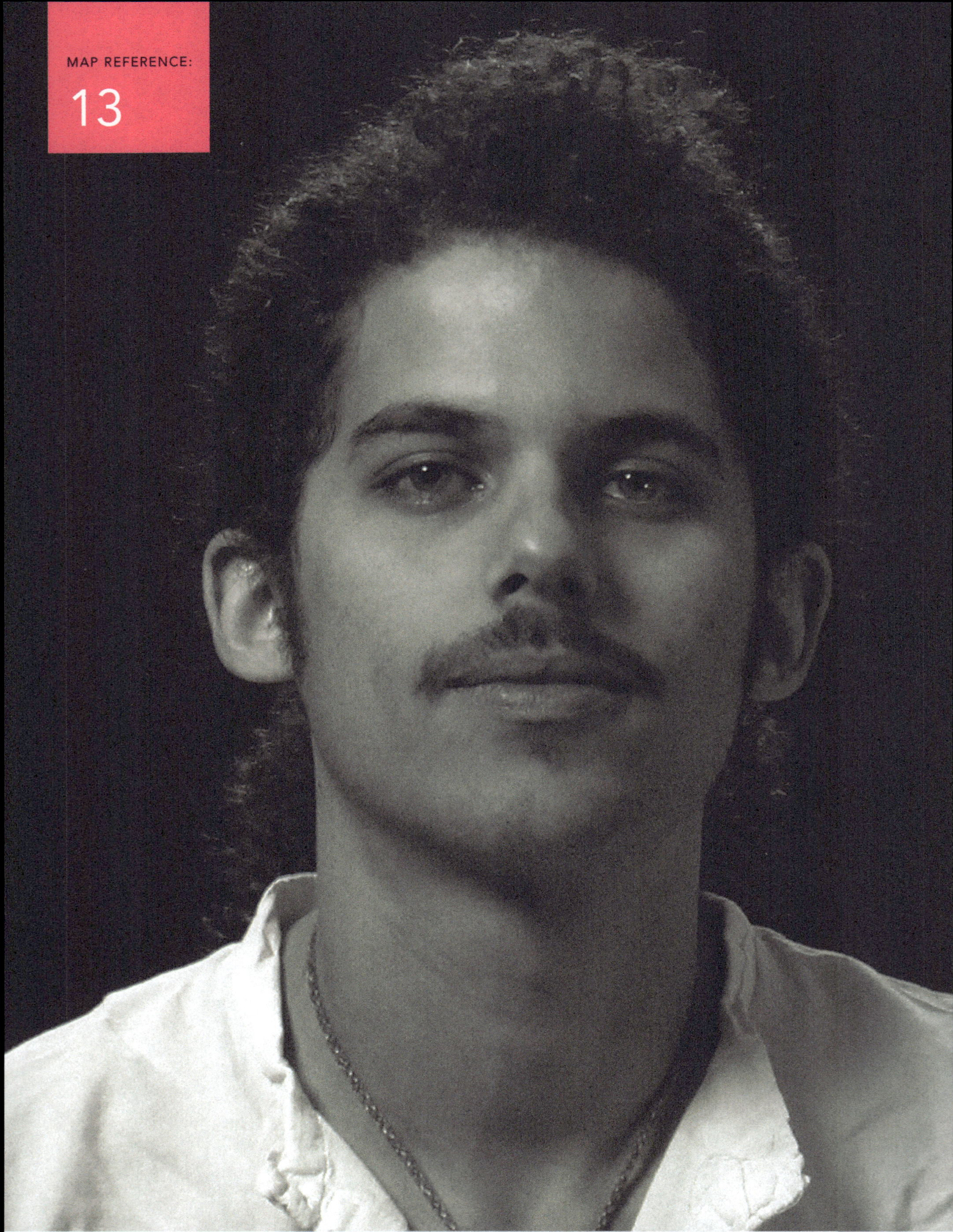

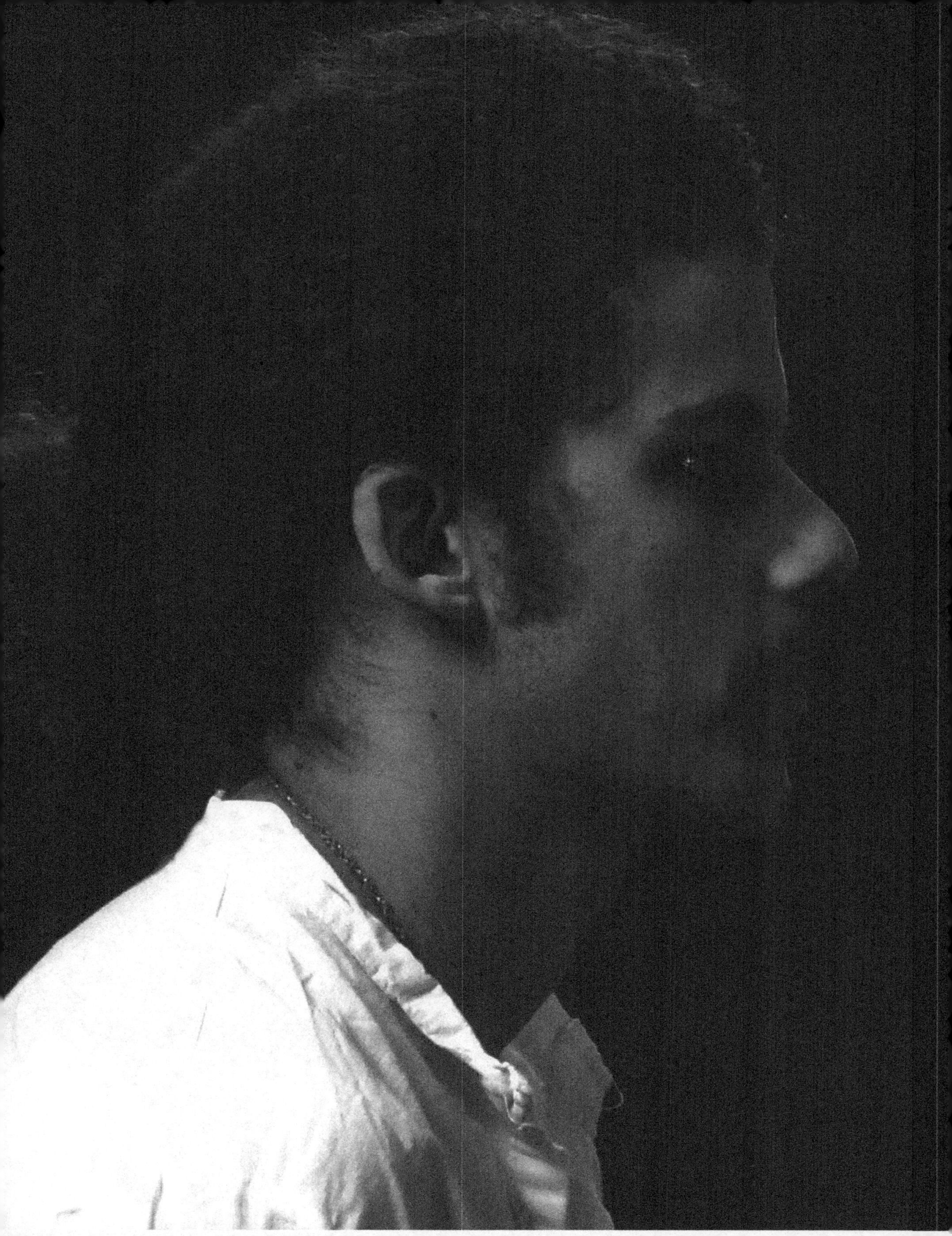

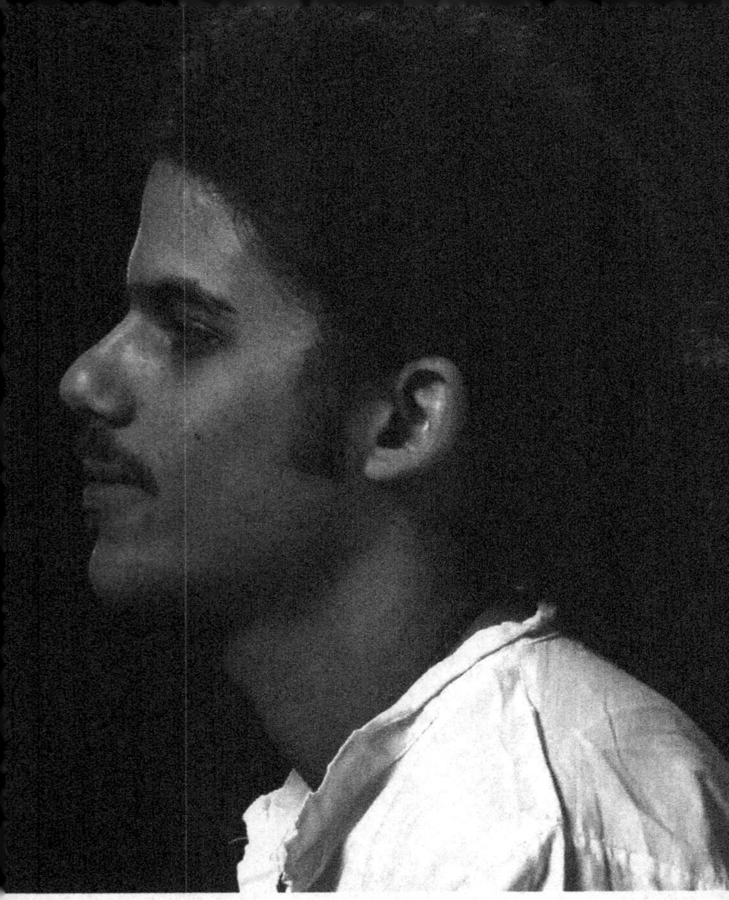

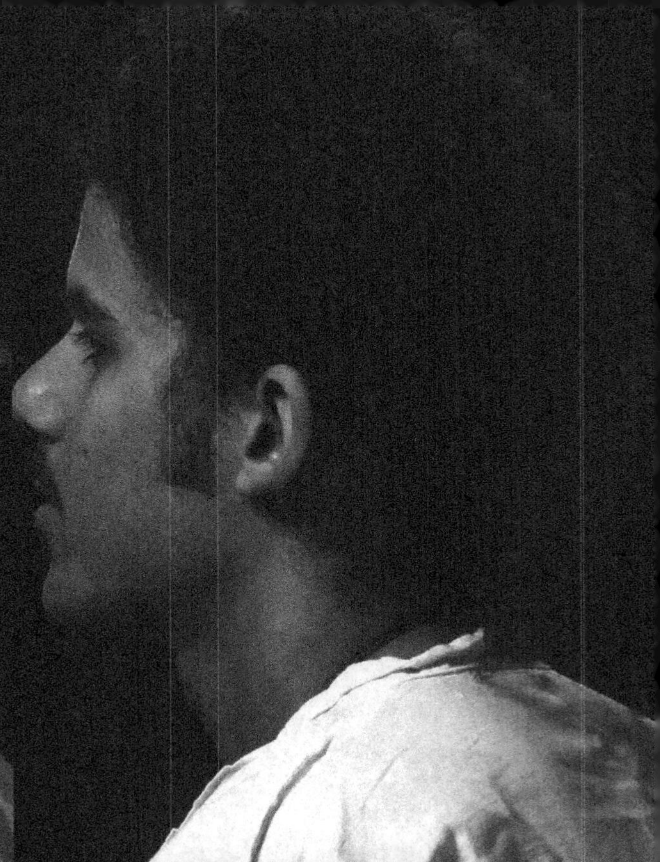

**Ethnicities claimed:**

Israel, Romania.

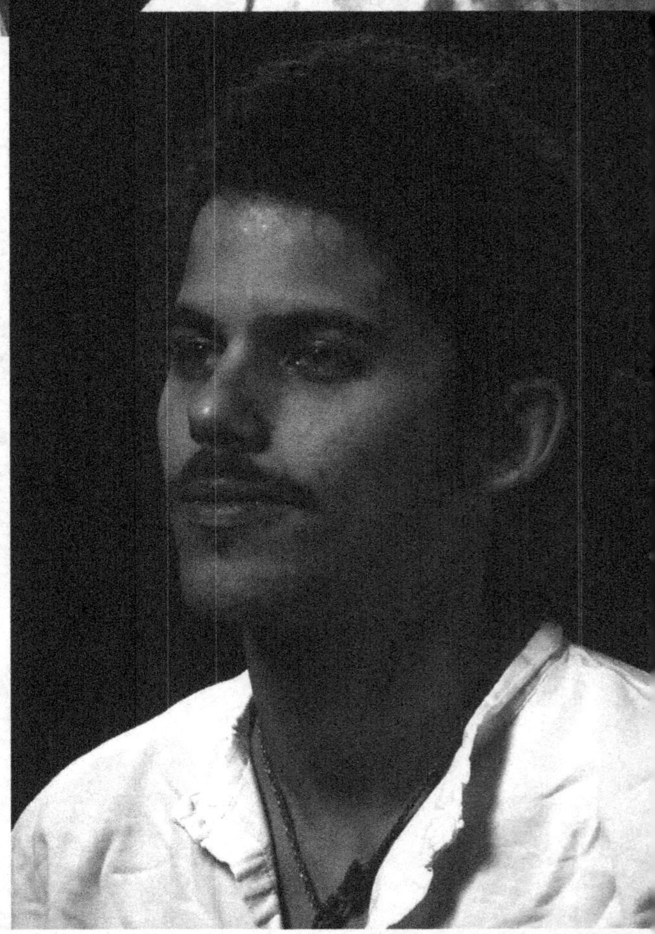

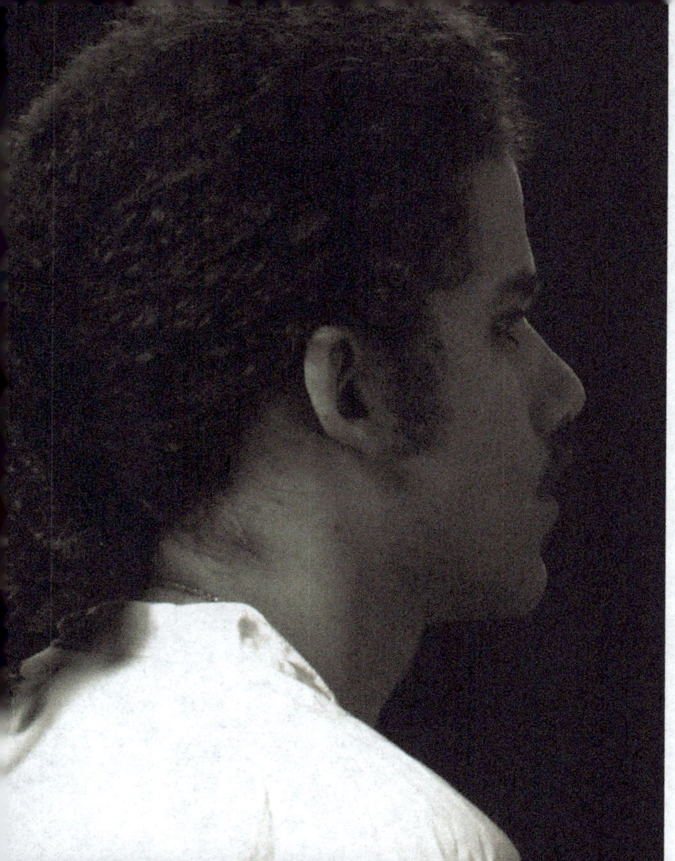

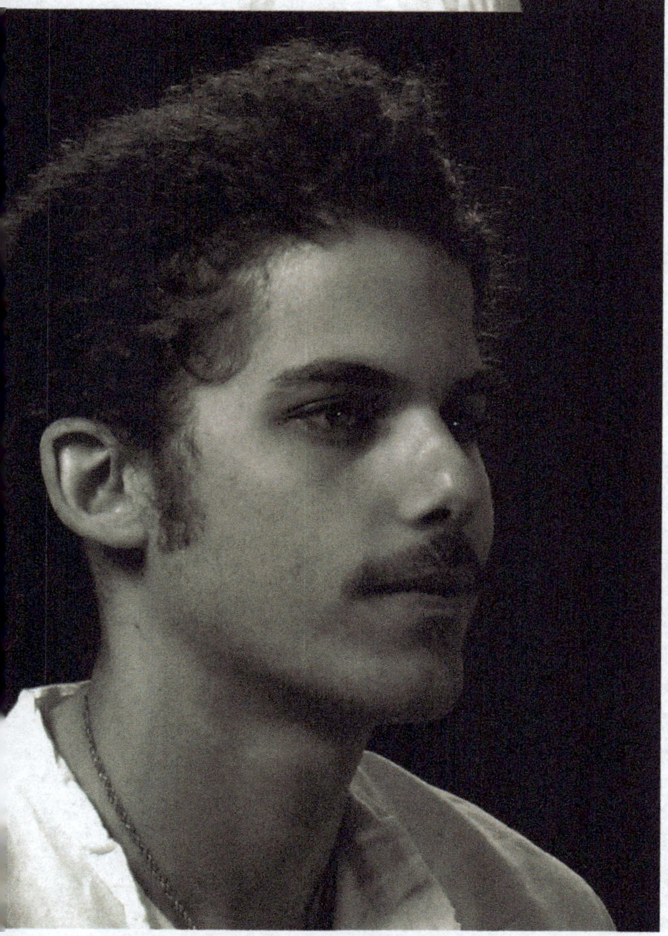

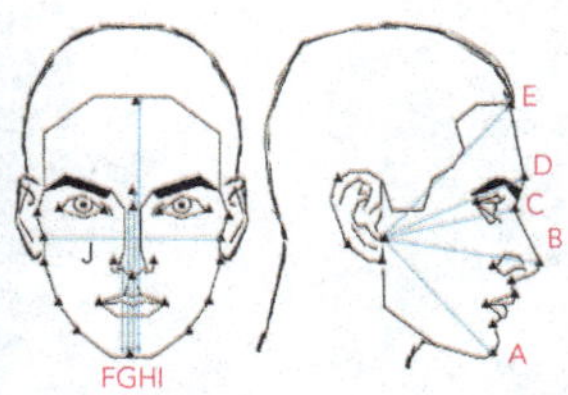


**Head measurements (in):**

A: 6

B: 5

C: 5 3/8

D: 5 3/8

E: 6 3/8

F: 4

G: 4 7/8

H: 5 3/8

I: 7 3/4

J: 5 3/4

MAP REFERENCE:

14

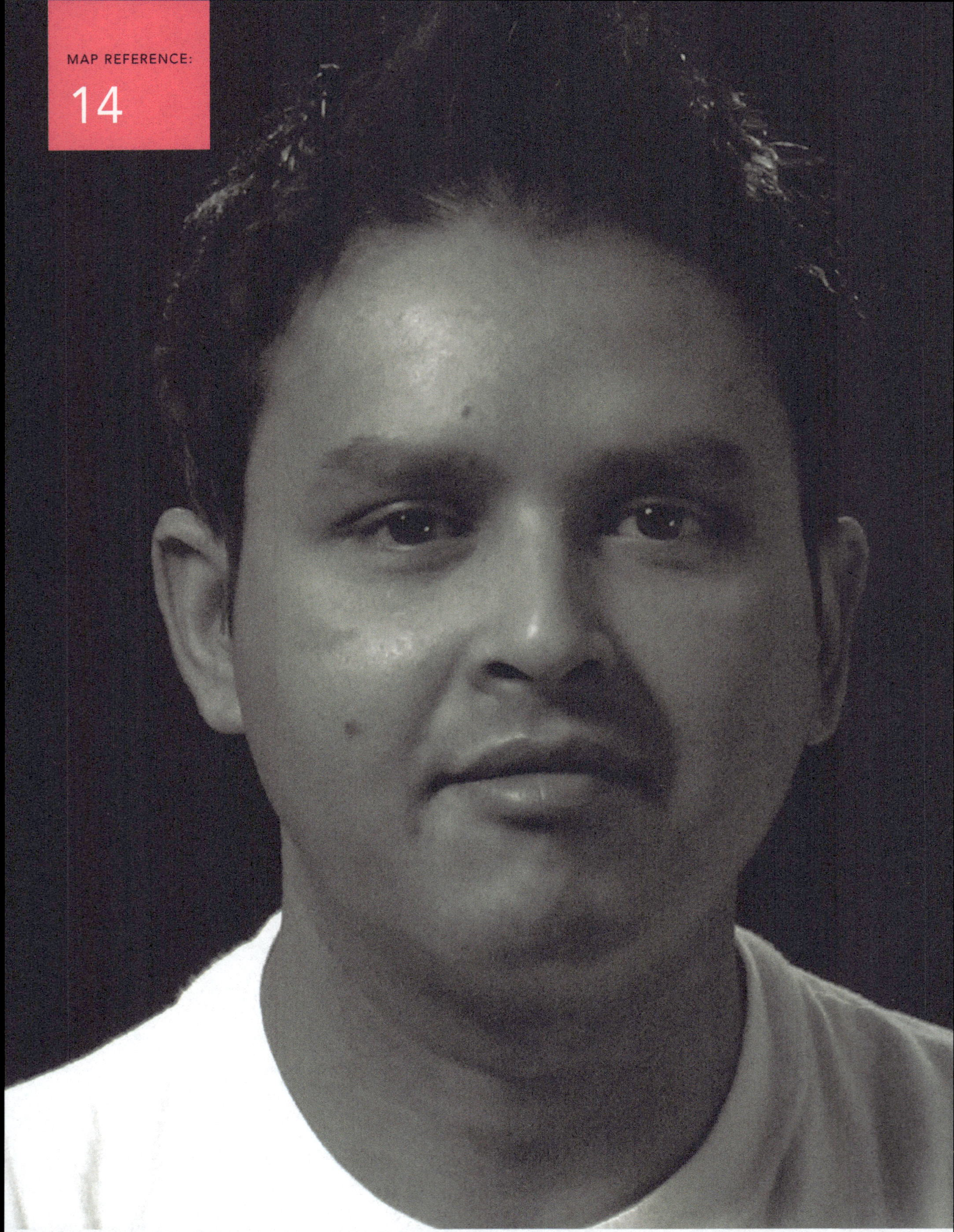

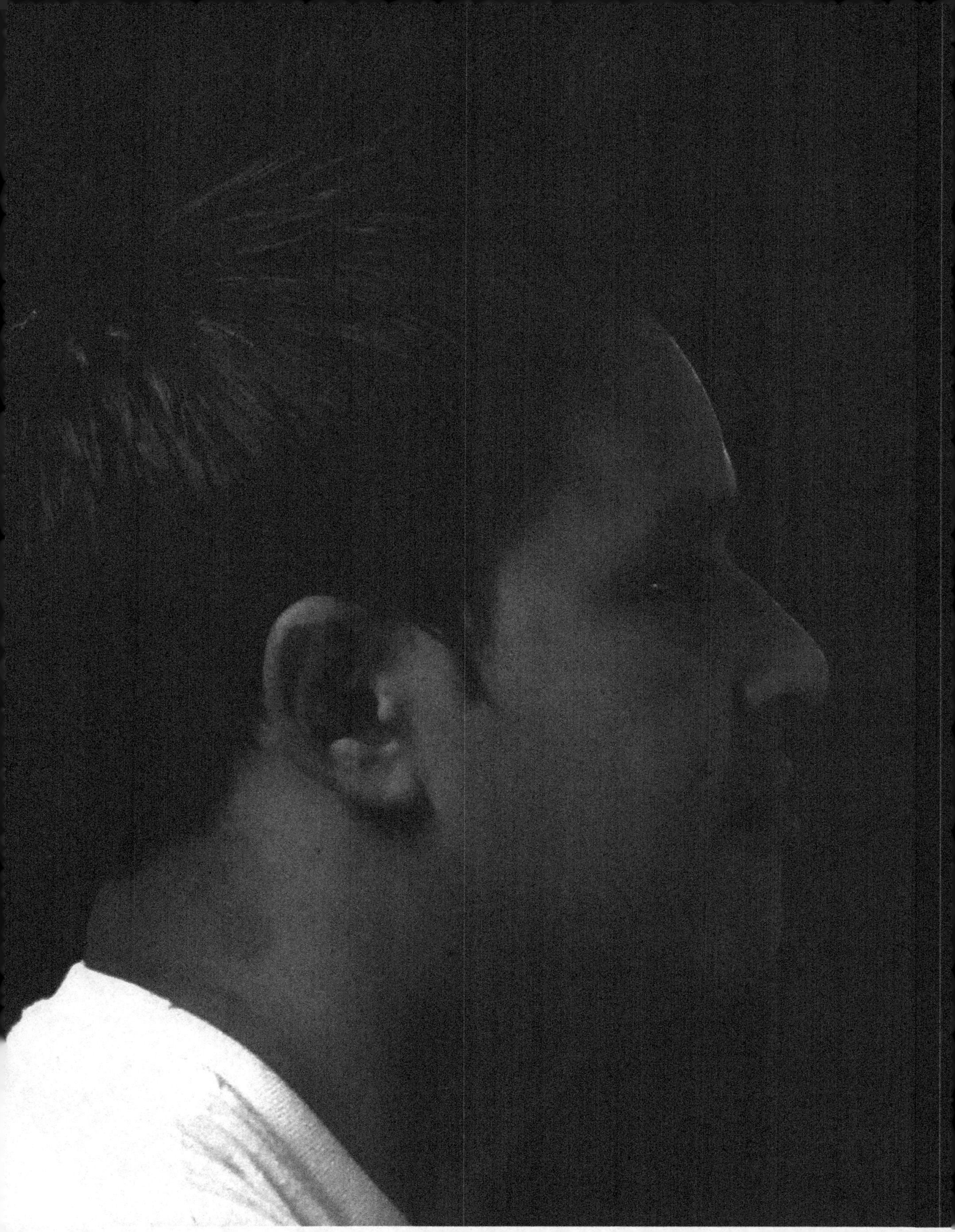

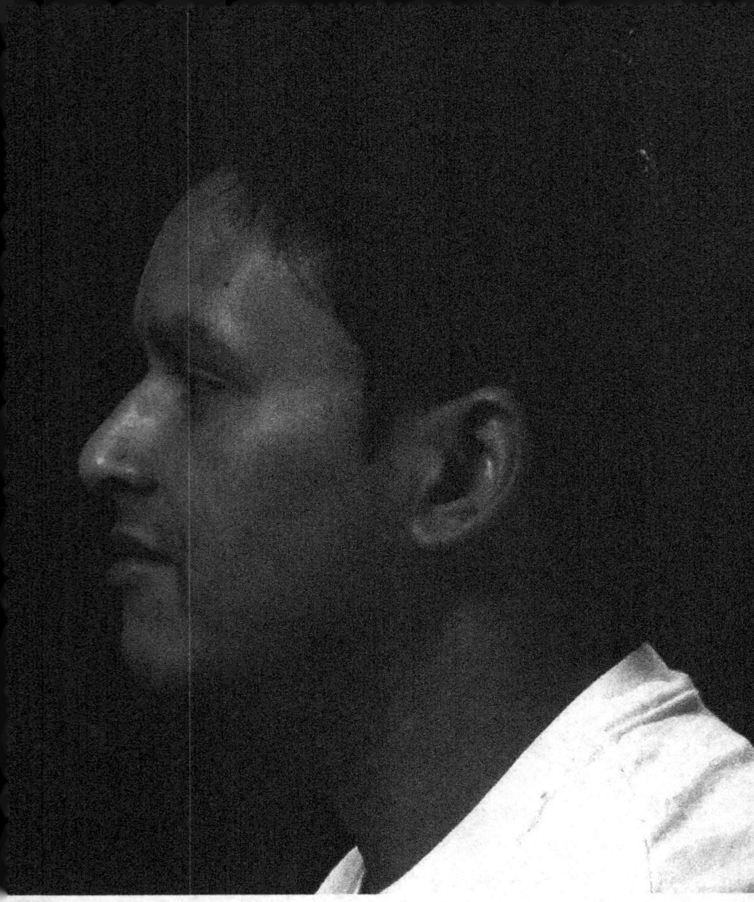

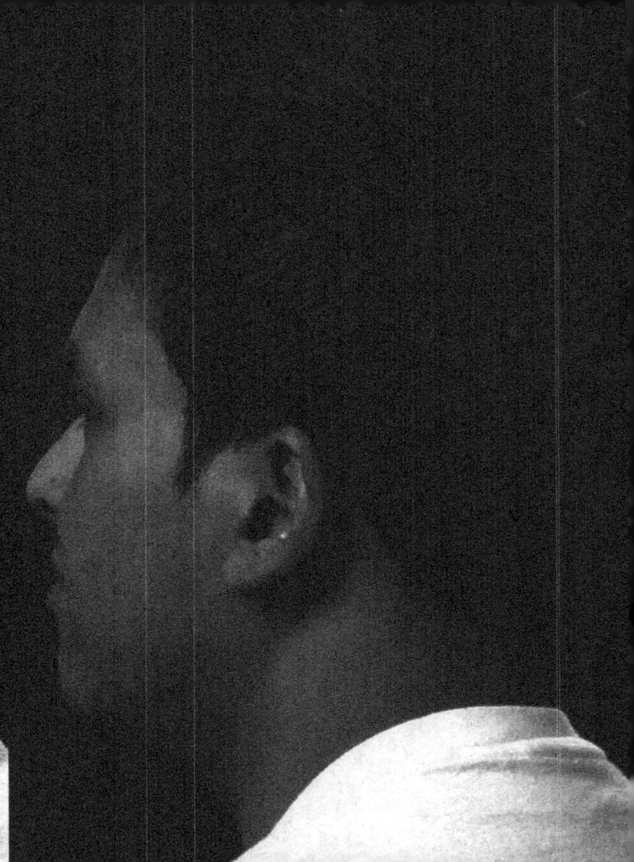

**Ethnicities claimed:**

Pakistan, Bangladesh.

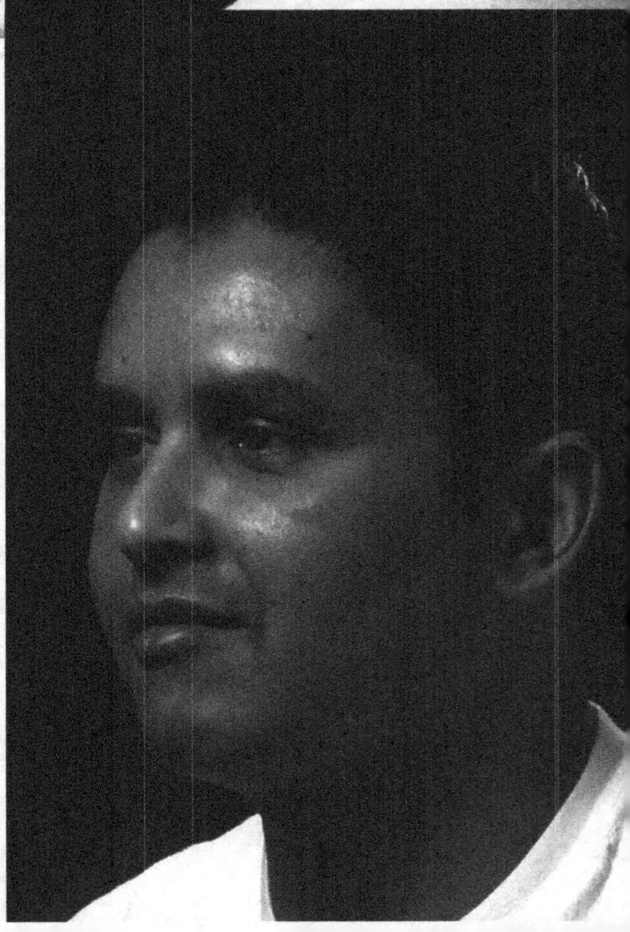

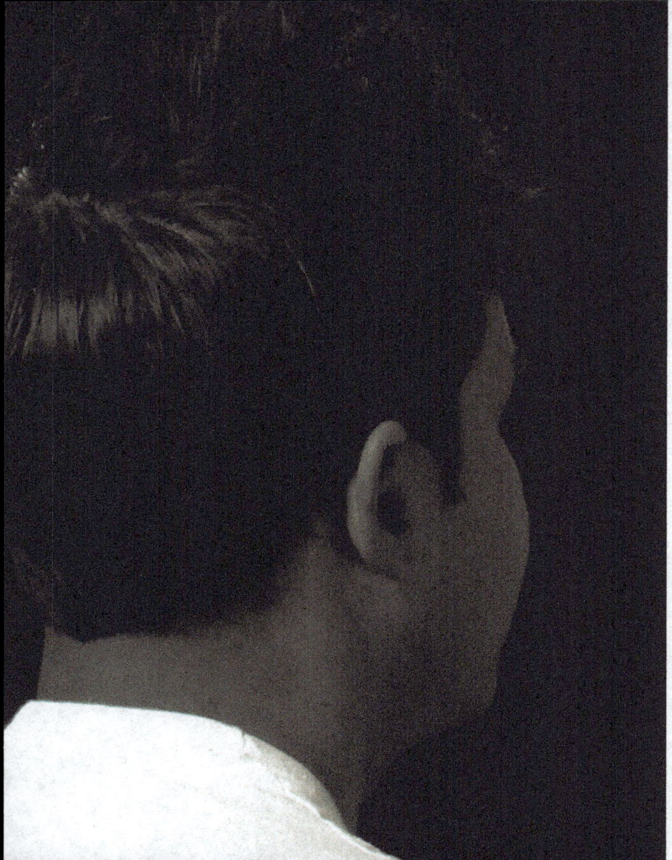

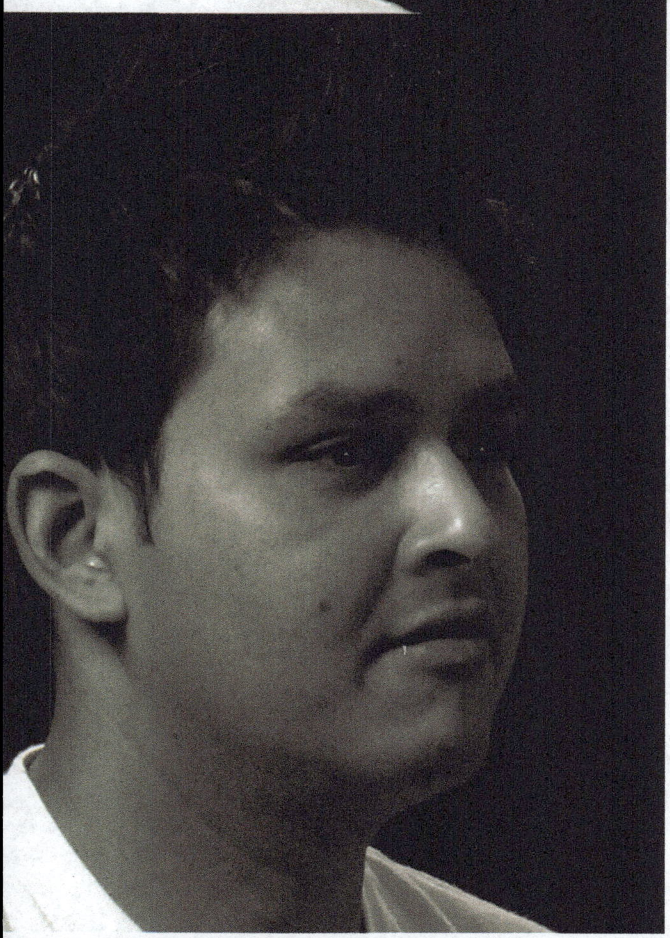

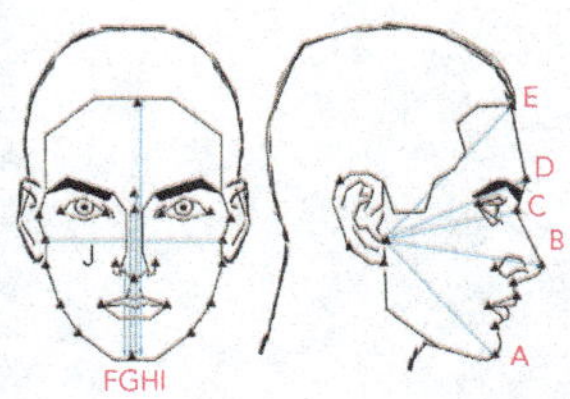


**Head measurements (in):**

A: 5
B: 5 1/4
C: 5 8
D: 5 1/4
E: 6 1/4
F: 3 7/8
G: 8 3/8
H: 5 3/8
I: 7 1/4
J: 6

MAP REFERENCE:

18

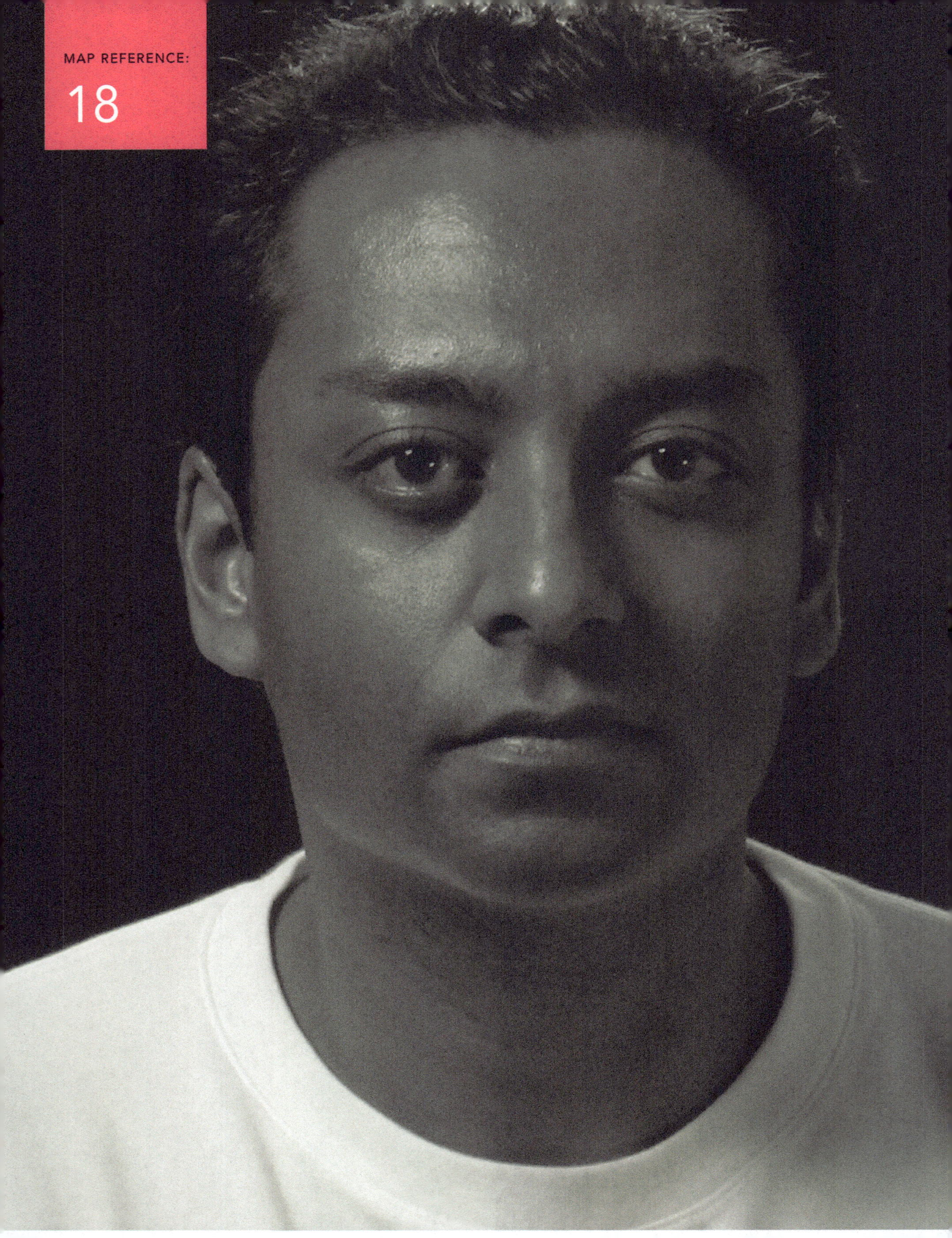

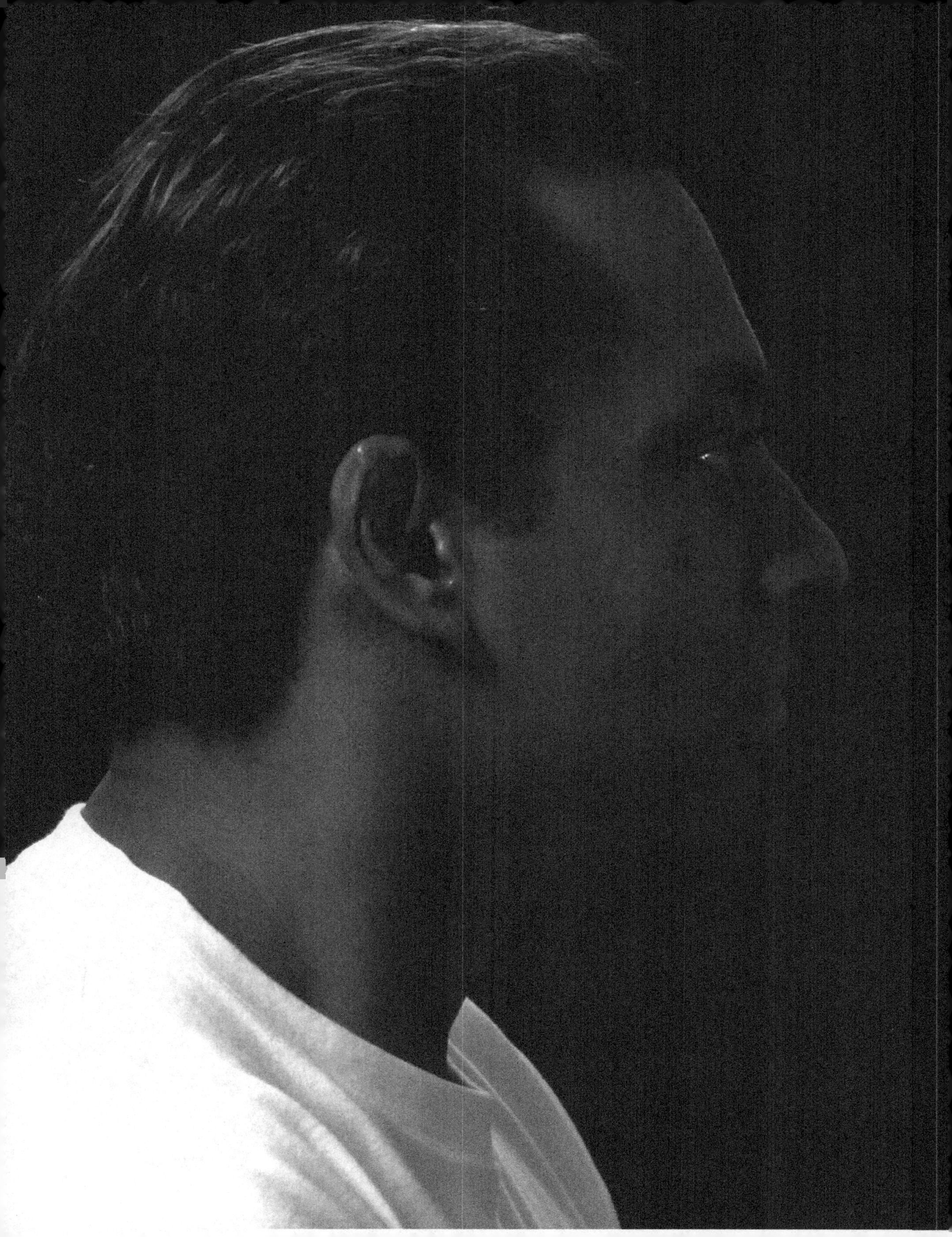

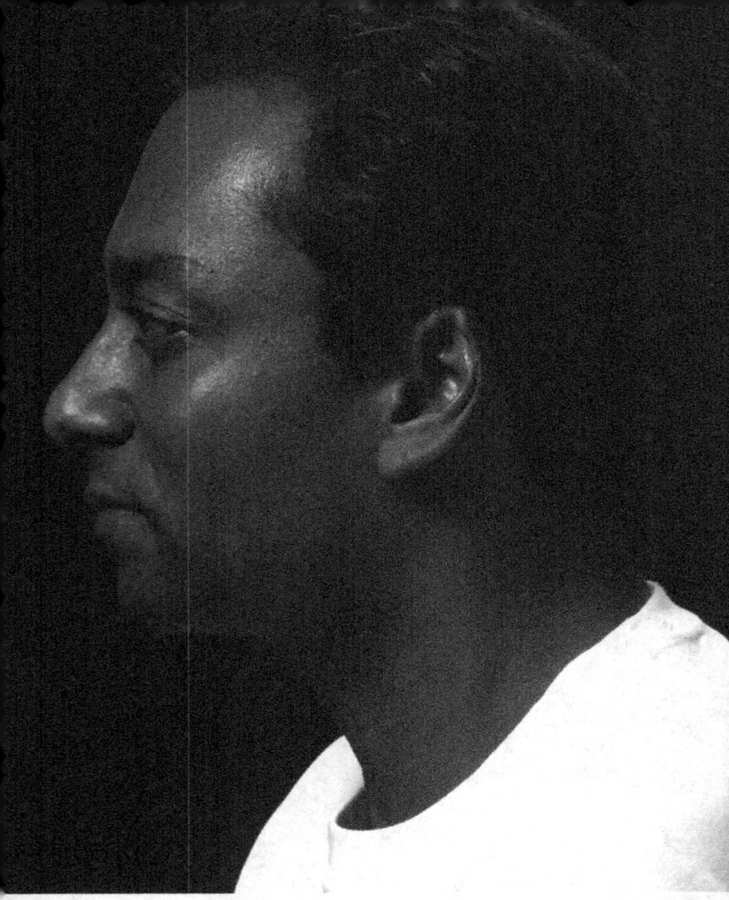

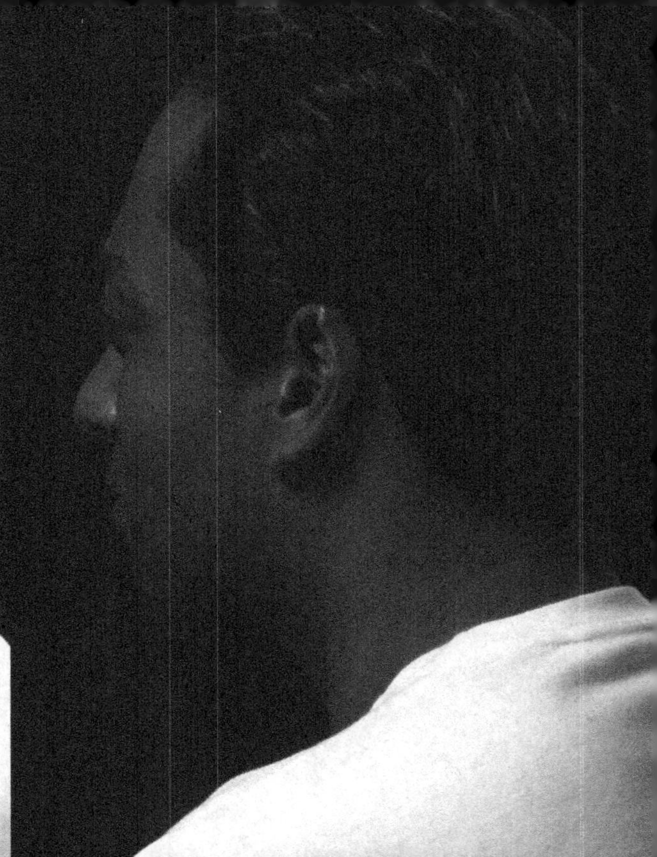

**Ethnicities claimed:**

East India—Tamil Nadu Province.

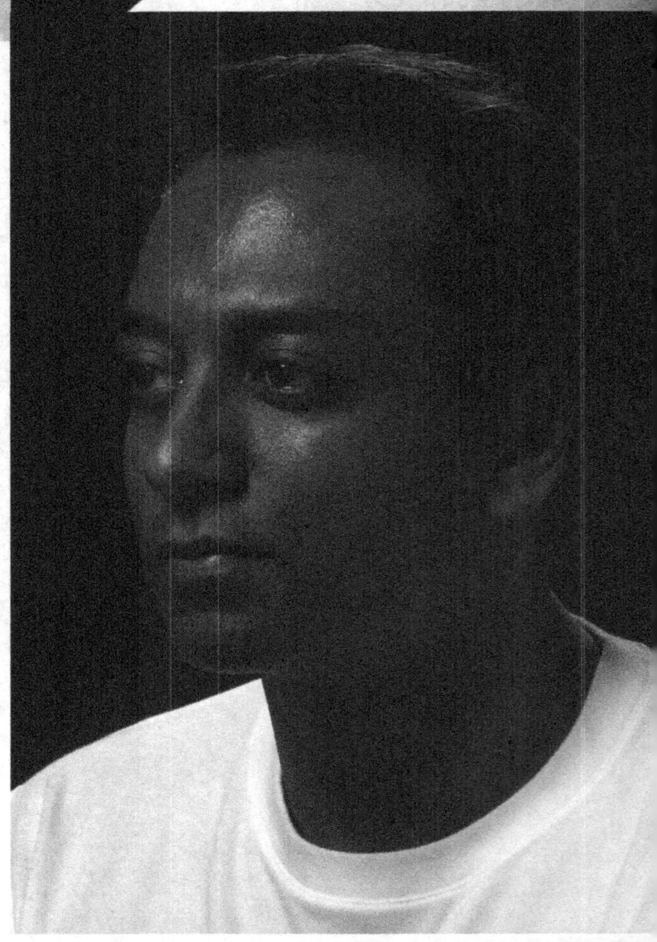

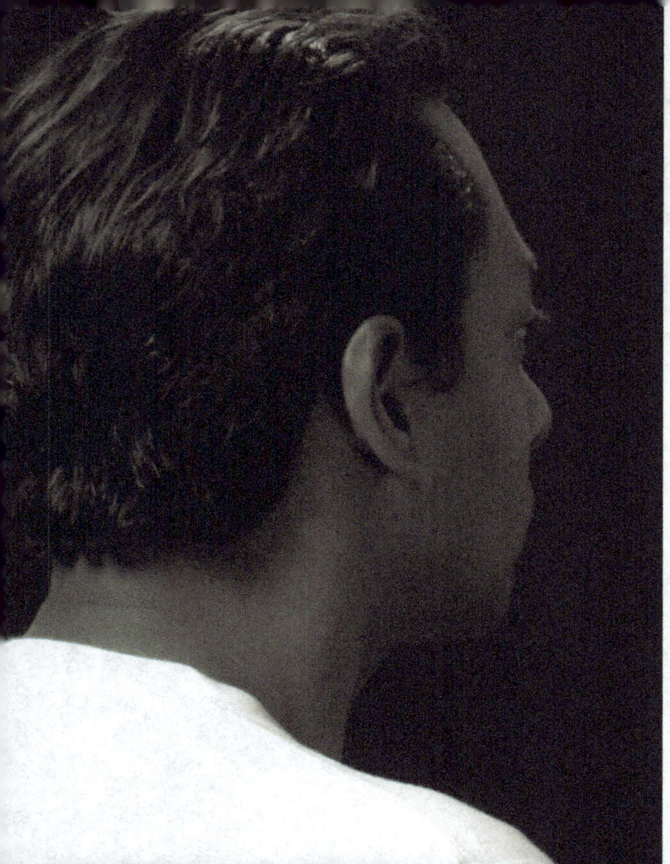

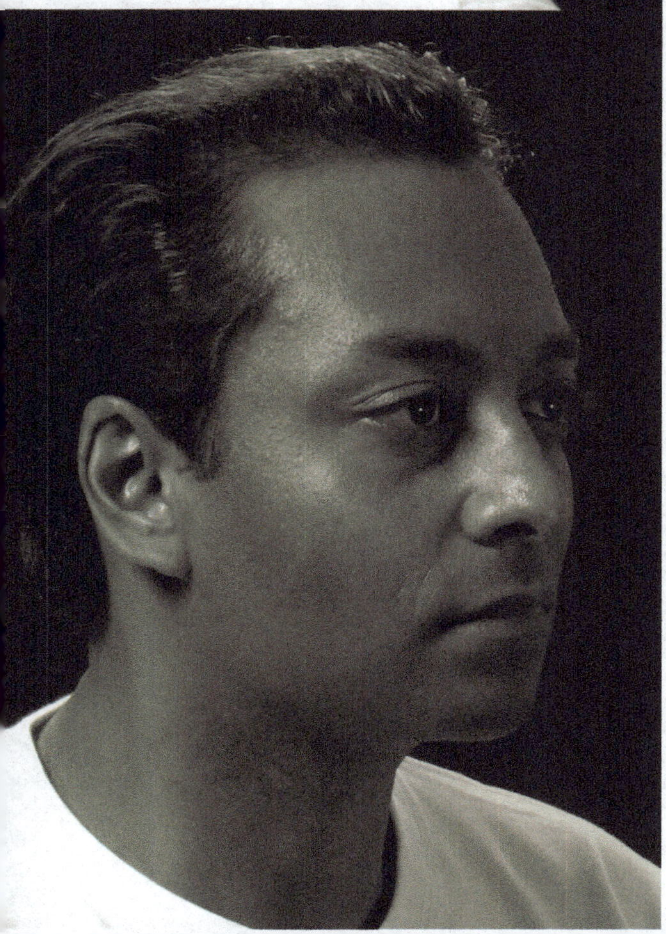

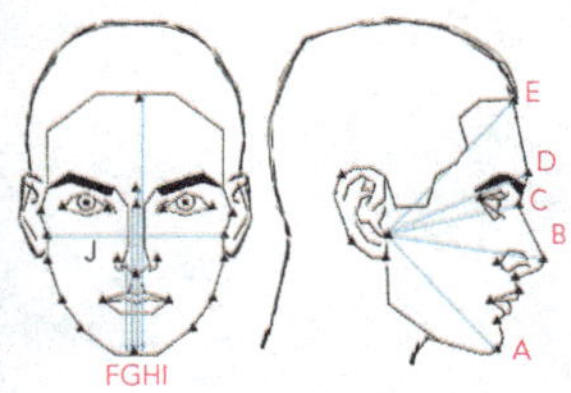


**Head measurements (in):**

A: 5 1/2
B: 5 1/4
C: 5 3/8
D: 5 3/4
E: 6 2/8
F: 3 3/8
G: 4 3/8
H: 5 1/4
I: 8
J: 5 3/4

MAP REFERENCE:

21

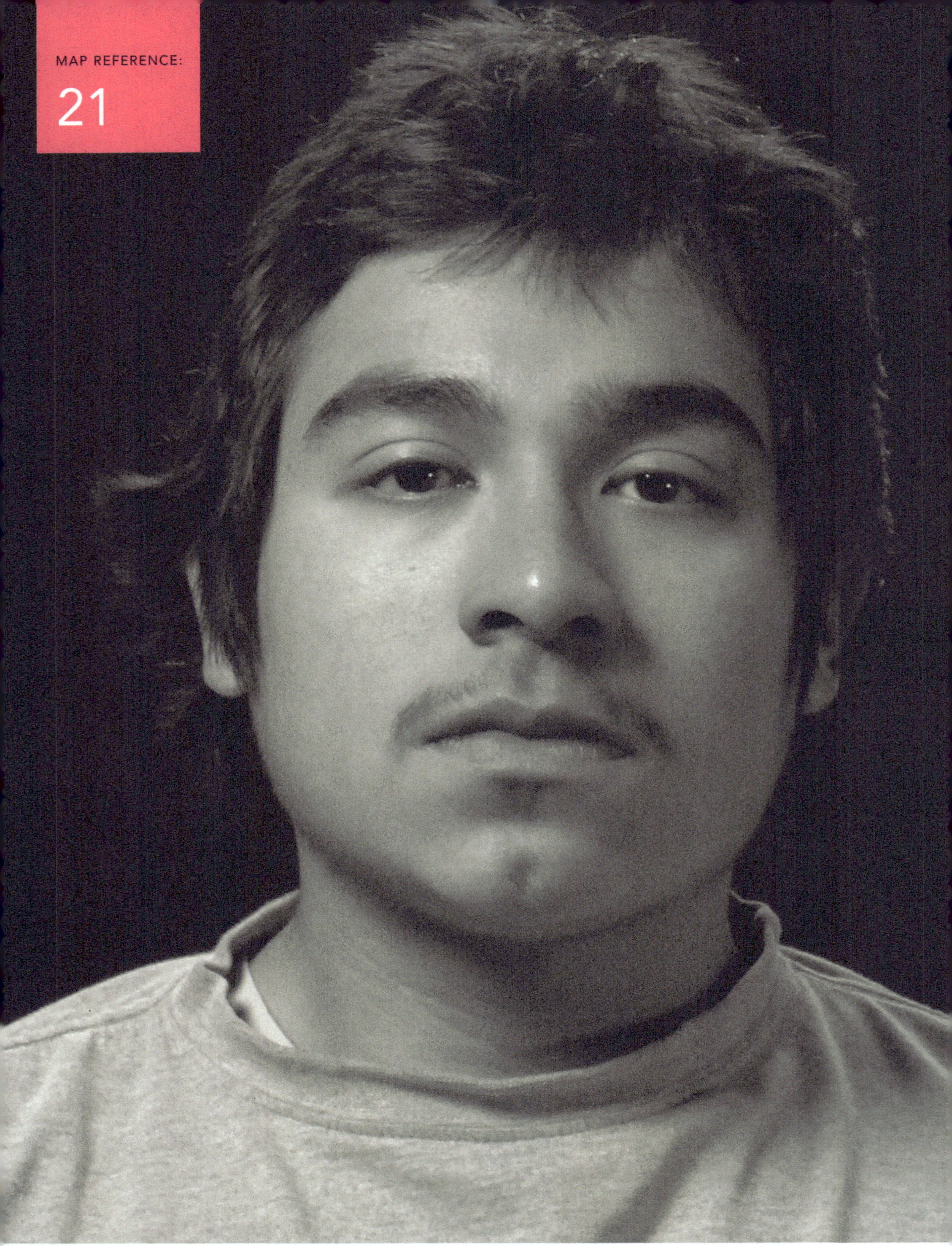

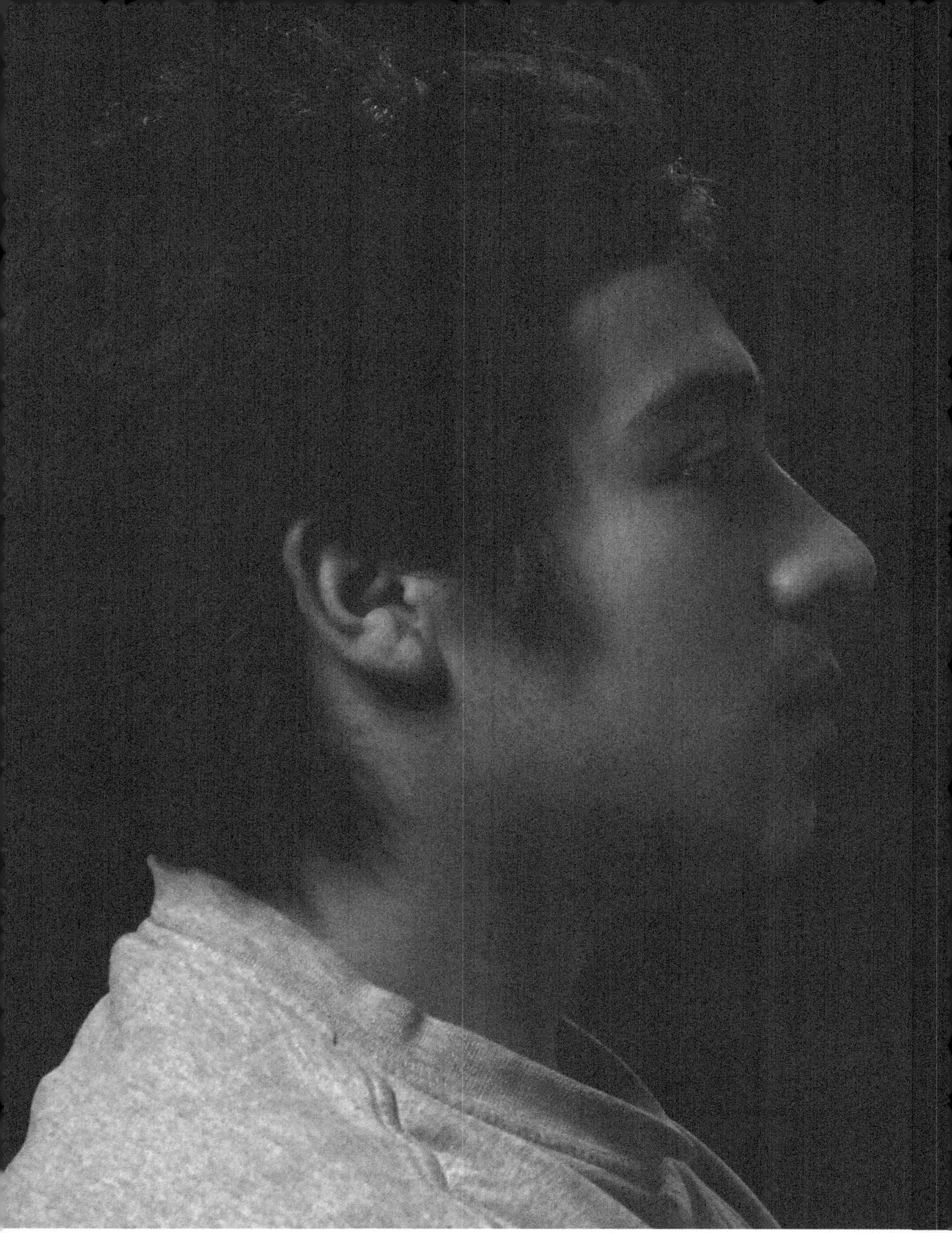

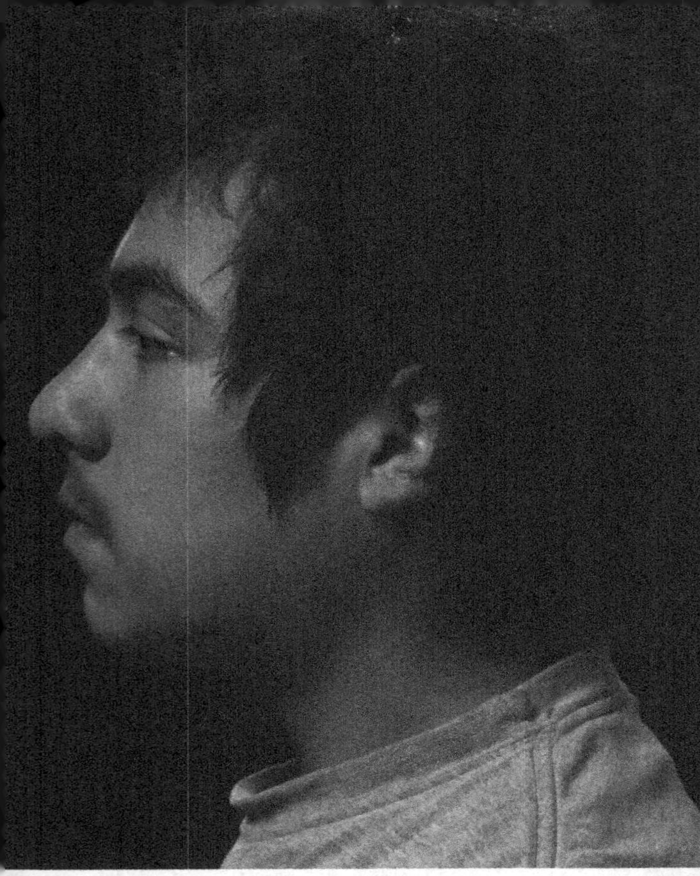

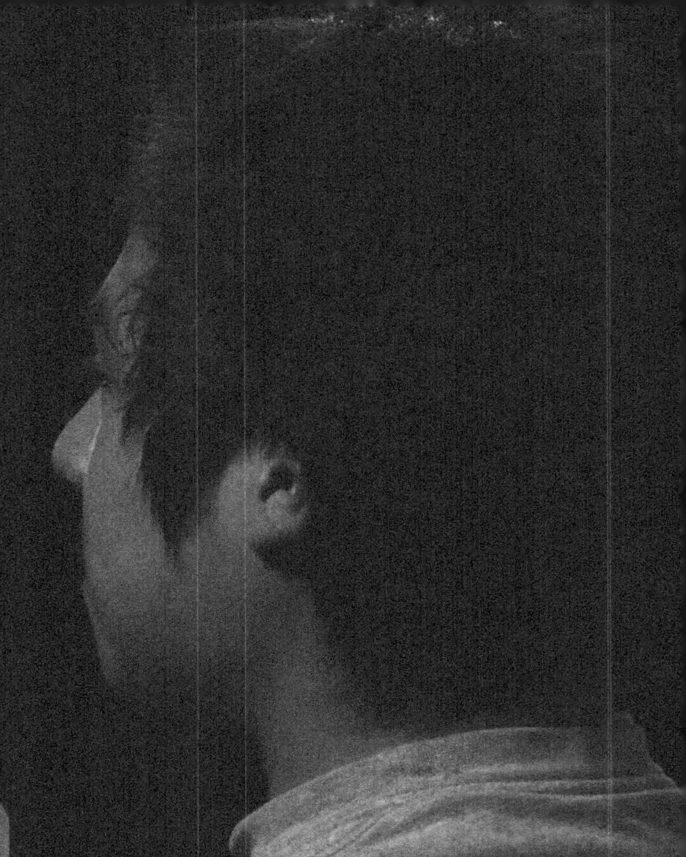

**Ethnicities claimed:**

Mexico.

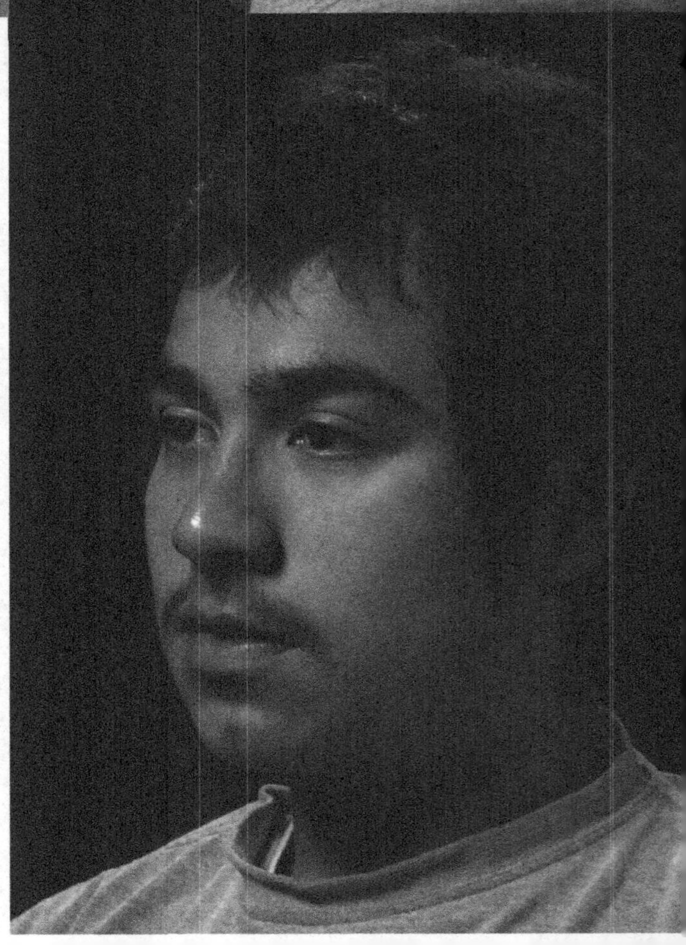

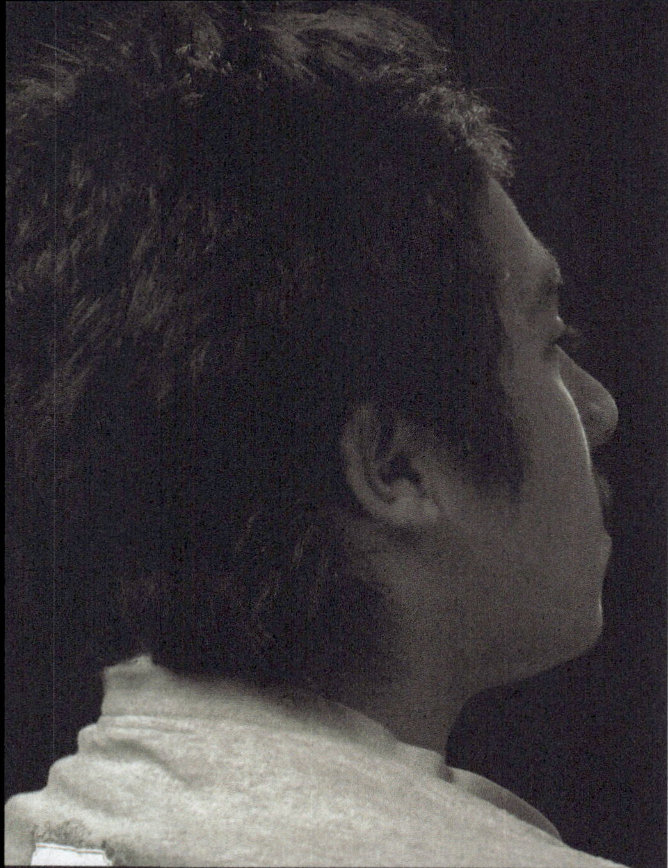

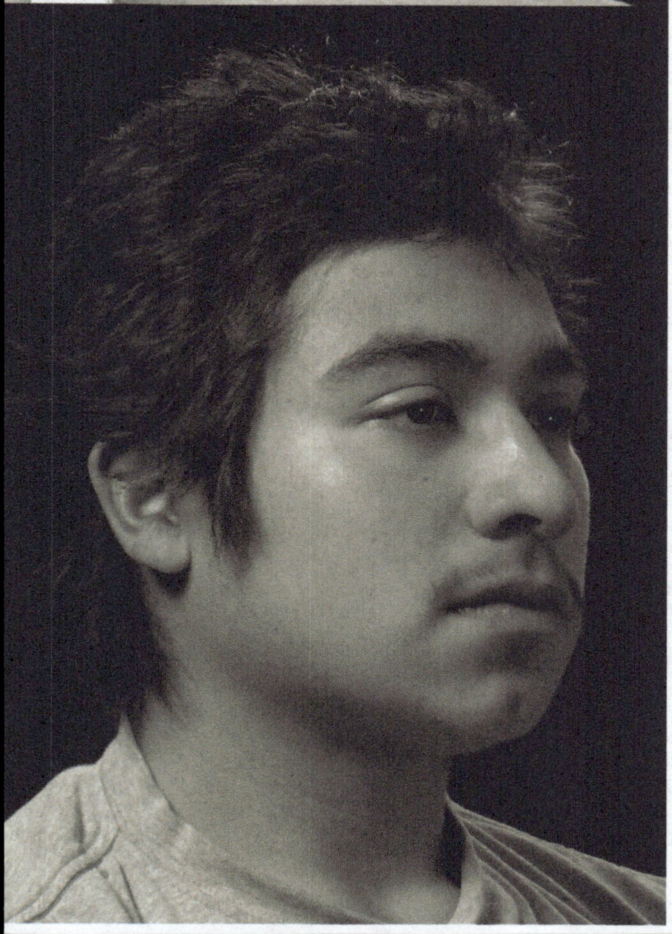

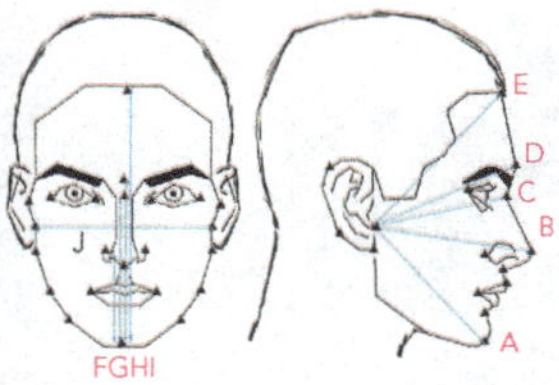


**Head measurements (in):**

A: 6 1/4
B: 6 1/8
C: 5 1/2
D: 5 7/8
E: 6 1/2
F: 3 5/8
G: 4 1/2
H: 5 1/2
I: 7 7/8
J: 6 1/2

MAP REFERENCE:
26

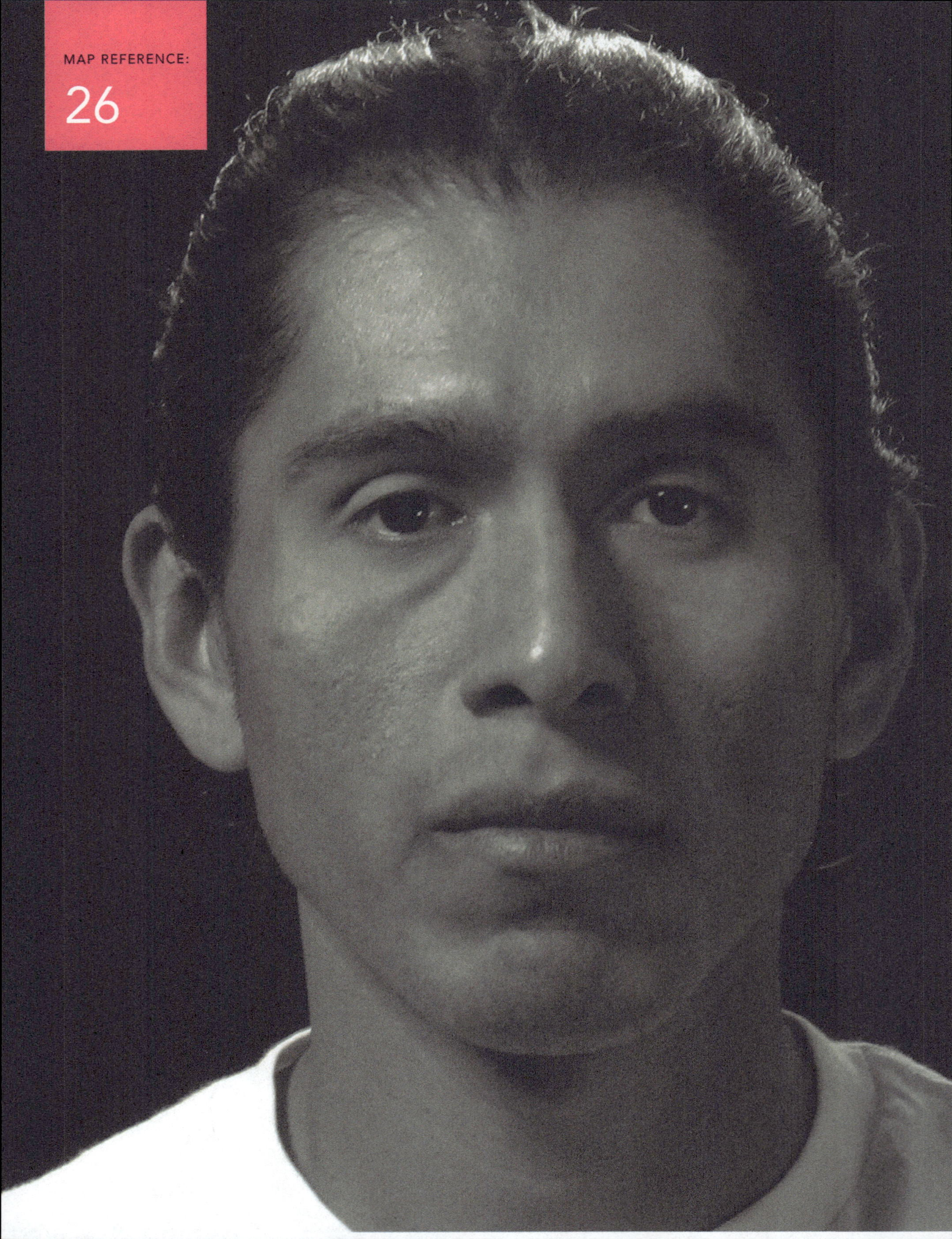

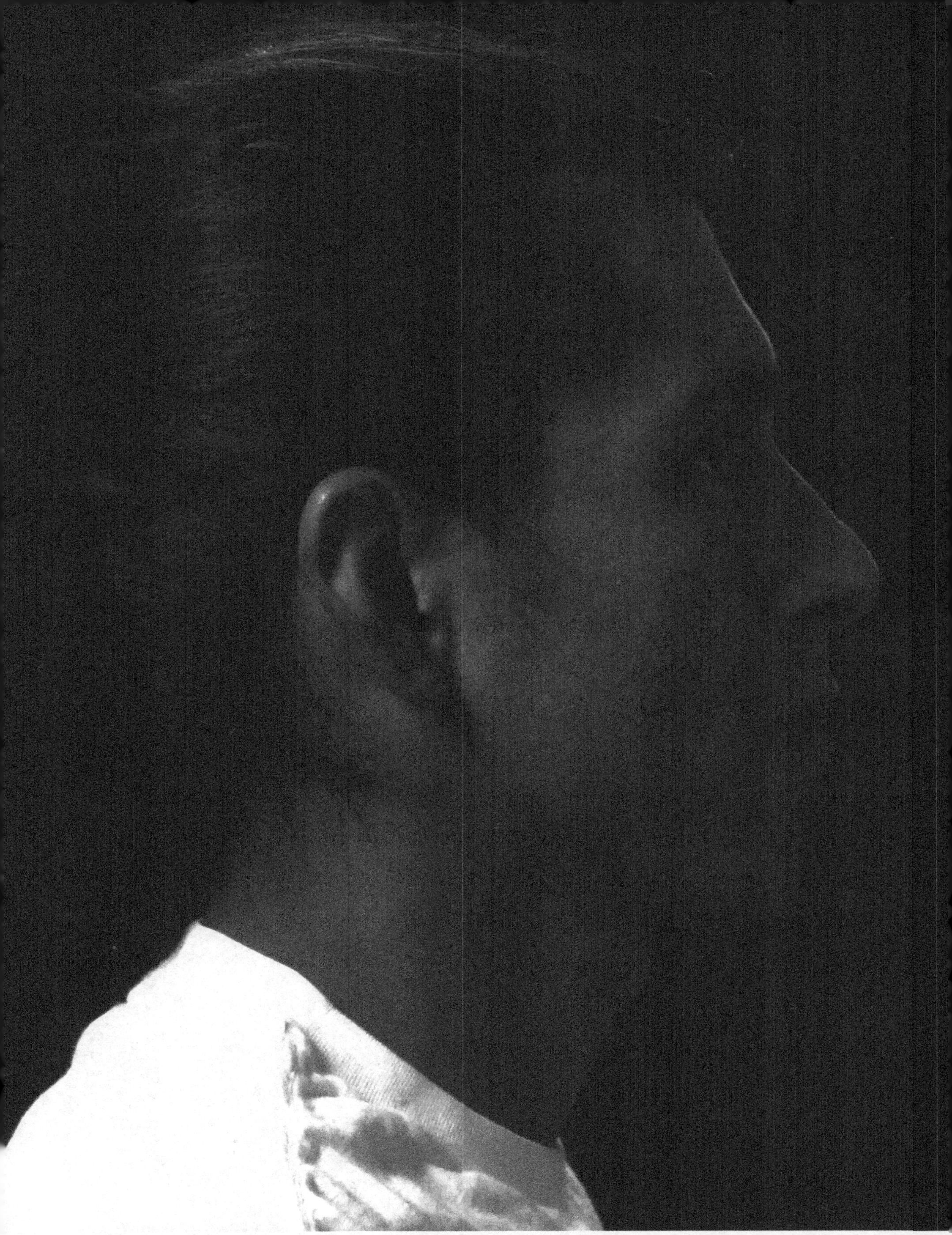

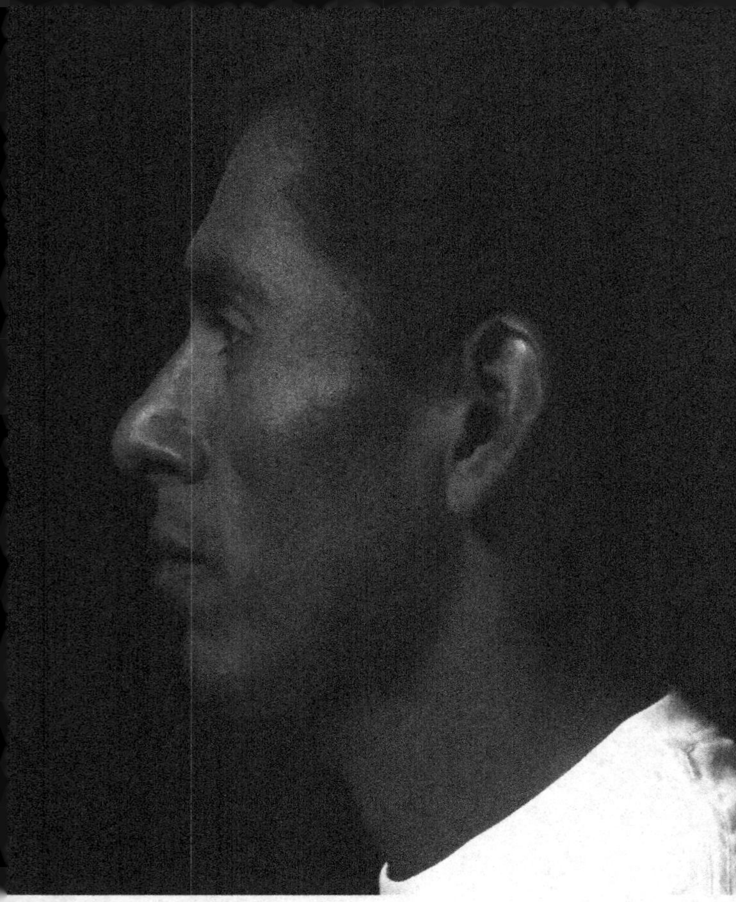

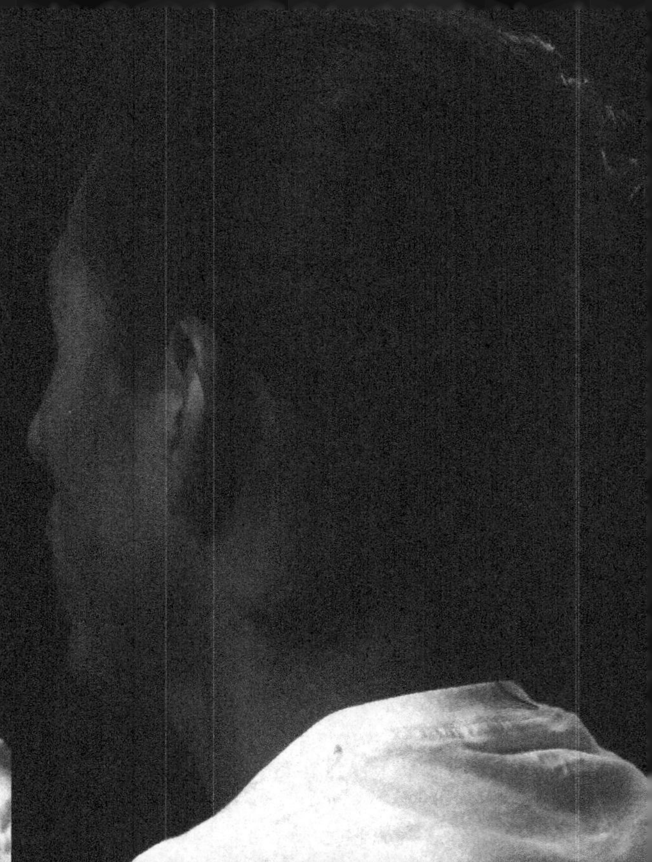

**Ethnicities claimed:**

Mexico.

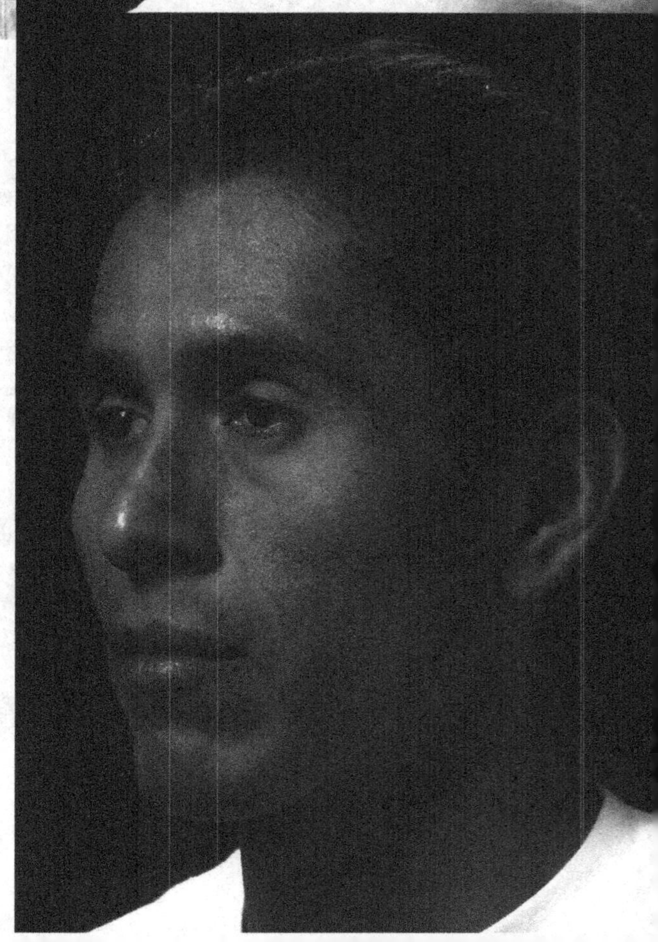

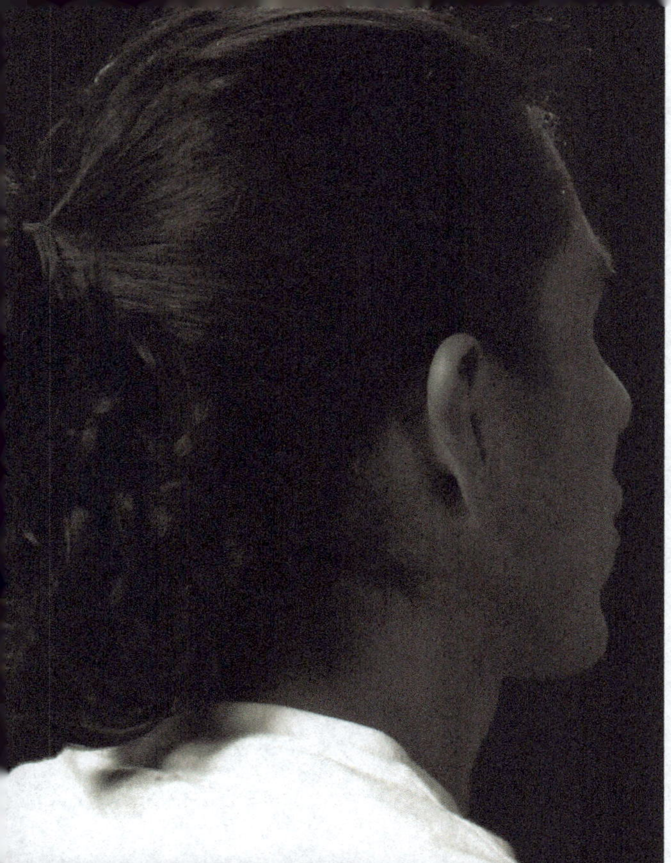

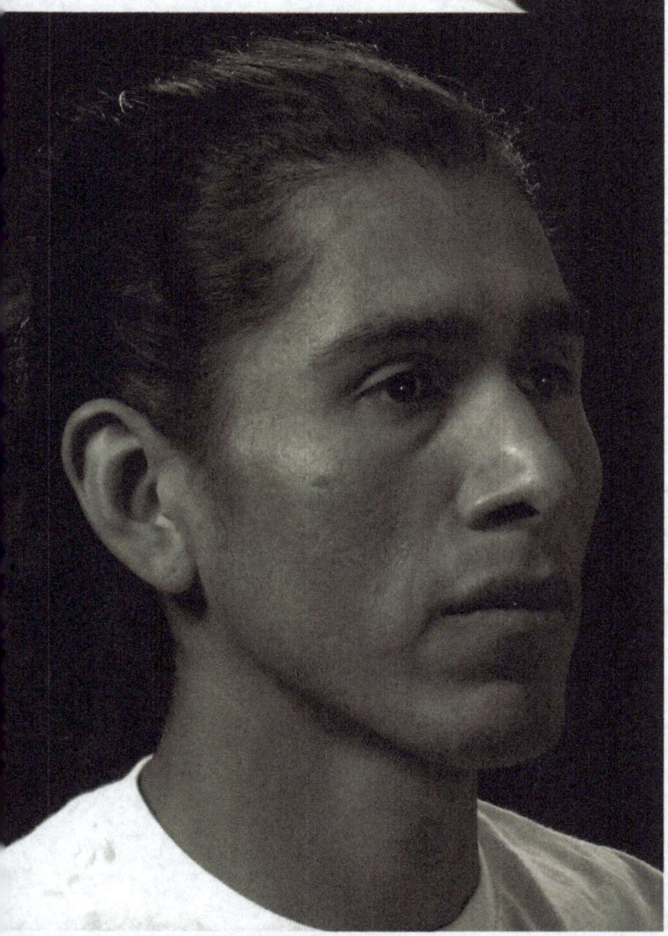

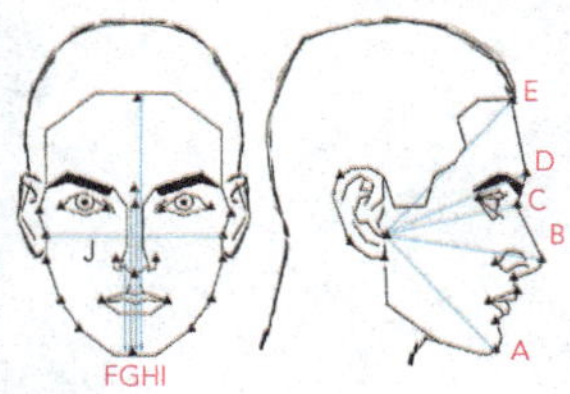


**Head measurements (in):**

A: 5 3/4
B: 4 3/4
C: 4 3/4
D: 5 3/8
E: 6 3/8
F: 3 3/4
G: 4 7/8
H: 5 5/8
I: 7 7/8
J: 6 1/8

MAP REFERENCE:

27

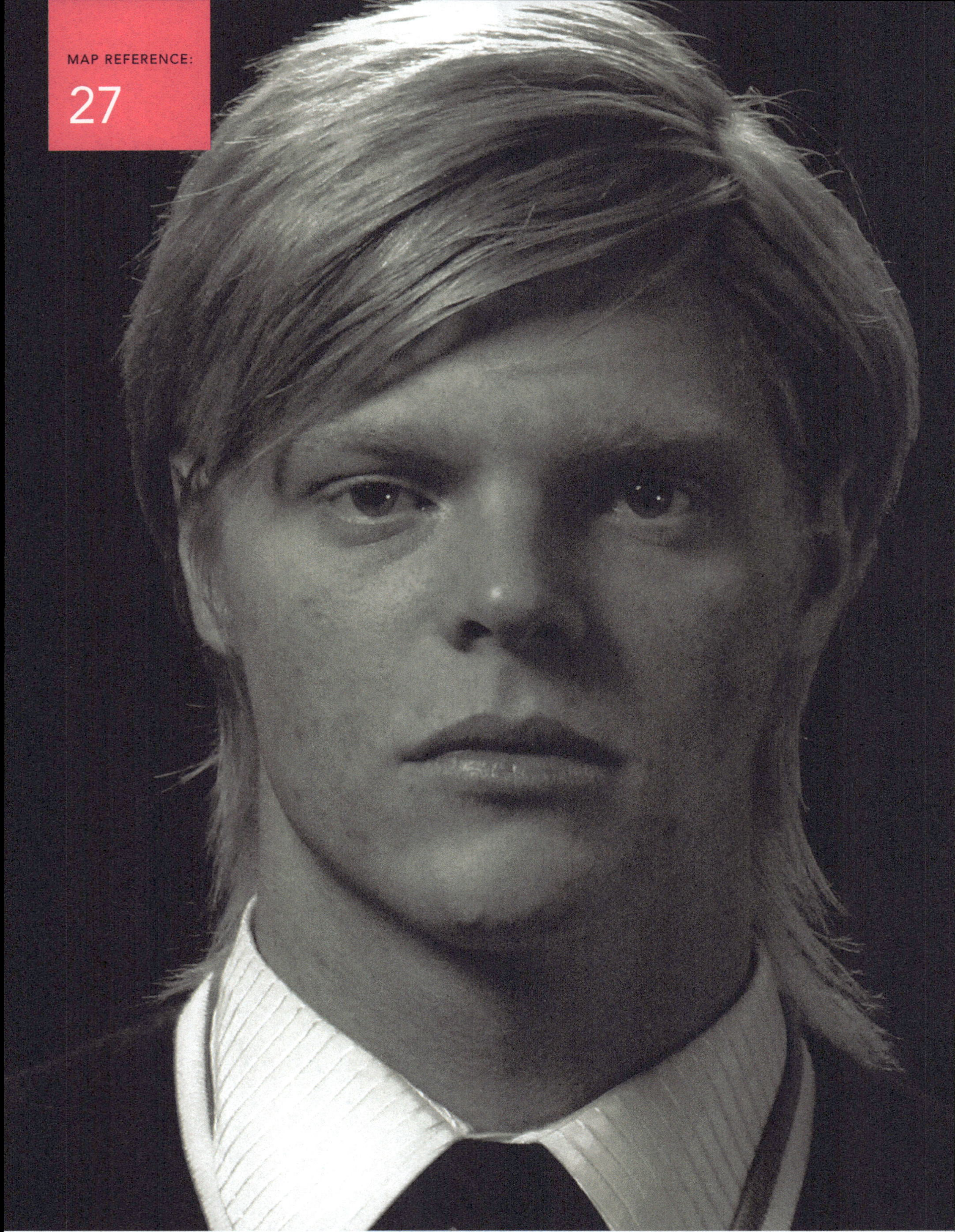

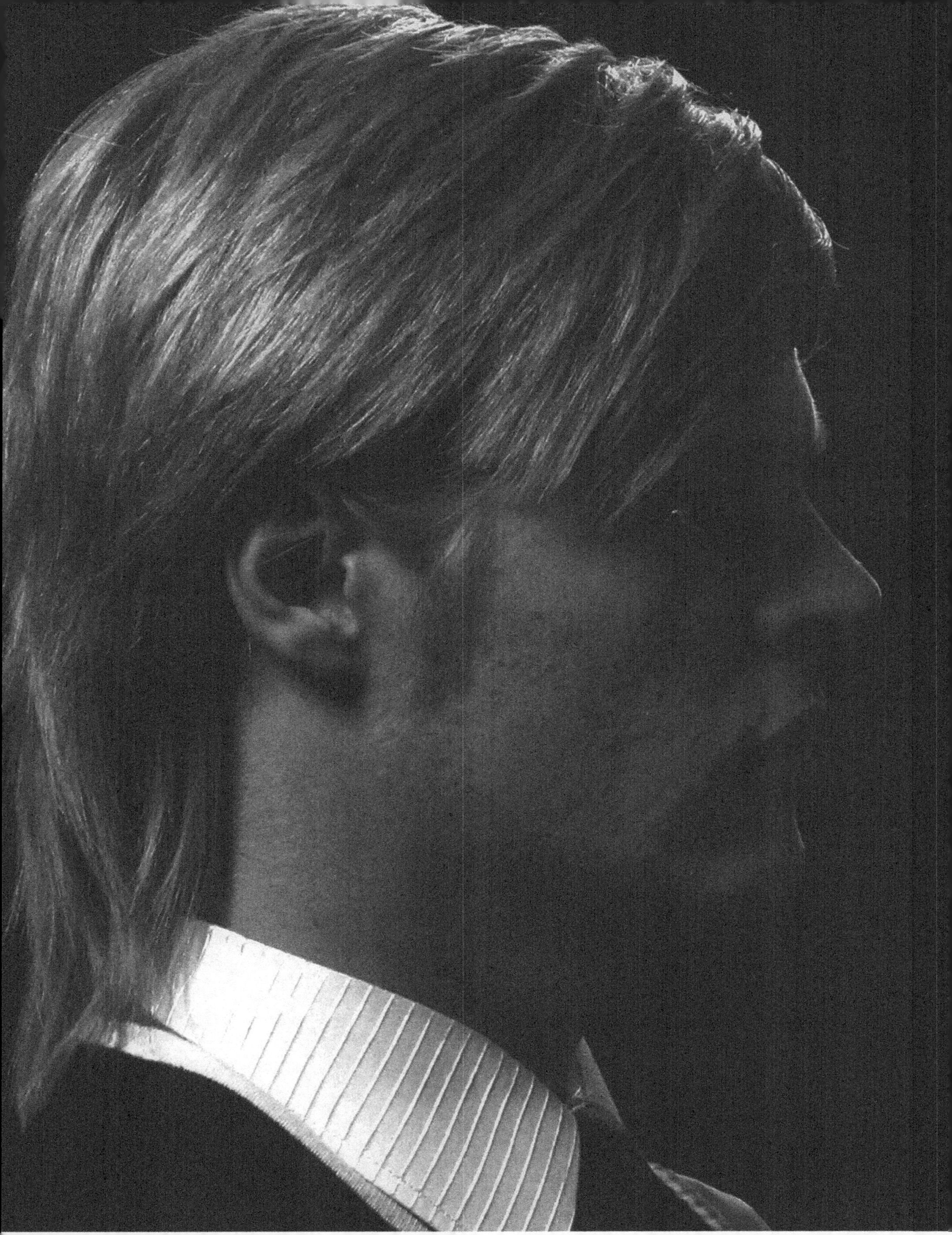

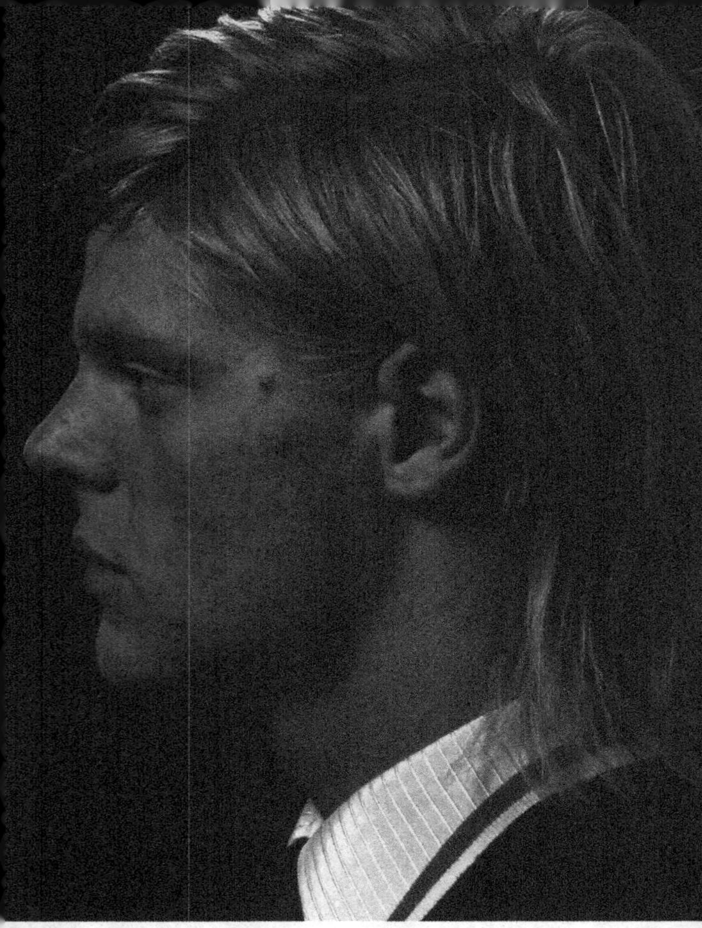

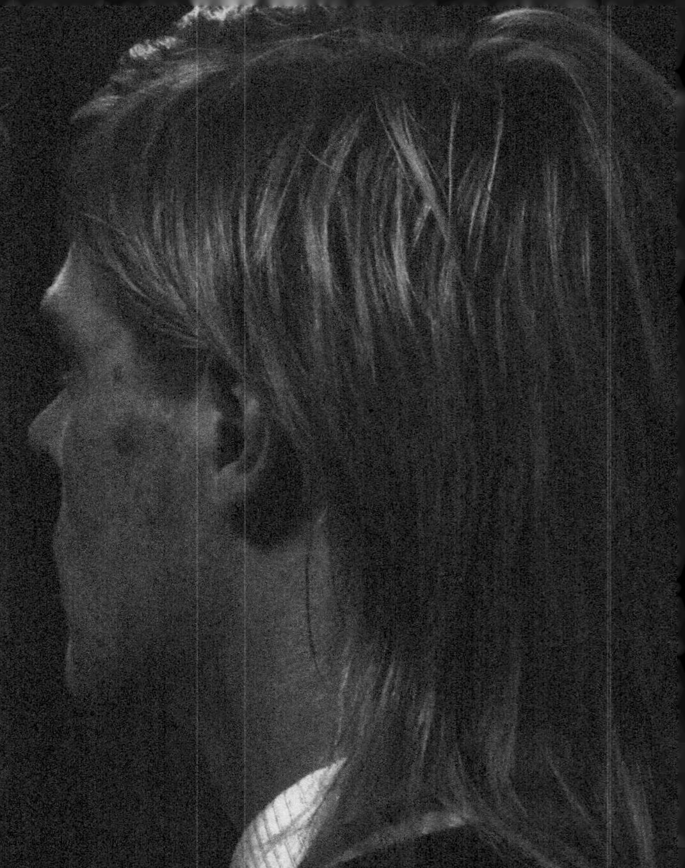

**Ethnicities claimed:**

Latvia.

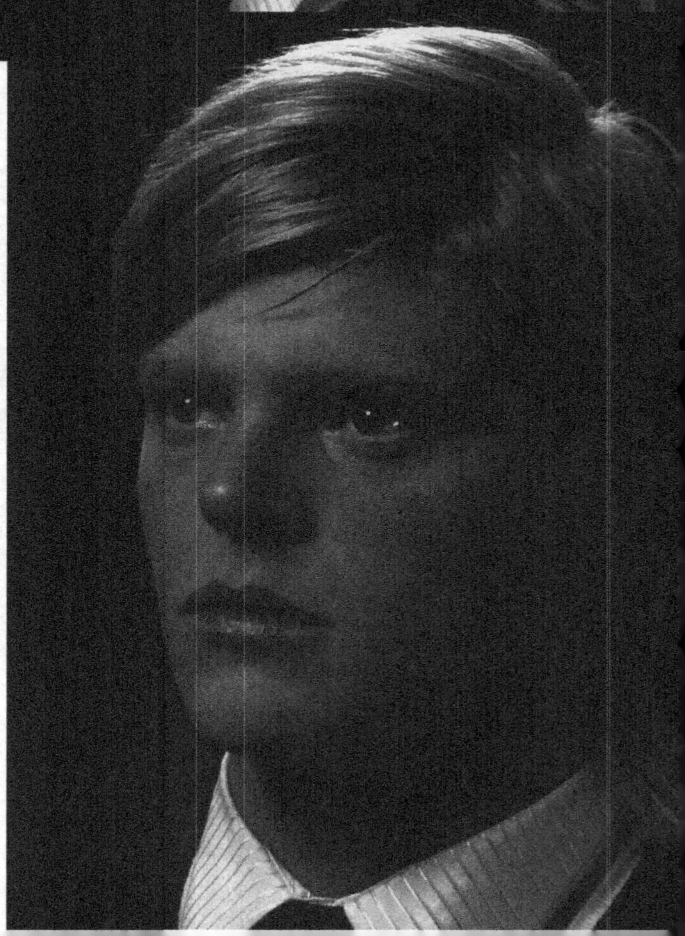

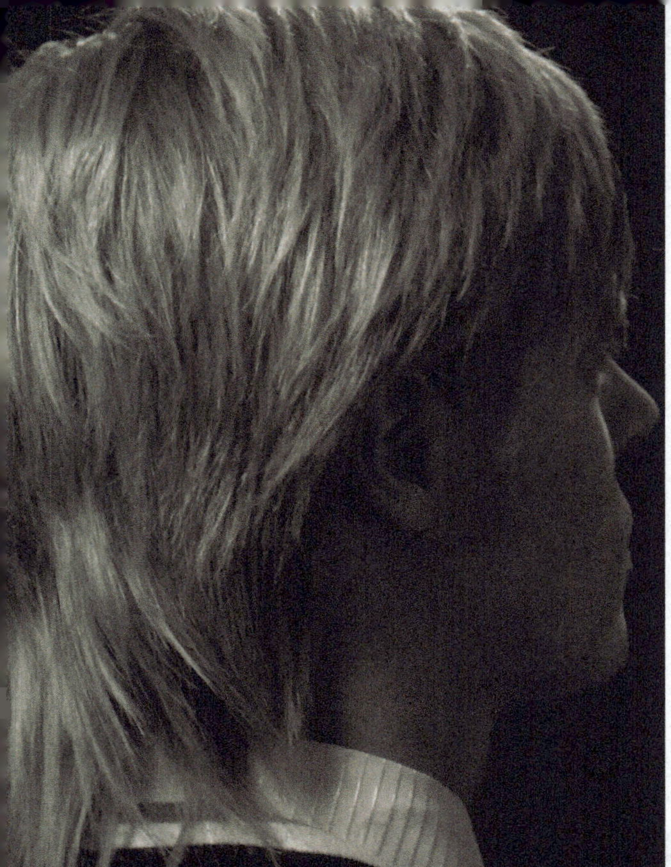

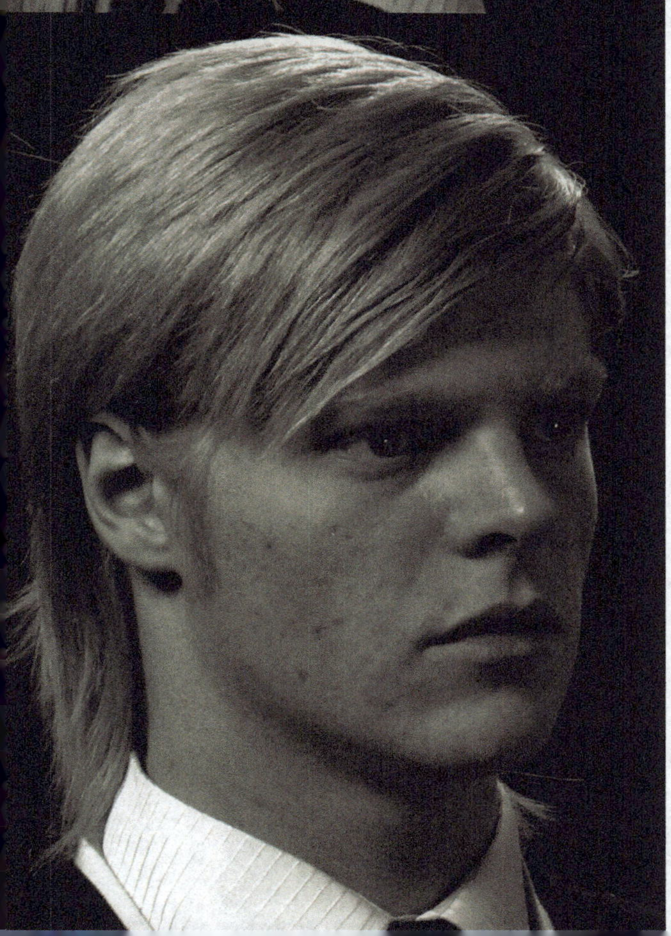

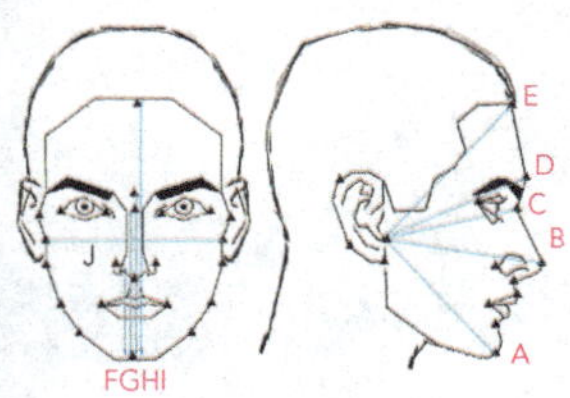


**Head measurements (in):**

A: 6 1/8
B: 5 3/4
C: 5 1/8
D: 5 3/4
E: 6 3/8
F: 3 7/8
G: 4 1/4
H: 5 1/8
I: 7 3/4
J: 6 1/8

MAP REFERENCE:

29

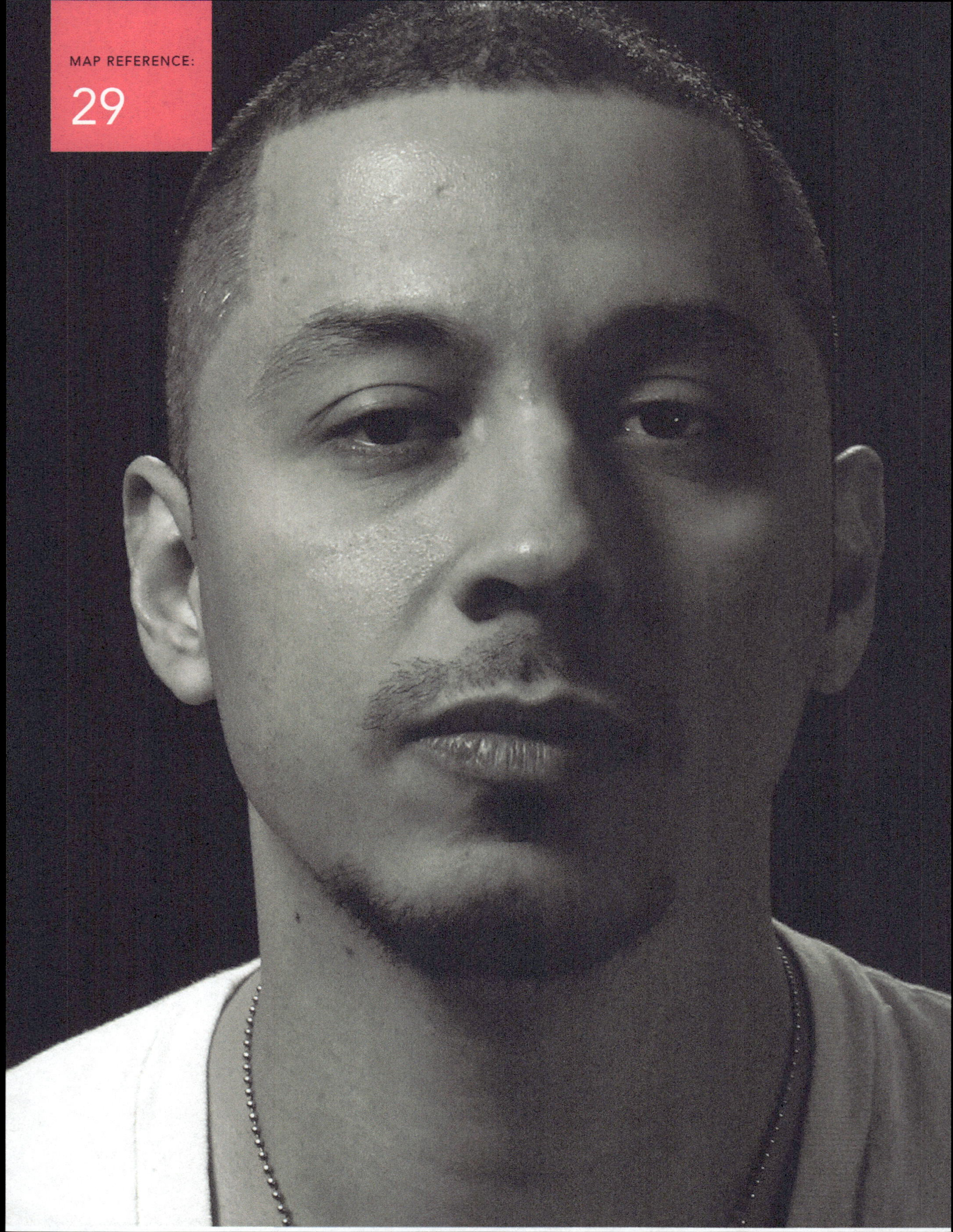

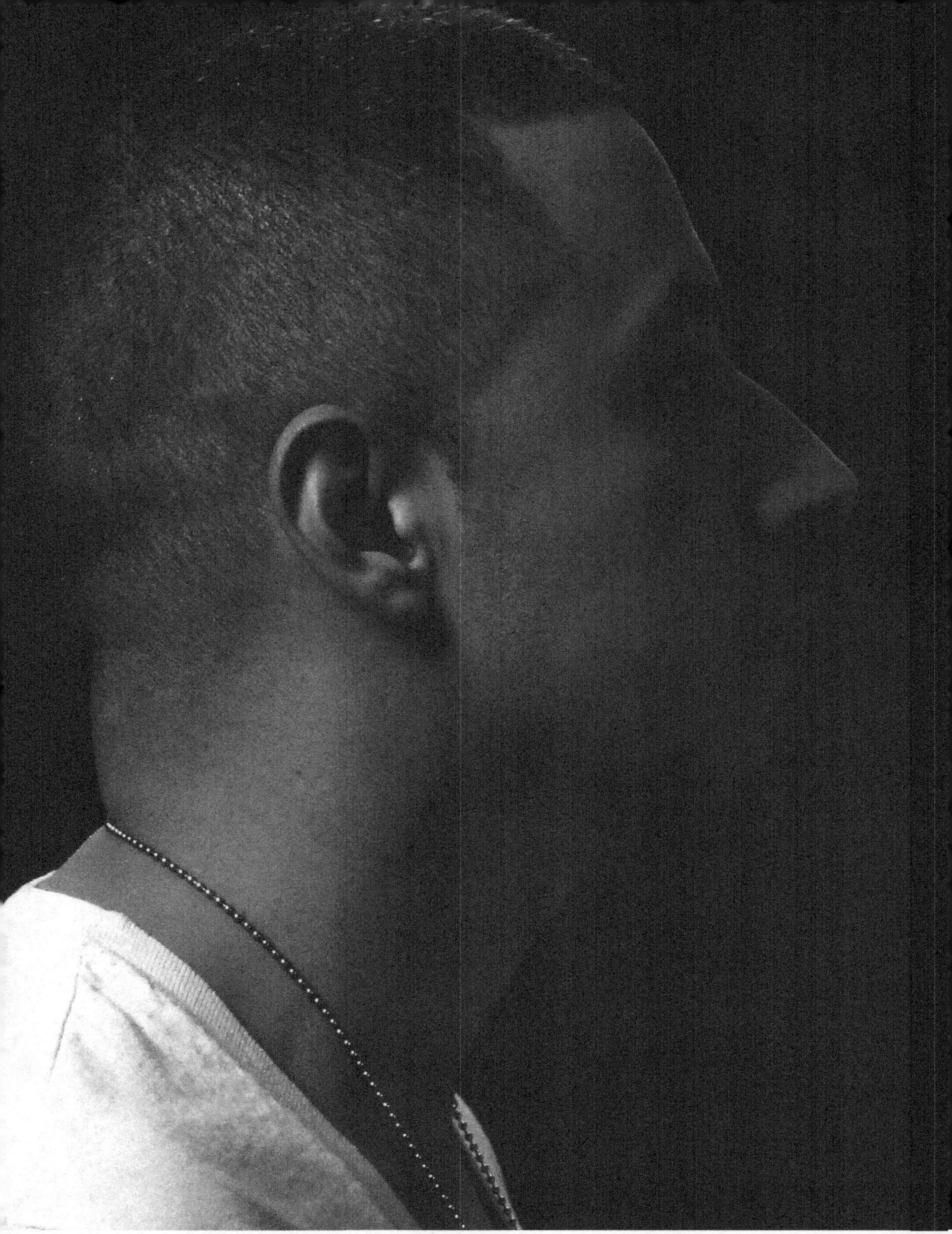

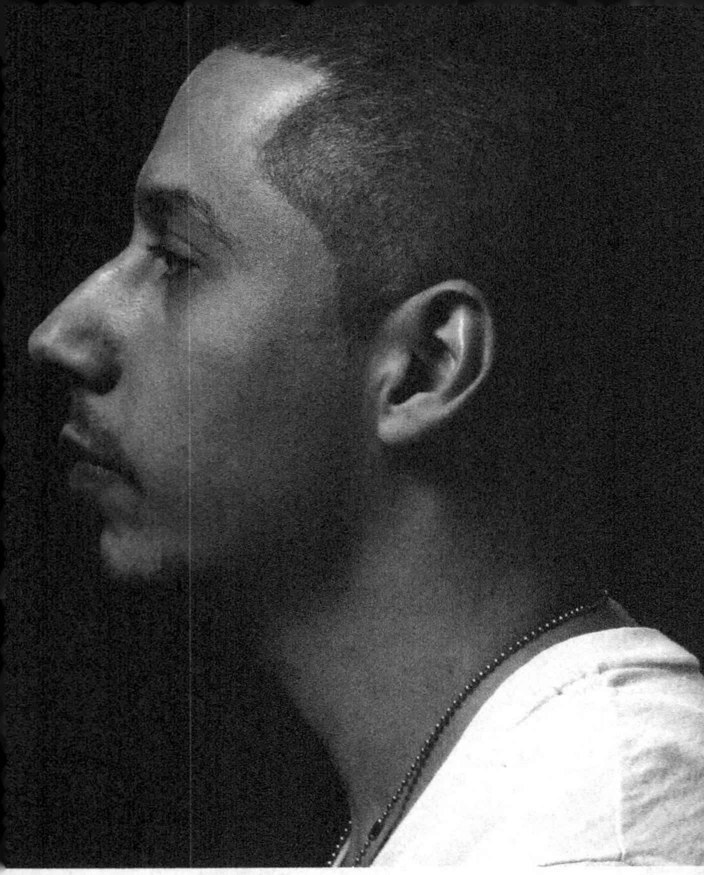

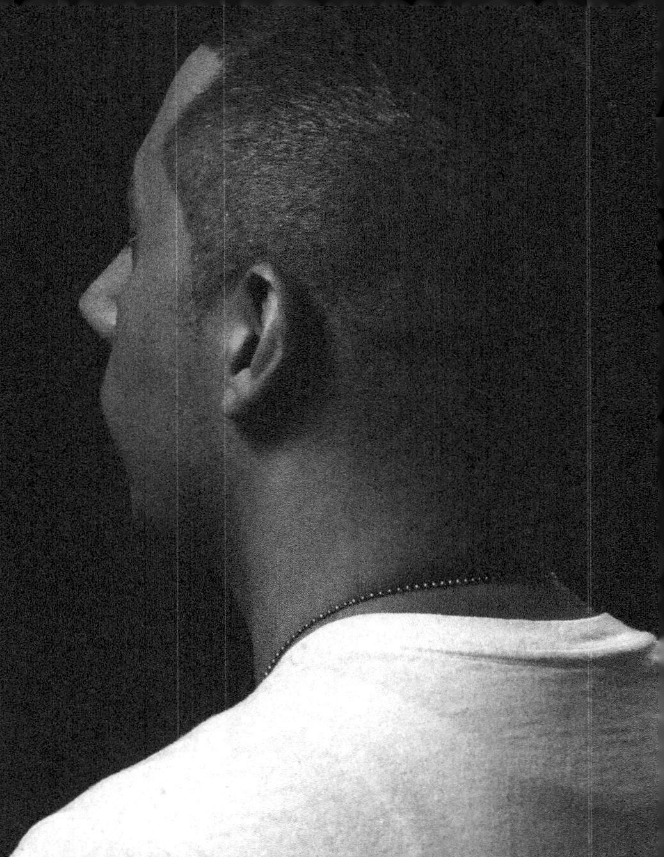

**Ethnicities claimed:**

Native American, Mexico.

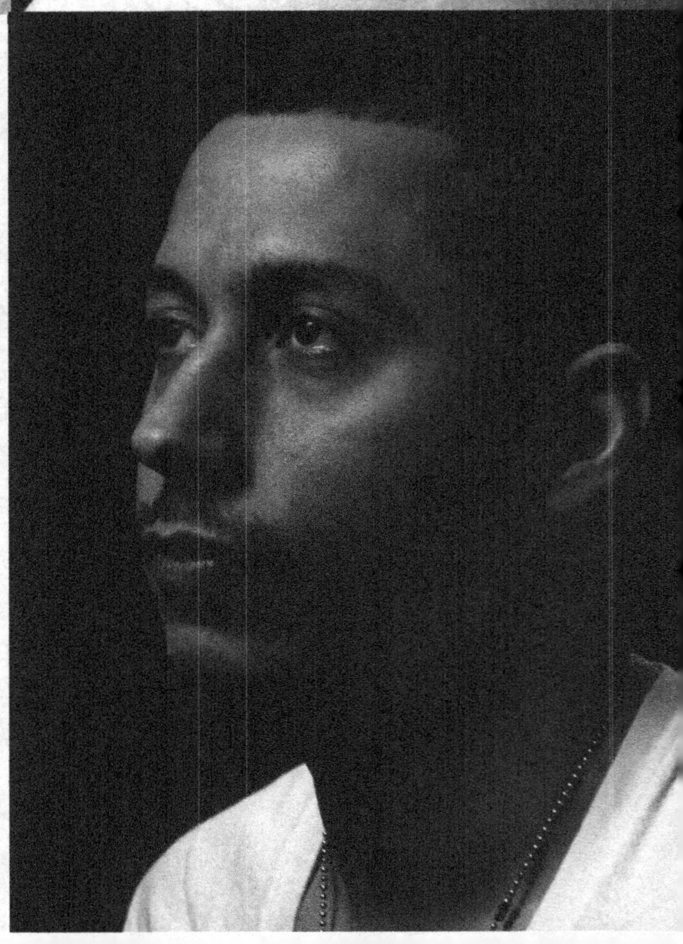

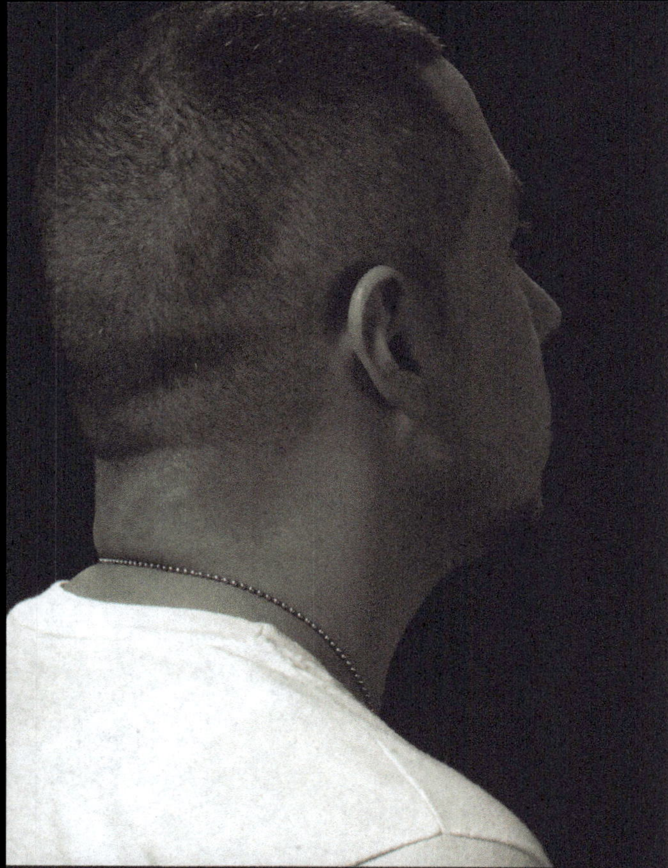

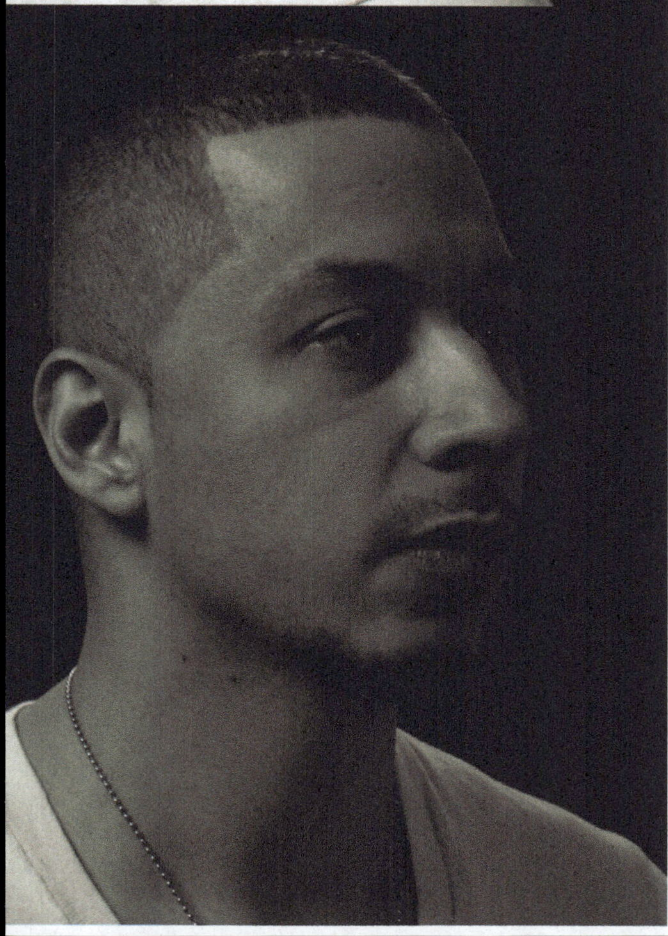

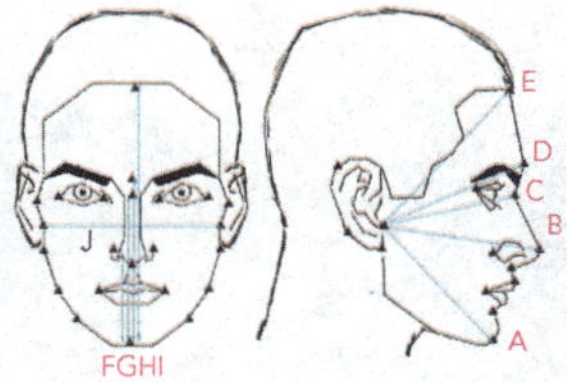


**Head measurements (in):**

A: 6 1/8
B: 5 3/4
C: 5 1/2
D: 5 5/8
E: 6 5/8
F: 3 7/8
G: 4 5/8
H: 5 5/8
I: 7 7/8
J: 6 1/8

MAP REFERENCE:

30

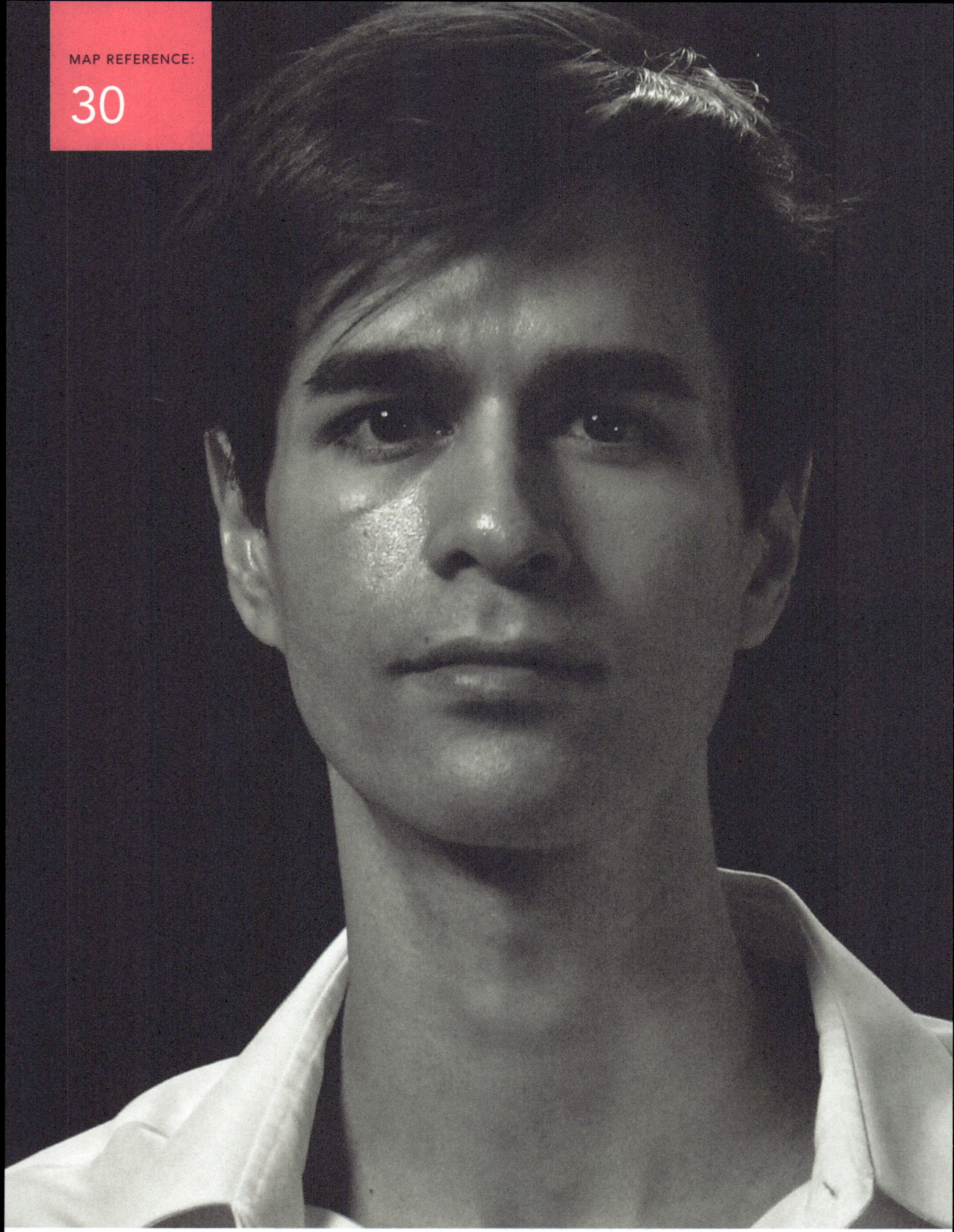

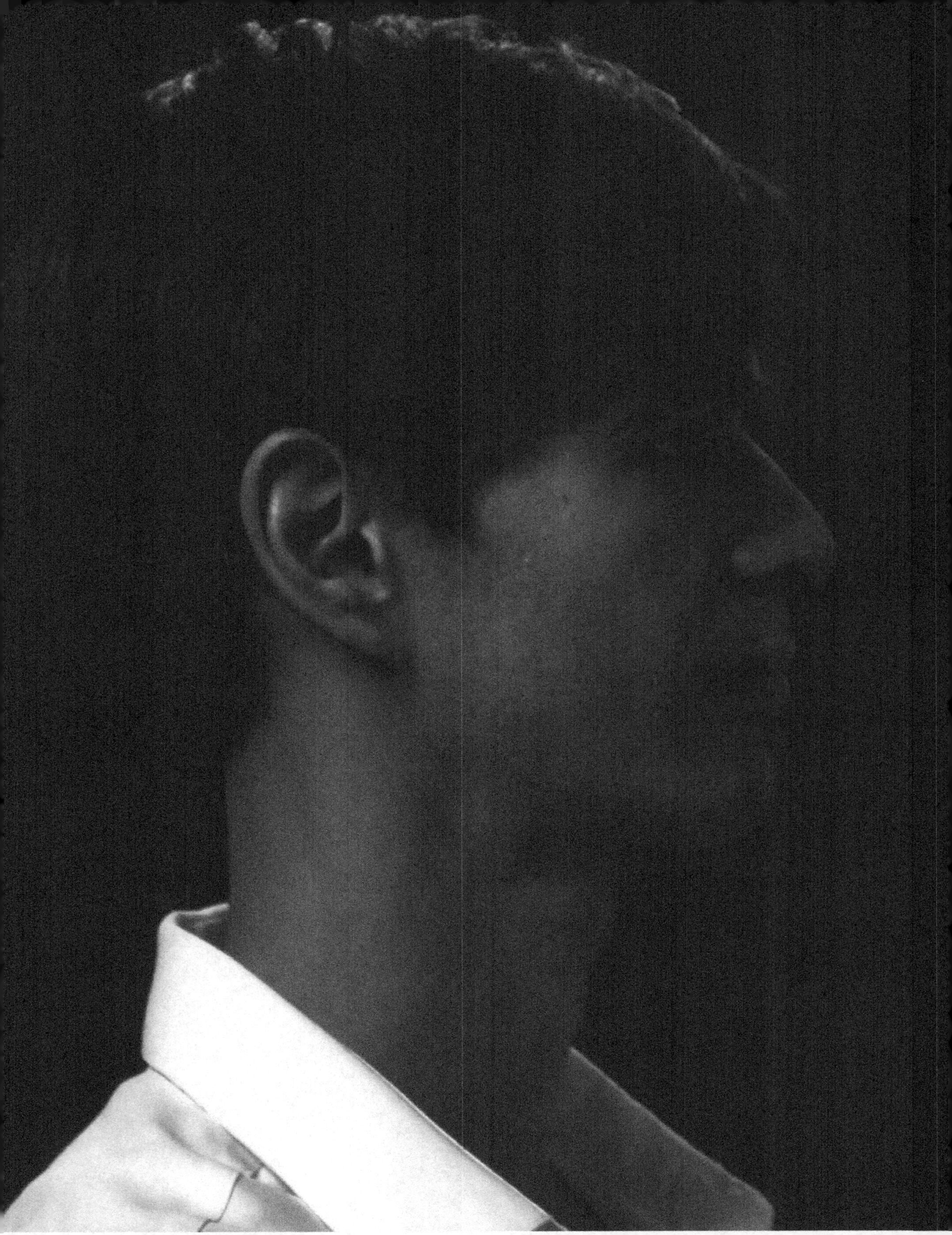

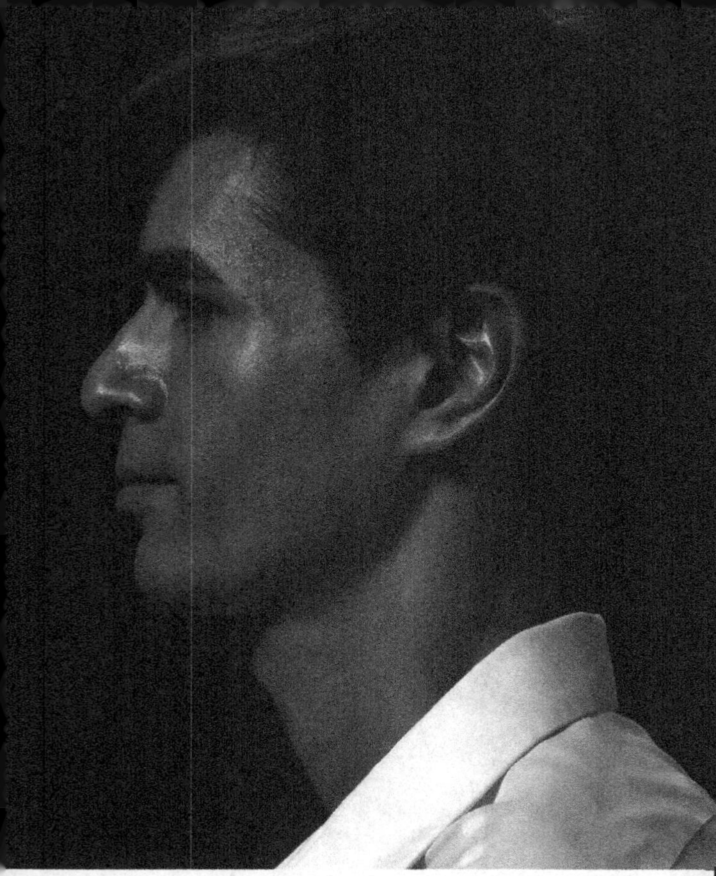
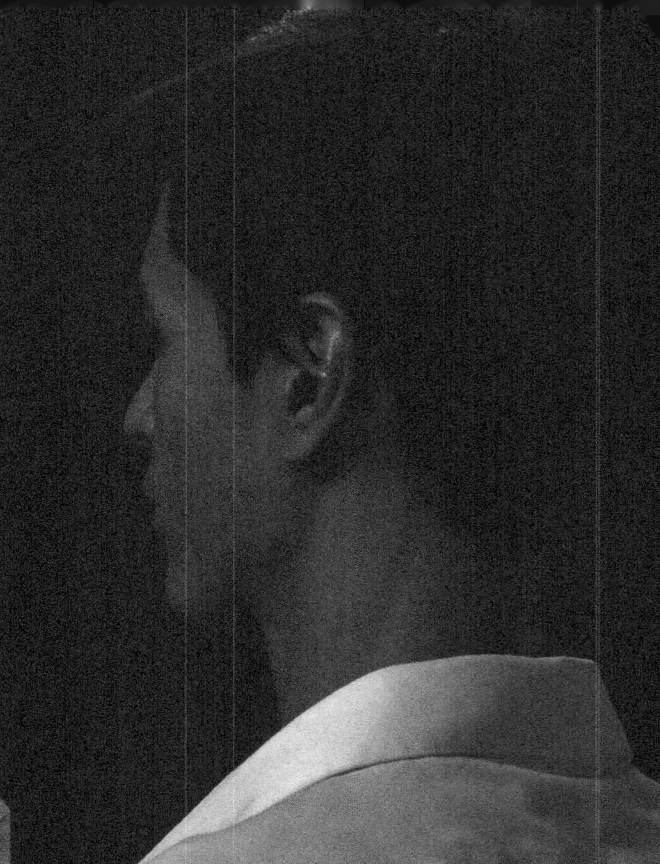

**Ethnicities claimed:**

Malaysia, Ireland.

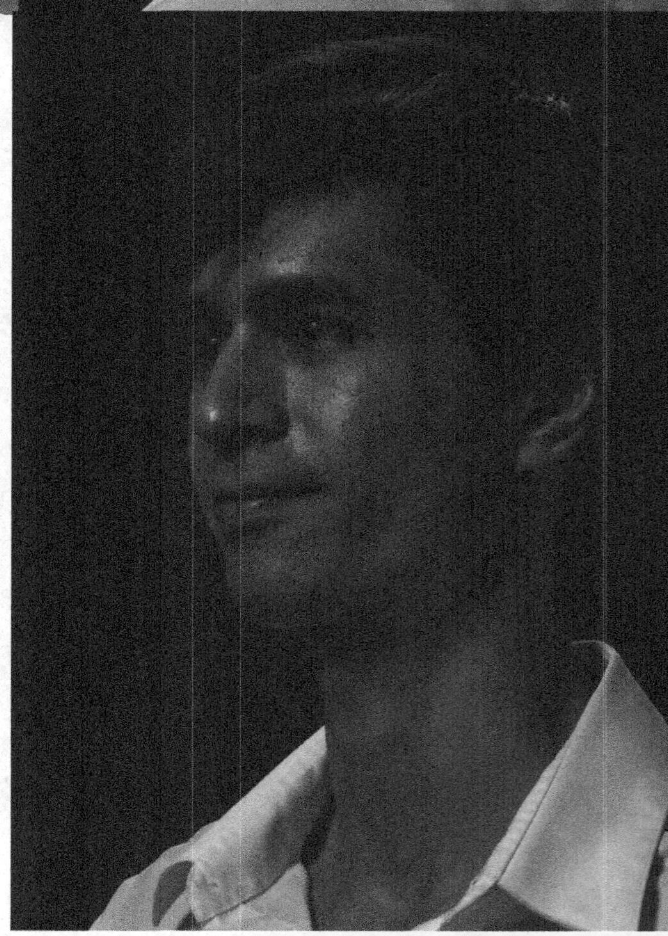

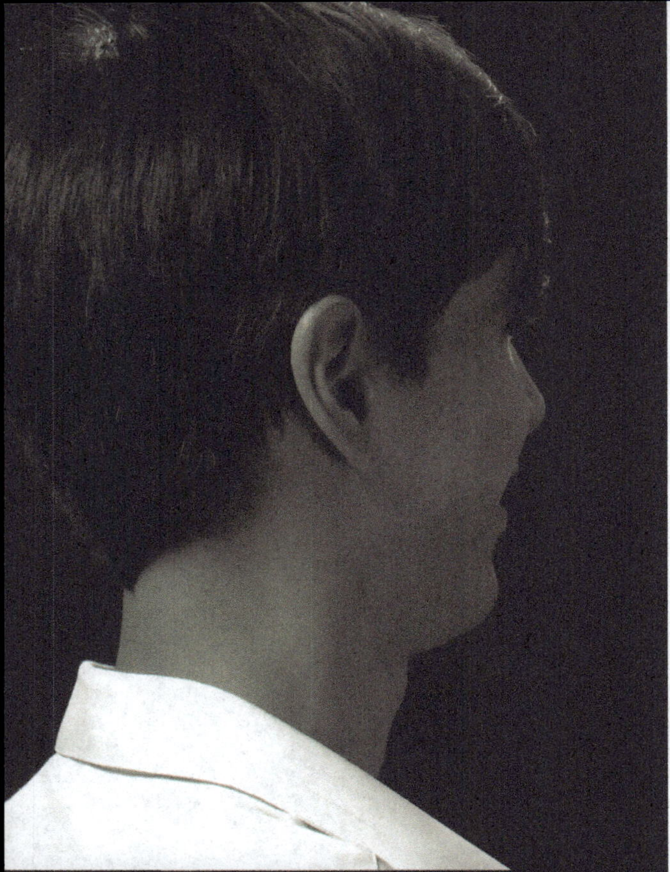

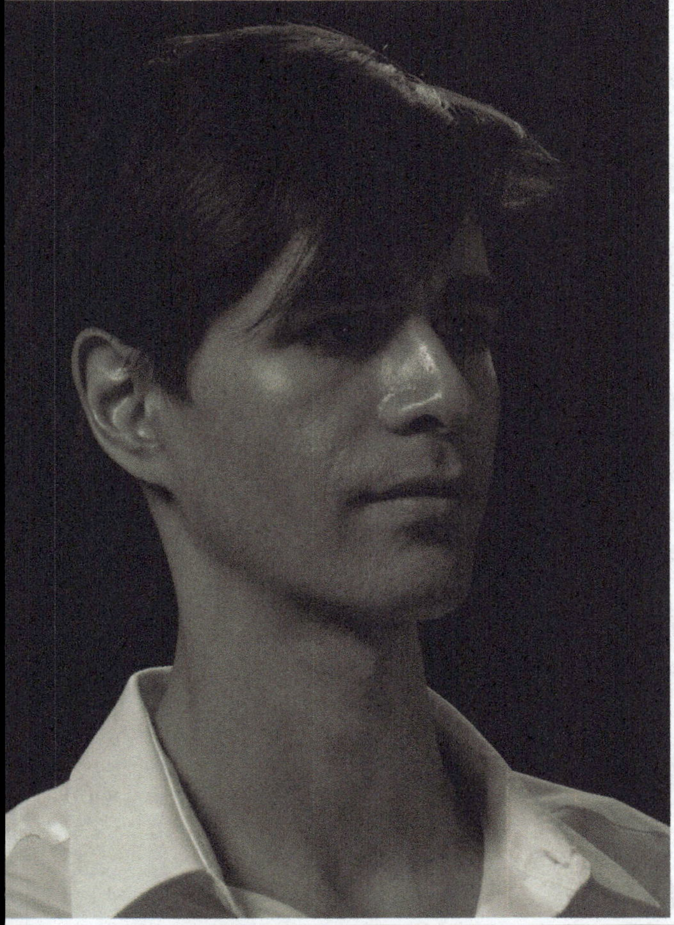

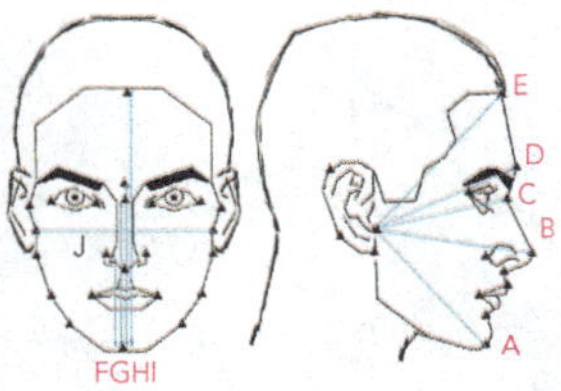


**Head measurements (in):**

A: 5 1/2
B: 6
C: 5 1/4
D: 5 1/2
E: 6 1/2
F: 3 3/8
G: 4 1/2
H: 5 1/4
I: 7 3/4
J: 5 3/4

MAP REFERENCE:
38

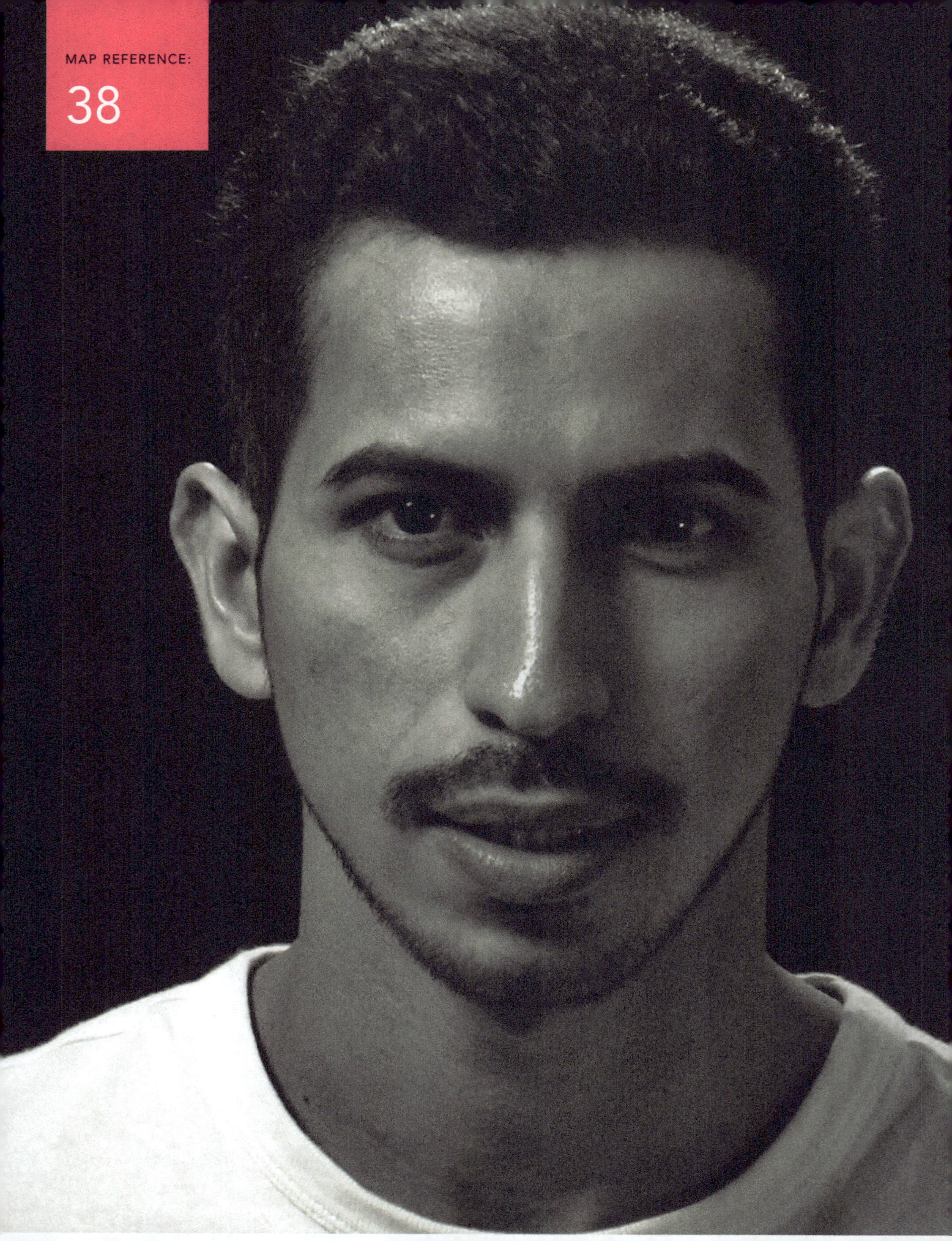

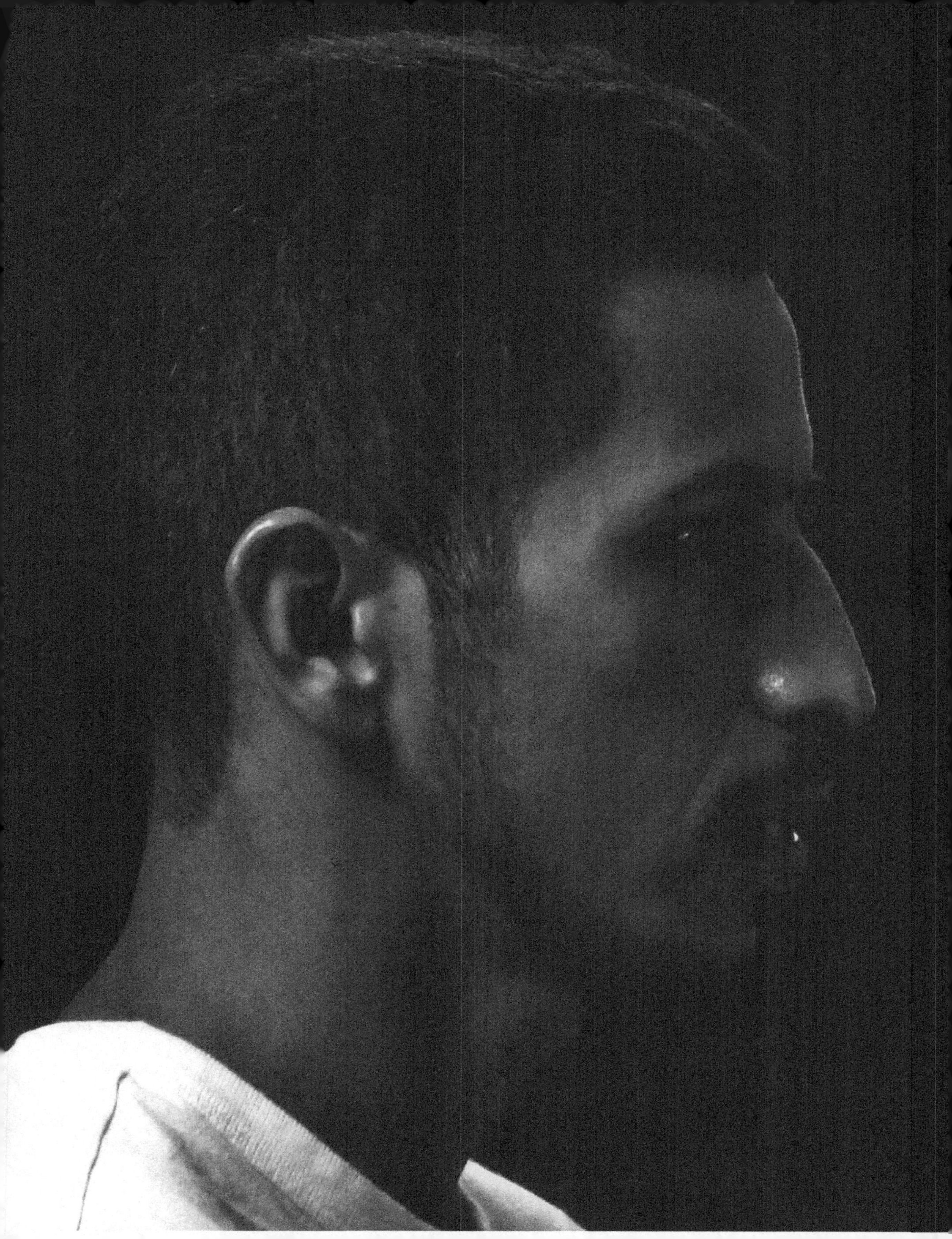

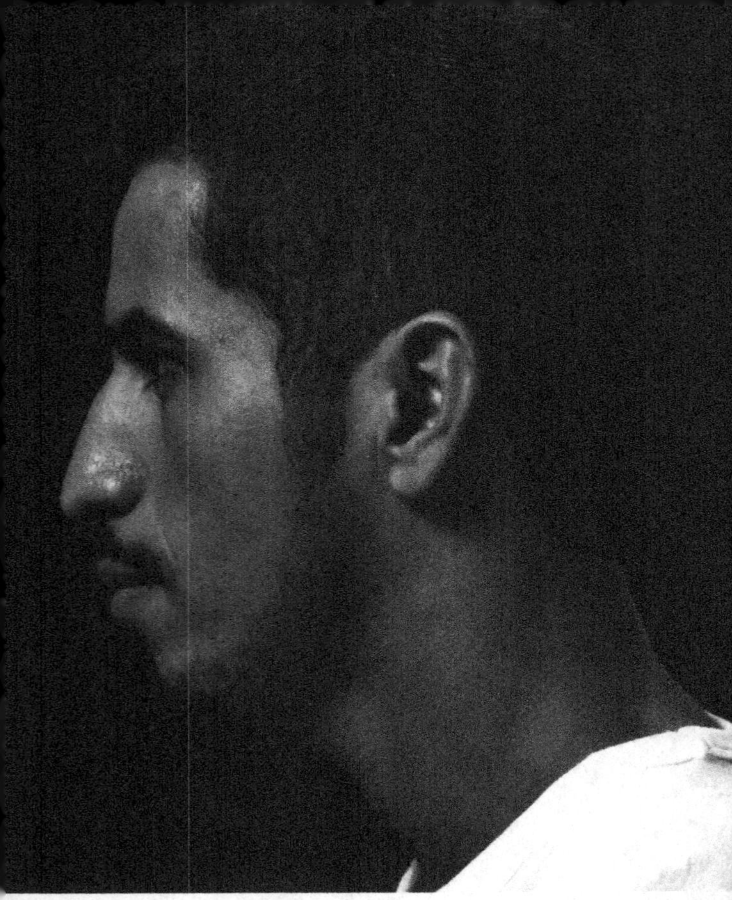

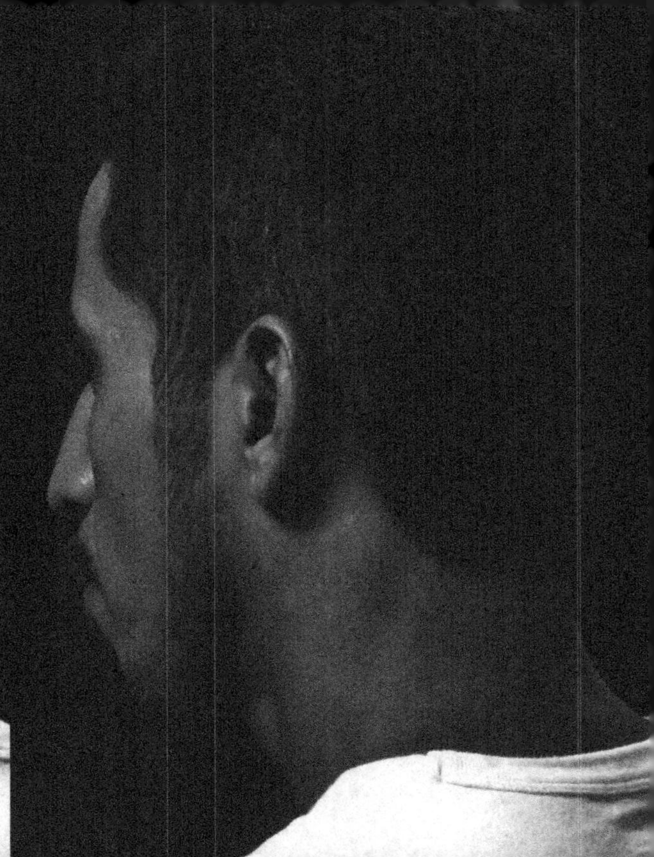

**Ethnicities claimed:**

El Salvador, Spain, India.

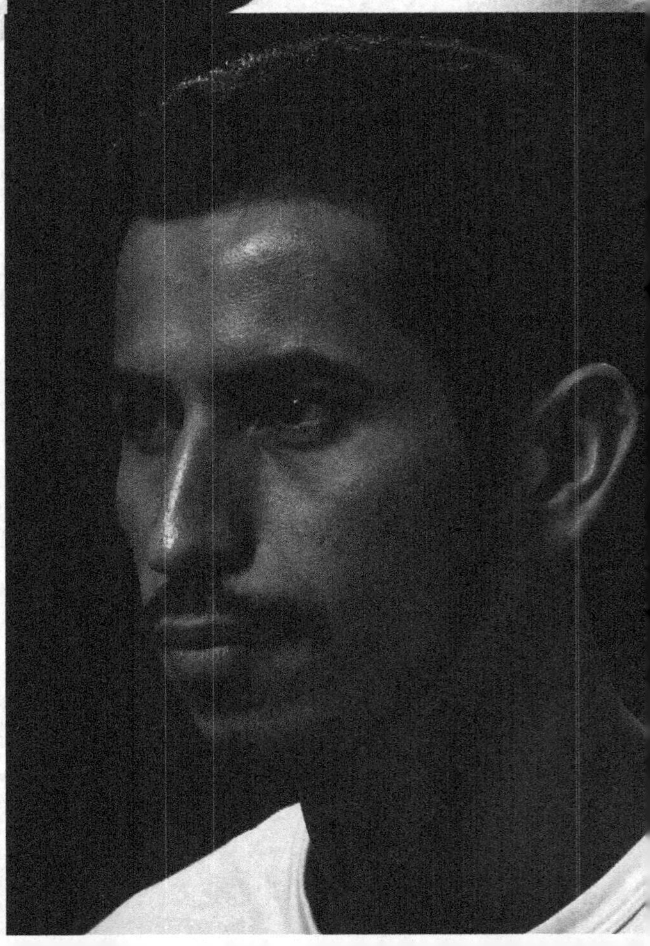

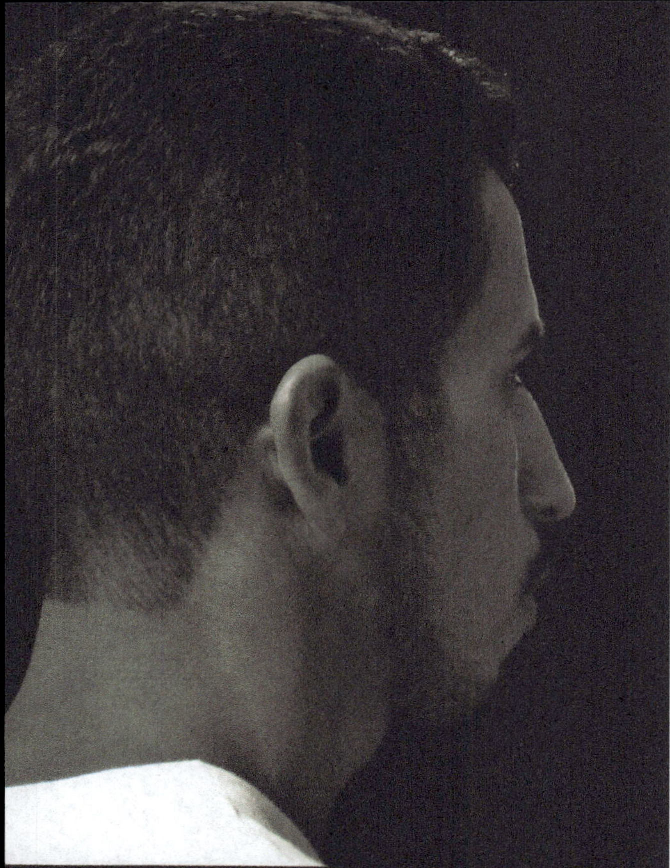

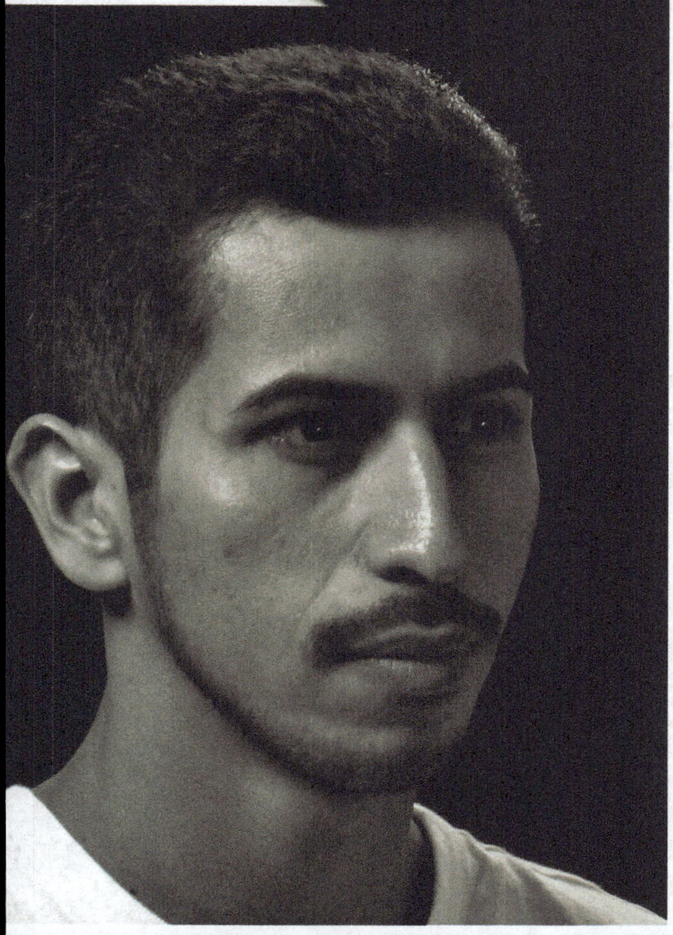

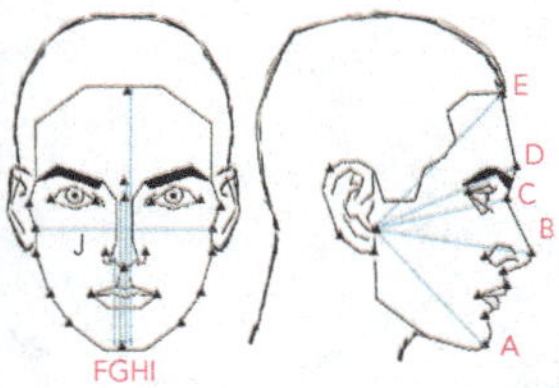


**Head measurements (in):**

A: 5 1/2
B: 5 1/4
C: 5 1/8
D: 5 1/8
E: 6 1/2
F: 3 3/8
G: 4 3/4
H: 5 5/8
I: 7 1/4
J: 5 3/8

MAP REFERENCE:

42

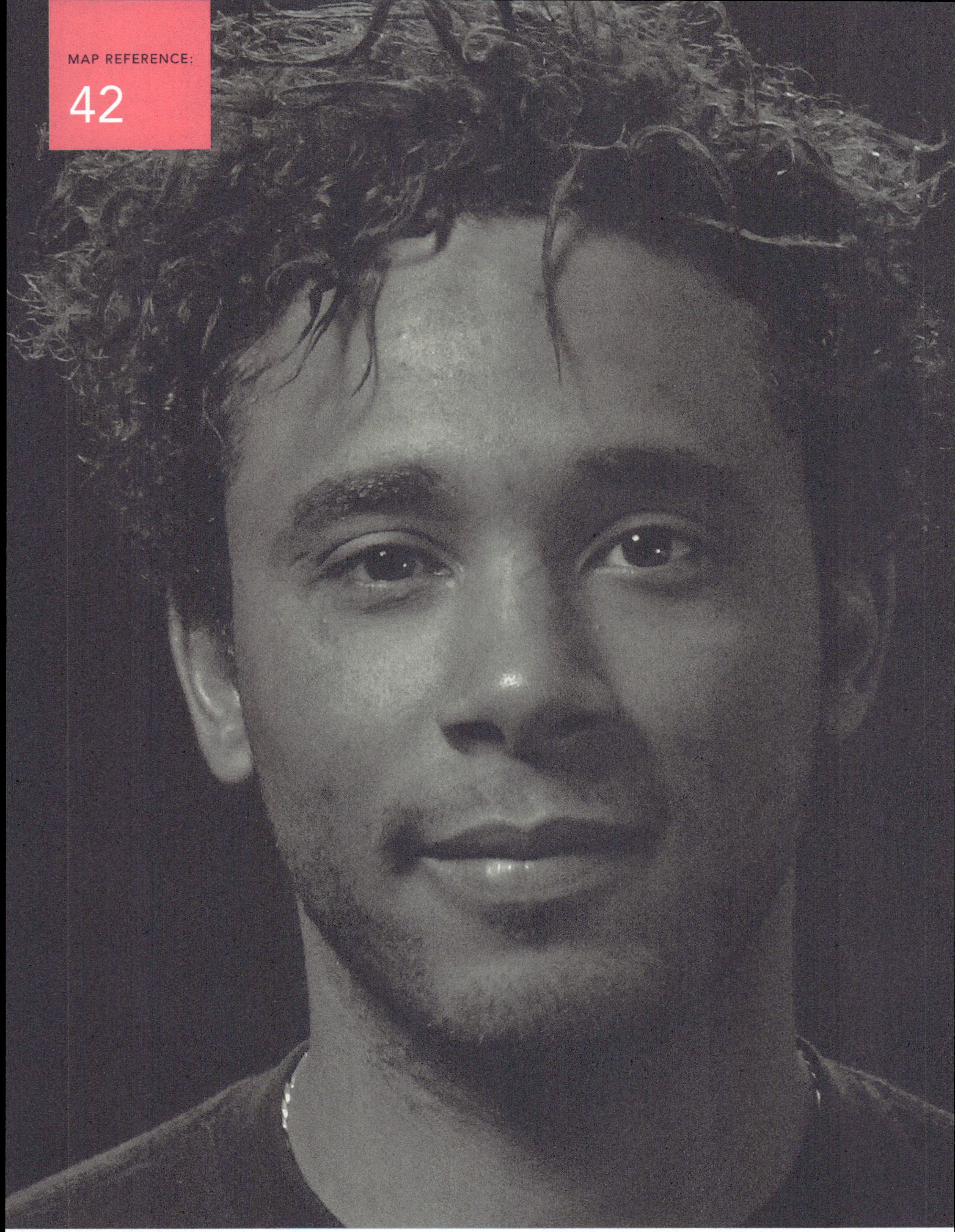

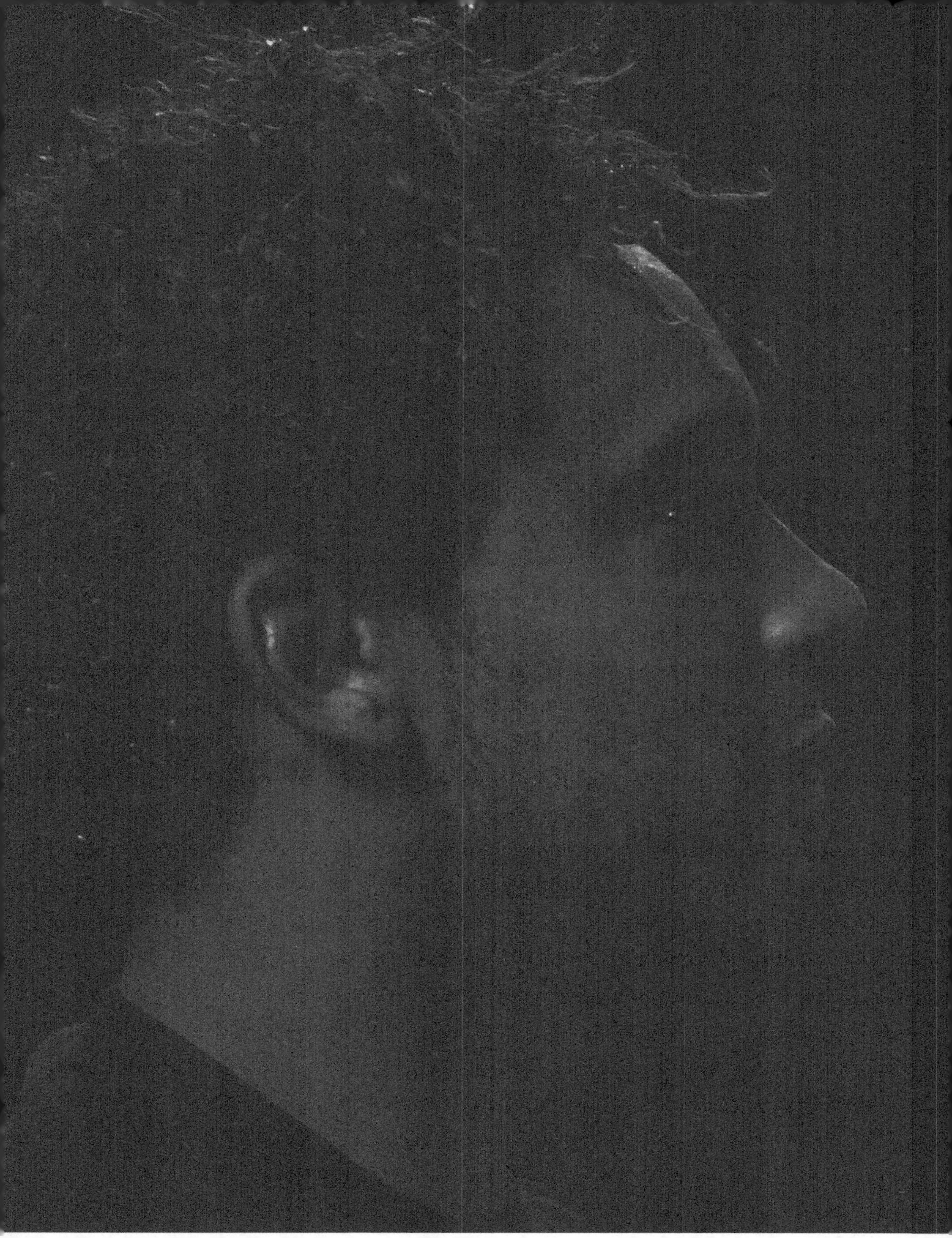

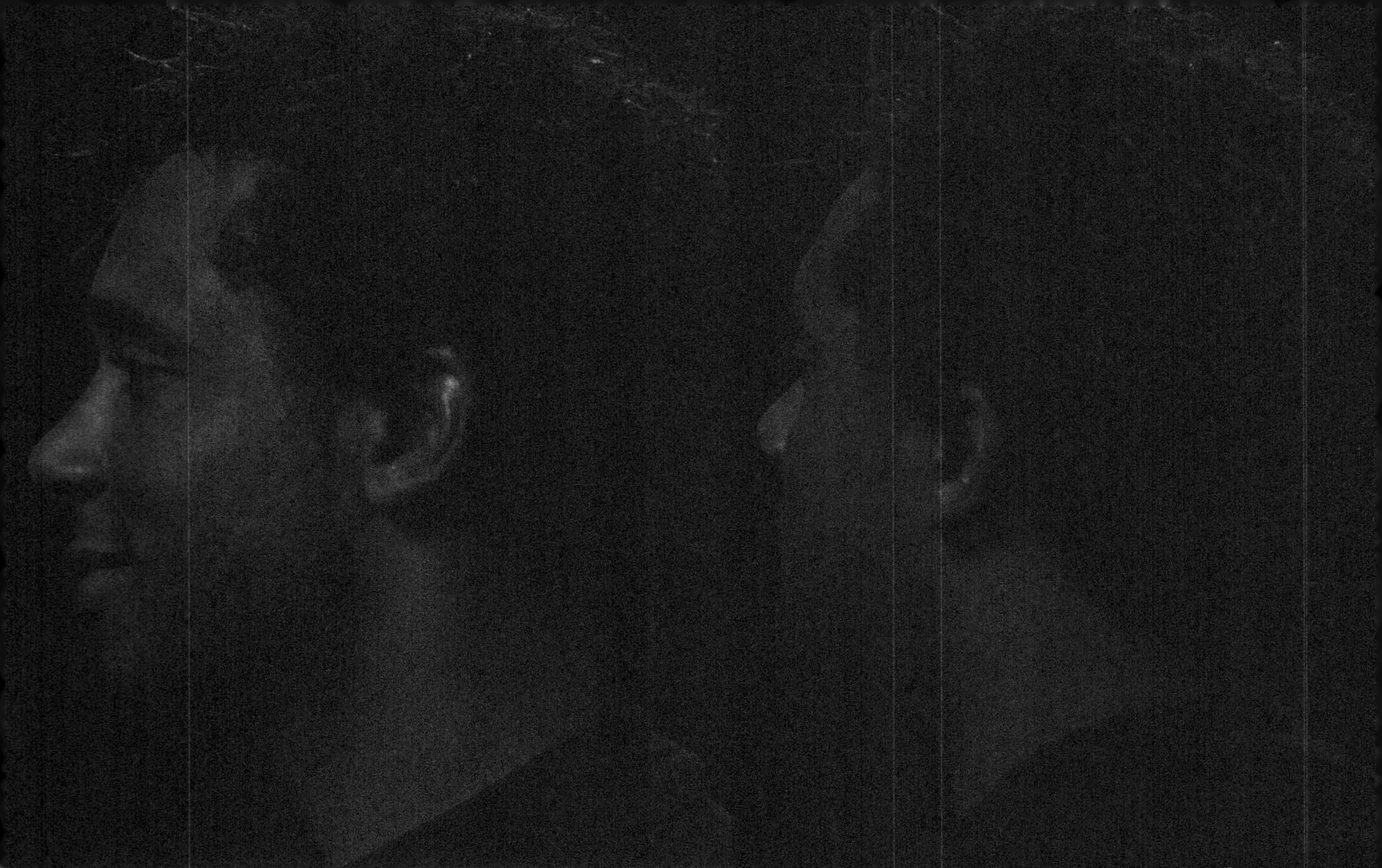

**Ethnicities claimed:**

Egypt.

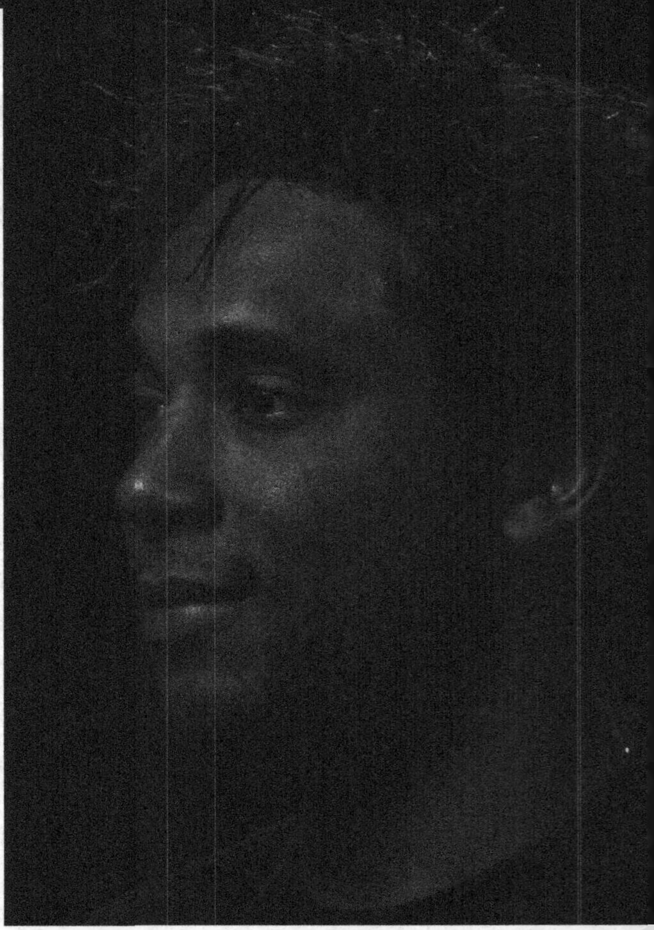

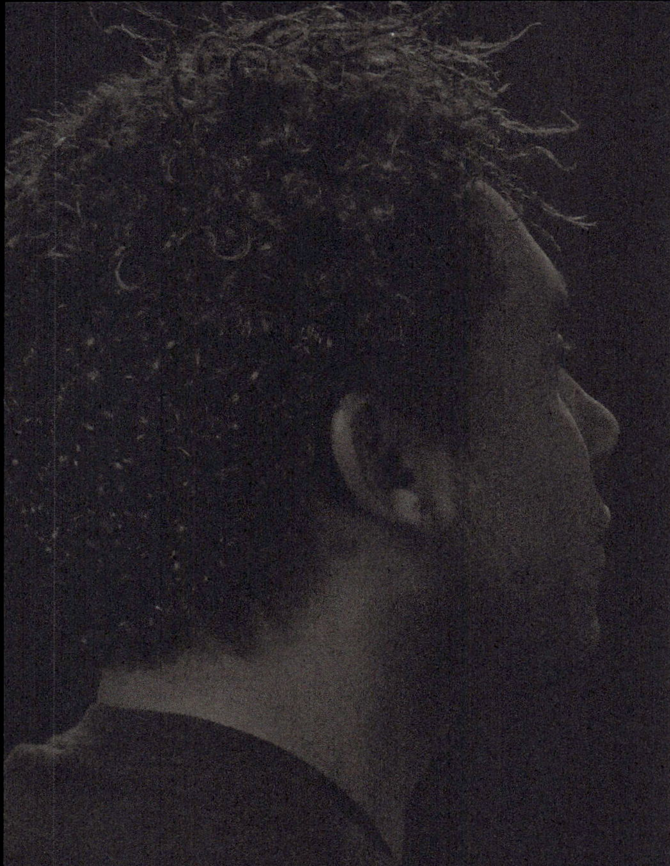

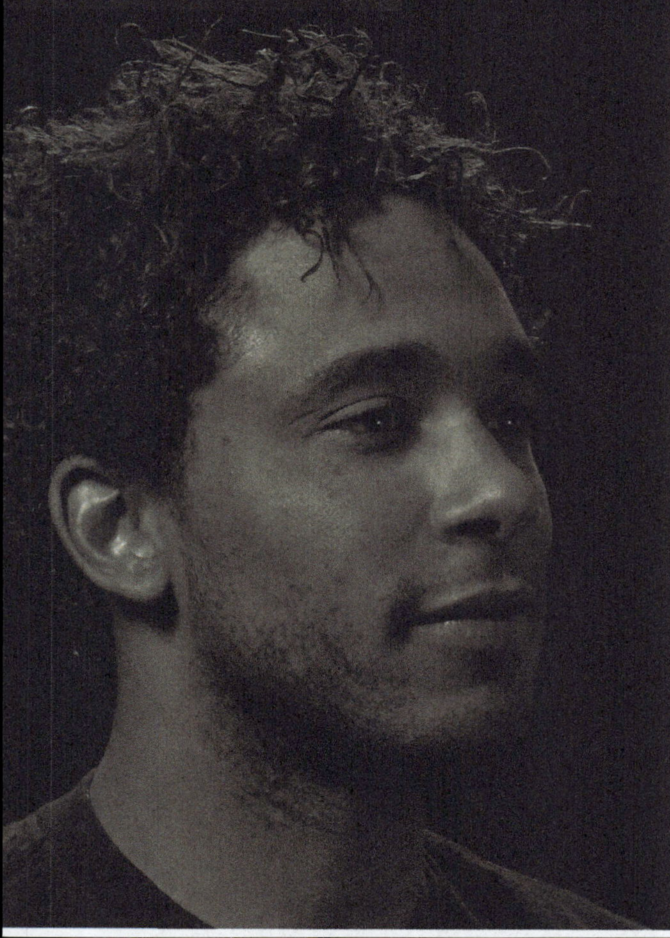

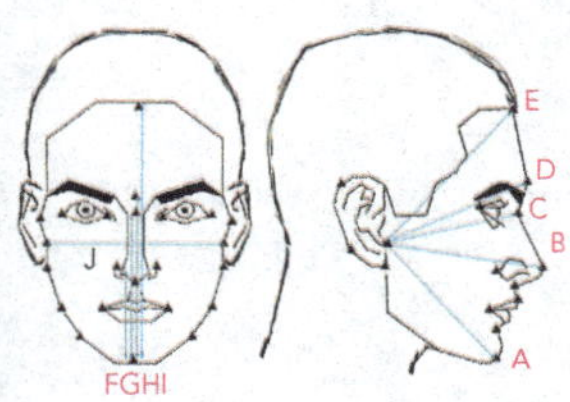


**Head measurements (in):**

A: 5 7/8
B: 5 5/8
C: 4 7/8
D: 5 5/8
E: 6 1/4
F: 4 3/8
G: 4 5/8
H: 5 5/8
I: 7 7/8
J: 5 7/8

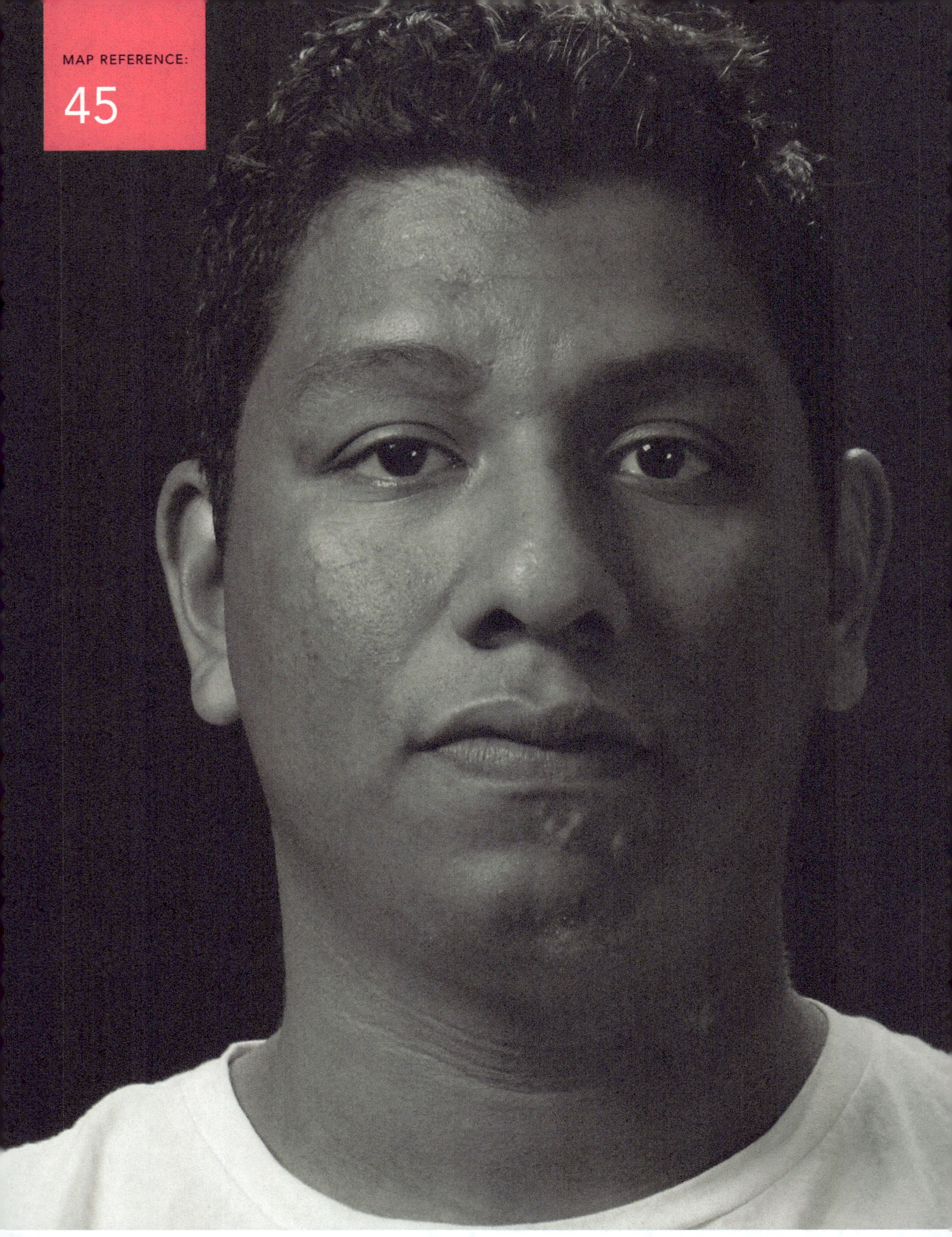
MAP REFERENCE:
45

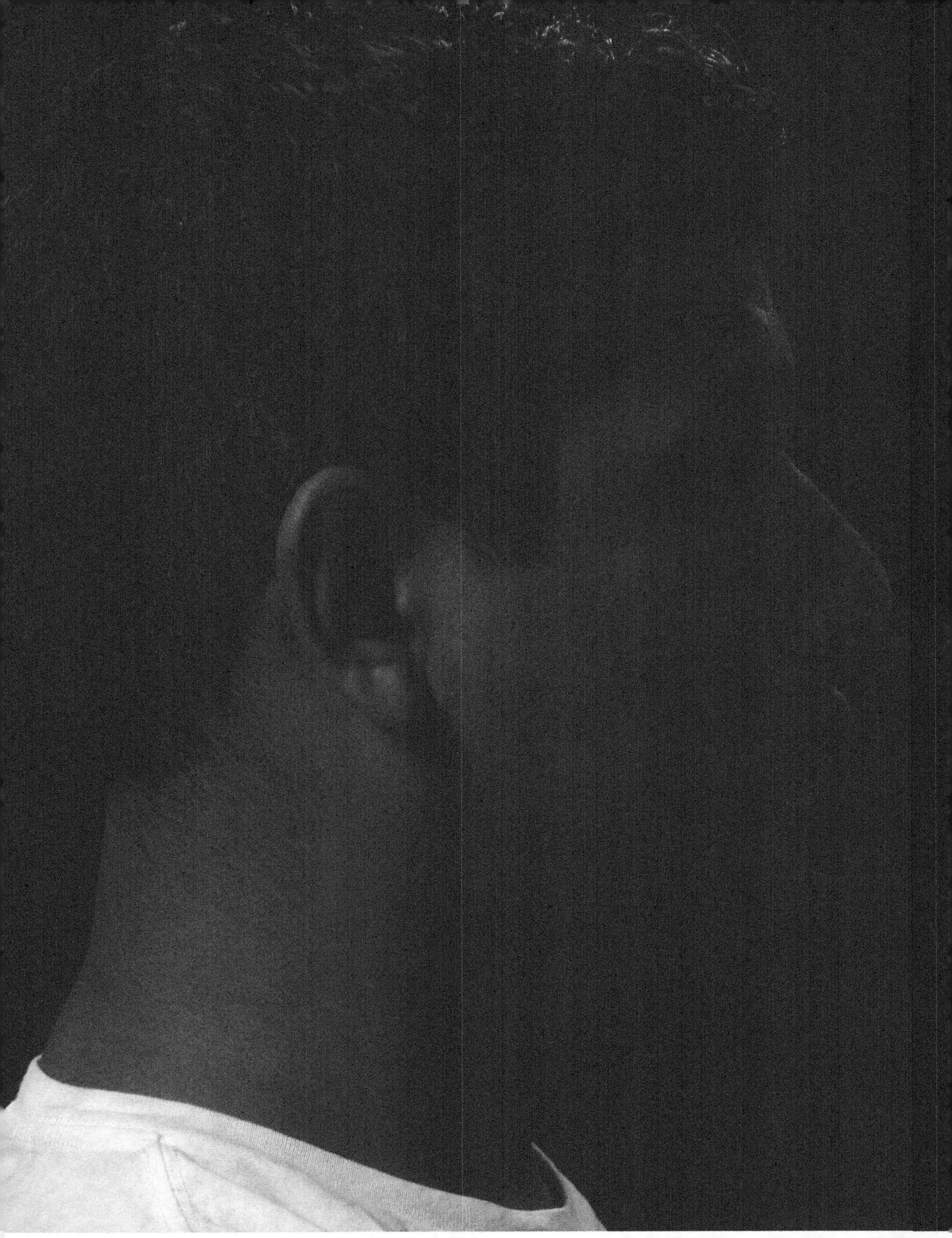

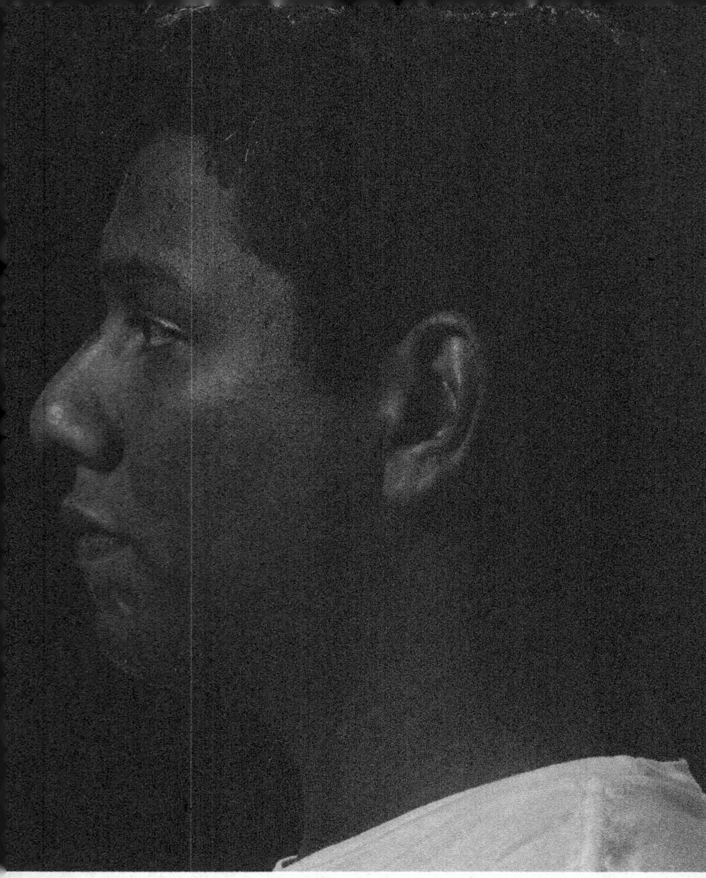

**Ethnicities claimed:**

Peru, Inca, Trinidad.

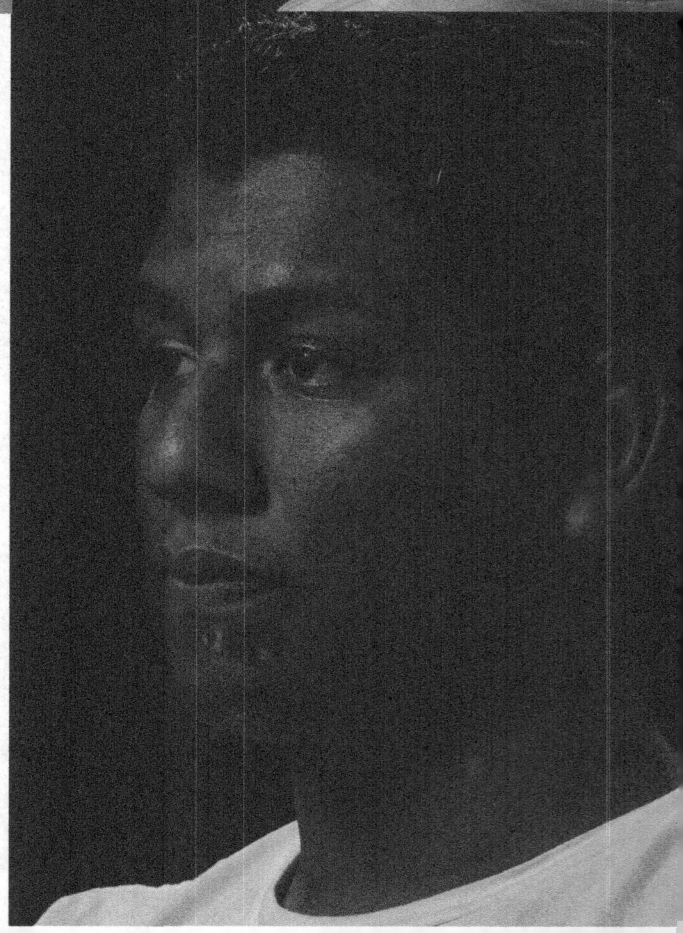

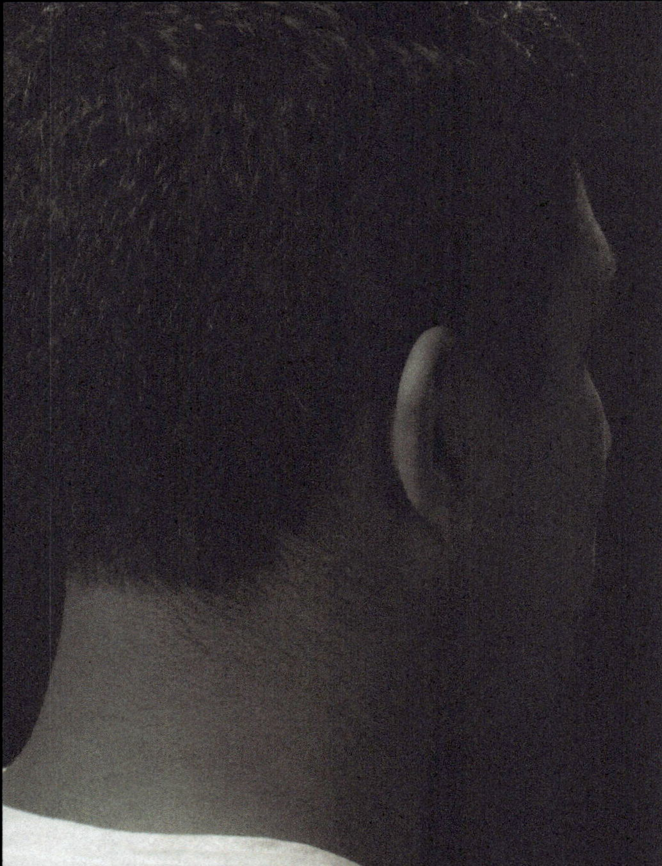

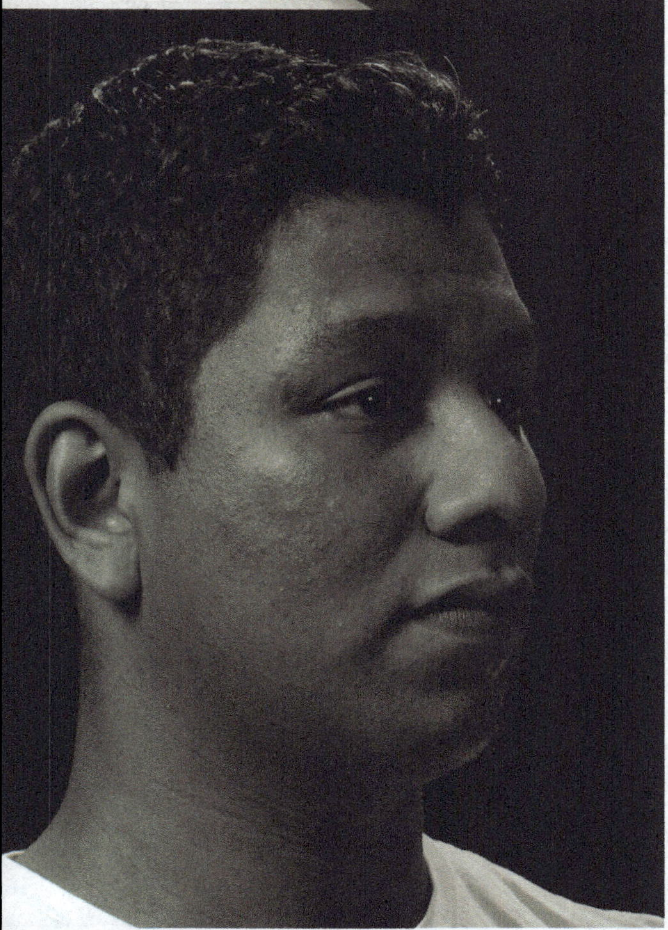

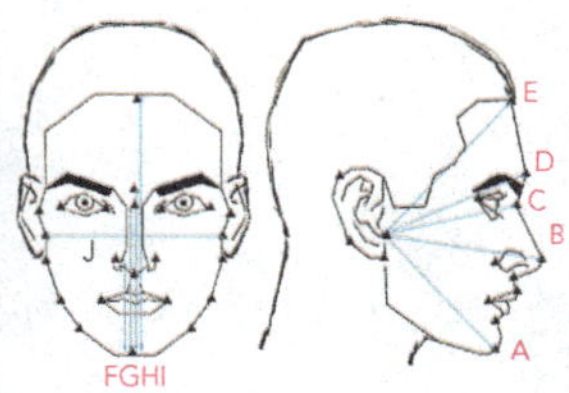


**Head measurements (in):**

A: 6 5/8
B: 6 3/8
C: 5 7/8
D: 5 5/8
E: 6 1/2
F: 4
G: 4 1/2
H: 5 5/8
I: 7 3/4
J: 6 5/8

MAP REFERENCE:

46

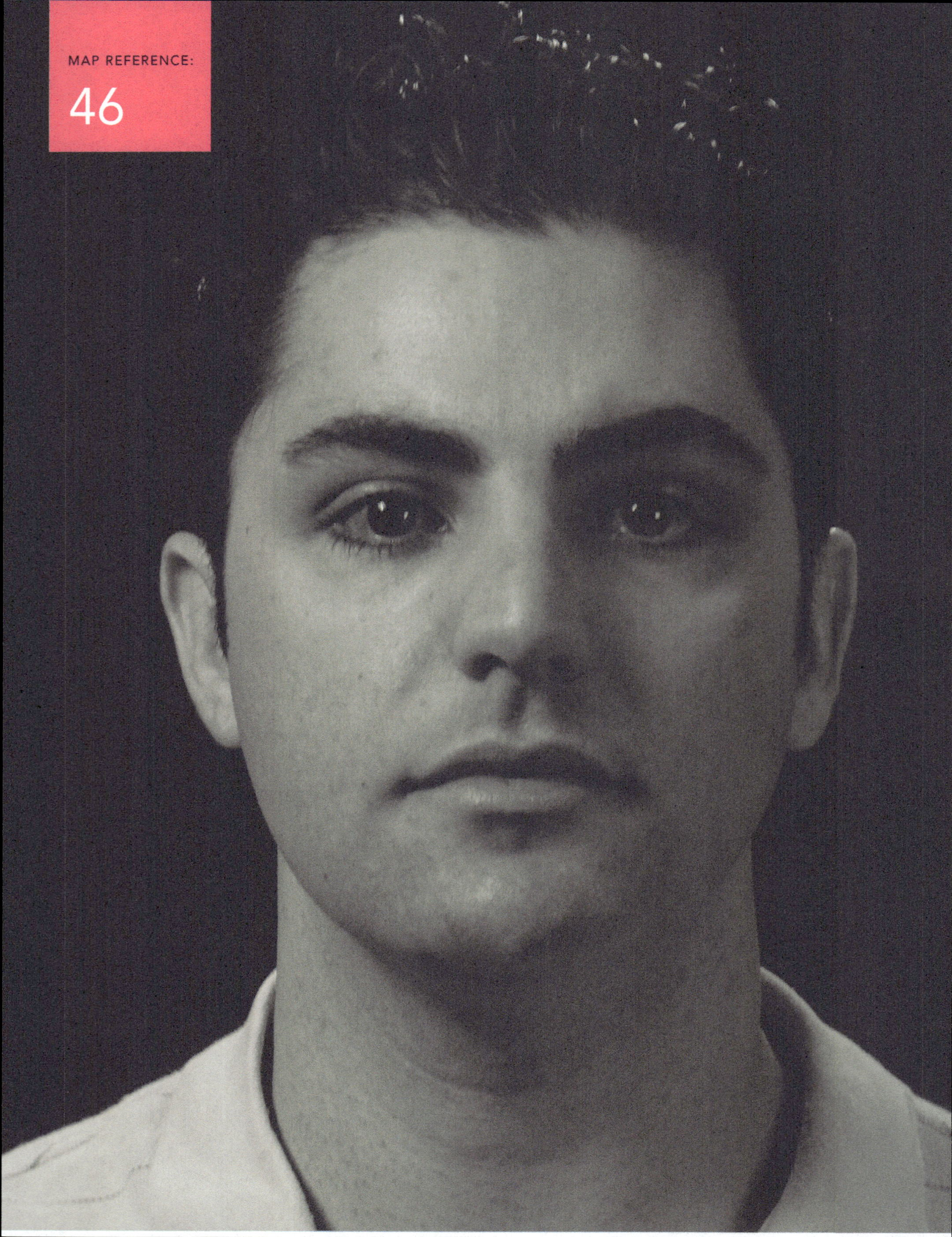

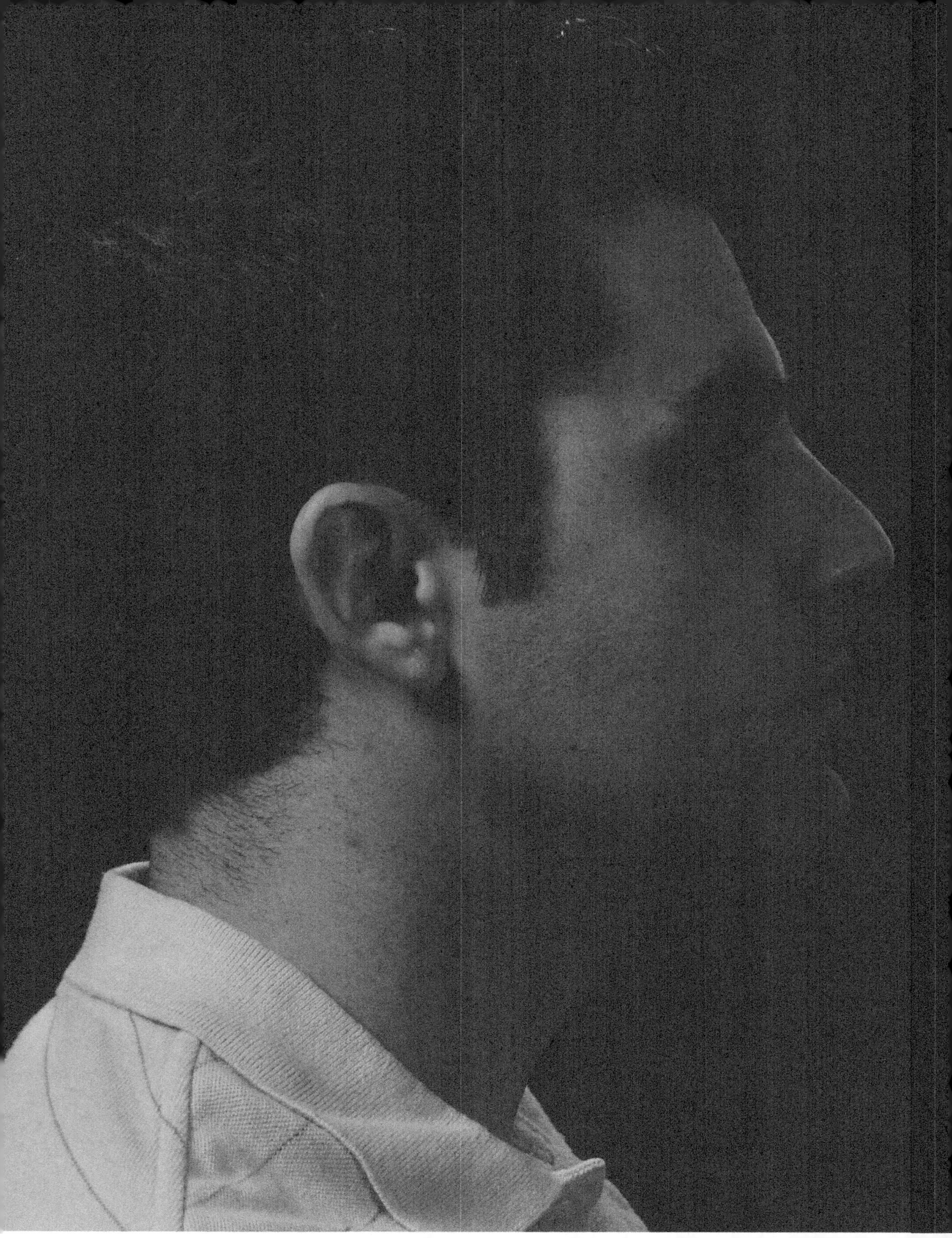

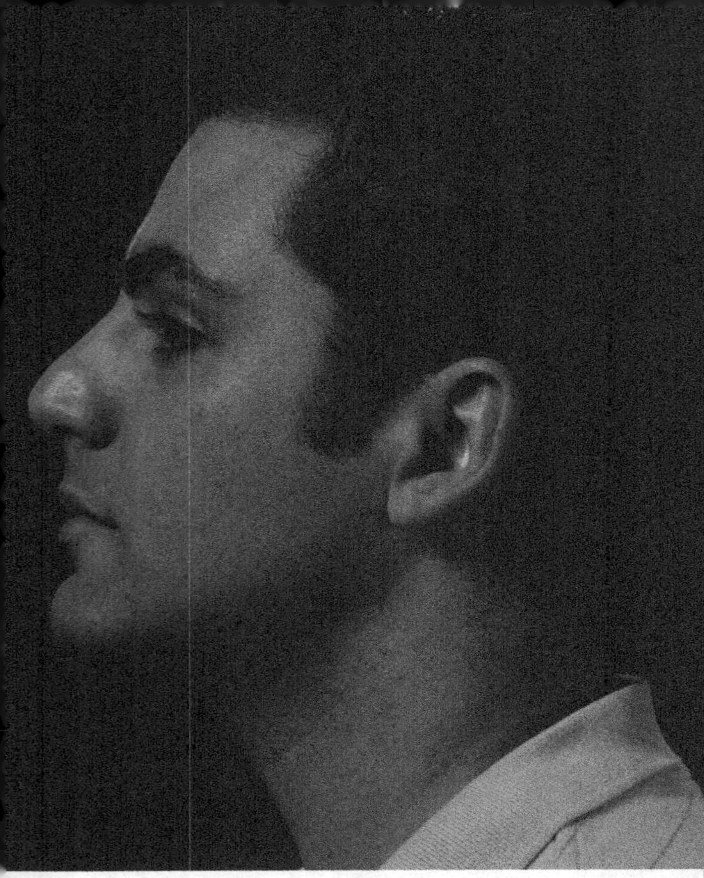

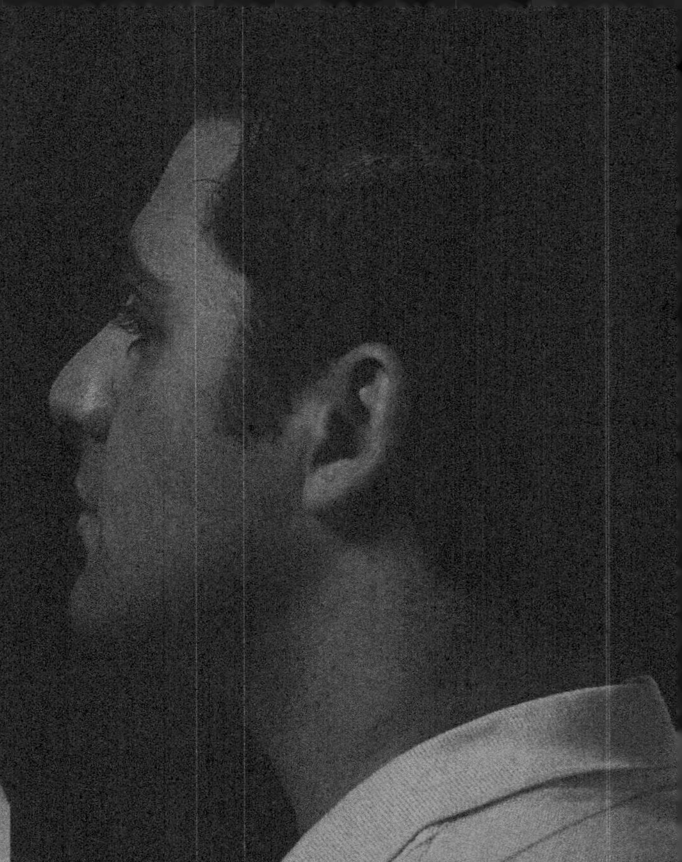

**Ethnicities claimed:**

Israel, Tunisia, Greece.

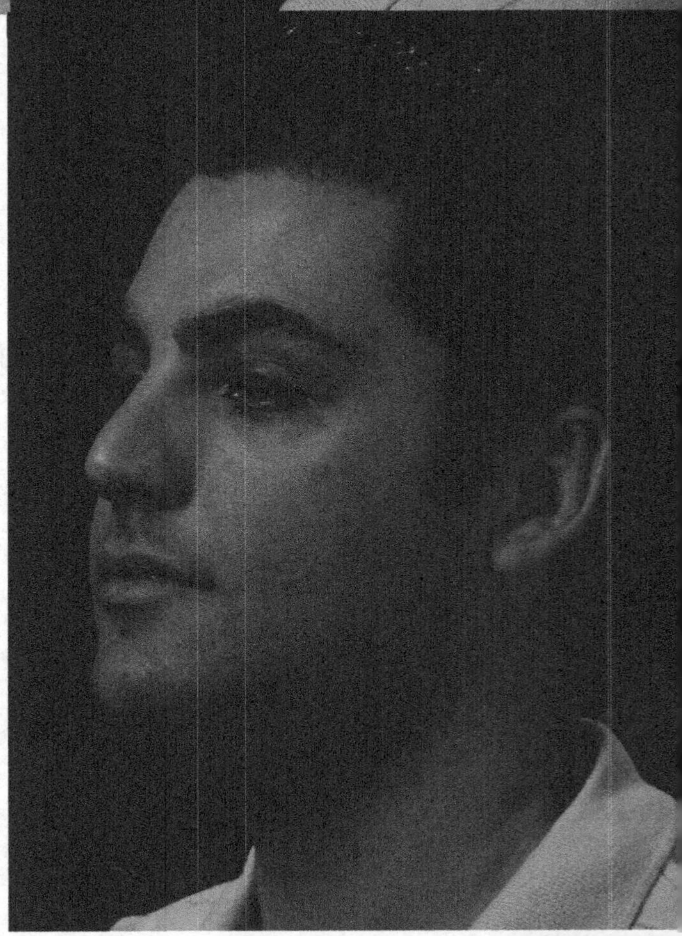

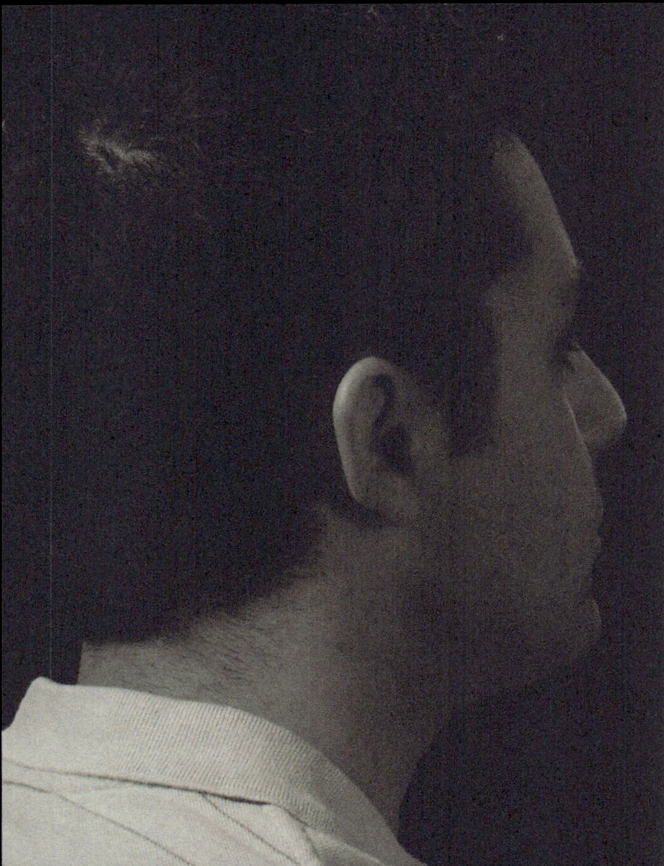

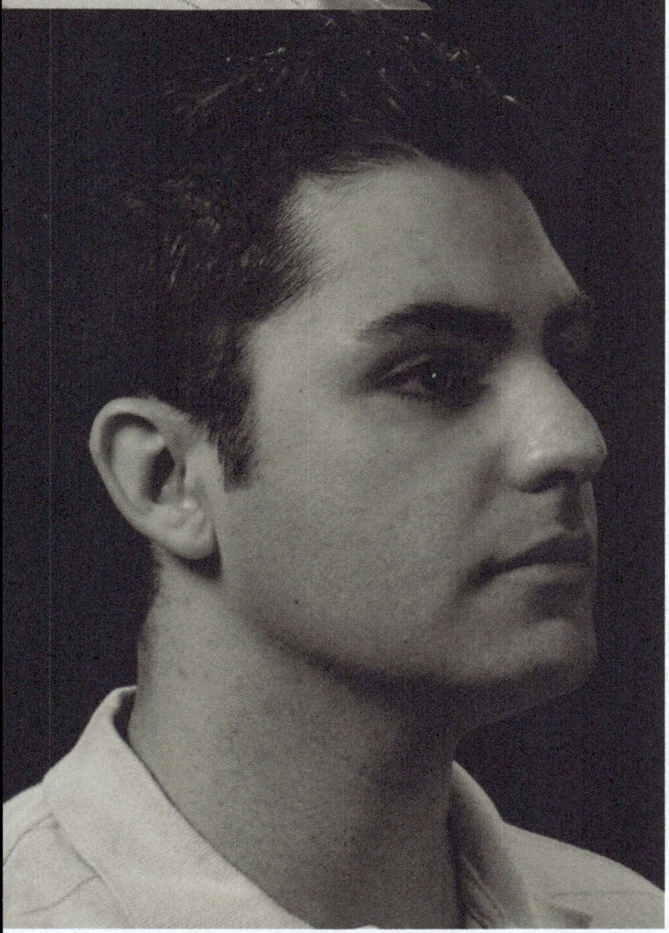

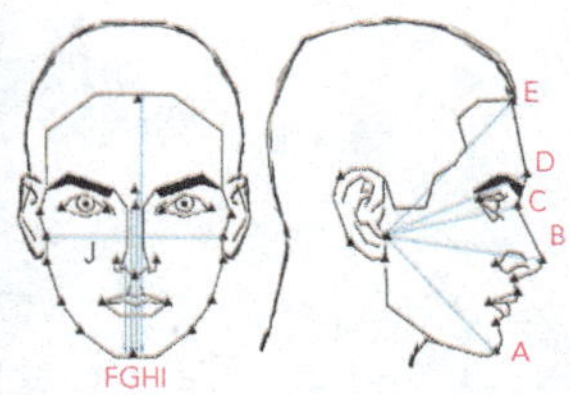


**Head measurements (in):**

A: 5 7/8
B: 5 5/8
C: 5 3/8
D: 5 1/2
E: 6 1/8
F: 3 3/8
G: 4 1/8
H: 5 1/4
I: 7 1/4
J: 5 7/8

MAP REFERENCE:
47

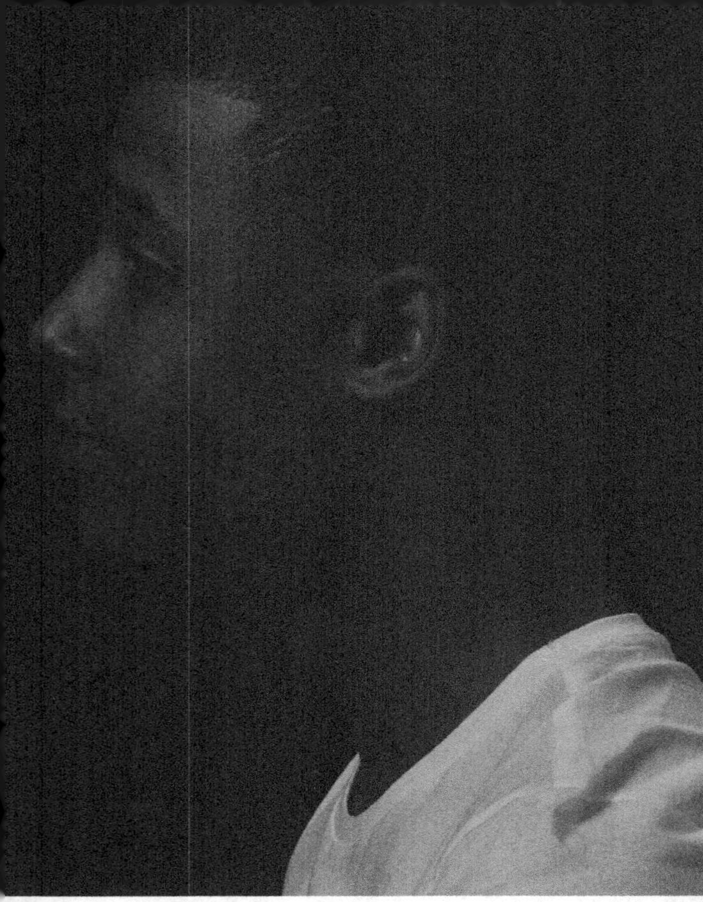

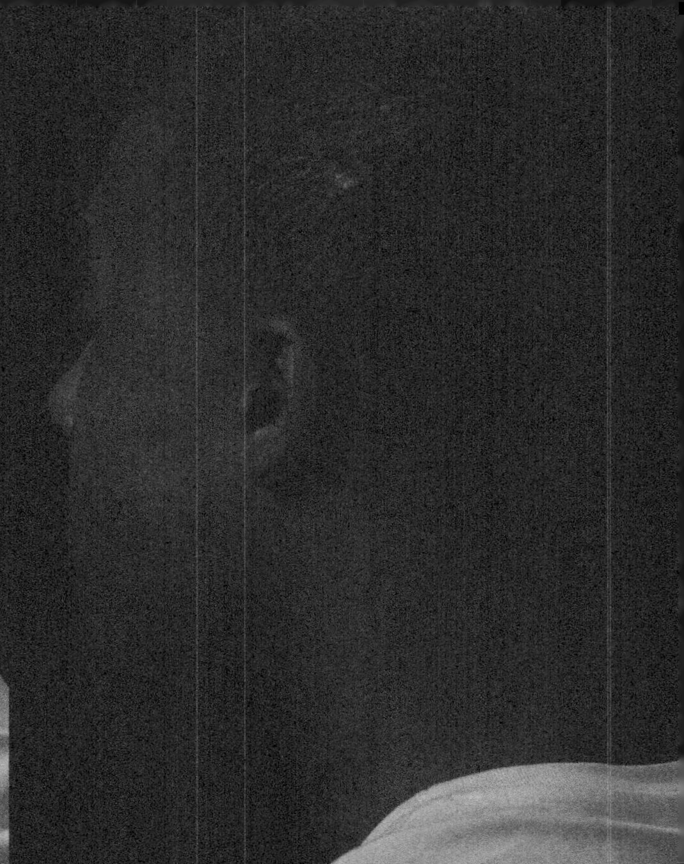

**Ethnicities claimed:**

American Indian—Cherokee, African American, Puerto Rico, France.

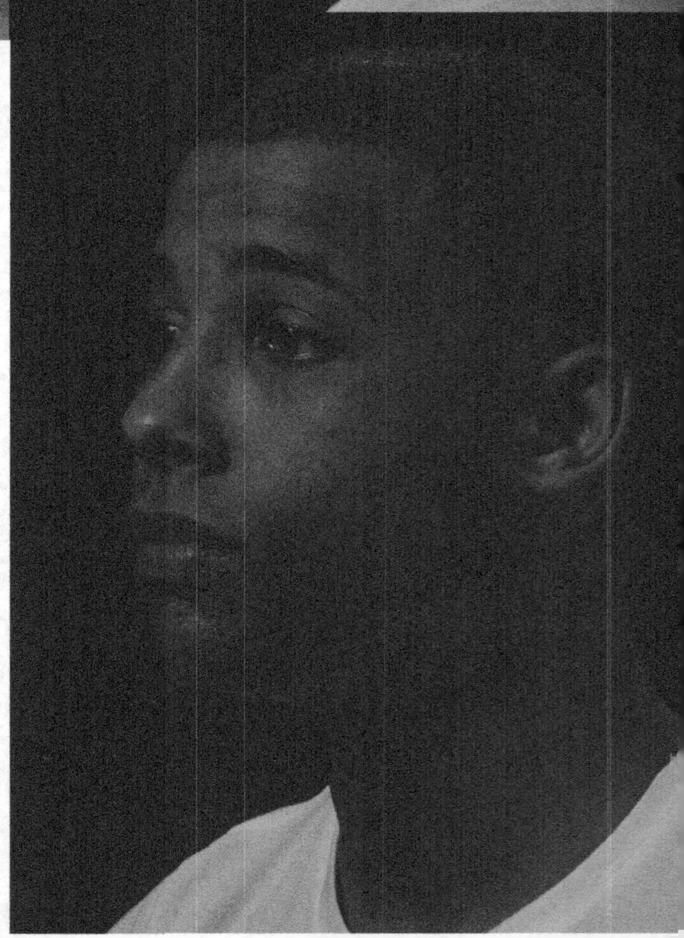

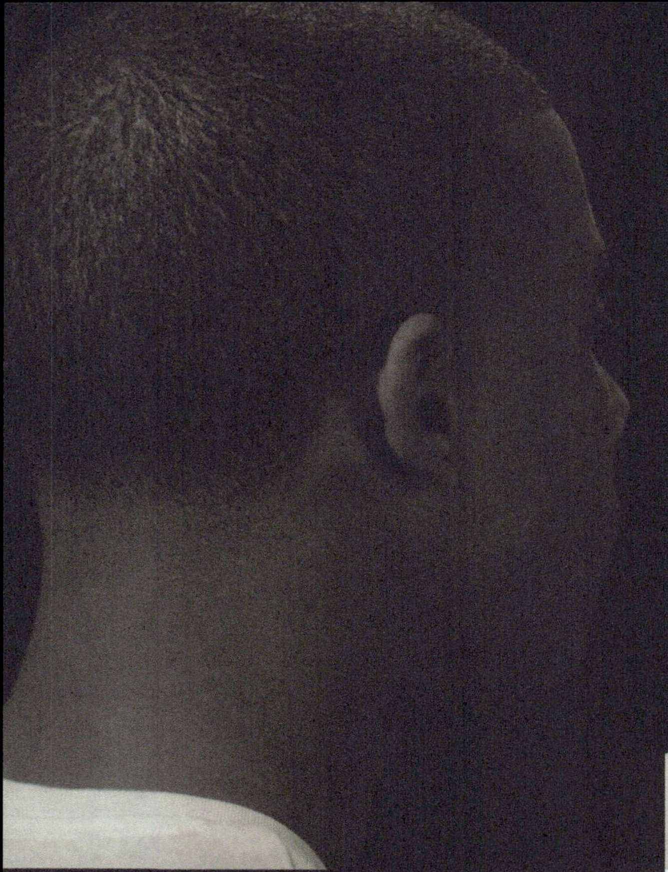

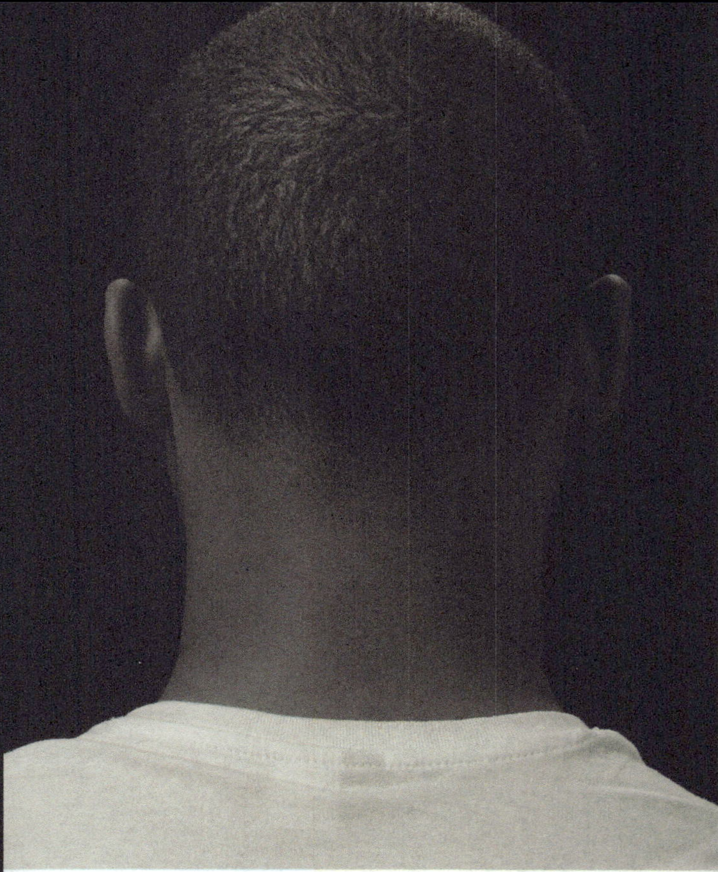

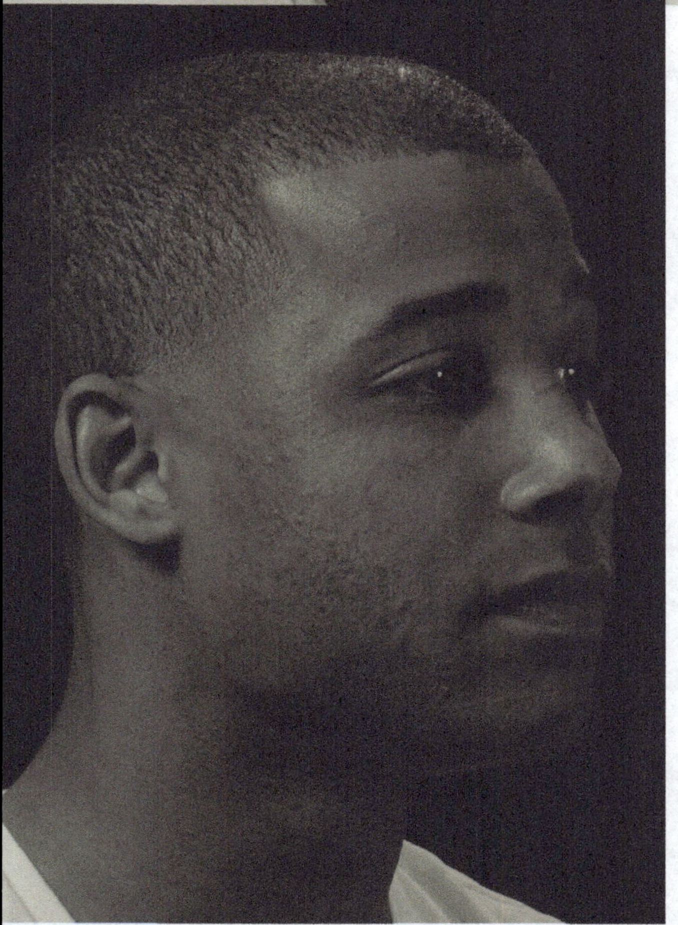

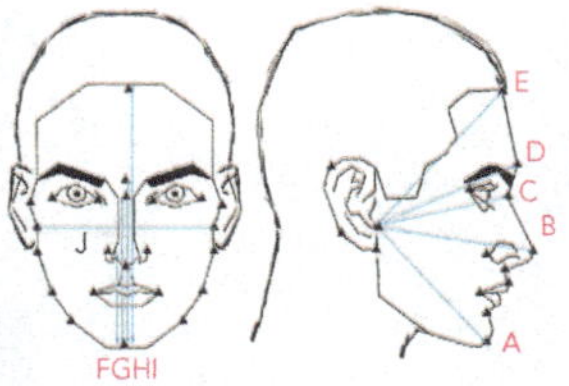


**Head measurements (in):**

A: 5 1/2
B: 5 3/8
C: 4 7/8
D: 5 3/8
E: 5 3/4
F: 3 1/2
G: 4 5/8
H: 5 1/4
I: 7
J: 5 5/8

MAP REFERENCE:

49

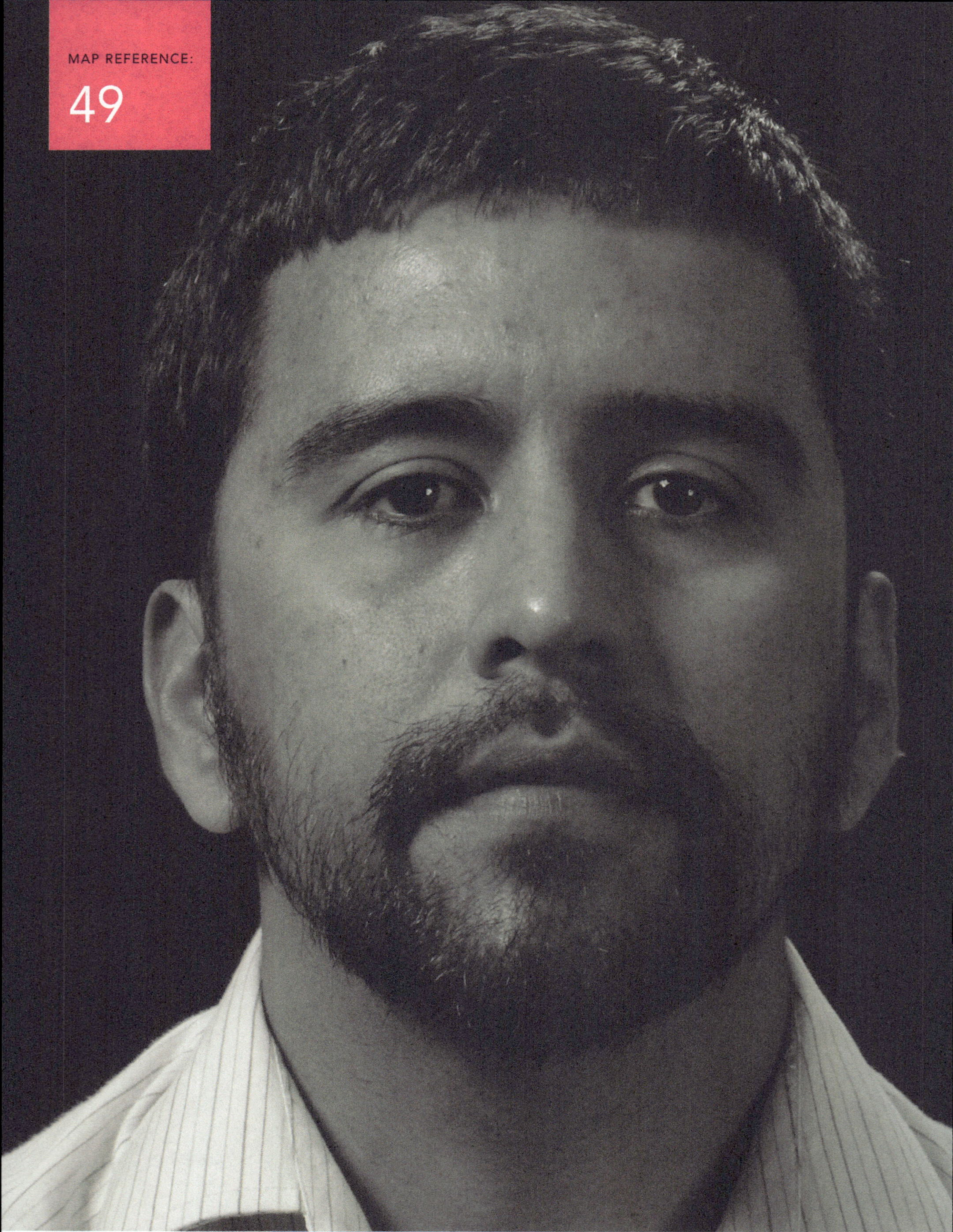

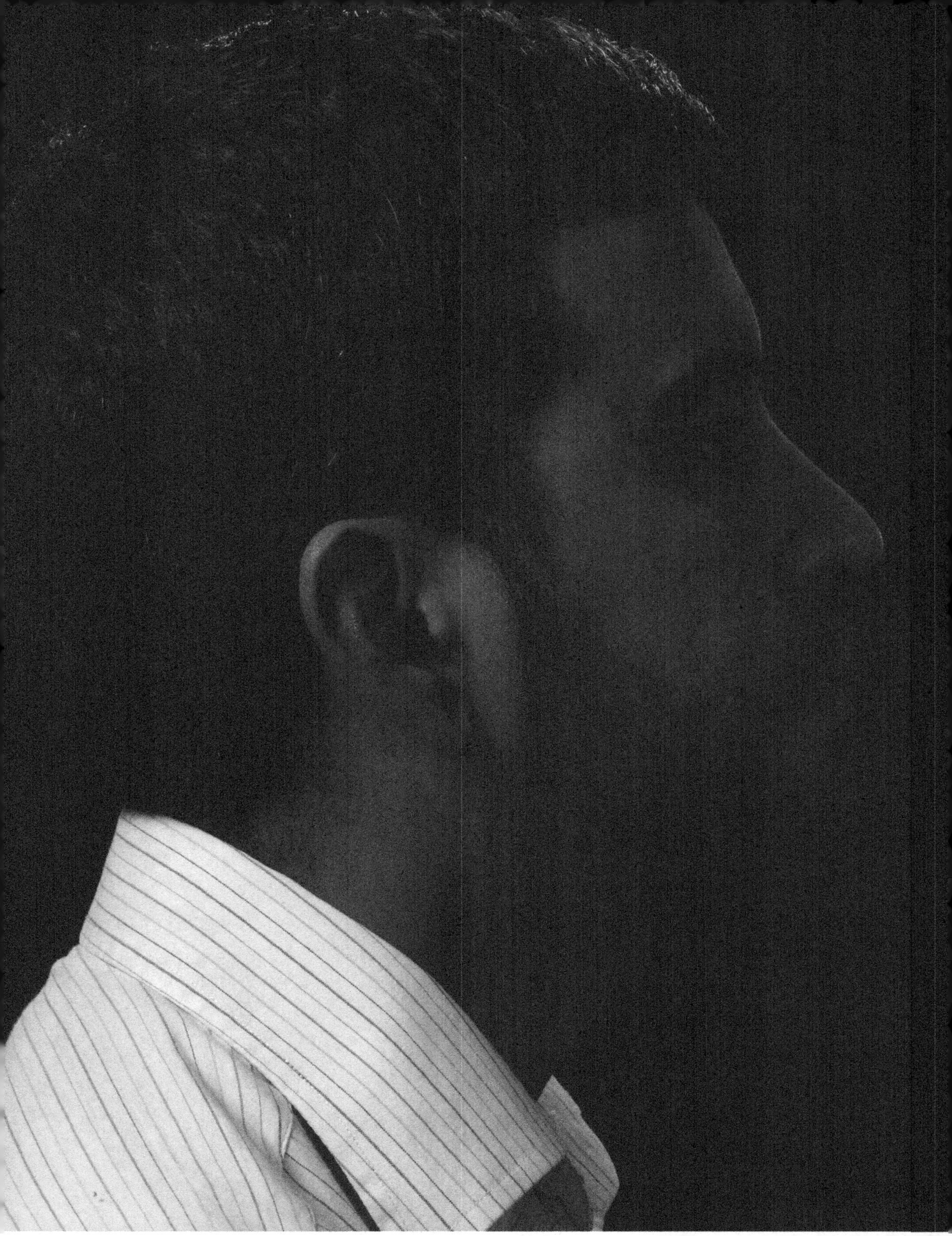

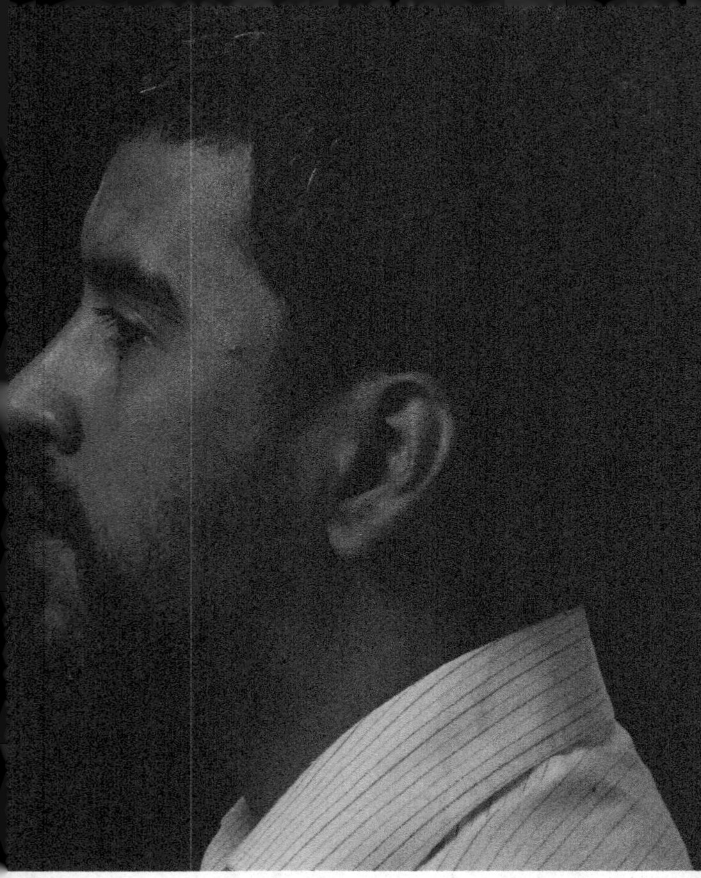

**Ethnicities claimed:**

Colombia, Spain, Arabian Peninsula, Guana Island.

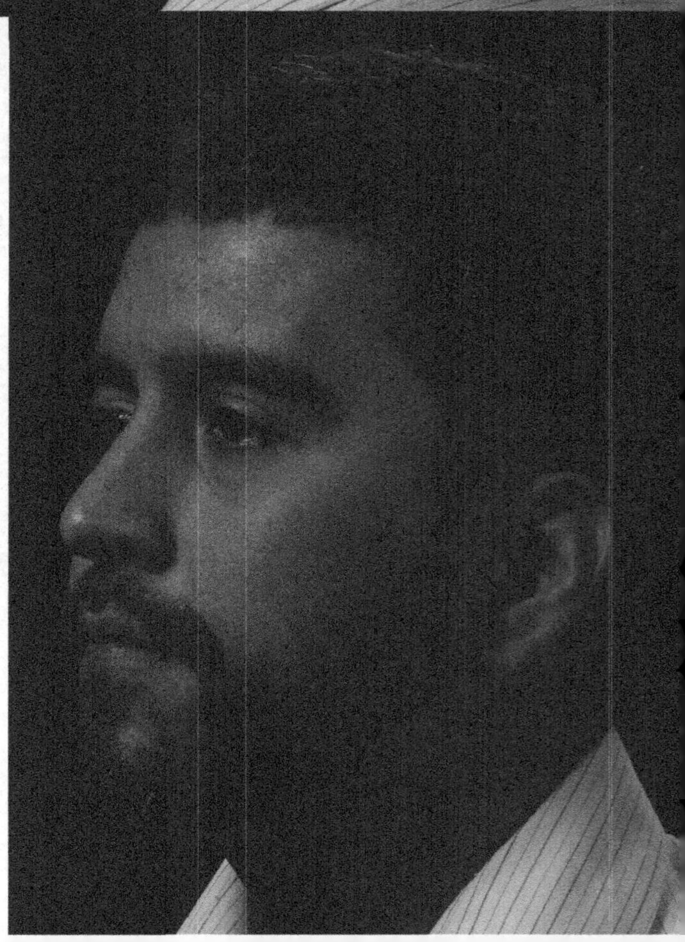

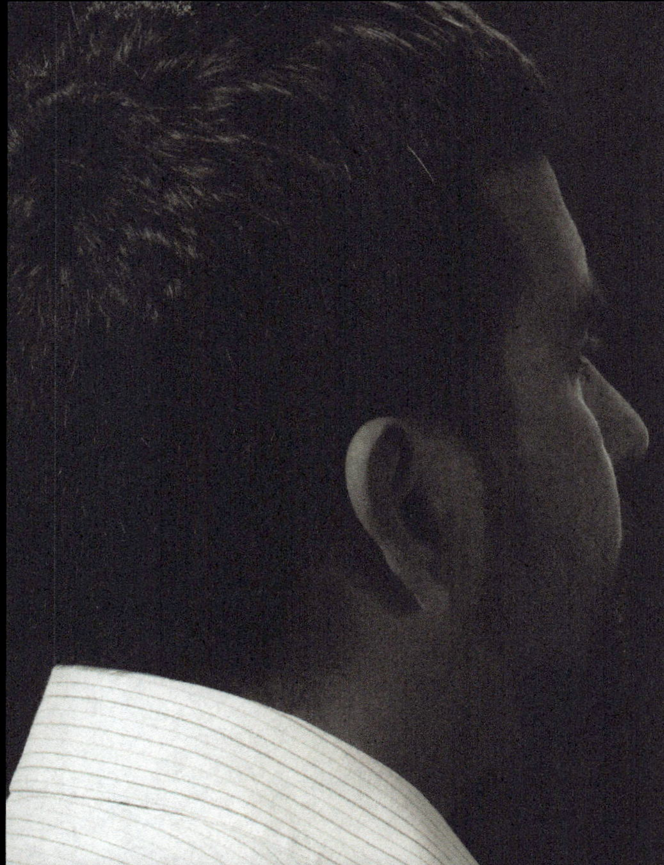

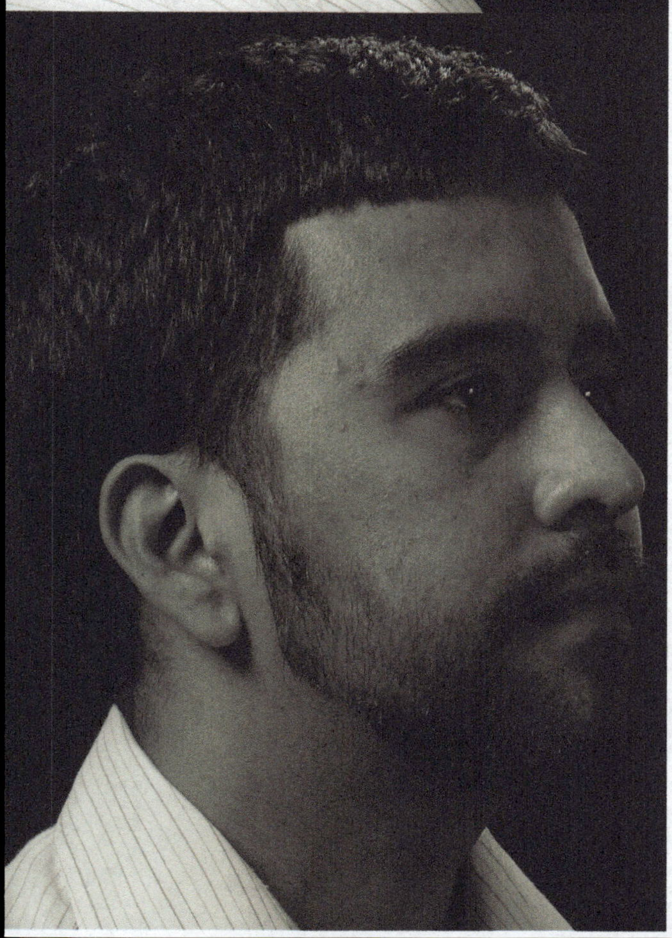

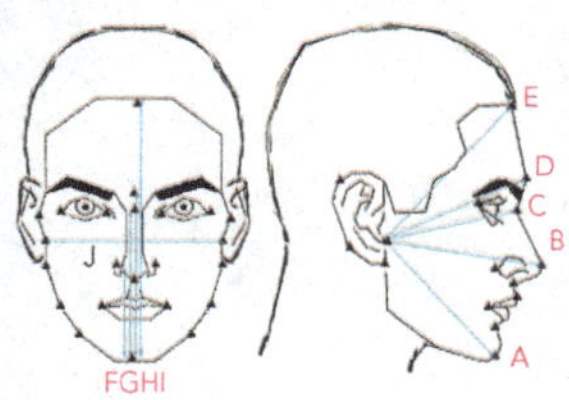


**Head measurements (in):**

A: 5 1/2
B: 5 1/2
C: 5 1/4
D: 5 3/4
E: 6 5/8
F: 4
G: 5
H: 5 3/4
I: 8 3/8
J: 5 5/8

MAP REFERENCE:

50

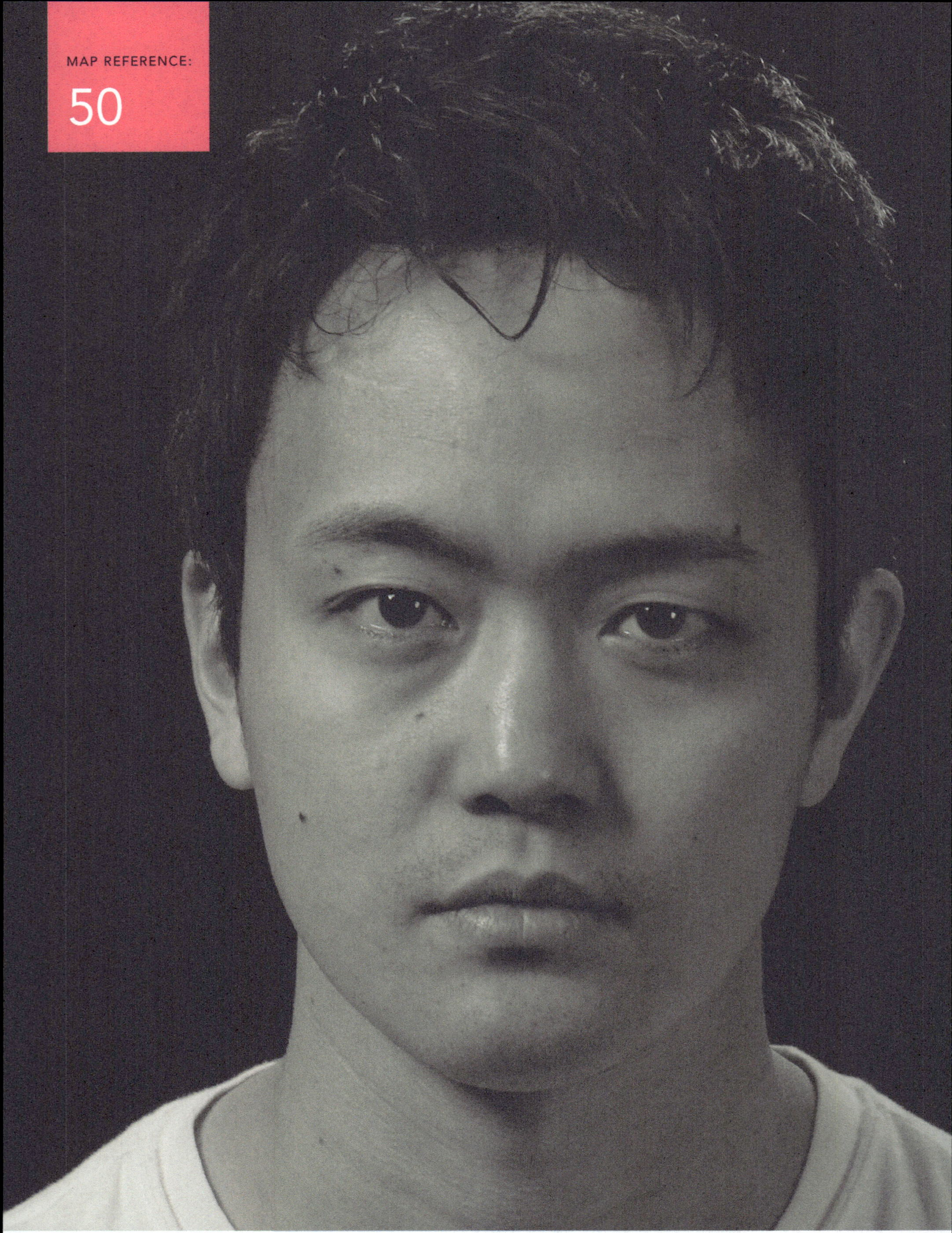

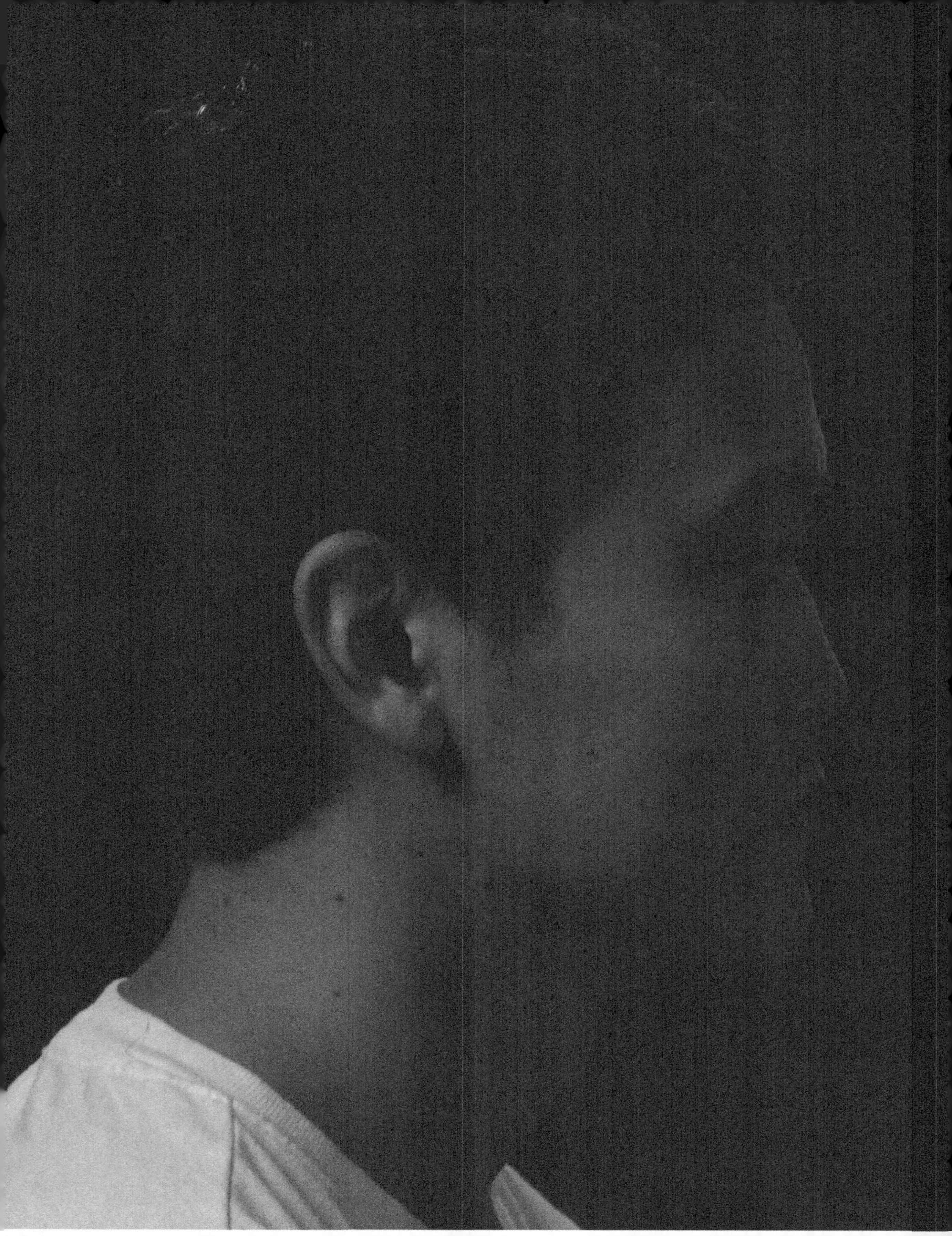

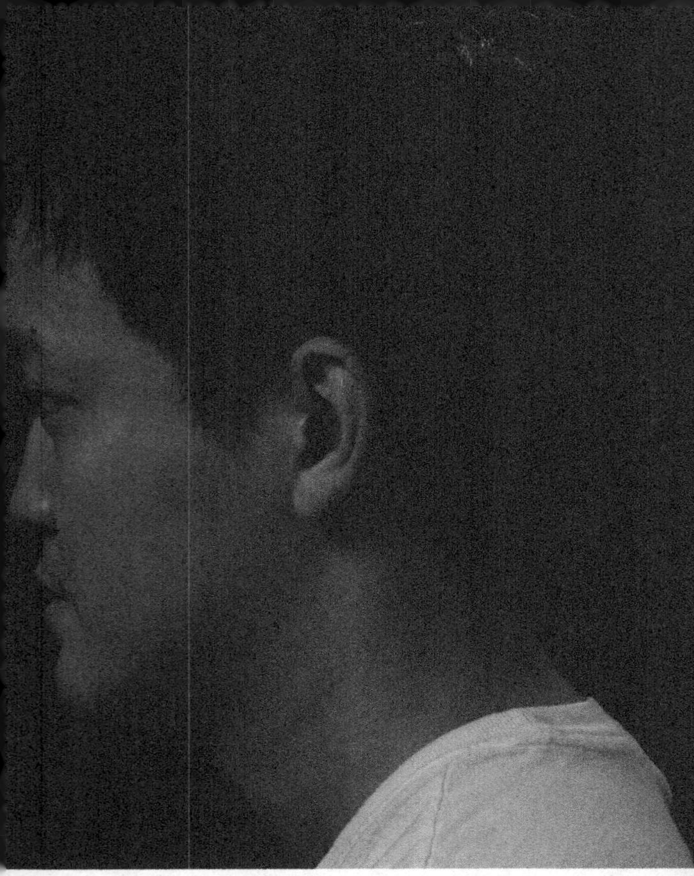

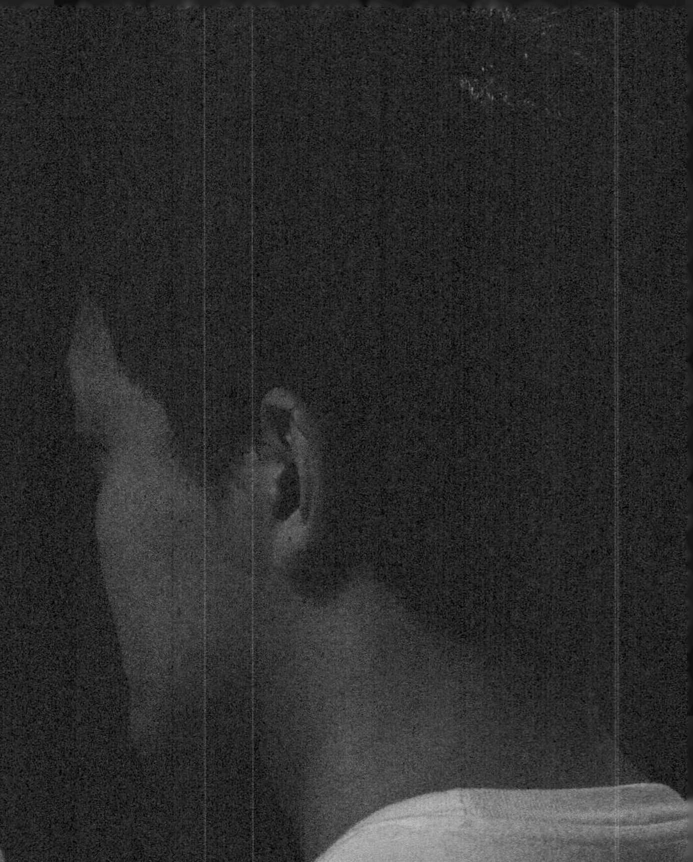

**Ethnicities claimed:**

Japan.

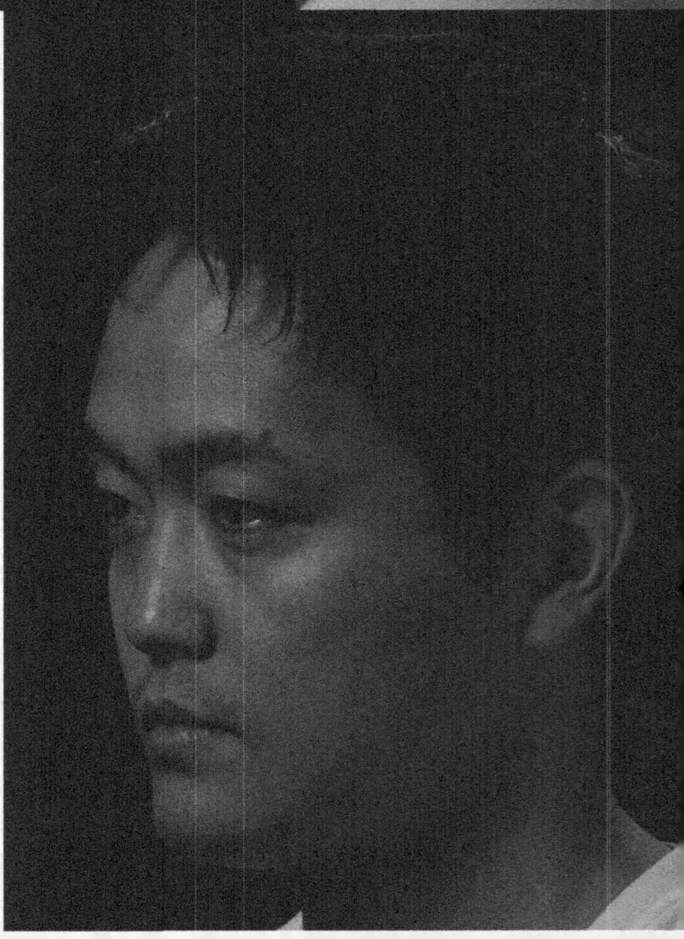

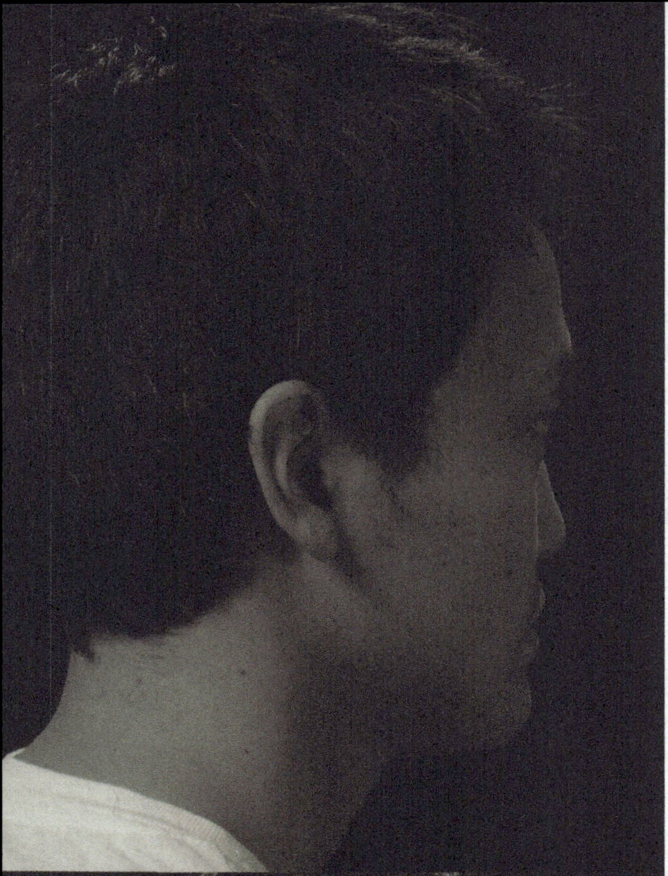

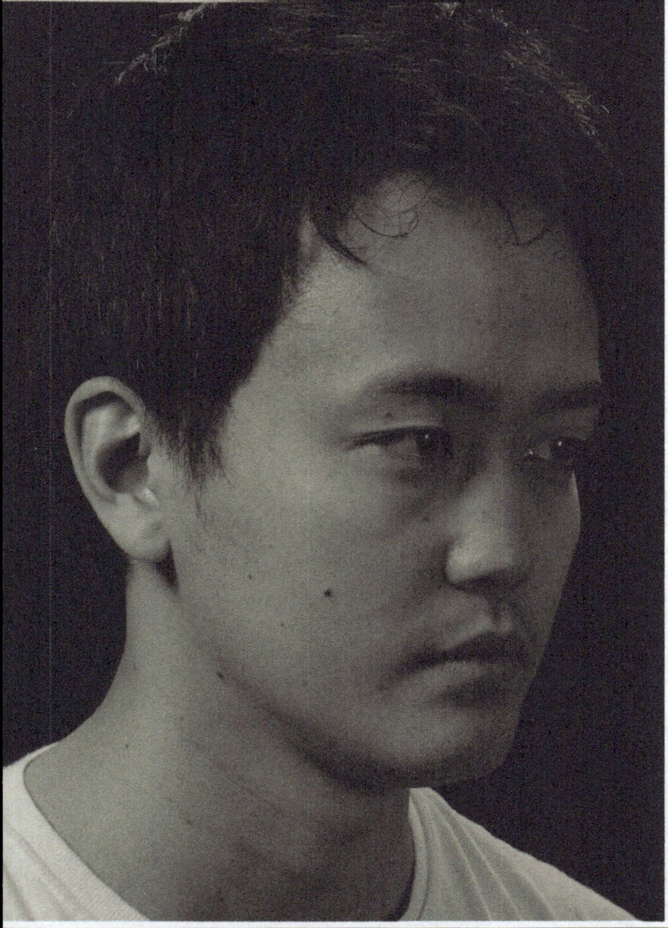

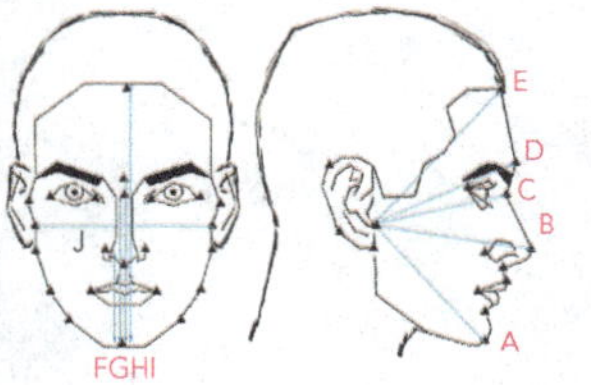


**Head measurements (in):**

A: 5 5/8
B: 5 1/2
C: 5 1/4
D: 5 5/8
E: 6 3/4
F: 3 3/8
G: 4 3/8
H: 5 1/8
I: 8 1/8
J: 6

MAP REFERENCE:

51

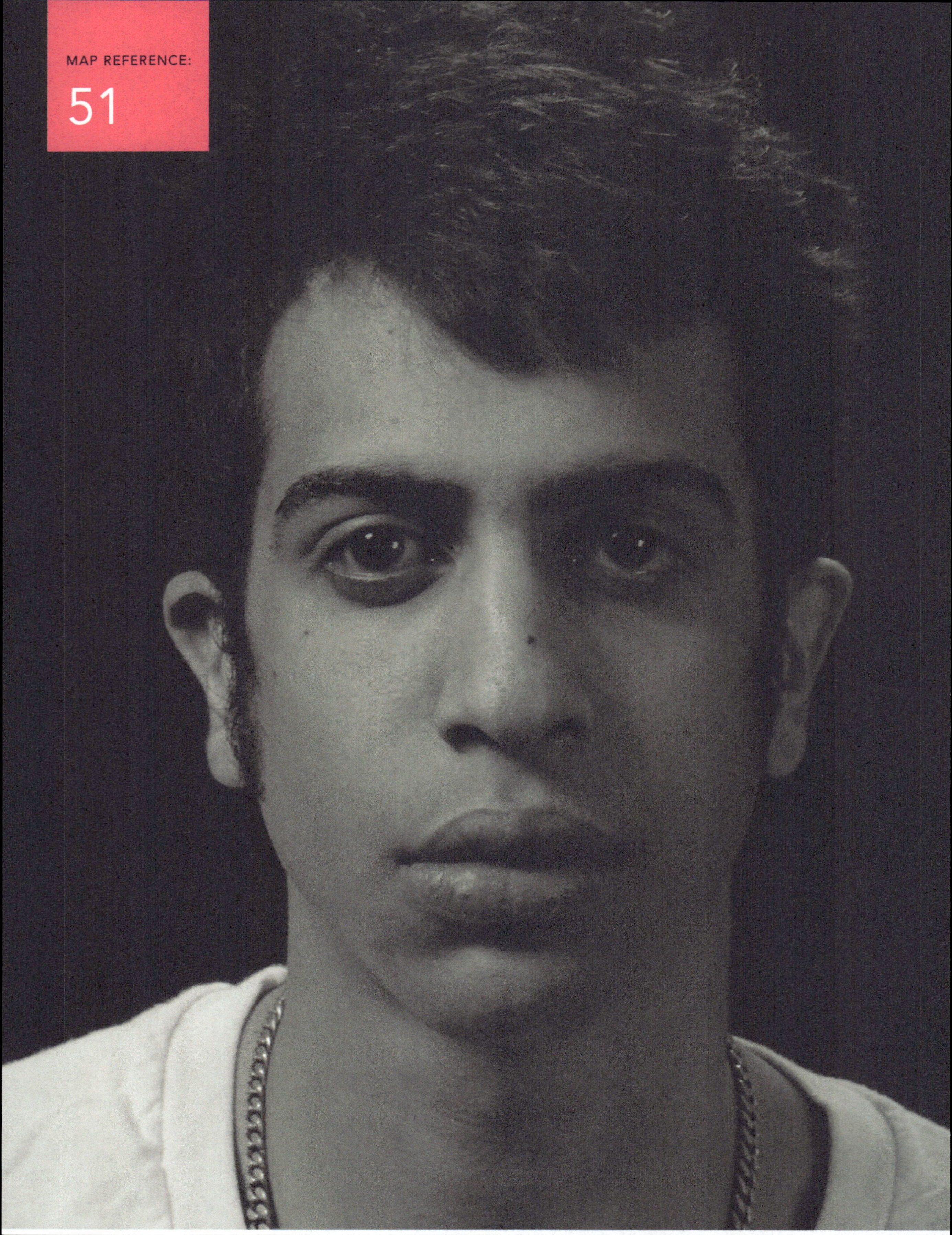

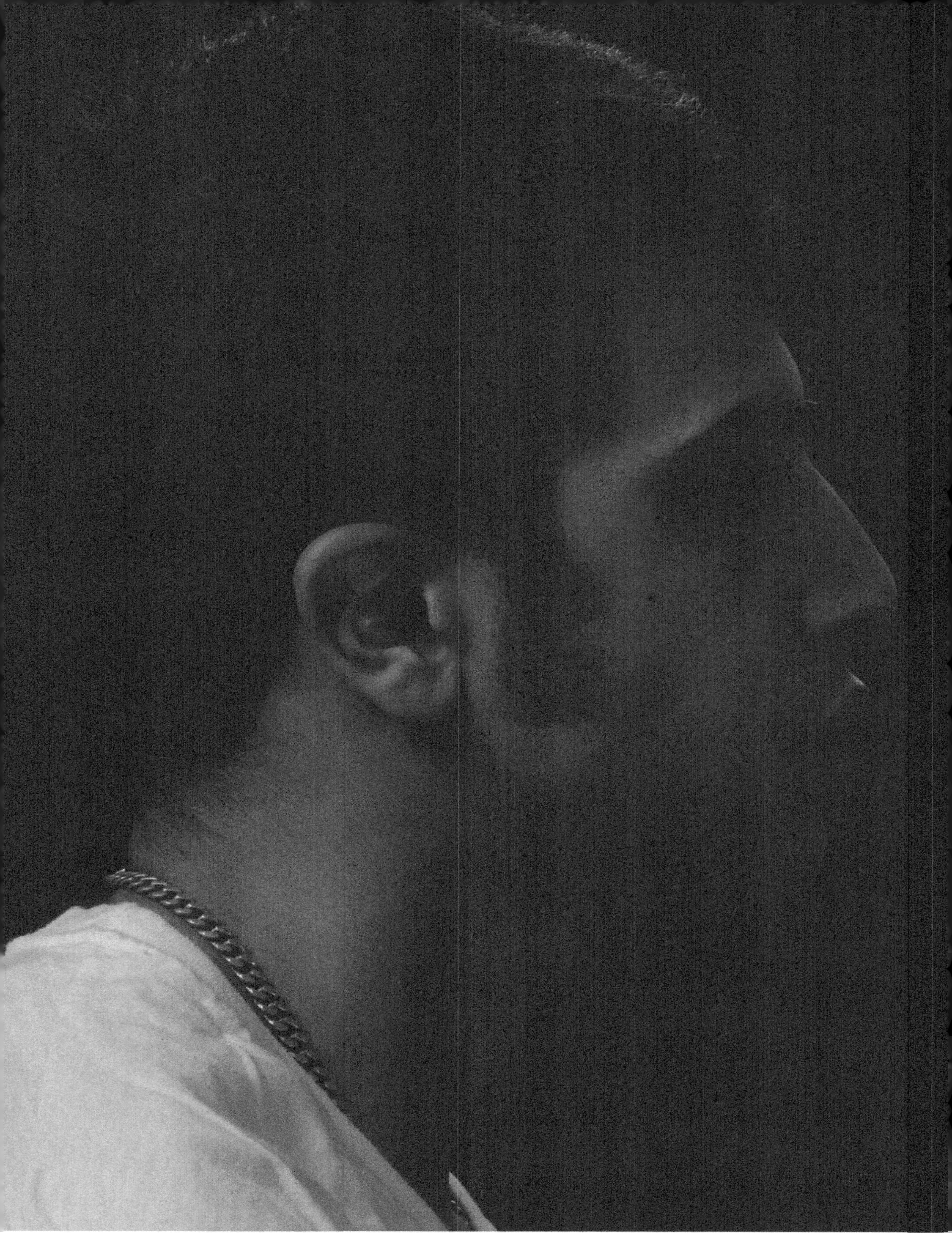

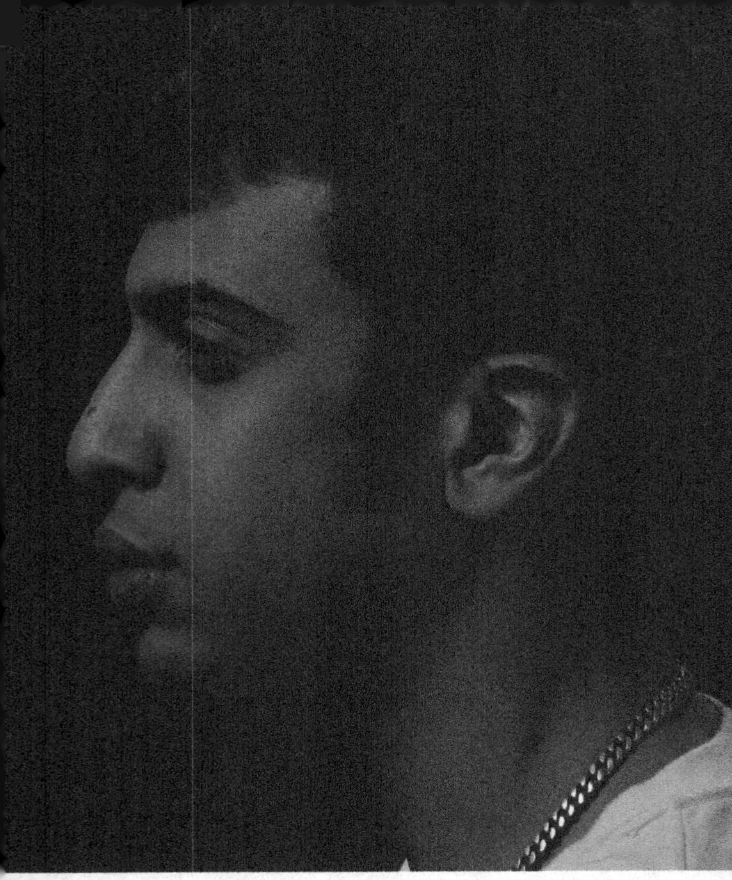

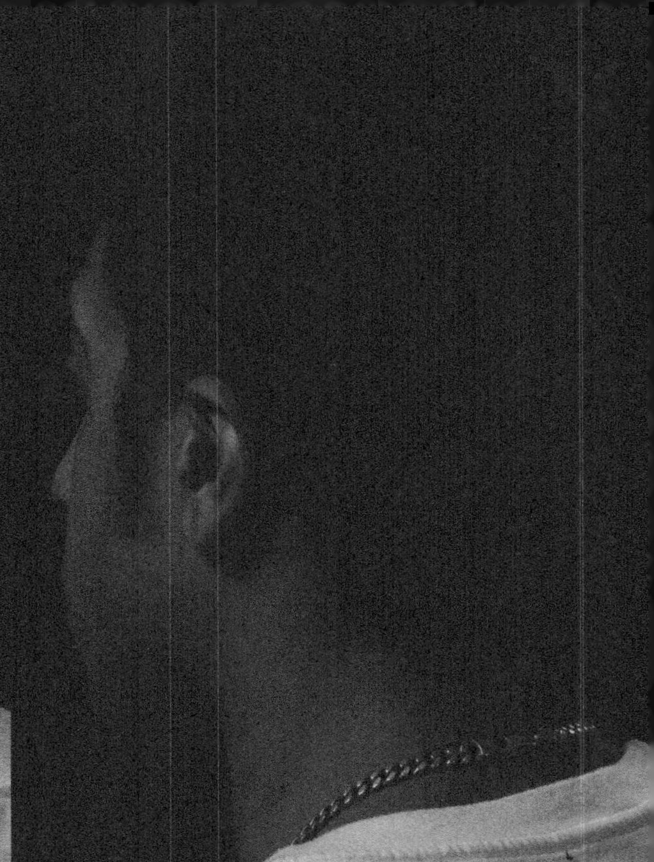

**Ethnicities claimed:**

African American, Iran.

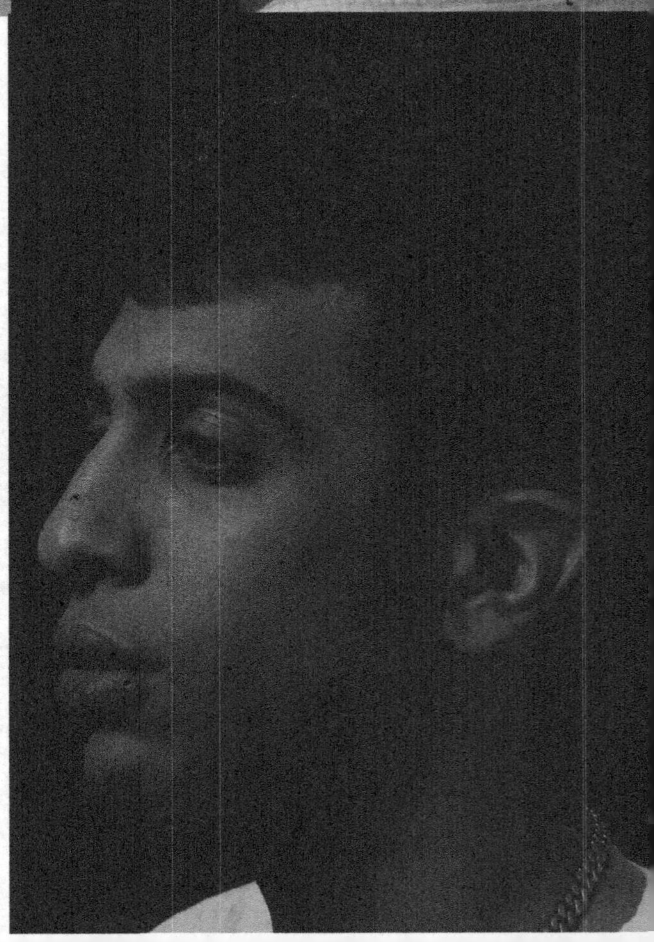

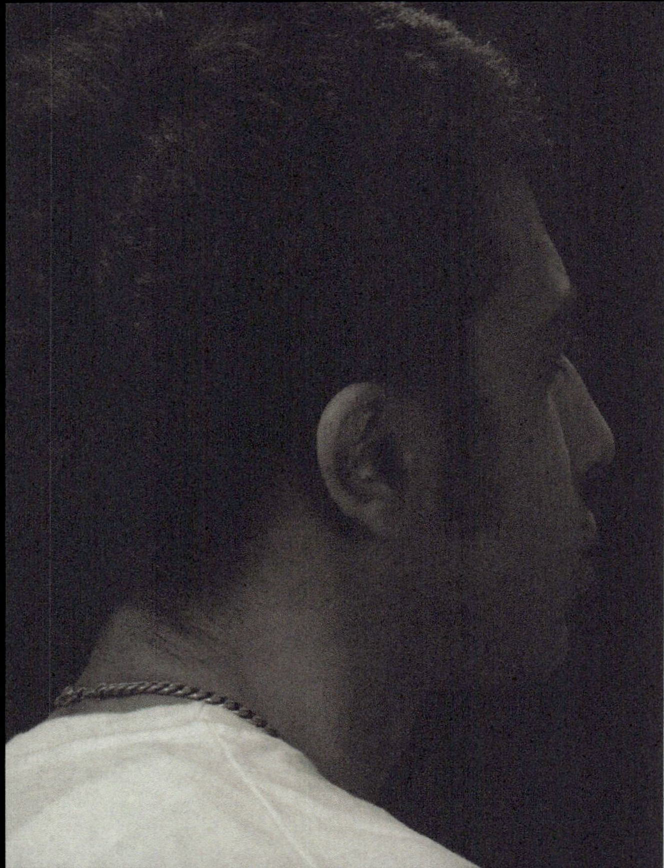

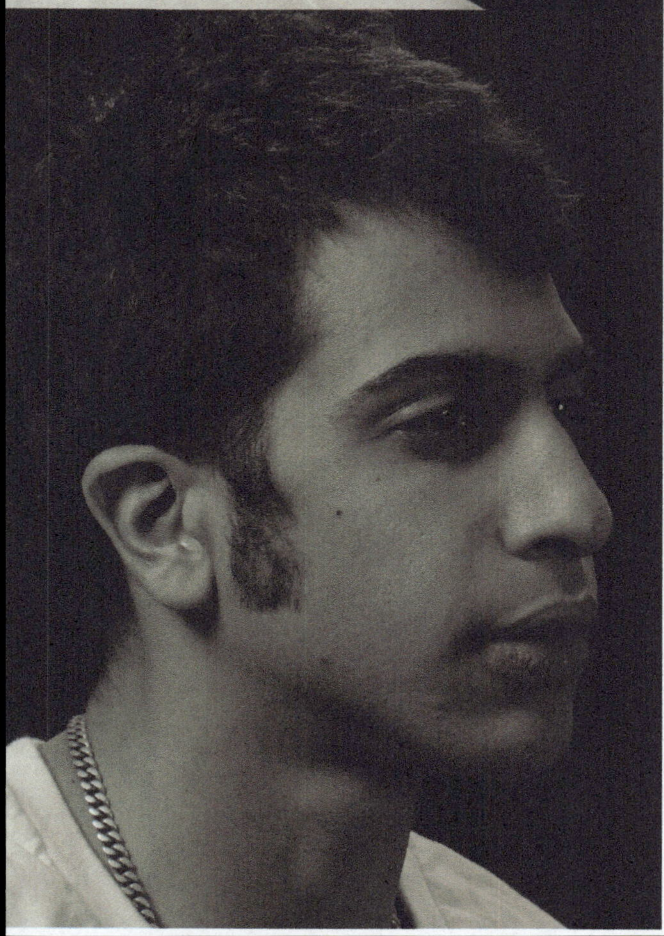

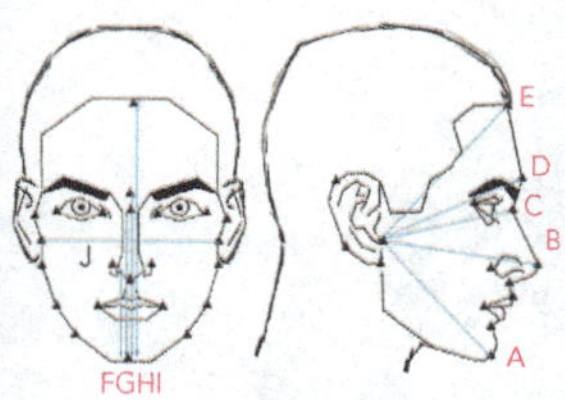


**Head measurements (in):**

A: 5 1/2
B: 5 5/8
C: 5
D: 5 3/4
E: 5 5/8
F: 3 5/8
G: 4 3/4
H: 5
I: 7 1/2
J: 5 1/8

MAP REFERENCE:
53

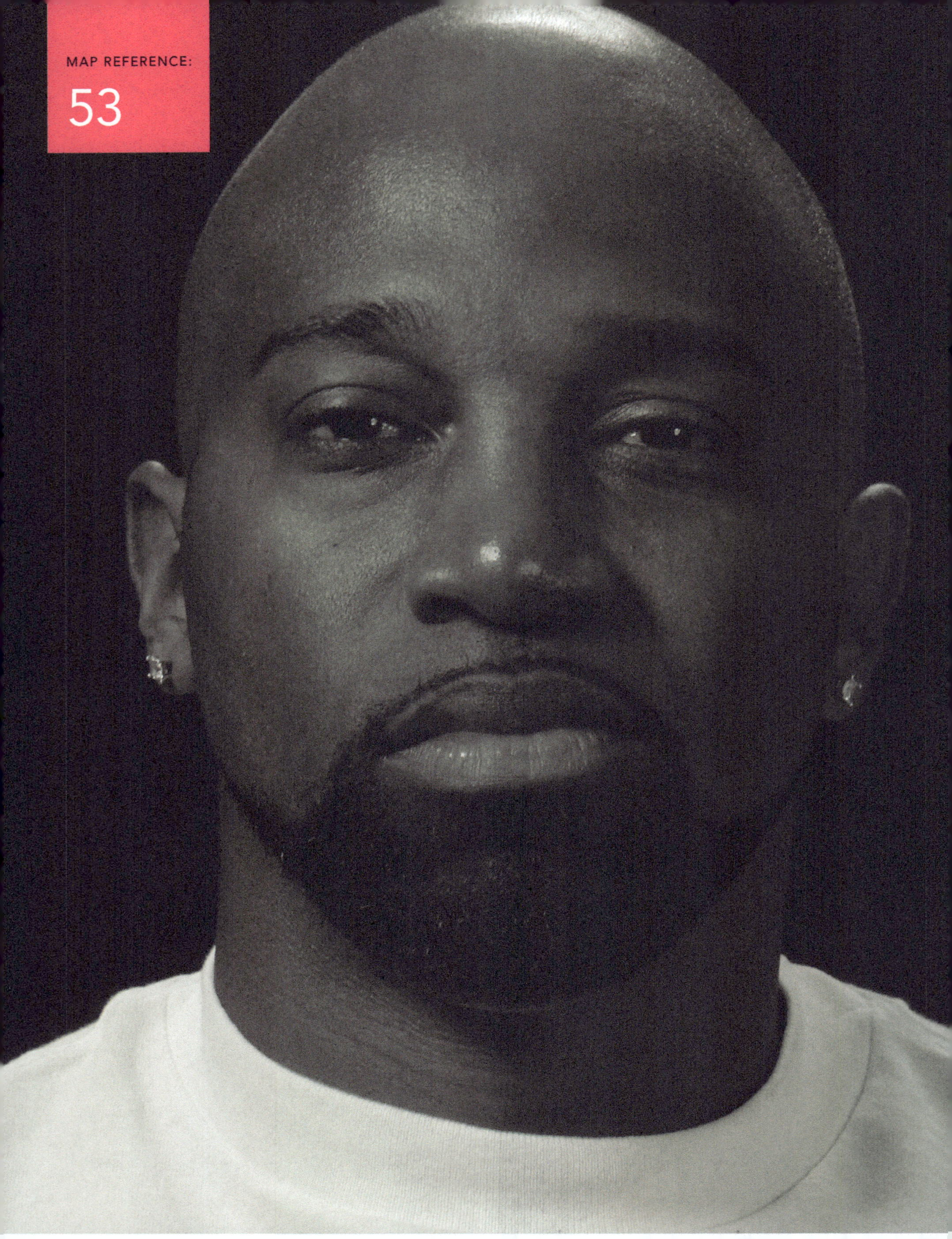

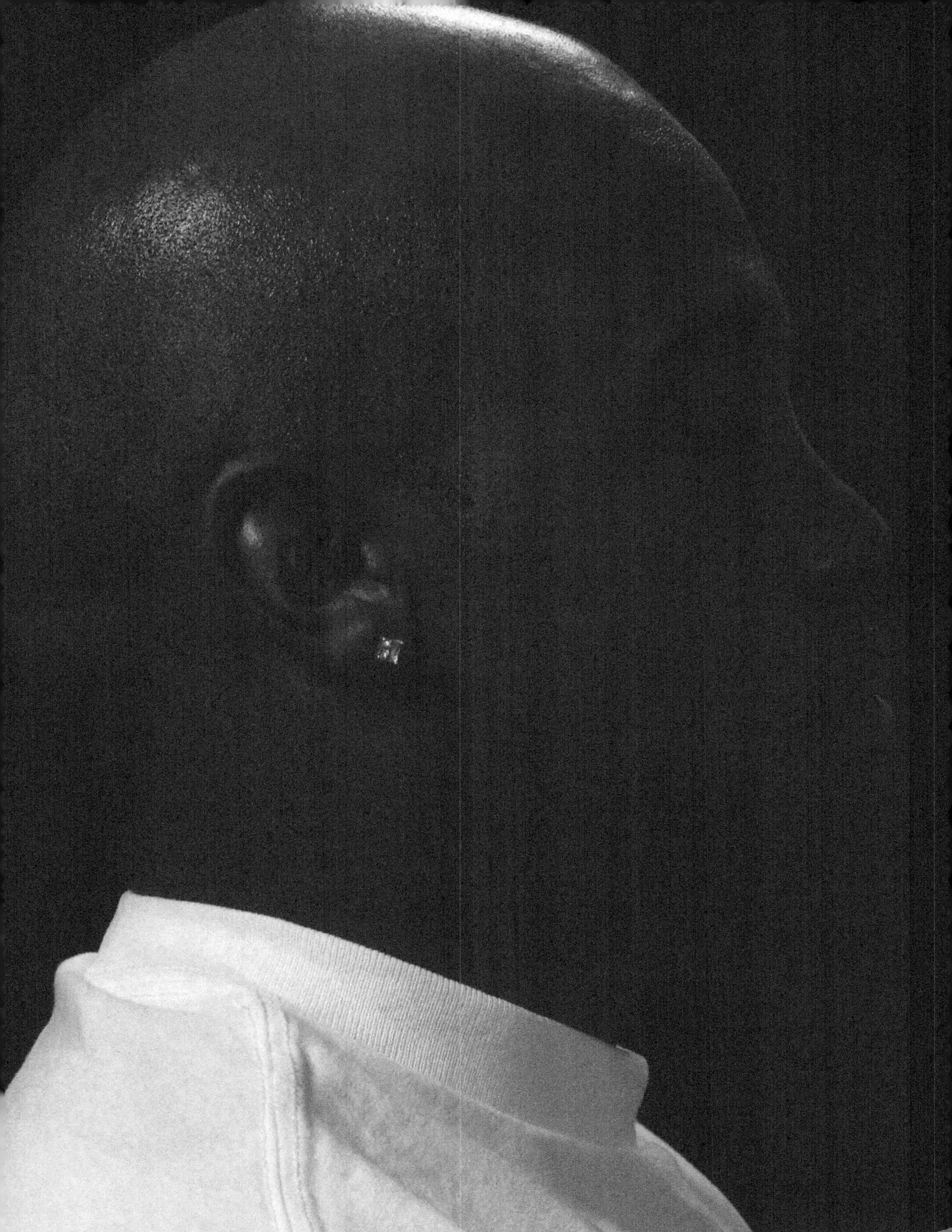

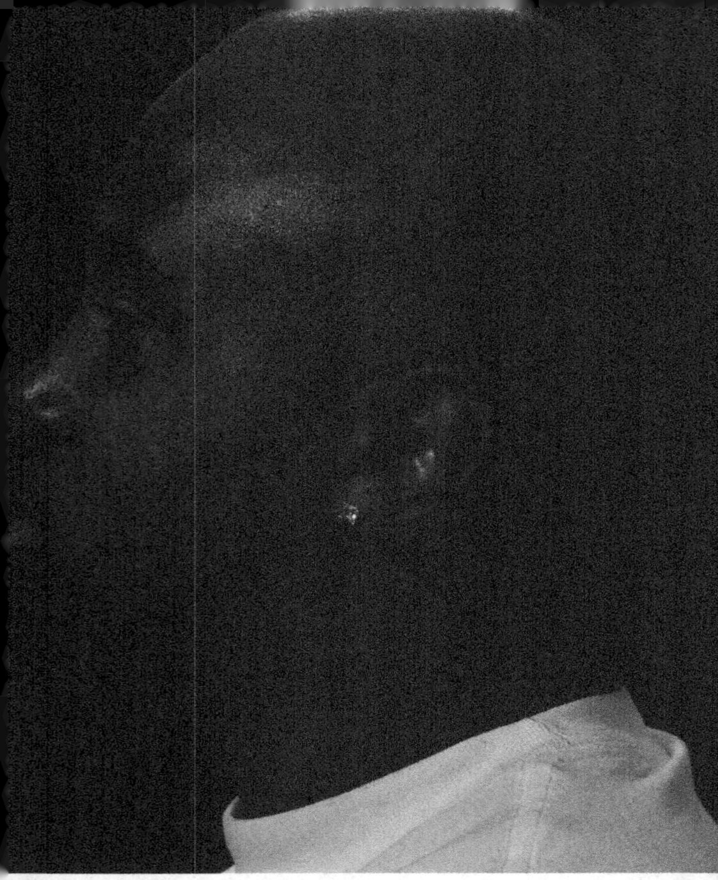

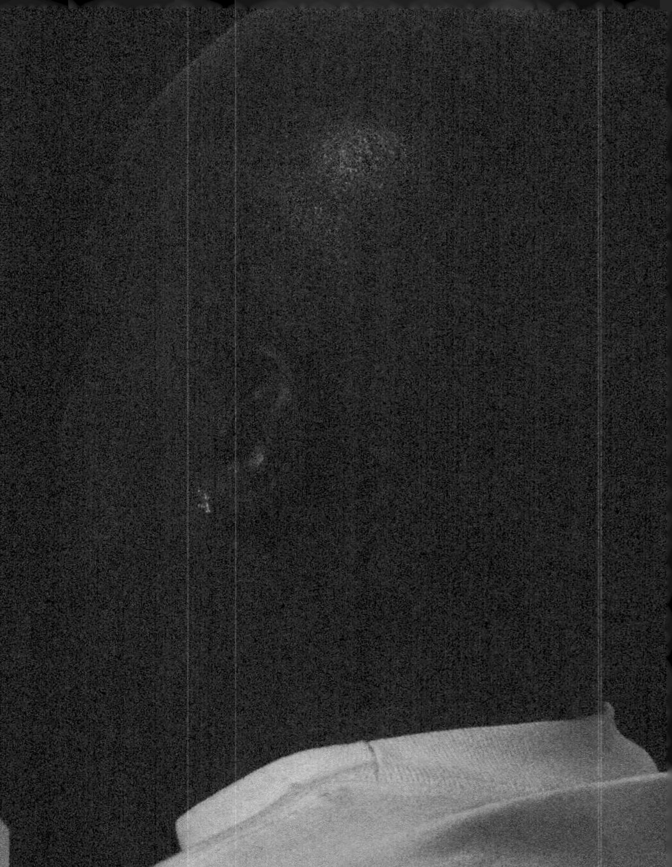

**Ethnicities claimed:**

Africa, France, American Indian, Garifuna, Caribbean.

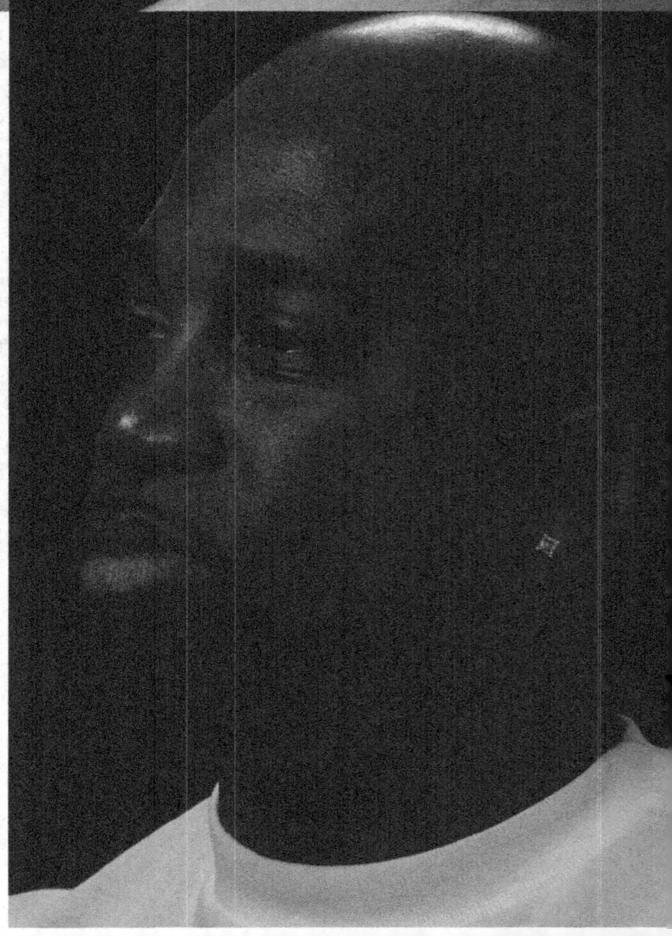

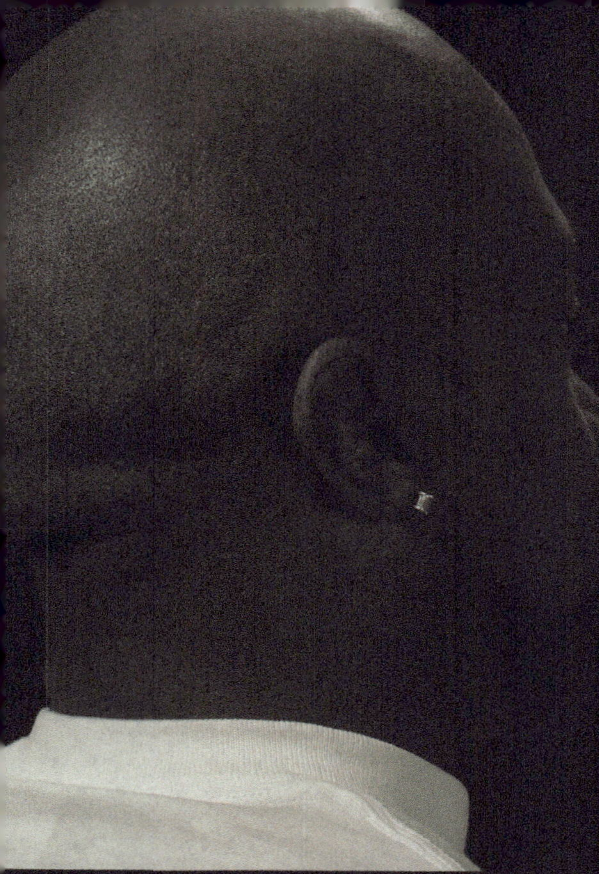

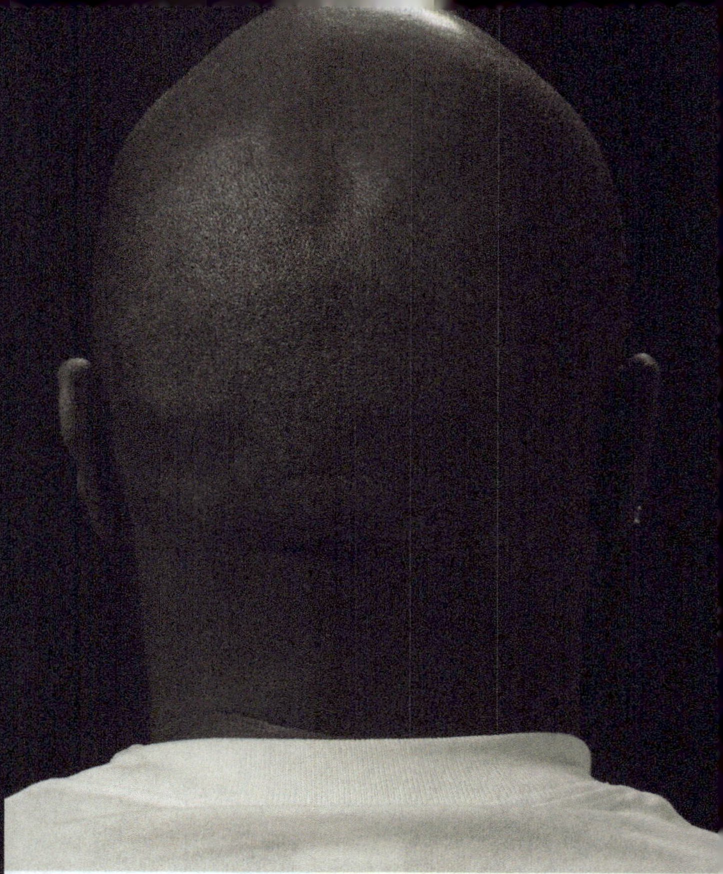

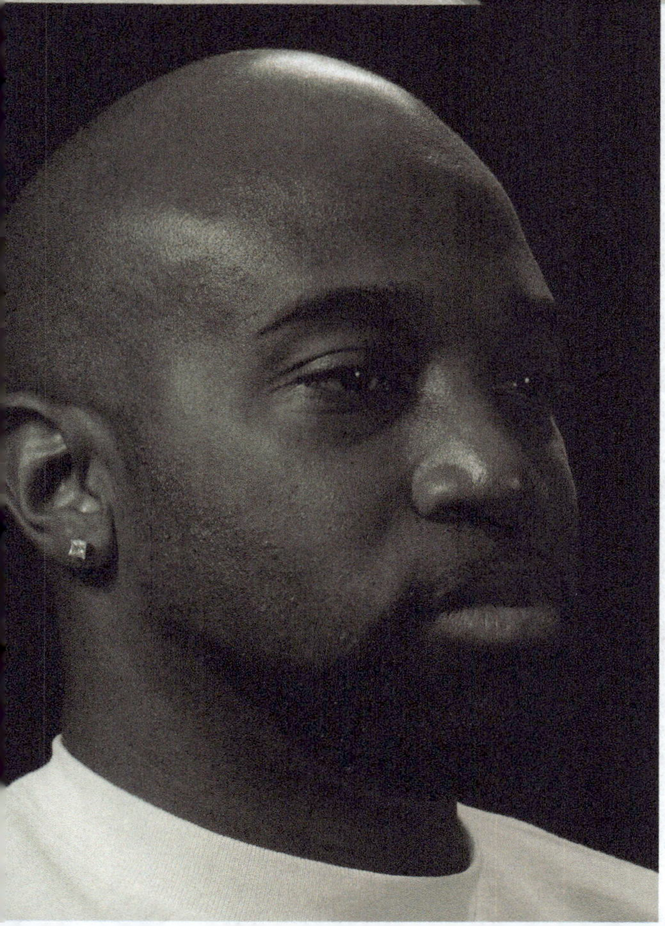

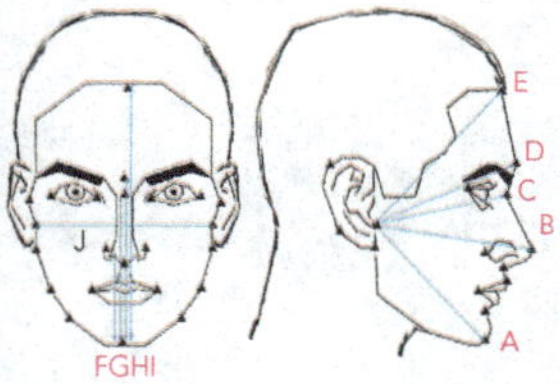


**Head measurements (in):**

A: 5 5/8
B: 5 1/8
C: 4 7/8
D: 5 1/4
E: 6
F: 3 3/4
G: 4 7/8
H: 5 1/2
I: 7 3/4
J: 6 1/8

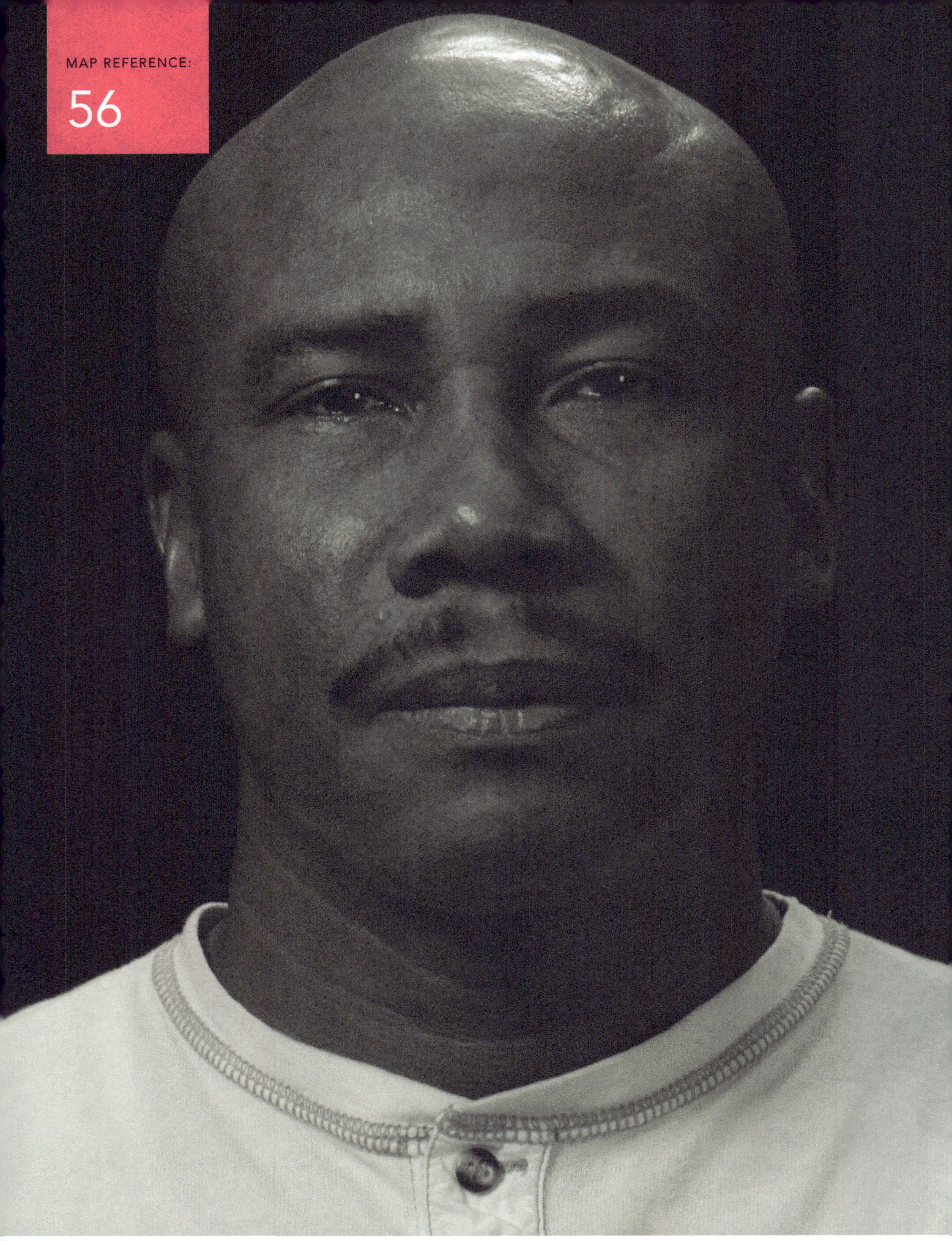
MAP REFERENCE:
56

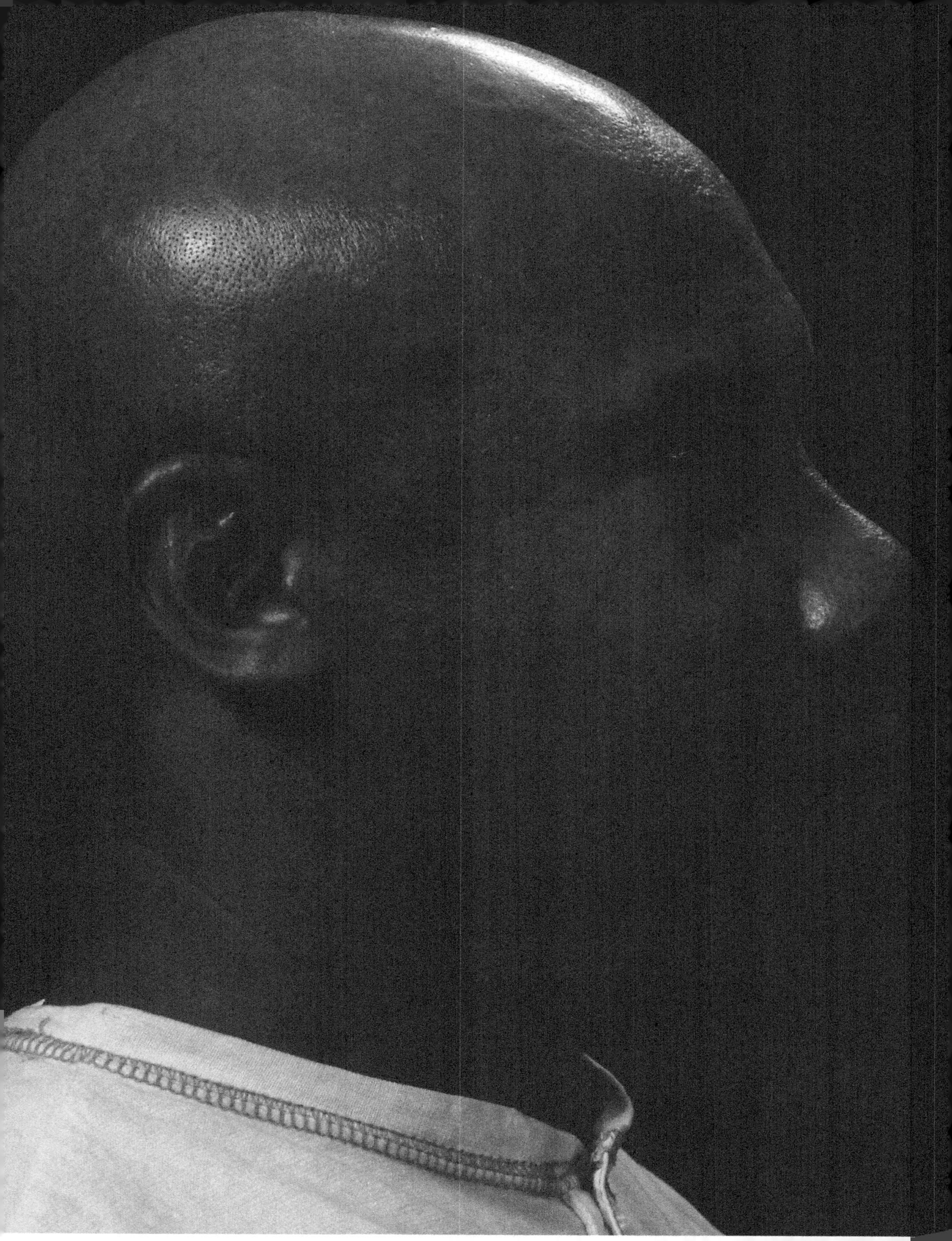

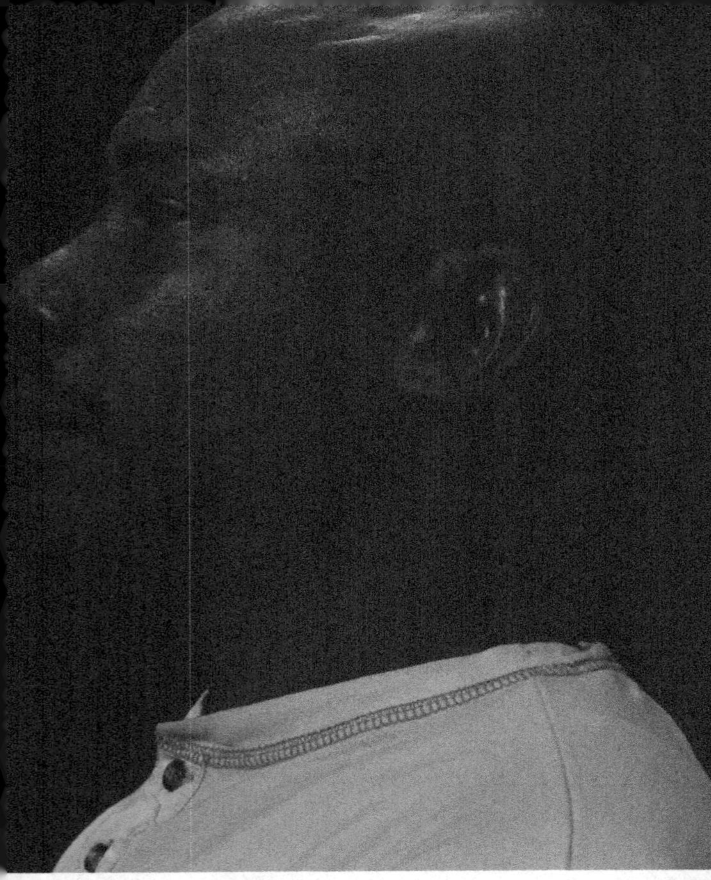

**Ethnicities claimed:**

Moorish American descended from North African.

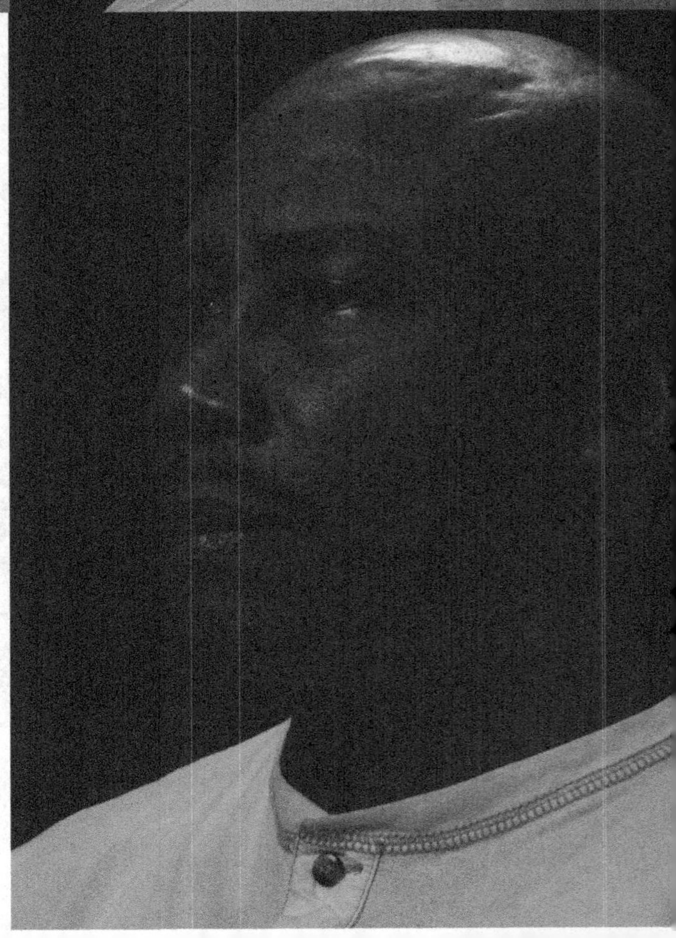

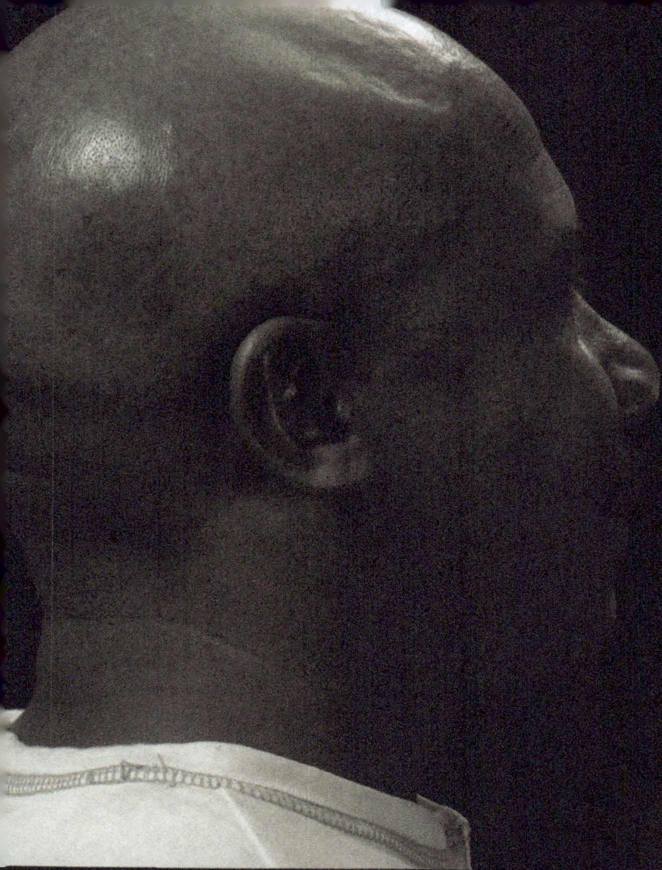

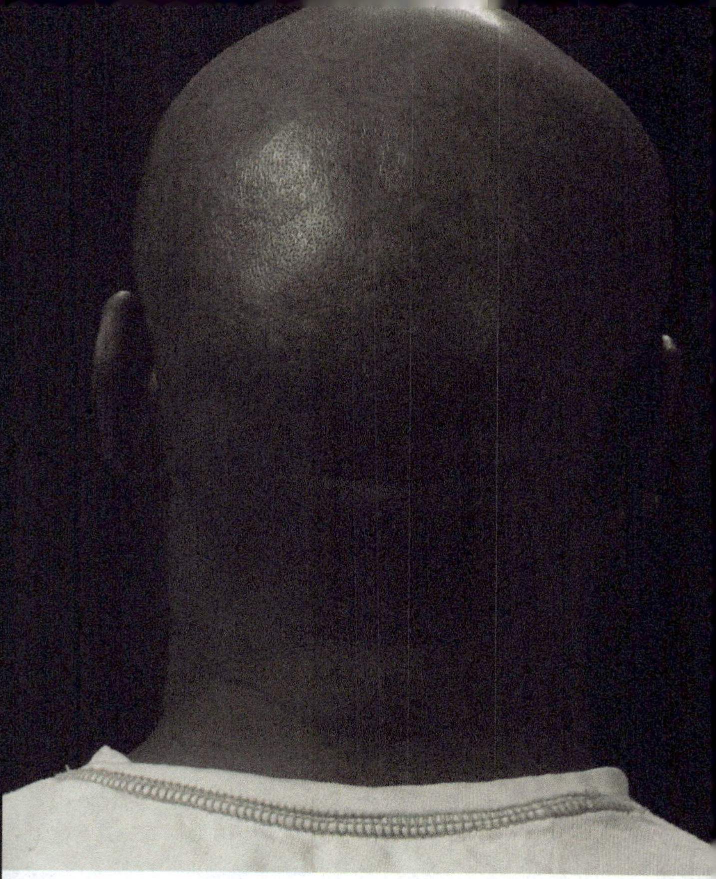

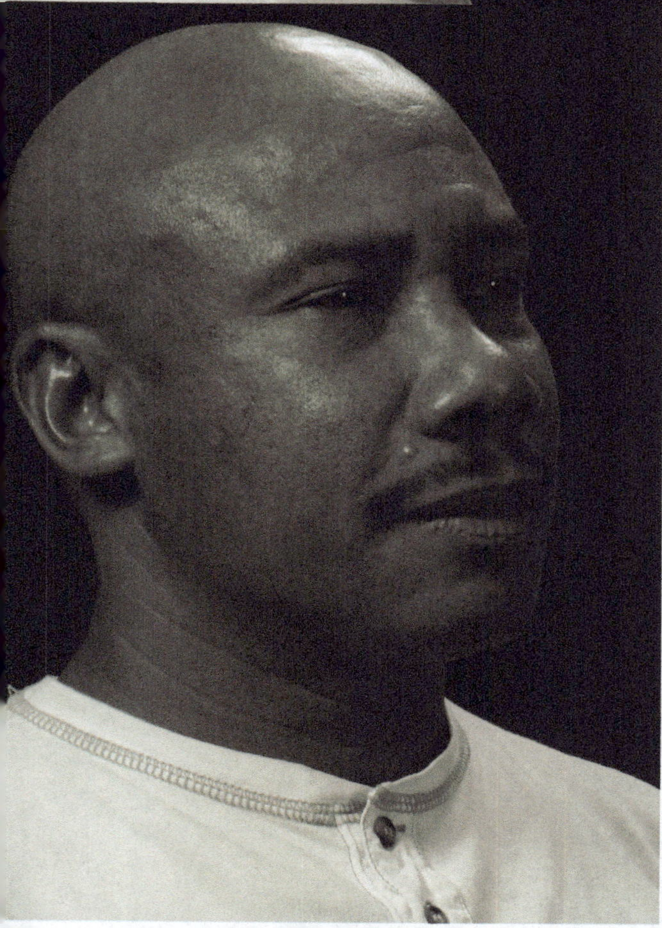

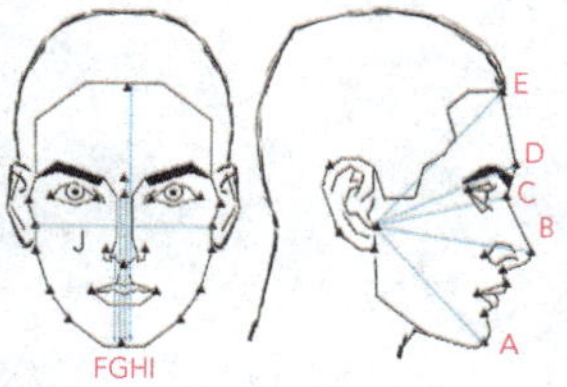


**Head measurements (in):**

A: 6 1/8
B: 6 1/8
C: 5 1/2
D: 5 1/2
E: 5 3/4
F: 3 7/8
G: 4 7/8
H: 5 1/2
I: 6 1/2
J: 5 1/2

MAP REFERENCE:

57

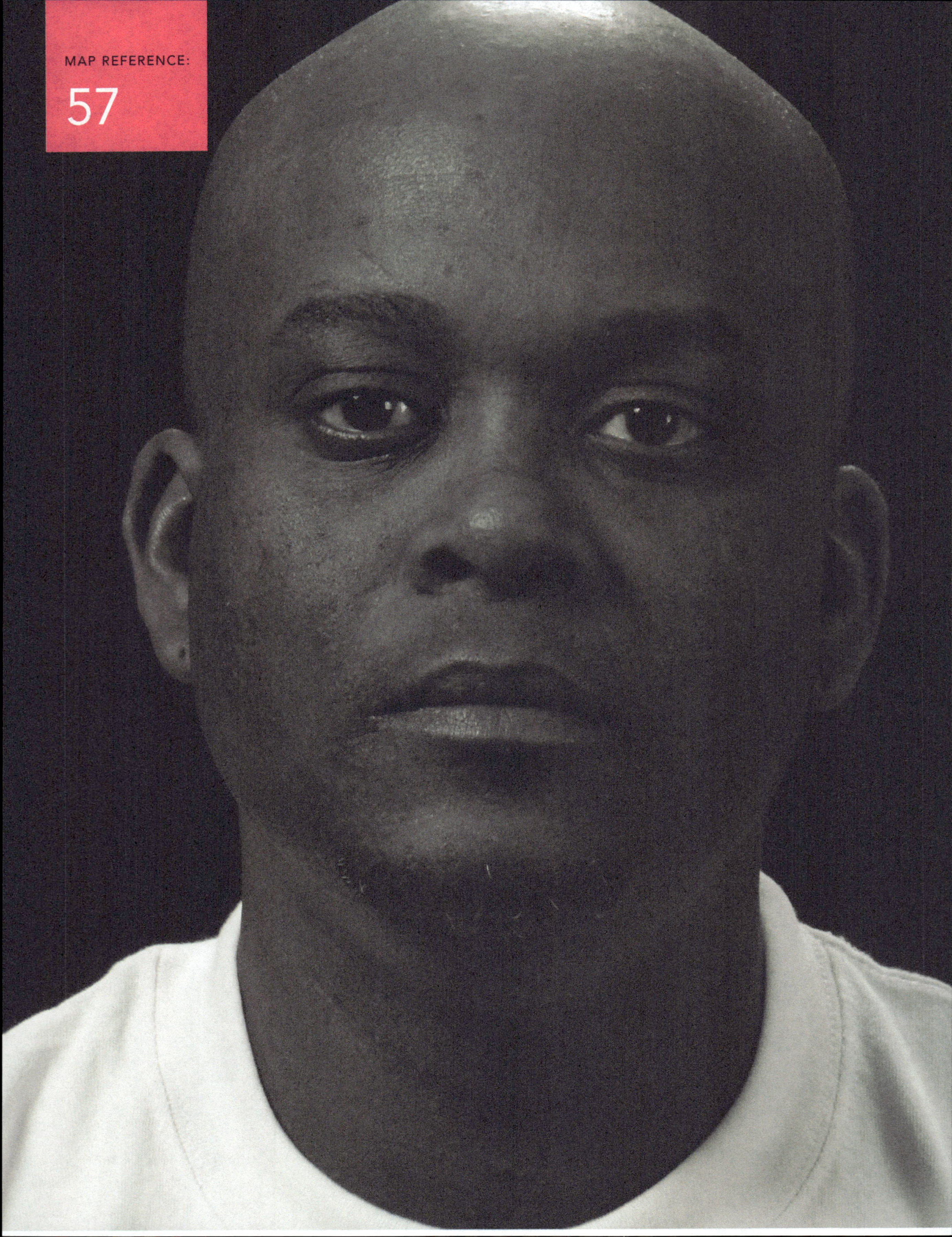

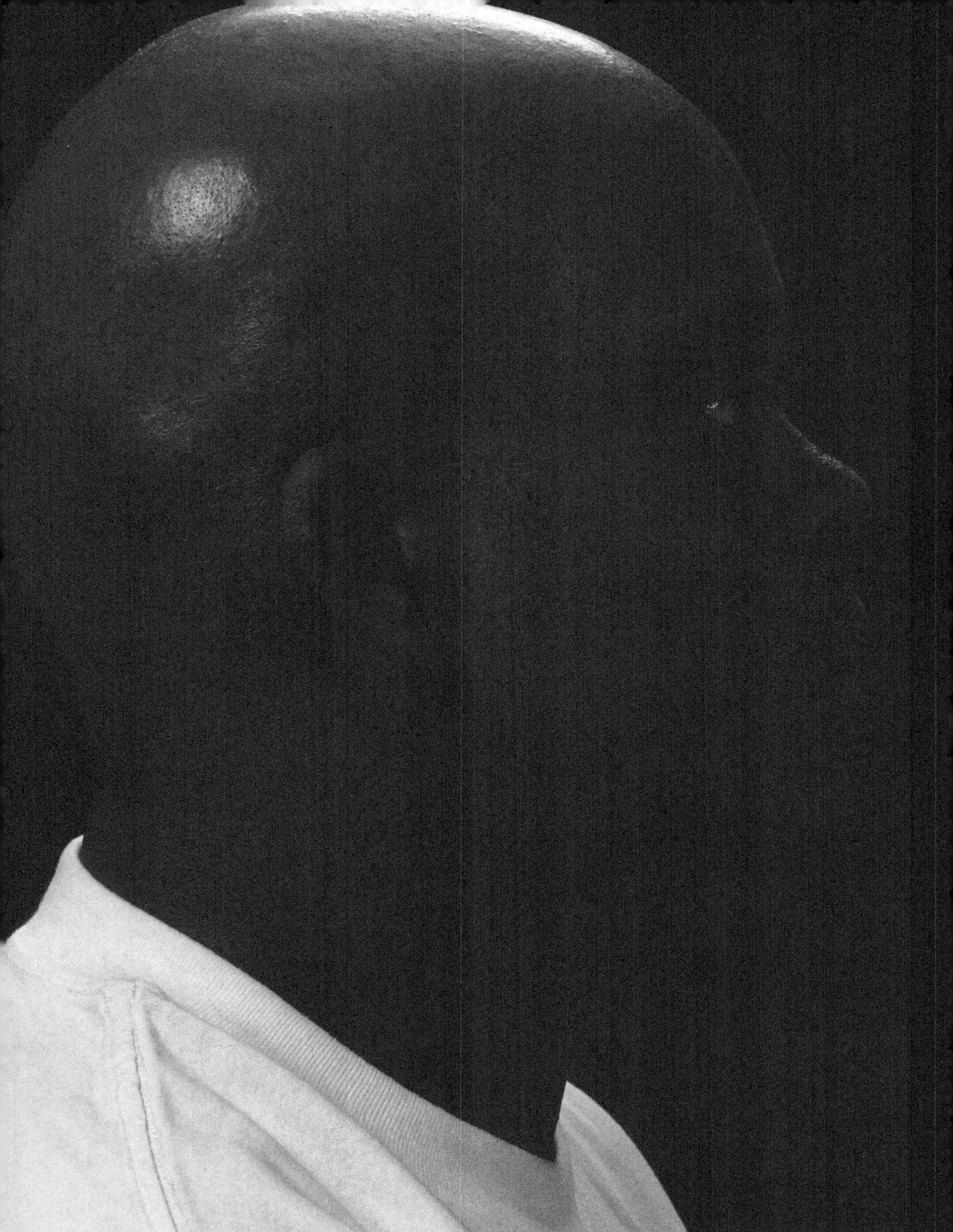

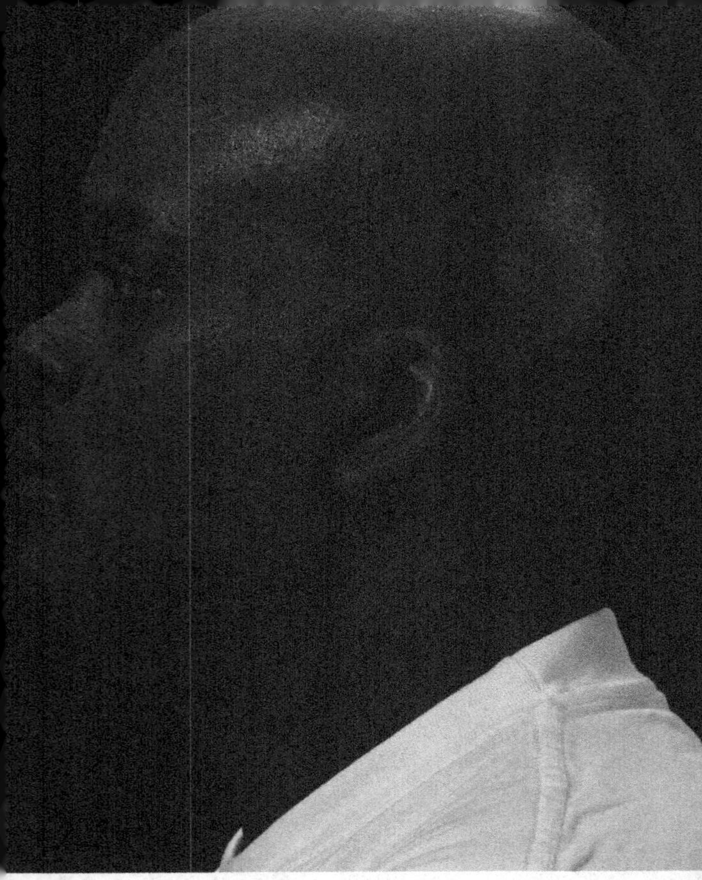

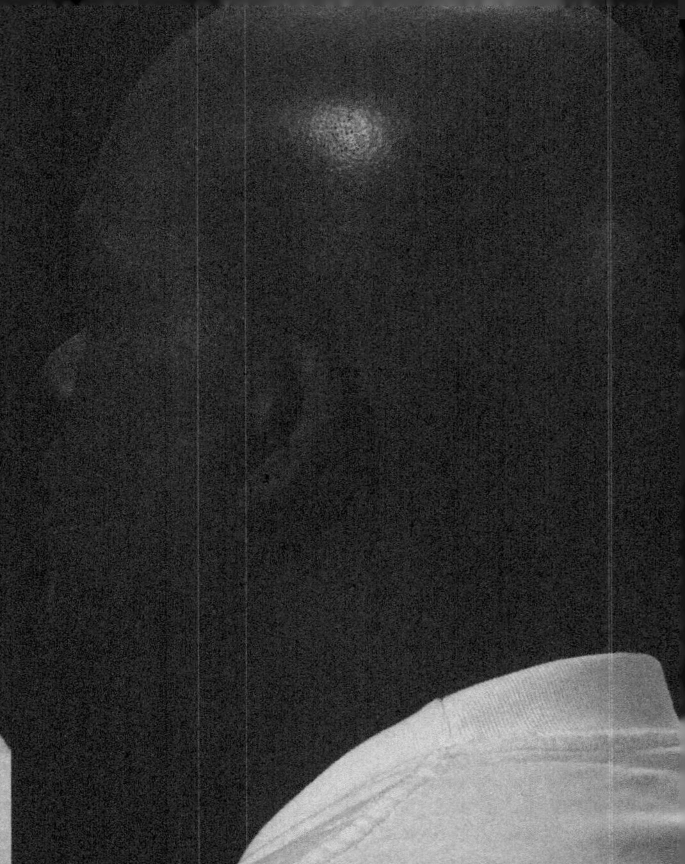

**Ethnicities claimed:**

Native American—Iroquois, Ireland, African American—east coast

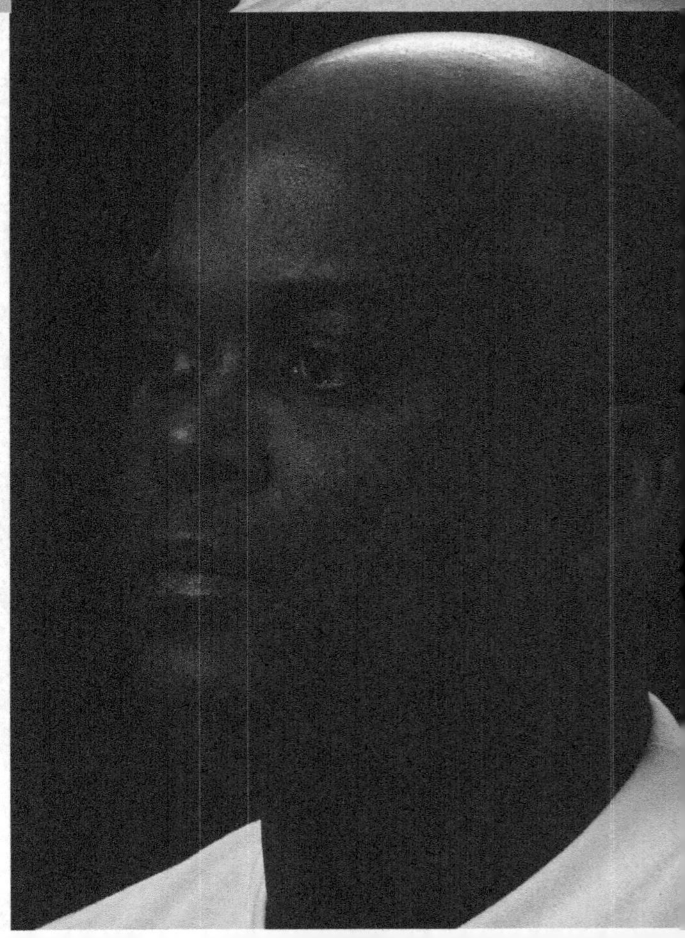

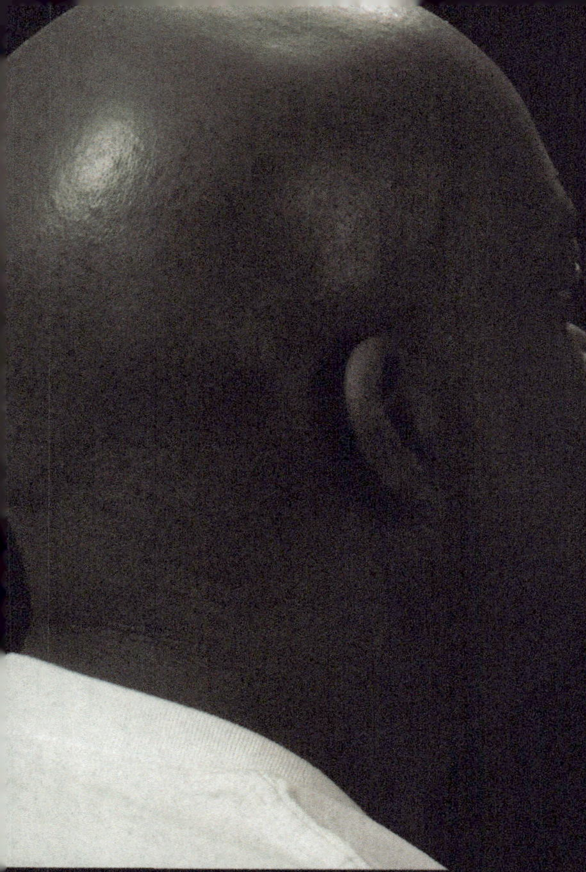

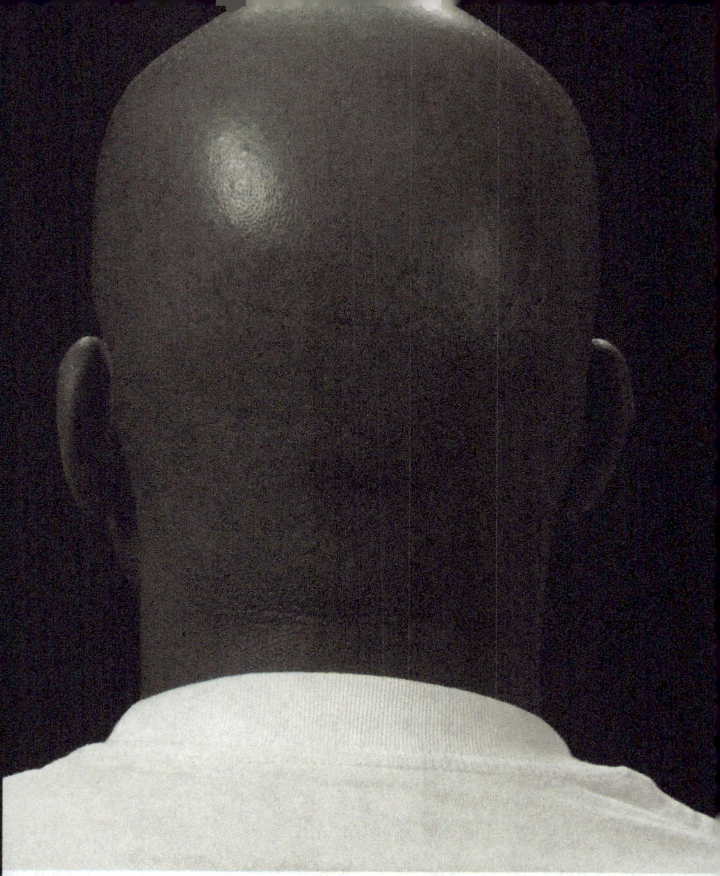

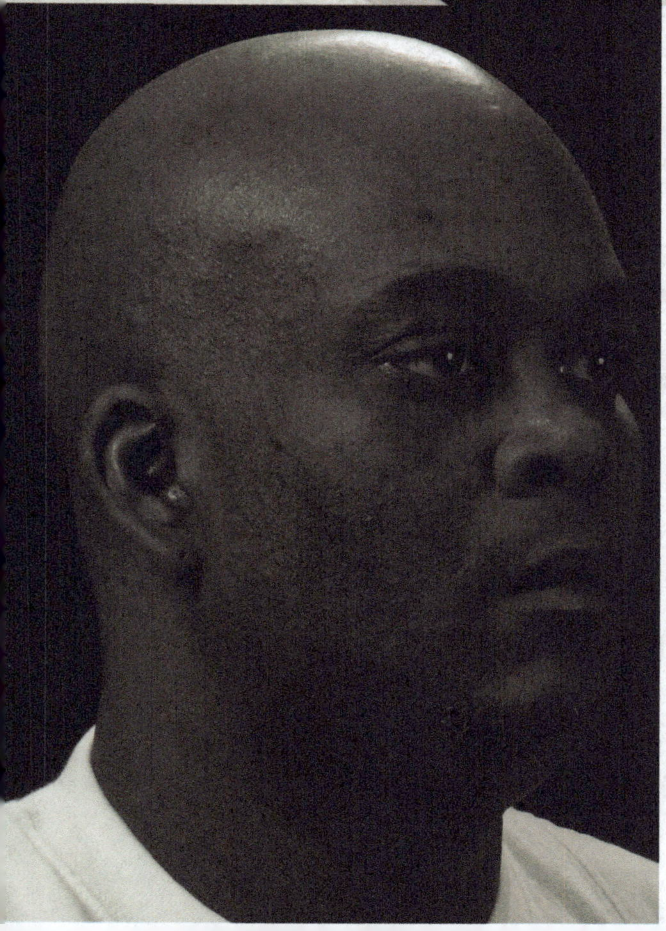

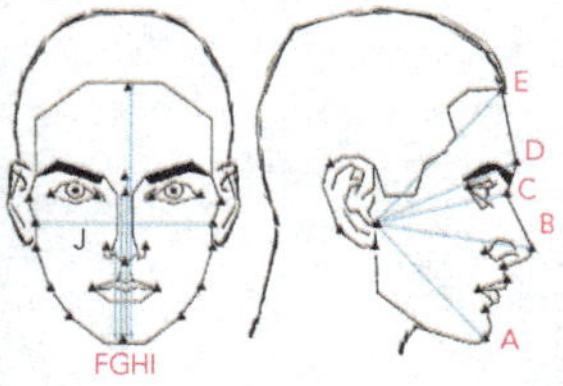


**Head measurements (in):**

A: 5 1/2
B: 5 3/8
C: 4 3/4
D: 5 1/4
E: 5 7/8
F: 3 1/2
G: 4 1/2
H: 5 1/2
I: 7 1/8
J: 5 5/8

MAP REFERENCE:

61

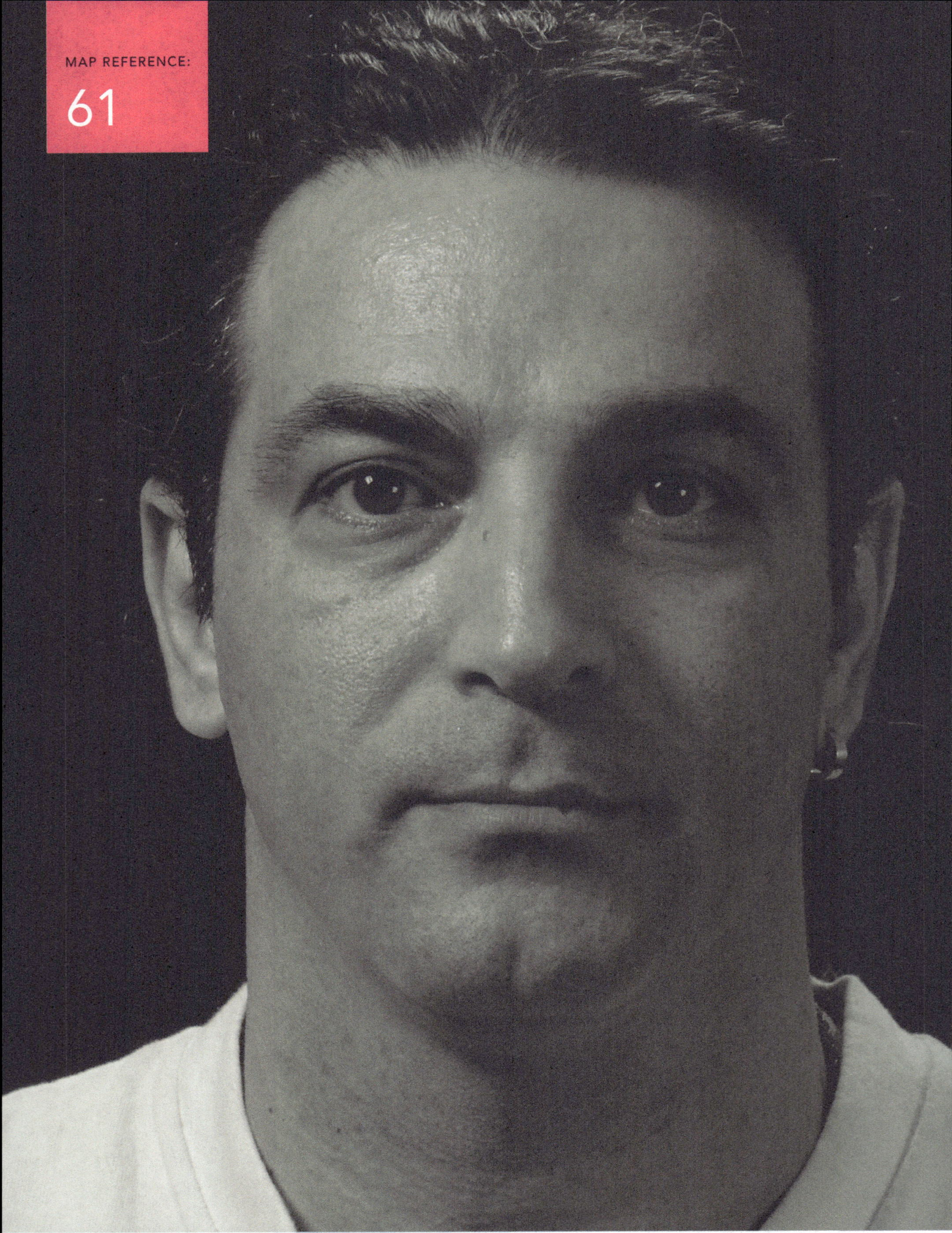

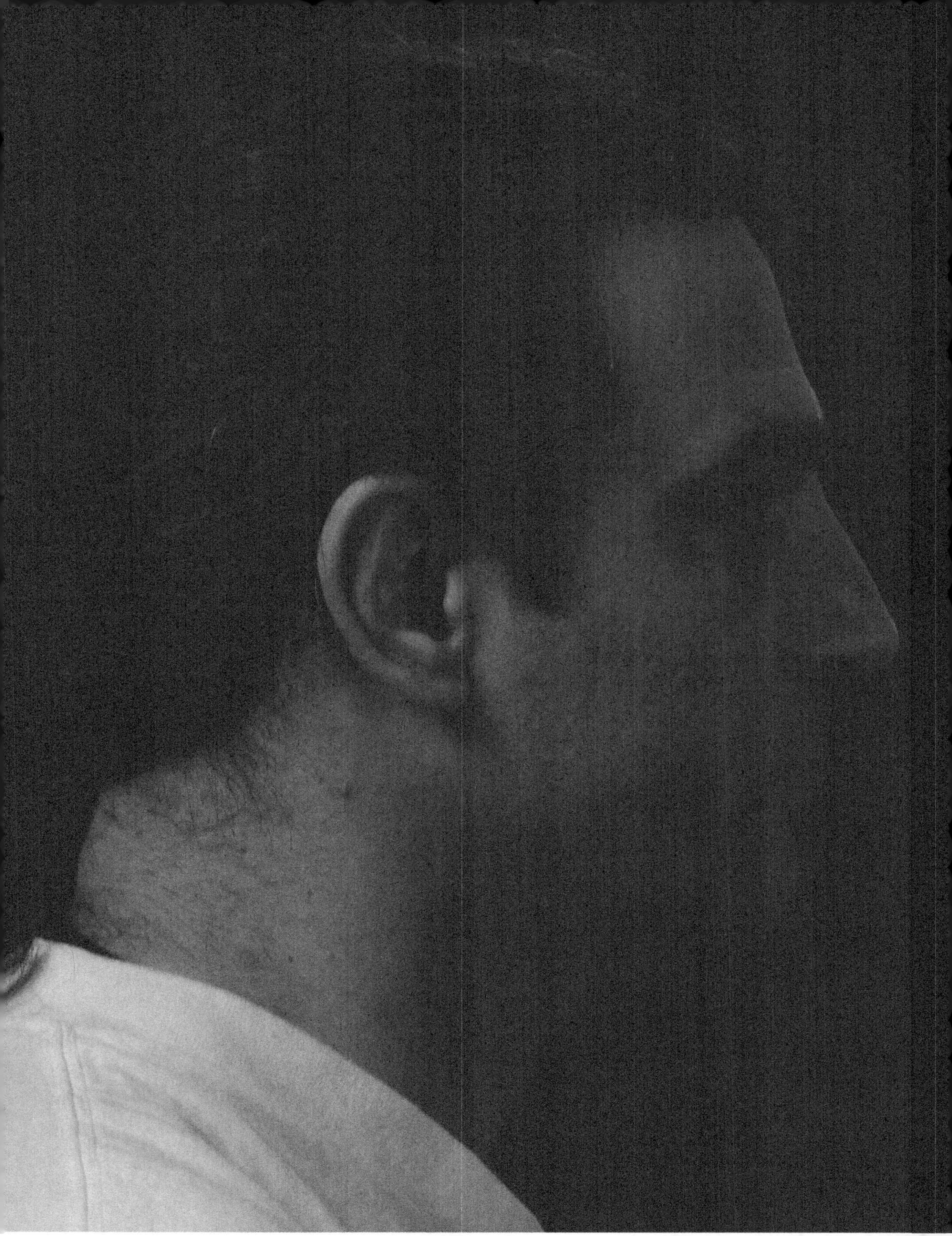

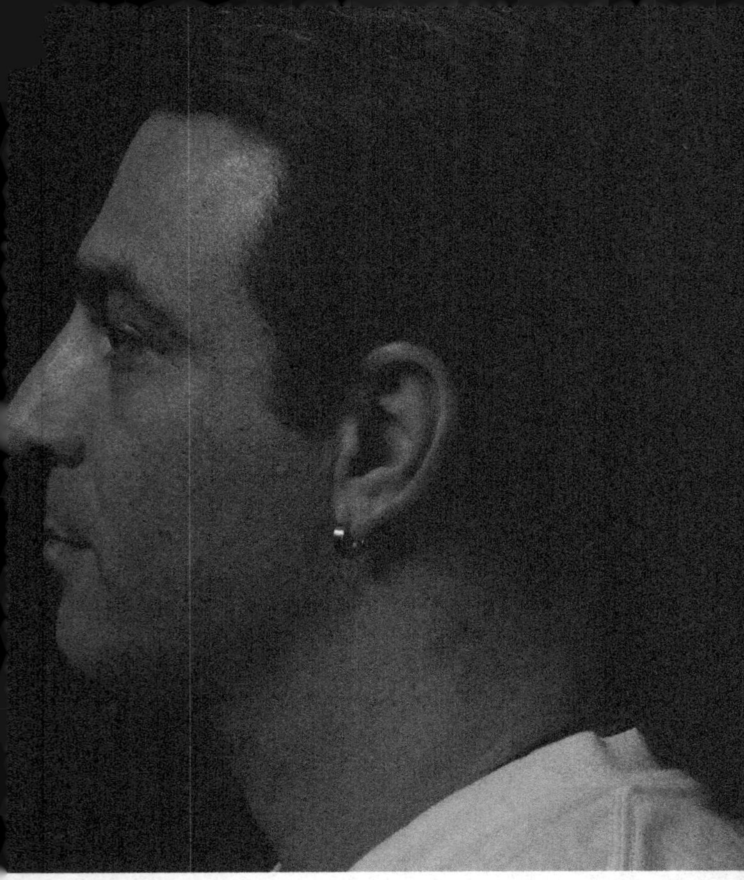

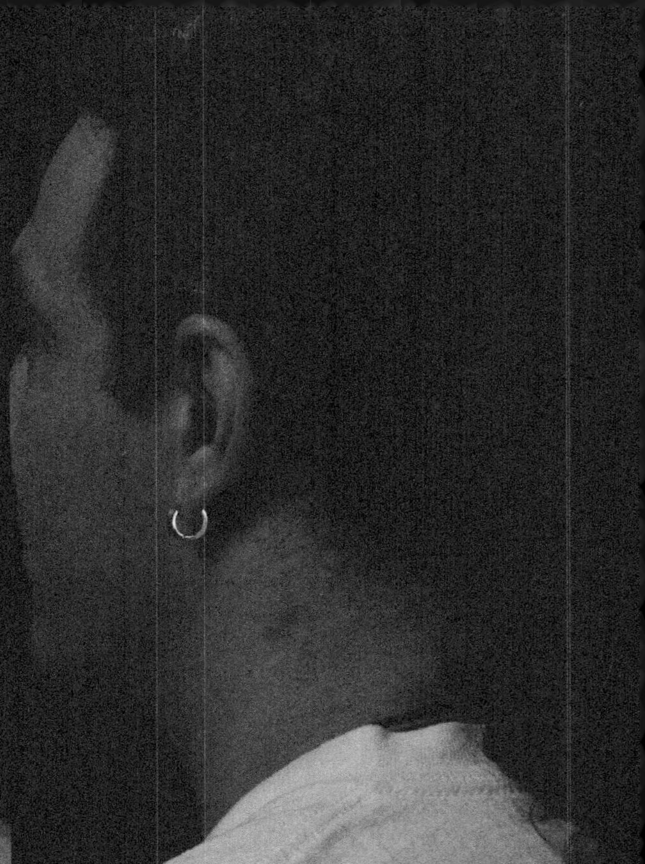

**Ethnicities claimed:**

Armenia, Iran, Greece.

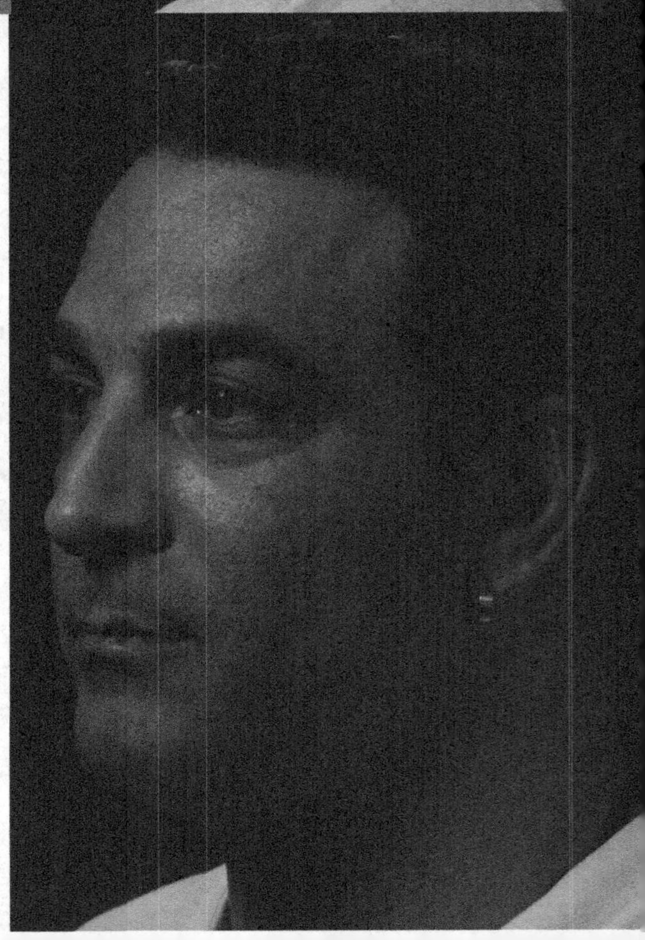

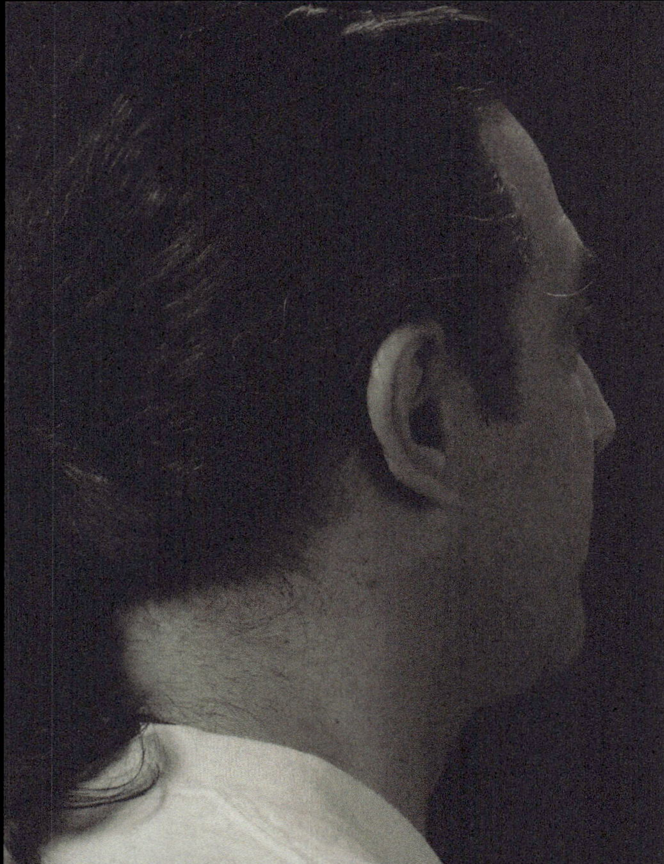

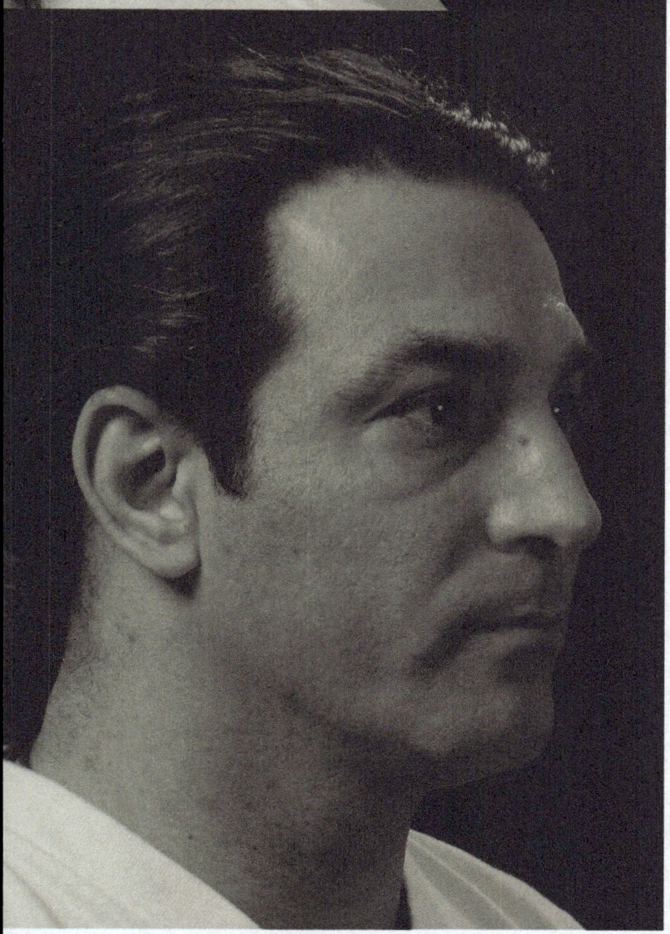

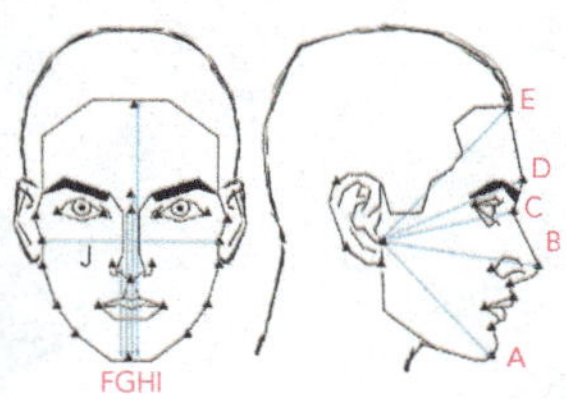


**Head measurements (in):**

A: 5 1/2 in
B: 5 1/2 in
C: 4 3/4 in
D: 5 1/8 in
E: 6 in
F: 3 7/8 in
G: 4 7/8 in
H: 5 3/8 in
I: 7 7/8 in
J: 5 1/8 in

MAP REFERENCE:

62

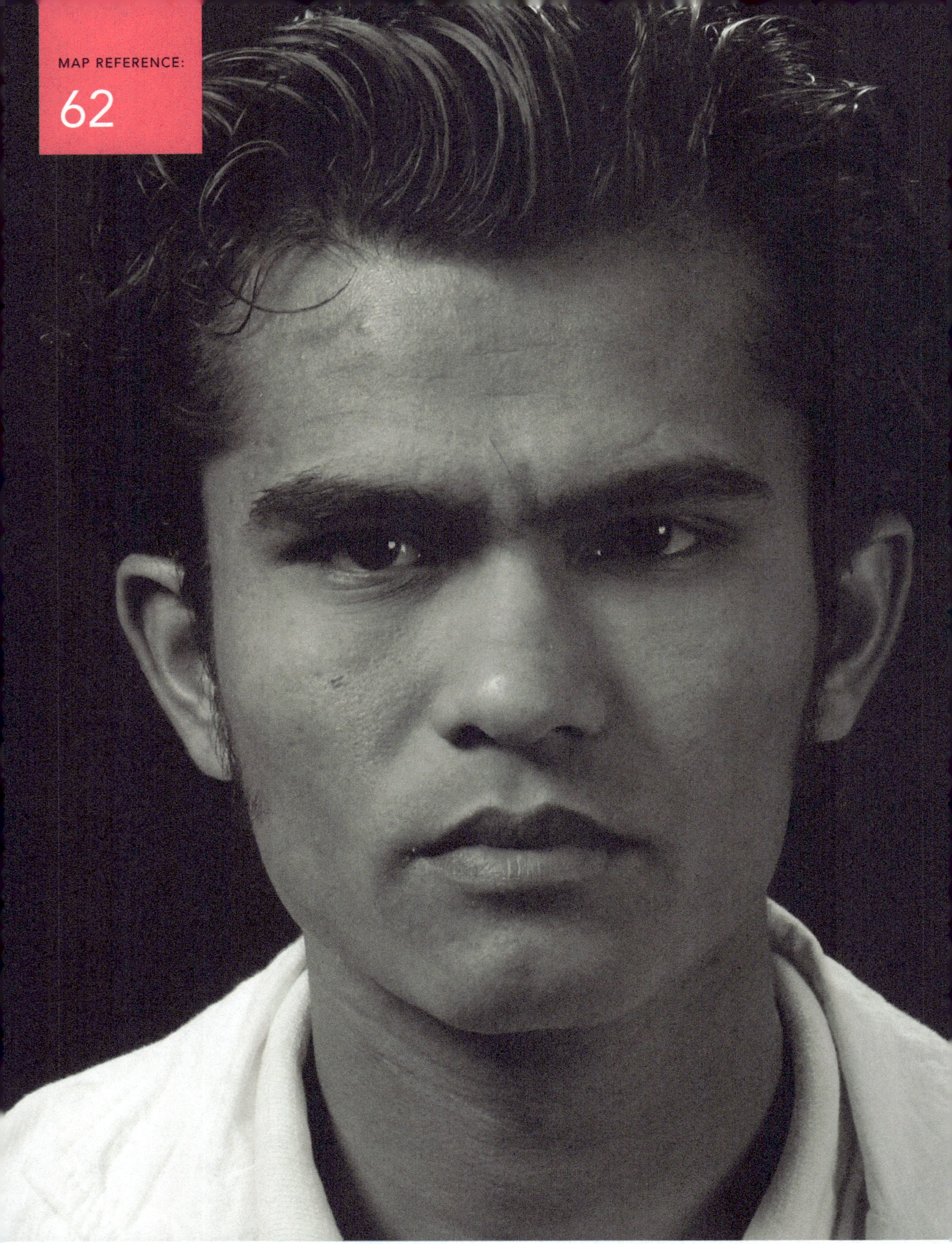

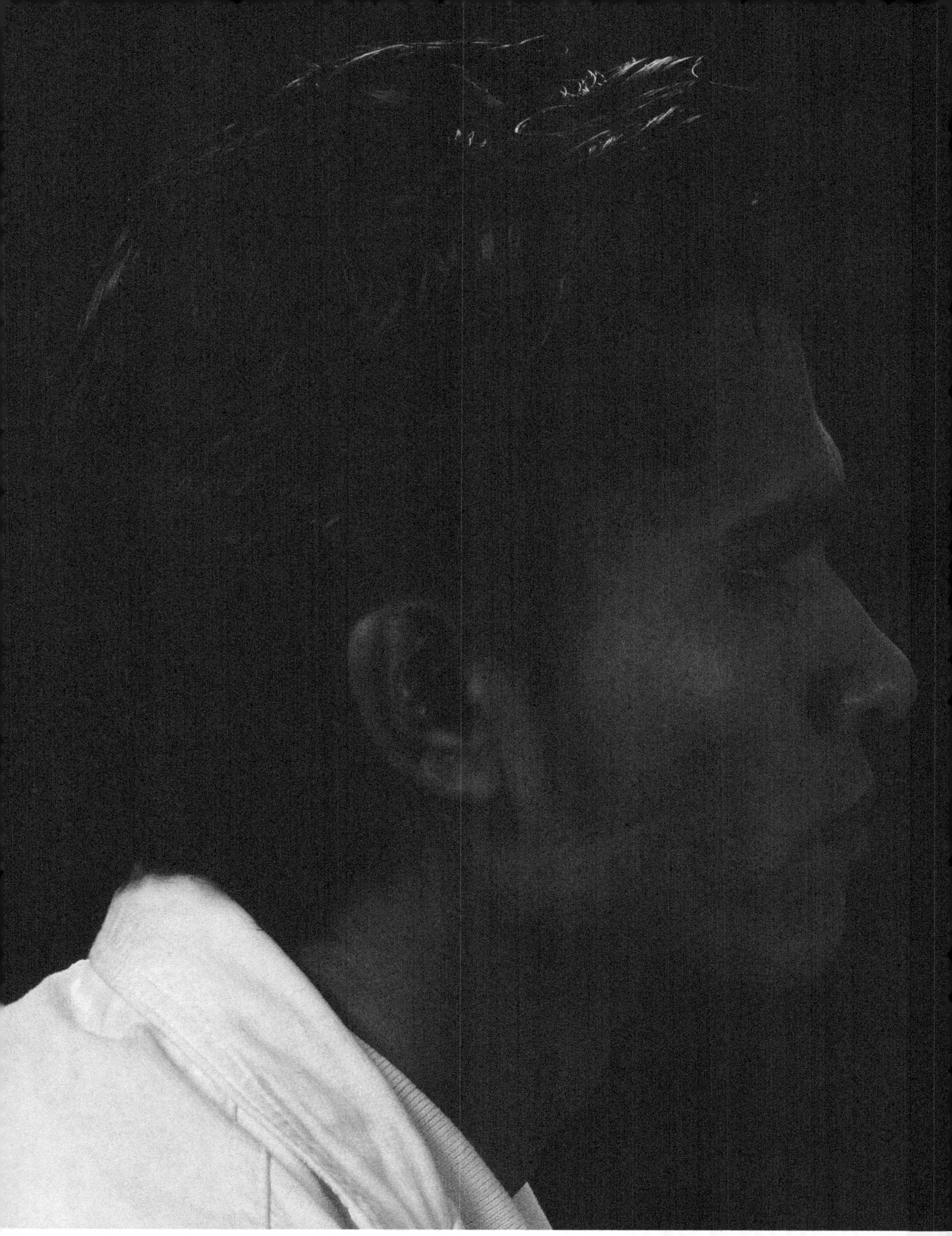

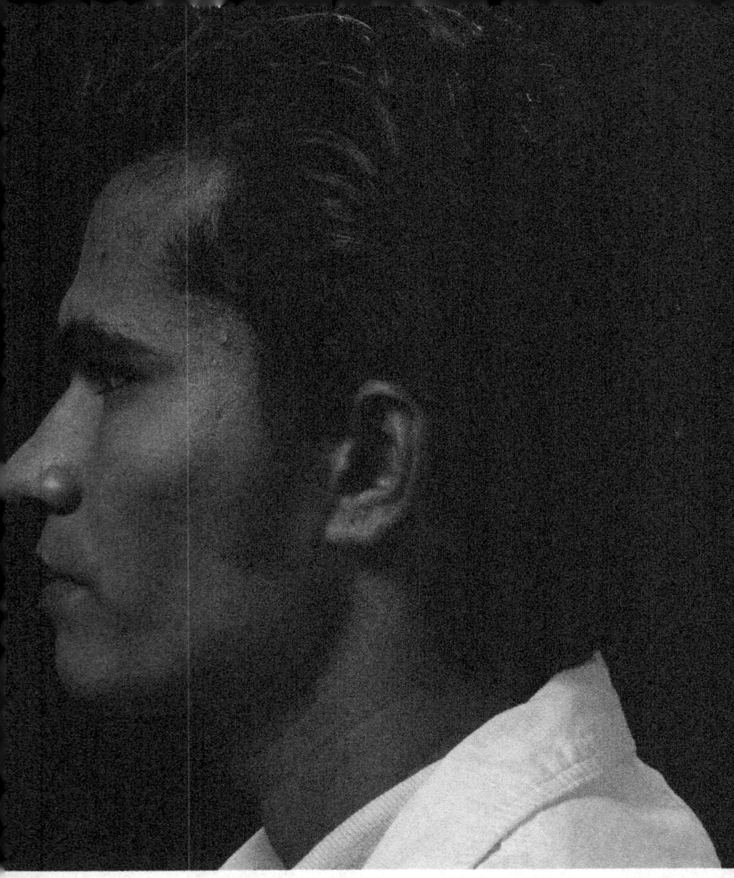

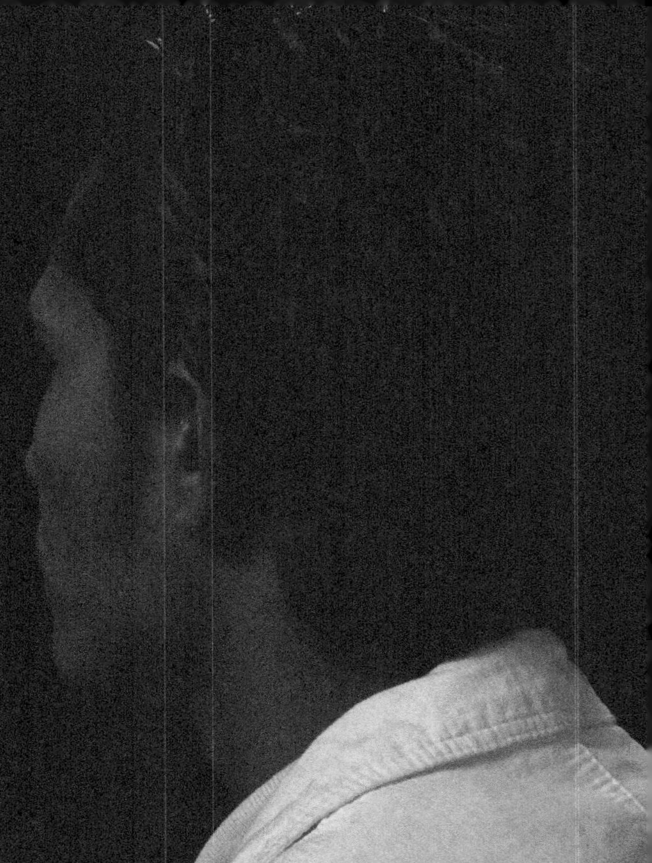

**Ethnicities claimed:**

Nepal.

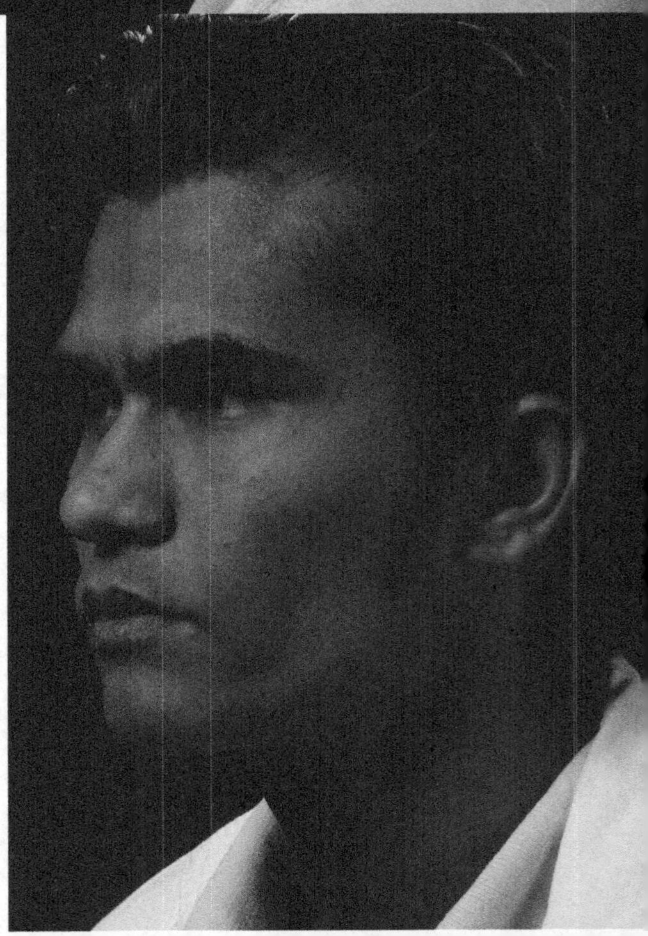

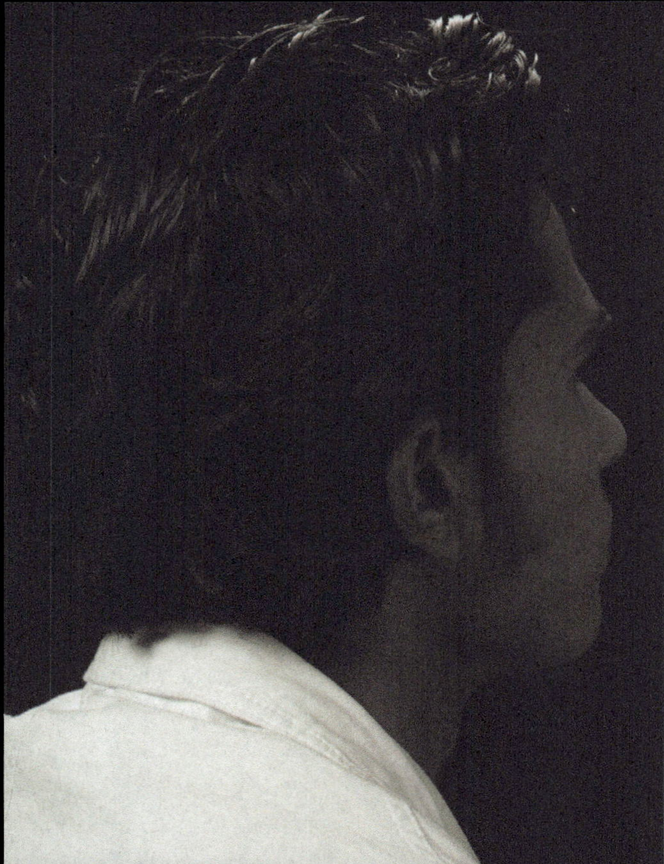

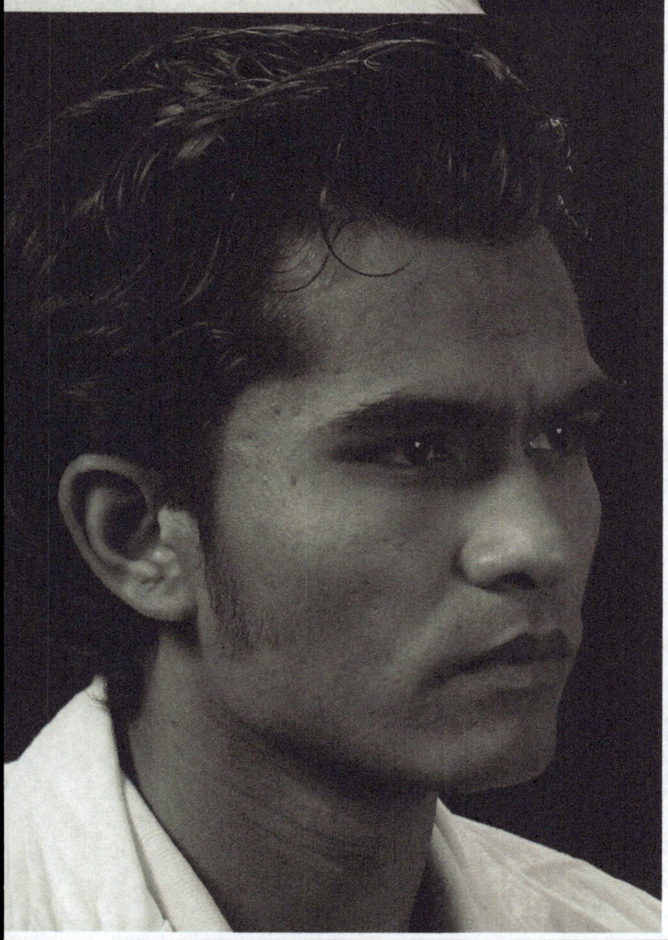

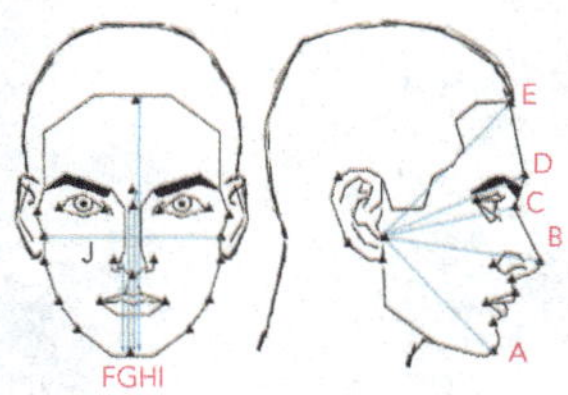


**Head measurements (in):**

A: 5 1/8
B: 5 1/8
C: 4 1/2
D: 4 5/8
E: 6
F: 3 3/8
G: 4 1/4
H: 4 7/8
I: 6 5/8
J: 5 1/2

MAP REFERENCE:

66

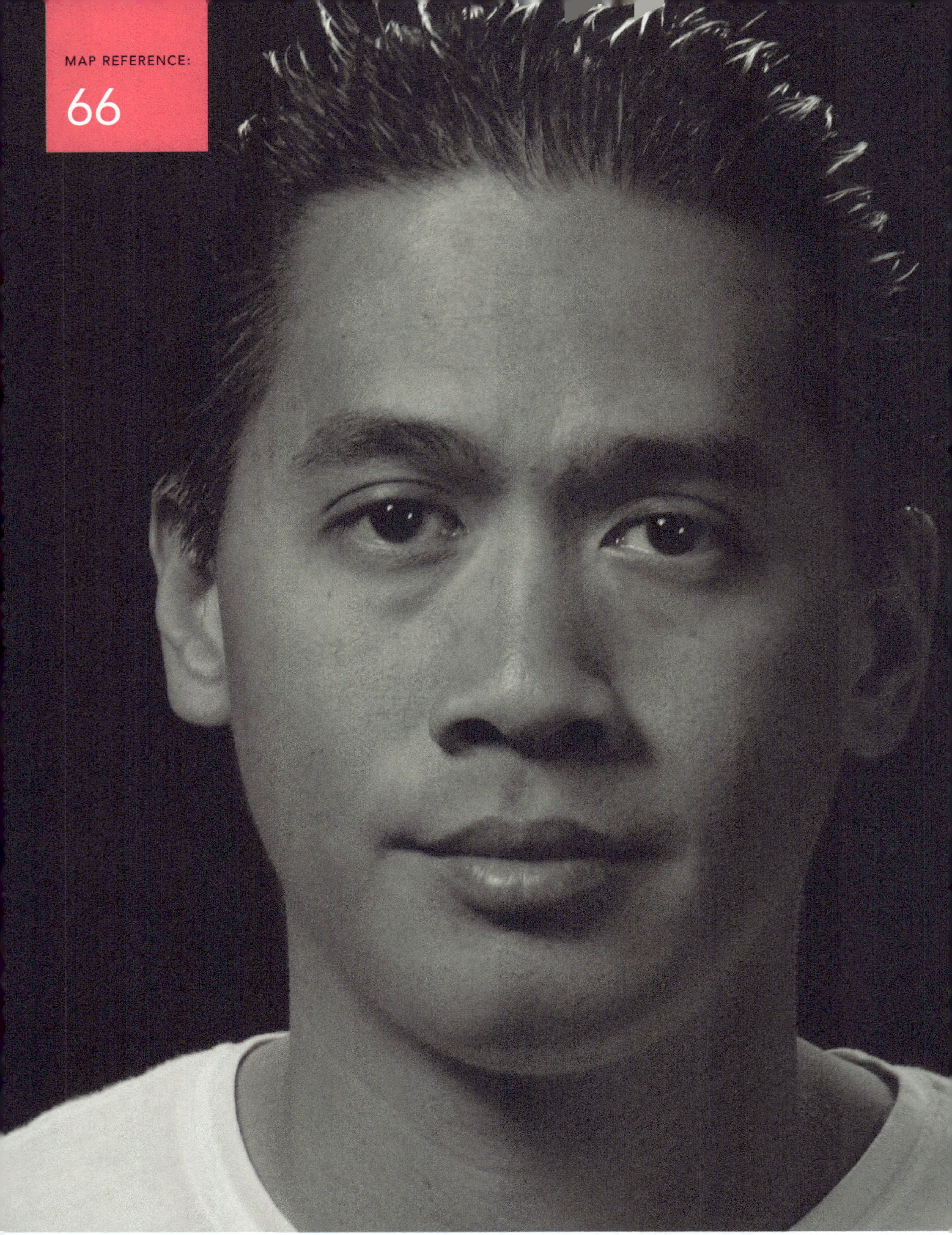

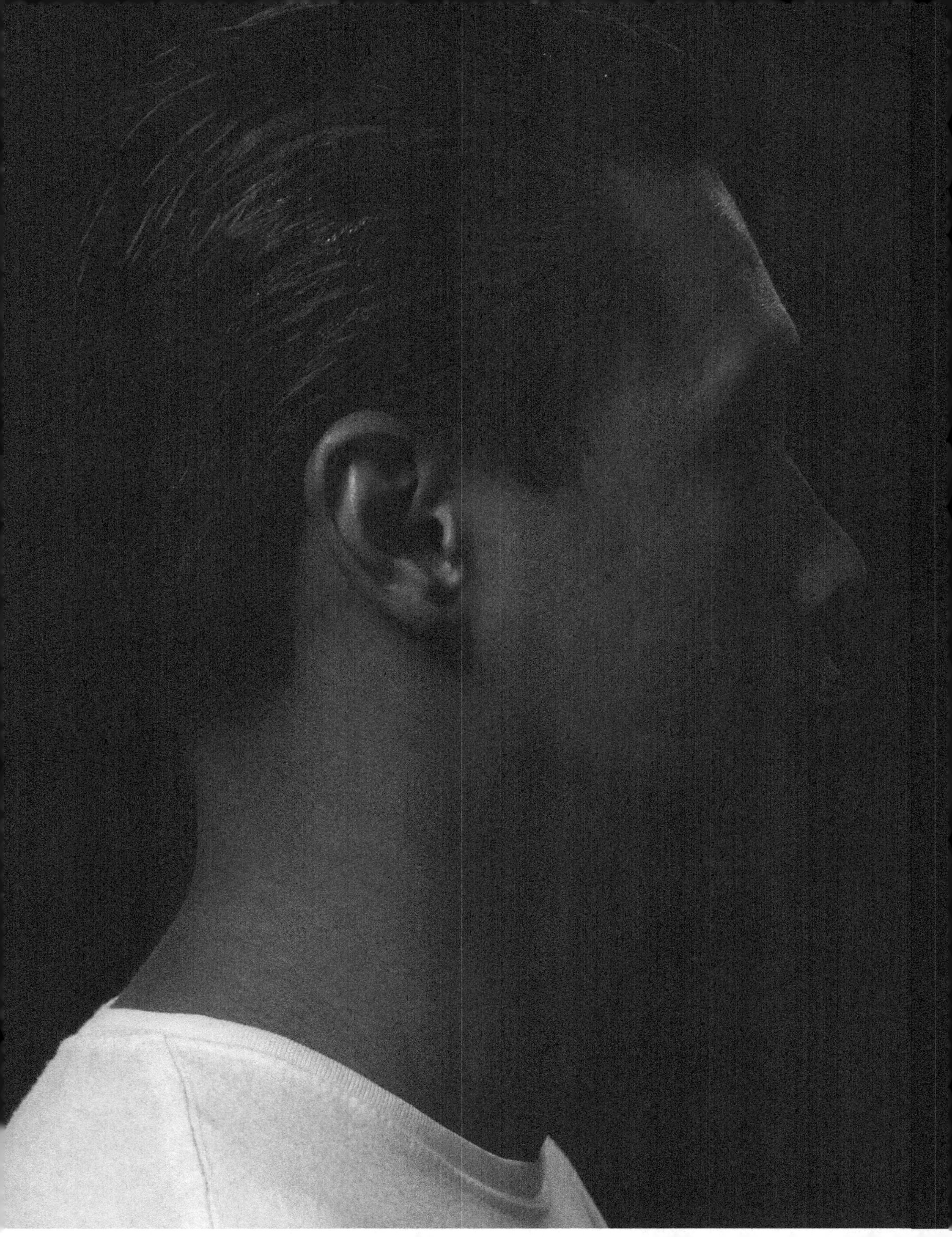

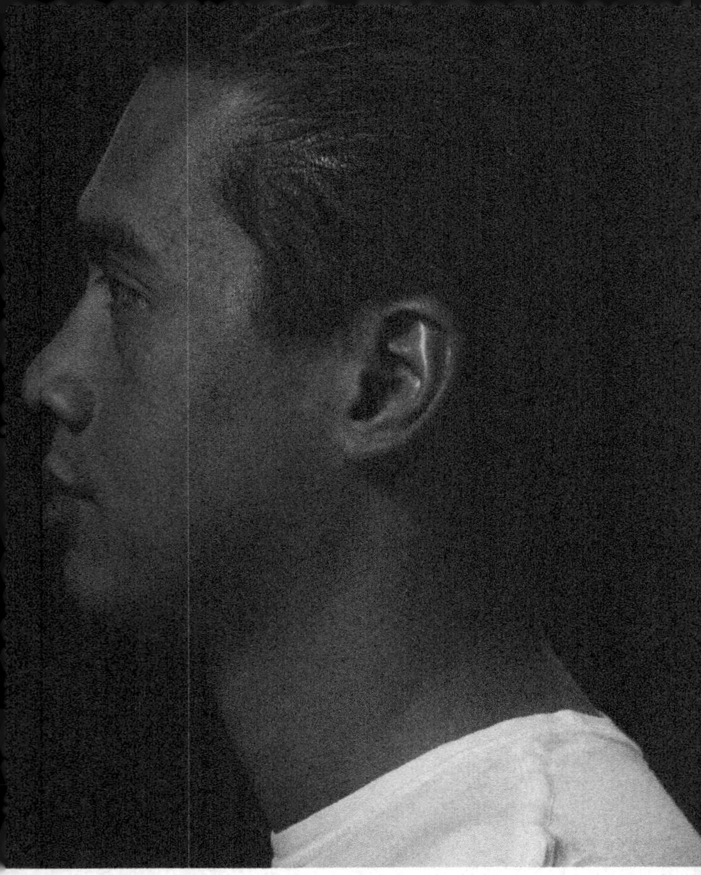

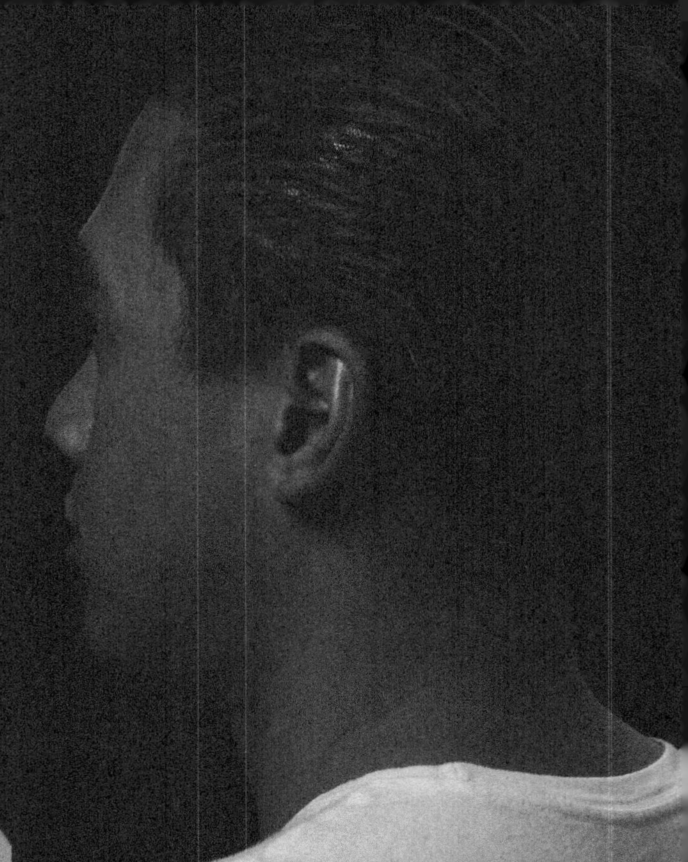

**Ethnicities claimed:**

Filipino, Chinese.

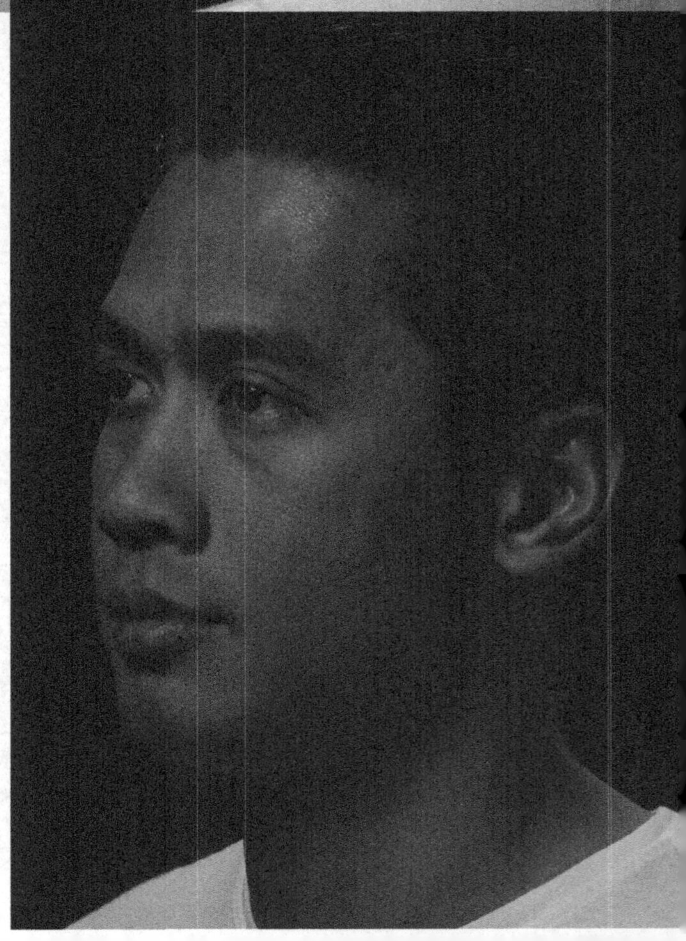

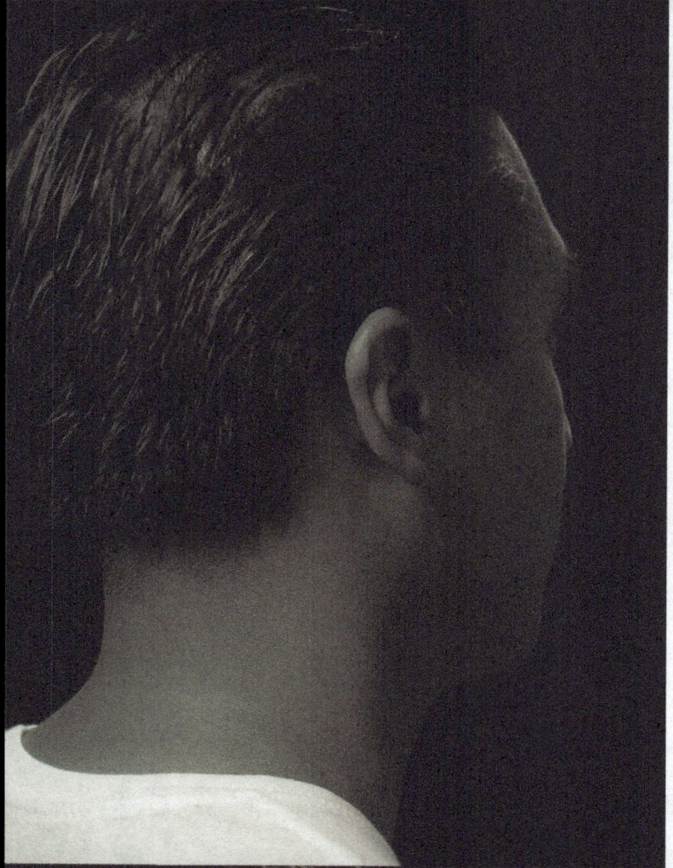

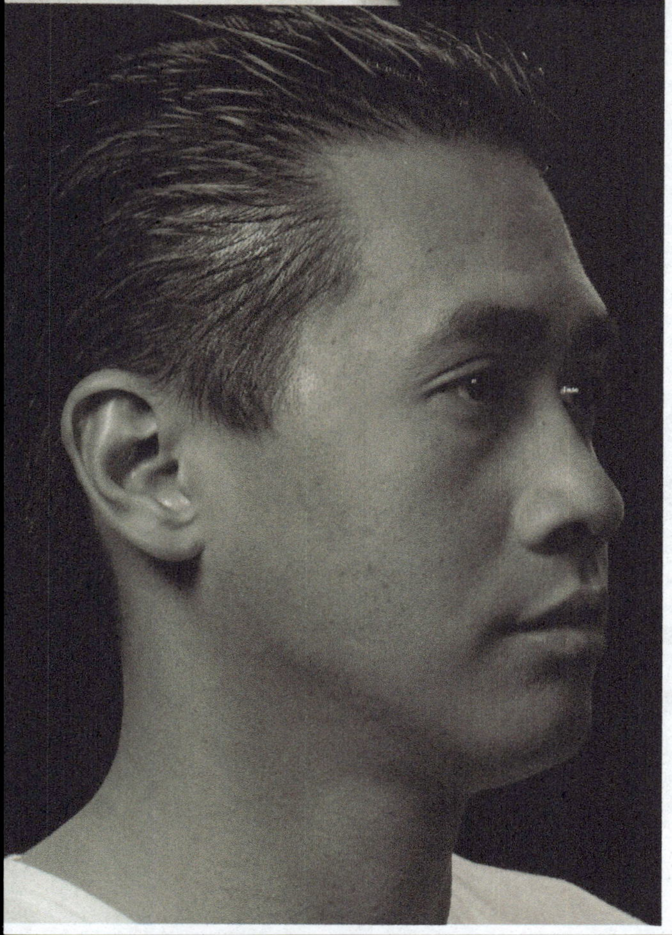

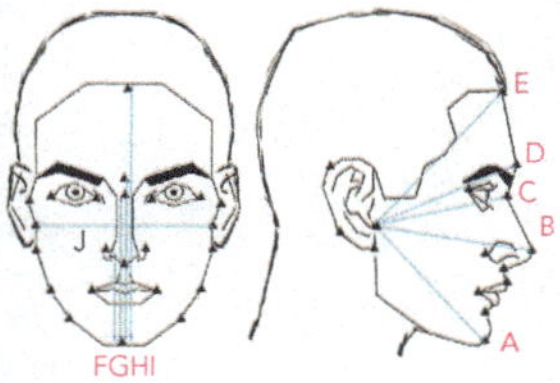


**Head measurements (in):**

A: 5 1/2
B: 5 1/2
C: 5 1/8
D: 5 3/8
E: 6 1/2
F: 3 1/4
G: 4 3/4
H: 5 1/8
I: 7 5/8
J: 6 1/8

MAP REFERENCE:

66

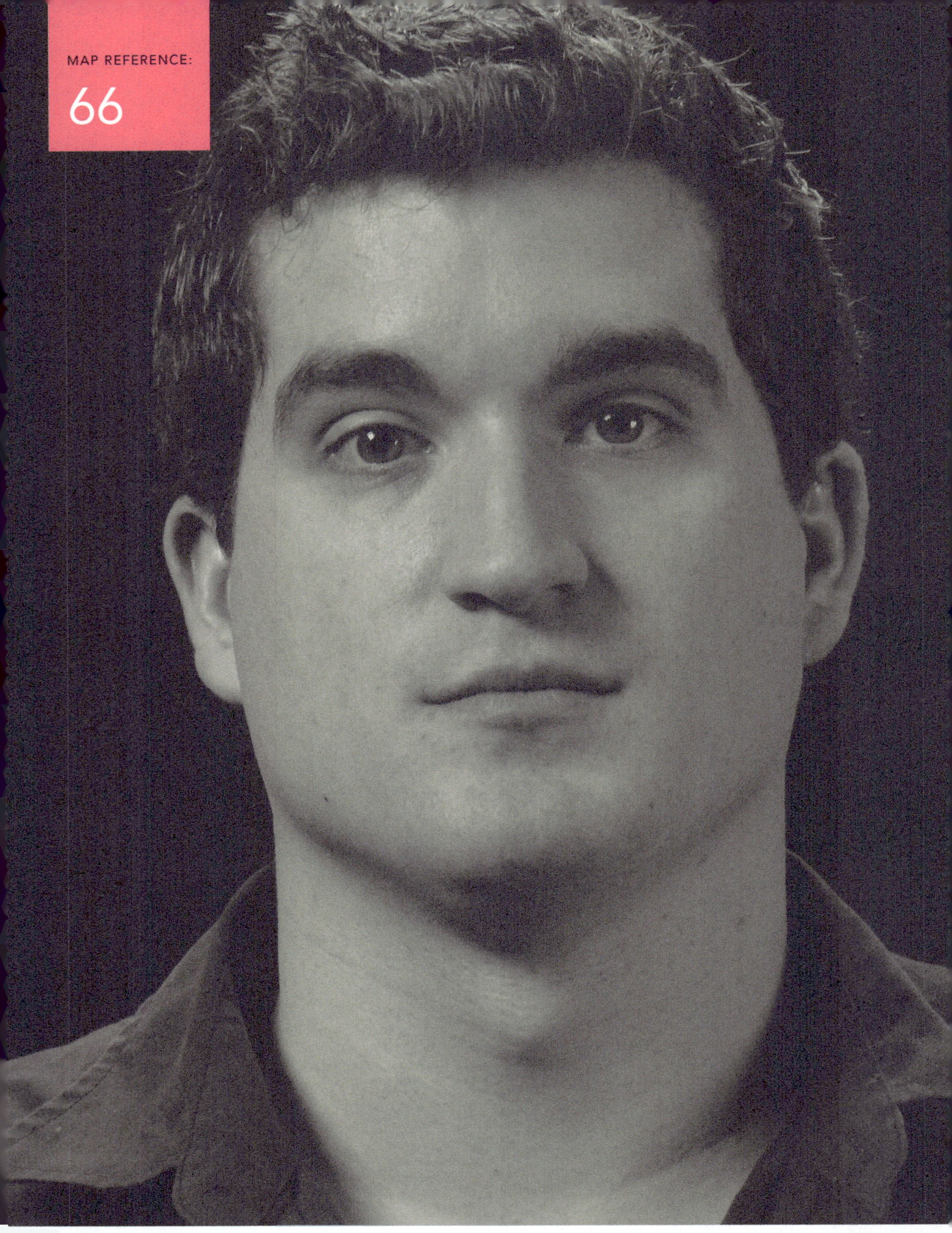

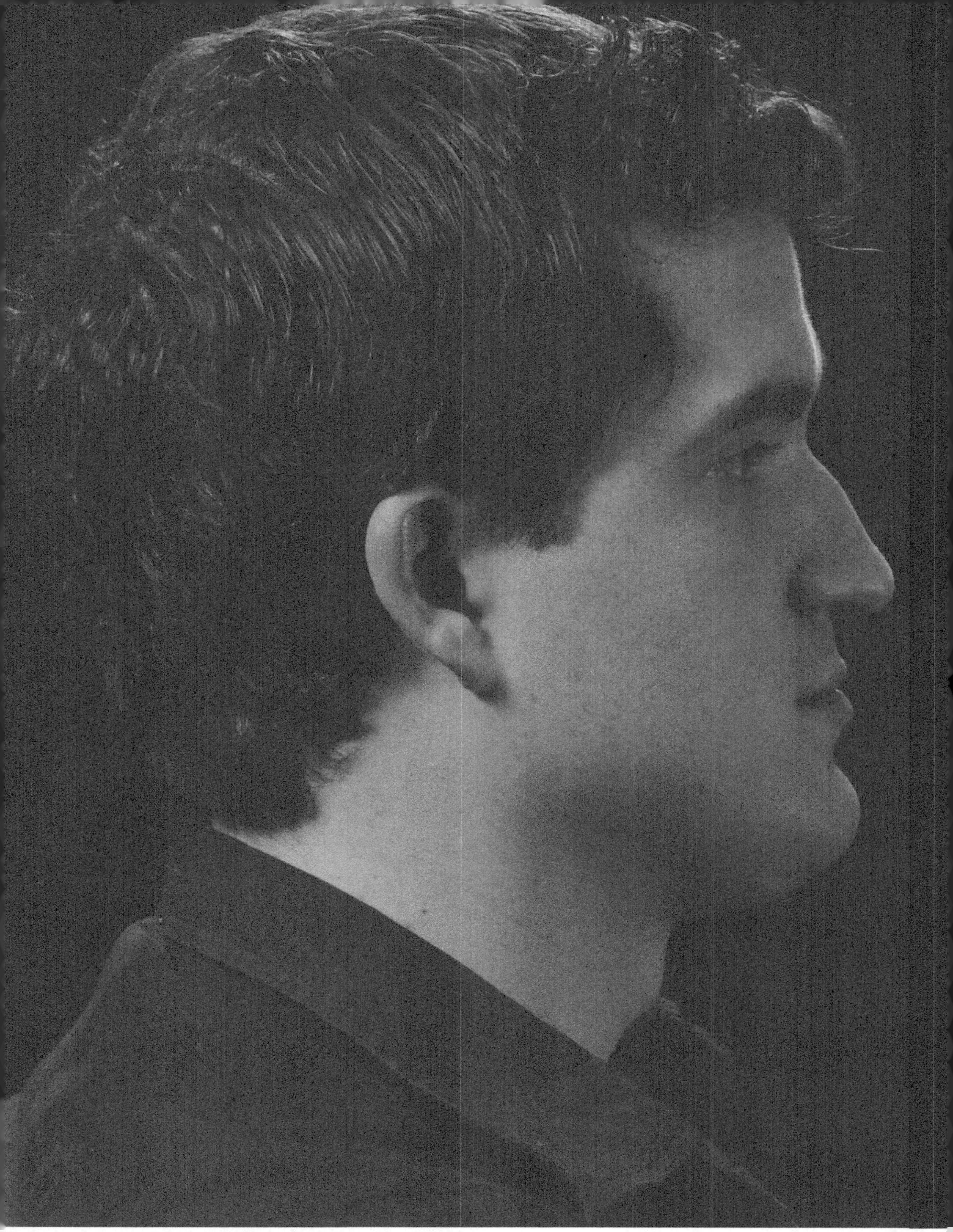

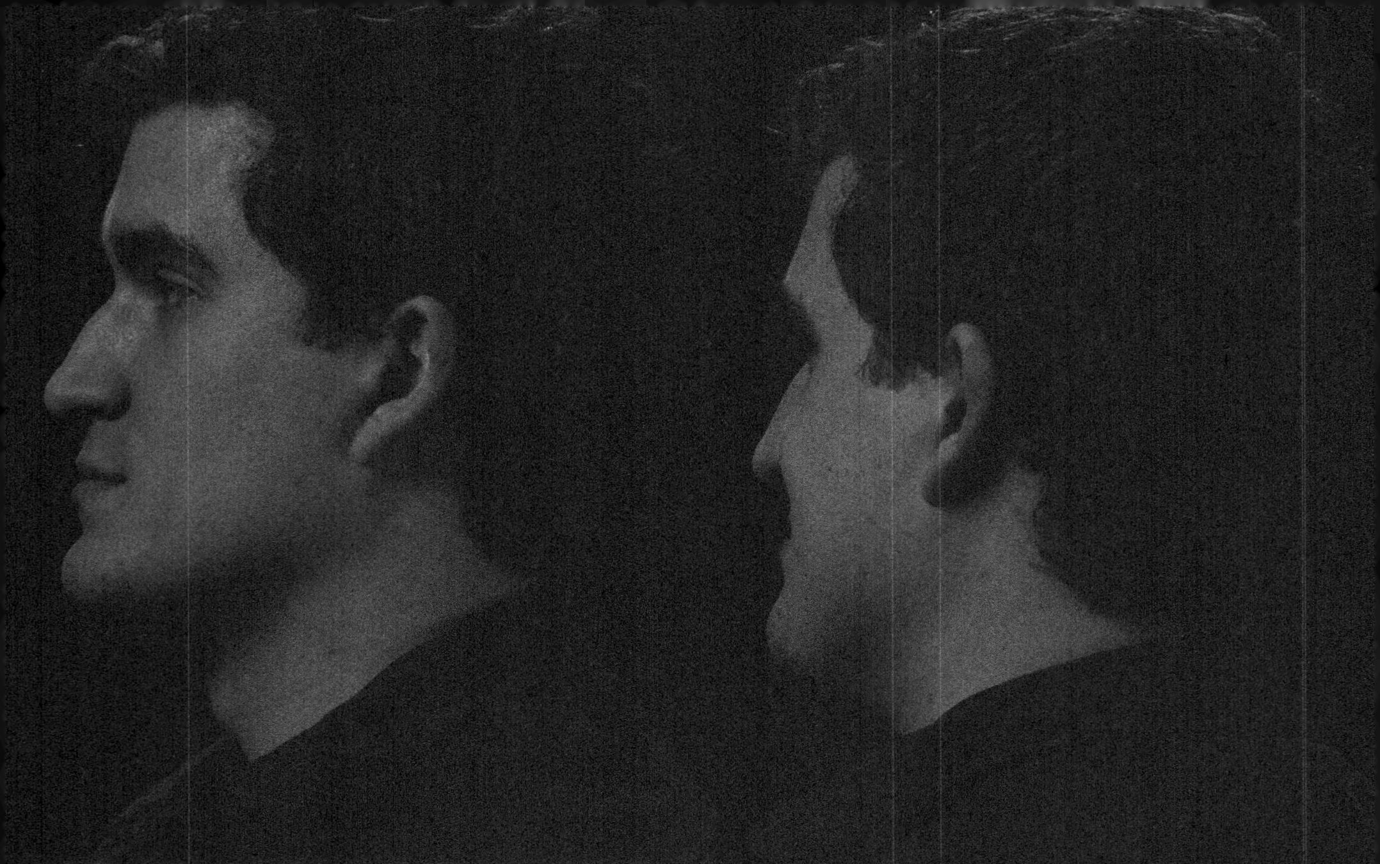

**Ethnicities claimed:**

Germany, Poland, Britain, Russia.

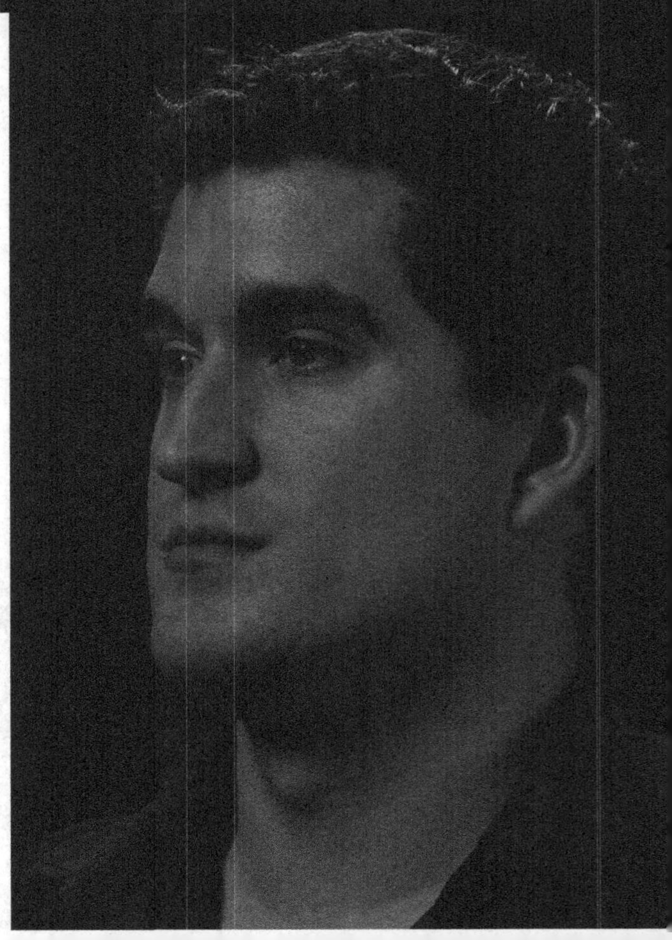

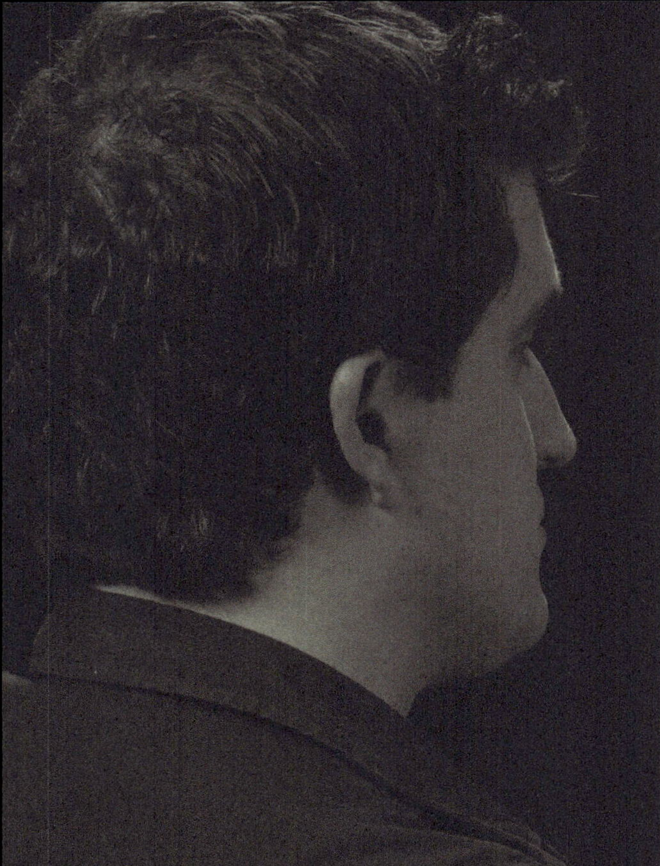

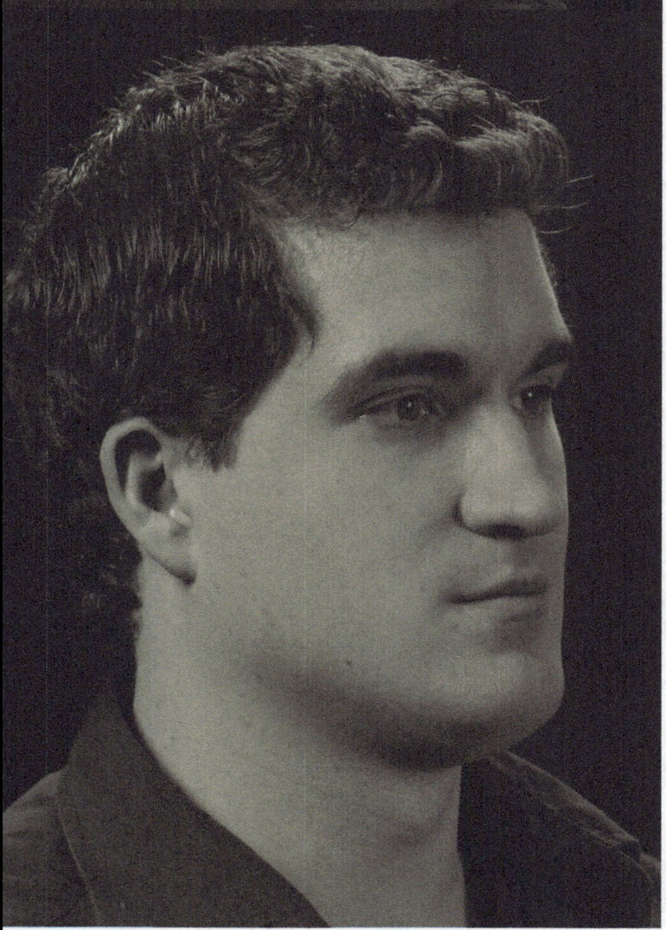

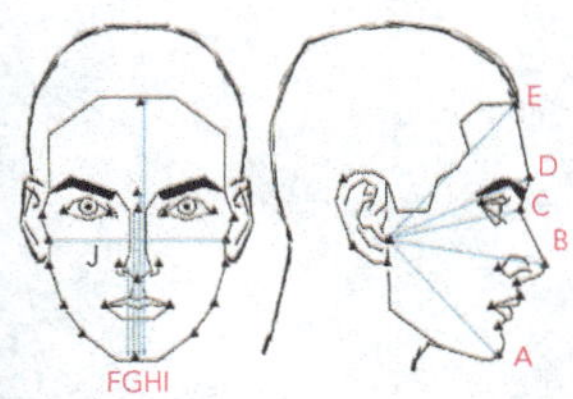


**Head measurements (in):**

A: 5 3/8 in
B: 5 3/8 in
C: 4 7/8 in
D: 5 1/4 in
E: 6 in
F: 3 5/8 in
G: 5 1/8 in
H: 5 3/4 in
I: 7 1/2 in
J: 6 1/8 in

MAP REFERENCE:

69

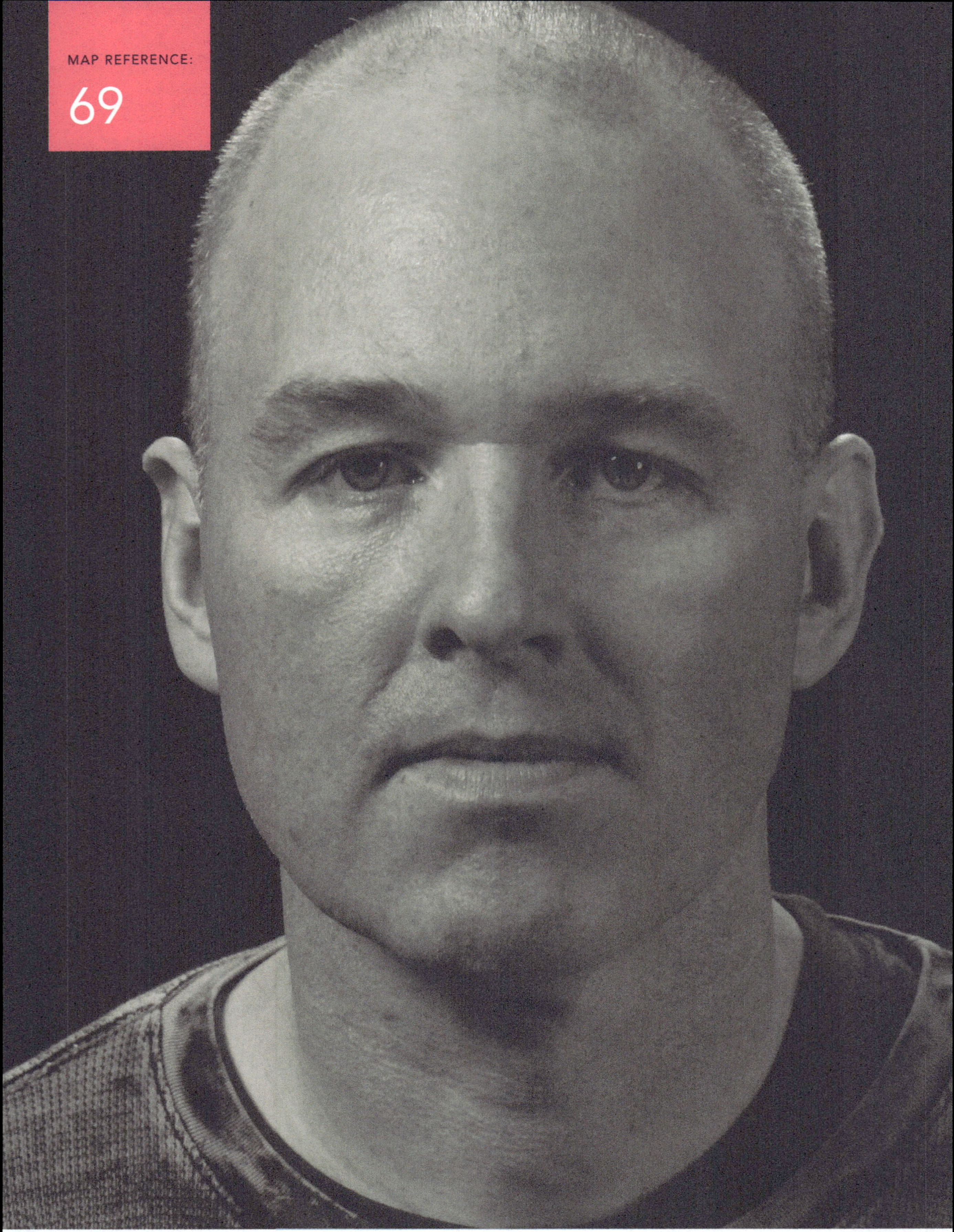

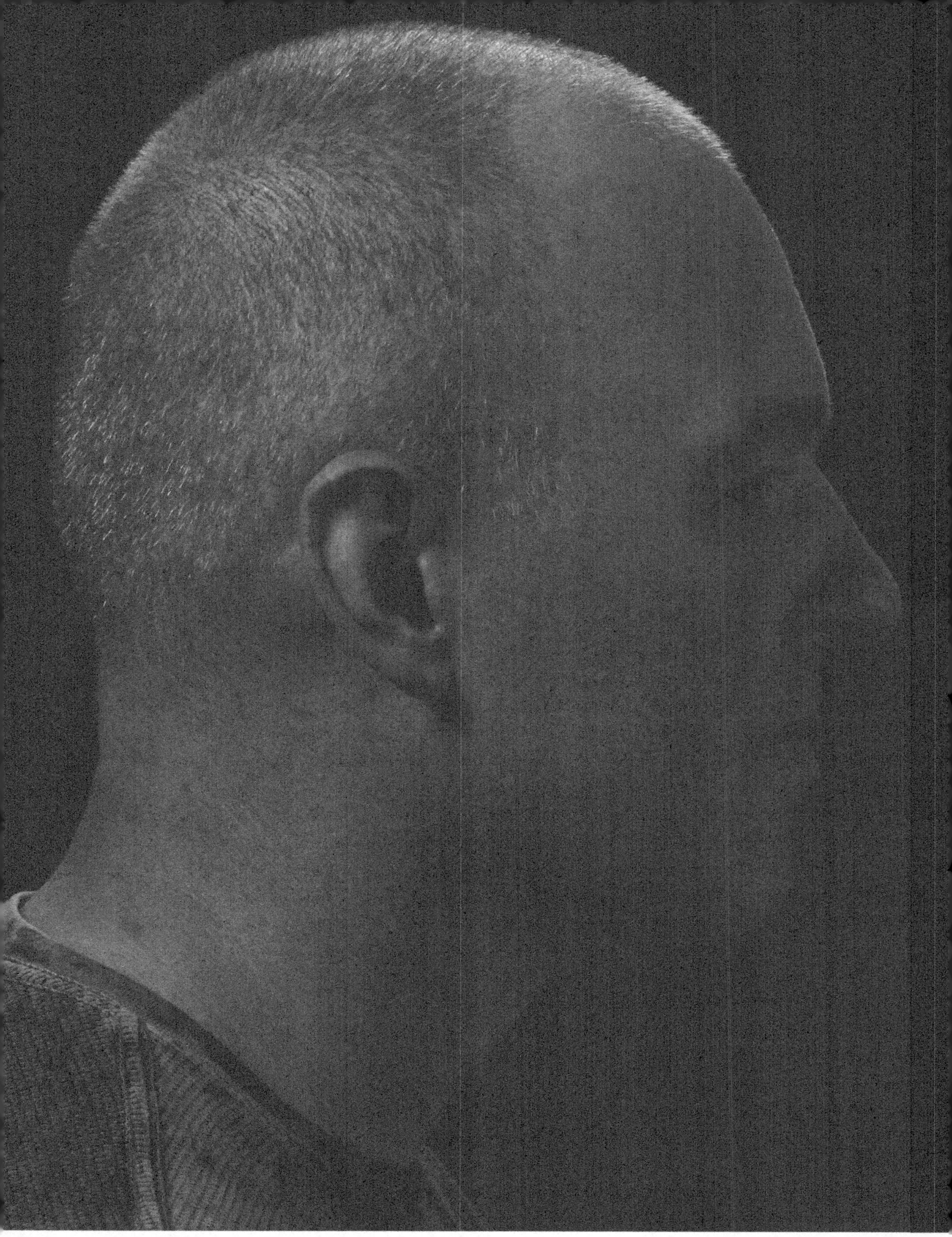

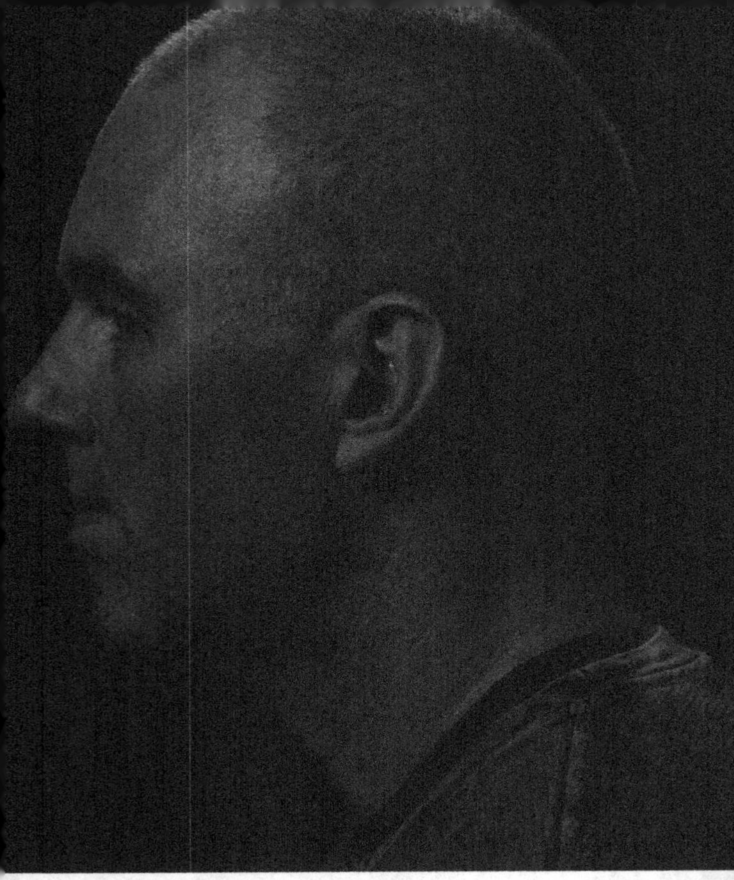
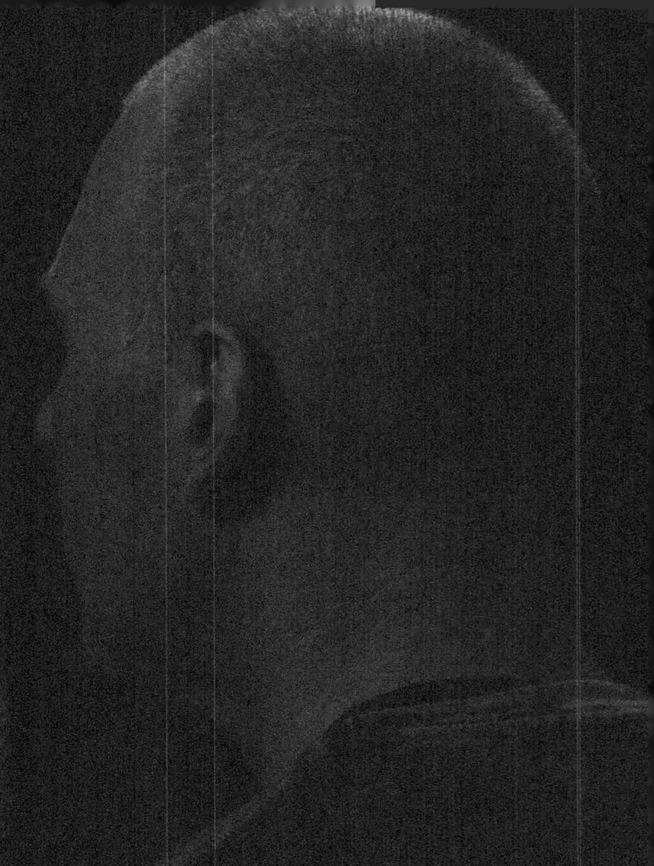

**Ethnicities claimed:**

English, Scottish, Irish.

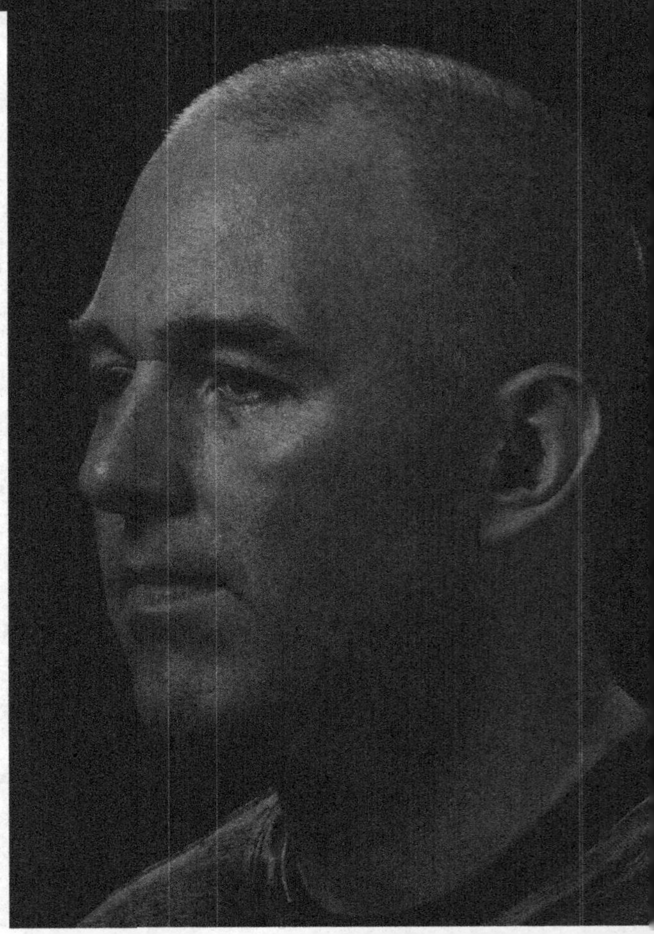

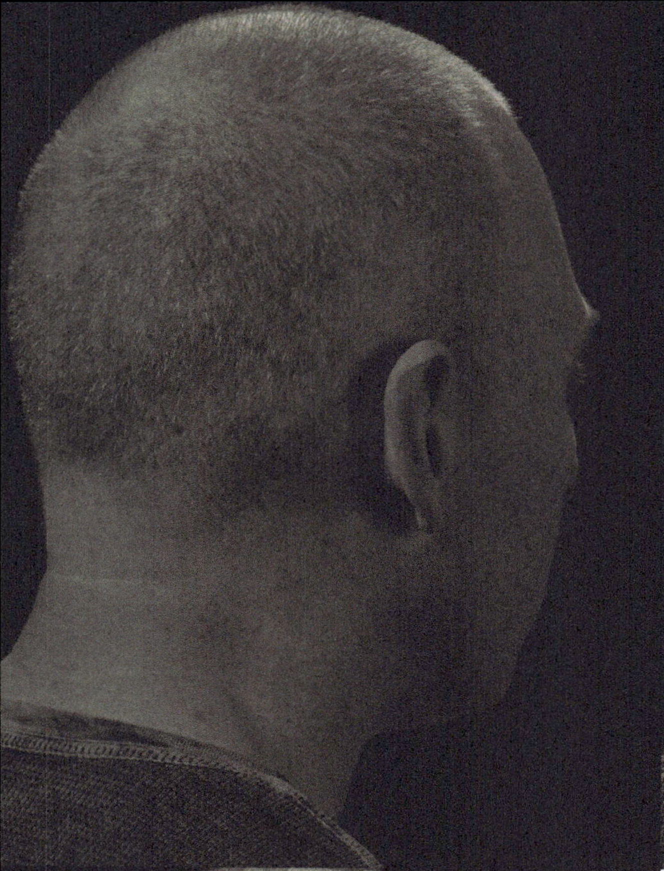

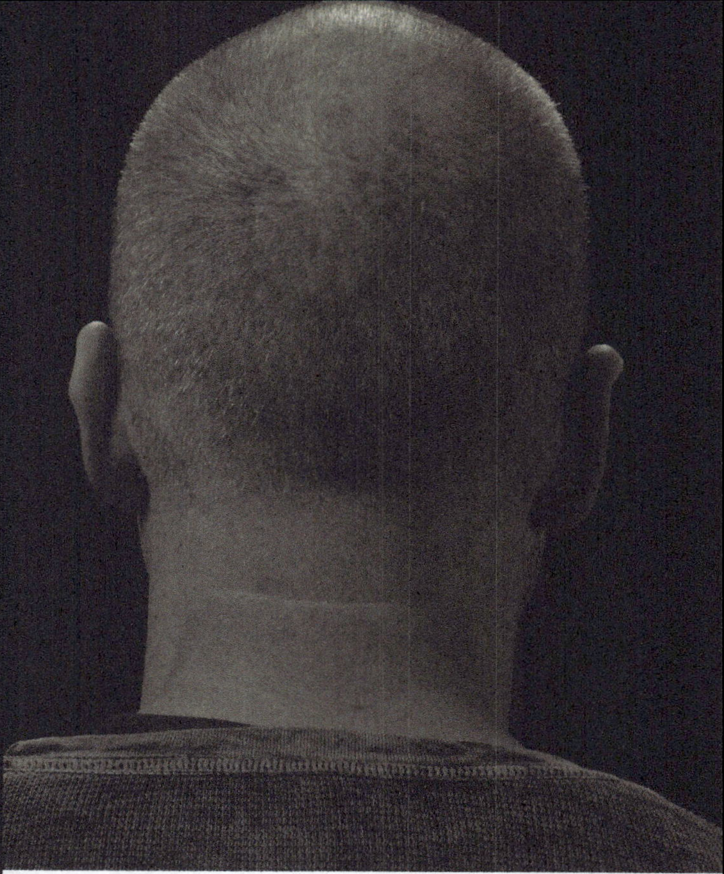

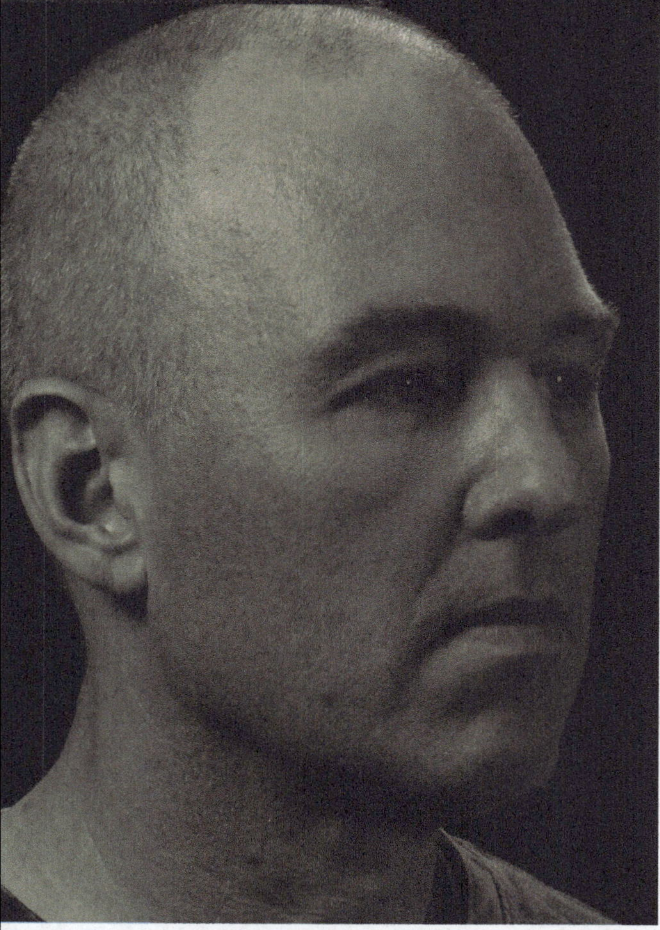

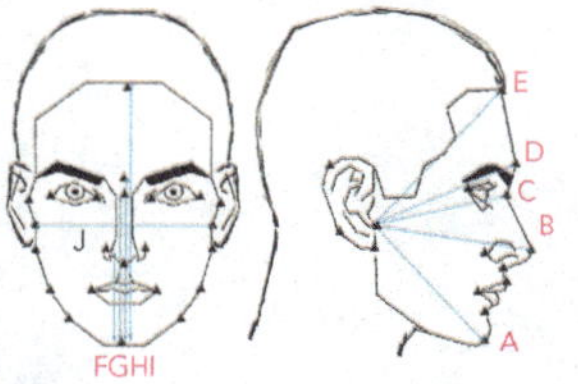


**Head measurements (in):**

A: 5 3/8
B: 5 9/16
C: 5 1/16
D: 5 3/4
E: 6 7/16
F: 3 5/8
G: 5
H: 6
I: 8 5/8
J: 5 5/8

MAP REFERENCE:

70

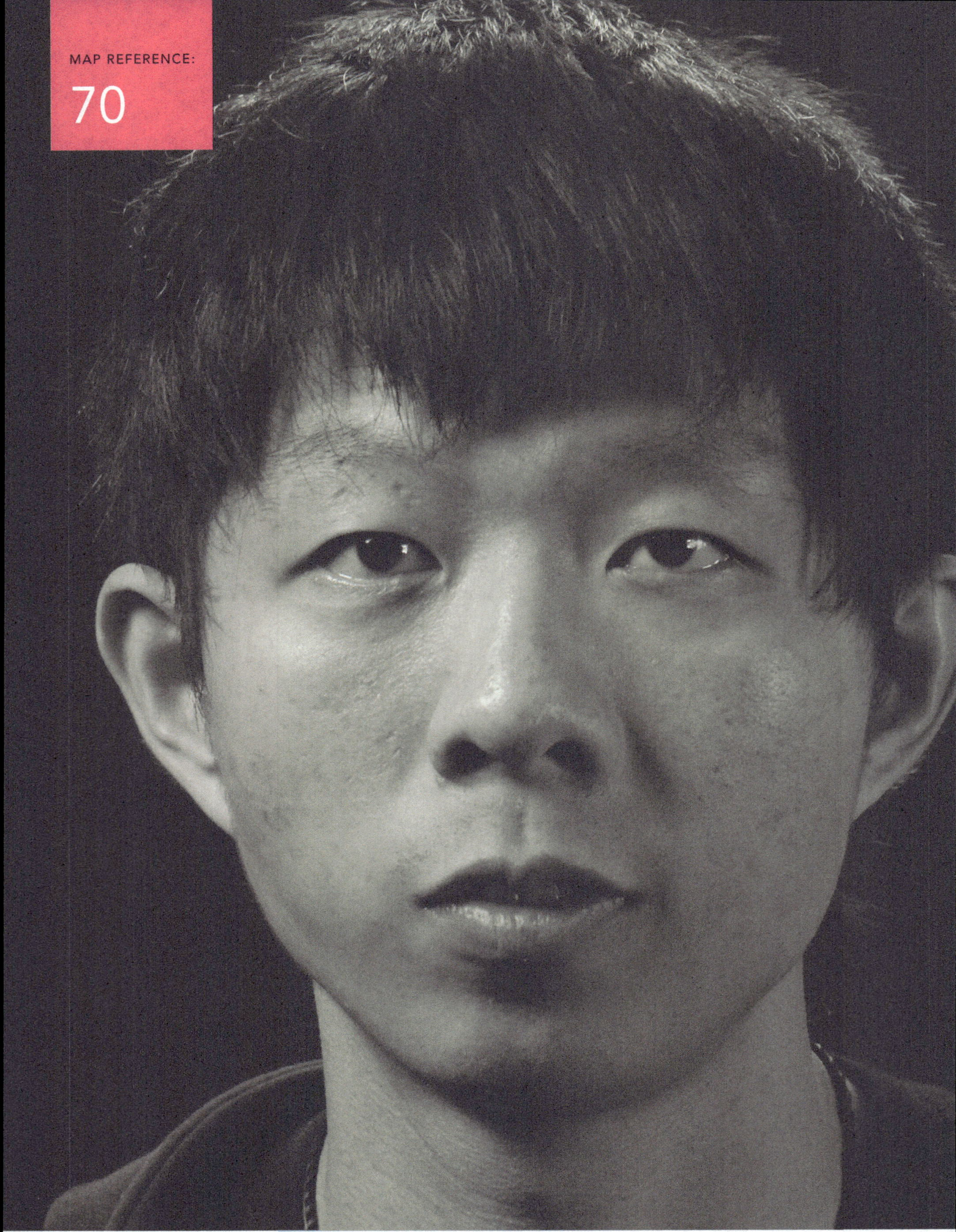

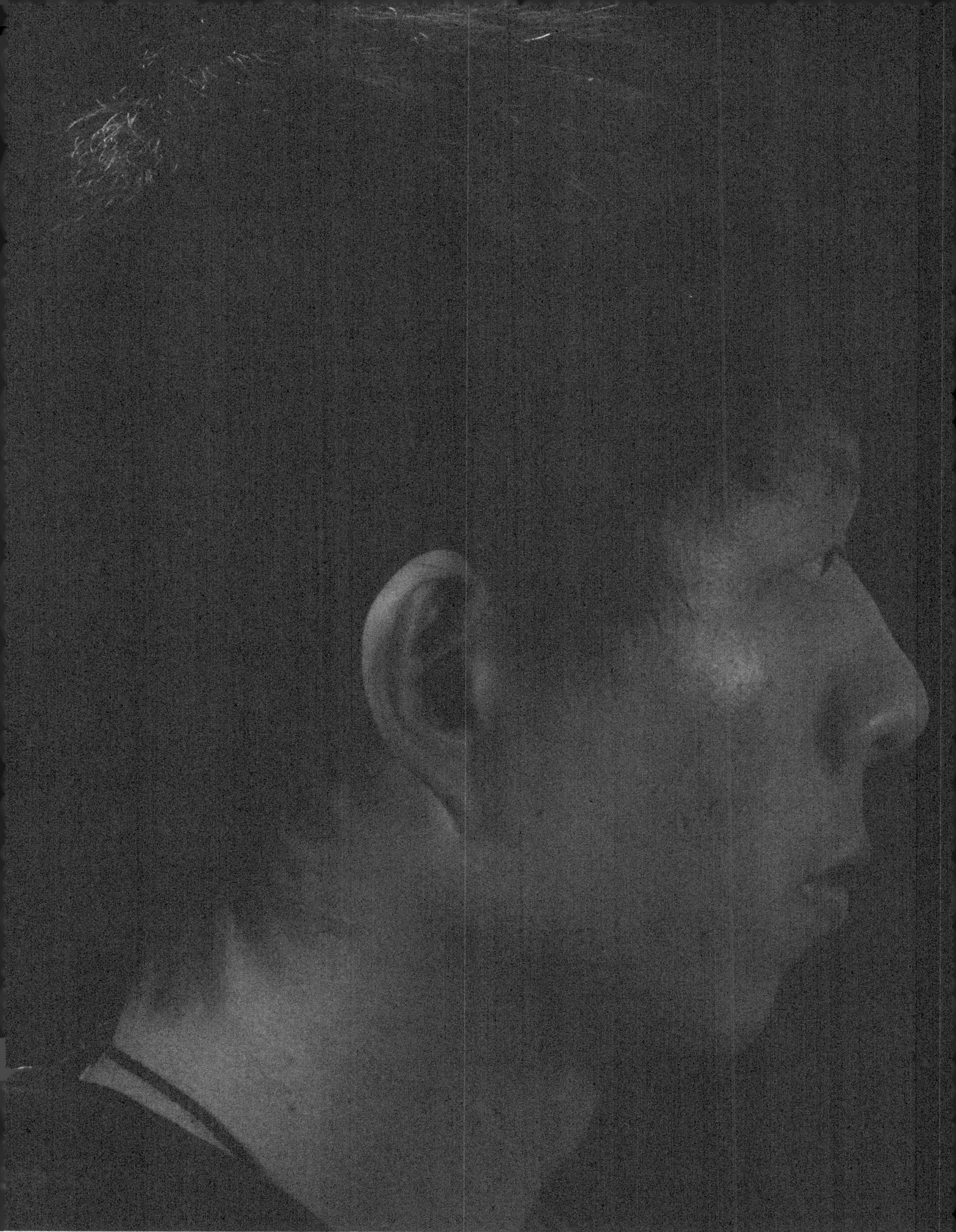

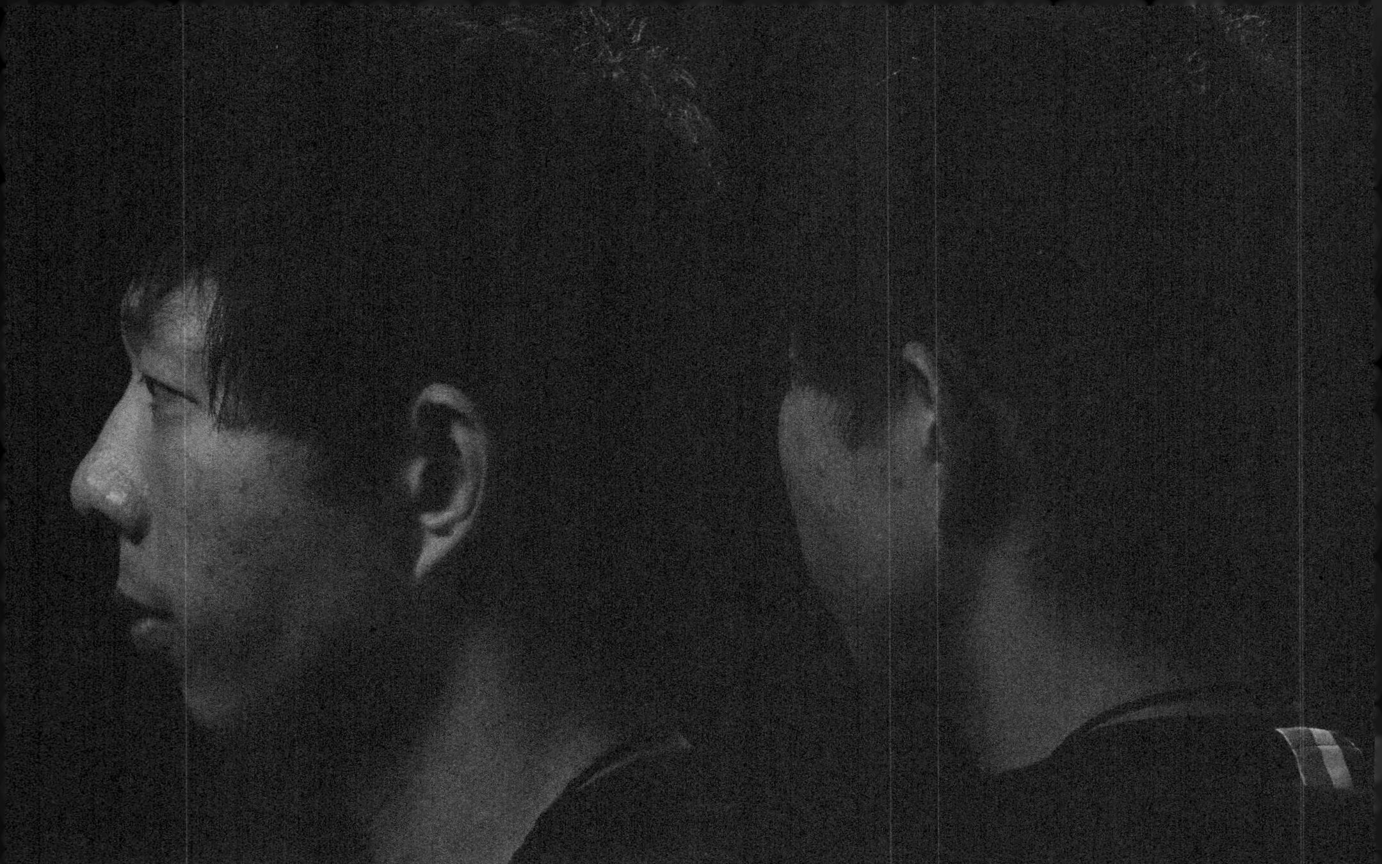

**Ethnicities claimed:**

China.

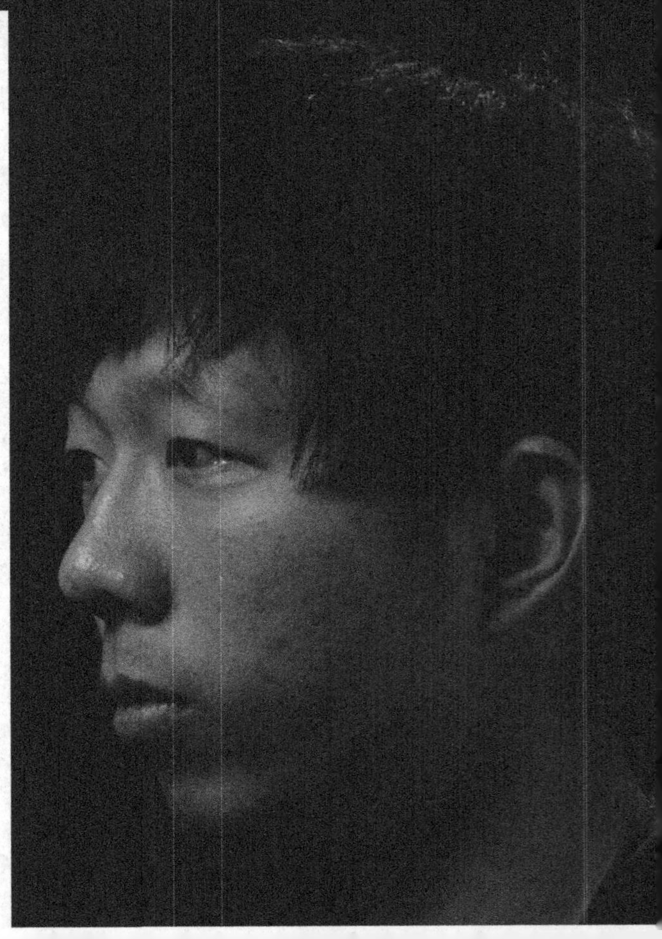

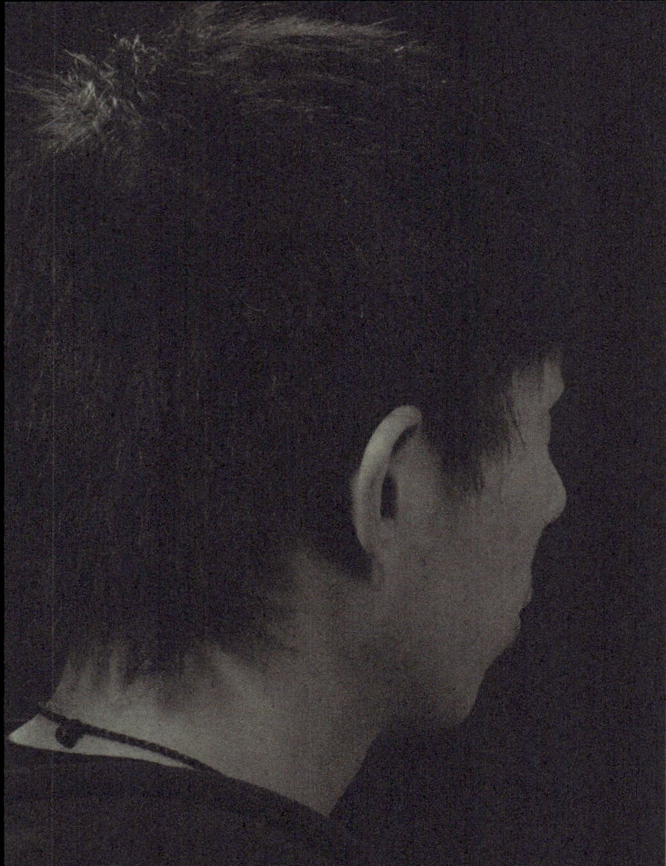

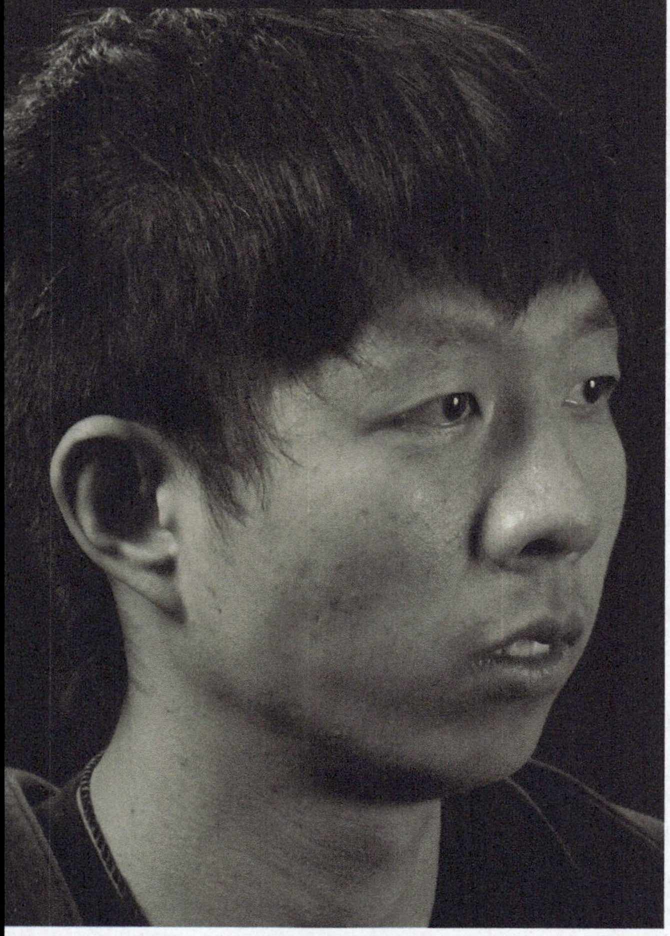

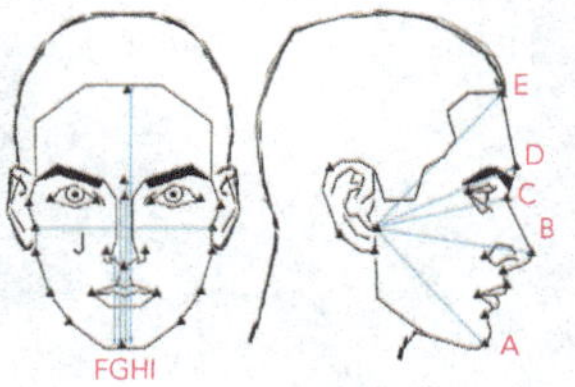


**Head measurements (in):**

A: 4 7/8
B: 4 3/4
C: 5
D: 5 3/8
E: 6 1/4
F: 3 5/8
G: 4 1/2
H: 5 3/4
I: 7 3/8
J: 5 5/8

MAP REFERENCE:

74

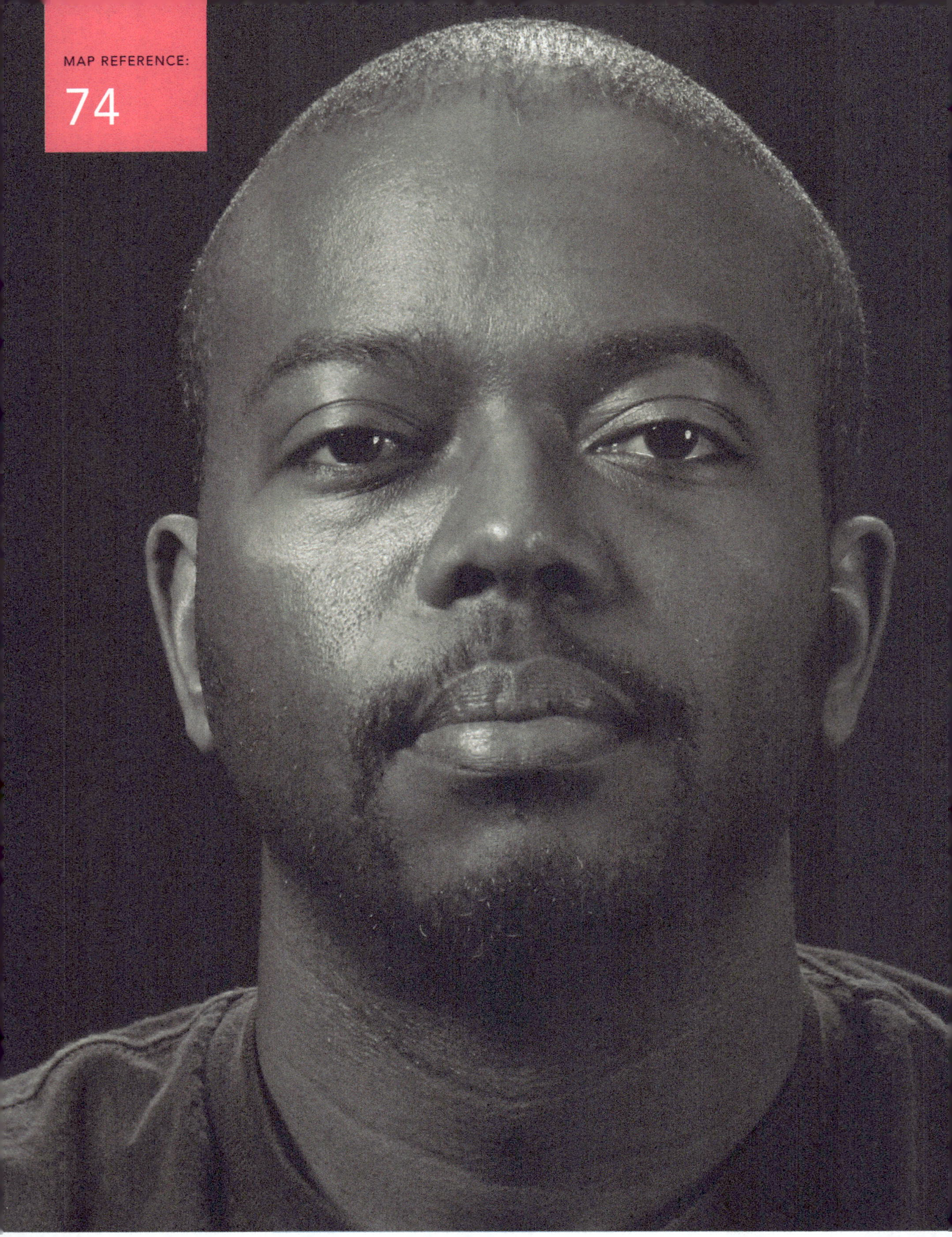

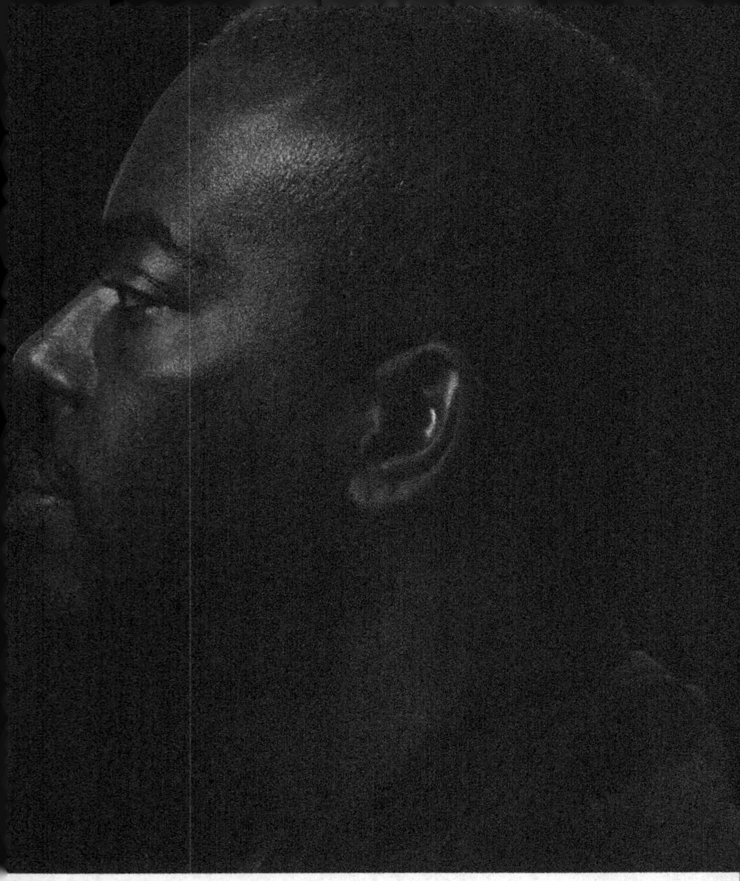

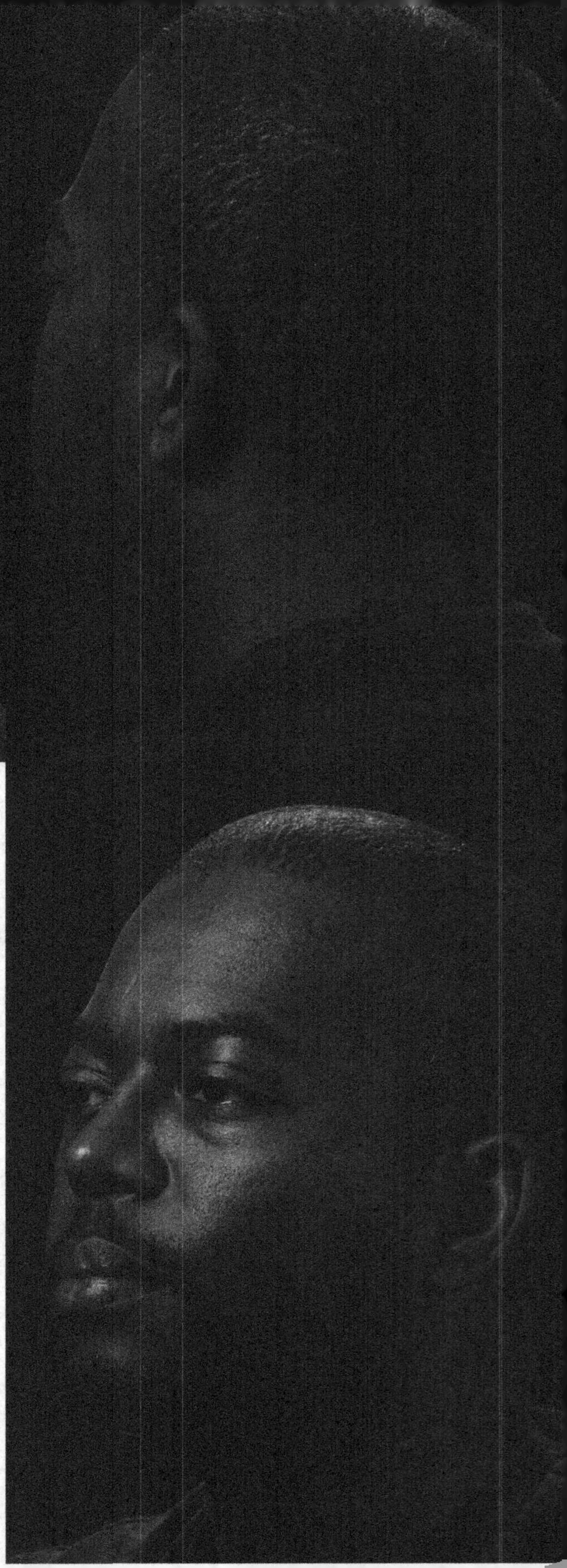

**Ethnicities claimed:**

African American.

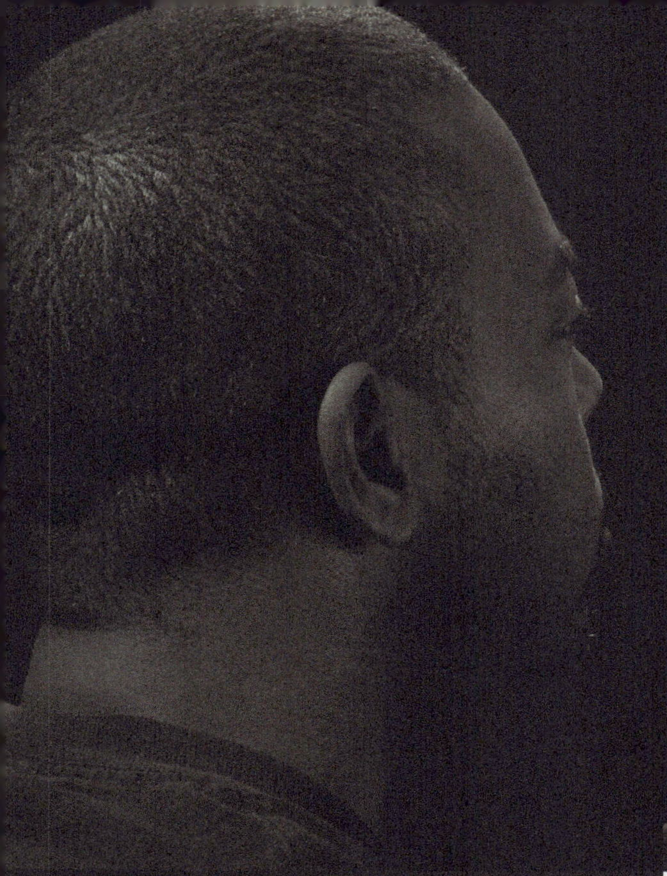

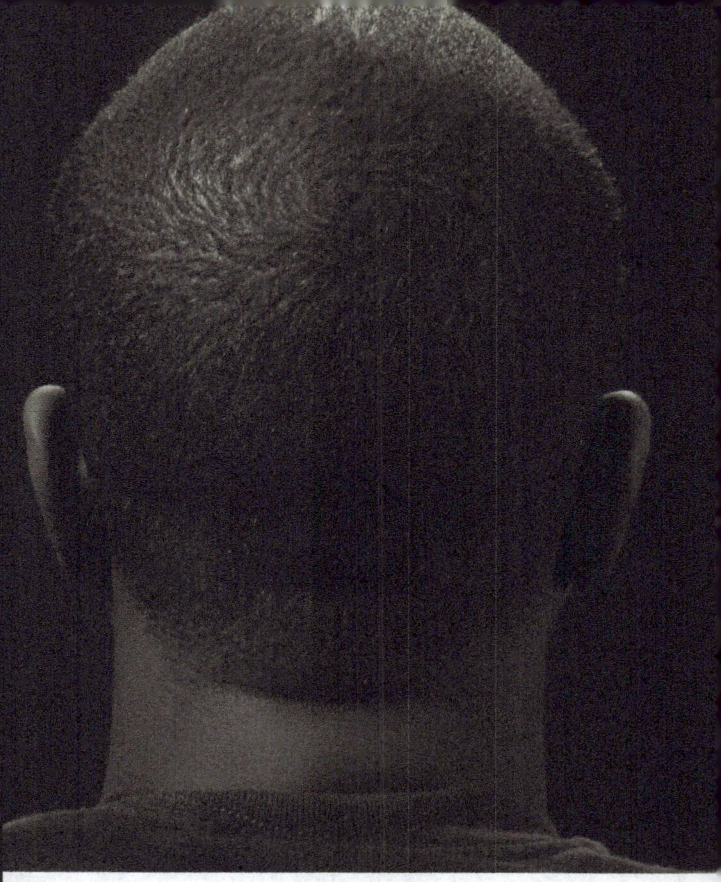

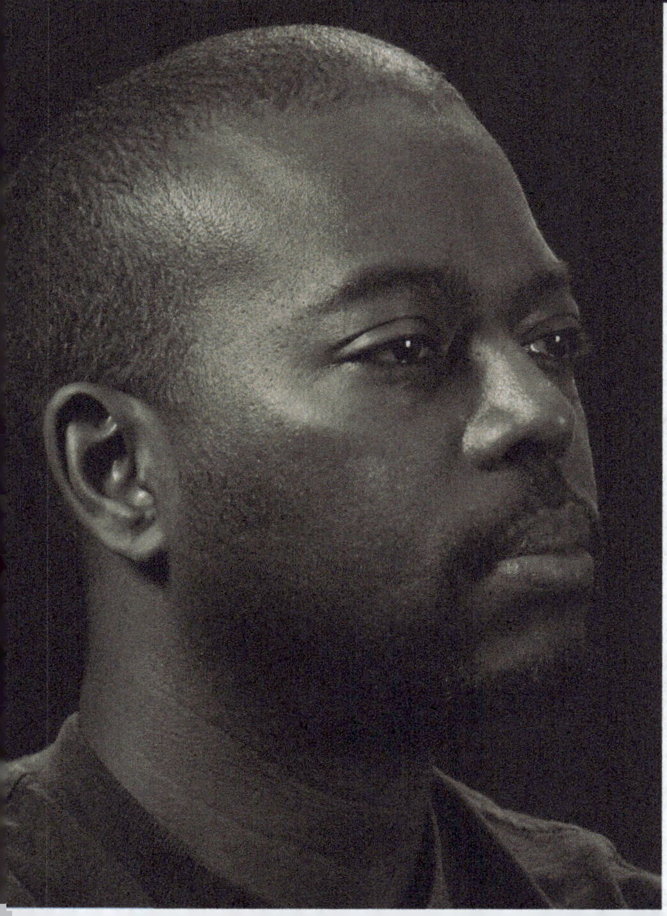

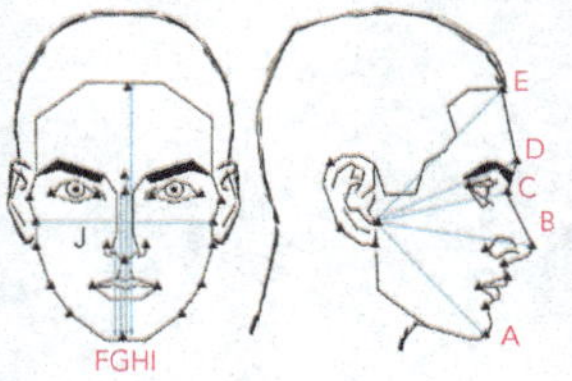


**Head measurements (in):**

A: 5 1/8
B: 5 5/8
C: 5 1/8
D: 5 3/8
E: 6 3/8
F: 3 7/8
G: 4 3/4
H: 5 3/8
I: 8
J: 5 5/8

CHAPTER 4:
3D TUTORIAL

# EYE TUTORIAL

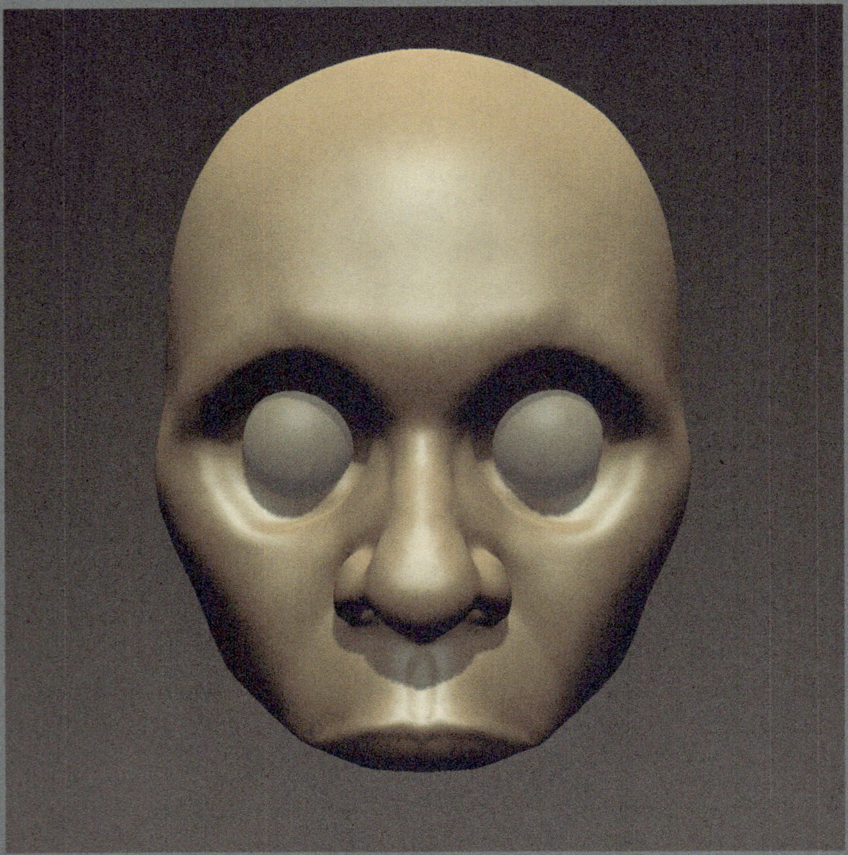

Eye-starter.obj file.

Load your model from the nose tutorial, or import from the companion website:

***/tutorials/eye_tutorial/eye_starter.obj***

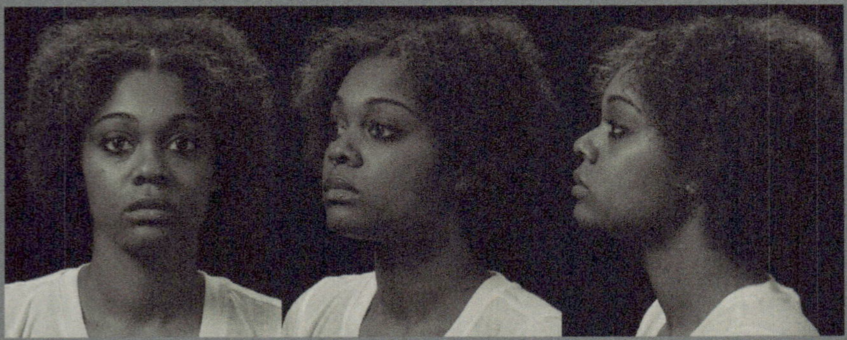

Female reference material.

Use the same reference images as in the nose tutorial:

***/tutorials/tutorial2/african_american_female.jpg***

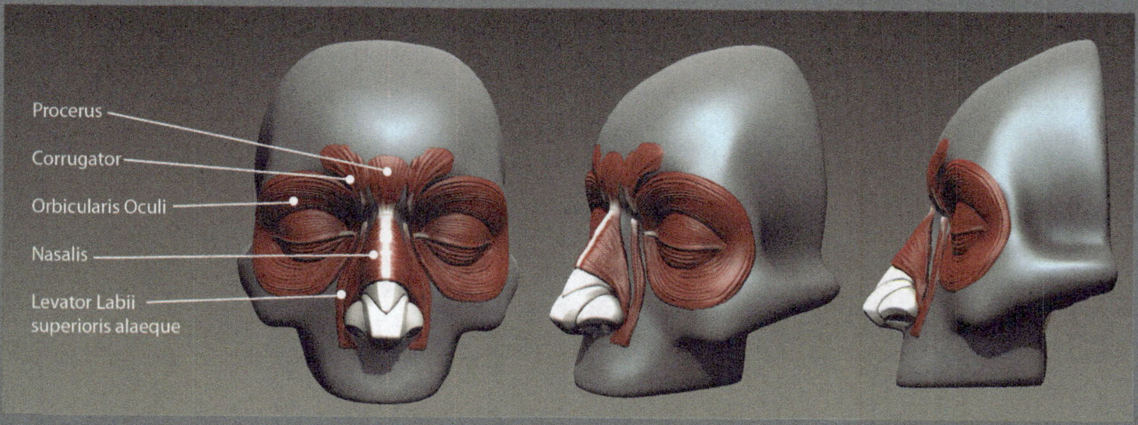


Let's quickly review the anatomy of the eye region.

*Eye region anatomy.*

When creating an eye, a few landmarks you want to keep in mind:

- The boney border of the orbital cavity, particularly the prominence of the edge next to the nasal bone
- The fleshy bulge of the Orbicular muscle, again on the inside edge of the orbital cavity below the eye.

We'll start by blocking in the basic form of the upper eyelid. Focus on treating the lids very basically to start.

*Blocking in the upper eyelid.*

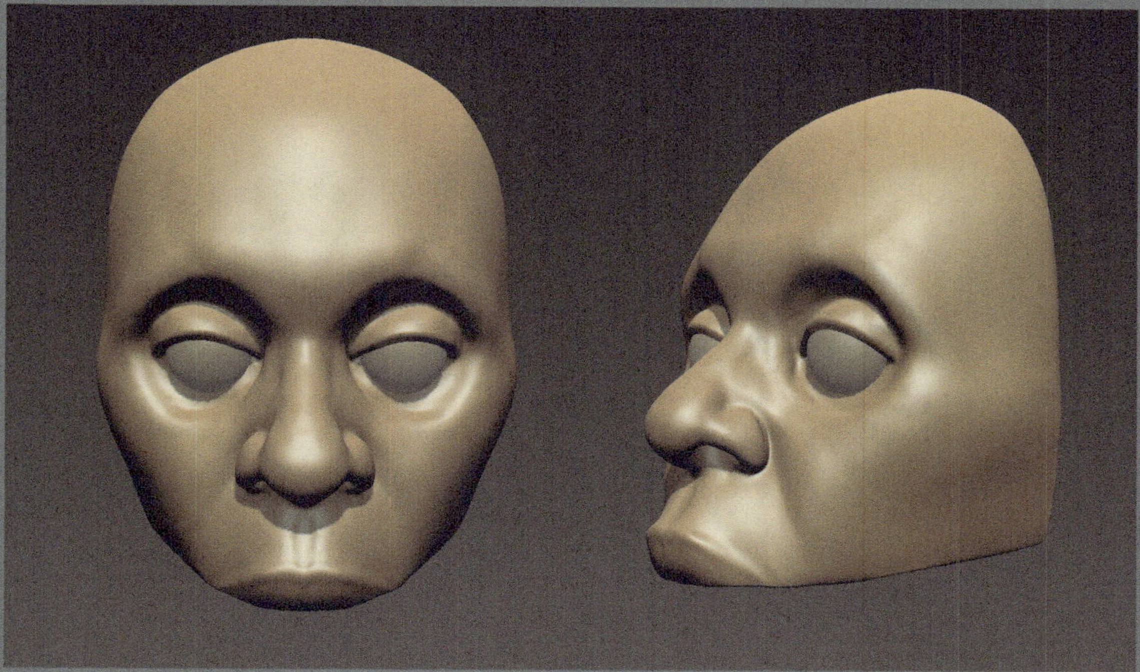

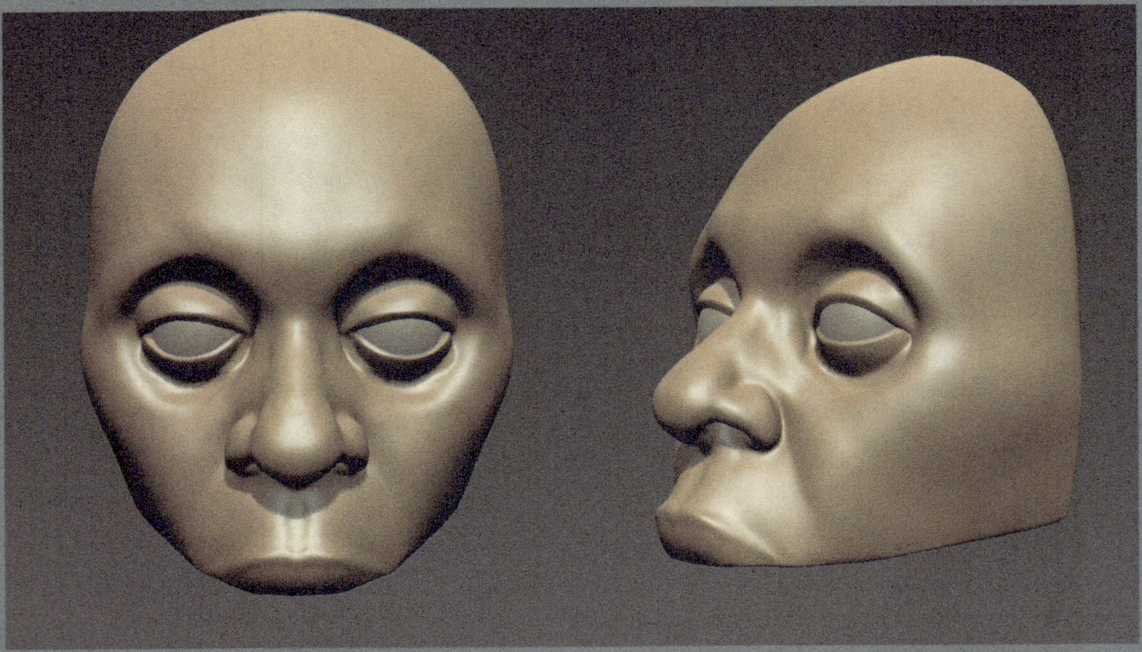

Next, sculpt in the basic form of the lower lid:

*Blocking in the lower eyelid.*

Now, referring to the model photos, rough in the tear duct as shown:

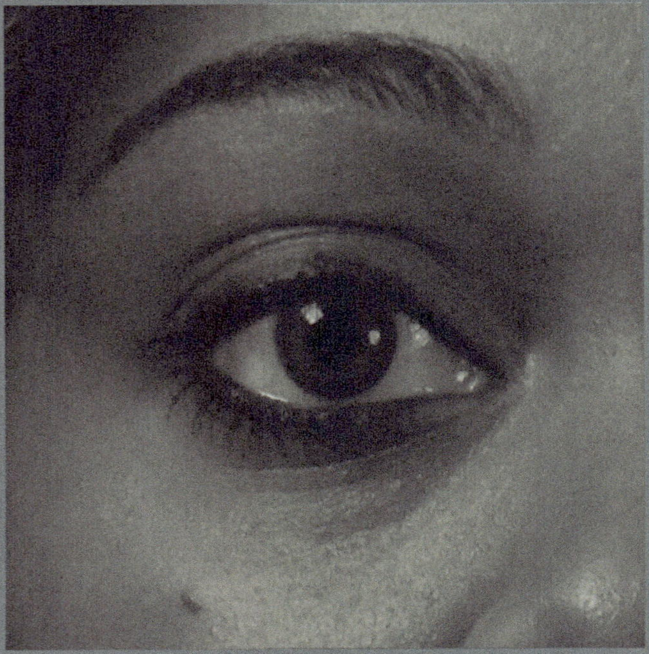

*Model reference of tear duct.*

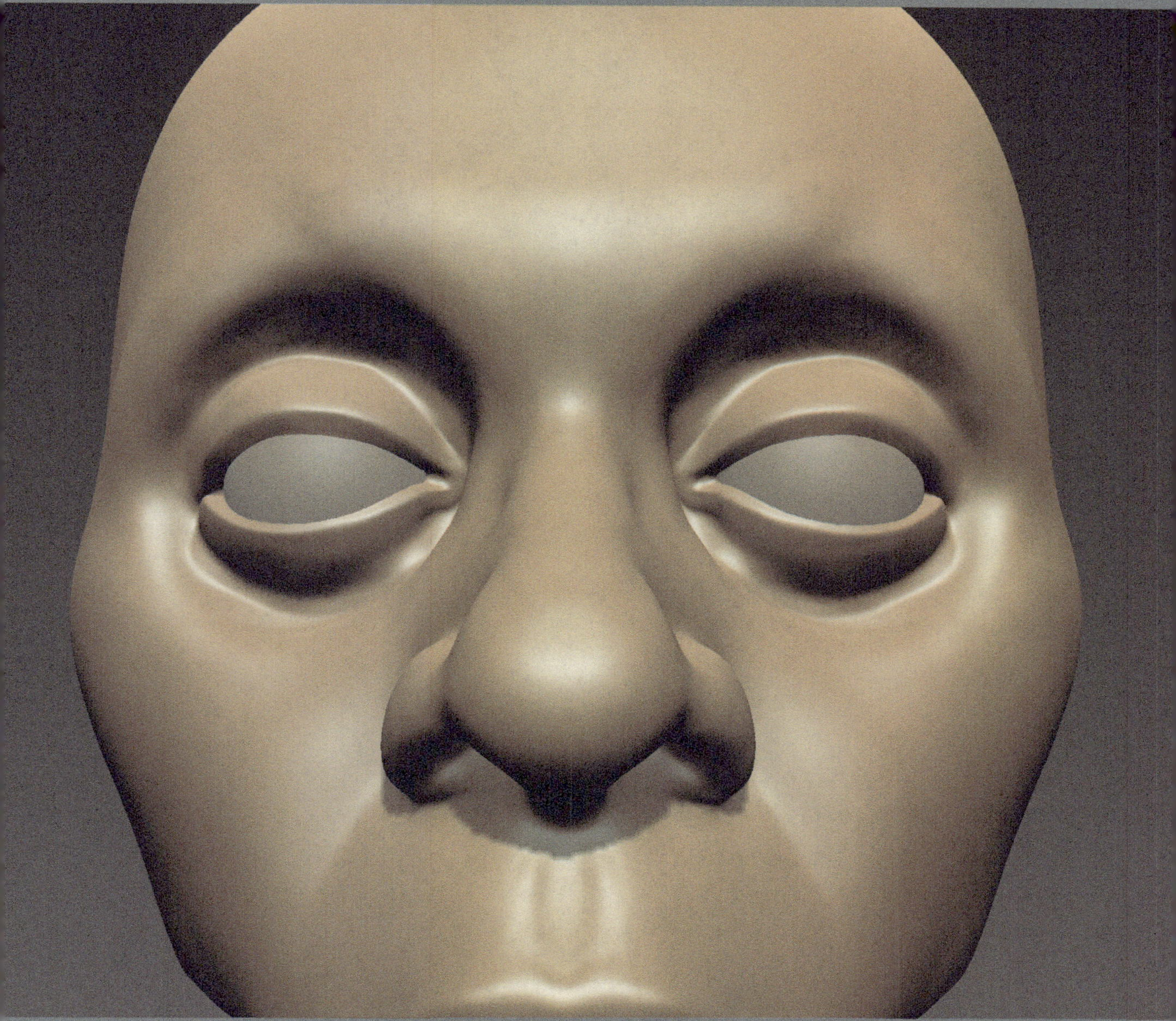

*Progress of tear duct.*

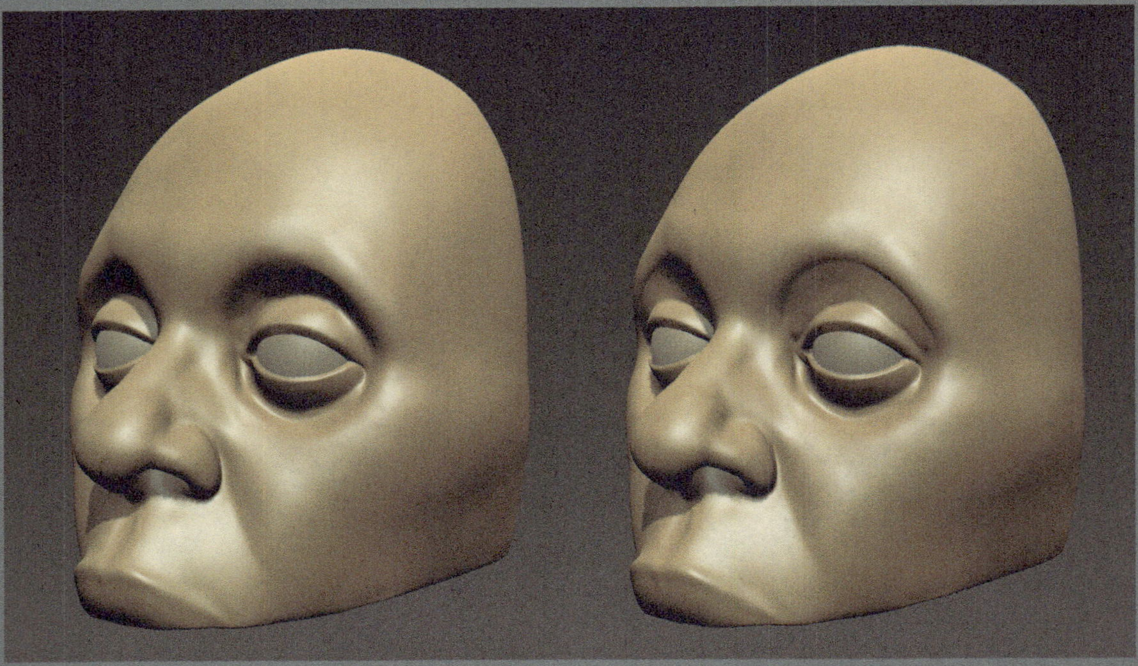

Cavity above eye.

Keep in mind we're roughing in form right now and there will be time to refine proportions and position once the surrounding area is blocked in. You want to focus on big shapes first.

Next, you are going to block in the area between the eye and the brow. The first step is to fill in the cavity above the eye as a flat plane:

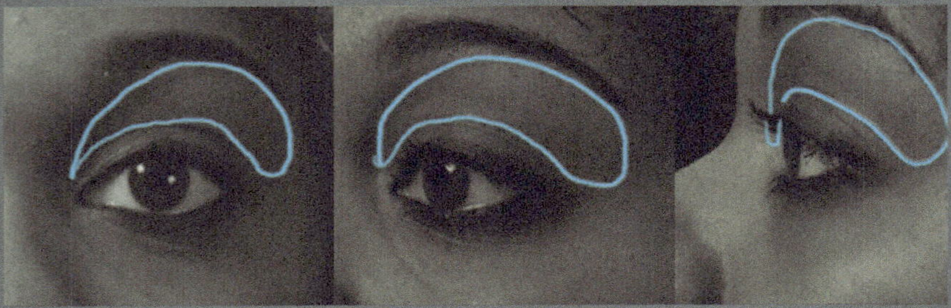

Model reference of flesh pockets.

Then create the flesh pocket that lies over the top of the eye, making the outer-upper corner the high point:

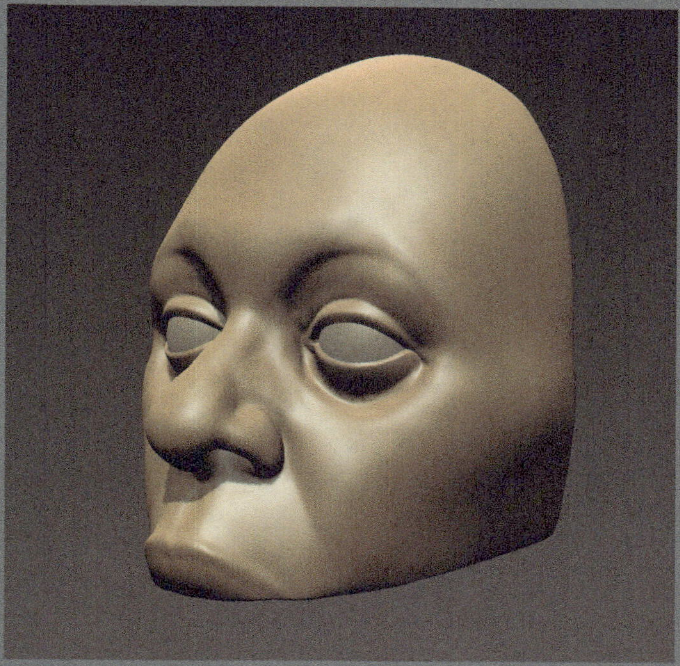

*Progress of model.*

Next, you will address the cavity below the lower lid.

Start as in the last step by filling in the cavity with a flat plane as shown:

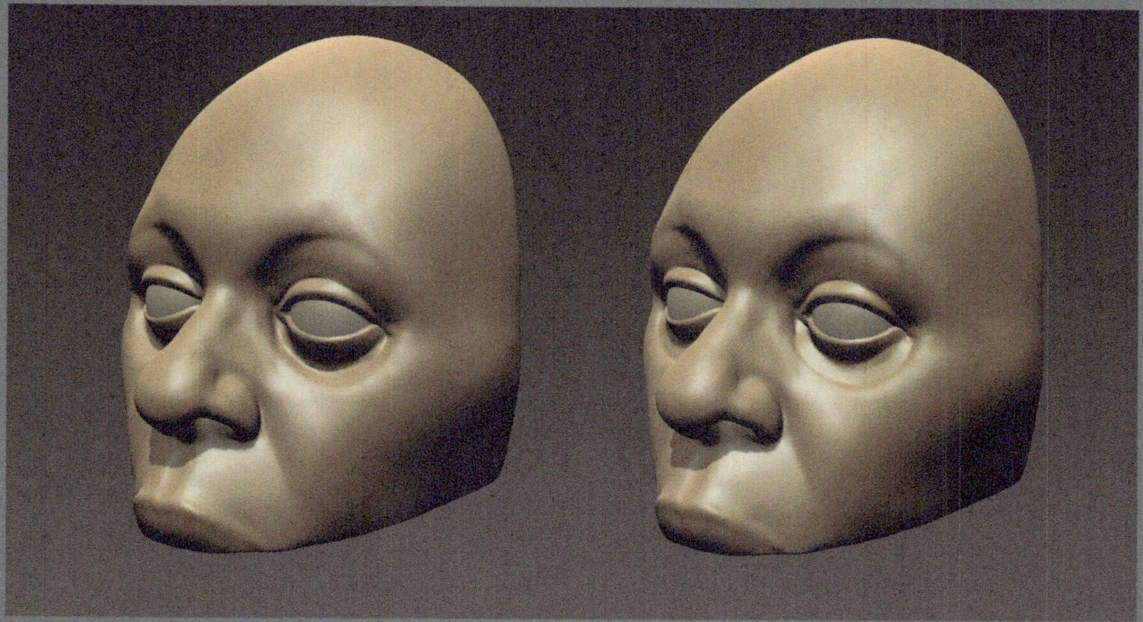

*Filling in the cavity.*

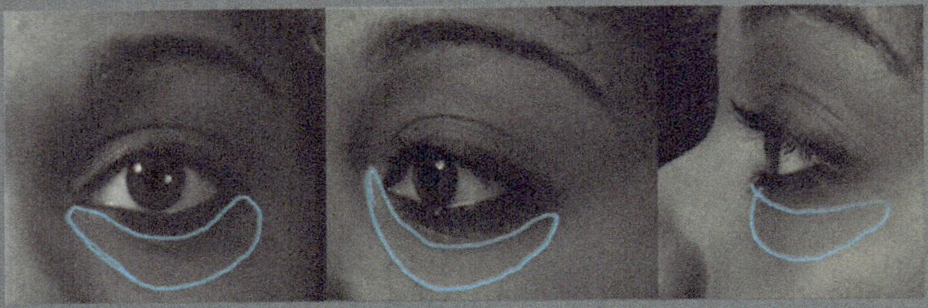

Model reference, fleshy pocket below eye.

Next, create the fleshy pocket between the lower eyelid and the edge of the orbital cavity. Pay particular attention to how it bulges on the side closest to the nose. Also, make sure you keep the inner edge of the orbital cavity clearly defined as it is an important structural landmark:

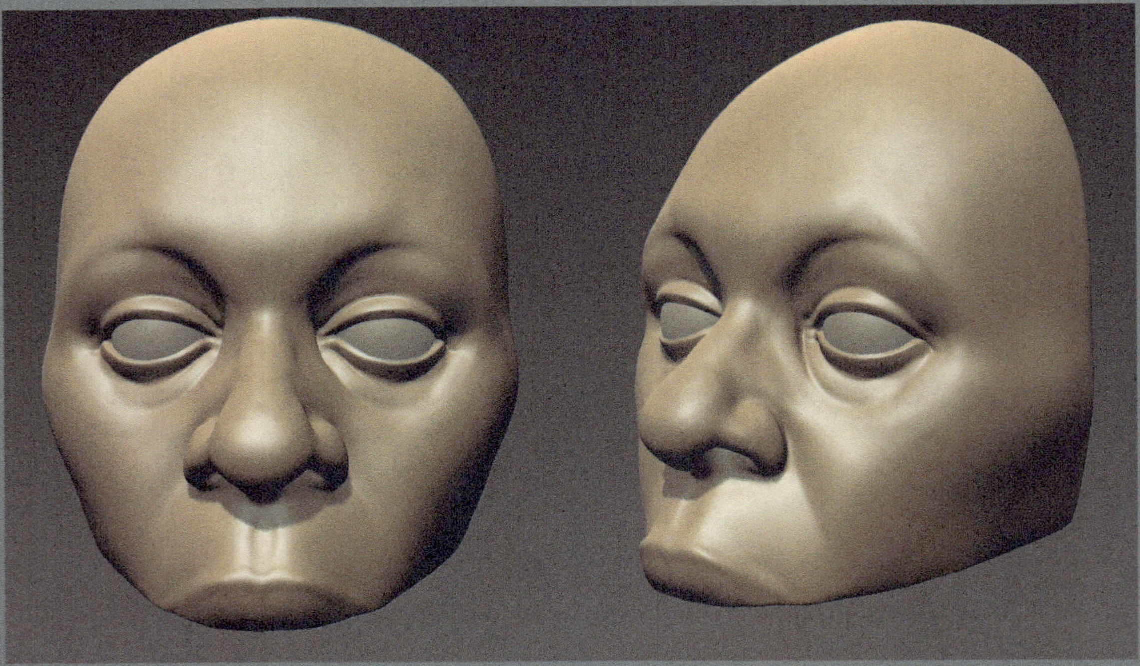

Evaluate progress.

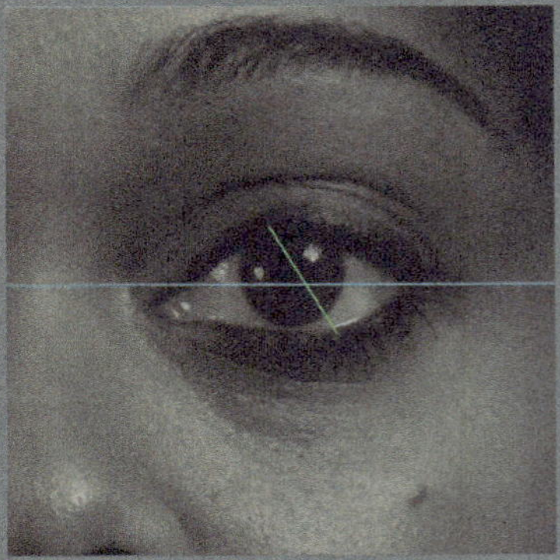

Model reference.

Before finishing up, look closely at the photo reference. You want to be sure to position the tear duct vertically, properly in relation to the outer corner of the eye. You also will notice that the high point of the upper lid and the low point of the lower lid are slightly offset: Make those adjustments now.

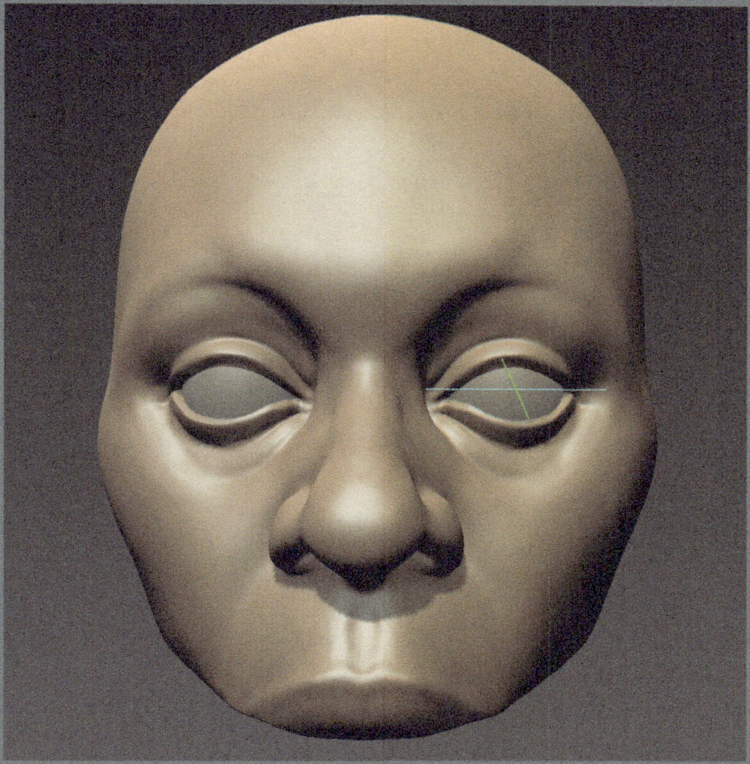

*Evaluate tear duct.*

Finally, take some time and evaluate the reference photographs and add or correct any forms you think are required. Pay attention to impacting forms, such as the subtle bulge of the fleshy area above the eye, impacting the upper eyelid. These types of details help aid in the realism of the final sculpt.

In the end, you should wind up with something that looks similar to the following images.

*Final output.*

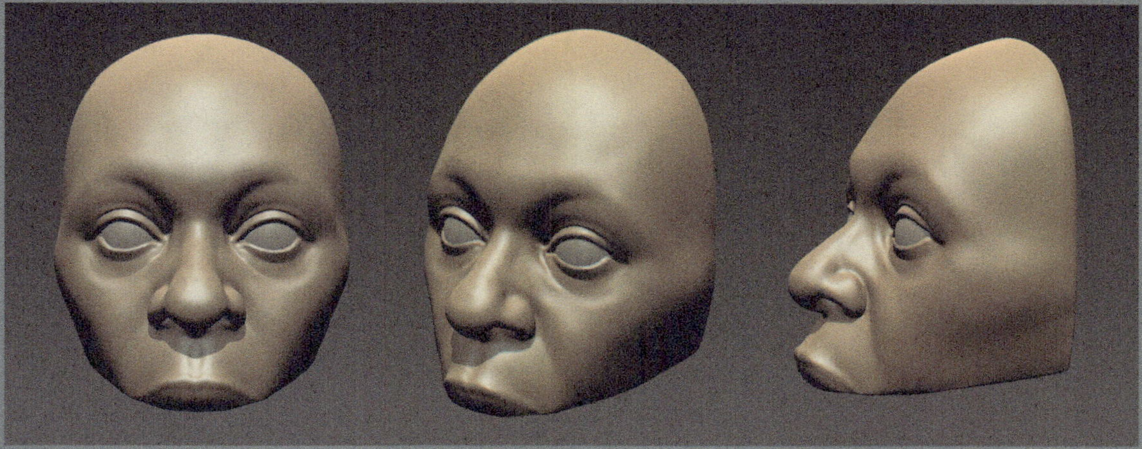

# 5

CHAPTER 5

# EXPRESSIONS

DOI: 10.1201/ 9781003484554-5

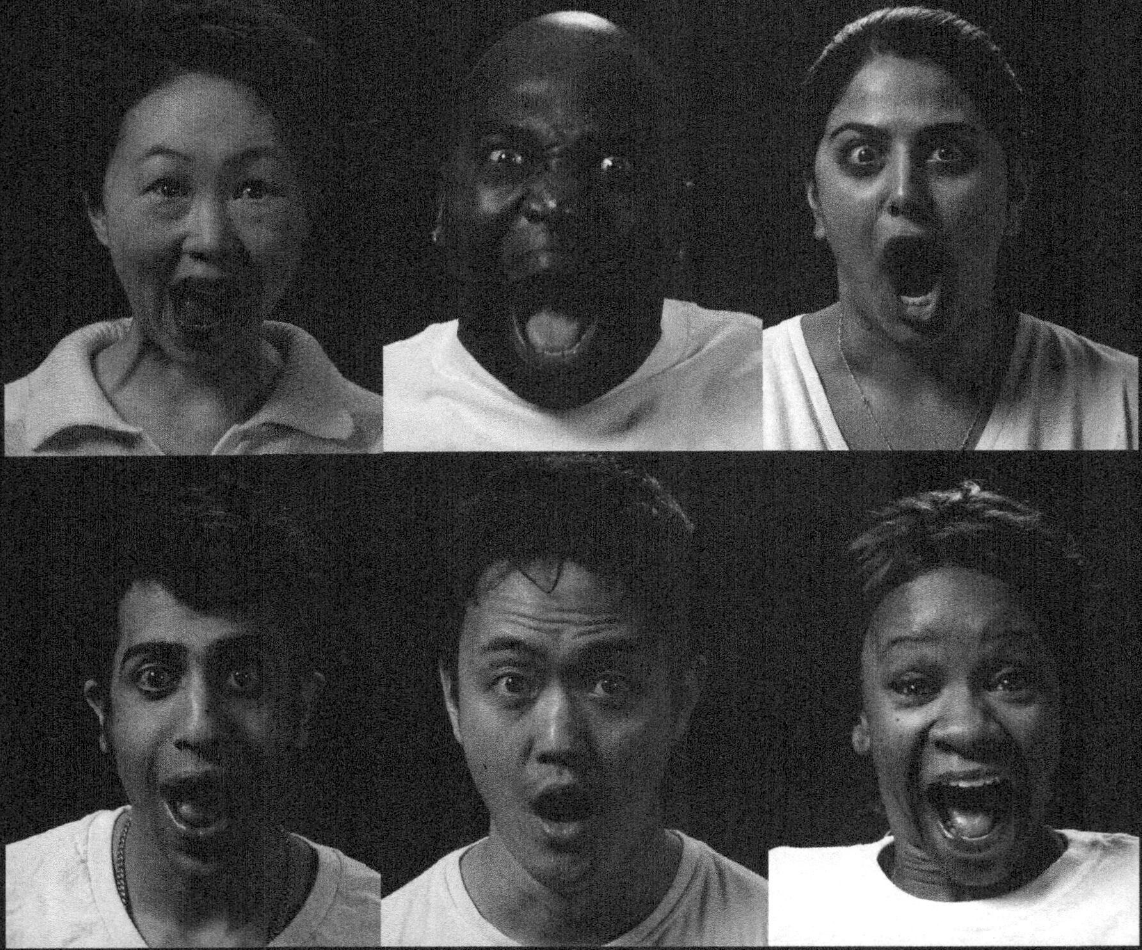

*And now for something completely different...*

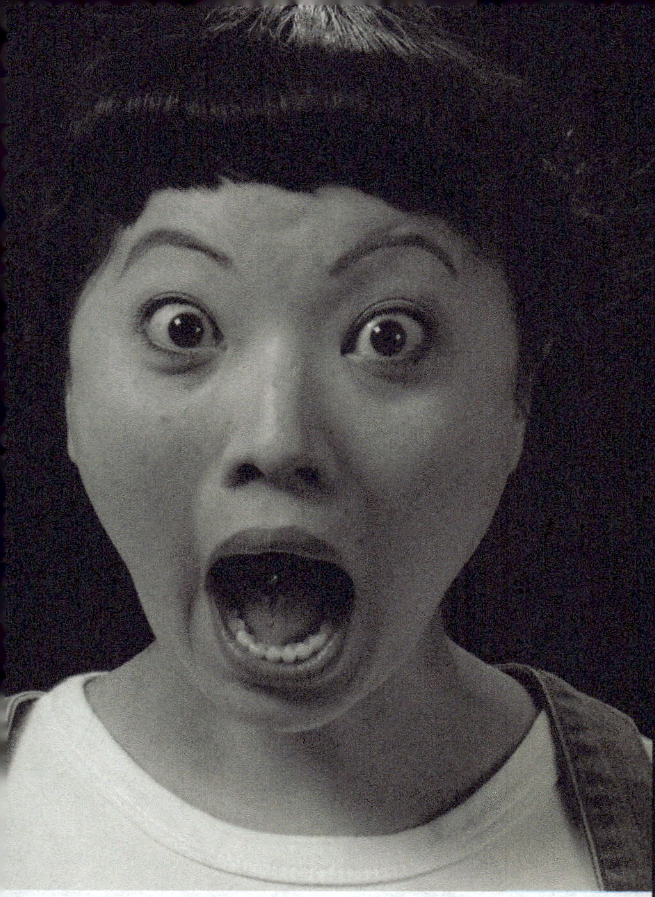

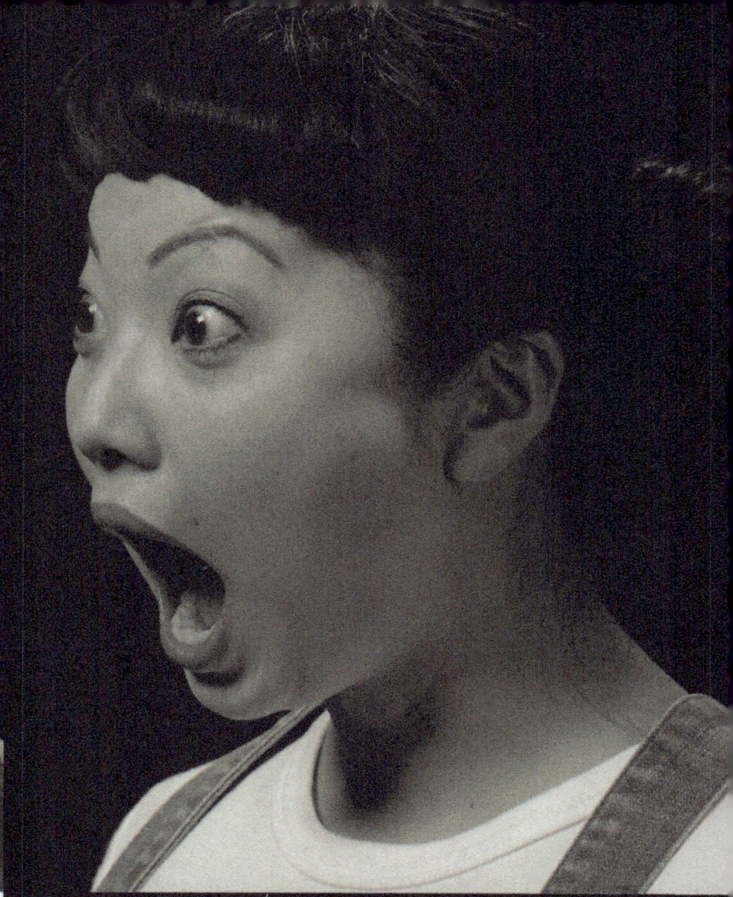

# HAPPY

MAP REFERENCE:

44

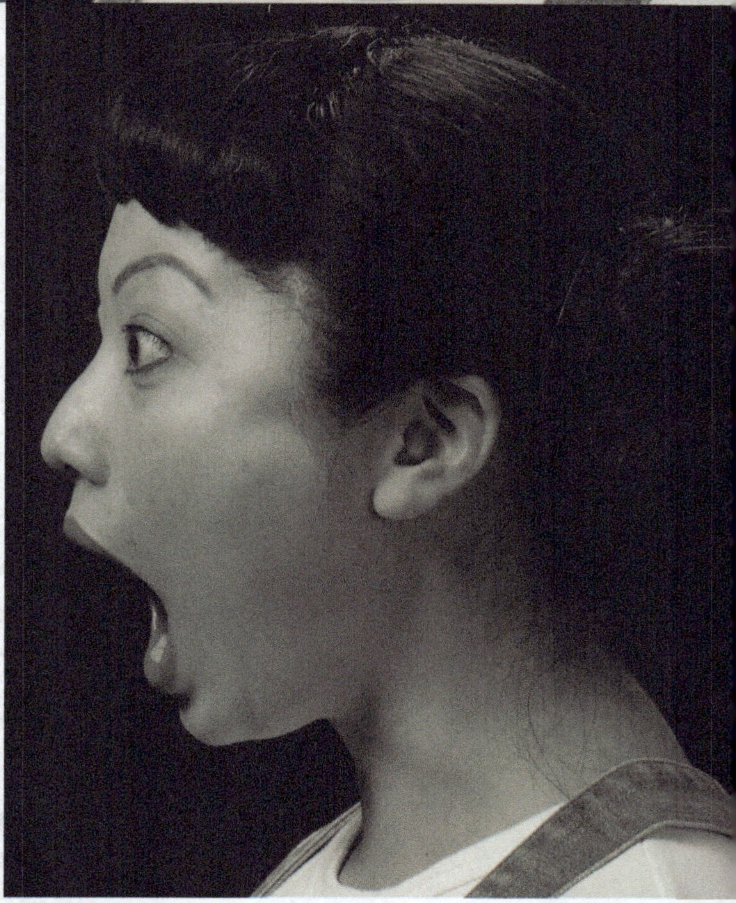

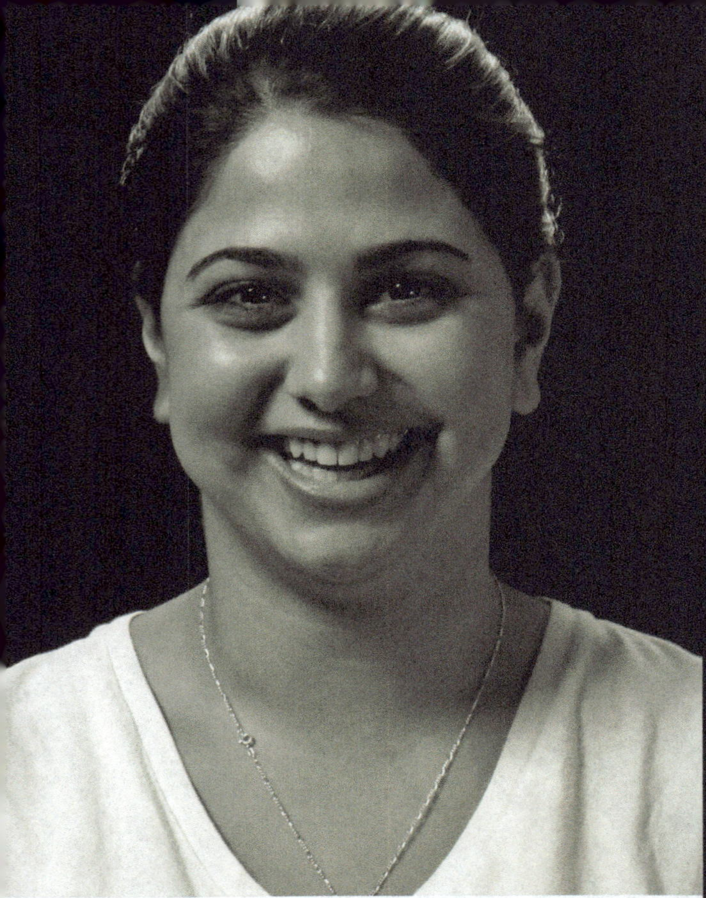

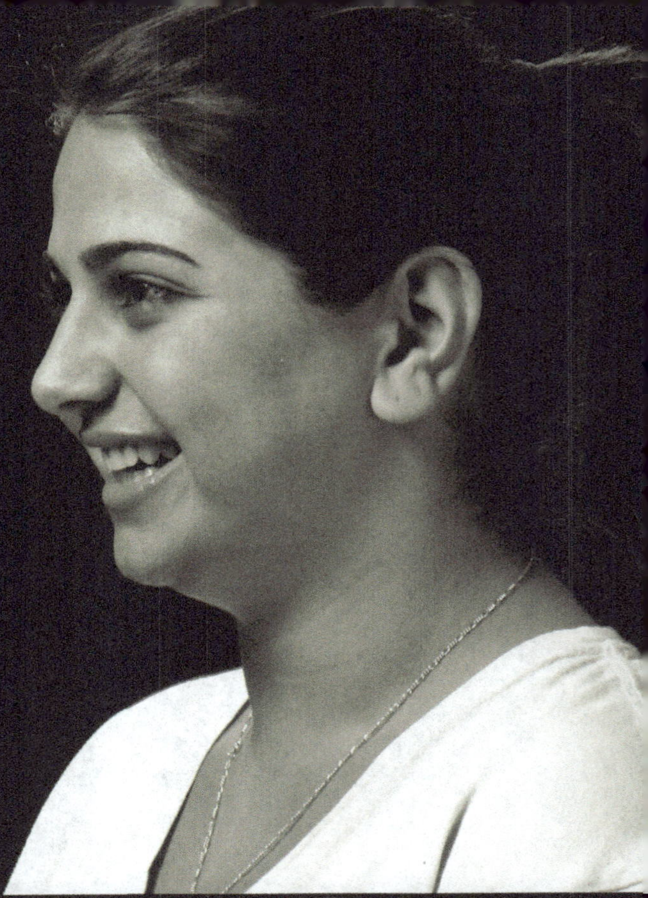

# HAPPY

MAP REFERENCE:

28

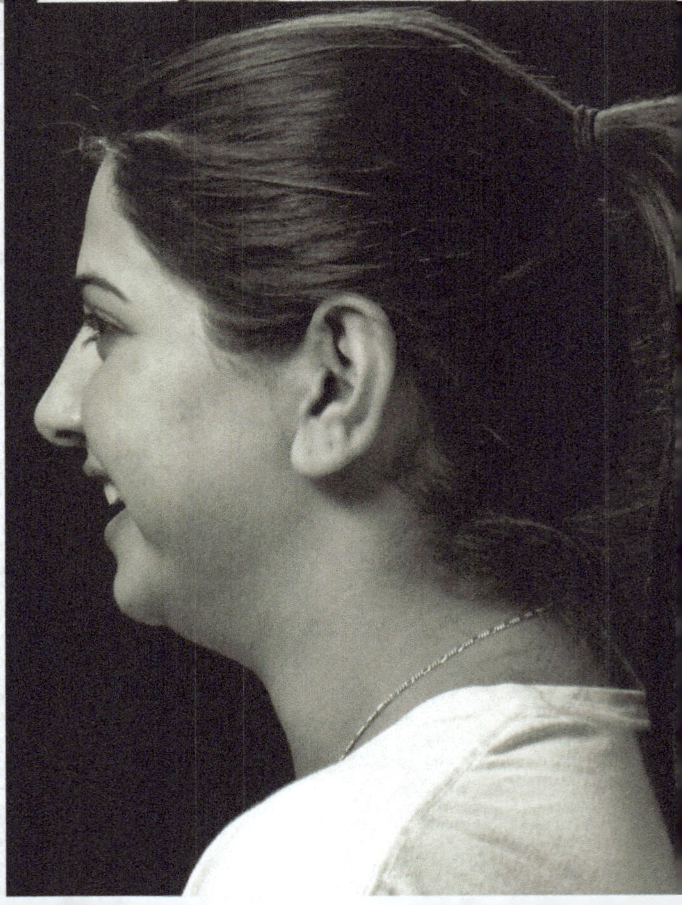

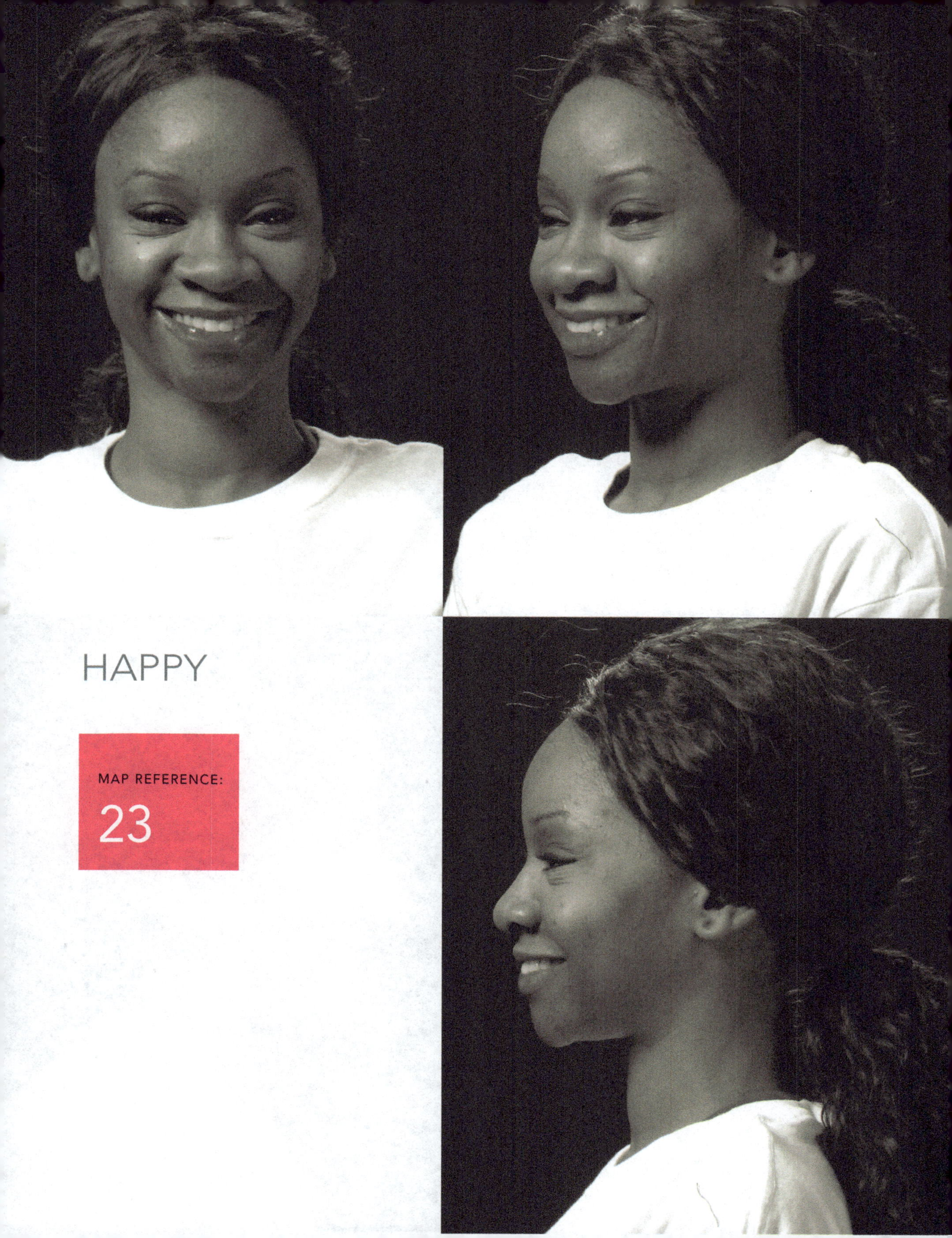

HAPPY

MAP REFERENCE:

23

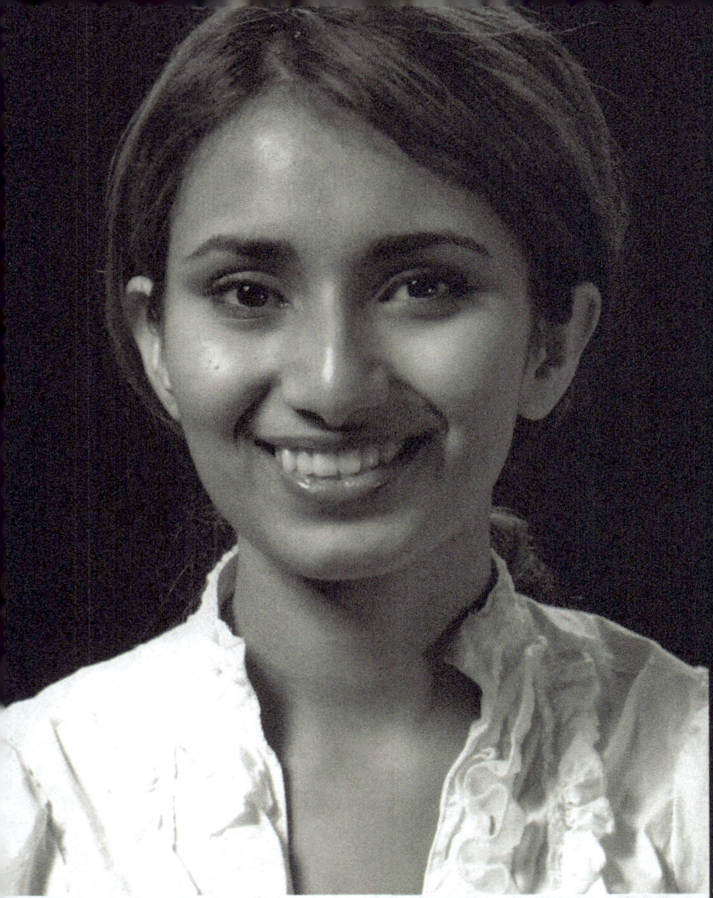

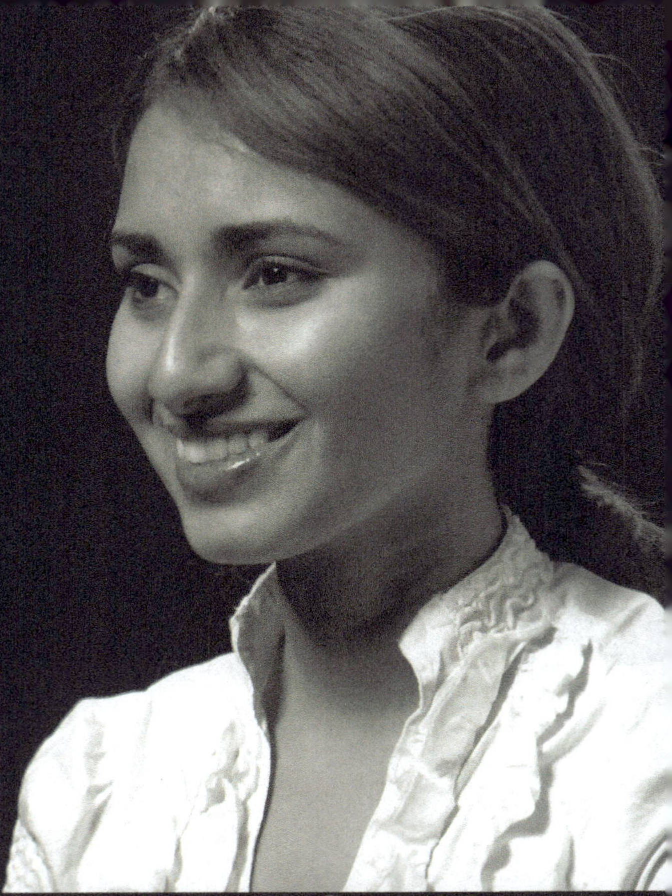

# HAPPY

MAP REFERENCE:

31

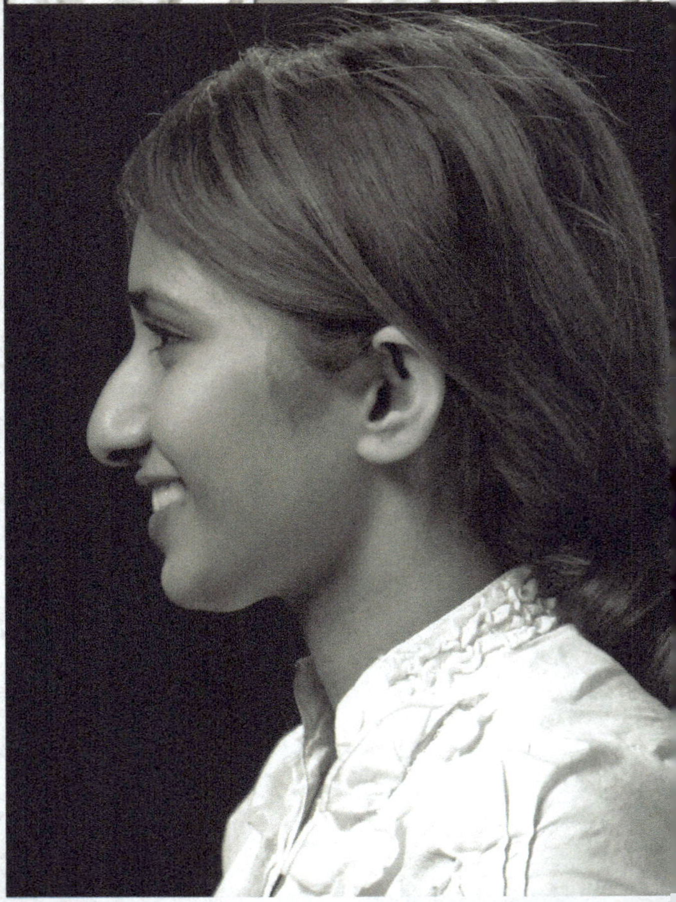

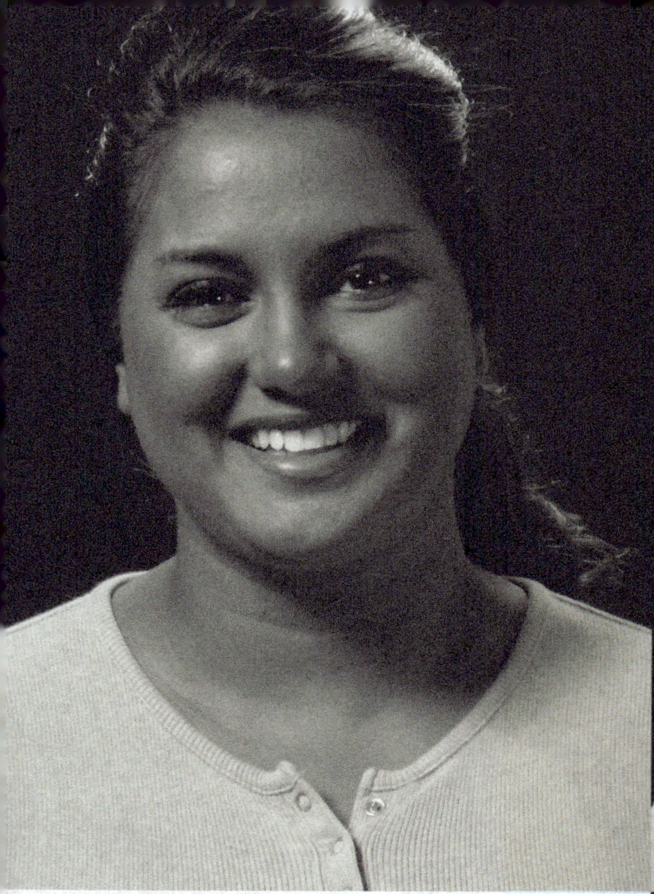

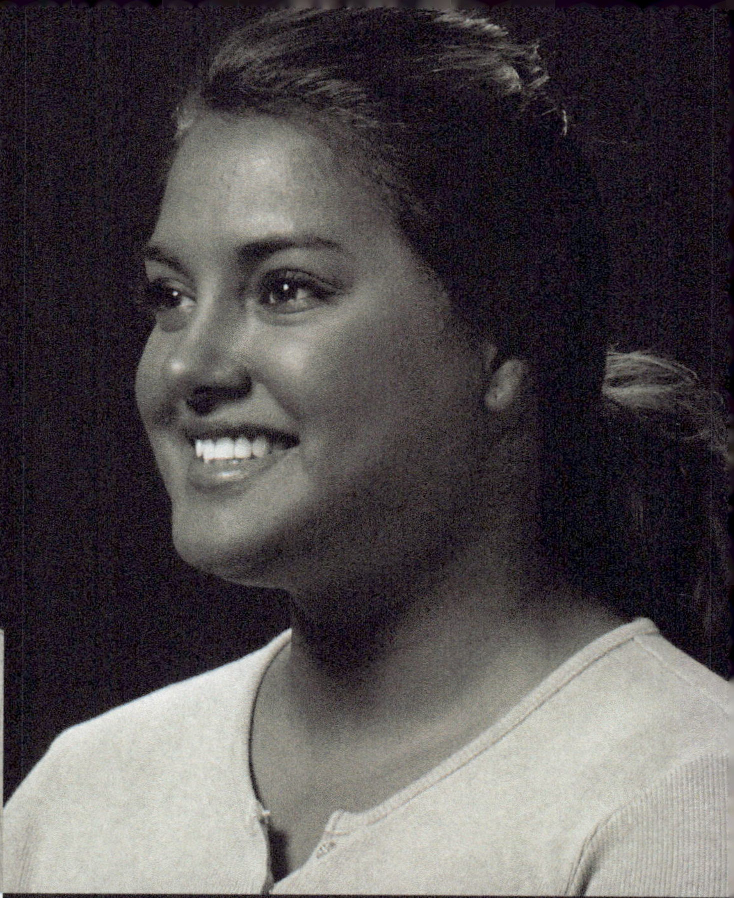

HAPPY

MAP REFERENCE:

39

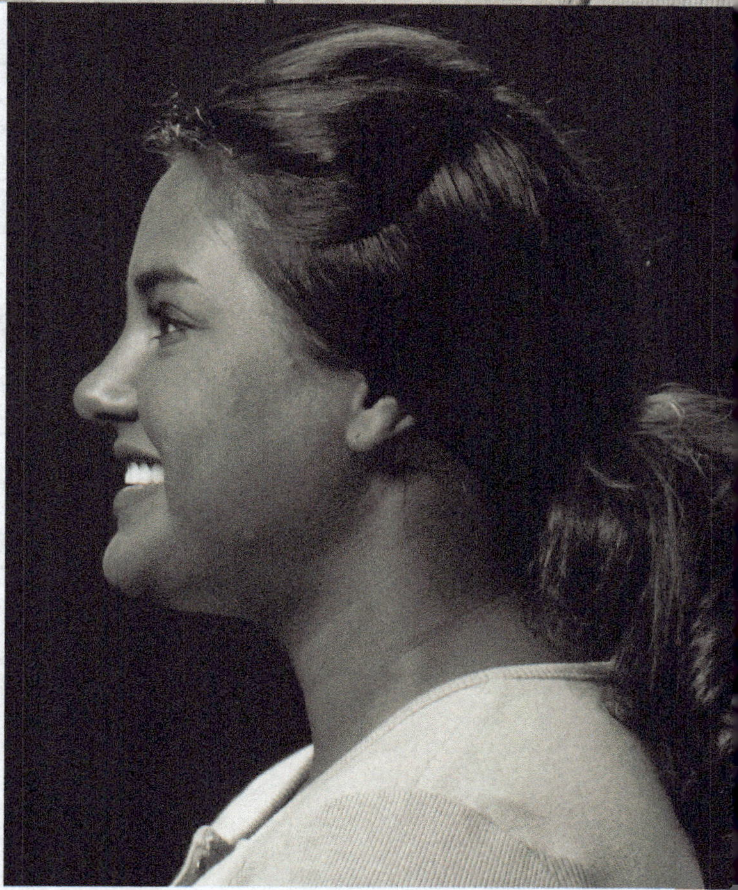

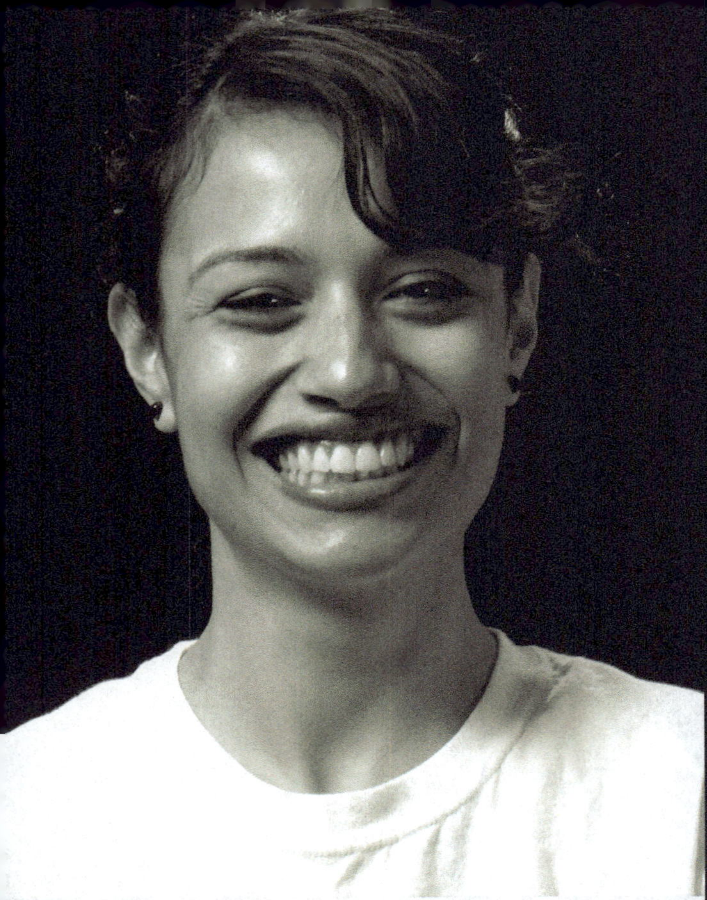

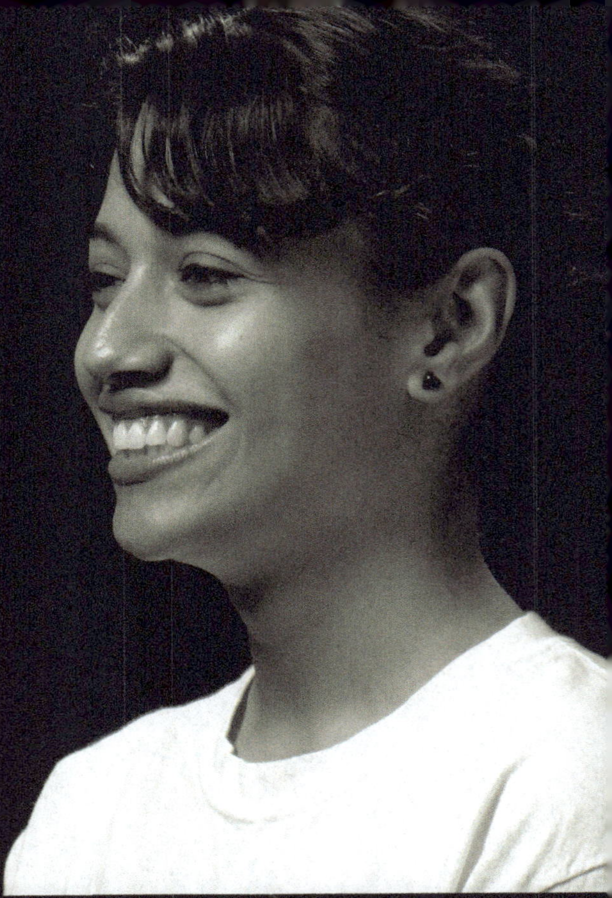

# HAPPY

MAP REFERENCE:

40

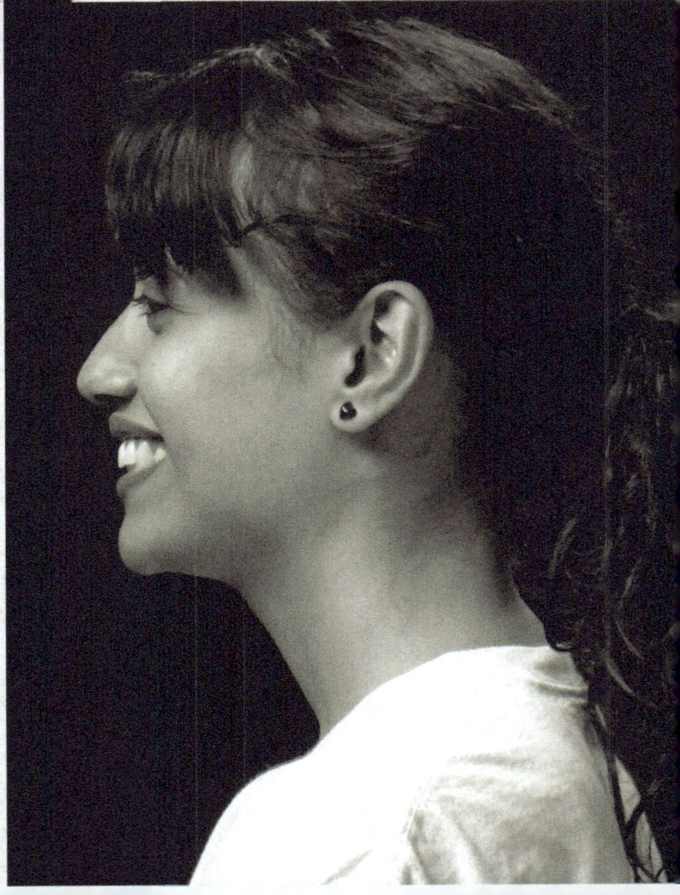

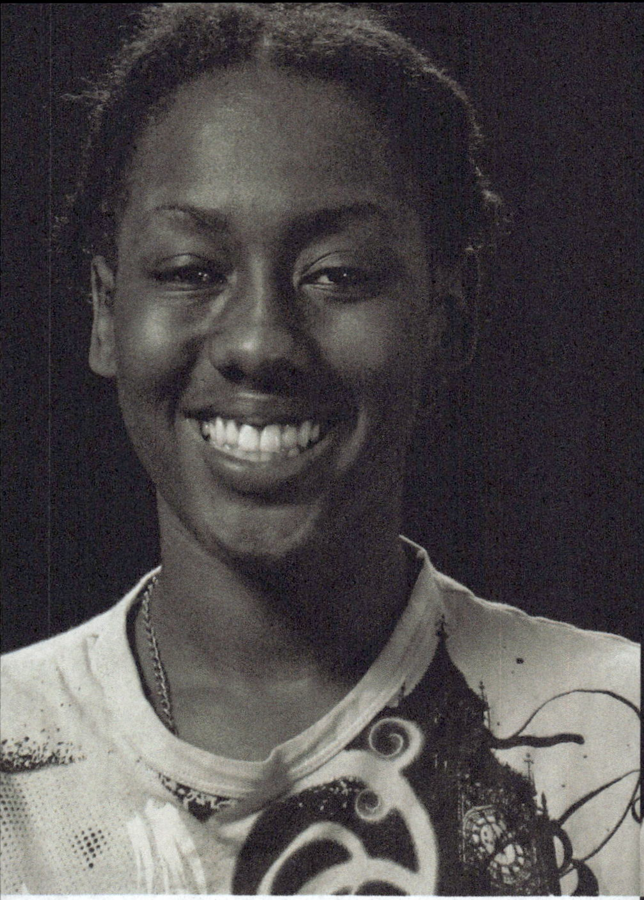

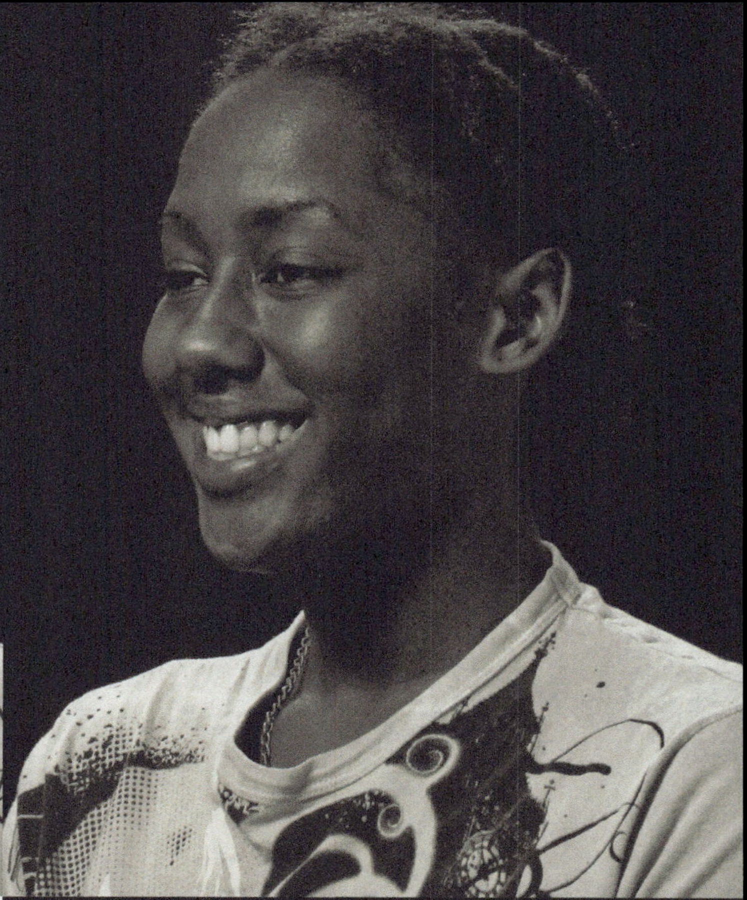

HAPPY

MAP REFERENCE:

43

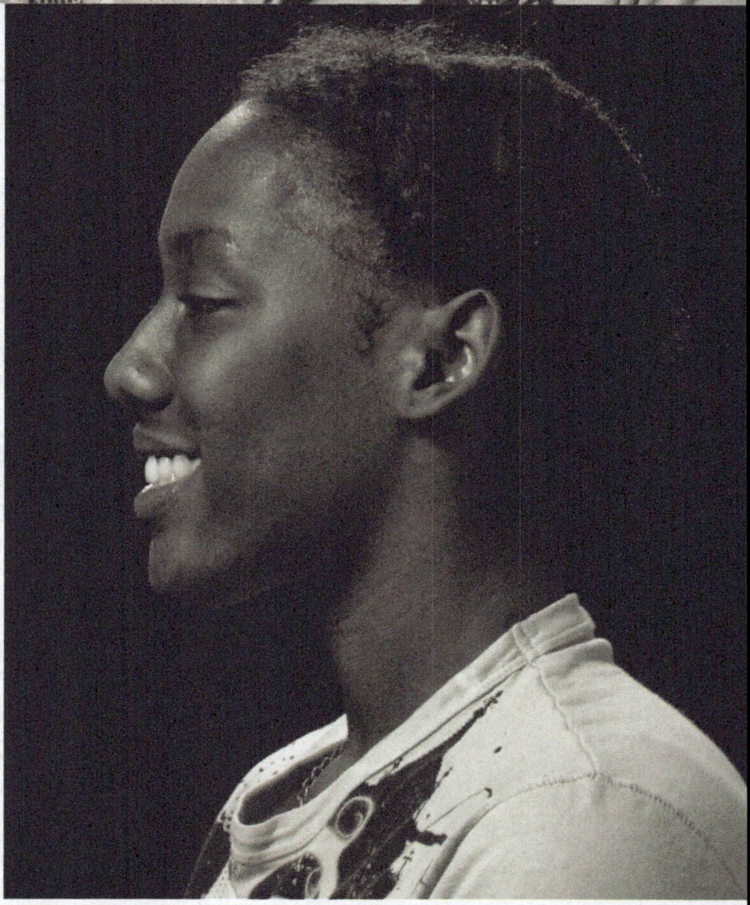

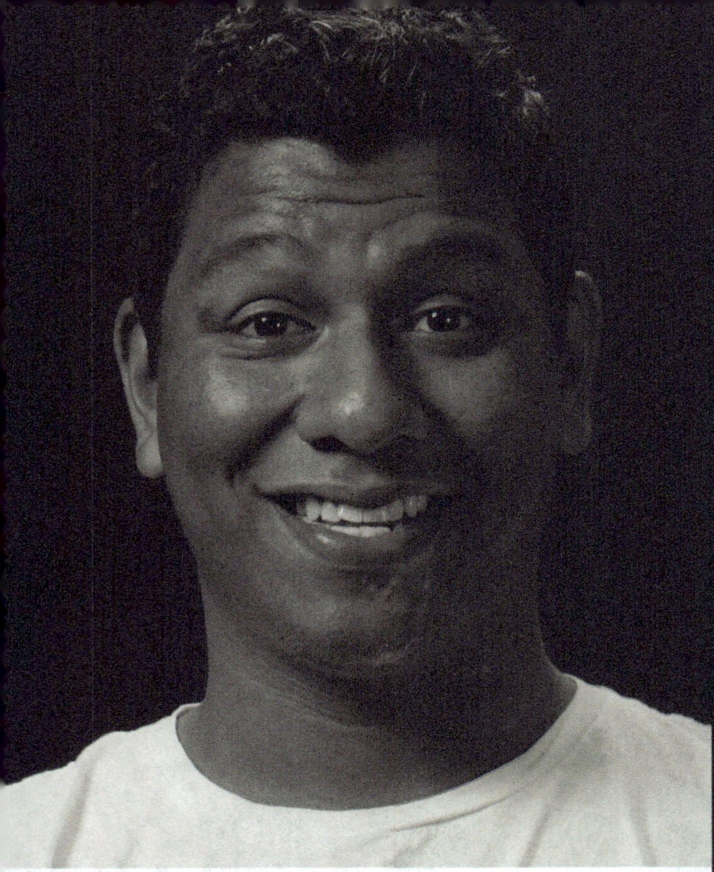

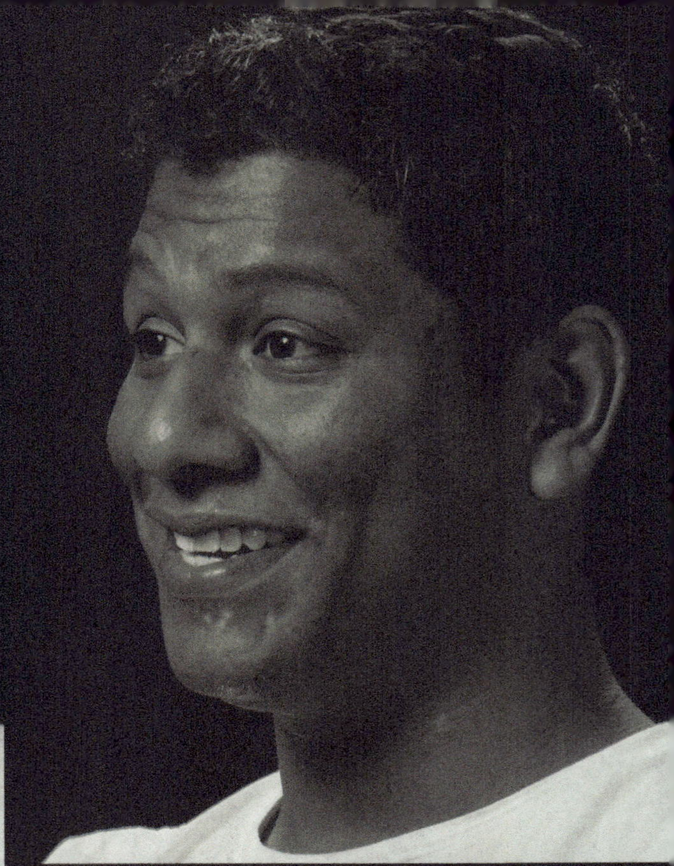

# HAPPY

MAP REFERENCE:

45

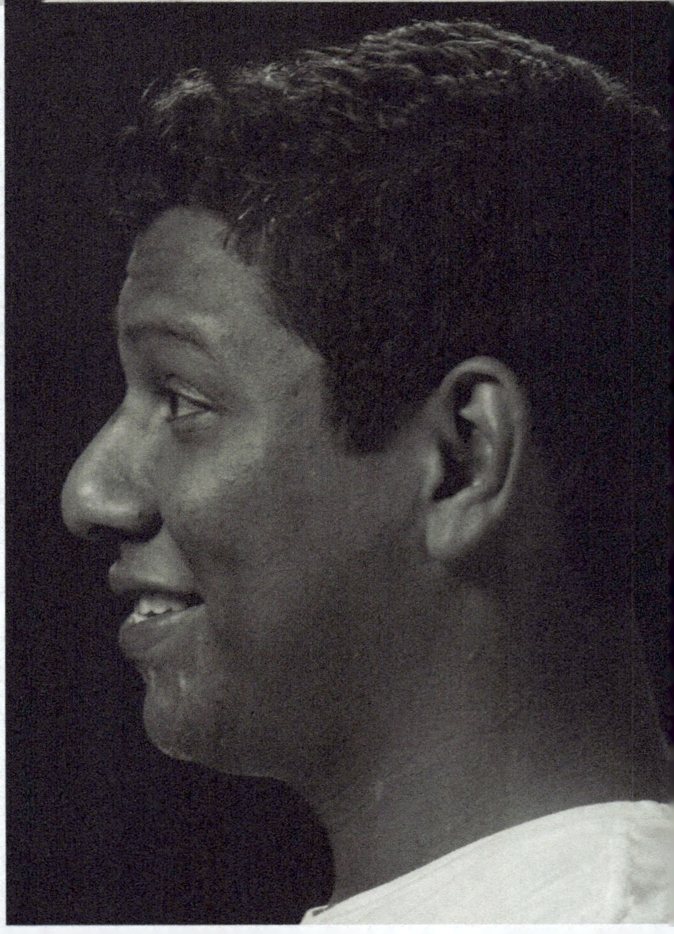

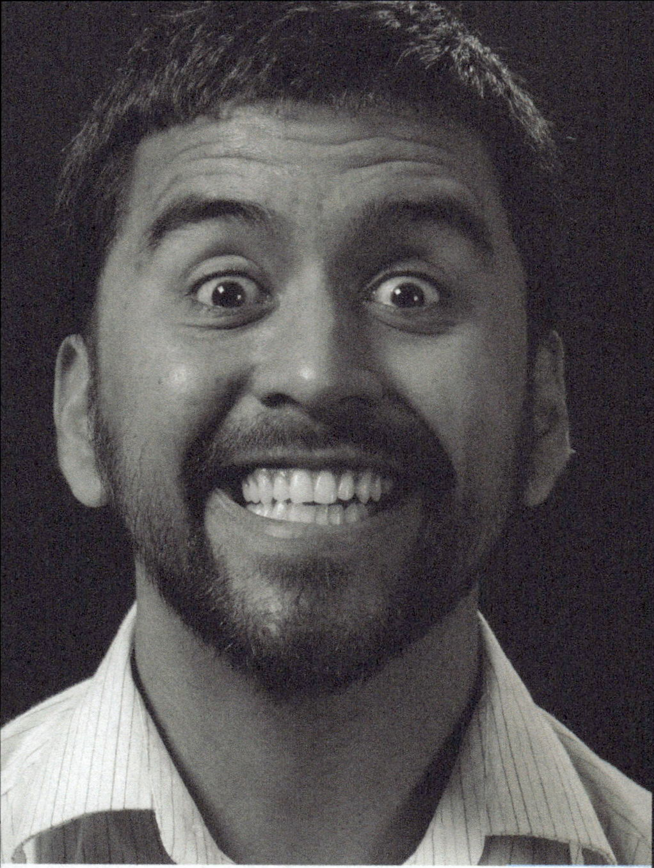

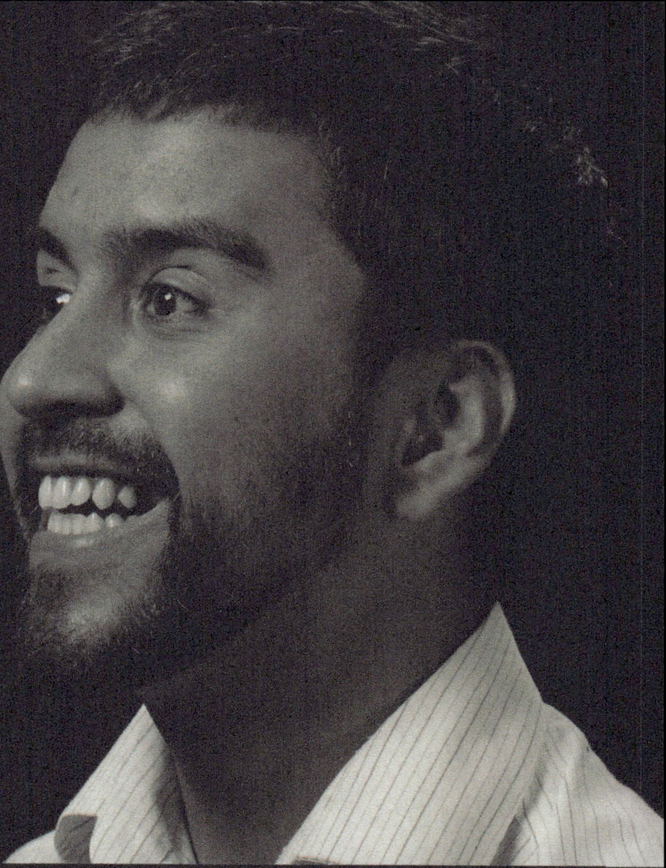

## HAPPY

MAP REFERENCE:

49

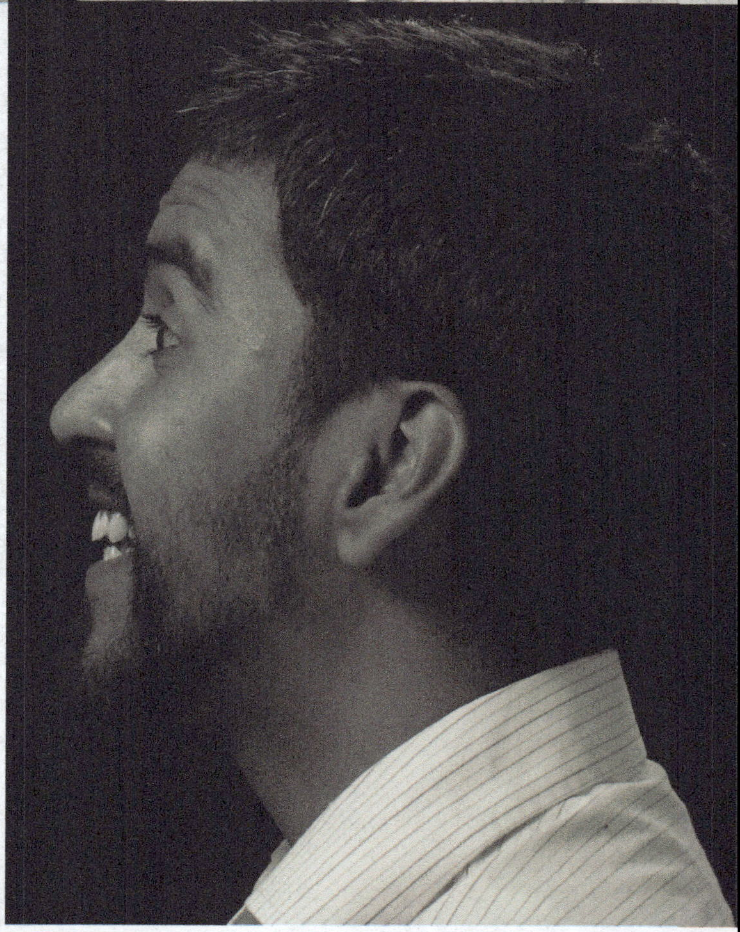

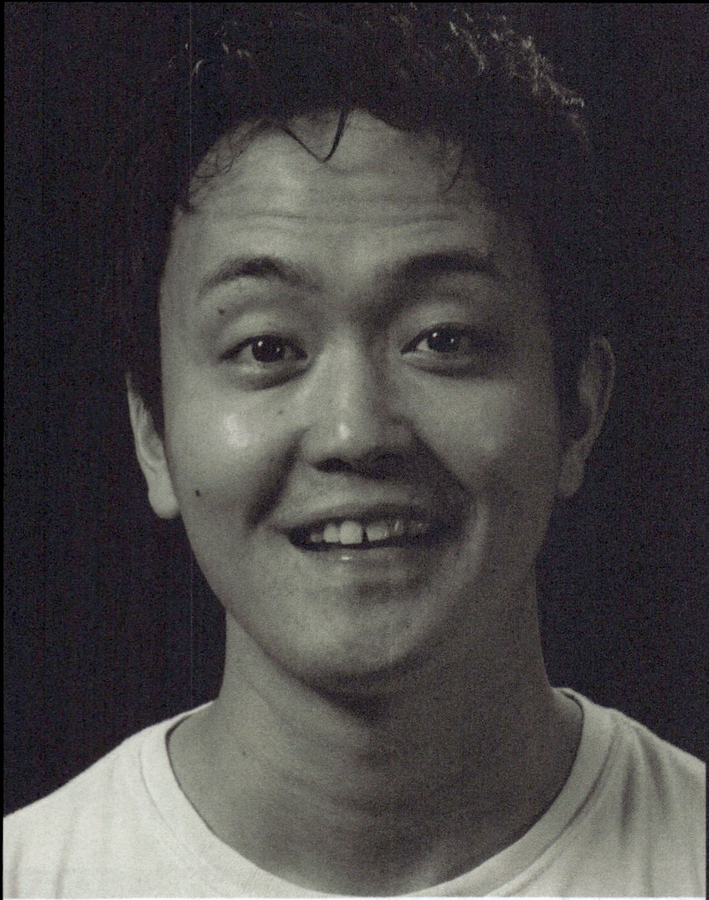

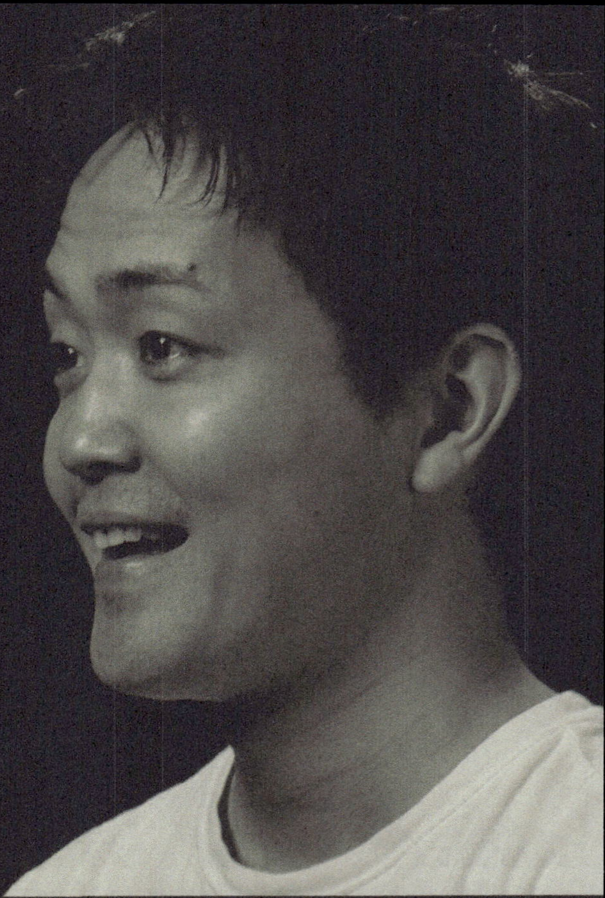

# HAPPY

MAP REFERENCE:

50

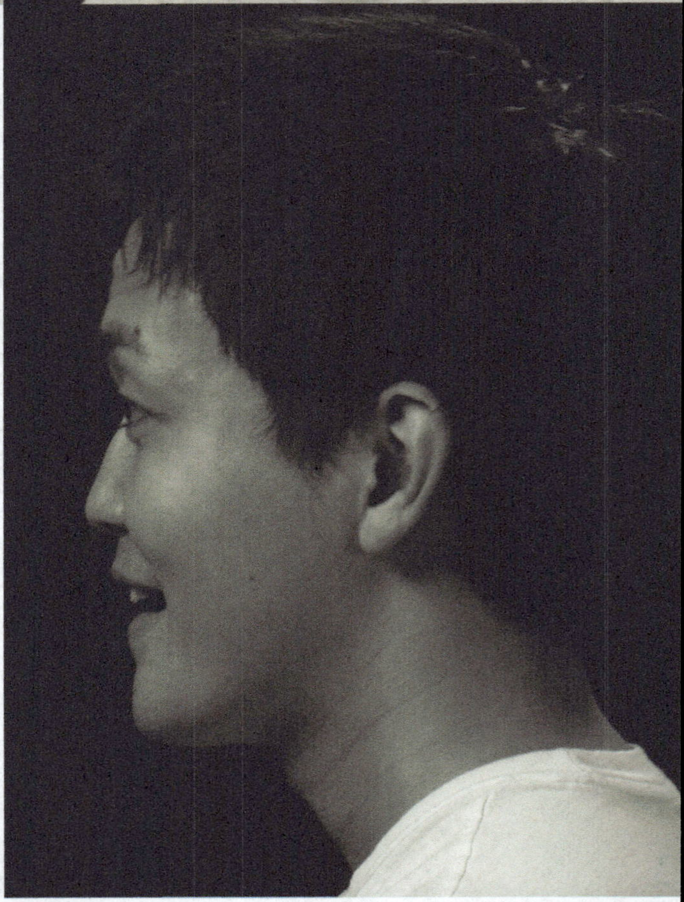

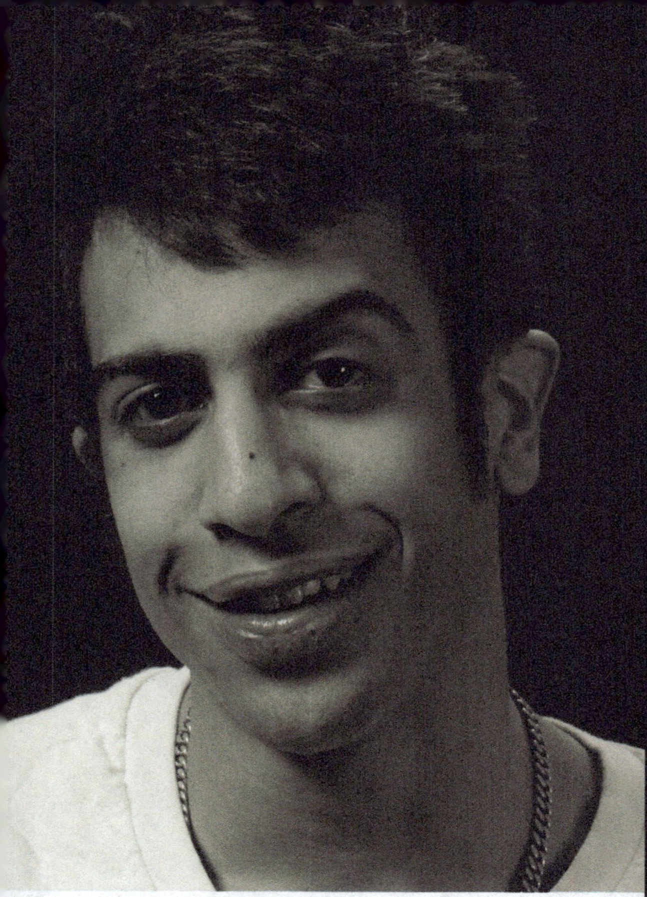

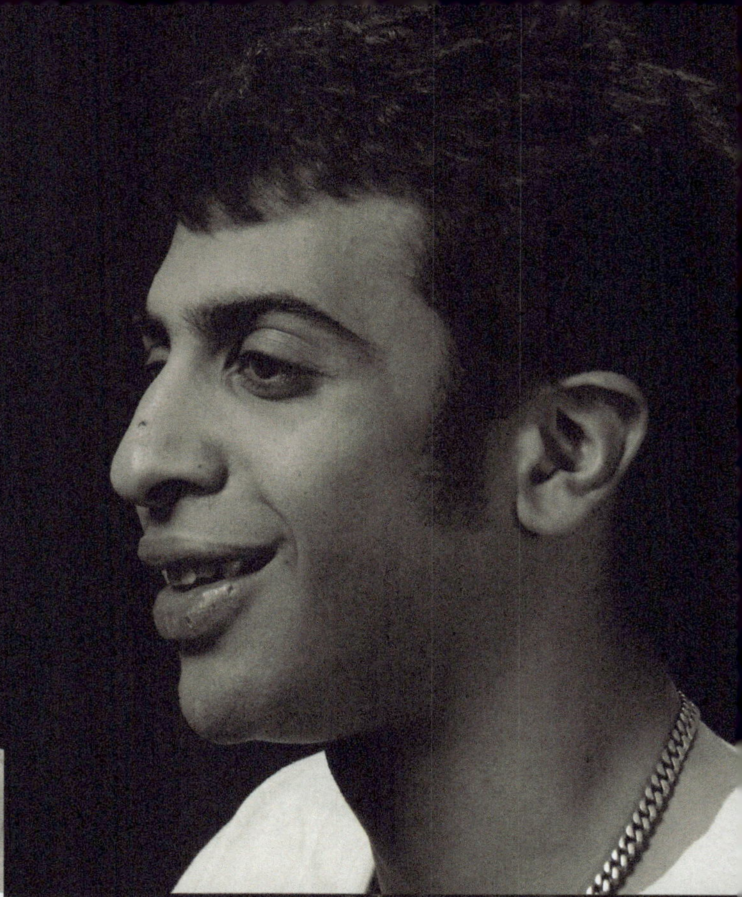

HAPPY

MAP REFERENCE:

51

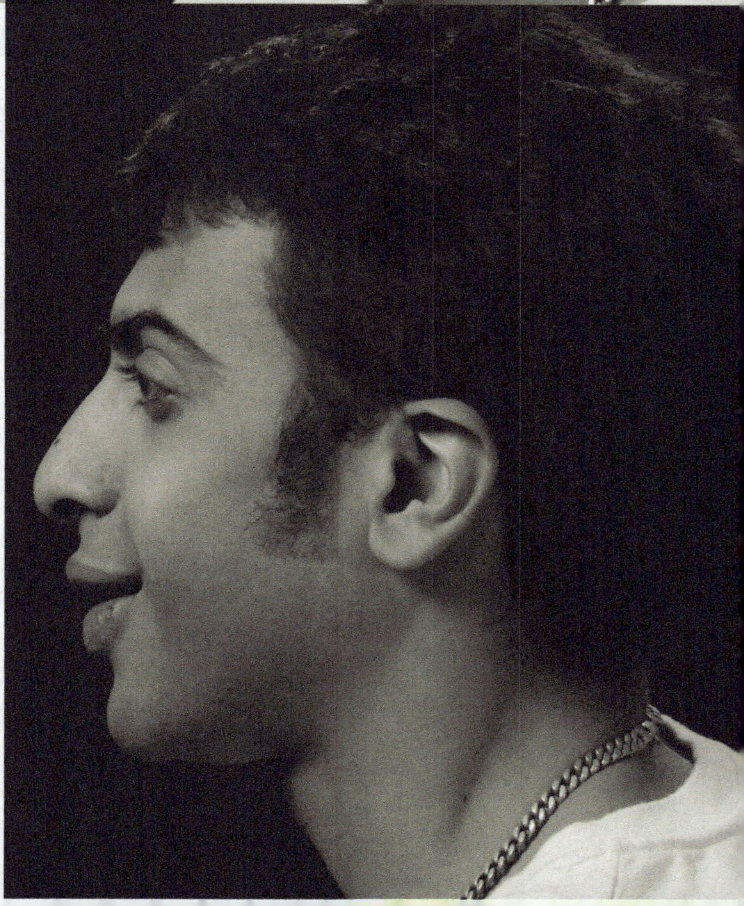

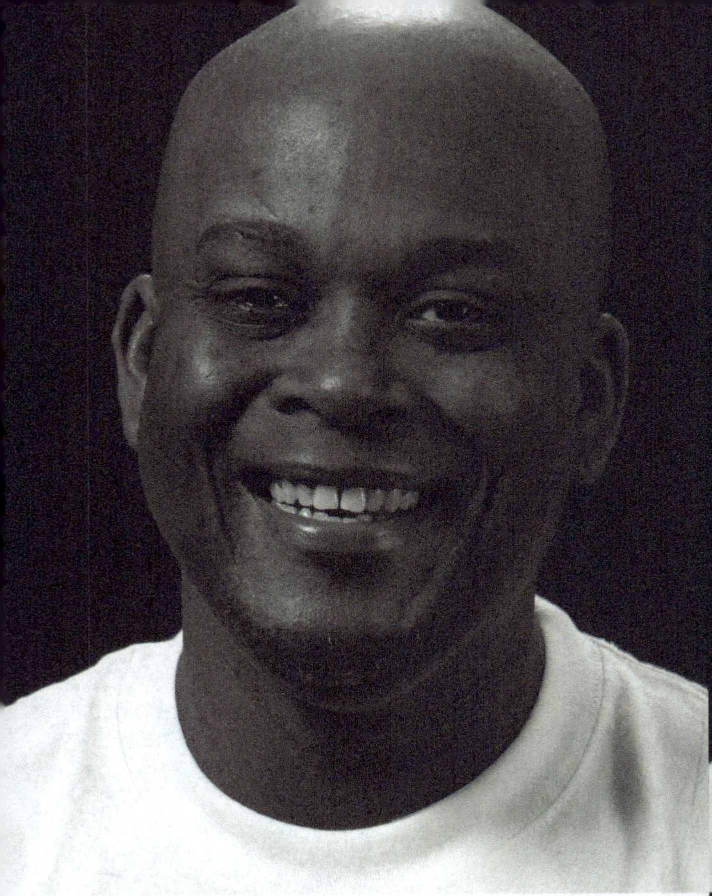
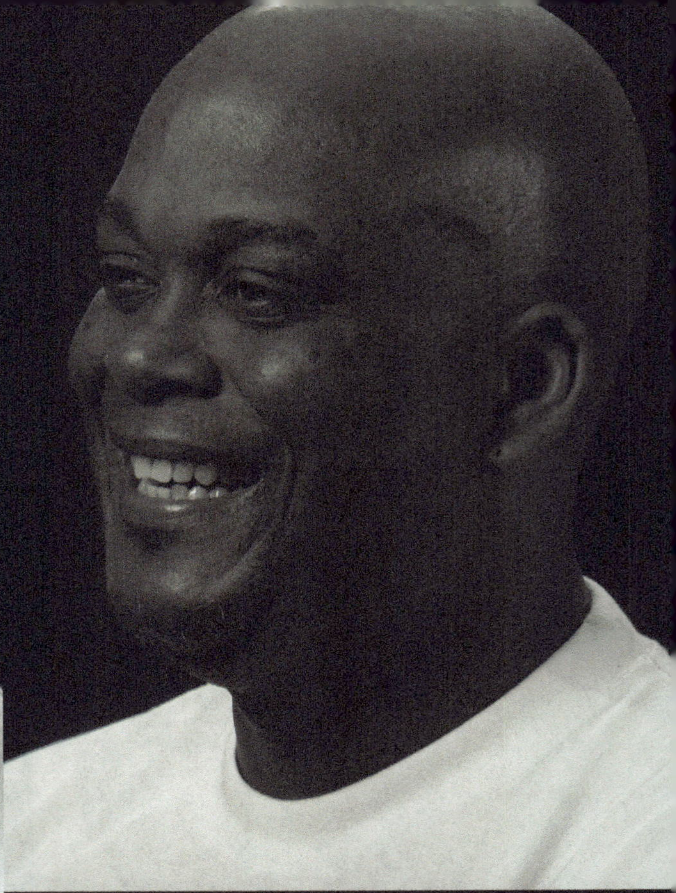

# HAPPY

MAP REFERENCE:

57

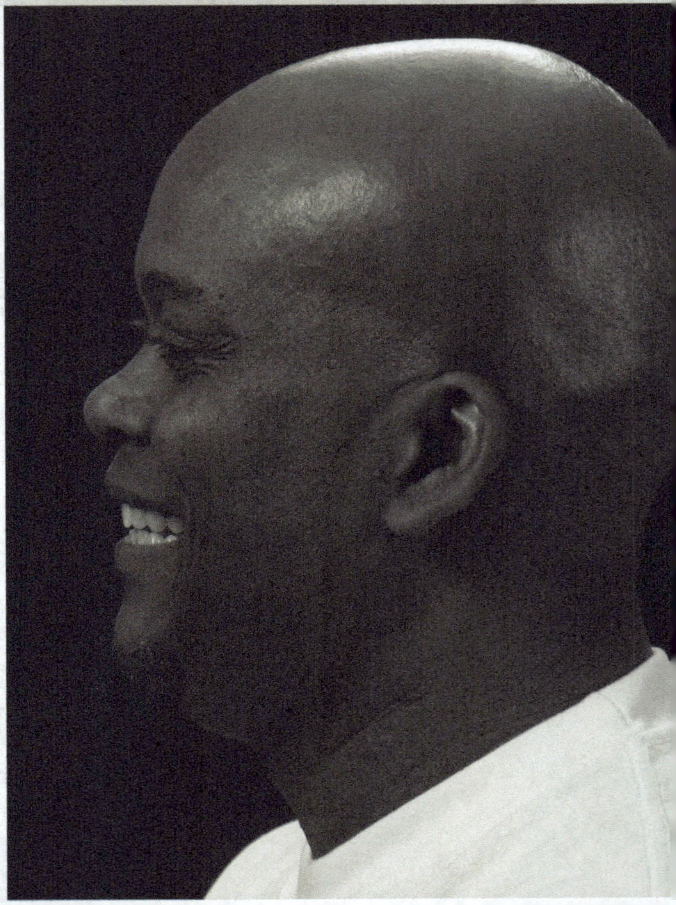

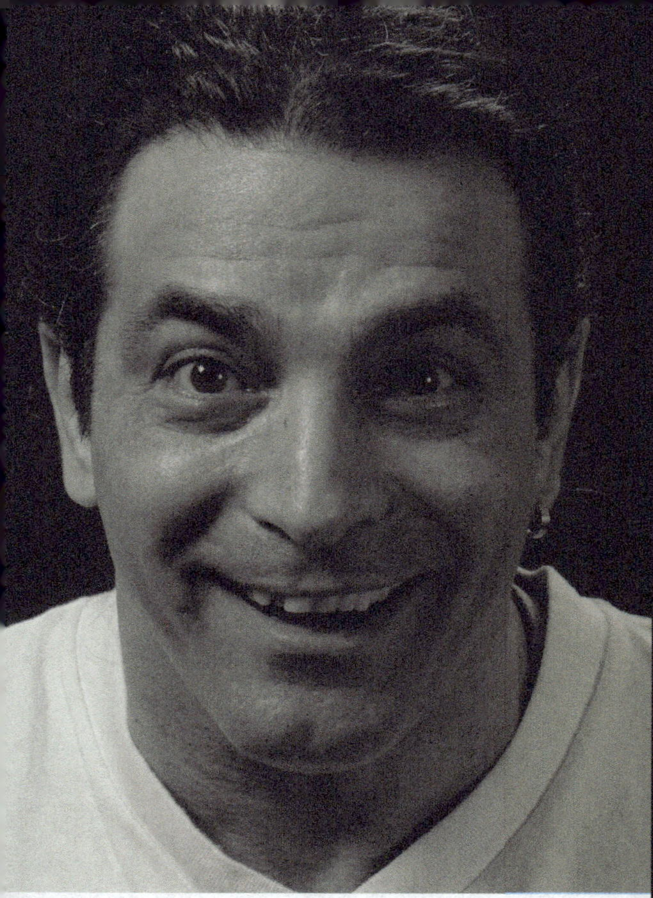

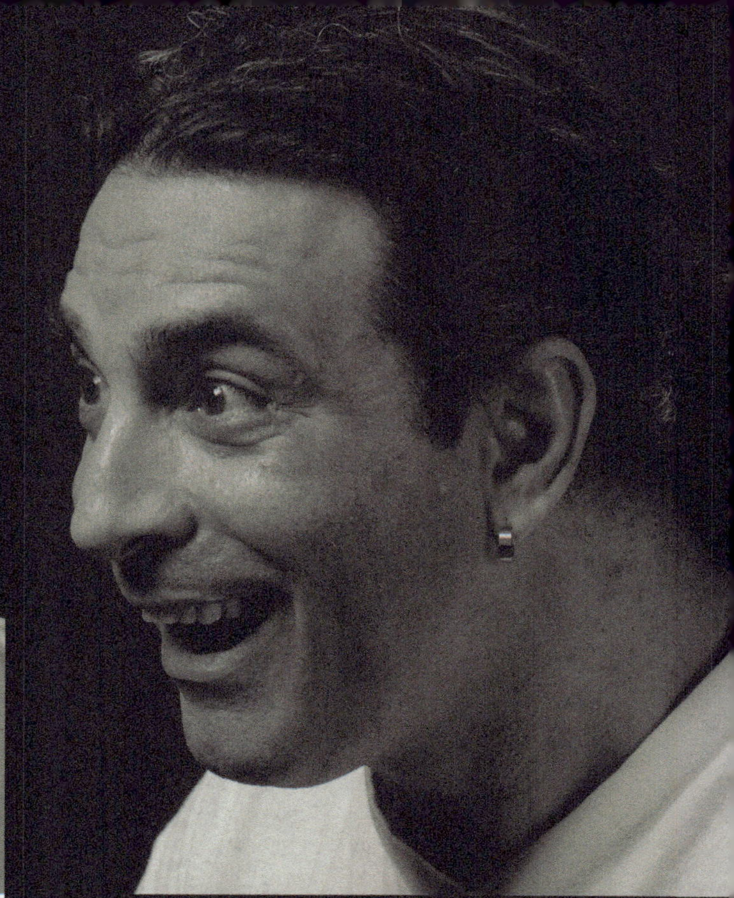

# HAPPY

MAP REFERENCE:

61

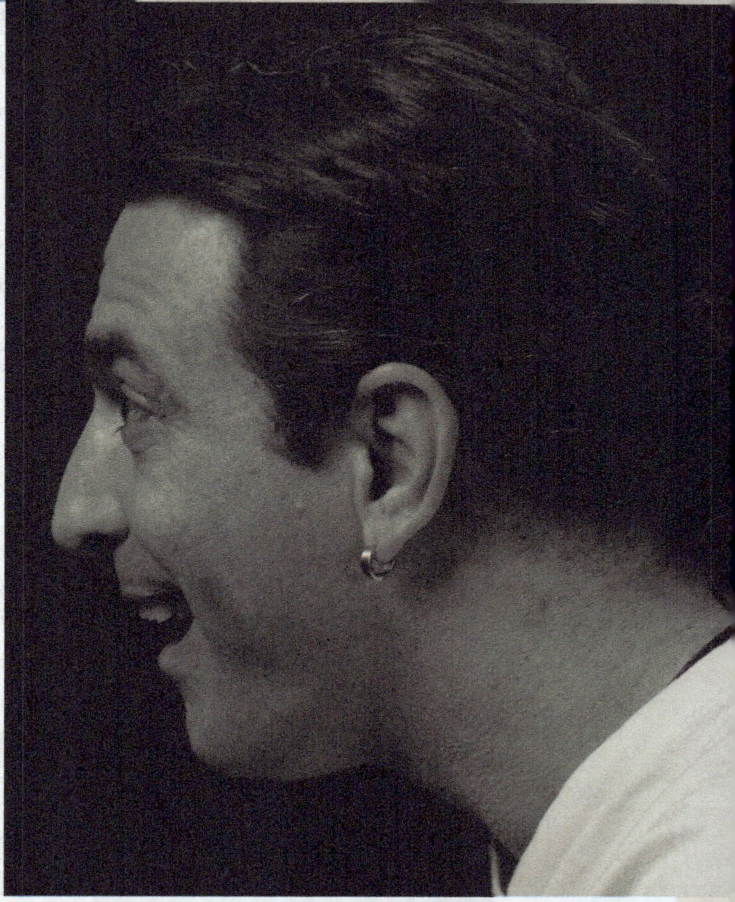

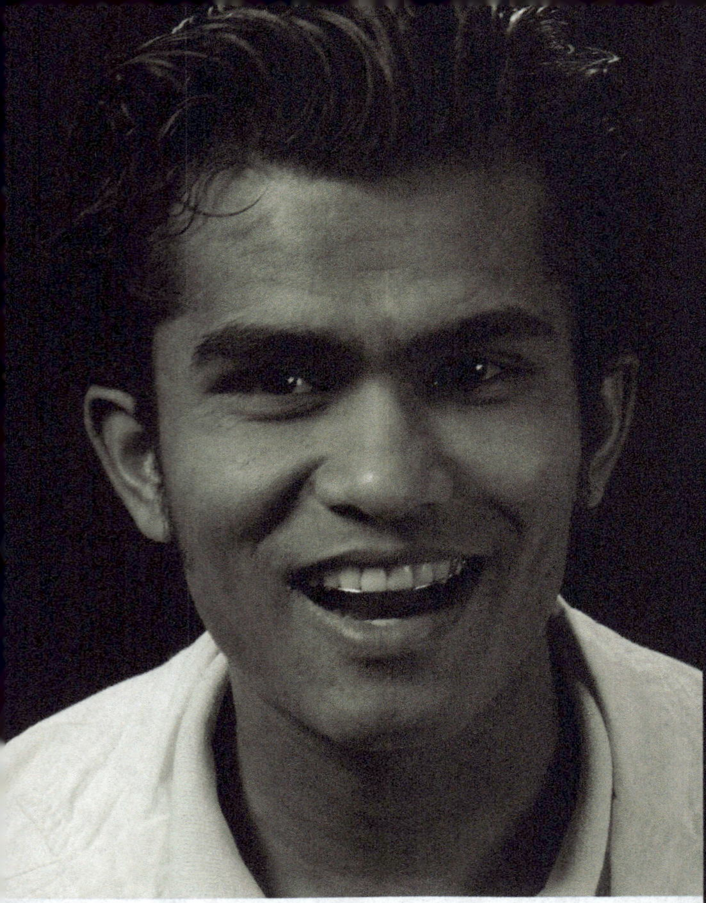

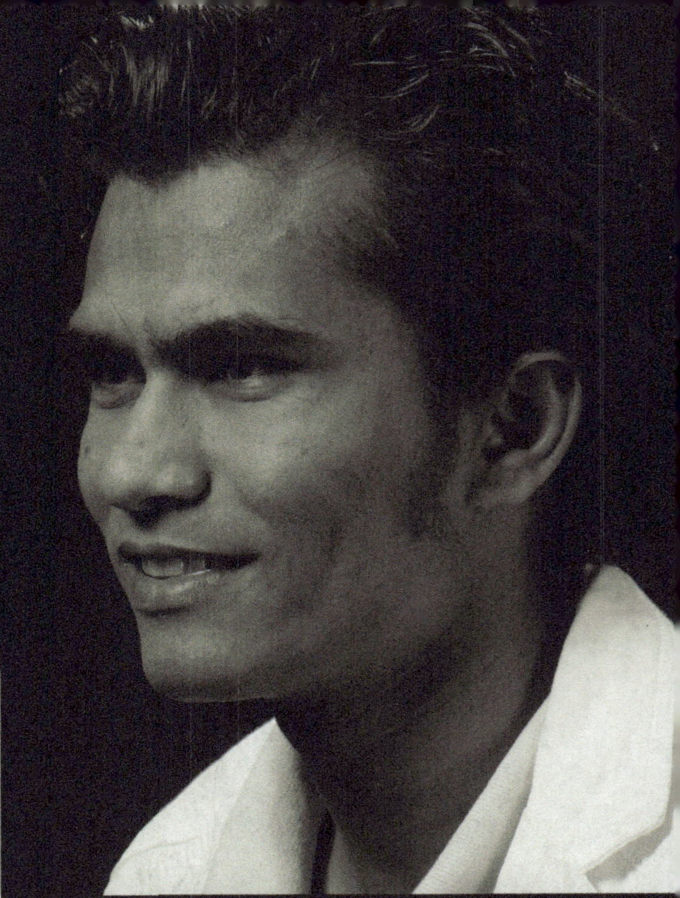

# HAPPY

MAP REFERENCE:
62

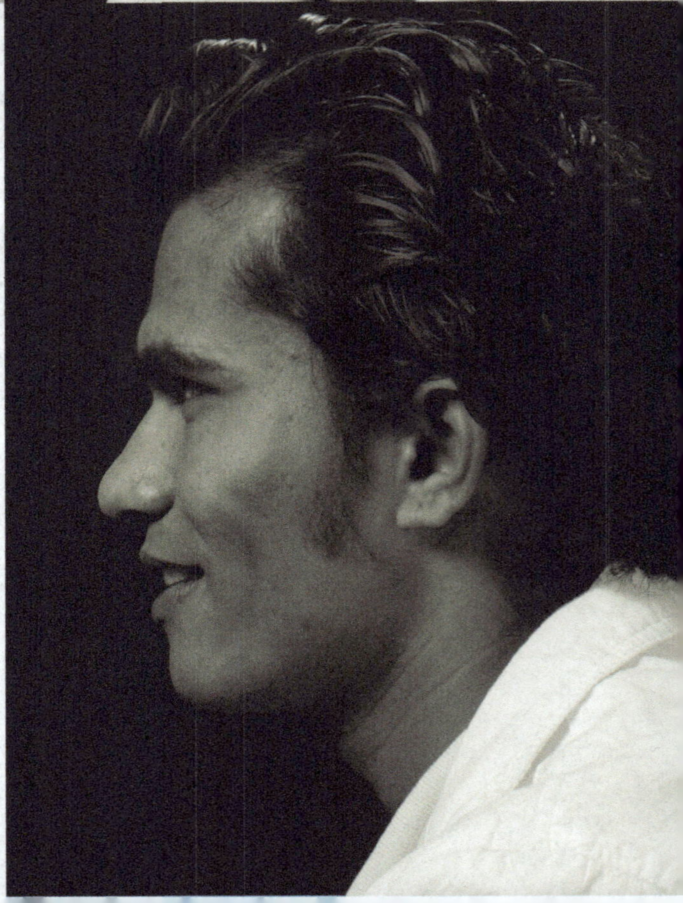

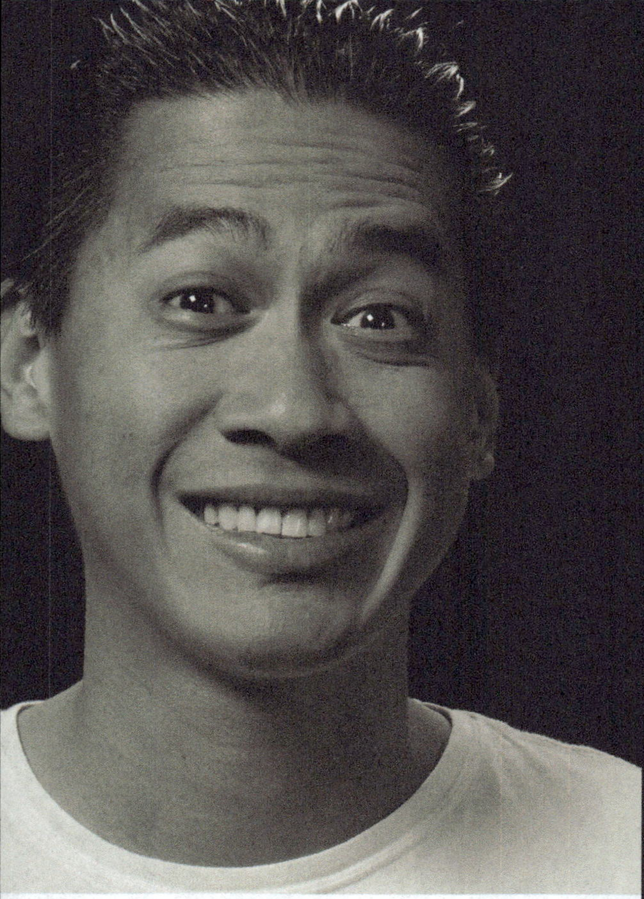

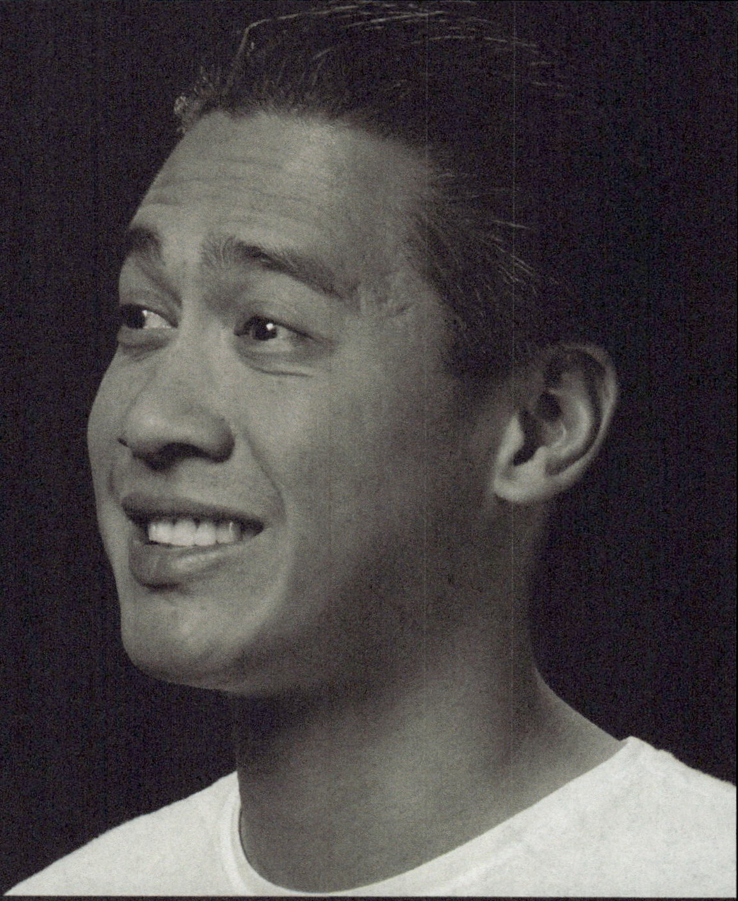

# HAPPY

MAP REFERENCE:

66

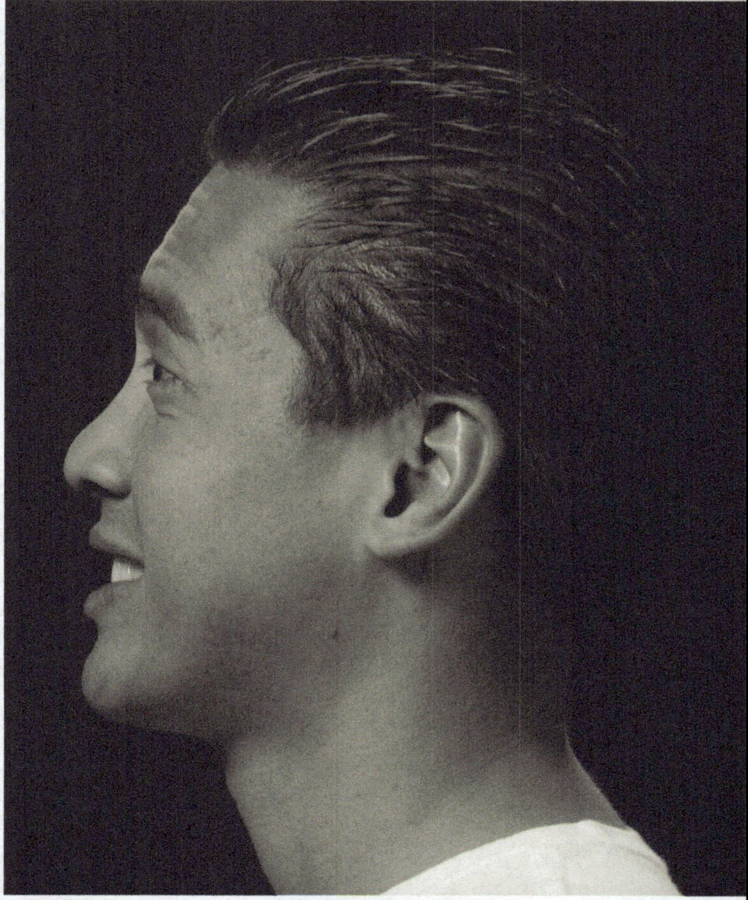

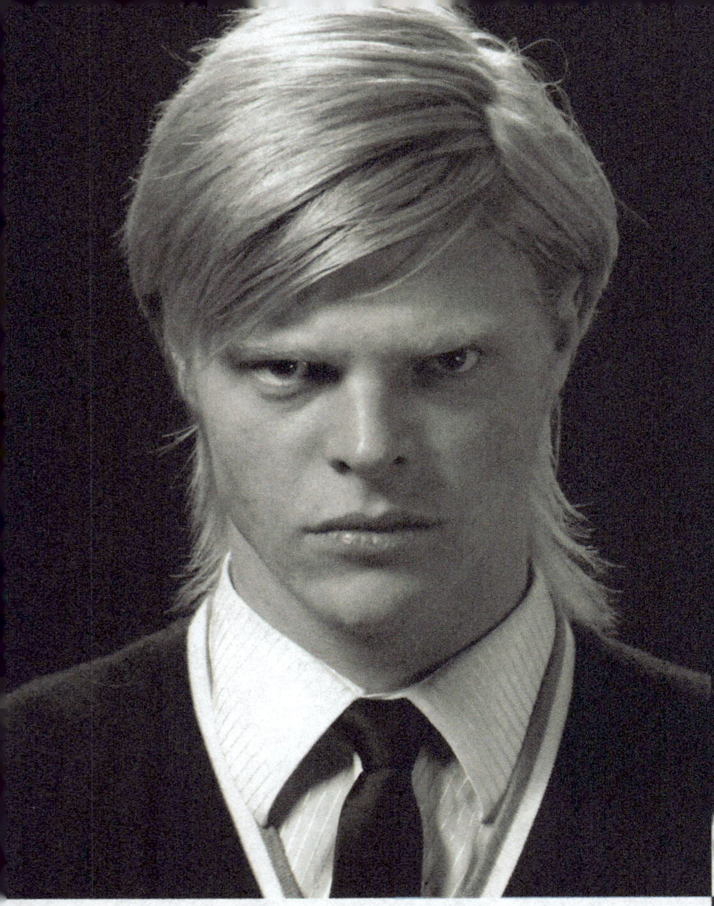

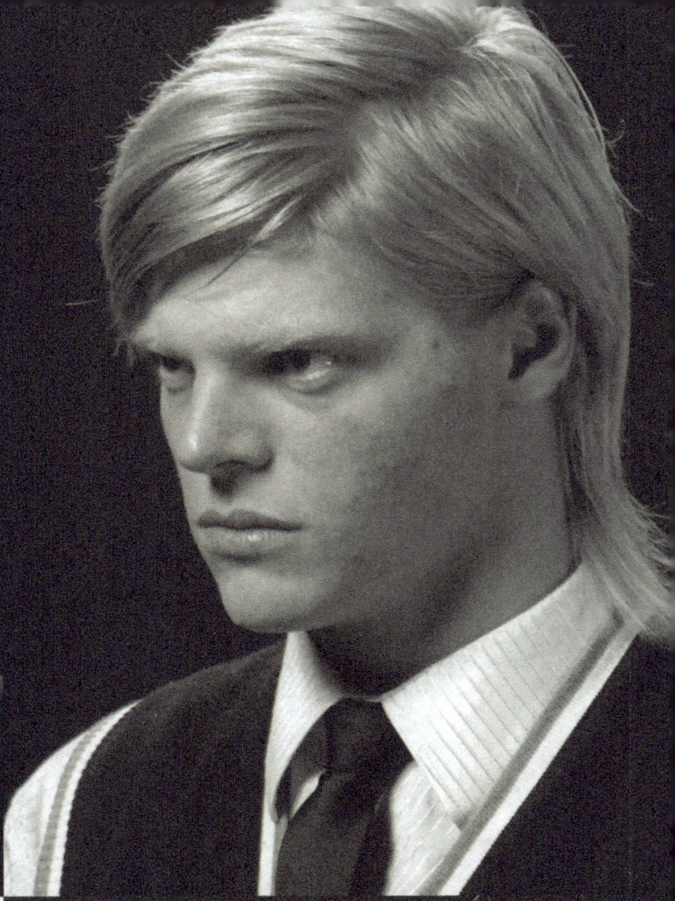

# ANGRY

MAP REFERENCE:

27

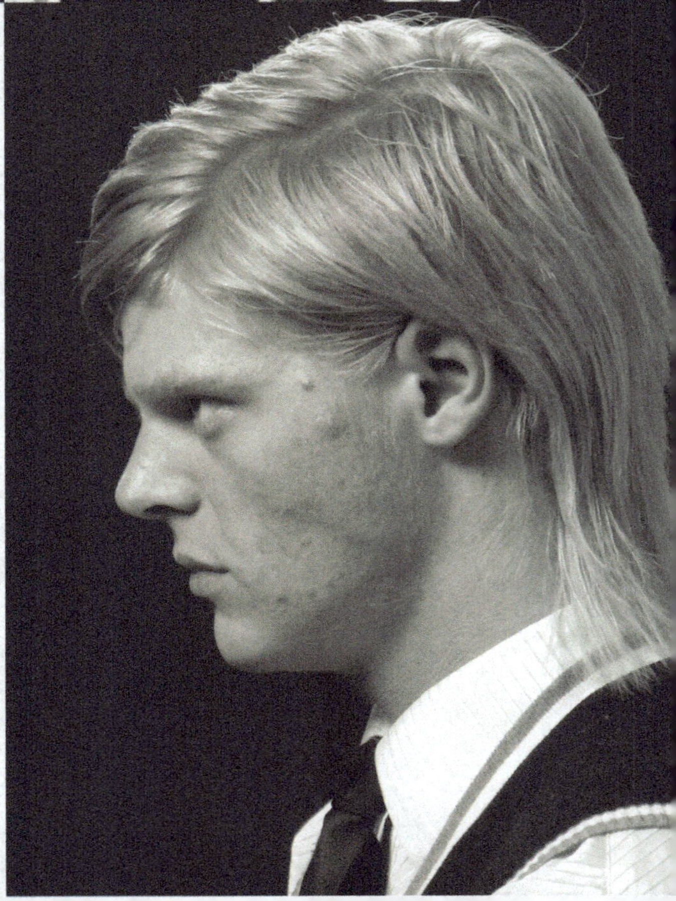

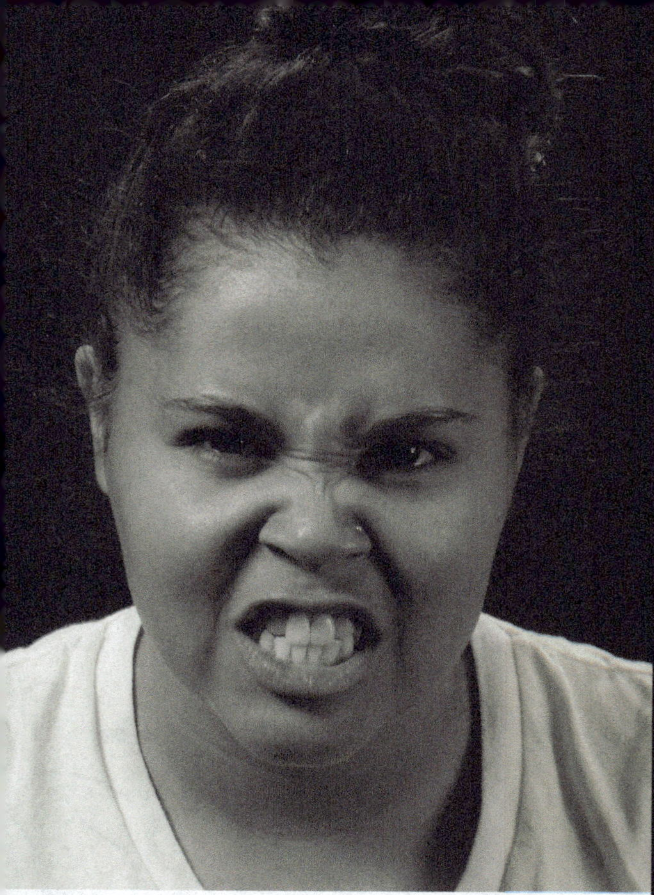

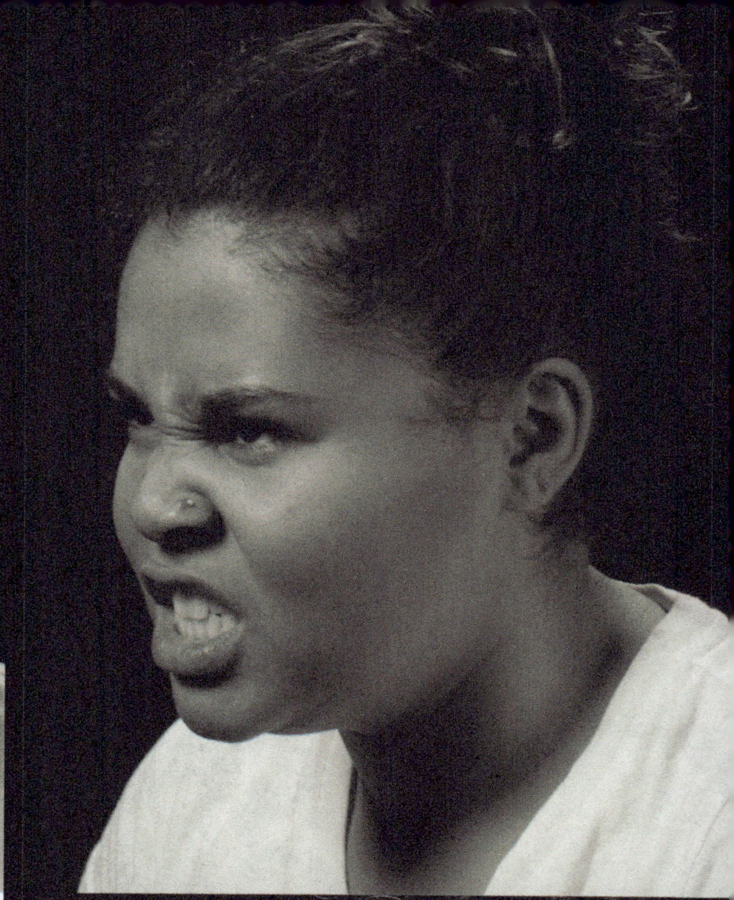

# ANGRY

MAP REFERENCE:
73

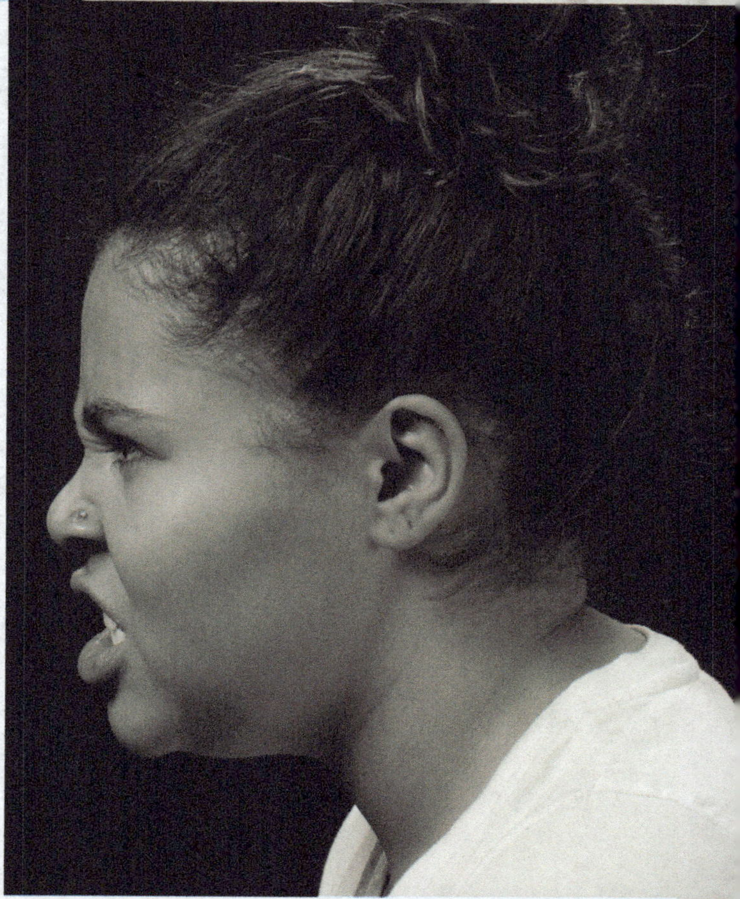

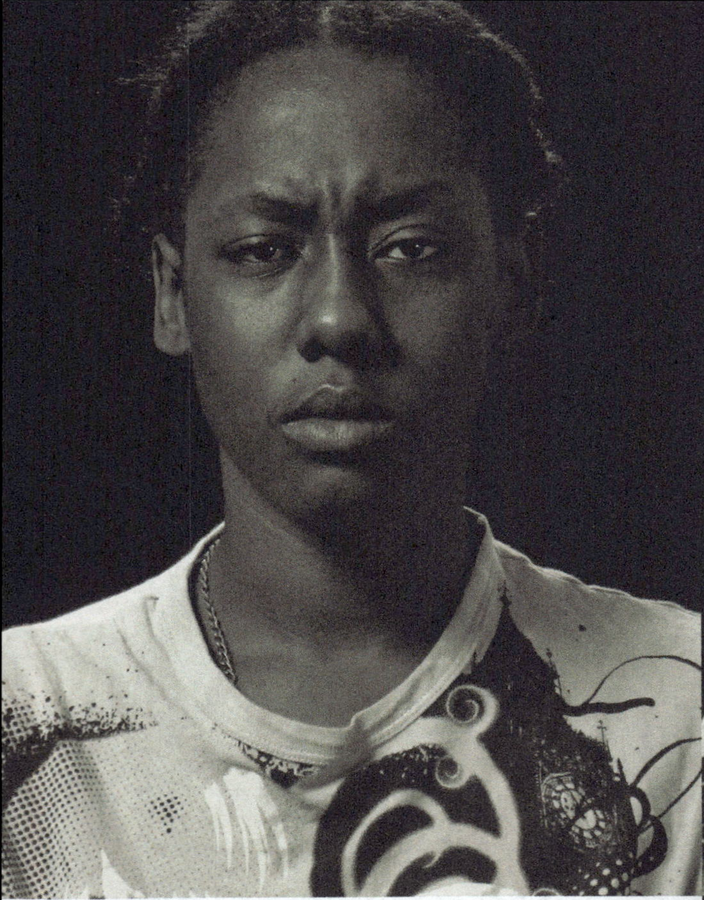

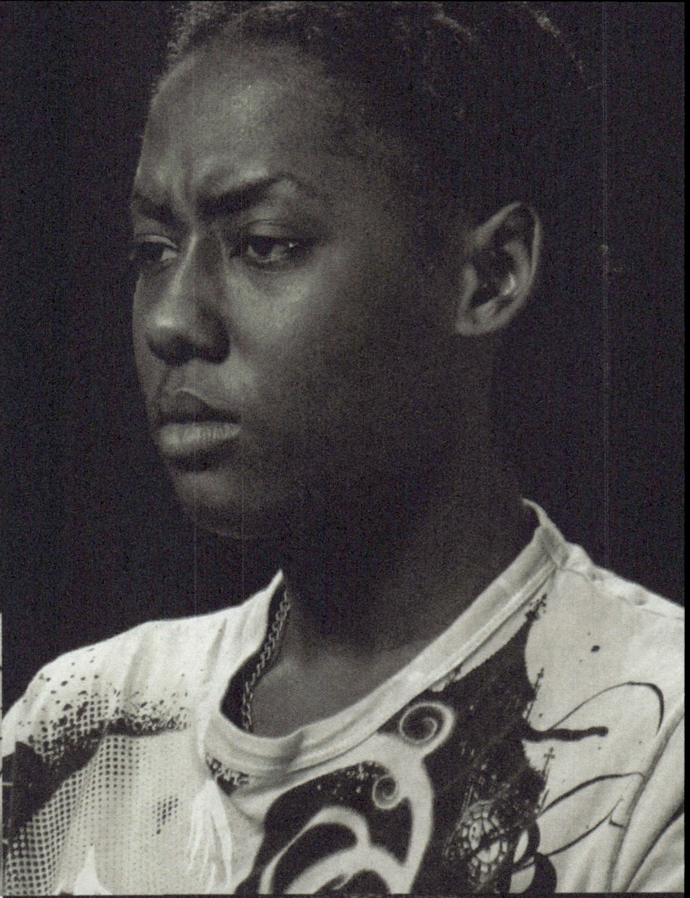

# ANGRY

MAP REFERENCE:

43

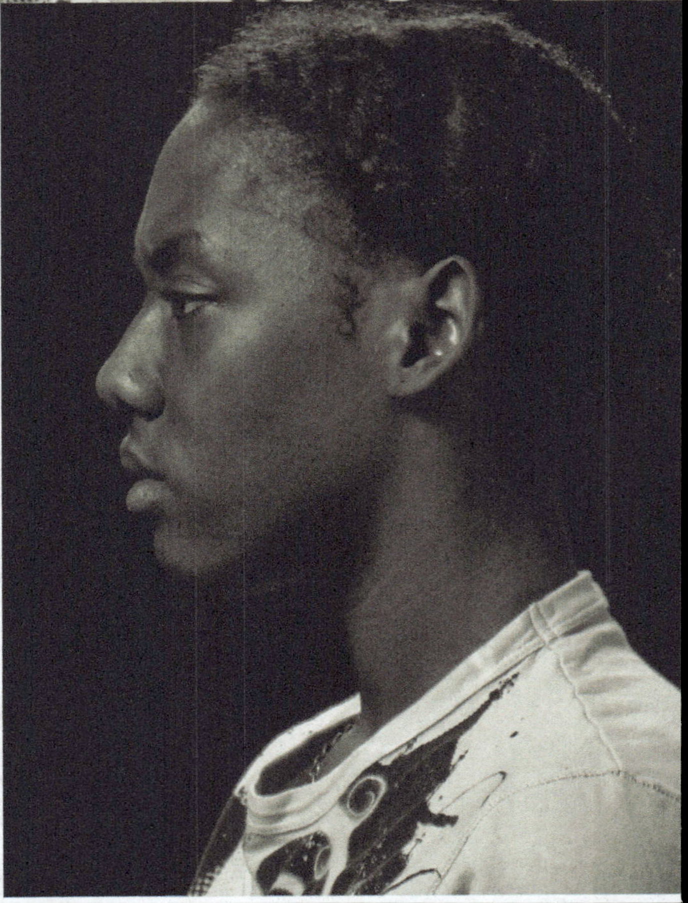

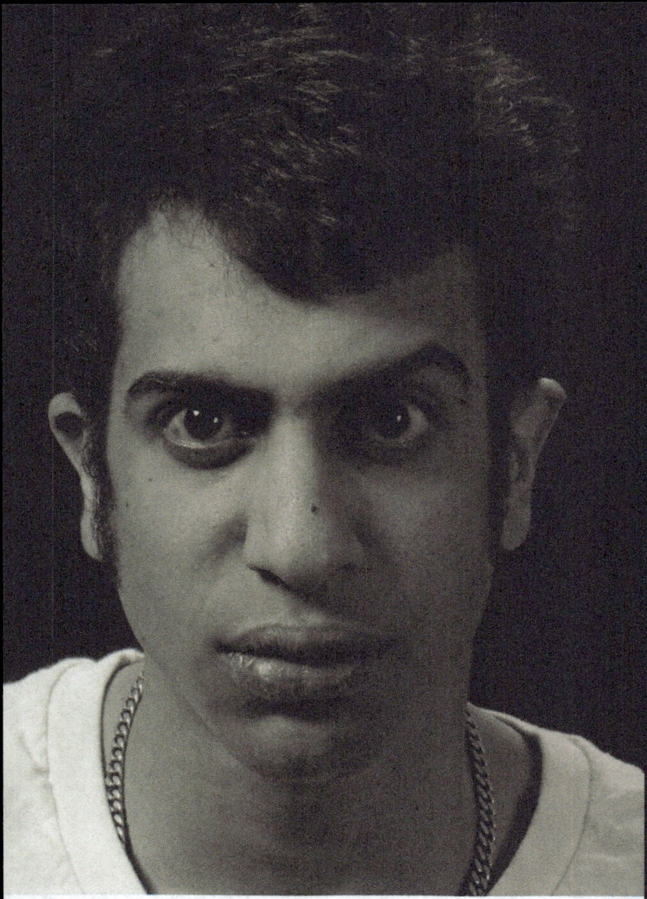

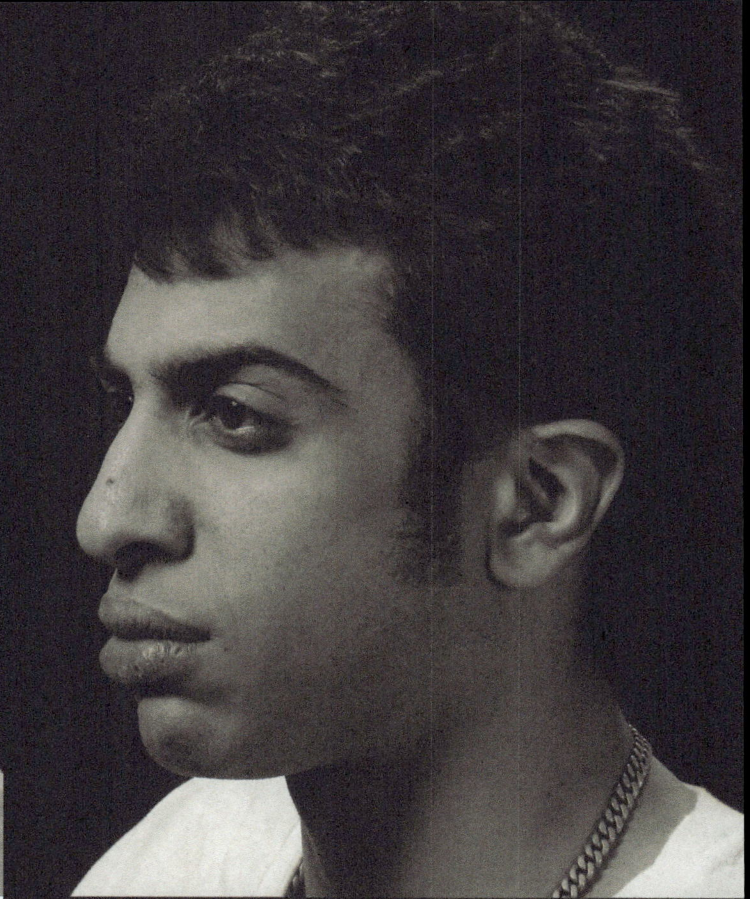

ANGRY

MAP REFERENCE:

51

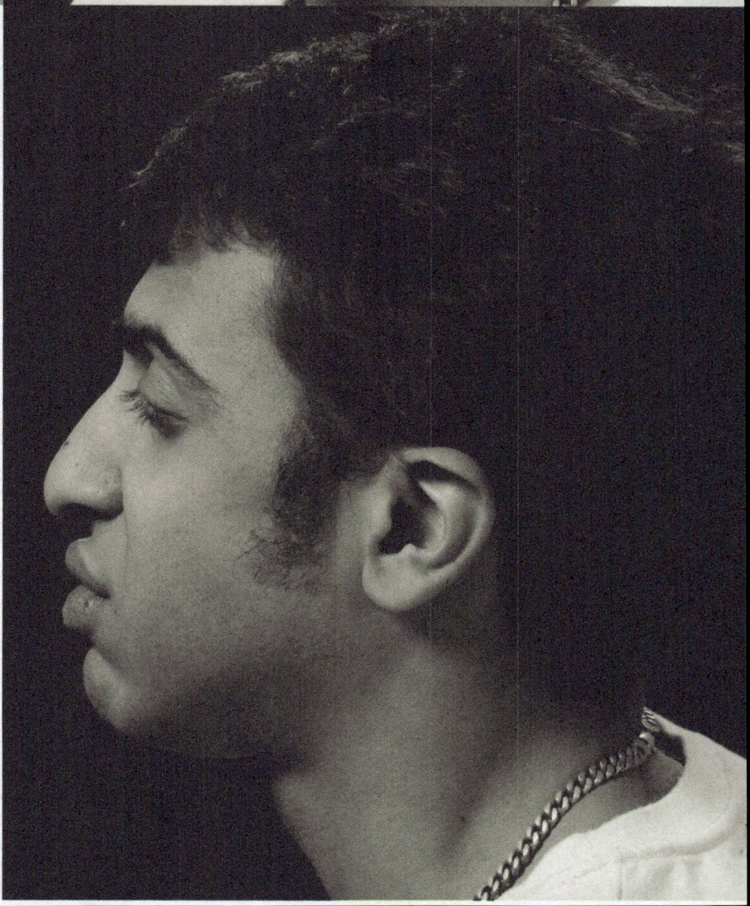

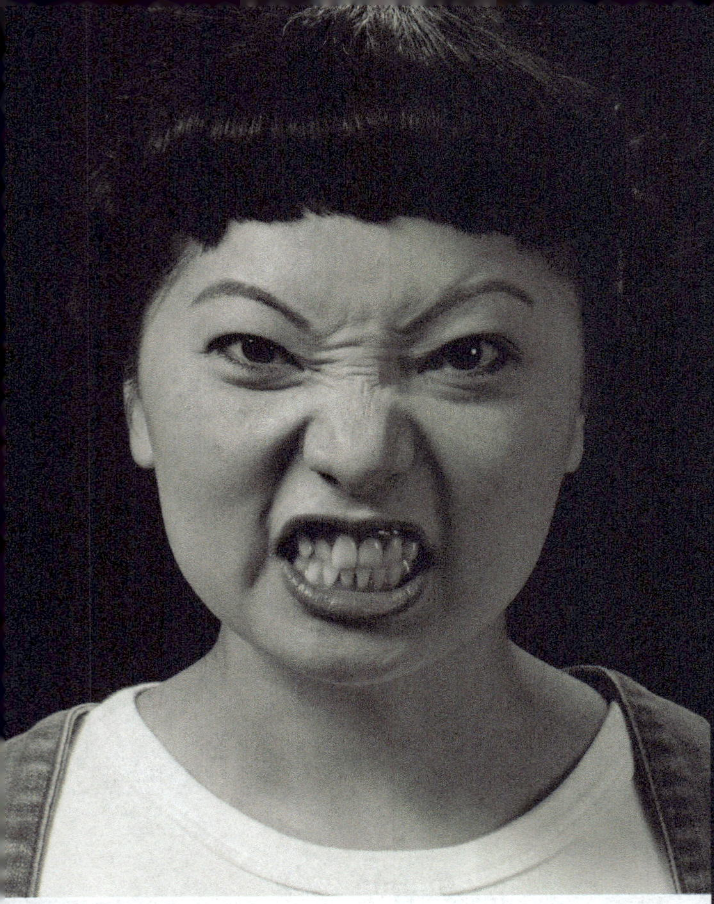

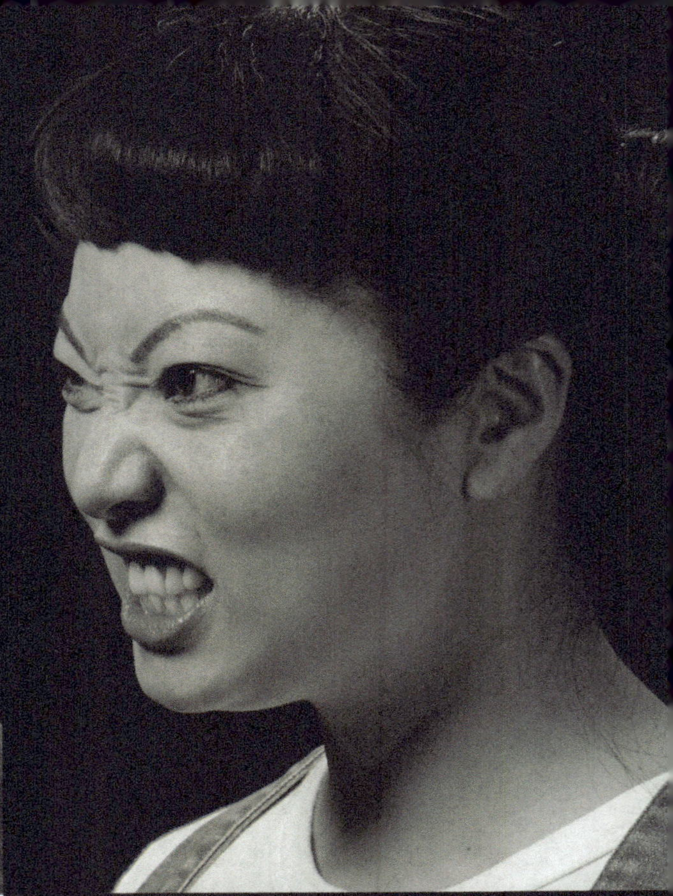

# ANGRY

MAP REFERENCE:

44

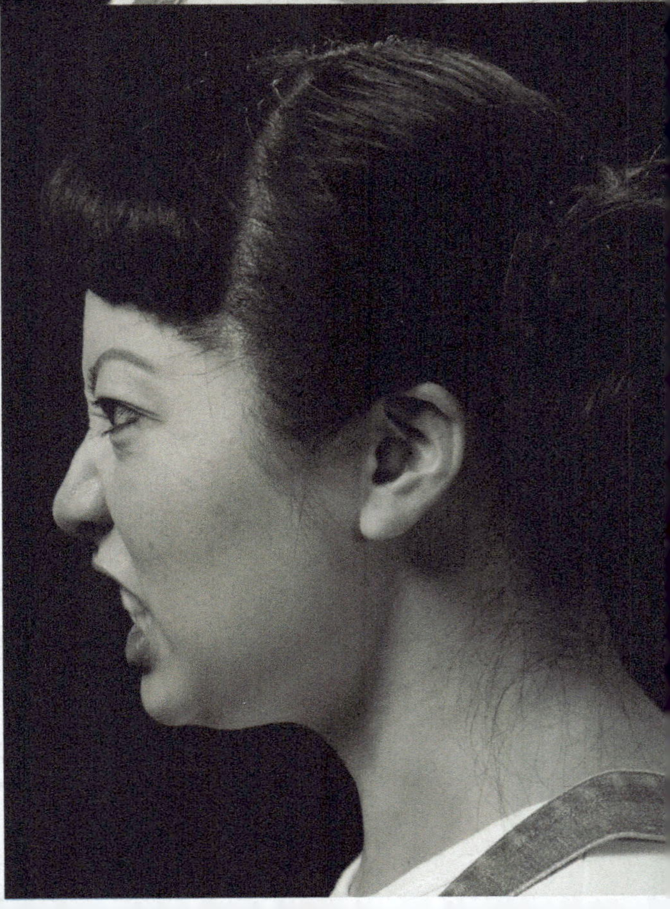

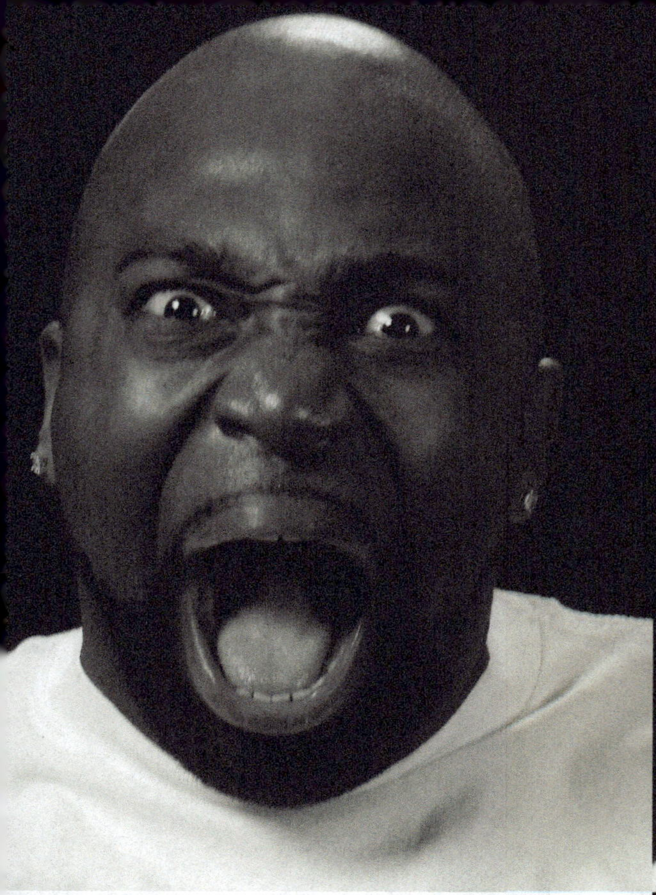

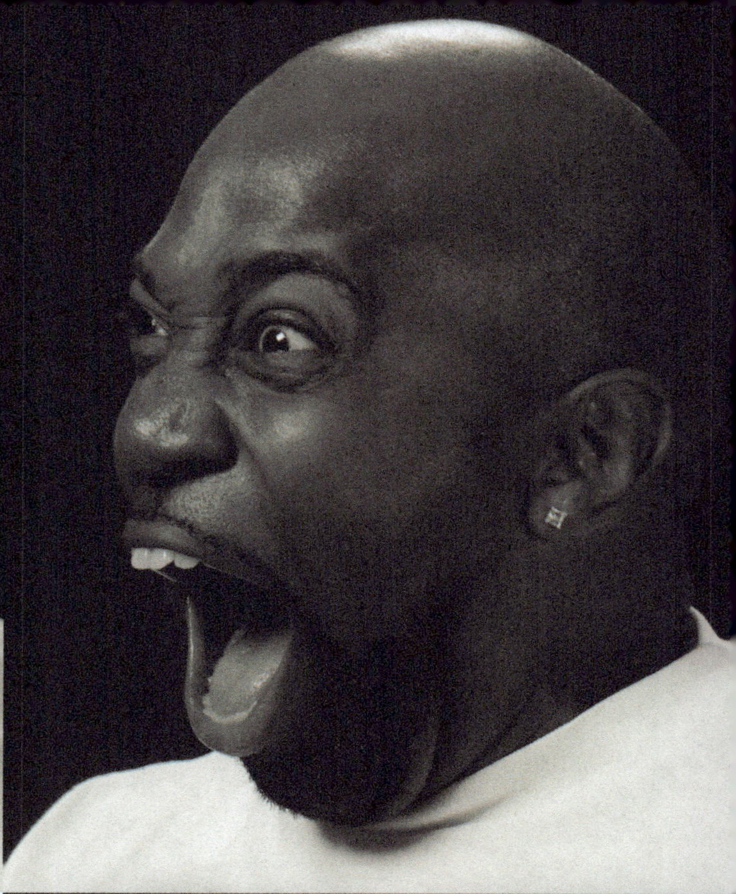

## ANGRY

MAP REFERENCE:

53

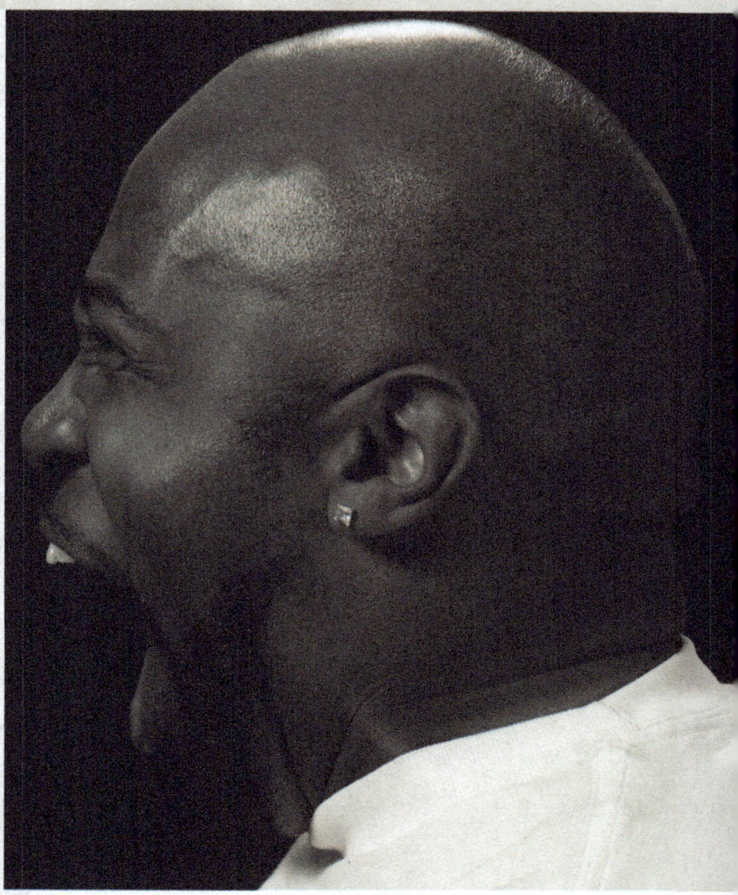

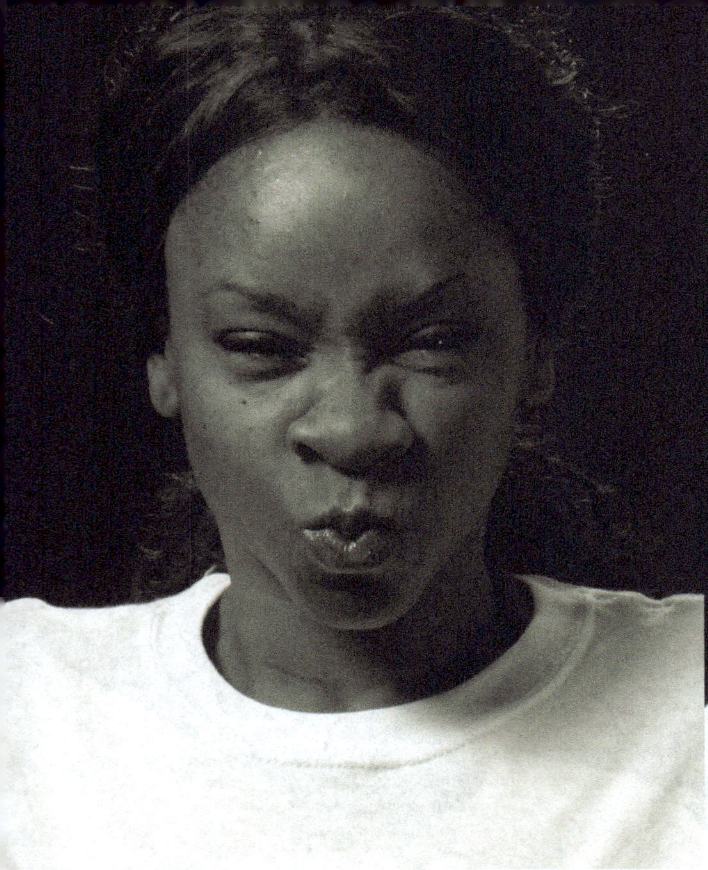

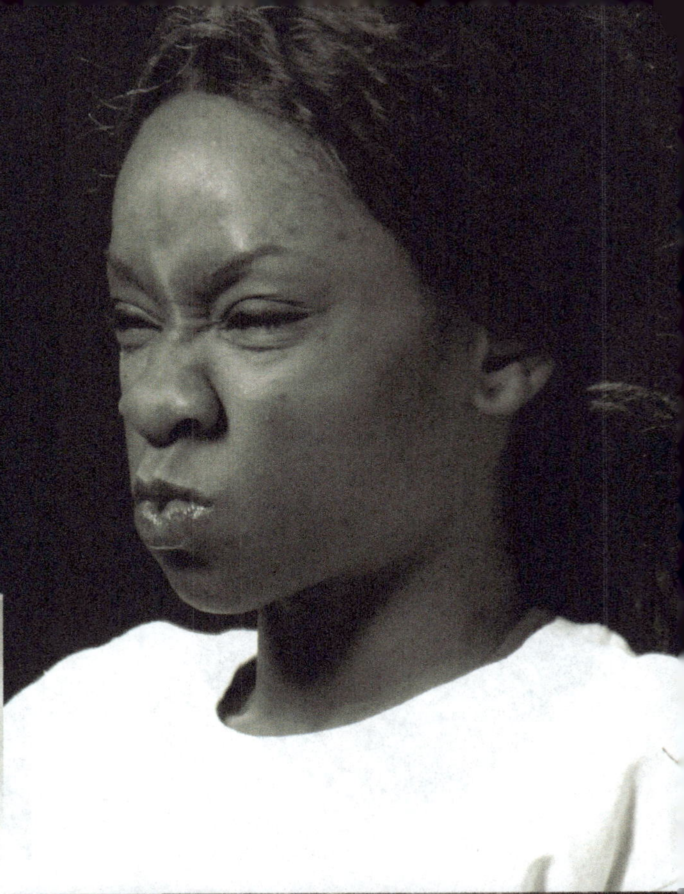

# ANGRY

MAP REFERENCE:

23

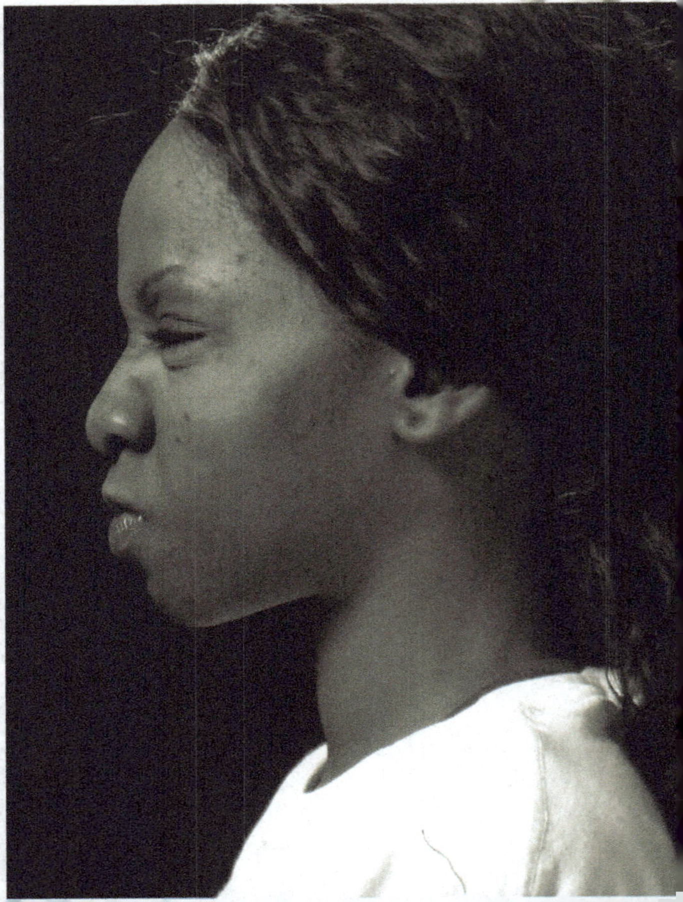

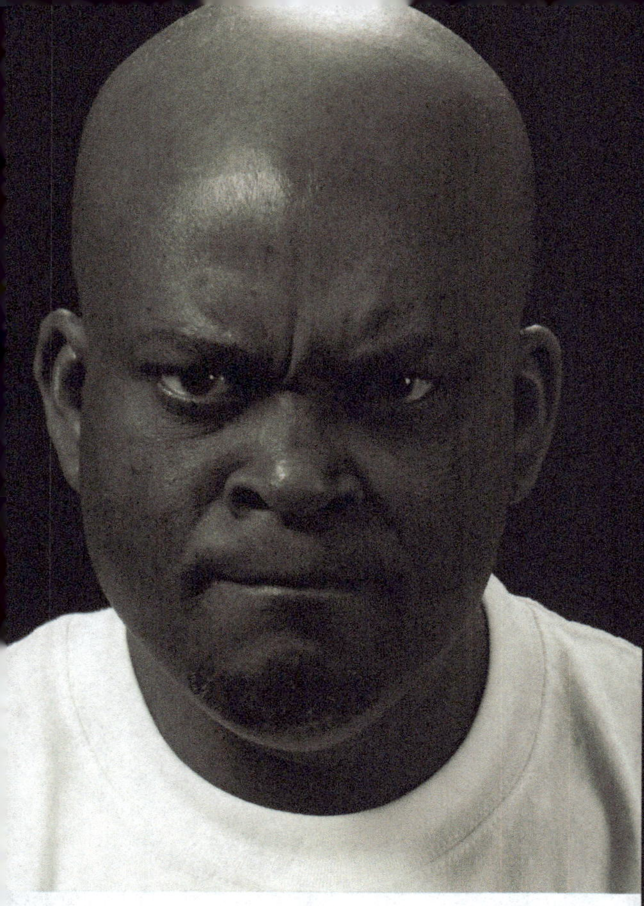

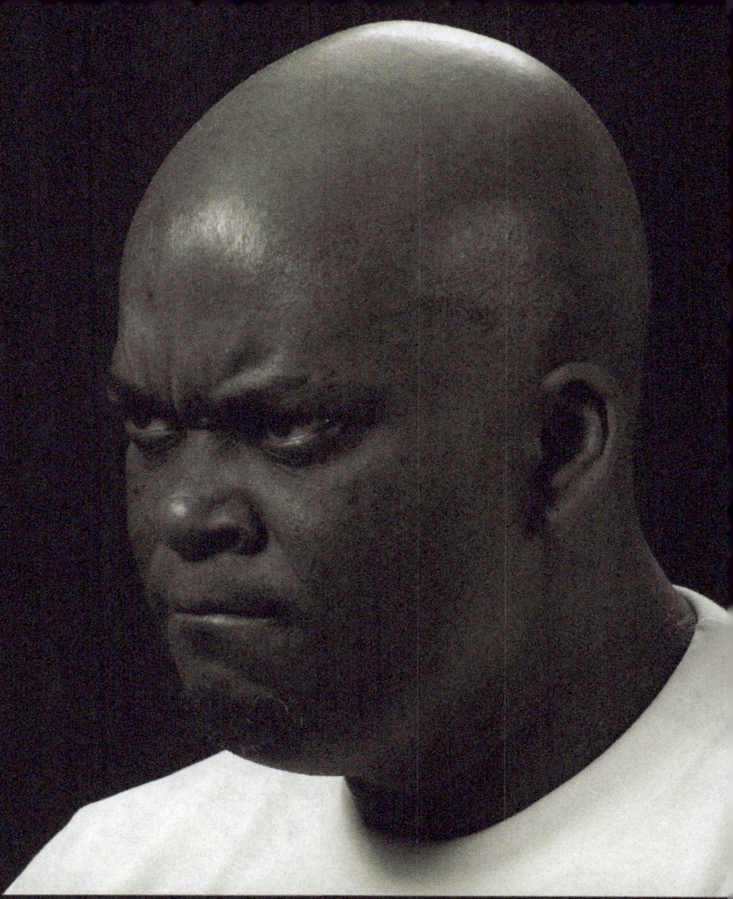

# ANGRY

MAP REFERENCE:

57

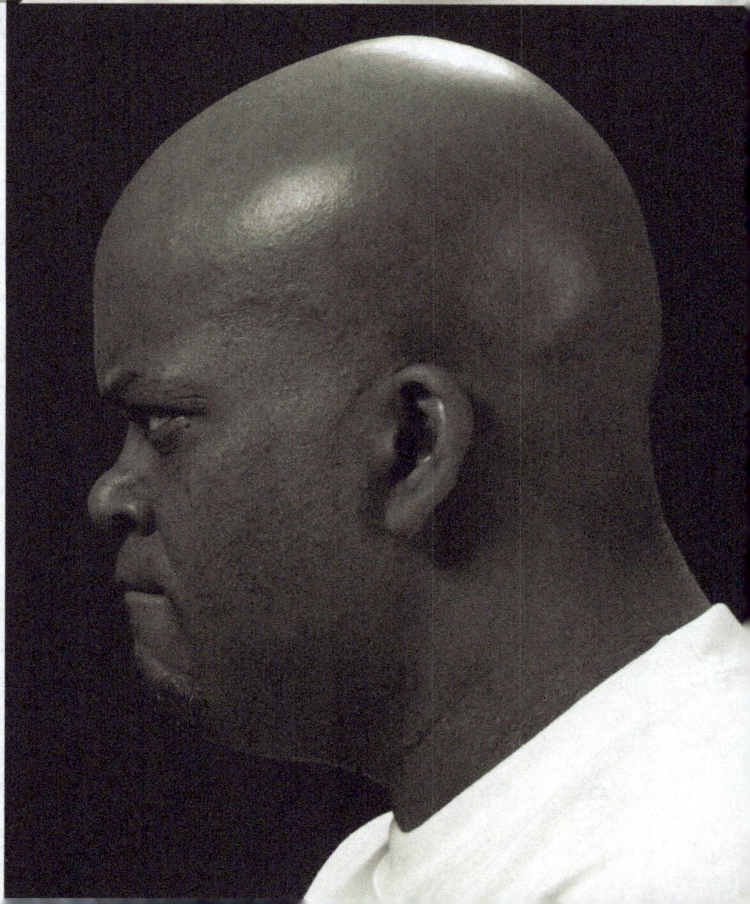

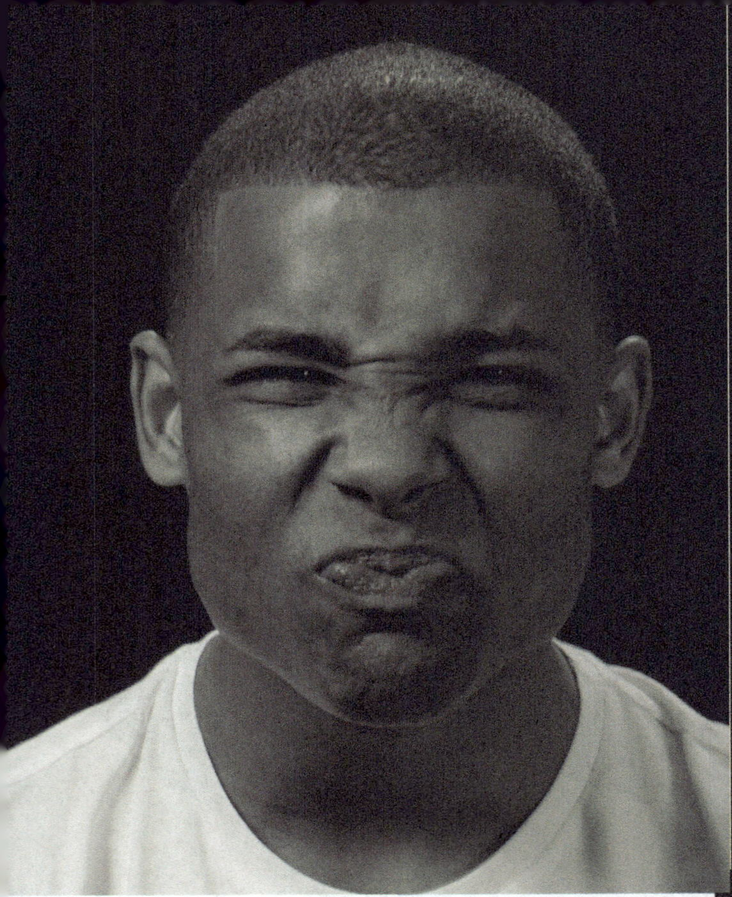

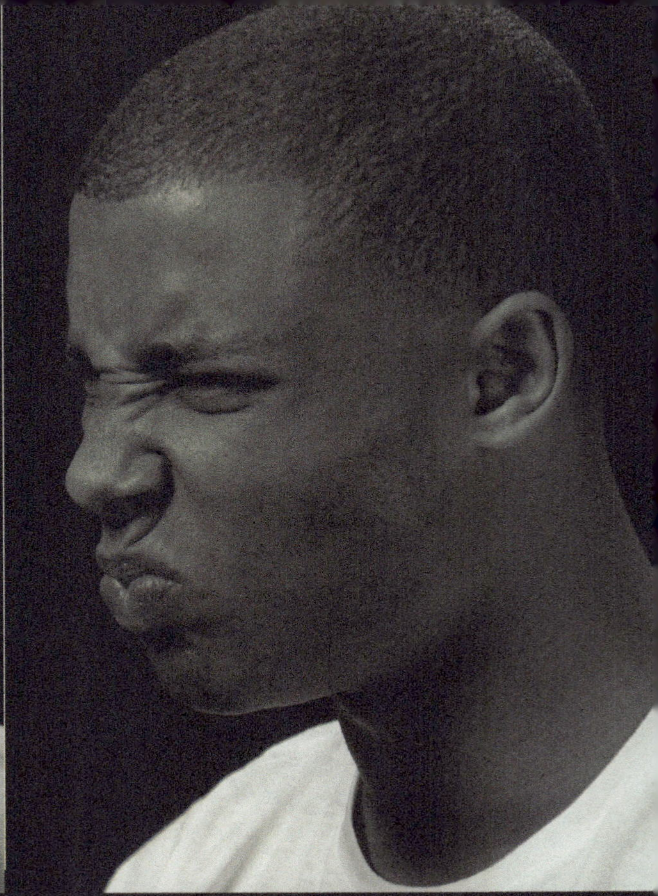

# ANGRY

MAP REFERENCE:

47

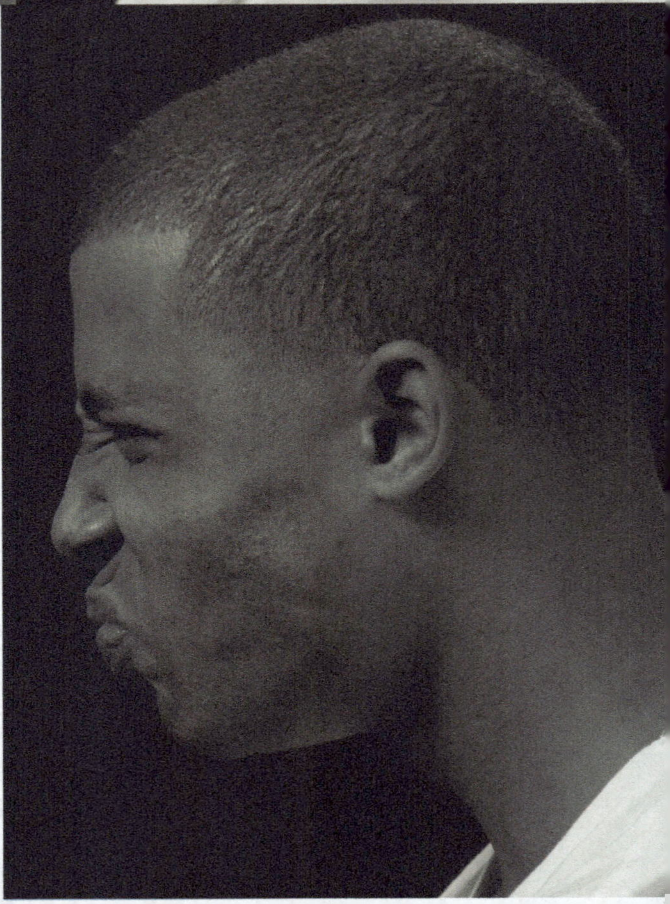

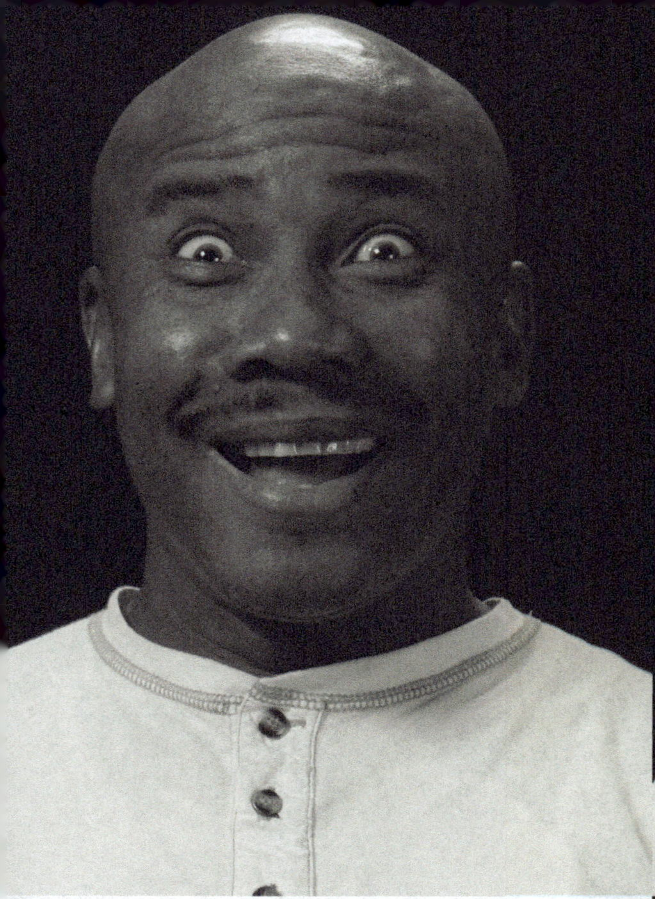

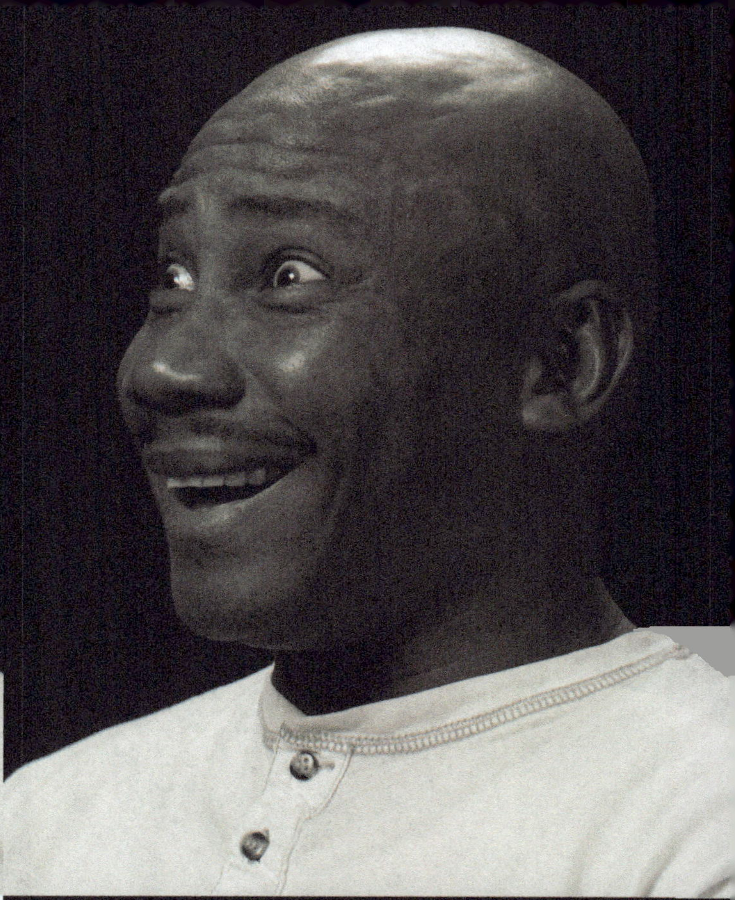

# SURPRISE

MAP REFERENCE:

56

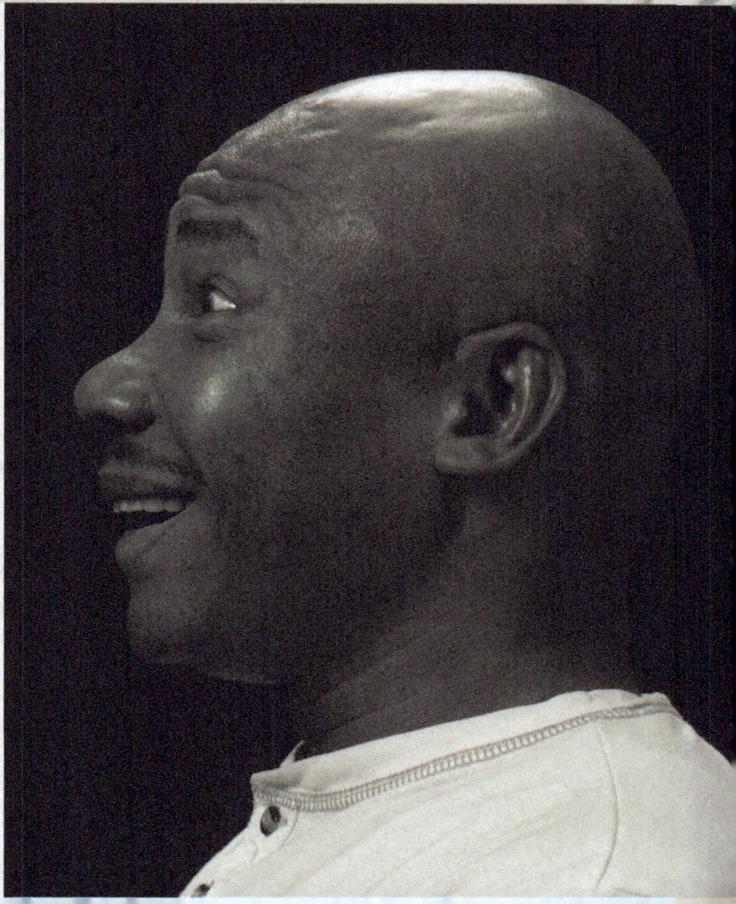

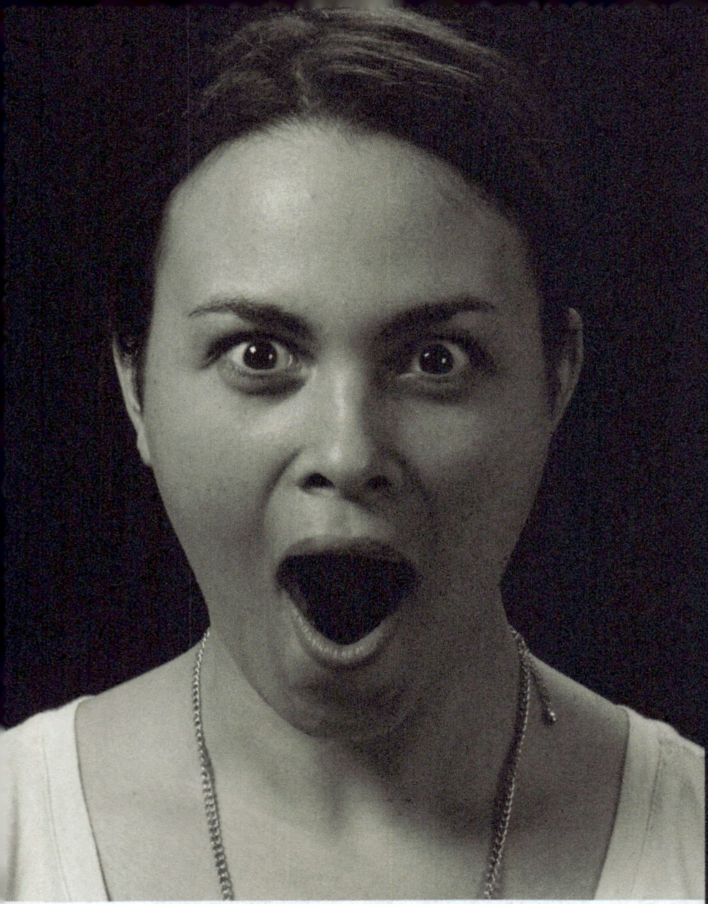

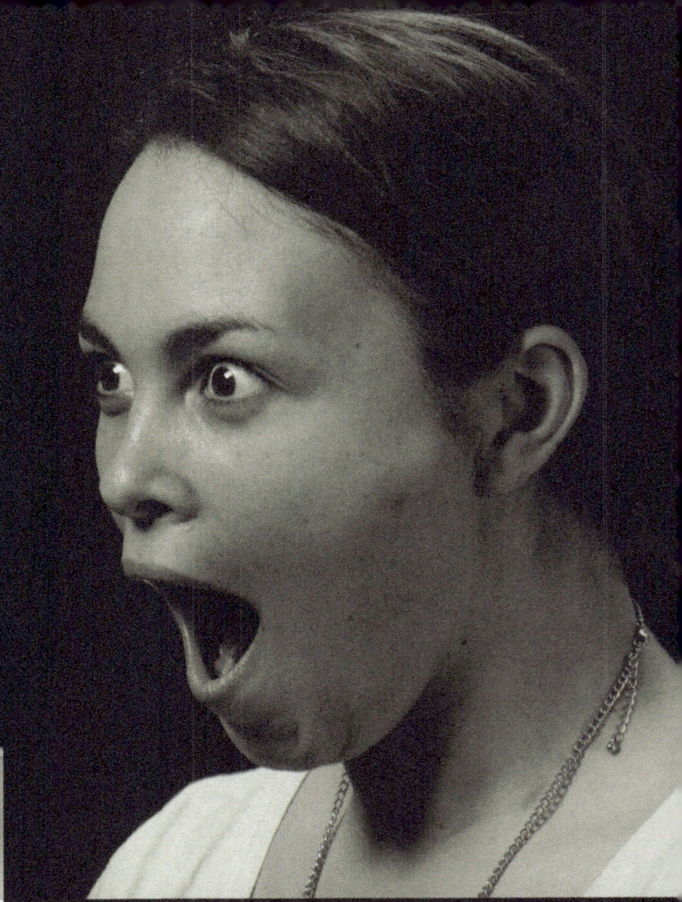

# SURPRISE

MAP REFERENCE:

48

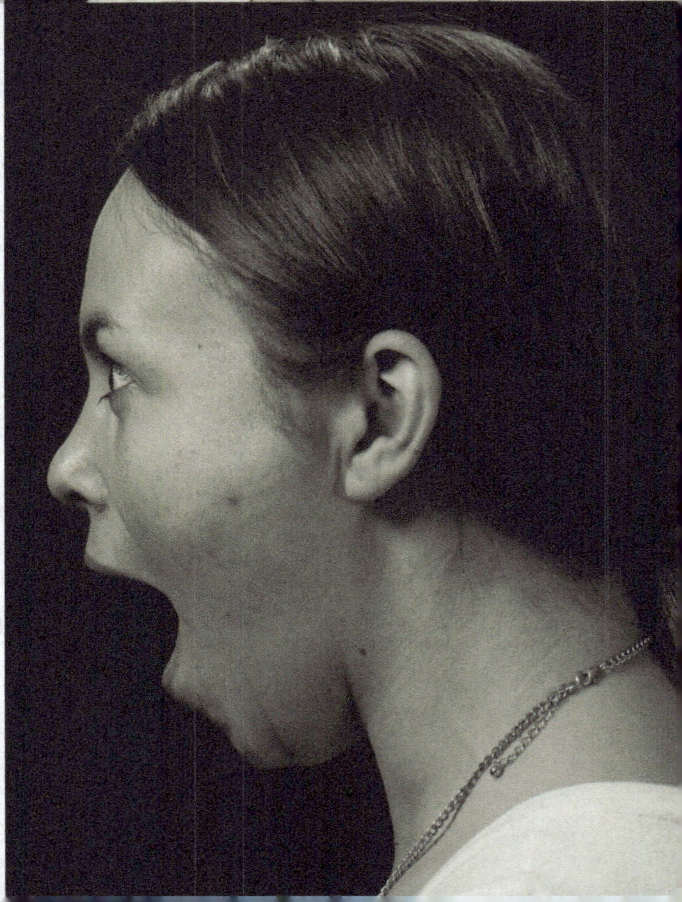

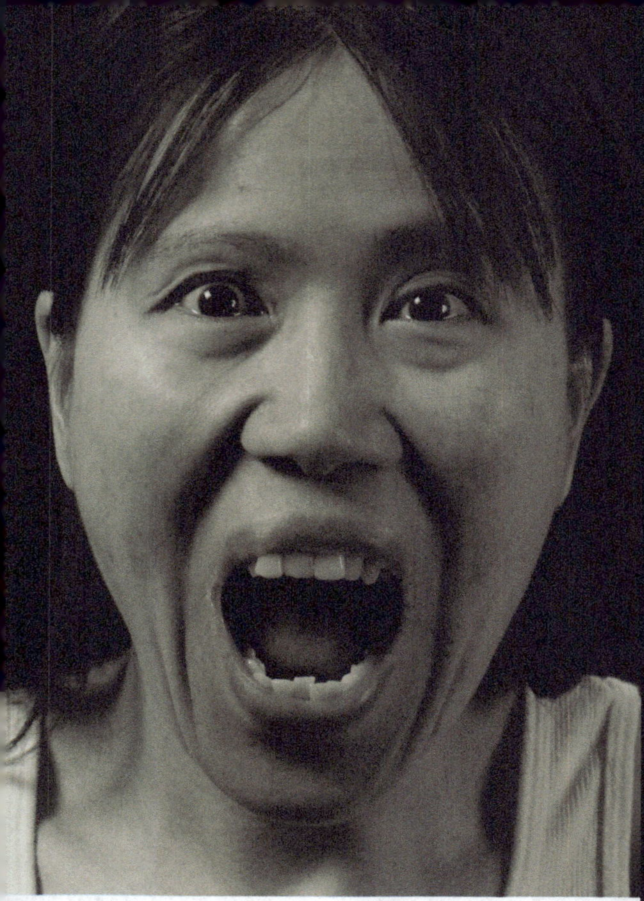

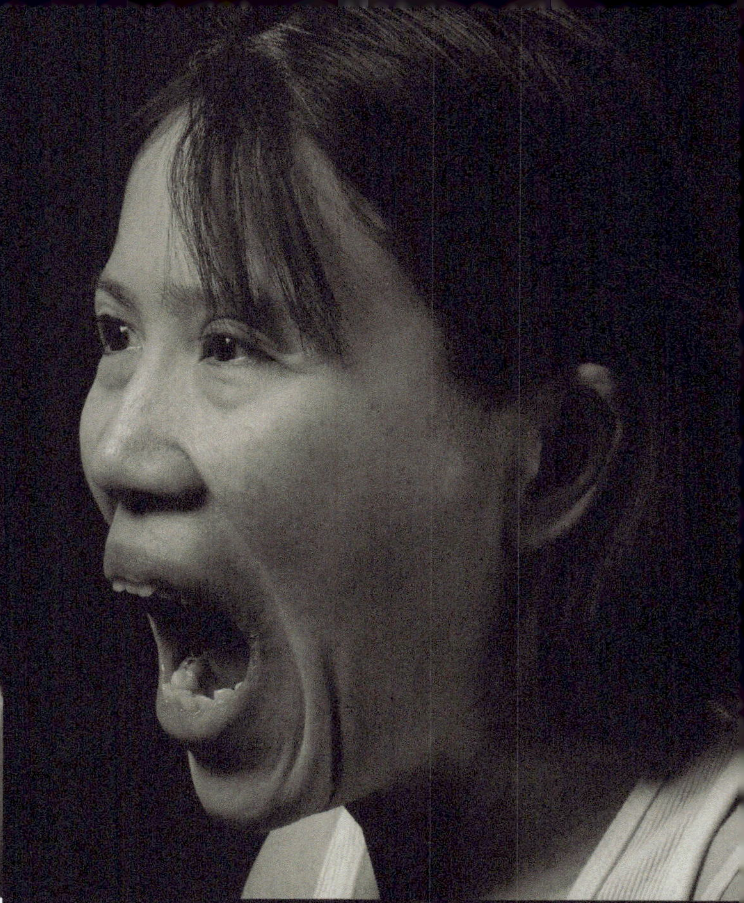

# SURPRISE

MAP REFERENCE:

63

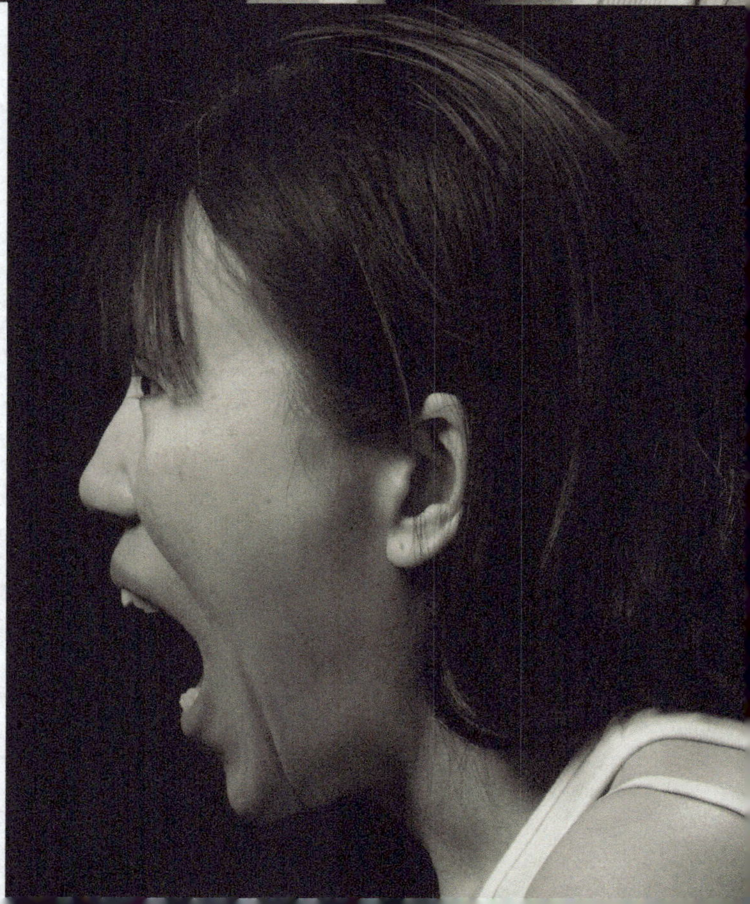

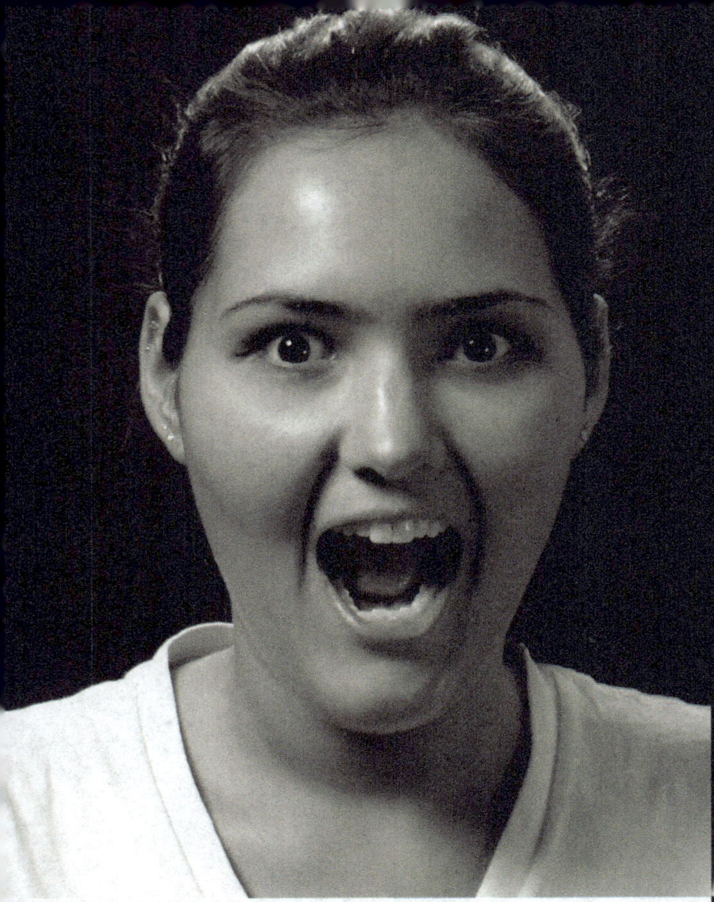

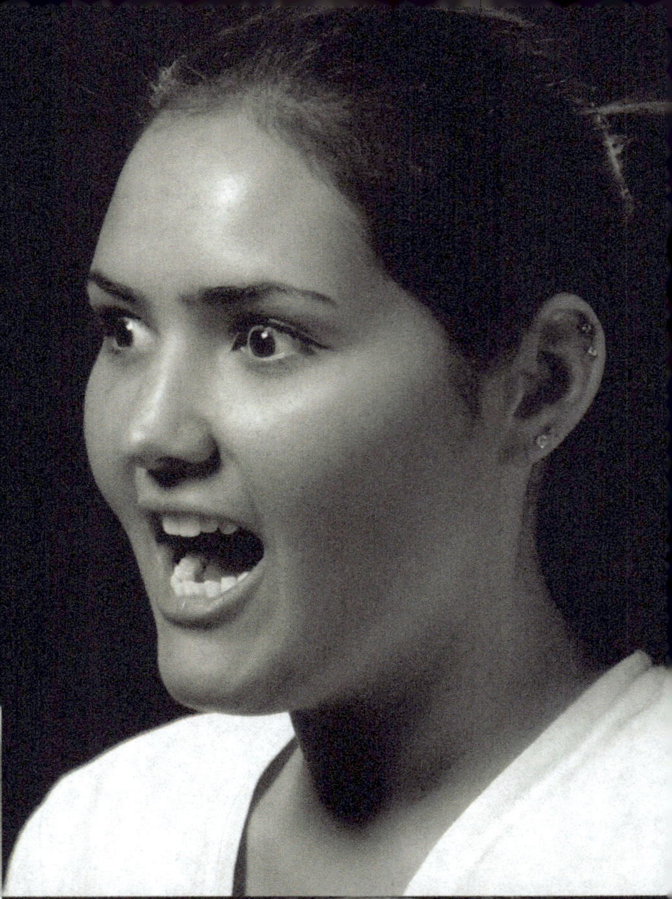

# SURPRISE

MAP REFERENCE:

34

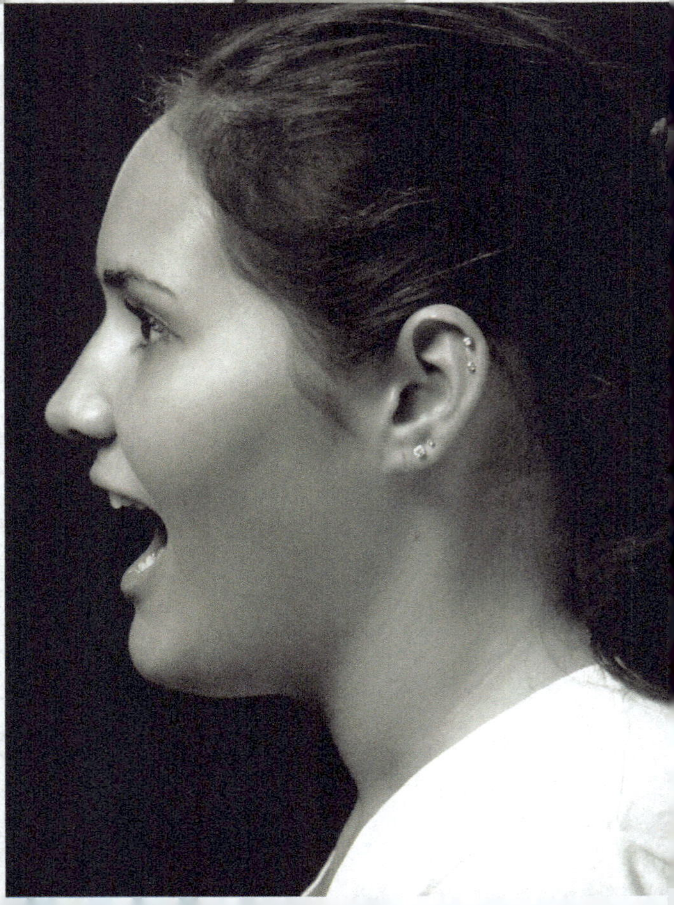

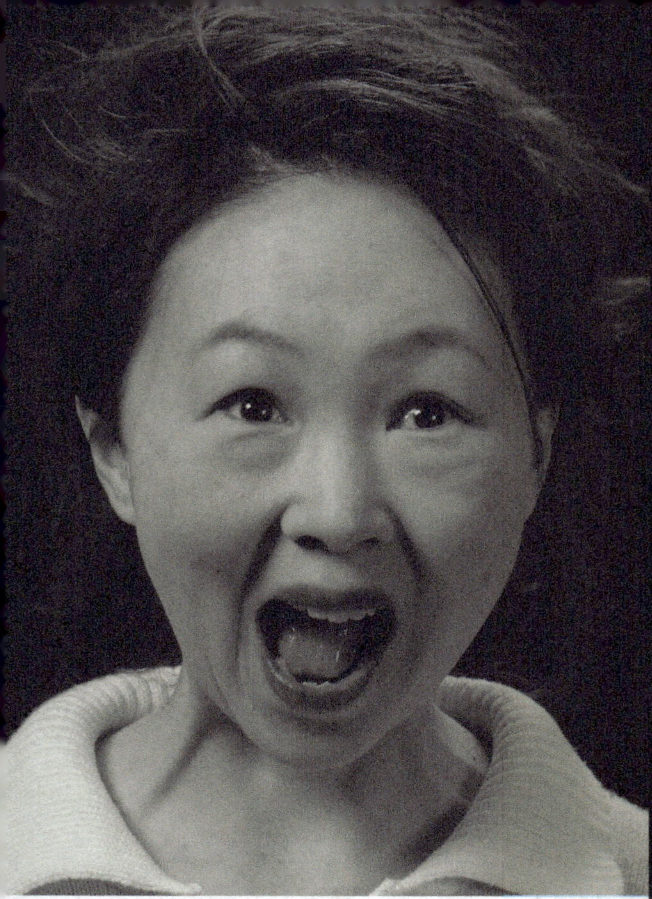

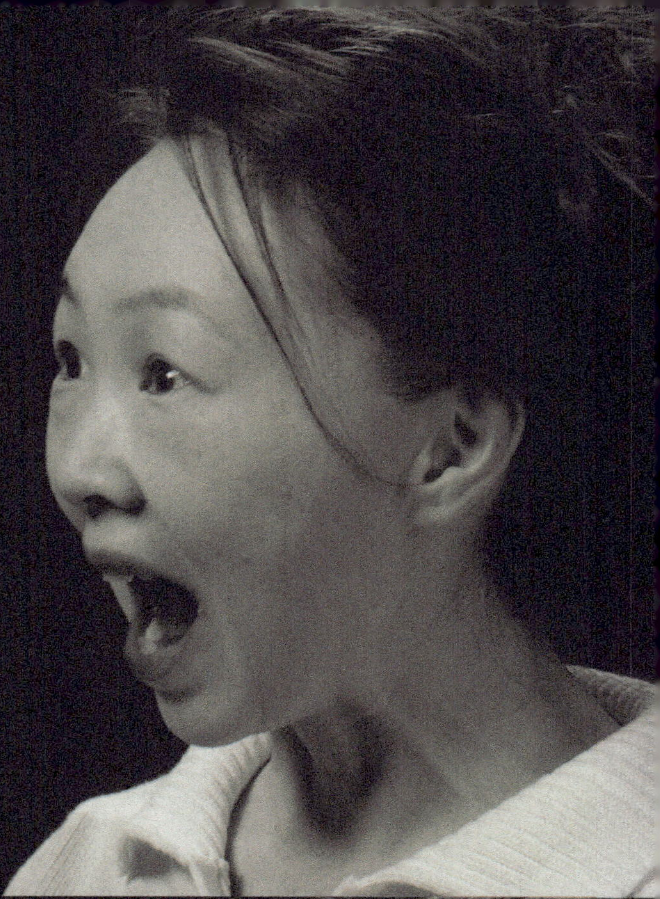

# SURPRISE

MAP REFERENCE:

52

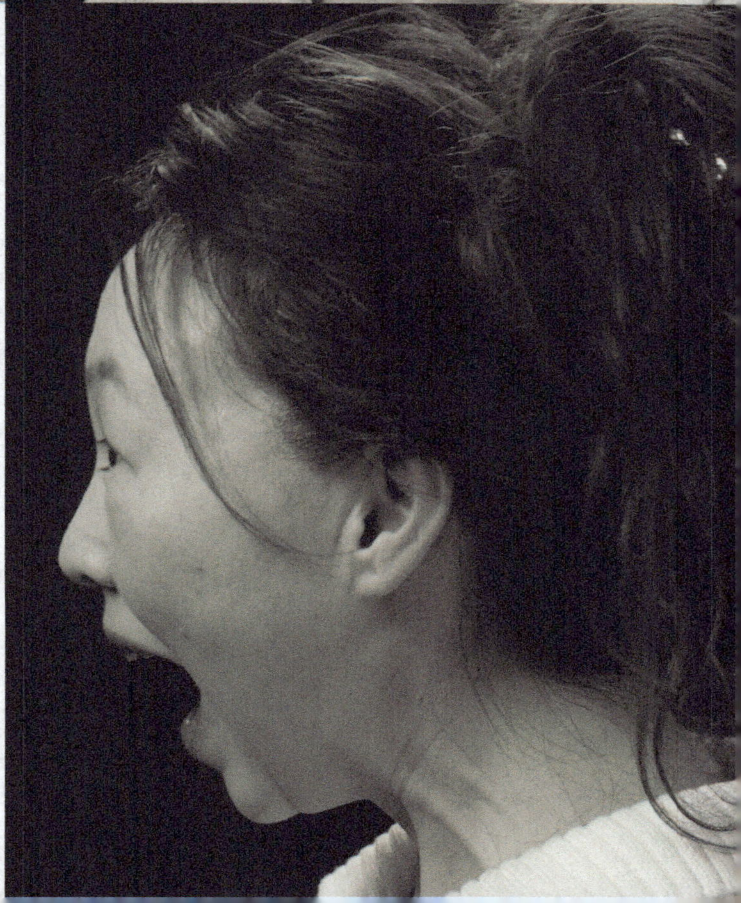

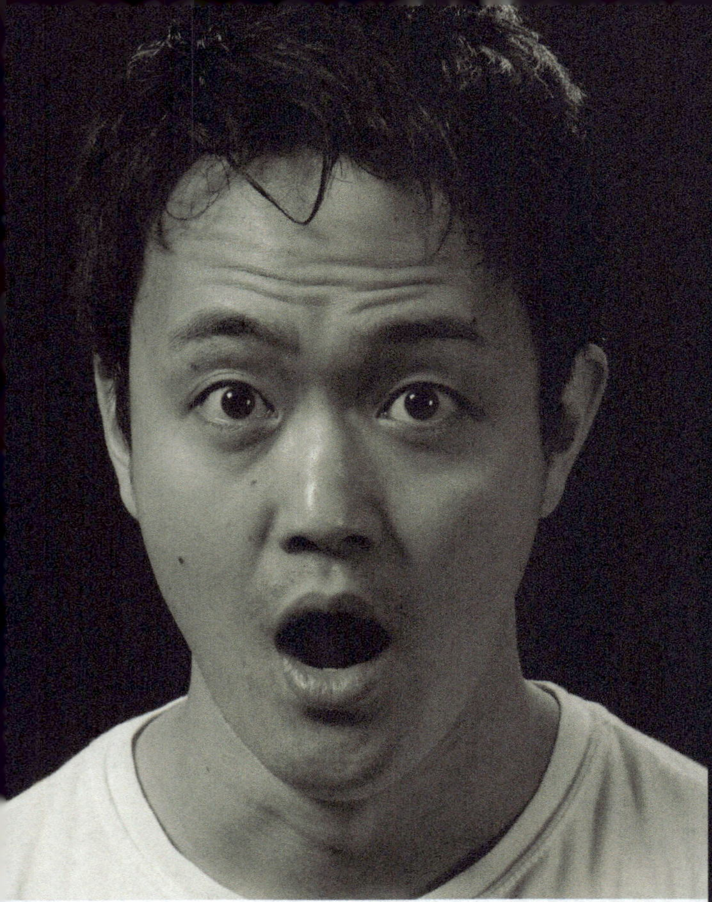

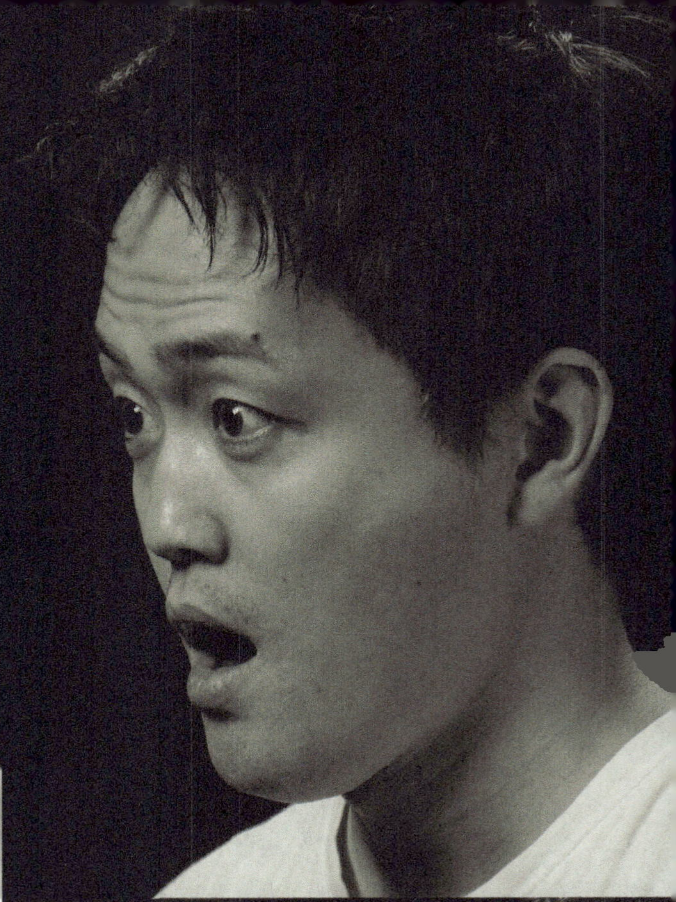

# SURPRISE

MAP REFERENCE:
50

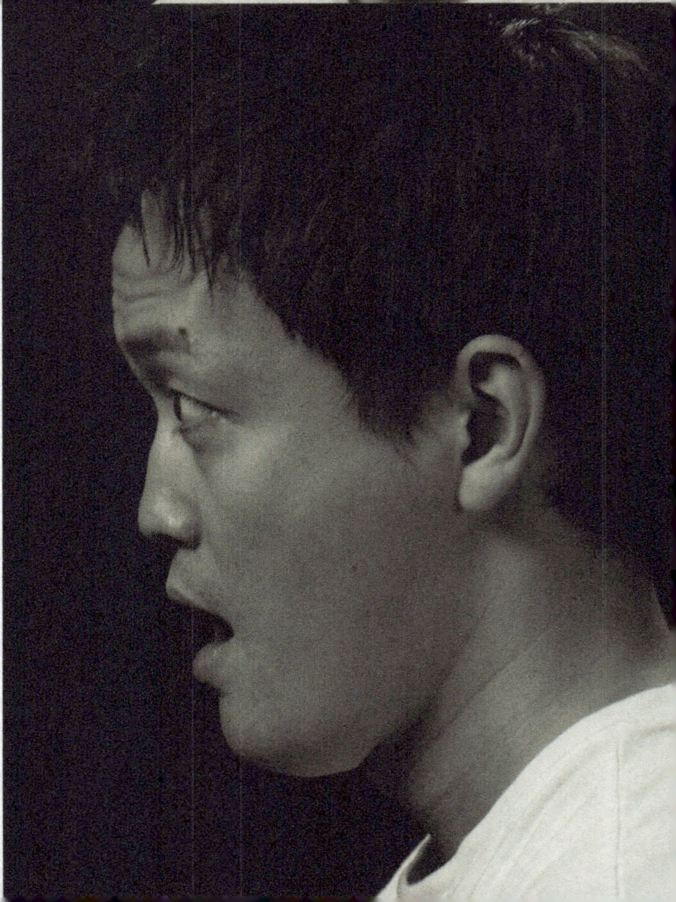

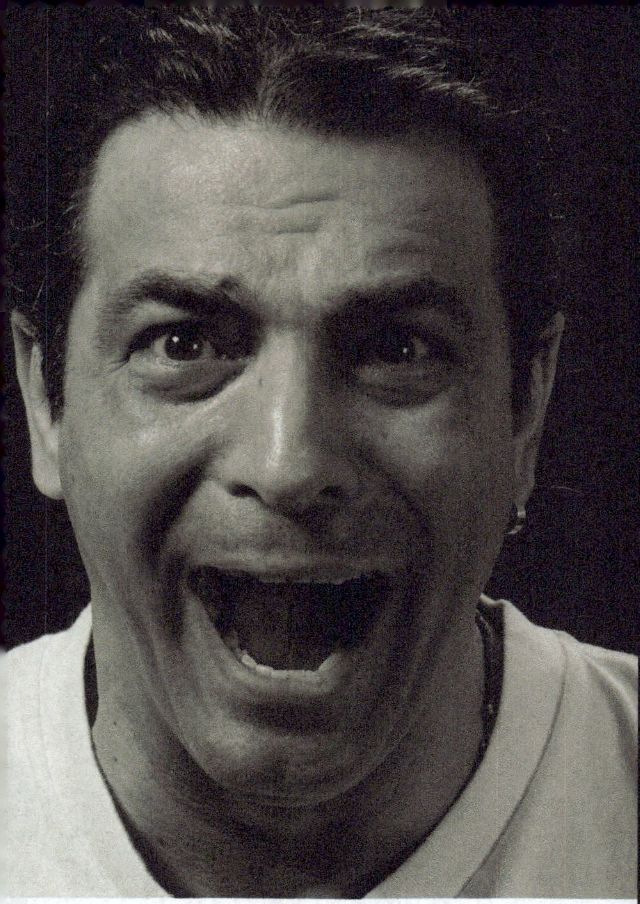

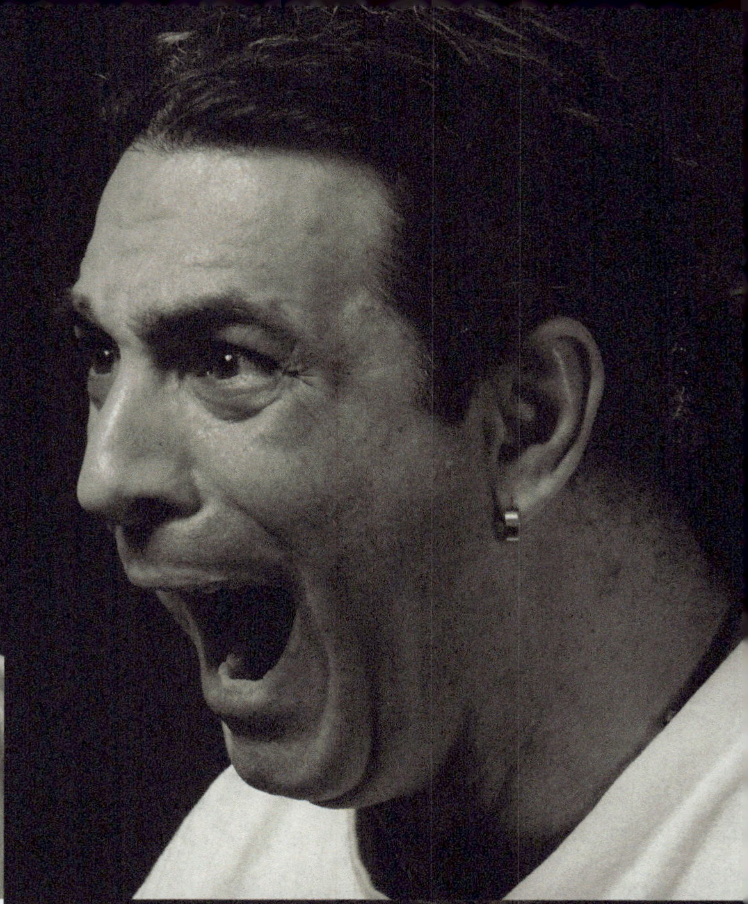

# SURPRISE

MAP REFERENCE:
61

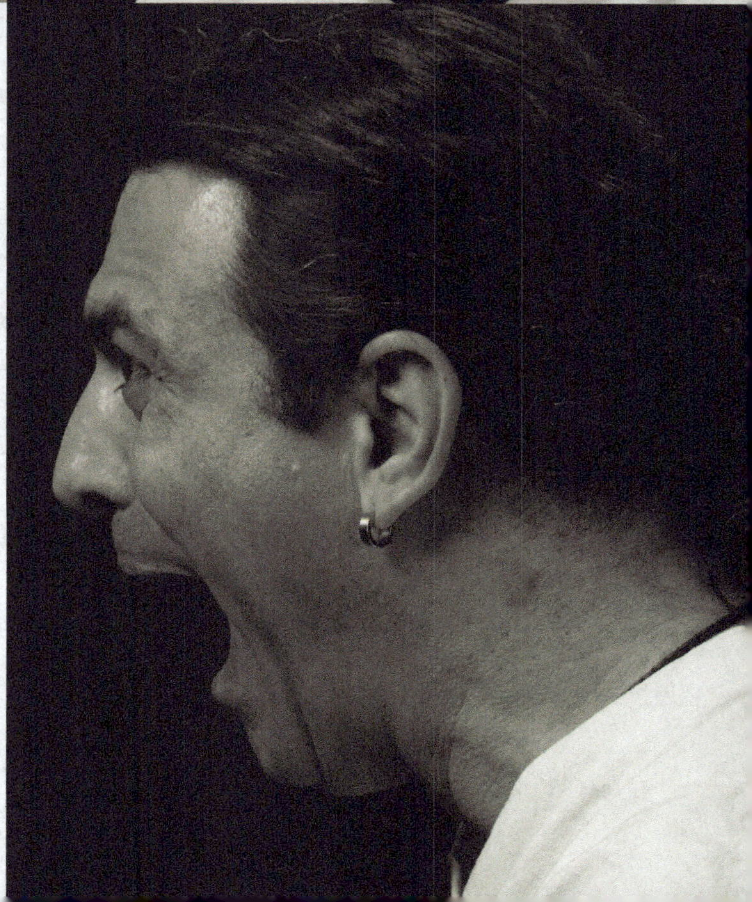

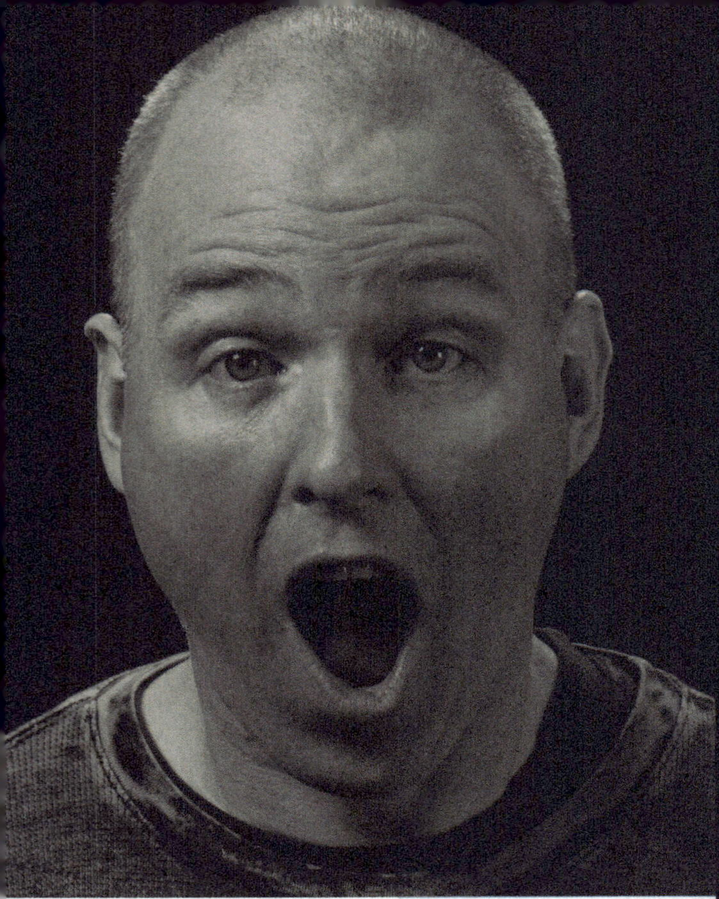

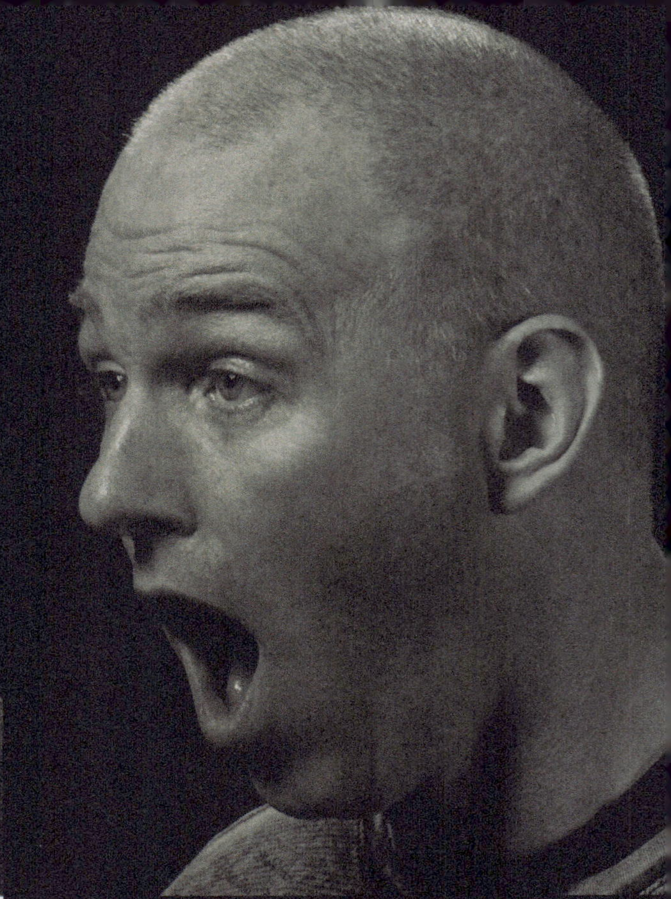

# SURPRISE

MAP REFERENCE:

69

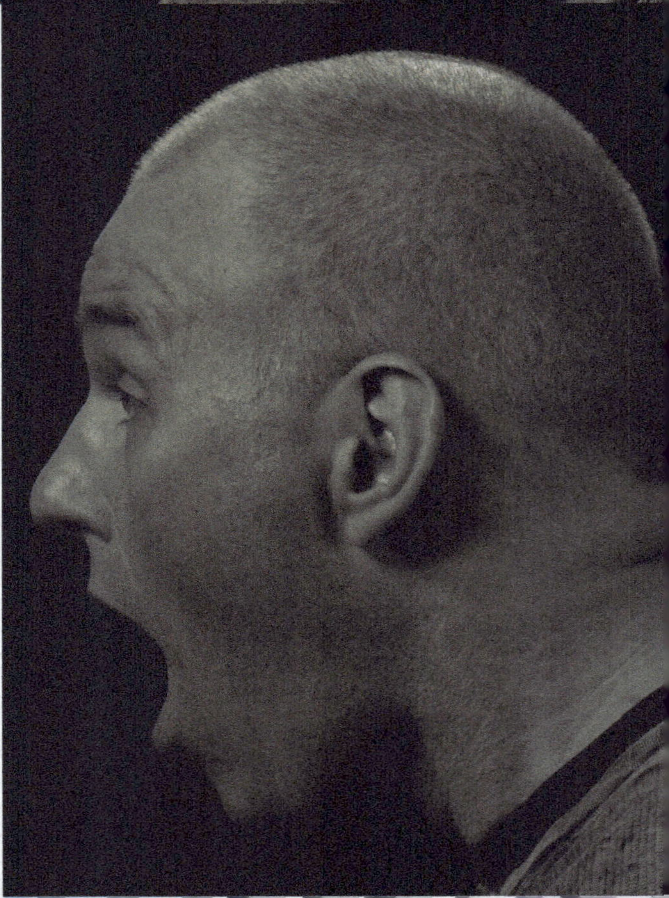

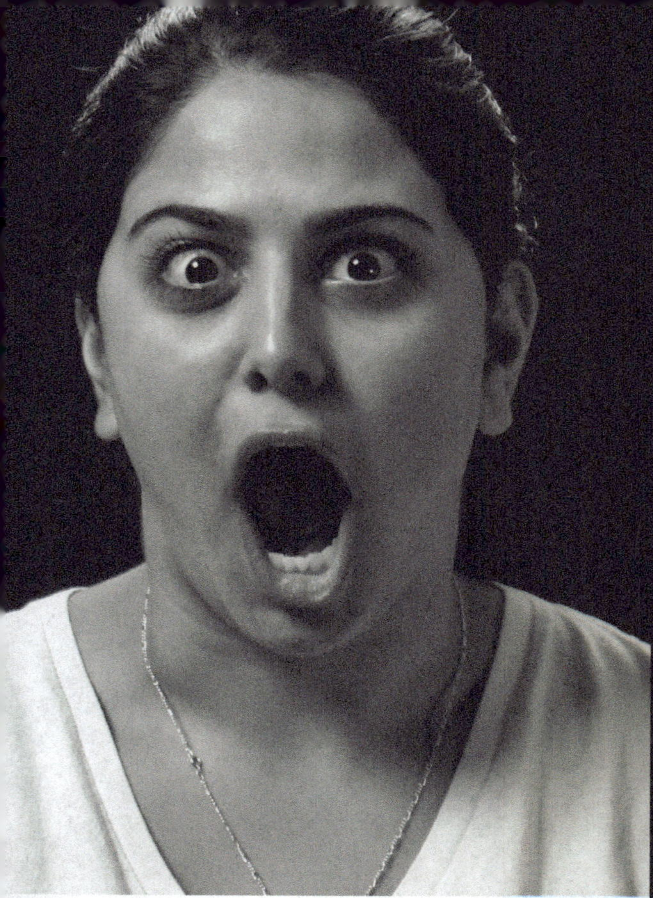

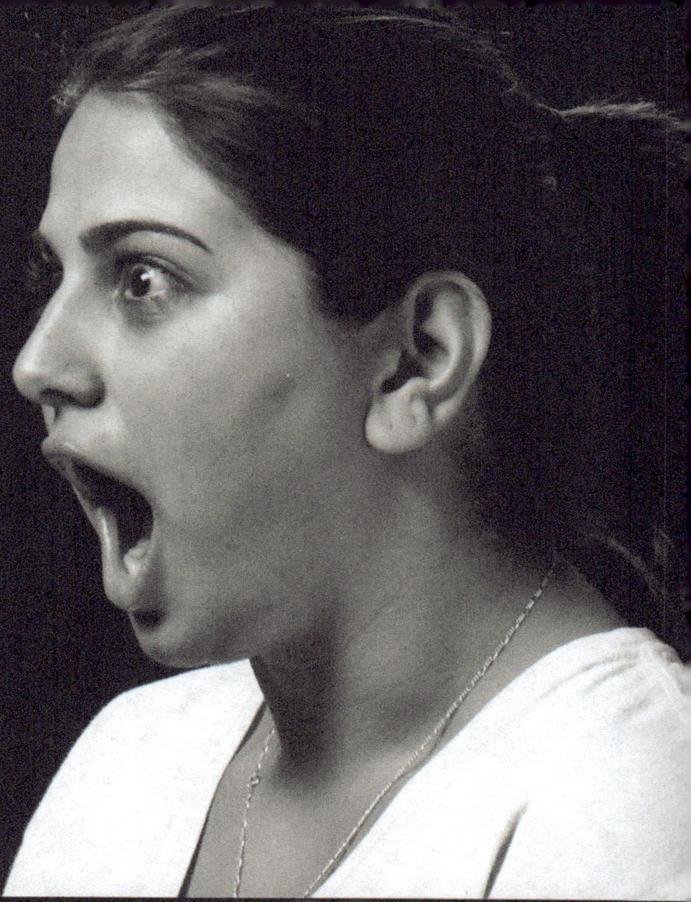

# SURPRISE

MAP REFERENCE:

28

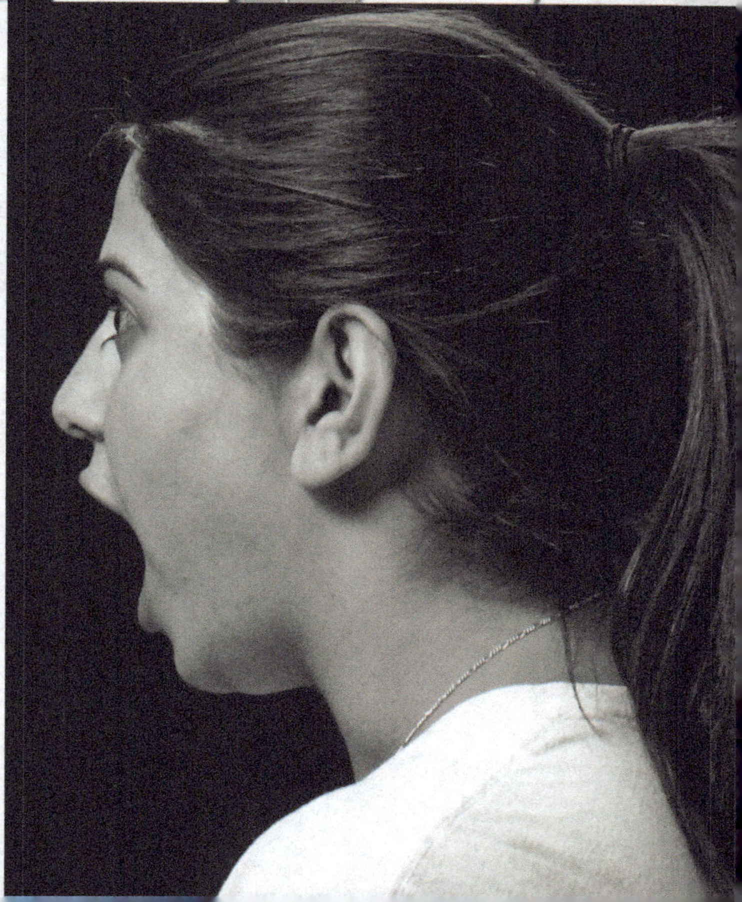

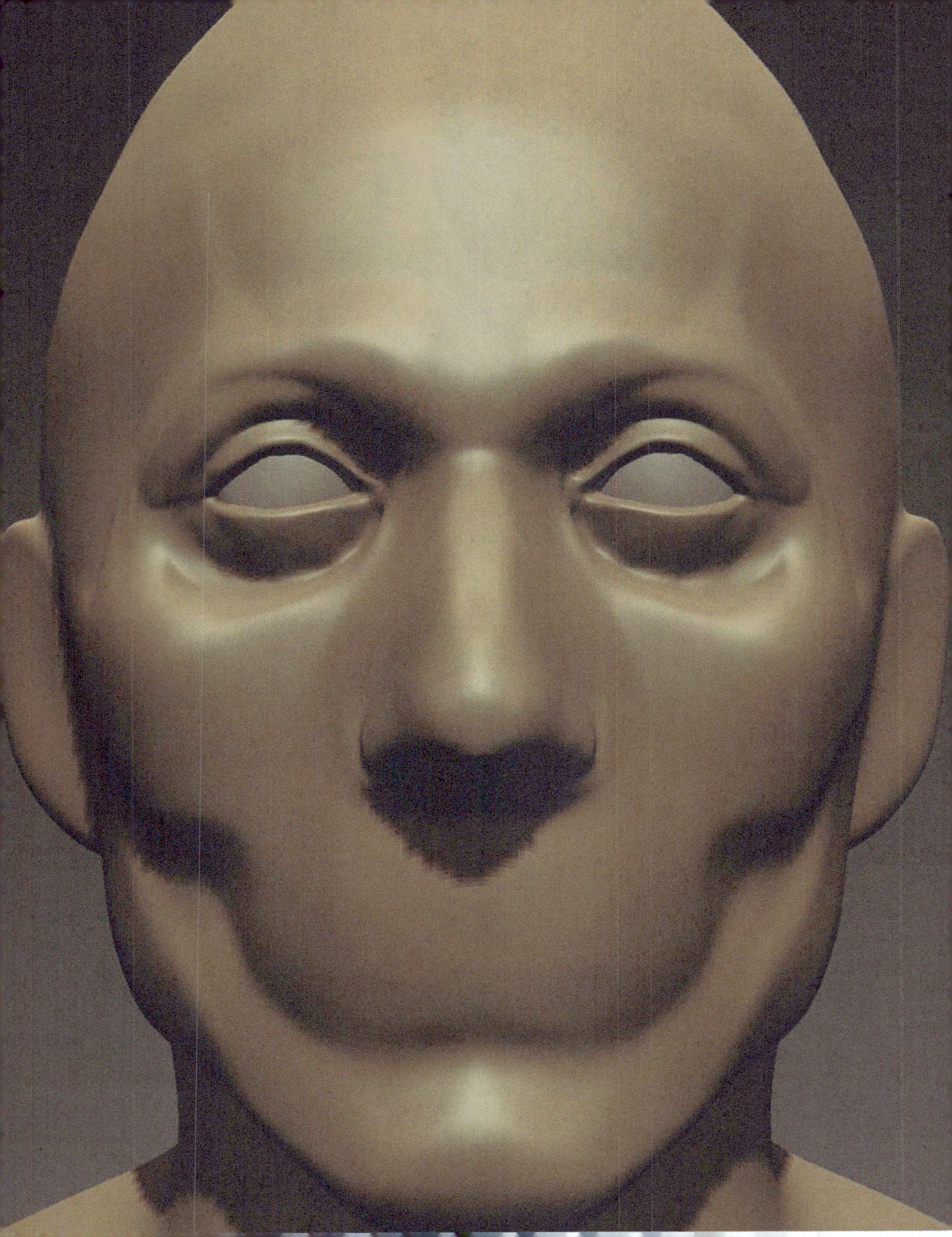

CHAPTER 5:
3D TUTORIAL

# SCULPTING THE HUMAN HEAD

In this tutorial, it is time to put all the things that have been talked about together and sculpt an entire head. You will be sculpting one of our models, a Latino male. We chose this individual because he possesses exceptionally well-defined anatomical forms in his face.

Import the tutorial four-base mesh into your sculpting application.

***/tutorials/tutorial4/starterhead.obj***

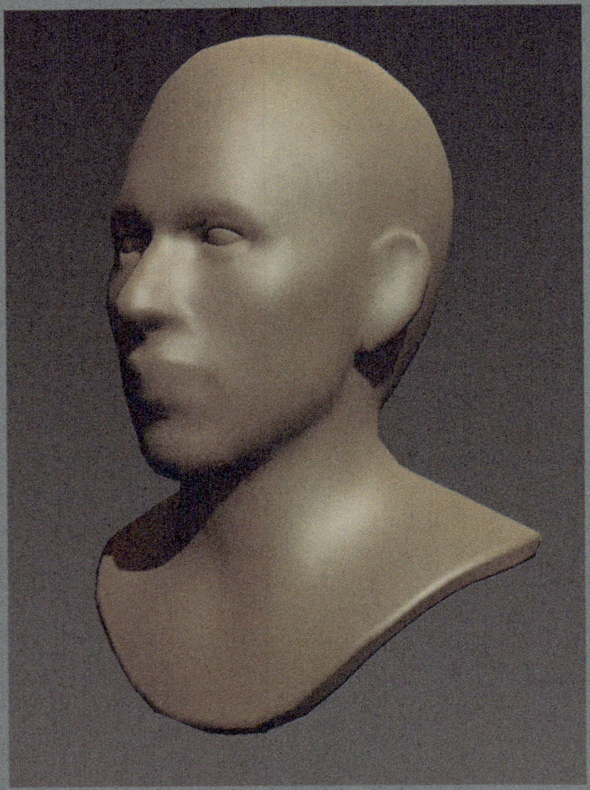

*Base mesh.*

Prepare the reference photography in the way you prefer (printouts, image planes, etc.). The images can be found:

***/tutorials/tutorial4/tut_4_front.jpg***

***/tutorials/tutorial4/tut_4_angle_fr.jpg***

***/tutorials/tutorial4/tut_4_side.jpg***

***/tutorials/tutorial4/tut_4_angle_bk.jpg***

The base mesh will approximately match the proportions of the model minus hair volume to give you a bit of a head start.

Next, block out the basic skull forms that you learned in tutorial 1.

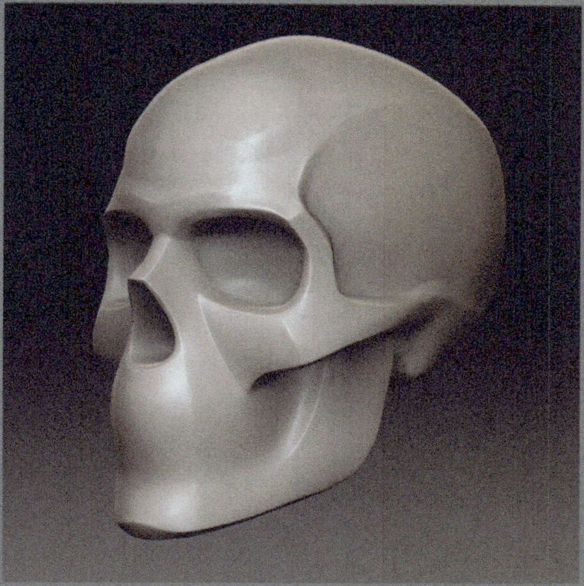

*Generic skull form.*

Carefully evaluate where the bone landmarks fall, based on the photo reference. You will want to wind up with something along the lines of Figure 4.4:

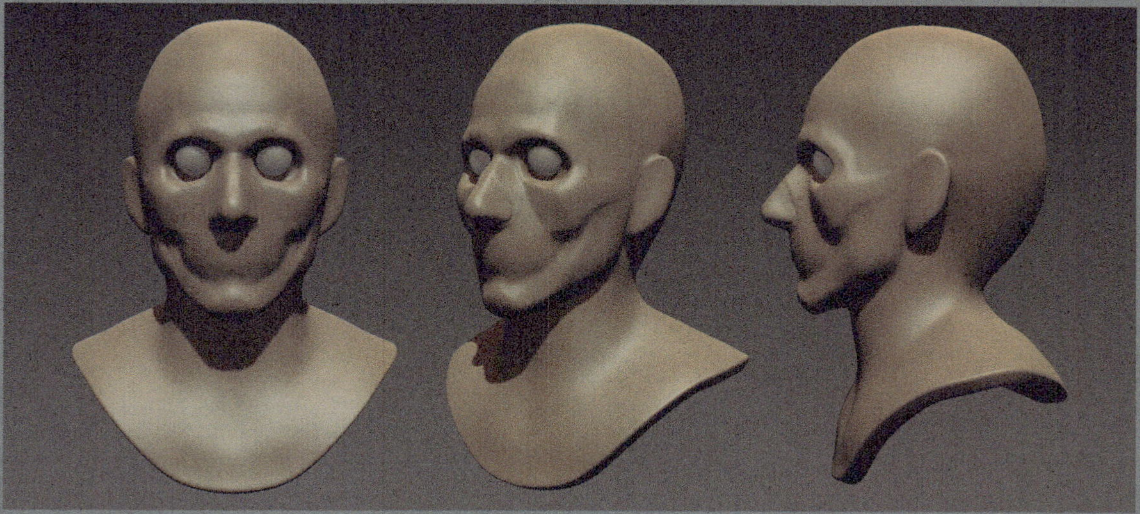

*Step 1 goal.*

Looking at the reference photos, you are trying to take your best educated guess where the bone forms lie. You will be constantly referring back to the photos as you add and refine the soft tissue, so do not be too concerned.

Next, you are going to begin to construct the eye region, keeping to basics at first. Follow the images below and your reference photography:

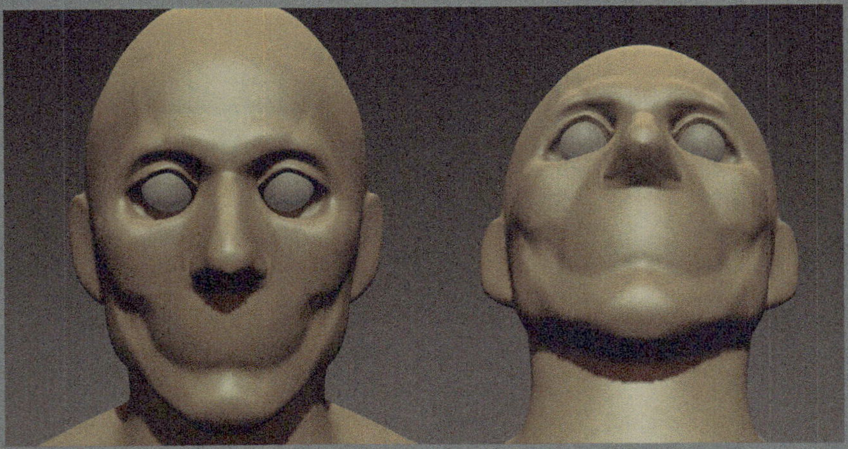

*Upper lid.*

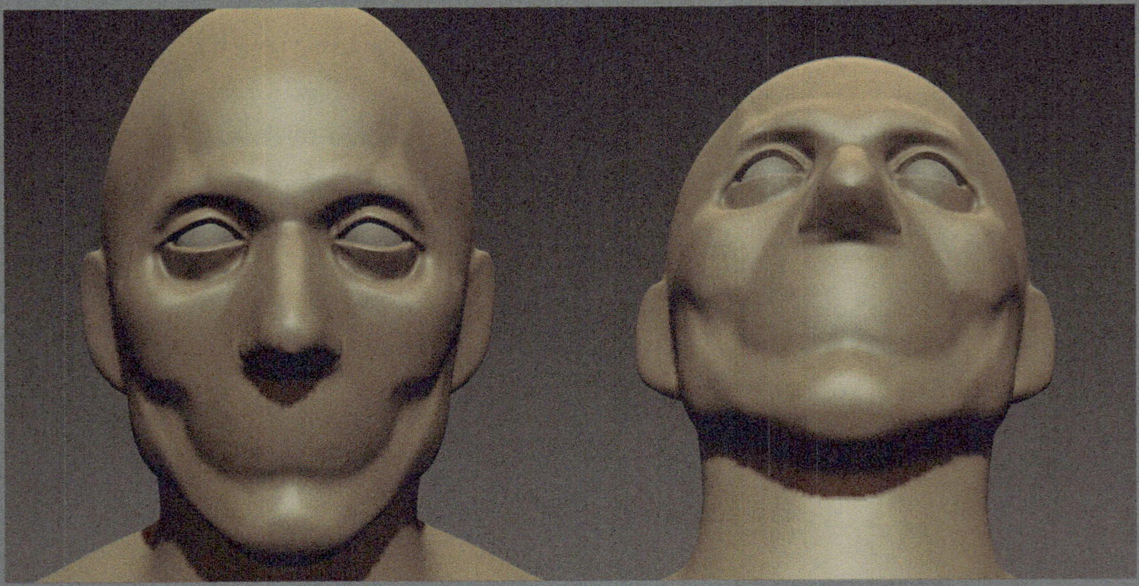

*Lower lid.*

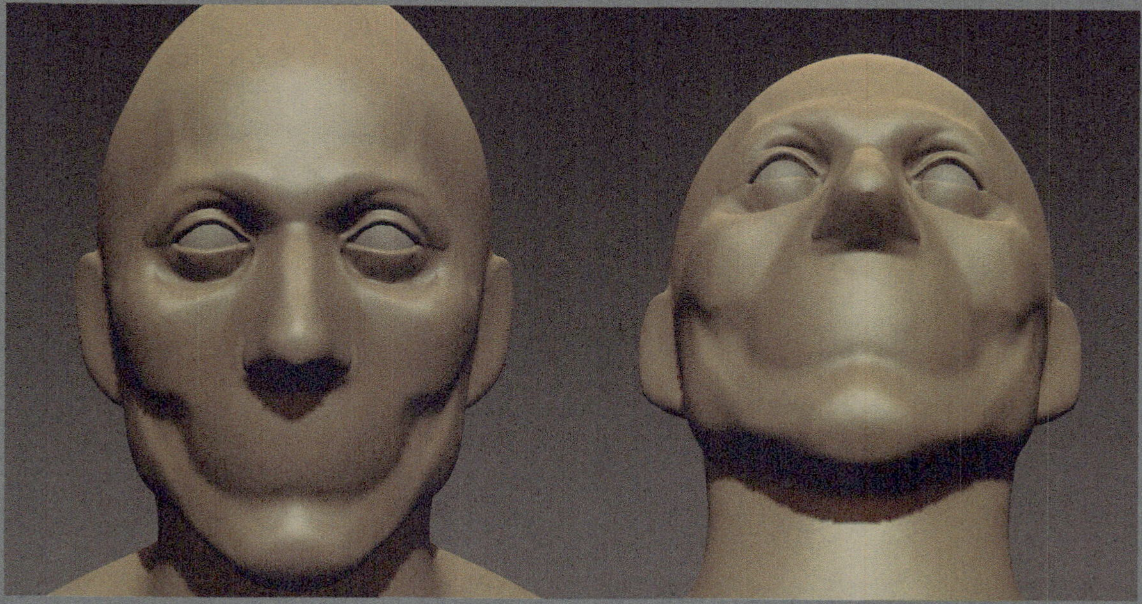

*Above eye.*

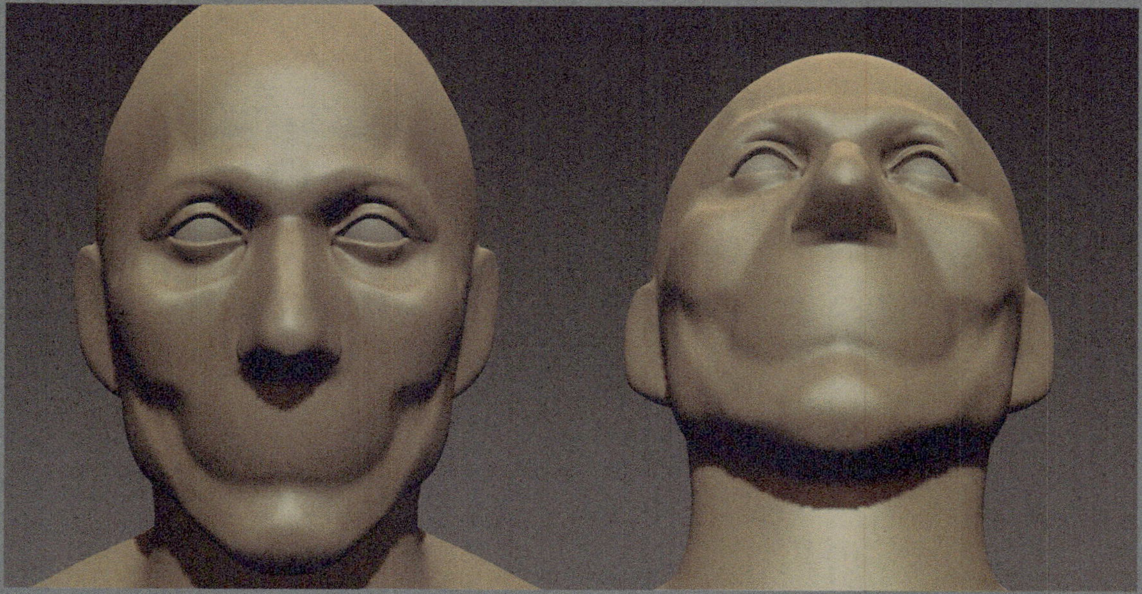

*Below eye.*

Now, you will focus on the mouth area. As before, follow the steps pictured next and refer to the model reference photography.

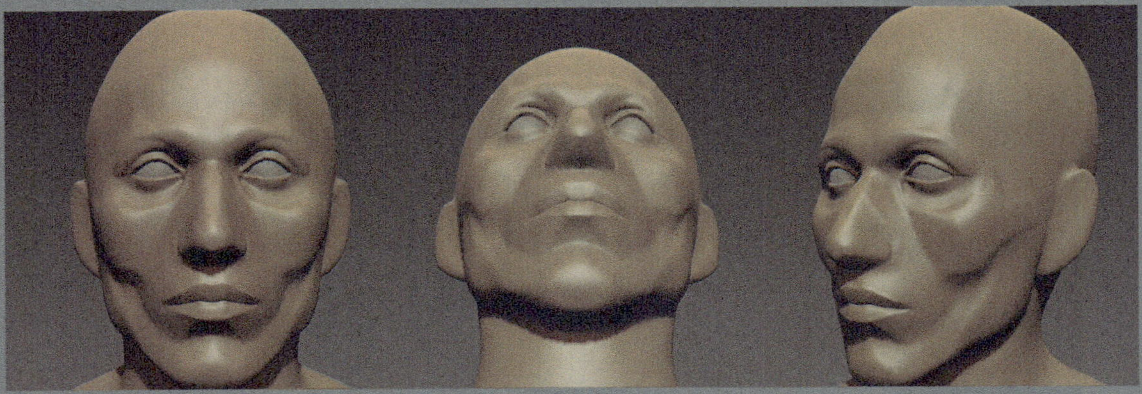

*Lips*

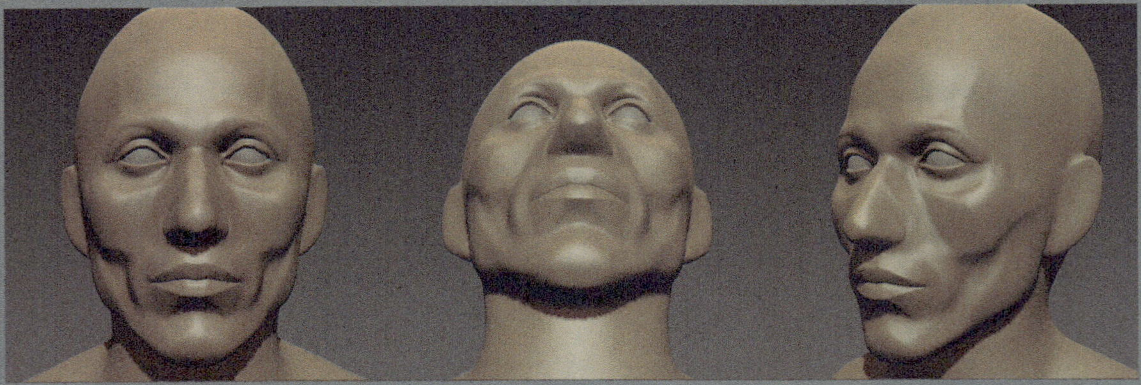

*Lips part 2.*

Now, move onto the basic geometric forms of the nose:

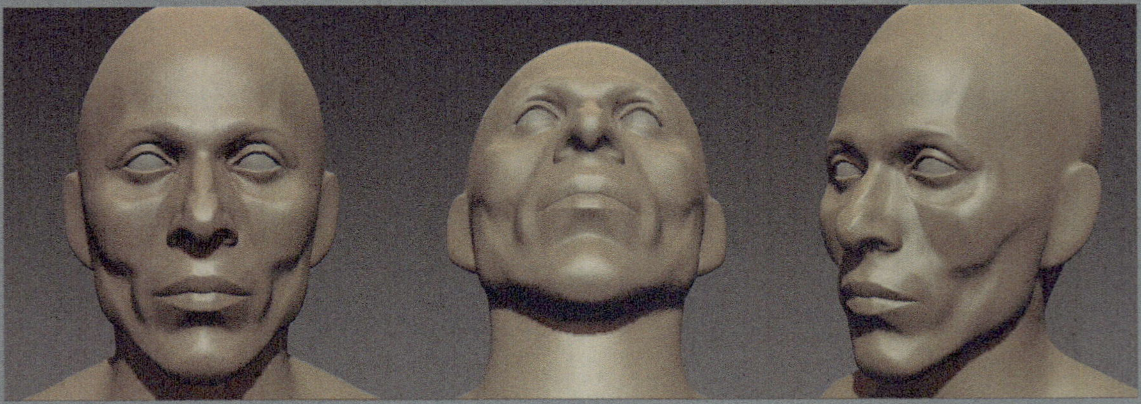

*Nose forms.*

From this point forward, you will be focusing on adding the more subtle details and attempting to capture the model's likeness as much as possible. One good technique for capturing the next level of detail without getting too bogged down in the fine details is to take a copy of the reference photos into Photoshop and use the Median filter on them:

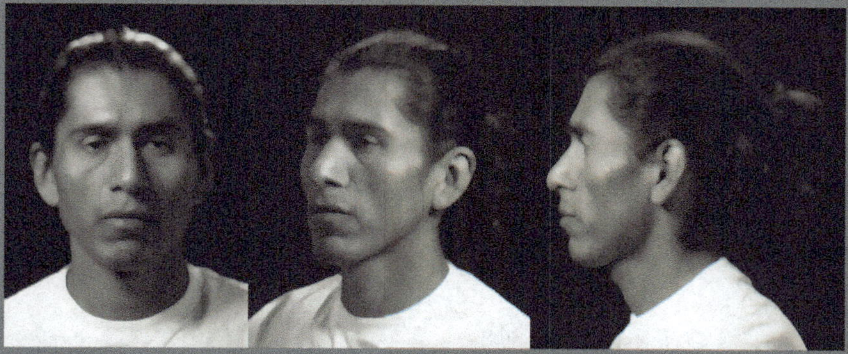

*Detail reduced in source photography using median filter.*

You will need to experiment with the value you set in the filter—its effect will vary based on the image resolution. What this does is simplify form and highlight shape so you can focus on the next level of detail while avoiding confusing high-frequency detail too early. Other filters can probably provide a similar result; you just want to wind up with a slightly less detailed painterly version of your images.

Using the Median-filtered source photos, start to refine the fleshy area below the eye, particularly the bulge of the orbicular muscle, leading away from the tear duct.

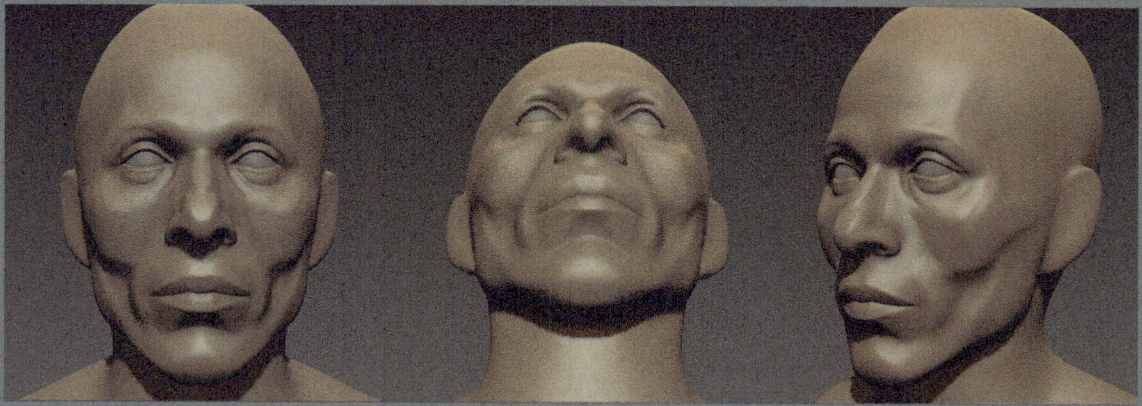

*Evaluate progress.*

Now, working downward, add the nasal labial fold. While you are at it, examine the reference photography closely, and you will notice the Alaeque is visible on the surface of his face. Add that form as well:

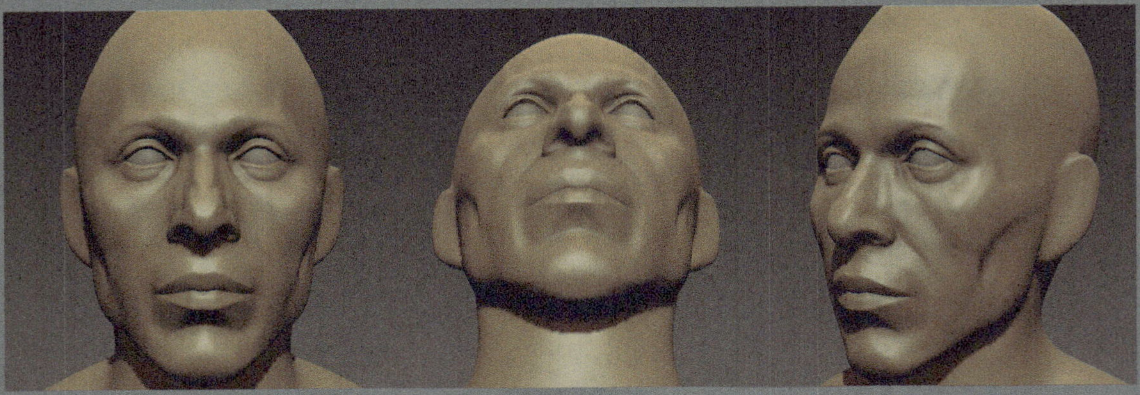

Evaluate progress.

Continuing downward, add the next level of detail to the lips:

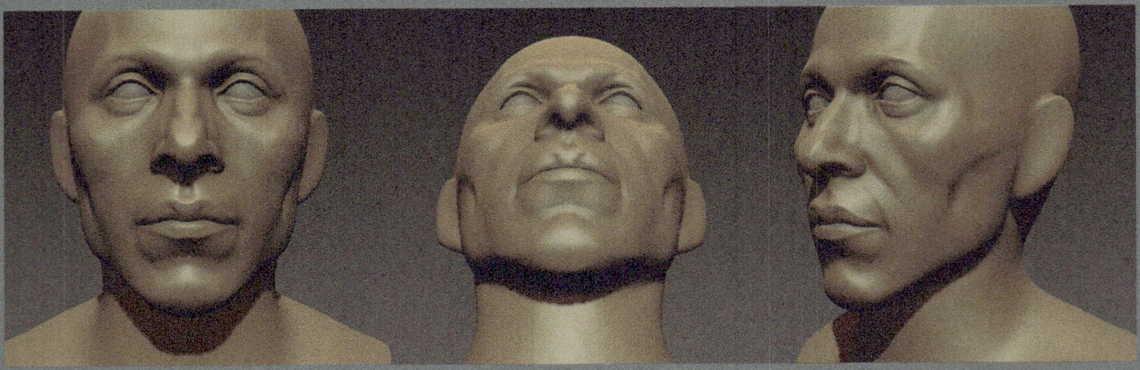

Lip refinement.

Now address the forehead region, blocking in the brow region and the frontal eminence:

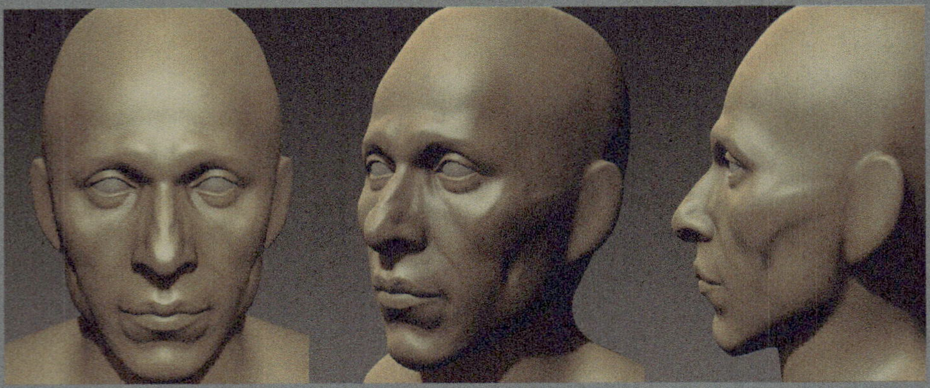

Forehead region.

Next, add the form of the nasal labial fold.

Next, refine the zygomatic and jaw region:

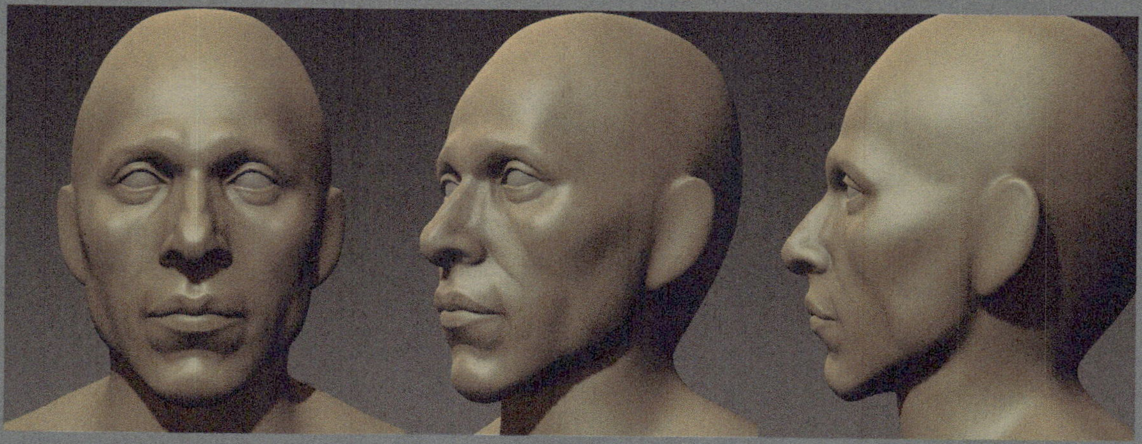

*Zygomatic jaw region.*

Now the basic forms of the ear:

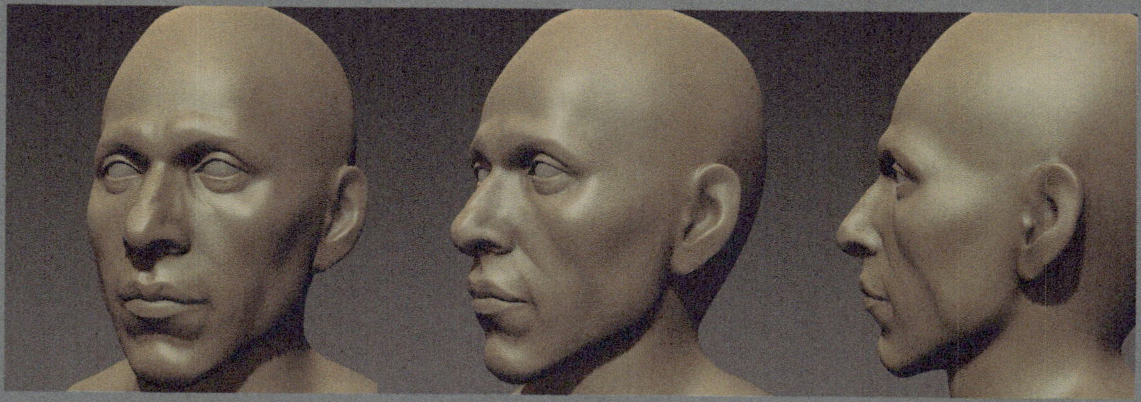

*Basic forms of ear.*

And refine:

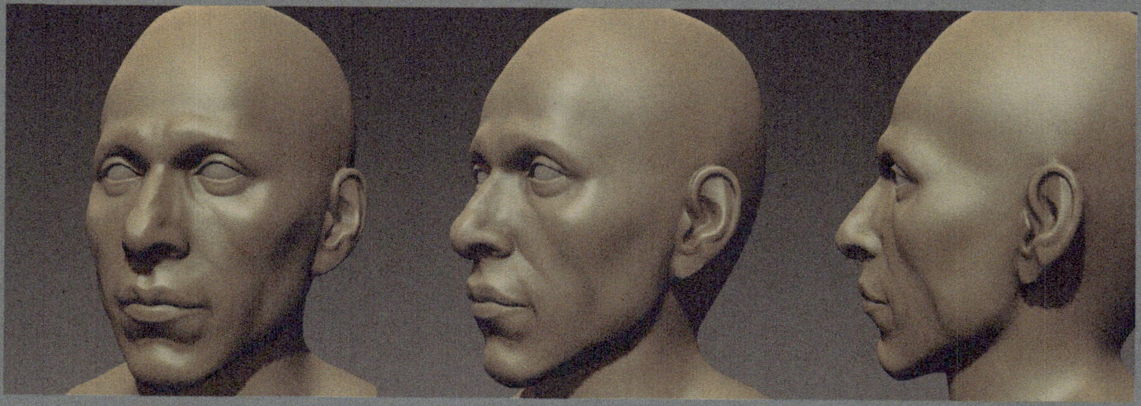

*Refining the ear.*

Before entering the final level of refinement, you should block in the hair form so that you can compare the overall proportions of your work to the reference photos.

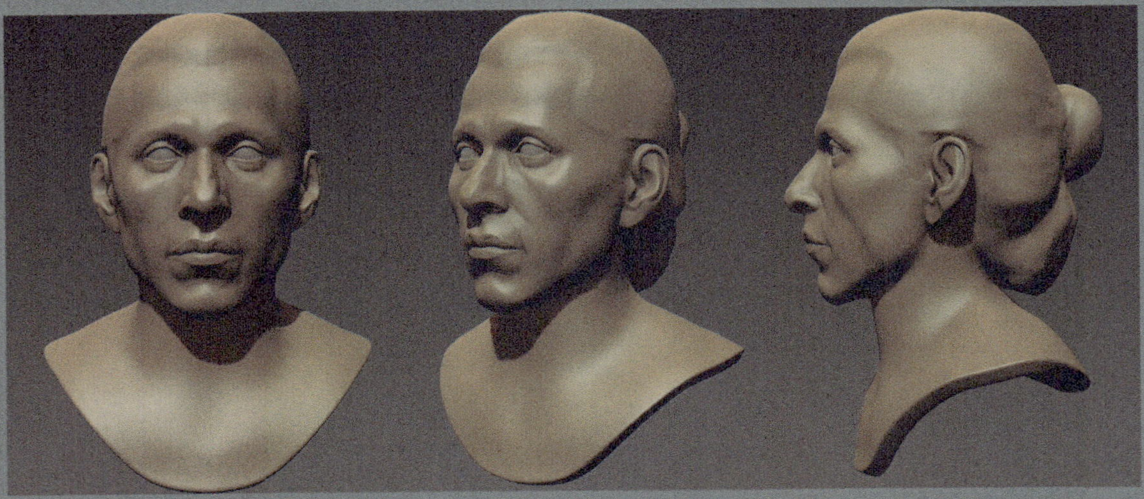

Basic hair form.

At this point, assess your portrait for likeness and anatomic forms. Make any corrections you feel you need before proceeding.

Now we will walk through each region again and finalize the detail. In some steps, the refinements are subtle.

Starting with the eye, examine the tutorial images (left is before refinement, right is after refinement) as well as your source photos to soften any forms that are too strong, adding the next level of refinement.

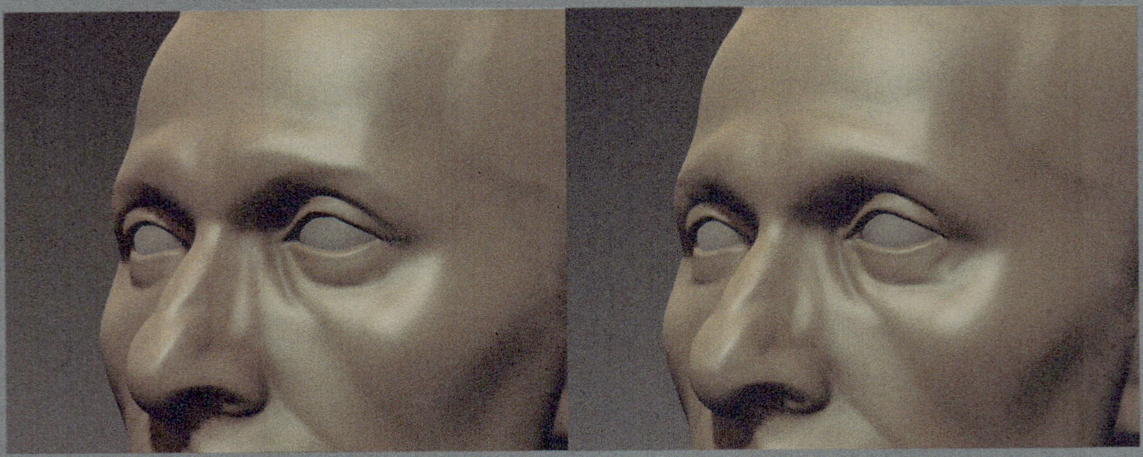

Refine.

The nose:

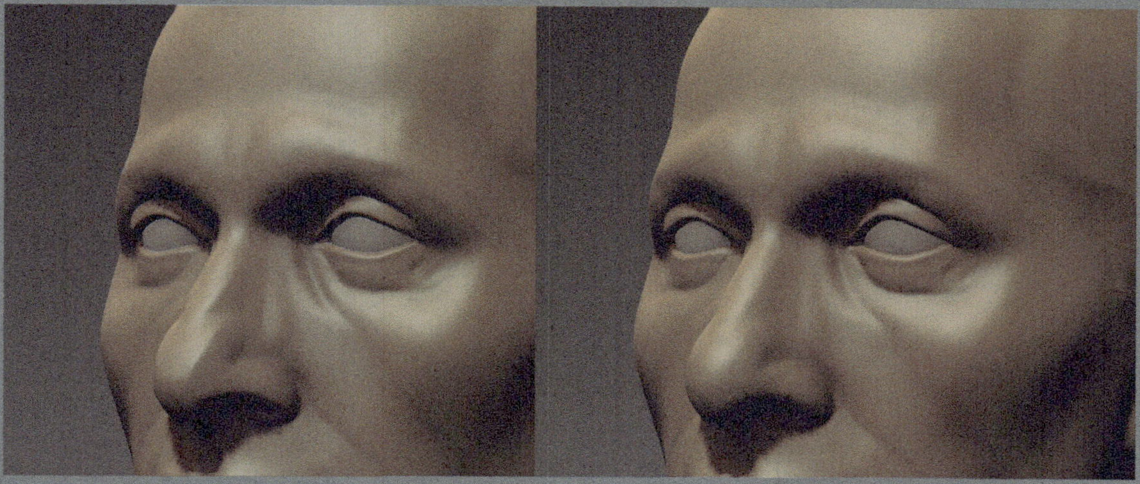

*Nose refinement.*

The mouth:

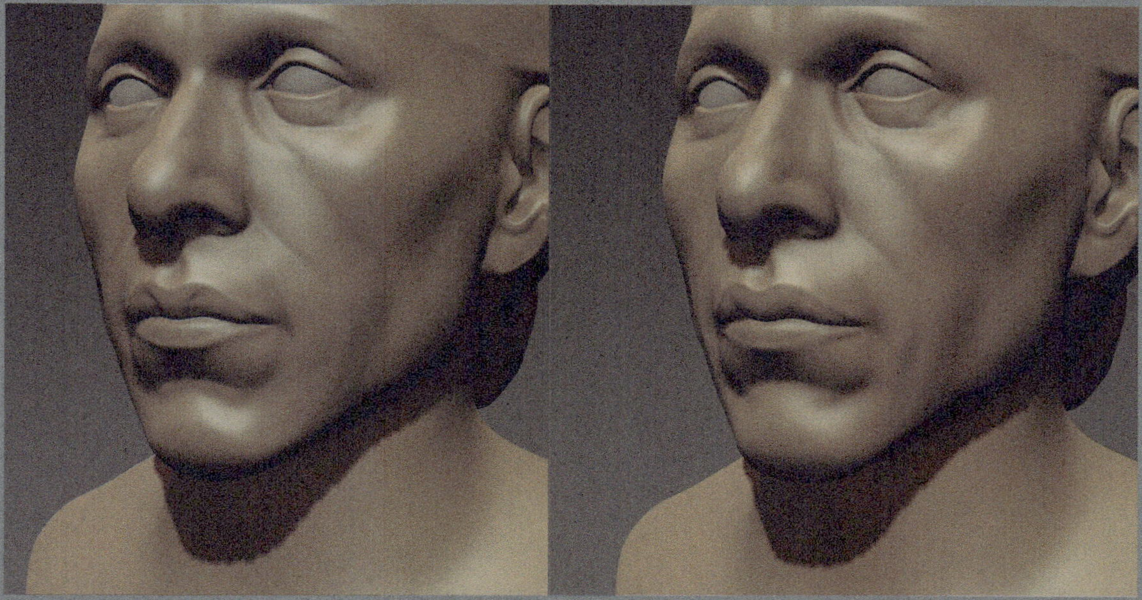

*Mouth refinement.*

The forehead:

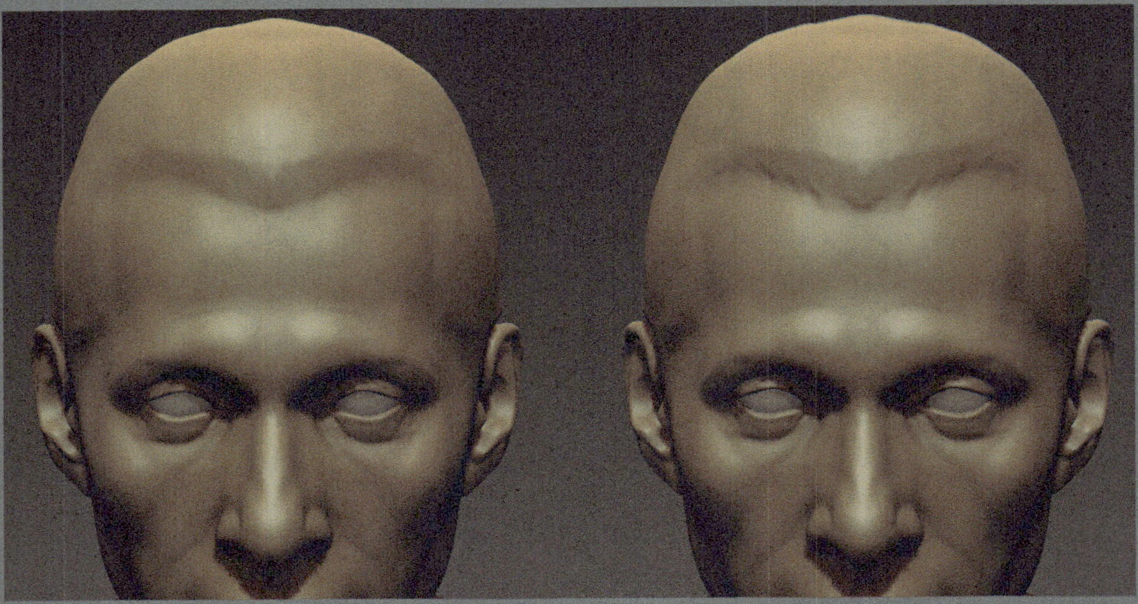

*Forehead refinement front view.*

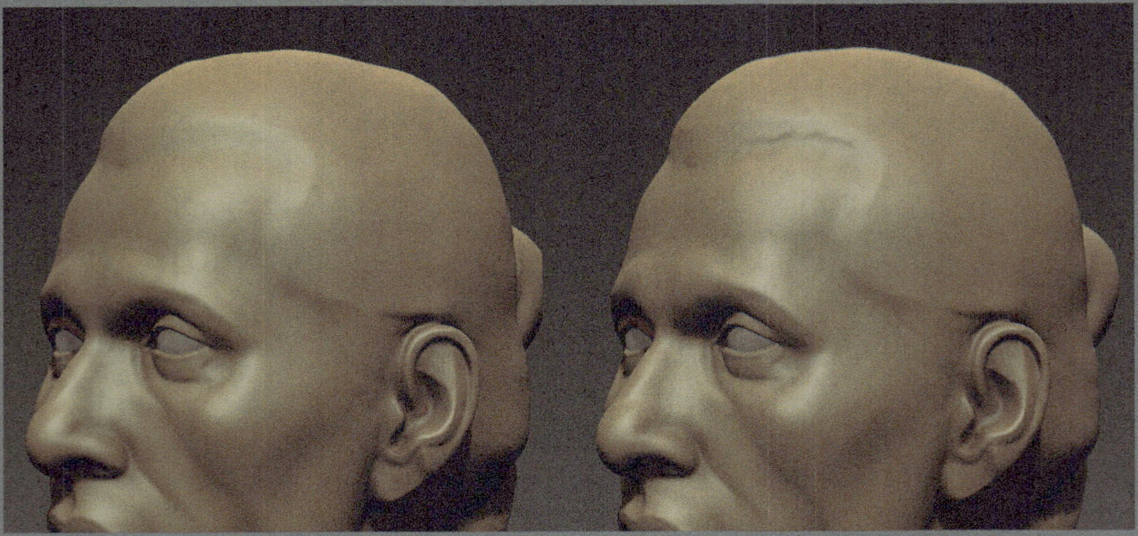

*forehead refinement front view.*

The ear:

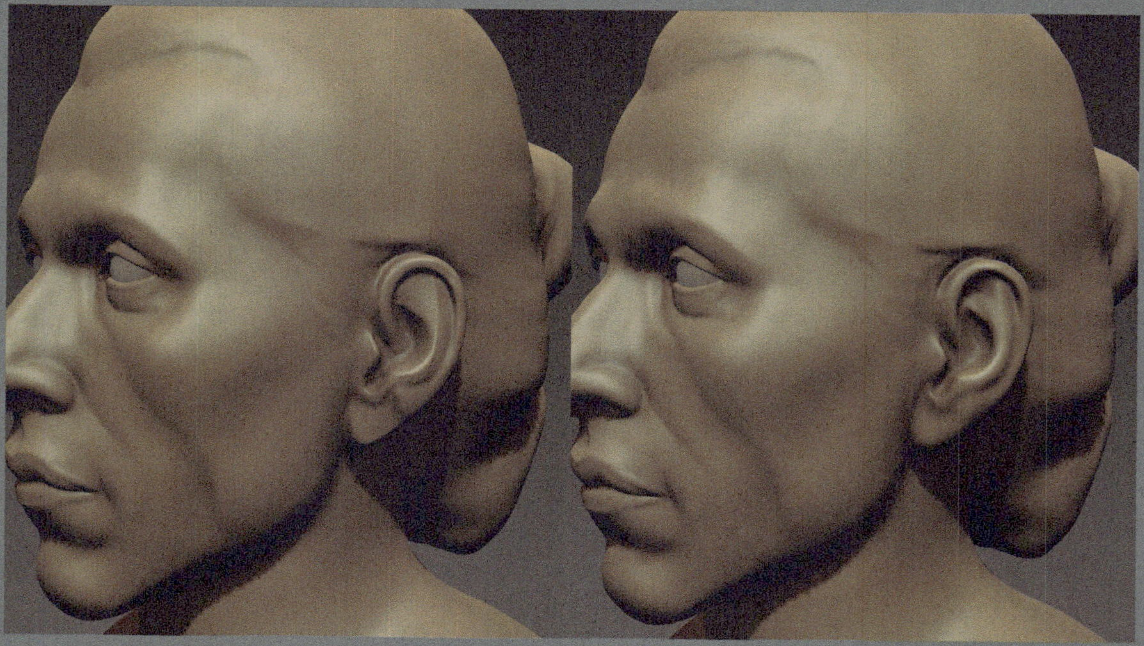

Ear refinement.

And finally, the jaw and chin region, paying attention to the flesh under the jaw that softens the jawline:

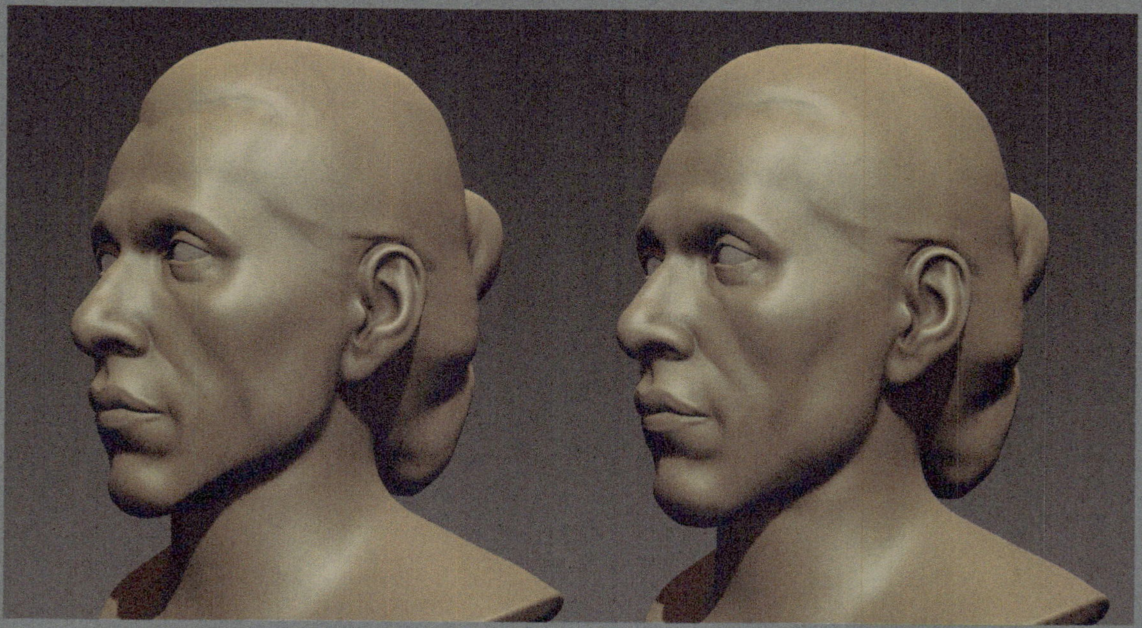

Jaw refinement.

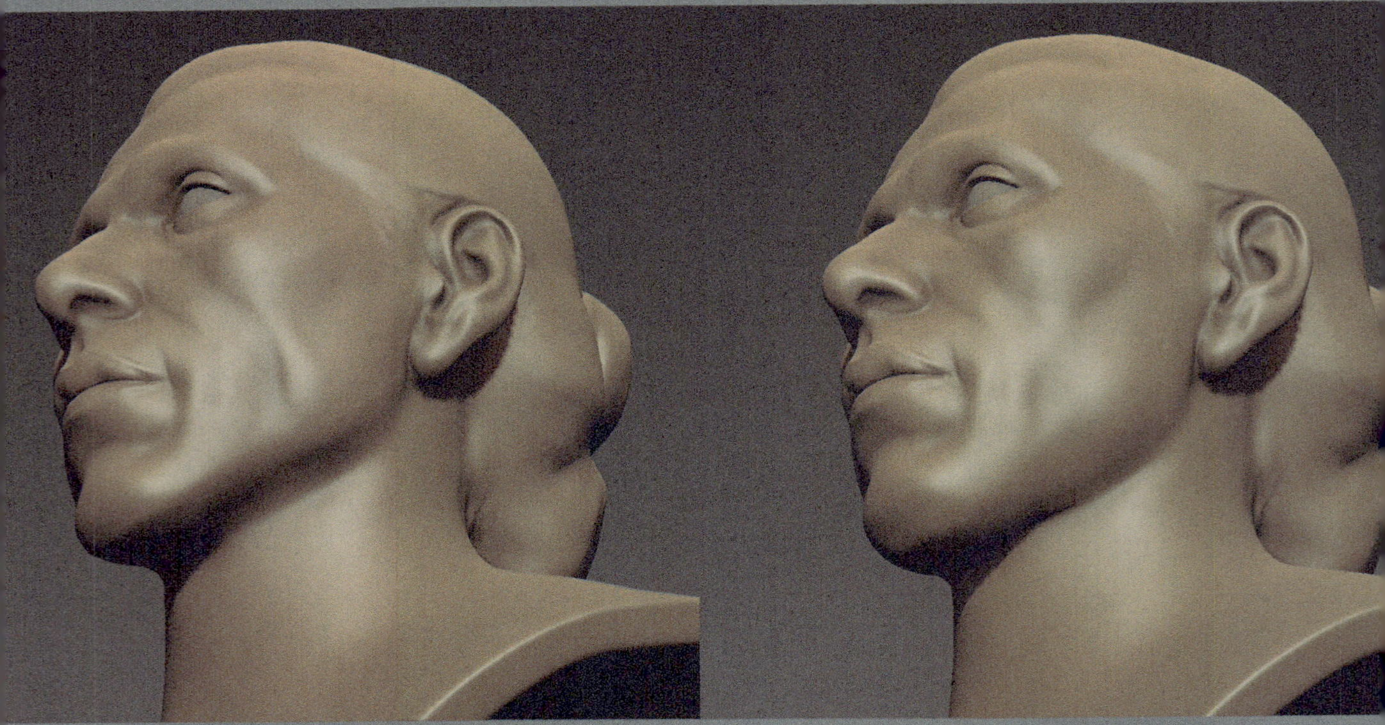

Refinement.

With some additional refinement and detail added to the hair and neck regions, hopefully you have something similar (or better!) than in Figure 4.29:

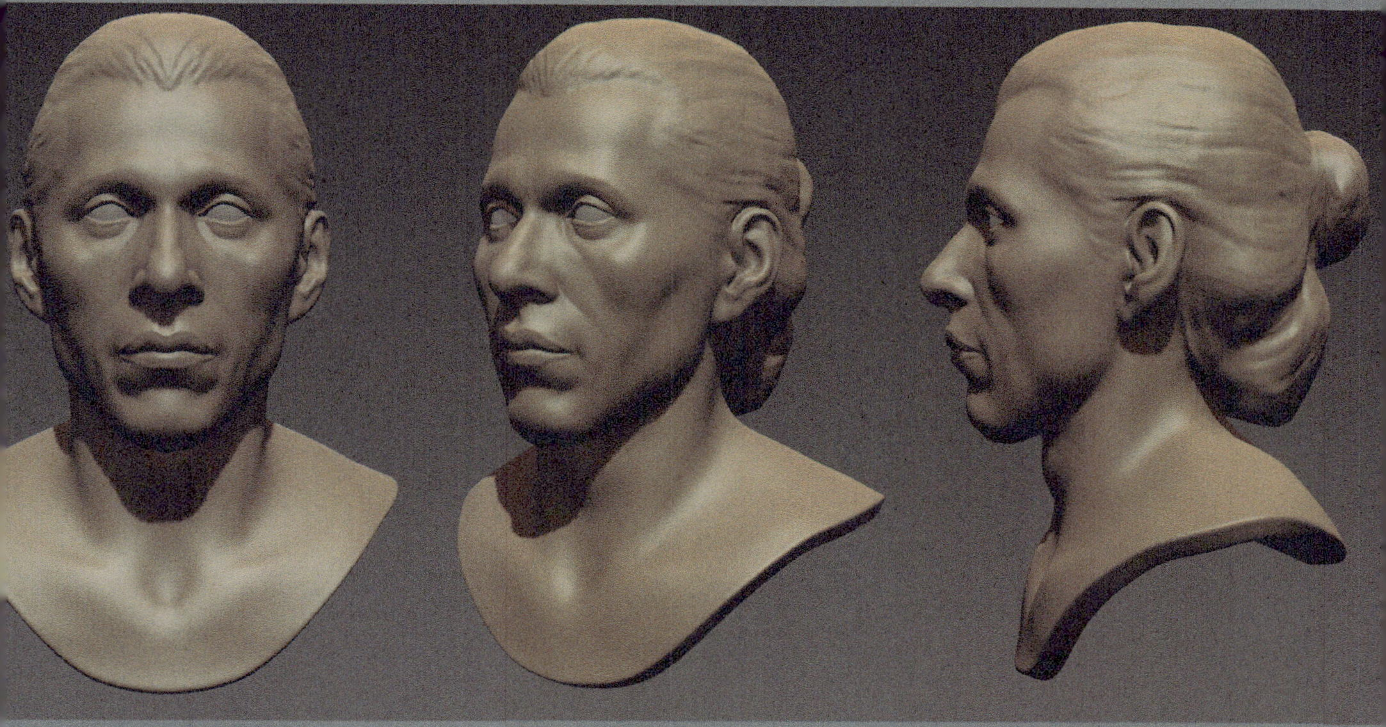

*Final product.*

# 6

CHAPTER 6

# FACIAL VARIATION OVER TIME

DOI: 10.1201/ 9781003484554-6

The skull changes over time. The facial mass construct is influenced by muscle and fat pads, facial fat migration, and aging, leading to facial variation beyond the skull.

The measurement of this variation is changing. Traditional research used simple methods like measuring distances between facial landmarks to study facial shape differences, like we did in this text using skulls. Newer methods of research use 3D imaging. Although these methods are straightforward, they might not be powerful enough to detect all the complex changes in the facial structure.

While we know that some facial features are strongly influenced by our genetics, we do not know all the details about which genes are involved. Diet, cultural practice, language, climate and other variables can change a cline characteristic in just one generation. Therefore, I will decline from identifying features as typical of an ethnicity and instead present the variables to consider and a sample of research on a wide variety of world populations provided by scientists. Most of this research is done by the medical community, interested in facial reconstruction and maintenance.

The various studies on cline characteristics will initiate a discussion about how we identify members of our cline and appreciate the unique representations of family lines across different cultures.

*I need to note that there are multiple ethnic groups within these basic sample ethnic classifications. Within each ethnic group, there is substantial morphological variation. In this sample of research, we are all struggling to find the answer—what makes you recognize someone from your cline?*

This chapter will provide a review of academic literature on informed character design, concerning the following subjects:

1. The growth of the human skull from infancy to old age
2. Variation in facial appearances beyond the skull
3. Facial fat migration
4. Comparison of male versus female aging
5. Academic resources on ethnicity and facial morphology

I encourage the reader to read the cited literature to expand their research in the subject area of choice.

# 6.1 THE GROWTH OF THE HUMAN SKULL FROM INFANCY TO OLD AGE

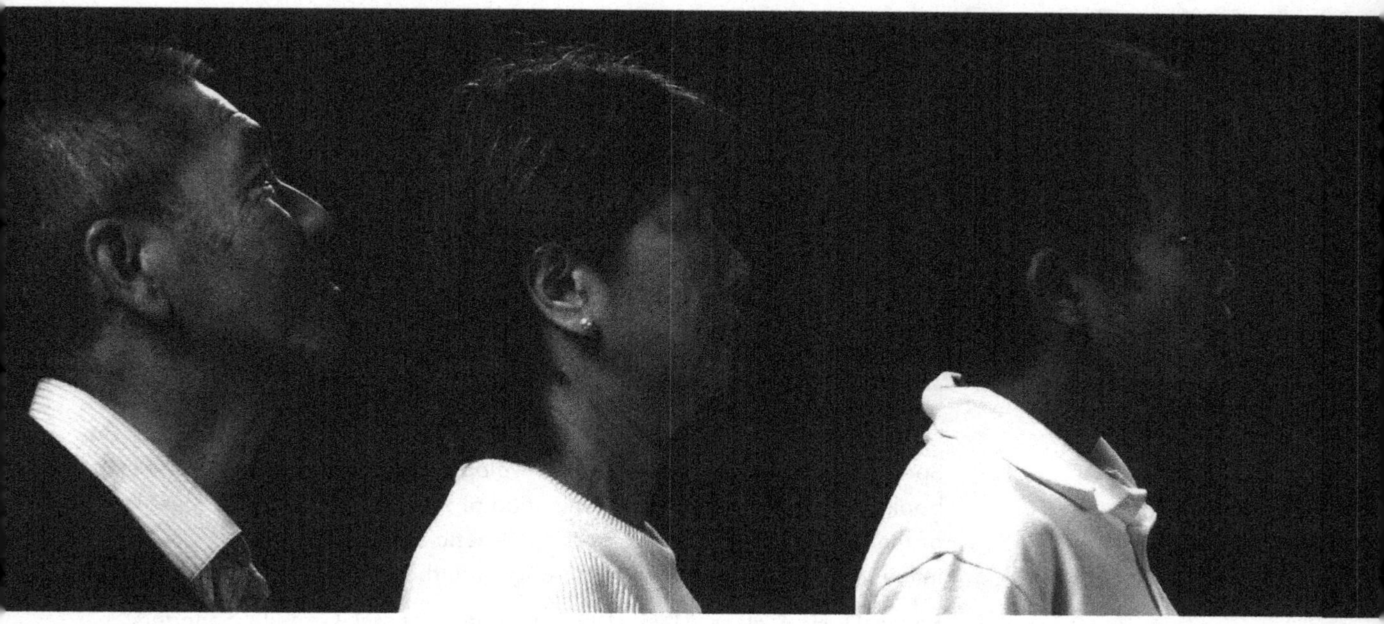

*the picture of the family.*

## 6.1.1 Infancy and Early Childhood

### 6.1.1.1 Rapid Growth

During the first two years of life, the human skull undergoes rapid growth, primarily driven by the rapid expansion of the brain. At birth, the brain is about 25% of its adult size, but by the age of two, it reaches approximately 75% of its adult size. Consequently, the skull must expand quickly to accommodate this growth. This rapid expansion is facilitated by the plasticity of the cranial bones and the presence of flexible joints known as sutures.

### 6.1.1.2 Fontanelles

Fontanelles, commonly referred to as "soft spots," are crucial during infancy. These are gaps between the cranial bones covered by tough membranes. The major fontanelles include the anterior, posterior, mastoid, and sphenoidal fontanelles. The presence of these fontanelles allows for the overlapping of bones during childbirth and the subsequent expansion of the skull as the brain grows. Over time, these fontanelles gradually ossify and close, with the posterior fontanelle typically closing by 2 to 3 months of age and the anterior fontanelle closing by 18 to 24 months. Research varies on the actual month these close.

#### 6.1.1.3 Cranial Sutures

Cranial sutures are fibrous joints that connect the bones of the skull. In infants and young children, these sutures are flexible, allowing the skull to expand as the brain grows. The major sutures include the coronal, sagittal, lambdoid, and squamosal sutures. As a child grows, these sutures begin to fuse, a process that typically starts in late childhood and continues into adolescence. This fusion process is critical for maintaining the structural integrity of the skull while allowing for brain growth during the early years.

### ACADEMIC RESOURCES ON CRANIOFACIAL DEVELOPMENT

1. Sperber, G. H. (2001). *Craniofacial development*. BC Decker Inc. This book provides an extensive examination of the developmental processes of the craniofacial complex, covering genetic and environmental influences from prenatal stages through adulthood.
2. Enlow, D. H., & Hans, M. G. (1996). *Essentials of facial growth*. Saunders. This resource offers a detailed understanding of the complex process of facial growth and development, highlighting the anatomical changes from birth through adolescence.
3. Moyers, R. E. (1988). *Handbook of orthodontics*. Year Book Medical Publishers. Although older, this book is a standard reference in orthodontics, providing foundational knowledge on the growth and developmental changes of the craniofacial skeleton.
4. Cowin, S. C., & Doty, S. B. (2007). *Tissue mechanics*. Springer. This book, while more focused on the mechanical aspects of tissue, includes discussions relevant to the biomechanics of craniofacial growth, particularly the mechanical forces involved in the development of cranial sutures.

### 6.1.2 Childhood to Adolescence

#### 6.1.2.1 Proportional Changes

As a child transitions from early childhood into adolescence, the proportions of the skull undergo significant changes. During this period, the cranial vault, which houses the brain, grows at a slower rate compared to the facial skeleton. Consequently, the face becomes more prominent relative to the cranial vault. This shift in proportion is due to the differential growth rates of various parts of the skull. The development of the jaw and nasal areas is particularly notable during this stage.

1. **Facial Development**: The maxilla (upper jaw) and mandible (lower jaw) both grow in size and prominence. The growth of the maxilla is influenced by the eruption of permanent teeth, while the mandible lengthens and changes shape to accommodate the growing facial structures.
2. **Nasal Development**: The nasal region also undergoes significant changes. The nasal bones lengthen, and the nasal bridge becomes more pronounced. This is partly due to the growth of the underlying cartilaginous structures and the development of the paranasal sinuses.

### 6.1.2.2 Growth Spurts

During puberty, adolescents experience a significant growth spurt, which also affects the skull, particularly the facial bones. This pubertal growth spurt is driven by hormonal changes, including increased levels of growth hormone, sex steroids, and thyroid hormones. These hormonal changes stimulate the growth of both the cranial base and the facial skeleton.

1. **Cranial Base**: The cranial base undergoes remodeling and growth during adolescence. This includes the sphenoid and occipital bones, which contribute to the overall shape and size of the skull.
2. **Facial Bones**: The facial bones, including the maxilla and mandible, experience accelerated growth during puberty. This results in increased facial height and the forward projection of the face. The growth of the mandible, in particular, contributes to changes in facial profile and the overall appearance of the lower face.
3. **Dental Changes**: The eruption of permanent teeth, especially the second molars, and, in some cases, the third molars (wisdom teeth) further influences the growth and development of the jaw and facial structure.

## ACADEMIC RESOURCES


1. Scheuer, L., & Black, S. (2000). *Developmental juvenile osteology*. Academic Press. This book provides comprehensive coverage of the growth and development of juvenile skeletons, including detailed descriptions of craniofacial growth patterns.
2. Enlow, D. H., & Hans, M. G. (2008). *Essentials of facial growth*. Needham Press; 2nd edition. This updated edition covers the principles of facial

growth, emphasizing the changes that occur during childhood and adolescence.

3. Nanda, R. (2009). *Current therapy in orthodontics*. Mosby. This text discusses the growth and development of the craniofacial complex with a focus on orthodontic implications, providing insights into the changes during puberty.
4. Broadbent, B. H., Broadbent, B. H. Jr., & Golden, W. H. (1975). *Bolton standards of dentofacial developmental growth*. This text is a seminal work that provides longitudinal data on dentofacial development, offering detailed norms for assessing and comparing craniofacial growth.

## 6.1.3 Old Age

*the picture of mother and daughter.*

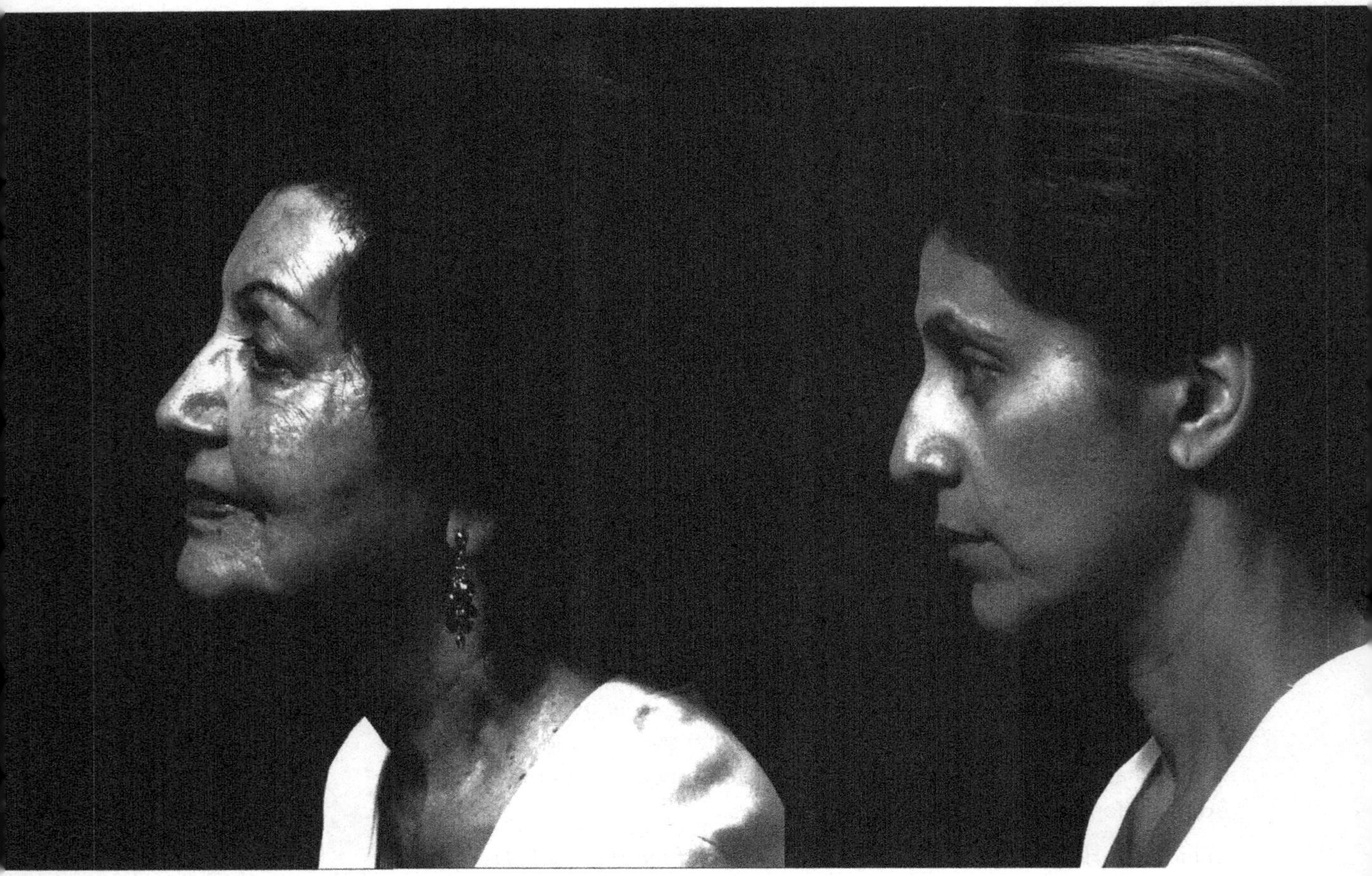

### 6.1.3.1 Bone Density Changes

As individuals age, there is a natural decline in bone density, known as osteoporosis. This decrease in bone density affects the thickness and structural integrity of the skull bones. Osteoporosis leads to the thinning of cranial bones, making them more fragile and susceptible to fractures. Additionally, the reduction in bone density impacts the overall shape and strength of the skull.

1. **Cranial Bone Thinning**: The thinning of cranial bones can result in a more pronounced appearance of the cranial sutures and other anatomical landmarks due to decreased bone mass and loss of bone mineral density (BMD).
2. **Impact on Facial Bones**: The facial bones, including the maxilla and mandible, also experience a reduction in density, leading to changes in facial structure and contour, potentially contributing to a more aged appearance.

### 6.1.3.2 Dental Changes

Dental changes in older adults can significantly impact the structure and proportions of the face, including tooth loss, changes in the alveolar bone (the bone that contains the tooth sockets), and alterations in the jaw structure.

1. **Tooth Loss**: Loss of teeth, whether due to periodontal disease, decay, or other factors, leads to the resorption of the alveolar bone. This resorption decreases the vertical dimension of the face, causing the lower third of the face to collapse inward, often referred to as "facial collapse."
2. **Changes in Jaw Structure**: The mandible and maxilla undergo remodeling in response to tooth loss and other age-related factors. The mandible can experience significant resorption, leading to a reduction in the height and width of the jawbone. This alters overall facial proportions and contributes to a more sunken or hollow appearance.
3. **Dentures and Implants**: The use of dentures or dental implants can help mitigate some of these changes. However, they may also affect facial proportions, depending on the fit and placement of the dental prosthetics.

## ACADEMIC RESOURCES

1. Clynes, M. A., Harvey, N. C., Curtis, E. M., Fuggle, N. R., Dennison, E. M., & Cooper, C. (2020). The epidemiology of osteoporosis. *British Medical*

*Bulletin, 133*(1), 105–117. https://doi.org/10.1093/bmb/ldaa005. This article discusses the impact of osteoporosis on aging populations, including changes in bone density and implications for cranial and facial structures.

2. Petersen, P. E., & Ogawa, H. (2018). Promoting oral health and quality of life of older people—the need for public health action. *Oral Health & Preventive Dentistry, 16*(2), 113–124. https://doi.org/10.3290/j.ohpd.a40309. This article explores the relationship between oral health and quality of life in older adults, highlighting dental changes and their impact on facial proportions.
3. Johnston, C. B., & Dagar, M. (2020). Osteoporosis in older adults. *The Medical Clinics of North America, 104*(5), 873–884. https://doi.org/10.1016/j.mcna.2020.06.004. This comprehensive review covers the clinical aspects of osteoporosis in older adults, including the effects on cranial and facial bones.

# 6.2 VARIATION IN FACIAL APPEARANCES BEYOND THE SKULL

The variation in facial appearance is influenced by several factors, including the underlying skull and muscles, as well as the distribution and characteristics of facial fat pads. Here is a bit more about how these elements contribute to facial appearance and their variations.

## 6.2.1 Skull and Muscles

### 6.2.1.1 Skull Structure

The shape and size of the skull form the foundation of the face. This includes the cranial base, facial bones such as the maxilla and mandible, and the overall cranial shape. The structure of the skull determines the contours and proportions of the face, influencing features such as forehead height, cheekbone prominence, and jawline definition.

Cranial Base: The cranial base supports the brain and the facial skeleton. Its growth and development during childhood and adolescence shape the overall facial structure.

Facial Bones: The maxilla (upper jaw) and mandible (lower jaw) are key components that define the midface and lower face. The maxilla supports the upper teeth and forms the base of the nose, while the mandible provides the foundation for the lower teeth and jawline.

#### 6.2.1.2 Muscles

Facial muscles overlay the skull and are responsible for expressions and movements. These muscles are connected to the skin and other soft tissues, enabling a wide range of facial expressions that convey emotions and contribute to individual identity.

Masseter Muscle: This muscle is one of the main muscles responsible for chewing. It is located at the angle of the jaw and contributes to the width of the lower face.

Temporalis Muscle: This muscle is involved in chewing and is located on the sides of the head, extending down to the jaw.

Orbicularis Oculi and Orbicularis Oris: These muscles surround the eyes and mouth, respectively, and are crucial for expressions such as smiling, frowning, and blinking.

#### ACADEMIC RESOURCES

1. Enlow, D. H., & Hans, M. G. (1996). *Facial growth.* This book is a classic and reliable source for understanding the complex process of facial growth and development, including the role of the skull and muscles. Of special interest is Chapter 11, The Structural Basis for Ethnic Variations in Facial Form.
2. Sperber, G. H. (2001). *Craniofacial development.* This text offers insights into the development of the craniofacial region from embryological stages through adulthood, detailing the interactions between skeletal structures and soft tissues.

## 6.2.2 Variations Influenced by Genetics, Age, and Weight

### 6.2.2.1 Genetics

Genetic factors play a significant role in determining the shape and size of the skull and the distribution of facial muscles. Genetic inheritance influences facial proportions, the prominence of facial features, and the overall harmony of the face. Specific genes regulate the growth and development of craniofacial structures, leading to variations in features such as nose size, cheekbone height, and jaw prominence among different individuals and populations. For example, certain genetic variants are associated with a higher likelihood of pronounced cheekbones or a stronger jawline, while others may influence the relative width or length of the face.

## ACADEMIC RESOURCES

Claes, P., Roosenboom, J., White, J. D., Swigut, T., Sero, D., Li, J., Lee, M. K., Zaidi, A., Mattern, B. C., Liebowitz, C., Pearson, L., González, T., Leslie, E. J., Carlson, J. C., Orlova, E., Suetens, P., Vandermeulen, D., Feingold, E., Marazita, M. L., . . . Weinberg, S. M. (2018). Genome-wide mapping of global-to-local genetic effects on human facial shape. *Nature Genetics*, *50*(3), 414–423. https://doi.org/10.1038/s41588-018-0057-4. You will find under the article similar articles that reach into multiple ethnic populations.

### 6.2.2.2 Age

As individuals age, the skull and facial muscles undergo changes that affect appearance. The skull may lose bone density, leading to a reduction in facial height and the appearance of a more pronounced jawline. Additionally, the resorption of bone in the jaw and chin area can lead to changes in the lower face's shape. Muscle tone and elasticity also decrease with age, contributing to sagging skin and the formation of wrinkles. The skin loses collagen and elastin, essential for maintaining firmness and elasticity, resulting in a more aged appearance. Fat pads in the face also shift and diminish, further impacting facial contours.

## ACADEMIC RESOURCES

Farkas, L. G., Katic, M. J., Forrest, C. R., Alt, K. W., Bagic, I., Baltadjiev, G., Cunha, E., Cvicelová, M., Davies, S., Erasmus, I., Gillett-Netting, R., Hajnis, K., Kemkes-Grottenthaler, A., Khomyakova, I., Kumi, A., Kgamphe, J. S., Kayo-daigo, N., Le, T., Malinowski, A., . . . Yahia, E. (2005). International anthropometric study of facial morphology in various ethnic groups/races. *The Journal of Craniofacial Surgery*, *16*(4), 615–646. https://doi.org/10.1097/01.scs.0000171847.58031.9e. You will find under the article similar articles that reach into multiple ethnic populations.

## 6.2.2.3 Weight

The fat under the skin of the face is divided into several separate sections. For example, the nasolabial fold, the line that runs from the nose to the mouth corners, is its own distinct section. What people call malar fat, found in the cheek area, actually consists of three parts: The medial, middle, and lateral temporal-cheek fat. The forehead also has three parts: Central, middle, and lateral temporal-cheek fat. Around the eyes, the fat is divided into three sections by thin membranes. The jowl fat, found at the bottom of the face, is the lowest section of subcutaneous fat. Some structures called "retaining ligaments" are just points where these sections meet and fuse together.

As we age, these separate fat sections change, contributing to the aging appearance of the face. The idea that the face has distinct fat compartments means that it does not age as a single unit. The manner of movement between these sections might also play a role in how the soft tissue changes position over time. Knowing about these separate compartments helps artists better understand and plan displacement to better accentuate age.

## ACADEMIC RESOURCES

1. Rohrich, R. J., & Pessa, J. E. (2007). The fat compartments of the face: Anatomy and clinical implications for cosmetic surgery. *Plastic and Reconstructive Surgery, 119*(7), 2219–2227. https://doi.org/10.1097/01.prs.0000265403.66886.54. This study explores the distinct fat compartments in the face, their anatomical boundaries, and implications for cosmetic surgery, particularly with changes in body weight.
2. Tchkonia, T., Thomou, T., Zhu, Y., Karagiannides, I., Pothoulakis, C., Jensen, M. D., & Kirkland, J. L. (2013). Mechanisms and metabolic implications of regional differences among fat depots. *Cell Metabolism, 17*(5), 644–656. https://doi.org/10.1016/j.cmet.2013.03.008. Although primarily focused on body fat, this paper provides insights into regional fat distribution, including facial areas, and discusses the physiological implications of fat changes.

# 6.3 FACIAL FAT MIGRATION

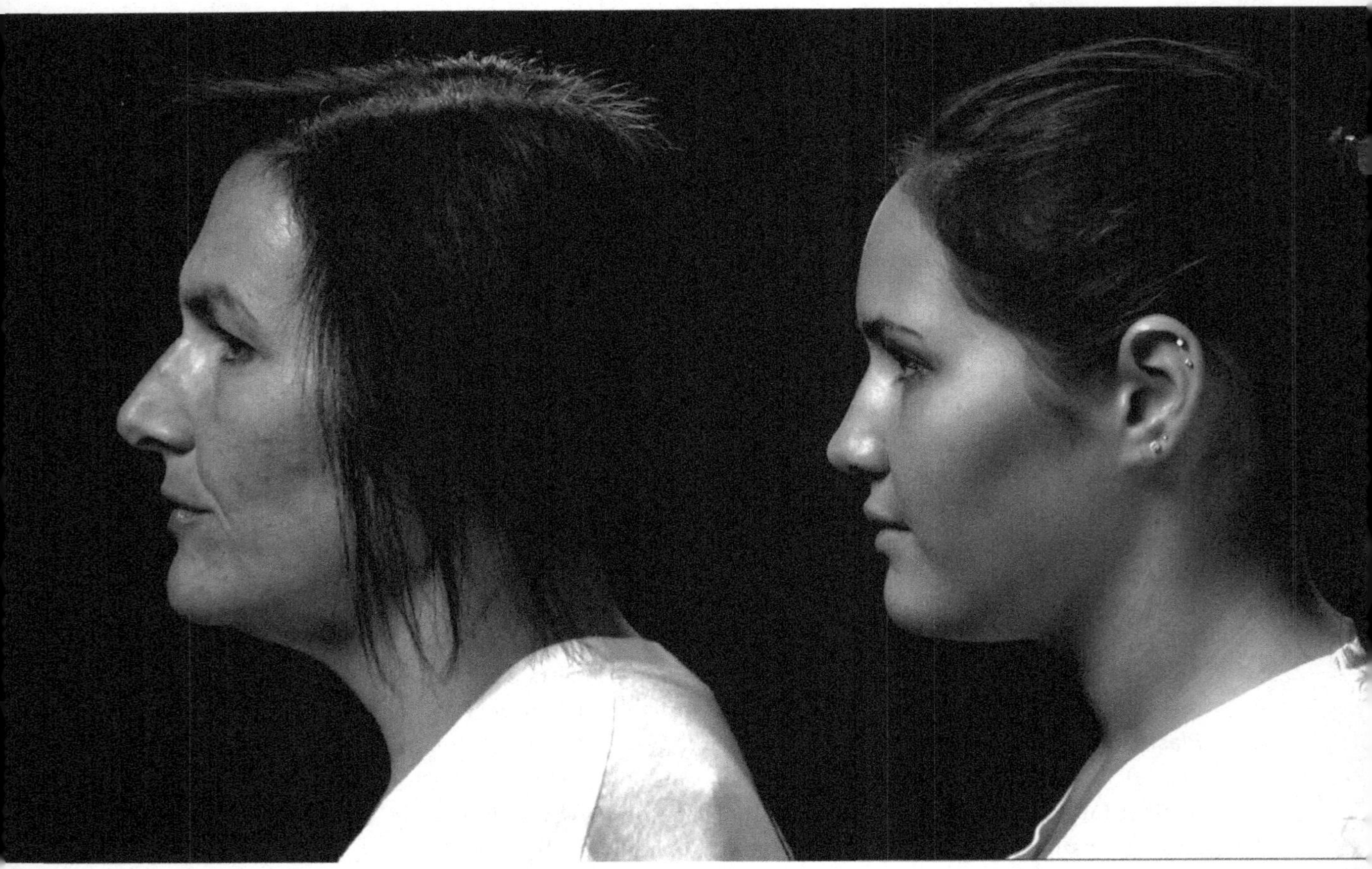

Facial fat migration is a crucial aspect of the aging process, impacting facial aesthetics significantly. This phenomenon involves the redistribution and atrophy of facial fat over time, leading to changes in facial contours and the overall appearance. Here, we delve into the mechanisms, stages, and contributing factors in greater detail.

## Mechanisms of Facial Fat Migration

1. Volume Loss and Redistribution:

   **Youthful Face**: In youth, facial fat is evenly distributed, providing a full, smooth appearance. Key fat compartments include the buccal fat pads (cheeks), malar fat pads (cheekbones), and submental fat (under the chin).

**Midface Changes**: With age, there is a reduction in the volume of the midface fat compartments. This results in a hollowed appearance under the eyes and flattening of the cheeks. Fat from the midface migrates downward due to gravity, creating deeper nasolabial folds.

**Lower Face Accumulation**: As midface fat descends, it often accumulates around the jawline and neck, forming jowls and contributing to a sagging, heavier lower face.

2. Impact of Gravity:

   **Midface Descent**: Gravity pulls down the fat pads in the cheeks and under the eyes, causing them to descend. This results in a more pronounced nasolabial fold and loss of cheek prominence.

   **Jowl Formation**: The migration of fat toward the lower face can lead to the formation of jowls, which disrupt the youthful V-shaped contour of the face.

3. Structural Changes:

   **Skin Elasticity**: Over time, the skin loses its elasticity due to decreased collagen and elastin production. This reduction in skin support exacerbates the effects of fat migration, leading to sagging and wrinkling.

   **Bone Resorption**: Age-related bone loss, particularly in the maxilla (upper jaw) and mandible (lower jaw), further reduces the structural support for the overlying soft tissues, enhancing the appearance of sagging and volume loss.

## Hormonal Changes

Menopause and Hormones: Hormonal changes, particularly during menopause, can accelerate facial fat loss and redistribution. Reduced estrogen levels contribute to decreased fat volume in the midface and increased fat deposition in the lower face and neck. This hormonal impact exacerbates the visual signs of aging.

## Other Factors

Weight Fluctuations: Significant changes in body weight can impact facial fat distribution. Weight gain typically leads to increased facial fat, resulting in a fuller face, while weight loss can cause a more hollowed and gaunt appearance.

Genetics: Genetic predisposition plays a significant role in determining the pattern and rate of facial fat migration. Some individuals may experience more pronounced changes due to their genetic makeup, impacting how and where fat is distributed and lost.

### 6.3.1 Detailed Stages of Facial Fat Migration

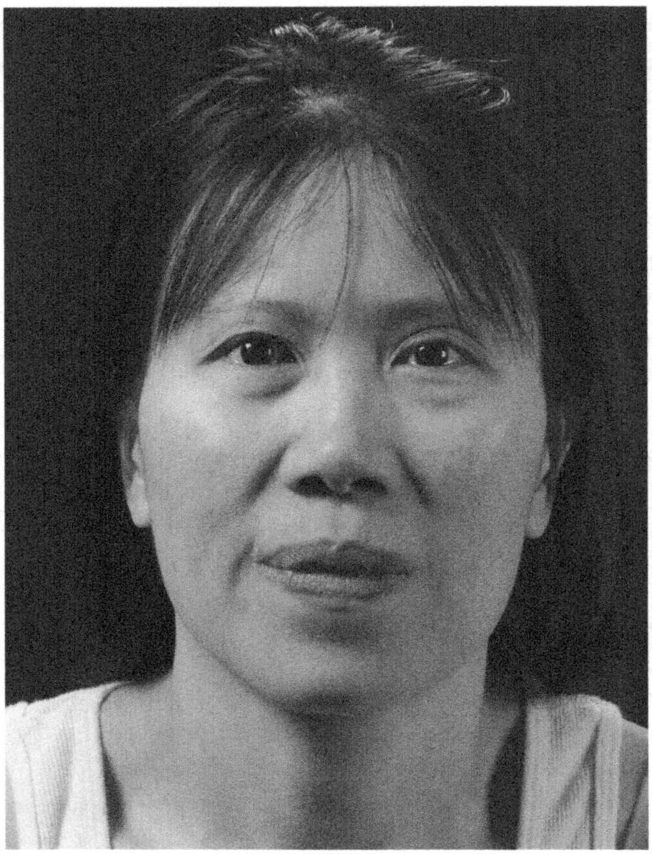

1. Twenties to thirties:

   **Minimal Changes**: During this period, the face generally retains its youthful fullness. However, early signs of aging may start to appear, such as slight hollowing under the eyes and minor sagging in the midface.

2. Forties to fifties:

   **Midface Volume Loss**: Noticeable volume loss in the midface, particularly in the cheeks and under the eyes, becomes evident. The descent of malar fat pads creates deeper nasolabial folds.

   **Emergence of Jowls**: Fat migration toward the lower face leads to the formation of jowls and a less-defined jawline. Skin elasticity continues to decrease, enhancing the sagging effect.

3. Sixties and Beyond:

   **Advanced Sagging and Volume Loss**: Significant sagging and volume loss occur in both the midface and lower face. The cheeks become more hollow, and jowls become more prominent.

   **Bone Density Reduction**: Age-related bone resorption reduces the structural support for facial fat and skin, exacerbating the appearance of aging.

## ACADEMIC RESOURCES

1. Donofrio, L. M. (2000). Fat distribution: A morphologic study of the aging face. *Dermatologic Surgery, 26*(12), 1107–1112.
2. Rohrich, R. J., & Pessa, J. E. (2007). The fat compartments of the face: Anatomy and clinical implications for cosmetic surgery. *Plastic and Reconstructive Surgery, 119*(7), 2219–2227. https://doi.org/10.1097/01.prs.0000265403.66886.54

These sources provide comprehensive insights into the mechanisms of facial fat migration, the anatomical changes involved, and the clinical implications for aesthetic treatments and interventions.

# 6.4 COMPARISON OF MALE AND FEMALE FACIAL AGING

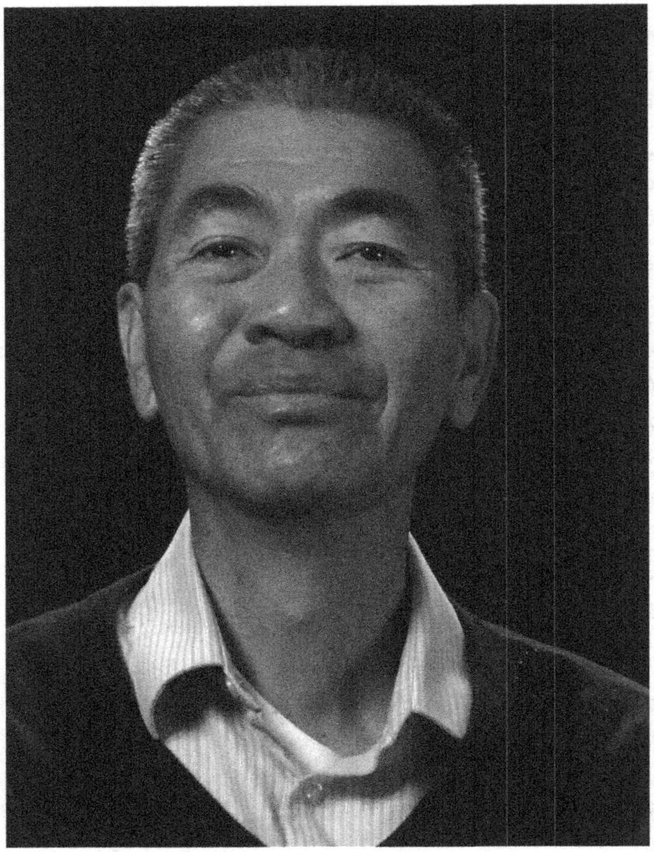

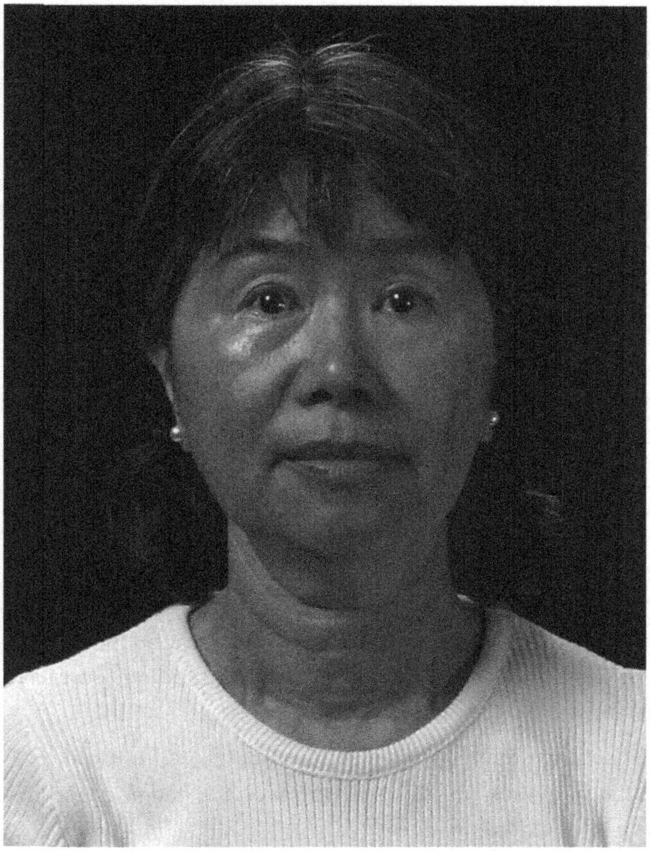

Facial aging differs between males and females due to a combination of genetic, hormonal, and environmental factors. Here is a detailed comparison of how facial aging manifests in men and women, highlighting the key differences in the aging process:

## 6.4.1 Bone Structure Changes

### 6.4.1.1 Male Facial Aging

**Bone Density**: Men typically have thicker and denser facial bones, providing a robust structure that supports the overlying soft tissues. As men age, they experience a slower rate of bone resorption compared to women, which helps maintain facial structure for a longer period.

**Jawline**: The male jawline remains relatively well-defined with age due to slower bone resorption. However, over time, men may still experience some loss of definition in the jawline and chin area.

#### 6.4.1.1.1 Female Facial Aging

**Bone Density**: Women experience a more rapid decline in bone density, particularly after menopause due to decreased estrogen levels. This accelerated bone resorption can lead to more noticeable changes in facial structure such as a receding jawline and decreased cheekbone prominence.

**Jawline**: Women often experience a more pronounced loss of jawline definition and chin prominence as they age, contributing to a more softened and rounded facial appearance.

## 6.4.2 Skin Characteristics

### 6.4.2.1 Male Facial Aging

**Thickness**: Male skin is generally thicker and contains more collagen than female skin, which provides better resistance to wrinkles and sagging. However, men tend to have coarser skin texture and larger pores.

**Oil Production**: Higher sebum production in men can keep their skin more moisturized, delaying the formation of fine lines. However, this can also lead to more issues with acne and enlarged pores.

### 6.4.2.2 Female Facial Aging

**Thickness**: Female skin is thinner and more delicate, making it more prone to fine lines, wrinkles, and sagging. Reduced collagen levels, especially post menopause, accelerate these aging signs.

**Oil Production**: Women generally have lower sebum production, which can lead to drier skin and more pronounced wrinkles. Hormonal changes can also impact skin hydration and elasticity.

## 6.4.3 Wrinkle Formation

### 6.4.3.1 Male Facial Aging

**Wrinkle Pattern**: Men typically develop deeper forehead lines and crow's feet around the eyes. Due to thicker skin and higher collagen content, their wrinkles may appear later but are often more profound.

**Expression Lines**: Men's facial muscles are stronger, leading to more pronounced expression lines such as nasolabial folds and marionette lines (lines running from the corners of the mouth to the chin).

#### 6.4.3.2 Female Facial Aging

**Wrinkle Pattern**: Women tend to develop finer lines around the eyes, mouth, and forehead earlier due to thinner skin and lower collagen levels. Vertical lines around the lips are more common in women.

**Expression Lines**: While women also develop expression lines, they tend to be less deep but more numerous compared to men.

### 6.4.4 Facial Fat Distribution

#### 6.4.4.1 Male Facial Aging

**Fat Loss**: Men tend to lose facial fat more uniformly, maintaining overall facial volume longer. However, they may experience significant fat loss in the midface and cheeks, leading to a hollowed appearance.

**Sagging**: Fat pads in men's faces tend to descend more slowly, resulting in less pronounced sagging compared to women.

#### 6.4.4.2 Female Facial Aging

**Fat Loss**: Women experience more significant fat loss in specific areas, such as the cheeks and around the eyes, leading to a more hollow and gaunt appearance. This uneven fat loss contributes to a more aged look.

**Sagging**: Women's facial fat pads descend more quickly, resulting in more noticeable sagging, particularly in the midface, jawline, and neck areas.

### 6.4.5 Hormonal Influences

#### 6.4.5.1 Male Facial Aging

**Testosterone**: Testosterone levels decrease gradually in men, leading to slower and more gradual facial aging. This hormone supports thicker skin and greater muscle mass, contributing to a more youthful appearance for a longer period.

#### 6.4.5.2 Female Facial Aging

**Estrogen**: Estrogen levels decline sharply during menopause, accelerating facial aging. This hormonal drop leads to decreased collagen production, increased skin dryness, and more rapid bone resorption, contributing to faster and more noticeable aging changes.

### 6.4.5.3 Effects on Skin

- Lower hormone levels lead to thinner, drier skin with less collagen and elasticity.
- Wound healing is slower in older men due to higher testosterone levels.
- Hormone changes affect sweat glands and hair follicles, leading to issues like male-pattern baldness (in men) and dry skin.

#### ACADEMIC RESOURCES


1. Farage, M. A., Miller, K. W., Zouboulis, C. C., Piérard, G. E., & Maibach, H. I. (2012). Gender differences in skin aging and the changing profile of the sex hormones with age. *Journal of Steroids and Hormonal Science*, *3*(2), 109.
2. Juul, A., & Skakkebæk, N. E. (2002, September 1). Androgens and the ageing male. *Human Reproduction Update*, *8*(5), 423–433. https://doi.org/10.1093/humupd/8.5.423
3. Thornton, M. J. (2013). Estrogens and aging skin. *Dermato-Endocrinology*, *5*(2), 264–270. https://doi.org/10.4161/derm.23872


## 6.4.6 Academic Resources on Ethnicity and Facial Morphology

Academic papers provide in-depth research on ethnicity and facial morphology. The following list is included to give you a place to start your research on a specific ethnic identity. If the ethnicity you are most interested in is not depicted in the research given here, use Google scholar and the keywords from these articles to find the most relevant papers available.

#### FACIAL MORPHOLOGY


1. Fang, F., Clapham, P. J., & Chung, K. C. (2011). A systematic review of interethnic variability in facial dimensions. *Plastic and Reconstructive Surgery*, *127*(2), 874–881. https://doi.org/10.1097/PRS.0b013e318200afdb
2. Farkas, L. G., Katic, M. J., Forrest, C. R., Alt, K. W., Bagic, I., Baltadjiev, G., Cunha, E., Cvicelová, M., Davies, S., Erasmus, I., Gillett-Netting, R., Hajnis, K., Kemkes-Grottenthaler, A., Khomyakova, I., Kumi, A.,

3. Kgamphe, J. S., Kayo-daigo, N., Le, T., Malinowski, A., . . . Yahia, E. (2005). International anthropometric study of facial morphology in various ethnic groups/races. *The Journal of Craniofacial Surgery*, *16*(4), 615–646. https://doi.org/10.1097/01.scs.0000171847.58031.9e

4. Farkas, L. G., Katic, M. J., Forrest, C. R., Alt, K. W., Bagic, I., Baltadjiev, G., . . . & Tóth, G. (2005). International anthropometric study of facial morphology in various ethnic groups/races. *Journal of Craniofacial Surgery*, *31*(6), 15851598. https://doi.org/10.1097/SCS.0000000000006694. This extensive study examines the anthropometric measurements of facial morphology across different ethnic groups, including Caucasian, African, East Asian, and others. Look up this paper to see the related papers that provide detailed measurements of more diverse populations.

5. Matts, P. J., Canfield, D. B. S., & D'Alessandro, B. (2021, December). A new model to simulate human facial appearance, accurately, and realistically, across age and ethnicity. *Plastic and Reconstructive Surgery*, *148*(6S), 14S–20S. https://doi.org/10.1097/PRS.0000000000008781

6. Salah, M., Higzi, M. A., Ali, R. W., & Naini, F. B. (2014). The Sudanese female face: Normative craniofacial measurements and comparison with African-American and North American White females. *Journal of Cranio-Maxillo-Facial Surgery: Official Publication of the European Association for Cranio-Maxillo-Facial Surgery*, *42*(8), 1704–1709. https://doi.org/10.1016/j.jcms.2014.06.003

7. Uppada, U. K., Tauro, D. P., & Senthilnathan, K. P. (2024). Anthropometric analysis of Indian faces: A systematic review. *Journal of Maxillofacial and Oral Surgery*, *23*(3), 451–461. https://doi.org/10.1007/s12663-024-02185-6

8. Zacharopoulos, G. V., Manios, A., Kau, C. H., Velagrakis, G., Tzanakakis, G. N., & de Bree, E. (2016). Anthropometric analysis of the face. *The Journal of Craniofacial Surgery*, *27*(1), e71–e75. https://doi.org/10.1097/SCS.0000000000002231

## FACIAL FAT

1. Gray, M. L., & Boahene, K. D. (2022). Facial rejuvenation in patients of color. *Current Otorhinolaryngology Reports*, *10*(3), 303–309.

2. Naik, M. (2023). Periorbital conditions in ethnic skin. In *Essentials for aesthetic dermatology in ethnic skin* (pp. 59–74). CRC Press.

3. Walker, J. M., Garcet, S., Aleman, J. O., Mason, C. E., Danko, D., Butler, D., . . . & Holt, P. R. (2020). Obesity and ethnicity alter gene expression in skin. *Scientific Reports, 10*(1), 14079.

## FACIAL MORPHOLOGY—EYES

1. Flament, F., Coubard, O., Cruz, R., & Flores, F. (2021). Changes in the eye contour signs due to age among Mexican women: Comparison with women of other ethnic origins. *International Journal of Cosmetic Science, 43*(1), 20–25.
2. Flament, F., Francois, G., Seyrek, I., & Saint-Leger, D. (2020). Age-related changes to characteristics of the human eyes in women from six different ethnicities. *Skin Research and Technology, 26*(4), 520–528.

## SKIN COLOR AND TYPE

1. Jablonski, N. G., & Chaplin, G. (2000). The evolution of human skin coloration. *Journal of Human Evolution, 39*(1), 57–106. https://doi.org/10.1006/jhev.2000.0403. This paper discusses the evolutionary aspects of skin color variation among different ethnicities and the influence of environmental factors on these variations.
2. Rawlings, A. V. (2006). Ethnic skin types: Are there differences in skin structure and function? *International Journal of Cosmetic Science, 28*(2), 79–93.

## AGING SKIN

1. Adler, S. C., Adler, E. T., & Carniol, P. J. (2009). The aging face in a multiethnic world. In *Aesthetic rejuvenation challenges and solutions* (pp. 55–63). CRC Press.
2. Alexis, A. F., & Obioha, J. O. (2017). Ethnicity and aging skin. *Journal of Drugs in Dermatology, 16*(6), Supplement Individual Articles, 77. Copyright © June 2017.
3. Chien, A. L., Qi, J., Cheng, N., Do, T. T., Mesfin, M., Egbers, R., . . . & Kang, S. (2016). Perioral wrinkles are associated with female gender, aging, and smoking: Development of a gender-specific photonumeric scale. *Journal of the American Academy of Dermatology, 74*(5), 924–930.
4. Flament, F., Abric, A., & Adam, A. S. (2021). Evaluating the respective weights of some facial signs on perceived ages in differently aged

women of five ethnic origins. *Journal of Cosmetic Dermatology, 20*(3), 842–853.

5. Grimes, P. E., Hexsel, D. M., Rutowitsch, M., & Grimes, P. E. (2008). The aging face in darker racial ethnic groups. In *Aesthetics and cosmetic surgery for darker skin types* (pp. 27–36).
6. Owen, C. M., Pal, L., Mumford, S. L., Freeman, R., Isaac, B., McDonald, L., . . . & Wolff, E. F. (2016). Effects of hormones on skin wrinkles and rigidity vary by race/ethnicity: Four-year follow-up from the ancillary skin study of the Kronos Early Estrogen Prevention Study. *Fertility and Sterility, 106*(5), 1170–1175.
7. Tschachler, E., & Morizot, F. (2006). Ethnic differences in skin aging. *Skin Aging*, 23–31.
8. Tsukahara, K., Hotta, M., Osanai, O., Fujimura, T., Kitahara, T., & Takema, Y. (2009). The effect of eye opening and closing on the result of facial wrinkle assessment. *Skin Research and Technology, 15*(4), 384–391.
9. Tsukahara, K., Sugata, K., Osanai, O., Ohuchi, A., Miyauchi, Y., Takizawa, M., . . . & Kitahara, T. (2007). Comparison of age-related changes in facial wrinkles and sagging in the skin of Japanese, Chinese and Thai women. *Journal of Dermatological Science, 47*(1), 19–28.
10. Vashi, N. A., de Castro Maymone, M. B., & Kundu, R. V. (2016). Aging differences in ethnic skin. *The Journal of Clinical and Aesthetic Dermatology, 9*(1), 31–38.

## FACE DATABASES

1. Juefei-Xu, F., & Savvides, M. (2014, September). Facial ethnic appearance synthesis. In *European conference on computer vision* (pp. 825–840). Springer International Publishing.
2. Monteiro, L. C. P., Ripardo, R. C., Torro-Alves, N., & Souza, G. S. (2023). Facial morphometric differences across face databases: Influence of ethnicities and sex. *Frontiers in Neuroscience, 17*, 1130867.
3. Riccio, D., Tortora, G., De Marsico, M., & Wechsler, H. (2012, September). EGA—Ethnicity, gender and age, a pre-annotated face database. In *2012 IEEE workshop on Biometric measurements and systems for security and medical applications (BIOMS) proceedings* (pp. 1–8). IEEE.
4. Xie, Y., Luu, K., & Savvides, M. (2012, September). A robust approach to facial ethnicity classification on large scale face databases. In *2012 IEEE fifth international conference on Biometrics: Theory, applications and systems (BTAS)* (pp. 143–149). IEEE.

## 6.4.7 Case Studies and Research on Ancestry versus Climate

Ancestry and climate both play significant roles in shaping facial morphology. Here are two studies that discuss the effect of genetics and climate on facial characteristics.

Zhang, M., Wu, S., Du, S., Qian, W., Chen, J., Qiao, L., Yang, Y., Tan, J., Yuan, Z., Peng, Q., Liu, Y., Navarro, N., Tang, K., Ruiz-Linares, A., Wang, J., Claes, P., Jin, L., Li, J., & Wang, S. (2022). Genetic variants underlying differences in facial morphology in East Asian and European populations. *Nature Genetics*, *54*(4), 403–411. https://doi.org/10.1038/s41588-022-01038-7

Past studies on the genetics of facial features mainly focused on people of European descent (EUR). By using advanced techniques to analyze 3D facial images of people with East Asian (EAS) ancestry, they found 244 genetic variations in 166 locations on the genome (62 of these are new discoveries), which are linked to typical facial differences. A new method they used shows that these genetic effects on facial shape in EAS can also apply to EUR. Additionally, they found 13 genetic variations that explain the differences in facial shape between EUR and EAS populations. Their evolutionary research suggests that the differences in nose shape between these groups are due to adaptation in Europeans. Overall, the study shows the genetic reasons for facial differences across populations.

Evteev, A., Cardini, A. L., Morozova, I., & O'Higgins, P. (2014). Extreme climate, rather than population history, explains mid-facial morphology of northern Asians. *American Journal of Biological Anthropology*, *153*, 449–462. https://doi.org/10.1002/ajpa.22444

Previous studies have looked at how people's faces adapt to cold weather in two different ways: By studying very different groups of humans who have been separated for tens of thousands of years or by studying closely related groups living in different climates. This study focused on one East Asian and seven North Asian populations to see how their faces might have adapted to very cold climates.

The results show that the shape of the midface (the area around the nose and cheeks) is strongly linked to the climate. East Asians, who live in a milder climate, have different midface shapes compared to North Asians, who live in a very cold and dry climate. This pattern holds true whether they look at the upper jaw or the nasal cavity alone. Even when they consider genetic differences, the connection between midface shape and climate remains significant.

The differences they found between populations match what one would expect based on how the body adapts to cold. However, among North Asians, they discovered some new features in the midface that seem to help them cope with extreme cold.

When they looked only at the seven North Asian groups, we find that their midface shapes are still strongly linked to the climate, especially the amount of winter precipitation. But when they account for genetic differences, the link is not as strong.

Overall, these findings suggest that modern humans have adapted their mid-faces to extreme cold climates, which could help us understand how ancient humans adapted during ice ages.

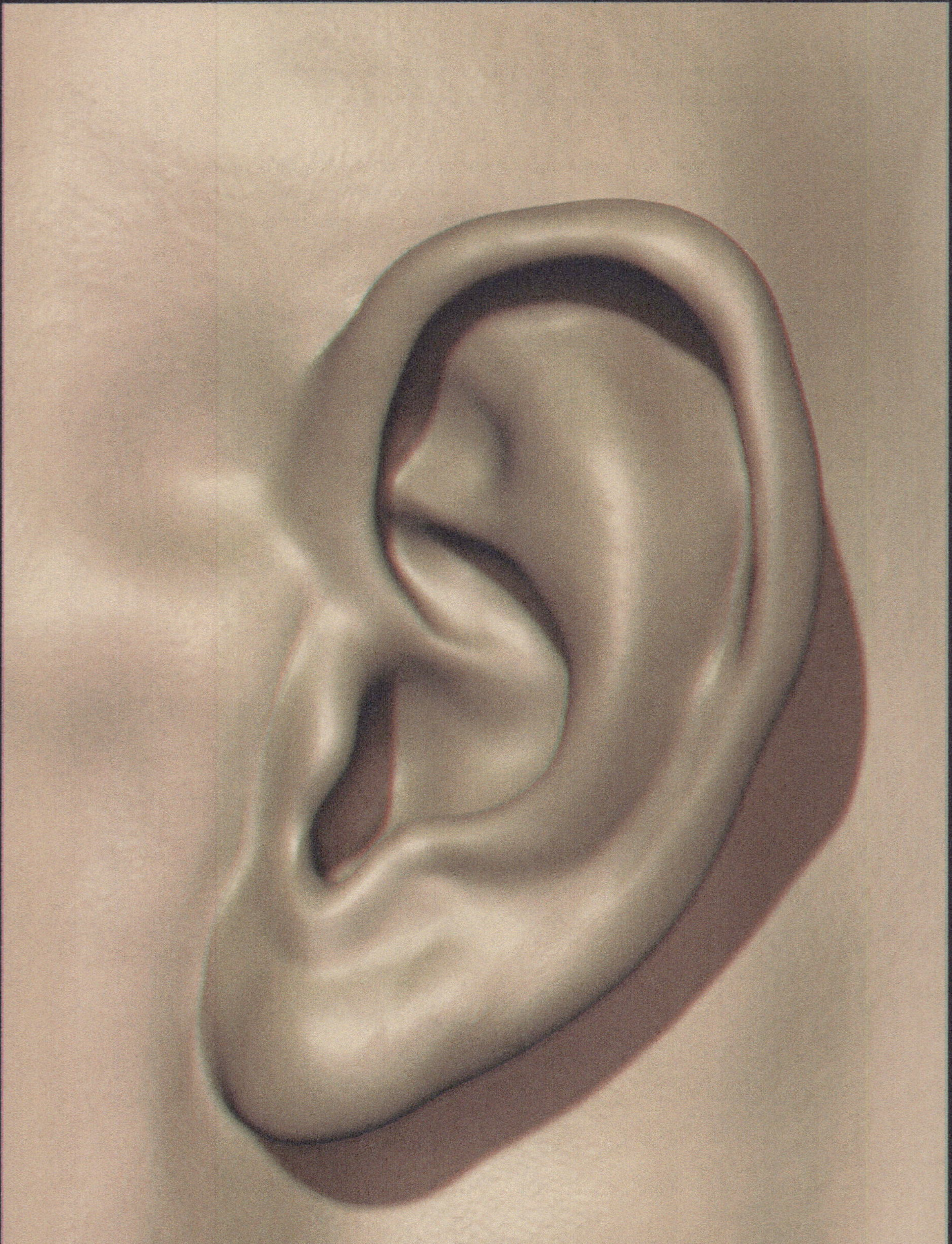

CHAPTER 6:
3D TUTORIAL

# THE EAR

# INTRODUCTION

The ear is one of the more potentially confusing anatomical structures within the human head. But, like a lot of artistic anatomy, once you learn to identify the basic anatomical subforms, how those subforms fit together, and the way the ear overall fits into the human skull, it becomes a much more solvable challenge.

Looking back at our skull forms, the *External Acoustic Meatus* is the opening that is the ear canal. It lies at approximately the halfway point between the front and the back of the skull, which will be approximately where the front border of the ear will be.

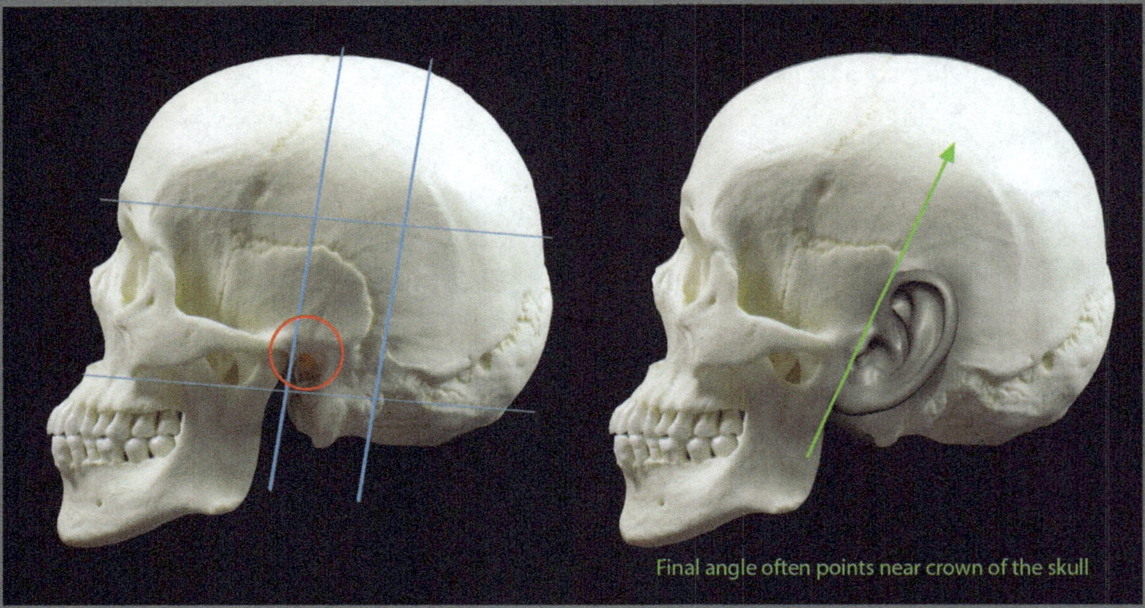


*Ear position on skull.*

A general rule of thumb is that the ear will vertically occupy the space between the line of the brows and the bottom of the nose.

Like all "rules," this is an average. Age, sex, ethnicity, and lifestyle may play some effect in variation away from this, so it is used as a guide to identify how a subject may be similar or different.

Let us look at the forms landmarks that make up the ear and approximately how to position the ear correctly on the human head, particularly in reference to the surrounding anatomy.

Your average healthy, unaltered ear will always have a combination of the same forms. What will vary will be proportional relationships between the forms and individual characteristics like prominence and arcs/angles. The basic anatomical forms are:

- Helix (red)
- Antihelix (light blue)
- Concha (purple)
- Tragus (blue)
- Antitragus (orange)
- Crux of the helix (yellow)
- Lobule (green)

*Landmarks of the ear.*

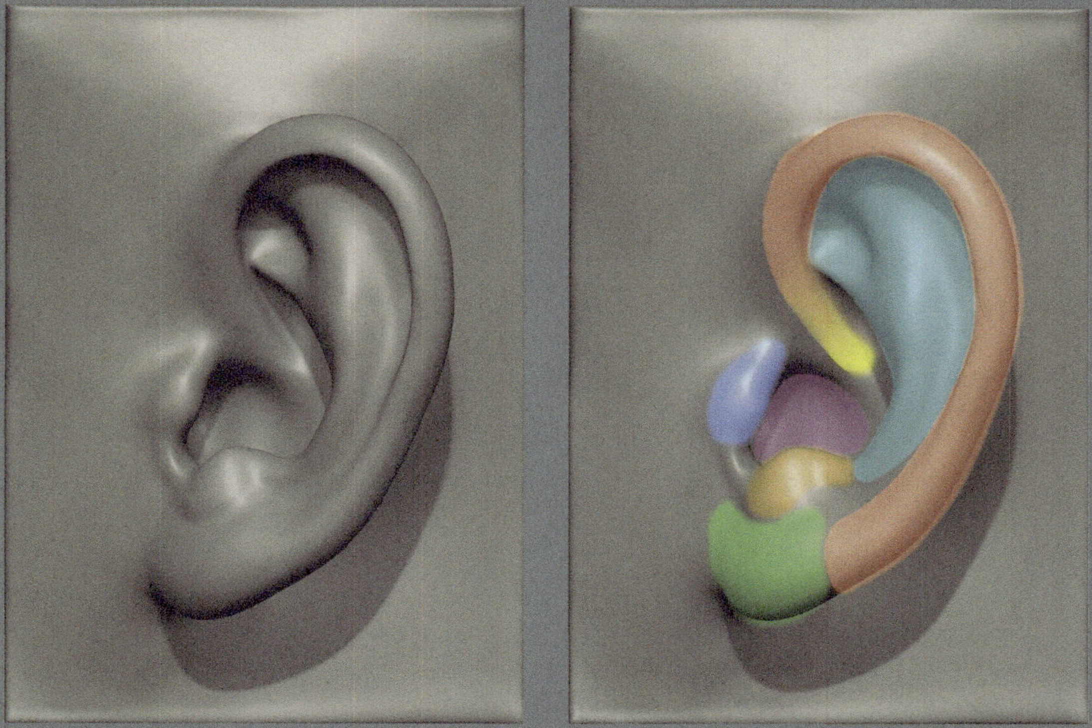

Things can be broken down a little more:

- Antihelix contains the superior and inferior crus (light blue)
- Scaphoid and triangular fossa (purple)
- Intertragal notch (red)
- Lobe can be attached or detached (green lines)

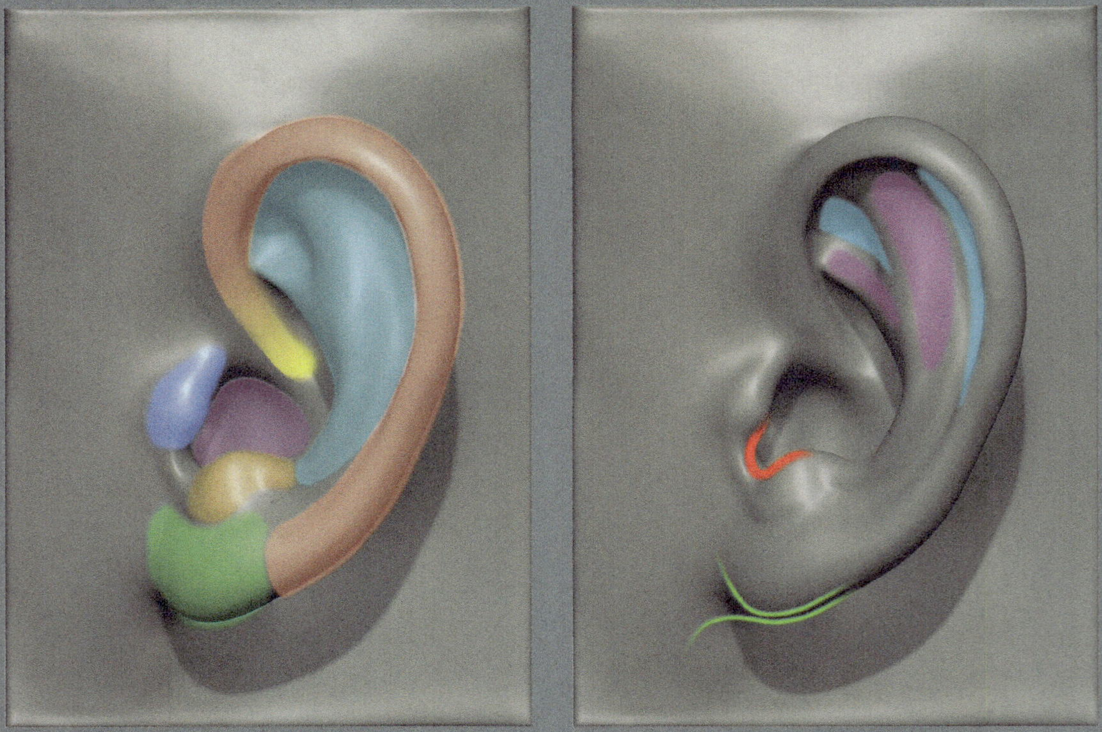

*Smaller forms.*

The ears forms are a series of arcs with a rhythm that you can observe in all ears. The scale of the arcs and their relationships will vary, but, in general, you should look for arcs represented in the following simplified illustration. You should also observe in the ears you study that the forms represented by each colored line tend to flow into one and other to a greater or lesser extent in each individual (helix into lobe and antihelix into antitragus and tragus)

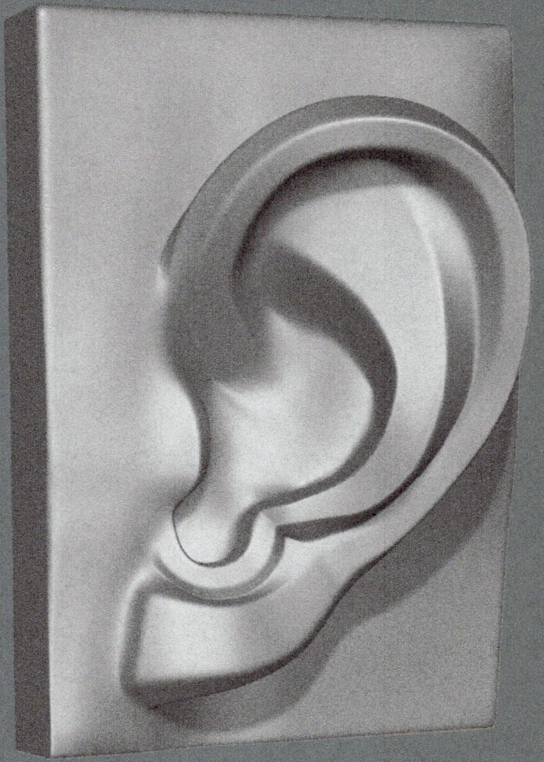

*Arcs.*

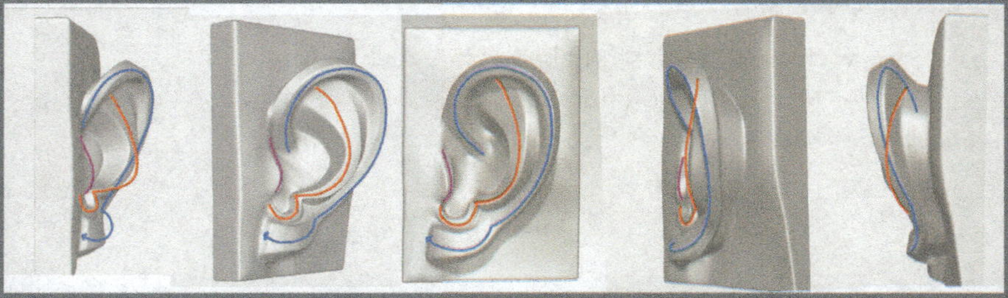

*Arcs from different angles.*

Some more observational techniques

Dividing the ear top to bottom into thirds is a good basic way to plot the arcs and important landmarks vertically. Observing the approximate angle of the ear by visualizing a trapezoidal bounding box with middle dividing lines can give clues for angle changes and relative horizontal positioning of features.

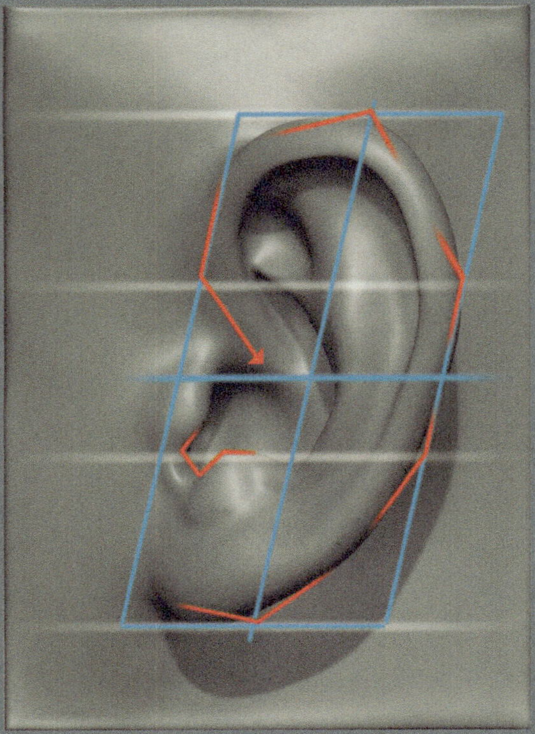

*Division points.*

In addition to these structural forms that make up every ear, it is important to consider how the ear fits within the surface forms of the head.

The zygomatic bones are the widest part of the front half of the skull, so the front border of the ear will usually be set in a bit from the widest point of the cheek. The skull behind the ear will be narrower than the width at the front edge of the ear.

*Skull widths.*

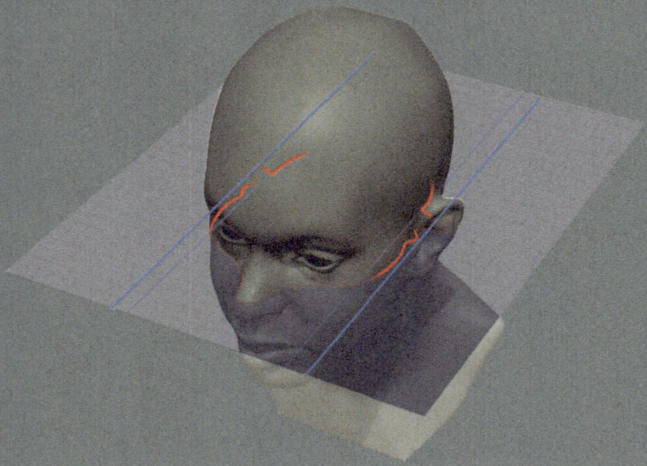

The occipital bone of the skull and temporalis muscles will widen the head above the ear.

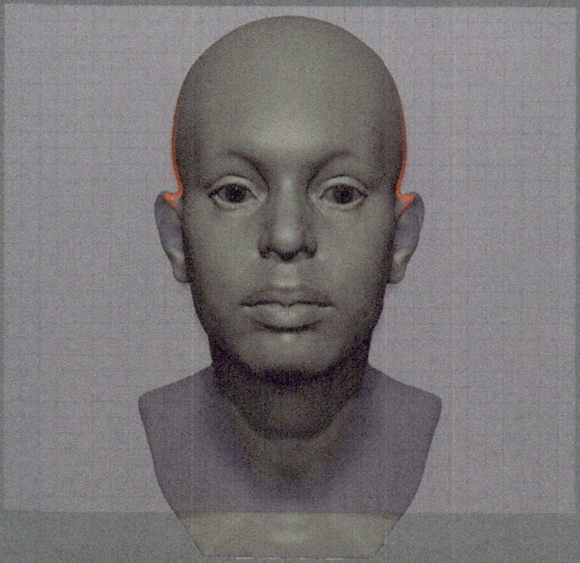

*Temporalis width.*

From the back, the skull will taper toward the neck; however, the mastoid process (blue circle) will generally cause a bulge that will give a bit of an "s" form to the point where the back of the ear contacts the skull.

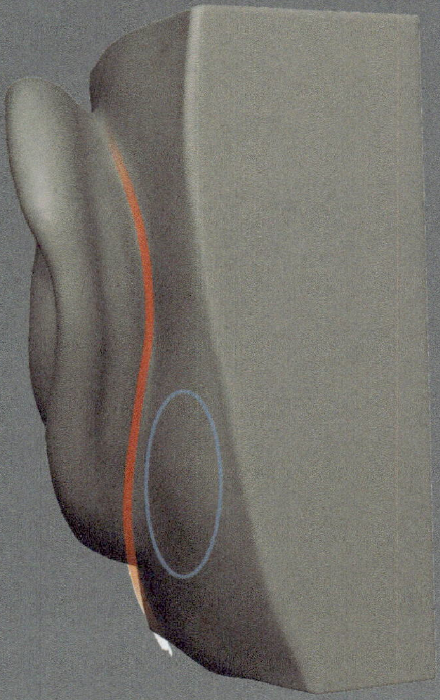

*Backside of ear details.*

The arcs of the ear forms and their interaction with the skull forms is where you can capture the natural gesture of the ear in your work.

You should also observe the direction the vertical axis of the front border of the ear points in; as a general guide if you draw a line along the front of the ear, it will tilt backwards, often pointing in the vicinity of the crown of the head (see Figure 6.1 at the beginning of this tutorial).

Between male and female ears, the main differences will generally be:

- Scale—female ears will tend to be a little smaller and protrude a bit less from the head
- Smaller lobe form
- Smaller fossa between the helix and antihelix

What you observe in your model can vary widely, so this "rule" is intended to give you a reference point to use to compare with your observations.

*Male and female ears.*

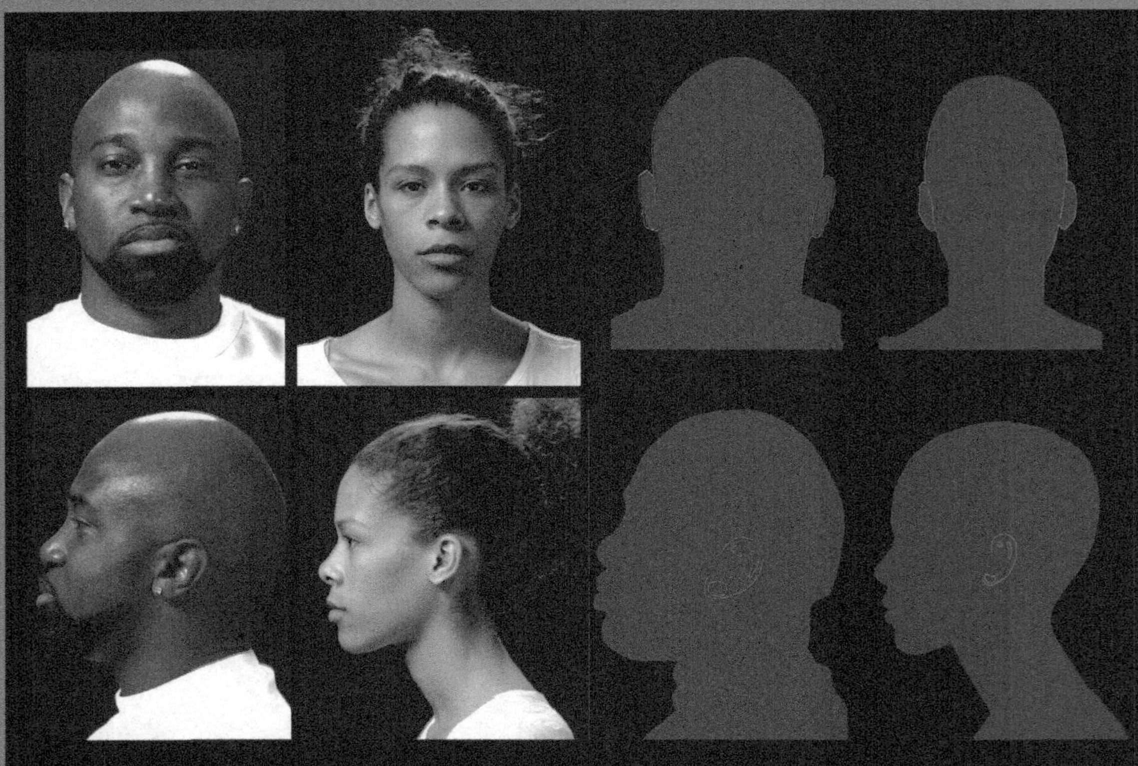

Sculpting the ear:

Load the zbrush project "earTutorialStarter.zprj" . Alternatively, you can load file "earStarter.obj" or start from scratch with clay or in your digital sculpting app. The instructions will assume that you are working in Zbrush, but everything should be simple and straightforward enough to be software/ medium-agnostic.

The easiest way to think of the ear starting out is a pair of stacked intersecting rounded rectangle shapes at slight angles to the plane of the side of the head.

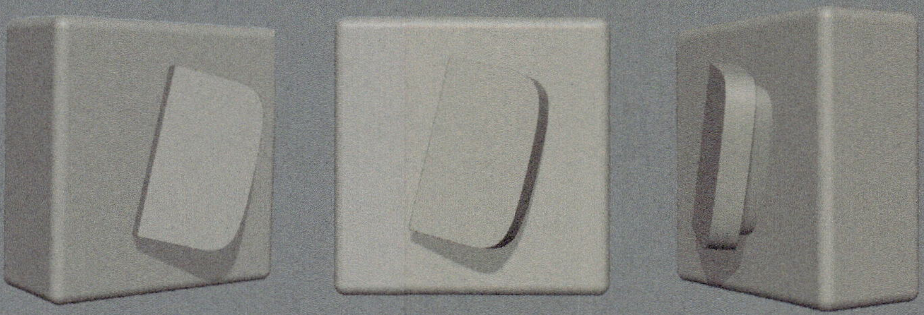

*Basic geometric forms.*

basic geometric starter forms

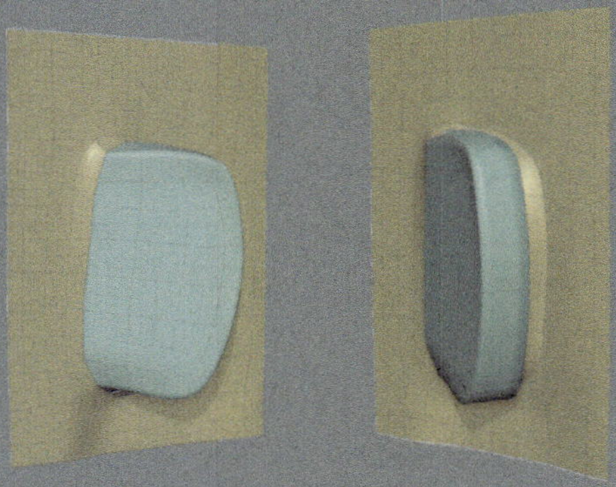

earTutorialStarter.zpr

Start by subdividing one level and shaping the silhouette of the ear to be generally more ear-like, referring back to the examples given earlier in this tutorial to define proportions and overall angle of the ear form. As you proceed through the tutorial, increase the resolution of your model as needed to support the required detail. Avoid increasing geometry density too quickly and try to work with the least amount of polygons needed to finish your current task,

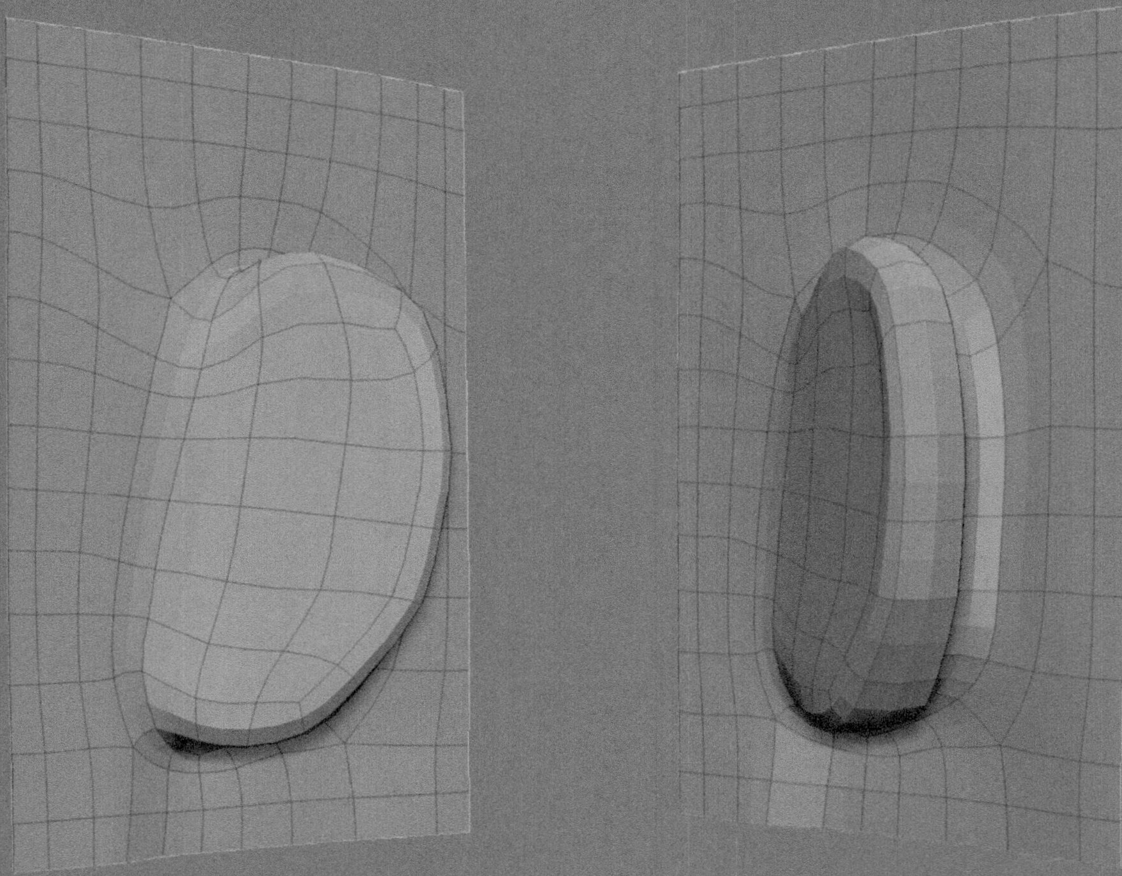

*Basic shaping.*

Next, define the deep cavity (concha). This is a deep recess, and a lot of artists represent it too shallow on the internal depth of the ear, resulting in something that does not feel quite natural, so go reasonably deep. You can always refine it later.

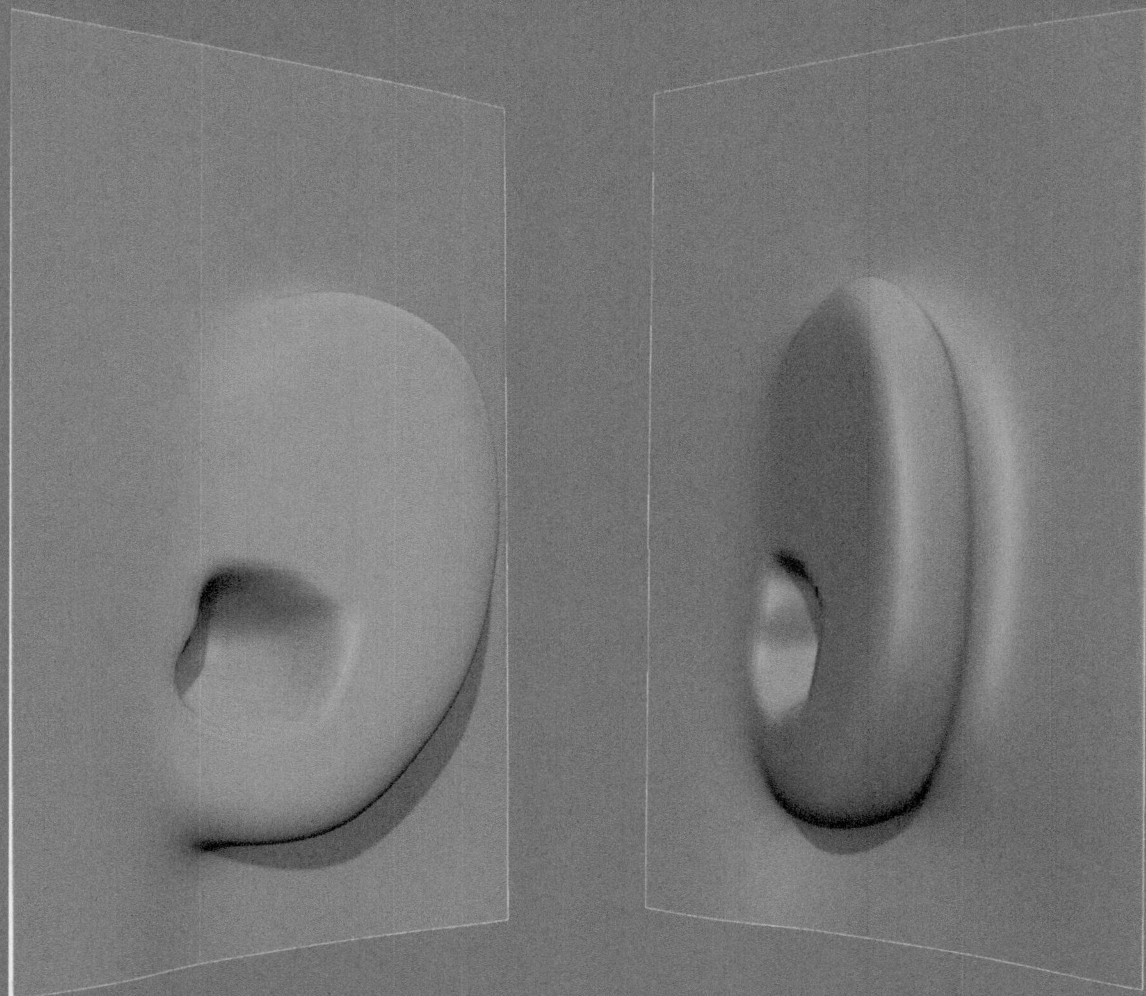

*Carve in concha.*

Next, carve in the basic landmarks of the ear forms (helix, antihelix, tragus, antitragus, lobe) paying attention to where they are in the examples presented earlier.

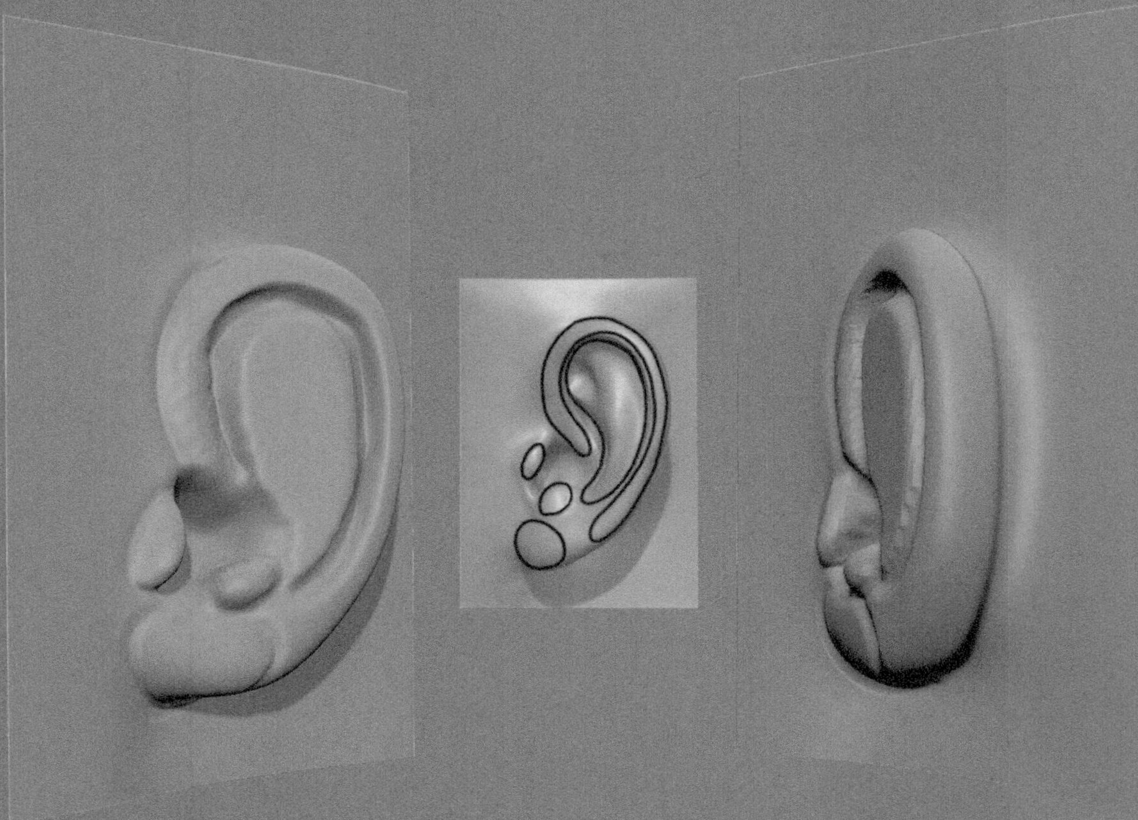

*Carve in landmark borders.*

Next, start to build up or carve in the helix, antihelix, lobe, and tragus forms to incorporate some of the arcs in the example given earlier while refining the shapes and proportions (still trying to stay with basic forms and not going into smaller details yet).

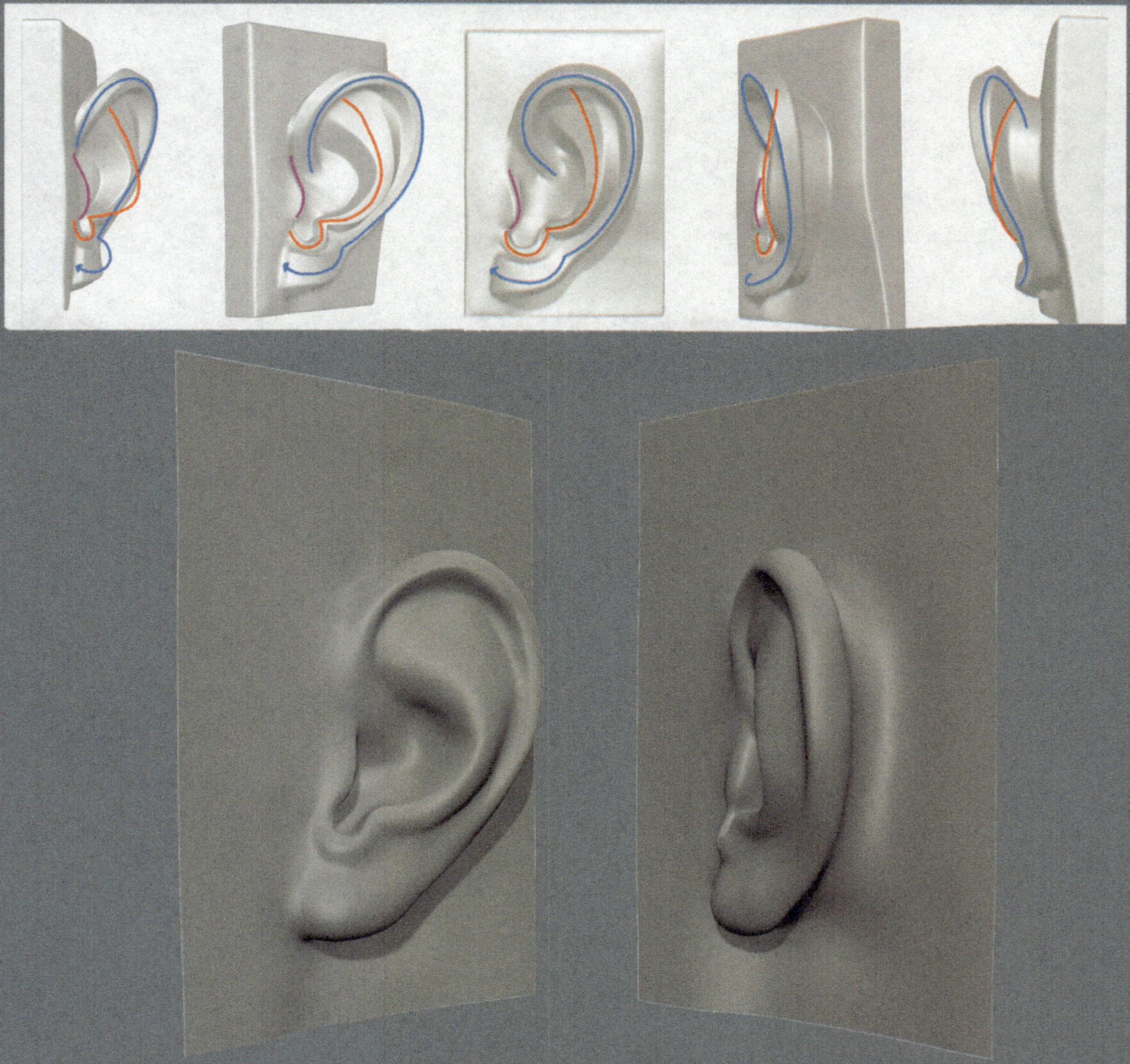

*Refine forms using arcs.*

Now, using what we know about the smaller forms, carve recesses into the antihelix for the superior and inferior crus and build up/refine the scaphoid and triangular fossa.

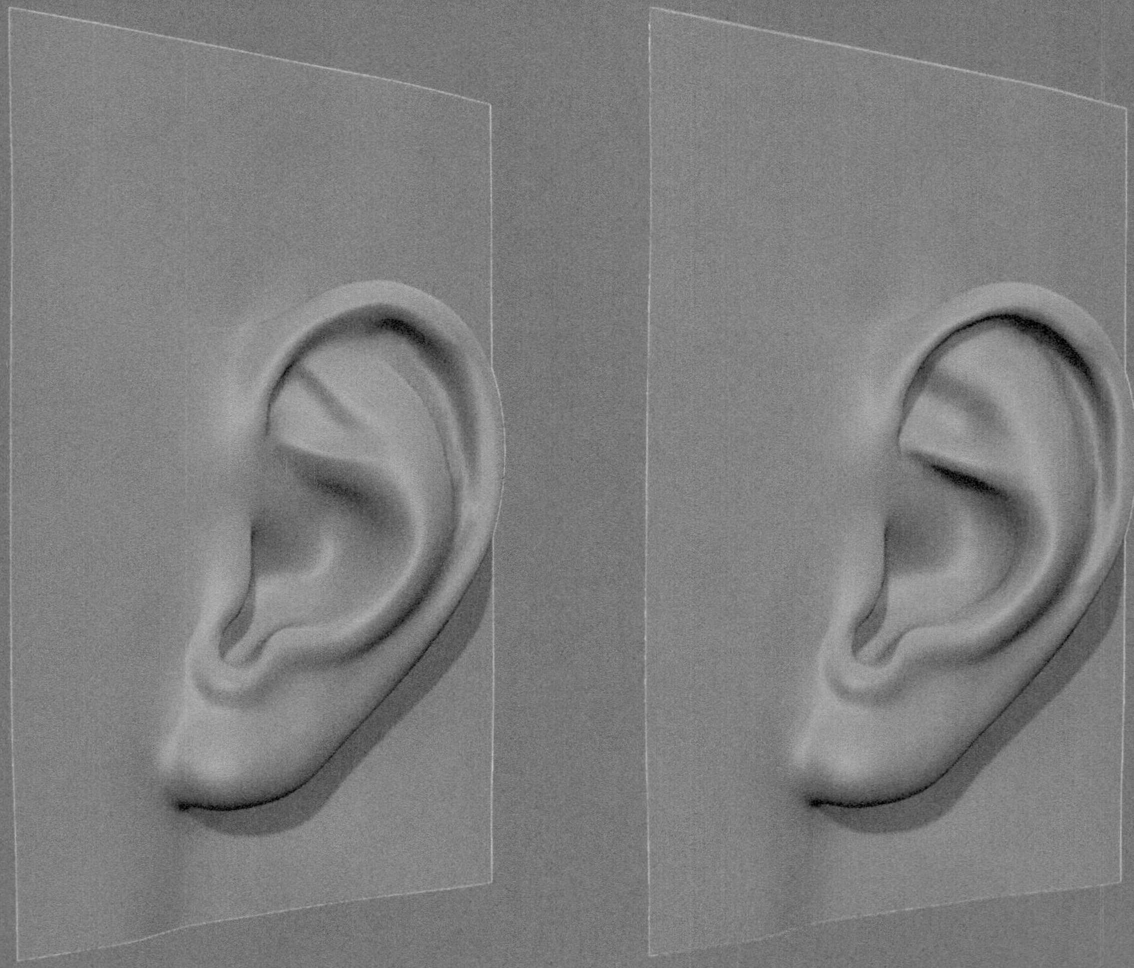

*Carve in crus and refine fossa.*

Considering the ear's function, you realize that it is a series of channels designed to capture and direct sound inward toward the ear canal. As a result, there will be undercuts in the helix and antihelix to create duct-like forms to accomplish that function. This is another area where not going deep enough in your sculpture can lead to ears lacking their natural depth which can lend to the ears feeling stuck on rather than integrated into the head.

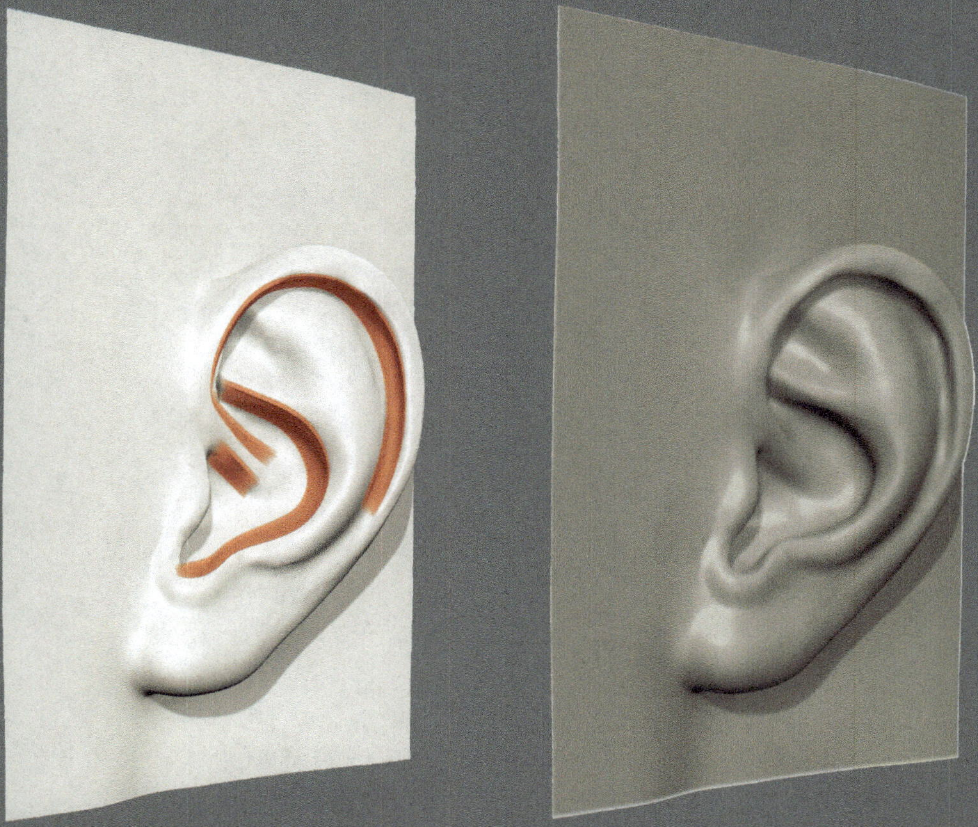

*Sculpt concave forms.*

Give the back of the ear as much attention as you give to the front. Remember that the recessed form on the back of the ear is the back side of the antihelix, so position it appropriately and consider the interaction of the surrounding anatomy discussed earlier.

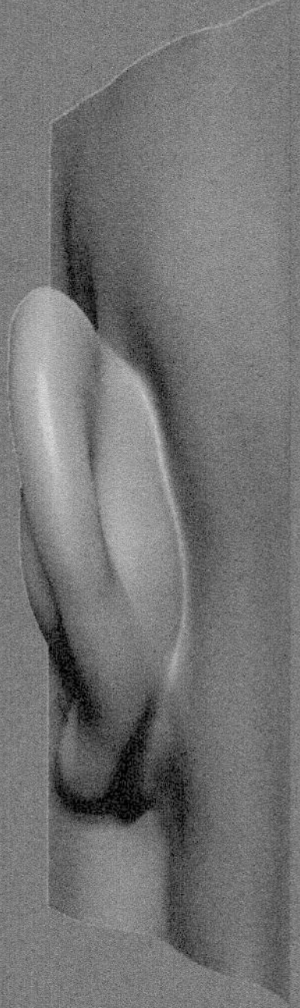

*Refine back of ear.*

Finally, make sure that you are looking at a live model or reference photography and add details you observe in life, paying close attention to how factors like age and the impact of surrounding anatomical forms affect the ear. There will also be interesting variation and irregularity that are unique to the individual, so look for those details in your model.

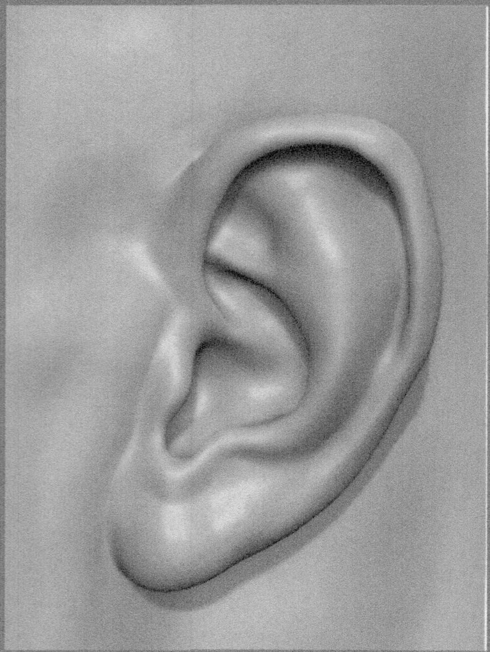

*Finished basic ear.*

# INDEX

# INDEX

# CREDITS

p. 23 - Australian Aboriginal Male Skull – Dr. Evan Matshes, BSc MD. Consultant Osteologist, Bone Clones

p. 27 - African American Female Skull – Dr. Evan Matshes, BSc MD. Consultant Osteologist, Bone Clones

p. 31 - African American Male Skull – Dr. Evan Matshes, BSc MD. Consultant Osteologist, Bone Clones

p. 35 - African Male Skull – Dr. Evan Matshes, BSc MD. Consultant Osteologist, Bone Clones

p. 39 - Asian Female Skull – Dr. Evan Matshes, BSc MD. Consultant Osteologist, Bone Clones

p. 43 - Asian Male Skull – Dr. Evan Matshes, BSc MD. Consultant Osteologist, Bone Clones

p. 47 - Asian Male Robust Skull – Dr. Karen Ramey Burns, PhD. Forensic Anthropologist

p. 51 - American Indian Female Skull – Dr. Evan Matshes, BSc MD. Consultant Osteologist, Bone Clones

p. 55 - European Female skull – Dr. Karen Ramey Burns, PhD. Consultant Osteologist, Bone Clones

p. 59 - European Male Skull – Dr. Karen Ramey Burns, PhD. Consultant Osteologist, Bone Clones

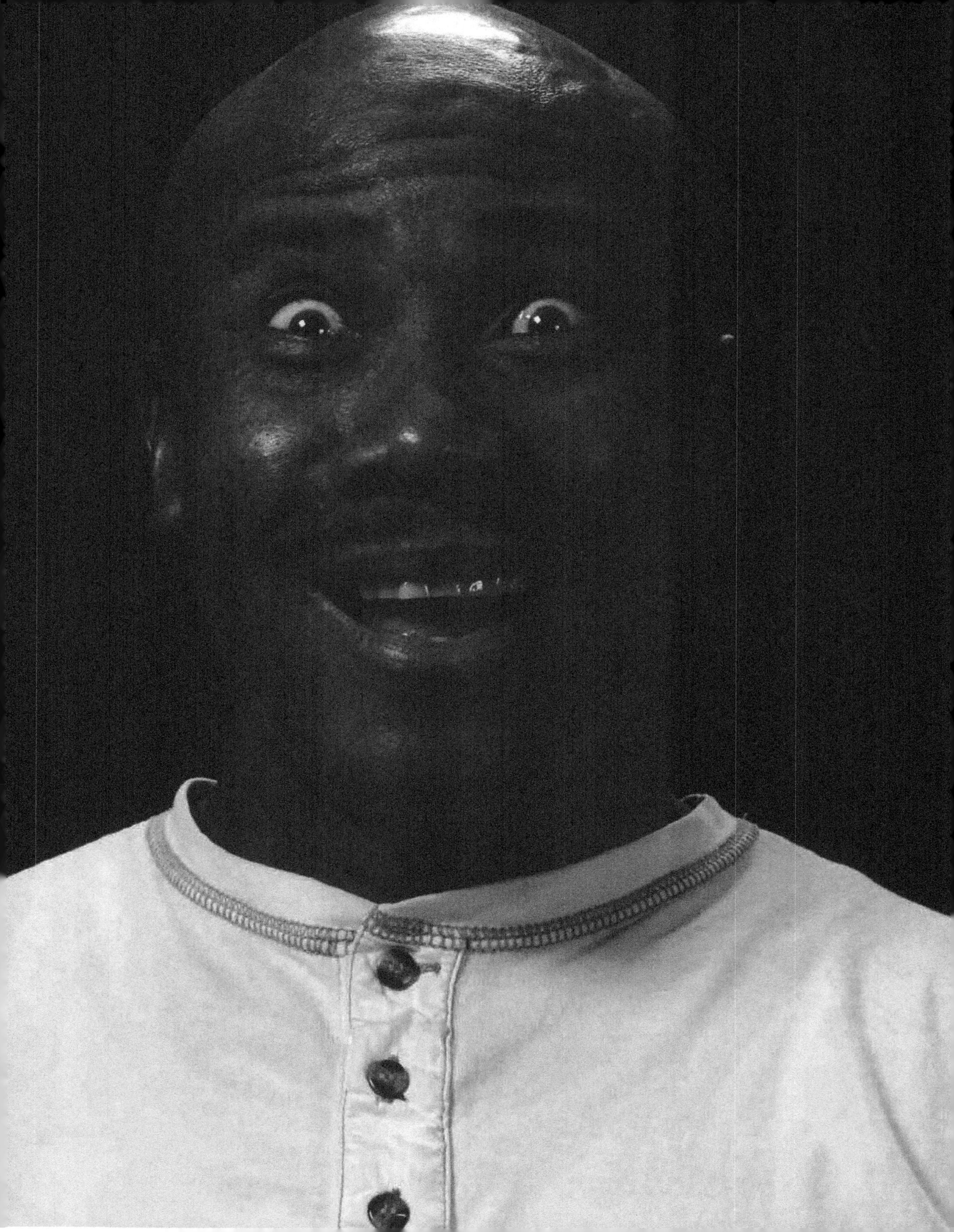

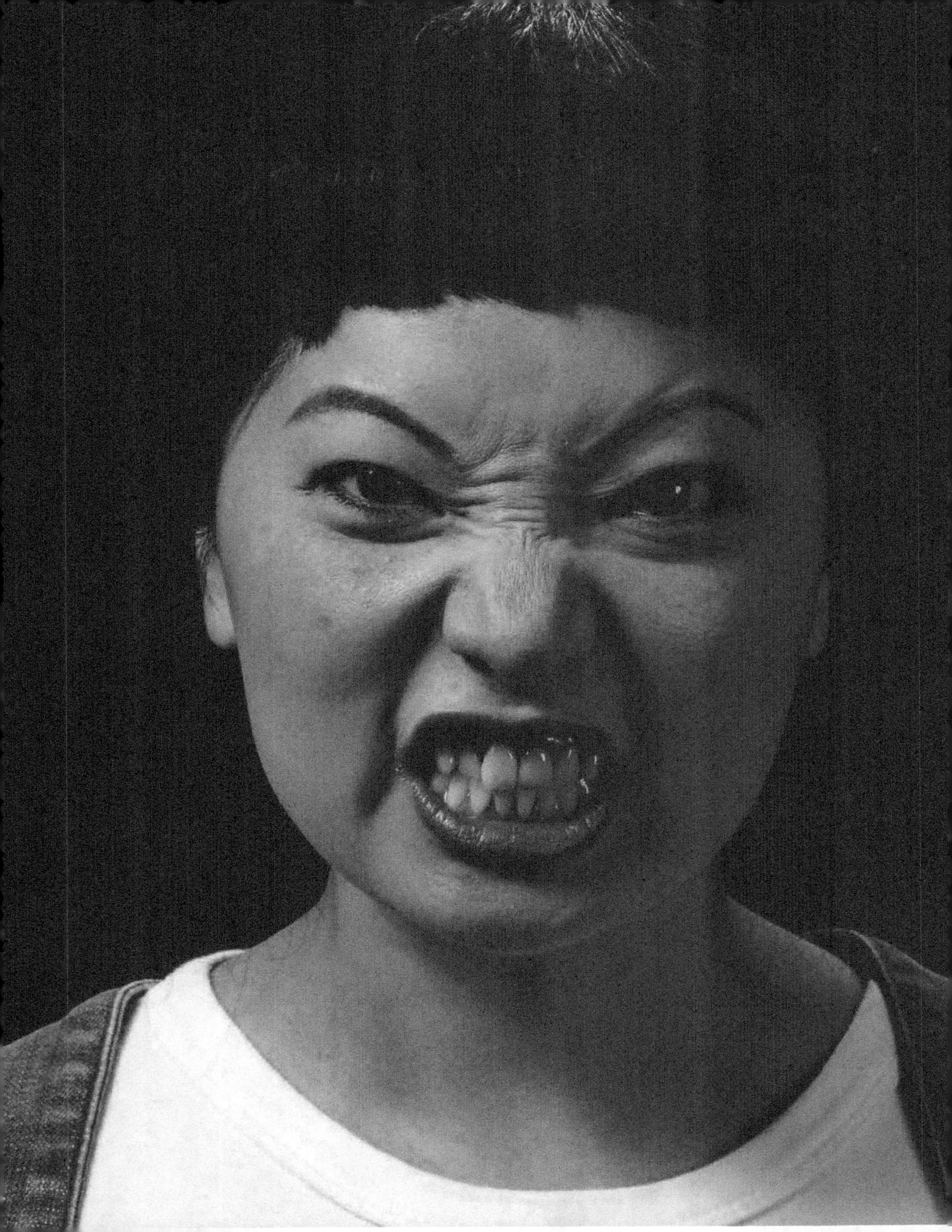

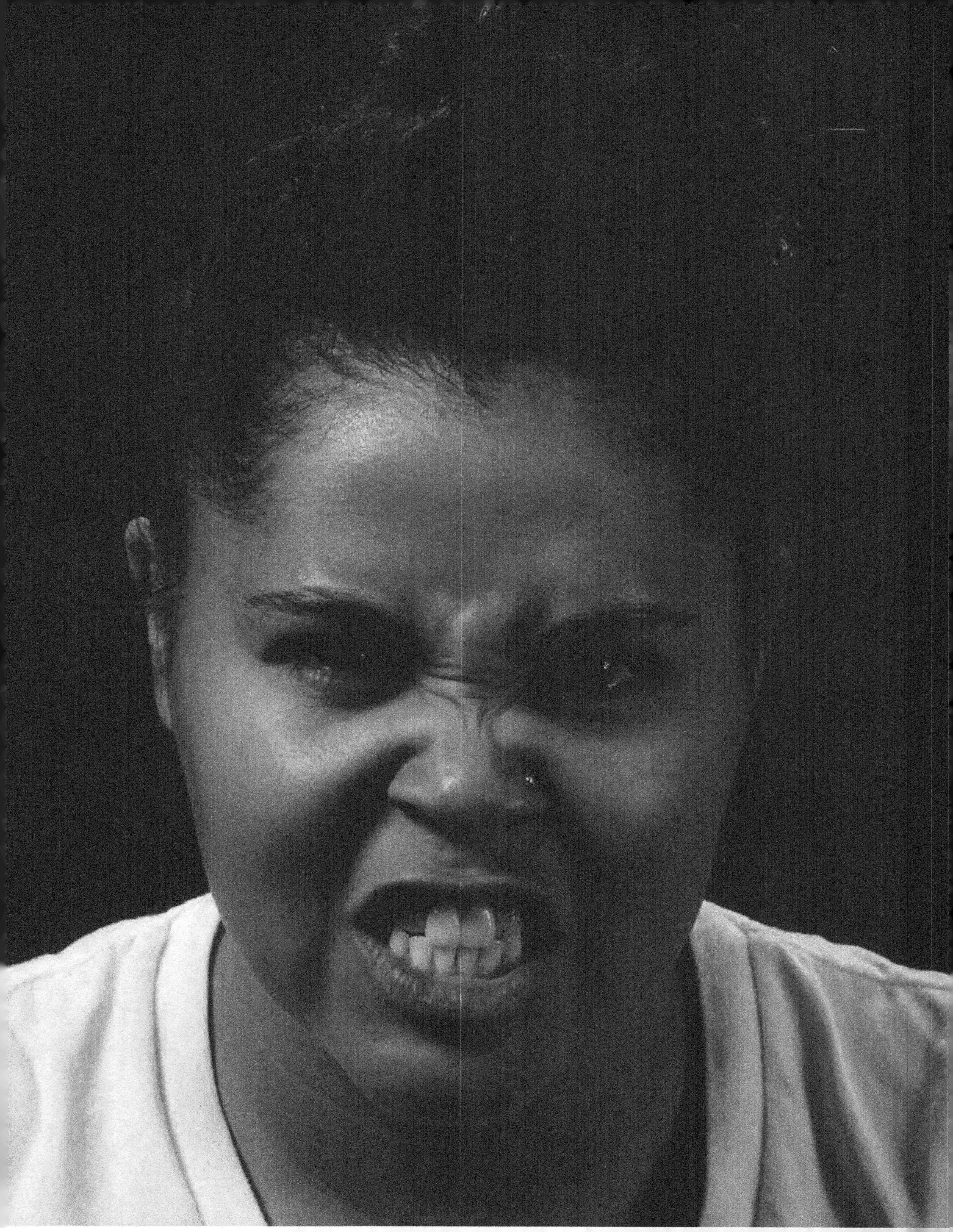

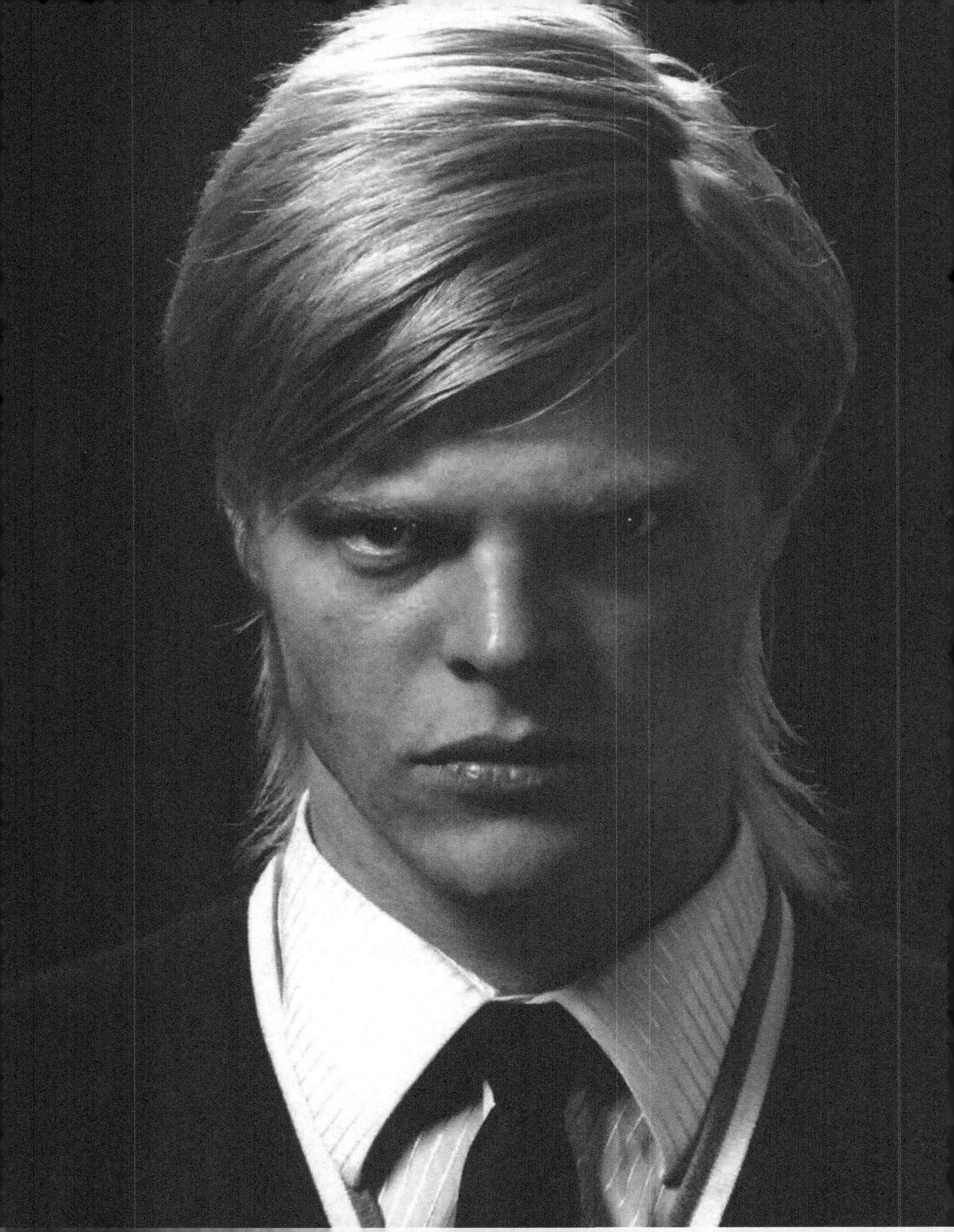

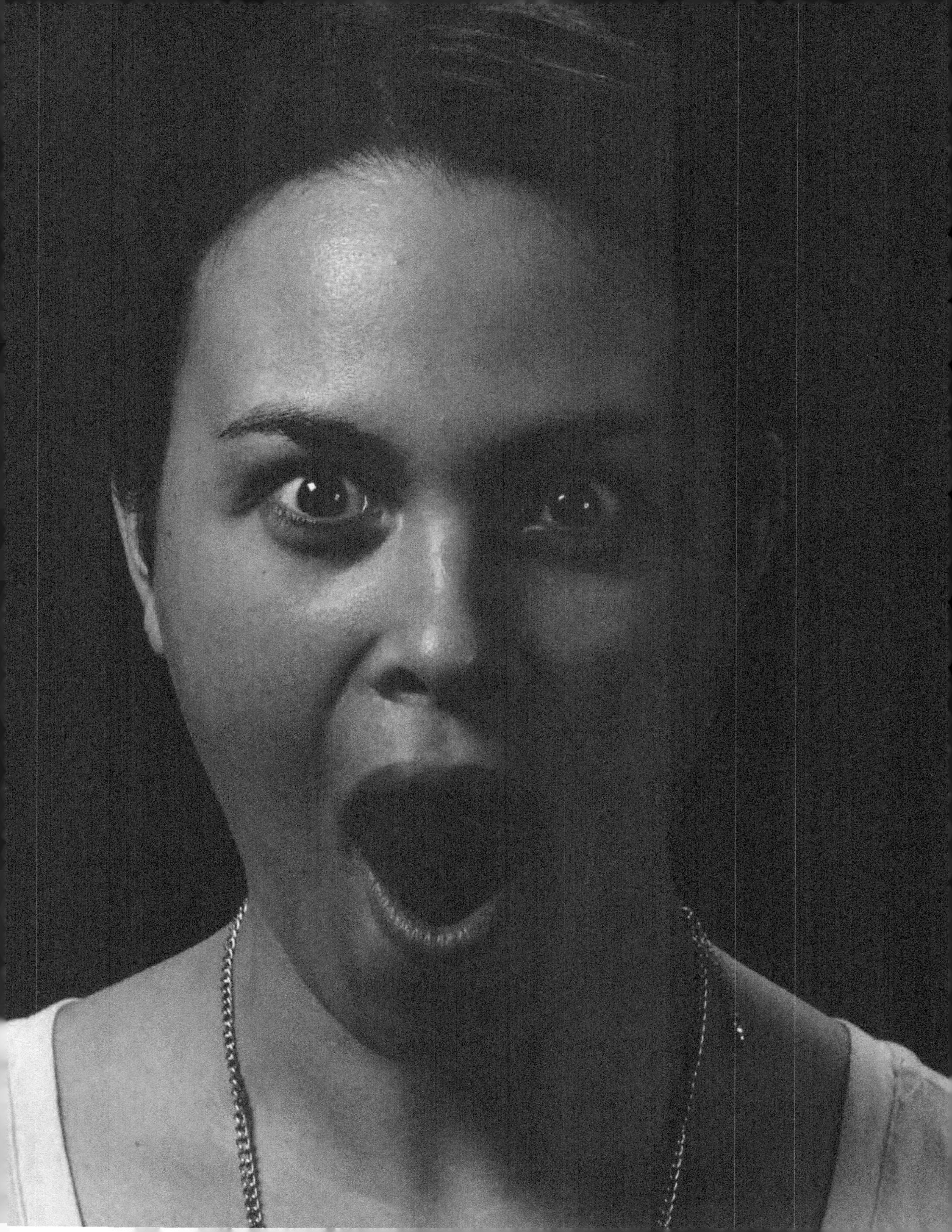

Made in United States
North Haven, CT
21 April 2026

10305270R00287